AMERICA VOTES 14

A HANDBOOK OF CONTEMPORARY
AMERICAN ELECTION STATISTICS

COMPILED AND EDITED BY

RICHARD M. SCAMMON

and

ALICE V. McGILLIVRAY

1980

ELECTIONS   RESEARCH   CENTER

CONGRESSIONAL QUARTERLY   WASHINGTON   1981

© **1981 ELECTIONS RESEARCH CENTER**
1619 Massachusetts Ave. N.W., Washington, D.C. 20036

Copies available from: Congressional Quarterly Inc., 1414 22nd St. N.W., Washington, D.C. 20037

Printed in the United States of America

Library of Congress Catalog Card Number: 56-10132
International Standard Book Number: 0-87187-218-8

CONTENTS

Cities will be found in their appropriate state sections.

INTRODUCTION

The fourteenth volume of AMERICA VOTES follows the general pattern used in the previous handbooks. Users will note a continuation of the state chapter system, including a "profile" sheet, maps, county and ward breakdowns of voting data, time sequence detail in the vote for Congress, and primary election figures. The Congressional figures, as in earlier volumes of AMERICA VOTES, are in the form of a time series, running back to the date of formation of each Congressional District in its present boundaries.

Attention of AMERICA VOTES 14 users is directed particularly to the note sections at the close of each state chapter. Many special situations develop in the politics of the various states, and these are detailed in the note sections. Distribution of the non-major-party vote, boundary changes, discrepancies or corrections in the canvassed returns — these and similar state peculiarities are listed here.

Originally the note section was intended to include for each state a source reference as well as comments on special state electoral situations, but this has appeared to be unnecessary. American elections data, organized as they are by the states rather than by Federal authority, come entirely from state sources. With a few exceptions, examples of which are North Carolina, Oklahoma, and Virginia, materials come from the Secretary of State, the official responsible in most states for election administration and election reporting. Some Secretaries report their elections voluminously, some in very limited detail, but all states make out at least a minimum type of reporting document.

The special section has been continued in the front of this volume to detail the voting in the 1972, 1976 and 1980 Presidential preference primaries along with the United States tables, by state, for the Presidential vote in the general elections from 1948 to 1980. Statistics of voting in New England by larger cities and towns have also been continued for 1980, as have the data for voting in cities of over one million population in which statistics are available by ward or district.

AMERICA VOTES 14 seeks to draw from all these sources the raw material of American elections behavior. From that raw material is built a national reference volume on American politics. To make this reference volume of maximum efficiency in meeting the needs of its users, suggestions as to new materials, together with any corrections of data in this volume, are solicited.

For AMERICA VOTES 14 as for its predecessors, it would be impossible to list all those to whom acknowledgment is due for aid in bringing this volume to the public. To all who have helped in gathering this material and preparing it for publication must go the gratitude of the Editors and of all those who will use this newest volume in the series AMERICA VOTES.

Richard M. Scammon
Alice V. McGillivray

Washington, D.C.
October 1981

UNITED STATES

POST ELECTION CHANGES

Following the 1980 elections several changes took place among the Governors and the members of Congress. Summarized below are all such changes up to September 15, 1981.

GOVERNORS

Connecticut. Governor Ella T. Grasso (D) resigned at the end of December 1980; succeeded by Lieutenant-Governor William A. O'Neill (D). Next full-term election in 1982.

SENATORS

Maine. Senator Edmund S. Muskie (D) had resigned prior to the 1980 election (in May 1980) to become Secretary of State in the Carter administration. His appointed successor — George J. Mitchell (D) — continues in this office until the next full-term election in 1982.

REPRESENTATIVES

1st Connecticut. Representative William R. Cotter (D) died in September 1981; this vacancy will be filled by a special vote in January 1982.

5th Maryland. The seat of Representative Gladys N. Spellman (D) was declared vacant; Steny Hoyer (D) was elected in May 1981 to succeed her.

4th Michigan. Representative Dave Stockman (R) resigned to join the Reagan administration; Mark Siljander (R) was elected in April 1981 to succeed him.

4th Mississippi. Representative Jon C. Hinson (R) resigned; Wayne Dowdy (D) was elected in July 1981 to succeed him.

4th Ohio. Representative Tennyson Guyer (R) died; Michael Oxley (R) was elected in June 1981 to succeed him.

3rd Pennsylvania. Representative Raymond F. Lederer (D) resigned; Joseph F. Smith was elected in July 1981 to succeed him. Though a Democrat, Smith was elected with ballot identifications as Republican and as Independent. However, he announced he would campaign as a Democrat and he now sits as a Democrat.

PRESIDENT 1948

The electoral votes of Alabama, Louisiana, Mississippi, and South Carolina were cast for the States Rights nominees. In addition, one of the 12 Democratic electors chosen in Tennessee cast his Electoral College vote for the States Rights nominees rather than for the national Democratic candidates.

In Alabama the Democratic electors were pledged to the States Rights candidates. There were no national Democratic electors on the ballot in that state.

The Republican figure in Mississippi includes votes cast for two elector tickets. In New York the Democratic figure includes Liberal votes.

The full list of candidates for President and Vice-President was:

24,179,345	Harry S. Truman and Alben W. Barkley, Democratic.
21,991,291	Thomas E. Dewey and Earl Warren, Republican.
1,176,125	Strom Thurmond and Fielding L. Wright, States Rights.
1,157,326	Henry A. Wallace and Glen H. Taylor, Progressive.
139,572	Norman Thomas and Tucker P. Smith, Socialist.
103,900	Claude A. Watson and Dale H. Learn, Prohibition.
29,241	Edward A. Teichert and Stephen Emery, Socialist Labor.
13,614	Farrell Dobbs and Grace Carlson, Socialist Workers.

In addition, 3,412 scattered votes were reported from various states.

UNITED STATES

PRESIDENT 1948

State	Electoral Vote Rep.	Electoral Vote Dem.	Electoral Vote Other	Total Vote	Republican	Democratic	Other	Plurality	Total Vote % Rep.	Total Vote % Dem.	Major Vote % Rep.	Major Vote % Dem.
Alabama			11	214,980	40,930		174,050	130,513 SR	19.0%		100.0%	
Alaska												
Arizona		4		177,065	77,597	95,251	4,217	17,654 D	43.8%	53.8%	44.9%	55.1%
Arkansas		9		242,475	50,959	149,659	41,857	98,700 D	21.0%	61.7%	25.4%	74.6%
California		25		4,021,538	1,895,269	1,913,134	213,135	17,865 D	47.1%	47.6%	49.8%	50.2%
Colorado		6		515,237	239,714	267,288	8,235	27,574 D	46.5%	51.9%	47.3%	52.7%
Connecticut	8			883,518	437,754	423,297	22,467	14,457 R	49.5%	47.9%	50.8%	49.2%
Delaware	3			139,073	69,588	67,813	1,672	1,775 R	50.0%	48.8%	50.6%	49.4%
Florida		8		577,643	194,280	281,988	101,375	87,708 D	33.6%	48.8%	40.8%	59.2%
Georgia		12		418,844	76,691	254,646	87,507	169,511 D	18.3%	60.8%	23.1%	76.9%
Hawaii												
Idaho		4		214,816	101,514	107,370	5,932	5,856 D	47.3%	50.0%	48.6%	51.4%
Illinois		28		3,984,046	1,961,103	1,994,715	28,228	33,612 D	49.2%	50.1%	49.6%	50.4%
Indiana	13			1,656,212	821,079	807,831	27,302	13,248 R	49.6%	48.8%	50.4%	49.6%
Iowa		10		1,038,264	494,018	522,380	21,866	28,362 D	47.6%	50.3%	48.6%	51.4%
Kansas	8			788,819	423,039	351,902	13,878	71,137 R	53.6%	44.6%	54.6%	45.4%
Kentucky		11		822,658	341,210	466,756	14,692	125,546 D	41.5%	56.7%	42.2%	57.8%
Louisiana			10	416,336	72,657	136,344	207,335	67,946 SR	17.5%	32.7%	34.8%	65.2%
Maine	5			264,787	150,234	111,916	2,637	38,318 R	56.7%	42.3%	57.3%	42.7%
Maryland	8			596,748	294,814	286,521	15,413	8,293 R	49.4%	48.0%	50.7%	49.3%
Massachusetts		16		2,107,146	909,370	1,151,788	45,988	242,418 D	43.2%	54.7%	44.1%	55.9%
Michigan	19			2,109,609	1,038,595	1,003,448	67,566	35,147 R	49.2%	47.6%	50.9%	49.1%
Minnesota		11		1,212,226	483,617	692,966	35,643	209,349 D	39.9%	57.2%	41.1%	58.9%
Mississippi			9	192,190	5,043	19,384	167,763	148,154 SR	2.6%	10.1%	20.6%	79.4%
Missouri		15		1,578,628	655,039	917,315	6,274	262,276 D	41.5%	58.1%	41.7%	58.3%
Montana		4		224,278	96,770	119,071	8,437	22,301 D	43.1%	53.1%	44.8%	55.2%
Nebraska	6			488,940	264,774	224,165	1	40,609 R	54.2%	45.8%	54.2%	45.8%
Nevada		3		62,117	29,357	31,291	1,469	1,934 D	47.3%	50.4%	48.4%	51.6%
New Hampshire	4			231,440	121,299	107,995	2,146	13,304 R	52.4%	46.7%	52.9%	47.1%
New Jersey	16			1,949,555	981,124	895,455	72,976	85,669 R	50.3%	45.9%	52.3%	47.7%
New Mexico		4		187,063	80,303	105,464	1,296	25,161 D	42.9%	56.4%	43.2%	56.8%
New York	47			6,177,337	2,841,163	2,780,204	555,970	60,959 R	46.0%	45.0%	50.5%	49.5%
North Carolina		14		791,209	258,572	459,070	73,567	200,498 D	32.7%	58.0%	36.0%	64.0%
North Dakota	4			220,716	115,139	95,812	9,765	19,327 R	52.2%	43.4%	54.6%	45.4%
Ohio		25		2,936,071	1,445,684	1,452,791	37,596	7,107 D	49.2%	49.5%	49.9%	50.1%
Oklahoma		10		721,599	268,817	452,782		183,965 D	37.3%	62.7%	37.3%	62.7%
Oregon	6			524,080	260,904	243,147	20,029	17,757 R	49.8%	46.4%	51.8%	48.2%
Pennsylvania	35			3,735,348	1,902,197	1,752,426	80,725	149,771 R	50.9%	46.9%	52.0%	48.0%
Rhode Island		4		327,702	135,787	188,736	3,179	52,949 D	41.4%	57.6%	41.8%	58.2%
South Carolina			8	142,571	5,386	34,423	102,762	68,184 SR	3.8%	24.1%	13.5%	86.5%
South Dakota	4			250,105	129,651	117,653	2,801	11,998 R	51.8%	47.0%	52.4%	47.6%
Tennessee		11	1	550,283	202,914	270,402	76,967	67,488 D	36.9%	49.1%	42.9%	57.1%
Texas		23		1,249,577	303,467	824,235	121,875	520,768 D	24.3%	66.0%	26.9%	73.1%
Utah		4		276,306	124,402	149,151	2,753	24,749 D	45.0%	54.0%	45.5%	54.5%
Vermont	3			123,382	75,926	45,557	1,899	30,369 R	61.5%	36.9%	62.5%	37.5%
Virginia		11		419,256	172,070	200,786	46,400	28,716 D	41.0%	47.9%	46.1%	53.9%
Washington		8		905,058	386,314	476,165	42,579	89,851 D	42.7%	52.6%	44.8%	55.2%
West Virginia		8		748,750	316,251	429,188	3,311	112,937 D	42.2%	57.3%	42.4%	57.6%
Wisconsin		12		1,276,800	590,959	647,310	38,531	56,351 D	46.3%	50.7%	47.7%	52.3%
Wyoming		3		101,425	47,947	52,354	1,124	4,407 D	47.3%	51.6%	47.8%	52.2%
United States	189	303	39	48,793,826	21,991,291	24,179,345	2,623,190	2,188,054 D	45.1%	49.6%	47.6%	52.4%

PRESIDENT 1952

The Republican figure in South Carolina includes votes cast for two elector tickets; in Mississippi the Republican total is the vote cast for an Independent elector ticket "pledged to vote for the nominees of the National Republican Party". In New York the Democratic figure includes Liberal votes.

The full list of candidates for President and Vice-President was:

33,936,234	Dwight D. Eisenhower and Richard M. Nixon, <u>Republican.</u>
27,314,992	Adlai E. Stevenson and John J. Sparkman, <u>Democratic.</u>
140,023	Vincent Hallinan and Charlotta Bass, <u>Progressive.</u>
72,949	Stuart Hamblen and Enoch A. Holtwick, <u>Prohibition.</u>
30,267	Eric Hass and Stephen Emery, <u>Socialist Labor.</u>
20,203	Darlington Hoopes and Samuel H. Friedman, <u>Socialist.</u>
10,312	Farrell Dobbs and Myra Tanner Weiss, <u>Socialist Workers.</u>
4,203	Henry B. Krajewski and Frank Jenkins, <u>Poor Man's Party.</u>

In addition, 17,205 votes were cast for various elector tickets filed on behalf of General Douglas MacArthur, including Christian Nationalist (with Jack B. Tenney as candidate for Vice-President), Constitution (with Vivien Kellems), and America First (with Senator Harry Flood Byrd). In California, Missouri, and Texas the MacArthur vote was cast for two elector tickets. 4,530 scattered votes were reported from various states.

UNITED STATES

PRESIDENT 1952

State	Electoral Vote Rep.	Dem.	Other	Total Vote	Republican	Democratic	Other	Plurality	Total Vote Rep.	Dem.	Major Vote Rep.	Dem.
Alabama		11		426,120	149,231	275,075	1,814	125,844 D	35.0%	64.6%	35.2%	64.8%
Alaska												
Arizona	4			260,570	152,042	108,528		43,514 R	58.3%	41.7%	58.3%	41.7%
Arkansas		8		404,800	177,155	226,300	1,345	49,145 D	43.8%	55.9%	43.9%	56.1%
California	32			5,141,849	2,897,310	2,197,548	46,991	699,762 R	56.3%	42.7%	56.9%	43.1%
Colorado	6			630,103	379,782	245,504	4,817	134,278 R	60.3%	39.0%	60.7%	39.3%
Connecticut	8			1,096,911	611,012	481,649	4,250	129,363 R	55.7%	43.9%	55.9%	44.1%
Delaware	3			174,025	90,059	83,315	651	6,744 R	51.8%	47.9%	51.9%	48.1%
Florida	10			989,337	544,036	444,950	351	99,086 R	55.0%	45.0%	55.0%	45.0%
Georgia		12		655,785	198,961	456,823	1	257,862 D	30.3%	69.7%	30.3%	69.7%
Hawaii												
Idaho	4			276,254	180,707	95,081	466	85,626 R	65.4%	34.4%	65.5%	34.5%
Illinois	27			4,481,058	2,457,327	2,013,920	9,811	443,407 R	54.8%	44.9%	55.0%	45.0%
Indiana	13			1,955,049	1,136,259	801,530	17,260	334,729 R	58.1%	41.0%	58.6%	41.4%
Iowa	10			1,268,773	808,906	451,513	8,354	357,393 R	63.8%	35.6%	64.2%	35.8%
Kansas	8			896,166	616,302	273,296	6,568	343,006 R	68.8%	30.5%	69.3%	30.7%
Kentucky		10		993,148	495,029	495,729	2,390	700 D	49.8%	49.9%	50.0%	50.0%
Louisiana		10		651,952	306,925	345,027		38,102 D	47.1%	52.9%	47.1%	52.9%
Maine	5			351,786	232,353	118,806	627	113,547 R	66.0%	33.8%	66.2%	33.8%
Maryland	9			902,074	499,424	395,337	7,313	104,087 R	55.4%	43.8%	55.8%	44.2%
Massachusetts	16			2,383,398	1,292,325	1,083,525	7,548	208,800 R	54.2%	45.5%	54.4%	45.6%
Michigan	20			2,798,592	1,551,529	1,230,657	16,406	320,872 R	55.4%	44.0%	55.8%	44.2%
Minnesota	11			1,379,483	763,211	608,458	7,814	154,753 R	55.3%	44.1%	55.6%	44.4%
Mississippi		8		285,532	112,966	172,566		59,600 D	39.6%	60.4%	39.6%	60.4%
Missouri	13			1,892,062	959,429	929,830	2,803	29,599 R	50.7%	49.1%	50.8%	49.2%
Montana	4			265,037	157,394	106,213	1,430	51,181 R	59.4%	40.1%	59.7%	40.3%
Nebraska	6			609,660	421,603	188,057		233,546 R	69.2%	30.8%	69.2%	30.8%
Nevada	3			82,190	50,502	31,688		18,814 R	61.4%	38.6%	61.4%	38.6%
New Hampshire	4			272,950	166,287	106,663		59,624 R	60.9%	39.1%	60.9%	39.1%
New Jersey	16			2,418,554	1,373,613	1,015,902	29,039	357,711 R	56.8%	42.0%	57.5%	42.5%
New Mexico	4			238,608	132,170	105,661	777	26,509 R	55.4%	44.3%	55.6%	44.4%
New York	45			7,128,239	3,952,813	3,104,601	70,825	848,212 R	55.5%	43.6%	56.0%	44.0%
North Carolina		14		1,210,910	558,107	652,803		94,696 D	46.1%	53.9%	46.1%	53.9%
North Dakota	4			270,127	191,712	76,694	1,721	115,018 R	71.0%	28.4%	71.4%	28.6%
Ohio	25			3,700,758	2,100,391	1,600,367		500,024 R	56.8%	43.2%	56.8%	43.2%
Oklahoma	8			948,984	518,045	430,939		87,106 R	54.6%	45.4%	54.6%	45.4%
Oregon	6			695,059	420,815	270,579	3,665	150,236 R	60.5%	38.9%	60.9%	39.1%
Pennsylvania	32			4,580,969	2,415,789	2,146,269	18,911	269,520 R	52.7%	46.9%	53.0%	47.0%
Rhode Island	4			414,498	210,935	203,293	270	7,642 R	50.9%	49.0%	50.9%	49.1%
South Carolina		8		341,087	168,082	173,004	1	4,922 D	49.3%	50.7%	49.3%	50.7%
South Dakota	4			294,283	203,857	90,426		113,431 R	69.3%	30.7%	69.3%	30.7%
Tennessee	11			892,553	446,147	443,710	2,696	2,437 R	50.0%	49.7%	50.1%	49.9%
Texas	24			2,075,946	1,102,878	969,228	3,840	133,650 R	53.1%	46.7%	53.2%	46.8%
Utah	4			329,554	194,190	135,364		58,826 R	58.9%	41.1%	58.9%	41.1%
Vermont	3			153,557	109,717	43,355	485	66,362 R	71.5%	28.2%	71.7%	28.3%
Virginia	12			619,689	349,037	268,677	1,975	80,360 R	56.3%	43.4%	56.5%	43.5%
Washington	9			1,102,708	599,107	492,845	10,756	106,262 R	54.3%	44.7%	54.9%	45.1%
West Virginia		8		873,548	419,970	453,578		33,608 D	48.1%	51.9%	48.1%	51.9%
Wisconsin	12			1,607,370	979,744	622,175	5,451	357,569 R	61.0%	38.7%	61.2%	38.8%
Wyoming	3			129,253	81,049	47,934	270	33,115 R	62.7%	37.1%	62.8%	37.2%
United States	442	89		61,550,918	33,936,234	27,314,992	299,692	6,621,242 R	55.1%	44.4%	55.4%	44.6%

PRESIDENT 1956

One of the 11 Democratic electors chosen in Alabama cast his Electoral College vote for Walter B. Jones and Herman Talmadge rather than for the national Democratic candidates.

The Republican figure in Mississippi includes votes cast for two elector tickets. In New York the Democratic figure includes Liberal votes.

The full list of candidates for President and Vice-President was:

35,590,472	Dwight D. Eisenhower and Richard M. Nixon, <u>Republican.</u>
26,022,752	Adlai E. Stevenson and Estes Kefauver, <u>Democratic.</u>
111,178	T. Coleman Andrews and Thomas H. Werdel, <u>States Rights.</u>
44,450	Eric Hass and Georgia Cozzini, <u>Socialist Labor.</u>
41,937	Enoch A. Holtwick and Edwin M. Cooper, <u>Prohibition.</u>
7,797	Farrell Dobbs and Myra Tanner Weiss, <u>Socialist Workers.</u>
2,657	Harry Flood Byrd and William E. Jenner, <u>States Rights.</u>
2,126	Darlington Hoopes and Samuel H. Friedman, <u>Socialist.</u>
1,829	Henry B. Krajewski and Anne Marie Yezo, <u>American Third Party.</u>
8	Gerald L. K. Smith and Charles F. Robertson, <u>Christian Nationalist.</u>

In addition, 196,318 votes were cast in Alabama, Louisiana, Mississippi, and South Carolina for Independent electors or for States Rights elector tickets not officially pledged to any candidate, and 5,384 scattered votes were reported from various states.

UNITED STATES

PRESIDENT 1956

State	Electoral Vote Rep.	Dem.	Other	Total Vote	Republican	Democratic	Other	Plurality	Total Vote Rep.	Dem.	Major Vote Rep.	Dem.
Alabama		10	1	496,861	195,694	280,844	20,323	85,150 D	39.4%	56.5%	41.1%	58.9%
Alaska												
Arizona	4			290,173	176,990	112,880	303	64,110 R	61.0%	38.9%	61.1%	38.9%
Arkansas		8		406,572	186,287	213,277	7,008	26,990 D	45.8%	52.5%	46.6%	53.4%
California	32			5,466,355	3,027,668	2,420,135	18,552	607,533 R	55.4%	44.3%	55.6%	44.4%
Colorado	6			657,074	394,479	257,997	4,598	136,482 R	60.0%	39.3%	60.5%	39.5%
Connecticut	8			1,117,121	711,837	405,079	205	306,758 R	63.7%	36.3%	63.7%	36.3%
Delaware	3			177,988	98,057	79,421	510	18,636 R	55.1%	44.6%	55.3%	44.7%
Florida	10			1,125,762	643,849	480,371	1,542	163,478 R	57.2%	42.7%	57.3%	42.7%
Georgia		12		669,655	222,778	444,688	2,189	221,910 D	33.3%	66.4%	33.4%	66.6%
Hawaii												
Idaho	4			272,989	166,979	105,868	142	61,111 R	61.2%	38.8%	61.2%	38.8%
Illinois	27			4,407,407	2,623,327	1,775,682	8,398	847,645 R	59.5%	40.3%	59.6%	40.4%
Indiana	13			1,974,607	1,182,811	783,908	7,888	398,903 R	59.9%	39.7%	60.1%	39.9%
Iowa	10			1,234,564	729,187	501,858	3,519	227,329 R	59.1%	40.7%	59.2%	40.8%
Kansas	8			866,243	566,878	296,317	3,048	270,561 R	65.4%	34.2%	65.7%	34.3%
Kentucky	10			1,053,805	572,192	476,453	5,160	95,739 R	54.3%	45.2%	54.6%	45.4%
Louisiana	10			617,544	329,047	243,977	44,520	85,070 R	53.3%	39.5%	57.4%	42.6%
Maine	5			351,706	249,238	102,468		146,770 R	70.9%	29.1%	70.9%	29.1%
Maryland	9			932,827	559,738	372,613	476	187,125 R	60.0%	39.9%	60.0%	40.0%
Massachusetts	16			2,348,506	1,393,197	948,190	7,119	445,007 R	59.3%	40.4%	59.5%	40.5%
Michigan	20			3,080,468	1,713,647	1,359,898	6,923	353,749 R	55.6%	44.1%	55.8%	44.2%
Minnesota	11			1,340,005	719,302	617,525	3,178	101,777 R	53.7%	46.1%	53.8%	46.2%
Mississippi		8		248,104	60,685	144,453	42,966	83,768 D	24.5%	58.2%	29.6%	70.4%
Missouri		13		1,832,562	914,289	918,273		3,984 D	49.9%	50.1%	49.9%	50.1%
Montana	4			271,171	154,933	116,238		38,695 R	57.1%	42.9%	57.1%	42.9%
Nebraska	6			577,137	378,108	199,029		179,079 R	65.5%	34.5%	65.5%	34.5%
Nevada	3			96,689	56,049	40,640		15,409 R	58.0%	42.0%	58.0%	42.0%
New Hampshire	4			266,994	176,519	90,364	111	86,155 R	66.1%	33.8%	66.1%	33.9%
New Jersey	16			2,484,312	1,606,942	850,337	27,033	756,605 R	64.7%	34.2%	65.4%	34.6%
New Mexico	4			253,926	146,788	106,098	1,040	40,690 R	57.8%	41.8%	58.0%	42.0%
New York	45			7,095,971	4,345,506	2,747,944	2,521	1,597,562 R	61.2%	38.4%	61.3%	38.7%
North Carolina		14		1,165,592	575,062	590,530		15,468 D	49.3%	50.7%	49.3%	50.7%
North Dakota	4			253,991	156,766	96,742	483	60,024 R	61.7%	38.1%	61.8%	38.2%
Ohio	25			3,702,265	2,262,610	1,439,655		822,955 R	61.1%	38.9%	61.1%	38.9%
Oklahoma	8			859,350	473,769	385,581		88,188 R	55.1%	44.9%	55.1%	44.9%
Oregon	6			736,132	406,393	329,204	535	77,189 R	55.2%	44.7%	55.2%	44.8%
Pennsylvania	32			4,576,503	2,585,252	1,981,769	9,482	603,483 R	56.5%	43.3%	56.6%	43.4%
Rhode Island	4			387,609	225,819	161,790		64,029 R	58.3%	41.7%	58.3%	41.7%
South Carolina		8		300,583	75,700	136,372	88,511	47,863 D	25.2%	45.4%	35.7%	64.3%
South Dakota	4			293,857	171,569	122,288		49,281 R	58.4%	41.6%	58.4%	41.6%
Tennessee	11			939,404	462,288	456,507	20,609	5,781 R	49.2%	48.6%	50.3%	49.7%
Texas	24			1,955,168	1,080,619	859,958	14,591	220,661 R	55.3%	44.0%	55.7%	44.3%
Utah	4			333,995	215,631	118,364		97,267 R	64.6%	35.4%	64.6%	35.4%
Vermont	3			152,978	110,390	42,549	39	67,841 R	72.2%	27.8%	72.2%	27.8%
Virginia	12			697,978	386,459	267,760	43,759	118,699 R	55.4%	38.4%	59.1%	40.9%
Washington	9			1,150,889	620,430	523,002	7,457	97,428 R	53.9%	45.4%	54.3%	45.7%
West Virginia	8			830,831	449,297	381,534		67,763 R	54.1%	45.9%	54.1%	45.9%
Wisconsin	12			1,550,558	954,844	586,768	8,946	368,076 R	61.6%	37.8%	61.9%	38.1%
Wyoming	3			124,127	74,573	49,554		25,019 R	60.1%	39.9%	60.1%	39.9%
United States	457	73	1	62,026,908	35,590,472	26,022,752	413,684	9,567,720 R	57.4%	42.0%	57.8%	42.2%

PRESIDENT 1960

Senator Harry Flood Byrd received 15 votes for President in the Electoral College; these were the votes of 6 of the 11 Democratic electors in Alabama, all 8 unpledged Democratic electors in Mississippi, and one of the 8 Republican electors in Oklahoma. The Alabama and Mississippi electors also cast 14 votes for Senator Strom Thurmond for Vice-President; the single Oklahoma elector voted for Senator Barry M. Goldwater for Vice-President.

In New York the Democratic figure includes Liberal votes.

The full list of candidates for President and Vice-President was:

34,226,731	John F. Kennedy and Lyndon B. Johnson, Democratic.
34,108,157	Richard M. Nixon and Henry Cabot Lodge, Republican.
47,522	Eric Hass and Georgia Cozzini, Socialist Labor.
46,203	Rutherford L. Decker and E. Harold Munn, Prohibition.
44,977	Orval E. Faubus and John G. Crommelin, National States Rights.
40,165	Farrell Dobbs and Myra Tanner Weiss, Socialist Workers.
18,162	Charles L. Sullivan and Merritt B. Curtis, Constitution.
8,708	J. Bracken Lee and Kent H. Courtney, Conservative.
4,204	C. Benton Coiner and Edward J. Silverman, Conservative.
1,767	Lar Daly and B. M. Miller, Tax Cut.
1,485	Clennon King and Reginald Carter, Independent Afro-American.
1,401	Merritt B. Curtis and B. M. Miller, Constitution.

In addition, 169,572 votes were cast in Louisiana for Independent electors and 116,248 in Mississippi for an unpledged Democratic elector ticket. 539 votes were cast in Michigan for an Independent American ticket and 2,378 scattered votes were reported from various states.

UNITED STATES

PRESIDENT 1960

State	Electoral Vote Rep.	Dem.	Other	Total Vote	Republican	Democratic	Other	Plurality	Total Vote Rep.	Dem.	Major Vote Rep.	Dem.
Alabama		5	6	570,225	237,981	324,050	8,194	86,069 D	41.7%	56.8%	42.3%	57.7%
Alaska	3			60,762	30,953	29,809		1,144 R	50.9%	49.1%	50.9%	49.1%
Arizona	4			398,491	221,241	176,781	469	44,460 R	55.5%	44.4%	55.6%	44.4%
Arkansas		8		428,509	184,508	215,049	28,952	30,541 D	43.1%	50.2%	46.2%	53.8%
California	32			6,506,578	3,259,722	3,224,099	22,757	35,623 R	50.1%	49.6%	50.3%	49.7%
Colorado	6			736,236	402,242	330,629	3,365	71,613 R	54.6%	44.9%	54.9%	45.1%
Connecticut		8		1,222,883	565,813	657,055	15	91,242 D	46.3%	53.7%	46.3%	53.7%
Delaware		3		196,683	96,373	99,590	720	3,217 D	49.0%	50.6%	49.2%	50.8%
Florida	10			1,544,176	795,476	748,700		46,776 R	51.5%	48.5%	51.5%	48.5%
Georgia		12		733,349	274,472	458,638	239	184,166 D	37.4%	62.5%	37.4%	62.6%
Hawaii		3		184,705	92,295	92,410		115 D	50.0%	50.0%	50.0%	50.0%
Idaho	4			300,450	161,597	138,853		22,744 R	53.8%	46.2%	53.8%	46.2%
Illinois		27		4,757,409	2,368,988	2,377,846	10,575	8,858 D	49.8%	50.0%	49.9%	50.1%
Indiana	13			2,135,360	1,175,120	952,358	7,882	222,762 R	55.0%	44.6%	55.2%	44.8%
Iowa	10			1,273,810	722,381	550,565	864	171,816 R	56.7%	43.2%	56.7%	43.3%
Kansas	8			928,825	561,474	363,213	4,138	198,261 R	60.4%	39.1%	60.7%	39.3%
Kentucky	10			1,124,462	602,607	521,855		80,752 R	53.6%	46.4%	53.6%	46.4%
Louisiana		10		807,891	230,980	407,339	169,572	176,359 D	28.6%	50.4%	36.2%	63.8%
Maine	5			421,767	240,608	181,159		59,449 R	57.0%	43.0%	57.0%	43.0%
Maryland		9		1,055,349	489,538	565,808	3	76,270 D	46.4%	53.6%	46.4%	53.6%
Massachusetts		16		2,469,480	976,750	1,487,174	5,556	510,424 D	39.6%	60.2%	39.6%	60.4%
Michigan		20		3,318,097	1,620,428	1,687,269	10,400	66,841 D	48.8%	50.9%	49.0%	51.0%
Minnesota		11		1,541,887	757,915	779,933	4,039	22,018 D	49.2%	50.6%	49.3%	50.7%
Mississippi			8	298,171	73,561	108,362	116,248	7,886 U	24.7%	36.3%	40.4%	59.6%
Missouri		13		1,934,422	962,221	972,201		9,980 D	49.7%	50.3%	49.7%	50.3%
Montana	4			277,579	141,841	134,891	847	6,950 R	51.1%	48.6%	51.3%	48.7%
Nebraska	6			613,095	380,553	232,542		148,011 R	62.1%	37.9%	62.1%	37.9%
Nevada		3		107,267	52,387	54,880		2,493 D	48.8%	51.2%	48.8%	51.2%
New Hampshire	4			295,761	157,989	137,772		20,217 R	53.4%	46.6%	53.4%	46.6%
New Jersey		16		2,773,111	1,363,324	1,385,415	24,372	22,091 D	49.2%	50.0%	49.6%	50.4%
New Mexico		4		311,107	153,733	156,027	1,347	2,294 D	49.4%	50.2%	49.6%	50.4%
New York		45		7,291,079	3,446,419	3,830,085	14,575	383,666 D	47.3%	52.5%	47.4%	52.6%
North Carolina		14		1,368,556	655,420	713,136		57,716 D	47.9%	52.1%	47.9%	52.1%
North Dakota	4			278,431	154,310	123,963	158	30,347 R	55.4%	44.5%	55.5%	44.5%
Ohio	25			4,161,859	2,217,611	1,944,248		273,363 R	53.3%	46.7%	53.3%	46.7%
Oklahoma	7		1	903,150	533,039	370,111		162,928 R	59.0%	41.0%	59.0%	41.0%
Oregon	6			776,421	408,060	367,402	959	40,658 R	52.6%	47.3%	52.6%	47.4%
Pennsylvania		32		5,006,541	2,439,956	2,556,282	10,303	116,326 D	48.7%	51.1%	48.8%	51.2%
Rhode Island		4		405,535	147,502	258,032	1	110,530 D	36.4%	63.6%	36.4%	63.6%
South Carolina		8		386,688	188,558	198,129	1	9,571 D	48.8%	51.2%	48.8%	51.2%
South Dakota	4			306,487	178,417	128,070		50,347 R	58.2%	41.8%	58.2%	41.8%
Tennessee	11			1,051,792	556,577	481,453	13,762	75,124 R	52.9%	45.8%	53.6%	46.4%
Texas		24		2,311,084	1,121,310	1,167,567	22,207	46,257 D	48.5%	50.5%	49.0%	51.0%
Utah	4			374,709	205,361	169,248	100	36,113 R	54.8%	45.2%	54.8%	45.2%
Vermont	3			167,324	98,131	69,186	7	28,945 R	58.6%	41.3%	58.6%	41.4%
Virginia	12			771,449	404,521	362,327	4,601	42,194 R	52.4%	47.0%	52.8%	47.2%
Washington	9			1,241,572	629,273	599,298	13,001	29,975 R	50.7%	48.3%	51.2%	48.8%
West Virginia		8		837,781	395,995	441,786		45,791 D	47.3%	52.7%	47.3%	52.7%
Wisconsin	12			1,729,082	895,175	830,805	3,102	64,370 R	51.8%	48.0%	51.9%	48.1%
Wyoming	3			140,782	77,451	63,331		14,120 R	55.0%	45.0%	55.0%	45.0%
United States	219	303	15	68,838,219	34,108,157	34,226,731	503,331	118,574 D	49.5%	49.7%	49.9%	50.1%

PRESIDENT 1964

In New York the Democratic figure includes Liberal votes.

The full list of candidates for President and Vice-President was:

43,129,566	Lyndon B. Johnson and Hubert H. Humphrey, <u>Democratic.</u>
27,178,188	Barry M. Goldwater and William E. Miller, <u>Republican.</u>
45,219	Eric Hass and Henning A. Blomen, <u>Socialist Labor.</u>
32,720	Clifton DeBerry and Edward Shaw, <u>Socialist Workers.</u>
23,267	E. Harold Munn and Mark R. Shaw, <u>Prohibition.</u>
6,953	John Kasper and J. B. Stoner, <u>National States Rights.</u>
5,060	Joseph B. Lightburn and T. C. Billings, <u>Constitution.</u>
19	James Hensley and John O. Hopkins, <u>Universal.</u>

In addition, 210,732 votes were cast in Alabama for an unpledged Democratic elector ticket and 12,868 scattered votes were reported from various states.

UNITED STATES

PRESIDENT 1964

State	Electoral Vote Rep.	Electoral Vote Dem.	Electoral Vote Other	Total Vote	Republican	Democratic	Other	Plurality	Total Vote Rep.	Total Vote Dem.	Major Vote Rep.	Major Vote Dem.
Alabama	10			689,818	479,085		210,733	268,353 R	69.5%		100.0%	
Alaska		3		67,259	22,930	44,329		21,399 D	34.1%	65.9%	34.1%	65.9%
Arizona	5			480,770	242,535	237,753	482	4,782 R	50.4%	49.5%	50.5%	49.5%
Arkansas		6		560,426	243,264	314,197	2,965	70,933 D	43.4%	56.1%	43.6%	56.4%
California		40		7,057,586	2,879,108	4,171,877	6,601	1,292,769 D	40.8%	59.1%	40.8%	59.2%
Colorado		6		776,986	296,767	476,024	4,195	179,257 D	38.2%	61.3%	38.4%	61.6%
Connecticut		8		1,218,578	390,996	826,269	1,313	435,273 D	32.1%	67.8%	32.1%	67.9%
Delaware		3		201,320	78,078	122,704	538	44,626 D	38.8%	60.9%	38.9%	61.1%
Florida		14		1,854,481	905,941	948,540		42,599 D	48.9%	51.1%	48.9%	51.1%
Georgia	12			1,139,335	616,584	522,556	195	94,028 R	54.1%	45.9%	54.1%	45.9%
Hawaii		4		207,271	44,022	163,249		119,227 D	21.2%	78.8%	21.2%	78.8%
Idaho		4		292,477	143,557	148,920		5,363 D	49.1%	50.9%	49.1%	50.9%
Illinois		26		4,702,841	1,905,946	2,796,833	62	890,887 D	40.5%	59.5%	40.5%	59.5%
Indiana		13		2,091,606	911,118	1,170,848	9,640	259,730 D	43.6%	56.0%	43.8%	56.2%
Iowa		9		1,184,539	449,148	733,030	2,361	283,822 D	37.9%	61.9%	38.0%	62.0%
Kansas		7		857,901	386,579	464,028	7,294	77,449 D	45.1%	54.1%	45.4%	54.6%
Kentucky		9		1,046,105	372,977	669,659	3,469	296,682 D	35.7%	64.0%	35.8%	64.2%
Louisiana	10			896,293	509,225	387,068		122,157 R	56.8%	43.2%	56.8%	43.2%
Maine		4		380,965	118,701	262,264		143,563 D	31.2%	68.8%	31.2%	68.8%
Maryland		10		1,116,457	385,495	730,912	50	345,417 D	34.5%	65.5%	34.5%	65.5%
Massachusetts		14		2,344,798	549,727	1,786,422	8,649	1,236,695 D	23.4%	76.2%	23.5%	76.5%
Michigan		21		3,203,102	1,060,152	2,136,615	6,335	1,076,463 D	33.1%	66.7%	33.2%	66.8%
Minnesota		10		1,554,462	559,624	991,117	3,721	431,493 D	36.0%	63.8%	36.1%	63.9%
Mississippi	7			409,146	356,528	52,618		303,910 R	87.1%	12.9%	87.1%	12.9%
Missouri		12		1,817,879	653,535	1,164,344		510,809 D	36.0%	64.0%	36.0%	64.0%
Montana		4		278,628	113,032	164,246	1,350	51,214 D	40.6%	58.9%	40.8%	59.2%
Nebraska		5		584,154	276,847	307,307		30,460 D	47.4%	52.6%	47.4%	52.6%
Nevada		3		135,433	56,094	79,339		23,245 D	41.4%	58.6%	41.4%	58.6%
New Hampshire		4		288,093	104,029	184,064		80,035 D	36.1%	63.9%	36.1%	63.9%
New Jersey		17		2,847,663	964,174	1,868,231	15,258	904,057 D	33.9%	65.6%	34.0%	66.0%
New Mexico		4		328,645	132,838	194,015	1,792	61,177 D	40.4%	59.0%	40.6%	59.4%
New York		43		7,166,275	2,243,559	4,913,102	9,614	2,669,543 D	31.3%	68.6%	31.3%	68.7%
North Carolina		13		1,424,983	624,844	800,139		175,295 D	43.8%	56.2%	43.8%	56.2%
North Dakota		4		258,389	108,207	149,784	398	41,577 D	41.9%	58.0%	41.9%	58.1%
Ohio		26		3,969,196	1,470,865	2,498,331		1,027,466 D	37.1%	62.9%	37.1%	62.9%
Oklahoma		8		932,499	412,665	519,834		107,169 D	44.3%	55.7%	44.3%	55.7%
Oregon		6		786,305	282,779	501,017	2,509	218,238 D	36.0%	63.7%	36.1%	63.9%
Pennsylvania		29		4,822,690	1,673,657	3,130,954	18,079	1,457,297 D	34.7%	64.9%	34.8%	65.2%
Rhode Island		4		390,091	74,615	315,463	13	240,848 D	19.1%	80.9%	19.1%	80.9%
South Carolina	8			524,779	309,048	215,723	8	93,325 R	58.9%	41.1%	58.9%	41.1%
South Dakota		4		293,118	130,108	163,010		32,902 D	44.4%	55.6%	44.4%	55.6%
Tennessee		11		1,143,946	508,965	634,947	34	125,982 D	44.5%	55.5%	44.5%	55.5%
Texas		25		2,626,811	958,566	1,663,185	5,060	704,619 D	36.5%	63.3%	36.6%	63.4%
Utah		4		401,413	181,785	219,628		37,843 D	45.3%	54.7%	45.3%	54.7%
Vermont		3		163,089	54,942	108,127	20	53,185 D	33.7%	66.3%	33.7%	66.3%
Virginia		12		1,042,267	481,334	558,038	2,895	76,704 D	46.2%	53.5%	46.3%	53.7%
Washington		9		1,258,556	470,366	779,881	8,309	309,515 D	37.4%	62.0%	37.6%	62.4%
West Virginia		7		792,040	253,953	538,087		284,134 D	32.1%	67.9%	32.1%	67.9%
Wisconsin		12		1,691,815	638,495	1,050,424	2,896	411,929 D	37.7%	62.1%	37.8%	62.2%
Wyoming		3		142,716	61,998	80,718		18,720 D	43.4%	56.6%	43.4%	56.6%
Dist. of Col.		3		198,597	28,801	169,796		140,995 D	14.5%	85.5%	14.5%	85.5%
United States	52	486		70,644,592	27,178,188	43,129,566	336,838	15,951,378 D	38.5%	61.1%	38.7%	61.3%

PRESIDENT 1968

In North Carolina one Republican elector voted in the Electoral College for the American Independent candidates for President and Vice-President.

In New York the Democratic figure includes Liberal votes and in Alabama the Democratic vote is the total of the Alabama Independent Democratic and National Democratic Party of Alabama vote. In certain states candidates appeared under variants of the party name used below and in most states the Vice-Presidential candidate of the American Independent party was listed as Marvin Griffin rather than Curtis E. LeMay.

The full list of candidates for President and Vice-President was:

31,785,480	Richard M. Nixon and Spiro T. Agnew, Republican.
31,275,166	Hubert H. Humphrey and Edmund S. Muskie, Democratic.
9,906,473	George C. Wallace and Curtis E. LeMay, American Independent.
52,588	Henning A. Blomen and George S. Taylor, Socialist Labor.
47,133	Dick Gregory, Peace and Freedom, with various Vice-Presidential candidates.
41,388	Fred Halstead and Paul Boutelle, Socialist Workers.
36,563	Eldridge Cleaver, Peace and Freedom, with various Vice-Presidential candidates.
25,552	Eugene J. McCarthy, under various titles and written-in, but without indication of Vice-Presidential candidates.
15,123	E. Harold Munn and Rolland E. Fisher, Prohibition.
1,519	Ventura Chavez and Adelicio Moya, People's Constitutional.
1,075	Charlene Mitchell and Michael Zagarell, Communist.
142	James Hensley and Roscoe B. MacKenna, Universal.
34	Richard K. Troxell and Merle Thayer, Constitution.
17	Kent M. Soeters and James P. Powers, Berkeley Defense Group.

In the vote listed above for Eldridge Cleaver, two states are included (California and Utah) in which only the party Vice-Presidential candidate appeared on the ballot.

In addition to these votes, 12,430 were cast for elector tickets for which there were no formal Presidential or Vice-Presidential candidates, and 11,192 scattered votes were reported from various states.

UNITED STATES

PRESIDENT 1968

State	Electoral Vote Rep.	Dem.	AIP	Total Vote	Republican	Democratic	AIP	Other	Plurality	Percentage Total Vote Rep.	Dem.	AIP
Alabama			10	1,049,922	146,923	196,579	691,425	14,995	494,846 A	14.0%	18.7%	65.9%
Alaska	3			83,035	37,600	35,411	10,024		2,189 R	45.3%	42.6%	12.1%
Arizona	5			486,936	266,721	170,514	46,573	3,128	96,207 R	54.8%	35.0%	9.6%
Arkansas			6	619,969	190,759	188,228	240,982		50,223 A	30.8%	30.4%	38.9%
California	40			7,251,587	3,467,664	3,244,318	487,270	52,335	223,346 R	47.8%	44.7%	6.7%
Colorado	6			811,199	409,345	335,174	60,813	5,867	74,171 R	50.5%	41.3%	7.5%
Connecticut		8		1,256,232	556,721	621,561	76,650	1,300	64,840 D	44.3%	49.5%	6.1%
Delaware	3			214,367	96,714	89,194	28,459		7,520 R	45.1%	41.6%	13.3%
Florida	14			2,187,805	886,804	676,794	624,207		210,010 R	40.5%	30.9%	28.5%
Georgia			12	1,250,266	380,111	334,440	535,550	165	155,439 A	30.4%	26.7%	42.8%
Hawaii		4		236,218	91,425	141,324	3,469		49,899 D	38.7%	59.8%	1.5%
Idaho	4			291,183	165,369	89,273	36,541		76,096 R	56.8%	30.7%	12.5%
Illinois	26			4,619,749	2,174,774	2,039,814	390,958	14,203	134,960 R	47.1%	44.2%	8.5%
Indiana	13			2,123,597	1,067,885	806,659	243,108	5,945	261,226 R	50.3%	38.0%	11.4%
Iowa	9			1,167,931	619,106	476,699	66,422	5,704	142,407 R	53.0%	40.8%	5.7%
Kansas	7			872,783	478,674	302,996	88,921	2,192	175,678 R	54.8%	34.7%	10.2%
Kentucky	9			1,055,893	462,411	397,541	193,098	2,843	64,870 R	43.8%	37.6%	18.3%
Louisiana			10	1,097,450	257,535	309,615	530,300		220,685 A	23.5%	28.2%	48.3%
Maine		4		392,936	169,254	217,312	6,370		48,058 D	43.1%	55.3%	1.6%
Maryland		10		1,235,039	517,995	538,310	178,734		20,315 D	41.9%	43.6%	14.5%
Massachusetts		14		2,331,752	766,844	1,469,218	87,088	8,602	702,374 D	32.9%	63.0%	3.7%
Michigan		21		3,306,250	1,370,665	1,593,082	331,968	10,535	222,417 D	41.5%	48.2%	10.0%
Minnesota		10		1,588,506	658,643	857,738	68,931	3,194	199,095 D	41.5%	54.0%	4.3%
Mississippi			7	654,509	88,516	150,644	415,349		264,705 A	13.5%	23.0%	63.5%
Missouri	12			1,809,502	811,932	791,444	206,126		20,488 R	44.9%	43.7%	11.4%
Montana	4			274,404	138,835	114,117	20,015	1,437	24,718 R	50.6%	41.6%	7.3%
Nebraska	5			536,851	321,163	170,784	44,904		150,379 R	59.8%	31.8%	8.4%
Nevada	3			154,218	73,188	60,598	20,432		12,590 R	47.5%	39.3%	13.2%
New Hampshire	4			297,298	154,903	130,589	11,173	633	24,314 R	52.1%	43.9%	3.8%
New Jersey	17			2,875,395	1,325,467	1,264,206	262,187	23,535	61,261 R	46.1%	44.0%	9.1%
New Mexico	4			327,350	169,692	130,081	25,737	1,840	39,611 R	51.8%	39.7%	7.9%
New York		43		6,791,688	3,007,932	3,378,470	358,864	46,422	370,538 D	44.3%	49.7%	5.3%
North Carolina	12		1	1,587,493	627,192	464,113	496,188		131,004 R	39.5%	29.2%	31.3%
North Dakota	4			247,882	138,669	94,769	14,244	200	43,900 R	55.9%	38.2%	5.7%
Ohio	26			3,959,698	1,791,014	1,700,586	467,495	603	90,428 R	45.2%	42.9%	11.8%
Oklahoma	8			943,086	449,697	301,658	191,731		148,039 R	47.7%	32.0%	20.3%
Oregon	6			819,622	408,433	358,866	49,683	2,640	49,567 R	49.8%	43.8%	6.1%
Pennsylvania		29		4,747,928	2,090,017	2,259,405	378,582	19,924	169,388 D	44.0%	47.6%	8.0%
Rhode Island		4		385,000	122,359	246,518	15,678	445	124,159 D	31.8%	64.0%	4.1%
South Carolina	8			666,978	254,062	197,486	215,430		38,632 R	38.1%	29.6%	32.3%
South Dakota	4			281,264	149,841	118,023	13,400		31,818 R	53.3%	42.0%	4.8%
Tennessee	11			1,248,617	472,592	351,233	424,792		47,800 R	37.8%	28.1%	34.0%
Texas		25		3,079,216	1,227,844	1,266,804	584,269	299	38,960 D	39.9%	41.1%	19.0%
Utah	4			422,568	238,728	156,665	26,906	269	82,063 R	56.5%	37.1%	6.4%
Vermont	3			161,404	85,142	70,255	5,104	903	14,887 R	52.8%	43.5%	3.2%
Virginia	12			1,361,491	590,319	442,387	321,833	6,952	147,932 R	43.4%	32.5%	23.6%
Washington		9		1,304,281	588,510	616,037	96,990	2,744	27,527 D	45.1%	47.2%	7.4%
West Virginia		7		754,206	307,555	374,091	72,560		66,536 D	40.8%	49.6%	9.6%
Wisconsin	12			1,691,538	809,997	748,804	127,835	4,902	61,193 R	47.9%	44.3%	7.6%
Wyoming	3			127,205	70,927	45,173	11,105		25,754 R	55.8%	35.5%	8.7%
Dist. of Col.		3		170,578	31,012	139,566			108,554 D	18.2%	81.8%	
United States	301	191	46	73,211,875	31,785,480	31,275,166	9,906,473	244,756	510,314 R	43.4%	42.7%	13.5%

PRESIDENT 1972

In Virginia one Republican elector voted in the Electoral College for the Libertarian candidates for President and Vice-President.

In New York the Republican figures include Conservative votes and the Democratic figures include Liberal votes. In Alabama the Democratic figures include votes cast on the National Democratic Party of Alabama ticket, and in South Carolina include United Citizens Party votes.

In certain states candidates appeared on the ballot under party names other than those used below; for the Socialist Workers party the votes listed for Jenness and Pulley were actually cast for substitute candidates (Reed and DeBerry) or without named candidates in several states.

The Democratic Vice-Presidential candidate originally was Senator Thomas F. Eagleton; on his withdrawal shortly after the party convention, R. Sargent Shriver was named by the Democratic National Committee as candidate.

The full list of candidates for President and Vice-President was:

47,169,911	Richard M. Nixon and Spiro T. Agnew, Republican.
29,170,383	George S. McGovern and R. Sargent Shriver, Democratic.
1,099,482	John G. Schmitz and Thomas J. Anderson, American.
78,756	Benjamin Spock and Julius Hobson, People's.
66,677	Linda Jenness and Andrew Pulley, Socialist Workers.
53,814	Louis Fisher and Genevieve Gunderson, Socialist Labor.
25,595	Gus Hall and Jarvis Tyner, Communist.
13,505	E. Harold Munn and Marshall E. Uncapher, Prohibition.
3,673	John Hospers and Theodora Nathan, Libertarian.
1,743	John V. Mahalchik and Irving Homer, America First.
220	Gabriel Green and Daniel Fry, Universal.

In addition to the above, 34,795 scattered votes were reported from various states.

Vice-President Agnew resigned in October 1973 and Representative Gerald R. Ford of Michigan was nominated by President Nixon to fill the vacancy. In November (Senate) and December (House of Representatives) this action was approved by Congress.

In August 1974 President Nixon resigned and was succeeded by Vice-President Ford. In the same month Nelson A. Rockefeller, former Governor of New York, was nominated to be Vice-President and was confirmed by Congress in December 1974.

UNITED STATES

PRESIDENT 1972

State	Electoral Vote Rep.	Dem.	Other	Total Vote	Republican	Democratic	Other	Plurality	Total Vote Rep.	Dem.	Major Vote Rep.	Dem.
Alabama	9			1,006,111	728,701	256,923	20,487	471,778 R	72.4%	25.5%	73.9%	26.1%
Alaska	3			95,219	55,349	32,967	6,903	22,382 R	58.1%	34.6%	62.7%	37.3%
Arizona	6			622,926	402,812	198,540	21,574	204,272 R	64.7%	31.9%	67.0%	33.0%
Arkansas	6			651,320	448,541	199,892	2,887	248,649 R	68.9%	30.7%	69.2%	30.8%
California	45			8,367,862	4,602,096	3,475,847	289,919	1,126,249 R	55.0%	41.5%	57.0%	43.0%
Colorado	7			953,884	597,189	329,980	26,715	267,209 R	62.6%	34.6%	64.4%	35.6%
Connecticut	8			1,384,277	810,763	555,498	18,016	255,265 R	58.6%	40.1%	59.3%	40.7%
Delaware	3			235,516	140,357	92,283	2,876	48,074 R	59.6%	39.2%	60.3%	39.7%
Florida	17			2,583,283	1,857,759	718,117	7,407	1,139,642 R	71.9%	27.8%	72.1%	27.9%
Georgia	12			1,174,772	881,496	289,529	3,747	591,967 R	75.0%	24.6%	75.3%	24.7%
Hawaii	4			270,274	168,865	101,409		67,456 R	62.5%	37.5%	62.5%	37.5%
Idaho	4			310,379	199,384	80,826	30,169	118,558 R	64.2%	26.0%	71.2%	28.8%
Illinois	26			4,723,236	2,788,179	1,913,472	21,585	874,707 R	59.0%	40.5%	59.3%	40.7%
Indiana	13			2,125,529	1,405,154	708,568	11,807	696,586 R	66.1%	33.3%	66.5%	33.5%
Iowa	8			1,225,944	706,207	496,206	23,531	210,001 R	57.6%	40.5%	58.7%	41.3%
Kansas	7			916,095	619,812	270,287	25,996	349,525 R	67.7%	29.5%	69.6%	30.4%
Kentucky	9			1,067,499	676,446	371,159	19,894	305,287 R	63.4%	34.8%	64.6%	35.4%
Louisiana	10			1,051,491	686,852	298,142	66,497	388,710 R	65.3%	28.4%	69.7%	30.3%
Maine	4			417,042	256,458	160,584		95,874 R	61.5%	38.5%	61.5%	38.5%
Maryland	10			1,353,812	829,305	505,781	18,726	323,524 R	61.3%	37.4%	62.1%	37.9%
Massachusetts		14		2,458,756	1,112,078	1,332,540	14,138	220,462 D	45.2%	54.2%	45.5%	54.5%
Michigan	21			3,489,727	1,961,721	1,459,435	68,571	502,286 R	56.2%	41.8%	57.3%	42.7%
Minnesota	10			1,741,652	898,269	802,346	41,037	95,923 R	51.6%	46.1%	52.8%	47.2%
Mississippi	7			645,963	505,125	126,782	14,056	378,343 R	78.2%	19.6%	79.9%	20.1%
Missouri	12			1,855,803	1,153,852	697,147	4,804	456,705 R	62.2%	37.6%	62.3%	37.7%
Montana	4			317,603	183,976	120,197	13,430	63,779 R	57.9%	37.8%	60.5%	39.5%
Nebraska	5			576,289	406,298	169,991		236,307 R	70.5%	29.5%	70.5%	29.5%
Nevada	3			181,766	115,750	66,016		49,734 R	63.7%	36.3%	63.7%	36.3%
New Hampshire	4			334,055	213,724	116,435	3,896	97,289 R	64.0%	34.9%	64.7%	35.3%
New Jersey	17			2,997,229	1,845,502	1,102,211	49,516	743,291 R	61.6%	36.8%	62.6%	37.4%
New Mexico	4			386,241	235,606	141,084	9,551	94,522 R	61.0%	36.5%	62.5%	37.5%
New York	41			7,165,919	4,192,778	2,951,084	22,057	1,241,694 R	58.5%	41.2%	58.7%	41.3%
North Carolina	13			1,518,612	1,054,889	438,705	25,018	616,184 R	69.5%	28.9%	70.6%	29.4%
North Dakota	3			280,514	174,109	100,384	6,021	73,725 R	62.1%	35.8%	63.4%	36.6%
Ohio	25			4,094,787	2,441,827	1,558,889	94,071	882,938 R	59.6%	38.1%	61.0%	39.0%
Oklahoma	8			1,029,900	759,025	247,147	23,728	511,878 R	73.7%	24.0%	75.4%	24.6%
Oregon	6			927,946	486,686	392,760	48,500	93,926 R	52.4%	42.3%	55.3%	44.7%
Pennsylvania	27			4,592,106	2,714,521	1,796,951	80,634	917,570 R	59.1%	39.1%	60.2%	39.8%
Rhode Island	4			415,808	220,383	194,645	780	25,738 R	53.0%	46.8%	53.1%	46.9%
South Carolina	8			673,960	477,044	186,824	10,092	290,220 R	70.8%	27.7%	71.9%	28.1%
South Dakota	4			307,415	166,476	139,945	994	26,531 R	54.2%	45.5%	54.3%	45.7%
Tennessee	10			1,201,182	813,147	357,293	30,742	455,854 R	67.7%	29.7%	69.5%	30.5%
Texas	26			3,471,281	2,298,896	1,154,289	18,096	1,144,607 R	66.2%	33.3%	66.6%	33.4%
Utah	4			478,476	323,643	126,284	28,549	197,359 R	67.6%	26.4%	71.9%	28.1%
Vermont	3			186,947	117,149	68,174	1,624	48,975 R	62.7%	36.5%	63.2%	36.8%
Virginia	11		1	1,457,019	988,493	438,887	29,639	549,606 R	67.8%	30.1%	69.3%	30.7%
Washington	9			1,470,847	837,135	568,334	65,378	268,801 R	56.9%	38.6%	59.6%	40.4%
West Virginia	6			762,399	484,964	277,435		207,529 R	63.6%	36.4%	63.6%	36.4%
Wisconsin	11			1,852,890	989,430	810,174	53,286	179,256 R	53.4%	43.7%	55.0%	45.0%
Wyoming	3			145,570	100,464	44,358	748	56,106 R	69.0%	30.5%	69.4%	30.6%
Dist. of Col.		3		163,421	35,226	127,627	568	92,401 D	21.6%	78.1%	21.6%	78.4%
United States	520	17	1	77,718,554	47,169,911	29,170,383	1,378,260	17,999,528 R	60.7%	37.5%	61.8%	38.2%

PRESIDENT 1976

In Washington, one Republican elector voted in the Electoral College for Ronald Reagan for President and Robert Dole for Vice-President.

In New York the Republican figures include Conservative votes and the Democratic figures include Liberal votes; in Vermont the Democratic figures include votes cast on the Independent Vermonters party ticket.

In a number of states candidates appeared on the ballot with variants of the party designations listed below and in several cases with entirely different party names.

The ballot designations for electors for Eugene J. McCarthy for President varied from state to state, as did the names of Vice-Presidential candidates running with him. In New Jersey, the Maddox Vice-Presidential candidate was Edmund O. Matzal.

The full list of candidates for President and Vice-President was:

40,830,763	Jimmy Carter and Walter F. Mondale, Democratic.
39,147,793	Gerald R. Ford and Robert Dole, Republican.
756,691	Eugene J. McCarthy with various Vice-Presidential candidates, Independent.
173,011	Roger L. MacBride and David D. Bergland, Libertarian.
170,531	Lester G. Maddox and William D. Dyke, American Independent.
160,773	Thomas J. Anderson and Rufus Shackelford, American.
91,314	Peter Camejo and Willie Mae Reid, Socialist Workers.
58,992	Gus Hall and Jarvis Tyner, Communist.
49,024	Margaret Wright and Benjamin Spock, People's.
40,043	Lyndon LaRouche and R. W. Evans, United States Labor.
15,934	Benjamin C. Bubar and Earl F. Dodge, Prohibition.
9,616	Julius Levin and Constance Blomen, Socialist Labor.
6,038	Frank P. Zeidler and J. Q. Brisben, Socialist.
361	Ernest L. Miller and Roy N. Eddy, Restoration.
36	Frank Taylor and Henry Swan, United American.

In addition to these votes, 39,861 scattered write-in votes were reported from various states and 5,108 votes were cast for "None of these Candidates" in Nevada.

UNITED STATES

PRESIDENT 1976

State	Electoral Vote Rep.	Dem.	Other	Total Vote	Republican	Democratic	Other	Plurality	Total Vote Rep.	Dem.	Major Vote Rep.	Dem.
Alabama		9		1,182,850	504,070	659,170	19,610	155,100 D	42.6%	55.7%	43.3%	56.7%
Alaska	3			123,574	71,555	44,058	7,961	27,497 R	57.9%	35.7%	61.9%	38.1%
Arizona	6			742,719	418,642	295,602	28,475	123,040 R	56.4%	39.8%	58.6%	41.4%
Arkansas		6		767,535	267,903	498,604	1,028	230,701 D	34.9%	65.0%	35.0%	65.0%
California	45			7,867,117	3,882,244	3,742,284	242,589	139,960 R	49.3%	47.6%	50.9%	49.1%
Colorado	7			1,081,554	584,367	460,353	36,834	124,014 R	54.0%	42.6%	55.9%	44.1%
Connecticut	8			1,381,526	719,261	647,895	14,370	71,366 R	52.1%	46.9%	52.6%	47.4%
Delaware		3		235,834	109,831	122,596	3,407	12,765 D	46.6%	52.0%	47.3%	52.7%
Florida		17		3,150,631	1,469,531	1,636,000	45,100	166,469 D	46.6%	51.9%	47.3%	52.7%
Georgia		12		1,467,458	483,743	979,409	4,306	495,666 D	33.0%	66.7%	33.1%	66.9%
Hawaii		4		291,301	140,003	147,375	3,923	7,372 D	48.1%	50.6%	48.7%	51.3%
Idaho	4			344,071	204,151	126,549	13,371	77,602 R	59.3%	36.8%	61.7%	38.3%
Illinois	26			4,718,914	2,364,269	2,271,295	83,350	92,974 R	50.1%	48.1%	51.0%	49.0%
Indiana	13			2,220,362	1,183,958	1,014,714	21,690	169,244 R	53.3%	45.7%	53.8%	46.2%
Iowa	8			1,279,306	632,863	619,931	26,512	12,932 R	49.5%	48.5%	50.5%	49.5%
Kansas	7			957,845	502,752	430,421	24,672	72,331 R	52.5%	44.9%	53.9%	46.1%
Kentucky		9		1,167,142	531,852	615,717	19,573	83,865 D	45.6%	52.8%	46.3%	53.7%
Louisiana		10		1,278,439	587,446	661,365	29,628	73,919 D	46.0%	51.7%	47.0%	53.0%
Maine	4			483,216	236,320	232,279	14,617	4,041 R	48.9%	48.1%	50.4%	49.6%
Maryland		10		1,439,897	672,661	759,612	7,624	86,951 D	46.7%	52.8%	47.0%	53.0%
Massachusetts		14		2,547,558	1,030,276	1,429,475	87,807	399,199 D	40.4%	56.1%	41.9%	58.1%
Michigan	21			3,653,749	1,893,742	1,696,714	63,293	197,028 R	51.8%	46.4%	52.7%	47.3%
Minnesota		10		1,949,931	819,395	1,070,440	60,096	251,045 D	42.0%	54.9%	43.4%	56.6%
Mississippi		7		769,361	366,846	381,309	21,206	14,463 D	47.7%	49.6%	49.0%	51.0%
Missouri		12		1,953,600	927,443	998,387	27,770	70,944 D	47.5%	51.1%	48.2%	51.8%
Montana	4			328,734	173,703	149,259	5,772	24,444 R	52.8%	45.4%	53.8%	46.2%
Nebraska	5			607,668	359,705	233,692	14,271	126,013 R	59.2%	38.5%	60.6%	39.4%
Nevada	3			201,876	101,273	92,479	8,124	8,794 R	50.2%	45.8%	52.3%	47.7%
New Hampshire	4			339,618	185,935	147,635	6,048	38,300 R	54.7%	43.5%	55.7%	44.3%
New Jersey	17			3,014,472	1,509,688	1,444,653	60,131	65,035 R	50.1%	47.9%	51.1%	48.9%
New Mexico	4			418,409	211,419	201,148	5,842	10,271 R	50.5%	48.1%	51.2%	48.8%
New York		41		6,534,170	3,100,791	3,389,558	43,821	288,767 D	47.5%	51.9%	47.8%	52.2%
North Carolina		13		1,678,914	741,960	927,365	9,589	185,405 D	44.2%	55.2%	44.4%	55.6%
North Dakota	3			297,188	153,470	136,078	7,640	17,392 R	51.6%	45.8%	53.0%	47.0%
Ohio		25		4,111,873	2,000,505	2,011,621	99,747	11,116 D	48.7%	48.9%	49.9%	50.1%
Oklahoma	8			1,092,251	545,708	532,442	14,101	13,266 R	50.0%	48.7%	50.6%	49.4%
Oregon	6			1,029,876	492,120	490,407	47,349	1,713 R	47.8%	47.6%	50.1%	49.9%
Pennsylvania		27		4,620,787	2,205,604	2,328,677	86,506	123,073 D	47.7%	50.4%	48.6%	51.4%
Rhode Island		4		411,170	181,249	227,636	2,285	46,387 D	44.1%	55.4%	44.3%	55.7%
South Carolina		8		802,583	346,149	450,807	5,627	104,658 D	43.1%	56.2%	43.4%	56.6%
South Dakota	4			300,678	151,505	147,068	2,105	4,437 R	50.4%	48.9%	50.7%	49.3%
Tennessee		10		1,476,345	633,969	825,879	16,497	191,910 D	42.9%	55.9%	43.4%	56.6%
Texas		26		4,071,884	1,953,300	2,082,319	36,265	129,019 D	48.0%	51.1%	48.4%	51.6%
Utah	4			541,198	337,908	182,110	21,180	155,798 R	62.4%	33.6%	65.0%	35.0%
Vermont	3			187,765	102,085	80,954	4,726	21,131 R	54.4%	43.1%	55.8%	44.2%
Virginia	12			1,697,094	836,554	813,896	46,644	22,658 R	49.3%	48.0%	50.7%	49.3%
Washington	8		1	1,555,534	777,732	717,323	60,479	60,409 R	50.0%	46.1%	52.0%	48.0%
West Virginia		6		750,964	314,760	435,914	290	121,154 D	41.9%	58.0%	41.9%	58.1%
Wisconsin		11		2,104,175	1,004,987	1,040,232	58,956	35,245 D	47.8%	49.4%	49.1%	50.9%
Wyoming	3			156,343	92,717	62,239	1,387	30,478 R	59.3%	39.8%	59.8%	40.2%
Dist. of Col.		3		168,830	27,873	137,818	3,139	109,945 D	16.5%	81.6%	16.8%	83.2%
United States	240	297	1	81,555,889	39,147,793	40,830,763	1,577,333	1,682,970 D	48.0%	50.1%	48.9%	51.1%

PRESIDENT 1980

In New York the Republican figures include Conservative votes and in a number of states candidates appeared on the ballot with variants of the party designations listed below, without any party designation, or with entirely different party names.

In several cases, Vice-Presidential nominees were different from those listed for most states and the Socialist Workers party nominee for President varied from state to state.

43,904,153	Ronald Reagan and George Bush, <u>Republican</u>.
35,483,883	Jimmy Carter and Walter F. Mondale, <u>Democratic</u>.
5,720,060	John B. Anderson and Patrick J. Lucey, <u>Independent</u>.
921,299	Edward E. Clark and David Koch, <u>Libertarian</u>.
234,294	Barry Commoner and LaDonna Harris, <u>Citizens</u>.
45,023	Gus Hall and Angela Davis, <u>Communist</u>.
41,268	John R. Rarick and Eileen M. Shearer, <u>American Independent</u>.
38,737	Clifton DeBerry and Matilde Zimmermann, <u>Socialist Workers</u>.
32,327	Ellen McCormack and Carroll Driscoll, <u>Right to Life</u>.
18,116	Maureen Smith and Elizabeth Barron, <u>Peace and Freedom</u>.
13,300	Deirdre Griswold and Larry Holmes, <u>Workers World</u>.
7,212	Benjamin C. Bubar and Earl F. Dodge, <u>Statesman</u>.
6,898	David McReynolds and Diane Drufenbrock, <u>Socialist</u>.
6,647	Percy L. Greaves and Frank L. Varnum, <u>American</u>.
6,272	Andrew Pulley and Matilde Zimmermann, <u>Socialist Workers</u>.
4,029	Richard Congress and Matilde Zimmermann, <u>Socialist Workers</u>.
3,694	Kurt Lynen and Harry Kieve, <u>Middle Class</u>.
1,718	Bill Gahres and J. F. Loughlin, <u>Down With Lawyers</u>.
1,555	Frank W. Shelton and George E. Jackson, <u>American</u>.
923	Martin E. Wendelken with no Vice-Presidential candidate, <u>Independent</u>.
296	Harley McLain and Jewelie Goeller, <u>Natural Peoples</u>.

In addition to these votes, 13,185 scattered write-in votes were reported from various states, 6,139 votes were cast in Minnesota for American party electors without designated national nominees, and 4,193 votes were cast for "None of these Candidates" in Nevada.

State-by-state vote details will be found in the individual state note sections and a supplementary state-by-state national table follows for all "other" candidates polling over 100,000 votes. An asterisk by the vote denotes write-in.

UNITED STATES

PRESIDENT 1980

State	Electoral Vote Rep.	Dem.	Other	Total Vote	Republican	Democratic	Other	Plurality	Percentage Total Vote Rep.	Dem.	Percentage Major Vote Rep.	Dem.
Alabama	9			1,341,929	654,192	636,730	51,007	17,462 R	48.8%	47.4%	50.7%	49.3%
Alaska	3			158,445	86,112	41,842	30,491	44,270 R	54.3%	26.4%	67.3%	32.7%
Arizona	6			873,945	529,688	246,843	97,414	282,845 R	60.6%	28.2%	68.2%	31.8%
Arkansas	6			837,582	403,164	398,041	36,377	5,123 R	48.1%	47.5%	50.3%	49.7%
California	45			8,587,063	4,524,858	3,083,661	978,544	1,441,197 R	52.7%	35.9%	59.5%	40.5%
Colorado	7			1,184,415	652,264	367,973	164,178	284,291 R	55.1%	31.1%	63.9%	36.1%
Connecticut	8			1,406,285	677,210	541,732	187,343	135,478 R	48.2%	38.5%	55.6%	44.4%
Delaware	3			235,900	111,252	105,754	18,894	5,498 R	47.2%	44.8%	51.3%	48.7%
Florida	17			3,686,930	2,046,951	1,419,475	220,504	627,476 R	55.5%	38.5%	59.1%	40.9%
Georgia		12		1,596,695	654,168	890,733	51,794	236,565 D	41.0%	55.8%	42.3%	57.7%
Hawaii		4		303,287	130,112	135,879	37,296	5,767 D	42.9%	44.8%	48.9%	51.1%
Idaho	4			437,431	290,699	110,192	36,540	180,507 R	66.5%	25.2%	72.5%	27.5%
Illinois	26			4,749,721	2,358,049	1,981,413	410,259	376,636 R	49.6%	41.7%	54.3%	45.7%
Indiana	13			2,242,033	1,255,656	844,197	142,180	411,459 R	56.0%	37.7%	59.8%	40.2%
Iowa	8			1,317,661	676,026	508,672	132,963	167,354 R	51.3%	38.6%	57.1%	42.9%
Kansas	7			979,795	566,812	326,150	86,833	240,662 R	57.9%	33.3%	63.5%	36.5%
Kentucky	9			1,294,627	635,274	616,417	42,936	18,857 R	49.1%	47.6%	50.8%	49.2%
Louisiana	10			1,548,591	792,853	708,453	47,285	84,400 R	51.2%	45.7%	52.8%	47.2%
Maine	4			523,011	238,522	220,974	63,515	17,548 R	45.6%	42.3%	51.9%	48.1%
Maryland		10		1,540,496	680,606	726,161	133,729	45,555 D	44.2%	47.1%	48.4%	51.6%
Massachusetts	14			2,524,298	1,057,631	1,053,802	412,865	3,829 R	41.9%	41.7%	50.1%	49.9%
Michigan	21			3,909,725	1,915,225	1,661,532	332,968	253,693 R	49.0%	42.5%	53.5%	46.5%
Minnesota		10		2,051,980	873,268	954,174	224,538	80,906 D	42.6%	46.5%	47.8%	52.2%
Mississippi	7			892,620	441,089	429,281	22,250	11,808 R	49.4%	48.1%	50.7%	49.3%
Missouri	12			2,099,824	1,074,181	931,182	94,461	142,999 R	51.2%	44.3%	53.6%	46.4%
Montana	4			363,952	206,814	118,032	39,106	88,782 R	56.8%	32.4%	63.7%	36.3%
Nebraska	5			640,854	419,937	166,851	54,066	253,086 R	65.5%	26.0%	71.6%	28.4%
Nevada	3			247,885	155,017	66,666	26,202	88,351 R	62.5%	26.9%	69.9%	30.1%
New Hampshire	4			383,990	221,705	108,864	53,421	112,841 R	57.7%	28.4%	67.1%	32.9%
New Jersey	17			2,975,684	1,546,557	1,147,364	281,763	399,193 R	52.0%	38.6%	57.4%	42.6%
New Mexico	4			456,971	250,779	167,826	38,366	82,953 R	54.9%	36.7%	59.9%	40.1%
New York	41			6,201,959	2,893,831	2,728,372	579,756	165,459 R	46.7%	44.0%	51.5%	48.5%
North Carolina	13			1,855,833	915,018	875,635	65,180	39,383 R	49.3%	47.2%	51.1%	48.9%
North Dakota	3			301,545	193,695	79,189	28,661	114,506 R	64.2%	26.3%	71.0%	29.0%
Ohio	25			4,283,603	2,206,545	1,752,414	324,644	454,131 R	51.5%	40.9%	55.7%	44.3%
Oklahoma	8			1,149,708	695,570	402,026	52,112	293,544 R	60.5%	35.0%	63.4%	36.6%
Oregon	6			1,181,516	571,044	456,890	153,582	114,154 R	48.3%	38.7%	55.6%	44.4%
Pennsylvania	27			4,561,501	2,261,872	1,937,540	362,089	324,332 R	49.6%	42.5%	53.9%	46.1%
Rhode Island		4		416,072	154,793	198,342	62,937	43,549 D	37.2%	47.7%	43.8%	56.2%
South Carolina	8			894,071	441,841	430,385	21,845	11,456 R	49.4%	48.1%	50.7%	49.3%
South Dakota	4			327,703	198,343	103,855	25,505	94,488 R	60.5%	31.7%	65.6%	34.4%
Tennessee	10			1,617,616	787,761	783,051	46,804	4,710 R	48.7%	48.4%	50.1%	49.9%
Texas	26			4,541,636	2,510,705	1,881,147	149,784	629,558 R	55.3%	41.4%	57.2%	42.8%
Utah	4			604,222	439,687	124,266	40,269	315,421 R	72.8%	20.6%	78.0%	22.0%
Vermont	3			213,299	94,628	81,952	36,719	12,676 R	44.4%	38.4%	53.6%	46.4%
Virginia	12			1,866,032	989,609	752,174	124,249	237,435 R	53.0%	40.3%	56.8%	43.2%
Washington	9			1,742,394	865,244	650,193	226,957	215,051 R	49.7%	37.3%	57.1%	42.9%
West Virginia		6		737,715	334,206	367,462	36,047	33,256 D	45.3%	49.8%	47.6%	52.4%
Wisconsin	11			2,273,221	1,088,845	981,584	202,792	107,261 R	47.9%	43.2%	52.6%	47.4%
Wyoming	3			176,713	110,700	49,427	16,586	61,273 R	62.6%	28.0%	69.1%	30.9%
Dist. of Col.		3		175,237	23,545	131,113	20,579	107,568 D	13.4%	74.8%	15.2%	84.8%
United States	489	49	—	86,515,221	43,904,153	35,483,883	7,127,185	8,420,270 R	50.7%	41.0%	55.3%	44.7%

UNITED STATES

OTHER VOTE 1980

State	Total Other Vote	Independent	Libertarian	Citizens	All Other
Alabama	51,007	16,481	13,318	517	20,691
Alaska	30,491	11,155	18,479		857
Arizona	97,414	76,952	18,784	551*	1,127
Arkansas	36,377	22,468	8,970	2,345	2,594
California	978,544	739,833	148,434	61,063	29,214
Colorado	164,178	130,633	25,744	5,614	2,187
Connecticut	187,343	171,807	8,570	6,130	836
Delaware	18,894	16,288	1,974	103*	529
Florida	220,504	189,692	30,524		288
Georgia	51,794	36,055	15,627	104*	8
Hawaii	37,296	32,021	3,269	1,548	458
Idaho	36,540	27,058	8,425		1,057
Illinois	410,259	346,754	38,939	10,692	13,874
Indiana	142,180	111,639	19,627	4,852	6,062
Iowa	132,963	115,633	13,123	2,273	1,934
Kansas	86,833	68,231	14,470		4,132
Kentucky	42,936	31,127	5,531	1,304	4,974
Louisiana	47,285	26,345	8,240	1,584	11,116
Maine	63,515	53,327	5,119	4,394	675
Maryland	133,729	119,537	14,192		
Massachusetts	412,865	382,539	22,038	2,056*	6,232
Michigan	332,968	275,223	41,597	11,930	4,218
Minnesota	224,538	174,990	31,592	8,407	9,549
Mississippi	22,250	12,036	5,465		4,749
Missouri	94,461	77,920	14,422	573*	1,546
Montana	39,106	29,281	9,825		
Nebraska	54,066	44,993	9,073		
Nevada	26,202	17,651	4,358		4,193
New Hampshire	53,421	49,693	2,064	1,320	344
New Jersey	281,763	234,632	20,652	8,203	18,276
New Mexico	38,366	29,459	4,365	2,202	2,340
New York	579,756	467,801	52,648	23,186	36,121
North Carolina	65,180	52,800	9,677	2,287	416
North Dakota	28,661	23,640	3,743	429	849
Ohio	324,644	254,472	49,033	8,564	12,575
Oklahoma	52,112	38,284	13,828		
Oregon	153,582	112,389	25,838	13,642	1,713
Pennsylvania	362,089	292,921	33,263	10,430	25,475
Rhode Island	62,937	59,819	2,458	67*	593
South Carolina	21,845	14,153	5,139		2,553
South Dakota	25,505	21,431	3,824		250
Tennessee	46,804	35,991	7,116	1,112	2,585
Texas	149,784	111,613	37,643	453*	75
Utah	40,269	30,284	7,226	1,009	1,750
Vermont	36,719	31,761	1,900	2,316	742
Virginia	124,249	95,418	12,821	14,024	1,986
Washington	226,957	185,073	29,213	9,403	3,268
West Virginia	36,047	31,691	4,356		
Wisconsin	202,792	160,657	29,135	7,767	5,233
Wyoming	16,586	12,072	4,514		
Dist. of Col.	20,579	16,337	1,114	1,840	1,288
United States	7,127,185	5,720,060	921,299	234,294	251,532

*Write-in

1972 PRESIDENTIAL PRIMARIES

In 1972 twenty states and the District of Columbia held preferential primaries. California, South Dakota and the District of Columbia held slate-type preferential primaries. In the other eighteen states the voter marked his ballot for his preference among the candidates listed and in some states could write in his choice if the candidate he preferred was not on the ballot. In a few states the voter had an additional option for uncommitted or for none of the listed candidates. In Alabama and New York, delegates to the national party conventions were elected in primaries, but neither state provided for a specific expression of Presidential preference by the voter, nor printed on the ballot any indication of the Presidential preference of the candidates for convention delegates.

In each state the vote used is the preferential vote if there was such a vote. In Ohio, where no specific preference vote was authorized, the major candidates ran state-wide at-large blocks of delegate candidates, and the vote given is that for the highest vote winner in each of these blocks. In several states there were both a preference and a delegate vote. In such cases the preference vote is indicated here, even though the delegate contest was controlling in terms of individuals chosen to go to the party national conventions in Miami Beach.

The tables included here give the vote in each state for those candidates on the ballot in ten or more states. Other votes, for ballot candidates or written-in, are included in the general "Other" category.

Republican candidates on the ballot in at least one state were John M. Ashbrook, Paul N. McCloskey, Richard M. Nixon, Patrick Paulsen.

Democratic candidates on the ballot in at least one state were Shirley Chisholm, Edward T. Coll, Walter E. Fauntroy, R. Vance Hartke, Hubert H. Humphrey, Henry M. Jackson, Edward M. Kennedy, John V. Lindsay, Eugene J. McCarthy, George S. McGovern, Wilbur D. Mills, Patsy Mink, Edmund S. Muskie, Terry Sanford, George C. Wallace, Samuel W. Yorty.

CALIFORNIA JUNE 6

Republican   2,058,825 Nixon slate; 224,922 Ashbrook slate; 175 scattered.

Democratic   1,550,652 McGovern slate; 1,375,064 Humphrey slate; 268,551 Wallace (write-in); 157,435 Chisholm slate; 72,701 Muskie slate; 50,745 Yorty slate; 34,203 McCarthy slate; 28,901 Jackson slate; 26,246 Lindsay slate; 20 scattered.

FLORIDA MARCH 14

Republican   360,278 Nixon; 36,617 Ashbrook; 17,312 McCloskey.

Democratic   526,651 Wallace; 234,658 Humphrey; 170,156 Jackson; 112,523 Muskie; 82,386 Lindsay; 78,232 McGovern; 43,989 Chisholm; 5,847 McCarthy; 4,539 Mills; 3,009 Hartke; 2,564 Yorty.

ILLINOIS MARCH 21

Republican   No Presidential candidates on the ballot. Write-in votes were 32,550 Nixon; 170 Ashbrook; 47 McCloskey; 802 scattered.

Democratic   766,914 Muskie; 444,260 McCarthy; 7,017 Wallace (write-in); 3,687 McGovern (write-in); 1,476 Humphrey (write-in); 777 Chisholm (write-in); 442 Jackson (write-in); 242 Kennedy (write-in); 118 Lindsay (write-in); 211 scattered.

INDIANA MAY 2

Republican   417,069 Nixon, unopposed.

Democratic   354,244 Humphrey; 309,495 Wallace; 87,719 Muskie.

1972 PRESIDENTIAL PRIMARIES

MARYLAND MAY 16

Republican   99,308 Nixon; 9,223 McCloskey; 6,718 Ashbrook.

Democratic   219,687 Wallace; 151,981 Humphrey; 126,978 McGovern; 17,728 Jackson; 13,584 Yorty; 13,363 Muskie; 12,602 Chisholm; 4,776 Mills; 4,691 McCarthy; 2,168 Lindsay; 573 Mink.

MASSACHUSETTS APRIL 25

Republican   99,150 Nixon; 16,435 McCloskey; 4,864 Ashbrook; 1,690 scattered.

Democratic   325,673 McGovern; 131,709 Muskie; 48,929 Humphrey; 45,807 Wallace; 22,398 Chisholm; 19,441 Mills; 8,736 McCarthy; 8,499 Jackson; 2,348 Kennedy (write-in); 2,107 Lindsay; 874 Hartke; 646 Yorty; 589 Coll; 760 scattered.

MICHIGAN MAY 16

Republican   321,652 Nixon; 9,691 McCloskey; 5,370 Uncommitted; 30 scattered.

Democratic   809,239 Wallace; 425,694 McGovern; 249,798 Humphrey; 44,090 Chisholm; 38,701 Muskie; 10,700 Uncommitted; 6,938 Jackson; 2,862 Hartke; 51 scattered.

NEBRASKA MAY 9

Republican   179,464 Nixon; 9,011 McCloskey; 4,996 Ashbrook; 801 scattered.

Democratic   79,309 McGovern; 65,968 Humphrey; 23,912 Wallace; 6,886 Muskie; 5,276 Jackson; 3,459 Yorty; 3,194 McCarthy; 1,763 Chisholm; 1,244 Lindsay; 377 Mills; 293 Kennedy (write-in); 249 Hartke; 207 scattered.

NEW HAMPSHIRE MARCH 7

Republican   79,239 Nixon; 23,190 McCloskey; 11,362 Ashbrook; 1,211 Paulsen; 2,206 scattered.

Democratic   41,235 Muskie; 33,007 McGovern; 5,401 Yorty; 3,563 Mills (write-in); 2,417 Hartke; 954 Kennedy (write-in); 348 Humphrey (write-in); 280 Coll; 197 Jackson (write-in); 175 Wallace (write-in); 1,277 scattered.

NEW JERSEY JUNE 6

Republican   No Presidential candidates on the ballot.

Democratic   51,433 Chisholm; 25,401 Sanford.

NEW MEXICO JUNE 6

Republican   49,067 Nixon; 3,367 McCloskey; 3,035 None of the Names Shown.

Democratic   51,011 McGovern; 44,843 Wallace; 39,768 Humphrey; 6,411 Muskie; 4,236 Jackson; 3,819 None of the Names Shown; 3,205 Chisholm.

1972 PRESIDENTIAL PRIMARIES

NORTH CAROLINA MAY 6

Republican   159,167 Nixon; 8,732 McCloskey.

Democratic   413,518 Wallace; 306,014 Sanford; 61,723 Chisholm; 30,739 Muskie; 9,416 Jackson.

OHIO MAY 2

Republican   692,828 Nixon, unopposed.

Democratic   499,680 Humphrey; 480,320 McGovern; 107,806 Muskie; 98,498 Jackson; 26,026 McCarthy.

OREGON MAY 23

Republican   231,151 Nixon; 29,365 McCloskey; 16,696 Ashbrook; 4,798 scattered.

Democratic   205,328 McGovern; 81,868 Wallace; 51,163 Humphrey; 22,042 Jackson; 12,673 Kennedy; 10,244 Muskie; 8,943 McCarthy; 6,500 Mink; 5,082 Lindsay; 2,975 Chisholm; 1,208 Mills; 618 scattered.

PENNSYLVANIA APRIL 25

Republican   No Presidential candidates on the ballot. Write-in votes were 153,886 Nixon; 30,915 scattered. Of the latter, most were for candidates for the Democratic nomination, including 20,472 Wallace.

Democratic   481,900 Humphrey; 292,437 Wallace; 280,861 McGovern; 279,983 Muskie; 38,767 Jackson; 306 Chisholm (write-in); 585 scattered.

RHODE ISLAND MAY 23

Republican   4,953 Nixon; 337 McCloskey; 175 Ashbrook; 146 Uncommitted.

Democratic   15,603 McGovern; 7,838 Muskie; 7,701 Humphrey; 5,802 Wallace; 490 Uncommitted; 245 McCarthy; 138 Jackson; 41 Mills; 6 Yorty.

SOUTH DAKOTA JUNE 6

Republican   52,820 Nixon slate, unopposed.

Democratic   28,017 McGovern slate, unopposed.

TENNESSEE MAY 4

Republican   109,696 Nixon; 2,419 Ashbrook; 2,370 McCloskey; 4 scattered.

Democratic   335,858 Wallace; 78,350 Humphrey; 35,551 McGovern; 18,809 Chisholm; 9,634 Muskie; 5,896 Jackson; 2,543 Mills; 2,267 McCarthy; 1,621 Hartke; 1,476 Lindsay; 692 Yorty; 24 scattered.

WEST VIRGINIA MAY 9

Republican   No Presidential candidates on the ballot.

Democratic   246,596 Humphrey; 121,888 Wallace.

1972 PRESIDENTIAL PRIMARIES

WISCONSIN APRIL 4

Republican   277,601 Nixon; 3,651 McCloskey; 2,604 Ashbrook; 2,315 None of the Names Shown; 273 scattered.

Democratic   333,528 McGovern; 248,676 Wallace; 233,748 Humphrey; 115,811 Muskie; 88,068 Jackson; 75,579 Lindsay; 15,543 McCarthy; 9,198 Chisholm; 2,450 None of the Names Shown; 2,349 Yorty; 1,213 Mink; 913 Mills; 766 Hartke; 183 Kennedy (write-in); 559 scattered.

DISTRICT OF COLUMBIA MAY 2

Republican   No slates entered.

Democratic   21,217 Fauntroy slate; 8,343 Uncommitted slate.

1972 REPUBLICAN PREFERENCE PRIMARIES

Date		State	Total Vote	Ashbrook	McCloskey	Nixon	Other
March	7	New Hampshire	117,208	11,362	23,190	79,239	3,417
	14	Florida	414,207	36,617	17,312	360,278	—
	21	Illinois	33,569	170	47	32,550	802
April	4	Wisconsin	286,444	2,604	3,651	277,601	2,588
	25	Massachusetts	122,139	4,864	16,435	99,150	1,690
	25	Pennsylvania	184,801	—	—	153,886	30,915
May	2	District of Columbia	No Slates Entered				
	2	Indiana	417,069	—	—	417,069	—
	2	Ohio	692,828	—	—	692,828	—
	4	Tennessee	114,489	2,419	2,370	109,696	4
	6	North Carolina	167,899	—	8,732	159,167	—
	9	Nebraska	194,272	4,996	9,011	179,464	801
	9	West Virginia	No Candidates Entered				
	16	Maryland	115,249	6,718	9,223	99,308	—
	16	Michigan	336,743	—	9,691	321,652	5,400
	23	Rhode Island	5,611	175	337	4,953	146
	23	Oregon	282,010	16,696	29,365	231,151	4,798
June	6	California	2,283,922	224,922	—	2,058,825	175
	6	New Jersey	No Candidates Entered				
	6	New Mexico	55,469	—	3,367	49,067	3,035
	6	South Dakota	52,820	—	—	52,820	—
			5,876,749	311,543	132,731	5,378,704	53,771

Other vote includes 1,211 Paulsen; 52,559 Uncommitted, None, and scattered.

1972 DEMOCRATIC PREFERENCE PRIMARIES

Date		State	Total Vote	Chisholm	Humphrey	Jackson	McCarthy	McGovern	Muskie	Wallace	Other
March	7	New Hampshire	88,854	—	348	197	—	33,007	41,235	175	13,892
	14	Florida	1,264,554	43,989	234,658	170,156	5,847	78,232	112,523	526,651	92,498
	21	Illinois	1,225,144	777	1,476	442	444,260	3,687	766,914	7,017	571
April	4	Wisconsin	1,128,584	9,198	233,748	88,068	15,543	333,528	115,811	248,676	84,012
	25	Massachusetts	618,516	22,398	48,929	8,499	8,736	325,673	131,709	45,807	26,765
	25	Pennsylvania	1,374,839	306	481,900	38,767	—	280,861	279,983	292,437	585
May	2	District of Columbia	29,560	—	—	—	—	—	—	—	29,560
	2	Indiana	751,458	—	354,244	—	—	—	87,719	309,495	—
	2	Ohio	1,212,330	—	499,680	98,498	26,026	480,320	107,806	—	—
	4	Tennessee	492,721	18,809	78,350	5,896	2,267	35,551	9,634	335,858	6,356
	6	North Carolina	821,410	61,723	—	9,416	—	—	30,739	413,518	306,014
	9	Nebraska	192,137	1,763	65,968	5,276	3,194	79,309	6,886	23,912	5,829
	9	West Virginia	368,484	—	246,596	—	—	—	—	121,888	—
	16	Maryland	568,131	12,602	151,981	17,728	4,691	126,978	13,363	219,687	21,101
	16	Michigan	1,588,073	44,090	249,798	6,938	—	425,694	38,701	809,239	13,613
	23	Rhode Island	37,864	—	7,701	138	245	15,603	7,838	5,802	537
	23	Oregon	408,644	2,975	51,163	22,042	8,943	205,328	10,244	81,868	26,081
June	6	California	3,564,518	157,435	1,375,064	28,901	34,203	1,550,652	72,701	268,551	77,011
	6	New Jersey	76,834	51,433	—	—	—	—	—	—	25,401
	6	New Mexico	153,293	3,205	39,768	4,236	—	51,011	6,411	44,843	3,819
	6	South Dakota	28,017	—	—	—	—	28,017	—	—	—
			15,993,965	430,703	4,121,372	505,198	553,955	4,053,451	1,840,217	3,755,424	733,645

Other vote includes 331,415 Sanford; 196,406 Lindsay; 79,446 Yorty; 37,401 Mills; 21,217 Fauntroy; 16,693 Kennedy; 11,798 Hartke; 8,286 Mink; 869 Coll; 30,114 Uncommitted, None, and scattered.

1976 PRESIDENTIAL PRIMARIES

In 1976 twenty-six states and the District of Columbia held preferential primaries. California and South Dakota held slate-type preferential primaries. In the District and the other twenty-four states the voter marked his ballot for his preference among the candidates listed and in some states could write in his choice if the candidate he preferred was not on the ballot. In a few states the voter had an additional option for uncommitted, no preference or none. In Alabama, New York and Texas delegates to the national party conventions were elected in primaries, but none of these states provided for a specific expression of Presidential preference by the voter save by an indication of the Presidential preference of the candidates for convention delegates.

In each state the vote used is the preferential vote if there was such a vote. In Ohio, the vote is for delegates at-large pledged to specific candidates and elected as a group. In several states there were both a preference and a delegate vote. In such cases the preference vote is indicated here, even though the delegate contest was controlling in terms of individuals chosen to go to the party national conventions in Kansas City and New York City.

The tables included here give the major party primary vote in each state for those candidates who were on the ballot in at least ten states or who polled a minimum of one percent of their party's total national Presidential preference vote.

Republican candidates on the ballot in at least one state were Lar Daly, Gerald R. Ford, Tommy Klein and Ronald Reagan.

Democratic candidates on the ballot in at least one state were Frank Ahern, Stanley N. Arnold, Birch Bayh, Lloyd Bentsen, Arthur O. Blessitt, Frank Bona, Edmund G. Brown, Jr., Robert C. Byrd, Jimmy Carter, Frank Church, Billy Joe Clegg, Gertrude W. Donahey, Abram Eisenman, John S. Gonas, Jesse Gray, Fred R. Harris, Hubert H. Humphrey, Henry M. Jackson, Robert L. Kelleher, Edward M. Kennedy, Rick Loewenherz, Frank Lomento, Floyd L. Lunger, Ellen McCormack, Fifi Rockefeller, George Roden, Ray Rollinson, Terry Sanford, Bernard B. Schechter, Milton Shapp, R. Sargent Shriver, Morris K. Udall and George C. Wallace.

ARKANSAS MAY 25

Republican   20,628 Reagan; 11,430 Ford; 483 Uncommitted.

Democratic   314,306 Carter; 83,005 Wallace; 57,152 Uncommitted; 37,783 Udall; 9,554 Jackson. Original uncorrected canvass gave the Uncommitted vote as 57,067.

CALIFORNIA JUNE 8

Republican   1,604,836 Reagan; 845,655 Ford; 20 scattered write-ins.

Democratic   2,013,210 Brown slate; 697,092 Carter slate; 250,581 Church slate; 171,501 Udall slate; 102,292 Wallace slate; 78,595 Uncommitted slate; 38,634 Jackson slate; 29,242 McCormack slate; 16,920 Harris slate; 11,419 Bayh slate; 215 scattered write-ins.

American Independent   3,447 Shea; 2,922 Rarick; 2,447 Watson; 1,719 Procell; 1,523 Goodloe; 7 scattered write-ins.

Peace & Freedom   4,351 Wright; 1,372 Zeidler; 12 scattered write-ins.

FLORIDA MARCH 9

Republican   321,982 Ford; 287,837 Reagan.

Democratic   448,844 Carter; 396,820 Wallace; 310,944 Jackson; 37,626 No Preference; 32,198 Shapp; 27,235 Udall; 8,750 Bayh; 7,889 Blessitt; 7,595 McCormack; 7,084 Shriver; 5,397 Harris; 5,042 Byrd; 4,906 Church.

1976 PRESIDENTIAL PRIMARIES

GEORGIA MAY 4

Republican   128,671 Reagan; 59,801 Ford.

Democratic   419,272 Carter; 57,594 Wallace; 9,755 Udall; 3,628 Byrd; 3,358 Jackson; 2,477 Church; 1,487 Ahern; 1,378 Shriver; 824 Bayh; 699 Harris; 635 McCormack; 351 Eisenman; 277 Bentsen; 263 Bona; 181 Shapp; 153 Roden; 139 Kelleher.

IDAHO MAY 25

Republican   66,743 Reagan; 22,323 Ford; 727 Uncommitted.

Democratic   58,570 Church; 8,818 Carter; 1,700 Humphrey; 1,453 Brown (write-in); 1,115 Wallace; 981 Udall; 964 Uncommitted; 485 Jackson; 319 Harris.

American   409 Rarick; 261 Anderson; 92 Uncommitted.

ILLINOIS MARCH 16

Republican   456,750 Ford; 311,295 Reagan; 7,582 Daly; 266 scattered write-ins.

Democratic   630,915 Carter; 361,798 Wallace; 214,024 Shriver; 98,862 Harris; 6,315 scattered write-ins.

INDIANA MAY 4

Republican   323,779 Reagan; 307,513 Ford.

Democratic   417,480 Carter; 93,121 Wallace; 72,080 Jackson; 31,708 McCormack.

KENTUCKY MAY 25

Republican   67,976 Ford; 62,683 Reagan; 1,781 Uncommitted; 1,088 Klein.

Democratic   181,690 Carter; 51,540 Wallace; 33,262 Udall; 17,061 McCormack; 11,962 Uncommitted; 8,186 Jackson; 2,305 Fifi Rockefeller.

MARYLAND MAY 18

Republican   96,291 Ford; 69,680 Reagan.

Democratic   286,672 Brown; 219,404 Carter; 32,790 Udall; 24,176 Wallace; 13,956 Jackson; 7,907 McCormack; 6,841 Harris.

MASSACHUSETTS MARCH 2

Republican   115,375 Ford; 63,555 Reagan; 6,000 No Preference; 3,519 scattered write-ins.

Democratic   164,393 Jackson; 130,440 Udall; 123,112 Wallace; 101,948 Carter; 55,701 Harris; 53,252 Shriver; 34,963 Bayh; 25,772 McCormack; 21,693 Shapp; 9,804 No Preference; 7,851 Humphrey (write-in); 1,623 Kennedy (write-in); 1,603 Kelleher; 364 Bentsen; 351 Sanford; 2,951 scattered write-ins.

American   No candidate names were printed on the ballot; there were 595 write-in votes including 86 for Wallace. In addition there were 98 No Preference votes.

1976 PRESIDENTIAL PRIMARIES

MICHIGAN MAY 18

Republican   690,180 Ford; 364,052 Reagan; 8,473 Uncommitted; 109 scattered write-ins.

Democratic   307,559 Carter; 305,134 Udall; 49,204 Wallace; 15,853 Uncommitted; 10,332 Jackson; 7,623 McCormack; 5,738 Shriver; 4,081 Harris; 3,142 scattered write-ins.

MONTANA JUNE 1

Republican   56,683 Reagan; 31,100 Ford; 1,996 No Preference.

Democratic   63,448 Church; 26,329 Carter; 6,708 Udall; 3,820 No Preference; 3,680 Wallace; 2,856 Jackson.

NEBRASKA MAY 11

Republican   113,493 Reagan; 94,542 Ford; 379 scattered write-ins.

Democratic   67,297 Church; 65,833 Carter; 12,685 Humphrey; 7,199 Kennedy; 6,033 McCormack; 5,567 Wallace; 4,688 Udall; 2,642 Jackson; 811 Harris; 407 Bayh; 384 Shriver; 1,467 scattered write-ins.

NEVADA MAY 25

Republican   31,637 Reagan; 13,747 Ford; 2,365 "None of these Candidates".

Democratic   39,671 Brown; 17,567 Carter; 6,778 Church; 4,603 "None of these Candidates"; 2,490 Wallace; 2,237 Udall; 1,896 Jackson.

NEW HAMPSHIRE FEBRUARY 24

Republican   55,156 Ford; 53,569 Reagan; 2,949 scattered write-ins.

Democratic   23,373 Carter; 18,710 Udall; 12,510 Bayh; 8,863 Harris; 6,743 Shriver; 4,596 Humphrey (write-in); 1,857 Jackson (write-in); 1,061 Wallace (write-in); 1,007 McCormack; 828 Blessitt; 371 Arnold; 174 Clegg; 173 Schechter; 135 Bona; 87 Kelleher; 53 Sanford; 49 Loewenherz; 1,791 scattered write-ins.

NEW JERSEY JUNE 8

Republican   242,122 Ford, unopposed.

Democratic   210,655 Carter; 49,034 Church; 31,820 Jackson; 31,183 Wallace; 21,774 McCormack; 3,935 Lunger; 3,574 Gray; 3,555 Lomento; 3,021 Rollinson; 2,288 Gonas.

NORTH CAROLINA MARCH 23

Republican   101,468 Reagan; 88,897 Ford; 3,362 No Preference.

Democratic   324,437 Carter; 210,166 Wallace; 25,749 Jackson; 22,850 No Preference; 14,032 Udall; 5,923 Harris; 1,675 Bentsen.

OHIO JUNE 8

Republican   516,111 Ford; 419,646 Reagan.

Democratic   593,130 Carter; 240,342 Udall; 157,884 Church; 63,953 Wallace; 43,661 Donahey; 35,404 Jackson.

1976 PRESIDENTIAL PRIMARIES

OREGON MAY 25

Republican   150,181 Ford; 136,691 Reagan; 11,663 scattered write-ins.

Democratic   145,394 Church; 115,310 Carter; 106,812 Brown (write-ins); 22,488 Humphrey; 11,747 Udall; 10,983 Kennedy; 5,797 Wallace; 5,298 Jackson; 3,753 McCormack; 1,344 Harris; 743 Bayh; 2,963 scattered write-ins.

PENNSYLVANIA APRIL 27

Republican   733,472 Ford; 40,510 Reagan (write-in); 22,678 scattered write-ins.

Democratic   511,905 Carter; 340,340 Jackson; 259,166 Udall; 155,902 Wallace; 38,800 McCormack; 32,947 Shapp; 15,320 Bayh; 13,067 Harris; 12,563 Humphrey (write-in); 5,032 scattered write-ins.

Constitutional 1,333 Cunningham; 87 scattered write-ins.

RHODE ISLAND JUNE 1

Republican   9,365 Ford; 4,480 Reagan; 507 Uncommitted.

Democratic   19,035 Uncommitted; 18,237 Carter; 16,423 Church; 2,543 Udall; 2,468 McCormack; 756 Jackson; 507 Wallace; 247 Bayh; 132 Shapp.

SOUTH DAKOTA JUNE 1

Republican   43,068 Reagan slate; 36,976 Ford slate; 4,033 No Preference slate.

Democratic   24,186 Carter slate; 19,510 Udall slate; 7,871 No Preference slate; 4,561 McCormack slate; 1,412 Wallace slate; 573 Harris slate; 558 Jackson slate.

TENNESSEE MAY 25

Republican   120,685 Ford; 118,997 Reagan; 2,756 Uncommitted; 97 scattered write-ins.

Democratic   259,243 Carter; 36,495 Wallace; 12,420 Udall; 8,026 Church; 6,148 Uncommitted; 5,672 Jackson; 1,782 McCormack; 1,628 Harris; 1,556 Brown (write-in); 507 Shapp; 109 Humphrey (write-in); 492 scattered write-ins, including all 424 write-ins in Shelby County.

VERMONT MARCH 2

Republican   27,014 Ford; 4,892 Reagan (write-in); 251 scattered.

Democratic   16,335 Carter; 10,699 Shriver; 4,893 Harris; 3,324 McCormack; 3,463 scattered.

Liberty
Union   965 Wright; 150 scattered.

WEST VIRGINIA MAY 11

Republican   88,386 Ford; 67,306 Reagan.

Democratic   331,639 Byrd; 40,938 Wallace.

1976 PRESIDENTIAL PRIMARIES

WISCONSIN APRIL 6

Republican   326,869 Ford; 262,126 Reagan; 2,234 "None of the Names Shown"; 583 scattered write-ins.

Democratic   271,220 Carter; 263,771 Udall; 92,460 Wallace; 47,605 Jackson; 26,982 McCormack; 8,185 Harris; 7,154 "None of the Names Shown"; 5,097 Shriver; 1,730 Bentsen; 1,255 Bayh; 596 Shapp; 14,473 scattered write-ins.

American   No candidate names were printed on the ballot; there were 1,033 write-in votes.

DISTRICT OF COLUMBIA MAY 4

Republican   No Presidential candidates on the ballot.

Democratic   10,521 Carter; 10,149 Uncommitted (Fauntroy slate); 6,999 Udall; 5,161 Uncommitted (Washington slate); 461 Harris.

1976 REPUBLICAN PREFERENCE PRIMARIES

Date		State	Total Vote	Ford	Reagan	Other
February	24	New Hampshire	111,674	55,156	53,569	2,949
March	2	Massachusetts	188,449	115,375	63,555	9,519
	2	Vermont	32,157	27,014	4,892	251
	9	Florida	609,819	321,982	287,837	—
	16	Illinois	775,893	456,750	311,295	7,848
	23	North Carolina	193,727	88,897	101,468	3,362
April	6	Wisconsin	591,812	326,869	262,126	2,817
	27	Pennsylvania	796,660	733,472	40,510	22,678
May	4	District of Columbia	No Primary			
	4	Georgia	188,472	59,801	128,671	—
	4	Indiana	631,292	307,513	323,779	—
	11	Nebraska	208,414	94,542	113,493	379
	11	West Virginia	155,692	88,386	67,306	—
	18	Maryland	165,971	96,291	69,680	—
	18	Michigan	1,062,814	690,180	364,052	8,582
	25	Arkansas	32,541	11,430	20,628	483
	25	Idaho	89,793	22,323	66,743	727
	25	Kentucky	133,528	67,976	62,683	2,869
	25	Nevada	47,749	13,747	31,637	2,365
	25	Oregon	298,535	150,181	136,691	11,663
	25	Tennessee	242,535	120,685	118,997	2,853
June	1	Montana	89,779	31,100	56,683	1,996
	1	Rhode Island	14,352	9,365	4,480	507
	1	South Dakota	84,077	36,976	43,068	4,033
	8	California	2,450,511	845,655	1,604,836	20
	8	New Jersey	242,122	242,122	—	—
	8	Ohio	935,757	516,111	419,646	—
			10,374,125	5,529,899	4,758,325	85,901

Other vote includes 7,582 Daly; 1,088 Klein; 42,514 scattered write-ins; 15,391 No Preference; 14,727 Uncommitted; 2,365 "None of These Candidates"; 2,234 "None of the Names Shown".

1976 DEMOCRATIC PREFERENCE PRIMARIES

Date	State	Total Vote	Bayh	Brown	Byrd	Carter	Church	Harris	Jackson	McCormack	Shriver	Udall	Wallace	Other
February 24	New Hampshire	82,381	12,510	—	—	23,373	—	8,863	1,857	1,007	6,743	18,710	1,061	8,257
March 2	Massachusetts	735,821	34,963	—	—	101,948	—	55,701	164,393	25,772	53,252	130,440	123,112	46,240
2	Vermont	38,714	—	—	—	16,335	—	4,893	—	3,324	10,699	—	—	3,463
9	Florida	1,300,330	8,750	—	5,042	448,844	4,906	5,397	310,944	7,595	7,084	27,235	396,820	77,713
16	Illinois	1,311,914	—	—	—	630,915	—	98,862	25,749	—	214,024	—	361,798	6,315
23	North Carolina	604,832	—	—	—	324,437	—	5,923	—	—	—	14,032	210,166	24,525
April 6	Wisconsin	740,528	1,255	—	—	271,220	—	8,185	47,605	26,982	5,097	263,771	92,460	23,953
27	Pennsylvania	1,385,042	15,320	—	—	511,905	—	13,067	340,340	38,800	—	259,166	155,902	50,542
May 4	District of Columbia	33,291	—	—	—	10,521	—	461	—	—	—	6,999	—	15,310
4	Georgia	502,471	824	—	3,628	419,272	2,477	699	3,358	635	1,378	9,755	57,594	2,851
4	Indiana	614,389	—	—	—	417,480	—	—	72,080	31,708	—	—	93,121	—
11	Nebraska	175,013	407	—	—	65,833	67,297	811	2,642	6,033	384	4,688	5,567	21,351
11	West Virginia	372,577	—	—	331,639	—	—	—	—	—	—	—	40,938	—
18	Maryland	591,746	—	286,672	—	219,404	—	6,841	13,956	7,907	—	32,790	24,176	—
18	Michigan	708,666	—	—	—	307,559	—	4,081	10,332	7,623	5,738	305,134	49,204	18,995
25	Arkansas	501,800	—	—	—	314,306	—	—	9,554	—	—	37,783	83,005	57,152
25	Idaho	74,405	—	1,453	—	8,818	58,570	319	485	—	—	981	1,115	2,664
25	Kentucky	306,006	—	—	—	181,690	—	—	8,186	17,061	—	33,262	51,540	14,267
25	Nevada	75,242	—	39,671	—	17,567	6,778	—	1,896	—	—	2,237	2,490	4,603
25	Oregon	432,632	743	106,812	—	115,310	145,394	1,344	5,298	3,753	—	11,747	5,797	36,434
25	Tennessee	334,078	—	1,556	—	259,243	8,026	1,628	5,672	1,782	—	12,420	36,495	7,256
June 1	Montana	106,841	—	—	—	26,329	63,448	—	2,856	—	—	6,708	3,680	3,820
1	Rhode Island	60,348	247	—	—	18,237	16,423	573	756	2,468	—	2,543	507	19,167
1	South Dakota	58,671	—	—	—	24,186	—	—	558	4,561	—	19,510	1,412	7,871
8	California	3,409,701	11,419	2,013,210	—	697,092	250,581	16,920	38,634	29,242	—	171,501	102,292	78,810
8	New Jersey	360,839	—	—	—	210,655	49,034	—	31,820	21,774	—	—	31,183	16,373
8	Ohio	1,134,374	—	—	—	593,130	157,884	—	35,404	—	—	240,342	63,953	43,661
		16,052,652	86,438	2,449,374	340,309	6,235,609	830,818	234,568	1,134,375	238,027	304,399	1,611,754	1,995,388	591,593

Other vote includes 88,254 Shapp; 61,992 Humphrey; 43,661 Donahey; 19,805 Kennedy; 8,717 Blessitt; 4,046 Bentsen; 3,935 Lunger; 3,574 Gray; 3,555 Lomento; 3,021 Rollinson; 2,305 Fifi Rockefeller; 2,288 Gonas; 1,829 Kelleher; 1,487 Ahern; 404 Sanford; 398 Bona; 371 Arnold; 351 Eisenman; 174 Clegg; 173 Schechter; 153 Roden; 49 Loewenherz; 205,019 Uncommitted; 81,971 No Preference; 42,304 scattered write-ins; 7,154 "None of the Names Shown"; 4,603 "None of These Candidates".

1980 PRESIDENTIAL PRIMARIES

In 1980 thirty-five states and the District of Columbia held Presidential primaries. California Democrats and South Dakota Republicans and Democrats held slate-type preferential primaries. In New York, Democrats had a Presidential preference, but Republicans held primaries for the selection of delegates only, without indication of Presidential preference. In Mississippi, Republicans elected delegates by Congressional Districts pledged to candidates and the vote indicated is for the highest of each slate's candidates in each CD. In Arkansas, the Republicans did not hold a primary although Democrats did. In South Carolina, the Democrats did not hold a primary but Republicans did. The vote in Ohio is for delegates at-large pledged to specific candidates and elected as a group.

The tables included here give the major party primary vote in each state for those candidates who were on the ballot in at least ten states and polled at least 25,000 votes.

Republican candidates on the ballot in at least one state were John B. Anderson, Donald Badgley, Howard H. Baker, Jr., Nick Belluso, George Bush, William E. Carlson, Alvin G. Carris, John B. Connally, Philip M. Crane, Robert Dole, Benjamin Fernandez, Alvin J. Jacobson, V. A. Kelley, C. Leon Pickett, Ronald Reagan, Harold E. Stassen, R. W. Yeager.

Democratic candidates on the ballot in at least one state were Frank Ahern, Edmund G. Brown, Jr., Jimmy Carter, Cliff Finch, Richard B. Kay, Edward M. Kennedy, Lyndon H. LaRouche, Bob Maddox, William L. Nuckols, Don Reaux, Ray Rollinson.

ALABAMA MARCH 11

Republican   147,352 Reagan; 54,730 Bush; 5,099 Crane; 1,963 Baker; 1,077 Connally; 544 Stassen; 447 Dole; 141 Belluso.

Democratic   193,734 Carter; 31,382 Kennedy; 9,529 Brown; 1,670 Uncommitted; 609 Nuckols; 540 Maddox.

ARKANSAS MAY 27

Republican   No Presidential primary held.

Democratic   269,375 Carter; 80,904 Uncommitted; 78,542 Kennedy; 19,469 Finch.

CALIFORNIA JUNE 3

Republican   2,057,923 Reagan; 349,315 Anderson; 125,113 Bush; 21,465 Crane; 10,242 Fernandez; 14 scattered.

Democratic   1,507,142 Kennedy slate; 1,266,276 Carter slate; 382,759 Unpledged slate; 135,962 Brown slate; 71,779 LaRouche slate; 51 scattered.

American Independent   10,838 Downey; 10,358 Rarick; 9 scattered.

Peace & Freedom   4,071 Spock; 2,494 Hall; 1,596 McReynolds; 1,330 Griswold; 3 scattered.

CONNECTICUT MARCH 25

Republican   70,367 Bush; 61,735 Reagan; 40,354 Anderson; 4,256 Uncommitted; 2,446 Baker; 1,887 Crane; 598 Connally; 333 Dole; 308 Fernandez.

Democratic   98,662 Kennedy; 87,207 Carter; 13,403 Uncommitted; 5,617 LaRouche; 5,386 Brown.

FLORIDA MARCH 11

Republican   345,699 Reagan; 185,996 Bush; 56,636 Anderson; 12,000 Crane; 6,345 Baker; 4,958 Connally, 1,377 Stassen; 1,086 Dole; 898 Fernandez.

Democratic   666,321 Carter; 254,727 Kennedy; 104,321 No Preference; 53,474 Brown; 19,160 Kay.

1980 PRESIDENTIAL PRIMARIES

GEORGIA MARCH 11

Republican   146,500 Reagan; 25,293 Bush; 16,853 Anderson; 6,308 Crane; 2,388 Connally; 1,571 Baker; 809 Fernandez; 249 Dole; 200 Stassen.

Democratic   338,772 Carter; 32,315 Kennedy; 7,255 Brown; 3,707 Uncommitted; 1,378 Finch; 840 Kay; 513 LaRouche.

IDAHO MAY 27

Republican   111,868 Reagan; 13,130 Anderson; 5,416 Bush; 3,441 Uncommitted; 1,024 Crane.

Democratic   31,383 Carter; 11,087 Kennedy; 5,934 Uncommitted; 2,078 Brown.

American   97 Rarick; 63 Uncommitted.

Libertarian   88 Clark; 39 Uncommitted.

ILLINOIS MARCH 18

Republican   547,355 Reagan; 415,193 Anderson; 124,057 Bush; 24,865 Crane; 7,051 Baker; 4,548 Connally; 3,757 Kelley; 1,843 Dole; 1,412 scattered.

Democratic   780,787 Carter; 359,875 Kennedy; 39,168 Brown; 19,192 LaRouche; 2,045 scattered.

INDIANA MAY 6

Republican   419,016 Reagan; 92,955 Bush; 56,342 Anderson.

Democratic   398,949 Carter; 190,492 Kennedy.

KANSAS APRIL 1

Republican   179,739 Reagan; 51,924 Anderson; 35,838 Bush; 3,603 Baker; 2,067 Connally; 1,650 Fernandez; 1,367 Crane; 1,063 Yeager; 483 Carris; 383 Stassen; 311 Carlson; 244 Badgley; 6,726 "None of the Names Shown".

Democratic   109,807 Carter; 61,318 Kennedy; 9,434 Brown; 632 Maddox; 629 Finch; 571 Ahern; 364 Rollinson; 11,163 "None of the Names Shown".

KENTUCKY MAY 27

Republican   78,072 Reagan; 6,861 Bush; 4,791 Anderson; 3,084 Uncommitted; 1,223 Stassen; 764 Fernandez.

Democratic   160,819 Carter; 55,167 Kennedy; 19,219 Uncommitted; 2,609 Kay; 2,517 Finch.

LOUISIANA APRIL 5

Republican   31,212 Reagan; 7,818 Bush; 2,221 Uncommitted; 155 Belluso; 126 Stassen; 84 Fernandez; 67 Pickett.

Democratic   199,956 Carter; 80,797 Kennedy; 41,614 Uncommitted; 16,774 Brown; 11,153 Finch; 3,362 Kay; 2,830 Maddox; 2,255 Reaux.

MARYLAND MAY 13

Republican   80,557 Reagan; 68,389 Bush; 16,244 Anderson; 2,113 Crane.

Democratic   226,528 Carter; 181,091 Kennedy; 45,879 Uncommitted; 14,313 Brown; 4,891 Finch; 4,388 LaRouche.

1980 PRESIDENTIAL PRIMARIES

MASSACHUSETTS MARCH 4

Republican   124,365 Bush; 122,987 Anderson; 115,334 Reagan; 19,366 Baker; 4,714 Connally; 4,669 Crane; 2,243 No Preference; 577 Dole; 374 Fernandez; 218 Stassen; 5,979 scattered.

Democratic   590,393 Kennedy; 260,401 Carter; 31,498 Brown; 19,663 No Preference; 5,368 scattered.

MICHIGAN MAY 20

Republican   341,998 Bush; 189,184 Regan; 48,947 Anderson; 10,265 Uncommitted; 2,248 Fernandez; 1,938 Stassen; 596 scattered.

Democratic   36,385 Uncommitted; 23,043 Brown; 8,948 LaRouche; 10,048 scattered.

MISSISSIPPI JUNE 3

Republican   23,028 Reagan slate; 2,105 Bush slate; 618 Unslated (CD's 3 and 4 only).

Democratic   No Presidential primary held.

MONTANA JUNE 3

Republican   68,744 Reagan; 7,665 Bush; 3,014 No Preference.

Democratic   66,922 Carter; 47,671 Kennedy; 15,466 No Preference.

NEBRASKA MAY 13

Republican   155,995 Reagan; 31,380 Bush; 11,879 Anderson; 1,420 Dole; 1,062 Crane; 799 Stassen; 400 Fernandez; 2,268 scattered.

Democratic   72,120 Carter; 57,826 Kennedy; 16,041 Uncommitted; 5,478 Brown; 1,169 LaRouche; 1,247 scattered.

NEVADA MAY 27

Republican   39,352 Reagan; 3,078 Bush; 4,965 "None of These Candidates".

Democratic   25,159 Carter; 19,296 Kennedy; 22,493 "None of These Candidates".

NEW HAMPSHIRE FEBRUARY 26

Republican   72,983 Reagan; 33,443 Bush; 18,943 Baker; 14,458 Anderson; 2,618 Crane; 2,239 Connally; 597 Dole; 1,876 scattered.

Democratic   52,692 Carter; 41,745 Kennedy; 10,743 Brown; 2,326 LaRouche; 566 Kay; 3,858 scattered.

NEW JERSEY JUNE 3

Republican   225,959 Reagan; 47,447 Bush; 4,571 Stassen.

Democratic   315,109 Kennedy; 212,387 Carter; 19,499 Uncommitted; 13,913 LaRouche.

1980 PRESIDENTIAL PRIMARIES

NEW MEXICO JUNE 3

Republican   37,982 Reagan; 7,171 Anderson; 5,892 Bush; 4,412 Crane, 1,795 Fernandez; 1,347 Uncommitted; 947 Stassen.

Democratic   73,721 Kennedy; 66,621 Carter; 9,734 Uncommitted; 4,798 LaRouche; 4,490 Finch.

NEW YORK MARCH 25

Republican   No Presidential primary was held. Delegates were elected, but without indication of Presidential preference.

Democratic   582,757 Kennedy; 406,305 Carter.

NORTH CAROLINA MAY 6

Republican   113,854 Reagan; 36,631 Bush; 8,542 Anderson; 4,538 No Preference; 2,543 Baker; 1,107 Connally; 629 Dole; 547 Crane.

Democratic   516,778 Carter; 130,684 Kennedy; 68,380 No Preference; 21,420 Brown.

OHIO JUNE 3

Republican   692,288 Reagan; 164,485 Bush.

Democratic   605,744 Carter; 523,874 Kennedy; 35,268 LaRouche; 21,524 Kay.

OREGON MAY 20

Republican   170,449 Reagan; 109,210 Bush; 32,118 Anderson; 2,324 Crane; 1,265 scattered.

Democratic   208,693 Carter; 114,651 Kennedy; 34,409 Brown; 10,569 scattered.

PENNSYLVANIA APRIL 22

Republican   626,759 Bush; 527,916 Reagan; 30,846 Baker; 26,890 Anderson (write-in); 10,656 Connally, 6,767 Stassen; 4,357 Jacobson; 2,521 Fernandez; 4,699 scattered.

Democratic   736,854 Kennedy; 732,332 Carter; 93,865 No Preference; 37,669 Brown; 12,831 scattered.

RHODE ISLAND JUNE 3

Republican   3,839 Reagan; 993 Bush; 348 Uncommitted; 107 Stassen; 48 Fernandez.

Democratic   26,179 Kennedy; 9,907 Carter; 1,160 LaRouche; 771 Uncommitted; 310 Brown.

SOUTH CAROLINA MARCH 8

Republican   79,549 Reagan; 43,113 Connally; 21,569 Bush; 773 Baker; 171 Fernandez; 150 Stassen; 117 Dole; 59 Belluso.

Democratic   No Presidential primary was held.

SOUTH DAKOTA JUNE 3

Republican   72,861 Reagan slate; 5,366 No Preference slate; 3,691 Bush slate; 987 Stassen slate.

Democratic   33,418 Kennedy slate; 31,251 Carter slate; 4,094 Uncommitted slate (in CD 1 only).

1980 PRESIDENTIAL PRIMARIES

TENNESSEE MAY 6

Republican   144,625 Reagan; 35,274 Bush; 8,722 Anderson; 4,976 Uncommitted; 1,574 Crane; 39 scattered.

Democratic   221,658 Carter; 53,258 Kennedy; 11,515 Uncommitted; 5,612 Brown; 1,663 Finch; 925 LaRouche; 49 scattered.

TEXAS MAY 3

Republican   268,798 Reagan; 249,819 Bush; 8,152 Uncommitted.

Democratic   770,390 Carter; 314,129 Kennedy; 257,250 Uncommitted; 35,585 Brown.

VERMONT MARCH 4

Republican   19,720 Reagan; 19,030 Anderson; 14,226 Bush; 8,055 Baker; 1,238 Crane; 884 Connally; 105 Stassen; 2,353 scattered.

Democratic   29,015 Carter; 10,135 Kennedy; 553 scattered.

Liberty Union 257 Gardner; 165 McReynolds; 76 Hall; 75 scattered.

WEST VIRGINIA JUNE 3

Republican   115,407 Reagan; 19,509 Bush; 3,100 Stassen.

Democratic   197,687 Carter; 120,247 Kennedy.

WISCONSIN APRIL 1

Republican   364,898 Reagan; 276,164 Bush; 248,623 Anderson; 3,298 Baker; 2,951 Crane; 2,312 Connally; 1,051 Fernandez; 1,010 Stassen; 2,595 ''None of the Names Shown''; 4,951 scattered.

Democratic   353,662 Carter; 189,520 Kennedy; 74,496 Brown; 6,896 LaRouche; 1,842 Finch; 2,694 ''None of the Names Shown''; 509 scattered.

DISTRICT OF COLUMBIA MAY 6

Republican   4,973 Bush; 2,025 Anderson; 270 Crane; 201 Stassen; 60 Fernandez.

Democratic   39,561 Kennedy; 23,697 Carter; 892 LaRouche.

1980 REPUBLICAN PREFERENCE PRIMARIES

Date		State	Total Vote	Anderson	Baker	Bush	Connally	Crane	Reagan	Other
Feb.	26	New Hampshire	147,157	14,458	18,943	33,443	2,239	2,618	72,983	2,473
Mar.	4	Massachusetts	400,826	122,987	19,366	124,365	4,714	4,669	115,334	9,391
	4	Vermont	65,611	19,030	8,055	14,226	884	1,238	19,720	2,458
	8	South Carolina	145,501	—	773	21,569	43,113	—	79,549	497
	11	Alabama	211,353	—	1,963	54,730	1,077	5,099	147,352	1,132
	11	Florida	614,995	56,636	6,345	185,996	4,958	12,000	345,699	3,361
	11	Georgia	200,171	16,853	1,571	25,293	2,388	6,308	146,500	1,258
	18	Illinois	1,130,081	415,193	7,051	124,057	4,548	24,865	547,355	7,012
	25	Connecticut	182,284	40,354	2,446	70,367	598	1,887	61,735	4,897
	25	New York	No Primary Held							
April	1	Kansas	285,398	51,924	3,603	35,838	2,067	1,367	179,739	10,860
	1	Wisconsin	907,853	248,623	3,298	276,164	2,312	2,951	364,898	9,607
	5	Louisiana	41,683	—	—	7,818	—	—	31,212	2,653
	22	Pennsylvania	1,241,411	26,890	30,846	626,759	10,656	—	527,916	18,344
May	3	Texas	526,769	—	—	249,819	—	—	268,798	8,152
	6	Indiana	568,313	56,342	—	92,955	—	—	419,016	—
	6	North Carolina	168,391	8,542	2,543	36,631	1,107	547	113,854	5,167
	6	Tennessee	195,210	8,722	—	35,274	—	1,574	144,625	5,015
	6	District of Columbia	7,529	2,025	—	4,973	—	270	—	261
	13	Maryland	167,303	16,244	—	68,389	—	2,113	80,557	—
	13	Nebraska	205,203	11,879	—	31,380	—	1,062	155,995	4,887
	20	Michigan	595,176	48,947	—	341,998	—	—	189,184	15,047
	20	Oregon	315,366	32,118	—	109,210	—	2,324	170,449	1,265
	27	Arkansas	No Primary Held							
	27	Idaho	134,879	13,130	5,416	—	—	1,024	111,868	3,441
	27	Kentucky	94,795	4,791	—	6,861	—	—	78,072	5,071
	27	Nevada	47,395	—	—	3,078	—	—	39,352	4,965
June	3	California	2,564,072	349,315	—	125,113	—	21,465	2,057,923	10,256
	3	Mississippi	25,751	—	—	2,105	—	—	23,028	618
	3	Montana	79,423	—	—	7,665	—	—	68,744	3,014
	3	New Jersey	277,977	—	—	47,447	—	—	225,959	4,571
	3	New Mexico	59,546	7,171	—	5,892	—	4,412	37,982	4,089
	3	Ohio	856,773	—	—	164,485	—	—	692,288	—
	3	Rhode Island	5,335	—	—	993	—	—	3,839	503
	3	South Dakota	82,905	—	—	3,691	—	—	72,861	6,353
	3	West Virginia	138,016	—	—	19,509	—	—	115,407	3,100
			12,690,451	1,572,174	112,219	2,958,093	80,661	97,793	7,709,793	159,718

Other vote includes 38,708 Uncommitted; 24,753 Stassen; 23,423 Fernandez; 15,161 No Preference; 9,321 "None of the Names Shown"; 7,298 Dole; 4,965 "None of These Candidates"; 4,357 Jacobson; 3,757 Kelley; 1,063 Yeager; 483 Carris; 355 Belluso; 311 Carlson; 244 Badgley; 67 Pickett; 25,452 scattered.

1980 DEMOCRATIC PREFERENCE PRIMARIES

Date		State	Total Vote	Brown	Carter	Kennedy	LaRouche	Other
Feb.	26	New Hampshire	111,930	10,743	52,692	41,745	2,326	4,424
Mar.	4	Massachusetts	907,323	31,498	260,401	590,393	—	25,031
	4	Vermont	39,703	—	29,015	10,135	—	553
	8	South Carolina	No Primary Held					
	11	Alabama	237,464	9,529	193,734	31,382	—	2,819
	11	Florida	1,098,003	53,474	666,321	254,727	—	123,481
	11	Georgia	384,780	7,255	338,772	32,315	513	5,925
	18	Illinois	1,201,067	39,168	780,787	359,875	19,192	2,045
	25	Connecticut	210,275	5,386	87,207	98,662	5,617	13,403
	25	New York	989,062	—	406,305	582,757	—	—
April	1	Kansas	193,918	9,434	109,807	61,318	—	13,359
	1	Wisconsin	629,619	74,496	353,662	189,520	6,896	5,045
	5	Louisiana	358,741	16,774	199,956	80,797	—	61,214
	22	Pennsylvania	1,613,551	37,669	732,332	736,854	—	106,696
May	3	Texas	1,377,354	35,585	770,390	314,129	—	257,250
	6	Indiana	589,441	—	398,949	190,492	—	—
	6	North Carolina	737,262	21,420	516,778	130,684	—	68,380
	6	Tennessee	294,680	5,612	221,658	53,258	925	13,227
	6	District of Columbia	64,150	—	23,697	39,561	892	—
	13	Maryland	477,090	14,313	226,528	181,091	4,388	50,770
	13	Nebraska	153,881	5,478	72,120	57,826	1,169	17,288
	20	Michigan	78,424	23,043	—	—	8,948	46,433
	20	Oregon	368,322	34,409	208,693	114,651	—	10,569
	27	Arkansas	448,290	—	269,375	78,542	—	100,373
	27	Idaho	50,482	2,078	31,383	11,087	—	5,934
	27	Kentucky	240,331	—	160,819	55,167	—	24,345
	27	Nevada	66,948	—	25,159	19,296	—	22,493
June	3	California	3,363,969	135,962	1,266,276	1,507,142	71,779	382,810
	3	Mississippi	No Primary Held					
	3	Montana	130,059	—	66,922	47,671	—	15,466
	3	New Jersey	560,908	—	212,387	315,109	13,913	19,499
	3	New Mexico	159,364	—	66,621	73,721	4,798	14,224
	3	Ohio	1,186,410	—	605,744	523,874	35,268	21,524
	3	Rhode Island	38,327	310	9,907	26,179	1,160	771
	3	South Dakota	68,763	—	31,251	33,418	—	4,094
	3	West Virginia	317,934	—	197,687	120,247	—	—
			18,747,825	573,636	9,593,335	6,963,625	177,784	1,439,445

Other vote includes 950,378 Uncommitted; 301,695 No Preference; 48,061 Kay; 48,032 Finch; 22,493 "None of These Candidates"; 13,857 "None of the Names Shown"; 4,002 Maddox; 2,255 Reaux; 609 Nuckols; 571 Ahern; 364 Rollinson; 47,128 Scattered.

ALABAMA

GOVERNOR
Forrest H. James (D). Elected 1978 to a four-year term.

SENATORS
Jeremiah Denton (R). Elected 1980 to a six-year term.

Howell Heflin (D). Elected 1978 to a six-year term.

REPRESENTATIVES
1. Jack Edwards (R)
2. William Dickinson (R)
3. Bill Nichols (D)
4. Tom Bevill (D)
5. Ronnie G. Flippo (D)
6. Albert L. Smith (R)
7. Richard C. Shelby (D)

POSTWAR VOTE FOR GOVERNOR

Year	Total Vote	Republican Vote	Republican Candidate	Democratic Vote	Democratic Candidate	Other Vote	Rep.-Dem. Plurality	Total Vote Rep.	Total Vote Dem.	Major Vote Rep.	Major Vote Dem.
1978	760,474	196,963	Hunt, Guy	551,886	James, Forrest H.	11,625	354,923 D	25.9%	72.6%	26.3%	73.7%
1974	598,305	88,381	McCary, Elvin	497,574	Wallace, George C.	12,350	409,193 D	14.8%	83.2%	15.1%	84.9%
1970	854,952	—	—	637,046	Wallace, George C.	217,906	637,046 D	—	74.5%	—	100.0%
1966	848,101	262,943	Martin, James D.	537,505	Wallace, Mrs. Lurleen	47,653	274,562 D	31.0%	63.4%	32.8%	67.2%
1962	315,776	—	—	303,987	Wallace, George C.	11,789	303,987 D	—	96.3%	—	100.0%
1958	270,952	30,415	Longshore, W. L.	239,633	Patterson, John	904	209,218 D	11.2%	88.4%	11.3%	88.7%
1954	333,090	88,688	Abernethy, Tom	244,401	Folsom, James E.	1	155,713 D	26.6%	73.4%	26.6%	73.4%
1950	170,541	15,127	Crowder, John S.	155,414	Persons, Gordon	—	140,287 D	8.9%	91.1%	8.9%	91.1%
1946	197,324	22,362	Ward, Lyman	174,962	Folsom, James E.	—	152,600 D	11.3%	88.7%	11.3%	88.7%

POSTWAR VOTE FOR SENATOR

Year	Total Vote	Republican Vote	Republican Candidate	Democratic Vote	Democratic Candidate	Other Vote	Rep.-Dem. Plurality	Total Vote Rep.	Total Vote Dem.	Major Vote Rep.	Major Vote Dem.
1980	1,296,757	650,362	Denton, Jeremiah	610,175	Folsom, James E., Jr.	36,220	40,187 R	50.2%	47.1%	51.6%	48.4%
1978	582,025	—	—	547,054	Heflin, Howell	34,971	547,054 D	—	94.0%	—	100.0%
1978s	731,614	316,170	Martin, James D.	401,852	Stewart, Donald W.	13,592	85,682 D	43.2%	54.9%	44.0%	56.0%
1974	523,290	—	—	501,541	Allen, James B.	21,749	501,541 D	—	95.8%	—	100.0%
1972	1,051,099	347,523	Blount, Winton M.	654,491	Sparkman, John J.	49,085	306,968 D	33.1%	62.3%	34.7%	65.3%
1968	912,708	201,227	Hooper, Perry	638,774	Allen, James B.	72,707	437,547 D	22.0%	70.0%	24.0%	76.0%
1966	802,608	313,018	Grenier, John	482,138	Sparkman, John J.	7,452	169,120 D	39.0%	60.1%	39.4%	60.6%
1962	397,079	195,134	Martin, James D.	201,937	Hill, Lister	8	6,803 D	49.1%	50.9%	49.1%	50.9%
1960	554,081	164,868	Elgin, Julian	389,196	Sparkman, John J.	17	224,328 D	29.8%	70.2%	29.8%	70.2%
1956	330,191	—	—	330,182	Hill, Lister	9	330,182 D	—	100.0%	—	100.0%
1954	314,459	55,110	Guin, J. Foy	259,348	Sparkman, John J.	1	204,238 D	17.5%	82.5%	17.5%	82.5%
1950	164,011	—	—	125,534	Hill, Lister	38,477	125,534 D	—	76.5%	—	100.0%
1948	220,875	35,341	Parsons, Paul G.	185,534	Sparkman, John J.	—	150,193 D	16.0%	84.0%	16.0%	84.0%
1946s	163,217	—	—	163,217	Sparkman, John J.	—	163,217 D	—	100.0%	—	100.0%

The 1946 election and one of the 1978 elections were for short terms to fill vacancies.

ALABAMA

Districts Established January 19, 1972

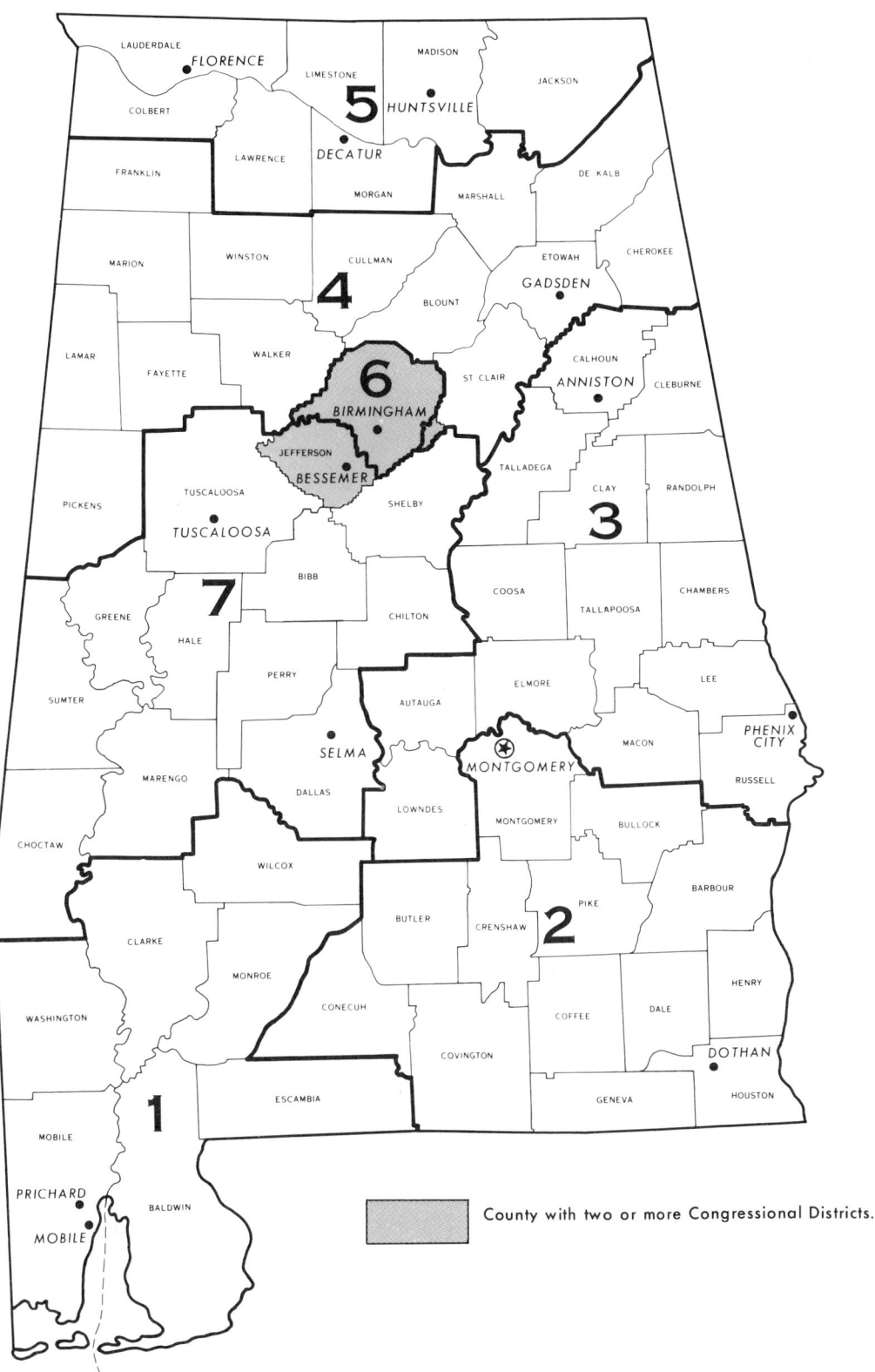

County with two or more Congressional Districts.

ALABAMA

PRESIDENT 1980

1980 Census Population	County	Total Vote	Republican	Democratic	Other	Rep.-Dem. Plurality	Percentage Total Vote Rep.	Dem.	Major Vote Rep.	Dem.
32,259	AUTAUGA	11,063	6,292	4,295	476	1,997 R	56.9%	38.8%	59.4%	40.6%
78,440	BALDWIN	28,353	18,652	8,448	1,253	10,204 R	65.8%	29.8%	68.8%	31.2%
24,756	BARBOUR	9,001	4,171	4,458	372	287 D	46.3%	49.5%	48.3%	51.7%
15,723	BIBB	5,623	2,491	3,097	35	606 D	44.3%	55.1%	44.6%	55.4%
36,459	BLOUNT	12,724	6,819	5,656	249	1,163 R	53.6%	44.5%	54.7%	45.3%
10,596	BULLOCK	5,637	1,446	3,960	231	2,514 D	25.7%	70.3%	26.7%	73.3%
21,680	BUTLER	8,368	3,810	4,156	402	346 D	45.5%	49.7%	47.8%	52.2%
116,936	CALHOUN	35,541	17,475	17,017	1,049	458 R	49.2%	47.9%	50.7%	49.3%
39,191	CHAMBERS	11,899	4,864	6,649	386	1,785 D	40.9%	55.9%	42.2%	57.8%
18,760	CHEROKEE	6,438	2,482	3,764	192	1,282 D	38.6%	58.5%	39.7%	60.3%
30,612	CHILTON	11,477	6,615	4,706	156	1,909 R	57.6%	41.0%	58.4%	41.6%
16,839	CHOCTAW	6,580	2,859	3,680	41	821 D	43.4%	55.9%	43.7%	56.3%
27,702	CLARKE	10,663	5,059	5,249	355	190 D	47.4%	49.2%	49.1%	50.9%
13,703	CLAY	5,747	2,764	2,858	125	94 D	48.1%	49.7%	49.2%	50.8%
12,595	CLEBURNE	4,526	2,389	2,050	87	339 R	52.8%	45.3%	53.8%	46.2%
38,533	COFFEEE	13,399	6,760	6,140	499	620 R	50.5%	45.8%	52.4%	47.6%
54,519	COLBERT	20,013	6,619	12,550	844	5,931 D	33.1%	62.7%	34.5%	65.5%
15,884	CONECUH	6,181	2,948	3,102	131	154 D	47.7%	50.2%	48.7%	51.3%
11,377	COOSA	4,209	1,714	2,383	112	669 D	40.7%	56.6%	41.8%	58.2%
36,850	COVINGTON	13,608	7,014	6,305	289	709 R	51.5%	46.3%	52.7%	47.3%
14,110	CRENSHAW	5,256	2,478	2,704	74	226 D	47.1%	51.4%	47.8%	52.2%
61,642	CULLMAN	22,240	10,212	11,525	503	1,313 D	45.9%	51.8%	47.0%	53.0%
47,821	DALE	12,573	7,247	4,936	390	2,311 R	57.6%	39.3%	59.5%	40.5%
53,981	DALLAS	18,147	7,647	9,770	730	2,123 D	42.1%	53.8%	43.9%	56.1%
53,658	DE KALB	18,690	9,673	8,820	197	853 R	51.8%	47.2%	52.3%	47.7%
43,390	ELMORE	15,190	8,688	5,947	555	2,741 R	57.2%	39.2%	59.4%	40.6%
38,392	ESCAMBIA	12,053	6,513	5,148	392	1,365 R	54.0%	42.7%	55.9%	44.1%
103,057	ETOWAH	37,806	16,177	20,790	839	4,613 D	42.8%	55.0%	43.8%	56.2%
18,809	FAYETTE	6,789	3,315	3,389	85	74 D	48.8%	49.9%	49.4%	50.6%
28,350	FRANKLIN	10,763	4,448	6,136	179	1,688 D	41.3%	57.0%	42.0%	58.0%
24,253	GENEVA	9,628	4,747	4,703	178	44 R	49.3%	48.8%	50.2%	49.8%
11,021	GREENE	4,538	1,034	3,474	30	2,440 D	22.8%	76.6%	22.9%	77.1%
15,604	HALE	5,979	2,074	3,583	322	1,509 D	34.7%	59.9%	36.7%	63.3%
15,302	HENRY	5,879	2,813	2,973	93	160 D	47.8%	50.6%	48.6%	51.4%
74,632	HOUSTON	23,238	14,884	7,848	506	7,036 R	64.1%	33.8%	65.5%	34.5%
51,407	JACKSON	14,203	4,897	8,776	530	3,879 D	34.5%	61.8%	35.8%	64.2%
671,197	JEFFERSON	259,512	132,612	113,069	13,831	19,543 D	51.1%	43.6%	54.0%	46.0%
16,453	LAMAR	6,186	2,778	3,366	42	588 D	44.9%	54.4%	45.2%	54.8%
80,504	LAUDERDALE	27,243	10,467	15,379	1,397	4,912 D	38.4%	56.5%	40.5%	59.5%
30,170	LAWRENCE	8,742	2,456	6,112	174	3,656 D	28.1%	69.9%	28.7%	71.3%
76,283	LEE	21,972	10,982	9,606	1,384	1,376 R	50.0%	43.7%	53.3%	46.7%
46,005	LIMESTONE	13,384	4,574	8,180	630	3,606 D	34.2%	61.1%	35.9%	64.1%
13,253	LOWNDES	5,329	1,524	3,577	228	2,053 D	28.6%	67.1%	29.9%	70.1%
26,829	MACON	8,774	1,259	7,028	487	5,769 D	14.3%	80.1%	15.2%	84.8%
196,966	MADISON	65,072	30,604	30,469	3,999	135 R	47.0%	46.8%	50.1%	49.9%
25,047	MARENGO	9,660	4,048	5,178	434	1,130 D	41.9%	53.6%	43.9%	56.1%
30,041	MARION	10,738	5,182	5,450	106	268 D	48.3%	50.8%	48.7%	51.3%
65,622	MARSHALL	19,933	8,159	10,854	920	2,695 D	40.9%	54.5%	42.9%	57.1%
364,379	MOBILE	116,992	67,515	46,180	3,297	21,335 R	57.7%	39.5%	59.4%	40.6%
22,651	MONROE	9,072	4,615	4,262	195	353 R	50.9%	47.0%	52.0%	48.0%
197,038	MONTGOMERY	66,504	35,745	28,018	2,741	7,727 R	53.7%	42.1%	56.1%	43.9%
90,231	MORGAN	29,271	13,214	14,703	1,354	1,489 D	45.1%	50.2%	47.3%	52.7%
15,012	PERRY	6,522	2,262	4,208	52	1,946 D	34.7%	64.5%	35.0%	65.0%
21,481	PICKENS	8,182	3,582	4,504	96	922 D	43.8%	55.0%	44.3%	55.7%
28,050	PIKE	9,991	5,220	4,417	354	803 R	52.2%	44.2%	54.2%	45.8%
20,075	RANDOLPH	7,094	3,279	3,378	437	99 D	46.2%	47.6%	49.3%	50.7%
47,356	RUSSELL	13,500	4,485	8,123	892	3,638 D	33.2%	60.2%	35.6%	64.4%
41,205	ST. CLAIR	13,654	7,768	5,236	650	2,532 R	56.9%	38.3%	59.7%	40.3%
66,298	SHELBY	23,267	14,957	7,396	914	7,561 R	64.3%	31.8%	66.9%	33.1%
16,908	SUMTER	7,199	2,104	5,015	80	2,911 D	29.2%	69.7%	29.6%	70.4%
73,826	TALLADEGA	20,641	9,902	10,159	580	257 D	48.0%	49.2%	49.4%	50.6%
38,676	TALLAPOOSA	13,603	5,958	7,260	385	1,302 D	43.8%	53.4%	45.1%	54.9%
137,473	TUSCALOOSA	40,720	19,750	19,103	1,867	647 R	48.5%	46.9%	50.8%	49.2%
68,660	WALKER	22,828	8,795	13,616	417	4,821 D	38.5%	59.6%	39.2%	60.8%
16,821	WASHINGTON	6,625	3,045	3,520	60	475 D	46.0%	53.1%	46.4%	53.6%
14,755	WILCOX	7,261	2,280	4,951	30	2,671 D	31.4%	68.2%	31.5%	68.5%
21,953	WINSTON	8,436	4,981	3,368	87	1,613 R	59.0%	39.9%	59.7%	40.3%
3,890,061	TOTAL	1,341,929	654,192	636,730	51,007	17,462 R	48.8%	47.4%	50.7%	49.3%

ALABAMA

SENATOR 1980

1980 Census Population	County	Total Vote	Republican	Democratic	Other	Rep.-Dem. Plurality	Percentage Total Vote Rep.	Dem.	Major Vote Rep.	Dem.
32,259	AUTAUGA	10,859	5,986	4,421	452	1,565 R	55.1%	40.7%	57.5%	42.5%
78,440	BALDWIN	28,396	19,575	7,879	942	11,696 R	68.9%	27.7%	71.3%	28.7%
24,756	BARBOUR	8,359	3,648	4,340	371	692 D	43.6%	51.9%	45.7%	54.3%
15,723	BIBB	5,522	2,077	3,393	52	1,316 D	37.6%	61.4%	38.0%	62.0%
36,459	BLOUNT	12,350	6,861	5,350	139	1,511 R	55.6%	43.3%	56.2%	43.8%
10,596	BULLOCK	5,496	1,257	4,009	230	2,752 D	22.9%	72.9%	23.9%	76.1%
21,680	BUTLER	8,045	3,605	4,109	331	504 D	44.8%	51.1%	46.7%	53.3%
116,936	CALHOUN	33,491	18,722	14,196	573	4,526 R	55.9%	42.4%	56.9%	43.1%
39,191	CHAMBERS	11,290	4,490	6,485	315	1,995 D	39.8%	57.4%	40.9%	59.1%
18,760	CHEROKEE	6,221	2,171	3,904	146	1,733 D	34.9%	62.8%	35.7%	64.3%
30,612	CHILTON	10,663	5,950	4,596	117	1,354 R	55.8%	43.1%	56.4%	43.6%
16,839	CHOCTAW	5,511	2,093	3,379	39	1,286 D	38.0%	61.3%	38.2%	61.8%
27,702	CLARKE	10,339	4,925	5,075	339	150 D	47.6%	49.1%	49.3%	50.8%
13,703	CLAY	5,181	2,292	2,703	186	411 D	44.2%	52.2%	45.9%	54.1%
12,595	CLEBURNE	4,127	1,910	2,144	73	234 D	46.3%	52.0%	47.1%	52.9%
38,533	COFFEEE	13,298	6,132	6,764	402	632 D	46.1%	50.9%	47.5%	52.5%
54,519	COLBERT	19,665	7,393	11,670	602	4,277 D	37.6%	59.3%	38.8%	61.2%
15,884	CONECUH	5,898	2,586	3,183	129	597 D	43.8%	54.0%	44.8%	55.2%
11,377	COOSA	4,170	1,528	2,489	153	961 D	36.6%	59.7%	38.0%	62.0%
36,850	COVINGTON	13,057	6,636	6,164	257	472 R	50.8%	47.2%	51.8%	48.2%
14,110	CRENSHAW	5,067	2,117	2,911	39	794 D	41.8%	57.5%	42.1%	57.9%
61,642	CULLMAN	21,283	9,241	11,833	209	2,592 D	43.4%	55.6%	43.9%	56.1%
47,821	DALE	12,246	6,786	5,149	311	1,637 R	55.4%	42.0%	56.9%	43.1%
53,981	DALLAS	17,515	6,979	9,929	607	2,950 D	39.8%	56.7%	41.3%	58.7%
53,658	DE KALB	18,441	9,663	8,721	57	942 R	52.4%	47.3%	52.6%	47.4%
43,390	ELMORE	14,804	8,217	6,174	413	2,043 R	55.5%	41.7%	57.1%	42.9%
38,392	ESCAMBIA	11,155	6,299	4,522	334	1,777 R	56.5%	40.5%	58.2%	41.8%
103,057	ETOWAH	36,699	16,796	19,359	544	2,563 D	45.8%	52.8%	46.5%	53.5%
18,809	FAYETTE	6,662	2,819	3,822	21	1,003 D	42.3%	57.4%	42.4%	57.6%
28,350	FRANKLIN	10,499	4,410	5,935	154	1,525 D	42.0%	56.5%	42.6%	57.4%
24,253	GENEVA	8,708	3,630	4,926	152	1,296 D	41.7%	56.6%	42.4%	57.6%
11,021	GREENE	4,139	945	3,150	44	2,205 D	22.8%	76.1%	23.1%	76.9%
15,604	HALE	5,569	1,721	3,680	168	1,959 D	30.9%	66.1%	31.9%	68.1%
15,302	HENRY	5,437	2,362	2,960	115	598 D	43.4%	54.4%	44.4%	55.6%
74,632	HOUSTON	22,006	13,099	8,503	404	4,596 R	59.5%	38.6%	60.6%	39.4%
51,407	JACKSON	13,663	4,368	8,920	375	4,552 D	32.0%	65.3%	32.9%	67.1%
671,197	JEFFERSON	252,003	136,115	105,777	10,111	30,338 R	54.0%	42.0%	56.3%	43.7%
16,453	LAMAR	5,880	2,293	3,564	23	1,271 D	39.0%	60.6%	39.1%	60.9%
80,504	LAUDERDALE	26,746	11,485	14,409	852	2,924 D	42.9%	53.9%	44.4%	55.6%
30,170	LAWRENCE	8,422	2,312	6,005	105	3,693 D	27.5%	71.3%	27.8%	72.2%
76,283	LEE	21,286	11,492	8,927	867	2,565 R	54.0%	41.9%	56.3%	43.7%
46,005	LIMESTONE	13,067	5,109	7,444	514	2,335 D	39.1%	57.0%	40.7%	59.3%
13,253	LOWNDES	5,076	1,340	3,507	229	2,167 D	26.4%	69.1%	27.6%	72.4%
26,829	MACON	8,472	1,220	6,820	432	5,600 D	14.4%	80.5%	15.2%	84.8%
196,966	MADISON	64,011	33,688	28,548	1,775	5,140 R	52.6%	44.6%	54.1%	45.9%
25,047	MARENGO	8,430	3,039	5,065	326	2,026 D	36.0%	60.1%	37.5%	62.5%
30,041	MARION	10,437	4,958	5,223	256	265 D	47.5%	50.0%	48.7%	51.3%
65,622	MARSHALL	19,608	8,815	10,103	690	1,288 D	45.0%	51.5%	46.6%	53.4%
364,379	MOBILE	113,368	71,548	39,568	2,252	31,980 R	63.1%	34.9%	64.4%	35.6%
22,651	MONROE	8,496	4,327	4,008	161	319 R	50.9%	47.2%	51.9%	48.1%
197,038	MONTGOMERY	66,191	35,515	28,787	1,889	6,728 R	53.7%	43.5%	55.2%	44.8%
90,231	MORGAN	28,842	13,871	14,143	828	272 D	48.1%	49.0%	49.5%	50.5%
15,012	PERRY	6,286	1,857	4,406	23	2,549 D	29.5%	70.1%	29.7%	70.3%
21,481	PICKENS	7,609	3,071	4,481	57	1,410 D	40.4%	58.9%	40.7%	59.3%
28,050	PIKE	9,838	4,515	5,065	258	550 D	45.9%	51.5%	47.1%	52.9%
20,075	RANDOLPH	6,650	2,552	3,727	371	1,175 D	38.4%	56.0%	40.6%	59.4%
47,356	RUSSELL	11,991	3,256	7,945	790	4,689 D	27.2%	66.3%	29.1%	70.9%
41,205	ST. CLAIR	13,586	7,941	5,057	588	2,884 R	58.4%	37.2%	61.1%	38.9%
66,298	SHELBY	23,017	15,230	7,218	569	8,012 R	66.2%	31.4%	67.8%	32.2%
16,908	SUMTER	4,976	1,744	3,167	65	1,423 D	35.0%	63.6%	35.5%	64.5%
73,826	TALLADEGA	19,367	9,413	9,580	374	167 D	48.6%	49.5%	49.6%	50.4%
38,676	TALLAPOOSA	13,320	5,828	7,101	391	1,273 D	43.8%	53.3%	45.1%	54.9%
137,473	TUSCALOOSA	40,010	19,882	18,920	1,208	962 D	49.7%	47.3%	51.2%	48.8%
68,660	WALKER	22,099	8,759	13,020	320	4,261 D	39.6%	58.9%	40.2%	59.8%
16,821	WASHINGTON	6,415	2,779	3,582	54	803 D	43.3%	55.8%	43.7%	56.3%
14,755	WILCOX	7,008	1,988	5,007	13	3,019 D	28.4%	71.4%	28.4%	71.6%
21,953	WINSTON	8,419	5,131	3,254	34	1,877 R	60.9%	38.7%	61.2%	38.8%
3,890,061	TOTAL	1,296,757	650,362	610,175	36,220	40,187 R	50.2%	47.1%	51.6%	48.4%

ALABAMA

CONGRESS

CD	Year	Total Vote	Republican Vote	Candidate	Democratic Vote	Candidate	Other Vote	Rep.-Dem. Plurality	Percentage Total Vote Rep.	Dem.	Major Vote Rep.	Dem.
1	1980	117,221	111,089	EDWARDS, JACK			6,132	111,089 R	94.8%		100.0%	
1	1978	112,161	71,711	EDWARDS, JACK	40,450	NOONAN, L. W.		31,261 R	63.9%	36.1%	63.9%	36.1%
1	1976	157,170	98,257	EDWARDS, JACK	58,906	DAVENPORT, BILL	7	39,351 R	62.5%	37.5%	62.5%	37.5%
1	1974	102,066	60,710	EDWARDS, JACK	37,718	WILSON, AUGUSTA E.	3,638	22,992 R	59.5%	37.0%	61.7%	38.3%
1	1972	136,710	104,606	EDWARDS, JACK	24,357	MCCRORY, O. W.	7,747	80,249 R	76.5%	17.8%	81.1%	18.9%
2	1980	172,962	104,796	DICKINSON, WILLIAM	63,447	WYATT, CECIL	4,719	41,349 R	60.6%	36.7%	62.3%	37.7%
2	1978	107,265	57,924	DICKINSON, WILLIAM	49,341	MITCHELL, WENDELL		8,583 R	54.0%	46.0%	54.0%	46.0%
2	1976	156,362	90,069	DICKINSON, WILLIAM	66,288	KEAHEY, J. CAROLE	5	23,781 R	57.6%	42.4%	57.6%	42.4%
2	1974	81,818	54,089	DICKINSON, WILLIAM	27,729	CHISLER, CLAIR		26,360 R	66.1%	33.9%	66.1%	33.9%
2	1972	146,508	80,362	DICKINSON, WILLIAM	60,769	REEVES, BEN C.	5,377	19,593 R	54.9%	41.5%	56.9%	43.1%
3	1980	107,654			107,654	NICHOLS, BILL		107,654 D	-	100.0%		100.0%
3	1978	74,897			74,895	NICHOLS, BILL	2	74,895 D		100.0%		100.0%
3	1976	108,048			106,935	NICHOLS, BILL	1,113	106,935 D		99.0%		100.0%
3	1974	66,312			63,582	NICHOLS, BILL	2,730	63,582 D		95.9%		100.0%
3	1972	132,383	27,253	KERR, ROBERT M.	100,045	NICHOLS, BILL	5,085	72,792 D	20.6%	75.6%	21.4%	78.6%
4	1980	132,086			129,365	BEVILL, TOM	2,721	129,365 D		97.9%		100.0%
4	1978	87,381			87,380	BEVILL, TOM	1	87,380 D		100.0%		100.0%
4	1976	176,022	34,531	WILSON, LEONARD	141,490	BEVILL, TOM	1	106,959 D	19.6%	80.4%	19.6%	80.4%
4	1974	78,118			77,925	BEVILL, TOM	193	77,925 D		99.8%		100.0%
4	1972	155,301	46,551	NELSON, ED	108,039	BEVILL, TOM	711	61,488 D	30.0%	69.6%	30.1%	69.9%
5	1980	124,967			117,626	FLIPPO, RONNIE G.	7,341	117,626 D		94.1%		100.0%
5	1978	71,236			68,985	FLIPPO, RONNIE G.	2,251	68,985 D		96.8%		100.0%
5	1976	113,560			113,553	FLIPPO, RONNIE G.	7	113,553 D		100.0%		100.0%
5	1974	56,381			56,375	JONES, ROBERT E.	6	56,375 D		100.0%		100.0%
5	1972	136,553	33,352	SCHRADER, DIETER J.	101,303	JONES, ROBERT E.	1,898	67,951 D	24.4%	74.2%	24.8%	75.2%
8	1970	90,058			76,413	JONES, ROBERT E.	13,645	76,413 D		84.8%		100.0%
8	1968	112,449			85,528	JONES, ROBERT E.	26,921	85,528 D		76.1%		100.0%
8	1966	91,386	25,404	MAYHALL, DONALD G.	65,982	JONES, ROBERT E.		40,578 D	27.8%	72.2%	27.8%	72.2%
8	1964	43,842			43,842	JONES, ROBERT E.		43,842 D		100.0%		100.0%
6	1980	187,982	95,019	SMITH, ALBERT L.	87,536	CLIFFORD, W. B.	5,427	7,483 R	50.5%	46.6%	52.0%	48.0%
6	1978	106,471	65,700	BUCHANAN, JOHN	40,771	HAWKINS, DON		24,929 R	61.7%	38.3%	61.7%	38.3%
6	1976	162,518	92,113	BUCHANAN, JOHN	69,384	BAILEY, MEL	1,021	22,729 R	56.7%	42.7%	57.0%	43.0%
6	1974	96,237	54,505	BUCHANAN, JOHN	39,444	MIGLIONICO, NINA	2,288	15,061 R	56.6%	41.0%	58.0%	42.0%
6	1972	153,133	91,499	BUCHANAN, JOHN	54,497	ERDREICH, BEN	7,137	37,002 R	59.8%	35.6%	62.7%	37.3%
7	1980	168,804	43,320	BACON, JAMES E.	122,505	SHELBY, RICHARD C.	2,979	79,185 D	25.7%	72.6%	26.1%	73.9%
7	1978	82,868	1,841	SCRUGGS, JAMES L.	77,742	SHELBY, RICHARD C.	3,285	75,901 D	2.2%	93.8%	2.3%	97.7%
7	1976	110,501			110,496	FLOWERS, WALTER	5	110,496 D		100.0%		100.0%
7	1974	80,468			73,203	FLOWERS, WALTER	7,265	73,203 D		91.0%		100.0%
7	1972	112,041			95,060	FLOWERS, WALTER	16,981	95,060 D		84.8%		100.0%

ALABAMA

1980 GENERAL ELECTION

President   Other vote was a 16,481 Anderson (Independent); 15,010 Rarick (Conservative); 13,318 Clark (Libertarian); 1,743 Bubar (Statesman); 1,629 Hall (Communist); 1,303 DeBerry (Socialist Workers); 1,006 McReynolds (Socialist); 517 Commoner (Citizens).

Senator   Other vote was 15,989 Erdey (Conservative); 13,098 Crew (Libertarian); 2,973 Hadnott (National Democratic); 2,649 Partain (Statesman); 1,511 Oliver (Socialist Workers).

Congress   Other vote was 6,130 Smith (Libertarian) and 2 scattered in CD 1; 4,103 Hand (Libertarian) and 616 Couch (Statesman) in CD 2; Killingsworth (Statesman) in CD 4; Benson (Libertarian) in CD 5; 3,218 Jacobson (Libertarian), 1,743 Lenud (National Democratic) and 466 Robey (Statesman) in CD 6; 2,132 Walker (Libertarian) and 847 Owensby (Statesman) in CD 7. In CD 3 Riley, the Statesman candidate, withdrew but his name appeared on the ballot in some counties in that district; his votes and the scattered votes were not certified by the state authorities. In CD 5 Beason, the Statesman candidate, withdrew but her name appeared on the ballot in some of the counties in that district; her votes were not certified by the state authorities.

1980 PRIMARIES

SEPTEMBER 2 REPUBLICAN

Senator   73,708 Jeremiah Denton; 41,825 Armistead Selden.

Congress   Unopposed in two CD's. No candidate in CD's 3, 4 and 5. Contested as follows:

  CD 6   25,857 Albert L. Smith; 20,855 John Buchanan.
  CD 7   5,175 James E. Bacon; 2,995 Robert W. Shores; 2,664 Fulton Gray.

SEPTEMBER 2 DEMOCRATIC

Senator   222,540 Donald W. Stewart; 163,196 James E. Folsom, Jr.; 51,260 Finis St. John; 20,582 Mrs. Frank R. Stewart.

Congress   Unopposed in five CD's. No candidate in CD 1. Contested as follows:

  CD 3   49,323 Bill Nichols; 8,608 Charlie Baker.

SEPTEMBER 23 REPUBLICAN RUN-OFF

Congress

  CD 7   744 James E. Bacon; 437 Robert W. Shores.

SEPTEMBER 23 DEMOCRATIC RUN-OFF

Senator   204,486 James E. Folsom, Jr.; 199,428 Donald W. Stewart.

ALASKA

GOVERNOR
Jay S. Hammond (R). Re-elected 1978 to a four-year term. Previously elected 1974.

SENATORS
Frank H. Murkowski (R). Elected 1980 to a six-year term.

Ted Stevens (R). Re-elected 1978 to a six-year term. Previously elected 1972, and in 1970 to fill out term vacated by the death of Senator E. L. Bartlett; had been appointed December 1968 to fill this vacancy.

REPRESENTATIVE
At-Large. Don Young (R)

POSTWAR VOTE FOR GOVERNOR

| | | | | | | Other | Rep.-Dem. | Percentage | | | |
| | Total | Republican | | Democratic | | | | Total Vote | | Major Vote | |
Year	Vote	Vote	Candidate	Vote	Candidate	Vote	Plurality	Rep.	Dem.	Rep.	Dem.
1978	126,910	49,580	Hammond, Jay S.	25,656	Croft, Chancy	51,674	23,924 R	39.1%	20.2%	65.9%	34.1%
1974	96,163	45,840	Hammond, Jay S.	45,553	Egan, William A.	4,770	287 R	47.7%	47.4%	50.2%	49.8%
1970	80,779	37,264	Miller, Keith	42,309	Egan, William A.	1,206	5,045 D	46.1%	52.4%	46.8%	53.2%
1966	66,294	33,145	Hickel, Walter J.	32,065	Egan, William A.	1,084	1,080 R	50.0%	48.4%	50.8%	49.2%
1962	56,681	27,054	Stepovich, Mike	29,627	Egan, William A.	—	2,573 D	47.7%	52.3%	47.7%	52.3%
1958	48,968	19,299	Butrovich, John	29,189	Egan, William A.	480	9,890 D	39.4%	59.6%	39.8%	60.2%

POSTWAR VOTE FOR SENATOR

| | | | | | | Other | Rep.-Dem. | Percentage | | | |
| | Total | Republican | | Democratic | | | | Total Vote | | Major Vote | |
Year	Vote	Vote	Candidate	Vote	Candidate	Vote	Plurality	Rep.	Dem.	Rep.	Dem.
1980	156,762	84,159	Murkowski, Frank H.	72,007	Gruening, Clark S.	596	12,152 R	53.7%	45.9%	53.9%	46.1%
1978	122,741	92,783	Stevens, Ted	29,574	Hobbs, Donald W.	384	63,209 R	75.6%	24.1%	75.8%	24.2%
1974	93,275	38,914	Lewis, C. R.	54,361	Gravel, Mike	—	15,447 D	41.7%	58.3%	41.7%	58.3%
1972	96,007	74,216	Stevens, Ted	21,791	Guess, Gene	—	52,425 R	77.3%	22.7%	77.3%	22.7%
1970s	80,364	47,908	Stevens, Ted	32,456	Kay, Wendell P.	—	15,452 R	59.6%	40.4%	59.6%	40.4%
1968	80,931	30,286	Rasmuson, Elmer	36,527	Gravel, Mike	14,118	6,241 D	37.4%	45.1%	45.3%	54.7%
1966	65,250	15,961	McKinley, Lee L.	49,289	Bartlett, E. L.	—	33,328 D	24.5%	75.5%	24.5%	75.5%
1962	58,181	24,354	Stevens, Ted	33,827	Gruening, Ernest	—	9,473 D	41.9%	58.1%	41.9%	58.1%
1960	59,978	21,937	McKinley, Lee L.	38,041	Bartlett, E. L.	—	16,104 D	36.6%	63.4%	36.6%	63.4%
1958s	49,525	23,462	Stepovich, Mike	26,063	Gruening, Ernest	—	2,601 D	47.4%	52.6%	47.4%	52.6%
1958s	48,837	7,299	Robertson, R. E.	40,939	Bartlett, E. L.	599	33,640 D	14.9%	83.8%	15.1%	84.9%

The two 1958 elections were held to indeterminate terms and the Senate later determined by lot that Senator Gruening would serve four years, Senator Bartlett two. The 1970 election was for a short term to fill a vacancy.

ALASKA

ALASKA

PRESIDENT 1980

1980 Census Population	District	Total Vote	Republican	Democratic	Other	Rep.-Dem. Plurality	Total Vote Rep.	Dem.	Major Vote Rep.	Dem.
15,138	DISTRICT 1	6,112	3,473	1,772	867	1,701 R	56.8%	29.0%	66.2%	33.8%
7,804	DISTRICT 2	3,368	1,612	1,256	500	356 R	47.9%	37.3%	56.2%	43.8%
8,742	DISTRICT 3	3,920	2,019	1,354	547	665 R	51.5%	34.5%	59.9%	40.1%
22,143	DISTRICT 4	11,489	5,345	3,899	2,245	1,446 R	46.5%	33.9%	57.8%	42.2%
10,702	DISTRICT 5	4,794	2,847	973	974	1,874 R	59.4%	20.3%	74.5%	25.5%
17,739	DISTRICT 6	8,176	5,008	1,316	1,852	3,692 R	61.3%	16.1%	79.2%	20.8%
27,827	DISTRICT 7	8,427	4,311	2,620	1,496	1,691 R	51.2%	31.1%	62.2%	37.8%
40,976	DISTRICT 8	12,605	7,432	2,860	2,313	4,572 R	59.0%	22.7%	72.2%	27.8%
12,337	DISTRICT 9	4,521	2,363	1,164	994	1,199 R	52.3%	25.7%	67.0%	33.0%
28,385	DISTRICT 10	12,388	7,659	2,778	1,951	4,881 R	61.8%	22.4%	73.4%	26.6%
37,511	DISTRICT 11	15,966	9,741	3,308	2,917	6,433 R	61.0%	20.7%	74.6%	25.4%
25,981	DISTRICT 12	12,009	7,450	2,456	2,103	4,994 R	62.0%	20.5%	75.2%	24.8%
22,241	DISTRICT 13	10,091	6,170	1,806	2,115	4,364 R	61.1%	17.9%	77.4%	22.6%
8,757	DISTRICT 14	2,983	1,473	844	666	629 R	49.4%	28.3%	63.6%	36.4%
9,472	DISTRICT 15	1,862	832	710	320	122 R	44.7%	38.1%	54.0%	46.0%
6,830	DISTRICT 16	2,286	869	1,083	334	214 D	38.0%	47.4%	44.5%	55.5%
8,790	DISTRICT 17	2,744	720	1,623	401	903 D	26.2%	59.1%	30.7%	69.3%
8,322	DISTRICT 18	2,386	769	1,327	290	558 D	32.2%	55.6%	36.7%	63.3%
9,168	DISTRICT 19	4,349	2,255	1,168	926	1,087 R	51.9%	26.9%	65.9%	34.1%
55,756	DISTRICT 20	22,999	11,673	5,310	6,016	6,363 R	50.8%	23.1%	68.7%	31.3%
8,152	DISTRICT 21	2,373	1,010	1,022	341	12 D	42.6%	43.1%	49.7%	50.3%
7,708	DISTRICT 22	2,597	1,081	1,193	323	112 D	41.6%	45.9%	47.5%	52.5%
400,481	TOTAL	158,445	86,112	41,842	30,491	44,270 R	54.3%	26.4%	67.3%	32.7%

ALASKA

SENATOR 1980

1980 Census Population	District	Total Vote	Republican	Democratic	Other	Rep.-Dem. Plurality	Total Vote Rep.	Dem.	Major Vote Rep.	Dem.
15,138	DISTRICT 1	6,200	3,337	2,857	6	480 R	53.8%	46.1%	53.9%	46.1%
7,804	DISTRICT 2	3,354	1,510	1,839	5	329 D	45.0%	54.8%	45.1%	54.9%
8,742	DISTRICT 3	3,910	1,508	2,394	8	886 D	38.6%	61.2%	38.6%	61.4%
22,143	DISTRICT 4	11,343	5,266	6,044	33	778 D	46.4%	53.3%	46.6%	53.4%
10,702	DISTRICT 5	4,788	2,908	1,864	16	1,044 R	60.7%	38.9%	60.9%	39.1%
17,739	DISTRICT 6	8,152	5,371	2,764	17	2,607 R	65.9%	33.9%	66.0%	34.0%
27,827	DISTRICT 7	8,257	3,956	4,261	40	305 D	47.9%	51.6%	48.1%	51.9%
40,976	DISTRICT 8	12,305	7,174	5,054	77	2,120 R	58.3%	41.1%	58.7%	41.3%
12,337	DISTRICT 9	4,458	2,229	2,197	32	32 R	50.0%	49.3%	50.4%	49.6%
28,385	DISTRICT 10	12,271	7,142	5,092	37	2,050 R	58.2%	41.5%	58.4%	41.6%
37,511	DISTRICT 11	15,804	9,171	6,593	40	2,578 R	58.0%	41.7%	58.2%	41.8%
25,981	DISTRICT 12	11,906	7,210	4,648	48	2,562 R	60.6%	39.0%	60.8%	39.2%
22,241	DISTRICT 13	10,038	6,436	3,591	11	2,845 R	64.1%	35.8%	64.2%	35.8%
8,757	DISTRICT 14	2,962	1,510	1,452		58 R	51.0%	49.0%	51.0%	49.0%
9,472	DISTRICT 15	1,840	668	1,172		504 D	36.3%	63.7%	36.3%	63.7%
6,830	DISTRICT 16	2,307	760	1,547		787 D	32.9%	67.1%	32.9%	67.1%
8,790	DISTRICT 17	2,740	635	2,100	5	1,465 D	23.2%	76.6%	23.2%	76.8%
8,322	DISTRICT 18	2,361	822	1,537	2	715 D	34.8%	65.1%	34.8%	65.2%
9,168	DISTRICT 19	4,301	2,217	2,078	6	139 R	51.5%	48.3%	51.6%	48.4%
55,756	DISTRICT 20	22,446	12,630	9,610	206	3,020 R	56.3%	42.8%	56.8%	43.2%
8,152	DISTRICT 21	2,391	801	1,586	4	785 D	33.5%	66.3%	33.6%	66.4%
7,708	DISTRICT 22	2,628	898	1,727	3	829 D	34.2%	65.7%	34.2%	65.8%
400,481	TOTAL	156,762	84,159	72,007	596	12,152 R	53.7%	45.9%	53.9%	46.1%

ALASKA

CONGRESS

CD	Year	Total Vote	Republican Vote	Republican Candidate	Democratic Vote	Democratic Candidate	Other Vote	Rep.-Dem. Plurality	Total Vote Rep.	Total Vote Dem.	Major Vote Rep.	Major Vote Dem.
AL	1980	154,618	114,089	YOUNG, DON	39,922	PARNELL, KEVIN	607	74,167 R	73.8%	25.8%	74.1%	25.9%
AL	1978	124,187	68,811	YOUNG, DON	55,176	RODEY, PATRICK	200	13,635 R	55.4%	44.4%	55.5%	44.5%
AL	1976	118,208	83,722	YOUNG, DON	34,194	HOPSON, EBEN	292	49,528 R	70.8%	28.9%	71.0%	29.0%
AL	1974	95,921	51,641	YOUNG, DON	44,280	HENSLEY, WILLIAM L.		7,361 R	53.8%	46.2%	53.8%	46.2%
AL	1972	95,401	41,750	YOUNG, DON	53,651	BEGICH, N. J.		11,901 D	43.8%	56.2%	43.8%	56.2%
AL	1970	80,084	35,947	MURKOWSKI, FRANK H.	44,137	BEGICH, N. J.		8,190 D	44.9%	55.1%	44.9%	55.1%
AL	1968	80,362	43,577	POLLOCK, HOWARD W.	36,785	BEGICH, N. J.		6,792 R	54.2%	45.8%	54.2%	45.8%
AL	1966	65,907	34,040	POLLOCK, HOWARD W.	31,867	RIVERS, RALPH J.		2,173 R	51.6%	48.4%	51.6%	48.4%
AL	1964	67,146	32,556	THOMAS, LOWELL	34,590	RIVERS, RALPH J.		2,034 D	48.5%	51.5%	48.5%	51.5%
AL	1962	58,591	26,638	THOMAS, LOWELL	31,953	RIVERS, RALPH J.		5,315 D	45.5%	54.5%	45.5%	54.5%
AL	1960	59,063	25,517	RETTIG, R. L.	33,546	RIVERS, RALPH J.		8,029 D	43.2%	56.8%	43.2%	56.8%
AL	1958	48,647	20,699	BENSON, HENRY A.	27,948	RIVERS, RALPH J.		7,249 D	42.5%	57.5%	42.5%	57.5%
AL	1956	28,266	9,332	GILLAM, BYRON A.	18,934	BARTLETT, E. L.		9,602 D	33.0%	67.0%	33.0%	67.0%
AL	1954	26,999	7,083	DIMOCK, BARBARA D.	19,916	BARTLETT, E. L.		12,833 D	26.2%	73.8%	26.2%	73.8%
AL	1952	25,112	10,893	REEVE, ROBERT C.	14,219	BARTLETT, E. L.		3,326 D	43.4%	56.6%	43.4%	56.6%
AL	1950	18,726	5,138	PETERSON, ALMER J.	13,588	BARTLETT, E. L.		8,450 D	27.4%	72.6%	27.4%	72.6%
AL	1948	22,309	4,789	STOCK, R. H.	17,520	BARTLETT, E. L.		12,731 D	21.5%	78.5%	21.5%	78.5%
AL	1946	16,384	4,868	PETERSON, ALMER J.	11,516	BARTLETT, E. L.		6,648 D	29.7%	70.3%	29.7%	70.3%

ALASKA

1980 GENERAL ELECTION

President   Other vote was 18,479 Clark (Libertarian); 11,155 Anderson (Independent); 857 scattered. Clark, the Libertarian candidate, ran second in District 6.

Senator   Other vote was scattered.

Congress   Other vote was scattered.

1980 PRIMARIES

AUGUST 26 REPUBLICAN

Senator   16,292 Frank H. Murkowski; 5,527 Arthur R. Kennedy; 3,635 Morris Thompson; 896 Donald L. Smith; 824 Donald R. Wright; 458 David J. Moe.

Congress   Unopposed at-large.

AUGUST 26 DEMOCRATIC

Senator   39,719 Clark S. Gruening; 31,504 Mike Gravel; 1,145 Michael J. Beasley.

Congress   Contested as follows:

AL   16,697 Kevin Parnell; 10,777 Richard Whittaker.

ARIZONA

GOVERNOR

Bruce Babbitt (D). Elected 1978 to a four-year term; had succeeded to the Governorship in March 1978 on the death of Governor Wesley Bolin, who himself had succeeded Governor Raul H. Castro on the latter's October 1977 appointment to be an Ambassador.

SENATORS

Dennis DeConcini (D). Elected 1976 to a six-year term.

Barry M. Goldwater (R). Re-elected 1980 to a six-year term. Previously elected 1974, 1968, 1958, 1952.

REPRESENTATIVES

1. John J. Rhodes (R)
2. Morris K. Udall (D)
3. Bob Stump (D)
4. Eldon Rudd (R)

POSTWAR VOTE FOR GOVERNOR

Year	Total Vote	Republican Vote	Candidate	Democratic Vote	Candidate	Other Vote	Rep.-Dem. Plurality	Total Vote Rep.	Total Vote Dem.	Major Vote Rep.	Major Vote Dem.
1978	538,556	241,093	Mecham, Evan	282,605	Babbitt, Bruce	14,858	41,512 D	44.8%	52.5%	46.0%	54.0%
1974	552,202	273,674	Williams, Russell	278,375	Castro, Raul H.	153	4,701 D	49.6%	50.4%	49.6%	50.4%
1970	411,409	209,522	Williams, John R.	201,887	Castro, Raul H.	—	7,635 R	50.9%	49.1%	50.9%	49.1%
1968	483,998	279,923	Williams, John R.	204,075	Goddard, Sam	—	75,848 R	57.8%	42.2%	57.8%	42.2%
1966	378,342	203,438	Williams, John R.	174,904	Goddard, Sam	—	28,534 R	53.8%	46.2%	53.8%	46.2%
1964	473,502	221,404	Kleindienst, Richard	252,098	Goddard, Sam	—	30,694 D	46.8%	53.2%	46.8%	53.2%
1962	365,841	200,578	Fannin, Paul	165,263	Goddard, Sam	—	35,315 R	54.8%	45.2%	54.8%	45.2%
1960	397,107	235,502	Fannin, Paul	161,605	Ackerman, Lee	—	73,897 R	59.3%	40.7%	59.3%	40.7%
1958	290,465	160,136	Fannin, Paul	130,329	Morrison, Robert	—	29,807 R	55.1%	44.9%	55.1%	44.9%
1956	288,592	116,744	Griffen, Horace B.	171,848	McFarland, Ernest W.	—	55,104 D	40.5%	59.5%	40.5%	59.5%
1954	243,970	115,866	Pyle, Howard	128,104	McFarland, Ernest W.	—	12,238 D	47.5%	52.5%	47.5%	52.5%
1952	260,285	156,592	Pyle, Howard	103,693	Haldiman, Joe C.	—	52,899 R	60.2%	39.8%	60.2%	39.8%
1950	195,227	99,109	Pyle, Howard	96,118	Frohmiller, Ana	—	2,991 D	50.8%	49.2%	50.8%	49.2%
1948	175,767	70,419	Brockett, Bruce	104,008	Garvey, Dan E.	1,340	33,589 D	40.1%	59.2%	40.4%	59.6%
1946	122,462	48,867	Brockett, Bruce	73,595	Osborn, Sidney P.	—	24,728 D	39.9%	60.1%	39.9%	60.1%

The term of office for Arizona's Governor was increased from two to four years effective with the 1970 election.

POSTWAR VOTE FOR SENATOR

Year	Total Vote	Republican Vote	Candidate	Democratic Vote	Candidate	Other Vote	Rep.-Dem. Plurality	Total Vote Rep.	Total Vote Dem.	Major Vote Rep.	Major Vote Dem.
1980	874,238	432,371	Goldwater, Barry M.	422,972	Schulz, Bill	18,895	9,399 R	49.5%	48.4%	50.5%	49.5%
1976	741,210	321,236	Steiger, Sam	400,334	DeConcini, Dennis	19,640	79,098 D	43.3%	54.0%	44.5%	55.5%
1974	549,919	320,396	Goldwater, Barry M.	229,523	Marshall, Jonathan	—	90,873 R	58.3%	41.7%	58.3%	41.7%
1970	407,796	228,284	Fannin, Paul	179,512	Grossman, Sam	—	48,772 R	56.0%	44.0%	56.0%	44.0%
1968	479,945	274,607	Goldwater, Barry M.	205,338	Elson, Roy L.	—	69,269 R	57.2%	42.8%	57.2%	42.8%
1964	468,801	241,089	Fannin, Paul	227,712	Elson, Roy L.	—	13,377 R	51.4%	48.6%	51.4%	48.6%
1962	362,605	163,388	Mecham, Evan	199,217	Hayden, Carl	—	35,829 D	45.1%	54.9%	45.1%	54.9%
1958	293,623	164,593	Goldwater, Barry M.	129,030	McFarland, Ernest W.	—	35,563 R	56.1%	43.9%	56.1%	43.9%
1956	278,263	107,447	Jones, Ross F.	170,816	Hayden, Carl	—	63,369 D	38.6%	61.4%	38.6%	61.4%
1952	257,401	132,063	Goldwater, Barry M.	125,338	McFarland, Ernest W.	—	6,725 R	51.3%	48.7%	51.3%	48.7%
1950	185,092	68,846	Brockett, Bruce	116,246	Hayden, Carl	—	47,400 D	37.2%	62.8%	37.2%	62.8%
1946	116,239	35,022	Powers, Ward S.	80,415	McFarland, Ernest W.	802	45,393 D	30.1%	69.2%	30.3%	69.7%

ARIZONA

Districts Established October 21, 1971

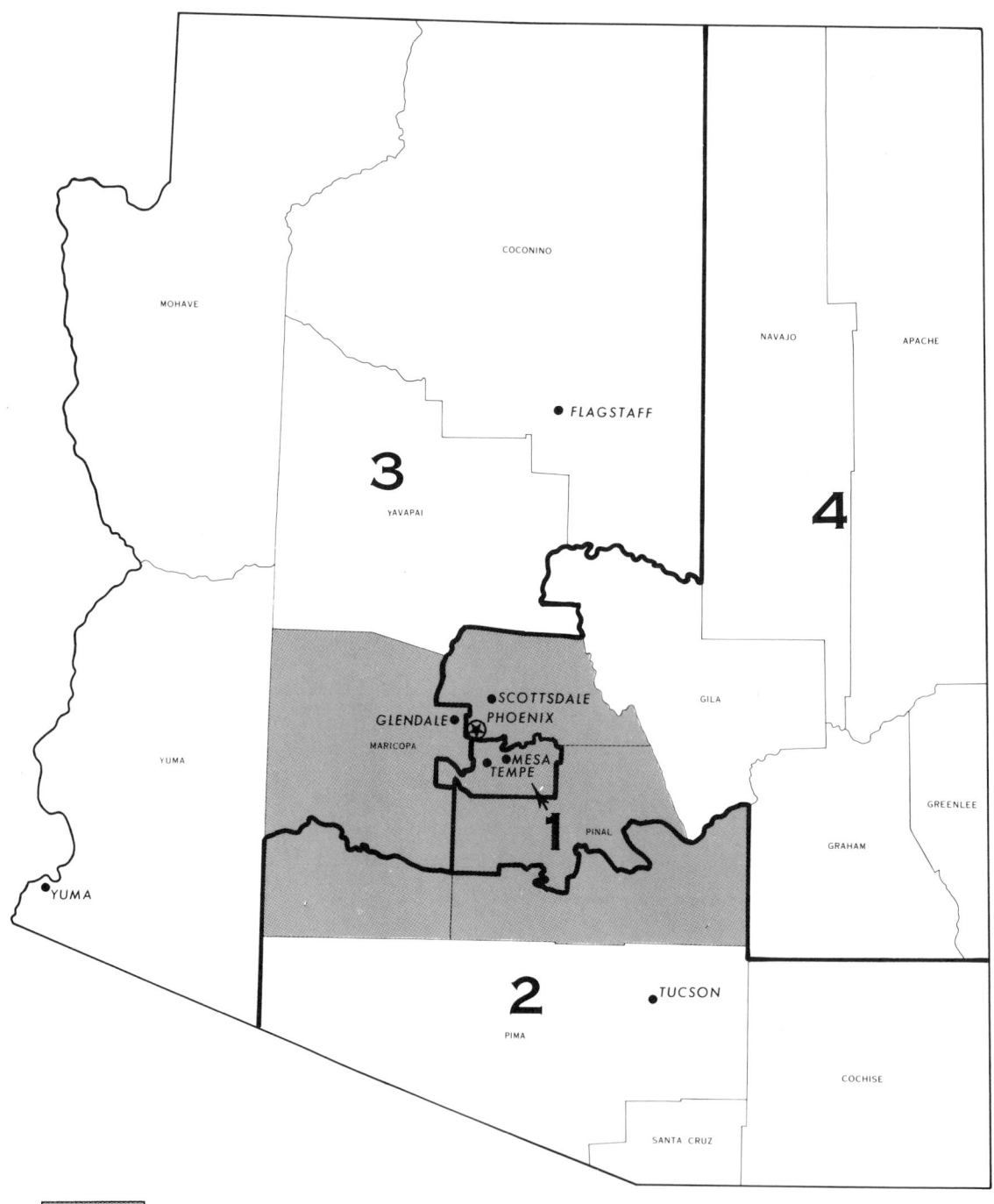

County with two or more Congressional Districts.

ARIZONA

PRESIDENT 1980

1980 Census Population	County	Total Vote	Republican	Democratic	Other	Rep.-Dem. Plurality	Percentage Total Vote Rep.	Dem.	Major Vote Rep.	Dem.
52,083	APACHE	10,595	5,991	3,917	687	2,074 R	56.5%	37.0%	60.5%	39.5%
86,717	COCHISE	22,445	13,351	7,028	2,066	6,323 R	59.5%	31.3%	65.5%	34.5%
74,947	COCONINO	26,199	14,613	7,832	3,754	6,781 R	55.8%	29.9%	65.1%	34.9%
37,080	GILA	13,399	7,405	5,068	926	2,337 R	55.3%	37.8%	59.4%	40.6%
22,862	GRAHAM	7,961	4,765	2,801	395	1,964 R	59.9%	35.2%	63.0%	37.0%
11,406	GREENLEE	3,782	1,537	2,043	202	506 D	40.6%	54.0%	42.9%	57.1%
1,508,030	MARICOPA	486,834	316,287	119,752	50,795	196,535 R	65.0%	24.6%	72.5%	27.5%
55,693	MOHAVE	20,054	13,809	4,900	1,345	8,909 R	68.9%	24.4%	73.8%	26.2%
67,709	NAVAJO	16,882	10,790	5,110	982	5,680 R	63.9%	30.3%	67.9%	32.1%
531,263	PIMA	187,057	93,055	64,418	29,584	28,637 R	49.7%	34.4%	59.1%	40.9%
90,918	PINAL	23,258	12,195	9,207	1,856	2,988 R	52.4%	39.6%	57.0%	43.0%
20,459	SANTA CRUZ	5,340	2,674	2,089	577	585 R	50.1%	39.1%	56.1%	43.9%
68,145	YAVAPAI	28,994	19,823	6,664	2,507	13,159 R	68.4%	23.0%	74.8%	25.2%
90,554	YUMA	21,145	13,393	6,014	1,738	7,379 R	63.3%	28.4%	69.0%	31.0%
2,717,866	TOTAL	873,945	529,688	246,843	97,414	282,845 R	60.6%	28.2%	68.2%	31.8%

ARIZONA

SENATOR 1980

1980 Census Population	County	Total Vote	Republican	Democratic	Other	Rep.-Dem. Plurality	Percentage Total Vote Rep.	Dem.	Major Vote Rep.	Dem.
52,083	APACHE	10,446	3,068	6,887	491	3,819 D	29.4%	65.9%	30.8%	69.2%
86,717	COCHISE	22,095	10,757	10,894	444	137 D	48.7%	49.3%	49.7%	50.3%
74,947	COCONINO	26,001	10,349	14,798	854	4,449 D	39.8%	56.9%	41.2%	58.8%
37,080	GILA	13,326	5,756	7,378	192	1,622 D	43.2%	55.4%	43.8%	56.2%
22,862	GRAHAM	7,802	3,677	3,939	186	262 D	47.1%	50.5%	48.3%	51.7%
11,406	GREENLEE	3,805	1,171	2,558	76	1,387 D	30.8%	67.2%	31.4%	68.6%
1,508,030	MARICOPA	490,329	264,951	215,284	10,094	49,667 R	54.0%	43.9%	55.2%	44.8%
55,693	MOHAVE	20,237	10,043	9,931	263	112 R	49.6%	49.1%	50.3%	49.7%
67,709	NAVAJO	16,764	7,296	9,176	292	1,880 D	43.5%	54.7%	44.3%	55.7%
531,263	PIMA	186,189	78,513	103,424	4,252	24,911 D	42.2%	55.5%	43.2%	56.8%
90,918	PINAL	22,931	9,321	13,093	517	3,772 D	40.6%	57.1%	41.6%	58.4%
20,459	SANTA CRUZ	5,131	2,024	2,874	233	850 D	39.4%	56.0%	41.3%	58.7%
68,145	YAVAPAI	28,399	15,781	12,011	607	3,770 R	55.6%	42.3%	56.8%	43.2%
90,554	YUMA	20,783	9,664	10,725	394	1,061 D	46.5%	51.6%	47.4%	52.6%
2,717,866	TOTAL	874,238	432,371	422,972	18,895	9,399 R	49.5%	48.4%	50.5%	49.5%

ARIZONA

CONGRESS

CD	Year	Total Vote	Republican Vote	Candidate	Democratic Vote	Candidate	Other Vote	Rep.-Dem. Plurality	Percentage Total Vote Rep.	Dem.	Major Vote Rep.	Dem.
1	1980	186,833	136,961	RHODES, JOHN J.	40,045	JANCEK, STEVE	9,827	96,916 R	73.3%	21.4%	77.4%	22.6%
1	1978	114,286	81,108	RHODES, JOHN J.	33,178	GRAVES, KEN		47,930 R	71.0%	29.0%	71.0%	29.0%
1	1976	168,119	96,397	RHODES, JOHN J.	68,404	FULLINWIDER, PATRICIA	3,318	27,993 R	57.3%	40.7%	58.5%	41.5%
1	1974	124,961	63,847	RHODES, JOHN J.	52,897	FULLINWIDER, PATRICIA	8,217	10,950 R	51.1%	42.3%	54.7%	45.3%
1	1972	140,353	80,453	RHODES, JOHN J.	59,900	POLLOCK, GERALD A.		20,553 R	57.3%	42.7%	57.3%	42.7%
2	1980	219,686	88,653	HUFF, RICHARD H.	127,736	UDALL, MORRIS K.	3,297	39,083 D	40.4%	58.1%	41.0%	59.0%
2	1978	129,197	58,697	RICHEY, TOM	67,878	UDALL, MORRIS K.	2,622	9,181 D	45.4%	52.5%	46.4%	53.6%
2	1976	182,128	71,765	GUTTERSEN, LAIRD	106,054	UDALL, MORRIS K.	4,309	34,289 D	39.4%	58.2%	40.4%	59.6%
2	1974	136,377	51,886	DOLGAARD, KEITH	84,491	UDALL, MORRIS K.		32,605 D	38.0%	62.0%	38.0%	62.0%
2	1972	153,804	56,188	SAVOIE, GENE	97,616	UDALL, MORRIS K.		41,428 D	36.5%	63.5%	36.5%	63.5%
3	1980	219,822	65,845	CROFT, BOB	141,448	STUMP, BOB	12,529	75,603 D	30.0%	64.3%	31.8%	68.2%
3	1978	131,663			111,850	STUMP, BOB	19,813	111,850 D		85.0%		100.0%
3	1976	187,165	79,162	KOORY, FRED	88,854	STUMP, BOB	19,149	9,692 D	42.3%	47.5%	47.1%	52.9%
3	1974	139,921	71,497	STEIGER, SAM	68,424	BOSCH, PAT	3,073	3,073 R	51.1%	48.9%	51.1%	48.9%
3	1972	143,930	90,710	STEIGER, SAM	53,220	WYCKOFF, TED		37,490 R	63.0%	37.0%	63.0%	37.0%
4	1980	227,611	142,565	RUDD, ELDON	85,046	MILLER, LES		57,519 R	62.6%	37.4%	62.6%	37.4%
4	1978	143,836	90,768	RUDD, ELDON	48,661	MCCORMICK, MICHAEL	4,407	42,107 R	63.1%	33.8%	65.1%	34.9%
4	1976	191,590	93,154	RUDD, ELDON	92,435	MASON, TONY	6,001	719 R	48.6%	48.2%	50.2%	49.8%
4	1974	142,564	78,887	CONLAN, JOHN B.	63,677	BROWN, BYRON T.		15,210 R	55.3%	44.7%	55.3%	44.7%
4	1972	155,820	82,511	CONLAN, JOHN B.	73,309	BROWN, JACK E.		9,202 R	53.0%	47.0%	53.0%	47.0%

ARIZONA

1980 GENERAL ELECTION

President   Other vote was 76,952 Anderson (Independent); 18,784 Clark (Libertarian); 1,100 DeBerry (Socialist Workers); 551 Commoner (write-in); 25 Hall (write-in); 2 Griswold (write-in).

Senator   Other vote was 12,008 Esser (Libertarian); 3,266 Otero (Socialist Workers); 3,608 Torrez (People Before Politics); 13 scattered.

Congress   Other vote was 7,784 Leitch (Libertarian)and 2,043 Roper (Socialist Workers) in CD 1; Stefanov (Libertarian) in CD 2; Hayse (Libertarian) in CD 3.

1980 PRIMARIES

SEPTEMBER 9 REPUBLICAN

Senator   Barry M. Goldwater, unopposed.

Congress   Unopposed in two CD's. In CD 3, no candidate appeared on the ballot; Bob Croft received 1,279 write-in votes and gained the nomination. Contested as follows:

  CD 4   35,515 Eldon Rudd; 4,718 Richard C. Rosberg.

SEPTEMBER 9 DEMOCRATIC

Senator   97,520 Bill Schulz; 58,894 Jim McNulty; 19,259 Frank DePaoli; 485 Frances Morgan (write-in).

Congress   Unopposed in three CD's. Contested as follows:

  CD 1   12,647 Steve Jancek; 8,943 Francis J. Killelea.

SEPTEMBER 9 LIBERTARIAN

Senator   Fred Esser, unopposed.

Congress   Unopposed in two CD's. No candidates in CD's 3 and 4. In CD 3 Sharon Hayse received 36 write-in votes and gained the nomination.

SEPTEMBER 9 SOCIALIST WORKERS

Senator   No candidate appeared on the ballot. Josefina Otero received 27 write-in votes and gained the nomination.

Congress   Unopposed in CD 1. No candidates in other CD's.

ARKANSAS

GOVERNOR
Frank D. White (R). Elected 1980 to a two-year term.

SENATORS
Dale Bumpers (D). Re-elected 1980 to a six-year term. Previously elected 1974.

David H. Pryor (D). Elected 1978 to a six-year term.

REPRESENTATIVES
1. William Alexander (D)
2. Ed Bethune (R)
3. John Hammerschmidt (R)
4. Beryl F. Anthony (D)

POSTWAR VOTE FOR GOVERNOR

Year	Total Vote	Republican Vote	Candidate	Democratic Vote	Candidate	Other Vote	Rep.-Dem. Plurality	Total Vote Rep.	Dem.	Major Vote Rep.	Dem.
1980	838,925	435,684	White, Frank D.	403,241	Clinton, Bill	—	32,443 R	51.9%	48.1%	51.9%	48.1%
1978	528,912	193,746	Lowe, A. Lynn	335,101	Clinton, Bill	65	141,355 D	36.6%	63.4%	36.6%	63.4%
1976	726,949	121,716	Griffith, Leon	605,083	Pryor, David H.	150	483,367 D	16.7%	83.2%	16.7%	83.3%
1974	545,974	187,872	Coon, Ken	358,018	Pryor, David H.	84	170,146 D	34.4%	65.6%	34.4%	65.6%
1972	648,069	159,177	Blaylock, Len E.	488,892	Bumpers, Dale	—	329,715 D	24.6%	75.4%	24.6%	75.4%
1970	609,198	197,418	Rockefeller, Winthrop	375,648	Bumpers, Dale	36,132	178,230 D	32.4%	61.7%	34.4%	65.6%
1968	615,595	322,782	Rockefeller, Winthrop	292,813	Crank, Marion	—	29,969 R	52.4%	47.6%	52.4%	47.6%
1966	563,527	306,324	Rockefeller, Winthrop	257,203	Johnson, James D.	—	49,121 R	54.4%	45.6%	54.4%	45.6%
1964	592,113	254,561	Rockefeller, Winthrop	337,489	Faubus, Orval E.	63	82,928 D	43.0%	57.0%	43.0%	57.0%
1962	308,092	82,349	Ricketts, Willis	225,743	Faubus, Orval E.	—	143,394 D	26.7%	73.3%	26.7%	73.3%
1960	421,985	129,921	Britt, Henry M.	292,064	Faubus, Orval E.	—	162,143 D	30.8%	69.2%	30.8%	69.2%
1958	286,886	50,288	Johnson, George W.	236,598	Faubus, Orval E.	—	186,310 D	17.5%	82.5%	17.5%	82.5%
1956	399,012	77,215	Mitchell, Roy	321,797	Faubus, Orval E.	—	244,582 D	19.4%	80.6%	19.4%	80.6%
1954	335,176	127,004	Remmel, Pratt C.	208,121	Faubus, Orval E.	51	81,117 D	37.9%	62.1%	37.9%	62.1%
1952	391,592	49,292	Speck, Jefferson W.	342,292	Cherry, Francis	8	293,000 D	12.6%	87.4%	12.6%	87.4%
1950	317,087	50,309	Speck, Jefferson W.	266,778	McMath, Sidney S.	—	216,469 D	15.9%	84.1%	15.9%	84.1%
1948	249,301	26,500	Black, Charles R.	222,801	McMath, Sidney S.	—	196,301 D	10.6%	89.4%	10.6%	89.4%
1946	152,162	24,133	Mills, W. T.	128,029	Laney, Ben T.	—	103,896 D	15.9%	84.1%	15.9%	84.1%

POSTWAR VOTE FOR SENATOR

Year	Total Vote	Republican Vote	Candidate	Democratic Vote	Candidate	Other Vote	Rep.-Dem. Plurality	Total Vote Rep.	Dem.	Major Vote Rep.	Dem.
1980	808,812	330,576	Clark, Bill	477,905	Bumpers, Dale	331	147,329 D	40.9%	59.1%	40.9%	59.1%
1978	522,239	84,722	Kelly, Tom	399,916	Pryor, David H.	37,601	315,194 D	16.2%	76.6%	17.5%	82.5%
1974	543,082	82,026	Jones, John H.	461,056	Bumpers, Dale	—	379,030 D	15.1%	84.9%	15.1%	84.9%
1972	634,636	248,238	Babbitt, Wayne H.	386,398	McClellan, John L.	—	138,160 D	39.1%	60.9%	39.1%	60.9%
1968	591,704	241,739	Bernard, Charles T.	349,965	Fulbright, J. W.	—	108,226 D	40.9%	59.1%	40.9%	59.1%
1966	—	—		—	McClellan, John L.	—	—	—	—	—	—
1962	312,880	98,013	Jones, Kenneth	214,867	Fulbright, J. W.	—	116,854 D	31.3%	68.7%	31.3%	68.7%
1960	—	—		—	McClellan, John L.	—	—	—	—	—	—
1956	399,695	68,016	Henley, Ben C.	331,679	Fulbright, J. W.	—	263,663 D	17.0%	83.0%	17.0%	83.0%
1954	291,058	—	—	291,058	McClellan, John L.	—	291,058 D	—	100.0%	—	100.0%
1950	302,582	—	—	302,582	Fulbright, J. W.	—	302,582 D	—	100.0%	—	100.0%
1948	216,401	—	—	216,401	McClellan, John L.	—	216,401 D	—	100.0%	—	100.0%

Senator McClellan was re-elected in 1966 and in 1960, but his vote was not canvassed in many counties.

ARKANSAS

Districts Established March 22, 1971

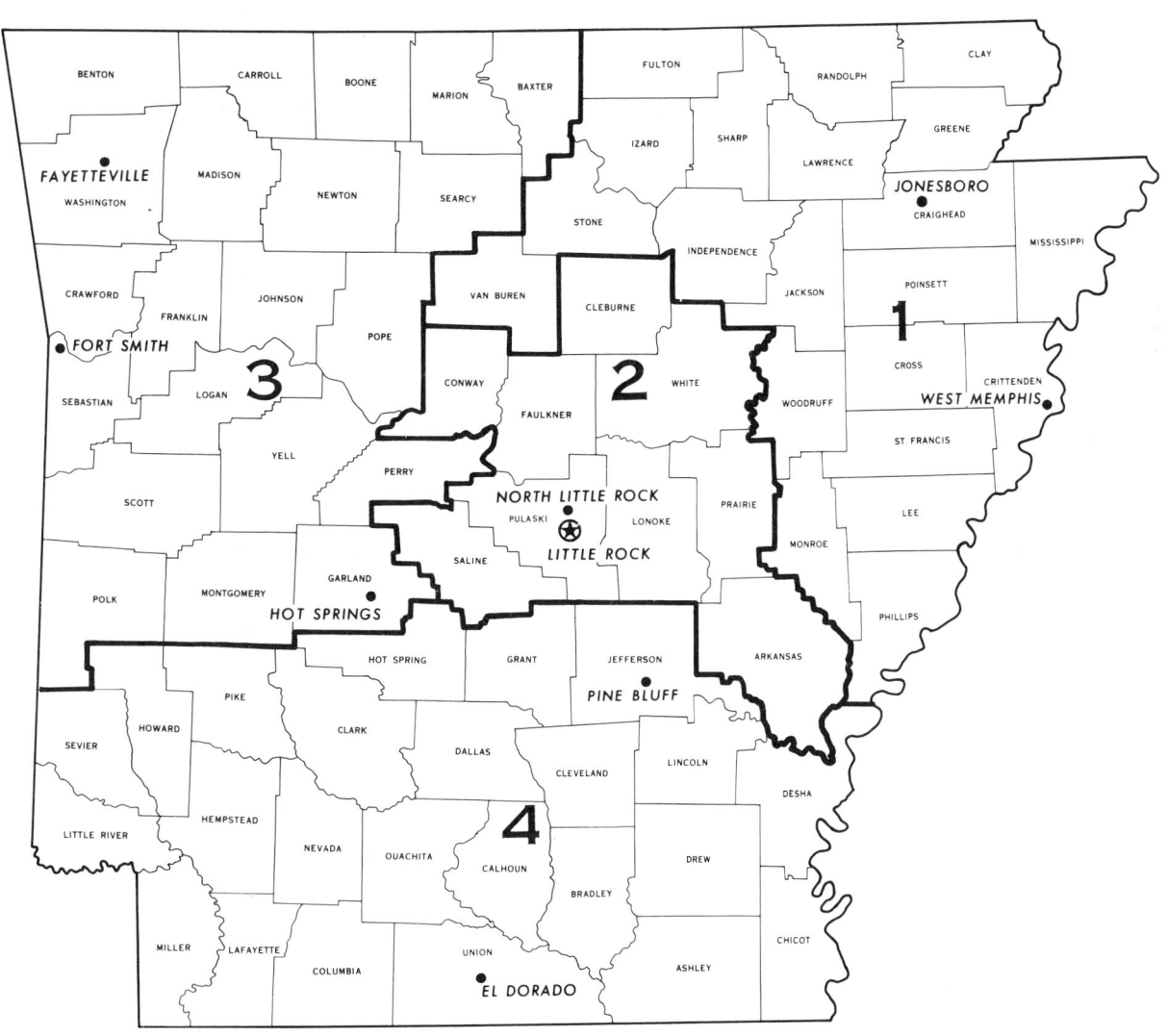

ARKANSAS

PRESIDENT 1980

1980 Census Population	County	Total Vote	Republican	Democratic	Other	Rep.-Dem. Plurality	Percentage Total Vote Rep.	Dem.	Major Vote Rep.	Dem.
24,175	ARKANSAS	7,985	3,409	4,303	273	894 D	42.7%	53.9%	44.2%	55.8%
26,538	ASHLEY	8,748	3,960	4,552	236	592 D	45.3%	52.0%	46.5%	53.5%
27,409	BAXTER	15,147	9,684	4,789	674	4,895 R	63.9%	31.6%	66.9%	33.1%
78,115	BENTON	29,440	18,830	9,231	1,379	9,599 R	64.0%	31.4%	67.1%	32.9%
26,067	BOONE	12,088	6,778	4,576	734	2,202 R	56.1%	37.9%	59.7%	40.3%
13,803	BRADLEY	4,890	1,650	3,139	101	1,489 D	33.7%	64.2%	34.5%	65.5%
6,079	CALHOUN	2,396	896	1,438	62	542 D	37.4%	60.0%	38.4%	61.6%
16,203	CARROLL	7,728	4,273	2,977	478	1,296 R	55.3%	38.5%	58.9%	41.1%
17,793	CHICOT	5,776	2,239	3,445	92	1,206 D	38.8%	59.6%	39.4%	60.6%
23,326	CLARK	9,153	2,743	6,122	288	3,379 D	30.0%	66.9%	30.9%	69.1%
20,616	CLAY	7,330	3,091	3,985	254	894 D	42.2%	54.4%	43.7%	56.3%
16,909	CLEBURNE	8,355	4,042	4,021	292	21 R	48.4%	48.1%	50.1%	49.9%
7,868	CLEVELAND	3,058	1,124	1,856	78	732 D	36.8%	60.7%	37.7%	62.3%
26,644	COLUMBIA	9,967	5,259	4,445	263	814 R	52.8%	44.6%	54.2%	45.8%
19,505	CONWAY	9,189	4,145	4,698	346	553 D	45.1%	51.1%	46.9%	53.1%
63,218	CRAIGHEAD	21,456	11,010	9,231	1,215	1,779 R	51.3%	43.0%	54.4%	45.6%
36,892	CRAWFORD	12,899	8,542	3,948	409	4,594 R	66.2%	30.6%	68.4%	31.6%
49,097	CRITTENDEN	13,823	6,248	7,022	553	774 D	45.2%	50.8%	47.1%	52.9%
20,434	CROSS	6,492	2,895	3,471	126	576 D	44.6%	53.5%	45.5%	54.5%
10,515	DALLAS	4,539	1,596	2,838	105	1,242 D	35.2%	62.5%	36.0%	64.0%
19,760	DESHA	6,037	2,057	3,748	232	1,691 D	34.1%	62.1%	35.4%	64.6%
17,910	DREW	6,184	2,272	3,757	155	1,485 D	36.7%	60.8%	37.7%	62.3%
46,192	FAULKNER	17,073	7,544	8,528	1,001	984 D	44.2%	50.0%	46.9%	53.1%
14,705	FRANKLIN	6,426	3,448	2,716	262	732 R	53.7%	42.3%	55.9%	44.1%
9,975	FULTON	4,257	2,101	2,037	119	64 R	49.4%	47.9%	50.8%	49.2%
69,916	GARLAND	29,717	15,739	12,515	1,463	3,224 R	53.0%	42.1%	55.7%	44.3%
13,008	GRANT	5,276	2,007	3,078	191	1,071 D	38.0%	58.3%	39.5%	60.5%
30,744	GREENE	10,841	4,514	5,996	331	1,482 D	41.6%	55.3%	42.9%	57.1%
23,635	HEMPSTEAD	8,628	3,852	4,671	105	819 D	44.6%	54.1%	45.2%	54.8%
26,819	HOT SPRING	10,817	3,561	6,897	359	3,336 D	32.9%	63.8%	34.1%	65.9%
13,459	HOWARD	5,064	2,386	2,564	114	178 D	47.1%	50.6%	48.2%	51.8%
30,147	INDEPENDENCE	11,125	5,076	5,683	366	607 D	45.6%	51.1%	47.2%	52.8%
10,768	IZARD	5,254	2,266	2,750	238	484 D	43.1%	52.3%	45.2%	54.8%
21,646	JACKSON	8,081	3,191	4,651	239	1,460 D	39.5%	57.6%	40.7%	59.3%
90,718	JEFFERSON	30,046	10,697	17,292	2,057	6,595 D	35.6%	57.6%	38.2%	61.8%
17,423	JOHNSON	7,636	3,619	3,709	308	90 D	47.4%	48.6%	49.4%	50.6%
10,213	LAFAYETTE	3,776	1,756	1,947	73	191 D	46.5%	51.6%	47.4%	52.6%
18,447	LAWRENCE	6,963	3,245	3,547	171	302 D	46.6%	50.9%	47.8%	52.2%
15,539	LEE	4,876	1,711	3,103	62	1,392 D	35.1%	63.6%	35.5%	64.5%
13,369	LINCOLN	3,849	1,243	2,517	89	1,274 D	32.3%	65.4%	33.1%	66.9%
13,952	LITTLE RIVER	5,024	2,272	2,631	121	359 D	45.2%	52.4%	46.3%	53.7%
20,144	LOGAN	8,913	4,511	4,098	304	413 R	50.6%	46.0%	52.4%	47.6%
34,518	LONOKE	11,585	5,619	5,605	361	14 R	48.5%	48.4%	50.1%	49.9%
11,373	MADISON	5,835	3,180	2,434	221	746 R	54.5%	41.7%	56.6%	43.4%
11,334	MARION	5,356	3,059	2,046	251	1,013 R	57.1%	38.2%	59.9%	40.1%
37,766	MILLER	12,921	6,770	5,996	155	774 R	52.4%	46.4%	53.0%	47.0%
59,517	MISSISSIPPI	16,417	7,170	8,908	339	1,738 D	43.7%	54.3%	44.6%	55.4%
14,052	MONROE	4,829	2,027	2,686	116	659 D	42.0%	55.6%	43.0%	57.0%
7,771	MONTGOMERY	3,612	1,585	1,878	149	293 D	43.9%	52.0%	45.8%	54.2%
11,097	NEVADA	4,440	1,697	2,631	112	934 D	38.2%	59.3%	39.2%	60.8%
7,756	NEWTON	4,033	2,423	1,436	174	987 R	60.1%	35.6%	62.8%	37.2%
30,541	OUACHITA	12,208	4,329	7,152	727	2,823 D	35.5%	58.6%	37.7%	62.3%
7,266	PERRY	3,186	1,459	1,606	121	147 D	45.8%	50.4%	47.6%	52.4%
34,772	PHILLIPS	11,146	4,270	6,642	234	2,372 D	38.3%	59.6%	39.1%	60.9%
10,373	PIKE	4,097	1,916	2,094	87	178 D	46.8%	51.1%	47.8%	52.2%
27,032	POINSETT	9,180	4,040	4,894	246	854 D	44.0%	53.3%	45.2%	54.8%
17,007	POLK	6,824	3,993	2,617	214	1,376 R	58.5%	38.3%	60.4%	39.6%
39,003	POPE	14,230	7,217	6,364	649	853 R	50.7%	44.7%	53.1%	46.9%
10,140	PRAIRIE	3,895	1,855	1,928	112	73 D	47.6%	49.5%	49.0%	51.0%
340,613	PULASKI	112,937	52,125	54,839	5,973	2,714 D	46.2%	48.6%	48.7%	51.3%
16,834	RANDOLPH	5,929	2,579	3,070	280	491 D	43.5%	51.8%	45.7%	54.3%
30,858	ST. FRANCIS	10,487	4,485	5,816	186	1,331 D	42.8%	55.5%	43.5%	56.5%
52,881	SALINE	19,555	8,330	10,368	857	2,038 D	42.6%	53.0%	44.6%	55.4%
9,685	SCOTT	4,626	2,228	2,236	162	8 D	48.2%	48.3%	49.9%	50.1%
8,847	SEARCY	4,183	2,459	1,536	188	923 R	58.8%	36.7%	61.6%	38.4%
94,930	SEBASTIAN	36,879	23,403	10,141	3,335	13,262 R	63.5%	27.5%	69.8%	30.2%
14,060	SEVIER	5,497	2,502	2,854	141	352 D	45.5%	51.9%	46.7%	53.3%
14,607	SHARP	6,416	3,420	2,774	222	646 R	53.3%	43.2%	55.2%	44.8%
9,022	STONE	3,975	1,793	1,968	214	175 D	45.1%	49.5%	47.7%	52.3%
49,988	UNION	17,063	9,401	6,852	810	2,549 R	55.1%	40.2%	57.8%	42.2%

ARKANSAS

PRESIDENT 1980

1980 Census Population	County	Total Vote	Republican	Democratic	Other	Rep.-Dem. Plurality	Percentage Total Vote Rep.	Dem.	Major Vote Rep.	Dem.
13,357	VAN BUREN	6,292	3,090	2,968	234	122 R	49.1%	47.2%	51.0%	49.0%
99,735	WASHINGTON	35,421	20,788	12,276	2,357	8,512 R	58.7%	34.7%	62.9%	37.1%
50,835	WHITE	17,313	8,079	8,750	484	671 D	46.7%	50.5%	48.0%	52.0%
11,222	WOODRUFF	3,756	1,204	2,452	100	1,248 D	32.1%	65.3%	32.9%	67.1%
17,026	YELL	7,137	3,187	3,702	248	515 D	44.7%	51.9%	46.3%	53.7%
2,285,513	TOTAL	837,582	403,164	398,041	36,377	5,123 R	48.1%	47.5%	50.3%	49.7%

ARKANSAS

GOVERNOR 1980

1980 Census Population	County	Total Vote	Republican	Democratic	Other	Rep.-Dem. Plurality	Percentage			
							Total Vote		Major Vote	
							Rep.	Dem.	Rep.	Dem.
24,175	ARKANSAS	8,579	3,301	5,278		1,977 D	38.5%	61.5%	38.5%	61.5%
26,538	ASHLEY	8,658	4,269	4,389		120 D	49.3%	50.7%	49.3%	50.7%
27,409	BAXTER	15,219	9,526	5,693		3,833 R	62.6%	37.4%	62.6%	37.4%
78,115	BENTON	29,339	17,400	11,939		5,461 R	59.3%	40.7%	59.3%	40.7%
26,067	BOONE	11,706	6,457	5,249		1,208 R	55.2%	44.8%	55.2%	44.8%
13,803	BRADLEY	4,925	2,000	2,925		925 D	40.6%	59.4%	40.6%	59.4%
6,079	CALHOUN	2,494	1,438	1,056		382 R	57.7%	42.3%	57.7%	42.3%
16,203	CARROLL	7,290	4,336	2,954		1,382 R	59.5%	40.5%	59.5%	40.5%
17,793	CHICOT	5,645	1,841	3,804		1,963 D	32.6%	67.4%	32.6%	67.4%
23,326	CLARK	9,395	3,266	6,129		2,863 D	34.8%	65.2%	34.8%	65.2%
20,616	CLAY	7,308	4,164	3,144		1,020 R	57.0%	43.0%	57.0%	43.0%
16,909	BYRNE	8,545	4,330	4,215		115 R	50.7%	49.3%	50.7%	49.3%
7,868	CLEVELAND	3,207	1,797	1,410		387 R	56.0%	44.0%	56.0%	44.0%
26,644	COLUMBIA	9,211	5,397	3,814		1,583 R	58.6%	41.4%	58.6%	41.4%
19,505	CONWAY	9,399	4,773	4,626		147 R	50.8%	49.2%	50.8%	49.2%
63,218	CRAIGHEAD	20,908	12,161	8,747		3,414 R	58.2%	41.8%	58.2%	41.8%
36,892	CRAWFORD	12,939	9,216	3,723		5,493 R	71.2%	28.8%	71.2%	28.8%
49,097	CRITTENDEN	12,435	5,057	7,378		2,321 D	40.7%	59.3%	40.7%	59.3%
20,434	CROSS	6,741	3,131	3,610		479 D	46.4%	53.6%	46.4%	53.6%
10,515	DALLAS	4,626	2,320	2,306		14 R	50.2%	49.8%	50.2%	49.8%
19,760	DESHA	5,761	1,763	3,998		2,235 D	30.6%	69.4%	30.6%	69.4%
17,910	DREW	6,301	2,423	3,878		1,455 D	38.5%	61.5%	38.5%	61.5%
46,192	FAULKNER	16,148	7,949	8,199		250 D	49.2%	50.8%	49.2%	50.8%
14,705	FRANKLIN	6,783	4,421	2,362		2,059 R	65.2%	34.8%	65.2%	34.8%
9,975	FULTON	4,332	2,572	1,760		812 R	59.4%	40.6%	59.4%	40.6%
69,916	GARLAND	29,432	15,279	14,153		1,126 R	51.9%	48.1%	51.9%	48.1%
13,008	GRANT	5,374	2,922	2,452		470 R	54.4%	45.6%	54.4%	45.6%
30,744	GREENE	10,897	5,825	5,072		753 R	53.5%	46.5%	53.5%	46.5%
23,635	HEMPSTEAD	8,748	4,147	4,601		454 D	47.4%	52.6%	47.4%	52.6%
26,819	HOT SPRING	10,716	5,363	5,353		10 R	50.0%	50.0%	50.0%	50.0%
13,459	HOWARD	5,037	3,085	1,952		1,133 R	61.2%	38.8%	61.2%	38.8%
30,147	INDEPENDENCE	11,253	5,988	5,265		723 R	53.2%	46.8%	53.2%	46.8%
10,768	IZARD	5,295	2,667	2,628		39 R	50.4%	49.6%	50.4%	49.6%
21,646	JACKSON	8,095	4,175	3,920		255 R	51.6%	48.4%	51.6%	48.4%
90,718	JEFFERSON	28,773	11,541	17,232		5,691 D	40.1%	59.9%	40.1%	59.9%
17,423	JOHNSON	7,857	4,614	3,243		1,371 R	58.7%	41.3%	58.7%	41.3%
10,213	LAFAYETTE	4,174	2,460	1,714		746 R	58.9%	41.1%	58.9%	41.1%
18,447	LAWRENCE	7,239	4,624	2,615		2,009 R	63.9%	36.1%	63.9%	36.1%
15,539	LEE	5,146	1,712	3,434		1,722 D	33.3%	66.7%	33.3%	66.7%
13,369	LINCOLN	3,962	1,516	2,446		930 D	38.3%	61.7%	38.3%	61.7%
13,952	LITTLE RIVER	5,104	2,512	2,592		80 D	49.2%	50.8%	49.2%	50.8%
20,144	LOGAN	9,110	5,402	3,708		1,694 R	59.3%	40.7%	59.3%	40.7%
34,518	LONOKE	11,751	6,287	5,464		823 R	53.5%	46.5%	53.5%	46.5%
11,373	MADISON	5,821	3,321	2,500		821 R	57.1%	42.9%	57.1%	42.9%
11,334	MARION	5,568	3,291	2,277		1,014 R	59.1%	40.9%	59.1%	40.9%
37,766	MILLER	13,396	7,787	5,609		2,178 R	58.1%	41.9%	58.1%	41.9%
59,517	MISSISSIPPI	16,549	8,058	8,491		433 D	48.7%	51.3%	48.7%	51.3%
14,052	MONROE	4,923	2,086	2,837		751 D	42.4%	57.6%	42.4%	57.6%
7,771	MONTGOMERY	3,600	2,023	1,577		446 R	56.2%	43.8%	56.2%	43.8%
11,097	NEVADA	4,722	2,185	2,537		352 D	46.3%	53.7%	46.3%	53.7%
7,756	NEWTON	4,135	2,514	1,621		893 R	60.8%	39.2%	60.8%	39.2%
30,541	OUACHITA	11,715	5,878	5,837		41 R	50.2%	49.8%	50.2%	49.8%
7,266	PERRY	3,352	1,878	1,474		404 R	56.0%	44.0%	56.0%	44.0%
34,772	PHILLIPS	11,383	3,840	7,543		3,703 D	33.7%	66.3%	33.7%	66.3%
10,373	PIKE	4,209	2,530	1,679		851 R	60.1%	39.9%	60.1%	39.9%
27,032	POINSETT	9,259	5,510	3,749		1,761 R	59.5%	40.5%	59.5%	40.5%
17,007	POLK	7,012	4,012	3,000		1,012 R	57.2%	42.8%	57.2%	42.8%
39,003	POPE	14,750	8,770	5,980		2,790 R	59.5%	40.5%	59.5%	40.5%
10,140	PRAIRIE	4,150	2,158	1,992		166 R	52.0%	48.0%	52.0%	48.0%
340,613	PULASKI	114,498	50,339	64,159		13,820 D	44.0%	56.0%	44.0%	56.0%
16,834	RANDOLPH	5,879	3,590	2,289		1,301 R	61.1%	38.9%	61.1%	38.9%
30,858	ST. FRANCIS	10,117	4,490	5,627		1,137 D	44.4%	55.6%	44.4%	55.6%
52,881	SALINE	19,968	9,830	10,138		308 D	49.2%	50.8%	49.2%	50.8%
9,685	SCOTT	4,625	3,150	1,475		1,675 R	68.1%	31.9%	68.1%	31.9%
8,847	SEARCY	4,603	3,041	1,562		1,479 R	66.1%	33.9%	66.1%	33.9%
94,930	SEBASTIAN	35,904	24,010	11,894		12,116 R	66.9%	33.1%	66.9%	33.1%
14,060	SEVIER	5,541	2,763	2,778		15 D	49.9%	50.1%	49.9%	50.1%
14,607	SHARP	6,737	3,768	2,969		799 R	55.9%	44.1%	55.9%	44.1%
9,022	STONE	4,206	2,470	1,736		734 R	58.7%	41.3%	58.7%	41.3%
49,988	UNION	15,949	10,117	5,832		4,285 R	63.4%	36.6%	63.4%	36.6%

ARKANSAS

GOVERNOR 1980

1980 Census Population	County	Total Vote	Republican	Democratic	Other	Rep.-Dem. Plurality	Percentage Total Vote Rep.	Dem.	Major Vote Rep.	Dem.
13,357	VAN BUREN	6,458	3,453	3,005		448 R	53.5%	46.5%	53.5%	46.5%
99,735	WASHINGTON	34,557	18,334	16,223		2,111 R	53.1%	46.9%	53.1%	46.9%
50,835	WHITE	17,988	9,245	8,743		502 R	51.4%	48.6%	51.4%	48.6%
11,222	WOODRUFF	3,902	1,351	2,551		1,200 D	34.6%	65.4%	34.6%	65.4%
17,026	YELL	7,592	4,465	3,127		1,338 R	58.8%	41.2%	58.8%	41.2%
2,285,513	TOTAL	838,925	435,684	403,241		32,443 R	51.9%	48.1%	51.9%	48.1%

ARKANSAS

SENATOR 1980

1980 Census Population	County	Total Vote	Republican	Democratic	Other	Rep.-Dem. Plurality	Total Vote Rep.	Total Vote Dem.	Major Vote Rep.	Major Vote Dem.
24,175	ARKANSAS	7,860	2,357	5,503		3,146 D	30.0%	70.0%	30.0%	70.0%
26,538	ASHLEY	8,511	3,306	5,205		1,899 D	38.8%	61.2%	38.8%	61.2%
27,409	BAXTER	15,142	8,094	7,048		1,046 R	53.5%	46.5%	53.5%	46.5%
78,115	BENTON	28,733	15,731	13,002		2,729 R	54.7%	45.3%	54.7%	45.3%
26,067	BOONE	10,471	5,060	5,411		351 D	48.3%	51.7%	48.3%	51.7%
13,803	BRADLEY	4,526	1,054	3,472		2,418 D	23.3%	76.7%	23.3%	76.7%
6,079	CALHOUN	2,439	752	1,687		935 D	30.8%	69.2%	30.8%	69.2%
16,203	CARROLL	7,042	3,001	4,041		1,040 D	42.6%	57.4%	42.6%	57.4%
17,793	CHICOT	5,630	1,348	4,282		2,934 D	23.9%	76.1%	23.9%	76.1%
23,326	CLARK	9,299	2,059	7,240		5,181 D	22.1%	77.9%	22.1%	77.9%
20,616	CLAY	7,083	2,613	4,470		1,857 D	36.9%	63.1%	36.9%	63.1%
16,909	CLEBURNE	8,497	3,415	5,082		1,667 D	40.2%	59.8%	40.2%	59.8%
7,868	CLEVELAND	3,210	915	2,295		1,380 D	28.5%	71.5%	28.5%	71.5%
26,644	COLUMBIA	8,160	4,341	3,819		522 R	53.2%	46.8%	53.2%	46.8%
19,505	CONWAY	9,150	3,150	6,000		2,850 D	34.4%	65.6%	34.4%	65.6%
63,218	CRAIGHEAD	19,744	8,869	10,875		2,006 D	44.9%	55.1%	44.9%	55.1%
36,892	CRAWFORD	12,843	9,156	3,687		5,469 R	71.3%	28.7%	71.3%	28.7%
49,097	CRITTENDEN	11,008	3,786	7,222		3,436 D	34.4%	65.6%	34.4%	65.6%
20,434	CROSS	6,629	2,125	4,504		2,379 D	32.1%	67.9%	32.1%	67.9%
10,515	DALLAS	4,575	1,328	3,247		1,919 D	29.0%	71.0%	29.0%	71.0%
19,760	DESHA	5,367	1,115	4,252		3,137 D	20.8%	79.2%	20.8%	79.2%
17,910	DREW	6,205	1,566	4,639		3,073 D	25.2%	74.8%	25.2%	74.8%
46,192	FAULKNER	15,709	5,450	10,259		4,809 D	34.7%	65.3%	34.7%	65.3%
14,705	FRANKLIN	6,762	3,996	2,766		1,230 R	59.1%	40.9%	59.1%	40.9%
9,975	FULTON	4,235	1,519	2,716		1,197 D	35.9%	64.1%	35.9%	64.1%
69,916	GARLAND	26,050	13,080	12,970		110 R	50.2%	49.8%	50.2%	49.8%
13,008	GRANT	5,357	1,865	3,492		1,627 D	34.8%	65.2%	34.8%	65.2%
30,744	GREENE	10,944	3,647	7,297		3,650 D	33.3%	66.7%	33.3%	66.7%
23,635	HEMPSTEAD	8,457	2,503	5,954		3,451 D	29.6%	70.4%	29.6%	70.4%
26,819	HOT SPRING	9,786	2,999	6,787		3,788 D	30.6%	69.4%	30.6%	69.4%
13,459	HOWARD	4,935	2,050	2,885		835 D	41.5%	58.5%	41.5%	58.5%
30,147	INDEPENDENCE	11,175	3,775	7,400		3,625 D	33.8%	66.2%	33.8%	66.2%
10,768	IZARD	5,176	1,900	3,276		1,376 D	36.7%	63.3%	36.7%	63.3%
21,646	JACKSON	7,980	2,493	5,486	1	2,993 D	31.2%	68.7%	31.2%	68.8%
90,718	JEFFERSON	27,433	8,422	19,011		10,589 D	30.7%	69.3%	30.7%	69.3%
17,423	JOHNSON	7,711	3,498	4,213		715 D	45.4%	54.6%	45.4%	54.6%
10,213	LAFAYETTE	4,047	1,247	2,800		1,553 D	30.8%	69.2%	30.8%	69.2%
18,447	LAWRENCE	7,184	3,022	4,162		1,140 D	42.1%	57.9%	42.1%	57.9%
15,539	LEE	5,043	1,127	3,916		2,789 D	22.3%	77.7%	22.3%	77.7%
13,369	LINCOLN	3,567	765	2,802		2,037 D	21.4%	78.6%	21.4%	78.6%
13,952	LITTLE RIVER	4,812	1,487	3,325		1,838 D	30.9%	69.1%	30.9%	69.1%
20,144	LOGAN	9,104	4,802	4,302		500 R	52.7%	47.3%	52.7%	47.3%
34,518	LONOKE	11,695	4,618	7,077		2,459 D	39.5%	60.5%	39.5%	60.5%
11,373	MADISON	5,479	2,739	2,740		1 D	50.0%	50.0%	50.0%	50.0%
11,334	MARION	5,500	2,466	3,034		568 D	44.8%	55.2%	44.8%	55.2%
37,766	MILLER	12,561	5,194	7,367		2,173 D	41.4%	58.6%	41.4%	58.6%
59,517	MISSISSIPPI	16,215	4,996	11,219		6,223 D	30.8%	69.2%	30.8%	69.2%
14,052	MONROE	4,660	1,401	3,259		1,858 D	30.1%	69.9%	30.1%	69.9%
7,771	MONTGOMERY	3,513	1,327	2,186		859 D	37.8%	62.2%	37.8%	62.2%
11,097	NEVADA	4,547	1,260	3,287		2,027 D	27.7%	72.3%	27.7%	72.3%
7,756	NEWTON	4,084	2,335	1,749		586 R	57.2%	42.8%	57.2%	42.8%
30,541	OUACHITA	10,849	3,247	7,602		4,355 D	29.9%	70.1%	29.9%	70.1%
7,266	PERRY	3,314	1,316	1,998		682 D	39.7%	60.3%	39.7%	60.3%
34,772	PHILLIPS	10,878	2,276	8,602		6,326 D	20.9%	79.1%	20.9%	79.1%
10,373	PIKE	4,171	1,659	2,512		853 D	39.8%	60.2%	39.8%	60.2%
27,032	POINSETT	9,085	3,129	5,956		2,827 D	34.4%	65.6%	34.4%	65.6%
17,007	POLK	6,877	3,398	3,479		81 D	49.4%	50.6%	49.4%	50.6%
39,003	POPE	14,636	6,191	8,445		2,254 D	42.3%	57.7%	42.3%	57.7%
10,140	PRAIRIE	4,100	1,344	2,756		1,412 D	32.8%	67.2%	32.8%	67.2%
340,613	PULASKI	113,123	39,836	72,987	300	33,151 D	35.2%	64.5%	35.3%	64.7%
16,834	RANDOLPH	5,908	2,410	3,498		1,088 D	40.8%	59.2%	40.8%	59.2%
30,858	ST. FRANCIS	9,870	3,372	6,498		3,126 D	34.2%	65.8%	34.2%	65.8%
52,881	SALINE	19,270	6,903	12,367		5,464 D	35.8%	64.2%	35.8%	64.2%
9,685	SCOTT	4,589	2,618	1,971		647 R	57.0%	43.0%	57.0%	43.0%
8,847	SEARCY	4,259	1,967	2,262	30	295 D	46.2%	53.1%	46.5%	53.5%
94,930	SEBASTIAN	34,452	24,289	10,163		14,126 R	70.5%	29.5%	70.5%	29.5%
14,060	SEVIER	5,412	1,844	3,568		1,724 D	34.1%	65.9%	34.1%	65.9%
14,607	SHARP	6,632	3,157	3,475		318 D	47.6%	52.4%	47.6%	52.4%
9,022	STONE	4,138	1,587	2,551		964 D	38.4%	61.6%	38.4%	61.6%
49,988	UNION	14,793	9,231	5,562		3,669 R	62.4%	37.6%	62.4%	37.6%

ARKANSAS

SENATOR 1980

1980 Census Population	County	Total Vote	Republican	Democratic	Other	Rep.-Dem. Plurality	Percentage Total Vote Rep.	Dem.	Major Vote Rep.	Dem.
13,357	VAN BUREN	6,026	2,417	3,609		1,192 D	40.1%	59.9%	40.1%	59.9%
99,735	WASHINGTON	31,713	16,313	15,400		913 R	51.4%	48.6%	51.4%	48.6%
50,835	WHITE	17,593	7,161	10,432		3,271 D	40.7%	59.3%	40.7%	59.3%
11,222	WOODRUFF	3,793	866	2,927		2,061 D	22.8%	77.2%	22.8%	77.2%
17,026	YELL	7,486	2,921	4,565		1,644 D	39.0%	61.0%	39.0%	61.0%
2,285,513	TOTAL	808,812	330,576	477,905	331	147,329 D	40.9%	59.1%	40.9%	59.1%

ARKANSAS

CONGRESS

CD	Year	Total Vote	Republican Vote	Candidate	Democratic Vote	Candidate	Other Vote	Rep.-Dem. Plurality	Total Vote Rep.	Total Vote Dem.	Major Vote Rep.	Major Vote Dem.
1	1980					ALEXANDER, WILLIAM						
1	1978					ALEXANDER, WILLIAM						
1	1976	168,782	52,565	HOLLEMAN, HARLAN	116,217	ALEXANDER, WILLIAM		63,652 D	31.1%	68.9%	31.1%	68.9%
1	1974	115,068	10,821	DAUER, JAMES L.	104,247	ALEXANDER, WILLIAM		93,426 D	9.4%	90.6%	9.4%	90.6%
1	1972					ALEXANDER, WILLIAM						
2	1980	201,655	159,148	BETHUNE, ED	42,278	REID, JAMES G.	229	116,870 R	78.9%	21.0%	79.0%	21.0%
2	1978	127,425	65,285	BETHUNE, ED	62,140	BRANDON, DOUG		3,145 R	51.2%	48.8%	51.2%	48.8%
2	1976	167,607	22,819	KELLY, JAMES J.	144,780	TUCKER, JIM GUY	8	121,961 D	13.6%	86.4%	13.6%	86.4%
2	1974	136,334	56,038	PETTY, JUDY	80,296	MILLS, WILBUR D.		24,258 D	41.1%	58.9%	41.1%	58.9%
2	1972					MILLS, WILBUR D.						
3	1980			HAMMERSCHMIDT, JOHN								
3	1978	165,834	130,086	HAMMERSCHMIDT, JOHN	35,748	MEARS, WILLIAM C.		94,338 R	78.4%	21.6%	78.4%	21.6%
3	1976			HAMMERSCHMIDT, JOHN								
3	1974	172,354	89,324	HAMMERSCHMIDT, JOHN	83,030	CLINTON, BILL		6,294 R	51.8%	48.2%	51.8%	48.2%
3	1972	187,052	144,571	HAMMERSCHMIDT, JOHN	42,481	HATFIELD, GUY W.		102,090 R	77.3%	22.7%	77.3%	22.7%
4	1980					ANTHONY, BERYL F.						
4	1978					ANTHONY, BERYL F.						
4	1976					THORNTON, RAY						
4	1974					THORNTON, RAY						
4	1972					THORNTON, RAY						

ARKANSAS

1980 GENERAL ELECTION

President   Other vote was 22,468 Anderson (Anderson Coalition); 8,970 Clark (Libertarian); 2,345 Commoner (Citizens); 1,350 Bubar (Statesman); 1,244 Hall (People Before Profits).

Governor

Senator   Other vote was McCarty (write-in).

Congress   Under present legislation, votes are not tallied in unopposed elections, so no total vote or candidate vote is available for unopposed Congressional districts. Other vote in CD 2 was Hubanks (write-in).

1980 PRIMARIES

MAY 27 REPUBLICAN

Governor   5,867 Frank D. White; 2,310 Marshall Chrisman.

Senator   Bill Clark, unopposed.

Congress   Unopposed in two CD's. No candidates in CD's 1 and 4.

MAY 27 DEMOCRATIC

Governor   306,735 Bill Clinton; 138,660 Monroe A. Schwarzlose.

Senator   Dale Bumpers, unopposed.

Congress   Unopposed in two CD's. No candidate in CD 3. Contested as follows:

  CD 2   50,556 James G. Reid; 34,946 J. R. Whitten.

CALIFORNIA

GOVERNOR
Edmund G. Brown, Jr. (D). Re-elected 1978 to a four-year term. Previously elected 1974.

SENATORS
Alan Cranston (D). Re-elected 1980 to a six-year term. Previously elected 1974, 1968.

S. I. Hayakawa (R). Elected 1976 to a six-year term.

REPRESENTATIVES

1. Eugene A. Chappie (R)
2. Don H. Clausen (R)
3. Robert T. Matsui (D)
4. Vic Fazio (D)
5. John Burton (D)
6. Phillip Burton (D)
7. George Miller (D)
8. Ronald V. Dellums (D)
9. Fortney Stark (D)
10. Don Edwards (D)
11. Tom Lantos (D)
12. Paul N. McCloskey (R)
13. Norman Y. Mineta (D)
14. Norman D. Shumway (R)
15. Tony Coelho (D)
16. Leon E. Panetta (D)
17. Charles Pashayan (R)
18. William M. Thomas (R)
19. Robert J. Lagomarsino (R)
20. Barry M. Goldwater, Jr. (R)
21. Bobbi Fiedler (R)
22. Carlos J. Moorhead (R)
23. Anthony C. Beilenson (D)
24. Henry A. Waxman (D)
25. Edward R. Roybal (D)
26. John H. Rousselot (R)
27. Robert K. Dornan (R)
28. Julian C. Dixon (D)
29. Augustus Hawkins (D)
30. George E. Danielson (D)
31. Mervyn M. Dymally (D)
32. Glenn M. Anderson (D)
33. Wayne Grisham (R)
34. Daniel E. Lungren (R)
35. David Dreier (R)
36. George E. Brown (D)
37. Jerry Lewis (R)
38. Jerry M. Patterson (D)
39. William E. Dannemeyer (R)
40. Robert E. Badham (R)
41. Bill Lowery (R)
42. Duncan L. Hunter (R)
43. Clair W. Burgener (R)

POSTWAR VOTE FOR GOVERNOR

Year	Total Vote	Republican Vote	Candidate	Democratic Vote	Candidate	Other Vote	Rep.-Dem. Plurality	Total Vote Rep.	Total Vote Dem.	Major Vote Rep.	Major Vote Dem.
1978	6,922,378	2,526,534	Younger, Evelle J.	3,878,812	Brown, Edmund G., Jr.	517,032	1,352,278 D	36.5%	56.0%	39.4%	60.6%
1974	6,248,070	2,952,954	Flournoy, Houston I.	3,131,648	Brown, Edmund G., Jr.	163,468	178,694 D	47.3%	50.1%	48.5%	51.5%
1970	6,510,072	3,439,664	Reagan, Ronald	2,938,607	Unruh, Jess	131,801	501,057 R	52.8%	45.1%	53.9%	46.1%
1966	6,503,445	3,742,913	Reagan, Ronald	2,749,174	Brown, Edmund G.	11,358	993,739 R	57.6%	42.3%	57.7%	42.3%
1962	5,853,270	2,740,351	Nixon, Richard M.	3,037,109	Brown, Edmund G.	75,810	296,758 D	46.8%	51.9%	47.4%	52.6%
1958	5,255,777	2,110,911	Knowland, William F.	3,140,076	Brown, Edmund G.	4,790	1,029,165 D	40.2%	59.7%	40.2%	59.8%
1954	4,030,368	2,290,519	Knight, Goodwin J.	1,739,368	Graves, Richard P.	481	551,151 R	56.8%	43.2%	56.8%	43.2%
1950	3,796,090	2,461,754	Warren, Earl	1,333,856	Roosevelt, James	480	1,127,898 R	64.8%	35.1%	64.9%	35.1%
1946	2,558,399	2,344,542	Warren, Earl	—	—	213,857	2,344,542 R	91.6%	—	100.0%	—

In 1946 the Republican candidate won both major party nominations.

POSTWAR VOTE FOR SENATOR

Year	Total Vote	Republican Vote	Candidate	Democratic Vote	Candidate	Other Vote	Rep.-Dem. Plurality	Total Vote Rep.	Total Vote Dem.	Major Vote Rep.	Major Vote Dem.
1980	8,327,481	3,093,426	Gann, Paul	4,705,399	Cranston, Alan	528,656	1,611,973 D	37.1%	56.5%	39.7%	60.3%
1976	7,472,268	3,748,973	Hayakawa, S. I.	3,502,862	Tunney, John V.	220,433	246,111 R	50.2%	46.9%	51.7%	48.3%
1974	6,102,432	2,210,267	Richardson, H. L.	3,693,160	Cranston, Alan	199,005	1,482,893 D	36.2%	60.5%	37.4%	62.6%
1970	6,492,157	2,877,617	Murphy, George	3,496,558	Tunney, John V.	117,982	618,941 D	44.3%	53.9%	45.1%	54.9%
1968	7,102,465	3,329,148	Rafferty, Max	3,680,352	Cranston, Alan	92,965	351,204 D	46.9%	51.8%	47.5%	52.5%
1964	7,041,821	3,628,555	Murphy, George	3,411,912	Salinger, Pierre	1,354	216,643 R	51.5%	48.5%	51.5%	48.5%
1962	5,647,952	3,180,483	Kuchel, Thomas H.	2,452,839	Richards, Richard	14,630	727,644 R	56.3%	43.4%	56.5%	43.5%
1958	5,135,221	2,204,337	Knight, Goodwin J.	2,927,693	Engle, Clair	3,191	723,356 D	42.9%	57.0%	43.0%	57.0%
1956	5,361,467	2,892,918	Kuchel, Thomas H.	2,445,816	Richards, Richard	22,733	447,102 R	54.0%	45.6%	54.2%	45.8%
1954s	3,929,668	2,090,836	Kuchel, Thomas H.	1,788,071	Yorty, Samuel W.	50,761	302,765 R	53.2%	45.5%	53.9%	46.1%
1952	4,542,548	3,982,448	Knowland, William F.	—	—	560,100	3,982,448 R	87.7%	—	100.0%	—
1950	3,686,315	2,183,454	Nixon, Richard M.	1,502,507	Douglas, Helen	354	680,947 R	59.2%	40.8%	59.2%	40.8%
1946	2,639,465	1,428,067	Knowland, William F.	1,167,161	Rogers, Will	44,237	260,906 R	54.1%	44.2%	55.0%	45.0%

The 1954 election was for a short term to fill a vacancy. In 1952 the Republican candidate won both major party nominations.

CALIFORNIA

Districts Established November 28, 1973

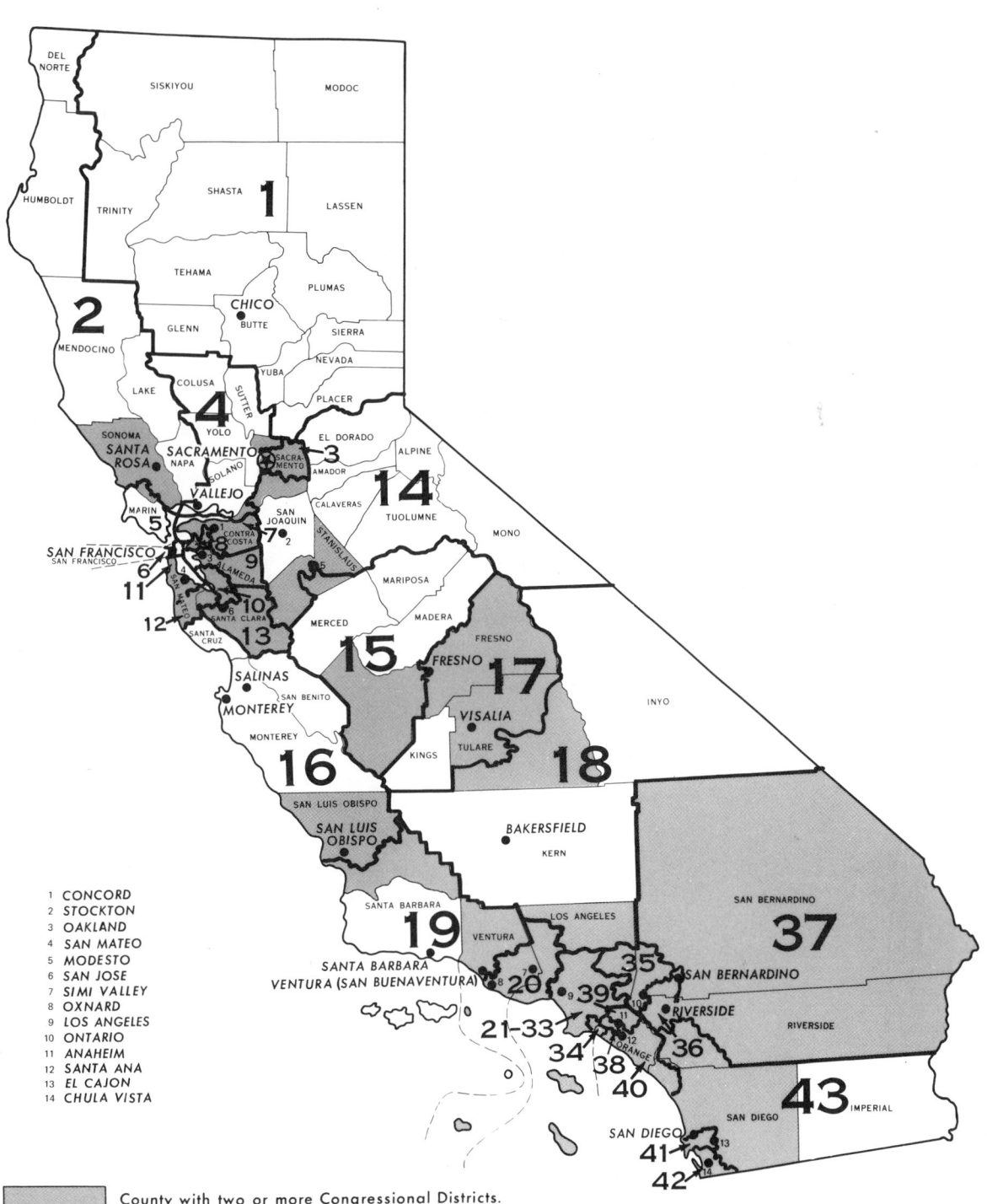

1 CONCORD
2 STOCKTON
3 OAKLAND
4 SAN MATEO
5 MODESTO
6 SAN JOSE
7 SIMI VALLEY
8 OXNARD
9 LOS ANGELES
10 ONTARIO
11 ANAHEIM
12 SANTA ANA
13 EL CAJON
14 CHULA VISTA

County with two or more Congressional Districts.

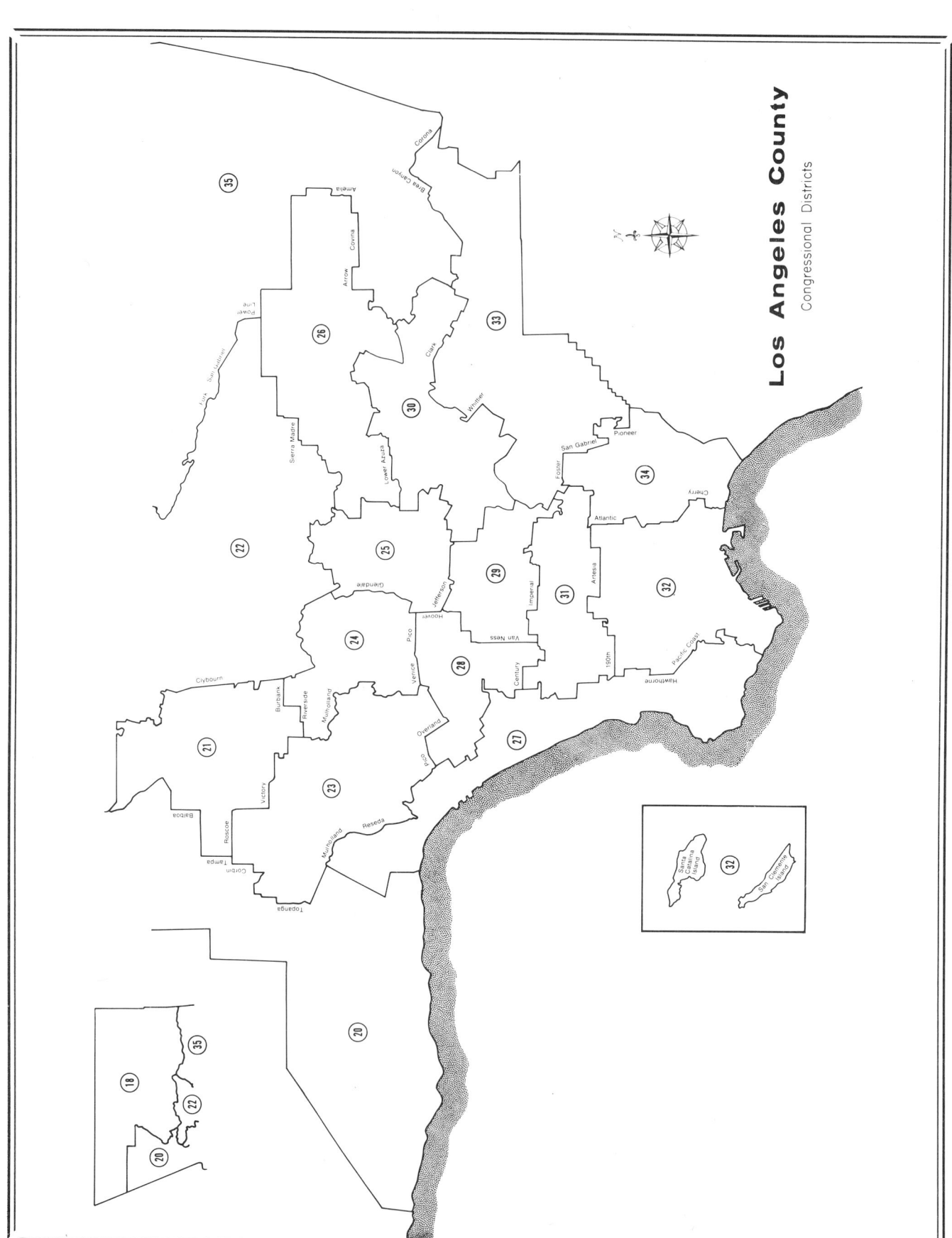

Los Angeles County
Congressional Districts

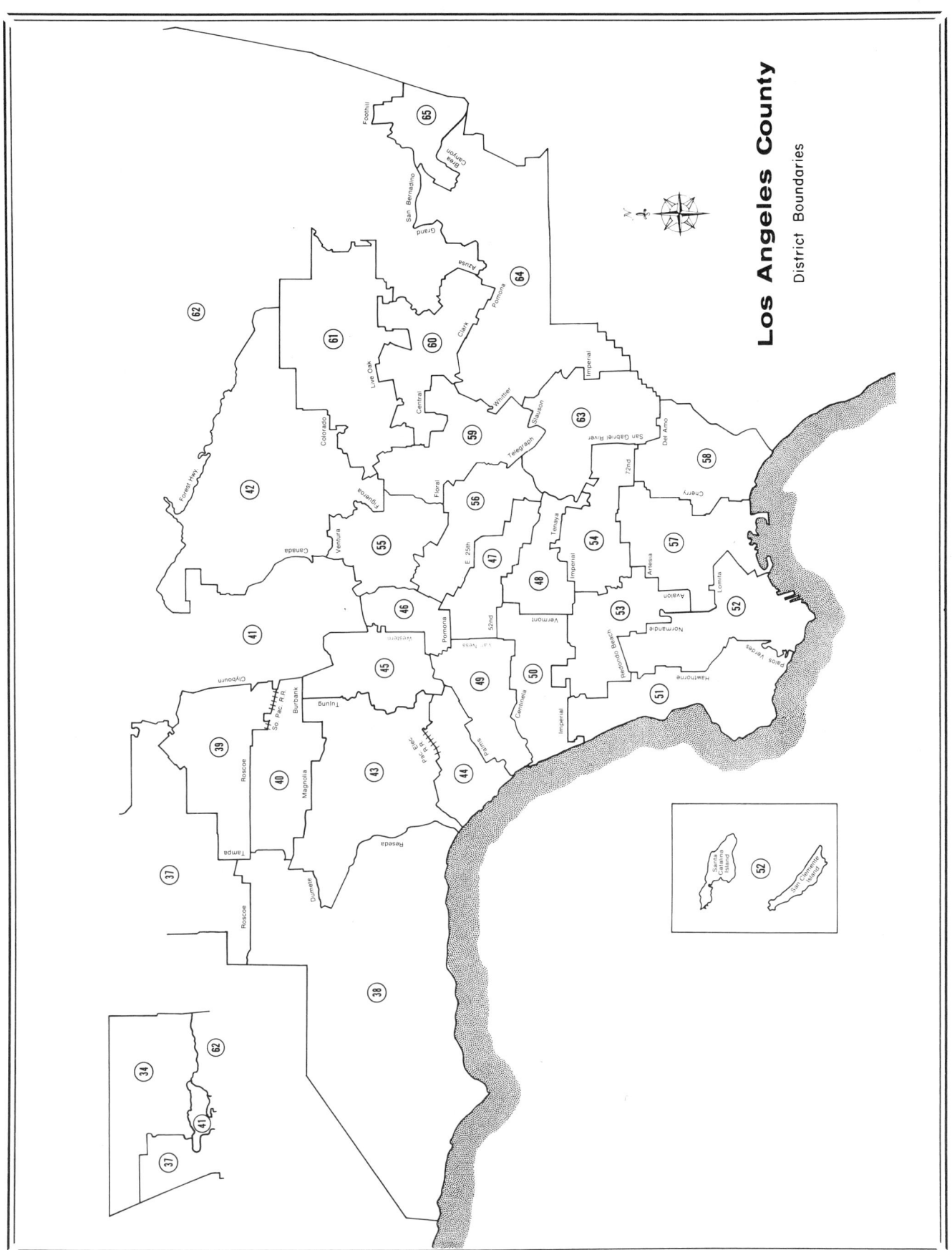

Los Angeles County
District Boundaries

CALIFORNIA

PRESIDENT 1980

1980 Census Population	County	Total Vote	Republican	Democratic	Other	Rep.-Dem. Plurality	Percentage Total Vote Rep.	Dem.	Major Vote Rep.	Dem.
1,105,379	ALAMEDA	417,617	158,531	201,720	57,366	43,189 D	38.0%	48.3%	44.0%	56.0%
1,097	ALPINE	461	254	133	74	121 R	55.1%	28.9%	65.6%	34.4%
19,314	AMADOR	9,670	5,401	3,191	1,078	2,210 R	55.9%	33.0%	62.9%	37.1%
143,851	BUTTE	66,012	38,188	19,520	8,304	18,668 R	57.9%	29.6%	66.2%	33.8%
20,710	CALAVERAS	10,275	6,054	3,076	1,145	2,978 R	58.9%	29.9%	66.3%	33.7%
12,791	COLUSA	4,995	2,897	1,605	493	1,292 R	58.0%	32.1%	64.3%	35.7%
657,252	CONTRA COSTA	287,545	144,112	107,398	36,035	36,714 R	50.1%	37.3%	57.3%	42.7%
18,217	DEL NORTE	6,987	4,016	2,338	633	1,678 R	57.5%	33.5%	63.2%	36.8%
85,812	EL DORADO	36,449	21,238	10,765	4,446	10,473 R	58.3%	29.5%	66.4%	33.6%
515,013	FRESNO	161,386	82,515	65,254	13,617	17,261 R	51.1%	40.4%	55.8%	44.2%
21,350	GLENN	8,312	5,386	2,227	699	3,159 R	64.8%	26.8%	70.7%	29.3%
108,024	HUMBOLDT	48,712	24,047	17,133	7,532	6,914 R	49.4%	35.2%	58.4%	41.6%
92,110	IMPERIAL	21,579	12,068	7,961	1,550	4,107 R	55.9%	36.9%	60.3%	39.7%
17,895	INYO	8,027	5,201	2,080	746	3,121 R	64.8%	25.9%	71.4%	28.6%
403,089	KERN	122,121	72,842	41,097	8,182	31,745 R	59.6%	33.7%	63.9%	36.1%
73,738	KINGS	19,021	10,531	7,299	1,191	3,232 R	55.4%	38.4%	59.1%	40.9%
36,366	LAKE	16,654	8,934	5,978	1,742	2,956 R	53.6%	35.9%	59.9%	40.1%
21,661	LASSEN	8,198	4,464	2,941	793	1,523 R	54.5%	35.9%	60.3%	39.7%
7,477,657	LOS ANGELES	2,440,185	1,224,533	979,830	235,822	244,703 R	50.2%	40.2%	55.6%	44.4%
63,116	MADERA	19,780	10,599	7,783	1,398	2,816 R	53.6%	39.3%	57.7%	42.3%
222,952	MARIN	108,507	49,678	39,231	19,598	10,447 R	45.8%	36.2%	55.9%	44.1%
11,108	MARIPOSA	5,608	3,082	1,889	637	1,193 R	55.0%	33.7%	62.0%	38.0%
66,738	MENDOCINO	28,224	12,432	10,784	5,008	1,648 R	44.0%	38.2%	53.5%	46.5%
134,560	MERCED	36,996	18,043	15,886	3,067	2,157 R	48.8%	42.9%	53.2%	46.8%
8,610	MODOC	4,000	2,579	1,046	375	1,533 R	64.5%	26.2%	71.1%	28.9%
8,577	MONO	3,421	2,132	865	424	1,267 R	62.3%	25.3%	71.1%	28.9%
290,444	MONTEREY	86,794	47,452	29,086	10,256	18,366 R	54.7%	33.5%	62.0%	38.0%
99,199	NAPA	44,035	23,632	14,898	5,505	8,734 R	53.7%	33.8%	61.3%	38.7%
51,645	NEVADA	26,261	15,207	7,605	3,449	7,602 R	57.9%	29.0%	66.7%	33.3%
1,931,570	ORANGE	780,212	529,797	176,704	73,711	353,093 R	67.9%	22.6%	75.0%	25.0%
117,247	PLACER	51,440	28,179	17,311	5,950	10,868 R	54.8%	33.7%	61.9%	38.1%
17,340	PLUMAS	8,161	4,182	2,911	1,068	1,271 R	51.2%	35.7%	59.0%	41.0%
663,923	RIVERSIDE	243,278	145,642	76,650	20,986	68,992 R	59.9%	31.5%	65.5%	34.5%
783,381	SACRAMENTO	322,120	153,721	130,031	38,368	23,690 R	47.7%	40.4%	54.2%	45.8%
25,005	SAN BENITO	7,602	4,054	2,749	799	1,305 R	53.3%	36.2%	59.6%	40.4%
893,157	SAN BERNARDINO	289,812	172,957	91,790	25,065	81,167 R	59.7%	31.7%	65.3%	34.7%
1,861,846	SAN DIEGO	716,866	435,910	195,410	85,546	240,500 R	60.8%	27.3%	69.0%	31.0%
678,974	SAN FRANCISCO	254,028	80,967	133,184	39,877	52,217 D	31.9%	52.4%	37.8%	62.2%
347,342	SAN JOAQUIN	116,863	64,718	41,551	10,594	23,167 R	55.4%	35.6%	60.9%	39.1%
155,345	SAN LUIS OBISPO	69,527	38,631	20,508	10,388	18,123 R	55.6%	29.5%	65.3%	34.7%
588,164	SAN MATEO	238,637	116,491	87,335	34,811	29,156 R	48.8%	36.6%	57.2%	42.8%
298,660	SANTA BARBARA	128,995	69,629	40,650	18,716	28,979 R	54.0%	31.5%	63.1%	36.9%
1,295,071	SANTA CLARA	477,003	229,048	166,995	80,960	62,053 R	48.0%	35.0%	57.8%	42.2%
188,141	SANTA CRUZ	85,804	37,347	32,346	16,111	5,001 R	43.5%	37.7%	53.6%	46.4%
115,715	SHASTA	47,418	27,547	15,364	4,507	12,183 R	58.1%	32.4%	64.2%	35.8%
3,073	SIERRA	1,718	855	651	212	204 R	49.8%	37.9%	56.8%	43.2%
39,732	SISKIYOU	16,738	9,331	5,664	1,743	3,667 R	55.7%	33.8%	62.2%	37.8%
235,203	SOLANO	80,676	40,919	30,952	8,805	9,967 R	50.7%	38.4%	56.9%	43.1%
299,827	SONOMA	125,985	60,722	45,596	19,667	15,126 R	48.2%	36.2%	57.1%	42.9%
265,902	STANISLAUS	84,186	41,595	33,683	8,908	7,912 R	49.4%	40.0%	55.3%	44.7%
52,246	SUTTER	18,557	11,778	5,103	1,676	6,675 R	63.5%	27.5%	69.8%	30.2%
38,888	TEHAMA	15,457	9,140	4,832	1,485	4,308 R	59.1%	31.3%	65.4%	34.6%
11,858	TRINITY	5,546	3,048	1,734	764	1,314 R	55.0%	31.3%	63.7%	36.3%
245,751	TULARE	70,846	41,317	25,155	4,374	16,162 R	58.3%	35.5%	62.2%	37.8%
33,920	TUOLUMNE	16,063	8,810	5,449	1,804	3,361 R	54.8%	33.9%	61.8%	38.2%
529,899	VENTURA	190,650	114,930	56,311	19,409	58,619 R	60.3%	29.5%	67.1%	32.9%
113,374	YOLO	49,690	19,603	21,527	8,560	1,924 D	39.5%	43.3%	47.7%	52.3%
49,733	YUBA	14,111	7,942	4,896	1,273	3,046 R	56.3%	34.7%	61.9%	38.1%
23,668,562	TOTAL	8,587,063	4,524,858	3,083,661	978,544	1,441,197 R	52.7%	35.9%	59.5%	40.5%

CALIFORNIA

SENATOR 1980

1980 Census Population	County	Total Vote	Republican	Democratic	Other	Rep.-Dem. Plurality	Percentage Total Vote Rep.	Dem.	Major Vote Rep.	Dem.
1,105,379	ALAMEDA	409,201	108,790	273,332	27,079	164,542 D	26.6%	66.8%	28.5%	71.5%
1,097	ALPINE	454	169	242	43	73 D	37.2%	53.3%	41.1%	58.9%
19,314	AMADOR	9,478	4,112	4,591	775	479 D	43.4%	48.4%	47.2%	52.8%
143,851	BUTTE	64,657	28,014	31,359	5,284	3,345 D	43.3%	48.5%	47.2%	52.8%
20,710	CALAVERAS	9,718	4,257	4,484	977	227 D	43.8%	46.1%	48.7%	51.3%
12,791	COLUSA	4,586	1,562	2,579	445	1,017 D	34.1%	56.2%	37.7%	62.3%
657,252	CONTRA COSTA	282,999	95,943	170,685	16,371	74,742 D	33.9%	60.3%	36.0%	64.0%
18,217	DEL NORTE	6,421	2,384	3,255	782	871 D	37.1%	50.7%	42.3%	57.7%
85,812	EL DORADO	35,762	16,345	16,305	3,112	40 R	45.7%	45.6%	50.1%	49.9%
515,013	FRESNO	155,976	54,073	94,164	7,739	40,091 D	34.7%	60.4%	36.5%	63.5%
21,350	GLENN	8,179	3,618	4,079	482	461 D	44.2%	49.9%	47.0%	53.0%
108,024	HUMBOLDT	47,848	15,610	27,698	4,540	12,088 D	32.6%	57.9%	36.0%	64.0%
92,110	IMPERIAL	21,869	7,355	12,946	1,568	5,591 D	33.6%	59.2%	36.2%	63.8%
17,895	INYO	7,906	4,172	3,179	555	993 R	52.8%	40.2%	56.8%	43.2%
403,089	KERN	120,359	44,997	66,943	8,419	21,946 D	37.4%	55.6%	40.2%	59.8%
73,738	KINGS	18,729	6,634	11,089	1,006	4,455 D	35.4%	59.2%	37.4%	62.6%
36,366	LAKE	16,479	6,543	8,723	1,213	2,180 D	39.7%	52.9%	42.9%	57.1%
21,661	LASSEN	7,787	2,872	4,220	695	1,348 D	36.9%	54.2%	40.5%	59.5%
7,477,657	LOS ANGELES	2,367,188	894,712	1,348,919	123,557	454,207 D	37.8%	57.0%	39.9%	60.1%
63,116	MADERA	18,170	6,505	10,562	1,103	4,057 D	35.8%	58.1%	38.1%	61.9%
222,952	MARIN	106,396	30,921	68,464	7,011	37,543 D	29.1%	64.3%	31.1%	68.9%
11,108	MARIPOSA	5,495	2,171	2,879	445	708 D	39.5%	52.4%	43.0%	57.0%
66,738	MENDOCINO	27,677	9,013	15,744	2,920	6,731 D	32.6%	56.9%	36.4%	63.6%
134,560	MERCED	33,687	10,590	20,053	3,044	9,463 D	31.4%	59.5%	34.6%	65.4%
8,610	MODOC	3,905	1,848	1,784	273	64 R	47.3%	45.7%	50.9%	49.1%
8,577	MONO	3,343	1,609	1,459	275	150 R	48.1%	43.6%	52.4%	47.6%
290,444	MONTEREY	84,203	26,966	52,180	5,057	25,214 D	32.0%	62.0%	34.1%	65.9%
99,199	NAPA	41,460	15,369	23,503	2,588	8,134 D	37.1%	56.7%	39.5%	60.5%
51,645	NEVADA	25,054	12,080	10,252	2,722	1,828 R	48.2%	40.9%	54.1%	45.9%
1,931,570	ORANGE	765,952	380,762	335,720	49,470	45,042 R	49.7%	43.8%	53.1%	46.9%
117,247	PLACER	49,752	20,950	24,373	4,429	3,423 D	42.1%	49.0%	46.2%	53.8%
17,340	PLUMAS	7,539	2,972	3,654	913	682 D	39.4%	48.5%	44.9%	55.1%
663,923	RIVERSIDE	239,640	103,583	121,407	14,650	17,824 D	43.2%	50.7%	46.0%	54.0%
783,381	SACRAMENTO	314,289	110,579	178,243	25,467	67,664 D	35.2%	56.7%	38.3%	61.7%
25,005	SAN BENITO	7,079	1,930	4,612	537	2,682 D	27.3%	65.2%	29.5%	70.5%
893,157	SAN BERNARDINO	282,980	123,024	143,992	15,964	20,968 D	43.5%	50.9%	46.1%	53.9%
1,861,846	SAN DIEGO	669,954	266,877	361,742	41,335	94,865 D	39.8%	54.0%	42.5%	57.5%
678,974	SAN FRANCISCO	249,135	46,415	188,239	14,481	141,824 D	18.6%	75.6%	19.8%	80.2%
347,342	SAN JOAQUIN	114,290	45,208	62,183	6,899	16,975 D	39.6%	54.4%	42.1%	57.9%
155,345	SAN LUIS OBISPO	67,994	23,863	38,995	5,136	15,132 D	35.1%	57.4%	38.0%	62.0%
588,164	SAN MATEO	228,262	61,810	145,208	21,244	83,398 D	27.1%	63.6%	29.9%	70.1%
298,660	SANTA BARBARA	125,464	44,451	73,570	7,443	29,119 D	35.4%	58.6%	37.7%	62.3%
1,295,071	SANTA CLARA	461,883	150,423	280,732	30,728	130,309 D	32.6%	60.8%	34.9%	65.1%
188,141	SANTA CRUZ	83,517	22,917	53,679	6,921	30,762 D	27.4%	64.3%	29.9%	70.1%
115,715	SHASTA	46,590	16,482	26,785	3,323	10,303 D	35.4%	57.5%	38.1%	61.9%
3,073	SIERRA	1,608	582	880	146	298 D	36.2%	54.7%	39.8%	60.2%
39,732	SISKIYOU	16,053	6,029	8,742	1,282	2,713 D	37.6%	54.5%	40.8%	59.2%
235,203	SOLANO	78,423	27,072	45,910	5,441	18,838 D	34.5%	58.5%	37.1%	62.9%
299,827	SONOMA	123,046	38,797	75,239	9,010	36,442 D	31.5%	61.1%	34.0%	66.0%
265,902	STANISLAUS	77,857	27,422	42,699	7,736	15,277 D	35.2%	54.8%	39.1%	60.9%
52,246	SUTTER	16,834	7,617	7,459	1,758	158 R	45.2%	44.3%	50.5%	49.5%
38,888	TEHAMA	15,184	5,713	8,236	1,235	2,523 D	37.6%	54.2%	41.0%	59.0%
11,858	TRINITY	5,422	1,964	2,887	571	923 D	36.2%	53.2%	40.5%	59.5%
245,751	TULARE	68,749	27,084	38,099	3,566	11,015 D	39.4%	55.4%	41.6%	58.4%
33,920	TUOLUMNE	15,670	6,358	8,177	1,135	1,819 D	40.6%	52.2%	43.7%	56.3%
529,899	VENTURA	187,458	84,379	91,104	11,975	6,725 D	45.0%	48.6%	48.1%	51.9%
113,374	YOLO	48,226	13,218	30,617	4,391	17,399 D	27.4%	63.5%	30.2%	69.8%
49,733	YUBA	13,472	5,711	6,544	1,217	833 D	42.4%	48.6%	46.6%	53.4%
23,668,562	TOTAL	8,327,481	3,093,426	4,705,399	528,656	1,611,973 D	37.1%	56.5%	39.7%	60.3%

LOS ANGELES COUNTY

PRESIDENT 1980

1980 Census Population	Assembly District	Total Vote	Republican	Democratic	Other	Rep.-Dem. Plurality	Total Vote Rep.	Total Vote Dem.	Major Vote Rep.	Major Vote Dem.
	DISTRICT 34 [PART]	40,804	29,011	8,744	3,049	20,267 R	71.1%	21.4%	76.8%	23.2%
	DISTRICT 37 [PART]	89,645	58,557	22,396	8,692	36,161 R	65.3%	25.0%	72.3%	27.7%
	DISTRICT 38 [PART]	101,856	60,228	28,947	12,681	31,281 R	59.1%	28.4%	67.5%	32.5%
261,575	DISTRICT 39	80,833	41,749	31,232	7,852	10,517 R	51.6%	38.6%	57.2%	42.8%
254,205	DISTRICT 40	93,007	47,118	34,639	11,250	12,479 R	50.7%	37.2%	57.6%	42.4%
252,328	DISTRICT 41	97,523	64,012	24,872	8,639	39,140 R	65.6%	25.5%	72.0%	28.0%
250,756	DISTRICT 42	109,080	61,613	35,710	11,757	25,903 R	56.5%	32.7%	63.3%	36.7%
256,887	DISTRICT 43	131,538	62,729	50,599	18,210	12,130 R	47.7%	38.5%	55.4%	44.6%
247,638	DISTRICT 44	110,469	43,660	50,713	16,096	7,053 D	39.5%	45.9%	46.3%	53.7%
265,872	DISTRICT 45	104,696	41,079	50,205	13,412	9,126 D	39.2%	48.0%	45.0%	55.0%
313,518	DISTRICT 46	58,744	23,725	28,693	6,326	4,968 D	40.4%	48.8%	45.3%	54.7%
285,567	DISTRICT 47	49,331	8,702	38,687	1,942	29,985 D	17.6%	78.4%	18.4%	81.6%
253,419	DISTRICT 48	52,421	10,169	40,506	1,746	30,337 D	19.4%	77.3%	20.1%	79.9%
252,429	DISTRICT 49	94,992	25,366	62,313	7,313	36,947 D	26.7%	65.6%	28.9%	71.1%
236,408	DISTRICT 50	77,358	21,291	51,684	4,383	30,393 D	27.5%	66.8%	29.2%	70.8%
250,315	DISTRICT 51	118,893	75,789	28,760	14,344	47,029 R	63.7%	24.2%	72.5%	27.5%
247,135	DISTRICT 52	81,707	45,767	28,575	7,365	17,192 R	56.0%	35.0%	61.6%	38.4%
250,245	DISTRICT 53	69,110	30,202	33,820	5,088	3,618 D	43.7%	48.9%	47.2%	52.8%
258,822	DISTRICT 54	58,560	17,356	38,371	2,833	21,015 D	29.6%	65.5%	31.1%	68.9%
269,216	DISTRICT 55	53,301	21,308	26,602	5,391	5,294 D	40.0%	49.9%	44.5%	55.5%
291,792	DISTRICT 56	32,563	9,314	20,962	2,287	11,648 D	28.6%	64.4%	30.8%	69.2%
262,042	DISTRICT 57	71,702	33,860	31,529	6,313	2,331 R	47.2%	44.0%	51.8%	48.2%
232,498	DISTRICT 58	104,234	60,516	32,302	11,416	28,214 R	58.1%	31.0%	65.2%	34.8%
269,649	DISTRICT 59	76,268	34,853	35,053	6,362	200 D	45.7%	46.0%	49.9%	50.1%
264,831	DISTRICT 60	54,946	26,987	23,548	4,411	3,439 R	49.1%	42.9%	53.4%	46.6%
249,743	DISTRICT 61	99,833	66,198	25,233	8,402	40,965 R	66.3%	25.3%	72.4%	27.6%
282,013	DISTRICT 62	108,816	69,772	28,887	10,157	40,885 R	64.1%	26.5%	70.7%	29.3%
274,104	DISTRICT 63	86,675	50,876	29,122	6,677	21,754 R	58.7%	33.6%	63.6%	36.4%
291,924	DISTRICT 64	108,596	71,685	27,621	9,290	44,064 R	66.0%	25.4%	72.2%	27.8%
	DISTRICT 65 [PART]	22,684	11,041	9,505	2,138	1,536 R	48.7%	41.9%	53.7%	46.3%
7,477,657	TOTAL	2,440,185	1,224,533	979,830	235,822	244,703 R	50.2%	40.2%	55.6%	44.4%

LOS ANGELES COUNTY

SENATOR 1980

1980 Census Population	Assembly District	Total Vote	Republican	Democratic	Other	Rep.-Dem. Plurality	Percentage Total Vote Rep.	Dem.	Major Vote Rep.	Dem.
	DISTRICT 34 [PART]	39,676	21,645	15,209	2,822	6,436 R	54.6%	38.3%	58.7%	41.3%
	DISTRICT 37 [PART]	87,412	44,007	39,044	4,361	4,963 R	50.3%	44.7%	53.0%	47.0%
	DISTRICT 38 [PART]	99,480	43,265	51,298	4,917	8,033 D	43.5%	51.6%	45.8%	54.2%
261,575	DISTRICT 39	78,742	29,440	45,058	4,244	15,618 D	37.4%	57.2%	39.5%	60.5%
254,205	DISTRICT 40	90,727	32,713	53,070	4,944	20,357 D	36.1%	58.5%	38.1%	61.9%
252,328	DISTRICT 41	94,654	49,268	40,473	4,913	8,795 R	52.1%	42.8%	54.9%	45.1%
250,756	DISTRICT 42	105,772	49,460	51,176	5,136	1,716 D	46.8%	48.4%	49.1%	50.9%
256,887	DISTRICT 43	127,980	39,153	83,204	5,623	44,051 D	30.6%	65.0%	32.0%	68.0%
247,638	DISTRICT 44	107,093	29,352	71,535	6,206	42,183 D	27.4%	66.8%	29.1%	70.9%
265,872	DISTRICT 45	101,783	27,468	68,407	5,908	40,939 D	27.0%	67.2%	28.6%	71.4%
313,518	DISTRICT 46	56,841	17,651	35,262	3,928	17,611 D	31.1%	62.0%	33.4%	66.6%
285,567	DISTRICT 47	46,146	6,970	36,967	2,209	29,997 D	15.1%	80.1%	15.9%	84.1%
253,419	DISTRICT 48	49,239	7,697	39,340	2,202	31,643 D	15.6%	79.9%	16.4%	83.6%
252,429	DISTRICT 49	91,728	17,828	70,126	3,774	52,298 D	19.4%	76.4%	20.3%	79.7%
236,408	DISTRICT 50	74,608	16,053	55,924	2,631	39,871 D	21.5%	75.0%	22.3%	77.7%
250,315	DISTRICT 51	115,697	58,038	51,434	6,225	6,604 R	50.2%	44.5%	53.0%	47.0%
247,135	DISTRICT 52	79,554	35,242	40,292	4,020	5,050 D	44.3%	50.6%	46.7%	53.3%
250,245	DISTRICT 53	67,188	21,444	41,995	3,749	20,551 D	31.9%	62.5%	33.8%	66.2%
258,822	DISTRICT 54	56,979	12,377	41,766	2,836	29,389 D	21.7%	73.3%	22.9%	77.1%
269,216	DISTRICT 55	51,863	15,955	32,764	3,144	16,809 D	30.8%	63.2%	32.7%	67.3%
291,792	DISTRICT 56	31,118	6,148	23,055	1,915	16,907 D	19.8%	74.1%	21.1%	78.9%
262,042	DISTRICT 57	69,254	25,083	40,625	3,546	15,542 D	36.2%	58.7%	38.2%	61.8%
232,498	DISTRICT 58	101,581	43,096	53,544	4,941	10,448 D	42.4%	52.7%	44.6%	55.4%
269,649	DISTRICT 59	74,044	24,100	45,962	3,982	21,862 D	32.5%	62.1%	34.4%	65.6%
264,831	DISTRICT 60	53,827	19,051	31,563	3,213	12,512 D	35.4%	58.6%	37.6%	62.4%
249,743	DISTRICT 61	96,723	51,322	40,322	5,079	11,000 R	53.1%	41.7%	56.0%	44.0%
282,013	DISTRICT 62	105,905	54,245	46,256	5,404	7,989 R	51.2%	43.7%	54.0%	46.0%
274,104	DISTRICT 63	84,042	35,759	43,472	4,811	7,713 D	42.5%	51.7%	45.1%	54.9%
291,924	DISTRICT 64	105,578	52,556	47,525	5,497	5,031 R	49.8%	45.0%	52.5%	47.5%
	DISTRICT 65 [PART]	21,954	8,326	12,251	1,377	3,925 D	37.9%	55.8%	40.5%	59.5%
7,477,657	TOTAL	2,367,188	894,712	1,348,919	123,557	454,207 D	37.8%	57.0%	39.9%	60.1%

CALIFORNIA

CONGRESS

CD	Year	Total Vote	Republican Vote	Candidate	Democratic Vote	Candidate	Other Vote	Rep.-Dem. Plurality	Total Vote Rep.	Total Vote Dem.	Major Vote Rep.	Major Vote Dem.
1	1980	271,075	145,585	CHAPPIE, EUGENE A.	107,993	JOHNSON, HAROLD T.	17,497	37,592 R	53.7%	39.8%	57.4%	42.6%
1	1978	210,812	85,690	TAYLOR, JAMES E.	125,122	JOHNSON, HAROLD T.		39,432 D	40.6%	59.4%	40.6%	59.4%
1	1976	217,016	56,539	TAYLOR, JAMES E.	160,477	JOHNSON, HAROLD T.		103,938 D	26.1%	73.9%	26.1%	73.9%
1	1974	160,963			138,082	JOHNSON, HAROLD T.	22,881	138,082 D		85.8%		100.0%
2	1980	261,674	141,698	CLAUSEN, DON H.	109,789	BORK, NORMA	10,187	31,909 R	54.2%	42.0%	56.3%	43.7%
2	1978	220,260	114,451	CLAUSEN, DON H.	99,712	BORK, NORMA	6,097	14,739 R	52.0%	45.3%	53.4%	46.6%
2	1976	216,563	121,290	CLAUSEN, DON H.	88,829	KLEE, OSCAR H.	6,444	32,461 R	56.0%	41.0%	57.7%	42.3%
2	1974	180,905	95,929	CLAUSEN, DON H.	77,232	KLEE, OSCAR H.	7,744	18,697 R	53.0%	42.7%	55.4%	44.6%
3	1980	241,865	64,215	MURPHY, JOSEPH	170,670	MATSUI, ROBERT T.	6,980	106,455 D	26.5%	70.6%	27.3%	72.7%
3	1978	197,503	91,966	SMOLEY, SANDY	105,537	MATSUI, ROBERT T.		13,571 D	46.6%	53.4%	46.6%	53.4%
3	1976	191,854	52,075	MARSH, GEORGE R.	139,779	MOSS, JOHN E.		87,704 D	27.1%	72.9%	27.1%	72.9%
3	1974	168,846	46,712	LENCI, IVALDO	122,134	MOSS, JOHN E.		75,422 D	27.7%	72.3%	27.7%	72.3%
4	1980	205,594	60,935	DEHR, ALBERT	133,853	FAZIO, VIC	10,806	72,918 D	29.6%	65.1%	31.3%	68.7%
4	1978	158,497	70,733	HIME, REX	87,764	FAZIO, VIC		17,031 D	44.6%	55.4%	44.6%	55.4%
4	1976	162,368	75,193	DEHR, ALBERT	75,844	LEGGETT, ROBERT L.	11,331	651 D	46.3%	46.7%	49.8%	50.2%
4	1974	101,152			101,152	LEGGETT, ROBERT L.		101,152 D		100.0%		100.0%
5	1980	197,821	89,624	MCQUAID, DENNIS	101,105	BURTON, JOHN	7,092	11,481 D	45.3%	51.1%	47.0%	53.0%
5	1978	158,649	52,603	SKORE, DOLORES	106,046	BURTON, JOHN		53,443 D	33.2%	66.8%	33.2%	66.8%
5	1976	167,754	64,008	FANNING, BRANWELL	103,746	BURTON, JOHN		39,738 D	38.2%	61.8%	38.2%	61.8%
5	1974	149,260	56,274	CAYLOR, THOMAS	88,909	BURTON, JOHN	4,077	32,635 D	37.7%	59.6%	38.8%	61.2%
6	1980	134,650	34,500	SPINOSA, TOM	93,400	BURTON, PHILLIP	6,750	58,900 D	25.6%	69.4%	27.0%	73.0%
6	1978	119,771	33,515	SPINOSA, TOM	81,801	BURTON, PHILLIP	4,455	48,286 D	28.0%	68.3%	29.1%	70.9%
6	1976	130,916	35,359	SPINOSA, TOM	86,493	BURTON, PHILLIP	9,064	51,134 D	27.0%	66.1%	29.0%	71.0%
6	1974	120,248	26,260	SPINOSA, TOM	85,712	BURTON, PHILLIP	8,276	59,452 D	21.8%	71.3%	23.5%	76.5%
7	1980	224,469	70,479	ST. CLAIR, GILES	142,044	MILLER, GEORGE	11,946	71,565 D	31.4%	63.3%	33.2%	66.8%
7	1978	172,865	58,332	GORDON, PAULA	109,676	MILLER, GEORGE	4,857	51,344 D	33.7%	63.4%	34.7%	65.3%
7	1976	196,816	45,863	VICKERS, ROBERT L.	147,064	MILLER, GEORGE	3,889	101,201 D	23.3%	74.7%	23.8%	76.2%
7	1974	149,379	66,325	FERNANDEZ, GARY	83,054	MILLER, GEORGE		16,729 D	44.4%	55.6%	44.4%	55.6%
8	1980	195,425	76,580	HUGHES, CHARLES V.	108,380	DELLUMS, RONALD V.	10,465	31,800 D	39.2%	55.5%	41.4%	58.6%
8	1978	165,305	70,481	HUGHES, CHARLES V.	94,824	DELLUMS, RONALD V.		24,343 D	42.6%	57.4%	42.6%	57.4%
8	1976	197,012	68,374	BRECK, PHILIP S.	122,342	DELLUMS, RONALD V.	6,296	53,968 D	34.7%	62.1%	35.9%	64.1%
8	1974	167,865	66,386	REDDEN, JACK	95,041	DELLUMS, RONALD V.	6,438	28,655 D	39.5%	56.6%	41.1%	58.9%
9	1980	163,592	67,265	KENNEDY, WILLIAM J.	90,504	STARK, FORTNEY	5,823	23,239 D	41.1%	55.3%	42.6%	57.4%
9	1978	134,879	41,138	ALLEN, ROBERT S.	88,179	STARK, FORTNEY	5,562	47,041 D	30.5%	65.4%	31.8%	68.2%
9	1976	164,391	44,607	MILLS, JAMES K.	116,398	STARK, FORTNEY	3,386	71,791 D	27.1%	70.8%	27.7%	72.3%
9	1974	130,957	38,521	ADAMS, EDSON	92,436	STARK, FORTNEY		53,915 D	29.4%	70.6%	29.4%	70.6%
10	1980	164,543	45,987	LUTTON, JOHN M.	102,231	EDWARDS, DON	16,325	56,244 D	27.9%	62.1%	31.0%	69.0%
10	1978	125,862	41,374	HANSEN, RUDY	84,488	EDWARDS, DON		43,114 D	32.9%	67.1%	32.9%	67.1%
10	1976	155,443	38,088	SMITH, HERB	111,992	EDWARDS, DON	5,363	73,904 D	24.5%	72.0%	25.4%	74.6%
10	1974	114,266	26,288	ENRIGHT, JOHN M.	87,978	EDWARDS, DON		61,690 D	23.0%	77.0%	23.0%	77.0%
11	1980	185,013	80,100	ROYER, BILL	85,823	LANTOS, TOM	19,090	5,723 D	43.3%	46.4%	48.3%	51.7%
11	1978	153,464	54,621	WELCH, DAVE	92,882	RYAN, LEO J.	5,961	38,261 D	35.6%	60.5%	37.0%	63.0%
11	1976	176,194	62,435	JONES, BOB	107,618	RYAN, LEO J.	6,141	45,183 D	35.4%	61.1%	36.7%	63.3%
11	1974	140,356	29,861	MERDINGER, BRAINARD G.	106,429	RYAN, LEO J.	4,066	76,568 D	21.3%	75.8%	21.9%	78.1%
12	1980	199,104	143,817	MCCLOSKEY, PAUL N.	37,009	OLSEN, KIRSTEN	18,278	106,808 R	72.2%	18.6%	79.5%	20.5%
12	1978	160,085	116,982	MCCLOSKEY, PAUL N.	34,472	OLSEN, KIRSTEN	8,631	82,510 R	73.1%	21.5%	77.2%	22.8%
12	1976	196,857	130,332	MCCLOSKEY, PAUL N.	61,526	HARRIS, DAVID	4,999	68,806 R	66.2%	31.3%	67.9%	32.1%
12	1974	150,075	103,692	MCCLOSKEY, PAUL N.	46,383	GILLMOR, GARY G.		57,309 R	69.1%	30.9%	69.1%	30.9%
13	1980	224,609	79,766	GAGNE, W. E.	132,246	MINETA, NORMAN Y.	12,597	52,480 D	35.5%	58.9%	37.6%	62.4%
13	1978	175,361	69,306	O'KEEFE, DAN	100,809	MINETA, NORMAN Y.	5,246	31,503 D	39.5%	57.5%	40.7%	59.3%
13	1976	202,611	63,130	KONNYU, ERNEST L.	135,291	MINETA, NORMAN Y.	4,190	72,161 D	31.2%	66.8%	31.8%	68.2%
13	1974	150,099	63,573	MILIAS, GEORGE W.	78,858	MINETA, NORMAN Y.	7,668	15,285 D	42.4%	52.5%	44.6%	55.4%
14	1980	220,579	133,979	SHUMWAY, NORMAN D.	79,883	CERNEY, ANN	6,717	54,096 R	60.7%	36.2%	62.6%	37.4%
14	1978	179,727	95,962	SHUMWAY, NORMAN D.	76,602	MCFALL, JOHN J.	7,163	19,360 R	53.4%	42.6%	55.6%	44.4%
14	1976	169,959	46,674	BLAIN, ROGER A.	123,285	MCFALL, JOHN J.		76,611 D	27.5%	72.5%	27.5%	72.5%
14	1974	144,078	34,775	GIBSON, CHARLES M.	102,180	MCFALL, JOHN J.	7,123	67,405 D	24.1%	70.9%	25.4%	74.6%
15	1980	150,491	37,895	SCHWARTZ, RON	108,072	COELHO, TONY	4,524	70,177 D	25.2%	71.8%	26.0%	74.0%
15	1978	125,126	49,914	PATTERAKIS, CHRIS	75,212	COELHO, TONY		25,298 D	39.9%	60.1%	39.9%	60.1%
15	1976	128,435	35,700	HARNER, CAROL O.	92,735	SISK, B. F.		57,035 D	27.8%	72.2%	27.8%	72.2%
15	1974	112,336	31,439	HARNER, CAROL O.	80,897	SISK, B. F.		49,458 D	28.0%	72.0%	28.0%	72.0%

CALIFORNIA

CONGRESS

CD	Year	Total Vote	Republican Vote	Republican Candidate	Democratic Vote	Democratic Candidate	Other Vote	Rep.-Dem. Plurality	Total Vote Rep.	Total Vote Dem.	Major Vote Rep.	Major Vote Dem.
16	1980	223,035	54,675	ROTH, W. A.	158,360	PANETTA, LEON E.	10,000	103,685 D	24.5%	71.0%	25.7%	74.3%
16	1978	170,358	65,808	SEASTRAND, ERIC	104,550	PANETTA, LEON E.		38,742 D	38.6%	61.4%	38.6%	61.4%
16	1976	195,705	91,160	TALCOTT, BURT L.	104,545	PANETTA, LEON E.		13,385 D	46.6%	53.4%	46.6%	53.4%
16	1974	155,113	76,356	TALCOTT, BURT L.	74,168	CAMACHO, JULIAN	4,589	2,188 R	49.2%	47.8%	50.7%	49.3%
17	1980	182,939	129,159	PASHAYAN, CHARLES	53,780	JOHNSON, WILLARD H.		75,379 R	70.6%	29.4%	70.6%	29.4%
17	1978	149,181	81,296	PASHAYAN, CHARLES	67,885	KREBS, JOHN		13,411 R	54.5%	45.5%	54.5%	45.5%
17	1976	158,168	54,270	ANDREAS, HENRY J.	103,898	KREBS, JOHN		49,628 D	34.3%	65.7%	34.3%	65.7%
17	1974	128,487	61,812	MATHIAS, ROBERT B.	66,675	KREBS, JOHN		4,863 R	48.1%	51.9%	48.1%	51.9%
18	1980	177,461	126,046	THOMAS, WILLIAM M.	51,415	TIMMERMANS, MARY		74,631 R	71.0%	29.0%	71.0%	29.0%
18	1978	144,585	85,663	THOMAS, WILLIAM M.	58,900	SOGGE, BOB	22	26,763 R	59.2%	40.7%	59.3%	40.7%
18	1976	158,341	101,658	KETCHUM, WILLIAM M.	56,683	CLOSE, DEAN		44,975 R	64.2%	35.8%	64.2%	35.8%
18	1974	128,383	67,650	KETCHUM, WILLIAM M.	60,733	SEIELSTAD, GEORGE A.		6,917 R	52.7%	47.3%	52.7%	47.3%
19	1980	209,609	162,854	LAGOMARSINO, ROBERT J.	36,990	LODISE, CARMEN	9,765	125,864 R	77.7%	17.6%	81.5%	18.5%
19	1978	171,751	123,192	LAGOMARSINO, ROBERT J.	41,672	ZAMOS, JERRY	6,887	81,520 R	71.7%	24.3%	74.7%	25.3%
19	1976	192,923	124,201	LAGOMARSINO, ROBERT J.	68,722	SISSON, DON		55,479 R	64.4%	35.6%	64.4%	35.6%
19	1974	149,718	84,249	LAGOMARSINO, ROBERT J.	65,469	LOEBL, JAMES D.		18,780 R	56.3%	43.7%	56.3%	43.7%
20	1980	253,311	199,681	GOLDWATER, BARRY M., JR.	43,025	MILLER, MATT	10,605	156,656 R	78.8%	17.0%	82.3%	17.7%
20	1978	195,453	129,714	GOLDWATER, BARRY M., JR.	65,695	LEAR, PAT	44	64,019 R	66.4%	33.6%	66.4%	33.6%
20	1976	217,351	146,158	GOLDWATER, BARRY M., JR.	71,193	CORMAN, PATTI L.		74,965 R	67.2%	32.8%	67.2%	32.8%
20	1974	160,736	98,410	GOLDWATER, BARRY M., JR.	62,326	MATHEWS, ARLINE		36,084 R	61.2%	38.8%	61.2%	38.8%
21	1980	153,770	74,843	FIEDLER, BOBBI	74,091	CORMAN, JAMES C.	4,836	752 R	48.7%	48.2%	50.3%	49.7%
21	1978	124,138	44,519	WALSH, G. ROD	73,869	CORMAN, JAMES C.	5,750	29,350 D	35.9%	59.5%	37.6%	62.4%
21	1976	153,109	44,094	HOGAN, ERWIN	101,837	CORMAN, JAMES C.	7,178	57,743 D	28.8%	66.5%	30.2%	69.8%
21	1974	120,957	32,038	NADELL, MEL	88,915	CORMAN, JAMES C.	4	56,877 D	26.5%	73.5%	26.5%	73.5%
22	1980	180,423	115,241	MOORHEAD, CARLOS J.	57,477	O'DONNELL, PIERCE	7,705	57,764 R	63.9%	31.9%	66.7%	33.3%
22	1978	153,944	99,502	MOORHEAD, CARLOS J.	54,442	HENRY, ROBERT S.		45,060 R	64.6%	35.4%	64.6%	35.4%
22	1976	183,312	114,769	MOORHEAD, CARLOS J.	68,543	SALLEY, ROBERT L.		46,226 R	62.6%	37.4%	62.6%	37.4%
22	1974	146,332	81,641	MOORHEAD, CARLOS J.	64,691	HALLIN, RICHARD		16,950 R	55.8%	44.2%	55.8%	44.2%
23	1980	199,385	62,742	WINCKLER, ROBERT	126,020	BEILENSON, ANTHONY C.	10,623	63,278 D	31.5%	63.2%	33.2%	66.8%
23	1978	178,994	61,496	BARBARA, JOSEPH	117,498	BEILENSON, ANTHONY C.		56,002 D	34.4%	65.6%	34.4%	65.6%
23	1976	217,053	86,434	BARTMAN, THOMAS F.	130,619	BEILENSON, ANTHONY C.		44,185 D	39.8%	60.2%	39.8%	60.2%
23	1974	170,902	48,826	ROBERTS, JACK E.	122,076	REES, THOMAS M.		73,250 D	28.6%	71.4%	28.6%	71.4%
24	1980	146,731	39,744	CAYARD, ROLAND	93,569	WAXMAN, HENRY A.	13,418	53,825 D	27.1%	63.8%	29.8%	70.2%
24	1978	135,771	44,243	SCHAEFER, HOWARD G.	85,075	WAXMAN, HENRY A.	6,453	40,832 D	32.6%	62.7%	34.2%	65.8%
24	1976	159,774	51,478	SIMMONS, DAVID I.	108,296	WAXMAN, HENRY A.		56,818 D	32.2%	67.8%	32.2%	67.8%
24	1974	136,722	45,128	GRAHAM, ELLIOTT S.	87,521	WAXMAN, HENRY A.	4,073	42,393 D	33.0%	64.0%	34.0%	66.0%
25	1980	74,365	21,116	FERRARO, RICHARD E.	49,080	ROYBAL, EDWARD R.	4,169	27,964 D	28.4%	66.0%	30.1%	69.9%
25	1978	68,108	22,205	WATSON, ROBERT K.	45,881	ROYBAL, EDWARD R.	22	23,676 D	32.6%	67.4%	32.6%	67.4%
25	1976	80,625	17,737	MADRID, JIM	57,966	ROYBAL, EDWARD R.	4,922	40,229 D	22.0%	71.9%	23.4%	76.6%
25	1974	45,163			45,059	ROYBAL, EDWARD R.	104	45,059 D		99.8%		100.0%
26	1980	164,514	116,715	ROUSSELOT, JOHN H.	40,099	LISONI, JOSEPH L.	7,700	76,616 R	70.9%	24.4%	74.4%	25.6%
26	1978	113,059	113,059	ROUSSELOT, JOHN H.				113,059 R	100.0%		100.0%	
26	1976	171,712	112,619	ROUSSELOT, JOHN H.	59,093	LATTA, BRUCE		53,526 R	65.6%	34.4%	65.6%	34.4%
26	1974	140,420	82,735	ROUSSELOT, JOHN H.	57,685	CONFORTI, PAUL A.		25,050 R	58.9%	41.1%	58.9%	41.1%
27	1980	215,316	109,807	DORNAN, ROBERT K.	100,061	PECK, CAREY	5,448	9,746 R	51.0%	46.5%	52.3%	47.7%
27	1978	175,272	89,392	DORNAN, ROBERT K.	85,880	PECK, CAREY		3,512 R	51.0%	49.0%	51.0%	49.0%
27	1976	209,611	114,623	DORNAN, ROBERT K.	94,988	FAMILIAN, GARY		19,635 R	54.7%	45.3%	54.7%	45.3%
27	1974	160,605	102,663	BELL, ALPHONZO E.	52,236	DALESSIO, JOHN	5,706	50,427 R	63.9%	32.5%	66.3%	33.7%
28	1980	137,304	23,179	REID, ROBERT	108,725	DIXON, JULIAN C.	5,400	85,546 D	16.9%	79.2%	17.6%	82.4%
28	1978	97,592			97,592	DIXON, JULIAN C.		97,592 D		100.0%		100.0%
28	1976	142,915	28,303	SKINNER, EDWARD S.	114,612	BURKE, YVONNE BRATHWAITE		86,309 D	19.8%	80.2%	19.8%	80.2%
28	1974	110,629	21,957	NEDDY, TOM	88,655	BURKE, YVONNE BRATHWAITE	17	66,698 D	19.8%	80.1%	19.9%	80.1%
29	1980	92,999	10,282	HIRT, MICHAEL A.	80,095	HAWKINS, AUGUSTUS	2,622	69,813 D	11.1%	86.1%	11.4%	88.6%
29	1978	76,726	11,512	FIELDS, URIAH J.	65,214	HAWKINS, AUGUSTUS		53,702 D	15.0%	85.0%	15.0%	85.0%
29	1976	96,602	10,852	GERMONPREZ, MICHAEL D.	82,515	HAWKINS, AUGUSTUS	3,235	71,663 D	11.2%	85.4%	11.6%	88.4%
29	1974	47,204			47,204	HAWKINS, AUGUSTUS		47,204 D		100.0%		100.0%
30	1980	102,735	24,136	PLATTEN, J. ARTHUR	74,119	DANIELSON, GEORGE E.	4,480	49,983 D	23.5%	72.1%	24.6%	75.4%
30	1978	92,752	26,511	ARES, HENRY	66,241	DANIELSON, GEORGE E.		39,730 D	28.6%	71.4%	28.6%	71.4%
30	1976	111,270	28,503	COUCH, HARRY	82,767	DANIELSON, GEORGE E.		54,264 D	25.6%	74.4%	25.6%	74.4%
30	1974	90,711	23,383	PEREZ, JOHN J.	67,328	DANIELSON, GEORGE E.		43,945 D	25.8%	74.2%	25.8%	74.2%

CALIFORNIA

CONGRESS

CD	Year	Total Vote	Republican Vote	Candidate	Democratic Vote	Candidate	Other Vote	Rep.-Dem. Plurality	Total Vote Rep.	Total Vote Dem.	Major Vote Rep.	Major Vote Dem.
31	1980	107,349	38,203	GRIMSHAW, DON	69,146	DYMALLY, MERVYN M.		30,943 D	35.6%	64.4%	35.6%	64.4%
31	1978	82,172	26,490	GRIMSHAW, DON	55,667	WILSON, CHARLES E.	15	29,177 D	32.2%	67.7%	32.2%	67.8%
31	1976	83,155			83,155	WILSON, CHARLES H.		83,155 D		100.0%		100.0%
31	1974	87,058	23,359	HODGES, NORMAN A.	61,322	WILSON, CHARLES H.	2,377	37,963 D	26.8%	70.4%	27.6%	72.4%
32	1980	127,526	39,260	ADLER, JOHN R.	84,057	ANDERSON, GLENN M.	4,209	44,797 D	30.8%	65.9%	31.8%	68.2%
32	1978	103,609	23,242	MATHISON, SONYA	74,004	ANDERSON, GLENN M.	6,363	50,762 D	22.4%	71.4%	23.9%	76.1%
32	1976	127,428	35,394	YOUNG, CLIFFORD O.	92,034	ANDERSON, GLENN M.		56,640 D	27.8%	72.2%	27.8%	72.2%
32	1974	96,265			84,428	ANDERSON, GLENN M.	11,837	84,428 D		87.7%		100.0%
33	1980	172,804	122,439	GRISHAM, WAYNE	50,365	ANDERSON, FRED L.		72,074 R	70.9%	29.1%	70.9%	29.1%
33	1978	142,073	79,533	GRISHAM, WAYNE	62,540	KAZARIAN, DENNIS S.		16,993 R	56.0%	44.0%	56.0%	44.0%
33	1976	173,205	95,398	CLAWSON, DEL	77,807	SNYDER, TED		17,591 R	55.1%	44.9%	55.1%	44.9%
33	1974	135,688	72,471	CLAWSON, DEL	58,492	WHITE, ROBERT E.	4,725	13,979 R	53.4%	43.1%	55.3%	44.7%
34	1980	192,171	138,024	LUNGREN, DANIEL E.	46,351	SIMONE	7,796	91,673 R	71.8%	24.1%	74.9%	25.1%
34	1978	168,572	90,554	LUNGREN, DANIEL E.	73,608	HANNAFORD, MARK W.	4,410	16,946 R	53.7%	43.7%	55.2%	44.8%
34	1976	199,191	98,147	LUNGREN, DANIEL E.	100,988	HANNAFORD, MARK W.	56	2,841 D	49.3%	50.7%	49.3%	50.7%
34	1974	163,003	75,426	BOND, BILL	81,151	HANNAFORD, MARK W.	6,426	5,725 D	46.3%	49.8%	48.2%	51.8%
35	1980	194,514	100,743	DREIER, DAVID	88,279	LLOYD, JIM	5,492	12,464 R	51.8%	45.4%	53.3%	46.7%
35	1978	148,830	68,442	DREIER, DAVID	80,388	LLOYD, JIM		11,946 D	46.0%	54.0%	46.0%	54.0%
35	1976	164,237	76,765	BRUTOCAO, LOUIS	87,472	LLOYD, JIM		10,707 D	46.7%	53.3%	46.7%	53.3%
35	1974	123,071	61,168	VEYSEY, VICTOR V.	61,903	LLOYD, JIM		735 D	49.7%	50.3%	49.7%	50.3%
36	1980	168,701	73,252	STARK, JOHN P.	88,634	BROWN, GEORGE E.	6,815	15,382 D	43.4%	52.5%	45.2%	54.8%
36	1978	127,865	47,417	CARMODY, DANA W.	80,448	BROWN, GEORGE E.		33,031 D	37.1%	62.9%	37.1%	62.9%
36	1976	147,556	49,368	CARNER, GRANT	90,830	BROWN, GEORGE E.	7,358	41,462 D	33.5%	61.6%	35.2%	64.8%
36	1974	111,415	35,938	OSGOOD, JIM	69,766	BROWN, GEORGE E.	5,711	33,828 D	32.3%	62.6%	34.0%	66.0%
37	1980	232,763	166,640	LEWIS, JERRY	58,462	RUSK, DONALD M.	7,661	108,178 R	71.6%	25.1%	74.0%	26.0%
37	1978	173,588	106,581	LEWIS, JERRY	60,463	CORCORAN, DAN	6,544	46,118 R	61.4%	34.8%	63.8%	36.2%
37	1976	188,007	133,634	PETTIS, SHIRLEY N.	49,021	NILSON, DOUGLAS C.	5,352	84,613 R	71.1%	26.1%	73.2%	26.8%
37	1974	142,202	89,849	PETTIS, JERRY L.	46,783	VINCENT, BOBBY RAY	5,570	43,066 R	63.2%	32.9%	65.8%	34.2%
38	1980	165,437	66,256	JACOBSON, ART	91,880	PATTERSON, JERRY M.	7,301	25,624 D	40.0%	55.5%	41.9%	58.1%
38	1978	128,769	53,298	GOEDEKE, DON	75,471	PATTERSON, JERRY M.		22,173 D	41.4%	58.6%	41.4%	58.6%
38	1976	162,409	59,092	COMBS, JAMES	103,317	PATTERSON, JERRY M.		44,225 D	36.4%	63.6%	36.4%	63.6%
38	1974	126,461	52,207	REHMANN, DAVID	68,335	PATTERSON, JERRY M.	5,919	16,128 D	41.3%	54.0%	43.3%	56.7%
39	1980	229,732	175,228	DANNEMEYER, WILLIAM E.	54,504	LAHTINEN, LEONARD L.		120,724 R	76.3%	23.7%	76.3%	23.7%
39	1978	176,051	112,160	DANNEMEYER, WILLIAM E.	63,891	FARRIS, WILLIAM E.		48,269 R	63.7%	36.3%	63.7%	36.3%
39	1976	209,402	122,657	WIGGINS, CHARLES E.	86,745	FARRIS, WILLIAM E.		35,912 R	58.6%	41.4%	58.6%	41.4%
39	1974	161,446	89,220	WIGGINS, CHARLES E.	65,170	FARRIS, WILLIAM E.	7,056	24,050 R	55.3%	40.4%	57.8%	42.2%
40	1980	305,053	213,999	BADHAM, ROBERT E.	66,512	DOW, MICHAEL F.	24,542	147,487 R	70.2%	21.8%	76.3%	23.7%
40	1978	224,240	147,882	BADHAM, ROBERT E.	76,358	MCGUY, JIM		71,524 R	65.9%	34.1%	65.9%	34.1%
40	1976	250,644	148,512	BADHAM, ROBERT E.	102,132	HALL, VIVIAN		46,380 R	59.3%	40.7%	59.3%	40.7%
40	1974	183,797	116,449	HINSHAW, ANDREW J.	56,850	WILSON, RODERICK J.	10,498	59,599 R	63.4%	30.9%	67.2%	32.8%
41	1980	233,927	123,187	LOWERY, BILL	101,101	WILSON, ROBERT	9,639	22,086 R	52.7%	43.2%	54.9%	45.1%
41	1978	185,225	107,685	WILSON, BOB	77,540	GOLDEN, KING		30,145 R	58.1%	41.9%	58.1%	41.9%
41	1976	223,374	128,784	WILSON, BOB	94,590	GOLDEN, KING		34,194 R	57.7%	42.3%	57.7%	42.3%
41	1974	173,886	94,709	WILSON, BOB	74,823	O'CONNOR, COLLEEN M.	4,354	19,886 R	54.5%	43.0%	55.9%	44.1%
42	1980	149,649	79,713	HUNTER, DUNCAN L.	69,936	VAN DEERLIN, LIONEL		9,777 R	53.3%	46.7%	53.3%	46.7%
42	1978	115,445	30,319	MATTERA, LAWRENCE C.	85,126	VAN DEERLIN, LIONEL		54,807 D	26.3%	73.7%	26.3%	73.7%
42	1976	135,627	32,565	MARDEN, WES	103,062	VAN DEERLIN, LIONEL		70,497 D	24.0%	76.0%	24.0%	76.0%
42	1974	101,014	30,435	MARDEN, WES	70,579	VAN DEERLIN, LIONEL		40,144 D	30.1%	69.9%	30.1%	69.9%
43	1980	345,715	299,037	BURGENER, CLAIR W.	46,383	METZGER, TOM	295	252,654 R	86.5%	13.4%	86.6%	13.4%
43	1978	243,458	167,150	BURGENER, CLAIR W.	76,308	BROOKS, RUBEN B.		90,842 R	68.7%	31.3%	68.7%	31.3%
43	1976	267,051	173,576	BURGENER, CLAIR W.	93,475	KELLY, PAT		80,101 R	65.0%	35.0%	65.0%	35.0%
43	1974	191,007	115,275	BURGENER, CLAIR W.	75,629	BANDES, BILL	103	39,646 R	60.4%	39.6%	60.4%	39.6%

CALIFORNIA

1980 GENERAL ELECTION

President   Other vote was 739,833 Anderson (Independent); 148,434 Clark (Libertarian); 61,063 Commoner (Independent); 18,116 Smith (Peace and Freedom); 9,856 Rarick (American Independent); 847 Hall (write-in); 231 Pulley (write-in); 87 Greaves (write-in); 36 Bubar (write-in); 15 Griswold (write-in); 26 scattered. State-wide total for other vote column includes these 1,242 scattered votes not reported by county.

Senator   Other vote was 202,481 Bergland (Libertarian); 196,354 Wald (Peace and Freedom); 129,648 Griffin (American Independent); 173 scattered. State-wide total for other vote column includes these 173 scattered votes not reported by county.

Congress   Other vote was McClarin (Libertarian) in CD 1; 6,833 Mosier (Libertarian) and 3,354 Wren (Peace and Freedom) in CD 2; Daniel (Libertarian) in CD 3; 10,267 Burnside (Libertarian) and 539 scattered in CD 4. Dougherty (Libertarian) in CD 5; Childs (Libertarian) in CD 6; 6,923 Snow (Libertarian) and 5,023 Thompson (American Independent) in CD 7; Mikuriya (Libertarian) in CD 8; Clanin (Libertarian) in CD 9; 11,904 Fuhrig (Libertarian) and 4,421 Kaiser (American Independent) in CD 10; 13,723 Branch (Peace and Freedom), 3,816 Wade (Libertarian), 1,550 Kudrovzeff (American Independent) and 1 scattered in CD 11; 15,073 Evers (Libertarian), 3,184 Fumino (Peace and Freedom) and 21 scattered in CD 12; 8,806 Strong (Libertarian) and 3,791 Goldsborough (Peace and Freedom) in CD 13; Housley (Libertarian) in CD 14; Pullen (Libertarian) in CD 15; 6,802 Bowers (Libertarian) and 3,198 Mauro (American Independent) in CD 16; Trotter (Libertarian) in CD 19; Darwin (Libertarian) in CD 20; 2,791 Lehmann (Libertarian) and 2,045 Tucker (Peace and Freedom) in CD 21; Susel (Libertarian) in CD 22; Lieb (Libertarian) in CD 23; 5,905 Feigin (Peace and Freedom), 5,172 Lehman (Libertarian) and 2,341 Smilowitz (American Independent) in CD 24; Mitchell (Libertarian) in CD 25; Wagener (Libertarian) in CD 26; Sievers (Libertarian) in CD 27; Ghermann (Libertarian) in CD 28; Smith (Libertarian) in CD 29; Hobbs (Libertarian) in CD 30; Cosgrove (Libertarian) in CD 32; 7,794 Donohue (Peace and Freedom) and 2 scattered in CD 34; Noonan (Peace and Freedom) in CD 35; Histen (Libertarian) in CD 36; Morris (Libertarian) in CD 37; Heiser (Libertarian) in CD 38; 24,486 Mahaffey (Libertarian) and 56 scattered in CD 40; 9,630 Alldredge (Libertarian) and 9 scattered in CD 41; scattered in CD 43.

LOS ANGELES COUNTY
Population data for Assembly Districts that are partially within Los Angeles county are not available at this time.

President   Other vote was 175,882 Anderson (Independent); 37,832 Clark (Libertarian); 14,970 Commoner (Independent); 4,921 Smith (Peace and Freedom); 2,217 Rarick (American Independent).

Senator   Other vote was 47,597 Bergland (Libertarian); 46,125 Wald (Peace and Freedom); 29,835 Griffin (American Independent).

1980 PRIMARIES

JUNE 3 REPUBLICAN

Senator   934,433 Paul Gann; 668,583 Samuel W. Yorty; 442,839 John G. Schmitz; 95,155 James A. Ware; 76,268 Ray Hanzlik; 68,790 Philip Schwartz; 50,122 Brian Hyndman.

Congress   Unopposed in twenty-four CD's. Contested as follows:

CD 3   27,763 Joseph Murphy; 14,935 Raymond E. Vandegriff; 13,344 George Marsh.
CD 4   20,947 Albert Dehr; 12,106 Harvey Taylor; 6,438 Terry J. Biffel.
CD 6   10,579 Tom Spinosa; 6,312 Gordon A. Bloyer.
CD 8   33,651 Charles V. Hughes; 6,377 Tertius Chandler.
CD 12   51,688 Paul N. McCloskey; 13,302 Royce M. Cole.
CD 18   48,215 William M. Thomas; 8,127 Michael D. Berry.
CD 21   23,980 Bobbi Fiedler; 8,580 Patrick L. O'Brien.

CALIFORNIA

CD 24   12,593 Roland Cayard; 12,437 Jerry Zerg.
CD 28   8,742 Robert Reid; 4,147 P. J. Gladnick.
CD 31   7,074 Don Grimshaw; 5,693 Arnold A. Johnston.
CD 32   14,580 John R. Adler; 9,138 Ida Bader.
CD 33   39,301 Wayne Grisham; 12,736 Mike Manicone.
CD 35   32,189 David Dreier; 8,720 Russ Blewett; 8,036 Frances M. Livingston; 4,046 Walter P. Hollywood; 4,004 Don Feldman; 3,547 Cecil F. Osoff.
CD 36   15,491 John P. Stark; 12,542 Ed Vallen; 11,672 W. Dennis Mansfield.
CD 37   67,694 Jerry Lewis; 5,802 A. J. Mathewson; 4,876 George Beardsley; 3,201 Charles Maciejerski.
CD 38   20,223 Art Jacobson; 15,143 E. L. Wiley.
CD 40   90,706 Robert E. Badham; 23,938 Richard G. Gardner; 5,435 Jack Utter.
CD 41   37,066 Bill Lowery; 34,236 Dan McKinnon; 2,084 Michael Gomez; 1,487 Quincy J. Workman.
CD 42   15,870 Duncan L. Hunter; 14,681 Michael T. McGuillen.

JUNE 3 DEMOCRATIC

Senator   2,608,746 Alan Cranston; 350,394 Richard Morgan; 195,351 Frank L. Thomas; 110,125 David T. Rees; 26 scattered.

Congress   Unopposed in twenty CD's. Contested as follows:

CD 1   80,687 Harold T. Johnson; 17,380 Tracy Murphy; 8,330 Tim Loree; 4,001 Joseph A. Gavagan.
CD 2   46,016 Norma Bork; 40,186 Brian Kahn; 15,198 Peter Windrem; 6,892 Dean Koethke.
CD 3   95,565 Robert T. Matsui; 11,967 Ivaldo Lenci.
CD 4   71,344 Vic Fazio; 18,100 Wayne D. Cowley.
CD 6   57,463 Phillip Burton; 8,128 Bob Barnes; 5,223 Tibor Uskert.
CD 7   81,956 George Miller; 14,253 Alexander W. Malick.
CD 12   34,586 Kirsten Olsen; 22,212 Marc Strassman.
CD 14   42,073 Ann Cerney; 36,733 Ronald C. Richards.
CD 17   39,236 Willard H. Johnson; 14,646 David L. Creighton; 12,914 Anthony G. Garza.
CD 18   37,596 Mary Timmermans; 19,138 Barry D. Gorelick.
CD 22   28,822 Pierce O'Donnell; 13,750 Stanley M. Sapiro.
CD 23   67,432 Anthony C. Beilenson; 11,588 Eileen Anderson.
CD 27   42,673 Carey Peck; 15,641 Gary Dubin; 7,134 David Alkire.
CD 31   29,916 Mervyn M. Dymally; 14,512 Mark W. Hannaford; 9,320 Charles H. Wilson; 4,953 B. E.Henschel; 2,239 Emanuel Gary.
CD 32   43,475 Glenn M. Anderson; 7,911 Edward Jamison.
CD 33   25,139 Fred L. Anderson; 21,920 Paul Servelle; 8,984 Nick Mull.
CD 34   20,533 Simone; 16,317 Ivan E. Lynch; 12,653 David Yachimowicz; 12,565 Jim McNab.
CD 35   48,534 Jim Lloyd; 17,472 Richard S. Anderson.
CD 36   51,494 George E. Brown; 17,657 Gary A. Wedge.
CD 40   34,248 Michael F. Dow; 28,360 Basil P. Roman.
CD 41   38,564 Robert Wilson (not to be confused with Republican Bob Wilson who was the Congressman from this district in prior years); 32,272 Jim Bates; 3,281 Arthur L. Sanders; 2,594 Ron Buckley.
CD 42   43,650 Lionel Van Deerlin; 7,107 Lois Bodle; 6,459 Samuel W. Bagwell.
CD 43   33,071 Tom Metzger; 32,679 Edward M. Skagen; 23,462 Bud Higgins.

JUNE 3 AMERICAN INDEPENDENT

Senator   James C. Griffin, unopposed.

Congress   Unopposed in all CD's in which candidates were entered.

CALIFORNIA

JUNE 3 PEACE AND FREEDOM

Senator   David Wald, unopposed.

Congress   Unopposed in all CD's in which candidates were entered.

JUNE 3 LIBERTARIAN

Senator   David Bergland, unopposed.

Congress   Unopposed in all CD's in which candidates were entered except CD 2 as follows:

  CD 2   247 Daniel Rosier; 189 Louis G. Beary.

COLORADO

GOVERNOR
Richard D. Lamm (D). Re-elected 1978 to a four-year term. Previously elected 1974.

SENATORS
William L. Armstrong (R). Elected 1978 to a six-year term.

Gary W. Hart (D). Elected 1980 to a six-year term. Previously elected 1974.

REPRESENTATIVES
1. Patricia Schroeder (D)
2. Timothy E. Wirth (D)
3. Ray Kogovsek (D)
4. Hank Brown (R)
5. Ken Kramer (R)

POSTWAR VOTE FOR GOVERNOR

Year	Total Vote	Republican Vote	Candidate	Democratic Vote	Candidate	Other Vote	Rep.-Dem. Plurality	Total Vote Rep.	Total Vote Dem.	Major Vote Rep.	Major Vote Dem.
1978	823,807	317,292	Strickland, Ted	483,985	Lamm, Richard D.	22,530	166,693 D	38.5%	58.7%	39.6%	60.4%
1974	828,968	378,698	Vanderhoof, John D.	441,408	Lamm, Richard D.	8,862	62,710 D	45.7%	53.2%	46.2%	53.8%
1970	668,496	350,690	Love, John A.	302,432	Hogan, Mark	15,374	48,258 R	52.5%	45.2%	53.7%	46.3%
1966	660,063	356,730	Love, John A.	287,132	Knous, Robert L.	16,201	69,598 R	54.0%	43.5%	55.4%	44.6%
1962	616,481	349,342	Love, John A.	262,890	McNichols, Stephen	4,249	86,452 R	56.7%	42.6%	57.1%	42.9%
1958	549,808	228,643	Burch, Palmer L.	321,165	McNichols, Stephen	—	92,522 D	41.6%	58.4%	41.6%	58.4%
1956	645,233	313,950	Brotzman, Donald G.	331,283	McNichols, Stephen	—	17,333 D	48.7%	51.3%	48.7%	51.3%
1954	489,540	227,335	Brotzman, Donald G.	262,205	Johnson, Ed C.	—	34,870 D	46.4%	53.6%	46.4%	53.6%
1952	613,034	349,924	Thornton, Dan	260,044	Metzger, John W.	3,066	89,880 R	57.1%	42.4%	57.1%	42.6%
1950	450,994	236,472	Thornton, Dan	212,976	Johnson, Walter	1,546	23,496 R	52.4%	47.2%	52.6%	47.4%
1948	501,680	168,928	Hamil, David A.	332,752	Knous, William Lee	—	163,824 D	33.7%	66.3%	33.7%	66.3%
1946	335,087	160,483	Lavington, Leon E.	174,604	Knous, William Lee	—	14,121 D	47.9%	52.1%	47.9%	52.1%

The term of office of Colorado's Governor was increased from two to four years effective with the 1958 election.

POSTWAR VOTE FOR SENATOR

Year	Total Vote	Republican Vote	Candidate	Democratic Vote	Candidate	Other Vote	Rep.-Dem. Plurality	Total Vote Rep.	Total Vote Dem.	Major Vote Rep.	Major Vote Dem.
1980	1,173,646	571,295	Buchanan, Mary E.	590,501	Hart, Gary W.	11,850	19,206 D	48.7%	50.3%	49.2%	50.8%
1978	819,150	480,596	Armstrong, William L.	330,247	Haskell, Floyd K.	8,307	150,349 R	58.7%	40.3%	59.3%	40.7%
1974	824,166	325,508	Dominick, Peter H.	471,691	Hart, Gary W.	26,967	146,183 D	39.5%	57.2%	40.8%	59.2%
1972	926,093	447,957	Allott, Gordon	457,545	Haskell, Floyd K.	20,591	9,588 D	48.4%	49.4%	49.5%	50.5%
1968	785,536	459,952	Dominick, Peter H.	325,584	McNichols, Stephen	—	134,368 R	58.6%	41.4%	58.6%	41.4%
1966	634,898	368,307	Allott, Gordon	266,259	Romer, Roy	332	102,048 R	58.0%	41.9%	58.0%	42.0%
1962	613,444	328,655	Dominick, Peter H.	279,586	Carroll, John A.	5,203	49,069 R	53.6%	45.6%	54.0%	46.0%
1960	727,633	389,428	Allott, Gordon	334,854	Knous, Robert L.	3,351	54,574 R	53.5%	46.0%	53.8%	46.2%
1956	636,974	317,102	Thornton, Dan	319,872	Carroll, John A.	—	2,770 D	49.8%	50.2%	49.8%	50.2%
1954	484,188	248,502	Allott, Gordon	235,686	Carroll, John A.	—	12,816 R	51.3%	48.7%	51.3%	48.7%
1950	450,176	239,734	Millikin, Eugene D.	210,442	Carroll, John A.	—	29,292 R	53.3%	46.7%	53.3%	46.7%
1948	510,121	165,069	Nicholson, W. F.	340,719	Johnson, Ed C.	4,333	175,650 D	32.4%	66.8%	32.6%	67.4%

COLORADO

Districts Established May 11, 1972

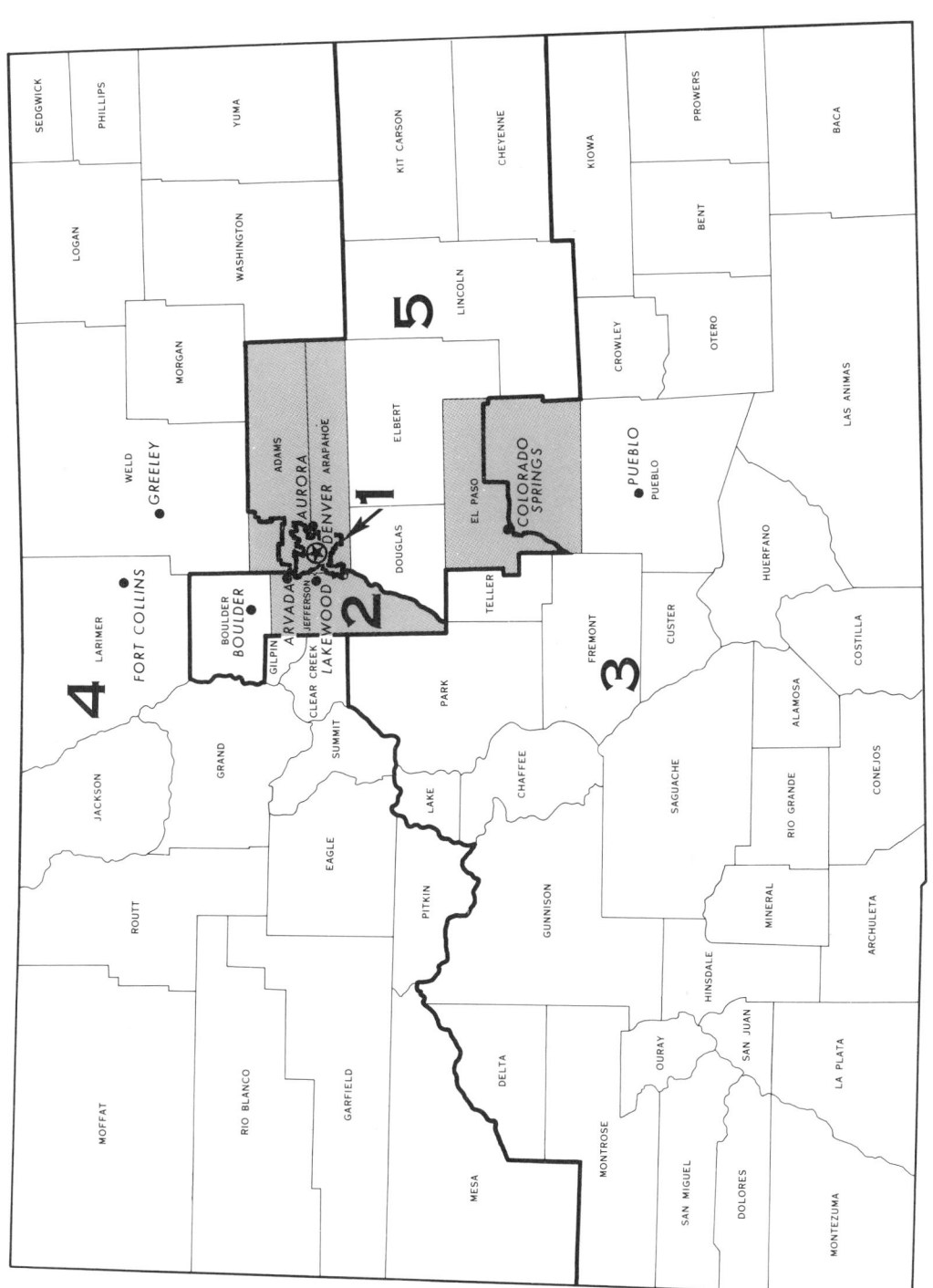

County with two or more Congressional Districts.

COLORADO

PRESIDENT 1980 .

1980 Census Population	County	Total Vote	Republican	Democratic	Other	Rep.-Dem. Plurality	Percentage Total Vote Rep.	Dem.	Major Vote Rep.	Dem.
245,944	ADAMS	84,975	42,916	31,357	10,702	11,559 R	50.5%	36.9%	57.8%	42.2%
11,799	ALAMOSA	4,828	2,601	1,821	406	780 R	53.9%	37.7%	58.8%	41.2%
293,621	ARAPAHOE	127,980	79,594	30,148	18,238	49,446 R	62.2%	23.6%	72.5%	27.5%
3,664	ARCHULETA	1,900	1,252	532	116	720 R	65.9%	28.0%	70.2%	29.8%
5,419	BACA	2,692	1,999	551	142	1,448 R	74.3%	20.5%	78.4%	21.6%
5,945	BENT	2,330	1,206	894	230	312 R	51.8%	38.4%	57.4%	42.6%
189,625	BOULDER	87,069	40,698	28,422	17,949	12,276 R	46.7%	32.6%	58.9%	41.1%
13,227	CHAFFEE	5,478	3,327	1,583	568	1,744 R	60.7%	28.9%	67.8%	32.2%
2,153	CHEYENNE	1,239	816	322	101	494 R	65.9%	26.0%	71.7%	28.3%
7,308	CLEAR CREEK	3,173	1,784	837	552	947 R	56.2%	26.4%	68.1%	31.9%
7,794	CONEJOS	3,232	1,597	1,503	132	94 R	49.4%	46.5%	51.5%	48.5%
3,071	COSTILLA	1,583	489	1,036	58	547 D	30.9%	65.4%	32.1%	67.9%
2,988	CROWLEY	1,473	926	472	75	454 R	62.9%	32.0%	66.2%	33.8%
1,528	CUSTER	1,010	674	231	105	443 R	66.7%	22.9%	74.5%	25.5%
21,225	DELTA	9,227	6,179	2,348	700	3,831 R	67.0%	25.4%	72.5%	27.5%
491,396	DENVER	209,508	88,398	85,903	35,207	2,495 R	42.2%	41.0%	50.7%	49.3%
1,658	DOLORES	817	615	157	45	458 R	75.3%	19.2%	79.7%	20.3%
25,153	DOUGLAS	11,596	8,126	2,108	1,362	6,018 R	70.1%	18.2%	79.4%	20.6%
13,171	EAGLE	5,816	3,061	1,608	1,147	1,453 R	52.6%	27.6%	65.6%	34.4%
6,850	ELBERT	3,122	2,107	698	317	1,409 R	67.5%	22.4%	75.1%	24.9%
309,424	EL PASO	103,990	66,199	27,463	10,328	38,736 R	63.7%	26.4%	70.7%	29.3%
28,676	FREMONT	12,113	7,162	3,952	999	3,210 R	59.1%	32.6%	64.4%	35.6%
22,514	GARFIELD	9,325	5,416	2,639	1,270	2,777 R	58.1%	28.3%	67.2%	32.8%
2,441	GILPIN	1,387	694	441	252	253 R	50.0%	31.8%	61.1%	38.9%
7,475	GRAND	3,481	2,133	820	528	1,313 R	61.3%	23.6%	72.2%	27.8%
10,689	GUNNISON	4,970	2,756	1,297	917	1,459 R	55.5%	26.1%	68.0%	32.0%
408	HINSDALE	336	232	76	28	156 R	69.0%	22.6%	75.3%	24.7%
6,440	HUERFANO	3,032	1,258	1,574	200	316 D	41.5%	51.9%	44.4%	55.6%
1,863	JACKSON	1,059	673	283	103	390 R	63.6%	26.7%	70.4%	29.6%
371,741	JEFFERSON	162,611	97,008	41,525	24,078	55,483 R	59.7%	25.5%	70.0%	30.0%
1,936	KIOWA	1,159	754	331	74	423 R	65.1%	28.6%	69.5%	30.5%
7,599	KIT CARSON	3,653	2,622	790	241	1,832 R	71.8%	21.6%	76.8%	23.2%
8,830	LAKE	3,025	1,375	1,213	437	162 R	45.5%	40.1%	53.1%	46.9%
27,424	LA PLATA	12,201	7,291	3,034	1,876	4,257 R	59.8%	24.9%	70.6%	29.4%
149,184	LARIMER	64,129	36,240	17,072	10,817	19,168 R	56.5%	26.6%	68.0%	32.0%
14,897	LAS ANIMAS	7,409	2,917	4,117	375	1,200 D	39.4%	55.6%	41.5%	58.5%
4,663	LINCOLN	2,371	1,535	602	234	933 R	64.7%	25.4%	71.8%	28.2%
19,800	LOGAN	8,293	5,238	2,332	723	2,906 R	63.2%	28.1%	69.2%	30.8%
81,530	MESA	32,916	22,686	7,549	2,681	15,137 R	68.9%	22.9%	75.0%	25.0%
804	MINERAL	450	271	125	54	146 R	60.2%	27.8%	68.4%	31.6%
13,133	MOFFAT	4,925	3,344	1,079	502	2,265 R	67.9%	21.9%	75.6%	24.4%
16,510	MONTEZUMA	6,006	4,120	1,467	419	2,653 R	68.6%	24.4%	73.7%	26.3%
24,352	MONTROSE	9,800	6,685	2,232	883	4,453 R	68.2%	22.8%	75.0%	25.0%
22,513	MORGAN	8,334	5,209	2,246	879	2,963 R	62.5%	26.9%	69.9%	30.1%
22,567	OTERO	8,801	4,801	3,294	706	1,507 R	54.6%	37.4%	59.3%	40.7%
1,925	OURAY	1,201	813	237	151	576 R	67.7%	19.7%	77.4%	22.6%
5,333	PARK	2,735	1,623	674	438	949 R	59.3%	24.6%	70.7%	29.3%
4,542	PHILLIPS	2,354	1,488	640	226	848 R	63.2%	27.2%	69.9%	30.1%
10,338	PITKIN	5,417	2,153	1,760	1,504	393 R	39.7%	32.5%	55.0%	45.0%
13,070	PROWERS	5,212	3,115	1,669	428	1,446 R	59.8%	32.0%	65.1%	34.9%
125,972	PUEBLO	46,441	20,770	21,874	3,797	1,104 D	44.7%	47.1%	48.7%	51.3%
6,255	RIO BLANCO	2,647	1,971	462	214	1,509 R	74.5%	17.5%	81.0%	19.0%
10,511	RIO GRANDE	4,488	2,844	1,370	274	1,474 R	63.4%	30.5%	67.5%	32.5%
13,404	ROUTT	6,702	3,574	1,944	1,184	1,630 R	53.3%	29.0%	64.8%	35.2%
3,935	SAGUACHE	2,135	1,124	893	118	231 R	52.6%	41.8%	55.7%	44.3%
833	SAN JUAN	549	268	146	135	122 R	48.8%	26.6%	64.7%	35.3%
3,192	SAN MIGUEL	1,809	774	651	384	123 R	42.8%	36.0%	54.3%	45.7%
3,266	SEDGWICK	1,708	1,151	438	119	713 R	67.4%	25.6%	72.4%	27.6%
8,848	SUMMIT	4,355	2,027	1,285	1,043	742 R	46.5%	29.5%	61.2%	38.8%
8,034	TELLER	3,707	2,457	802	448	1,655 R	66.3%	21.6%	75.4%	24.6%
5,304	WASHINGTON	2,811	2,007	568	236	1,439 R	71.4%	20.2%	77.9%	22.1%
123,438	WELD	40,646	23,901	11,433	5,312	12,468 R	58.8%	28.1%	67.6%	32.4%
9,682	YUMA	4,674	3,220	1,043	411	2,177 R	68.9%	22.3%	75.5%	24.5%
2,888,834	TOTAL	1,184,415	652,264	367,973	164,178	284,291 R	55.1%	31.1%	63.9%	36.1%

COLORADO

SENATOR 1980

1980 Census Population	County	Total Vote	Republican	Democratic	Other	Rep.-Dem. Plurality	Percentage Total Vote Rep.	Dem.	Major Vote Rep.	Dem.
245,944	ADAMS	84,977	39,167	44,786	1,024	5,619 D	46.1%	52.7%	46.7%	53.3%
11,799	ALAMOSA	4,824	2,461	2,322	41	139 R	51.0%	48.1%	51.5%	48.5%
293,621	ARAPAHOE	126,047	65,854	58,723	1,470	7,131 R	52.2%	46.6%	52.9%	47.1%
3,664	ARCHULETA	1,862	1,092	757	13	335 R	58.6%	40.7%	59.1%	40.9%
5,419	BACA	2,683	1,758	906	19	852 R	65.5%	33.8%	66.0%	34.0%
5,945	BENT	2,178	1,208	953	17	255 R	55.5%	43.8%	55.9%	44.1%
189,625	BOULDER	91,041	38,608	51,770	663	13,162 D	42.4%	56.9%	42.7%	57.3%
13,227	CHAFFEE	5,298	2,970	2,246	82	724 R	56.1%	42.4%	56.9%	43.1%
2,153	CHEYENNE	1,229	726	487	16	239 R	59.1%	39.6%	59.9%	40.1%
7,308	CLEAR CREEK	3,159	1,648	1,477	34	171 R	52.2%	46.8%	52.7%	47.3%
7,794	CONEJOS	3,350	1,775	1,547	28	228 R	53.0%	46.2%	53.4%	46.6%
3,071	COSTILLA	1,563	508	1,050	5	542 D	32.5%	67.2%	32.6%	67.4%
2,988	CROWLEY	1,483	902	576	5	326 R	60.8%	38.8%	61.0%	39.0%
1,528	CUSTER	1,014	669	333	12	336 R	66.0%	32.8%	66.8%	33.2%
21,225	DELTA	9,241	5,315	3,870	56	1,445 R	57.5%	41.9%	57.9%	42.1%
491,396	DENVER	202,179	74,337	125,136	2,706	50,799 D	36.8%	61.9%	37.3%	62.7%
1,658	DOLORES	786	449	331	6	118 R	57.1%	42.1%	57.6%	42.4%
25,153	DOUGLAS	11,562	7,230	4,256	76	2,974 R	62.5%	36.8%	62.9%	37.1%
13,171	EAGLE	5,799	2,919	2,841	39	78 R	50.3%	49.0%	50.7%	49.3%
6,850	ELBERT	3,135	1,901	1,202	32	699 R	60.6%	38.3%	61.3%	38.7%
309,424	EL PASO	97,961	58,376	38,897	688	19,479 R	59.6%	39.7%	60.0%	40.0%
28,676	FREMONT	11,443	6,275	5,026	142	1,249 R	54.8%	43.9%	55.5%	44.5%
22,514	GARFIELD	9,028	4,638	4,294	96	344 R	51.4%	47.6%	51.9%	48.1%
2,441	GILPIN	1,352	619	716	17	97 D	45.8%	53.0%	46.4%	53.6%
7,475	GRAND	3,476	1,989	1,464	23	525 R	57.2%	42.1%	57.6%	42.4%
10,689	GUNNISON	4,849	2,591	2,181	77	410 R	53.4%	45.0%	54.3%	45.7%
408	HINSDALE	337	236	99	2	137 R	70.0%	29.4%	70.4%	29.6%
6,440	HUERFANO	3,064	1,411	1,637	16	226 D	46.1%	53.4%	46.3%	53.7%
1,863	JACKSON	1,061	663	392	6	271 R	62.5%	36.9%	62.8%	37.2%
371,741	JEFFERSON	161,045	81,766	77,764	1,515	4,002 R	50.8%	48.3%	51.3%	48.7%
1,936	KIOWA	1,155	658	487	10	171 R	57.0%	42.2%	57.5%	42.5%
7,599	KIT CARSON	3,646	2,240	1,380	26	860 R	61.4%	37.8%	61.9%	38.1%
8,830	LAKE	2,958	1,379	1,519	60	140 D	46.6%	51.4%	47.6%	52.4%
27,424	LA PLATA	12,094	6,293	5,732	69	561 R	52.0%	47.4%	52.3%	47.7%
149,184	LARIMER	64,243	31,151	32,564	528	1,413 D	48.5%	50.7%	48.9%	51.1%
14,897	LAS ANIMAS	7,498	3,299	4,158	41	859 D	44.0%	55.5%	44.2%	55.8%
4,663	LINCOLN	2,391	1,455	920	16	535 R	60.9%	38.5%	61.3%	38.7%
19,800	LOGAN	8,339	4,854	3,444	41	1,410 R	58.2%	41.3%	58.5%	41.5%
81,530	MESA	33,263	18,790	14,222	251	4,568 R	56.5%	42.8%	56.9%	43.1%
804	MINERAL	446	305	137	4	168 R	68.4%	30.7%	69.0%	31.0%
13,133	MOFFAT	4,772	2,647	2,005	120	642 R	55.5%	42.0%	56.9%	43.1%
16,510	MONTEZUMA	5,913	3,346	2,502	65	844 R	56.6%	42.3%	57.2%	42.8%
24,352	MONTROSE	9,797	6,391	3,348	58	3,043 R	65.2%	34.2%	65.6%	34.4%
22,513	MORGAN	8,063	4,460	3,472	131	988 R	55.3%	43.1%	56.2%	43.8%
22,567	OTERO	8,436	4,662	3,621	153	1,041 R	55.3%	42.9%	56.3%	43.7%
1,925	OURAY	1,204	771	426	7	345 R	64.0%	35.4%	64.4%	35.6%
5,333	PARK	2,678	1,517	1,105	56	412 R	56.6%	41.3%	57.9%	42.1%
4,542	PHILLIPS	2,356	1,246	1,096	14	150 R	52.9%	46.5%	53.2%	46.8%
10,338	PITKIN	5,408	2,269	3,115	24	846 D	42.0%	57.6%	42.1%	57.9%
13,070	PROWERS	5,000	2,679	2,216	105	463 R	53.6%	44.3%	54.7%	45.3%
125,972	PUEBLO	48,493	19,746	28,167	580	8,421 D	40.7%	58.1%	41.2%	58.8%
6,255	RIO BLANCO	2,526	1,542	952	32	590 R	61.0%	37.7%	61.8%	38.2%
10,511	RIO GRANDE	4,510	2,698	1,778	34	920 R	59.8%	39.4%	60.3%	39.7%
13,404	ROUTT	6,696	3,655	2,986	55	669 R	54.6%	44.6%	55.0%	45.0%
3,935	SAGUACHE	2,109	1,017	1,075	17	58 D	48.2%	51.0%	48.6%	51.4%
833	SAN JUAN	551	286	261	4	25 R	51.9%	47.4%	52.3%	47.7%
3,192	SAN MIGUEL	1,801	808	984	9	176 D	44.9%	54.6%	45.1%	54.9%
3,266	SEDGWICK	1,695	1,045	646	4	399 R	61.7%	38.1%	61.8%	38.2%
8,848	SUMMIT	4,355	1,985	2,331	39	346 D	45.6%	53.5%	46.0%	54.0%
8,034	TELLER	3,760	2,427	1,300	33	1,127 R	64.5%	34.6%	65.1%	34.9%
5,304	WASHINGTON	2,796	1,739	1,031	26	708 R	62.2%	36.9%	62.8%	37.2%
123,438	WELD	43,008	21,224	21,503	281	279 D	49.3%	50.0%	49.7%	50.3%
9,682	YUMA	4,660	2,650	1,979	31	671 R	56.9%	42.5%	57.2%	42.8%
2,888,834	TOTAL	1,173,646	571,295	590,501	11,850	19,206 D	48.7%	50.3%	49.2%	50.8%

COLORADO

CONGRESS

CD	Year	Total Vote	Republican Vote	Republican Candidate	Democratic Vote	Democratic Candidate	Other Vote	Rep.-Dem. Plurality	Total Vote Rep.	Total Vote Dem.	Major Vote Rep.	Major Vote Dem.
1	1980	179,622	67,804	BRADFORD, NAOMI	107,364	SCHROEDER, PATRICIA	4,454	39,560 D	37.7%	59.8%	38.7%	61.3%
1	1978	134,630	49,845	HUTCHESON, GENE	82,742	SCHROEDER, PATRICIA	2,043	32,897 D	37.0%	61.5%	37.6%	62.4%
1	1976	193,610	89,384	FRIEDMAN, DON	103,037	SCHROEDER, PATRICIA	1,189	13,653 D	46.2%	53.2%	46.5%	53.5%
1	1974	161,734	66,046	SOUTHWORTH, FRANK	94,583	SCHROEDER, PATRICIA	1,105	28,537 D	40.8%	58.5%	41.1%	58.9%
1	1972	197,495	93,733	MCKEVITT, JAMES D.	101,832	SCHROEDER, PATRICIA	1,930	8,099 D	47.5%	51.6%	47.9%	52.1%
2	1980	272,295	111,825	MCELDERRY, JOHN	153,618	WIRTH, TIMOTHY E.	6,852	41,793 D	41.1%	56.4%	42.1%	57.9%
2	1978	186,961	88,072	SCOTT, ED	98,889	WIRTH, TIMOTHY E.		10,817 D	47.1%	52.9%	47.1%	52.9%
2	1976	240,272	118,936	SCOTT, ED	121,336	WIRTH, TIMOTHY E.		2,400 D	49.5%	50.5%	49.5%	50.5%
2	1974	180,500	86,720	BROTZMAN, DONALD G.	93,728	WIRTH, TIMOTHY E.	52	7,008 D	48.0%	51.9%	48.1%	51.9%
2	1972	199,983	132,562	BROTZMAN, DONALD G.	66,817	BRUSH, FRANCIS W.	604	65,745 R	66.3%	33.4%	66.5%	33.5%
3	1980	192,782	84,292	MCCORMICK, HAROLD L.	105,820	KOGOVSEK, RAY	2,670	21,528 D	43.7%	54.9%	44.3%	55.7%
3	1978	141,442	69,303	MCCORMICK, HAROLD L.	69,669	KOGOVSEK, RAY	2,470	366 D	49.0%	49.3%	49.9%	50.1%
3	1976	175,184	82,269	TAKAKI, MELVIN H.	89,308	EVANS, FRANK E.	3,607	7,039 D	47.0%	51.0%	47.9%	52.1%
3	1974	135,081	38,688	RECORDS, E. KEITH	96,393	EVANS, FRANK E.		57,705 D	28.6%	71.4%	28.6%	71.4%
3	1972	162,067	54,556	BRADY, CHUCK	107,511	EVANS, FRANK E.		52,955 D	33.7%	66.3%	33.7%	66.3%
4	1980	260,491	178,221	BROWN, HANK	76,849	BARRAGAN, POLLY B.	5,421	101,372 R	68.4%	29.5%	69.9%	30.1%
4	1978	168,362	103,121	JOHNSON, JAMES P.	65,241	SMITH, MORGAN		37,880 R	61.2%	38.8%	61.2%	38.8%
4	1976	222,328	119,408	JOHNSON, JAMES P.	78,355	OGDEN, DAN	24,565	41,053 R	53.7%	35.2%	60.4%	39.6%
4	1974	159,434	82,608	JOHNSON, JAMES P.	76,826	CARROLL, JOHN		5,782 R	51.8%	48.2%	51.8%	48.2%
4	1972	186,145	94,994	JOHNSON, JAMES P.	91,151	MERSON, ALAN		3,843 R	51.0%	49.0%	51.0%	49.0%
5	1980	244,900	177,319	KRAMER, KEN	62,003	SCHREIBER, ED	5,578	115,316 R	72.4%	25.3%	74.1%	25.9%
5	1978	153,780	91,933	KRAMER, KEN	52,914	FRANK, GERRY	8,933	39,019 R	59.8%	34.4%	63.5%	36.5%
5	1976	190,851	126,784	ARMSTRONG, WILLIAM L.	64,067	HORES, DOROTHY		62,717 R	66.4%	33.6%	66.4%	33.6%
5	1974	147,794	85,326	ARMSTRONG, WILLIAM L.	56,888	GALLOWAY, BEN	5,580	28,438 R	57.7%	38.5%	60.0%	40.0%
5	1972	167,190	104,214	ARMSTRONG, WILLIAM L.	60,948	JOHNSON, BYRON L.	2,028	43,266 R	62.3%	36.5%	63.1%	36.9%

COLORADO

1980 GENERAL ELECTION

President   Other vote was 130,633 Anderson (National Unity Campaign); 25,744 Clark (Libertarian); 5,614 Commoner (Citizens); 1,180 Bubar (Statesman); 520 Pulley (Socialist Workers); 487 Hall (Communist).

Senator   Other vote was 7,265 Higgerson (Statesman); 4,081 Olshaw (Unaffiliated American); 499 Phelps (write-in); 3 Sagona (write-in); 2 Osburn (write-in).

Congress   Other vote was 3,888 Mason (Libertarian) and 566 Sudmeyer (Socialist Workers) in CD 1; 4,633 Grant (Libertarian) and 2,219 McFarland (Citizens) in CD 2; Glennie (Libertarian) in CD 3; Molson-Smith (Libertarian) in CD 4; Lanning (Libertarian) in CD 5. Early returns gave the vote in CD 2 as 111,868 McElderry (Republican); 153,550 Wirth (Democratic).

1980 PRIMARIES

SEPTEMBER 9 REPUBLICAN

Senator   65,803 Mary E. Buchanan; 64,256 Howard W. Callaway; 42,629 Sam Zakhem; 40,651 John M. Cogswell.

Congress   Unopposed in four CD's. Contested as follows:

  CD 2   23,342 John McElderry; 22,008 Ben Loye.

SEPTEMBER 9 DEMOCRATIC

Senator   Gary W. Hart, unopposed.

Congress   Unopposed in all five CD's.

CONNECTICUT

GOVERNOR
William A. O'Neill (D). Elected Lieutenant-Governor in 1978 and became Governor in December 1980 on the resignation of Governor Ella T. Grasso. Next election in 1982.

SENATORS
Christopher J. Dodd (D). Elected 1980 to a six-year term.

Lowell P. Weicker (R). Re-elected 1976 to a six-year term. Previously elected 1970.

REPRESENTATIVES
1. William R. Cotter (D)
   (see page 1)
2. Samuel Gejdenson (D)
3. Lawrence J. DeNardis (R)
4. Stewart B. McKinney (R)
5. William Ratchford (D)
6. Anthony T. Moffett (D)

POSTWAR VOTE FOR GOVERNOR

Year	Total Vote	Republican Vote	Candidate	Democratic Vote	Candidate	Other Vote	Rep.-Dem. Plurality	Total Vote Rep.	Total Vote Dem.	Major Vote Rep.	Major Vote Dem.
1978	1,036,608	422,316	Sarasin, Ronald A.	613,109	Grasso, Ella T.	1,183	190,793 D	40.7%	59.1%	40.8%	59.2%
1974	1,102,773	440,169	Steele, Robert H.	643,490	Grasso, Ella T.	19,114	203,321 D	39.9%	58.4%	40.6%	59.4%
1970	1,082,797	582,160	Meskill, Thomas J.	500,561	Daddario, Emilio	76	81,599 R	53.8%	46.2%	53.8%	46.2%
1966	1,008,557	446,536	Gengras, E. Clayton	561,599	Dempsey, John N.	422	115,063 D	44.3%	55.7%	44.3%	55.7%
1962	1,031,902	482,852	Alsop, John	549,027	Dempsey, John N.	23	66,175 D	46.8%	53.2%	46.8%	53.2%
1958	974,509	360,644	Zeller, Fred R.	607,012	Ribicoff, Abraham A.	6,853	246,368 D	37.0%	62.3%	37.3%	62.7%
1954	936,753	460,528	Lodge, John D.	463,643	Ribicoff, Abraham A.	12,582	3,115 D	49.2%	49.5%	49.8%	50.2%
1950	878,735	436,418	Lodge, John D.	419,404	Bowles, Chester	22,913	17,014 R	49.7%	47.7%	51.0%	49.0%
1948	875,170	429,071	Shannon, James C.	431,296	Bowles, Chester	14,803	2,225 D	49.0%	49.3%	49.9%	50.1%
1946	683,831	371,852	McConaughy, J. L.	276,335	Snow, Wilbert	35,644	95,517 R	54.4%	40.4%	57.4%	42.6%

The term of office of Connecticut's Governor was increased from two to four years effective with the 1950 election.

POSTWAR VOTE FOR SENATOR

Year	Total Vote	Republican Vote	Candidate	Democratic Vote	Candidate	Other Vote	Rep.-Dem. Plurality	Total Vote Rep.	Total Vote Dem.	Major Vote Rep.	Major Vote Dem.
1980	1,356,075	581,884	Buckley, James L.	763,969	Dodd, Christopher J.	10,222	182,085 D	42.9%	56.3%	43.2%	56.8%
1976	1,361,666	785,683	Weicker, Lowell P.	561,018	Schaffer, Gloria	14,965	224,665 R	57.7%	41.2%	58.3%	41.7%
1974	1,084,918	372,055	Brannen, James H.	690,820	Ribicoff, Abraham A.	22,043	318,765 D	34.3%	63.7%	35.0%	65.0%
1970	1,089,353	454,721	Weicker, Lowell P.	368,111	Duffey, Joseph D.	266,521	86,610 R	41.7%	33.8%	55.3%	44.7%
1968	1,206,537	551,455	May, Edwin H.	655,043	Ribicoff, Abraham A.	39	103,588 D	45.7%	54.3%	45.7%	54.3%
1964	1,208,163	426,939	Lodge, John D.	781,008	Dodd, Thomas J.	216	354,069 D	35.3%	64.6%	35.3%	64.7%
1962	1,029,301	501,694	Seely-Brown, Horace	527,522	Ribicoff, Abraham A.	85	25,828 D	48.7%	51.3%	48.7%	51.3%
1958	965,463	410,622	Purtell, William A.	554,841	Dodd, Thomas J.	—	144,219 D	42.5%	57.5%	42.5%	57.5%
1956	1,113,819	610,829	Bush, Prescott	479,460	Dodd, Thomas J.	23,530	131,369 R	54.8%	43.0%	56.0%	44.0%
1952	1,093,467	573,854	Purtell, William A.	485,066	Benton, William	34,547	88,788 R	52.5%	44.4%	54.2%	45.8%
1952s	1,093,268	559,465	Bush, Prescott	530,505	Ribicoff, Abraham A.	3,298	28,960 R	51.2%	48.5%	51.3%	48.7%
1950	877,827	409,053	Talbot, Joseph E.	453,646	McMahon, Brien	15,128	44,593 D	46.6%	51.7%	47.4%	52.6%
1950s	877,135	430,311	Bush, Prescott	431,413	Benton, William	15,411	1,102 D	49.1%	49.2%	49.9%	50.1%
1946	682,921	381,328	Baldwin, Raymond	276,424	Tone, Joseph M.	25,169	104,904 R	55.8%	40.5%	58.0%	42.0%

One each of the 1952 and 1950 elections was for a short term to fill a vacancy.

CONNECTICUT

Districts Established July 18, 1972

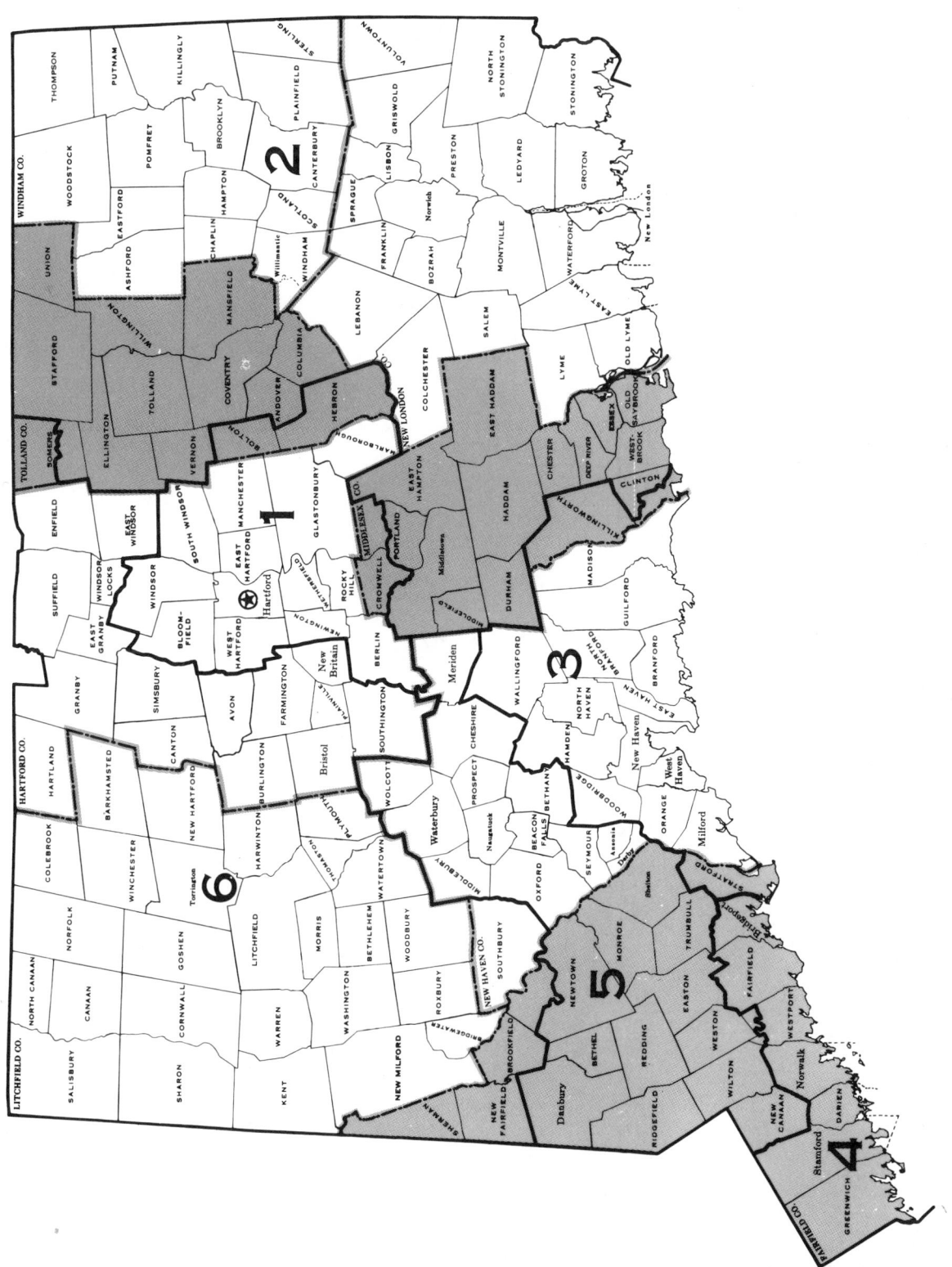

CONNECTICUT

PRESIDENT 1980

1980 Census Population	County	Total Vote	Republican	Democratic	Other	Rep.-Dem. Plurality	Percentage Total Vote Rep.	Dem.	Major Vote Rep.	Dem.
807,143	FAIRFIELD	368,098	201,997	124,074	42,027	77,923 R	54.9%	33.7%	61.9%	38.1%
807,766	HARTFORD	371,380	150,265	164,643	56,472	14,378 D	40.5%	44.3%	47.7%	52.3%
156,769	LITCHFIELD	76,354	38,725	26,705	10,924	12,020 R	50.7%	35.0%	59.2%	40.8%
129,017	MIDDLESEX	63,672	28,989	24,768	9,915	4,221 R	45.5%	38.9%	53.9%	46.1%
761,337	NEW HAVEN	337,732	169,038	130,913	37,781	38,125 R	50.1%	38.8%	56.4%	43.6%
238,409	NEW LONDON	98,448	47,217	36,628	14,603	10,589 R	48.0%	37.2%	56.3%	43.7%
114,823	TOLLAND	50,346	22,127	18,557	9,662	3,570 R	43.9%	36.9%	54.4%	45.6%
92,312	WINDHAM	39,419	18,852	15,444	5,123	3,408 R	47.8%	39.2%	55.0%	45.0%
3,107,576	TOTAL	1,406,285	677,210	541,732	187,343	135,478 R	48.2%	38.5%	55.6%	44.4%

CONNECTICUT

PRESIDENT 1980

1980 Census Population	City/Town	Total Vote	Republican	Democratic	Other	Rep.-Dem. Plurality	Percentage Total Vote Rep.	Dem.	Major Vote Rep.	Dem.
19,039	ANSONIA	8,498	4,064	3,696	738	368 R	47.8%	43.5%	52.4%	47.6%
23,363	BRANFORD	11,706	6,432	3,827	1,447	2,605 R	54.9%	32.7%	62.7%	37.3%
142,546	BRIDGEPORT	45,875	19,185	23,505	3,185	4,320 D	41.8%	51.2%	44.9%	55.1%
57,370	BRISTOL	24,012	9,583	11,123	3,306	1,540 D	39.9%	46.3%	46.3%	53.7%
21,788	CHESHIRE	11,211	6,541	3,038	1,632	3,503 R	58.3%	27.1%	68.3%	31.7%
60,470	DANBURY	23,414	11,308	9,374	2,732	1,934 R	48.3%	40.0%	54.7%	45.3%
18,892	DARIEN	10,714	7,245	1,990	1,479	5,255 R	67.6%	18.6%	78.5%	21.5%
52,563	EAST HARTFORD	23,157	8,487	11,416	3,254	2,929 D	36.6%	49.3%	42.6%	57.4%
25,028	EAST HAVEN	10,647	5,870	3,942	835	1,928 R	55.1%	37.0%	59.8%	40.2%
42,695	ENFIELD	18,019	7,227	8,023	2,769	796 D	40.1%	44.5%	47.4%	52.6%
54,849	FAIRFIELD TOWN	30,273	17,406	9,169	3,698	8,237 R	57.5%	30.3%	65.5%	34.5%
24,327	GLASTONBURY	13,916	7,019	4,283	2,614	2,736 R	50.4%	30.8%	62.1%	37.9%
59,578	GREENWICH	31,819	19,379	8,670	3,770	10,709 R	60.9%	27.2%	69.1%	30.9%
41,062	GROTON	12,811	6,131	4,523	2,157	1,608 R	47.9%	35.3%	57.5%	42.5%
51,071	HAMDEN	26,078	13,729	9,515	2,834	4,214 R	52.6%	36.5%	59.1%	40.9%
136,392	HARTFORD CITY	39,652	8,138	27,657	3,857	19,519 D	20.5%	69.7%	22.7%	77.3%
49,761	MANCHESTER	24,642	10,839	9,459	4,344	1,380 R	44.0%	38.4%	53.4%	46.6%
20,634	MANSFIELD	6,213	2,096	2,633	1,484	537 D	33.7%	42.4%	44.3%	55.7%
57,118	MERIDEN	23,568	10,186	10,255	3,127	69 D	43.2%	43.5%	49.8%	50.2%
39,040	MIDDLETOWN	17,458	6,186	8,753	2,519	2,567 D	35.4%	50.1%	41.4%	58.6%
50,898	MILFORD	22,417	12,419	7,450	2,548	4,969 R	55.4%	33.2%	62.5%	37.5%
26,456	NAUGATUCK	11,069	5,914	3,863	1,292	2,051 R	53.4%	34.9%	60.5%	39.5%
73,840	NEW BRITAIN	29,411	10,292	15,649	3,470	5,357 D	35.0%	53.2%	39.7%	60.3%
126,109	NEW HAVEN CITY	45,690	14,388	26,648	4,654	12,260 D	31.5%	58.3%	35.1%	64.9%
28,841	NEWINGTON	15,273	6,493	6,369	2,411	124 R	42.5%	41.7%	50.5%	49.5%
28,842	NEW LONDON CITY	10,309	3,788	5,010	1,511	1,222 D	36.7%	48.6%	43.1%	56.9%
22,080	NORTH HAVEN	11,807	6,971	3,666	1,170	3,305 R	59.0%	31.0%	65.5%	34.5%
77,767	NORWALK	32,381	16,969	11,785	3,627	5,184 R	52.4%	36.4%	59.0%	41.0%
38,074	NORWICH	14,326	6,767	5,853	1,706	914 R	47.2%	40.9%	53.6%	46.4%
20,120	RIDGEFIELD	10,685	6,542	2,591	1,552	3,951 R	61.2%	24.2%	71.6%	28.4%
31,314	SHELTON	13,821	8,393	4,084	1,344	4,309 R	60.7%	29.5%	67.3%	32.7%
21,161	SIMSBURY	12,081	6,654	3,101	2,326	3,553 R	55.1%	25.7%	68.2%	31.8%
36,879	SOUTHINGTON	15,573	6,849	6,590	2,134	259 R	44.0%	42.3%	51.0%	49.0%
102,453	STAMFORD	45,982	23,250	17,633	5,099	5,617 R	50.6%	38.3%	56.9%	43.1%
50,541	STRATFORD	25,039	13,489	9,187	2,363	4,302 R	53.9%	36.7%	59.5%	40.5%
30,987	TORRINGTON	15,264	6,538	6,783	1,943	245 D	42.8%	44.4%	49.1%	50.9%
32,989	TRUMBULL	17,478	10,782	4,880	1,816	5,902 R	61.7%	27.9%	68.8%	31.2%
27,974	VERNON	12,439	5,372	4,784	2,283	588 R	43.2%	38.5%	52.9%	47.1%
37,274	WALLINGFORD	16,710	8,351	6,213	2,146	2,138 R	50.0%	37.2%	57.3%	42.7%
103,266	WATERBURY	41,588	19,461	17,922	4,205	1,539 R	46.8%	43.1%	52.1%	47.9%
61,301	WEST HARTFORD	38,462	16,590	14,662	7,210	1,928 R	43.1%	38.1%	53.1%	46.9%
53,184	WEST HAVEN	23,905	11,844	9,964	2,097	1,880 R	49.5%	41.7%	54.3%	45.7%
25,290	WESTPORT	14,476	7,810	4,381	2,285	3,429 R	54.0%	30.3%	64.1%	35.9%
26,013	WINDHAM TOWN	15,568	7,066	6,295	2,207	771 R	45.4%	40.4%	52.9%	47.1%
21,062	WETHERSFIELD	8,367	3,571	3,603	1,193	32 D	42.7%	43.1%	49.8%	50.2%
25,204	WINDSOR	12,492	5,126	5,404	1,962	278 D	41.0%	43.3%	48.7%	51.3%

CONNECTICUT

SENATOR 1980

1980 Census Population	County	Total Vote	Republican	Democratic	Other	Rep.-Dem. Plurality	Percentage Total Vote Rep.	Dem.	Major Vote Rep.	Dem.
807,143	FAIRFIELD	352,013	186,695	162,789	2,529	23,906 R	53.0%	46.2%	53.4%	46.6%
807,766	HARTFORD	359,475	125,806	231,149	2,520	105,343 D	35.0%	64.3%	35.2%	64.8%
156,769	LITCHFIELD	74,040	34,355	39,134	551	4,779 D	46.4%	52.9%	46.7%	53.3%
129,017	MIDDLESEX	62,060	23,293	38,178	589	14,885 D	37.5%	61.5%	37.9%	62.1%
761,337	NEW HAVEN	325,137	142,873	179,735	2,529	36,862 D	43.9%	55.3%	44.3%	55.7%
238,409	NEW LONDON	96,102	35,536	60,030	536	24,494 D	37.0%	62.5%	37.2%	62.8%
114,823	TOLLAND	49,105	17,889	30,702	514	12,813 D	36.4%	62.5%	36.8%	63.2%
92,312	WINDHAM	38,029	15,437	22,252	340	6,815 D	40.6%	58.5%	41.0%	59.0%
3,107,576	TOTAL	1,356,075	581,884	763,969	10,222	182,085 D	42.9%	56.3%	43.2%	56.8%

CONNECTICUT

SENATOR 1980

1980 Census Population	City/Town	Total Vote	Republican	Democratic	Other	Rep.-Dem. Plurality	Percentage Total Vote Rep.	Dem.	Major Vote Rep.	Dem.
19,039	ANSONIA	8,215	3,244	4,930	41	1,686 D	39.5%	60.0%	39.7%	60.3%
23,363	BRANFORD	11,322	5,677	5,561	84	116 R	50.1%	49.1%	50.5%	49.5%
142,546	BRIDGEPORT	43,110	16,404	26,452	254	10,048 D	38.1%	61.4%	38.3%	61.7%
57,370	BRISTOL	23,306	7,633	15,495	178	7,862 D	32.8%	66.5%	33.0%	67.0%
21,788	CHESHIRE	10,857	5,517	5,253	87	264 R	50.8%	48.4%	51.2%	48.8%
60,470	DANBURY	22,432	10,717	11,558	157	841 D	47.8%	51.5%	48.1%	51.9%
18,892	DARIEN	10,231	7,295	2,852	84	4,443 R	71.3%	27.9%	71.9%	28.1%
52,563	EAST HARTFORD	22,555	6,758	15,673	124	8,915 D	30.0%	69.5%	30.1%	69.9%
25,028	EAST HAVEN	10,310	4,943	5,324	43	381 D	47.9%	51.6%	48.1%	51.9%
42,695	ENFIELD	17,464	5,643	11,703	118	6,060 D	32.3%	67.0%	32.5%	67.5%
54,849	FAIRFIELD TOWN	29,328	15,936	13,193	199	2,743 R	54.3%	45.0%	54.7%	45.3%
24,327	GLASTONBURY	13,600	6,263	7,233	104	970 D	46.1%	53.2%	46.4%	53.6%
59,578	GREENWICH	30,373	19,400	10,748	225	8,652 R	63.9%	35.4%	64.3%	35.7%
41,062	GROTON	12,533	4,736	7,726	71	2,990 D	37.8%	61.6%	38.0%	62.0%
51,071	HAMDEN	25,208	11,562	13,501	145	1,939 D	45.9%	53.6%	46.1%	53.9%
136,392	HARTFORD CITY	37,864	6,932	30,591	341	23,659 D	18.3%	80.8%	18.5%	81.5%
49,761	MANCHESTER	23,876	9,030	14,686	160	5,656 D	37.8%	61.5%	38.1%	61.9%
20,634	MANSFIELD	6,027	1,688	4,230	109	2,542 D	28.0%	70.2%	28.5%	71.5%
57,118	MERIDEN	23,008	8,643	14,158	207	5,515 D	37.6%	61.5%	37.9%	62.1%
39,040	MIDDLETOWN	16,925	4,692	12,054	179	7,362 D	27.7%	71.2%	28.0%	72.0%
50,898	MILFORD	21,669	10,546	11,009	114	463 D	48.7%	50.8%	48.9%	51.1%
26,456	NAUGATUCK	10,624	4,680	5,867	77	1,187 D	44.1%	55.2%	44.4%	55.6%
73,840	NEW BRITAIN	27,768	7,931	19,658	179	11,727 D	28.6%	70.8%	28.7%	71.3%
126,109	NEW HAVEN CITY	42,299	11,839	29,831	629	17,992 D	28.0%	70.5%	28.4%	71.6%
28,841	NEWINGTON	14,780	5,220	9,489	71	4,269 D	35.3%	64.2%	35.5%	64.5%
28,842	NEW LONDON CITY	9,972	2,765	7,139	68	4,374 D	27.7%	71.6%	27.9%	72.1%
22,080	NORTH HAVEN	11,466	5,781	5,614	71	167 R	50.4%	49.0%	50.7%	49.3%
77,767	NORWALK	30,754	15,792	14,704	258	1,088 R	51.3%	47.8%	51.8%	48.2%
38,074	NORWICH	14,097	4,920	9,096	81	4,176 D	34.9%	64.5%	35.1%	64.9%
20,120	RIDGEFIELD	10,243	6,429	3,705	109	2,724 R	62.8%	36.2%	63.4%	36.6%
31,314	SHELTON	13,084	6,585	6,418	81	167 R	50.3%	49.1%	50.6%	49.4%
21,161	SIMSBURY	11,803	6,310	5,407	86	903 R	53.5%	45.8%	53.9%	46.1%
36,879	SOUTHINGTON	15,079	5,335	9,634	110	4,299 D	35.4%	63.9%	35.6%	64.4%
102,453	STAMFORD	43,726	20,614	22,832	276	2,222 D	47.1%	52.2%	47.4%	52.6%
50,541	STRATFORD	24,214	11,820	12,285	109	465 D	48.8%	50.7%	49.0%	51.0%
30,987	TORRINGTON	14,807	5,380	9,340	87	3,960 D	36.3%	63.1%	36.5%	63.5%
32,989	TRUMBULL	16,917	9,695	7,150	72	2,545 R	57.3%	42.3%	57.6%	42.4%
27,974	VERNON	12,162	4,311	7,769	82	3,458 D	35.4%	63.9%	35.7%	64.3%
37,274	WALLINGFORD	16,294	6,689	9,510	95	2,821 D	41.1%	58.4%	41.3%	58.7%
103,266	WATERBURY	40,123	16,796	23,019	308	6,223 D	41.9%	57.4%	42.2%	57.8%
61,301	WEST HARTFORD	37,375	14,214	22,923	238	8,709 D	38.0%	61.3%	38.3%	61.7%
53,184	WEST HAVEN	23,276	9,751	13,391	134	3,640 D	41.9%	57.5%	42.1%	57.9%
25,290	WESTPORT	13,874	7,570	6,127	177	1,443 R	54.6%	44.2%	55.3%	44.7%
26,013	WINDHAM TOWN	15,194	5,969	9,146	79	3,177 D	39.3%	60.2%	39.5%	60.5%
21,062	WETHERSFIELD	8,072	2,662	5,324	86	2,662 D	33.0%	66.0%	33.3%	66.7%
25,204	WINDSOR	12,130	4,285	7,746	99	3,461 D	35.3%	63.9%	35.6%	64.4%

CONNECTICUT

CONGRESS

CD	Year	Total Vote	Republican Vote	Republican Candidate	Democratic Vote	Democratic Candidate	Other Vote	Rep.-Dem. Plurality	Total Vote Rep.	Total Vote Dem.	Major Vote Rep.	Major Vote Dem.
1	1980	218,694	80,816	ANDERSON, MARJORIE D.	137,849	COTTER, WILLIAM R.	29	57,033 D	37.0%	63.0%	37.0%	63.0%
1	1978	172,564	67,828	ANDREWS, BEN F.	102,749	COTTER, WILLIAM R.	1,987	34,921 D	39.3%	59.5%	39.8%	60.2%
1	1976	225,076	94,106	DI FAZIO, LUCIEN	128,479	COTTER, WILLIAM R.	2,491	34,373 D	41.8%	57.1%	42.3%	57.7%
1	1974	186,772	67,080	BUCKLEY, F. MAC	117,038	COTTER, WILLIAM R.	2,654	49,958 D	35.9%	62.7%	36.4%	63.6%
1	1972	229,682	96,188	RITTENBAND, RICHARD M.	130,701	COTTER, WILLIAM R.	2,793	34,513 D	41.9%	56.9%	42.4%	57.6%
2	1980	223,311	104,107	GUGLIELMO, TONY	119,176	GEJDENSON, SAMUEL	28	15,069 D	46.6%	53.4%	46.6%	53.4%
2	1978	166,814	50,167	CONNELL, THOMAS H.	116,624	DODD, CHRISTOPHER J.	23	66,457 D	30.1%	69.9%	30.1%	69.9%
2	1976	219,308	74,743	JACKSON, RICHARD M.	142,684	DODD, CHRISTOPHER J.	1,881	67,941 D	34.1%	65.1%	34.4%	65.6%
2	1974	176,949	69,380	HELLIER, SAMUEL B.	104,436	DODD, CHRISTOPHER J.	3,133	35,056 D	39.2%	59.0%	39.9%	60.1%
2	1972	215,512	142,094	STEELE, ROBERT H.	73,400	HILSMAN, ROGER	18	68,694 R	65.9%	34.1%	65.9%	34.1%
3	1980	223,648	117,024	DENARDIS, LAWRENCE J.	103,903	LIEBERMAN, JOSEPH I.	2,721	13,121 R	52.3%	46.5%	53.0%	47.0%
3	1978	166,587	66,663	PUCCIANO, JOHN G.	96,830	GIAIMO, ROBERT N.	3,094	30,167 D	40.0%	58.1%	40.8%	59.2%
3	1976	222,643	96,714	PUCCIANO, JOHN G.	121,623	GIAIMO, ROBERT N.	4,306	24,909 D	43.4%	54.6%	44.3%	55.7%
3	1974	175,507	55,177	ALTHAM, JAMES	114,316	GIAIMO, ROBERT N.	6,014	59,139 D	31.4%	65.1%	32.6%	67.4%
3	1972	227,561	106,313	POVINELLI, HENRY A.	121,217	GIAIMO, ROBERT N.	31	14,904 D	46.7%	53.3%	46.7%	53.3%
4	1980	198,625	124,285	MCKINNEY, STEWART B.	74,326	PHILLIPS, JOHN A.	14	49,959 R	62.6%	37.4%	62.6%	37.4%
4	1978	143,919	83,990	MCKINNEY, STEWART B.	59,918	MORGAN, MICHAEL G.	11	24,072 R	58.4%	41.6%	58.4%	41.6%
4	1976	207,058	126,314	MCKINNEY, STEWART B.	76,722	PETERSON, GEOFFREY	4,022	49,592 R	61.0%	37.1%	62.2%	37.8%
4	1974	157,235	83,630	MCKINNEY, STEWART B.	71,047	KELLIS, JAMES G.	2,558	12,583 R	53.2%	45.2%	54.1%	45.9%
4	1972	215,433	135,883	MCKINNEY, STEWART B.	79,515	MCLOUGHLIN, JAMES P.	35	56,368 R	63.1%	36.9%	63.1%	36.9%
5	1980	232,943	115,614	DONAHUE, EDWARD M.	117,316	RATCHFORD, WILLIAM	13	1,702 D	49.6%	50.4%	49.6%	50.4%
5	1978	184,913	88,162	GUIDERA, GEORGE C.	96,738	RATCHFORD, WILLIAM	13	8,576 D	47.7%	52.3%	47.7%	52.3%
5	1976	236,087	157,009	SARASIN, RONALD A.	77,308	ADANTI, MICHAEL J.	1,770	79,701 R	66.5%	32.7%	67.0%	33.0%
5	1974	188,489	94,998	SARASIN, RONALD A.	90,407	RATCHFORD, WILLIAM	3,084	4,591 R	50.4%	48.0%	51.2%	48.8%
5	1972	229,731	117,578	SARASIN, RONALD A.	112,142	MONAGAN, JOHN S.	11	5,436 R	51.2%	48.8%	51.2%	48.8%
6	1980	242,024	98,331	SCHAUS, NICHOLAS	142,685	MOFFETT, ANTHONY T.	1,008	44,354 D	40.6%	59.0%	40.8%	59.2%
6	1978	186,224	66,664	MACKINNON, DANIEL F.	119,537	MOFFETT, ANTHONY T.	23	52,873 D	35.8%	64.2%	35.8%	64.2%
6	1976	238,300	102,364	UPSON, THOMAS F.	134,914	MOFFETT, ANTHONY T.	1,022	32,550 D	43.0%	56.6%	43.1%	56.9%
6	1974	193,581	69,942	PISCOPO, PATSY J.	122,785	MOFFETT, ANTHONY T.	854	52,843 D	36.1%	63.4%	36.3%	63.7%
6	1972	233,082	92,783	WALSH, JOHN F.	140,290	GRASSO, ELLA T.	9	47,507 D	39.8%	60.2%	39.8%	60.2%

CONNECTICUT

1980 GENERAL ELECTION

In addition to the county-by-county figures, data are presented for selected Connecticut communities. Since not all jurisdictions of the state are listed in this special tabulation, state-wide totals are shown only with the county-by-county statistics.

President   Other vote was 171,807 Anderson (Anderson Coalition); 8,570 Clark (Libertarian); 6,130 Commoner (Citizens); 836 scattered. State-wide total for other vote column includes these 836 scattered votes not published by county.

Senator   Other vote was 5,336 Brennan (Libertarian); 4,772 Zemel (Citizens); 114 scattered. State-wide total for other vote column includes these 114 scattered votes not published by county.

Congress   Other vote was scattered in CD's 1, 2, 4 and 5; 2,711 Fishman (Communist) and 10 scattered in CD 3; 995 Marietta (Independent) and 13 scattered in CD 6.

1980 PRIMARIES

Party conventions nominate Connecticut candidates, subject to a system of "challenge" primaries. Any candidate who receives more than 20 percent of the convention vote is entitled to challenge the endorsed candidate in a primary.

SEPTEMBER 9 REPUBLICAN

Senator   64,962 James L. Buckley; 50,096 Richard C. Bozzuto.

Congress   Challenge primaries were held in four of the six CD's as follows:

CD 2   8,095 Tony Guglielmo; 7,517 Michael M. Connery.
CD 3   8,749 Lawrence J. DeNardis; 5,679 Henry A. Povinelli.
CD 5   11,506 Edward M. Donahue; 6,977 Charles R. Feld.
CD 6   14,073 Nicholas Schaus; 6,336 Paul M. Rosenberg.

SEPTEMBER 9 DEMOCRATIC

Senator   Christopher J. Dodd, nominated by convention.

Congress   Challenge primaries were held in two of the six CD's as follows:

CD 2   18,746 Samuel Gejdenson; 11,654 John N. Dempsey, Jr.
CD 4   11,351 John A. Phillips; 9,670 Wayne Konitshek.

DELAWARE

GOVERNOR
Pierre duPont (R). Re-elected 1980 to a four-year term. Previously elected 1976.

SENATORS
Joseph R. Biden (D). Re-elected 1978 to a six-year term. Previously elected 1972.

William V. Roth (R). Re-elected 1976 to a six-year term. Previously elected 1970.

REPRESENTATIVE
At-Large. Thomas B. Evans (R)

POSTWAR VOTE FOR GOVERNOR

Year	Total Vote	Republican Vote	Candidate	Democratic Vote	Candidate	Other Vote	Rep.-Dem. Plurality	Total Vote Rep.	Dem.	Major Vote Rep.	Dem.
1980	225,081	159,004	duPont, Pierre	64,217	Gordy, William J.	1,860	94,787 R	70.6%	28.5%	71.2%	28.8%
1976	229,563	130,531	duPont, Pierre	97,480	Tribbitt, Sherman W.	1,552	33,051 R	56.9%	42.5%	57.2%	42.8%
1972	228,722	109,583	Peterson, Russell W.	117,274	Tribbitt, Sherman W.	1,865	7,691 D	47.9%	51.3%	48.3%	51.7%
1968	206,834	104,474	Peterson, Russell W.	102,360	Terry, Charles L.	—	2,114 R	50.5%	49.5%	50.5%	49.5%
1964	200,171	97,374	Buckson, David P.	102,797	Terry, Charles L.	—	5,423 D	48.6%	51.4%	48.6%	51.4%
1960	194,835	94,043	Rollins, John W.	100,792	Carvel, Elbert N.	—	6,749 D	48.3%	51.7%	48.3%	51.7%
1956	177,012	91,965	Boggs, J. Caleb	85,047	McConnell, J. H. T.	—	6,918 R	52.0%	48.0%	52.0%	48.0%
1952	170,749	88,977	Boggs, J. Caleb	81,772	Carvel, Elbert N.	—	7,205 R	52.1%	47.9%	52.1%	47.9%
1948	140,335	64,996	George, Hyland P.	75,339	Carvel, Elbert N.	—	10,343 D	46.3%	53.7%	46.3%	53.7%

POSTWAR VOTE FOR SENATOR

Year	Total Vote	Republican Vote	Candidate	Democratic Vote	Candidate	Other Vote	Rep.-Dem. Plurality	Total Vote Rep.	Dem.	Major Vote Rep.	Dem.
1978	162,072	66,479	Baxter, James H.	93,930	Biden, Joseph R.	1,663	27,451 D	41.0%	58.0%	41.4%	58.6%
1976	224,859	125,502	Roth, William V.	98,055	Maloney, Thomas C.	1,302	27,447 R	55.8%	43.6%	56.1%	43.9%
1972	229,828	112,844	Boggs, J. Caleb	116,006	Biden, Joseph R.	978	3,162 D	49.1%	50.5%	49.3%	50.7%
1970	161,439	94,979	Roth, William V.	64,740	Zimmerman, Jacob	1,720	30,239 R	58.8%	40.1%	59.5%	40.5%
1966	164,549	97,268	Boggs, J. Caleb	67,281	Tunnell, James M., Jr.	—	29,987 R	59.1%	40.9%	59.1%	40.9%
1964	200,703	103,782	Williams, John J.	96,850	Carvel, Elbert N.	71	6,932 R	51.7%	48.3%	51.7%	48.3%
1960	194,964	98,874	Boggs, J. Caleb	96,090	Frear, J. Allen	—	2,784 R	50.7%	49.3%	50.7%	49.3%
1958	154,432	82,280	Williams, John J.	72,152	Carvel, Elbert N.	—	10,128 R	53.3%	46.7%	53.3%	46.7%
1954	144,900	62,389	Warburton, H. B.	82,511	Frear, J. Allen	—	20,122 D	43.1%	56.9%	43.1%	56.9%
1952	170,705	93,020	Williams, John J.	77,685	Bayard, A. I. duP.	—	15,335 R	54.5%	45.5%	54.5%	45.5%
1948	141,362	68,246	Buck, C. Douglas	71,888	Frear, J. Allen	1,228	3,642 D	48.3%	50.9%	48.7%	51.3%
1946	113,513	62,603	Williams, John J.	50,910	Tunnell, James M.	—	11,693 R	55.2%	44.8%	55.2%	44.8%

DELAWARE

WILMINGTON •

NEW CASTLE

⊛ DOVER

KENT

SUSSEX

DELAWARE

PRESIDENT 1980

1980 Census Population	County	Total Vote	Republican	Democratic	Other	Rep.-Dem. Plurality	Percentage Total Vote Rep.	Dem.	Major Vote Rep.	Dem.
98,219	KENT	29,878	14,882	12,884	2,112	1,998 R	49.8%	43.1%	53.6%	46.4%
399,002	NEW CASTLE	168,638	76,898	76,897	14,843	1 R	45.6%	45.6%	50.0%	50.0%
98,004	SUSSEX	37,384	19,472	15,973	1,939	3,499 R	52.1%	42.7%	54.9%	45.1%
595,225	TOTAL	235,900	111,252	105,754	18,894	5,498 R	47.2%	44.8%	51.3%	48.7%

DELAWARE

GOVERNOR 1980

1980 Census Population	County	Total Vote	Republican	Democratic	Other	Rep.-Dem. Plurality	Percentage Total Vote Rep.	Dem.	Major Vote Rep.	Dem.
98,219	KENT	28,742	19,895	8,666	181	11,229 R	69.2%	30.2%	69.7%	30.3%
399,002	NEW CASTLE	160,510	115,150	43,821	1,539	71,329 R	71.7%	27.3%	72.4%	27.6%
98,004	SUSSEX	35,829	23,959	11,730	140	12,229 R	66.9%	32.7%	67.1%	32.9%
595,225	TOTAL	225,081	159,004	64,217	1,860	94,787 R	70.6%	28.5%	71.2%	28.8%

DELAWARE

CONGRESS

CD	Year	Total Vote	Republican Vote	Candidate	Democratic Vote	Candidate	Other Vote	Rep.-Dem. Plurality	Percentage Total Vote Rep.	Dem.	Major Vote Rep.	Dem.
AL	1980	216,629	133,842	EVANS, THOMAS B.	81,227	MAXWELL, ROBERT L.	1,560	52,615 R	61.8%	37.5%	62.2%	37.8%
AL	1978	157,566	91,689	EVANS, THOMAS B.	64,863	HINDES, GARY E.	1,014	26,826 R	58.2%	41.2%	58.6%	41.4%
AL	1976	214,799	110,677	EVANS, THOMAS B.	102,431	SHIPLEY,SAMUEL L.	1,691	8,246 R	51.5%	47.7%	51.9%	48.1%
AL	1974	160,328	93,826	DUPONT, PIERRE	63,490	SOLES, JAMES	3,012	30,336 R	58.5%	39.6%	59.6%	40.4%
AL	1972	225,851	141,237	DUPONT, PIERRE	83,230	HANDLOFF, NORMA	1,384	58,007 R	62.5%	36.9%	62.9%	37.1%
AL	1970	160,313	86,125	DUPONT, PIERRE	71,429	DANIELLO, JOHN D.	2,759	14,696 R	53.7%	44.6%	54.7%	45.3%
AL	1968	200,820	117,827	ROTH, WILLIAM V.	82,993	MCDOWELL, HARRIS B.		34,834 R	58.7%	41.3%	58.7%	41.3%
AL	1966	163,103	90,961	ROTH, WILLIAM V.	72,142	MCDOWELL, HARRIS B.		18,819 R	55.8%	44.2%	55.8%	44.2%
AL	1964	198,691	86,254	SNOWDEN, JAMES H.	112,361	MCDOWELL, HARRIS B.	76	26,107 D	43.4%	56.6%	43.4%	56.6%
AL	1962	153,356	71,934	WILLIAMS, WILMER F.	81,166	MCDOWELL, HARRIS B.	256	9,232 D	46.9%	52.9%	47.0%	53.0%
AL	1960	194,564	96,337	MCKINSTRY, JAMES T.	98,227	MCDOWELL, HARRIS B.		1,890 D	49.5%	50.5%	49.5%	50.5%
AL	1958	152,896	76,099	HASKELL, HARRY G.	76,797	MCDOWELL, HARRIS B.		698 D	49.8%	50.2%	49.8%	50.2%
AL	1956	176,182	91,538	HASKELL, HARRY G.	84,644	MCDOWELL, HARRIS B.		6,894 R	52.0%	48.0%	52.0%	48.0%
AL	1954	144,236	65,035	MARTIN, LILLIAN	79,201	MCDOWELL, HARRIS B.		14,166 D	45.1%	54.9%	45.1%	54.9%
AL	1952	170,015	88,285	MARBURTON, H. B.	81,730	SCANNELL, JOSEPH S.		6,555 R	51.9%	48.1%	51.9%	48.1%
AL	1950	129,404	73,313	BOGGS, J. CALEB	56,091	WINCHESTER, H. M.		17,222 R	56.7%	43.3%	56.7%	43.3%
AL	1948	140,535	71,127	BOGGS, J. CALEB	68,909	MCGUIGAN, J. CARL	499	2,218 R	50.6%	49.0%	50.8%	49.2%
AL	1946	112,621	63,516	BOGGS, J. CALEB	49,105	TRAYNOR, PHILIP A.		14,411 R	56.4%	43.6%	56.4%	43.6%

DELAWARE

1980 GENERAL ELECTION

President   Other vote was 16,288 Anderson (Anderson Party); 1,974 Clark (Libertarian); 400 Greaves (American); 103 Commoner (write-in); 13 Hall (write-in); 6 Bubar (write-in); 4 Pulley (write-in); 3 Griswold (write-in); 2 McCormack (write-in); 101 scattered.

Governor   Other vote was 1,815 Levy (Libertarian) and 45 scattered.

Congress   Other vote was 1,506 Sullivan (Libertarian) and 54 scattered.

1980 PRIMARIES

Since 1978, Delaware has made nominations on a direct primary basis.

SEPTEMBER 6 REPUBLICAN

Governor   Pierre duPont, unopposed.

Congress   Unopposed at-large.

SEPTEMBER 6 DEMOCRATIC

Governor   William J. Gordy, unopposed.

Congress   Unopposed at-large.

FLORIDA

GOVERNOR
Robert Graham (D). Elected 1978 to a four-year term.

SENATORS
Lawton Chiles (D). Re-elected 1976 to a six-year term. Previously elected 1970.

Paula Hawkins (R). Elected 1980 to a six-year term.

REPRESENTATIVES
1. Earl D. Hutto (D)
2. Don Fuqua (D)
3. Charles E. Bennett (D)
4. William V. Chappell (D)
5. Bill McCollum (R)
6. C. W. Young (R)
7. Sam M. Gibbons (D)
8. Andrew P. Ireland (D)
9. Bill Nelson (D)
10. L. A. Bafalis (R)
11. Dan Mica (D)
12. Clay Shaw (R)
13. William Lehman (D)
14. Claude Pepper (D)
15. Dante B. Fascell (D)

POSTWAR VOTE FOR GOVERNOR

Year	Total Vote	Republican Vote	Republican Candidate	Democratic Vote	Democratic Candidate	Other Vote	Rep.-Dem. Plurality	Total Vote Rep.	Total Vote Dem.	Major Vote Rep.	Major Vote Dem.
1978	2,530,468	1,123,888	Eckerd, Jack M.	1,406,580	Graham, Robert	—	282,692 D	44.4%	55.6%	44.4%	55.6%
1974	1,828,392	709,438	Thomas, Jerry	1,118,954	Askew, Reubin	—	409,516 D	38.8%	61.2%	38.8%	61.2%
1970	1,730,813	746,243	Kirk, Claude R.	984,305	Askew, Reubin	265	238,062 D	43.1%	56.9%	43.1%	56.9%
1966	1,489,661	821,190	Kirk, Claude R.	668,233	High, Robert King	238	152,957 R	55.1%	44.9%	55.1%	44.9%
1964s	1,663,481	686,297	Holley, Charles R.	933,554	Burns, Haydon	43,630	247,257 D	41.3%	56.1%	42.4%	57.6%
1960	1,419,343	569,936	Petersen, George C.	849,407	Bryant, Farris	—	279,471 D	40.2%	59.8%	40.2%	59.8%
1956	1,014,733	266,980	Washburne, W. A.	747,753	Collins, LeRoy	—	480,773 D	26.3%	73.7%	26.3%	73.7%
1954s	357,783	69,852	Watson, J. Tom	287,769	Collins, LeRoy	162	217,917 D	19.5%	80.4%	19.5%	80.5%
1952	834,518	210,009	Swan, Harry S.	624,463	McCarty, Dan	46	414,454 D	25.2%	74.8%	25.2%	74.8%
1948	457,638	76,153	Acker, Bert Lee	381,459	Warren, Fuller	26	305,306 D	16.6%	83.4%	16.6%	83.4%

The 1954 election was for a short term to fill a vacancy. The 1964 vote was for a two-year term to permit shifting the vote for Governor to non-Presidential years.

POSTWAR VOTE FOR SENATOR

Year	Total Vote	Republican Vote	Republican Candidate	Democratic Vote	Democratic Candidate	Other Vote	Rep.-Dem. Plurality	Total Vote Rep.	Total Vote Dem.	Major Vote Rep.	Major Vote Dem.
1980	3,528,028	1,822,460	Hawkins, Paula	1,705,409	Gunter, Bill	159	117,051 R	51.7%	48.3%	51.7%	48.3%
1976	2,857,534	1,057,886	Grady, John	1,799,518	Chiles, Lawton	130	741,632 D	37.0%	63.0%	37.0%	63.0%
1974	1,800,539	736,674	Eckerd, Jack M.	781,031	Stone, Richard	282,834	44,357 D	40.9%	43.4%	48.5%	51.5%
1970	1,675,378	772,817	Cramer, William C.	902,438	Chiles, Lawton	123	129,621 D	46.1%	53.9%	46.1%	53.9%
1968	2,024,136	1,131,499	Gurney, Edward J.	892,637	Collins, LeRoy	—	238,862 R	55.9%	44.1%	55.9%	44.1%
1964	1,560,337	562,212	Kirk, Claude R.	997,585	Holland, Spessard L.	540	435,373 D	36.0%	63.9%	36.0%	64.0%
1962	939,207	281,381	Rupert, Emerson H.	657,633	Smathers, George A.	193	376,252 D	30.0%	70.0%	30.0%	70.0%
1958	542,069	155,956	Hyzer, Leland	386,113	Holland, Spessard L.	—	230,157 D	28.8%	71.2%	28.8%	71.2%
1956	655,418	—	—	655,418	Smathers, George A.	—	655,418 D	—	100.0%	—	100.0%
1952	617,800	—	—	616,665	Holland, Spessard L.	1,135	616,665 D	—	99.8%	—	100.0%
1950	313,487	74,228	Booth, John P.	238,987	Smathers, George A.	272	164,759 D	23.7%	76.2%	23.7%	76.3%
1946	198,640	42,408	Schad, J. Harry	156,232	Holland, Spessard L.	—	113,824 D	21.3%	78.7%	21.3%	78.7%

FLORIDA

Districts Established April 26, 1972

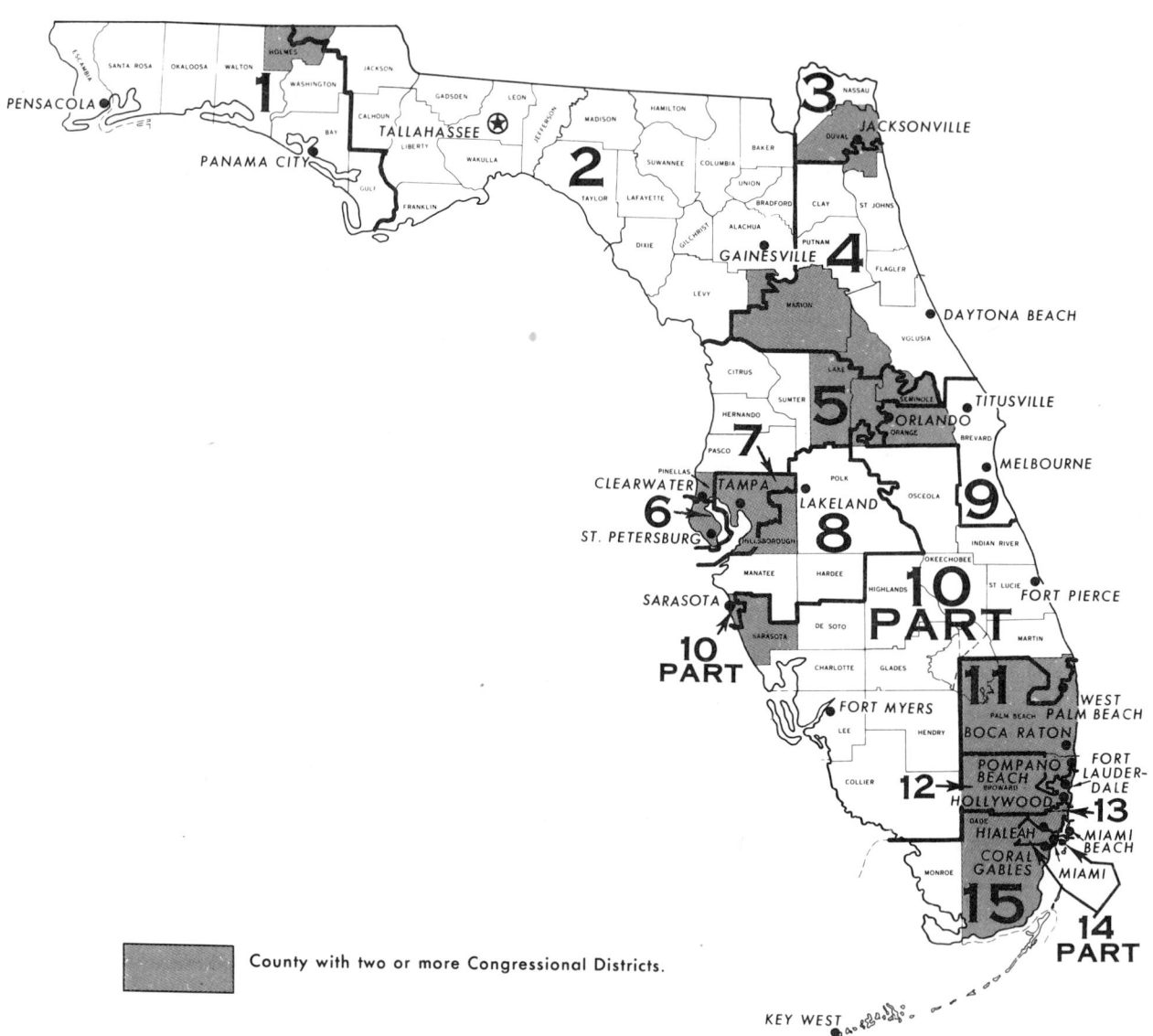

PENSACOLA

PANAMA CITY

1

TALLAHASSEE

2

GAINESVILLE

3 JACKSONVILLE

4

DAYTONA BEACH

TITUSVILLE

5 ORLANDO

7

CLEARWATER TAMPA

6

ST. PETERSBURG

SARASOTA

10
PART

MELBOURNE

9

LAKELAND

8

10
PART

FORT MYERS

11 WEST PALM BEACH

BOCA RATON

POMPANO BEACH

HOLLYWOOD

12

FORT LAUDERDALE

13

HIALEAH

CORAL GABLES

MIAMI BEACH

MIAMI

15

14
PART

KEY WEST

County with two or more Congressional Districts.

FLORIDA

PRESIDENT 1980

1980 Census Population	County	Total Vote	Republican	Democratic	Other	Rep.-Dem. Plurality	Percentage Total Vote Rep.	Dem.	Major Vote Rep.	Dem.
151,348	ALACHUA	51,355	19,804	26,849	4,702	7,045 D	38.6%	52.3%	42.4%	57.6%
15,289	BAKER	4,976	2,283	2,611	82	328 D	45.9%	52.5%	46.6%	53.4%
97,740	BAY	34,561	20,948	12,389	1,224	8,559 R	60.6%	35.8%	62.8%	37.2%
20,023	BRADFORD	6,243	2,778	3,347	118	569 D	44.5%	53.6%	45.4%	54.6%
272,959	BREVARD	115,636	69,460	39,007	7,169	30,453 R	60.1%	33.7%	64.0%	36.0%
1,014,043	BROWARD	410,561	229,693	146,323	34,545	83,370 R	55.9%	35.6%	61.1%	38.9%
9,294	CALHOUN	3,884	1,504	2,300	80	796 D	38.7%	59.2%	39.5%	60.5%
59,115	CHARLOTTE	31,700	20,486	9,769	1,445	10,717 R	64.6%	30.8%	67.7%	32.3%
54,703	CITRUS	24,430	14,286	9,162	982	5,124 R	58.5%	37.5%	60.9%	39.1%
67,052	CLAY	24,122	15,643	7,630	849	8,013 R	64.8%	31.6%	67.2%	32.8%
85,791	COLLIER	33,613	23,900	7,739	1,974	16,161 R	71.1%	23.0%	75.5%	24.5%
35,399	COLUMBIA	11,648	5,643	5,680	325	37 D	48.4%	48.8%	49.8%	50.2%
1,625,979	DADE	524,896	265,888	210,868	48,140	55,020 R	50.7%	40.2%	55.8%	44.2%
19,039	DESOTO	6,285	3,356	2,713	216	643 R	53.4%	43.2%	55.3%	44.7%
7,751	DIXIE	3,173	1,101	2,010	62	909 D	34.7%	63.3%	35.4%	64.6%
570,981	DUVAL	195,545	98,664	90,466	6,415	8,198 R	50.5%	46.3%	52.2%	47.8%
233,794	ESCAMBIA	88,559	51,794	33,513	3,252	18,281 R	58.5%	37.8%	60.7%	39.3%
10,913	FLAGLER	5,600	2,895	2,503	202	392 R	51.7%	44.7%	53.6%	46.4%
7,661	FRANKLIN	3,382	1,508	1,775	99	267 D	44.6%	52.5%	45.9%	54.1%
41,565	GADSDEN	12,225	3,718	8,222	285	4,504 D	30.4%	67.3%	31.1%	68.9%
5,767	GILCHRIST	2,793	1,093	1,627	73	534 D	39.1%	58.3%	40.2%	59.8%
5,992	GLADES	2,389	1,098	1,203	88	105 D	46.0%	50.4%	47.7%	52.3%
10,658	GULF	4,926	2,127	2,700	99	573 D	43.2%	54.8%	44.1%	55.9%
8,761	HAMILTON	3,280	1,301	1,923	56	622 D	39.7%	58.6%	40.4%	59.6%
19,379	HARDEE	5,332	2,603	2,599	130	4 R	48.8%	48.7%	50.0%	50.0%
18,599	HENDRY	5,414	2,703	2,543	168	160 R	49.9%	47.0%	51.5%	48.5%
44,469	HERNANDO	22,032	12,115	8,858	1,059	3,257 R	55.0%	40.2%	57.8%	42.2%
47,526	HIGHLANDS	19,249	11,925	6,688	636	5,237 R	62.0%	34.7%	64.1%	35.9%
646,960	HILLSBOROUGH	205,314	106,160	88,271	10,883	17,889 R	51.7%	43.0%	54.6%	45.4%
14,723	HOLMES	6,137	3,221	2,767	149	454 R	52.5%	45.1%	53.8%	46.2%
59,896	INDIAN RIVER	24,717	15,568	7,759	1,390	7,809 R	63.0%	31.4%	66.7%	33.3%
39,154	JACKSON	14,181	6,348	7,567	266	1,219 D	44.8%	53.4%	45.6%	54.4%
10,703	JEFFERSON	4,141	1,623	2,367	151	744 D	39.2%	57.2%	40.7%	59.3%
4,035	LAFAYETTE	1,863	795	1,034	34	239 D	42.7%	55.5%	43.5%	56.5%
104,870	LAKE	41,528	26,798	13,128	1,602	13,670 R	64.5%	31.6%	67.1%	32.9%
205,266	LEE	94,613	61,033	28,125	5,455	32,908 R	64.5%	29.7%	68.5%	31.5%
148,655	LEON	57,308	24,919	28,450	3,939	3,531 D	43.5%	49.6%	46.7%	53.3%
19,870	LEVY	7,596	3,210	4,170	216	960 D	42.3%	54.9%	43.5%	56.5%
4,260	LIBERTY	2,052	899	1,114	39	215 D	43.8%	54.3%	44.7%	55.3%
14,894	MADISON	5,509	2,280	3,134	95	854 D	41.4%	56.9%	42.1%	57.9%
148,442	MANATEE	65,576	40,535	21,679	3,362	18,856 R	61.8%	33.1%	65.2%	34.8%
122,488	MARION	40,592	23,743	15,400	1,449	8,343 R	58.5%	37.9%	60.7%	39.3%
64,014	MARTIN	30,154	20,521	8,087	1,546	12,434 R	68.1%	26.8%	71.7%	28.3%
63,098	MONROE	21,806	11,644	7,920	2,242	3,724 R	53.4%	36.3%	59.5%	40.5%
32,894	NASSAU	10,751	5,440	5,074	237	366 R	50.6%	47.2%	51.7%	48.3%
109,920	OKALOOSA	40,323	28,072	10,845	1,406	17,227 R	69.6%	26.9%	72.1%	27.9%
20,264	OKEECHOBEE	6,210	2,783	3,228	199	445 D	44.8%	52.0%	46.3%	53.7%
471,660	ORANGE	143,201	87,454	48,767	6,980	38,687 R	61.1%	34.1%	64.2%	35.8%
49,287	OSCEOLA	18,205	10,863	6,603	739	4,260 R	59.7%	36.3%	62.2%	37.8%
573,125	PALM BEACH	252,930	143,639	91,991	17,300	51,648 R	56.8%	36.4%	61.0%	39.0%
194,123	PASCO	88,445	50,120	34,054	4,271	16,066 R	56.7%	38.5%	59.5%	40.5%
728,409	PINELLAS	345,003	185,728	138,428	20,847	47,300 R	53.8%	40.1%	57.3%	42.7%
321,652	POLK	106,315	59,651	43,327	3,337	16,324 R	56.1%	40.8%	57.9%	42.1%
50,549	PUTNAM	17,727	8,273	8,906	548	633 D	46.7%	50.2%	48.2%	51.8%
51,303	ST. JOHNS	18,826	11,234	6,898	694	4,336 R	59.7%	36.6%	62.0%	38.0%
87,182	ST. LUCIE	29,830	18,126	10,347	1,357	7,779 R	60.8%	34.7%	63.7%	36.3%
55,988	SANTA ROSA	21,590	13,802	6,964	824	6,838 R	63.9%	32.3%	66.5%	33.5%
202,251	SARASOTA	99,238	68,065	25,621	5,552	42,444 R	68.6%	25.8%	72.7%	27.3%
179,752	SEMINOLE	60,439	39,989	17,443	3,007	22,546 R	66.2%	28.9%	69.6%	30.4%
24,272	SUMTER	8,267	3,671	4,380	216	709 D	44.4%	53.0%	45.6%	54.4%
22,287	SUWANNEE	8,436	3,899	4,345	192	446 D	46.2%	51.5%	47.3%	52.7%
16,532	TAYLOR	5,868	2,776	2,963	129	187 D	47.3%	50.5%	48.4%	51.6%
10,166	UNION	2,423	1,123	1,237	63	114 D	46.3%	51.1%	47.6%	52.4%
258,762	VOLUSIA	101,882	52,663	44,513	4,706	8,150 R	51.7%	43.7%	54.2%	45.8%
10,887	WAKULLA	4,276	2,021	2,082	173	61 D	47.3%	48.7%	49.3%	50.7%
21,300	WALTON	9,336	4,694	4,360	282	334 R	50.3%	46.7%	51.8%	48.2%
14,509	WASHINGTON	6,513	3,251	3,110	152	141 R	49.9%	47.8%	51.1%	48.9%
9,739,992	TOTAL	3,686,930	2,046,951	1,419,475	220,504	627,476 R	55.5%	38.5%	59.1%	40.9%

FLORIDA

SENATOR 1980

1980 Census Population	County	Total Vote	Republican	Democratic	Other	Rep.-Dem. Plurality	Percentage Total Vote Rep.	Dem.	Major Vote Rep.	Dem.
151,348	ALACHUA	48,222	19,063	29,153	6	10,090 D	39.5%	60.5%	39.5%	60.5%
15,289	BAKER	4,769	1,687	3,082		1,395 D	35.4%	64.6%	35.4%	64.6%
97,740	BAY	31,918	17,276	14,642		2,634 R	54.1%	45.9%	54.1%	45.9%
20,023	BRADFORD	6,076	2,182	3,894		1,712 D	35.9%	64.1%	35.9%	64.1%
272,959	BREVARD	113,706	59,357	54,340	9	5,017 R	52.2%	47.8%	52.2%	47.8%
1,014,043	BROWARD	395,598	210,849	184,749		26,100 R	53.3%	46.7%	53.3%	46.7%
9,294	CALHOUN	3,447	1,320	2,127		807 D	38.3%	61.7%	38.3%	61.7%
59,115	CHARLOTTE	28,351	17,510	10,841		6,669 R	61.8%	38.2%	61.8%	38.2%
54,703	CITRUS	21,686	10,560	11,126		566 D	48.7%	51.3%	48.7%	51.3%
67,052	CLAY	23,349	13,140	10,209		2,931 R	56.3%	43.7%	56.3%	43.7%
85,791	COLLIER	32,953	23,050	9,902	1	13,148 R	69.9%	30.0%	70.0%	30.0%
35,399	COLUMBIA	11,011	4,729	6,282		1,553 D	42.9%	57.1%	42.9%	57.1%
1,625,979	DADE	502,966	243,652	259,300	14	15,648 D	48.4%	51.6%	48.4%	51.6%
19,039	DESOTO	5,930	2,887	3,043		156 D	48.7%	51.3%	48.7%	51.3%
7,751	DIXIE	3,107	680	2,427		1,747 D	21.9%	78.1%	21.9%	78.1%
570,981	DUVAL	183,960	86,725	97,234	1	10,509 D	47.1%	52.9%	47.1%	52.9%
233,794	ESCAMBIA	83,036	39,659	43,365	12	3,706 D	47.8%	52.2%	47.8%	52.2%
10,913	FLAGLER	5,065	2,186	2,879		693 D	43.2%	56.8%	43.2%	56.8%
7,661	FRANKLIN	3,047	1,161	1,886		725 D	38.1%	61.9%	38.1%	61.9%
41,565	GADSDEN	10,110	3,508	6,602		3,094 D	34.7%	65.3%	34.7%	65.3%
5,767	GILCHRIST	2,753	660	2,093		1,433 D	24.0%	76.0%	24.0%	76.0%
5,992	GLADES	2,350	993	1,357		364 D	42.3%	57.7%	42.3%	57.7%
10,658	GULF	4,465	1,647	2,818		1,171 D	36.9%	63.1%	36.9%	63.1%
8,761	HAMILTON	2,686	871	1,815		944 D	32.4%	67.6%	32.4%	67.6%
19,379	HARDEE	5,010	2,252	2,758		506 D	45.0%	55.0%	45.0%	55.0%
18,599	HENDRY	5,035	2,549	2,486		63 R	50.6%	49.4%	50.6%	49.4%
44,469	HERNANDO	20,129	9,965	10,164		199 D	49.5%	50.5%	49.5%	50.5%
47,526	HIGHLANDS	18,768	10,606	8,162		2,444 R	56.5%	43.5%	56.5%	43.5%
646,960	HILLSBOROUGH	203,322	98,458	104,862	2	6,404 D	48.4%	51.6%	48.4%	51.6%
14,723	HOLMES	5,832	2,192	3,640		1,448 D	37.6%	62.4%	37.6%	62.4%
59,896	INDIAN RIVER	22,950	14,140	8,810		5,330 R	61.6%	38.4%	61.6%	38.4%
39,154	JACKSON	12,977	4,865	8,112		3,247 D	37.5%	62.5%	37.5%	62.5%
10,703	JEFFERSON	3,674	1,388	2,286		898 D	37.8%	62.2%	37.8%	62.2%
4,035	LAFAYETTE	1,875	433	1,442		1,009 D	23.1%	76.9%	23.1%	76.9%
104,870	LAKE	39,837	22,596	17,241		5,355 R	56.7%	43.3%	56.7%	43.3%
205,266	LEE	86,029	53,263	32,759	7	20,504 R	61.9%	38.1%	61.9%	38.1%
148,655	LEON	54,716	25,296	29,404	16	4,108 D	46.2%	53.7%	46.2%	53.8%
19,870	LEVY	6,996	2,381	4,615		2,234 D	34.0%	66.0%	34.0%	66.0%
4,260	LIBERTY	1,875	661	1,214		553 D	35.3%	64.7%	35.3%	64.7%
14,894	MADISON	5,401	1,629	3,772		2,143 D	30.2%	69.8%	30.2%	69.8%
148,442	MANATEE	64,796	36,866	27,930		8,936 R	56.9%	43.1%	56.9%	43.1%
122,488	MARION	40,228	20,686	19,542		1,144 R	51.4%	48.6%	51.4%	48.6%
64,014	MARTIN	27,815	16,968	10,846	1	6,122 R	61.0%	39.0%	61.0%	39.0%
63,098	MONROE	19,662	10,893	8,769		2,124 R	55.4%	44.6%	55.4%	44.6%
32,894	NASSAU	9,999	4,347	5,652		1,305 D	43.5%	56.5%	43.5%	56.5%
109,920	OKALOOSA	39,044	21,426	17,618		3,808 R	54.9%	45.1%	54.9%	45.1%
20,264	OKEECHOBEE	5,642	2,395	3,247		852 D	42.4%	57.6%	42.4%	57.6%
471,660	ORANGE	136,243	69,232	66,972	39	2,260 R	50.8%	49.2%	50.8%	49.2%
49,287	OSCEOLA	16,970	9,164	7,806		1,358 R	54.0%	46.0%	54.0%	46.0%
573,125	PALM BEACH	249,517	141,029	108,487	1	32,542 R	56.5%	43.5%	56.5%	43.5%
194,123	PASCO	86,202	45,259	40,943		4,316 R	52.5%	47.5%	52.5%	47.5%
728,409	PINELLAS	326,206	176,409	149,749	48	26,660 R	54.1%	45.9%	54.1%	45.9%
321,652	POLK	100,513	52,005	48,507	1	3,498 R	51.7%	48.3%	51.7%	48.3%
50,549	PUTNAM	16,631	6,762	9,869		3,107 D	40.7%	59.3%	40.7%	59.3%
51,303	ST. JOHNS	18,018	10,191	7,827		2,364 R	56.6%	43.4%	56.6%	43.4%
87,182	ST. LUCIE	29,011	16,432	12,579		3,853 R	56.6%	43.4%	56.6%	43.4%
55,988	SANTA ROSA	20,798	9,758	11,040		1,282 D	46.9%	53.1%	46.9%	53.1%
202,251	SARASOTA	98,985	60,169	38,815	1	21,354 R	60.8%	39.2%	60.8%	39.2%
179,752	SEMINOLE	59,741	34,137	25,604		8,533 R	57.1%	42.9%	57.1%	42.9%
24,272	SUMTER	7,559	2,988	4,571		1,583 D	39.5%	60.5%	39.5%	60.5%
22,287	SUWANNEE	8,015	2,364	5,651		3,287 D	29.5%	70.5%	29.5%	70.5%
16,532	TAYLOR	5,492	1,808	3,684		1,876 D	32.9%	67.1%	32.9%	67.1%
10,166	UNION	2,384	806	1,578		772 D	33.8%	66.2%	33.8%	66.2%
258,762	VOLUSIA	94,690	44,769	49,921		5,152 D	47.3%	52.7%	47.3%	52.7%
10,887	WAKULLA	4,021	1,864	2,157		293 D	46.4%	53.6%	46.4%	53.6%
21,300	WALTON	8,749	3,364	5,385		2,021 D	38.5%	61.5%	38.5%	61.5%
14,509	WASHINGTON	6,110	2,343	3,767		1,424 D	38.3%	61.7%	38.3%	61.7%
9,739,992	TOTAL	3,528,028	1,822,460	1,705,409	159	117,051 R	51.7%	48.3%	51.7%	48.3%

FLORIDA

CONGRESS

CD	Year	Total Vote	Republican Vote	Republican Candidate	Democratic Vote	Democratic Candidate	Other Vote	Rep.-Dem. Plurality	Total Vote Rep.	Total Vote Dem.	Major Vote Rep.	Major Vote Dem.
1	1980	195,768	75,939	BRIGGS, WARREN	119,829	HUTTO, EARL D.		43,890 D	38.8%	61.2%	38.8%	61.2%
1	1978	135,323	49,715	BRIGGS, WARREN	85,608	HUTTO, EARL D.		35,893 D	36.7%	63.3%	36.7%	63.3%
1	1976					SIKES, ROBERT L. F.						
1	1974					SIKES, ROBERT L. F.						
1	1972					SIKES, ROBERT L. F.						
2	1980	195,840	57,588	LACAPRA, JOHN R.	138,252	FUQUA, DON		80,664 D	29.4%	70.6%	29.4%	70.6%
2	1978	137,797	25,148	BRATHWAITE, PETER	112,649	FUQUA, DON		87,501 D	18.3%	81.7%	18.3%	81.7%
2	1976					FUQUA, DON						
2	1974					FUQUA, DON						
2	1972					FUQUA, DON						
3	1980	135,880	31,208	RADCLIFFE, HARRY	104,672	BENNETT, CHARLES E.		73,464 D	23.0%	77.0%	23.0%	77.0%
3	1978					BENNETT, CHARLES E.						
3	1976					BENNETT, CHARLES E.						
3	1974					BENNETT, CHARLES E.						
3	1972	123,660	22,219	BOWEN, JOHN F.	101,441	BENNETT, CHARLES E.		79,222 D	18.0%	82.0%	18.0%	82.0%
4	1980	224,699	76,924	DILLARD, BARNEY E.	147,775	CHAPPELL, WILLIAM V.		70,851 D	34.2%	65.8%	34.2%	65.8%
4	1978	154,949	41,647	BONEY, TOM	113,302	CHAPPELL, WILLIAM V.		71,655 D	26.9%	73.1%	26.9%	73.1%
4	1976					CHAPPELL, WILLIAM V.						
4	1974	109,587	34,867	HAUSER, WARREN	74,720	CHAPPELL, WILLIAM V.		39,853 D	31.8%	68.2%	31.8%	68.2%
4	1972	165,501	72,960	FLEUCHAUS, P. T.	92,541	CHAPPELL, WILLIAM V.		19,581 D	44.1%	55.9%	44.1%	55.9%
5	1980	318,506	177,603	MCCOLLUM, BILL	140,903	BEST, DAVID R.		36,700 R	55.8%	44.2%	55.8%	44.2%
5	1978	208,186	106,319	KELLY, RICHARD	101,867	BEST, DAVID R.		4,452 R	51.1%	48.9%	51.1%	48.9%
5	1976	234,631	138,371	KELLY, RICHARD	96,260	SAUNDERS, JOANN		42,111 R	59.0%	41.0%	59.0%	41.0%
5	1974	142,088	74,954	KELLY, RICHARD	63,610	SAUNDERS, JOANN	3,524	11,344 R	52.8%	44.8%	54.1%	45.9%
5	1972	176,380	78,468	INSCO, JACK P.	97,902	GUNTER, WILLIAM D.	10	19,434 D	44.5%	55.5%	44.5%	55.5%
6	1980			YOUNG, C. W.								
6	1978	191,348	150,694	YOUNG, C. W.	40,654	CHRISTISON, JAMES A.		110,040 R	78.8%	21.2%	78.8%	21.2%
6	1976	232,218	151,371	YOUNG, C. W.	80,821	CAZARES, GABRIEL	26	70,550 R	65.2%	34.8%	65.2%	34.8%
6	1974	144,188	109,302	YOUNG, C. W.	34,886	MONROSE, MICKEY		74,416 R	75.8%	24.2%	75.8%	24.2%
6	1972	205,549	156,150	YOUNG, C. W.	49,399	PLUNKETT, MICHAEL O.		106,751 R	76.0%	24.0%	76.0%	24.0%
7	1980	184,667	52,138	JONES, CHARLES P.	132,529	GIBBONS, SAM M.		80,391 D	28.2%	71.8%	28.2%	71.8%
7	1978					GIBBONS, SAM M.						
7	1976	156,338	53,599	OWENS, DUSTY	102,739	GIBBONS, SAM M.		49,140 D	34.3%	65.7%	34.3%	65.7%
7	1974					GIBBONS, SAM M.						
7	1972	135,274	43,343	CARTER, ROBERT A.	91,931	GIBBONS, SAM M.		48,588 D	32.0%	68.0%	32.0%	68.0%
8	1980	218,913	61,820	NICHOLSON, SCOTT	151,613	IRELAND, ANDREW P.	5,480	89,793 D	28.2%	69.3%	29.0%	71.0%
8	1978					IRELAND, ANDREW P.						
8	1976	178,154	74,794	JOHNSON, ROBERT	103,360	IRELAND, ANDREW P.		28,566 D	42.0%	58.0%	42.0%	58.0%
8	1974	111,523	48,240	LOVINGOOD, JOE Z.	63,283	HALEY, JAMES A.		15,043 D	43.3%	56.7%	43.3%	56.7%
8	1972	153,988	64,920	THOMPSON, ROY	89,068	HALEY, JAMES A.		24,148 D	42.2%	57.8%	42.2%	57.8%
9	1980	198,202	58,734	DOWIAT, STAN	139,468	NELSON, BILL		80,734 D	29.6%	70.4%	29.6%	70.4%
9	1978	145,617	56,074	GURNEY, EDWARD J.	89,543	NELSON, BILL		33,469 D	38.5%	61.5%	38.5%	61.5%
9	1976	167,139	130,509	FREY, LOUIS	36,630	ROSIER, JOSEPH A.		93,879 R	78.1%	21.9%	78.1%	21.9%
9	1974	112,481	86,226	FREY, LOUIS	26,255	ROWLAND, WILLIAM D.		59,971 R	76.7%	23.3%	76.7%	23.3%
9	1972			FREY, LOUIS								
10	1980	345,039	272,393	BAFALIS, L. A.	72,646	SPARKMAN, RICHARD D.		199,747 R	78.9%	21.1%	78.9%	21.1%
10	1978			BAFALIS, L. A.								
10	1976	247,686	164,273	BAFALIS, L. A.	83,413	SIKES, BILL		80,860 R	66.3%	33.7%	66.3%	33.7%
10	1974	159,293	117,368	BAFALIS, L. A.	41,925	TUCKER, EVELYN		75,443 R	73.7%	26.3%	73.7%	26.3%
10	1972	182,963	113,461	BAFALIS, L. A.	69,502	SIKES, BILL		43,959 R	62.0%	38.0%	62.0%	38.0%
11	1980	339,233	137,520	COOGLER, AL	201,713	MICA, DAN		64,193 D	40.5%	59.5%	40.5%	59.5%
11	1978	223,103	99,757	JAMES, BILL	123,346	MICA, DAN		23,589 D	44.7%	55.3%	44.7%	55.3%
11	1976	218,437			199,031	ROGERS, PAUL G.	19,406	199,031 D		91.1%		100.0%
11	1974					ROGERS, PAUL G.						
11	1972	192,896	76,739	GUSTAFSON, JOEL KARL	116,157	ROGERS, PAUL G.		39,418 D	39.8%	60.2%	39.8%	60.2%
12	1980	235,725	128,561	SHAW, CLAY	107,164	BECKER, ALAN S.		21,397 R	54.5%	45.5%	54.5%	45.5%
12	1978	173,647	66,610	BURKE, J. HERBERT	107,037	STACK, EDWARD J.		40,427 D	38.4%	61.6%	38.4%	61.6%
12	1976	199,076	107,268	BURKE, J. HERBERT	91,749	FRIEDMAN, CHARLES	59	15,519 R	53.9%	46.1%	53.9%	46.1%
12	1974	120,090	61,191	BURKE, J. HERBERT	58,899	FRIEDMAN, CHARLES		2,292 R	51.0%	49.0%	51.0%	49.0%
12	1972	176,276	110,750	BURKE, J. HERBERT	65,526	STEPHANIS, JAMES T.		45,224 R	62.8%	37.2%	62.8%	37.2%

FLORIDA

CONGRESS

CD	Year	Total Vote	Republican Vote	Republican Candidate	Democratic Vote	Democratic Candidate	Other Vote	Rep.-Dem. Plurality	Total Vote Rep.	Total Vote Dem.	Major Vote Rep.	Major Vote Dem.
13	1980	170,658	42,830	ENTIN, ALVIN E.	127,828	LEHMAN, WILLIAM		84,998 D	25.1%	74.9%	25.1%	74.9%
13	1978					LEHMAN, WILLIAM						
13	1976	163,179	35,357	SPIEGELMAN, LEE A.	127,822	LEHMAN, WILLIAM		92,465 D	21.7%	78.3%	21.7%	78.3%
13	1974					LEHMAN, WILLIAM						
13	1972	149,676	57,418	BETHEL, PAUL D.	92,258	LEHMAN, WILLIAM		34,840 D	38.4%	61.6%	38.4%	61.6%
14	1980	127,847	32,027	ESTRELLA, EVELIO S.	95,820	PEPPER, CLAUDE		63,793 D	25.1%	74.9%	25.1%	74.9%
14	1978	103,283	38,081	CARDENAS, AL	65,202	PEPPER, CLAUDE		27,121 D	36.9%	63.1%	36.9%	63.1%
14	1976	113,439	30,774	ESTRELLA, EVELIO S.	82,665	PEPPER, CLAUDE		51,891 D	27.1%	72.9%	27.1%	72.9%
14	1974	65,862	20,383	CARRICARTE, MICHAEL A.	45,479	PEPPER, CLAUDE		25,096 D	30.9%	69.1%	30.9%	69.1%
14	1972	111,066	35,935	ESTRELLA, EVELIO S.	75,131	PEPPER, CLAUDE		39,196 D	32.4%	67.6%	32.4%	67.6%
15	1980	203,385	70,433	HOODWIN, HERBERT J.	132,952	FASCELL, DANTE B.		62,519 D	34.6%	65.4%	34.6%	65.4%
15	1978	146,734	37,897	HOODWIN, HERBERT J.	108,837	FASCELL, DANTE B.		70,940 D	25.8%	74.2%	25.8%	74.2%
15	1976	172,233	50,941	COBB, PAUL R.	121,292	FASCELL, DANTE B.		70,351 D	29.6%	70.4%	29.6%	70.4%
15	1974	96,508	28,444	CAPUA, S. PETER	68,064	FASCELL, DANTE B.		39,620 D	29.5%	70.5%	29.5%	70.5%
15	1972	158,281	68,320	RUBIN, ELLIS S.	89,961	FASCELL, DANTE B.		21,641 D	43.2%	56.8%	43.2%	56.8%

FLORIDA

1980 GENERAL ELECTION

President   Other vote was 189,692 Anderson (Independent); 30,524 Clark (Libertarian); 123 Hall (write-in); 116 McReynolds (write-in); 41 DeBerry (write-in); 8 Griswold (write-in). County and state-wide totals include absentee votes counted separately by court order.

Senator   Other vote was Baron (write-in). County and state-wide totals include absentee votes counted separately by court order.

Congress   Under present legislation, votes are not tallied in unopposed elections, so no total vote or candidate vote is available for unopposed Congressional districts. Other vote in CD 8 was Rebholz (Independent).

1980 PRIMARIES

SEPTEMBER 9 REPUBLICAN

Senator   209,856 Paula Hawkins; 119,834 Louis Frey; 54,767 Ander Crenshaw; 19,990 Ellis Rubin; 16,341 John T. Ware; 15,174 Lewis Dinkins.

Congress   Unopposed in thirteen CD's. Contested as follows:

CD 5   26,152 Bill McCollum; 23,942 Vince Fechtel; 10,889 Richard Kelly.
CD 11   24,283 Al Coogler; 12,309 Norman E. Leonard.

SEPTEMBER 9 DEMOCRATIC

Senator   355,287 Richard Stone; 335,859 Bill Gunter; 272,538 Buddy MacKay; 108,154 Richard A. Pettigrew; 18,118 James L. Miller; 17,410 John B. Coffey.

Congress   Unopposed in eleven CD's. No candidate in CD 6. Contested as follows:

CD 5   56,368 David R. Best; 32,143 Dick Fischer.
CD 12   28,364 Alan S. Becker; 20,178 Edward J. Stack.
CD 14   26,800 Claude Pepper; 7,012 Douglas MacKenzie.

OCTOBER 7 REPUBLICAN RUN-OFF

Senator   293,600 Paula Hawkins; 182,911 Louis Frey.

Congress

CD 5   34,875 Bill McCollum; 29,229 Vince Fechtel.

OCTOBER 7 DEMOCRATIC RUN-OFF

Senator   594,676 Bill Gunter; 554,268 Richard Stone.

GEORGIA

GOVERNOR
George Busbee (D). Re-elected 1978 to a four-year term. Previously elected 1974.

SENATORS
Mack Mattingly (R). Elected 1980 to a six-year term.

Sam Nunn (D). Re-elected 1978 to a six-year term. Previously elected 1972.

REPRESENTATIVES
1. Ronald B. Ginn (D)
2. Charles Hatcher (D)
3. Jack Brinkley (D)
4. Elliott H. Levitas (D)
5. Wyche Fowler (D)
6. Newt Gingrich (R)
7. Larry McDonald (D)
8. Billy Lee Evans (D)
9. Ed Jenkins (D)
10. Doug Barnard (D)

POSTWAR VOTE FOR GOVERNOR

Year	Total Vote	Republican Vote	Candidate	Democratic Vote	Candidate	Other Vote	Rep.-Dem. Plurality	Total Vote Rep.	Total Vote Dem.	Major Vote Rep.	Major Vote Dem.
1978	662,862	128,139	Cook, Rodney M.	534,572	Busbee, George	151	406,433 D	19.3%	80.6%	19.3%	80.7%
1974	936,438	289,113	Thompson, Ronnie	646,777	Busbee, George	548	357,664 D	30.9%	69.1%	30.9%	69.1%
1970	1,046,663	424,983	Suit, Hal	620,419	Carter, Jimmy	1,261	195,436 D	40.6%	59.3%	40.7%	59.3%
1966	975,019	453,665	Callaway, Howard H.	450,626	Maddox, Lester	70,728	3,039 R	46.5%	46.2%	50.2%	49.8%
1962	311,691	—	—	311,524	Sanders, Carl E.	167	311,524 D	—	99.9%	—	100.0%
1958	168,497	—	—	168,414	Vandiver, Ernest	83	168,414 D	—	100.0%	—	100.0%
1954	331,966	—	—	331,899	Griffin, Marvin	67	331,899 D	—	100.0%	—	100.0%
1950	234,430	—	—	230,771	Talmadge, Herman	3,659	230,771 D	—	98.4%	—	100.0%
1948s	363,763	—	—	354,711	Talmadge, Herman	9,052	354,711 D	—	97.5%	—	100.0%
1946	145,403	—	—	143,279	Talmadge, Eugene	2,124	143,279 D	—	98.5%	—	100.0%

The 1948 election was for a short term to fill a vacancy. In 1966, in the absence of a majority for any candidate, the state legislature elected Lester Maddox to a four-year term.

POSTWAR VOTE FOR SENATOR

Year	Total Vote	Republican Vote	Candidate	Democratic Vote	Candidate	Other Vote	Rep.-Dem. Plurality	Total Vote Rep.	Total Vote Dem.	Major Vote Rep.	Major Vote Dem.
1980	1,580,340	803,686	Mattingly, Mack	776,143	Talmadge, Herman	511	27,543 R	50.9%	49.1%	50.9%	49.1%
1978	645,164	108,808	Stokes, John W.	536,320	Nunn, Sam	36	427,512 D	16.9%	83.1%	16.9%	83.1%
1974	874,555	246,866	Johnson, Jerry R.	627,376	Talmadge, Herman	313	380,510 D	28.2%	71.7%	28.2%	71.8%
1972	1,178,708	542,331	Thompson, Fletcher	635,970	Nunn, Sam	407	93,639 D	46.0%	54.0%	46.0%	54.0%
1968	1,141,889	256,796	Patton, E. Earl	885,093	Talmadge, Herman	—	628,297 D	22.5%	77.5%	22.5%	77.5%
1966	622,371	—	—	622,043	Russell, Richard B.	328	622,043 D	—	99.9%	—	100.0%
1962	306,250	—	—	306,250	Talmadge, Herman	—	306,250 D	—	100.0%	—	100.0%
1960	576,495	—	—	576,140	Russell, Richard B.	355	576,140 D	—	99.9%	—	100.0%
1956	541,267	—	—	541,094	Talmadge, Herman	173	541,094 D	—	100.0%	—	100.0%
1954	333,936	—	—	333,917	Russell, Richard B.	19	333,917 D	—	100.0%	—	100.0%
1950	261,293	—	—	261,290	George, Walter F.	3	261,290 D	—	100.0%	—	100.0%
1948	362,504	—	—	362,104	Russell, Richard B.	400	362,104 D	—	99.9%	—	100.0%

GEORGIA

Districts Established March 16, 1972

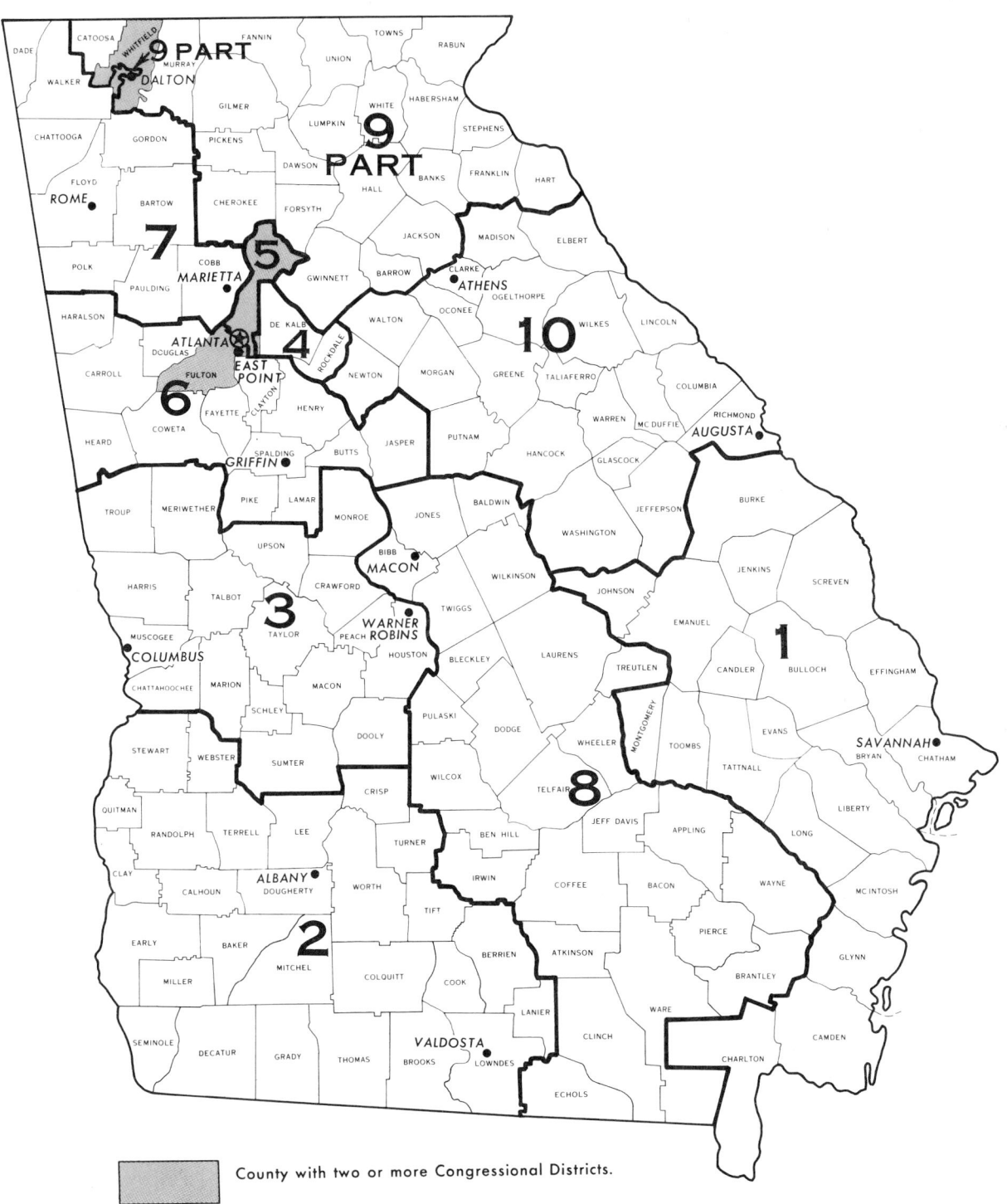

County with two or more Congressional Districts.

GEORGIA

PRESIDENT 1980

1980 Census Population	County	Total Vote	Republican	Democratic	Other	Rep.-Dem. Plurality	Total Vote Rep.	Total Vote Dem.	Major Vote Rep.	Major Vote Dem.
15,565	APPLING	5,007	1,961	2,985	61	1,024 D	39.2%	59.6%	39.6%	60.4%
6,141	ATKINSON	2,222	747	1,449	26	702 D	33.6%	65.2%	34.0%	66.0%
9,379	BACON	3,106	1,427	1,622	57	195 D	45.9%	52.2%	46.8%	53.2%
3,808	BAKER	1,564	510	1,035	19	525 D	32.6%	66.2%	33.0%	67.0%
34,686	BALDWIN	8,326	3,639	4,368	319	729 D	43.7%	52.5%	45.4%	54.6%
8,702	BANKS	2,868	746	2,091	31	1,345 D	26.0%	72.9%	26.3%	73.7%
21,293	BARROW	6,309	2,284	3,876	149	1,592 D	36.2%	61.4%	37.1%	62.9%
40,760	BARTOW	10,853	3,135	7,490	228	4,355 D	28.9%	69.0%	29.5%	70.5%
16,000	BEN HILL	4,067	1,459	2,544	64	1,085 D	35.9%	62.6%	36.4%	63.6%
13,525	BERRIEN	4,404	1,487	2,869	48	1,382 D	33.8%	65.1%	34.1%	65.9%
151,085	BIBB	48,130	15,175	31,770	1,185	16,595 D	31.5%	66.0%	32.3%	67.7%
10,767	BLECKLEY	3,440	1,261	2,014	165	753 D	36.7%	58.5%	38.5%	61.5%
8,701	BRANTLEY	2,977	882	2,066	29	1,184 D	29.6%	69.4%	29.9%	70.1%
15,255	BROOKS	3,827	1,546	2,230	51	684 D	40.4%	58.3%	40.9%	59.1%
10,175	BRYAN	3,235	1,212	1,966	57	754 D	37.5%	60.8%	38.1%	61.9%
35,785	BULLOCH	8,921	3,750	4,921	250	1,171 D	42.0%	55.2%	43.2%	56.8%
19,349	BURKE	4,991	1,871	3,047	73	1,176 D	37.5%	61.0%	38.0%	62.0%
13,665	BUTTS	3,845	1,210	2,574	61	1,364 D	31.5%	66.9%	32.0%	68.0%
5,717	CALHOUN	2,087	652	1,414	21	762 D	31.2%	67.8%	31.6%	68.4%
13,371	CAMDEN	4,443	1,439	2,924	80	1,485 D	32.4%	65.8%	33.0%	67.0%
7,518	CANDLER	2,421	1,030	1,358	33	328 D	42.5%	56.1%	43.1%	56.9%
56,346	CARROLL	14,475	5,815	8,202	458	2,387 D	40.2%	56.7%	41.5%	58.5%
36,991	CATOOSA	11,059	5,962	4,921	176	1,041 R	53.9%	44.5%	54.8%	45.2%
7,343	CHARLTON	2,286	779	1,469	38	690 D	34.1%	64.3%	34.7%	65.3%
202,226	CHATHAM	56,781	26,499	28,413	1,369	1,914 D	46.7%	50.0%	48.3%	51.7%
21,732	CHATTAHOOCHEE	752	256	476	20	220 D	34.0%	63.3%	35.0%	65.0%
21,856	CHATTOOGA	6,330	1,946	4,279	105	2,333 D	30.7%	67.6%	31.3%	68.7%
51,699	CHEROKEE	11,678	5,250	6,020	408	770 D	45.0%	51.5%	46.6%	53.4%
74,498	CLARKE	19,899	8,094	10,519	1,286	2,425 D	40.7%	52.9%	43.5%	56.5%
3,553	CLAY	1,241	316	909	16	593 D	25.5%	73.2%	25.8%	74.2%
150,357	CLAYTON	38,051	19,160	17,540	1,351	1,620 R	50.4%	46.1%	52.2%	47.8%
6,660	CLINCH	1,864	513	1,325	26	812 D	27.5%	71.1%	27.9%	72.1%
297,694	COBB	95,816	51,977	39,157	4,682	12,820 R	54.2%	40.9%	57.0%	43.0%
26,894	COFFEE	6,621	2,499	4,038	84	1,539 D	37.7%	61.0%	38.2%	61.8%
35,376	COLQUITT	9,069	3,593	5,353	123	1,760 D	39.6%	59.0%	40.2%	59.8%
40,118	COLUMBIA	11,938	6,293	5,335	310	958 R	52.7%	44.7%	54.1%	45.9%
13,490	COOK	3,684	1,188	2,461	35	1,273 D	32.2%	66.8%	32.6%	67.4%
39,268	COWETA	10,422	4,480	5,697	245	1,217 D	43.0%	54.7%	44.0%	56.0%
7,684	CRAWFORD	2,375	642	1,673	60	1,031 D	27.0%	70.4%	27.7%	72.3%
19,489	CRISP	5,347	1,861	3,403	83	1,542 D	34.8%	63.6%	35.4%	64.6%
12,318	DADE	3,929	2,114	1,735	80	379 R	53.8%	44.2%	54.9%	45.1%
4,774	DAWSON	1,837	729	1,072	36	343 D	39.7%	58.4%	40.5%	59.5%
25,495	DECATUR	6,243	2,919	3,242	82	323 D	46.8%	51.9%	47.4%	52.6%
483,024	DE KALB	167,405	74,904	82,743	9,758	7,839 D	44.7%	49.4%	47.5%	52.5%
16,955	DODGE	6,453	1,719	4,635	99	2,916 D	26.6%	71.8%	27.1%	72.9%
10,826	DOOLY	3,502	1,083	2,364	55	1,281 D	30.9%	67.5%	31.4%	68.6%
100,978	DOUGHERTY	26,615	12,726	13,430	459	704 D	47.8%	50.5%	48.7%	51.3%
54,573	DOUGLAS	14,238	6,945	6,807	486	138 R	48.8%	47.8%	50.5%	49.5%
13,158	EARLY	3,682	1,538	2,110	34	572 D	41.8%	57.3%	42.2%	57.8%
2,297	ECHOLS	783	259	515	9	256 D	33.1%	65.8%	33.5%	66.5%
18,327	EFFINGHAM	5,377	2,528	2,783	66	255 D	47.0%	51.8%	47.6%	52.4%
18,758	ELBERT	6,061	1,967	4,014	80	2,047 D	32.5%	66.2%	32.9%	67.1%
20,795	EMANUEL	6,251	2,199	3,971	81	1,772 D	35.2%	63.5%	35.6%	64.4%
8,428	EVANS	2,575	1,090	1,456	29	366 D	42.3%	56.5%	42.8%	57.2%
14,748	FANNIN	5,829	3,196	2,526	107	670 R	54.8%	43.3%	55.9%	44.1%
29,043	FAYETTE	10,549	6,351	3,798	400	2,553 R	60.2%	36.0%	62.6%	37.4%
79,800	FLOYD	23,596	9,220	13,710	666	4,490 D	39.1%	58.1%	40.2%	59.8%
27,958	FORSYTH	7,736	3,157	4,325	254	1,168 D	40.8%	55.9%	42.2%	57.8%
15,185	FRANKLIN	4,960	1,387	3,528	45	2,141 D	28.0%	71.1%	28.2%	71.8%
589,904	FULTON	192,723	64,909	118,748	9,066	53,839 D	33.7%	61.6%	35.3%	64.7%
11,110	GILMER	4,537	2,170	2,246	121	76 D	47.8%	49.5%	49.1%	50.9%
2,382	GLASCOCK	1,138	510	614	14	104 D	44.8%	54.0%	45.4%	54.6%
54,981	GLYNN	15,173	7,214	7,540	419	326 D	47.5%	49.7%	48.9%	51.1%
30,070	GORDON	8,542	3,107	5,199	236	2,092 D	36.4%	60.9%	37.4%	62.6%
19,845	GRADY	5,117	2,018	3,023	76	1,005 D	39.4%	59.1%	40.0%	60.0%
11,391	GREENE	3,573	961	2,571	41	1,610 D	26.9%	72.0%	27.2%	72.8%
166,903	GWINNETT	51,452	27,185	21,958	2,309	5,227 R	52.8%	42.7%	55.3%	44.7%
25,020	HABERSHAM	6,781	2,224	4,394	163	2,170 D	32.8%	64.8%	33.6%	66.4%
75,649	HALL	20,521	7,760	12,124	637	4,364 D	37.8%	59.1%	39.0%	61.0%
9,466	HANCOCK	2,809	573	2,205	31	1,632 D	20.4%	78.5%	20.6%	79.4%

GEORGIA

PRESIDENT 1980

1980 Census Population	County	Total Vote	Republican	Democratic	Other	Rep.-Dem. Plurality	Percentage Total Vote Rep.	Dem.	Major Vote Rep.	Dem.
18,422	HARALSON	5,960	2,229	3,606	125	1,377 D	37.4%	60.5%	38.2%	61.8%
15,464	HARRIS	4,942	2,001	2,807	134	806 D	40.5%	56.8%	41.6%	58.4%
18,585	HART	6,215	1,577	4,539	99	2,962 D	25.4%	73.0%	25.8%	74.2%
6,520	HEARD	2,283	875	1,348	60	473 D	38.3%	59.0%	39.4%	60.6%
36,309	HENRY	11,268	5,326	5,635	307	309 D	47.3%	50.0%	48.6%	51.4%
77,605	HOUSTON	20,695	9,005	10,915	775	1,910 D	43.5%	52.7%	45.2%	54.8%
8,988	IRWIN	2,632	1,056	1,555	21	499 D	40.1%	59.1%	40.4%	59.6%
25,343	JACKSON	6,949	2,209	4,591	149	2,382 D	31.8%	66.1%	32.5%	67.5%
7,553	JASPER	2,484	879	1,546	59	667 D	35.4%	62.2%	36.2%	63.8%
11,473	JEFF DAVIS	3,311	1,191	2,059	61	868 D	36.0%	62.2%	36.6%	63.4%
18,403	JEFFERSON	4,978	1,605	3,305	68	1,700 D	32.2%	66.4%	32.7%	67.3%
8,841	JENKINS	2,493	824	1,632	37	808 D	33.1%	65.5%	33.6%	66.4%
8,660	JOHNSON	3,029	1,123	1,854	52	731 D	37.1%	61.2%	37.7%	62.3%
16,579	JONES	5,220	1,828	3,239	153	1,411 D	35.0%	62.0%	36.1%	63.9%
12,215	LAMAR	3,828	1,298	2,453	77	1,155 D	33.9%	64.1%	34.6%	65.4%
5,654	LANIER	1,604	470	1,116	18	646 D	29.3%	69.6%	29.6%	70.4%
36,990	LAURENS	12,523	4,392	7,860	271	3,468 D	35.1%	62.8%	35.8%	64.2%
11,684	LEE	3,661	1,942	1,670	49	272 R	53.0%	45.6%	53.8%	46.2%
37,583	LIBERTY	4,683	1,507	3,099	77	1,592 D	32.2%	66.2%	32.7%	67.3%
6,949	LINCOLN	2,440	806	1,617	17	811 D	33.0%	66.3%	33.3%	66.7%
4,524	LONG	1,743	514	1,202	27	688 D	29.5%	69.0%	30.0%	70.0%
67,972	LOWNDES	12,912	6,622	5,989	301	633 R	51.3%	46.4%	52.5%	47.5%
10,762	LUMPKIN	3,085	1,024	1,951	110	927 D	33.2%	63.2%	34.4%	65.6%
18,546	MCDUFFIE	4,683	1,928	2,667	88	739 D	41.2%	57.0%	42.0%	58.0%
8,046	MCINTOSH	3,049	876	2,104	69	1,228 D	28.7%	69.0%	29.4%	70.6%
14,003	MACON	3,979	894	3,025	60	2,131 D	22.5%	76.0%	22.8%	77.2%
17,747	MADISON	5,401	2,330	2,980	91	650 D	43.1%	55.2%	43.9%	56.1%
5,297	MARION	1,773	567	1,174	32	607 D	32.0%	66.2%	32.6%	67.4%
21,229	MERIWETHER	5,805	1,838	3,876	91	2,038 D	31.7%	66.8%	32.2%	67.8%
7,038	MILLER	2,053	900	1,127	26	227 D	43.8%	54.9%	44.4%	55.6%
21,114	MITCHELL	5,856	2,231	3,566	59	1,335 D	38.1%	60.9%	38.5%	61.5%
14,610	MONROE	3,860	1,242	2,542	76	1,300 D	32.2%	65.9%	32.8%	67.2%
7,011	MONTGOMERY	2,640	948	1,663	29	715 D	35.9%	63.0%	36.3%	63.7%
11,572	MORGAN	3,671	1,323	2,276	72	953 D	36.0%	62.0%	36.8%	63.2%
19,685	MURRAY	4,701	1,538	3,094	69	1,556 D	32.7%	65.8%	33.2%	66.8%
170,108	MUSCOGEE	39,566	15,203	23,272	1,091	8,069 D	38.4%	58.8%	39.5%	60.5%
34,489	NEWTON	9,056	3,206	5,611	239	2,405 D	35.4%	62.0%	36.4%	63.6%
12,427	OCONEE	4,367	2,065	2,141	161	76 D	47.3%	49.0%	49.1%	50.9%
8,929	OGLETHORPE	2,856	1,187	1,611	58	424 D	41.6%	56.4%	42.4%	57.6%
26,042	PAULDING	7,717	2,845	4,686	186	1,841 D	36.9%	60.7%	37.8%	62.2%
19,151	PEACH	5,170	1,642	3,415	113	1,773 D	31.8%	66.1%	32.5%	67.5%
11,652	PICKENS	4,077	1,612	2,358	107	746 D	39.5%	57.8%	40.6%	59.4%
11,897	PIERCE	2,985	1,027	1,918	40	891 D	34.4%	64.3%	34.9%	65.1%
8,937	PIKE	3,094	1,271	1,755	68	484 D	41.1%	56.7%	42.0%	58.0%
32,386	POLK	8,562	2,949	5,421	192	2,472 D	34.4%	63.3%	35.2%	64.8%
8,950	PULASKI	3,232	1,153	1,997	82	844 D	35.7%	61.8%	36.6%	63.4%
10,295	PUTNAM	3,177	1,166	1,951	60	785 D	36.7%	61.4%	37.4%	62.6%
2,357	QUITMAN	837	240	589	8	349 D	28.7%	70.4%	29.0%	71.0%
10,466	RABUN	3,495	1,070	2,327	98	1,257 D	30.6%	66.6%	31.5%	68.5%
9,599	RANDOLPH	2,743	879	1,861	3	982 D	32.0%	67.8%	32.1%	67.9%
181,629	RICHMOND	44,871	19,619	24,104	1,148	4,485 D	43.7%	53.7%	44.9%	55.1%
36,747	ROCKDALE	10,067	5,300	4,395	372	905 R	52.6%	43.7%	54.7%	45.3%
3,433	SCHLEY	1,085	453	613	19	160 D	41.8%	56.5%	42.5%	57.5%
14,043	SCREVEN	3,664	1,490	2,117	57	627 D	40.7%	57.8%	41.3%	58.7%
9,057	SEMINOLE	2,936	1,117	1,794	25	677 D	38.0%	61.1%	38.4%	61.6%
47,899	SPALDING	12,331	4,809	7,176	346	2,367 D	39.0%	58.2%	40.1%	59.9%
21,763	STEPHENS	6,692	2,045	4,529	118	2,484 D	30.6%	67.7%	31.1%	68.9%
5,896	STEWART	2,087	611	1,440	36	829 D	29.3%	69.0%	29.8%	70.2%
29,360	SUMTER	8,060	2,957	4,956	147	1,999 D	36.7%	61.5%	37.4%	62.6%
6,536	TALBOT	2,243	572	1,635	36	1,063 D	25.5%	72.9%	25.9%	74.1%
2,032	TALIAFERRO	954	270	670	14	400 D	28.3%	70.2%	28.7%	71.3%
18,134	TATTNALL	5,002	2,082	2,864	56	782 D	41.6%	57.3%	42.1%	57.9%
7,902	TAYLOR	2,698	815	1,845	38	1,030 D	30.2%	68.4%	30.6%	69.4%
11,445	TELFAIR	3,941	1,173	2,700	68	1,527 D	29.8%	68.5%	30.3%	69.7%
12,017	TERRELL	3,420	1,378	2,010	32	632 D	40.3%	58.8%	40.7%	59.3%
38,098	THOMAS	10,161	4,294	5,695	172	1,401 D	42.3%	56.0%	43.0%	57.0%
32,862	TIFT	8,022	3,280	4,572	170	1,292 D	40.9%	57.0%	41.8%	58.2%
22,592	TOOMBS	6,197	2,835	3,255	107	420 D	45.7%	52.5%	46.6%	53.4%
5,638	TOWNS	3,065	1,475	1,510	80	35 D	48.1%	49.3%	49.4%	50.6%
6,087	TRUETLEN	2,004	668	1,307	29	639 D	33.3%	65.2%	33.8%	66.2%

GEORGIA

PRESIDENT 1980

1980 Census Population	County	Total Vote	Republican	Democratic	Other	Rep.-Dem. Plurality	Percentage Total Vote Rep.	Dem.	Major Vote Rep.	Dem.
50,003	TROUP	13,429	5,398	7,716	315	2,318 D	40.2%	57.5%	41.2%	58.8%
9,510	TURNER	2,921	898	1,990	33	1,092 D	30.7%	68.1%	31.1%	68.9%
9,354	TWIGGS	2,980	747	2,213	20	1,466 D	25.1%	74.3%	25.2%	74.8%
9,390	UNION	3,311	1,546	1,700	65	154 D	46.7%	51.3%	47.6%	52.4%
25,998	UPSON	7,635	2,788	4,713	134	1,925 D	36.5%	61.7%	37.2%	62.8%
56,470	WALKER	14,132	7,088	6,809	235	279 R	50.2%	48.2%	51.0%	49.0%
31,211	WALTON	7,303	2,618	4,525	160	1,907 D	35.8%	62.0%	36.7%	63.3%
37,180	WARE	10,137	3,715	6,307	115	2,592 D	36.6%	62.2%	37.1%	62.9%
6,583	WARREN	2,321	779	1,517	25	738 D	33.6%	65.4%	33.9%	66.1%
18,842	WASHINGTON	5,364	1,822	3,452	90	1,630 D	34.0%	64.4%	34.5%	65.5%
20,750	WAYNE	6,157	2,213	3,843	101	1,630 D	35.9%	62.4%	36.5%	63.5%
2,341	WEBSTER	940	312	608	20	296 D	33.2%	64.7%	33.9%	66.1%
5,155	WHEELER	2,186	550	1,599	37	1,049 D	25.2%	73.1%	25.6%	74.4%
10,120	WHITE	3,287	1,175	2,017	95	842 D	35.7%	61.4%	36.8%	63.2%
65,780	WHITFIELD	16,439	6,404	9,691	344	3,287 D	39.0%	59.0%	39.8%	60.2%
7,682	WILCOX	2,630	827	1,780	23	953 D	31.4%	67.7%	31.7%	68.3%
10,951	WILKES	3,623	1,212	2,350	61	1,138 D	33.5%	64.9%	34.0%	66.0%
10,368	WILKINSON	3,532	1,116	2,365	51	1,249 D	31.6%	67.0%	32.1%	67.9%
18,064	WORTH	4,695	2,076	2,567	52	491 D	44.2%	54.7%	44.7%	55.3%
5,464,265	TOTAL	1,596,695	654,168	890,733	51,794	236,565 D	41.0%	55.8%	42.3%	57.7%

GEORGIA

SENATOR 1980

1980 Census Population	County	Total Vote	Republican	Democratic	Other	Rep.-Dem. Plurality	Percentage			
							Total Vote		Major Vote	
							Rep.	Dem.	Rep.	Dem.
15,565	APPLING	4,720	1,622	3,098		1,476 D	34.4%	65.6%	34.4%	65.6%
6,141	ATKINSON	2,048	531	1,517		986 D	25.9%	74.1%	25.9%	74.1%
9,379	BACON	3,068	1,021	2,047		1,026 D	33.3%	66.7%	33.3%	66.7%
3,808	BAKER	1,431	178	1,253		1,075 D	12.4%	87.6%	12.4%	87.6%
34,686	BALDWIN	8,102	3,926	4,176		250 D	48.5%	51.5%	48.5%	51.5%
8,702	BANKS	2,859	660	2,199		1,539 D	23.1%	76.9%	23.1%	76.9%
21,293	BARROW	6,353	2,475	3,878		1,403 D	39.0%	61.0%	39.0%	61.0%
40,760	BARTOW	9,904	3,771	6,133		2,362 D	38.1%	61.9%	38.1%	61.9%
16,000	BEN HILL	4,374	1,225	3,149		1,924 D	28.0%	72.0%	28.0%	72.0%
13,525	BERRIEN	4,479	1,225	3,254		2,029 D	27.3%	72.7%	27.3%	72.7%
151,085	BIBB	43,589	19,610	23,979		4,369 D	45.0%	55.0%	45.0%	55.0%
10,767	BLECKLEY	3,388	1,098	2,290		1,192 D	32.4%	67.6%	32.4%	67.6%
8,701	BRANTLEY	2,871	725	2,146		1,421 D	25.3%	74.7%	25.3%	74.7%
15,255	BROOKS	3,564	1,146	2,418		1,272 D	32.2%	67.8%	32.2%	67.8%
10,175	BRYAN	3,043	1,066	1,977		911 D	35.0%	65.0%	35.0%	65.0%
35,785	BULLOCH	8,262	3,325	4,937		1,612 D	40.2%	59.8%	40.2%	59.8%
19,349	BURKE	4,677	1,343	3,334		1,991 D	28.7%	71.3%	28.7%	71.3%
13,665	BUTTS	3,931	1,198	2,733		1,535 D	30.5%	69.5%	30.5%	69.5%
5,717	CALHOUN	2,055	474	1,581		1,107 D	23.1%	76.9%	23.1%	76.9%
13,371	CAMDEN	3,126	1,107	2,019		912 D	35.4%	64.6%	35.4%	64.6%
7,518	CANDLER	2,331	830	1,501		671 D	35.6%	64.4%	35.6%	64.4%
56,346	CARROLL	15,697	7,441	8,256		815 D	47.4%	52.6%	47.4%	52.6%
36,991	CATOOSA	10,711	6,167	4,544		1,623 R	57.6%	42.4%	57.6%	42.4%
7,343	CHARLTON	1,827	543	1,284		741 D	29.7%	70.3%	29.7%	70.3%
202,226	CHATHAM	56,755	28,728	28,027		701 R	50.6%	49.4%	50.6%	49.4%
21,732	CHATTAHOOCHEE	710	268	442		174 D	37.7%	62.3%	37.7%	62.3%
21,856	CHATTOOGA	6,430	2,255	4,175		1,920 D	35.1%	64.9%	35.1%	64.9%
51,699	CHEROKEE	11,888	6,417	5,471		946 R	54.0%	46.0%	54.0%	46.0%
74,498	CLARKE	19,363	11,838	7,525		4,313 R	61.1%	38.9%	61.1%	38.9%
3,553	CLAY	1,129	201	928		727 D	17.8%	82.2%	17.8%	82.2%
150,357	CLAYTON	38,545	23,123	15,422		7,701 R	60.0%	40.0%	60.0%	40.0%
6,660	CLINCH	1,704	440	1,264		824 D	25.8%	74.2%	25.8%	74.2%
297,694	COBB	99,506	70,293	29,213		41,080 R	70.6%	29.4%	70.6%	29.4%
26,894	COFFEE	6,408	2,523	3,885		1,362 D	39.4%	60.6%	39.4%	60.6%
35,376	COLQUITT	8,810	3,179	5,631		2,452 D	36.1%	63.9%	36.1%	63.9%
40,118	COLUMBIA	12,258	7,475	4,783		2,692 R	61.0%	39.0%	61.0%	39.0%
13,490	COOK	3,735	1,138	2,597		1,459 D	30.5%	69.5%	30.5%	69.5%
39,268	COWETA	10,604	5,821	4,783		1,038 R	54.9%	45.1%	54.9%	45.1%
7,684	CRAWFORD	2,322	617	1,705		1,088 D	26.6%	73.4%	26.6%	73.4%
19,489	CRISP	5,142	1,480	3,662		2,182 D	28.8%	71.2%	28.8%	71.2%
12,318	DADE	3,455	1,894	1,561		333 R	54.8%	45.2%	54.8%	45.2%
4,774	DAWSON	1,798	652	1,146		494 D	36.3%	63.7%	36.3%	63.7%
25,495	DECATUR	5,794	2,107	3,687		1,580 D	36.4%	63.6%	36.4%	63.6%
483,024	DE KALB	166,567	115,684	50,883		64,801 R	69.5%	30.5%	69.5%	30.5%
16,955	DODGE	6,496	1,492	5,004		3,512 D	23.0%	77.0%	23.0%	77.0%
10,826	DOOLY	3,163	690	2,473		1,783 D	21.8%	78.2%	21.8%	78.2%
100,978	DOUGHERTY	26,459	13,577	12,882		695 R	51.3%	48.7%	51.3%	48.7%
54,573	DOUGLAS	14,479	8,059	6,420		1,639 R	55.7%	44.3%	55.7%	44.3%
13,158	EARLY	3,632	864	2,768		1,904 D	23.8%	76.2%	23.8%	76.2%
2,297	ECHOLS	762	160	602		442 D	21.0%	79.0%	21.0%	79.0%
18,327	EFFINGHAM	5,305	2,321	2,984		663 D	43.8%	56.2%	43.8%	56.2%
18,758	ELBERT	6,185	1,862	4,323		2,461 D	30.1%	69.9%	30.1%	69.9%
20,795	EMANUEL	5,703	1,865	3,838		1,973 D	32.7%	67.3%	32.7%	67.3%
8,428	EVANS	2,467	850	1,617		767 D	34.5%	65.5%	34.5%	65.5%
14,748	FANNIN	5,670	3,435	2,235		1,200 R	60.6%	39.4%	60.6%	39.4%
29,043	FAYETTE	11,455	7,666	3,789		3,877 R	66.9%	33.1%	66.9%	33.1%
79,800	FLOYD	23,621	12,230	11,391		839 R	51.8%	48.2%	51.8%	48.2%
27,958	FORSYTH	7,928	3,973	3,955		18 R	50.1%	49.9%	50.1%	49.9%
15,185	FRANKLIN	4,810	1,260	3,550		2,290 D	26.2%	73.8%	26.2%	73.8%
589,904	FULTON	192,165	109,513	82,652		26,861 R	57.0%	43.0%	57.0%	43.0%
11,110	GILMER	4,117	2,161	1,956		205 R	52.5%	47.5%	52.5%	47.5%
2,382	GLASCOCK	1,057	283	774		491 D	26.8%	73.2%	26.8%	73.2%
54,981	GLYNN	16,429	9,898	6,531		3,367 R	60.2%	39.8%	60.2%	39.8%
30,070	GORDON	8,283	3,947	4,336		389 D	47.7%	52.3%	47.7%	52.3%
19,845	GRADY	4,883	1,398	3,485		2,087 D	28.6%	71.4%	28.6%	71.4%
11,391	GREENE	3,624	758	2,866		2,108 D	20.9%	79.1%	20.9%	79.1%
166,903	GWINNETT	53,013	36,074	16,939		19,135 R	68.0%	32.0%	68.0%	32.0%
25,020	HABERSHAM	6,623	2,656	3,967		1,311 D	40.1%	59.9%	40.1%	59.9%
75,649	HALL	20,726	10,275	10,451		176 D	49.6%	50.4%	49.6%	50.4%
9,466	HANCOCK	2,122	546	1,576		1,030 D	25.7%	74.3%	25.7%	74.3%

GEORGIA

SENATOR 1980

1980 Census Population	County	Total Vote	Republican	Democratic	Other	Rep.-Dem. Plurality		Percentage Total Vote		Major Vote	
								Rep.	Dem.	Rep.	Dem.
18,422	HARALSON	6,076	2,393	3,683		1,290	D	39.4%	60.6%	39.4%	60.6%
15,464	HARRIS	4,630	2,433	2,197		236	R	52.5%	47.5%	52.5%	47.5%
18,585	HART	5,651	1,430	4,221		2,791	D	25.3%	74.7%	25.3%	74.7%
6,520	HEARD	2,343	674	1,669		995	D	28.8%	71.2%	28.8%	71.2%
36,309	HENRY	11,701	5,797	5,904		107	D	49.5%	50.5%	49.5%	50.5%
77,605	HOUSTON	21,194	11,219	9,975		1,244	R	52.9%	47.1%	52.9%	47.1%
8,988	IRWIN	2,615	646	1,969		1,323	D	24.7%	75.3%	24.7%	75.3%
25,343	JACKSON	7,188	2,326	4,862		2,536	D	32.4%	67.6%	32.4%	67.6%
7,553	JASPER	2,485	764	1,721		957	D	30.7%	69.3%	30.7%	69.3%
11,473	JEFF DAVIS	3,198	1,014	2,184		1,170	D	31.7%	68.3%	31.7%	68.3%
18,403	JEFFERSON	4,394	1,355	3,039		1,684	D	30.8%	69.2%	30.8%	69.2%
8,841	JENKINS	2,462	615	1,847		1,232	D	25.0%	75.0%	25.0%	75.0%
8,660	JOHNSON	3,048	862	2,186		1,324	D	28.3%	71.7%	28.3%	71.7%
16,579	JONES	5,379	1,882	3,497		1,615	D	35.0%	65.0%	35.0%	65.0%
12,215	LAMAR	3,676	1,339	2,337		998	D	36.4%	63.6%	36.4%	63.6%
5,654	LANIER	1,493	329	1,164		835	D	22.0%	78.0%	22.0%	78.0%
36,990	LAURENS	11,229	3,997	7,232		3,235	D	35.6%	64.4%	35.6%	64.4%
11,684	LEE	3,584	1,708	1,876		168	D	47.7%	52.3%	47.7%	52.3%
37,583	LIBERTY	4,337	1,488	2,849		1,361	D	34.3%	65.7%	34.3%	65.7%
6,949	LINCOLN	2,456	689	1,767		1,078	D	28.1%	71.9%	28.1%	71.9%
4,524	LONG	1,687	506	1,181		675	D	30.0%	70.0%	30.0%	70.0%
67,972	LOWNDES	14,406	7,336	7,070		266	R	50.9%	49.1%	50.9%	49.1%
10,762	LUMPKIN	3,059	1,202	1,857		655	D	39.3%	60.7%	39.3%	60.7%
18,546	MCDUFFIE	4,395	2,081	2,314		233	D	47.3%	52.7%	47.3%	52.7%
8,046	MCINTOSH	2,790	861	1,929		1,068	D	30.9%	69.1%	30.9%	69.1%
14,003	MACON	3,631	959	2,672		1,713	D	26.4%	73.6%	26.4%	73.6%
17,747	MADISON	5,334	1,942	3,392		1,450	D	36.4%	63.6%	36.4%	63.6%
5,297	MARION	1,559	501	1,058		557	D	32.1%	67.9%	32.1%	67.9%
21,229	MERIWETHER	5,675	1,765	3,910		2,145	D	31.1%	68.9%	31.1%	68.9%
7,038	MILLER	1,948	401	1,547		1,146	D	20.6%	79.4%	20.6%	79.4%
21,114	MITCHELL	5,716	1,549	4,167		2,618	D	27.1%	72.9%	27.1%	72.9%
14,610	MONROE	3,437	1,367	2,070		703	D	39.8%	60.2%	39.8%	60.2%
7,011	MONTGOMERY	2,528	598	1,930		1,332	D	23.7%	76.3%	23.7%	76.3%
11,572	MORGAN	3,615	1,190	2,425		1,235	D	32.9%	67.1%	32.9%	67.1%
19,685	MURRAY	4,615	1,993	2,622		629	D	43.2%	56.8%	43.2%	56.8%
170,108	MUSCOGEE	36,956	21,565	15,391		6,174	R	58.4%	41.6%	58.4%	41.6%
34,489	NEWTON	8,968	3,642	5,326		1,684	D	40.6%	59.4%	40.6%	59.4%
12,427	OCONEE	4,262	2,112	2,150		38	D	49.6%	50.4%	49.6%	50.4%
8,929	OGLETHORPE	2,831	966	1,865		899	D	34.1%	65.9%	34.1%	65.9%
26,042	PAULDING	7,657	2,753	4,904		2,151	D	36.0%	64.0%	36.0%	64.0%
19,151	PEACH	5,241	1,840	3,401		1,561	D	35.1%	64.9%	35.1%	64.9%
11,652	PICKENS	3,916	1,556	2,360		804	D	39.7%	60.3%	39.7%	60.3%
11,897	PIERCE	3,019	846	2,173		1,327	D	28.0%	72.0%	28.0%	72.0%
8,937	PIKE	3,038	1,126	1,912		786	D	37.1%	62.9%	37.1%	62.9%
32,386	POLK	8,510	3,107	5,403		2,296	D	36.5%	63.5%	36.5%	63.5%
8,950	PULASKI	3,174	856	2,318		1,462	D	27.0%	73.0%	27.0%	73.0%
10,295	PUTNAM	3,055	1,041	2,014		973	D	34.1%	65.9%	34.1%	65.9%
2,357	QUITMAN	705	185	520		335	D	26.2%	73.8%	26.2%	73.8%
10,466	RABUN	3,448	1,462	1,986		524	D	42.4%	57.6%	42.4%	57.6%
9,599	RANDOLPH	2,693	510	2,183		1,673	D	18.9%	81.1%	18.9%	81.1%
181,629	RICHMOND	45,382	24,254	21,128		3,126	R	53.4%	46.6%	53.4%	46.6%
36,747	ROCKDALE	9,971	5,833	4,138		1,695	R	58.5%	41.5%	58.5%	41.5%
3,433	SCHLEY	1,030	362	668		306	D	35.1%	64.9%	35.1%	64.9%
14,043	SCREVEN	3,499	1,208	2,291		1,083	D	34.5%	65.5%	34.5%	65.5%
9,057	SEMINOLE	2,917	604	2,313		1,709	D	20.7%	79.3%	20.7%	79.3%
47,899	SPALDING	12,331	5,972	6,359		387	D	48.4%	51.6%	48.4%	51.6%
21,763	STEPHENS	6,476	2,480	3,996		1,516	D	38.3%	61.7%	38.3%	61.7%
5,896	STEWART	1,762	539	1,223		684	D	30.6%	69.4%	30.6%	69.4%
29,360	SUMTER	7,972	3,191	4,781		1,590	D	40.0%	60.0%	40.0%	60.0%
6,536	TALBOT	1,943	637	1,306		669	D	32.8%	67.2%	32.8%	67.2%
2,032	TALIAFERRO	851	177	674		497	D	20.8%	79.2%	20.8%	79.2%
18,134	TATTNALL	4,879	1,538	3,341		1,803	D	31.5%	68.5%	31.5%	68.5%
7,902	TAYLOR	2,554	620	1,934		1,314	D	24.3%	75.7%	24.3%	75.7%
11,445	TELFAIR	4,074	748	3,326		2,578	D	18.4%	81.6%	18.4%	81.6%
12,017	TERRELL	3,134	946	2,188		1,242	D	30.2%	69.8%	30.2%	69.8%
38,098	THOMAS	9,799	4,100	5,699		1,599	D	41.8%	58.2%	41.8%	58.2%
32,862	TIFT	7,782	3,380	4,402		1,022	D	43.4%	56.6%	43.4%	56.6%
22,592	TOOMBS	6,121	2,315	3,806		1,491	D	37.8%	62.2%	37.8%	62.2%
5,638	TOWNS	3,238	1,699	1,539		160	R	52.5%	47.5%	52.5%	47.5%
6,087	TRUETLEN	2,042	500	1,542		1,042	D	24.5%	75.5%	24.5%	75.5%

GEORGIA

SENATOR 1980

1980 Census Population	County	Total Vote	Republican	Democratic	Other	Rep.-Dem. Plurality	Percentage Total Vote Rep.	Dem.	Major Vote Rep.	Dem.
50,003	TROUP	13,442	6,211	7,231		1,020 D	46.2%	53.8%	46.2%	53.8%
9,510	TURNER	2,980	596	2,384		1,788 D	20.0%	80.0%	20.0%	80.0%
9,354	TWIGGS	2,818	603	2,215		1,612 D	21.4%	78.6%	21.4%	78.6%
9,390	UNION	3,313	1,538	1,775		237 D	46.4%	53.6%	46.4%	53.6%
25,998	UPSON	7,641	2,631	5,010		2,379 D	34.4%	65.6%	34.4%	65.6%
56,470	WALKER	13,868	7,489	6,379		1,110 R	54.0%	46.0%	54.0%	46.0%
31,211	WALTON	7,172	2,643	4,529		1,886 D	36.9%	63.1%	36.9%	63.1%
37,180	WARE	9,934	3,710	6,224		2,514 D	37.3%	62.7%	37.3%	62.7%
6,583	WARREN	2,064	626	1,438		812 D	30.3%	69.7%	30.3%	69.7%
18,842	WASHINGTON	5,053	1,564	3,489		1,925 D	31.0%	69.0%	31.0%	69.0%
20,750	WAYNE	5,752	2,331	3,421		1,090 D	40.5%	59.5%	40.5%	59.5%
2,341	WEBSTER	809	170	639		469 D	21.0%	79.0%	21.0%	79.0%
5,155	WHEELER	2,419	456	1,963		1,507 D	18.9%	81.1%	18.9%	81.1%
10,120	WHITE	3,245	1,371	1,874		503 D	42.2%	57.8%	42.2%	57.8%
65,780	WHITFIELD	16,375	8,878	7,497		1,381 R	54.2%	45.8%	54.2%	45.8%
7,682	WILCOX	2,658	498	2,160		1,662 D	18.7%	81.3%	18.7%	81.3%
10,951	WILKES	3,474	1,233	2,241		1,008 D	35.5%	64.5%	35.5%	64.5%
10,368	WILKINSON	3,146	1,096	2,050		954 D	34.8%	65.2%	34.8%	65.2%
18,064	WORTH	4,392	1,508	2,884		1,376 D	34.3%	65.7%	34.3%	65.7%
5,464,265	TOTAL	1,580,340	803,686	776,143	511	27,543 R	50.9%	49.1%	50.9%	49.1%

GEORGIA

CONGRESS

CD	Year	Total Vote	Republican Vote	Republican Candidate	Democratic Vote	Democratic Candidate	Other Vote	Rep.-Dem. Plurality	Percentage Total Vote Rep.	Total Vote Dem.	Major Vote Rep.	Major Vote Dem.
1	1980	82,146			82,145	GINN, RONALD B.	1	82,145 D		100.0%		100.0%
1	1978	36,962			36,961	GINN, RONALD B.	1	36,961 D		100.0%		100.0%
1	1976	73,888			73,826	GINN, RONALD B.	62	73,826 D		99.9%		100.0%
1	1974	75,444	10,485	GOWAN, WILLIAM L.	64,958	GINN, RONALD B.	1	54,473 D	13.9%	86.1%	13.9%	86.1%
1	1972	55,267			55,256	GINN, RONALD B.	11	55,256 D		100.0%		100.0%
2	1980	125,372	33,107	HARRELL, JACK E.	92,264	HATCHER, CHARLES	1	59,157 D	26.4%	73.6%	26.4%	73.6%
2	1978	42,246			42,234	MATHIS, DAWSON	12	42,234 D		100.0%		100.0%
2	1976	96,026			95,807	MATHIS, DAWSON	219	95,807 D		99.8%		100.0%
2	1974	59,515			59,514	MATHIS, DAWSON	1	59,514 D		100.0%		100.0%
2	1972	65,999			65,997	MATHIS, DAWSON	2	65,997 D		100.0%		100.0%
3	1980	89,070			89,040	BRINKLEY, JACK	30	89,040 D		100.0%		100.0%
3	1978	54,882			54,881	BRINKLEY, JACK	1	54,881 D		100.0%		100.0%
3	1976	105,004	11,829	DUGAN, STEVE	93,174	BRINKLEY, JACK	1	81,345 D	11.3%	88.7%	11.3%	88.7%
3	1974	76,891	9,453	SAVAGE, CARL P.	67,438	BRINKLEY, JACK		57,985 D	12.3%	87.7%	12.3%	87.7%
3	1972	71,763			71,756	BRINKLEY, JACK	7	71,756 D		100.0%		100.0%
4	1980	168,650	51,546	BILLINGTON, BARRY	117,091	LEVITAS, ELLIOTT H.	13	65,545 D	30.6%	69.4%	30.6%	69.4%
4	1978	74,513	14,221	CHEUNG, HOMER	60,284	LEVITAS, ELLIOTT H.	8	46,063 D	19.1%	80.9%	19.1%	80.9%
4	1976	161,412	51,140	WARREN, GEORGE	110,261	LEVITAS, ELLIOTT H.	11	59,121 D	31.7%	68.3%	31.7%	68.3%
4	1974	111,139	49,922	BLACKBURN, BEN B.	61,211	LEVITAS, ELLIOTT H.	6	11,289 D	44.9%	55.1%	44.9%	55.1%
4	1972	135,886	103,155	BLACKBURN, BEN B.	32,731	WELBORN, F. ODELL		70,424 R	75.9%	24.1%	75.9%	24.1%
5	1980	137,302	35,640	DOWDA, F. WILLIAM	101,646	FOWLER, WYCHE	16	66,006 D	26.0%	74.0%	26.0%	74.0%
5	1978	69,875	17,132	BOWLES, THOMAS P.	52,739	FOWLER, WYCHE	4	35,607 D	24.5%	75.5%	24.5%	75.5%
5	1976	144,063	47,998	GADRIX, EDWARD W.	96,056	YOUNG, ANDREW	9	48,058 D	33.3%	66.7%	33.3%	66.7%
5	1974	96,667	27,397	LOWE, WYMAN C.	69,221	YOUNG, ANDREW	49	41,824 D	28.3%	71.6%	28.4%	71.6%
5	1972	136,810	64,495	COOK, RODNEY M.	72,289	YOUNG, ANDREW	26	7,794 D	47.1%	52.8%	47.2%	52.8%
6	1980	162,685	96,071	GINGRICH, NEWT	66,606	DAVIS, DOCK H.	8	29,465 R	59.1%	40.9%	59.1%	40.9%
6	1978	86,540	47,078	GINGRICH, NEWT	39,451	SHAPARD, VIRGINIA	11	7,627 R	54.4%	45.6%	54.4%	45.6%
6	1976	149,944	72,400	GINGRICH, NEWT	77,532	FLYNT, JOHN J.	12	5,132 D	48.3%	51.7%	48.3%	51.7%
6	1974	95,395	46,308	GINGRICH, NEWT	49,082	FLYNT, JOHN J.	5	2,774 D	48.5%	51.5%	48.5%	51.5%
6	1972	70,617			70,586	FLYNT, JOHN J.	31	70,586 D		100.0%		100.0%
7	1980	170,142	54,242	CASTELLUCIS, RICHARD	115,892	MCDONALD, LARRY	8	61,650 D	31.9%	68.1%	31.9%	68.1%
7	1978	70,827	23,698	NORSWORTHY, ERNIE	47,090	MCDONALD, LARRY	39	23,392 D	33.5%	66.5%	33.5%	66.5%
7	1976	153,554	68,947	COLLINS, QUINCY	84,587	MCDONALD, LARRY	20	15,640 D	44.9%	55.1%	44.9%	55.1%
7	1974	95,477	47,450	COLLINS, QUINCY	47,993	MCDONALD, LARRY	34	543 D	49.7%	50.3%	49.7%	50.3%
7	1972	101,306	42,265	SHERRILL, CHARLES B.	59,031	DAVIS, JOHN W.	10	16,766 D	41.7%	58.3%	41.7%	58.3%
8	1980	122,138	31,033	CARTER, DARWIN	91,103	EVANS, BILLY LEE	2	60,070 D	25.4%	74.6%	25.4%	74.6%
8	1978	41,193			41,184	EVANS, BILLY LEE	9	41,184 D		100.0%		100.0%
8	1976	130,978	39,623	ADAMS, BILLY	91,351	EVANS, BILLY LEE	4	51,728 D	30.3%	69.7%	30.3%	69.7%
8	1974	59,195			59,182	STUCKEY, W. S.	13	59,182 D		100.0%		100.0%
8	1972	114,272	42,986	THOMPSON, RONNIE	71,283	STUCKEY, W. S.	3	28,297 D	37.6%	62.4%	37.6%	62.4%
9	1980	169,918	54,341	ASHWORTH, DAVID G.	115,576	JENKINS, ED	1	61,235 D	32.0%	68.0%	32.0%	68.0%
9	1978	61,437	14,172	ASHWORTH, DAVID G.	47,264	JENKINS, ED	1	33,092 D	23.1%	76.9%	23.1%	76.9%
9	1976	143,357	29,954	WOFFORD, LOUISE	113,245	JENKINS, ED	158	83,291 D	20.9%	79.0%	20.9%	79.1%
9	1974	85,642	21,540	REEVES, RONALD D.	64,096	LANDRUM, PHIL M.	6	42,556 D	25.2%	74.8%	25.2%	74.8%
9	1972	71,809			71,801	LANDRUM, PHIL M.	8	71,801 D		100.0%		100.0%
10	1980	127,378	25,194	NEUBAUER, BRUCE J.	102,177	BARNARD, DOUG	7	76,983 D	19.8%	80.2%	19.8%	80.2%
10	1978	50,130			50,122	BARNARD, DOUG	8	50,122 D		100.0%		100.0%
10	1976	94,864			94,782	BARNARD, DOUG	82	94,782 D		99.9%		100.0%
10	1974	67,058	21,214	PLEGER, GARY	45,843	STEPHENS, ROBERT G.	1	24,629 D	31.6%	68.4%	31.6%	68.4%
10	1972	68,097			68,096	STEPHENS, ROBERT G.	1	68,096 D		100.0%		100.0%

GEORGIA

1980 GENERAL ELECTION

President   Other vote was 36,055 Anderson (Independent); 15,627 Clark (Libertarian); 104 Commoner (write-in); 4 Pulley (write-in); 1 Griswold (write-in); 3 scattered. State-wide total for other vote column includes the 112 write-in votes not reported by county. There were 742 other scattered votes reported by the state authorities which were cast for individuals and not for full slates of electors. Original uncorrected returns gave the Carter (Democratic) vote as 890,955.

Senator   State-wide total for other vote column represents scattered votes not reported by county. Original uncorrected returns gave the Mattingly (Republican) vote as 803,677 and the Talmadge (Democratic) vote as 776,025.

Congress   Other vote was scattered in all CD's.

1980 PRIMARIES

AUGUST 5 REPUBLICAN

Senator   28,191 Mack Mattingly; 6,082 E. J. Bagley; 3,999 Hulon M. Madeley; 3,219 Dean Parkison, 2,947 Nick M. Belluso; 2,700 J. W. Tibbs.

Congress   Unopposed in eight CD's. No candidates in CD's 1 and 3.

AUGUST 5 DEMOCRATIC

Senator   432,215 Herman Talmadge; 247,766 Zell Miller; 183,683 Norman Underwood; 133,729 Dawson Mathis; 19,664 J. B. Stoner; 12,243 John F. Collins.

Congress   Unopposed in six CD's. Contested as follows:

CD 2   40,315 Charles Hatcher; 15,976 Julian Holland; 15,747 Hanson Carter; 13,119 J. David Halstead; 8,520 Walter Stephens; 6,032 Wesley Patrick; 2,724 W. R. Connell; 1,882 H. R. McNease; 1,516 Opal S. Brewer. These figures are the recount tabulations.
CD 5   52,547 Wyche Fowler; 8,760 Doug Steele.
CD 6   50,245 Dock H. Davis; 32,569 Jim Huffman.
CD 7   67,463 Larry McDonald; 31,729 Jack Bade.

AUGUST 26 DEMOCRATIC RUN-OFF

Senator   559,615 Herman Talmadge; 395,773 Zell Miller.

Congress

CD 2   49,144 Charles Hatcher; 44,397 Julian Holland.

HAWAII

GOVERNOR
George R. Ariyoshi (D). Re-elected 1978 to a four-year term. Previously elected 1974.

SENATORS
Daniel K. Inouye (D). Re-elected 1980 to a six-year term. Previously elected 1974, 1968, 1962.

Spark M. Matsunaga (D). Elected 1976 to a six-year term.

REPRESENTATIVES
1. Cecil Heftel (D)   2. Daniel K. Akaka (D)

POSTWAR VOTE FOR GOVERNOR

Year	Total Vote	Republican Vote	Candidate	Democratic Vote	Candidate	Other Vote	Rep.-Dem. Plurality	Total Vote Rep.	Dem.	Major Vote Rep.	Dem.
1978	281,587	124,610	Leopold, John	153,394	Ariyoshi, George R.	3,583	28,784 D	44.3%	54.5%	44.8%	55.2%
1974	249,650	113,388	Crossley, Randolph	136,262	Ariyoshi, George R.	—	22,874 D	45.4%	54.6%	45.4%	54.6%
1970	239,061	101,249	King, Samuel P.	137,812	Burns, John A.	—	36,563 D	42.4%	57.6%	42.4%	57.6%
1966	213,164	104,324	Crossley, Randolph	108,840	Burns, John A.	—	4,516 D	48.9%	51.1%	48.9%	51.1%
1962	196,015	81,707	Quinn, William F.	114,308	Burns, John A.	—	32,601 D	41.7%	58.3%	41.7%	58.3%
1959	168,662	86,213	Quinn, William F.	82,074	Burns, John A.	375	4,139 R	51.1%	48.7%	51.2%	48.8%

POSTWAR VOTE FOR SENATOR

Year	Total Vote	Republican Vote	Candidate	Democratic Vote	Candidate	Other Vote	Rep.-Dem. Plurality	Total Vote Rep.	Dem.	Major Vote Rep.	Dem.
1980	288,006	53,068	Brown, Cooper	224,485	Inouye, Daniel K.	10,453	171,417 D	18.4%	77.9%	19.1%	80.9%
1976	302,092	122,724	Quinn, William F.	162,305	Matsunaga, Spark M.	17,063	39,581 D	40.6%	53.7%	43.1%	56.9%
1974	250,221	—	—	207,454	Inouye, Daniel K.	42,767	207,454 D	—	82.9%	—	100.0%
1970	240,760	124,163	Fong, Hiram L.	116,597	Heftel, Cecil	—	7,566 R	51.6%	48.4%	51.6%	48.4%
1968	226,927	34,008	Thiessen, Wayne C.	189,248	Inouye, Daniel K.	3,671	155,240 D	15.0%	83.4%	15.2%	84.8%
1964	208,814	110,747	Fong, Hiram L.	96,789	Gill, Thomas P.	1,278	13,958 R	53.0%	46.4%	53.4%	46.6%
1962	196,361	60,067	Dillingham, Ben F.	136,294	Inouye, Daniel K.	—	76,227 D	30.6%	69.4%	30.6%	69.4%
1959s	164,808	87,161	Fong, Hiram L.	77,647	Fasi, Frank F.	—	9,514 R	52.9%	47.1%	52.9%	47.1%
1959s	163,875	79,123	Tsukiyama, W. C.	83,700	Long, Oren E.	1,052	4,577 D	48.3%	51.1%	48.6%	51.4%

The two 1959 elections were held to indeterminate terms and the Senate later determined by lot that Senator Long would serve a short term, Senator Fong a long term.

HAWAII

Districts Established July 14, 1969

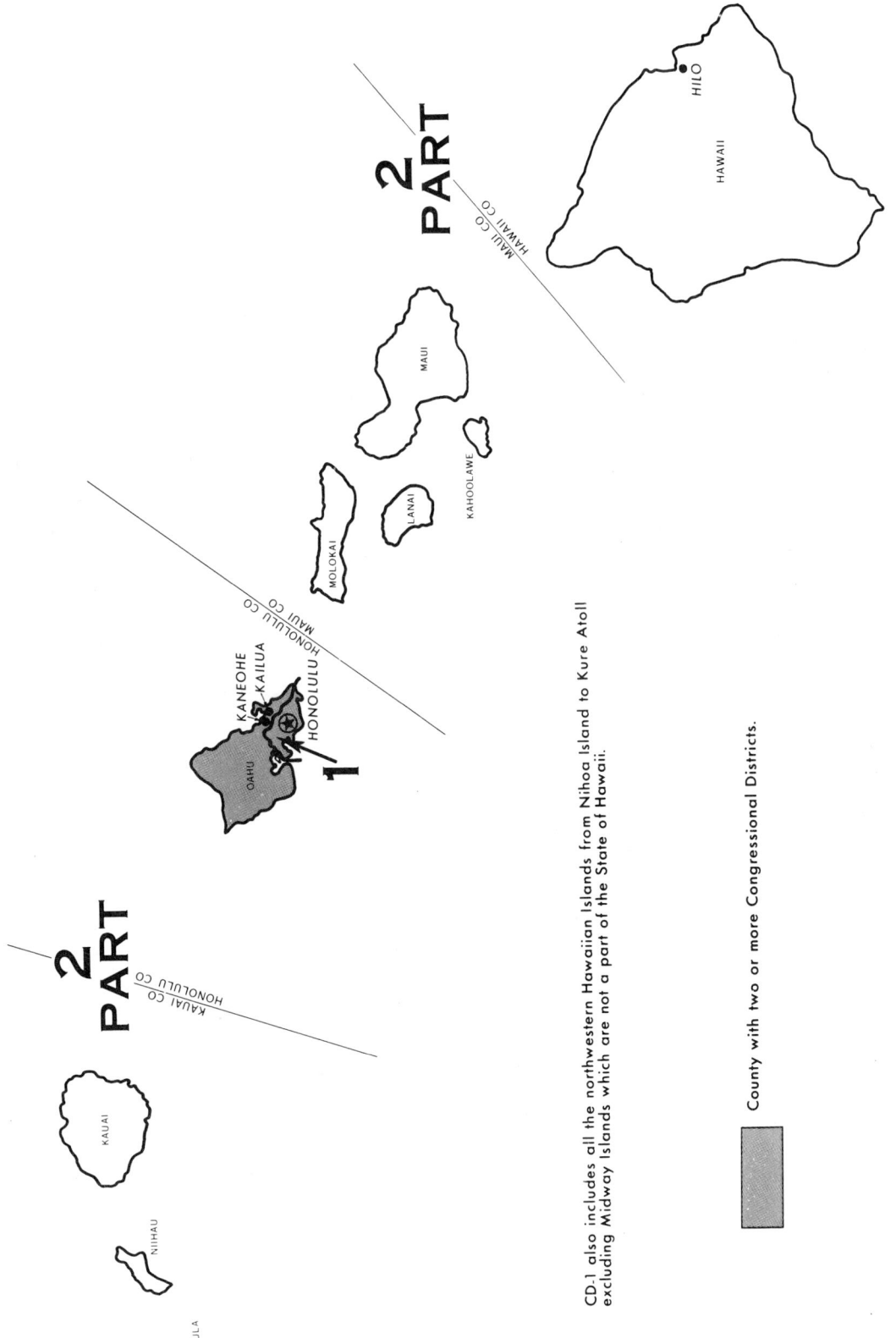

CD-1 also includes all the northwestern Hawaiian Islands from Nihoa Island to Kure Atoll excluding Midway Islands which are not a part of the State of Hawaii.

County with two or more Congressional Districts.

HAWAII

PRESIDENT 1980

1980 Census Population	County	Total Vote	Republican	Democratic	Other	Rep.-Dem. Plurality	Percentage Total Vote Rep.	Dem.	Major Vote Rep.	Dem.
92,053	HAWAII	35,861	14,247	17,630	3,984	3,383 D	39.7%	49.2%	44.7%	55.3%
762,874	HONOLULU	224,995	99,596	96,472	28,927	3,124 R	44.3%	42.9%	50.8%	49.2%
39,082	KAUAI	16,621	5,883	9,081	1,657	3,198 D	35.4%	54.6%	39.3%	60.7%
70,991	MAUI	25,751	10,359	12,674	2,718	2,315 D	40.2%	49.2%	45.0%	55.0%
	OVERSEAS VOTE	59	27	22	10	5 R	45.8%	37.3%	55.1%	44.9%
965,000	TOTAL	303,287	130,112	135,879	37,296	5,767 D	42.9%	44.8%	48.9%	51.1%

HAWAII

SENATOR 1980

1980 Census Population	County	Total Vote	Republican	Democratic	Other	Rep.-Dem. Plurality	Percentage Total Vote Rep.	Dem.	Major Vote Rep.	Dem.
92,053	HAWAII	34,230	6,386	26,495	1,349	20,109 D	18.7%	77.4%	19.4%	80.6%
762,874	HONOLULU	215,079	40,681	166,634	7,764	125,953 D	18.9%	77.5%	19.6%	80.4%
39,082	KAUAI	15,095	1,898	12,808	389	10,910 D	12.6%	84.8%	12.9%	87.1%
70,991	MAUI	23,550	4,091	18,513	946	14,422 D	17.4%	78.6%	18.1%	81.9%
	OVERSEAS VOTE	52	12	35	5	23 D	23.1%	67.3%	25.5%	74.5%
965,000	TOTAL	288,006	53,068	224,485	10,453	171,417 D	18.4%	77.9%	19.1%	80.9%

HAWAII

CONGRESS

CD	Year	Total Vote	Republican Vote	Republican Candidate	Democratic Vote	Democratic Candidate	Other Vote	Rep.-Dem. Plurality	Total Vote Rep.	Total Vote Dem.	Major Vote Rep.	Major Vote Dem.
1	1980	123,181	19,819	NOBLE, ALOMA K.	98,256	HEFTEL, CECIL	5,106	78,437 D	16.1%	79.8%	16.8%	83.2%
1	1978	115,412	24,470	SPILLANE, WILLIAM D.	84,552	HEFTEL, CECIL	6,390	60,082 D	21.2%	73.3%	22.4%	77.6%
1	1976	137,602	53,745	ROHLFING, FRED W.	60,050	HEFTEL, CECIL	23,807	6,305 D	39.1%	43.6%	47.2%	52.8%
1	1974	120,617	49,065	PAUL, WILIAM B.	71,552	MATSUNAGA, SPARK M.		22,487 D	40.7%	59.3%	40.7%	59.3%
1	1972	134,964	61,138	ROHLFING, FRED W.	73,826	MATSUNAGA, SPARK M.		12,688 D	45.3%	54.7%	45.3%	54.7%
1	1970	117,175	31,764	COCKEY, RICHARD K.	85,411	MATSUNAGA, SPARK M.		53,647 D	27.1%	72.9%	27.1%	72.9%
2	1980	157,380			141,477	AKAKA, DANIEL K.	15,903	141,477 D		89.9%		100.0%
2	1978	137,957	15,697	ISAAK, CHARLES	118,272	AKAKA, DANIEL K.	3,988	102,575 D	11.4%	85.7%	11.7%	88.3%
2	1976	156,099	23,917	INOUYE, HANK	124,116	AKAKA, DANIEL K.	8,066	100,199 D	15.3%	79.5%	16.2%	83.8%
2	1974	138,810	51,894	CORAY, CARLA W.	86,916	MINK, PATSY		35,022 D	37.4%	62.6%	37.4%	62.6%
2	1972	139,899	60,043	HANSEN, DIANA	79,856	MINK, PATSY		19,813 D	42.9%	57.1%	42.9%	57.1%
2	1970	91,038			91,038	MINK, PATSY		91,038 D		100.0%		100.0%

HAWAII

1980 GENERAL ELECTION

President   Other vote was 32,021 Anderson (Independent); 3,269 Clark (Libertarian); 1,548 Commoner (Citizens); 458 Hall (Hawaii Hall Committee).

Senator   Other vote was Shasteen (Libertarian).

Congress   Other vote was Johnson (Libertarian) in CD 1; Smith (Libertarian) in CD 2.

1980 PRIMARIES

SEPTEMBER 20 REPUBLICAN

Senator   3,219 Cooper Brown; 2,586 Lawrence I. Weisman; 1,854 Dan Dew; 584 E. F. Bernier-Nachtwey.

Congress   Unopposed in CD 1. No candidate in CD 2.

SEPTEMBER 20 DEMOCRATIC

Senator   198,468 Daniel K. Inouye; 15,361 Kamuela Price; 12,929 John P. Fritz.

Congress   Unopposed in CD 2. Contested as follows:

CD 1   73,162 Cecil Heftel; 26,024 Charles M. Campbell; 2,031 Romey J. Ramolete.

SEPTEMBER 20 LIBERTARIAN

Senator   H. E. Shasteen, unopposed.

Congress   Unopposed in both CD's.

IDAHO

GOVERNOR
John V. Evans (D). Elected 1978 to a four-year term. Elected as Lieutenant-Governor in 1974 and succeeded upon the resignation of Governor Cecil D. Andrus in January 1977.

SENATORS
James A. McClure (R). Re-elected 1978 to a six-year term. Previously elected 1972.

Steven D. Symms (R). Elected 1980 to a six-year term.

REPRESENTATIVES
1. Larry Craig (R)
2. George V. Hansen (R)

POSTWAR VOTE FOR GOVERNOR

Year	Total Vote	Republican Vote	Candidate	Democratic Vote	Candidate	Other Vote	Rep.-Dem. Plurality	Total Vote Rep.	Total Vote Dem.	Major Vote Rep.	Major Vote Dem.
1978	288,566	114,149	Larsen, Allan	169,540	Evans, John V.	4,877	55,391 D	39.6%	58.8%	40.2%	59.8%
1974	259,632	68,731	Murphy, Jack M.	184,142	Andrus, Cecil D.	6,759	115,411 D	26.5%	70.9%	27.2%	72.8%
1970	245,112	117,108	Samuelson, Don	128,004	Andrus, Cecil D.	—	10,896 D	47.8%	52.2%	47.8%	52.2%
1966	252,593	104,586	Samuelson, Don	93,744	Andrus, Cecil D.	54,263	10,842 R	41.4%	37.1%	52.7%	47.3%
1962	255,454	139,578	Smylie, Robert E.	115,876	Smith, Vernon K.	—	23,702 R	54.6%	45.4%	54.6%	45.4%
1958	239,046	121,810	Smylie, Robert E.	117,236	Derr, A. M.	—	4,574 R	51.0%	49.0%	51.0%	49.0%
1954	228,685	124,038	Smylie, Robert E.	104,647	Hamilton, Clark	—	19,391 R	54.2%	45.8%	54.2%	45.8%
1950	204,792	107,642	Jordan, Len B.	97,150	Wright, Calvin E.	—	10,492 R	52.6%	47.4%	52.6%	47.4%
1946	181,364	102,233	Robins, C. A.	79,131	Williams, Arnold	—	23,102 R	56.4%	43.6%	56.4%	43.6%

POSTWAR VOTE FOR SENATOR

Year	Total Vote	Republican Vote	Candidate	Democratic Vote	Candidate	Other Vote	Rep.-Dem. Plurality	Total Vote Rep.	Total Vote Dem.	Major Vote Rep.	Major Vote Dem.
1980	439,647	218,701	Symms, Steven D.	214,439	Church, Frank	6,507	4,262 R	49.7%	48.8%	50.5%	49.5%
1978	284,047	194,412	McClure, James A.	89,635	Jensen, Dwight	—	104,777 R	68.4%	31.6%	68.4%	31.6%
1974	258,847	109,072	Smith, Robert L.	145,140	Church, Frank	4,635	36,068 D	42.1%	56.1%	42.9%	57.1%
1972	309,602	161,804	McClure, James A.	140,913	Davis, William E.	6,885	20,891 R	52.3%	45.5%	53.5%	46.5%
1968	287,876	114,394	Hansen, George V.	173,482	Church, Frank	—	59,088 D	39.7%	60.3%	39.7%	60.3%
1966	252,456	139,819	Jordan, Len B.	112,637	Harding, Ralph R.	—	27,182 R	55.4%	44.6%	55.4%	44.6%
1962	258,786	117,129	Hawley, Jack	141,657	Church, Frank	—	24,528 D	45.3%	54.7%	45.3%	54.7%
1962s	257,677	131,279	Jordan, Len B.	126,398	Pfost, Gracie	—	4,881 R	50.9%	49.1%	50.9%	49.1%
1960	292,096	152,648	Dworshak, Henry C.	139,448	McLaughlin, Bob	—	13,200 R	52.3%	47.7%	52.3%	47.7%
1956	265,292	102,781	Welker, Herman	149,096	Church, Frank	13,415	46,315 D	38.7%	56.2%	40.8%	59.2%
1954	226,408	142,269	Dworshak, Henry C.	84,139	Taylor, Glen H.	—	58,130 R	62.8%	37.2%	62.8%	37.2%
1950	201,417	124,237	Welker, Herman	77,180	Clark, D. Worth	—	47,057 R	61.7%	38.3%	61.7%	38.3%
1950s	201,970	104,068	Dworshak, Henry C.	97,902	Burtenshaw, Claude	—	6,166 R	51.5%	48.5%	51.5%	48.5%
1948	214,188	103,868	Dworshak, Henry C.	107,000	Miller, Bert H.	3,320	3,132 D	48.5%	50.0%	49.3%	50.7%
1946s	180,152	105,523	Dworshak, Henry C.	74,629	Donart, George E.	—	30,894 R	58.6%	41.4%	58.6%	41.4%

The 1946 election and one each of the 1962 and 1950 elections were for short terms to fill vacancies.

120

IDAHO

Districts Established April 13, 1971

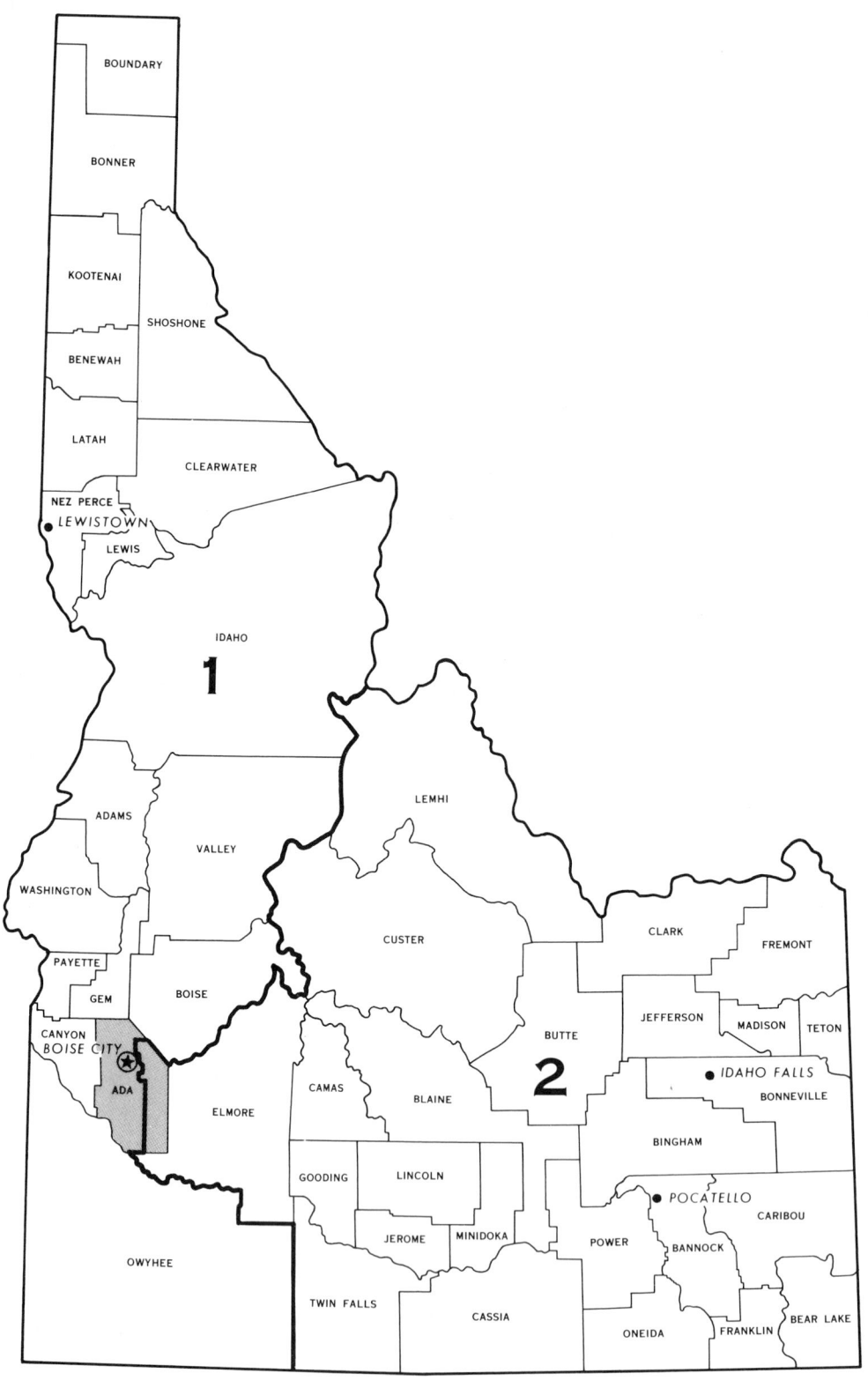

County with two or more Congressional Districts.

IDAHO

PRESIDENT 1980

1980 Census Population	County	Total Vote	Republican	Democratic	Other	Rep.-Dem. Plurality	Percentage Total Vote Rep.	Dem.	Major Vote Rep.	Dem.
173,036	ADA	86,544	55,205	21,324	10,015	33,881 R	63.8%	24.6%	72.1%	27.9%
3,347	ADAMS	1,897	1,189	590	118	599 R	62.7%	31.1%	66.8%	33.2%
65,421	BANNOCK	29,859	18,477	8,639	2,743	9,838 R	61.9%	28.9%	68.1%	31.9%
6,931	BEAR LAKE	3,567	2,941	508	118	2,433 R	82.5%	14.2%	85.3%	14.7%
8,292	BENEWAH	3,846	2,111	1,361	374	750 R	54.9%	35.4%	60.8%	39.2%
36,489	BINGHAM	15,487	11,781	2,933	773	8,848 R	76.1%	18.9%	80.1%	19.9%
9,841	BLAINE	5,529	2,716	1,840	973	876 R	49.1%	33.3%	59.6%	40.4%
2,999	BOISE	1,846	1,134	518	194	616 R	61.4%	28.1%	68.6%	31.4%
24,163	BONNER	11,940	6,727	4,060	1,153	2,667 R	56.3%	34.0%	62.4%	37.6%
65,980	BONNEVILLE	31,869	24,715	5,052	2,102	19,663 R	77.6%	15.9%	83.0%	17.0%
7,289	BOUNDARY	3,513	2,088	1,087	338	1,001 R	59.4%	30.9%	65.8%	34.2%
3,342	BUTTE	1,765	1,275	424	66	851 R	72.2%	24.0%	75.0%	25.0%
818	CAMAS	530	360	145	25	215 R	67.9%	27.4%	71.3%	28.7%
83,756	CANYON	36,016	24,375	9,172	2,469	15,203 R	67.7%	25.5%	72.7%	27.3%
8,695	CARIBOU	3,892	3,234	481	177	2,753 R	83.1%	12.4%	87.1%	12.9%
19,427	CASSIA	8,259	6,511	1,369	379	5,142 R	78.8%	16.6%	82.6%	17.4%
798	CLARK	483	379	87	17	292 R	78.5%	18.0%	81.3%	18.7%
10,390	CLEARWATER	4,314	2,178	1,699	437	479 R	50.5%	39.4%	56.2%	43.8%
3,385	CUSTER	1,902	1,398	398	106	1,000 R	73.5%	20.9%	77.8%	22.2%
21,565	ELMORE	6,157	3,994	1,760	403	2,234 R	64.9%	28.6%	69.4%	30.6%
8,895	FRANKLIN	4,301	3,669	511	121	3,158 R	85.3%	11.9%	87.8%	12.2%
10,813	FREMONT	5,253	4,167	926	160	3,241 R	79.3%	17.6%	81.8%	18.2%
11,972	GEM	5,726	3,766	1,613	347	2,153 R	65.8%	28.2%	70.0%	30.0%
11,874	GOODING	5,695	3,897	1,481	317	2,416 R	68.4%	26.0%	72.5%	27.5%
14,769	IDAHO	7,073	4,425	2,078	570	2,347 R	62.6%	29.4%	68.0%	32.0%
15,304	JEFFERSON	6,933	5,860	833	240	5,027 R	84.5%	12.0%	87.6%	12.4%
14,840	JEROME	6,625	4,962	1,368	295	3,594 R	74.9%	20.6%	78.4%	21.6%
59,770	KOOTENAI	26,912	17,022	7,521	2,369	9,501 R	63.3%	27.9%	69.4%	30.6%
28,749	LATAH	14,892	6,967	5,037	2,888	1,930 R	46.8%	33.8%	58.0%	42.0%
7,460	LEMHI	3,699	2,646	794	259	1,852 R	71.5%	21.5%	76.9%	23.1%
4,118	LEWIS	2,053	1,088	774	191	314 R	53.0%	37.7%	58.4%	41.6%
3,436	LINCOLN	1,872	1,294	462	116	832 R	69.1%	24.7%	73.7%	26.3%
19,480	MADISON	7,414	6,555	728	131	5,827 R	88.4%	9.8%	90.0%	10.0%
19,718	MINIDOKA	8,131	6,035	1,689	407	4,346 R	74.2%	20.8%	78.1%	21.9%
33,220	NEZ PERCE	15,744	7,495	6,565	1,684	930 R	47.6%	41.7%	53.3%	46.7%
3,258	ONEIDA	1,970	1,461	434	75	1,027 R	74.2%	22.0%	77.1%	22.9%
8,272	OWYHEE	3,140	2,257	732	151	1,525 R	71.9%	23.3%	75.5%	24.5%
15,722	PAYETTE	6,714	4,508	1,828	378	2,680 R	67.1%	27.2%	71.1%	28.9%
6,844	POWER	3,143	2,235	727	181	1,508 R	71.1%	23.1%	75.5%	24.5%
19,226	SHOSHONE	7,675	3,994	3,102	579	892 R	52.0%	40.4%	56.3%	43.7%
2,897	TETON	1,686	1,227	360	99	867 R	72.8%	21.4%	77.3%	22.7%
52,927	TWIN FALLS	23,708	17,425	4,835	1,448	12,590 R	73.5%	20.4%	78.3%	21.7%
5,604	VALLEY	3,272	2,041	926	305	1,115 R	62.4%	28.3%	68.8%	31.2%
8,803	WASHINGTON	4,585	2,915	1,421	249	1,494 R	63.6%	31.0%	67.2%	32.8%
943,935	TOTAL	437,431	290,699	110,192	36,540	180,507 R	66.5%	25.2%	72.5%	27.5%

IDAHO

SENATOR 1980

1980 Census Population	County	Total Vote	Republican	Democratic	Other	Rep.-Dem. Plurality	Percentage Total Vote Rep.	Dem.	Major Vote Rep.	Dem.
173,036	ADA	87,311	42,977	42,928	1,406	49 R	49.2%	49.2%	50.0%	50.0%
3,347	ADAMS	1,895	1,115	769	11	346 R	58.8%	40.6%	59.2%	40.8%
65,421	BANNOCK	30,133	11,651	17,661	821	6,010 D	38.7%	58.6%	39.7%	60.3%
6,931	BEAR LAKE	3,526	2,479	1,033	14	1,446 R	70.3%	29.3%	70.6%	29.4%
8,292	BENEWAH	3,808	1,697	2,083	28	386 D	44.6%	54.7%	44.9%	55.1%
36,489	BINGHAM	15,656	7,780	7,584	292	196 R	49.7%	48.4%	50.6%	49.4%
9,841	BLAINE	5,571	1,651	3,827	93	2,176 D	29.6%	68.7%	30.1%	69.9%
2,999	BOISE	1,830	885	923	22	38 D	48.4%	50.4%	48.9%	51.1%
24,163	BONNER	11,804	4,751	6,955	98	2,204 D	40.2%	58.9%	40.6%	59.4%
65,980	BONNEVILLE	32,197	17,391	14,271	535	3,120 R	54.0%	44.3%	54.9%	45.1%
7,289	BOUNDARY	3,515	1,625	1,862	28	237 D	46.2%	53.0%	46.6%	53.4%
3,342	BUTTE	1,762	847	893	22	46 D	48.1%	50.7%	48.7%	51.3%
818	CAMAS	525	290	231	4	59 R	55.2%	44.0%	55.7%	44.3%
83,756	CANYON	36,400	20,842	15,069	489	5,773 R	57.3%	41.4%	58.0%	42.0%
8,695	CARIBOU	3,823	2,735	1,054	34	1,681 R	71.5%	27.6%	72.2%	27.8%
19,427	CASSIA	8,336	4,988	3,213	135	1,775 R	59.8%	38.5%	60.8%	39.2%
798	CLARK	479	282	196	1	86 R	58.9%	40.9%	59.0%	41.0%
10,390	CLEARWATER	4,376	1,685	2,637	54	952 D	38.5%	60.3%	39.0%	61.0%
3,385	CUSTER	1,886	1,204	660	22	544 R	63.8%	35.0%	64.6%	35.4%
21,565	ELMORE	6,090	2,765	3,259	66	494 D	45.4%	53.5%	45.9%	54.1%
8,895	FRANKLIN	4,329	3,260	1,026	43	2,234 R	75.3%	23.7%	76.1%	23.9%
10,813	FREMONT	5,214	3,029	2,145	40	884 R	58.1%	41.1%	58.5%	41.5%
11,972	GEM	5,795	2,846	2,845	104	1 R	49.1%	49.1%	50.0%	50.0%
11,874	GOODING	5,617	2,711	2,840	66	129 D	48.3%	50.6%	48.8%	51.2%
14,769	IDAHO	7,020	3,993	2,961	66	1,032 R	56.9%	42.2%	57.4%	42.6%
15,304	JEFFERSON	6,988	4,689	2,149	150	2,540 R	67.1%	30.8%	68.6%	31.4%
14,840	JEROME	6,561	3,633	2,869	59	764 R	55.4%	43.7%	55.9%	44.1%
59,770	KOOTENAI	27,087	13,219	13,403	465	184 D	48.8%	49.5%	49.7%	50.3%
28,749	LATAH	15,120	4,680	10,214	226	5,534 D	31.0%	67.6%	31.4%	68.6%
7,460	LEMHI	3,635	2,341	1,248	46	1,093 R	64.4%	34.3%	65.2%	34.8%
4,118	LEWIS	2,031	826	1,188	17	362 D	40.7%	58.5%	41.0%	59.0%
3,436	LINCOLN	1,851	826	1,004	21	178 D	44.6%	54.2%	45.1%	54.9%
19,480	MADISON	7,454	4,811	2,561	82	2,250 R	64.5%	34.4%	65.3%	34.7%
19,718	MINIDOKA	8,211	4,062	4,029	120	33 R	49.5%	49.1%	50.2%	49.8%
33,220	NEZ PERCE	15,919	5,215	10,466	238	5,251 D	32.8%	65.7%	33.3%	66.7%
3,258	ONEIDA	1,901	1,104	780	17	324 R	58.1%	41.0%	58.6%	41.4%
8,272	OWYHEE	3,121	1,941	1,157	23	784 R	62.2%	37.1%	62.7%	37.3%
15,722	PAYETTE	6,777	3,591	3,106	80	485 R	53.0%	45.8%	53.6%	46.4%
6,844	POWER	3,070	1,315	1,711	44	396 D	42.8%	55.7%	43.5%	56.5%
19,226	SHOSHONE	7,787	2,993	4,692	102	1,699 D	38.4%	60.3%	38.9%	61.1%
2,897	TETON	1,668	888	762	18	126 R	53.2%	45.7%	53.8%	46.2%
52,927	TWIN FALLS	23,801	13,104	10,437	260	2,667 R	55.1%	43.9%	55.7%	44.3%
5,604	VALLEY	3,237	1,772	1,444	21	328 R	54.7%	44.6%	55.1%	44.9%
8,803	WASHINGTON	4,530	2,212	2,294	24	82 D	48.8%	50.6%	49.1%	50.9%
943,935	TOTAL	439,647	218,701	214,439	6,507	4,262 R	49.7%	48.8%	50.5%	49.5%

IDAHO

CONGRESS

CD	Year	Total Vote	Republican Vote	Republican Candidate	Democratic Vote	Democratic Candidate	Other Vote	Rep.-Dem. Plurality	Total Vote Rep.	Total Vote Dem.	Major Vote Rep.	Major Vote Dem.
1	1980	217,542	116,845	CRAIG, LARRY	100,697	NICHOLS, GLENN W.		16,148 R	53.7%	46.3%	53.7%	46.3%
1	1978	144,652	86,680	SYMMS, STEVEN D.	57,972	TRUBY, ROY		28,708 R	59.9%	40.1%	59.9%	40.1%
1	1976	175,495	95,833	SYMMS, STEVEN D.	79,662	PURSLEY, KEN		16,171 R	54.6%	45.4%	54.6%	45.4%
1	1974	129,405	75,404	SYMMS, STEVEN D.	54,001	COX, J. RAY		21,403 R	58.3%	41.7%	58.3%	41.7%
1	1972	153,376	85,270	SYMMS, STEVEN D.	68,106	WILLIAMS, ED		17,164 R	55.6%	44.4%	55.6%	44.4%
2	1980	197,560	116,196	HANSEN, GEORGE V.	81,364	BILYEU, DIANE		34,832 R	58.8%	41.2%	58.8%	41.2%
2	1978	140,631	80,591	HANSEN, GEORGE V.	60,040	KRESS, STAN		20,551 R	57.3%	42.7%	57.3%	42.7%
2	1976	166,412	84,175	HANSEN, GEORGE V.	82,237	KRESS, STAN		1,938 R	50.6%	49.4%	50.6%	49.4%
2	1974	120,873	67,274	HANSEN, GEORGE V.	53,599	HANSON, MAX		13,675 R	55.7%	44.3%	55.7%	44.3%
2	1972	148,178	102,537	HANSEN, ORVAL H.	40,081	LUDLOW, WILLIS	5,560	62,456 R	69.2%	27.0%	71.9%	28.1%

IDAHO

1980 GENERAL ELECTION

President   Other vote was 27,058 Anderson (Independent); 8,425 Clark (Libertarian); 1,057 Rarick (American).

Senator   Other vote was Fullmer (Libertarian).

Congress

1980 PRIMARIES

MAY 27 REPUBLICAN

Senator   Steven D. Symms, unopposed.

Congress   Contested as follows:

    CD 1   29,525 Larry Craig; 26,454 Wayne L. Kidwell.
    CD 2   41,718 George V. Hansen; 30,729 James T. Jones.

MAY 27 DEMOCRATIC

Senator   Frank Church, unopposed.

Congress   Unopposed in CD 2. Contested as follows:

    CD 1   14,858 Glenn W. Nichols; 12,923 Terry McKay.

MAY 27 LIBERTARIAN

Senator   Larry Fullmer, unopposed.

Congress   No candidate in either CD.

ILLINOIS

GOVERNOR
James R. Thompson (R). Re-elected 1978 to a four-year term. Previously elected 1976 to a two-year term.

SENATORS
Alan J. Dixon (D). Elected 1980 to a six-year term.

Charles H. Percy (R). Re-elected 1978 to a six-year term. Previously elected 1972, 1966.

REPRESENTATIVES
1. Harold Washington (D)
2. Gus Savage (D)
3. Martin A. Russo (D)
4. Edward J. Derwinski (R)
5. John G. Fary (D)
6. Henry J. Hyde (R)
7. Cardiss Collins (D)
8. Daniel Rostenkowski (D)
9. Sidney R. Yates (D)
10. John E. Porter (R)
11. Frank Annunzio (D)
12. Philip M. Crane (R)
13. Robert McClory (R)
14. John N. Erlenborn (R)
15. Tom Corcoran (R)
16. Lynn Martin (R)
17. George M. O'Brien (R)
18. Robert H. Michel (R)
19. Tom Railsback (R)
20. Paul Findley (R)
21. Edward R. Madigan (R)
22. Daniel B. Crane (R)
23. Melvin Price (D)
24. Paul Simon (D)

POSTWAR VOTE FOR GOVERNOR

Year	Total Vote	Republican Vote	Candidate	Democratic Vote	Candidate	Other Vote	Rep.-Dem. Plurality	Total Vote Rep.	Total Vote Dem.	Major Vote Rep.	Major Vote Dem.
1978	3,150,095	1,859,684	Thompson, James R.	1,263,134	Bakalis, Michael	27,277	596,550 R	59.0%	40.1%	59.6%	40.4%
1976s	4,638,997	3,000,395	Thompson, James R.	1,610,258	Howlett, Michael J.	28,344	1,390,137 R	64.7%	34.7%	65.1%	34.9%
1972	4,678,804	2,293,809	Ogilvie, Richard B.	2,371,303	Walker, Daniel	13,692	77,494 D	49.0%	50.7%	49.2%	50.8%
1968	4,506,000	2,307,295	Ogilvie, Richard B.	2,179,501	Shapiro, Samuel H.	19,204	127,794 R	51.2%	48.4%	51.4%	48.6%
1964	4,657,500	2,239,095	Percy, Charles H.	2,418,394	Kerner, Otto	11	179,299 D	48.1%	51.9%	48.1%	51.9%
1960	4,674,187	2,070,479	Stratton, William G.	2,594,731	Kerner, Otto	8,977	524,252 D	44.3%	55.5%	44.4%	55.6%
1956	4,314,611	2,171,786	Stratton, William G.	2,134,909	Austin, Richard B.	7,916	36,877 R	50.3%	49.5%	50.4%	49.6%
1952	4,415,864	2,317,363	Stratton, William G.	2,089,721	Dixon, Sherwood	8,780	227,642 R	52.5%	47.3%	52.6%	47.4%
1948	3,940,257	1,678,007	Green, Dwight H.	2,250,074	Stevenson, Adlai E.	12,176	572,067 D	42.6%	57.1%	42.7%	57.3%

The 1976 vote was for a two-year term to permit shifting the vote for Governor to non-Presidential years.

POSTWAR VOTE FOR SENATOR

Year	Total Vote	Republican Vote	Candidate	Democratic Vote	Candidate	Other Vote	Rep.-Dem. Plurality	Total Vote Rep.	Total Vote Dem.	Major Vote Rep.	Major Vote Dem.
1980	4,580,029	1,946,296	O'Neal, David C.	2,565,302	Dixon, Alan J.	68,431	619,006 D	42.5%	56.0%	43.1%	56.9%
1978	3,184,764	1,698,711	Percy, Charles H.	1,448,187	Seith, Alex	37,866	250,524 R	53.3%	45.5%	54.0%	46.0%
1974	2,914,666	1,084,884	Burditt, George M.	1,811,496	Stevenson, Adlai E., III	18,286	726,612 D	37.2%	62.2%	37.5%	62.5%
1972	4,608,380	2,867,078	Percy, Charles H.	1,721,031	Pucinski, Roman C.	20,271	1,146,047 R	62.2%	37.3%	62.5%	37.5%
1970s	3,599,272	1,519,718	Smith, Ralph T.	2,065,054	Stevenson, Adlai E., III	14,500	545,336 D	42.2%	57.4%	42.4%	57.6%
1968	4,449,757	2,358,947	Dirksen, Everett M.	2,073,242	Clark, William G.	17,568	285,705 R	53.0%	46.6%	53.2%	46.8%
1966	3,822,725	2,100,449	Percy, Charles H.	1,678,147	Douglas, Paul H.	44,129	422,302 R	54.9%	43.9%	55.6%	44.4%
1962	3,709,216	1,961,202	Dirksen, Everett M.	1,748,007	Yates, Sidney R.	7	213,195 R	52.9%	47.1%	52.9%	47.1%
1960	4,632,796	2,093,846	Witwer, Samuel W.	2,530,943	Douglas, Paul H.	8,007	437,097 D	45.2%	54.6%	45.3%	54.7%
1956	4,264,830	2,307,352	Dirksen, Everett M.	1,949,883	Stengel, Richard	7,595	357,469 R	54.1%	45.7%	54.2%	45.8%
1954	3,368,025	1,563,683	Meek, Joseph T.	1,804,338	Douglas, Paul H.	4	240,655 D	46.4%	53.6%	46.4%	53.6%
1950	3,622,673	1,951,984	Dirksen, Everett M.	1,657,630	Lucas, Scott W.	13,059	294,354 R	53.9%	45.8%	54.1%	45.9%
1948	3,900,285	1,740,026	Brooks, C. Wayland	2,147,754	Douglas, Paul H.	12,505	407,728 D	44.6%	55.1%	44.8%	55.2%

The 1970 election was for a short term to fill a vacancy.

ILLINOIS

Districts Established September 20, 1971

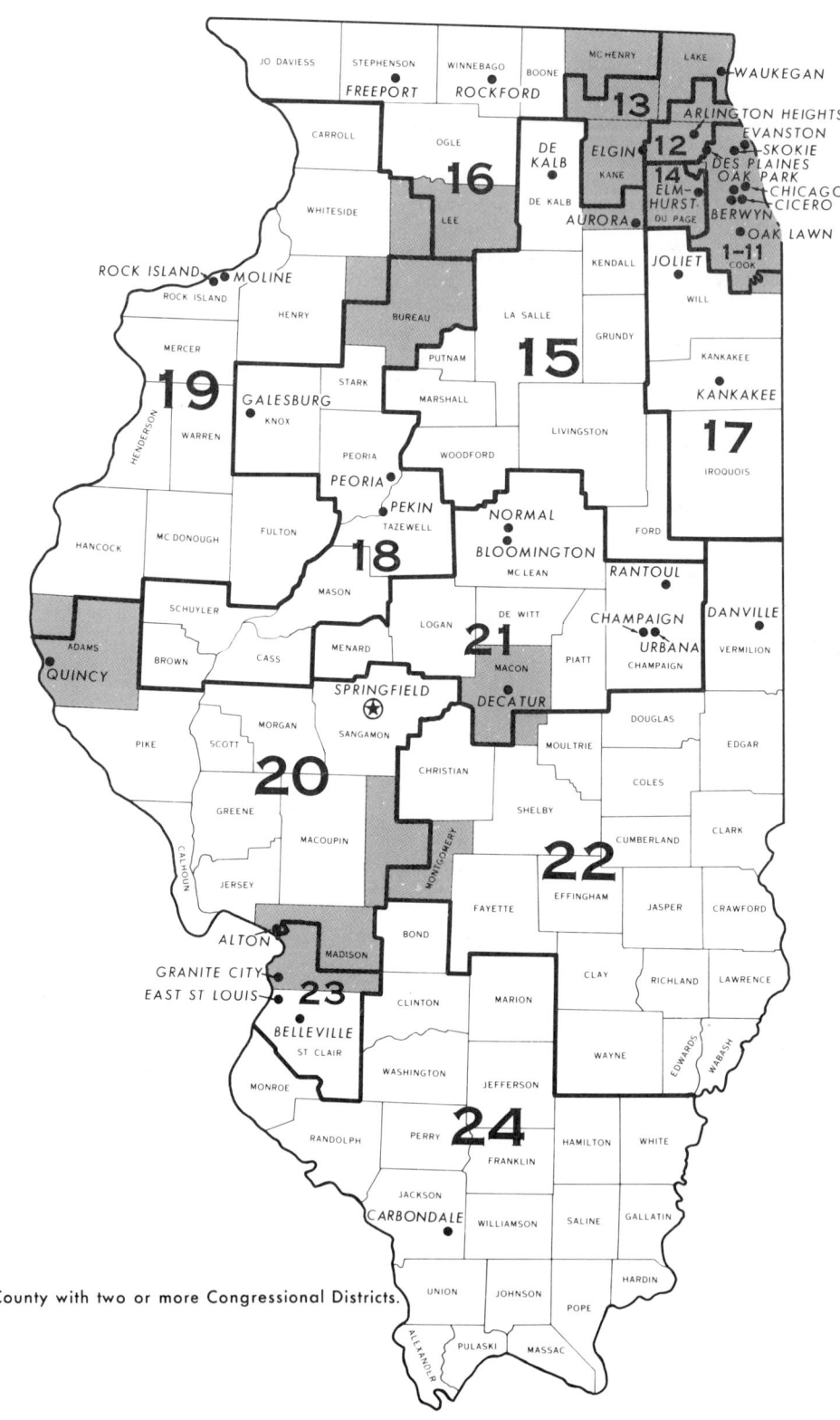

County with two or more Congressional Districts.

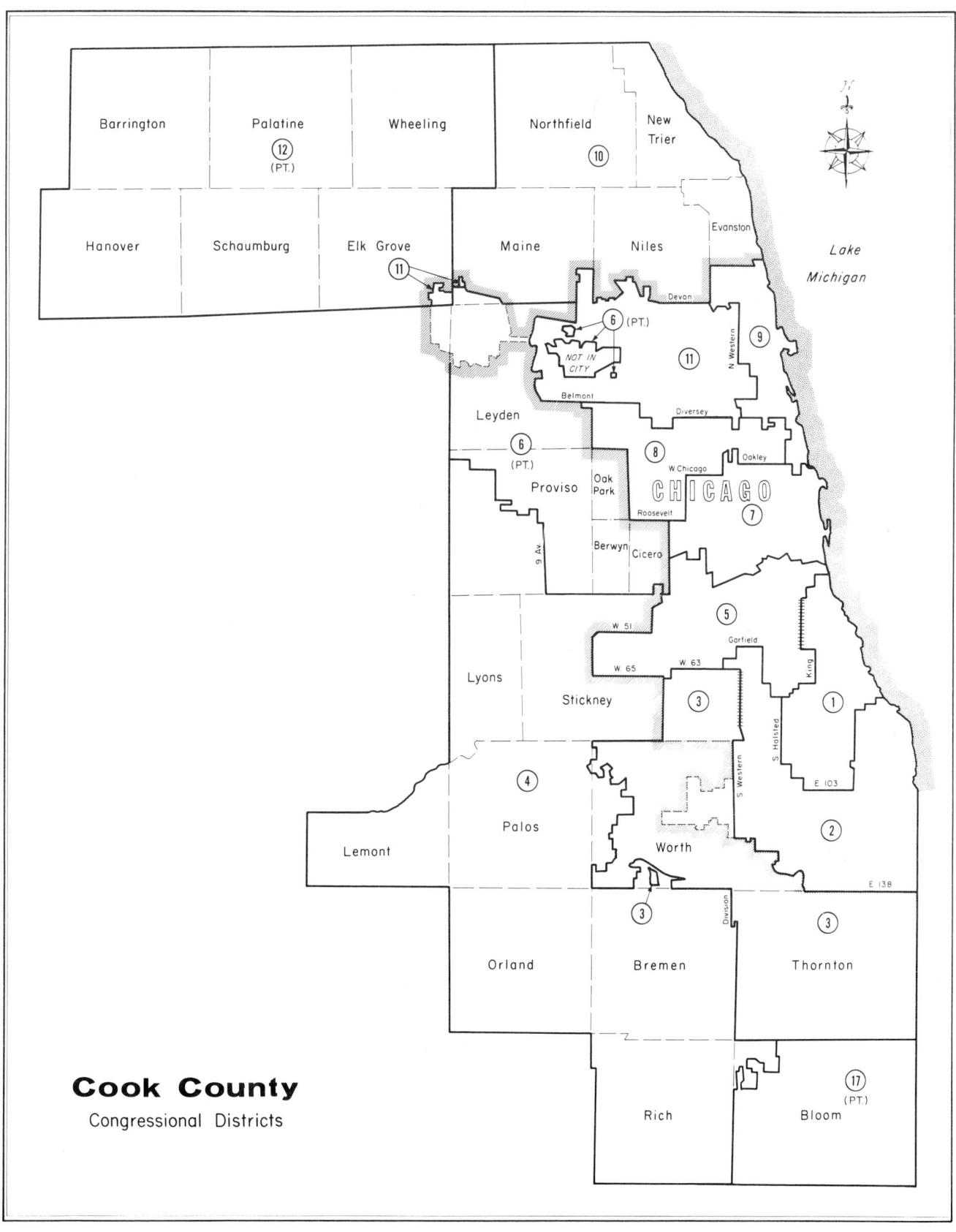

Cook County

Congressional Districts

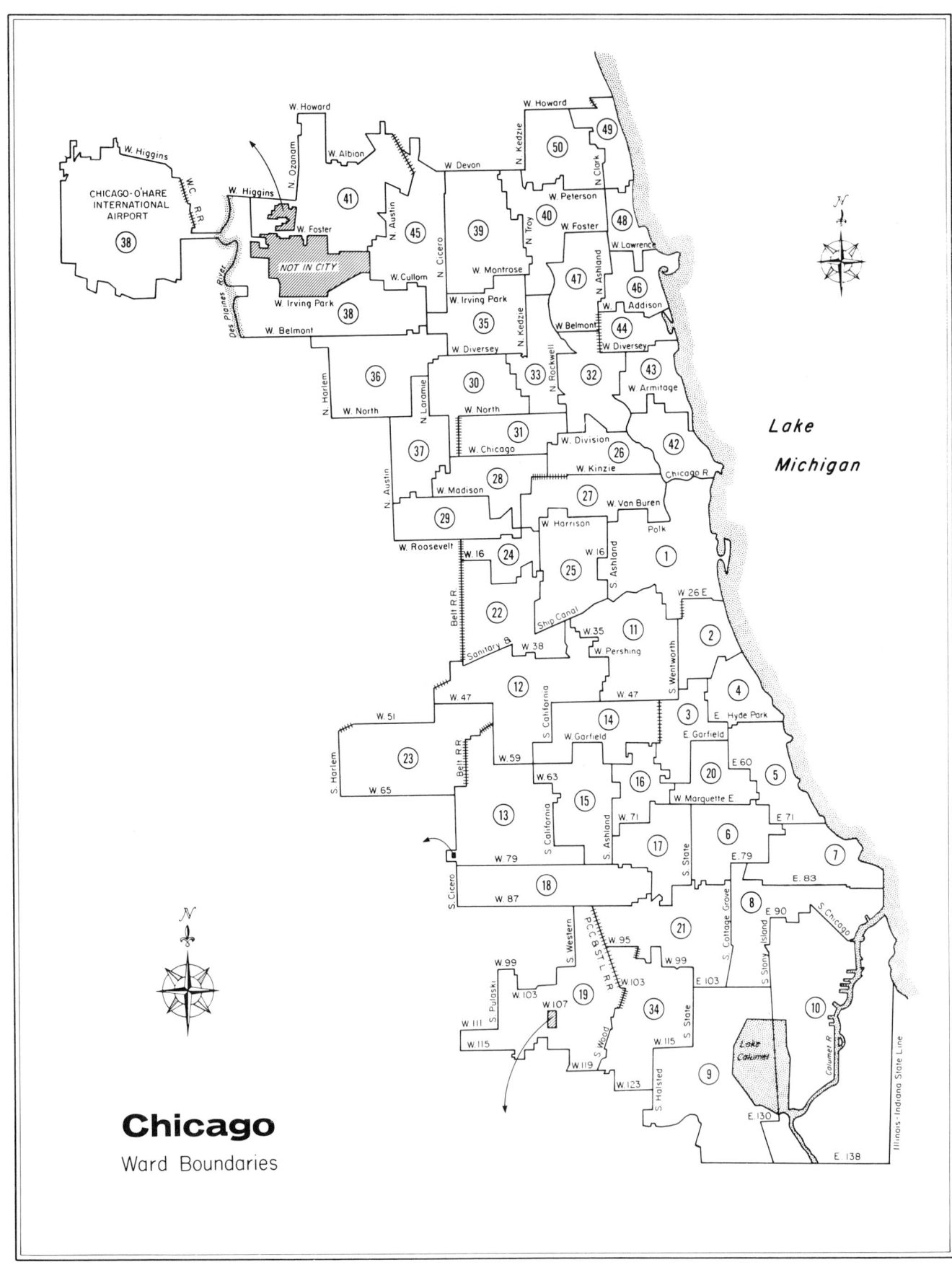

Chicago
Ward Boundaries

ILLINOIS

PRESIDENT 1980

1980 Census Population	County	Total Vote	Republican	Democratic	Other	Rep.-Dem. Plurality	Percentage Total Vote		Major Vote	
							Rep.	Dem.	Rep.	Dem.
71,622	ADAMS	31,917	19,842	10,606	1,469	9,236 R	62.2%	33.2%	65.2%	34.8%
12,264	ALEXANDER	5,678	2,650	2,925	103	275 D	46.7%	51.5%	47.5%	52.5%
16,224	BOND	7,532	4,398	2,834	300	1,564 R	58.4%	37.6%	60.8%	39.2%
28,630	BOONE	11,614	6,697	3,175	1,742	3,522 R	57.7%	27.3%	67.8%	32.2%
5,411	BROWN	2,692	1,660	950	82	710 R	61.7%	35.3%	63.6%	36.4%
39,114	BUREAU	18,587	11,484	5,753	1,350	5,731 R	61.8%	31.0%	66.6%	33.4%
5,867	CALHOUN	2,895	1,591	1,208	96	383 R	55.0%	41.7%	56.8%	43.2%
18,779	CARROLL	8,023	5,084	2,154	785	2,930 R	63.4%	26.8%	70.2%	29.8%
15,084	CASS	6,770	3,965	2,543	262	1,422 R	58.6%	37.6%	60.9%	39.1%
168,392	CHAMPAIGN	65,360	33,329	21,017	11,014	12,312 R	51.0%	32.2%	61.3%	38.7%
36,446	CHRISTIAN	16,036	8,770	6,625	641	2,145 R	54.7%	41.3%	57.0%	43.0%
16,913	CLARK	8,666	5,476	2,855	335	2,621 R	63.2%	32.9%	65.7%	34.3%
15,283	CLAY	7,266	4,447	2,587	232	1,860 R	61.2%	35.6%	63.2%	36.8%
32,617	CLINTON	13,593	8,500	4,470	623	4,030 R	62.5%	32.9%	65.5%	34.5%
52,992	COLES	20,671	11,994	6,743	1,934	5,251 R	58.0%	32.6%	64.0%	36.0%
5,253,190	COOK	2,163,097	856,574	1,124,584	181,939	268,010 D	39.6%	52.0%	43.2%	56.8%
20,818	CRAWFORD	9,710	5,894	3,372	444	2,522 R	60.7%	34.7%	63.6%	36.4%
11,062	CUMBERLAND	5,289	3,159	1,892	238	1,267 R	59.7%	35.8%	62.5%	37.5%
74,624	DE KALB	30,365	16,370	8,913	5,082	7,457 R	53.9%	29.4%	64.7%	35.3%
18,108	DE WITT	7,344	4,648	2,262	434	2,386 R	63.3%	30.8%	67.3%	32.7%
19,774	DOUGLAS	8,294	5,330	2,564	400	2,766 R	64.3%	30.9%	67.5%	32.5%
658,177	DU PAGE	284,749	182,308	68,991	33,450	113,317 R	64.0%	24.2%	72.5%	27.5%
21,725	EDGAR	10,515	6,639	3,394	482	3,245 R	63.1%	32.3%	66.2%	33.8%
7,961	EDWARDS	3,751	2,556	1,041	154	1,515 R	68.1%	27.8%	71.1%	28.9%
30,944	EFFINGHAM	13,808	9,104	4,229	475	4,875 R	65.9%	30.6%	68.3%	31.7%
22,167	FAYETTE	10,408	6,523	3,614	271	2,909 R	62.7%	34.7%	64.3%	35.7%
15,265	FORD	7,214	5,024	1,803	387	3,221 R	69.6%	25.0%	73.6%	26.4%
43,201	FRANKLIN	19,856	9,731	9,425	700	306 R	49.0%	47.5%	50.8%	49.2%
43,687	FULTON	18,957	10,316	7,481	1,160	2,835 R	54.4%	39.5%	58.0%	42.0%
7,590	GALLATIN	3,466	1,700	1,678	88	22 R	49.0%	48.4%	50.3%	49.7%
16,661	GREENE	7,120	4,224	2,607	289	1,617 R	59.3%	36.6%	61.8%	38.2%
30,582	GRUNDY	13,204	8,397	3,970	837	4,427 R	63.6%	30.1%	67.9%	32.1%
9,172	HAMILTON	5,456	3,254	1,990	212	1,264 R	59.6%	36.5%	62.1%	37.9%
23,877	HANCOCK	10,585	6,597	3,522	466	3,075 R	62.3%	33.3%	65.2%	34.8%
5,383	HARDIN	3,114	1,721	1,314	79	407 R	55.3%	42.2%	56.7%	43.3%
9,114	HENDERSON	4,246	2,443	1,609	194	834 R	57.5%	37.9%	60.3%	39.7%
57,968	HENRY	24,206	14,506	7,977	1,723	6,529 R	59.9%	33.0%	64.5%	35.5%
32,976	IROQUOIS	15,327	11,247	3,362	718	7,885 R	73.4%	21.9%	77.0%	23.0%
61,522	JACKSON	23,829	10,505	10,291	3,033	214 R	44.1%	43.2%	50.5%	49.5%
11,318	JASPER	5,612	3,548	1,846	218	1,702 R	63.2%	32.9%	65.8%	34.2%
36,354	JEFFERSON	16,340	8,972	6,761	607	2,211 R	54.9%	41.4%	57.0%	43.0%
20,538	JERSEY	8,985	5,266	3,324	395	1,942 R	58.6%	37.0%	61.3%	38.7%
23,520	JO DAVIESS	8,971	5,186	2,678	1,107	2,508 R	57.8%	29.9%	65.9%	34.1%
9,624	JOHNSON	4,888	3,201	1,586	101	1,615 R	65.5%	32.4%	66.9%	33.1%
278,405	KANE	103,784	64,106	29,015	10,663	35,091 R	61.8%	28.0%	68.8%	31.2%
102,926	KANKAKEE	40,873	23,810	14,626	2,437	9,184 R	58.3%	35.8%	61.9%	38.1%
37,202	KENDALL	14,327	10,028	3,143	1,156	6,885 R	70.0%	21.9%	76.1%	23.9%
61,607	KNOX	26,198	14,907	8,749	2,542	6,158 R	56.9%	33.4%	63.0%	37.0%
440,372	LAKE	164,853	96,350	48,287	20,216	48,063 R	58.4%	29.3%	66.6%	33.4%
109,139	LA SALLE	47,835	27,323	16,818	3,694	10,505 R	57.1%	35.2%	61.9%	38.1%
17,807	LAWRENCE	7,856	4,453	3,030	373	1,423 R	56.7%	38.6%	59.5%	40.5%
36,328	LEE	15,438	11,373	3,170	895	8,203 R	73.7%	20.5%	78.2%	21.8%
41,381	LIVINGSTON	16,823	11,544	4,111	1,168	7,433 R	68.6%	24.4%	73.7%	26.3%
31,802	LOGAN	14,366	9,681	3,916	769	5,765 R	67.4%	27.3%	71.2%	28.8%
37,236	MCDONOUGH	14,589	8,995	4,093	1,501	4,902 R	61.7%	28.1%	68.7%	31.3%
147,724	MCHENRY	61,655	40,045	14,540	7,070	25,505 R	65.0%	23.6%	73.4%	26.6%
119,149	MCLEAN	49,232	30,096	13,587	5,549	16,509 R	61.1%	27.6%	68.9%	31.1%
131,375	MACON	53,956	28,298	22,325	3,333	5,973 R	52.4%	41.4%	55.9%	44.1%
49,384	MACOUPIN	22,354	12,131	9,116	1,107	3,015 R	54.3%	40.8%	57.1%	42.9%
247,671	MADISON	100,124	51,160	43,860	5,104	7,300 R	51.1%	43.8%	53.8%	46.2%
43,523	MARION	18,678	10,969	6,990	719	3,979 R	58.7%	37.4%	61.1%	38.9%
14,479	MARSHALL	6,711	4,349	1,903	459	2,446 R	64.8%	28.4%	69.6%	30.4%
19,492	MASON	7,693	4,644	2,680	369	1,964 R	60.4%	34.8%	63.4%	36.6%
14,990	MASSAC	7,272	4,284	2,821	167	1,463 R	58.9%	38.8%	60.3%	39.7%
11,700	MENARD	5,534	3,622	1,589	323	2,033 R	65.4%	28.7%	69.5%	30.5%
19,286	MERCER	9,156	5,144	3,361	651	1,783 R	56.2%	36.7%	60.5%	39.5%
20,117	MONROE	9,924	6,315	3,121	488	3,194 R	63.6%	31.4%	66.9%	33.1%
31,686	MONTGOMERY	15,415	8,947	5,721	747	3,226 R	58.0%	37.1%	61.0%	39.0%
37,502	MORGAN	16,997	10,406	5,483	1,108	4,923 R	61.2%	32.3%	65.5%	34.5%
14,546	MOULTRIE	6,161	3,495	2,332	334	1,163 R	56.7%	37.9%	60.0%	40.0%

ILLINOIS

PRESIDENT 1980

| 1980 Census Population | County | Total Vote | Republican | Democratic | Other | Rep.-Dem. Plurality | Percentage | | | |
| | | | | | | | Total Vote | | Major Vote | |
							Rep.	Dem.	Rep.	Dem.
46,338	OGLE	18,871	12,533	4,067	2,271	8,466 R	66.4%	21.6%	75.5%	24.5%
200,466	PEORIA	83,510	47,815	28,276	7,419	19,539 R	57.3%	33.9%	62.8%	37.2%
21,714	PERRY	10,610	5,888	4,337	385	1,551 R	55.5%	40.9%	57.6%	42.4%
16,581	PIATT	7,818	4,867	2,421	530	2,446 R	62.3%	31.0%	66.8%	33.2%
18,896	PIKE	9,361	5,301	3,695	365	1,606 R	56.6%	39.5%	58.9%	41.1%
4,404	POPE	2,455	1,501	880	74	621 R	61.1%	35.8%	63.0%	37.0%
8,840	PULASKI	4,099	2,083	1,955	61	128 R	50.8%	47.7%	51.6%	48.4%
6,085	PUTNAM	3,414	1,959	1,158	297	801 R	57.4%	33.9%	62.8%	37.2%
35,566	RANDOLPH	15,494	8,810	6,052	632	2,758 R	56.9%	39.1%	59.3%	40.7%
17,587	RICHLAND	8,126	5,241	2,463	422	2,778 R	64.5%	30.3%	68.0%	32.0%
165,968	ROCK ISLAND	71,775	34,788	30,045	6,942	4,743 R	48.5%	41.9%	53.7%	46.3%
265,469	ST. CLAIR	100,673	46,063	50,046	4,564	3,983 D	45.8%	49.7%	47.9%	52.1%
27,360	SALINE	13,265	7,157	5,683	425	1,474 R	54.0%	42.8%	55.7%	44.3%
176,089	SANGAMON	85,200	49,372	29,354	6,474	20,018 R	57.9%	34.5%	62.7%	37.3%
8,365	SCHUYLER	4,460	2,799	1,445	216	1,354 R	62.8%	32.4%	66.0%	34.0%
6,142	SCOTT	3,042	1,990	941	111	1,049 R	65.4%	30.9%	67.9%	32.1%
23,923	SHELBY	10,894	6,441	3,988	465	2,453 R	59.1%	36.6%	61.8%	38.2%
7,389	STARK	3,380	2,358	806	216	1,552 R	69.8%	23.8%	74.5%	25.5%
49,536	STEPHENSON	20,388	10,779	6,195	3,414	4,584 R	52.9%	30.4%	63.5%	36.5%
132,078	TAZEWELL	56,462	35,481	16,924	4,057	18,557 R	62.8%	30.0%	67.7%	32.3%
16,851	UNION	8,441	4,289	3,781	371	508 R	50.8%	44.8%	53.1%	46.9%
95,222	VERMILION	39,567	22,579	14,498	2,490	8,081 R	57.1%	36.6%	60.9%	39.1%
13,713	WABASH	5,837	3,571	1,975	291	1,596 R	61.2%	33.8%	64.4%	35.6%
21,943	WARREN	9,071	5,667	2,756	648	2,911 R	62.5%	30.4%	67.3%	32.7%
15,472	WASHINGTON	7,762	5,354	2,158	250	3,196 R	69.0%	27.8%	71.3%	28.7%
18,059	WAYNE	9,557	6,013	3,258	286	2,755 R	62.9%	34.1%	64.9%	35.1%
17,864	WHITE	9,072	5,279	3,463	330	1,816 R	58.2%	38.2%	60.4%	39.6%
65,970	WHITESIDE	26,064	17,389	7,191	1,484	10,198 R	66.7%	27.6%	70.7%	29.3%
324,460	WILL	120,658	69,310	41,975	9,373	27,335 R	57.4%	34.8%	62.3%	37.7%
56,538	WILLIAMSON	26,228	14,451	10,779	998	3,672 R	55.1%	41.1%	57.3%	42.7%
250,884	WINNEBAGO	105,089	48,825	32,384	23,880	16,441 R	46.5%	30.8%	60.1%	39.9%
33,320	WOODFORD	15,268	10,791	3,552	925	7,239 R	70.7%	23.3%	75.2%	24.8%
11,418,461	TOTAL	4,749,721	2,358,049	1,981,413	410,259	376,636 R	49.6%	41.7%	54.3%	45.7%

ILLINOIS

SENATOR 1980

1980 Census Population	County	Total Vote	Republican	Democratic	Other	Rep.-Dem. Plurality	Percentage Total Vote Rep.	Dem.	Major Vote Rep.	Dem.
71,622	ADAMS	31,101	13,479	17,328	294	3,849 D	43.3%	55.7%	43.8%	56.2%
12,264	ALEXANDER	5,446	2,076	3,332	38	1,256 D	38.1%	61.2%	38.4%	61.6%
16,224	BOND	7,340	3,779	3,525	36	254 R	51.5%	48.0%	51.7%	48.3%
28,630	BOONE	11,387	6,489	4,773	125	1,716 R	57.0%	41.9%	57.6%	42.4%
5,411	BROWN	2,636	1,104	1,520	12	416 D	41.9%	57.7%	42.1%	57.9%
39,114	BUREAU	18,287	9,222	8,856	209	366 R	50.4%	48.4%	51.0%	49.0%
5,867	CALHOUN	2,790	1,164	1,607	19	443 D	41.7%	57.6%	42.0%	58.0%
18,779	CARROLL	7,904	4,312	3,507	85	805 R	54.6%	44.4%	55.1%	44.9%
15,084	CASS	6,653	3,069	3,545	39	476 D	46.1%	53.3%	46.4%	53.6%
168,392	CHAMPAIGN	64,180	30,242	31,402	2,536	1,160 D	47.1%	48.9%	49.1%	50.9%
36,446	CHRISTIAN	15,868	7,503	8,270	95	767 D	47.3%	52.1%	47.6%	52.4%
16,913	CLARK	8,406	4,103	4,235	68	132 D	48.8%	50.4%	49.2%	50.8%
15,283	CLAY	7,033	3,518	3,462	53	56 R	50.0%	49.2%	50.4%	49.6%
32,617	CLINTON	13,292	7,212	5,975	105	1,237 R	54.3%	45.0%	54.7%	45.3%
52,992	COLES	20,624	10,695	9,714	215	981 R	51.9%	47.1%	52.4%	47.6%
5,253,190	COOK	2,042,584	676,877	1,330,507	35,200	653,630 D	33.1%	65.1%	33.7%	66.3%
20,818	CRAWFORD	9,498	4,571	4,820	107	249 D	48.1%	50.7%	48.7%	51.3%
11,062	CUMBERLAND	5,168	2,488	2,631	49	143 D	48.1%	50.9%	48.6%	51.4%
74,624	DE KALB	30,206	14,909	14,492	805	417 R	49.4%	48.0%	50.7%	49.3%
18,108	DE WITT	7,213	4,223	2,914	76	1,309 R	58.5%	40.4%	59.2%	40.8%
19,774	DOUGLAS	8,184	4,641	3,490	53	1,151 R	56.7%	42.6%	57.1%	42.9%
658,177	DU PAGE	281,708	159,287	118,272	4,149	41,015 R	56.5%	42.0%	57.4%	42.6%
21,725	EDGAR	10,362	5,400	4,901	61	499 R	52.1%	47.3%	52.4%	47.6%
7,961	EDWARDS	3,601	2,075	1,496	30	579 R	57.6%	41.5%	58.1%	41.9%
30,944	EFFINGHAM	13,829	7,229	6,524	76	705 R	52.3%	47.2%	52.6%	47.4%
22,167	FAYETTE	9,796	5,329	4,450	17	879 R	54.4%	45.4%	54.5%	45.5%
15,265	FORD	7,119	4,535	2,534	50	2,001 R	63.7%	35.6%	64.2%	35.8%
43,201	FRANKLIN	19,039	6,972	11,881	186	4,909 D	36.6%	62.4%	37.0%	63.0%
43,687	FULTON	18,757	9,244	9,310	203	66 D	49.3%	49.6%	49.8%	50.2%
7,590	GALLATIN	3,290	1,261	2,013	16	752 D	38.3%	61.2%	38.5%	61.5%
16,661	GREENE	6,975	3,033	3,895	47	862 D	43.5%	55.8%	43.8%	56.2%
30,582	GRUNDY	13,035	6,983	5,949	103	1,034 R	53.6%	45.6%	54.0%	46.0%
9,172	HAMILTON	5,111	2,456	2,634	21	178 D	48.1%	51.5%	48.3%	51.7%
23,877	HANCOCK	10,392	5,168	5,140	84	28 R	49.7%	49.5%	50.1%	49.9%
5,383	HARDIN	2,952	1,313	1,628	11	315 D	44.5%	55.1%	44.6%	55.4%
9,114	HENDERSON	4,165	2,046	2,070	49	24 D	49.1%	49.7%	49.7%	50.3%
57,968	HENRY	23,795	12,089	11,416	290	673 R	50.8%	48.0%	51.4%	48.6%
32,976	IROQUOIS	15,049	9,126	5,819	104	3,307 R	60.6%	38.7%	61.1%	38.9%
61,522	JACKSON	23,258	8,853	13,424	981	4,571 D	38.1%	57.7%	39.7%	60.3%
11,318	JASPER	5,483	2,457	2,974	52	517 D	44.8%	54.2%	45.2%	54.8%
36,354	JEFFERSON	15,850	7,420	8,305	125	885 D	46.8%	52.4%	47.2%	52.8%
20,538	JERSEY	8,722	3,968	4,688	66	720 D	45.5%	53.7%	45.8%	54.2%
23,520	JO DAVIESS	8,610	4,241	4,235	134	6 R	49.3%	49.2%	50.0%	50.0%
9,624	JOHNSON	4,524	2,458	2,054	12	404 R	54.3%	45.4%	54.5%	45.5%
278,405	KANE	102,761	54,998	46,094	1,669	8,904 R	53.5%	44.9%	54.4%	45.6%
102,926	KANKAKEE	39,333	19,821	19,087	425	734 R	50.4%	48.5%	50.9%	49.1%
37,202	KENDALL	14,219	8,707	5,333	179	3,374 R	61.2%	37.5%	62.0%	38.0%
61,607	KNOX	25,840	13,214	12,187	439	1,027 R	51.1%	47.2%	52.0%	48.0%
440,372	LAKE	161,562	82,216	76,370	2,976	5,846 R	50.9%	47.3%	51.8%	48.2%
109,139	LA SALLE	47,209	22,308	24,344	557	2,036 D	47.3%	51.6%	47.8%	52.2%
17,807	LAWRENCE	7,630	3,461	4,082	87	621 D	45.4%	53.5%	45.9%	54.1%
36,328	LEE	15,283	9,339	5,825	119	3,514 R	61.1%	38.1%	61.6%	38.4%
41,381	LIVINGSTON	16,655	9,904	6,638	113	3,266 R	59.5%	39.9%	59.9%	40.1%
31,802	LOGAN	14,271	8,346	5,832	93	2,514 R	58.5%	40.9%	58.9%	41.1%
37,236	MCDONOUGH	14,211	7,380	6,564	267	816 R	51.9%	46.2%	52.9%	47.1%
147,724	MCHENRY	60,868	35,407	24,409	1,052	10,998 R	58.2%	40.1%	59.2%	40.8%
119,149	MCLEAN	48,678	26,523	21,389	766	5,134 R	54.5%	43.9%	55.4%	44.6%
131,375	MACON	53,111	23,942	28,614	555	4,672 D	45.1%	53.9%	45.6%	54.4%
49,384	MACOUPIN	21,879	9,628	12,081	170	2,453 D	44.0%	55.2%	44.4%	55.6%
247,671	MADISON	98,678	41,751	56,034	893	14,283 D	42.3%	56.8%	42.7%	57.3%
43,523	MARION	18,120	8,715	9,273	132	558 D	48.1%	51.2%	48.4%	51.6%
14,479	MARSHALL	6,659	3,856	2,714	89	1,142 R	57.9%	40.8%	58.7%	41.3%
19,492	MASON	7,603	3,891	3,649	63	242 R	51.2%	48.0%	51.6%	48.4%
14,990	MASSAC	7,008	3,276	3,688	44	412 D	46.7%	52.6%	47.0%	53.0%
11,700	MENARD	5,452	3,137	2,273	42	864 R	57.5%	41.7%	58.0%	42.0%
19,286	MERCER	9,023	4,441	4,521	61	80 D	49.2%	50.1%	49.6%	50.4%
20,117	MONROE	9,718	5,184	4,471	63	713 R	53.3%	46.0%	53.7%	46.3%
31,686	MONTGOMERY	15,137	7,313	7,674	150	361 D	48.3%	50.7%	48.8%	51.2%
37,502	MORGAN	16,779	7,450	9,186	143	1,736 D	44.4%	54.7%	44.8%	55.2%
14,546	MOULTRIE	6,051	3,065	2,941	45	124 R	50.7%	48.6%	51.0%	49.0%

ILLINOIS

SENATOR 1980

1980 Census Population	County	Total Vote	Republican	Democratic	Other	Rep.-Dem. Plurality	Percentage Total Vote Rep.	Dem.	Major Vote Rep.	Dem.
46,338	OGLE	18,507	11,057	7,245	205	3,812 R	59.7%	39.1%	60.4%	39.6%
200,466	PEORIA	82,768	40,593	40,915	1,260	322 D	49.0%	49.4%	49.8%	50.2%
21,714	PERRY	10,363	4,809	5,496	58	687 D	46.4%	53.0%	46.7%	53.3%
16,581	PIATT	7,713	4,163	3,481	69	682 R	54.0%	45.1%	54.5%	45.5%
18,896	PIKE	9,117	3,624	5,416	77	1,792 D	39.7%	59.4%	40.1%	59.9%
4,404	POPE	2,358	1,194	1,151	13	43 R	50.6%	48.8%	50.9%	49.1%
8,840	PULASKI	3,705	1,615	2,079	11	464 D	43.6%	56.1%	43.7%	56.3%
6,085	PUTNAM	3,354	1,652	1,662	40	10 D	49.3%	49.6%	49.8%	50.2%
35,566	RANDOLPH	15,382	7,252	8,022	108	770 D	47.1%	52.2%	47.5%	52.5%
17,587	RICHLAND	7,668	3,848	3,796	24	52 R	50.2%	49.5%	50.3%	49.7%
165,968	ROCK ISLAND	67,107	27,915	38,372	820	10,457 D	41.6%	57.2%	42.1%	57.9%
265,469	ST. CLAIR	98,417	40,176	57,615	626	17,439 D	40.8%	58.5%	41.1%	58.9%
27,360	SALINE	12,774	5,312	7,352	110	2,040 D	41.6%	57.6%	41.9%	58.1%
176,089	SANGAMON	84,644	40,780	42,718	1,146	1,938 D	48.2%	50.5%	48.8%	51.2%
8,365	SCHUYLER	4,392	2,161	2,199	32	38 D	49.2%	50.1%	49.6%	50.4%
6,142	SCOTT	2,962	1,374	1,564	24	190 D	46.4%	52.8%	46.8%	53.2%
23,923	SHELBY	10,705	5,478	5,148	79	330 R	51.2%	48.1%	51.6%	48.4%
7,389	STARK	3,309	1,923	1,338	48	585 R	58.1%	40.4%	59.0%	41.0%
49,536	STEPHENSON	20,012	9,973	9,782	257	191 R	49.8%	48.9%	50.5%	49.5%
132,078	TAZEWELL	55,847	30,471	24,589	787	5,882 R	54.6%	44.0%	55.3%	44.7%
16,851	UNION	8,175	3,177	4,912	86	1,735 D	38.9%	60.1%	39.3%	60.7%
95,222	VERMILION	38,885	19,763	18,761	361	1,002 R	50.8%	48.2%	51.3%	48.7%
13,713	WABASH	5,647	2,659	2,929	59	270 D	47.1%	51.9%	47.6%	52.4%
21,943	WARREN	8,834	5,018	3,675	141	1,343 R	56.8%	41.6%	57.7%	42.3%
15,472	WASHINGTON	7,608	4,844	2,740	24	2,104 R	63.7%	36.0%	63.9%	36.1%
18,059	WAYNE	9,145	4,795	4,286	64	509 R	52.4%	46.9%	52.8%	47.2%
17,864	WHITE	8,747	4,253	4,433	61	180 D	48.6%	50.7%	49.0%	51.0%
65,970	WHITESIDE	25,580	13,871	11,432	277	2,439 R	54.2%	44.7%	54.8%	45.2%
324,460	WILL	119,114	56,558	61,311	1,245	4,753 D	47.5%	51.5%	48.0%	52.0%
56,538	WILLIAMSON	23,886	10,987	12,690	209	1,703 D	46.0%	53.1%	46.4%	53.6%
250,884	WINNEBAGO	103,285	49,675	51,969	1,641	2,294 D	48.1%	50.3%	48.9%	51.1%
33,320	WOODFORD	15,059	9,434	5,434	191	4,000 R	62.6%	36.1%	63.5%	36.5%
11,418,461	TOTAL	4,580,029	1,946,296	2,565,302	68,431	619,006 D	42.5%	56.0%	43.1%	56.9%

CHICAGO

PRESIDENT 1980

1980 Census Population	Ward	Total Vote	Republican	Democratic	Other	Rep.-Dem. Plurality	Percentage Total Vote Rep.	Dem.	Major Vote Rep.	Dem.
66,600	WARD 1	16,932	3,132	12,932	868	9,800 D	18.5%	76.4%	19.5%	80.5%
60,205	WARD 2	18,704	895	17,084	725	16,189 D	4.8%	91.3%	5.0%	95.0%
44,854	WARD 3	14,379	405	13,622	352	13,217 D	2.8%	94.7%	2.9%	97.1%
48,284	WARD 4	17,691	1,093	15,733	865	14,640 D	6.2%	88.9%	6.5%	93.5%
56,683	WARD 5	22,466	2,507	17,380	2,579	14,873 D	11.2%	77.4%	12.6%	87.4%
56,615	WARD 6	22,958	710	21,874	374	21,164 D	3.1%	95.3%	3.1%	96.9%
69,521	WARD 7	19,228	1,962	16,492	774	14,530 D	10.2%	85.8%	10.6%	89.4%
65,959	WARD 8	27,490	860	26,051	579	25,191 D	3.1%	94.8%	3.2%	96.8%
71,328	WARD 9	22,116	1,287	20,249	580	18,962 D	5.8%	91.6%	6.0%	94.0%
63,753	WARD 10	27,928	8,237	18,262	1,429	10,025 D	29.5%	65.4%	31.1%	68.9%
56,662	WARD 11	26,855	5,497	20,379	979	14,882 D	20.5%	75.9%	21.2%	78.8%
58,703	WARD 12	26,708	10,170	14,782	1,756	4,612 D	38.1%	55.3%	40.8%	59.2%
60,350	WARD 13	34,627	15,507	16,916	2,204	1,409 D	44.8%	48.9%	47.8%	52.2%
63,942	WARD 14	21,193	5,498	14,500	1,195	9,002 D	25.9%	68.4%	27.5%	72.5%
72,255	WARD 15	24,832	4,815	19,031	986	14,216 D	19.4%	76.6%	20.2%	79.8%
48,067	WARD 16	16,056	405	15,176	475	14,771 D	2.5%	94.5%	2.6%	97.4%
52,922	WARD 17	18,718	489	17,884	345	17,395 D	2.6%	95.5%	2.7%	97.3%
61,409	WARD 18	30,728	9,604	19,698	1,426	10,094 D	31.3%	64.1%	32.8%	67.2%
59,786	WARD 19	34,365	15,441	16,109	2,815	668 D	44.9%	46.9%	48.9%	51.1%
49,498	WARD 20	17,301	546	16,331	424	15,785 D	3.2%	94.4%	3.2%	96.8%
61,554	WARD 21	28,248	739	27,017	492	26,278 D	2.6%	95.6%	2.7%	97.3%
74,008	WARD 22	14,575	2,986	10,974	615	7,988 D	20.5%	75.3%	21.4%	78.6%
58,775	WARD 23	31,932	14,034	15,690	2,208	1,656 D	43.9%	49.1%	47.2%	52.8%
40,995	WARD 24	13,247	396	12,536	315	12,140 D	3.0%	94.6%	3.1%	96.9%
57,211	WARD 25	13,469	2,098	10,880	491	8,782 D	15.6%	80.8%	16.2%	83.8%
55,457	WARD 26	15,832	3,802	11,338	692	7,536 D	24.0%	71.6%	25.1%	74.9%
45,339	WARD 27	14,656	765	13,508	383	12,743 D	5.2%	92.2%	5.4%	94.6%
52,376	WARD 28	14,709	433	13,783	493	13,350 D	2.9%	93.7%	3.0%	97.0%
55,548	WARD 29	15,514	716	14,354	444	13,638 D	4.6%	92.5%	4.8%	95.2%
68,049	WARD 30	22,089	7,190	13,425	1,474	6,235 D	32.6%	60.8%	34.9%	65.1%
61,022	WARD 31	17,481	2,864	13,992	625	11,128 D	16.4%	80.0%	17.0%	83.0%
54,718	WARD 32	17,389	3,921	12,247	1,221	8,326 D	22.5%	70.4%	24.3%	75.7%
63,151	WARD 33	18,955	5,526	12,021	1,408	6,495 D	29.2%	63.4%	31.5%	68.5%
68,395	WARD 34	27,006	732	25,756	518	25,024 D	2.7%	95.4%	2.8%	97.2%
61,652	WARD 35	24,010	9,921	12,102	1,987	2,181 D	41.3%	50.4%	45.0%	55.0%
63,924	WARD 36	32,678	14,123	16,272	2,283	2,149 D	43.2%	49.8%	46.5%	53.5%
77,394	WARD 37	20,456	2,444	17,320	692	14,876 D	11.9%	84.7%	12.4%	87.6%
57,925	WARD 38	32,463	15,243	14,787	2,433	456 R	47.0%	45.6%	50.8%	49.2%
63,059	WARD 39	24,724	10,744	11,631	2,349	887 D	43.5%	47.0%	48.0%	52.0%
63,383	WARD 40	24,475	9,710	12,214	2,551	2,504 D	39.7%	49.9%	44.3%	55.7%
67,056	WARD 41	38,787	20,284	15,248	3,255	5,036 R	52.3%	39.3%	57.1%	42.9%
63,325	WARD 42	29,667	10,891	15,565	3,211	4,674 D	36.7%	52.5%	41.2%	58.8%
61,955	WARD 43	33,063	12,270	15,279	5,514	3,009 D	37.1%	46.2%	44.5%	55.5%
54,776	WARD 44	24,404	7,259	13,554	3,591	6,295 D	29.7%	55.5%	34.9%	65.1%
60,706	WARD 45	33,511	16,210	14,561	2,740	1,649 R	48.4%	43.5%	52.7%	47.3%
56,627	WARD 46	20,402	5,863	12,238	2,301	6,375 D	28.7%	60.0%	32.4%	67.6%
60,969	WARD 47	25,198	8,872	14,068	2,258	5,196 D	35.2%	55.8%	38.7%	61.3%
63,060	WARD 48	21,898	7,126	12,499	2,273	5,373 D	32.5%	57.1%	36.3%	63.7%
61,769	WARD 49	23,355	6,761	12,972	3,622	6,211 D	28.9%	55.5%	34.3%	65.7%
62,308	WARD 50	30,420	9,990	16,781	3,649	6,791 D	32.8%	55.2%	37.3%	62.7%
	SPECIAL BALLOTS	282	68	165	49	97 D	24.1%	58.5%	29.2%	70.8%
3,005,072	TOTAL	1,166,170	303,041	785,262	77,867	482,221 D	26.0%	67.3%	27.8%	72.2%

CHICAGO

SENATOR 1980

1980 Census Population	Ward	Total Vote	Republican	Democratic	Other	Rep.-Dem. Plurality	Percentage Total Vote Rep.	Dem.	Major Vote Rep.	Dem.
66,600	WARD 1	15,774	2,425	13,088	261	10,663 D	15.4%	83.0%	15.6%	84.4%
60,205	WARD 2	16,295	895	14,989	411	14,094 D	5.5%	92.0%	5.6%	94.4%
44,854	WARD 3	12,833	459	12,089	285	11,630 D	3.6%	94.2%	3.7%	96.3%
48,284	WARD 4	15,855	1,013	14,395	447	13,382 D	6.4%	90.8%	6.6%	93.4%
56,683	WARD 5	20,276	2,271	16,734	1,271	14,463 D	11.2%	82.5%	11.9%	88.1%
56,615	WARD 6	21,842	1,132	20,399	311	19,267 D	5.2%	93.4%	5.3%	94.7%
69,521	WARD 7	17,363	1,738	15,196	429	13,458 D	10.0%	87.5%	10.3%	89.7%
65,959	WARD 8	25,621	1,229	24,060	332	22,831 D	4.8%	93.9%	4.9%	95.1%
71,328	WARD 9	18,748	1,267	17,123	358	15,856 D	6.8%	91.3%	6.9%	93.1%
63,753	WARD 10	24,875	5,633	18,884	358	13,251 D	22.6%	75.9%	23.0%	77.0%
56,662	WARD 11	24,470	3,006	21,281	183	18,275 D	12.3%	87.0%	12.4%	87.6%
58,703	WARD 12	23,630	6,728	16,543	359	9,815 D	28.5%	70.0%	28.9%	71.1%
60,350	WARD 13	31,744	10,328	21,132	284	10,804 D	32.5%	66.6%	32.8%	67.2%
63,942	WARD 14	18,740	3,820	14,679	241	10,859 D	20.4%	78.3%	20.6%	79.4%
72,255	WARD 15	22,794	3,637	18,806	351	15,169 D	16.0%	82.5%	16.2%	83.8%
48,067	WARD 16	13,858	497	13,005	356	12,508 D	3.6%	93.8%	3.7%	96.3%
52,922	WARD 17	16,461	845	15,325	291	14,480 D	5.1%	93.1%	5.2%	94.8%
61,409	WARD 18	28,599	6,590	21,702	307	15,112 D	23.0%	75.9%	23.3%	76.7%
59,786	WARD 19	31,804	10,357	21,016	431	10,659 D	32.6%	66.1%	33.0%	67.0%
49,498	WARD 20	15,778	648	14,836	294	14,188 D	4.1%	94.0%	4.2%	95.8%
61,554	WARD 21	26,965	1,314	25,302	349	23,988 D	4.9%	93.8%	4.9%	95.1%
74,008	WARD 22	13,214	2,191	10,779	244	8,588 D	16.6%	81.6%	16.9%	83.1%
58,775	WARD 23	28,843	9,331	19,156	356	9,825 D	32.4%	66.4%	32.8%	67.2%
40,995	WARD 24	11,873	437	11,193	243	10,756 D	3.7%	94.3%	3.8%	96.2%
57,211	WARD 25	12,670	1,618	10,898	154	9,280 D	12.8%	86.0%	12.9%	87.1%
55,457	WARD 26	14,089	2,644	11,196	249	8,552 D	18.8%	79.5%	19.1%	80.9%
45,339	WARD 27	13,408	688	12,474	246	11,786 D	5.1%	93.0%	5.2%	94.8%
52,376	WARD 28	12,836	486	11,979	371	11,493 D	3.8%	93.3%	3.9%	96.1%
55,548	WARD 29	13,954	646	12,974	334	12,328 D	4.6%	93.0%	4.7%	95.3%
68,049	WARD 30	19,908	5,101	14,462	345	9,361 D	25.6%	72.6%	26.1%	73.9%
61,022	WARD 31	16,040	2,089	13,691	260	11,602 D	13.0%	85.4%	13.2%	86.8%
54,718	WARD 32	15,951	3,055	12,515	381	9,460 D	19.2%	78.5%	19.6%	80.4%
63,151	WARD 33	16,994	4,234	12,350	410	8,116 D	24.9%	72.7%	25.5%	74.5%
68,395	WARD 34	24,181	981	22,804	396	21,823 D	4.1%	94.3%	4.1%	95.9%
61,652	WARD 35	21,562	7,671	13,547	344	5,876 D	35.6%	62.8%	36.2%	63.8%
63,924	WARD 36	29,228	9,913	18,912	403	8,999 D	33.9%	64.7%	34.4%	65.6%
77,394	WARD 37	19,175	1,976	16,888	311	14,912 D	10.3%	88.1%	10.5%	89.5%
57,925	WARD 38	29,247	10,968	17,966	313	6,998 D	37.5%	61.4%	37.9%	62.1%
63,059	WARD 39	22,694	7,973	14,325	396	6,352 D	35.1%	63.1%	35.8%	64.2%
63,383	WARD 40	22,607	7,231	14,921	455	7,690 D	32.0%	66.0%	32.6%	67.4%
67,056	WARD 41	35,350	14,658	20,267	425	5,609 D	41.5%	57.3%	42.0%	58.0%
63,325	WARD 42	27,345	8,218	18,555	572	10,337 D	30.1%	67.9%	30.7%	69.3%
61,955	WARD 43	30,299	9,325	19,868	1,106	10,543 D	30.8%	65.6%	31.9%	68.1%
54,776	WARD 44	22,182	5,471	15,758	953	10,287 D	24.7%	71.0%	25.8%	74.2%
60,706	WARD 45	31,121	11,929	18,843	349	6,914 D	38.3%	60.5%	38.8%	61.2%
56,627	WARD 46	18,030	4,480	12,823	727	8,343 D	24.8%	71.1%	25.9%	74.1%
60,969	WARD 47	23,192	7,042	15,630	520	8,588 D	30.4%	67.4%	31.1%	68.9%
63,060	WARD 48	19,828	5,684	13,558	586	7,874 D	28.7%	68.4%	29.5%	70.5%
61,769	WARD 49	21,494	5,432	15,079	983	9,647 D	25.3%	70.2%	26.5%	73.5%
62,308	WARD 50	27,647	6,438	20,585	624	14,147 D	23.3%	74.5%	23.8%	76.2%
	SPECIAL BALLOTS	267	62	196	9	134 D	23.2%	73.4%	24.0%	76.0%
3,005,072	TOTAL	1,059,554	223,804	814,776	20,974	590,972 D	21.1%	76.9%	21.5%	78.5%

ILLINOIS

CONGRESS

CD	Year	Total Vote	Republican Vote	Candidate	Democratic Vote	Candidate	Other Vote	Rep.-Dem. Plurality	Total Vote Rep.	Total Vote Dem.	Major Vote Rep.	Major Vote Dem.
1	1980	125,223	5,660	WILLIAMS, GEORGE	119,562	WASHINGTON, HAROLD	1	113,902 D	4.5%	95.5%	4.5%	95.5%
1	1978	81,279	33,540	RAYNER, A. A.	47,581	STEWART, BENNETT M.	158	14,041 D	41.3%	58.5%	41.3%	58.7%
1	1976	137,193	10,147	RAYNER, A. A.	126,632	METCALFE, RALPH H.	414	116,485 D	7.4%	92.3%	7.4%	92.6%
1	1974	80,225	4,399	HAYNES, OSCAR H.	75,206	METCALFE, RALPH H.	620	70,807 D	5.5%	93.7%	5.5%	94.5%
1	1972	149,634	12,877	COGGS, LOUIS	136,755	METCALFE, RALPH H.	2	123,878 D	8.6%	91.4%	8.6%	91.4%
2	1980	147,302	17,428	HARRIS, MARSHA A.	129,771	SAVAGE, GUS	103	112,343 D	11.8%	88.1%	11.8%	88.2%
2	1978	94,077	11,104	WOGNUM, JAMES P.	80,906	MURPHY, MORGAN F.	2,067	69,802 D	11.8%	86.0%	12.1%	87.9%
2	1976	150,335	23,037	LEAK, SPENCER	127,297	MURPHY, MORGAN F.	1	104,260 D	15.3%	84.7%	15.3%	84.7%
2	1974	75,198	9,386	GINDERSKE, JAMES J.	65,812	MURPHY, MORGAN F.		56,426 D	12.5%	87.5%	12.5%	87.5%
2	1972	153,698	38,391	DOYLE, JAMES E.	115,306	MURPHY, MORGAN F.	1	76,915 D	25.0%	75.0%	25.0%	75.0%
3	1980	199,240	61,955	SARSOUN, LAWRENCE C.	137,283	RUSSO, MARTIN A.	2	75,328 D	31.1%	68.9%	31.1%	68.9%
3	1978	146,800	51,098	DUNNE, ROBERT L.	95,701	RUSSO, MARTIN A.	1	44,603 D	34.8%	65.2%	34.8%	65.2%
3	1976	196,365	79,434	BUIKEMA, RONALD	115,591	RUSSO, MARTIN A.	1,340	36,157 D	40.5%	58.9%	40.7%	59.3%
3	1974	124,227	58,891	HANRAHAN, ROBERT	65,336	RUSSO, MARTIN A.		6,445 D	47.4%	52.6%	47.4%	52.6%
3	1972	206,147	128,329	HANRAHAN, ROBERT	77,814	COMAN, DANIEL P.	4	50,515 R	62.3%	37.7%	62.3%	37.7%
4	1980	224,192	152,377	DERWINSKI, EDWARD J.	71,814	JALOVEC, RICHARD S.	1	80,563 R	68.0%	32.0%	68.0%	32.0%
4	1978	141,229	94,435	DERWINSKI, EDWARD J.	46,788	THOMAS, ANDREW D.	6	47,647 R	66.9%	33.1%	66.9%	33.1%
4	1976	189,772	124,847	DERWINSKI, EDWARD J.	64,924	RODGER, RONALD A.	1	59,923 R	65.8%	34.2%	65.8%	34.2%
4	1974	115,524	68,428	DERWINSKI, EDWARD J.	47,096	RODGER, RONALD A.		21,332 R	59.2%	40.8%	59.2%	40.8%
4	1972	200,463	141,402	DERWINSKI, EDWARD J.	59,057	DORE, C. F.	4	82,345 R	70.5%	29.5%	70.5%	29.5%
5	1980	133,279	27,136	KOTOWSKI, ROBERT V.	106,142	FARY, JOHN G.	1	79,006 D	20.4%	79.6%	20.4%	79.6%
5	1978	117,506	18,802	BARRACCA, JOSEPH A.	98,702	FARY, JOHN G.	2	79,900 D	16.0%	84.0%	16.0%	84.0%
5	1976	155,092	35,756	KROK, VINCENT S.	119,336	FARY, JOHN G.		83,580 D	23.1%	76.9%	23.1%	76.9%
5	1974	108,177	15,108	TOMS, WILLIAM	93,069	KLUCZYNSKI, JOHN C.		77,961 D	14.0%	86.0%	14.0%	86.0%
5	1972	166,544	45,264	JARZAB, LEONARD C.	121,278	KLUCZYNSKI, JOHN C.	2	76,014 D	27.2%	72.8%	27.2%	72.8%
6	1980	184,550	123,593	HYDE, HENRY J.	60,951	REDA, MARIO R.	6	62,642 R	67.0%	33.0%	67.0%	33.0%
6	1978	131,737	87,193	HYDE, HENRY J.	44,543	QUINN, JEANNE P.	1	42,650 R	66.2%	33.8%	66.2%	33.8%
6	1976	176,027	106,667	HYDE, HENRY J.	69,359	CLANCY, MARILYN D.	1	37,308 R	60.6%	39.4%	60.6%	39.4%
6	1974	123,681	66,027	HYDE, HENRY J.	57,654	HANRAHAN, EDWARD V.		8,373 R	53.4%	46.6%	53.4%	46.6%
6	1972	203,501	124,486	COLLIER, HAROLD R.	79,002	GALASSO, MICHAEL R.	13	45,484 R	61.2%	38.8%	61.2%	38.8%
7	1980	94,097	14,041	HOOPER, RUTH	80,056	COLLINS, CARDISS		66,015 D	14.9%	85.1%	14.9%	85.1%
7	1978	74,989	10,273	HOLT, JAMES C.	64,716	COLLINS, CARDISS		54,443 D	13.7%	86.3%	13.7%	86.3%
7	1976	104,094	15,854	WARD, NEWELL	88,239	COLLINS, CARDISS	1	72,385 D	15.2%	84.8%	15.2%	84.8%
7	1974	72,762	8,800	METZGER, DONALD L.	63,962	COLLINS, CARDISS		55,162 D	12.1%	87.9%	12.1%	87.9%
7	1972	114,778	19,758	LENTO, THOMAS J.	95,018	COLLINS, GEORGE W.	2	75,260 D	17.2%	82.8%	17.2%	82.8%
8	1980	116,373	17,845	ZILKE, WALTER F.	98,524	ROSTENKOWSKI, DANIEL	4	80,679 D	15.3%	84.7%	15.3%	84.7%
8	1978	94,762	13,302	LODICO, CARL C.	81,457	ROSTENKOWSKI, DANIEL	3	68,155 D	14.0%	86.0%	14.0%	86.0%
8	1976	131,107	25,512	URBASZEWSKI, JOHN F.	105,595	ROSTENKOWSKI, DANIEL		80,083 D	19.5%	80.5%	19.5%	80.5%
8	1974	86,675	11,664	ODDO, SALVATORE E.	75,011	ROSTENKOWSKI, DANIEL		63,347 D	13.5%	86.5%	13.5%	86.5%
8	1972	149,219	38,758	STEPNOWSKI, EDWARD L.	110,457	ROSTENKOWSKI, DANIEL	4	71,699 D	26.0%	74.0%	26.0%	74.0%
9	1980	145,788	39,244	ANDRICA, JOHN D.	106,543	YATES, SIDNEY R.	1	67,299 D	26.9%	73.1%	26.9%	73.1%
9	1978	116,217	28,673	COLLINS, JOHN M.	87,543	YATES, SIDNEY R.	1	58,870 D	24.7%	75.3%	24.7%	75.3%
9	1976	168,983	47,054	WAJERSKI, THOMAS J.	121,915	YATES, SIDNEY R.	14	74,861 D	27.8%	72.1%	27.8%	72.2%
9	1974	93,864			93,864	YATES, SIDNEY R.		93,864 D		100.0%		100.0%
9	1972	192,862	61,083	FETRIDGE, CLARK W.	131,777	YATES, SIDNEY R.	2	70,694 D	31.7%	68.3%	31.7%	68.3%
10	1980	226,733	137,707	PORTER, JOHN E.	89,008	WEINBERGER, ROBERT A.	18	48,699 R	60.7%	39.3%	60.7%	39.3%
10	1978	178,309	88,829	PORTER, JOHN E.	89,479	MIKVA, ABNER J.	1	650 D	49.8%	50.2%	49.8%	50.2%
10	1976	213,414	106,603	YOUNG, SAMUEL H.	106,804	MIKVA, ABNER J.	7	201 D	50.0%	50.0%	50.0%	50.0%
10	1974	164,054	80,597	YOUNG, SAMUEL H.	83,457	MIKVA, ABNER J.		2,860 D	49.1%	50.9%	49.1%	50.9%
10	1972	233,929	120,681	YOUNG, SAMUEL H.	113,222	MIKVA, ABNER J.	26	7,459 R	51.6%	48.4%	51.6%	48.4%
11	1980	173,587	52,417	ZANILLO, MICHAEL R.	121,166	ANNUNZIO, FRANK	4	68,749 D	30.2%	69.8%	30.2%	69.8%
11	1978	152,412	40,044	HOEGER, JOHN	112,365	ANNUNZIO, FRANK	3	72,321 D	26.3%	73.7%	26.3%	73.7%
11	1976	201,440	65,680	REBER, DANIEL C.	135,755	ANNUNZIO, FRANK	5	70,075 D	32.6%	67.4%	32.6%	67.4%
11	1974	141,723	39,182	ZADROZNY, MITCHELL G.	102,541	ANNUNZIO, FRANK		63,359 D	27.6%	72.4%	27.6%	72.4%
11	1972	222,415	103,773	HOELLEN, JOHN J.	118,637	ANNUNZIO, FRANK	5	14,864 D	46.7%	53.3%	46.7%	53.3%
12	1980	249,818	185,080	CRANE, PHILIP M.	64,729	MCCARTNEY, DAVID	9	120,351 R	74.1%	25.9%	74.1%	25.9%
12	1978	138,935	110,503	CRANE, PHILIP M.	28,424	BOGEN, GILBERT	8	82,079 R	79.5%	20.5%	79.5%	20.5%
12	1976	208,553	151,899	CRANE, PHILIP M.	56,644	FRANK, EDWIN L.	10	95,255 R	72.8%	27.2%	72.8%	27.2%
12	1974	115,780	70,731	CRANE, PHILIP M.	45,049	SPENCE, BETTY C.		25,682 R	61.1%	38.9%	61.1%	38.9%
12	1972	206,000	152,938	CRANE, PHILIP M.	53,055	FRANK, EDWIN L.	7	99,883 R	74.2%	25.8%	74.2%	25.8%

ILLINOIS

CONGRESS

CD	Year	Total Vote	Republican Vote	Republican Candidate	Democratic Vote	Democratic Candidate	Other Vote	Rep.-Dem. Plurality	Total Vote Rep.	Total Vote Dem.	Major Vote Rep.	Major Vote Dem.
13	1980	183,458	131,448	MCCLORY, ROBERT	52,000	REESE, MICHAEL	10	79,448 R	71.7%	28.3%	71.7%	28.3%
13	1978	104,738	64,060	MCCLORY, ROBERT	40,675	STEFFEN, FREDERICK J.	3	23,385 R	61.2%	38.8%	61.2%	38.8%
12	1976	164,266	109,726	MCCLORY, ROBERT	49,777	CUMMINGS, JAMES J.	4,763	59,949 R	66.8%	30.3%	68.8%	31.2%
13	1974	94,313	51,405	MCCLORY, ROBERT	42,903	BEETHAM, STANLEY W.	5	8,502 R	54.5%	45.5%	54.5%	45.5%
13	1972	159,738	98,201	MCCLORY, ROBERT	61,537	BEETHAM, STANLEY W.		36,664 R	61.5%	38.5%	61.5%	38.5%
14	1980	263,828	202,583	ERLENBORN, JOHN N.	61,224	KENNEL, LEROY E.	21	141,359 R	76.8%	23.2%	76.8%	23.2%
14	1978	158,179	118,741	ERLENBORN, JOHN N.	39,438	ROMANYAK, JAMES A.		79,303 R	75.1%	24.9%	75.1%	24.9%
14	1976	236,588	176,076	ERLENBORN, JOHN N.	60,505	FESE, MARIE A.	7	115,571 R	74.4%	25.6%	74.4%	25.6%
14	1974	116,699	77,718	ERLENBORN, JOHN N.	38,981	RENSHAW, ROBERT H.		38,737 R	66.6%	33.4%	66.6%	33.4%
14	1972	212,668	154,794	ERLENBORN, JOHN N.	57,874	WALL, JAMES M.		96,920 R	72.8%	27.2%	72.8%	27.2%
15	1980	196,619	150,898	CORCORAN, TOM	45,721	QUILLIN, JOHN P.		105,177 R	76.7%	23.3%	76.7%	23.3%
15	1978	129,612	80,856	CORCORAN, TOM	48,756	HALL, TIM L.		32,100 R	62.4%	37.6%	62.4%	37.6%
15	1976	190,231	102,555	CORCORAN, TOM	87,676	HALL, TIM L.		14,879 R	53.9%	46.1%	53.9%	46.1%
15	1974	119,007	54,278	CARLSON, CLIFFARD D.	61,912	HALL, TIM L.	2,817	7,634 D	45.6%	52.0%	46.7%	53.3%
15	1972	193,950	111,022	ARENDS, LESLIE C.	82,925	HALL, TIM L.	3	28,097 R	57.2%	42.8%	57.2%	42.8%
16	1980	197,147	132,905	MARTIN, LYNN	64,224	AURAND, DOUGLAS R.	18	68,681 R	67.4%	32.6%	67.4%	32.6%
16	1978	117,309	76,752	ANDERSON, JOHN B.	40,471	DAHLIN, ERNEST W.	86	36,281 R	65.4%	34.5%	65.5%	34.5%
16	1976	168,328	114,324	ANDERSON, JOHN B.	54,002	EYTALIS, STEPHEN	2	60,322 R	67.9%	32.1%	67.9%	32.1%
16	1974	117,481	65,175	ANDERSON, JOHN B.	33,724	HUNGNESS, MARSHALL	18,582	31,451 R	55.5%	28.7%	65.9%	34.1%
16	1972	180,291	129,640	ANDERSON, JOHN B.	50,649	DEVINE, JOHN E.	2	78,991 R	71.9%	28.1%	71.9%	28.1%
17	1980	191,111	125,806	O'BRIEN, GEORGE M.	65,305	MURER, MICHAEL A		60,501 R	65.8%	34.2%	65.8%	34.2%
17	1978	133,635	94,375	O'BRIEN, GEORGE M.	39,260	SINCLAIR, CLIFFORD J.		55,115 R	70.6%	29.4%	70.6%	29.4%
17	1976	194,365	113,145	O'BRIEN, GEORGE M.	81,220	KARLOCK, MERLIN		31,925 R	58.2%	41.8%	58.2%	41.8%
17	1974	116,525	59,984	O'BRIEN, GEORGE M.	56,541	HOULIHAN, JOHN J.		3,443 R	51.5%	48.5%	51.5%	48.5%
17	1972	180,016	100,175	O'BRIEN, GEORGE M.	79,840	HOULIHAN, JOHN J.	1	20,335 R	55.6%	44.4%	55.6%	44.4%
18	1980	202,043	125,561	MICHEL, ROBERT H.	76,471	KNUPPEL, JOHN L.	11	49,090 R	62.1%	37.8%	62.1%	37.9%
18	1978	130,514	85,973	MICHEL, ROBERT H.	44,527	GRUNKEMEYER, VIRGIL R.	14	41,446 R	65.9%	34.1%	65.9%	34.1%
18	1976	187,130	108,028	MICHEL, ROBERT H.	79,102	RYAN, MATTHEW		28,926 R	57.7%	42.3%	57.7%	42.3%
18	1974	130,906	71,681	MICHEL, ROBERT H.	59,225	NORDVALL, STEPHEN L.		12,456 R	54.8%	45.2%	54.8%	45.2%
18	1972	191,921	124,407	MICHEL, ROBERT H.	67,514	NORDVALL, STEPHEN L.		56,893 R	64.8%	35.2%	64.8%	35.2%
19	1980	194,369	142,616	RAILSBACK, TOM	51,753	HAND, THOMAS J.		90,863 R	73.4%	26.6%	73.4%	26.6%
19	1978	89,790	89,770	RAILSBACK, TOM			20	89,770 R	100.0%		100.0%	
19	1976	193,539	132,571	RAILSBACK, TOM	60,967	CRAVER, JOHN	1	71,604 R	68.5%	31.5%	68.5%	31.5%
19	1974	128,728	84,049	RAILSBACK, TOM	44,677	GENDE, JIM	2	39,372 R	65.3%	34.7%	65.3%	34.7%
19	1972	138,123	138,123	RAILSBACK, TOM				138,123 R	100.0%		100.0%	
20	1980	220,377	123,427	FINDLEY, PAUL	96,950	ROBINSON, DAVID		26,477 R	56.0%	44.0%	56.0%	44.0%
20	1978	159,480	111,054	FINDLEY, PAUL	48,426	ROBERTS, VIC		62,628 R	69.6%	30.4%	69.6%	30.4%
20	1976	215,857	137,223	FINDLEY, PAUL	78,634	MACK, PETER F.		58,589 R	63.6%	36.4%	63.6%	36.4%
20	1974	153,987	84,426	FINDLEY, PAUL	69,551	MACK, PETER F.	10	14,875 R	54.8%	45.2%	54.8%	45.2%
20	1972	215,868	148,419	FINDLEY, PAUL	67,445	O'SHEA, ROBERT S.	4	80,974 R	68.8%	31.2%	68.8%	31.2%
21	1980	195,662	132,186	MADIGAN, EDWARD R.	63,476	SEVERNS, PENNY L.		68,710 R	67.6%	32.4%	67.6%	32.4%
21	1978	124,527	97,473	MADIGAN, EDWARD R.	27,054	BAUGHMAN, KEN		70,419 R	78.3%	21.7%	78.3%	21.7%
21	1976	184,035	137,037	MADIGAN, EDWARD R.	46,996	SCOTT, ANNA W.	2	90,041 R	74.5%	25.5%	74.5%	25.5%
21	1974	119,536	78,640	MADIGAN, EDWARD R.	40,896	SMALL, RICHARD N.		37,744 R	65.8%	34.2%	65.8%	34.2%
21	1972	182,496	99,966	MADIGAN, EDWARD R.	82,523	JOHNSON, LAWRENCE E.	7	17,443 R	54.8%	45.2%	54.8%	45.2%
22	1980	212,079	146,014	CRANE, DANIEL B.	66,065	VOELZ, PETER M.		79,949 R	68.8%	31.2%	68.8%	31.2%
22	1978	159,383	86,051	CRANE, DANIEL B.	73,331	BRUCE, TERRY L.	1	12,720 R	54.0%	46.0%	54.0%	46.0%
22	1976	210,289	81,102	MCGINNIS, RALPH Y.	129,187	SHIPLEY, GEORGE E.		48,085 D	38.6%	61.4%	38.6%	61.4%
22	1974	163,652	65,731	YOUNG, WILLIAM A.	97,921	SHIPLEY, GEORGE E.		32,190 D	40.2%	59.8%	40.2%	59.8%
22	1972	220,368	90,390	LAMKIN, ROBERT B.	124,589	SHIPLEY, GEORGE E.	5,389	34,199 D	41.0%	56.5%	42.0%	58.0%
23	1980	167,430	59,644	DAVINROY, RONALD L.	107,786	PRICE, MELVIN		48,142 D	35.6%	64.4%	35.6%	64.4%
23	1978	100,105	25,858	STACK, DANIEL J.	74,247	PRICE, MELVIN		48,389 D	25.8%	74.2%	25.8%	74.2%
23	1976	162,938	34,825	DRENOVAC, SAM P.	128,113	PRICE, MELVIN		93,288 D	21.4%	78.6%	21.4%	78.6%
23	1974	97,334	18,987	RANDOLPH, SCOTT R.	78,347	PRICE, MELVIN		59,360 D	19.5%	80.5%	19.5%	80.5%
23	1972	162,116	40,428	MAYS, ROBERT	121,682	PRICE, MELVIN	6	81,254 D	24.9%	75.1%	24.9%	75.1%
24	1980	228,296	110,176	ANDERSON, JOHN T.	112,134	SIMON, PAUL	5,986	1,958 D	48.3%	49.1%	49.6%	50.4%
24	1978	168,061	57,763	ANDERSON, JOHN T.	110,298	SIMON, PAUL		52,535 D	34.4%	65.6%	34.4%	65.6%
24	1976	226,110	73,766	PRINEAS, PETER G.	152,344	SIMON PAUL		78,578 D	32.6%	67.4%	32.6%	67.4%
24	1974	182,051	73,634	OSHEL, VAL	108,417	SIMON, PAUL		34,783 D	40.4%	59.6%	40.4%	59.6%
24	1972	148,278			138,867	GRAY, KENNETH J.	9,411	138,867 D		93.7%		100.0%

ILLINOIS

1980 GENERAL ELECTION

President   Other vote was 346,754 Anderson (Independent); 38,939 Clark (Libertarian); 10,692 Commoner (Citizens); 9,711 Hall (Communist); 2,257 Griswold (Workers World); 1,302 DeBerry (Socialist Workers); 604 scattered.

Senator   Other vote was 29,328 Green (Libertarian); 19,213 Lens (Citizens); 11,453 Wilson (Communist); 5,626 Soriano (Workers World); 2,715 Artz (Socialist Workers); 96 scattered.

Congress   Other vote was 5,985 Barrett (Constitution) and 1 scattered in CD 24; scattered in all other CD's.

CHICAGO

Population figures are unofficial hand tallies done in the Chicago regional office of the Census Bureau and do not represent final, official tabulations.

President   Other vote was 58,413 Anderson (Independent); 6,884 Hall (Communist); 6,598 Clark (Libertarian); 3,730 Commoner (Citizens); 1,629 Griswold (Workers World); 613 DeBerry (Socialist Workers). Special Ballots were absentee votes arriving too late to be counted in individual precincts and therefore tallied centrally by the Board of Election Commissioners.

Senator   Other vote was 6,819 Wilson (Communist); 6,190 Lens (Citizens); 4,702 Green (Libertarian); 2,299 Soriano (Workers World); 964 Artz (Socialist Workers). See note above on Special Ballots.

1980 PRIMARIES

MARCH 18 REPUBLICAN

Senator   424,634 David C. O'Neal; 352,138 William J. Scott; 245,668 Richard E. Carver; 141 scattered.

Congress   Unopposed in fifteen CD's. Contested as follows:

CD 1   No candidates appeared on the ballot; there were 3 write-in votes for George Williams and 4 scattered.
CD 4   40,593 Edward J. Derwinski; 8,118 Joseph P. Savard; 1 scattered.
CD 5   2,471 Robert V. Kotowski; 1,651 Walter F. Brenart.
CD 7   No candidates appeared on the ballot; there were 6 write-in votes for Ruth Hooper.
CD 13   40,335 Robert McClory; 26,668 Cal Skinner; 6 scattered.
CD 14   73,801 John N. Erlenborn; 16,938 William P. Grossklas; 2 scattered.
CD 16   36,291 Lynn Martin; 20,643 Don Lyon; 9,493 Dick Crosby; 9,294 Steve Anderson; 4,975 William E. Sisler; 1 scattered.
CD 20   31,894 Paul Findley; 25,499 David Nuessen; 1 scattered.
CD 23   9,789 Ronald L. Davinroy; 8,870 Phil Montalvo; 1 scattered.

MARCH 18 DEMOCRATIC

Senator   671,746 Alan J. Dixon; 190,339 Alex Seith; 64,037 Robert A. Wallace; 39,711 Anthony R. Martin-Trigona; 38,388 Dakin Williams; 153 scattered.

Congress   Unopposed in ten CD's. Contested as follows:

CD 1   30,522 Harold Washington; 12,356 Ralph H. Metcalfe, Jr.; 10,810 Bennett M. Stewart; 10,284 John H. Stroger; 11 scattered.
CD 2   28,359 Gus Savage; 21,243 Reginald V. Brown; 8,709 Bob Unger; 5,284 Leon Davis; 2 scattered.
CD 5   51,281 John G. Fary; 19,510 Melanie Kluczynski; 38 scattered.
CD 7   29,420 Cardiss Collins; 8,306 Mary R. Turner; 1 scattered.
CD 8   43,081 Daniel Rostenkowski; 5,286 Willie May; 1 scattered.

ILLINOIS

CD 9   44,341 Sidney R. Yates; 6,608 Sam S. Fried; 14 scattered.

CD 10   26,046 Robert A. Weinberger; 6,076 Thomas W. Flynn; 3,877 Marshall J. Hartman; 8 scattered.

CD 13   9,720 Michael Reese; 4,467 Edward J. LaFlamme; 2 scattered.

CD 16   9,595 Douglas R. Aurand; 7,221 Conn B. Hickey; 4,619 Robert E. Brinkmeier; 2 scattered.

CD 18   No candidates appeared on the ballot; there were 181 write-in votes for John L. Knuppel and 62 scattered.

CD 20   37,105 David Robinson; 4,903 Gregory Harutunian.

CD 22   No candidates appeared on the ballot; there were 1,200 write-in votes for Peter M. Voelz and 31 scattered.

CD 23   39,193 Melvin Price; 4,555 Vic Darnell; 1,889 Sam P. Drenovac; 1 scattered.

CD 24   38,005 Paul Simon; 14,183 Edwin Arentsen; 1 scattered.

INDIANA

GOVERNOR
Robert D. Orr (R). Elected 1980 to a four-year term.

SENATORS
Richard G. Lugar (R). Elected 1976 to a six-year term.

J. Danforth Quayle (R). Elected 1980 to a six-year term.

REPRESENTATIVES
1. Adam Benjamin (D)
2. Floyd Fithian (D)
3. John P. Hiler (R)
4. Daniel R. Coats (R)
5. Elwood H. Hillis (R)
6. David W. Evans (D)
7. John T. Myers (R)
8. H. Joel Deckard (R)
9. Lee H. Hamilton (D)
10. Philip R. Sharp (D)
11. Andrew Jacobs, Jr. (D)

POSTWAR VOTE FOR GOVERNOR

| | | | | | | | | | Percentage | | | |
| | Total | Republican | | Democratic | | Other | Rep.-Dem. | Total Vote | | Major Vote | |
Year	Vote	Vote	Candidate	Vote	Candidate	Vote	Plurality	Rep.	Dem.	Rep.	Dem.
1980	2,178,403	1,257,383	Orr, Robert D.	913,116	Hillenbrand, John A.	7,904	344,267 R	57.7%	41.9%	57.9%	42.1%
1976	2,175,324	1,236,555	Bowen, Otis R.	927,243	Conrad, Larry A.	11,526	309,312 R	56.8%	42.6%	57.1%	42.9%
1972	2,120,847	1,203,903	Bowen, Otis R.	900,489	Welsh, Matthew E.	16,455	303,414 R	56.8%	42.5%	57.2%	42.8%
1968	2,049,072	1,080,271	Whitcomb, Edgar D.	965,816	Rock, Robert L.	2,985	114,455 R	52.7%	47.1%	52.8%	47.2%
1964	2,072,915	901,342	Ristine, Richard O.	1,164,620	Branigin, Roger D.	6,953	263,278 D	43.5%	56.2%	43.6%	56.4%
1960	2,128,965	1,049,540	Parker, Crawford F.	1,072,717	Welsh, Matthew E.	6,708	23,177 D	49.3%	50.4%	49.5%	50.5%
1956	1,954,290	1,086,868	Handley, Harold W.	859,393	Tucker, Ralph	8,029	227,475 R	55.6%	44.0%	55.8%	44.2%
1952	1,931,869	1,075,685	Craig, George N.	841,984	Watkins, John A.	14,200	233,701 R	55.7%	43.6%	56.1%	43.9%
1948	1,652,321	745,892	Creighton, Hobart	884,995	Schricker, Henry F.	21,434	139,103 D	45.1%	53.6%	45.7%	54.3%

POSTWAR VOTE FOR SENATOR

| | | | | | | | | | Percentage | | | |
| | Total | Republican | | Democratic | | Other | Rep.-Dem. | Total Vote | | Major Vote | |
Year	Vote	Vote	Candidate	Vote	Candidate	Vote	Plurality	Rep.	Dem.	Rep.	Dem.
1980	2,198,376	1,182,414	Quayle, J. Danforth	1,015,962	Bayh, Birch	—	166,452 R	53.8%	46.2%	53.8%	46.2%
1976	2,171,187	1,275,833	Lugar, Richard G.	878,522	Hartke, R. Vance	16,832	397,311 R	58.8%	40.5%	59.2%	40.8%
1974	1,752,978	814,117	Lugar, Richard G.	889,269	Bayh, Birch	49,592	75,152 D	46.4%	50.7%	47.8%	52.2%
1970	1,737,697	866,707	Roudebush, Richard	870,990	Hartke, R. Vance	—	4,283 D	49.9%	50.1%	49.9%	50.1%
1968	2,053,118	988,571	Ruckelshaus, William	1,060,456	Bayh, Birch	4,091	71,885 D	48.1%	51.7%	48.2%	51.8%
1964	2,076,963	941,519	Bontrager, D. Russell	1,128,505	Hartke, R. Vance	6,939	186,986 D	45.3%	54.3%	45.5%	54.5%
1962	1,800,038	894,547	Capehart, Homer E.	905,491	Bayh, Birch	—	10,944 D	49.7%	50.3%	49.7%	50.3%
1958	1,724,598	731,635	Handley, Harold W.	973,636	Hartke, R. Vance	19,327	242,001 D	42.4%	56.5%	42.9%	57.1%
1956	1,963,986	1,084,262	Capehart, Homer E.	871,781	Wickard, Claude	7,943	212,481 R	55.2%	44.4%	55.4%	44.6%
1952	1,946,118	1,020,605	Jenner, William E.	911,169	Schricker, Henry F.	14,344	109,436 R	52.4%	46.8%	52.8%	47.2%
1950	1,598,724	844,303	Capehart, Homer E.	741,025	Campbell, Alex M.	13,396	103,278 R	52.8%	46.4%	53.3%	46.7%
1946	1,347,434	739,809	Jenner, William E.	584,288	Townsend, M. Clifford	23,337	155,521 R	54.9%	43.4%	55.9%	44.1%

INDIANA

Districts Established February 16, 1972

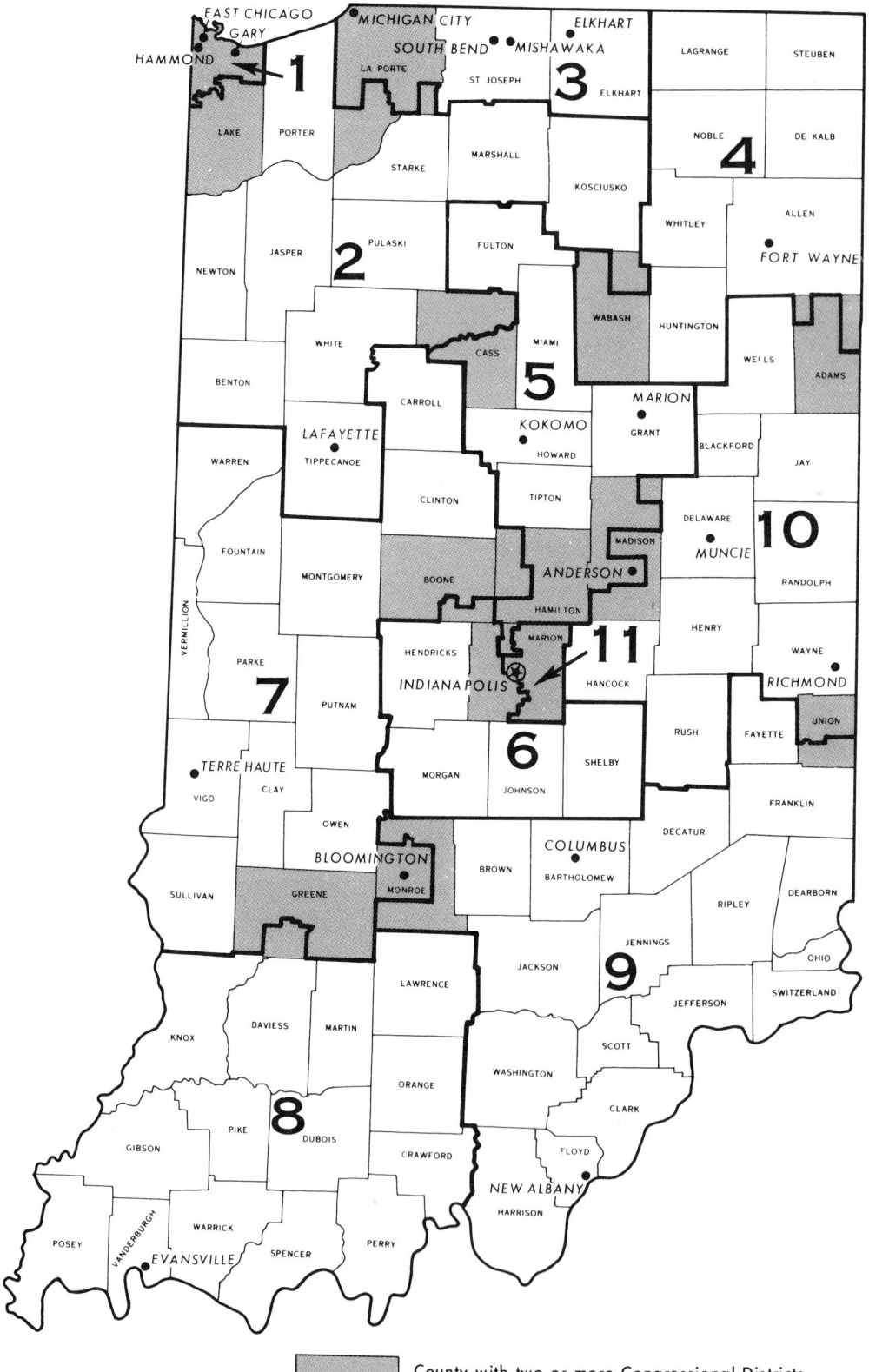

County with two or more Congressional Districts.

INDIANA

PRESIDENT 1980

1980 Census Population	County	Total Vote	Republican	Democratic	Other	Rep.-Dem. Plurality	Percentage Total Vote Rep.	Dem.	Major Vote Rep.	Dem.
29,619	ADAMS	11,978	6,368	4,673	937	1,695 R	53.2%	39.0%	57.7%	42.3%
294,335	ALLEN	118,898	68,524	37,765	12,609	30,759 R	57.6%	31.8%	64.5%	35.5%
65,088	BARTHOLOMEW	26,974	15,801	9,260	1,913	6,541 R	58.6%	34.3%	63.1%	36.9%
10,218	BENTON	4,963	3,189	1,520	254	1,669 R	64.3%	30.6%	67.7%	32.3%
15,570	BLACKFORD	5,962	3,168	2,431	363	737 R	53.1%	40.8%	56.6%	43.4%
36,446	BOONE	15,859	10,484	4,535	840	5,949 R	66.1%	28.6%	69.8%	30.2%
12,377	BROWN	5,291	2,884	2,014	393	870 R	54.5%	38.1%	58.9%	41.1%
19,722	CARROLL	8,699	5,262	2,966	471	2,296 R	60.5%	34.1%	64.0%	36.0%
40,936	CASS	18,274	11,500	5,838	936	5,662 R	62.9%	31.9%	66.3%	33.7%
88,838	CLARK	31,181	15,508	14,137	1,536	1,371 R	49.7%	45.3%	52.3%	47.7%
24,862	CLAY	11,812	6,980	4,363	469	2,617 R	59.1%	36.9%	61.5%	38.5%
31,545	CLINTON	13,962	8,158	5,258	546	2,900 R	58.4%	37.7%	60.8%	39.2%
9,820	CRAWFORD	4,864	2,554	2,130	180	424 R	52.5%	43.8%	54.5%	45.5%
27,836	DAVIESS	11,532	7,022	4,057	453	2,965 R	60.9%	35.2%	63.4%	36.6%
34,291	DEARBORN	13,249	7,467	5,135	647	2,332 R	56.4%	38.8%	59.3%	40.7%
23,841	DECATUR	9,951	5,819	3,646	486	2,173 R	58.5%	36.6%	61.5%	38.5%
33,606	DE KALB	13,950	7,886	4,911	1,153	2,975 R	56.5%	35.2%	61.6%	38.4%
128,587	DELAWARE	52,647	28,342	20,923	3,382	7,419 R	53.8%	39.7%	57.5%	42.5%
34,238	DUBOIS	14,276	6,775	6,700	801	75 R	47.5%	46.9%	50.3%	49.7%
137,330	ELKHART	48,994	30,081	14,883	4,030	15,198 R	61.4%	30.4%	66.9%	33.1%
28,272	FAYETTE	10,732	6,004	4,304	424	1,700 R	55.9%	40.1%	58.2%	41.8%
61,169	FLOYD	25,467	12,456	11,543	1,468	913 R	48.9%	45.3%	51.9%	48.1%
19,033	FOUNTAIN	8,506	5,289	2,845	372	2,444 R	62.2%	33.4%	65.0%	35.0%
19,612	FRANKLIN	7,701	4,551	2,834	316	1,717 R	59.1%	36.8%	61.6%	38.4%
19,335	FULTON	8,728	5,458	2,788	482	2,670 R	62.5%	31.9%	66.2%	33.8%
33,156	GIBSON	15,189	7,643	6,834	712	809 R	50.3%	45.0%	52.8%	47.2%
80,934	GRANT	30,909	19,078	10,390	1,441	8,688 R	61.7%	33.6%	64.7%	35.3%
30,416	GREENE	14,098	7,452	6,027	619	1,425 R	52.9%	42.8%	55.3%	44.7%
82,381	HAMILTON	35,327	26,218	7,036	2,073	19,182 R	74.2%	19.9%	78.8%	21.2%
43,939	HANCOCK	18,138	12,093	5,124	921	6,969 R	66.7%	28.3%	70.2%	29.8%
27,276	HARRISON	11,594	6,287	4,865	442	1,422 R	54.2%	42.0%	56.4%	43.6%
69,804	HENDRICKS	28,117	19,366	7,412	1,339	11,954 R	68.9%	26.4%	72.3%	27.7%
53,336	HENRY	21,196	12,724	7,626	846	5,098 R	60.0%	36.0%	62.5%	37.5%
86,896	HOWARD	35,910	21,272	12,916	1,722	8,356 R	59.2%	36.0%	62.2%	37.8%
35,596	HUNTINGTON	15,937	9,497	5,415	1,025	4,082 R	59.6%	34.0%	63.7%	36.3%
36,523	JACKSON	15,942	8,903	6,425	614	2,478 R	55.8%	40.3%	58.1%	41.9%
26,138	JASPER	9,276	6,316	2,544	416	3,772 R	68.1%	27.4%	71.3%	28.7%
23,239	JAY	9,217	5,351	3,256	610	2,095 R	58.1%	35.3%	62.2%	37.8%
30,419	JEFFERSON	13,087	6,831	5,496	760	1,335 R	52.2%	42.0%	55.4%	44.6%
22,854	JENNINGS	9,822	5,498	3,931	393	1,567 R	56.0%	40.0%	58.3%	41.7%
77,240	JOHNSON	30,174	20,018	8,445	1,711	11,573 R	66.3%	28.0%	70.3%	29.7%
41,838	KNOX	18,822	10,083	7,829	910	2,254 R	53.6%	41.6%	56.3%	43.7%
59,555	KOSCIUSKO	22,730	15,633	5,684	1,413	9,949 R	68.8%	25.0%	73.3%	26.7%
25,550	LAGRANGE	6,815	4,259	2,095	461	2,164 R	62.5%	30.7%	67.0%	33.0%
522,965	LAKE	207,339	95,408	101,145	10,786	5,737 D	46.0%	48.8%	48.5%	51.5%
108,632	LA PORTE	40,538	22,424	15,387	2,727	7,037 R	55.3%	38.0%	59.3%	40.7%
42,472	LAWRENCE	17,296	10,846	5,826	624	5,020 R	62.7%	33.7%	65.1%	34.9%
139,336	MADISON	62,092	35,582	23,554	2,956	12,028 R	57.3%	37.9%	60.2%	39.8%
765,233	MARION	314,269	168,680	126,103	19,486	42,577 R	53.7%	40.1%	57.2%	42.8%
39,155	MARSHALL	16,411	10,209	5,113	1,089	5,096 R	62.2%	31.2%	66.6%	33.4%
11,001	MARTIN	5,779	3,082	2,479	218	603 R	53.3%	42.9%	55.4%	44.6%
39,820	MIAMI	14,304	8,672	4,927	705	3,745 R	60.6%	34.4%	63.8%	36.2%
98,387	MONROE	36,894	18,233	13,316	5,345	4,917 R	49.4%	36.1%	57.8%	42.2%
35,501	MONTGOMERY	14,917	9,936	4,158	823	5,778 R	66.6%	27.9%	70.5%	29.5%
51,999	MORGAN	19,438	13,321	5,439	678	7,882 R	68.5%	28.0%	71.0%	29.0%
14,844	NEWTON	5,763	3,850	1,649	264	2,201 R	66.8%	28.6%	70.0%	30.0%
35,443	NOBLE	13,282	7,624	4,721	937	2,903 R	57.4%	35.5%	61.8%	38.2%
5,114	OHIO	2,420	1,264	1,074	82	190 R	52.2%	44.4%	54.1%	45.9%
18,677	ORANGE	8,558	5,073	3,228	257	1,845 R	59.3%	37.7%	61.1%	38.9%
15,840	OWEN	6,212	3,632	2,325	255	1,307 R	58.5%	37.4%	61.0%	39.0%
16,372	PARKE	7,315	4,595	2,432	288	2,163 R	62.8%	33.2%	65.4%	34.6%
19,346	PERRY	9,468	4,350	4,540	578	190 D	45.9%	48.0%	48.9%	51.1%
13,465	PIKE	6,952	3,343	3,346	263	3 D	48.1%	48.1%	50.0%	50.0%
119,816	PORTER	46,816	30,055	12,869	3,892	17,186 R	64.2%	27.5%	70.0%	30.0%
26,414	POSEY	11,354	6,096	4,465	793	1,631 R	53.7%	39.3%	57.7%	42.3%
13,258	PULASKI	6,310	3,916	2,092	302	1,824 R	62.1%	33.2%	65.2%	34.8%
29,163	PUTNAM	11,748	7,090	3,996	662	3,094 R	60.4%	34.0%	64.0%	36.0%
29,997	RANDOLPH	12,390	7,762	4,025	603	3,737 R	62.6%	32.5%	65.9%	34.1%
24,398	RIPLEY	10,233	5,770	4,022	441	1,748 R	56.4%	39.3%	58.9%	41.1%
19,604	RUSH	7,511	4,829	2,388	294	2,441 R	64.3%	31.8%	66.9%	33.1%

INDIANA

PRESIDENT 1980

1980 Census Population	County	Total Vote	Republican	Democratic	Other	Rep.-Dem. Plurality	Percentage			
							Total Vote		Major Vote	
							Rep.	Dem.	Rep.	Dem.
241,617	ST. JOSEPH	103,114	50,607	44,218	8,289	6,389 R	49.1%	42.9%	53.4%	46.6%
20,422	SCOTT	7,329	3,432	3,694	203	262 D	46.8%	50.4%	48.2%	51.8%
39,887	SHELBY	17,150	10,496	5,861	793	4,635 R	61.2%	34.2%	64.2%	35.8%
19,361	SPENCER	9,705	5,284	4,153	268	1,131 R	54.4%	42.8%	56.0%	44.0%
21,997	STARKE	9,110	5,035	3,615	460	1,420 R	55.3%	39.7%	58.2%	41.8%
24,694	STEUBEN	9,008	5,670	2,606	732	3,064 R	62.9%	28.9%	68.5%	31.5%
21,107	SULLIVAN	9,103	4,465	4,335	303	130 R	49.0%	47.6%	50.7%	49.3%
7,153	SWITZERLAND	3,360	1,584	1,704	72	120 D	47.1%	50.7%	48.2%	51.8%
121,702	TIPPECANOE	48,470	27,589	14,636	6,245	12,953 R	56.9%	30.2%	65.3%	34.7%
16,819	TIPTON	8,071	5,150	2,547	374	2,603 R	63.8%	31.6%	66.9%	33.1%
6,860	UNION	2,780	1,766	898	116	868 R	63.5%	32.3%	66.3%	33.7%
167,515	VANDERBURGH	70,982	36,248	29,930	4,804	6,318 R	51.1%	42.2%	54.8%	45.2%
18,229	VERMILLION	8,400	4,195	3,793	412	402 R	49.9%	45.2%	52.5%	47.5%
112,385	VIGO	46,527	24,133	19,261	3,133	4,872 R	51.9%	41.4%	55.6%	44.4%
36,640	WABASH	14,368	8,738	4,620	1,010	4,118 R	60.8%	32.2%	65.4%	34.6%
8,976	WARREN	4,157	2,665	1,287	205	1,378 R	64.1%	31.0%	67.4%	32.6%
41,474	WARRICK	16,570	8,681	6,845	1,044	1,836 R	52.4%	41.3%	55.9%	44.1%
21,932	WASHINGTON	9,297	5,234	3,663	400	1,571 R	56.3%	39.4%	58.8%	41.2%
76,058	WAYNE	28,052	16,981	9,599	1,472	7,382 R	60.5%	34.2%	63.9%	36.1%
25,401	WELLS	10,445	5,864	3,760	821	2,104 R	56.1%	36.0%	60.9%	39.1%
23,867	WHITE	10,855	6,999	3,247	609	3,752 R	64.5%	29.9%	68.3%	31.7%
26,215	WHITLEY	12,821	7,146	4,497	1,178	2,649 R	55.7%	35.1%	61.4%	38.6%
5,490,179	TOTAL	2,242,033	1,255,656	844,197	142,180	411,459 R	56.0%	37.7%	59.8%	40.2%

INDIANA

GOVERNOR 1980

1980 Census Population	County	Total Vote	Republican	Democratic	Other	Rep.-Dem. Plurality	Total Vote Rep.	Total Vote Dem.	Major Vote Rep.	Major Vote Dem.
29,619	ADAMS	11,755	6,369	5,316	70	1,053 R	54.2%	45.2%	54.5%	45.5%
294,335	ALLEN	115,654	71,230	43,878	546	27,352 R	61.6%	37.9%	61.9%	38.1%
65,088	BARTHOLOMEW	26,588	16,588	9,956	44	6,632 R	62.4%	37.4%	62.5%	37.5%
10,218	BENTON	4,729	3,051	1,654	24	1,397 R	64.5%	35.0%	64.8%	35.2%
15,570	BLACKFORD	5,812	3,481	2,310	21	1,171 R	59.9%	39.7%	60.1%	39.9%
36,446	BOONE	15,778	10,823	4,938	17	5,885 R	68.6%	31.3%	68.7%	31.3%
12,377	BROWN	5,191	2,910	2,265	16	645 R	56.1%	43.6%	56.2%	43.8%
19,722	CARROLL	8,574	5,140	3,421	13	1,719 R	59.9%	39.9%	60.0%	40.0%
40,936	CASS	17,949	10,527	7,335	87	3,192 R	58.6%	40.9%	58.9%	41.1%
88,838	CLARK	28,965	15,226	13,550	189	1,676 R	52.6%	46.8%	52.9%	47.1%
24,862	CLAY	11,533	6,084	5,436	13	648 R	52.8%	47.1%	52.8%	47.2%
31,545	CLINTON	13,674	8,526	5,137	11	3,389 R	62.4%	37.6%	62.4%	37.6%
9,820	CRAWFORD	4,678	2,495	2,172	11	323 R	53.3%	46.4%	53.5%	46.5%
27,836	DAVIESS	11,279	6,380	4,899		1,481 R	56.6%	43.4%	56.6%	43.4%
34,291	DEARBORN	12,707	5,977	6,674	56	697 D	47.0%	52.5%	47.2%	52.8%
23,841	DECATUR	9,847	5,322	4,510	15	812 R	54.0%	45.8%	54.1%	45.9%
33,606	DE KALB	13,621	7,971	5,588	62	2,383 R	58.5%	41.0%	58.8%	41.2%
128,587	DELAWARE	51,111	30,651	20,157	303	10,494 R	60.0%	39.4%	60.3%	39.7%
34,238	DUBOIS	13,908	6,289	7,547	72	1,258 D	45.2%	54.3%	45.5%	54.5%
137,330	ELKHART	47,893	31,681	16,006	206	15,675 R	66.1%	33.4%	66.4%	33.6%
28,272	FAYETTE	10,811	5,966	4,817	28	1,149 R	55.2%	44.6%	55.3%	44.7%
61,169	FLOYD	24,350	12,604	11,601	145	1,003 R	51.8%	47.6%	52.1%	47.9%
19,033	FOUNTAIN	8,179	5,048	3,094	37	1,954 R	61.7%	37.8%	62.0%	38.0%
19,612	FRANKLIN	7,498	2,773	4,714	11	1,941 D	37.0%	62.9%	37.0%	63.0%
19,335	FULTON	8,514	4,509	3,974	31	535 R	53.0%	46.7%	53.2%	46.8%
33,156	GIBSON	14,543	6,613	7,908	22	1,295 D	45.5%	54.4%	45.5%	54.5%
80,934	GRANT	30,231	19,323	10,767	141	8,556 R	63.9%	35.6%	64.2%	35.8%
30,416	GREENE	13,689	6,724	6,867	98	143 D	49.1%	50.2%	49.5%	50.5%
82,381	HAMILTON	34,296	26,880	7,367	49	19,513 R	78.4%	21.5%	78.5%	21.5%
43,939	HANCOCK	17,622	12,061	5,498	63	6,563 R	68.4%	31.2%	68.7%	31.3%
27,276	HARRISON	11,174	6,090	5,025	59	1,065 R	54.5%	45.0%	54.8%	45.2%
69,804	HENDRICKS	27,841	19,571	8,235	35	11,336 R	70.3%	29.6%	70.4%	29.6%
53,336	HENRY	21,006	12,700	8,288	18	4,412 R	60.5%	39.5%	60.5%	39.5%
86,896	HOWARD	35,417	20,892	14,441	84	6,451 R	59.0%	40.8%	59.1%	40.9%
35,596	HUNTINGTON	15,543	9,426	6,052	65	3,374 R	60.6%	38.9%	60.9%	39.1%
36,523	JACKSON	15,571	8,376	7,149	46	1,227 R	53.8%	45.9%	54.0%	46.0%
26,138	JASPER	8,818	6,111	2,645	62	3,466 R	69.3%	30.0%	69.8%	30.2%
23,239	JAY	8,938	5,746	3,155	37	2,591 R	64.3%	35.3%	64.6%	35.4%
30,419	JEFFERSON	12,483	6,846	5,556	81	1,290 R	54.8%	44.5%	55.2%	44.8%
22,854	JENNINGS	9,609	4,771	4,806	32	35 D	49.7%	50.0%	49.8%	50.2%
77,240	JOHNSON	29,655	20,444	9,092	119	11,352 R	68.9%	30.7%	69.2%	30.8%
41,838	KNOX	18,366	9,199	9,071	96	128 R	50.1%	49.4%	50.4%	49.6%
59,555	KOSCIUSKO	22,489	15,590	6,798	101	8,792 R	69.3%	30.2%	69.6%	30.4%
25,550	LAGRANGE	6,703	4,211	2,480	12	1,731 R	62.8%	37.0%	62.9%	37.1%
522,965	LAKE	190,806	83,571	106,570	665	22,999 D	43.8%	55.9%	44.0%	56.0%
108,632	LA PORTE	39,451	23,707	15,445	299	8,262 R	60.1%	39.1%	60.6%	39.4%
42,472	LAWRENCE	16,800	10,156	6,562	82	3,594 R	60.5%	39.1%	60.7%	39.3%
139,336	MADISON	60,852	36,758	23,852	242	12,906 R	60.4%	39.2%	60.6%	39.4%
765,233	MARION	311,433	182,257	128,613	563	53,644 R	58.5%	41.3%	58.6%	41.4%
39,155	MARSHALL	16,077	10,160	5,823	94	4,337 R	63.2%	36.2%	63.6%	36.4%
11,001	MARTIN	5,638	2,744	2,886	8	142 D	48.7%	51.2%	48.7%	51.3%
39,820	MIAMI	13,963	7,949	5,950	64	1,999 R	56.9%	42.6%	57.2%	42.8%
98,387	MONROE	35,472	20,895	14,424	153	6,471 R	58.9%	40.7%	59.2%	40.8%
35,501	MONTGOMERY	14,549	10,034	4,466	49	5,568 R	69.0%	30.7%	69.2%	30.8%
51,999	MORGAN	19,137	12,960	6,149	28	6,811 R	67.7%	32.1%	67.8%	32.2%
14,844	NEWTON	5,491	3,529	1,916	46	1,613 R	64.3%	34.9%	64.8%	35.2%
35,443	NOBLE	13,086	7,408	5,607	71	1,801 R	56.6%	42.8%	56.9%	43.1%
5,114	OHIO	2,331	1,097	1,224	10	127 D	47.1%	52.5%	47.3%	52.7%
18,677	ORANGE	8,231	4,870	3,329	32	1,541 R	59.2%	40.4%	59.4%	40.6%
15,840	OWEN	6,057	3,458	2,591	8	867 R	57.1%	42.8%	57.2%	42.8%
16,372	PARKE	7,164	4,398	2,731	35	1,667 R	61.4%	38.1%	61.7%	38.3%
19,346	PERRY	9,263	4,038	5,204	21	1,166 D	43.6%	56.2%	43.7%	56.3%
13,465	PIKE	6,742	2,913	3,801	28	888 D	43.2%	56.4%	43.4%	56.6%
119,816	PORTER	45,785	30,355	15,081	349	15,274 R	66.3%	32.9%	66.8%	33.2%
26,414	POSEY	11,073	5,799	5,235	39	564 R	52.4%	47.3%	52.6%	47.4%
13,258	PULASKI	6,123	3,565	2,510	48	1,055 R	58.2%	41.0%	58.7%	41.3%
29,163	PUTNAM	11,558	7,274	4,233	51	3,041 R	62.9%	36.6%	63.2%	36.8%
29,997	RANDOLPH	12,206	8,096	4,035	75	4,061 R	66.3%	33.1%	66.7%	33.3%
24,398	RIPLEY	9,448	3,726	5,684	38	1,958 D	39.4%	60.2%	39.6%	60.4%
19,604	RUSH	7,327	4,626	2,682	19	1,944 R	63.1%	36.6%	63.3%	36.7%

INDIANA

GOVERNOR 1980

1980 Census Population	County	Total Vote	Republican	Democratic	Other	Rep.-Dem. Plurality	Percentage Total Vote Rep.	Dem.	Major Vote Rep.	Dem.
241,617	ST. JOSEPH	99,915	53,572	46,080	263	7,492 R	53.6%	46.1%	53.8%	46.2%
20,422	SCOTT	6,565	3,105	3,437	23	332 D	47.3%	52.4%	47.5%	52.5%
39,887	SHELBY	16,914	10,282	6,595	37	3,687 R	60.8%	39.0%	60.9%	39.1%
19,361	SPENCER	9,661	5,173	4,474	14	699 R	53.5%	46.3%	53.6%	46.4%
21,997	STARKE	8,800	4,516	4,187	97	329 R	51.3%	47.6%	51.9%	48.1%
24,694	STEUBEN	8,857	5,695	3,127	35	2,568 R	64.3%	35.3%	64.6%	35.4%
21,107	SULLIVAN	8,540	3,680	4,845	15	1,165 D	43.1%	56.7%	43.2%	56.8%
7,153	SWITZERLAND	3,142	1,358	1,772	12	414 D	43.2%	56.4%	43.4%	56.6%
121,702	TIPPECANOE	47,283	30,347	16,817	119	13,530 R	64.2%	35.6%	64.3%	35.7%
16,819	TIPTON	7,936	5,040	2,865	31	2,175 R	63.5%	36.1%	63.8%	36.2%
6,860	UNION	2,719	1,670	1,039	10	631 R	61.4%	38.2%	61.6%	38.4%
167,515	VANDERBURGH	70,209	39,009	31,022	178	7,987 R	55.6%	44.2%	55.7%	44.3%
18,229	VERMILLION	8,099	3,938	4,111	50	173 D	48.6%	50.8%	48.9%	51.1%
112,385	VIGO	45,591	22,251	23,120	220	869 D	48.8%	50.7%	49.0%	51.0%
36,640	WABASH	14,241	8,941	5,288	12	3,653 R	62.8%	37.1%	62.8%	37.2%
8,976	WARREN	4,044	2,488	1,525	31	963 R	61.5%	37.7%	62.0%	38.0%
41,474	WARRICK	16,104	8,171	7,869	64	302 R	50.7%	48.9%	50.9%	49.1%
21,932	WASHINGTON	8,768	4,925	3,739	104	1,186 R	56.2%	42.6%	56.8%	43.2%
76,058	WAYNE	27,087	17,273	9,708	106	7,565 R	63.8%	35.8%	64.0%	36.0%
25,401	WELLS	10,320	6,143	4,127	50	2,016 R	59.5%	40.0%	59.8%	40.2%
23,867	WHITE	10,479	6,992	3,452	35	3,540 R	66.7%	32.9%	66.9%	33.1%
26,215	WHITLEY	12,474	7,276	5,165	33	2,111 R	58.3%	41.4%	58.5%	41.5%
5,490,179	TOTAL	2,178,403	1,257,383	913,116	7,904	344,267 R	57.7%	41.9%	57.9%	42.1%

INDIANA

SENATOR 1980

1980 Census Population	County	Total Vote	Republican	Democratic	Other	Rep.-Dem. Plurality	Percentage Total Vote Rep.	Dem.	Major Vote Rep.	Dem.
29,619	ADAMS	11,880	6,185	5,695		490 R	52.1%	47.9%	52.1%	47.9%
294,335	ALLEN	116,800	68,308	48,492		19,816 R	58.5%	41.5%	58.5%	41.5%
65,088	BARTHOLOMEW	26,710	15,673	11,037		4,636 R	58.7%	41.3%	58.7%	41.3%
10,218	BENTON	4,807	2,844	1,963		881 R	59.2%	40.8%	59.2%	40.8%
15,570	BLACKFORD	5,880	3,053	2,827		226 R	51.9%	48.1%	51.9%	48.1%
36,446	BOONE	15,815	10,374	5,441		4,933 R	65.6%	34.4%	65.6%	34.4%
12,377	BROWN	5,269	2,818	2,451		367 R	53.5%	46.5%	53.5%	46.5%
19,722	CARROLL	8,655	5,040	3,615		1,425 R	58.2%	41.8%	58.2%	41.8%
40,936	CASS	18,053	10,896	7,157		3,739 R	60.4%	39.6%	60.4%	39.6%
88,838	CLARK	30,510	14,814	15,696		882 D	48.6%	51.4%	48.6%	51.4%
24,862	CLAY	11,736	6,409	5,327		1,082 R	54.6%	45.4%	54.6%	45.4%
31,545	CLINTON	13,853	7,825	6,028		1,797 R	56.5%	43.5%	56.5%	43.5%
9,820	CRAWFORD	4,818	2,362	2,456		94 D	49.0%	51.0%	49.0%	51.0%
27,836	DAVIESS	11,433	6,356	5,077		1,279 R	55.6%	44.4%	55.6%	44.4%
34,291	DEARBORN	12,868	6,238	6,630		392 D	48.5%	51.5%	48.5%	51.5%
23,841	DECATUR	9,847	5,875	3,972		1,903 R	59.7%	40.3%	59.7%	40.3%
33,606	DE KALB	13,753	7,730	6,023		1,707 R	56.2%	43.8%	56.2%	43.8%
128,587	DELAWARE	52,129	27,554	24,575		2,979 R	52.9%	47.1%	52.9%	47.1%
34,238	DUBOIS	14,106	6,380	7,726		1,346 D	45.2%	54.8%	45.2%	54.8%
137,330	ELKHART	48,263	30,587	17,676		12,911 R	63.4%	36.6%	63.4%	36.6%
28,272	FAYETTE	10,890	5,948	4,942		1,006 R	54.6%	45.4%	54.6%	45.4%
61,169	FLOYD	24,735	12,034	12,701		667 D	48.7%	51.3%	48.7%	51.3%
19,033	FOUNTAIN	8,436	4,956	3,480		1,476 R	58.7%	41.3%	58.7%	41.3%
19,612	FRANKLIN	7,500	3,753	3,747		6 R	50.0%	50.0%	50.0%	50.0%
19,335	FULTON	8,506	5,107	3,399		1,708 R	60.0%	40.0%	60.0%	40.0%
33,156	GIBSON	14,955	6,339	8,616		2,277 D	42.4%	57.6%	42.4%	57.6%
80,934	GRANT	30,508	17,614	12,894		4,720 R	57.7%	42.3%	57.7%	42.3%
30,416	GREENE	13,988	6,539	7,449		910 D	46.7%	53.3%	46.7%	53.3%
82,381	HAMILTON	34,829	25,700	9,129		16,571 R	73.8%	26.2%	73.8%	26.2%
43,939	HANCOCK	17,870	11,358	6,512		4,846 R	63.6%	36.4%	63.6%	36.4%
27,276	HARRISON	11,480	5,733	5,747		14 D	49.9%	50.1%	49.9%	50.1%
69,804	HENDRICKS	27,961	18,484	9,477		9,007 R	66.1%	33.9%	66.1%	33.9%
53,336	HENRY	20,998	11,678	9,320		2,358 R	55.6%	44.4%	55.6%	44.4%
86,896	HOWARD	35,607	19,712	15,895		3,817 R	55.4%	44.6%	55.4%	44.6%
35,596	HUNTINGTON	15,684	9,248	6,436		2,812 R	59.0%	41.0%	59.0%	41.0%
36,523	JACKSON	15,693	8,680	7,013		1,667 R	55.3%	44.7%	55.3%	44.7%
26,138	JASPER	9,023	5,753	3,270		2,483 R	63.8%	36.2%	63.8%	36.2%
23,239	JAY	8,585	4,899	3,686		1,213 R	57.1%	42.9%	57.1%	42.9%
30,419	JEFFERSON	12,784	6,629	6,155		474 R	51.9%	48.1%	51.9%	48.1%
22,854	JENNINGS	9,617	5,053	4,564		489 R	52.5%	47.5%	52.5%	47.5%
77,240	JOHNSON	29,984	19,124	10,860		8,264 R	63.8%	36.2%	63.8%	36.2%
41,838	KNOX	18,599	9,646	8,953		693 R	51.9%	48.1%	51.9%	48.1%
59,555	KOSCIUSKO	22,644	15,592	7,052		8,540 R	68.9%	31.1%	68.9%	31.1%
25,550	LAGRANGE	6,789	4,341	2,448		1,893 R	63.9%	36.1%	63.9%	36.1%
522,965	LAKE	197,740	80,346	117,394		37,048 D	40.6%	59.4%	40.6%	59.4%
108,632	LA PORTE	39,715	21,437	18,278		3,159 R	54.0%	46.0%	54.0%	46.0%
42,472	LAWRENCE	17,127	10,089	7,038		3,051 R	58.9%	41.1%	58.9%	41.1%
139,336	MADISON	61,203	34,106	27,097		7,009 R	55.7%	44.3%	55.7%	44.3%
765,233	MARION	311,899	166,190	145,709		20,481 R	53.3%	46.7%	53.3%	46.7%
39,155	MARSHALL	16,121	9,766	6,355		3,411 R	60.6%	39.4%	60.6%	39.4%
11,001	MARTIN	5,748	2,842	2,906		64 D	49.4%	50.6%	49.4%	50.6%
39,820	MIAMI	14,190	8,040	6,150		1,890 R	56.7%	43.3%	56.7%	43.3%
98,387	MONROE	36,295	18,003	18,292		289 D	49.6%	50.4%	49.6%	50.4%
35,501	MONTGOMERY	14,738	9,721	5,017		4,704 R	66.0%	34.0%	66.0%	34.0%
51,999	MORGAN	19,251	12,598	6,653		5,945 R	65.4%	34.6%	65.4%	34.6%
14,844	NEWTON	5,642	3,139	2,503		636 R	55.6%	44.4%	55.6%	44.4%
35,443	NOBLE	13,326	7,477	5,849		1,628 R	56.1%	43.9%	56.1%	43.9%
5,114	OHIO	2,378	1,046	1,332		286 D	44.0%	56.0%	44.0%	56.0%
18,677	ORANGE	8,449	4,578	3,871		707 R	54.2%	45.8%	54.2%	45.8%
15,840	OWEN	6,169	3,256	2,913		343 R	52.8%	47.2%	52.8%	47.2%
16,372	PARKE	7,314	4,415	2,899		1,516 R	60.4%	39.6%	60.4%	39.6%
19,346	PERRY	9,378	3,941	5,437		1,496 D	42.0%	58.0%	42.0%	58.0%
13,465	PIKE	6,927	2,829	4,098		1,269 D	40.8%	59.2%	40.8%	59.2%
119,816	PORTER	46,407	26,774	19,633		7,141 R	57.7%	42.3%	57.7%	42.3%
26,414	POSEY	11,355	5,283	6,072		789 D	46.5%	53.5%	46.5%	53.5%
13,258	PULASKI	6,163	3,731	2,432		1,299 R	60.5%	39.5%	60.5%	39.5%
29,163	PUTNAM	11,731	6,803	4,928		1,875 R	58.0%	42.0%	58.0%	42.0%
29,997	RANDOLPH	12,304	7,201	5,103		2,098 R	58.5%	41.5%	58.5%	41.5%
24,398	RIPLEY	9,927	4,572	5,355		783 D	46.1%	53.9%	46.1%	53.9%
19,604	RUSH	7,436	4,617	2,819		1,798 R	62.1%	37.9%	62.1%	37.9%

INDIANA

SENATOR 1980

1980 Census Population	County	Total Vote	Republican	Democratic	Other	Rep.-Dem. Plurality	Percentage			
							Total Vote		Major Vote	
							Rep.	Dem.	Rep.	Dem.
241,617	ST. JOSEPH	101,374	49,076	52,298		3,222 D	48.4%	51.6%	48.4%	51.6%
20,422	SCOTT	7,016	3,218	3,798		580 D	45.9%	54.1%	45.9%	54.1%
39,887	SHELBY	16,964	9,681	7,283		2,398 R	57.1%	42.9%	57.1%	42.9%
19,361	SPENCER	9,669	5,004	4,665		339 R	51.8%	48.2%	51.8%	48.2%
21,997	STARKE	8,895	4,439	4,456		17 D	49.9%	50.1%	49.9%	50.1%
24,694	STEUBEN	8,698	5,470	3,228		2,242 R	62.9%	37.1%	62.9%	37.1%
21,107	SULLIVAN	8,942	3,690	5,252		1,562 D	41.3%	58.7%	41.3%	58.7%
7,153	SWITZERLAND	3,111	1,285	1,826		541 D	41.3%	58.7%	41.3%	58.7%
121,702	TIPPECANOE	47,914	27,975	19,939		8,036 R	58.4%	41.6%	58.4%	41.6%
16,819	TIPTON	7,957	4,889	3,068		1,821 R	61.4%	38.6%	61.4%	38.6%
6,860	UNION	2,783	1,629	1,154		475 R	58.5%	41.5%	58.5%	41.5%
167,515	VANDERBURGH	61,232	27,813	33,419		5,606 D	45.4%	54.6%	45.4%	54.6%
18,229	VERMILLION	8,413	4,027	4,386		359 D	47.9%	52.1%	47.9%	52.1%
112,385	VIGO	46,498	21,763	24,735		2,972 D	46.8%	53.2%	46.8%	53.2%
36,640	WABASH	14,265	8,614	5,651		2,963 R	60.4%	39.6%	60.4%	39.6%
8,976	WARREN	4,155	2,422	1,733		689 R	58.3%	41.7%	58.3%	41.7%
41,474	WARRICK	16,430	7,314	9,116		1,802 D	44.5%	55.5%	44.5%	55.5%
21,932	WASHINGTON	9,008	5,108	3,900		1,208 R	56.7%	43.3%	56.7%	43.3%
76,058	WAYNE	27,464	15,771	11,693		4,078 R	57.4%	42.6%	57.4%	42.6%
25,401	WELLS	10,476	5,685	4,791		894 R	54.3%	45.7%	54.3%	45.7%
23,867	WHITE	10,747	6,510	4,237		2,273 R	60.6%	39.4%	60.6%	39.4%
26,215	WHITLEY	12,582	6,990	5,592		1,398 R	55.6%	44.4%	55.6%	44.4%
5,490,179	TOTAL	2,198,376	1,182,414	1,015,962		166,452 R	53.8%	46.2%	53.8%	46.2%

INDIANA

CONGRESS

CD	Year	Total Vote	Republican Vote	Candidate	Democratic Vote	Candidate	Other Vote	Rep.-Dem. Plurality	Total Vote Rep.	Total Vote Dem.	Major Vote Rep.	Major Vote Dem.
1	1980	155,553	43,537	HARKIN, JOSEPH D.	112,016	BENJAMIN, ADAM		68,479 D	28.0%	72.0%	28.0%	72.0%
1	1978	90,170	17,419	CRUMPACKER, OWEN W.	72,367	BENJAMIN, ADAM	384	54,948 D	19.3%	80.3%	19.4%	80.6%
1	1976	169,911	48,756	BILLINGS, ROBERT J.	121,155	BENJAMIN, ADAM		72,399 D	28.7%	71.3%	28.7%	71.3%
1	1974	104,552	32,793	HARKIN, JOSEPH D.	71,759	MADDEN, RAY J.		38,966 D	31.4%	68.6%	31.4%	68.6%
1	1972	168,535	72,662	HALLER, BRUCE R.	95,873	MADDEN, RAY J.		23,211 D	43.1%	56.9%	43.1%	56.9%
2	1980	226,283	103,957	NIEMEYER, ERNEST	122,326	FITHIAN, FLOYD		18,369 D	45.9%	54.1%	45.9%	54.1%
2	1978	145,778	52,842	OPPENHEIM, J. PHILIP	82,402	FITHIAN, FLOYD	10,534	29,560 D	36.2%	56.5%	39.1%	60.9%
2	1976	214,795	95,505	ERWIN, WILLIAM W.	117,617	FITHIAN, FLOYD	1,673	22,112 D	44.5%	54.8%	44.8%	55.2%
2	1974	166,806	64,950	LANDGREBE, EARL F.	101,856	FITHIAN, FLOYD		36,906 D	38.9%	61.1%	38.9%	61.1%
2	1972	201,939	110,406	LANDGREBE, EARL F.	91,533	FITHIAN, FLOYD		18,873 R	54.7%	45.3%	54.7%	45.3%
3	1980	189,108	103,972	HILER, JOHN P.	85,136	BRADEMAS, JOHN		18,836 R	55.0%	45.0%	55.0%	45.0%
3	1978	115,862	50,145	THORSON, THOMAS L.	64,336	BRADEMAS, JOHN	1,381	14,191 D	43.3%	55.5%	43.8%	56.2%
3	1976	178,871	77,094	THORSON, THOMAS L.	101,777	BRADEMAS, JOHN		24,683 D	43.1%	56.9%	43.1%	56.9%
3	1974	139,422	50,116	BLACK, VIRGINIA R.	89,306	BRADEMAS, JOHN		39,190 D	35.9%	64.1%	35.9%	64.1%
3	1972	188,202	81,369	NEWMAN, DON M.	103,949	BRADEMAS, JOHN	2,884	22,580 D	43.2%	55.2%	43.9%	56.1%
4	1980	198,342	120,055	COATS, DANIEL R.	77,542	WALDA, JOHN D.	745	42,513 R	60.5%	39.1%	60.8%	39.2%
4	1978	125,117	80,527	QUAYLE, J. DANFORTH	42,238	WALDA, JOHN D.	2,352	38,289 R	64.4%	33.8%	65.6%	34.4%
4	1976	198,183	107,762	QUAYLE, J. DANFORTH	88,361	ROUSH, J. EDWARD	2,060	19,401 R	54.4%	44.6%	54.9%	45.1%
4	1974	161,219	75,031	HELMKE, WALTER P.	83,604	ROUSH, J. EDWARD	2,584	8,573 D	46.5%	51.9%	47.3%	52.7%
4	1972	194,819	94,492	BLOOM, ALLAN	100,327	ROUSH, J. EDWARD		5,835 D	48.5%	51.5%	48.5%	51.5%
5	1980	209,852	129,474	HILLIS, ELWOOD H.	80,378	ACKERSON, NELS J.		49,096 R	61.7%	38.3%	61.7%	38.3%
5	1978	140,429	94,950	HILLIS, ELWOOD H.	45,479	HEISS, MAX E.		49,471 R	67.6%	32.4%	67.6%	32.4%
5	1976	206,001	127,194	HILLIS, ELWOOD H.	78,807	STOUT, WILLIAM C.		48,387 R	61.7%	38.3%	61.7%	38.3%
5	1974	168,570	95,331	HILLIS, ELWOOD H.	73,239	SEBREE, WILLIAM T.		22,092 R	56.6%	43.4%	56.6%	43.4%
5	1972	194,438	124,692	HILLIS, ELWOOD H.	69,746	WILLIAMS, KATHLEEN Z.		54,946 R	64.1%	35.9%	64.1%	35.9%
6	1980	196,064	97,582	CRANE, DAVID G.	98,482	EVANS, DAVID W.		900 D	49.8%	50.2%	49.8%	50.2%
6	1978	127,282	60,630	CRANE, DAVID G.	66,421	EVANS, DAVID W.	231	5,791 D	47.6%	52.2%	47.7%	52.3%
6	1976	192,627	86,854	CRANE, DAVID G.	105,773	EVANS, DAVID W.		18,919 D	45.1%	54.9%	45.1%	54.9%
6	1974	149,548	71,134	BRAY, WILLIAM G.	78,414	EVANS, DAVID W.		7,280 D	47.6%	52.4%	47.6%	52.4%
6	1972	173,595	112,525	BRAY, WILLIAM G.	61,070	EVANS, DAVID W.		51,455 R	64.8%	35.2%	64.8%	35.2%
7	1980	208,264	137,604	MYERS, JOHN T.	69,051	CARROLL, PATRICK D.	1,609	68,553 R	66.1%	33.2%	66.6%	33.4%
7	1978	154,424	86,955	MYERS, JOHN T.	67,469	ZIETLOW, CHARLOTTE		19,486 R	56.3%	43.7%	56.3%	43.7%
7	1976	207,360	130,005	MYERS, JOHN T.	77,355	TIPTON, JOHN E.		52,650 R	62.7%	37.3%	62.7%	37.3%
7	1974	175,351	100,128	MYERS, JOHN T.	73,802	TIPTON, ELDEN	1,421	26,326 R	57.1%	42.1%	57.6%	42.4%
7	1972	208,833	128,688	MYERS, JOHN T.	80,145	HENEGAR, WARREN		48,543 R	61.6%	38.4%	61.6%	38.4%
8	1980	216,474	119,415	DECKARD, H. JOEL	97,059	SNIDER, KENNETH C.		22,356 R	55.2%	44.8%	55.2%	44.8%
8	1978	159,673	83,019	DECKARD, H. JOEL	76,654	CORNWELL, DAVID L.		6,365 R	52.0%	48.0%	52.0%	48.0%
8	1976	216,026	107,013	BELL, BELDEN	109,013	CORNWELL, DAVID L.		2,000 D	49.5%	50.5%	49.5%	50.5%
8	1974	187,417	87,296	ZION, ROGER H.	100,121	HAYES, PHILIP H.		12,825 D	46.6%	53.4%	46.6%	53.4%
8	1972	211,221	133,850	ZION, ROGER H.	77,371	DEEN, RICHARD L.		56,479 R	63.4%	36.6%	63.4%	36.6%
9	1980	212,175	75,601	MEYER, GEORGE	136,574	HAMILTON, LEE H.		60,973 D	35.6%	64.4%	35.6%	64.4%
9	1978	151,945	52,218	HAMILTON, FRANK I.	99,727	HAMILTON, LEE H.		47,509 D	34.4%	65.6%	34.4%	65.6%
9	1976	136,056	136,056		136,056	HAMILTON, LEE H.		136,056 D		100.0%		100.0%
9	1974	165,529	47,881	COX, DELSON	117,648	HAMILTON, LEE H.		69,767 D	28.9%	71.1%	28.9%	71.1%
9	1972	195,023	72,325	JOHNSON, WILLIAM A.	122,698	HAMILTON, LEE H.		50,373 D	37.1%	62.9%	37.1%	62.9%
10	1980	193,134	90,051	FRAZIER, WILLIAM G.	103,083	SHARP, PHILIP R.		13,032 D	46.6%	53.4%	46.6%	53.4%
10	1978	130,742	55,999	FRAZIER, WILLIAM G.	73,343	SHARP, PHILIP R.	1,400	17,344 D	42.8%	56.1%	43.3%	56.7%
10	1976	191,449	76,890	FRAZIER, WILLIAM G.	114,559	SHARP, PHILIP R.		37,669 D	40.2%	59.8%	40.2%	59.8%
10	1974	157,119	71,701	DENNIS, DAVID W.	85,418	SHARP, PHILIP R.		13,717 D	45.6%	54.4%	45.6%	54.4%
10	1972	186,554	106,798	DENNIS, DAVID W.	79,756	SHARP, PHILIP R.		27,042 R	57.2%	42.8%	57.2%	42.8%
11	1980	184,211	78,743	SUESS, SHEILA	105,468	JACOBS, ANDREW, JR.		26,725 D	42.7%	57.3%	42.7%	57.3%
11	1978	107,441	45,809	BOSMA, CHARLES F.	61,504	JACOBS, ANDREW, JR.	128	15,695 D	42.6%	57.2%	42.7%	57.3%
11	1976	191,859	74,829	BUELL, LAWRENCE L.	115,895	JACOBS, ANDREW, JR.	1,135	41,066 D	39.0%	60.4%	39.2%	60.8%
11	1974	155,301	73,793	HUDNUT, WILLIAM H.	81,508	JACOBS, ANDREW, JR.		7,715 D	47.5%	52.5%	47.5%	52.5%
11	1972	187,077	95,839	HUDNUT, WILLIAM H.	91,238	JACOBS, ANDREW, JR.		4,601 R	51.2%	48.8%	51.2%	48.8%

INDIANA

1980 GENERAL ELECTION

President   Other vote was 111,639 Anderson (Independent); 19,627 Clark (Libertarian); 4,852 Commoner (Citizens); 4,750 Greaves (American); 702 Hall (Communist); 610 DeBerry (Socialist Workers).

Governor   Other vote was Artist (American).

Senator

Congress   Other vote was Hope (Independent) in CD 4; Tescione (Independent) in CD 7. The data presented for CD 6 are for the recount; original canvass report was 99,089 Evans and 98,302 Crane.

1980 PRIMARIES

MAY 6 REPUBLICAN

Governor   Robert D. Orr, unopposed.

Senator   397,273 J. Danforth Quayle; 118,273 Roger F. Marsh.

Congress   Unopposed in three CD's. Contested as follows:

CD 1   6,285 Joseph D. Harkin; 3,940 Owen W. Crumpacker; 1,485 Damian J. Santay.
CD 2   21,634 Ernest Niemeyer; 21,136 John Bradshaw; 10,321 William Conover; 4,991 Sara K. Florek; 4,158 Dewey M. Conley; 3,223 James H. Logan.
CD 3   23,548 John P. Hiler; 15,567 Richard Pfeil; 1,582 Thomas N. Zorno.
CD 4   35,138 Daniel R. Coats; 14,550 Paul Helmke; 10,808 Elmer MacDonald.
CD 6   47,554 David G. Crane; 6,731 Ros Stovall; 4,668 Chester Coomer.
CD 9   22,391 George Meyer; 8,826 Thomas A. Zeig.
CD 10   26,271 William G. Frazier; 13,811 William DuBois; 6,571 Morris F. Evans; 4,222 Mark A. Hoelscher; 2,894 Robert J. Luellen.
CD 11   16,832 Sheila Suess; 10,734 Frederick Monschein; 5,278 James C. Cummings; 4,372 Clarence Hodges; 4,148 Eugene Barnett.

MAY 6 DEMOCRATIC

Governor   284,182 John A. Hillenbrand; 257,779 W. Wayne Townsend.

Senator   Birch Bayh, unopposed.

Congress   Unopposed in four CD's. Contested as follows:

CD 3   35,218 John Brademas; 7,490 Richard V. Meller; 5,919 Mary Hipsak.
CD 5   24,680 Nels J. Ackerson; 16,283 Betty J. Phelps.
CD 6   32,602 David W. Evans; 2,364 Joe L. Turner.
CD 7   28,873 Patrick D. Carroll; 13,844 Raymond R. Cronin; 10,179 Marc Haggerty.
CD 8   28,920 Kenneth C. Snider; 10,507 Thomas E. Fisher; 9,393 Samuel P. Adams; 9,418 Milton W. Harvey.
CD 9   62,160 Lee H. Hamilton; 6,883 Lendall B. Terry.
CD 10   43,142 Philip R. Sharp; 2,773 Robert L. Murphy; 2,284 Randall S. Harmon.

IOWA

GOVERNOR
Robert Ray (R). Re-elected 1978 to a four-year term. Previously elected 1974 to a four-year term and in 1972, 1970, 1968 to two-year terms.

SENATORS
Charles E. Grassley (R). Elected 1980 to a six-year term.

Roger W. Jepsen (R). Elected 1978 to a six-year term.

REPRESENTATIVES
1. James A. Leach (R)
2. Tom Tauke (R)
3. Cooper Evans (R)
4. Neal Smith (D)
5. Tom Harkin (D)
6. Berkley Bedell (D)

POSTWAR VOTE FOR GOVERNOR

Year	Total Vote	Republican Vote	Candidate	Democratic Vote	Candidate	Other Vote	Rep.-Dem. Plurality	Total Vote Rep.	Total Vote Dem.	Major Vote Rep.	Major Vote Dem.
1978	843,190	491,713	Ray, Robert	345,519	Fitzgerald, Jerome D.	5,958	146,194 R	58.3%	41.0%	58.7%	41.3%
1974	920,458	534,518	Ray, Robert	377,553	Schaben, James F.	8,387	156,965 R	58.1%	41.0%	58.6%	41.4%
1972	1,210,222	707,177	Ray, Robert	487,282	Franzenburg, Paul	15,763	219,895 R	58.4%	40.3%	59.2%	40.8%
1970	791,241	403,394	Ray, Robert	368,911	Fulton, Robert	18,936	34,483 R	51.0%	46.6%	52.2%	47.8%
1968	1,136,489	614,328	Ray, Robert	521,216	Franzenburg, Paul	945	93,112 R	54.1%	45.9%	54.1%	45.9%
1966	893,175	394,518	Murray, William G.	494,259	Hughes, Harold E.	4,398	99,741 D	44.2%	55.3%	44.4%	55.6%
1964	1,167,734	365,131	Hultman, Evan	794,610	Hughes, Harold E.	7,993	429,479 D	31.3%	68.0%	31.5%	68.5%
1962	819,854	388,955	Erbe, Norman A.	430,899	Hughes, Harold E.	—	41,944 D	47.4%	52.6%	47.4%	52.6%
1960	1,237,089	645,026	Erbe, Norman A.	592,063	McManus, E. J.	—	52,963 R	52.1%	47.9%	52.1%	47.9%
1958	859,095	394,071	Murray, William G.	465,024	Loveless, Herschel C.	—	70,953 D	45.9%	54.1%	45.9%	54.1%
1956	1,204,235	587,383	Hoegh, Leo A.	616,852	Loveless, Herschel C.	—	29,469 D	48.8%	51.2%	48.8%	51.2%
1954	848,592	435,944	Hoegh, Leo A.	410,255	Herring, Clyde E.	2,393	25,689 R	51.4%	48.3%	51.5%	48.5%
1952	1,230,045	638,388	Beardsley, William	587,671	Loveless, Herschel C.	3,986	50,717 R	51.9%	47.8%	52.1%	47.9%
1950	857,213	506,642	Beardsley, William	347,176	Gillette, Lester S.	3,395	159,466 R	59.1%	40.5%	59.3%	40.7%
1948	994,833	553,900	Beardsley, William	434,432	Switzer, Carroll O.	6,501	119,468 R	55.7%	43.7%	56.0%	44.0%
1946	631,681	362,592	Blue, Robert D.	266,190	Miles, Frank	2,899	96,402 R	57.4%	42.1%	57.7%	42.3%

The term of office of Iowa's Governor was increased from two to four years effective with the 1974 election.

POSTWAR VOTE FOR SENATOR

Year	Total Vote	Republican Vote	Candidate	Democratic Vote	Candidate	Other Vote	Rep.-Dem. Plurality	Total Vote Rep.	Total Vote Dem.	Major Vote Rep.	Major Vote Dem.
1980	1,277,034	683,014	Grassley, Charles E.	581,545	Culver, John C.	12,475	101,469 R	53.5%	45.5%	54.0%	46.0%
1978	824,654	421,598	Jepsen, Roger W.	395,066	Clark, Richard	7,990	26,532 R	51.1%	47.9%	51.6%	48.4%
1974	889,561	420,546	Stanley, David M.	462,947	Culver, John C.	6,068	42,401 D	47.3%	52.0%	47.6%	52.4%
1972	1,203,333	530,525	Miller, Jack	662,637	Clark, Richard	10,171	132,112 D	44.1%	55.1%	44.5%	55.5%
1968	1,144,086	568,469	Stanley, David M.	574,884	Hughes, Harold E.	733	6,415 D	49.7%	50.2%	49.7%	50.3%
1966	857,496	522,339	Miller, Jack	324,114	Smith, E. B.	11,043	198,225 R	60.9%	37.8%	61.7%	38.3%
1962	807,972	431,364	Hickenlooper, Bourke B.	376,602	Smith, E. B.	6	54,762 R	53.4%	46.6%	53.4%	46.6%
1960	1,237,582	642,463	Miller, Jack	595,119	Loveless, Herschel C.	—	47,344 R	51.9%	48.1%	51.9%	48.1%
1956	1,178,655	635,499	Hickenlooper, Bourke B.	543,156	Evans, R. M.	—	92,343 R	53.9%	46.1%	53.9%	46.1%
1954	847,355	442,409	Martin, Thomas E.	402,712	Gillette, Guy	2,234	39,697 R	52.2%	47.5%	52.3%	47.7%
1950	858,523	470,613	Hickenlooper, Bourke B.	383,766	Loveland, A. J.	4,144	86,847 R	54.8%	44.7%	55.1%	44.9%
1948	1,000,412	415,778	Wilson, George A.	578,226	Gillette, Guy	6,408	162,448 D	41.6%	57.8%	41.8%	58.2%

IOWA

Districts Established March 6,1971

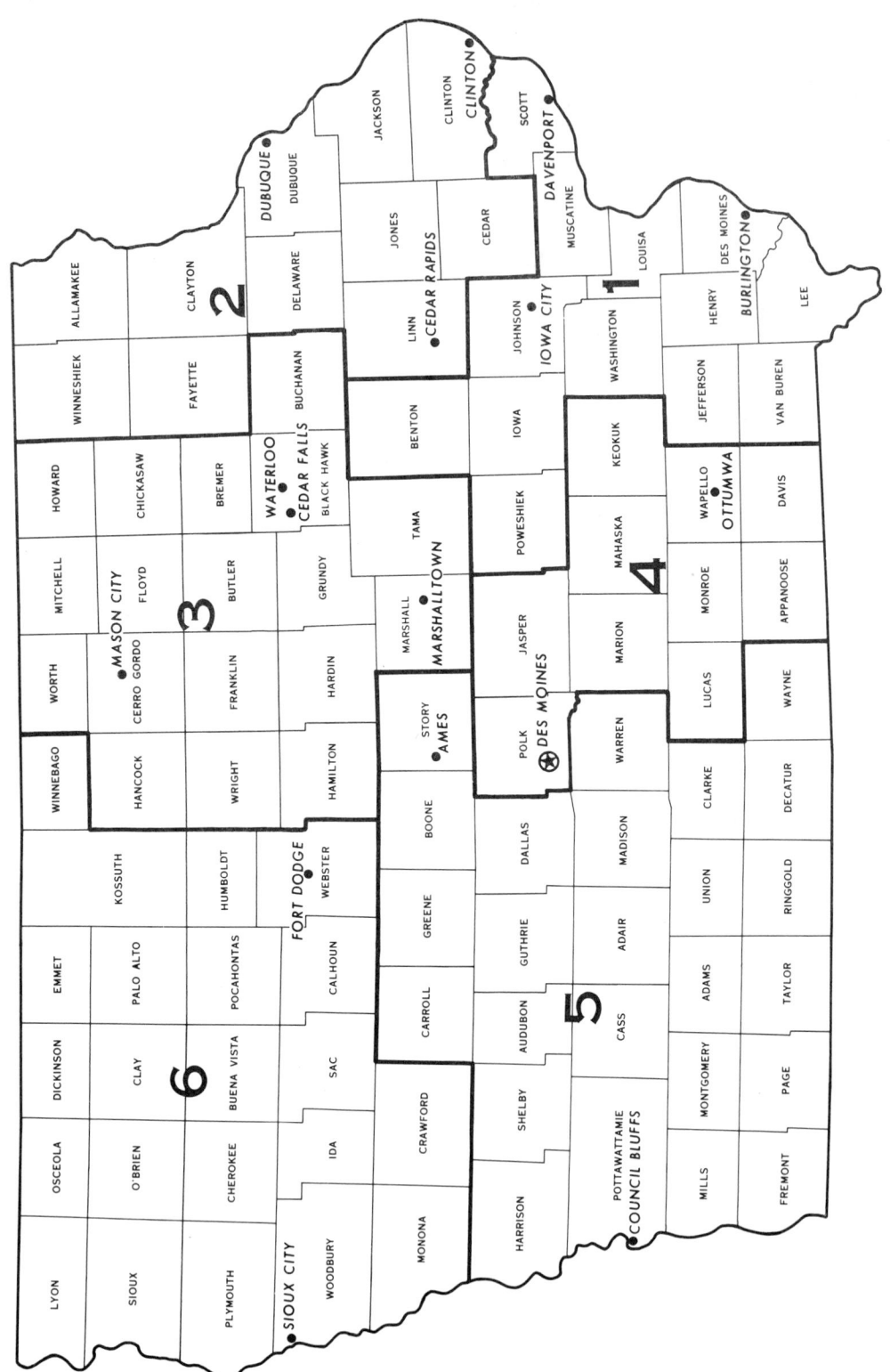

IOWA

PRESIDENT 1980

1980 Census Population	County	Total Vote	Republican	Democratic	Other	Rep.-Dem. Plurality	Total Vote Rep.	Total Vote Dem.	Major Vote Rep.	Major Vote Dem.
9,509	ADAIR	4,689	2,821	1,454	414	1,367 R	60.2%	31.0%	66.0%	34.0%
5,731	ADAMS	2,984	1,779	940	265	839 R	59.6%	31.5%	65.4%	34.6%
15,108	ALLAMAKEE	6,586	4,000	2,170	416	1,830 R	60.7%	32.9%	64.8%	35.2%
15,511	APPANOOSE	6,728	3,544	2,769	415	775 R	52.7%	41.2%	56.1%	43.9%
8,559	AUDUBON	4,353	2,523	1,546	284	977 R	58.0%	35.5%	62.0%	38.0%
23,649	BENTON	10,635	5,329	4,223	1,083	1,106 R	50.1%	39.7%	55.8%	44.2%
137,961	BLACK HAWK	63,722	29,627	27,443	6,652	2,184 R	46.5%	43.1%	51.9%	48.1%
26,184	BOONE	12,087	5,732	5,126	1,229	606 R	47.4%	42.4%	52.8%	47.2%
24,820	BREMER	11,318	6,706	3,527	1,085	3,179 R	59.3%	31.2%	65.5%	34.5%
22,900	BUCHANAN	9,422	5,041	3,605	776	1,436 R	53.5%	38.3%	58.3%	41.7%
20,774	BUENA VISTA	9,676	5,272	3,468	936	1,804 R	54.5%	35.8%	60.3%	39.7%
17,668	BUTLER	7,177	4,730	1,990	457	2,740 R	65.9%	27.7%	70.4%	29.6%
13,542	CALHOUN	6,328	3,633	2,150	545	1,483 R	57.4%	34.0%	62.8%	37.2%
22,951	CARROLL	9,737	5,017	3,885	835	1,132 R	51.5%	39.9%	56.4%	43.6%
16,932	CASS	8,126	5,391	2,176	559	3,215 R	66.3%	26.8%	71.2%	28.8%
18,635	CEDAR	7,797	4,398	2,589	810	1,809 R	56.4%	33.2%	62.9%	37.1%
48,458	CERRO GORDO	22,828	11,189	9,363	2,276	1,826 R	49.0%	41.0%	54.4%	45.6%
16,238	CHEROKEE	7,500	4,087	2,719	694	1,368 R	54.5%	36.3%	60.0%	40.0%
15,437	CHICKASAW	7,433	3,929	2,935	569	994 R	52.9%	39.5%	57.2%	42.8%
8,612	CLARKE	4,404	2,417	1,614	373	803 R	54.9%	36.6%	60.0%	40.0%
19,576	CLAY	8,764	4,479	3,179	1,106	1,300 R	51.1%	36.3%	58.5%	41.5%
21,098	CLAYTON	9,206	5,115	3,297	794	1,818 R	55.6%	35.8%	60.8%	39.2%
57,122	CLINTON	25,211	13,025	9,698	2,488	3,327 R	51.7%	38.5%	57.3%	42.7%
18,935	CRAWFORD	8,002	4,883	2,500	619	2,383 R	61.0%	31.2%	66.1%	33.9%
29,513	DALLAS	12,964	6,296	5,310	1,358	986 R	48.6%	41.0%	54.2%	45.8%
9,104	DAVIS	3,930	2,003	1,689	238	314 R	51.0%	43.0%	54.3%	45.7%
9,794	DECATUR	4,640	2,212	2,048	380	164 R	47.7%	44.1%	51.9%	48.1%
18,933	DELAWARE	7,794	4,316	2,671	807	1,645 R	55.4%	34.3%	61.8%	38.2%
46,203	DES MOINES	20,417	9,158	9,977	1,282	819 D	44.9%	48.9%	47.9%	52.1%
15,629	DICKINSON	7,442	4,028	2,620	794	1,408 R	54.1%	35.2%	60.6%	39.4%
93,745	DUBUQUE	41,539	18,649	18,689	4,201	40 D	44.9%	45.0%	49.9%	50.1%
13,336	EMMET	5,724	3,062	2,153	509	909 R	53.5%	37.6%	58.7%	41.3%
25,488	FAYETTE	11,523	6,374	4,377	772	1,997 R	55.3%	38.0%	59.3%	40.7%
19,597	FLOYD	9,118	4,665	3,634	819	1,031 R	51.2%	39.9%	56.2%	43.8%
13,036	FRANKLIN	5,682	3,290	1,920	472	1,370 R	57.9%	33.8%	63.1%	36.9%
9,401	FREMONT	4,131	2,693	1,203	235	1,490 R	65.2%	29.1%	69.1%	30.9%
12,119	GREENE	5,939	3,154	2,210	575	944 R	53.1%	37.2%	58.8%	41.2%
14,366	GRUNDY	7,026	4,644	1,869	513	2,775 R	66.1%	26.6%	71.3%	28.7%
11,983	GUTHRIE	5,514	3,214	1,866	434	1,348 R	58.3%	33.8%	63.3%	36.7%
17,862	HAMILTON	8,266	4,745	2,741	780	2,004 R	57.4%	33.2%	63.4%	36.6%
13,833	HANCOCK	6,092	3,681	1,918	493	1,763 R	60.4%	31.5%	65.7%	34.3%
21,776	HARDIN	9,920	5,329	3,757	834	1,572 R	53.7%	37.9%	58.7%	41.3%
16,348	HARRISON	7,053	4,502	2,152	399	2,350 R	63.8%	30.5%	67.7%	32.3%
18,890	HENRY	8,462	4,430	3,317	715	1,113 R	52.4%	39.2%	57.2%	42.8%
11,114	HOWARD	5,576	2,975	2,214	387	761 R	53.4%	39.7%	57.3%	42.7%
12,246	HUMBOLDT	5,899	3,575	1,840	484	1,735 R	60.6%	31.2%	66.0%	34.0%
8,908	IDA	4,354	2,825	1,235	294	1,590 R	64.9%	28.4%	69.6%	30.4%
15,429	IOWA	7,522	4,153	2,606	763	1,547 R	55.2%	34.6%	61.4%	38.6%
22,503	JACKSON	8,754	4,479	3,518	757	961 R	51.2%	40.2%	56.0%	44.0%
36,425	JASPER	16,966	8,286	7,258	1,422	1,028 R	48.8%	42.8%	53.3%	46.7%
16,316	JEFFERSON	7,299	4,099	2,577	623	1,522 R	56.2%	35.3%	61.4%	38.6%
81,717	JOHNSON	42,997	13,642	20,122	9,233	6,480 D	31.7%	46.8%	40.4%	59.6%
20,401	JONES	8,913	4,506	3,521	886	985 R	50.6%	39.5%	56.1%	43.9%
12,921	KEOKUK	5,975	3,145	2,390	440	755 R	52.6%	40.0%	56.8%	43.2%
21,891	KOSSUTH	10,262	5,568	3,810	884	1,758 R	54.3%	37.1%	59.4%	40.6%
43,106	LEE	18,265	8,793	8,204	1,268	589 R	48.1%	44.9%	51.7%	48.3%
169,775	LINN	78,224	36,254	31,950	10,020	4,304 R	46.3%	40.8%	53.2%	46.8%
12,055	LOUISA	4,584	2,530	1,700	354	830 R	55.2%	37.1%	59.8%	40.2%
10,313	LUCAS	4,929	2,593	1,989	347	604 R	52.6%	40.4%	56.6%	43.4%
12,896	LYON	6,208	4,349	1,431	428	2,918 R	70.1%	23.1%	75.2%	24.8%
12,597	MADISON	6,411	3,320	2,496	595	824 R	51.8%	38.9%	57.1%	42.9%
22,507	MAHASKA	10,363	5,650	3,968	745	1,682 R	54.5%	38.3%	58.7%	41.3%
29,669	MARION	13,518	6,665	5,490	1,363	1,175 R	49.3%	40.6%	54.8%	45.2%
41,652	MARSHALL	19,626	10,707	7,114	1,805	3,593 R	54.6%	36.2%	60.1%	39.9%
13,406	MILLS	5,183	3,581	1,244	358	2,337 R	69.1%	24.0%	74.2%	25.8%
12,329	MITCHELL	5,864	3,401	2,040	423	1,361 R	58.0%	34.8%	62.5%	37.5%
11,692	MONONA	5,284	3,268	1,660	356	1,608 R	61.8%	31.4%	66.3%	33.7%
9,209	MONROE	4,117	2,003	1,866	248	137 R	48.7%	45.3%	51.8%	48.2%
13,413	MONTGOMERY	6,054	4,115	1,556	383	2,559 R	68.0%	25.7%	72.6%	27.4%
40,436	MUSCATINE	15,145	7,829	5,597	1,719	2,232 R	51.7%	37.0%	58.3%	41.7%

IOWA

PRESIDENT 1980

1980 Census Population	County	Total Vote	Republican	Democratic	Other	Rep.-Dem. Plurality	Percentage Total Vote Rep.	Dem.	Major Vote Rep.	Dem.
16,972	O'BRIEN	7,761	4,937	2,210	614	2,727 R	63.6%	28.5%	69.1%	30.9%
8,371	OSCEOLA	3,486	2,177	1,051	258	1,126 R	62.4%	30.1%	67.4%	32.6%
19,063	PAGE	7,810	5,618	1,772	420	3,846 R	71.9%	22.7%	76.0%	24.0%
12,721	PALO ALTO	5,968	3,025	2,463	480	562 R	50.7%	41.3%	55.1%	44.9%
24,743	PLYMOUTH	10,346	6,515	2,965	866	3,550 R	63.0%	28.7%	68.7%	31.3%
11,369	POCAHONTAS	5,686	3,194	1,959	533	1,235 R	56.2%	34.5%	62.0%	38.0%
303,170	POLK	143,758	64,156	61,984	17,618	2,172 R	44.6%	43.1%	50.9%	49.1%
86,500	POTTAWATTAMIE	33,170	20,222	10,709	2,239	9,513 R	61.0%	32.3%	65.4%	34.6%
19,306	POWESHIEK	9,102	4,598	3,529	975	1,069 R	50.5%	38.8%	56.6%	43.4%
6,112	RINGGOLD	3,251	1,884	1,150	217	734 R	58.0%	35.4%	62.1%	37.9%
14,118	SAC	6,264	3,725	1,976	563	1,749 R	59.5%	31.5%	65.3%	34.7%
160,022	SCOTT	67,926	34,701	26,391	6,834	8,310 R	51.1%	38.9%	56.8%	43.2%
15,043	SHELBY	6,477	4,147	1,892	438	2,255 R	64.0%	29.2%	68.7%	31.3%
30,813	SIOUX	14,167	10,768	2,698	701	8,070 R	76.0%	19.0%	80.0%	20.0%
72,326	STORY	37,371	15,829	13,529	8,013	2,300 R	42.4%	36.2%	53.9%	46.1%
19,533	TAMA	8,602	4,840	3,049	713	1,791 R	56.3%	35.4%	61.4%	38.6%
8,353	TAYLOR	4,213	2,715	1,226	272	1,489 R	64.4%	29.1%	68.9%	31.1%
13,858	UNION	5,979	3,372	2,182	425	1,190 R	56.4%	36.5%	60.7%	39.3%
8,626	VAN BUREN	3,680	2,142	1,311	227	831 R	58.2%	35.6%	62.0%	38.0%
40,241	WAPELLO	17,668	7,475	8,923	1,270	1,448 D	42.3%	50.5%	45.6%	54.4%
34,878	WARREN	15,519	7,360	6,610	1,549	750 R	47.4%	42.6%	52.7%	47.3%
20,141	WASHINGTON	7,627	3,967	2,877	783	1,090 R	52.0%	37.7%	58.0%	42.0%
8,199	WAYNE	4,104	2,221	1,627	256	594 R	54.1%	39.6%	57.7%	42.3%
45,953	WEBSTER	21,030	10,438	9,001	1,591	1,437 R	49.6%	42.8%	53.7%	46.3%
13,010	WINNEBAGO	6,479	3,808	2,208	463	1,600 R	58.8%	34.1%	63.3%	36.7%
21,876	WINNESHIEK	9,304	5,033	3,201	1,070	1,832 R	54.1%	34.4%	61.1%	38.9%
100,884	WOODBURY	43,275	23,553	15,930	3,792	7,623 R	54.4%	36.8%	59.7%	40.3%
9,075	WORTH	4,310	2,247	1,721	342	526 R	52.1%	39.9%	56.6%	43.4%
16,319	WRIGHT	7,147	3,936	2,645	566	1,291 R	55.1%	37.0%	59.8%	40.2%
2,913,387	TOTAL	1,317,661	676,026	508,672	132,963	167,354 R	51.3%	38.6%	57.1%	42.9%

IOWA

SENATOR 1980

1980 Census Population	County	Total Vote	Republican	Democratic	Other	Rep.-Dem. Plurality	Percentage Total Vote Rep.	Dem.	Major Vote Rep.	Dem.
9,509	ADAIR	4,559	2,786	1,742	31	1,044 R	61.1%	38.2%	61.5%	38.5%
5,731	ADAMS	2,789	1,755	1,023	11	732 R	62.9%	36.7%	63.2%	36.8%
15,108	ALLAMAKEE	6,398	4,254	2,109	35	2,145 R	66.5%	33.0%	66.9%	33.1%
15,511	APPANOOSE	6,477	3,550	2,811	116	739 R	54.8%	43.4%	55.8%	44.2%
8,559	AUDUBON	4,149	2,500	1,623	26	877 R	60.3%	39.1%	60.6%	39.4%
23,649	BENTON	10,468	5,977	4,374	117	1,603 R	57.1%	41.8%	57.7%	42.3%
137,961	BLACK HAWK	62,795	33,918	28,415	462	5,503 R	54.0%	45.3%	54.4%	45.6%
26,184	BOONE	11,609	5,647	5,832	130	185 D	48.6%	50.2%	49.2%	50.8%
24,820	BREMER	11,170	7,822	3,301	47	4,521 R	70.0%	29.6%	70.3%	29.7%
22,900	BUCHANAN	9,049	5,340	3,682	27	1,658 R	59.0%	40.7%	59.2%	40.8%
20,774	BUENA VISTA	9,311	5,158	4,031	122	1,127 R	55.4%	43.3%	56.1%	43.9%
17,668	BUTLER	7,123	5,422	1,676	25	3,746 R	76.1%	23.5%	76.4%	23.6%
13,542	CALHOUN	6,174	3,716	2,359	99	1,357 R	60.2%	38.2%	61.2%	38.8%
22,951	CARROLL	9,227	5,059	4,029	139	1,030 R	54.8%	43.7%	55.7%	44.3%
16,932	CASS	7,608	5,242	2,312	54	2,930 R	68.9%	30.4%	69.4%	30.6%
18,603	CEDAR	7,575	4,561	2,941	73	1,620 R	60.2%	38.8%	60.8%	39.2%
48,458	CERRO GORDO	22,252	12,444	9,677	131	2,767 R	55.9%	43.5%	56.3%	43.7%
16,238	CHEROKEE	7,193	4,131	3,003	59	1,128 R	57.4%	41.7%	57.9%	42.1%
15,437	CHICKASAW	7,289	4,692	2,580	17	2,112 R	64.4%	35.4%	64.5%	35.5%
8,612	CLARKE	4,266	2,329	1,913	24	416 R	54.6%	44.8%	54.9%	45.1%
19,576	CLAY	8,269	4,481	3,697	91	784 R	54.2%	44.7%	54.8%	45.2%
21,098	CLAYTON	9,020	5,132	3,834	54	1,298 R	56.9%	42.5%	57.2%	42.8%
57,122	CLINTON	24,430	12,796	11,422	212	1,374 R	52.4%	46.8%	52.8%	47.2%
18,935	CRAWFORD	7,460	4,901	2,490	69	2,411 R	65.7%	33.4%	66.3%	33.7%
29,513	DALLAS	12,701	6,084	6,522	95	438 D	47.9%	51.4%	48.3%	51.7%
9,104	DAVIS	3,845	2,035	1,784	26	251 R	52.9%	46.4%	53.3%	46.7%
9,794	DECATUR	4,495	2,287	2,179	29	108 R	50.9%	48.5%	51.2%	48.8%
18,933	DELAWARE	7,581	4,613	2,905	63	1,708 R	60.8%	38.3%	61.4%	38.6%
46,203	DES MOINES	19,721	9,286	10,251	184	965 D	47.1%	52.0%	47.5%	52.5%
15,629	DICKINSON	6,951	3,864	2,997	90	867 R	55.6%	43.1%	56.3%	43.7%
93,745	DUBUQUE	40,321	19,172	20,877	272	1,705 D	47.5%	51.8%	47.9%	52.1%
13,336	EMMET	5,370	2,863	2,431	76	432 R	53.3%	45.3%	54.1%	45.9%
25,488	FAYETTE	11,414	6,702	4,642	70	2,060 R	58.7%	40.7%	59.1%	40.9%
19,597	FLOYD	8,902	5,246	3,590	66	1,656 R	58.9%	40.3%	59.4%	40.6%
13,036	FRANKLIN	5,579	3,888	1,654	37	2,234 R	69.7%	29.6%	70.2%	29.8%
9,401	FREMONT	3,873	2,611	1,224	38	1,387 R	67.4%	31.6%	68.1%	31.9%
12,119	GREENE	5,672	3,070	2,535	67	535 R	54.1%	44.7%	54.8%	45.2%
14,366	GRUNDY	6,930	5,309	1,592	29	3,717 R	76.6%	23.0%	76.9%	23.1%
11,983	GUTHRIE	5,337	3,070	2,228	39	842 R	57.5%	41.7%	57.9%	42.1%
17,862	HAMILTON	8,106	5,218	2,814	74	2,404 R	64.4%	34.7%	65.0%	35.0%
13,833	HANCOCK	5,957	4,044	1,879	34	2,165 R	67.9%	31.5%	68.3%	31.7%
21,776	HARDIN	9,536	5,822	3,626	88	2,196 R	61.1%	38.0%	61.6%	38.4%
16,348	HARRISON	6,750	4,478	2,255	17	2,223 R	66.3%	33.4%	66.5%	33.5%
18,890	HENRY	8,147	4,598	3,515	34	1,083 R	56.4%	43.1%	56.7%	43.3%
11,114	HOWARD	5,525	3,742	1,778	5	1,964 R	67.7%	32.2%	67.8%	32.2%
12,246	HUMBOLDT	5,731	3,469	2,198	64	1,271 R	60.5%	38.4%	61.2%	38.8%
8,908	IDA	4,156	2,765	1,365	26	1,400 R	66.5%	32.8%	66.9%	33.1%
15,429	IOWA	7,319	4,476	2,775	68	1,701 R	61.2%	37.9%	61.7%	38.3%
22,503	JACKSON	8,426	4,515	3,806	105	709 R	53.6%	45.2%	54.3%	45.7%
36,425	JASPER	16,581	8,496	7,902	183	594 R	51.2%	47.7%	51.8%	48.2%
16,316	JEFFERSON	7,018	4,200	2,743	75	1,457 R	59.8%	39.1%	60.5%	39.5%
81,717	JOHNSON	42,135	13,311	28,412	412	15,101 D	31.6%	67.4%	31.9%	68.1%
20,401	JONES	8,745	4,784	3,899	62	885 R	54.7%	44.6%	55.1%	44.9%
12,921	KEOKUK	5,796	3,324	2,378	94	946 R	57.3%	41.0%	58.3%	41.7%
21,891	KOSSUTH	9,717	5,848	3,784	85	2,064 R	60.2%	38.9%	60.7%	39.3%
43,106	LEE	17,498	8,297	8,990	211	693 D	47.4%	51.4%	48.0%	52.0%
169,775	LINN	77,098	35,829	40,460	809	4,631 D	46.5%	52.5%	47.0%	53.0%
12,055	LOUISA	4,493	2,697	1,769	27	928 R	60.0%	39.4%	60.4%	39.6%
10,313	LUCAS	4,788	2,668	2,089	31	579 R	55.7%	43.6%	56.1%	43.9%
12,896	LYON	5,835	4,303	1,487	45	2,816 R	73.7%	25.5%	74.3%	25.7%
12,597	MADISON	6,009	3,140	2,838	31	302 R	52.3%	47.2%	52.5%	47.5%
22,507	MAHASKA	10,068	5,696	4,259	113	1,437 R	56.6%	42.3%	57.2%	42.8%
29,669	MARION	13,029	6,764	6,106	159	658 R	51.9%	46.9%	52.6%	47.4%
41,652	MARSHALL	19,234	11,560	7,492	182	4,068 R	60.1%	39.0%	60.7%	39.3%
13,406	MILLS	4,874	3,533	1,295	46	2,238 R	72.5%	26.6%	73.2%	26.8%
12,329	MITCHELL	5,765	3,903	1,816	46	2,087 R	67.7%	31.5%	68.2%	31.8%
11,692	MONONA	4,938	3,098	1,801	39	1,297 R	62.7%	36.5%	63.2%	36.8%
9,209	MONROE	3,980	1,942	2,013	25	71 D	48.8%	50.6%	49.1%	50.9%
13,413	MONTGOMERY	5,650	4,087	1,510	53	2,577 R	72.3%	26.7%	73.0%	27.0%
40,436	MUSCATINE	14,603	8,110	6,290	203	1,820 R	55.5%	43.1%	56.3%	43.7%

IOWA

SENATOR 1980

1980 Census Population	County	Total Vote	Republican	Democratic	Other	Rep.-Dem. Plurality	Percentage Total Vote Rep.	Dem.	Major Vote Rep.	Dem.
16,972	O'BRIEN	7,302	4,794	2,443	65	2,351 R	65.7%	33.5%	66.2%	33.8%
8,371	OSCEOLA	3,289	2,034	1,217	38	817 R	61.8%	37.0%	62.6%	37.4%
19,063	PAGE	7,409	5,423	1,947	39	3,476 R	73.2%	26.3%	73.6%	26.4%
12,721	PALO ALTO	5,547	2,814	2,650	83	164 R	50.7%	47.8%	51.5%	48.5%
24,743	PLYMOUTH	9,715	6,358	3,243	114	3,115 R	65.4%	33.4%	66.2%	33.8%
11,369	POCAHONTAS	5,501	3,090	2,313	98	777 R	56.2%	42.0%	57.2%	42.8%
303,170	POLK	139,914	59,965	78,300	1,649	18,335 D	42.9%	56.0%	43.4%	56.6%
86,500	POTTAWATTAMIE	31,400	18,921	12,150	329	6,771 R	60.3%	38.7%	60.9%	39.1%
19,306	POWESHIEK	8,898	4,615	4,213	70	402 R	51.9%	47.3%	52.3%	47.7%
6,112	RINGGOLD	3,151	1,921	1,217	13	704 R	61.0%	38.6%	61.2%	38.8%
14,118	SAC	5,857	3,627	2,145	85	1,482 R	61.9%	36.6%	62.8%	37.2%
160,022	SCOTT	66,809	33,653	32,228	928	1,425 R	50.4%	48.2%	51.1%	48.9%
15,043	SHELBY	6,203	4,220	1,940	43	2,280 R	68.0%	31.3%	68.5%	31.5%
30,813	SIOUX	13,561	10,691	2,794	76	7,897 R	78.8%	20.6%	79.3%	20.7%
72,326	STORY	36,427	15,848	20,191	388	4,343 D	43.5%	55.4%	44.0%	56.0%
19,533	TAMA	8,897	5,637	3,182	78	2,455 R	63.4%	35.8%	63.9%	36.1%
8,353	TAYLOR	3,914	2,620	1,283	11	1,337 R	66.9%	32.8%	67.1%	32.9%
13,858	UNION	5,682	3,237	2,389	56	848 R	57.0%	42.0%	57.5%	42.5%
8,626	VAN BUREN	3,559	2,183	1,364	12	819 R	61.3%	38.3%	61.5%	38.5%
40,241	WAPELLO	17,063	7,242	9,530	291	2,288 D	42.4%	55.9%	43.2%	56.8%
34,878	WARREN	15,180	7,200	7,834	146	634 D	47.4%	51.6%	47.9%	52.1%
20,141	WASHINGTON	7,384	4,192	3,120	72	1,072 R	56.8%	42.3%	57.3%	42.7%
8,199	WAYNE	3,849	2,216	1,604	29	612 R	57.6%	41.7%	58.0%	42.0%
45,953	WEBSTER	20,129	9,673	10,128	328	455 D	48.1%	50.3%	48.9%	51.1%
13,010	WINNEBAGO	6,264	3,941	2,311	12	1,630 R	62.9%	36.9%	63.0%	37.0%
21,876	WINNESHIEK	8,976	5,478	3,420	78	2,058 R	61.0%	38.1%	61.6%	38.4%
100,884	WOODBURY	41,065	22,093	18,484	488	3,609 R	53.8%	45.0%	54.4%	45.6%
9,075	WORTH	4,211	2,472	1,723	16	749 R	58.7%	40.9%	58.9%	41.1%
16,319	WRIGHT	7,019	4,426	2,551	42	1,875 R	63.1%	36.3%	63.4%	36.6%
2,913,387	TOTAL	1,277,034	683,014	581,545	12,475	101,469 R	53.5%	45.5%	54.0%	46.0%

IOWA

CONGRESS

CD	Year	Total Vote	Republican		Democratic		Other Vote	Rep.-Dem. Plurality	Percentage Total Vote		Major Vote	
			Vote	Candidate	Vote	Candidate			Rep.	Dem.	Rep.	Dem.
1	1980	208,127	133,349	LEACH, JAMES A.	72,602	LAREW, JIM	2,176	60,747 R	64.1%	34.9%	64.7%	35.3%
1	1978	125,962	79,940	LEACH, JAMES A.	45,037	MYERS, DICK	985	34,903 R	63.5%	35.8%	64.0%	36.0%
1	1976	211,204	109,694	LEACH, JAMES A.	101,024	MEZVINSKY, EDWARD	486	8,670 R	51.9%	47.8%	52.1%	47.9%
1	1974	139,240	63,540	LEACH, JAMES A.	75,687	MEZVINSKY, EDWARD	13	12,147 D	45.6%	54.4%	45.6%	54.4%
1	1972	200,633	91,609	SCHWENGEL, FRED	107,099	MEZVINSKY, EDWARD	1,925	15,490 D	45.7%	53.4%	46.1%	53.9%
2	1980	206,637	111,587	TAUKE, TOM	93,175	SOVERN, STEVE	1,875	18,412 R	54.0%	45.1%	54.5%	45.5%
2	1978	138,982	72,644	TAUKE, TOM	65,450	BLOUIN, MICHAEL	888	7,194 R	52.3%	47.1%	52.6%	47.4%
2	1976	204,556	100,344	RILEY, TOM	102,980	BLOUIN, MICHAEL	1,232	2,636 D	49.1%	50.3%	49.4%	50.6%
2	1974	143,628	69,088	RILEY, TOM	73,416	BLOUIN, MICHAEL	1,124	4,328 D	48.1%	51.1%	48.5%	51.5%
2	1972	195,156	79,667	ELLSWORTH, THEODORE R.	115,489	CULVER, JOHN C.		35,822 D	40.8%	59.2%	40.8%	59.2%
3	1980	209,948	107,869	EVANS, COOPER	101,735	CUTLER, LYNN G.	344	6,134 R	51.4%	48.5%	51.5%	48.5%
3	1978	138,578	103,659	GRASSLEY, CHARLES E.	34,880	KNUDSON, JOHN	39	68,779 R	74.8%	25.2%	74.8%	25.2%
3	1976	208,943	117,957	GRASSLEY, CHARLES E.	90,981	RAPP, STEPHEN J.	5	26,976 R	56.5%	43.5%	56.5%	43.5%
3	1974	152,371	77,468	GRASSLEY, CHARLES E.	74,895	RAPP, STEPHEN J.	8	2,573 R	50.8%	49.2%	50.8%	49.2%
3	1972	195,965	109,113	GROSS, H. R.	86,848	TAYLOR, LYLE D.	4	22,265 R	55.7%	44.3%	55.7%	44.3%
4	1980	218,627	100,335	YOUNG, DONALD C.	117,896	SMITH, NEAL	396	17,561 D	45.9%	53.9%	46.0%	54.0%
4	1978	136,855	48,308	MINOR, CHARLES E.	88,526	SMITH, NEAL	21	40,218 D	35.3%	64.7%	35.3%	64.7%
4	1976	210,364	65,013	MINOR, CHARLES E.	145,343	SMITH, NEAL	8	80,330 D	30.9%	69.1%	30.9%	69.1%
4	1974	151,429	53,756	DICK, CHUCK	96,755	SMITH, NEAL	918	42,999 D	35.5%	63.9%	35.7%	64.3%
4	1972	210,588	85,156	KYL, JOHN	125,431	SMITH, NEAL	1	40,275 D	40.4%	59.6%	40.4%	59.6%
5	1980	212,370	84,472	HULTMAN, CAL	127,895	HARKIN, TOM	3	43,423 D	39.8%	60.2%	39.8%	60.2%
5	1978	139,716	57,377	GARRETT, JULIAN B.	82,333	HARKIN, TOM	6	24,956 D	41.1%	58.9%	41.1%	58.9%
5	1976	209,062	71,377	FULK, KENNETH R.	135,600	HARKIN, TOM	2,085	64,223 D	34.1%	64.9%	34.5%	65.5%
5	1974	158,835	77,683	SCHERLE, WILLIAM J.	81,146	HARKIN, TOM	6	3,463 D	48.9%	51.1%	48.9%	51.1%
5	1972	196,536	108,596	SCHERLE, WILLIAM J.	87,937	HARKIN, TOM	3	20,659 R	55.3%	44.7%	55.3%	44.7%
6	1980	201,327	71,866	CARNEY, CLARENCE S.	129,460	BEDELL, BERKLEY	1	57,594 D	35.7%	64.3%	35.7%	64.3%
6	1978	131,462	44,320	JUNKER, WILLIS E.	87,139	BEDELL, BERKLEY	3	42,819 D	33.7%	66.3%	33.7%	66.3%
6	1976	198,012	62,292	SOPER, JOANNE D.	133,507	BEDELL, BERKLEY	2,213	71,215 D	31.5%	67.4%	31.8%	68.2%
6	1974	158,012	71,695	MAYNE, WILEY	86,315	BEDELL, BERKLEY	2	14,620 D	45.4%	54.6%	45.4%	54.6%
6	1972	196,858	103,284	MAYNE, WILEY	93,574	BEDELL, BERKLEY		9,710 R	52.5%	47.5%	52.5%	47.5%

IOWA

1980 GENERAL ELECTION

President   Other vote was 115,633 Anderson (by petition); 13,123 Clark (Libertarian); 2,273 Commoner (Citizens); 534 McReynolds (Socialist); 298 Hall (Communist); 244 DeBerry (Socialist Workers); 189 Greaves (American); 150 Bubar (Statesman); 519 scattered.

Senator   Other vote was 5,858 DeYoung (by petition); 4,233 Hengerer (Libertarian); 2,336 Henderson (by petition); 48 scattered.

Congress   Other vote was 1,091 Williams (Socialist), 1,069 Grant (Libertarian) and 16 scattered in CD 1; 985 Miller (Libertarian), 887 Roberson (by petition) and 3 scattered in CD 2; 341 Suppus (American) and 3 scattered in CD 3; 389 Saadig (Socialist) and 7 scattered in CD 4; scattered in CD 5 and 6.

1980 PRIMARIES

JUNE 3 REPUBLICAN

Senator   170,120 Charles E. Grassley; 89,409 Tom Stoner.

Congress   Unopposed in four CD's. Contested as follows:

CD 3   26,480 Cooper Evans; 20,460 Jim West; 10,871 Bill Hansen; 1,372 Paul E. Sires; 1 scattered.
CD 4   21,432 Donald C. Young; 7,755 Jack Heidel; 5,065 George Cosson; 6 scattered.

JUNE 3 DEMOCRATIC

Senator   John C. Culver, unopposed.

Congress   Unopposed in five CD's. Contested as follows:

CD 1   11,485 Jim Larew; 5,549 Rick Nielsen; 9 scattered.

KANSAS

GOVERNOR
John Carlin (D). Elected 1978 to a four-year term.

SENATORS
Robert Dole (R). Re-elected 1980 to a six-year term. Previously elected 1974, 1968.

Nancy Landon Kassebaum (R). Elected 1978 to a six-year term.

REPRESENTATIVES
1. Pat Roberts (R)
2. Jim Jeffries (R)
3. Larry Winn (R)
4. Dan Glickman (D)
5. Robert Whittaker (R)

POSTWAR VOTE FOR GOVERNOR

| | | | | | | | | | Percentage | | | |
| | Total | Republican | | Democratic | | Other | Rep.-Dem. | Total Vote | | Major Vote | |
Year	Vote	Vote	Candidate	Vote	Candidate	Vote	Plurality	Rep.	Dem.	Rep.	Dem.
1978	736,246	348,015	Bennett, Robert F.	363,835	Carlin, John	24,396	15,820 D	47.3%	49.4%	48.9%	51.1%
1974	783,875	387,792	Bennett, Robert F.	384,115	Miller, Vern	11,968	3,677 R	49.5%	49.0%	50.2%	49.8%
1972	921,552	341,440	Kay, Morris	571,256	Docking, Robert	8,856	229,816 D	37.1%	62.0%	37.4%	62.6%
1970	745,196	333,227	Frizzell, Kent	404,611	Docking, Robert	7,358	71,384 D	44.7%	54.3%	45.2%	54.8%
1968	862,473	410,673	Harman, Rick	447,269	Docking, Robert	4,531	36,596 D	47.6%	51.9%	47.9%	52.1%
1966	692,955	304,325	Avery, William H.	380,030	Docking, Robert	8,600	75,705 D	43.9%	54.8%	44.5%	55.5%
1964	850,414	432,667	Avery, William H.	400,264	Wiles, Harry G.	17,483	32,403 R	50.9%	47.1%	51.9%	48.1%
1962	638,798	341,257	Anderson, John	291,285	Saffels, Dale E.	6,256	49,972 R	53.4%	45.6%	54.0%	46.0%
1960	922,522	511,534	Anderson, John	402,261	Docking, George	8,727	109,273 R	55.4%	43.6%	56.0%	44.0%
1958	735,939	313,036	Reed, Clyde M.	415,506	Docking, George	7,397	102,470 D	42.5%	56.5%	43.0%	57.0%
1956	864,935	364,340	Shaw, Warren W.	479,701	Docking, George	20,894	115,361 D	42.1%	55.5%	43.2%	56.8%
1954	622,633	329,868	Hall, Fred	286,218	Docking, George	6,547	43,650 R	53.0%	46.0%	53.5%	46.5%
1952	872,139	491,338	Arn, Edward F.	363,482	Rooney, Charles	17,319	127,856 R	56.3%	41.7%	57.5%	42.5%
1950	619,310	333,001	Arn, Edward F.	275,494	Anderson, Kenneth	10,815	57,507 R	53.8%	44.5%	54.7%	45.3%
1948	760,407	433,396	Carlson, Frank	307,485	Carpenter, Randolph	19,526	125,911 R	57.0%	40.4%	58.5%	41.5%
1946	577,694	309,064	Carlson, Frank	254,283	Woodring, Harry H.	14,347	54,781 R	53.5%	44.0%	54.9%	45.1%

The term of office of Kansas' Governor was increased from two to four years effective with the 1974 election.

POSTWAR VOTE FOR SENATOR

| | | | | | | | | | Percentage | | | |
| | Total | Republican | | Democratic | | Other | Rep.-Dem. | Total Vote | | Major Vote | |
Year	Vote	Vote	Candidate	Vote	Candidate	Vote	Plurality	Rep.	Dem.	Rep.	Dem.
1980	938,957	598,686	Dole, Robert	340,271	Simpson, John	—	258,415 R	63.8%	36.2%	63.8%	36.2%
1978	748,839	403,354	Kassebaum, Nancy Landon	317,602	Roy, William R.	27,883	85,752 R	53.9%	42.4%	55.9%	44.1%
1974	794,437	403,983	Dole, Robert	390,451	Roy, William R.	3	13,532 R	50.9%	49.1%	50.9%	49.1%
1972	871,722	622,591	Pearson, James B.	200,764	Tetzlaff, Arch O.	48,367	421,827 R	71.4%	23.0%	75.6%	24.4%
1968	817,096	490,911	Dole, Robert	315,911	Robinson, William I.	10,274	175,000 R	60.1%	38.7%	60.8%	39.2%
1966	671,345	350,077	Pearson, James B.	303,223	Breeding, J. Floyd	18,045	46,854 R	52.1%	45.2%	53.6%	46.4%
1962	622,232	388,500	Carlson, Frank	223,630	Smith, K. L.	10,102	164,870 R	62.4%	35.9%	63.5%	36.5%
1962s	613,250	344,689	Pearson, James B.	260,756	Aylward, Paul L.	7,805	83,933 R	56.2%	42.5%	56.9%	43.1%
1960	888,592	485,499	Schoeppel, Andrew F.	388,895	Theis, Frank	14,198	96,604 R	54.6%	43.8%	55.5%	44.5%
1956	825,280	477,822	Carlson, Frank	333,939	Hart, George	13,519	143,883 R	57.9%	40.5%	58.9%	41.1%
1954	618,063	348,144	Schoeppel, Andrew F.	258,575	McGill, George	11,344	89,569 R	56.3%	41.8%	57.4%	42.6%
1950	619,104	335,880	Carlson, Frank	271,365	Aiken, Paul	11,859	64,515 R	54.3%	43.8%	55.3%	44.7%
1948	716,342	393,412	Schoeppel, Andrew F.	305,987	McGill, George	·16,943	87,425 R	54.9%	42.7%	56.3%	43.7%

One of the 1962 elections was for a short term to fill a vacancy.

KANSAS

Districts Established March 30, 1971

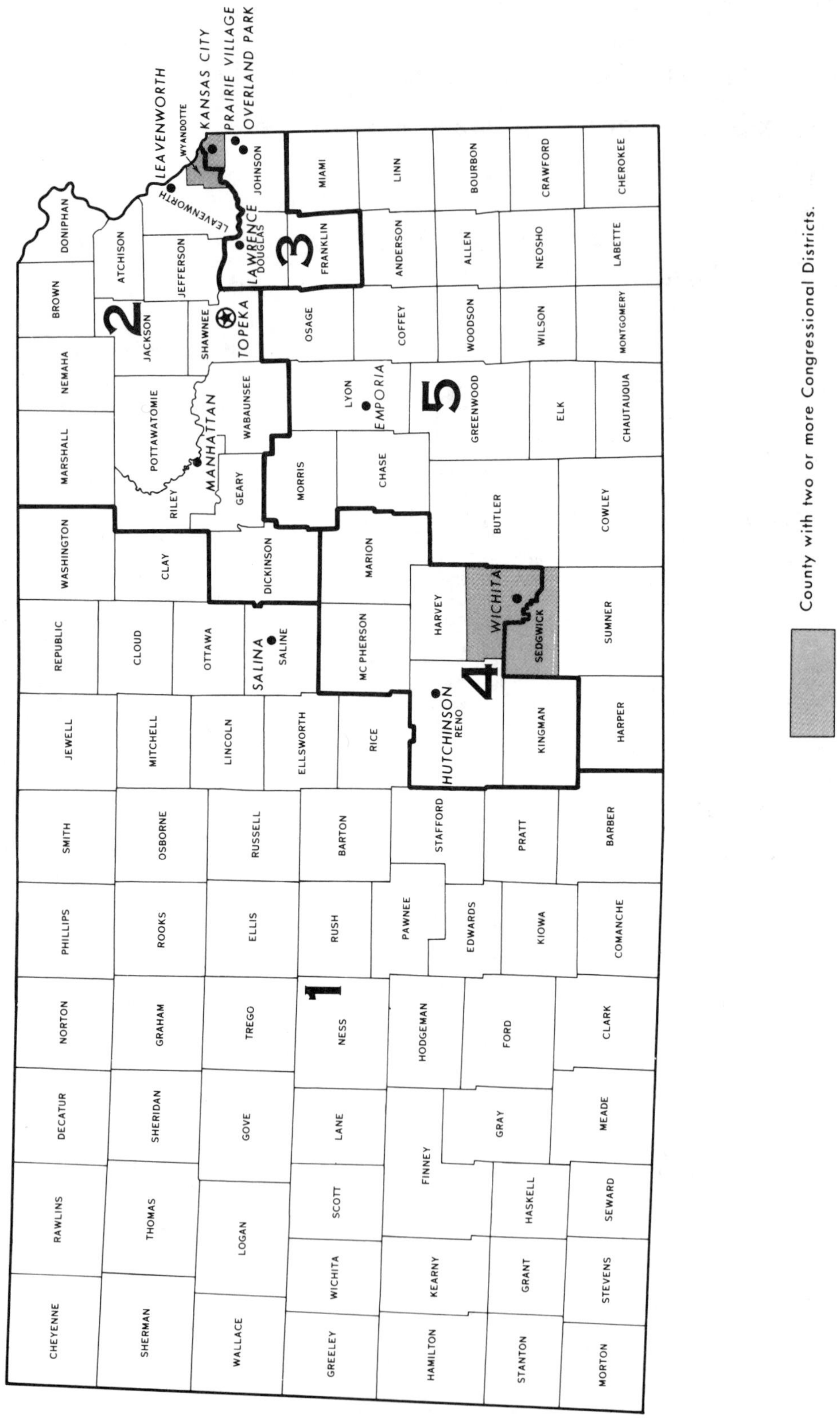

County with two or more Congressional Districts.

KANSAS

PRESIDENT 1980

1980 Census Population	County	Total Vote	Republican	Democratic	Other	Rep.-Dem. Plurality	Percentage Total Vote Rep.	Dem.	Major Vote Rep.	Dem.
15,654	ALLEN	6,317	3,811	2,009	497	1,802 R	60.3%	31.8%	65.5%	34.5%
8,749	ANDERSON	3,773	2,363	1,170	240	1,193 R	62.6%	31.0%	66.9%	33.1%
18,397	ATCHISON	7,581	4,084	3,063	434	1,021 R	53.9%	40.4%	57.1%	42.9%
6,548	BARBER	2,994	1,872	914	208	958 R	62.5%	30.5%	67.2%	32.8%
31,343	BARTON	13,852	9,147	3,663	1,042	5,484 R	66.0%	26.4%	71.4%	28.6%
15,969	BOURBON	7,199	4,263	2,605	331	1,658 R	59.2%	36.2%	62.1%	37.9%
11,955	BROWN	5,322	3,598	1,370	354	2,228 R	67.6%	25.7%	72.4%	27.6%
44,782	BUTLER	18,453	10,210	6,875	1,368	3,335 R	55.3%	37.3%	59.8%	40.2%
3,309	CHASE	1,603	1,073	413	117	660 R	66.9%	25.8%	72.2%	27.8%
5,016	CHAUTAUQUA	2,187	1,566	543	78	1,023 R	71.6%	24.8%	74.3%	25.7%
22,304	CHEROKEE	9,662	5,296	3,969	397	1,327 R	54.8%	41.1%	57.2%	42.8%
3,678	CHEYENNE	1,800	1,330	358	112	972 R	73.9%	19.9%	78.8%	21.2%
2,599	CLARK	1,417	901	430	86	471 R	63.6%	30.3%	67.7%	32.3%
9,802	CLAY	4,667	3,449	932	286	2,517 R	73.9%	20.0%	78.7%	21.3%
12,494	CLOUD	5,817	3,581	1,793	443	1,788 R	61.6%	30.8%	66.6%	33.4%
9,370	COFFEY	3,602	2,491	938	173	1,553 R	69.2%	26.0%	72.6%	27.4%
2,554	COMANCHE	1,340	877	393	70	484 R	65.4%	29.3%	69.1%	30.9%
36,824	COWLEY	15,312	8,749	5,474	1,089	3,275 R	57.1%	35.7%	61.5%	38.5%
37,916	CRAWFORD	16,855	8,058	7,658	1,139	400 R	47.8%	45.4%	51.3%	48.7%
4,509	DECATUR	2,250	1,642	443	165	1,199 R	73.0%	19.7%	78.8%	21.2%
20,175	DICKINSON	8,359	5,654	2,108	597	3,546 R	67.6%	25.2%	72.8%	27.2%
9,268	DONIPHAN	3,719	2,523	1,001	195	1,522 R	67.8%	26.9%	71.6%	28.4%
67,640	DOUGLAS	28,784	14,106	9,360	5,318	4,746 R	49.0%	32.5%	60.1%	39.9%
4,271	EDWARDS	2,204	1,409	616	179	793 R	63.9%	27.9%	69.6%	30.4%
3,918	ELK	1,837	1,280	482	75	798 R	69.7%	26.2%	72.6%	27.4%
26,098	ELLIS	10,724	5,634	3,940	1,150	1,694 R	52.5%	36.7%	58.8%	41.2%
6,640	ELLSWORTH	3,270	2,155	886	229	1,269 R	65.9%	27.1%	70.9%	29.1%
23,825	FINNEY	8,246	4,831	2,689	726	2,142 R	58.6%	32.6%	64.2%	35.8%
24,315	FORD	9,661	5,686	3,194	781	2,492 R	58.9%	33.1%	64.0%	36.0%
21,813	FRANKLIN	8,808	5,525	2,726	557	2,799 R	62.7%	30.9%	67.0%	33.0%
29,852	GEARY	6,304	3,534	2,357	413	1,177 R	56.1%	37.4%	60.0%	40.0%
3,726	GOVE	1,776	1,263	396	117	867 R	71.1%	22.3%	76.1%	23.9%
3,995	GRAHAM	2,045	1,450	473	122	977 R	70.9%	23.1%	75.4%	24.6%
6,977	GRANT	2,592	1,711	683	198	1,028 R	66.0%	26.4%	71.5%	28.5%
5,138	GRAY	2,057	1,310	583	164	727 R	63.7%	28.3%	69.2%	30.8%
1,845	GREELEY	947	600	235	112	365 R	63.4%	24.8%	71.9%	28.1%
8,764	GREENWOOD	4,155	2,685	1,241	229	1,444 R	64.6%	29.9%	68.4%	31.6%
2,514	HAMILTON	1,375	889	402	84	487 R	64.7%	29.2%	68.9%	31.1%
7,778	HARPER	3,512	2,254	990	268	1,264 R	64.2%	28.2%	69.5%	30.5%
30,531	HARVEY	12,912	7,045	4,173	1,694	2,872 R	54.6%	32.3%	62.8%	37.2%
3,814	HASKELL	1,499	1,014	374	111	640 R	67.6%	24.9%	73.1%	26.9%
2,269	HODGEMAN	1,256	831	339	86	492 R	66.2%	27.0%	71.0%	29.0%
11,644	JACKSON	5,070	3,211	1,537	322	1,674 R	63.3%	30.3%	67.6%	32.4%
15,207	JEFFERSON	6,263	4,046	1,776	441	2,270 R	64.6%	28.4%	69.5%	30.5%
5,241	JEWELL	2,849	2,074	578	197	1,496 R	72.8%	20.3%	78.2%	21.8%
270,269	JOHNSON	123,983	78,048	33,210	12,725	44,838 R	63.0%	26.8%	70.2%	29.8%
3,435	KEARNY	1,392	924	375	93	549 R	66.4%	26.9%	71.1%	28.9%
8,960	KINGMAN	4,102	2,610	1,133	359	1,477 R	63.6%	27.6%	69.7%	30.3%
4,046	KIOWA	1,986	1,433	438	115	995 R	72.2%	22.1%	76.6%	23.4%
25,682	LABETTE	9,921	5,244	3,947	730	1,297 R	52.9%	39.8%	57.1%	42.9%
2,472	LANE	1,368	924	321	123	603 R	67.5%	23.5%	74.2%	25.8%
54,809	LEAVENWORTH	16,656	9,157	6,354	1,145	2,803 R	55.0%	38.1%	59.0%	41.0%
4,145	LINCOLN	2,335	1,685	528	122	1,157 R	72.2%	22.6%	76.1%	23.9%
8,234	LINN	3,710	2,407	1,157	146	1,250 R	64.9%	31.2%	67.5%	32.5%
3,478	LOGAN	1,730	1,261	358	111	903 R	72.9%	20.7%	77.9%	22.1%
35,108	LYON	14,551	8,431	4,680	1,440	3,751 R	57.9%	32.2%	64.3%	35.7%
26,855	MCPHERSON	11,631	6,843	3,340	1,448	3,503 R	58.8%	28.7%	67.2%	32.8%
13,522	MARION	6,150	3,960	1,569	621	2,391 R	64.4%	25.5%	71.6%	28.4%
12,720	MARSHALL	6,097	4,127	1,555	415	2,572 R	67.7%	25.5%	72.6%	27.4%
4,788	MEADE	2,258	1,618	482	158	1,136 R	71.7%	21.3%	77.0%	23.0%
21,618	MIAMI	8,301	4,740	3,071	490	1,669 R	57.1%	37.0%	60.7%	39.3%
8,117	MITCHELL	3,953	2,821	876	256	1,945 R	71.4%	22.2%	76.3%	23.7%
42,281	MONTGOMERY	16,915	10,856	5,282	777	5,574 R	64.2%	31.2%	67.3%	32.7%
6,419	MORRIS	2,949	1,933	810	206	1,123 R	65.5%	27.5%	70.5%	29.5%
3,454	MORTON	1,662	1,157	414	91	743 R	69.6%	24.9%	73.6%	26.4%
11,211	NEMAHA	5,456	3,546	1,600	310	1,946 R	65.0%	29.3%	68.9%	31.1%
18,967	NEOSHO	8,077	4,613	2,923	541	1,690 R	57.1%	36.2%	61.2%	38.8%
4,498	NESS	2,455	1,657	616	182	1,041 R	67.5%	25.1%	72.9%	27.1%
6,689	NORTON	3,477	2,625	666	186	1,959 R	75.5%	19.2%	79.8%	20.2%
15,319	OSAGE	6,324	3,817	2,088	419	1,729 R	60.4%	33.0%	64.6%	35.4%

KANSAS

PRESIDENT 1980

1980 Census Population	County	Total Vote	Republican	Democratic	Other	Rep.-Dem. Plurality	Percentage Total Vote Rep.	Dem.	Major Vote Rep.	Dem.
5,959	OSBORNE	2,984	2,188	620	176	1,568 R	73.3%	20.8%	77.9%	22.1%
5,971	OTTAWA	2,947	2,118	630	199	1,488 R	71.9%	21.4%	77.1%	22.9%
8,065	PAWNEE	3,691	2,170	1,184	337	986 R	58.8%	32.1%	64.7%	35.3%
7,406	PHILLIPS	3,667	2,731	748	188	1,983 R	74.5%	20.4%	78.5%	21.5%
14,782	POTTAWATOMIE	6,144	3,895	1,724	525	2,171 R	63.4%	28.1%	69.3%	30.7%
10,275	PRATT	4,683	2,866	1,369	448	1,497 R	61.2%	29.2%	67.7%	32.3%
4,105	RAWLINS	2,076	1,524	427	125	1,097 R	73.4%	20.6%	78.1%	21.9%
64,983	RENO	26,121	13,804	9,615	2,702	4,189 R	52.8%	36.8%	58.9%	41.1%
7,569	REPUBLIC	4,120	3,031	850	239	2,181 R	73.6%	20.6%	78.1%	21.9%
11,900	RICE	5,568	3,211	1,847	510	1,364 R	57.7%	33.2%	63.5%	36.5%
63,505	RILEY	16,818	8,904	5,224	2,690	3,680 R	52.9%	31.1%	63.0%	37.0%
7,006	ROOKS	3,187	2,275	725	187	1,550 R	71.4%	22.7%	75.8%	24.2%
4,516	RUSH	2,572	1,840	557	175	1,283 R	71.5%	21.7%	76.8%	23.2%
8,868	RUSSELL	4,437	3,241	910	286	2,331 R	73.0%	20.5%	78.1%	21.9%
48,905	SALINE	21,169	12,758	6,382	2,029	6,376 R	60.3%	30.1%	66.7%	33.3%
5,782	SCOTT	2,418	1,829	456	133	1,373 R	75.6%	18.9%	80.0%	20.0%
366,531	SEDGWICK	145,431	75,317	55,105	15,009	20,212 R	51.8%	37.9%	57.7%	42.3%
17,071	SEWARD	6,191	4,385	1,460	346	2,925 R	70.8%	23.6%	75.0%	25.0%
154,916	SHAWNEE	67,776	36,290	24,852	6,634	11,438 R	53.5%	36.7%	59.4%	40.6%
3,544	SHERIDAN	1,693	1,202	391	100	811 R	71.0%	23.1%	75.5%	24.5%
7,759	SHERMAN	3,362	2,315	779	268	1,536 R	68.9%	23.2%	74.8%	25.2%
5,947	SMITH	3,368	2,415	719	234	1,696 R	71.7%	21.3%	77.1%	22.9%
5,539	STAFFORD	2,976	1,865	872	239	993 R	62.7%	29.3%	68.1%	31.9%
2,339	STANTON	992	672	231	89	441 R	67.7%	23.3%	74.4%	25.6%
4,736	STEVENS	2,085	1,502	478	105	1,024 R	72.0%	22.9%	75.9%	24.1%
24,928	SUMNER	10,496	6,038	3,761	697	2,277 R	57.5%	35.8%	61.6%	38.4%
8,451	THOMAS	4,202	2,789	1,045	368	1,744 R	66.4%	24.9%	72.7%	27.3%
4,165	TREGO	2,048	1,340	523	185	817 R	65.4%	25.5%	71.9%	28.1%
6,867	WABAUNSEE	3,317	2,255	853	209	1,402 R	68.0%	25.7%	72.6%	27.4%
2,045	WALLACE	1,036	811	167	58	644 R	78.3%	16.1%	82.9%	17.1%
8,543	WASHINGTON	4,083	3,058	784	241	2,274 R	74.9%	19.2%	79.6%	20.4%
3,041	WICHITA	1,258	880	303	75	577 R	70.0%	24.1%	74.4%	25.6%
12,128	WILSON	4,801	3,328	1,205	268	2,123 R	69.3%	25.1%	73.4%	26.6%
4,600	WOODSON	2,189	1,435	646	108	789 R	65.6%	29.5%	69.0%	31.0%
172,335	WYANDOTTE	60,223	23,012	32,763	4,448	9,751 D	38.2%	54.4%	41.3%	58.7%
2,363,208	TOTAL	979,795	566,812	326,150	86,833	240,662 R	57.9%	33.3%	63.5%	36.5%

KANSAS

SENATOR 1980

1980 Census Population	County	Total Vote	Republican	Democratic	Other	Rep.-Dem. Plurality	Total Vote Rep.	Total Vote Dem.	Major Vote Rep.	Major Vote Dem.
15,654	ALLEN	6,214	4,139	2,075		2,064 R	66.6%	33.4%	66.6%	33.4%
8,749	ANDERSON	3,746	2,473	1,273		1,200 R	66.0%	34.0%	66.0%	34.0%
18,397	ATCHISON	7,407	4,572	2,835		1,737 R	61.7%	38.3%	61.7%	38.3%
6,548	BARBER	2,903	2,068	835		1,233 R	71.2%	28.8%	71.2%	28.8%
31,343	BARTON	13,748	9,693	4,055		5,638 R	70.5%	29.5%	70.5%	29.5%
15,969	BOURBON	7,069	4,531	2,538		1,993 R	64.1%	35.9%	64.1%	35.9%
11,955	BROWN	5,167	3,808	1,359		2,449 R	73.7%	26.3%	73.7%	26.3%
44,782	BUTLER	16,469	10,012	6,457		3,555 R	60.8%	39.2%	60.8%	39.2%
3,309	CHASE	1,545	1,065	480		585 R	68.9%	31.1%	68.9%	31.1%
5,016	CHAUTAUQUA	1,826	1,457	369		1,088 R	79.8%	20.2%	79.8%	20.2%
22,304	CHEROKEE	9,565	5,664	3,901		1,763 R	59.2%	40.8%	59.2%	40.8%
3,678	CHEYENNE	1,759	1,359	400		959 R	77.3%	22.7%	77.3%	22.7%
2,599	CLARK	1,394	993	401		592 R	71.2%	28.8%	71.2%	28.8%
9,802	CLAY	4,565	3,374	1,191		2,183 R	73.9%	26.1%	73.9%	26.1%
12,494	CLOUD	5,767	3,535	2,232		1,303 R	61.3%	38.7%	61.3%	38.7%
9,370	COFFEY	3,533	2,462	1,071		1,391 R	69.7%	30.3%	69.7%	30.3%
2,554	COMANCHE	1,330	940	390		550 R	70.7%	29.3%	70.7%	29.3%
36,824	COWLEY	14,981	9,390	5,591		3,799 R	62.7%	37.3%	62.7%	37.3%
37,916	CRAWFORD	16,533	9,544	6,989		2,555 R	57.7%	42.3%	57.7%	42.3%
4,509	DECATUR	2,228	1,639	589		1,050 R	73.6%	26.4%	73.6%	26.4%
20,175	DICKINSON	8,283	5,756	2,527		3,229 R	69.5%	30.5%	69.5%	30.5%
9,268	DONIPHAN	3,580	2,710	870		1,840 R	75.7%	24.3%	75.7%	24.3%
67,640	DOUGLAS	28,196	16,203	11,993		4,210 R	57.5%	42.5%	57.5%	42.5%
4,271	EDWARDS	2,161	1,410	751		659 R	65.2%	34.8%	65.2%	34.8%
3,918	ELK	1,533	1,094	439		655 R	71.4%	28.6%	71.4%	28.6%
26,098	ELLIS	10,683	5,825	4,858		967 R	54.5%	45.5%	54.5%	45.5%
6,640	ELLSWORTH	3,255	2,109	1,146		963 R	64.8%	35.2%	64.8%	35.2%
23,825	FINNEY	8,200	5,534	2,666		2,868 R	67.5%	32.5%	67.5%	32.5%
24,315	FORD	9,541	6,143	3,398		2,745 R	64.4%	35.6%	64.4%	35.6%
21,813	FRANKLIN	8,689	5,737	2,952		2,785 R	66.0%	34.0%	66.0%	34.0%
29,852	GEARY	6,226	3,880	2,346		1,534 R	62.3%	37.7%	62.3%	37.7%
3,726	GOVE	1,727	1,181	546		635 R	68.4%	31.6%	68.4%	31.6%
3,995	GRAHAM	2,023	1,447	576		871 R	71.5%	28.5%	71.5%	28.5%
6,977	GRANT	2,617	1,879	738		1,141 R	71.8%	28.2%	71.8%	28.2%
5,138	GRAY	2,007	1,355	652		703 R	67.5%	32.5%	67.5%	32.5%
1,845	GREELEY	917	689	228		461 R	75.1%	24.9%	75.1%	24.9%
8,764	GREENWOOD	4,143	2,861	1,282		1,579 R	69.1%	30.9%	69.1%	30.9%
2,514	HAMILTON	1,338	895	443		452 R	66.9%	33.1%	66.9%	33.1%
7,778	HARPER	3,442	2,517	925		1,592 R	73.1%	26.9%	73.1%	26.9%
30,531	HARVEY	12,764	7,961	4,803		3,158 R	62.4%	37.6%	62.4%	37.6%
3,814	HASKELL	1,485	1,098	387		711 R	73.9%	26.1%	73.9%	26.1%
2,269	HODGEMAN	1,231	907	324		583 R	73.7%	26.3%	73.7%	26.3%
11,644	JACKSON	5,043	3,216	1,827		1,389 R	63.8%	36.2%	63.8%	36.2%
15,207	JEFFERSON	6,073	3,754	2,319		1,435 R	61.8%	38.2%	61.8%	38.2%
5,241	JEWELL	2,791	2,113	678		1,435 R	75.7%	24.3%	75.7%	24.3%
270,269	JOHNSON	119,619	83,514	36,105		47,409 R	69.8%	30.2%	69.8%	30.2%
3,435	KEARNY	1,343	963	380		583 R	71.7%	28.3%	71.7%	28.3%
8,960	KINGMAN	4,010	2,749	1,261		1,488 R	68.6%	31.4%	68.6%	31.4%
4,046	KIOWA	1,939	1,464	475		989 R	75.5%	24.5%	75.5%	24.5%
25,682	LABETTE	9,755	5,886	3,869		2,017 R	60.3%	39.7%	60.3%	39.7%
2,472	LANE	1,304	1,005	299		706 R	77.1%	22.9%	77.1%	22.9%
54,809	LEAVENWORTH	16,449	10,306	6,143		4,163 R	62.7%	37.3%	62.7%	37.3%
4,145	LINCOLN	2,269	1,640	629		1,011 R	72.3%	27.7%	72.3%	27.7%
8,234	LINN	3,503	2,438	1,065		1,373 R	69.6%	30.4%	69.6%	30.4%
3,478	LOGAN	1,705	1,213	492		721 R	71.1%	28.9%	71.1%	28.9%
35,108	LYON	13,817	7,910	5,907		2,003 R	57.2%	42.8%	57.2%	42.8%
26,855	MCPHERSON	11,425	7,532	3,893		3,639 R	65.9%	34.1%	65.9%	34.1%
13,522	MARION	5,897	4,287	1,610		2,677 R	72.7%	27.3%	72.7%	27.3%
12,720	MARSHALL	6,018	3,984	2,034		1,950 R	66.2%	33.8%	66.2%	33.8%
4,788	MEADE	2,172	1,588	584		1,004 R	73.1%	26.9%	73.1%	26.9%
21,618	MIAMI	8,095	4,918	3,177		1,741 R	60.8%	39.2%	60.8%	39.2%
8,117	MITCHELL	3,891	2,706	1,185		1,521 R	69.5%	30.5%	69.5%	30.5%
42,281	MONTGOMERY	16,492	11,115	5,377		5,738 R	67.4%	32.6%	67.4%	32.6%
6,419	MORRIS	2,913	1,903	1,010		893 R	65.3%	34.7%	65.3%	34.7%
3,454	MORTON	1,600	1,144	456		688 R	71.5%	28.5%	71.5%	28.5%
11,211	NEMAHA	5,342	3,301	2,041		1,260 R	61.8%	38.2%	61.8%	38.2%
18,967	NEOSHO	7,830	4,966	2,864		2,102 R	63.4%	36.6%	63.4%	36.6%
4,498	NESS	2,437	1,679	758		921 R	68.9%	31.1%	68.9%	31.1%
6,689	NORTON	3,250	2,479	771		1,708 R	76.3%	23.7%	76.3%	23.7%
15,319	OSAGE	6,220	3,666	2,554		1,112 R	58.9%	41.1%	58.9%	41.1%

KANSAS

SENATOR 1980

1980 Census Population	County	Total Vote	Republican	Democratic	Other	Rep.-Dem. Plurality	Percentage Total Vote Rep.	Dem.	Major Vote Rep.	Dem.
5,959	OSBORNE	2,942	2,102	840		1,262 R	71.4%	28.6%	71.4%	28.6%
5,971	OTTAWA	2,938	2,022	916		1,106 R	68.8%	31.2%	68.8%	31.2%
8,065	PAWNEE	3,636	2,333	1,303		1,030 R	64.2%	35.8%	64.2%	35.8%
7,406	PHILLIPS	3,609	2,733	876		1,857 R	75.7%	24.3%	75.7%	24.3%
14,782	POTTAWATOMIE	6,068	4,001	2,067		1,934 R	65.9%	34.1%	65.9%	34.1%
10,275	PRATT	4,635	3,122	1,513		1,609 R	67.4%	32.6%	67.4%	32.6%
4,105	RAWLINS	2,029	1,526	503		1,023 R	75.2%	24.8%	75.2%	24.8%
64,983	RENO	25,805	14,550	11,255		3,295 R	56.4%	43.6%	56.4%	43.6%
7,569	REPUBLIC	3,951	2,795	1,156		1,639 R	70.7%	29.3%	70.7%	29.3%
11,900	RICE	5,427	3,344	2,083		1,261 R	61.6%	38.4%	61.6%	38.4%
63,505	RILEY	16,515	10,710	5,805		4,905 R	64.9%	35.1%	64.9%	35.1%
7,006	ROOKS	3,085	2,187	898		1,289 R	70.9%	29.1%	70.9%	29.1%
4,516	RUSH	2,562	1,743	819		924 R	68.0%	32.0%	68.0%	32.0%
8,868	RUSSELL	4,448	3,538	910		2,628 R	79.5%	20.5%	79.5%	20.5%
48,905	SALINE	21,019	12,450	8,569		3,881 R	59.2%	40.8%	59.2%	40.8%
5,782	SCOTT	2,359	1,742	617		1,125 R	73.8%	26.2%	73.8%	26.2%
366,531	SEDGWICK	131,757	81,480	50,277		31,203 R	61.8%	38.2%	61.8%	38.2%
17,071	SEWARD	6,068	4,500	1,568		2,932 R	74.2%	25.8%	74.2%	25.8%
154,916	SHAWNEE	65,991	37,798	28,193		9,605 R	57.3%	42.7%	57.3%	42.7%
3,544	SHERIDAN	1,624	1,153	471		682 R	71.0%	29.0%	71.0%	29.0%
7,759	SHERMAN	3,192	2,262	930		1,332 R	70.9%	29.1%	70.9%	29.1%
5,947	SMITH	3,327	2,480	847		1,633 R	74.5%	25.5%	74.5%	25.5%
5,539	STAFFORD	2,953	1,995	958		1,037 R	67.6%	32.4%	67.6%	32.4%
2,339	STANTON	975	706	269		437 R	72.4%	27.6%	72.4%	27.6%
4,736	STEVENS	2,044	1,514	530		984 R	74.1%	25.9%	74.1%	25.9%
24,928	SUMNER	10,257	6,278	3,979		2,299 R	61.2%	38.8%	61.2%	38.8%
8,451	THOMAS	4,146	2,935	1,211		1,724 R	70.8%	29.2%	70.8%	29.2%
4,165	TREGO	2,022	1,381	641		740 R	68.3%	31.7%	68.3%	31.7%
6,867	WABAUNSEE	3,285	2,242	1,043		1,199 R	68.2%	31.8%	68.2%	31.8%
2,045	WALLACE	1,024	799	225		574 R	78.0%	22.0%	78.0%	22.0%
8,543	WASHINGTON	3,949	2,983	966		2,017 R	75.5%	24.5%	75.5%	24.5%
3,041	WICHITA	1,252	928	324		604 R	74.1%	25.9%	74.1%	25.9%
12,128	WILSON	4,600	3,265	1,335		1,930 R	71.0%	29.0%	71.0%	29.0%
4,600	WOODSON	2,146	1,439	707		732 R	67.1%	32.9%	67.1%	32.9%
172,335	WYANDOTTE	52,325	26,302	26,023		279 R	50.3%	49.7%	50.3%	49.7%
2,363,208	TOTAL	938,957	598,686	340,271		258,415 R	63.8%	36.2%	63.8%	36.2%

KANSAS

CONGRESS

CD	Year	Total Vote	Republican Vote	Candidate	Democratic Vote	Candidate	Other Vote	Rep.-Dem. Plurality	Percentage Total Vote Rep.	Dem.	Major Vote Rep.	Dem.
1	1980	195,131	121,545	ROBERTS, PAT	73,586	MARTIN, PHIL		47,959 R	62.3%	37.7%	62.3%	37.7%
1	1978	131,037	131,037	SEBELIUS, KEITH				131,037 R	100.0%		100.0%	
1	1976	194,772	142,311	SEBELIUS, KEITH	52,459	YOWELL, RANDY	2	89,852 R	73.1%	26.9%	73.1%	26.9%
1	1974	173,868	101,565	SEBELIUS, KEITH	57,326	SMITH, DONALD C.	14,977	44,239 R	58.4%	33.0%	63.9%	36.1%
1	1972	188,658	145,712	SEBELIUS, KEITH	40,678	COOVER, MORRIS	2,268	105,034 R	77.2%	21.6%	78.2%	21.8%
2	1980	170,977	92,107	JEFFRIES, JIM	78,859	KEYS, SAM	11	13,248 R	53.9%	46.1%	53.9%	46.1%
2	1978	146,879	76,419	JEFFRIES, JIM	70,460	KEYS, MARTHA		5,959 R	52.0%	48.0%	52.0%	48.0%
2	1976	174,861	82,946	FREEMAN, ROSS R.	88,645	KEYS, MARTHA	3,270	5,699 D	47.4%	50.7%	48.3%	51.7%
2	1974	154,239	67,650	PETERSON, JOHN C.	84,864	KEYS, MARTHA	1,725	17,214 D	43.9%	55.0%	44.4%	55.6%
2	1972	175,345	65,071	MCATEE, CHARLES D.	106,276	ROY, WILLIAM R.	3,998	41,205 D	37.1%	60.6%	38.0%	62.0%
3	1980	197,046	109,294	WINN, LARRY	82,414	WATKINS, DAN	5,338	26,880 R	55.5%	41.8%	57.0%	43.0%
3	1978	103,265	103,265	WINN, LARRY				103,265 R	100.0%		100.0%	
3	1976	179,865	123,578	WINN, LARRY	52,110	RHOADS, PHILIP S.	4,177	71,468 R	68.7%	29.0%	70.3%	29.7%
3	1974	142,650	89,694	WINN, LARRY	49,976	WELLS, SAMUEL J.	2,980	39,718 R	62.9%	35.0%	64.2%	35.8%
3	1972	172,406	122,358	WINN, LARRY	43,777	BARSOTTI, CHARLES	6,271	78,581 R	71.0%	25.4%	73.6%	26.4%
4	1980	179,913	55,899	HUNTER, CLAY	124,014	GLICKMAN, DAN		68,115 D	31.1%	68.9%	31.1%	68.9%
4	1978	143,993	43,854	LITSEY, JAMES P.	100,139	GLICKMAN, DAN		56,285 D	30.5%	69.5%	30.5%	69.5%
4	1976	179,168	86,832	SHRIVER, GARNER E.	90,067	GLICKMAN, DAN	2,269	3,235 D	48.5%	50.3%	49.1%	50.9%
4	1974	144,131	70,401	SHRIVER, GARNER E.	61,210	CHANEY, BERT	12,520	9,191 R	48.8%	42.5%	53.5%	46.5%
4	1972	164,127	120,120	SHRIVER, GARNER E.	40,753	STEVENS, JOHN S.	3,254	79,367 R	73.2%	24.8%	74.7%	25.3%
5	1980	190,047	141,029	WHITTAKER, ROBERT	45,676	MILLER, DAVID L.	3,342	95,353 R	74.2%	24.0%	75.5%	24.5%
5	1978	150,766	86,011	WHITTAKER, ROBERT	62,402	ALLEGRUCCI, DONALD L.	2,353	23,609 R	57.0%	41.4%	58.0%	42.0%
5	1976	180,625	109,573	SKUBITZ, JOE	65,340	OLSON, VIRGIL L.	5,712	44,233 R	60.7%	36.2%	62.6%	37.4%
5	1974	160,670	88,646	SKUBITZ, JOE	72,024	GAINES, FRANK		16,622 R	55.2%	44.8%	55.2%	44.8%
5	1972	177,829	128,639	SKUBITZ, JOE	49,169	KITCH, LLOYD L.	21	79,470 R	72.3%	27.6%	72.3%	27.7%

KANSAS

1980 GENERAL ELECTION

President   Other vote was 68,231 Anderson (Independent); 14,470 Clark (Independent); 1,555 Shelton (American); 967 Hall (Independent); 821 Bubar (Statesman); 789 Rarick (Conservative).

Senator

Congress   Other vote was scattered in CD 2; Stewart (Conservative) in CD 3; Blackwell (Statesman) in CD 5.

1980 PRIMARIES

AUGUST 5 REPUBLICAN

Senator   201,484 Robert Dole; 44,674 Jim H. Grainge.

Congress   Unopposed in three CD's. Contested as follows:

    CD 1   37,389 Pat Roberts; 24,231 Steve Pratt; 5,649 Donald R. Nicholson.
    CD 2   26,269 Jim Jeffries; 16,901 Bill McCormick; 10,318 Larry Abeldt.

AUGUST 5 DEMOCRATIC

Senator   52,004 John Simpson; 46,322 James Maher; 16,466 John A. Barnes; 14,218 Ken North; 8,838 Ed Phillips; 7,461 Howard C. Lee.

Congress   Unopposed in two CD's. Contested as follows:

    CD 1   17,912 Phil Martin; 13,175 Jeff Harsh.
    CD 2   15,193 Sam Keys; 10,213 H. J. Yount; 7,645 Bob Wootton.
    CD 3   15,237 Dan Watkins; 9,484 Jack Weyforth.

KENTUCKY

GOVERNOR
J. Y. Brown, Jr. (D). Elected 1979 to a four-year term.

SENATORS
Wendell H. Ford (D). Re-elected 1980 to a six-year term. Previously elected 1974.

Walter Huddleston (D). Re-elected 1978 to a six-year term. Previously elected 1972.

REPRESENTATIVES
1. Carroll Hubbard (D)
2. William H. Natcher (D)
3. Romano L. Mazzoli (D)
4. M. G. Snyder (R)
5. Harold Rogers (R)
6. Larry J. Hopkins (R)
7. Carl D. Perkins (D)

POSTWAR VOTE FOR GOVERNOR

Year	Total Vote	Republican Vote	Candidate	Democratic Vote	Candidate	Other Vote	Rep.-Dem. Plurality	Total Vote Rep.	Total Vote Dem.	Major Vote Rep.	Major Vote Dem.
1979	939,366	381,278	Nunn, Louie B.	558,088	Brown, J. Y., Jr.	—	176,810 D	40.6%	59.4%	40.6%	59.4%
1975	748,157	277,998	Gable, Robert E.	470,159	Carroll, Julian	—	192,161 D	37.2%	62.8%	37.2%	62.8%
1971	930,790	412,653	Emberton, Thomas	470,720	Ford, Wendell H.	47,417	58,067 D	44.3%	50.6%	46.7%	53.3%
1967	886,946	454,123	Nunn, Louie B.	425,674	Ward, Henry	7,149	28,449 R	51.2%	48.0%	51.6%	48.4%
1963	886,047	436,496	Nunn, Louie B.	449,551	Breathitt, Edward T.	—	13,055 D	49.3%	50.7%	49.3%	50.7%
1959	853,005	336,456	Robsion, John M.	516,549	Combs, Bert T.	—	180,093 D	39.4%	60.6%	39.4%	60.6%
1955	778,488	322,671	Denney, Edwin R.	451,647	Chandler, Albert B.	4,170	128,976 D	41.4%	58.0%	41.7%	58.3%
1951	634,359	288,014	Siler, Eugene	346,345	Wetherby, Lawrence	—	58,331 D	45.4%	54.6%	45.4%	54.6%
1947	672,372	287,130	Dummit, Eldon S.	385,242	Clements, Earle C.	—	98,112 D	42.7%	57.3%	42.7%	57.3%

POSTWAR VOTE FOR SENATOR

Year	Total Vote	Republican Vote	Candidate	Democratic Vote	Candidate	Other Vote	Rep.-Dem. Plurality	Total Vote Rep.	Total Vote Dem.	Major Vote Rep.	Major Vote Dem.
1980	1,106,890	386,029	Foust, Mary Louise	720,861	Ford, Wendell H.	—	334,832 D	34.9%	65.1%	34.9%	65.1%
1978	476,783	175,766	Guenthner, Louie	290,730	Huddleston, Walter	10,287	114,964 D	36.9%	61.0%	37.7%	62.3%
1974	745,994	328,982	Cook, Marlow W.	399,406	Ford, Wendell H.	17,606	70,424 D	44.1%	53.5%	45.2%	54.8%
1972	1,037,861	494,337	Nunn, Louie B.	528,550	Huddleston, Walter	14,974	34,213 D	47.6%	50.9%	48.3%	51.7%
1968	942,865	484,260	Cook, Marlow W.	448,960	Peden, Katherine	9,645	35,300 R	51.4%	47.6%	51.9%	48.1%
1966	749,884	483,805	Cooper, John Sherman	266,079	Brown, J. Y.	—	217,726 R	64.5%	35.5%	64.5%	35.5%
1962	820,088	432,648	Morton, Thruston B.	387,440	Wyatt, Wilson W.	—	45,208 R	52.8%	47.2%	52.8%	47.2%
1960	1,088,377	644,087	Cooper, John Sherman	444,290	Johnson, Keen	—	199,797 R	59.2%	40.8%	59.2%	40.8%
1956	1,006,825	506,903	Morton, Thruston B.	499,922	Clements, Earle C.	—	6,981 R	50.3%	49.7%	50.3%	49.7%
1956s	1,011,645	538,505	Cooper, John Sherman	473,140	Wetherby, Lawrence	—	65,365 R	53.2%	46.8%	53.2%	46.8%
1954	797,057	362,948	Cooper, John Sherman	434,109	Barkley, Alben W.	—	71,161 D	45.5%	54.5%	45.5%	54.5%
1952s	960,228	494,576	Cooper, John Sherman	465,652	Underwood, Thomas R.	—	28,924 R	51.5%	48.5%	51.5%	48.5%
1950	617,121	278,368	Dawson, Charles L.	334,249	Clements, Earle C.	4,504	55,881 D	45.1%	54.2%	45.4%	54.6%
1948	794,469	383,776	Cooper, John Sherman	408,256	Chapman, Virgil	2,437	24,480 D	48.3%	51.4%	48.5%	51.5%
1946s	615,119	327,652	Cooper, John Sherman	285,829	Brown, J. Y.	1,638	41,823 R	53.3%	46.5%	53.4%	46.6%

One of the elections in 1956 and those in 1952 and 1946 were for short terms to fill vacancies.

KENTUCKY

Districts Established June 27, 1972

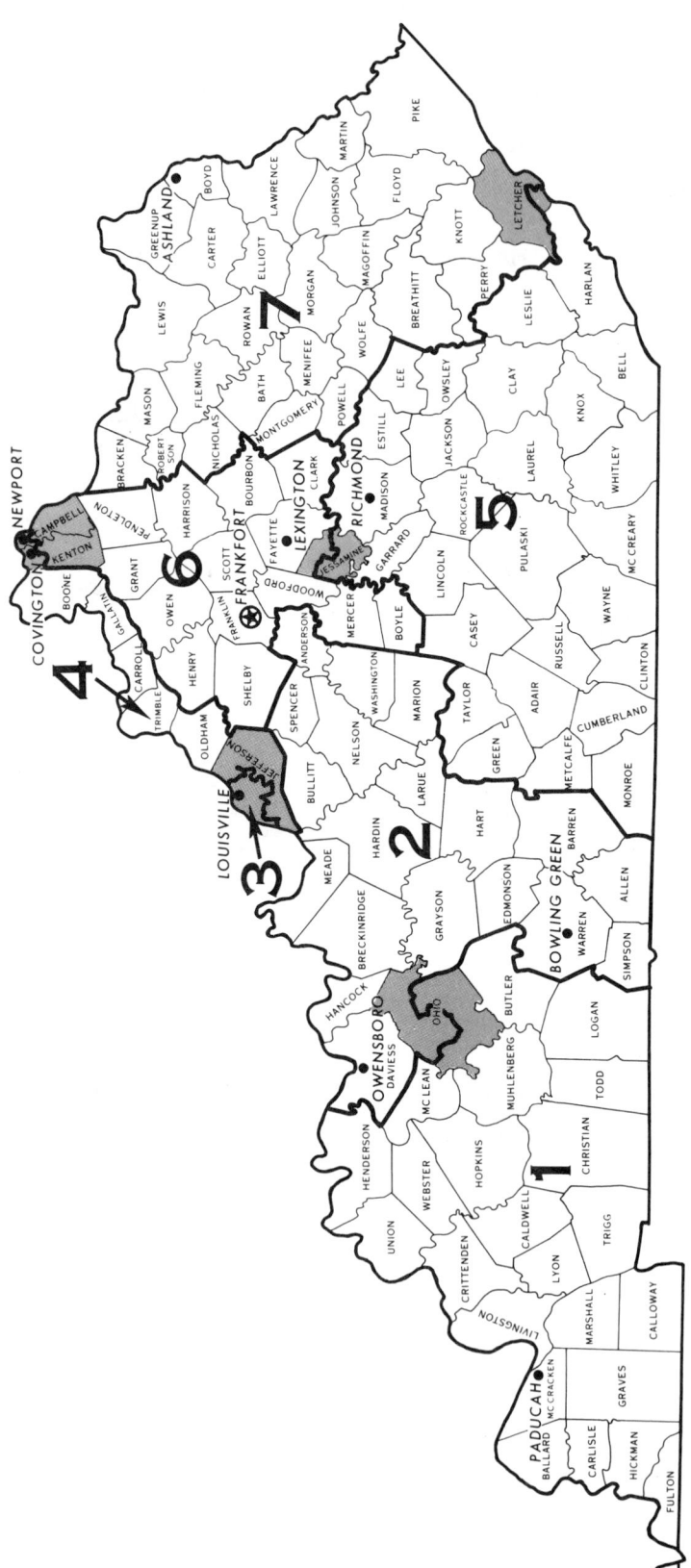

County with two or more Congressional Districts.

KENTUCKY

PRESIDENT 1980

1980 Census Population	County	Total Vote	Republican	Democratic	Other	Rep.-Dem. Plurality	Percentage Total Vote Rep.	Dem.	Major Vote Rep.	Dem.
15,233	ADAIR	6,418	4,051	2,285	82	1,766 R	63.1%	35.6%	63.9%	36.1%
14,128	ALLEN	5,278	3,186	2,010	82	1,176 R	60.4%	38.1%	61.3%	38.7%
12,567	ANDERSON	4,764	2,052	2,567	145	515 D	43.1%	53.9%	44.4%	55.6%
8,798	BALLARD	3,826	1,190	2,583	53	1,393 D	31.1%	67.5%	31.5%	68.5%
34,009	BARREN	11,933	6,405	5,285	243	1,120 R	53.7%	44.3%	54.8%	45.2%
10,025	BATH	3,698	1,463	2,174	61	711 D	39.6%	58.8%	40.2%	59.8%
34,330	BELL	12,088	5,433	6,362	293	929 D	44.9%	52.6%	46.1%	53.9%
45,842	BOONE	14,148	8,263	5,374	511	2,889 R	58.4%	38.0%	60.6%	39.4%
19,405	BOURBON	6,346	2,475	3,641	230	1,166 D	39.0%	57.4%	40.5%	59.5%
55,513	BOYD	21,695	10,367	10,702	626	335 D	47.8%	49.3%	49.2%	50.8%
25,066	BOYLE	8,574	3,848	4,429	297	581 D	44.9%	51.7%	46.5%	53.5%
7,738	BRACKEN	2,644	1,154	1,420	70	266 D	43.6%	53.7%	44.8%	55.2%
17,004	BREATHITT	5,532	1,532	3,916	84	2,384 D	27.7%	70.8%	28.1%	71.9%
16,861	BRECKINRIDGE	6,891	3,629	3,163	99	466 R	52.7%	45.9%	53.4%	46.6%
43,346	BULLITT	12,576	6,364	5,884	328	480 R	50.6%	46.8%	52.0%	48.0%
11,064	BUTLER	4,450	3,129	1,274	47	1,855 R	70.3%	28.6%	71.1%	28.9%
13,473	CALDWELL	5,645	2,609	2,924	112	315 D	46.2%	51.8%	47.2%	52.8%
30,031	CALLOWAY	11,964	4,498	6,809	657	2,311 D	37.6%	56.9%	39.8%	60.2%
83,317	CAMPBELL	29,208	16,743	11,059	1,406	5,684 R	57.3%	37.9%	60.2%	39.8%
5,487	CARLISLE	2,545	975	1,542	28	567 D	38.3%	60.6%	38.7%	61.3%
9,270	CARROLL	3,328	1,076	2,127	125	1,051 D	32.3%	63.9%	33.6%	66.4%
25,060	CARTER	7,839	3,934	3,782	123	152 R	50.2%	48.2%	51.0%	49.0%
14,818	CASEY	5,632	4,239	1,298	95	2,941 R	75.3%	23.0%	76.6%	23.4%
66,878	CHRISTIAN	15,512	8,209	7,048	255	1,161 R	52.9%	45.4%	53.8%	46.2%
28,322	CLARK	9,685	4,302	5,071	312	769 D	44.4%	52.4%	45.9%	54.1%
22,752	CLAY	6,778	4,594	2,121	63	2,473 R	67.8%	31.3%	68.4%	31.6%
9,321	CLINTON	4,590	3,539	1,000	51	2,539 R	77.1%	21.8%	78.0%	22.0%
9,207	CRITTENDEN	3,771	2,219	1,508	44	711 R	58.8%	40.0%	59.5%	40.5%
7,289	CUMBERLAND	3,081	2,216	821	44	1,395 R	71.9%	26.6%	73.0%	27.0%
85,949	DAVIESS	30,717	14,643	14,902	1,172	259 D	47.7%	48.5%	49.6%	50.4%
9,962	EDMONSON	4,233	2,913	1,252	68	1,661 R	68.8%	29.6%	69.9%	30.1%
6,908	ELLIOTT	2,241	551	1,668	22	1,117 D	24.6%	74.4%	24.8%	75.2%
14,495	ESTILL	4,861	2,818	1,965	78	853 R	58.0%	40.4%	58.9%	41.1%
204,165	FAYETTE	71,817	35,349	30,511	5,957	4,838 R	49.2%	42.5%	53.7%	46.3%
12,323	FLEMING	4,315	2,189	2,051	75	138 R	50.7%	47.5%	51.6%	48.4%
48,764	FLOYD	15,385	4,179	10,975	231	6,796 D	27.2%	71.3%	27.6%	72.4%
41,830	FRANKLIN	18,530	6,455	11,193	882	4,738 D	34.8%	60.4%	36.6%	63.4%
8,971	FULTON	3,547	1,462	2,016	69	554 D	41.2%	56.8%	42.0%	58.0%
4,842	GALLATIN	1,704	684	988	32	304 D	40.1%	58.0%	40.9%	59.1%
10,853	GARRARD	4,480	2,585	1,774	121	811 R	57.7%	39.6%	59.3%	40.7%
13,308	GRANT	4,183	1,779	2,272	132	493 D	42.5%	54.3%	43.9%	56.1%
34,049	GRAVES	13,816	6,556	6,999	261	443 D	47.5%	50.7%	48.4%	51.6%
20,854	GRAYSON	8,076	5,084	2,788	204	2,296 R	63.0%	34.5%	64.6%	35.4%
11,043	GREEN	4,587	2,775	1,758	54	1,017 R	60.5%	38.3%	61.2%	38.8%
39,132	GREENUP	14,275	6,857	7,126	292	269 D	48.0%	49.9%	49.0%	51.0%
7,742	HANCOCK	3,004	1,367	1,530	107	163 D	45.5%	50.9%	47.2%	52.8%
88,917	HARDIN	18,738	9,779	8,339	620	1,440 R	52.2%	44.5%	54.0%	46.0%
41,889	HARLAN	14,457	5,460	8,798	199	3,338 D	37.8%	60.9%	38.3%	61.7%
15,166	HARRISON	5,645	2,184	3,319	142	1,135 D	38.7%	58.8%	39.7%	60.3%
15,402	HART	6,204	3,129	3,005	70	124 R	50.4%	48.4%	51.0%	49.0%
40,849	HENDERSON	13,659	5,074	8,082	503	3,008 D	37.1%	59.2%	38.6%	61.4%
12,740	HENRY	4,810	1,723	2,999	88	1,276 D	35.8%	62.3%	36.5%	63.5%
6,065	HICKMAN	2,668	1,143	1,456	69	313 D	42.8%	54.6%	44.0%	56.0%
46,174	HOPKINS	15,355	6,238	8,810	307	2,572 D	40.6%	57.4%	41.5%	58.5%
11,996	JACKSON	4,123	3,379	702	42	2,677 R	82.0%	17.0%	82.8%	17.2%
684,793	JEFFERSON	265,286	127,254	125,844	12,188	1,410 R	48.0%	47.4%	50.3%	49.7%
26,653	JESSAMINE	8,530	4,809	3,310	411	1,499 R	56.4%	38.8%	59.2%	40.8%
24,432	JOHNSON	8,329	5,039	3,142	148	1,897 R	60.5%	37.7%	61.6%	38.4%
137,058	KENTON	46,232	25,965	17,907	2,360	8,058 R	56.2%	38.7%	59.2%	40.8%
17,940	KNOTT	7,065	1,602	5,405	58	3,803 D	22.7%	76.5%	22.9%	77.1%
30,239	KNOX	9,240	5,539	3,543	158	1,996 R	59.9%	38.3%	61.0%	39.0%
11,983	LARUE	4,249	2,000	2,183	66	183 D	47.1%	51.4%	47.8%	52.2%
38,982	LAUREL	12,997	8,868	3,969	160	4,899 R	68.2%	30.5%	69.1%	30.9%
14,121	LAWRENCE	4,980	2,564	2,362	54	202 R	51.5%	47.4%	52.1%	47.9%
7,754	LEE	2,726	1,650	1,017	59	633 R	60.5%	37.3%	61.9%	38.1%
14,882	LESLIE	4,921	3,536	1,327	58	2,209 R	71.9%	27.0%	72.7%	27.3%
30,687	LETCHER	7,818	3,426	4,280	112	854 D	43.8%	54.7%	44.5%	55.5%
14,545	LEWIS	4,393	2,802	1,543	48	1,259 R	63.8%	35.1%	64.5%	35.5%
19,053	LINCOLN	6,105	3,034	2,991	80	43 R	49.7%	49.0%	50.4%	49.6%
9,219	LIVINGSTON	4,008	1,670	2,287	51	617 D	41.7%	57.1%	42.2%	57.8%

KENTUCKY

PRESIDENT 1980

1980 Census Population	County	Total Vote	Republican	Democratic	Other	Rep.-Dem. Plurality		Percentage Total Vote Rep.	Dem.	Major Vote Rep.	Dem.
24,138	LOGAN	7,781	3,366	4,264	151	898	D	43.3%	54.8%	44.1%	55.9%
6,490	LYON	2,527	968	1,496	63	528	D	38.3%	59.2%	39.3%	60.7%
61,310	MCCRACKEN	24,325	10,281	13,365	679	3,084	D	42.3%	54.9%	43.5%	56.5%
15,634	MCCREARY	5,312	3,786	1,377	149	2,409	R	71.3%	25.9%	73.3%	26.7%
10,090	MCLEAN	3,710	1,497	2,147	66	650	D	40.4%	57.9%	41.1%	58.9%
53,352	MADISON	17,671	8,437	8,208	1,026	229	R	47.7%	46.4%	50.7%	49.3%
13,515	MAGOFFIN	5,297	2,265	2,986	46	721	D	42.8%	56.4%	43.1%	56.9%
17,910	MARION	5,816	2,126	3,577	113	1,451	D	36.6%	61.5%	37.3%	62.7%
25,637	MARSHALL	10,779	4,403	6,231	145	1,828	D	40.8%	57.8%	41.4%	58.6%
13,925	MARTIN	4,430	2,793	1,567	70	1,226	R	63.0%	35.4%	64.1%	35.9%
17,760	MASON	6,287	2,926	3,181	180	255	D	46.5%	50.6%	47.9%	52.1%
22,854	MEADE	6,059	2,740	3,205	114	465	D	45.2%	52.9%	46.1%	53.9%
5,117	MENIFEE	1,543	547	966	30	419	D	35.5%	62.6%	36.2%	63.8%
19,011	MERCER	6,970	3,275	3,528	167	253	D	47.0%	50.6%	48.1%	51.9%
9,484	METCALFE	3,707	2,013	1,628	66	385	R	54.3%	43.9%	55.3%	44.7%
12,353	MONROE	5,813	4,592	1,156	65	3,436	R	79.0%	19.9%	79.9%	20.1%
20,046	MONTGOMERY	6,418	2,869	3,391	158	522	D	44.7%	52.8%	45.8%	54.2%
12,103	MORGAN	4,199	1,450	2,698	51	1,248	D	34.5%	64.3%	35.0%	65.0%
32,238	MUHLENBERG	11,706	4,893	6,616	197	1,723	D	41.8%	56.5%	42.5%	57.5%
27,584	NELSON	9,114	3,349	5,514	251	2,165	D	36.7%	60.5%	37.8%	62.2%
7,157	NICHOLAS	2,351	915	1,349	87	434	D	38.9%	57.4%	40.4%	59.6%
21,765	OHIO	8,921	5,272	3,486	163	1,786	R	59.1%	39.1%	60.2%	39.8%
28,094	OLDHAM	9,510	5,586	3,487	437	2,099	R	58.7%	36.7%	61.6%	38.4%
8,924	OWEN	3,344	944	2,323	77	1,379	D	28.2%	69.5%	28.9%	71.1%
5,709	OWSLEY	1,699	1,250	437	12	813	R	73.6%	25.7%	74.1%	25.9%
10,989	PENDLETON	3,866	1,757	1,992	117	235	D	45.4%	51.5%	46.9%	53.1%
33,763	PERRY	10,367	4,226	6,031	110	1,805	D	40.8%	58.2%	41.2%	58.8%
81,123	PIKE	25,720	10,550	14,878	292	4,328	D	41.0%	57.8%	41.5%	58.5%
11,101	POWELL	3,767	1,716	2,006	45	290	D	45.6%	53.3%	46.1%	53.9%
45,803	PULASKI	19,919	12,970	6,570	379	6,400	R	65.1%	33.0%	66.4%	33.6%
2,270	ROBERTSON	999	416	562	21	146	D	41.6%	56.3%	42.5%	57.5%
13,973	ROCKCASTLE	4,947	3,543	1,345	59	2,198	R	71.6%	27.2%	72.5%	27.5%
19,049	ROWAN	5,987	2,758	2,975	254	217	D	46.1%	49.7%	48.1%	51.9%
13,708	RUSSELL	5,540	3,804	1,693	43	2,111	R	68.7%	30.6%	69.2%	30.8%
21,813	SCOTT	6,667	2,868	3,531	268	663	D	43.0%	53.0%	44.8%	55.2%
23,328	SHELBY	8,108	3,423	4,429	256	1,006	D	42.2%	54.6%	43.6%	56.4%
14,673	SIMPSON	4,819	2,020	2,713	86	693	D	41.9%	56.3%	42.7%	57.3%
5,929	SPENCER	2,200	935	1,216	49	281	D	42.5%	55.3%	43.5%	56.5%
21,178	TAYLOR	7,768	4,243	3,400	125	843	R	54.6%	43.8%	55.5%	44.5%
11,874	TODD	3,981	1,945	1,956	80	11	D	48.9%	49.1%	49.9%	50.1%
9,384	TRIGG	4,605	1,913	2,619	73	706	D	41.5%	56.9%	42.2%	57.8%
6,253	TRIMBLE	2,392	824	1,478	90	654	D	34.4%	61.8%	35.8%	64.2%
17,821	UNION	5,437	1,847	3,479	111	1,632	D	34.0%	64.0%	34.7%	65.3%
71,828	WARREN	22,604	12,184	9,643	777	2,541	R	53.9%	42.7%	55.8%	44.2%
10,764	WASHINGTON	4,249	2,008	2,147	94	139	D	47.3%	50.5%	48.3%	51.7%
17,022	WAYNE	6,716	3,972	2,673	71	1,299	R	59.1%	39.8%	59.8%	40.2%
14,832	WEBSTER	5,535	1,939	3,506	90	1,567	D	35.0%	63.3%	35.6%	64.4%
33,396	WHITLEY	11,077	7,007	3,889	181	3,118	R	63.3%	35.1%	64.3%	35.7%
6,698	WOLFE	2,805	951	1,814	40	863	D	33.9%	64.7%	34.4%	65.6%
17,778	WOODFORD	6,515	3,105	3,122	288	17	D	47.7%	47.9%	49.9%	50.1%
3,661,433	TOTAL	1,294,627	635,274	616,417	42,936	18,857	R	49.1%	47.6%	50.8%	49.2%

KENTUCKY

GOVERNOR 1979

1980 Census Population	County	Total Vote	Republican	Democratic	Other	Rep.-Dem. Plurality	Percentage Total Vote Rep.	Dem.	Major Vote Rep.	Dem.
15,233	ADAIR	5,990	3,569	2,421		1,148 R	59.6%	40.4%	59.6%	40.4%
14,128	ALLEN	4,502	2,512	1,990		522 R	55.8%	44.2%	55.8%	44.2%
12,567	ANDERSON	4,046	1,634	2,412		778 D	40.4%	59.6%	40.4%	59.6%
8,798	BALLARD	2,597	598	1,999		1,401 D	23.0%	77.0%	23.0%	77.0%
34,009	BARREN	10,019	5,498	4,521		977 R	54.9%	45.1%	54.9%	45.1%
10,025	BATH	3,030	820	2,210		1,390 D	27.1%	72.9%	27.1%	72.9%
34,330	BELL	8,891	3,799	5,092		1,293 D	42.7%	57.3%	42.7%	57.3%
45,842	BOONE	8,737	3,809	4,928		1,119 D	43.6%	56.4%	43.6%	56.4%
19,405	BOURBON	4,490	1,301	3,189		1,888 D	29.0%	71.0%	29.0%	71.0%
55,513	BOYD	16,697	6,279	10,418		4,139 D	37.6%	62.4%	37.6%	62.4%
25,066	BOYLE	6,717	2,514	4,203		1,689 D	37.4%	62.6%	37.4%	62.6%
7,738	BRACKEN	2,056	727	1,329		602 D	35.4%	64.6%	35.4%	64.6%
17,004	BREATHITT	3,932	1,079	2,853		1,774 D	27.4%	72.6%	27.4%	72.6%
16,861	BRECKINRIDGE	5,605	2,707	2,898		191 D	48.3%	51.7%	48.3%	51.7%
43,346	BULLITT	8,096	2,625	5,471		2,846 D	32.4%	67.6%	32.4%	67.6%
11,064	BUTLER	3,395	2,133	1,262		871 R	62.8%	37.2%	62.8%	37.2%
13,473	CALDWELL	4,528	1,943	2,585		642 D	42.9%	57.1%	42.9%	57.1%
30,031	CALLOWAY	7,204	2,303	4,901		2,598 D	32.0%	68.0%	32.0%	68.0%
83,317	CAMPBELL	22,768	10,383	12,385		2,002 D	45.6%	54.4%	45.6%	54.4%
5,487	CARLISLE	1,863	686	1,177		491 D	36.8%	63.2%	36.8%	63.2%
9,270	CARROLL	2,322	639	1,683		1,044 D	27.5%	72.5%	27.5%	72.5%
25,060	CARTER	6,126	2,851	3,275		424 D	46.5%	53.5%	46.5%	53.5%
14,818	CASEY	4,333	3,049	1,284		1,765 R	70.4%	29.6%	70.4%	29.6%
66,878	CHRISTIAN	9,270	2,898	6,372		3,474 D	31.3%	68.7%	31.3%	68.7%
28,322	CLARK	6,487	1,994	4,493		2,499 D	30.7%	69.3%	30.7%	69.3%
22,752	CLAY	5,889	3,452	2,437		1,015 R	58.6%	41.4%	58.6%	41.4%
9,321	CLINTON	3,961	2,875	1,086		1,789 R	72.6%	27.4%	72.6%	27.4%
9,207	CRITTENDEN	2,861	1,508	1,353		155 R	52.7%	47.3%	52.7%	47.3%
7,289	CUMBERLAND	3,031	2,196	835		1,361 R	72.5%	27.5%	72.5%	27.5%
85,949	DAVIESS	20,488	8,147	12,341		4,194 D	39.8%	60.2%	39.8%	60.2%
9,962	EDMONSON	4,150	2,405	1,745		660 R	58.0%	42.0%	58.0%	42.0%
6,908	ELLIOTT	1,821	641	1,180		539 D	35.2%	64.8%	35.2%	64.8%
14,495	ESTILL	3,820	2,125	1,695		430 R	55.6%	44.4%	55.6%	44.4%
204,165	FAYETTE	52,677	20,259	32,418		12,159 D	38.5%	61.5%	38.5%	61.5%
12,323	FLEMING	3,480	1,460	2,020		560 D	42.0%	58.0%	42.0%	58.0%
48,764	FLOYD	13,968	4,169	9,799		5,630 D	29.8%	70.2%	29.8%	70.2%
41,830	FRANKLIN	16,490	5,032	11,458		6,426 D	30.5%	69.5%	30.5%	69.5%
8,971	FULTON	2,313	865	1,448		583 D	37.4%	62.6%	37.4%	62.6%
4,842	GALLATIN	1,215	384	831		447 D	31.6%	68.4%	31.6%	68.4%
10,853	GARRARD	3,796	2,191	1,605		586 R	57.7%	42.3%	57.7%	42.3%
13,308	GRANT	2,760	1,014	1,746		732 D	36.7%	63.3%	36.7%	63.3%
34,049	GRAVES	9,403	3,323	6,080		2,757 D	35.3%	64.7%	35.3%	64.7%
20,854	GRAYSON	6,792	3,743	3,049		694 R	55.1%	44.9%	55.1%	44.9%
11,043	GREEN	4,484	2,370	2,114		256 R	52.9%	47.1%	52.9%	47.1%
39,132	GREENUP	11,168	4,295	6,873		2,578 D	38.5%	61.5%	38.5%	61.5%
7,742	HANCOCK	1,881	746	1,135		389 D	39.7%	60.3%	39.7%	60.3%
88,917	HARDIN	13,603	5,385	8,218		2,833 D	39.6%	60.4%	39.6%	60.4%
41,889	HARLAN	11,089	4,203	6,886		2,683 D	37.9%	62.1%	37.9%	62.1%
15,166	HARRISON	3,770	1,021	2,749		1,728 D	27.1%	72.9%	27.1%	72.9%
15,402	HART	6,509	3,573	2,936		637 R	54.9%	45.1%	54.9%	45.1%
40,849	HENDERSON	8,586	2,503	6,083		3,580 D	29.2%	70.8%	29.2%	70.8%
12,740	HENRY	3,778	1,180	2,598		1,418 D	31.2%	68.8%	31.2%	68.8%
6,065	HICKMAN	2,042	871	1,171		300 D	42.7%	57.3%	42.7%	57.3%
46,174	HOPKINS	9,027	3,436	5,591		2,155 D	38.1%	61.9%	38.1%	61.9%
11,996	JACKSON	2,922	2,329	593		1,736 R	79.7%	20.3%	79.7%	20.3%
684,793	JEFFERSON	187,663	62,551	125,112		62,561 D	33.3%	66.7%	33.3%	66.7%
26,653	JESSAMINE	5,065	2,255	2,810		555 D	44.5%	55.5%	44.5%	55.5%
24,432	JOHNSON	6,336	3,887	2,449		1,438 R	61.3%	38.7%	61.3%	38.7%
137,058	KENTON	31,261	14,839	16,422		1,583 D	47.5%	52.5%	47.5%	52.5%
17,940	KNOTT	4,030	1,063	2,967		1,904 D	26.4%	73.6%	26.4%	73.6%
30,239	KNOX	7,119	3,781	3,338		443 R	53.1%	46.9%	53.1%	46.9%
11,983	LARUE	3,492	1,665	1,827		162 D	47.7%	52.3%	47.7%	52.3%
38,982	LAUREL	8,287	4,775	3,512		1,263 R	57.6%	42.4%	57.6%	42.4%
14,121	LAWRENCE	3,354	1,803	1,551		252 R	53.8%	46.2%	53.8%	46.2%
7,754	LEE	2,386	1,329	1,057		272 R	55.7%	44.3%	55.7%	44.3%
14,882	LESLIE	3,716	2,557	1,159		1,398 R	68.8%	31.2%	68.8%	31.2%
30,687	LETCHER	5,765	2,427	3,338		911 D	42.1%	57.9%	42.1%	57.9%
14,545	LEWIS	3,327	2,008	1,319		689 R	60.4%	39.6%	60.4%	39.6%
19,053	LINCOLN	4,966	2,407	2,559		152 D	48.5%	51.5%	48.5%	51.5%
9,219	LIVINGSTON	2,782	850	1,932		1,082 D	30.6%	69.4%	30.6%	69.4%

KENTUCKY

GOVERNOR 1979

1980 Census Population	County	Total Vote	Republican	Democratic	Other	Rep.-Dem. Plurality		Percentage Total Vote Rep.	Dem.	Major Vote Rep.	Dem.
24,138	LOGAN	5,048	2,257	2,791		534	D	44.7%	55.3%	44.7%	55.3%
6,490	LYON	1,874	618	1,256		638	D	33.0%	67.0%	33.0%	67.0%
61,310	MCCRACKEN	16,696	4,388	12,308		7,920	D	26.3%	73.7%	26.3%	73.7%
15,634	MCCREARY	2,592	1,520	1,072		448	R	58.6%	41.4%	58.6%	41.4%
10,090	MCLEAN	2,578	845	1,733		888	D	32.8%	67.2%	32.8%	67.2%
53,352	MADISON	12,080	4,489	7,591		3,102	D	37.2%	62.8%	37.2%	62.8%
13,515	MAGOFFIN	4,913	2,589	2,324		265	R	52.7%	47.3%	52.7%	47.3%
17,910	MARION	4,859	1,325	3,534		2,209	D	27.3%	72.7%	27.3%	72.7%
25,637	MARSHALL	7,195	2,010	5,185		3,175	D	27.9%	72.1%	27.9%	72.1%
13,925	MARTIN	2,353	1,203	1,150		53	R	51.1%	48.9%	51.1%	48.9%
17,760	MASON	4,543	1,566	2,977		1,411	D	34.5%	65.5%	34.5%	65.5%
22,854	MEADE	4,305	1,656	2,649		993	D	38.5%	61.5%	38.5%	61.5%
5,117	MENIFEE	1,168	363	805		442	D	31.1%	68.9%	31.1%	68.9%
19,011	MERCER	5,739	2,355	3,384		1,029	D	41.0%	59.0%	41.0%	59.0%
9,484	METCALFE	3,830	1,937	1,893		44	R	50.6%	49.4%	50.6%	49.4%
12,353	MONROE	5,319	3,963	1,356		2,607	R	74.5%	25.5%	74.5%	25.5%
20,046	MONTGOMERY	4,322	1,568	2,754		1,186	D	36.3%	63.7%	36.3%	63.7%
12,103	MORGAN	3,212	1,436	1,776		340	D	44.7%	55.3%	44.7%	55.3%
32,238	MUHLENBERG	8,184	2,703	5,481		2,778	D	33.0%	67.0%	33.0%	67.0%
27,584	NELSON	6,389	2,077	4,312		2,235	D	32.5%	67.5%	32.5%	67.5%
7,157	NICHOLAS	1,748	528	1,220		692	D	30.2%	69.8%	30.2%	69.8%
21,765	OHIO	6,501	3,111	3,390		279	D	47.9%	52.1%	47.9%	52.1%
28,094	OLDHAM	5,814	2,322	3,492		1,170	D	39.9%	60.1%	39.9%	60.1%
8,924	OWEN	2,423	701	1,722		1,021	D	28.9%	71.1%	28.9%	71.1%
5,709	OWSLEY	1,539	1,095	444		651	R	71.2%	28.8%	71.2%	28.8%
10,989	PENDLETON	2,558	982	1,576		594	D	38.4%	61.6%	38.4%	61.6%
33,763	PERRY	7,300	3,405	3,895		490	D	46.6%	53.4%	46.6%	53.4%
81,123	PIKE	18,074	8,048	10,026		1,978	D	44.5%	55.5%	44.5%	55.5%
11,101	POWELL	3,233	1,231	2,002		771	D	38.1%	61.9%	38.1%	61.9%
45,803	PULASKI	12,744	7,435	5,309		2,126	R	58.3%	41.7%	58.3%	41.7%
2,270	ROBERTSON	878	306	572		266	D	34.9%	65.1%	34.9%	65.1%
13,973	ROCKCASTLE	4,008	2,490	1,518		972	R	62.1%	37.9%	62.1%	37.9%
19,049	ROWAN	5,073	1,892	3,181		1,289	D	37.3%	62.7%	37.3%	62.7%
13,708	RUSSELL	4,947	2,898	2,049		849	R	58.6%	41.4%	58.6%	41.4%
21,813	SCOTT	4,693	1,520	3,173		1,653	D	32.4%	67.6%	32.4%	67.6%
23,328	SHELBY	5,918	2,116	3,802		1,686	D	35.8%	64.2%	35.8%	64.2%
14,673	SIMPSON	2,962	1,352	1,610		258	D	45.6%	54.4%	45.6%	54.4%
5,929	SPENCER	1,538	624	914		290	D	40.6%	59.4%	40.6%	59.4%
21,178	TAYLOR	5,930	2,983	2,947		36	R	50.3%	49.7%	50.3%	49.7%
11,874	TODD	2,515	1,036	1,479		443	D	41.2%	58.8%	41.2%	58.8%
9,384	TRIGG	3,224	995	2,229		1,234	D	30.9%	69.1%	30.9%	69.1%
6,253	TRIMBLE	1,552	562	990		428	D	36.2%	63.8%	36.2%	63.8%
17,821	UNION	3,652	1,132	2,520		1,388	D	31.0%	69.0%	31.0%	69.0%
71,828	WARREN	15,262	5,257	10,005		4,748	D	34.4%	65.6%	34.4%	65.6%
10,764	WASHINGTON	3,305	1,348	1,957		609	D	40.8%	59.2%	40.8%	59.2%
17,022	WAYNE	5,821	2,881	2,940		59	D	49.5%	50.5%	49.5%	50.5%
14,832	WEBSTER	3,717	1,134	2,583		1,449	D	30.5%	69.5%	30.5%	69.5%
33,396	WHITLEY	7,021	3,831	3,190		641	R	54.6%	45.4%	54.6%	45.4%
6,698	WOLFE	2,228	1,191	1,037		154	R	53.5%	46.5%	53.5%	46.5%
17,778	WOODFORD	4,965	1,756	3,209		1,453	D	35.4%	64.6%	35.4%	64.6%
3,661,433	TOTAL	939,366	381,278	558,088		176,810	D	40.6%	59.4%	40.6%	59.4%

KENTUCKY

SENATOR 1980

1980 Census Population	County	Total Vote	Republican	Democratic	Other	Rep.-Dem. Plurality	Percentage Total Vote Rep.	Dem.	Major Vote Rep.	Dem.
15,233	ADAIR	5,416	2,817	2,599		218 R	52.0%	48.0%	52.0%	48.0%
14,128	ALLEN	4,725	2,354	2,371		17 D	49.8%	50.2%	49.8%	50.2%
12,567	ANDERSON	4,365	1,325	3,040		1,715 D	30.4%	69.6%	30.4%	69.6%
8,798	BALLARD	3,472	564	2,908		2,344 D	16.2%	83.8%	16.2%	83.8%
34,009	BARREN	10,287	3,869	6,418		2,549 D	37.6%	62.4%	37.6%	62.4%
10,025	BATH	3,191	891	2,300		1,409 D	27.9%	72.1%	27.9%	72.1%
34,330	BELL	9,997	3,607	6,390		2,783 D	36.1%	63.9%	36.1%	63.9%
45,842	BOONE	12,575	5,083	7,492		2,409 D	40.4%	59.6%	40.4%	59.6%
19,405	BOURBON	5,184	1,236	3,948		2,712 D	23.8%	76.2%	23.8%	76.2%
55,513	BOYD	18,947	6,032	12,915		6,883 D	31.8%	68.2%	31.8%	68.2%
25,066	BOYLE	7,431	2,124	5,307		3,183 D	28.6%	71.4%	28.6%	71.4%
7,738	BRACKEN	2,289	581	1,708		1,127 D	25.4%	74.6%	25.4%	74.6%
17,004	BREATHITT	4,937	860	4,077		3,217 D	17.4%	82.6%	17.4%	82.6%
16,861	BRECKINRIDGE	6,270	2,138	4,132		1,994 D	34.1%	65.9%	34.1%	65.9%
43,346	BULLITT	11,588	4,279	7,309		3,030 D	36.9%	63.1%	36.9%	63.1%
11,064	BUTLER	4,003	2,475	1,528		947 R	61.8%	38.2%	61.8%	38.2%
13,473	CALDWELL	4,669	1,337	3,332		1,995 D	28.6%	71.4%	28.6%	71.4%
30,031	CALLOWAY	9,835	2,387	7,448		5,061 D	24.3%	75.7%	24.3%	75.7%
83,317	CAMPBELL	24,932	10,287	14,645		4,358 D	41.3%	58.7%	41.3%	58.7%
5,487	CARLISLE	2,080	373	1,707		1,334 D	17.9%	82.1%	17.9%	82.1%
9,270	CARROLL	2,781	548	2,233		1,685 D	19.7%	80.3%	19.7%	80.3%
25,060	CARTER	6,603	2,446	4,157		1,711 D	37.0%	63.0%	37.0%	63.0%
14,818	CASEY	4,606	2,969	1,637		1,332 R	64.5%	35.5%	64.5%	35.5%
66,878	CHRISTIAN	11,921	3,640	8,281		4,641 D	30.5%	69.5%	30.5%	69.5%
28,322	CLARK	8,049	1,861	6,188		4,327 D	23.1%	76.9%	23.1%	76.9%
22,752	CLAY	5,607	2,872	2,735		137 R	51.2%	48.8%	51.2%	48.8%
9,321	CLINTON	3,430	2,382	1,048		1,334 R	69.4%	30.6%	69.4%	30.6%
9,207	CRITTENDEN	3,264	1,292	1,972		680 D	39.6%	60.4%	39.6%	60.4%
7,289	CUMBERLAND	2,270	1,463	807		656 R	64.4%	35.6%	64.4%	35.6%
85,949	DAVIESS	28,450	5,923	22,527		16,604 D	20.8%	79.2%	20.8%	79.2%
9,962	EDMONSON	3,790	2,328	1,462		866 R	61.4%	38.6%	61.4%	38.6%
6,908	ELLIOTT	1,973	371	1,602		1,231 D	18.8%	81.2%	18.8%	81.2%
14,495	ESTILL	4,323	2,030	2,293		263 D	47.0%	53.0%	47.0%	53.0%
204,165	FAYETTE	60,548	19,852	40,696		20,844 D	32.8%	67.2%	32.8%	67.2%
12,323	FLEMING	3,552	1,292	2,260		968 D	36.4%	63.6%	36.4%	63.6%
48,764	FLOYD	13,204	2,259	10,945		8,686 D	17.1%	82.9%	17.1%	82.9%
41,830	FRANKLIN	15,849	2,594	13,255		10,661 D	16.4%	83.6%	16.4%	83.6%
8,971	FULTON	2,911	615	2,296		1,681 D	21.1%	78.9%	21.1%	78.9%
4,842	GALLATIN	1,429	360	1,069		709 D	25.2%	74.8%	25.2%	74.8%
10,853	GARRARD	4,134	2,020	2,114		94 D	48.9%	51.1%	48.9%	51.1%
13,308	GRANT	3,172	966	2,206		1,240 D	30.5%	69.5%	30.5%	69.5%
34,049	GRAVES	11,116	2,520	8,596		6,076 D	22.7%	77.3%	22.7%	77.3%
20,854	GRAYSON	7,285	3,778	3,507		271 R	51.9%	48.1%	51.9%	48.1%
11,043	GREEN	4,207	2,133	2,074		59 R	50.7%	49.3%	50.7%	49.3%
39,132	GREENUP	12,548	4,241	8,307		4,066 D	33.8%	66.2%	33.8%	66.2%
7,742	HANCOCK	2,703	822	1,881		1,059 D	30.4%	69.6%	30.4%	69.6%
88,917	HARDIN	16,328	5,453	10,875		5,422 D	33.4%	66.6%	33.4%	66.6%
41,889	HARLAN	11,161	3,172	7,989		4,817 D	28.4%	71.6%	28.4%	71.6%
15,166	HARRISON	4,945	1,041	3,904		2,863 D	21.1%	78.9%	21.1%	78.9%
15,402	HART	5,602	2,215	3,387		1,172 D	39.5%	60.5%	39.5%	60.5%
40,849	HENDERSON	12,160	2,650	9,510		6,860 D	21.8%	78.2%	21.8%	78.2%
12,740	HENRY	4,348	1,009	3,339		2,330 D	23.2%	76.8%	23.2%	76.8%
6,065	HICKMAN	2,165	471	1,694		1,223 D	21.8%	78.2%	21.8%	78.2%
46,174	HOPKINS	12,963	2,823	10,140		7,317 D	21.8%	78.2%	21.8%	78.2%
11,996	JACKSON	3,103	2,172	931		1,241 R	70.0%	30.0%	70.0%	30.0%
684,793	JEFFERSON	238,988	92,110	146,878		54,768 D	38.5%	61.5%	38.5%	61.5%
26,653	JESSAMINE	6,991	2,580	4,411		1,831 D	36.9%	63.1%	36.9%	63.1%
24,432	JOHNSON	6,173	2,489	3,684		1,195 D	40.3%	59.7%	40.3%	59.7%
137,058	KENTON	37,616	15,293	22,323		7,030 D	40.7%	59.3%	40.7%	59.3%
17,940	KNOTT	5,352	691	4,661		3,970 D	12.9%	87.1%	12.9%	87.1%
30,239	KNOX	6,551	2,814	3,737		923 D	43.0%	57.0%	43.0%	57.0%
11,983	LARUE	3,853	1,245	2,608		1,363 D	32.3%	67.7%	32.3%	67.7%
38,982	LAUREL	9,112	4,539	4,573		34 D	49.8%	50.2%	49.8%	50.2%
14,121	LAWRENCE	4,158	1,584	2,574		990 D	38.1%	61.9%	38.1%	61.9%
7,754	LEE	2,447	1,185	1,262		77 D	48.4%	51.6%	48.4%	51.6%
14,882	LESLIE	3,706	2,346	1,360		986 R	63.3%	36.7%	63.3%	36.7%
30,687	LETCHER	6,414	1,988	4,426		2,438 D	31.0%	69.0%	31.0%	69.0%
14,545	LEWIS	3,883	2,035	1,848		187 R	52.4%	47.6%	52.4%	47.6%
19,053	LINCOLN	5,618	2,136	3,482		1,346 D	38.0%	62.0%	38.0%	62.0%
9,219	LIVINGSTON	3,480	830	2,650		1,820 D	23.9%	76.1%	23.9%	76.1%

KENTUCKY

SENATOR 1980

1980 Census Population	County	Total Vote	Republican	Democratic	Other	Rep.-Dem. Plurality	Percentage Total Vote		Major Vote	
							Rep.	Dem.	Rep.	Dem.
24,138	LOGAN	6,731	1,994	4,737		2,743 D	29.6%	70.4%	29.6%	70.4%
6,490	LYON	2,262	531	1,731		1,200 D	23.5%	76.5%	23.5%	76.5%
61,310	MCCRACKEN	21,045	5,158	15,887		10,729 D	24.5%	75.5%	24.5%	75.5%
15,634	MCCREARY	3,378	2,042	1,336		706 R	60.4%	39.6%	60.4%	39.6%
10,090	MCLEAN	3,464	857	2,607		1,750 D	24.7%	75.3%	24.7%	75.3%
53,352	MADISON	14,017	4,906	9,111		4,205 D	35.0%	65.0%	35.0%	65.0%
13,515	MAGOFFIN	4,411	1,524	2,887		1,363 D	34.5%	65.5%	34.5%	65.5%
17,910	MARION	5,209	1,103	4,106		3,003 D	21.2%	78.8%	21.2%	78.8%
25,637	MARSHALL	9,992	2,368	7,624		5,256 D	23.7%	76.3%	23.7%	76.3%
13,925	MARTIN	2,892	1,420	1,472		52 D	49.1%	50.9%	49.1%	50.9%
17,760	MASON	5,328	1,707	3,621		1,914 D	32.0%	68.0%	32.0%	68.0%
22,854	MEADE	5,404	1,443	3,961		2,518 D	26.7%	73.3%	26.7%	73.3%
5,117	MENIFEE	1,311	334	977		643 D	25.5%	74.5%	25.5%	74.5%
19,011	MERCER	5,902	1,955	3,947		1,992 D	33.1%	66.9%	33.1%	66.9%
9,484	METCALFE	3,147	1,356	1,791		435 D	43.1%	56.9%	43.1%	56.9%
12,353	MONROE	4,190	2,808	1,382		1,426 R	67.0%	33.0%	67.0%	33.0%
20,046	MONTGOMERY	5,301	1,256	4,045		2,789 D	23.7%	76.3%	23.7%	76.3%
12,103	MORGAN	3,480	824	2,656		1,832 D	23.7%	76.3%	23.7%	76.3%
32,238	MUHLENBERG	9,668	2,844	6,824		3,980 D	29.4%	70.6%	29.4%	70.6%
27,584	NELSON	7,868	1,711	6,157		4,446 D	21.7%	78.3%	21.7%	78.3%
7,157	NICHOLAS	2,059	503	1,556		1,053 D	24.4%	75.6%	24.4%	75.6%
21,765	OHIO	7,959	3,332	4,627		1,295 D	41.9%	58.1%	41.9%	58.1%
28,094	OLDHAM	8,843	3,719	5,124		1,405 D	42.1%	57.9%	42.1%	57.9%
8,924	OWEN	2,834	537	2,297		1,760 D	18.9%	81.1%	18.9%	81.1%
5,709	OWSLEY	1,468	877	591		286 R	59.7%	40.3%	59.7%	40.3%
10,989	PENDLETON	2,198	916	1,282		366 D	41.7%	58.3%	41.7%	58.3%
33,763	PERRY	8,585	2,758	5,827		3,069 D	32.1%	67.9%	32.1%	67.9%
81,123	PIKE	21,552	7,060	14,492		7,432 D	32.8%	67.2%	32.8%	67.2%
11,101	POWELL	3,090	1,019	2,071		1,052 D	33.0%	67.0%	33.0%	67.0%
45,803	PULASKI	15,974	7,457	8,517		1,060 D	46.7%	53.3%	46.7%	53.3%
2,270	ROBERTSON	896	262	634		372 D	29.2%	70.8%	29.2%	70.8%
13,973	ROCKCASTLE	4,394	2,701	1,693		1,008 R	61.5%	38.5%	61.5%	38.5%
19,049	ROWAN	5,288	1,869	3,419		1,550 D	35.3%	64.7%	35.3%	64.7%
13,708	RUSSELL	4,639	2,522	2,117		405 R	54.4%	45.6%	54.4%	45.6%
21,813	SCOTT	5,660	1,514	4,146		2,632 D	26.7%	73.3%	26.7%	73.3%
23,328	SHELBY	7,298	2,150	5,148		2,998 D	29.5%	70.5%	29.5%	70.5%
14,673	SIMPSON	3,985	992	2,993		2,001 D	24.9%	75.1%	24.9%	75.1%
5,929	SPENCER	1,875	504	1,371		867 D	26.9%	73.1%	26.9%	73.1%
21,178	TAYLOR	6,963	2,525	4,438		1,913 D	36.3%	63.7%	36.3%	63.7%
11,874	TODD	3,033	914	2,119		1,205 D	30.1%	69.9%	30.1%	69.9%
9,384	TRIGG	3,750	941	2,809		1,868 D	25.1%	74.9%	25.1%	74.9%
6,253	TRIMBLE	2,107	452	1,655		1,203 D	21.5%	78.5%	21.5%	78.5%
17,821	UNION	4,929	884	4,045		3,161 D	17.9%	82.1%	17.9%	82.1%
71,828	WARREN	19,547	7,274	12,273		4,999 D	37.2%	62.8%	37.2%	62.8%
10,764	WASHINGTON	3,795	1,357	2,438		1,081 D	35.8%	64.2%	35.8%	64.2%
17,022	WAYNE	5,854	2,976	2,878		98 R	50.8%	49.2%	50.8%	49.2%
14,832	WEBSTER	4,731	824	3,907		3,083 D	17.4%	82.6%	17.4%	82.6%
33,396	WHITLEY	7,810	3,926	3,884		42 R	50.3%	49.7%	50.3%	49.7%
6,698	WOLFE	2,188	515	1,673		1,158 D	23.5%	76.5%	23.5%	76.5%
17,778	WOODFORD	5,551	1,541	4,010		2,469 D	27.8%	72.2%	27.8%	72.2%
3,661,433	TOTAL	1,106,890	386,029	720,861		334,832 D	34.9%	65.1%	34.9%	65.1%

KENTUCKY

CONGRESS

CD	Year	Total Vote	Republican Vote	Republican Candidate	Democratic Vote	Democratic Candidate	Other Vote	Rep.-Dem. Plurality	Total Vote Rep.	Total Vote Dem.	Major Vote Rep.	Major Vote Dem.
1	1980	118,565			118,565	HUBBARD, CARROLL		118,565 D		100.0%		100.0%
1	1978	44,097			44,090	HUBBARD, CARROLL	7	44,090 D		100.0%		100.0%
1	1976	144,985	26,089	BERSKY, BOB	118,886	HUBBARD, CARROLL	10	92,797 D	18.0%	82.0%	18.0%	82.0%
1	1974	90,465	16,937	BANKEN, CHARLES T.	70,723	HUBBARD, CARROLL	2,805	53,786 D	18.7%	78.2%	19.3%	80.7%
1	1972	125,662	42,286	BANKEN, CHARLES T.	81,456	STUBBLEFIELD, FRANK	1,920	39,170 D	33.7%	64.8%	34.2%	65.8%
2	1980	151,780	52,110	WATSON, MARK T.	99,670	NATCHER, WILLIAM H.		47,560 D	34.3%	65.7%	34.3%	65.7%
2	1978	36,459			36,441	NATCHER, WILLIAM H.	18	36,441 D		100.0%		100.0%
2	1976	130,920	51,900	BAKER, WALTER A.	79,016	NATCHER, WILLIAM H.	4	27,116 D	39.6%	60.4%	39.6%	60.4%
2	1974	77,400	18,312	EDDLEMAN, ART	56,502	NATCHER, WILLIAM H.	2,586	38,190 D	23.7%	73.0%	24.5%	75.5%
2	1972	123,307	47,436	CARTER, J. C.	75,871	NATCHER, WILLIAM H.		28,435 D	38.5%	61.5%	38.5%	61.5%
3	1980	134,724	46,681	CESLER, RICHARD	85,873	MAZZOLI, ROMANO L.	2,170	39,192 D	34.6%	63.7%	35.2%	64.8%
3	1978	56,871	17,785	LEVERONNE, NORBERT D.	37,346	MAZZOLI, ROMANO L.	1,740	19,561 D	31.3%	65.7%	32.3%	67.7%
3	1976	140,744	58,019	RAMSEY, DENZIL J.	80,496	MAZZOLI, ROMANO L.	2,229	22,477 D	41.2%	57.2%	41.9%	58.1%
3	1974	108,475	28,813	BARCLAY, VINCENT N.	75,571	MAZZOLI, ROMANO L.	4,091	46,758 D	26.6%	69.7%	27.6%	72.4%
3	1972	139,671	51,634	KAELIN, PHIL	86,810	MAZZOLI, ROMANO L.	1,227	35,176 D	37.0%	62.2%	37.3%	62.7%
4	1980	188,187	126,049	SNYDER, M. G.	62,138	MCGARY, PHIL M.		63,911 R	67.0%	33.0%	67.0%	33.0%
4	1978	94,299	62,087	SNYDER, M. G.	32,212	MARTIN, GEORGE C.		29,875 R	65.8%	34.2%	65.8%	34.2%
4	1976	174,502	97,493	SNYDER, M. G.	77,009	WINTERBERG, EDWARD J.		20,484 R	55.9%	44.1%	55.9%	44.1%
4	1974	123,384	63,845	SNYDER, M. G.	59,539	HUBBARD, KYLE T.		4,306 R	51.7%	48.3%	51.7%	48.3%
4	1972	150,234	110,902	SNYDER, M. G.	39,332	ROGERS, JAMES W.		71,570 R	73.8%	26.2%	73.8%	26.2%
5	1980	166,120	112,093	ROGERS, HAROLD	54,027	MARCUM, TED R.		58,066 R	67.5%	32.5%	67.5%	32.5%
5	1978	75,458	59,743	CARTER, TIM LEE	15,714	RAMEY, JESSE M.	1	44,029 R	79.2%	20.8%	79.2%	20.8%
5	1976	150,473	100,204	CARTER, TIM LEE	49,128	SMITH, CHARLES C.	1,141	51,076 R	66.6%	32.6%	67.1%	32.9%
5	1974	97,882	66,709	CARTER, TIM LEE	28,706	WILLIS, LYLE LEONARD	2,467	38,003 R	68.2%	29.3%	69.9%	30.1%
5	1972	148,565	109,264	CARTER, TIM LEE	39,301	WILLIS, LYLE LEONARD		69,963 R	73.5%	26.5%	73.5%	26.5%
6	1980	179,051	105,376	HOPKINS, LARRY J.	72,473	EASTERLY, TOM	1,202	32,903 R	58.9%	40.5%	59.3%	40.7%
6	1978	102,857	52,092	HOPKINS, LARRY J.	47,436	EASTERLY, TOM	3,329	4,656 R	50.6%	46.1%	52.3%	47.7%
6	1976	96,493			90,695	BRECKINRIDGE, JOHN	5,798	90,695 D		94.0%		100.0%
6	1974	87,416	21,039	ROGERS, THOMAS F.	63,010	BRECKINRIDGE, JOHN	3,367	41,971 D	24.1%	72.1%	25.0%	75.0%
6	1972	145,412	68,012	JACKSON, LABAN P.	76,185	BRECKINRIDGE, JOHN	1,215	8,173 D	46.8%	52.4%	47.2%	52.8%
7	1980	117,665			117,665	PERKINS, CARL D.		117,665 D		100.0%		100.0%
7	1978	67,420	15,861	THOMAS, GRANVILLE	51,559	PERKINS, CARL D.		35,698 D	23.5%	76.5%	23.5%	76.5%
7	1976	150,831	40,381	THOMAS, GRANVILLE	110,450	PERKINS, CARL D.		70,069 D	26.8%	73.2%	26.8%	73.2%
7	1974	94,203	22,982	THOMAS, GRANVILLE	71,221	PERKINS, CARL D.		48,239 D	24.4%	75.6%	24.4%	75.6%
7	1972	153,126	58,286	HOLCOMB, ROBERT	94,840	PERKINS, CARL D.		36,554 D	38.1%	61.9%	38.1%	61.9%

KENTUCKY

1979 GENERAL ELECTION

Governor

1980 GENERAL ELECTION

President   Other vote was 31,127 Anderson (Anderson Coalition); 5,531 Clark (Libertarian); 4,233 McCormack (Respect for Life); 1,304 Commoner (Citizens); 393 Pulley (Socialist Workers); 348 Hall (Communist). Original uncorrected returns gave the Carter (Democratic) state-wide total vote as 617,417.

Senator   Original uncorrected returns gave the Ford (Democratic) state-wide total as 720,891.

Congress   Other vote was 1,272 Cumbler (Citizens), 468 Vessels (American) and 430 Logsdon (Independent) in CD 3; Pratt (Independent) in CD 6.

1979 PRIMARIES

MAY 29 REPUBLICAN

Governor   106,006 Louie B. Nunn; 18,514 Ray B. White; 5,106 Elmer Begley; 3,499 Thurman J. Hamlin.

MAY 29 DEMOCRATIC

Governor   165,158 J. Y. Brown, Jr.; 139,713 Harvey Sloane; 131,530 Terry McBrayer; 68,577 Carroll Hubbard; 47,633 Thelma L. Stovall; 5,349 Lyle Leonard Willis; 3,810 George Atkins; 2,580 Doris S. Binion; 2,436 John J. Weikel.

1980 PRIMARIES

MAY 27 REPUBLICAN

Senator   25,717 Mary Louise Foust; 10,246 Granville Thomas; 8,382 Jackson M. Andrews; 6,418 Tommy Klein; 5,669 Yale J. Lubkin; 4,848 DeSota Vaught.

Congress   Unopposed in two CD's. No candidates in CD's 1 and 7. Contested as follows:

CD 2   2,347 Mark T. Watson; 2,003 Rex N. Agers.
CD 3   2,795 Richard Cesler; 1,720 Norbert D. Leveronne.
CD 5   13,266 Harold Rogers; 10,576 Tom Emberton; 9,595 Gene Huff; 7,439 John D. Rogers; 5,171 Raymond Overstreet; 3,703 Eddie C. Lovelace; 3,681 Elmer Patrick; 2,246 Henry S. Garrison; 753 Phillip Connley; 192 Elmer Begley; 131 Thurman J. Hamlin.

MAY 27 DEMOCRATIC

Senator   188,047 Wendell H. Ford; 28,202 Flora T. Stuart.

Congress   Unopposed in CD 2. Contested as follows:

CD 1   35,708 Carroll Hubbard; 5,046 Clara Humphrey; 2,525 Kenneth P. Rains.
CD 3   18,734 Romano L. Mazzoli; 2,142 George Tolhurst; 1,852 William Gibbs; 904 John A. Knouse.
CD 4   11,578 Phil M. McGary; 9,145 James Moss; 4,568 Ken Heil.
CD 5   7,840 Ted R. Marcum; 2,984 Lyle Leonard Willis; 2,491 Charles W. Harris; 2,213 Jesse M. Ramey.
CD 6   29,022 Tom Easterly; 12,534 J. Y. Brown, Sr.; 7,895 Edwin E. Miller; 1,322 David M. Lee.
CD 7   30,722 Carl D. Perkins; 5,056 Ray Adkins.

LOUISIANA

GOVERNOR
David C. Treen (R). Elected December 1979 to a four-year term.

SENATORS
J. Bennett Johnston (D). Re-elected 1978 to a six-year term. Previously elected 1972.

Russell B. Long (D). Re-elected 1980 to a six-year term. Previously elected 1974, 1968, 1962, 1956, 1950, and in 1948 to fill out term vacated by the death of Senator John H. Overton.

REPRESENTATIVES
1. Bob Livingston (R)
2. Lindy Boggs (D)
3. W. J. Tauzin (D)
4. Charles Roemer (D)
5. Jerry Huckaby (D)
6. W. Henson Moore (R)
7. John B. Breaux (D)
8. Gillis W. Long (D)

POSTWAR VOTE FOR GOVERNOR

Year	Total Vote	Republican Vote	Candidate	Democratic Vote	Candidate	Other Vote	Rep.-Dem. Plurality	Total Vote Rep.	Total Vote Dem.	Major Vote Rep.	Major Vote Dem.
1979	1,371,825	690,691	Treen, David C.	681,134	Lambert, Louis	—	9,557 R	50.3%	49.7%	50.3%	49.7%
1975	430,095	—	—	430,095	Edwards, Edwin W.	—	430,095 D	—	100.0%	—	100.0%
1972	1,121,570	480,424	Treen, David C.	641,146	Edwards, Edwin W.	—	160,722 D	42.8%	57.2%	42.8%	57.2%
1968	372,762	—	—	372,762	McKeithen, John J.	—	372,762 D	—	100.0%	—	100.0%
1964	773,390	297,753	Lyons, C. H.	469,589	McKeithen, John J.	6,048	171,836 D	38.5%	60.7%	38.8%	61.2%
1960	506,562	86,135	Grevemberg, F. C.	407,907	Davis, Jimmie H.	12,520	321,772 D	17.0%	80.5%	17.4%	82.6%
1956	172,291	—	—	172,291	Long, Earl K.	—	172,291 D	—	100.0%	—	100.0%
1952	123,681	4,958	Bagwell, Harrison G.	118,723	Kennon, Robert F.	—	113,765 D	4.0%	96.0%	4.0%	96.0%
1948	76,566			76,566	Long, Earl K.	—	76,566 D	—	100.0%	—	100.0%

POSTWAR VOTE FOR SENATOR

Year	Total Vote	Republican Vote	Candidate	Democratic Vote	Candidate	Other Vote	Rep.-Dem. Plurality	Total Vote Rep.	Total Vote Dem.	Major Vote Rep.	Major Vote Dem.
1980	—	—	—	—	Long, Russell B.	—	—	—	—	—	—
1978	—	—	—	—	Johnston, J. Bennett	—	—	—	—	—	—
1974	434,643	—	—	434,643	Long, Russell B.	—	434,643 D	—	100.0%	—	100.0%
1972	1,084,904	206,846	Toledano, Ben C.	598,987	Johnston, J. Bennett	279,071	392,141 D	19.1%	55.2%	25.7%	74.3%
1968	518,586	—	—	518,586	Long, Russell B.	—	518,586 D	—	100.0%	—	100.0%
1966	437,695	—	—	437,695	Ellender, Allen J.	—	437,695 D	—	100.0%	—	100.0%
1962	421,904	103,066	O'Hearn, Taylor W.	318,838	Long, Russell B.	—	215,772 D	24.4%	75.6%	24.4%	75.6%
1960	541,928	109,698	Reese, George W.	432,228	Ellender, Allen J.	2	322,530 D	20.2%	79.8%	20.2%	79.8%
1956	335,564	—	—	335,564	Long, Russell B.	—	335,564 D	—	100.0%	—	100.0%
1954	207,115	—	—	207,115	Ellender, Allen J.	—	207,115 D	—	100.0%	—	100.0%
1950	251,838	30,931	Gerth, Charles S.	220,907	Long, Russell B.	—	189,976 D	12.3%	87.7%	12.3%	87.7%
1948	330,124	—	—	330,115	Ellender, Allen J.	9	330,115 D	—	100.0%	—	100.0%
1948s	408,667	102,331	Clarke, Clem S.	306,336	Long, Russell B.	—	204,005 D	25.0%	75.0%	25.0%	75.0%

One of the 1948 elections was for a short term to fill a vacancy. For 1978 and 1980, see primary note section; no run-off general election was required.

LOUISIANA

Districts Established June 1, 1972

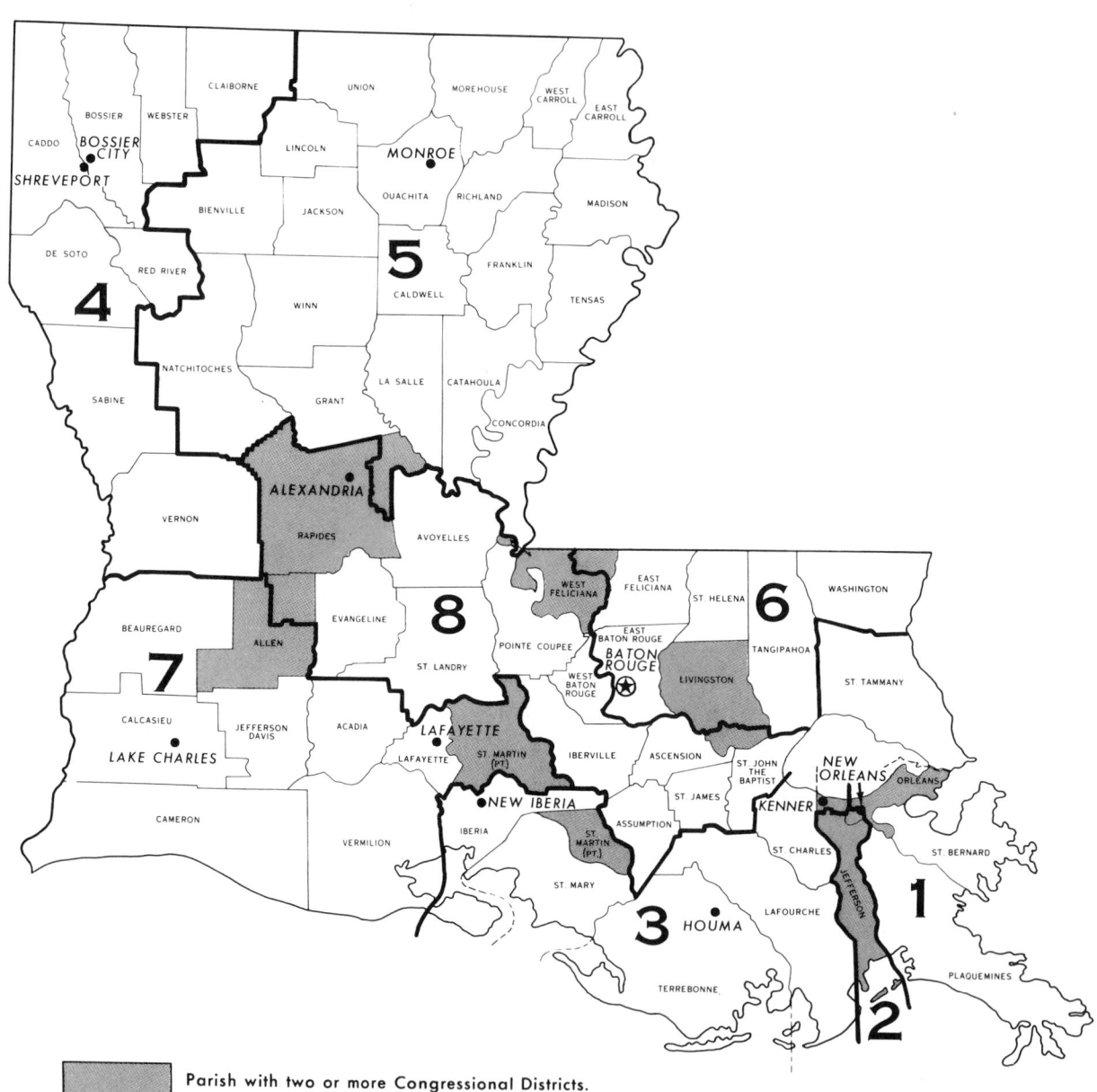

Parish with two or more Congressional Districts.

LOUISIANA

PRESIDENT 1980

1980 Census Population	Parish	Total Vote	Republican	Democratic	Other	Rep.-Dem. Plurality	Percentage Total Vote Rep.	Dem.	Major Vote Rep.	Dem.
56,427	ACADIA	22,100	11,533	9,948	619	1,585 R	52.2%	45.0%	53.7%	46.3%
21,390	ALLEN	9,564	3,328	6,057	179	2,729 D	34.8%	63.3%	35.5%	64.5%
50,068	ASCENSION	20,200	7,238	12,381	581	5,143 D	35.8%	61.3%	36.9%	63.1%
22,084	ASSUMPTION	9,073	4,001	4,679	393	678 D	44.1%	51.6%	46.1%	53.9%
41,393	AVOYELLES	16,071	8,216	7,174	681	1,042 R	51.1%	44.6%	53.4%	46.6%
29,692	BEAUREGARD	11,059	5,250	5,556	253	306 D	47.5%	50.2%	48.6%	51.4%
16,387	BIENVILLE	7,770	3,508	4,123	139	615 D	45.1%	53.1%	46.0%	54.0%
80,721	BOSSIER	26,339	16,515	9,377	447	7,138 R	62.7%	35.6%	63.8%	36.2%
252,294	CADDO	89,184	51,202	36,422	1,560	14,780 R	57.4%	40.8%	58.4%	41.6%
167,048	CALCASIEU	64,859	27,600	35,446	1,813	7,846 D	42.6%	54.7%	43.8%	56.2%
10,761	CALDWELL	4,581	2,653	1,786	142	867 R	57.9%	39.0%	59.8%	40.2%
9,336	CAMERON	3,798	1,449	2,221	128	772 D	38.2%	58.5%	39.5%	60.5%
12,287	CATAHOULA	5,531	2,942	2,414	175	528 R	53.2%	43.6%	54.9%	45.1%
17,095	CLAIBORNE	7,074	3,538	3,443	93	95 R	50.0%	48.7%	50.7%	49.3%
22,981	CONCORDIA	9,102	4,933	3,956	213	977 R	54.2%	43.5%	55.5%	44.5%
25,664	DE SOTO	10,327	4,349	5,861	117	1,512 D	42.1%	56.8%	42.6%	57.4%
366,164	EAST BATON ROUGE	133,168	71,063	57,442	4,663	13,621 R	53.4%	43.1%	55.3%	44.7%
11,772	EAST CARROLL	4,231	1,867	2,283	81	416 D	44.1%	54.0%	45.0%	55.0%
19,015	EAST FELICIANA	6,873	2,650	4,033	190	1,383 D	38.6%	58.7%	39.7%	60.3%
33,343	EVANGELINE	14,461	7,412	6,722	327	690 R	51.3%	46.5%	52.4%	47.6%
24,141	FRANKLIN	9,748	5,301	4,177	270	1,124 R	54.4%	42.8%	55.9%	44.1%
16,703	GRANT	7,148	3,611	3,290	247	321 R	50.5%	46.0%	52.3%	47.7%
63,752	IBERIA	25,028	14,273	9,681	1,074	4,592 R	57.0%	38.7%	59.6%	40.4%
32,159	IBERVILLE	14,135	4,463	9,361	311	4,898 R	31.6%	66.2%	32.3%	67.7%
17,321	JACKSON	7,730	3,923	3,609	198	314 R	50.8%	46.7%	52.1%	47.9%
454,592	JEFFERSON	155,111	99,403	50,870	4,838	48,533 R	64.1%	32.8%	66.1%	33.9%
32,168	JEFFERSON DAVIS	12,127	5,667	6,140	320	473 D	46.7%	50.6%	48.0%	52.0%
150,017	LAFAYETTE	53,526	31,429	19,694	2,403	11,735 R	58.7%	36.8%	61.5%	38.5%
82,483	LAFOURCHE	30,818	14,951	14,222	1,645	729 R	48.5%	46.1%	51.2%	48.8%
17,004	LA SALLE	6,634	3,792	2,665	177	1,127 R	57.2%	40.2%	58.7%	41.3%
39,763	LINCOLN	13,470	7,515	5,598	357	1,917 R	55.8%	41.6%	57.3%	42.7%
58,655	LIVINGSTON	22,609	10,666	11,319	624	653 D	47.2%	50.1%	48.5%	51.5%
14,733	MADISON	5,928	2,531	3,264	133	733 D	42.7%	55.1%	43.7%	56.3%
34,803	MOREHOUSE	12,397	7,254	4,856	287	2,398 R	58.5%	39.2%	59.9%	40.1%
39,863	NATCHITOCHES	14,189	6,668	7,102	419	434 D	47.0%	50.1%	48.4%	51.6%
557,482	ORLEANS	187,904	74,302	106,858	6,744	32,556 D	39.5%	56.9%	41.0%	59.0%
139,241	OUACHITA	47,314	29,799	16,306	1,209	13,493 R	63.0%	34.5%	64.6%	35.4%
26,049	PLAQUEMINES	10,079	5,489	4,318	272	1,171 R	54.5%	42.8%	56.0%	44.0%
24,045	POINTE COUPEE	10,263	3,667	6,395	201	2,728 D	35.7%	62.3%	36.4%	63.6%
135,282	RAPIDES	46,302	25,576	19,436	1,290	6,140 R	55.2%	42.0%	56.8%	43.2%
10,433	RED RIVER	4,986	2,147	2,776	63	629 D	43.1%	55.7%	43.6%	56.4%
22,187	RICHLAND	8,744	4,772	3,745	227	1,027 R	54.6%	42.8%	56.0%	44.0%
25,280	SABINE	9,585	4,265	5,100	220	835 D	44.5%	53.2%	45.5%	54.5%
64,097	ST. BERNARD	32,065	19,410	11,367	1,288	8,043 R	60.5%	35.4%	63.1%	36.9%
37,259	ST. CHARLES	15,123	6,779	7,898	446	1,119 D	44.8%	52.2%	46.2%	53.8%
9,827	ST. HELENA	4,852	1,531	3,183	138	1,652 D	31.6%	65.6%	32.5%	67.5%
21,495	ST. JAMES	9,824	3,429	6,206	189	2,777 D	34.9%	63.2%	35.6%	64.4%
31,924	ST. JOHN THE BAPTIST	13,861	5,819	7,647	395	1,828 D	42.0%	55.2%	43.2%	56.8%
84,128	ST. LANDRY	32,678	14,940	17,125	613	2,185 D	45.7%	52.4%	46.6%	53.4%
40,214	ST. MARTIN	15,040	6,701	7,760	579	1,059 D	44.6%	51.6%	46.3%	53.7%
64,395	ST. MARY	21,606	10,378	10,506	722	128 D	48.0%	48.6%	49.7%	50.3%
110,554	ST. TAMMANY	42,698	27,214	14,161	1,323	13,053 R	63.7%	33.2%	65.8%	34.2%
80,698	TANGIPAHOA	31,342	15,187	15,272	883	85 D	48.5%	48.7%	49.9%	50.1%
8,525	TENSAS	3,785	1,645	2,046	94	401 D	43.5%	54.1%	44.6%	55.4%
94,393	TERREBONNE	28,681	16,644	10,804	1,233	5,840 R	58.0%	37.7%	60.6%	39.4%
21,167	UNION	9,198	5,130	3,841	227	1,289 R	55.8%	41.8%	57.2%	42.8%
48,458	VERMILION	21,409	10,481	9,743	1,185	738 R	49.0%	45.5%	51.8%	48.2%
53,475	VERNON	13,436	5,869	7,198	369	1,329 D	43.7%	53.6%	44.9%	55.1%
44,207	WASHINGTON	19,472	8,681	10,413	378	1,732 D	44.6%	53.5%	45.5%	54.5%
43,631	WEBSTER	17,647	8,865	8,568	214	297 R	50.2%	48.6%	50.9%	49.1%
19,086	WEST BATON ROUGE	7,753	2,828	4,739	186	1,911 D	36.5%	61.1%	37.4%	62.6%
12,922	WEST CARROLL	5,712	3,430	2,118	164	1,312 R	60.0%	37.1%	61.8%	38.2%
12,186	WEST FELICIANA	3,722	1,237	2,341	144	1,104 D	33.2%	62.9%	34.6%	65.4%
17,253	WINN	7,547	3,944	3,411	192	533 R	52.3%	45.2%	53.6%	46.4%
4,203,972	TOTAL	1,548,591	792,853	708,453	47,285	84,400 R	51.2%	45.7%	52.8%	47.2%

LOUISIANA

GOVERNOR 1979

1980 Census Population	Parish	Total Vote	Republican	Democratic	Other	Rep.-Dem. Plurality	Total Vote Rep.	Total Vote Dem.	Major Vote Rep.	Major Vote Dem.
56,427	ACADIA	19,483	9,822	9,661		161 R	50.4%	49.6%	50.4%	49.6%
21,390	ALLEN	9,763	3,267	6,496		3,229 D	33.5%	66.5%	33.5%	66.5%
50,068	ASCENSION	20,020	3,008	17,012		14,004 D	15.0%	85.0%	15.0%	85.0%
22,084	ASSUMPTION	9,172	3,497	5,675		2,178 D	38.1%	61.9%	38.1%	61.9%
41,393	AVOYELLES	16,788	7,020	9,768		2,748 D	41.8%	58.2%	41.8%	58.2%
29,692	BEAUREGARD	9,321	4,848	4,473		375 R	52.0%	48.0%	52.0%	48.0%
16,387	BIENVILLE	6,885	2,999	3,886		887 D	43.6%	56.4%	43.6%	56.4%
80,721	BOSSIER	19,749	11,731	8,018		3,713 R	59.4%	40.6%	59.4%	40.6%
252,294	CADDO	70,296	41,337	28,959		12,378 R	58.8%	41.2%	58.8%	41.2%
167,048	CALCASIEU	56,039	26,678	29,361		2,683 D	47.6%	52.4%	47.6%	52.4%
10,761	CALDWELL	4,699	2,176	2,523		347 D	46.3%	53.7%	46.3%	53.7%
9,336	CAMERON	4,040	1,979	2,061		82 D	49.0%	51.0%	49.0%	51.0%
12,287	CATAHOULA	5,682	2,388	3,294		906 D	42.0%	58.0%	42.0%	58.0%
17,095	CLAIBORNE	6,325	3,093	3,232		139 D	48.9%	51.1%	48.9%	51.1%
22,981	CONCORDIA	9,230	4,327	4,903		576 D	46.9%	53.1%	46.9%	53.1%
25,664	DE SOTO	9,164	3,758	5,406		1,648 D	41.0%	59.0%	41.0%	59.0%
366,164	EAST BATON ROUGE	111,968	57,666	54,302		3,364 R	51.5%	48.5%	51.5%	48.5%
11,772	EAST CARROLL	3,793	1,675	2,118		443 D	44.2%	55.8%	44.2%	55.8%
19,015	EAST FELICIANA	7,176	2,014	5,162		3,148 D	28.1%	71.9%	28.1%	71.9%
33,343	EVANGELINE	15,934	7,021	8,913		1,892 D	44.1%	55.9%	44.1%	55.9%
24,141	FRANKLIN	9,838	4,660	5,178		518 D	47.4%	52.6%	47.4%	52.6%
16,703	GRANT	7,147	2,964	4,183		1,219 D	41.5%	58.5%	41.5%	58.5%
63,752	IBERIA	20,612	13,616	6,996		6,620 R	66.1%	33.9%	66.1%	33.9%
32,159	IBERVILLE	14,820	3,573	11,247		7,674 D	24.1%	75.9%	24.1%	75.9%
17,321	JACKSON	7,994	3,050	4,944		1,894 D	38.2%	61.8%	38.2%	61.8%
454,592	JEFFERSON	129,146	83,099	46,047		37,052 R	64.3%	35.7%	64.3%	35.7%
32,168	JEFFERSON DAVIS	11,893	6,473	5,420		1,053 R	54.4%	45.6%	54.4%	45.6%
150,017	LAFAYETTE	43,456	30,008	13,448		16,560 R	69.1%	30.9%	69.1%	30.9%
82,483	LAFOURCHE	29,147	17,433	11,714		5,719 R	59.8%	40.2%	59.8%	40.2%
17,004	LA SALLE	6,268	3,286	2,982		304 R	52.4%	47.6%	52.4%	47.6%
39,763	LINCOLN	11,188	6,760	4,428		2,332 R	60.4%	39.6%	60.4%	39.6%
58,655	LIVINGSTON	22,018	5,674	16,344		10,670 D	25.8%	74.2%	25.8%	74.2%
14,733	MADISON	5,027	2,022	3,005		983 D	40.2%	59.8%	40.2%	59.8%
34,803	MOREHOUSE	11,939	5,847	6,092		245 D	49.0%	51.0%	49.0%	51.0%
39,863	NATCHITOCHES	12,587	5,969	6,618		649 D	47.4%	52.6%	47.4%	52.6%
557,482	ORLEANS	153,733	74,676	79,057		4,381 D	48.6%	51.4%	48.6%	51.4%
139,241	OUACHITA	41,872	23,840	18,032		5,808 R	56.9%	43.1%	56.9%	43.1%
26,049	PLAQUEMINES	7,593	5,443	2,150		3,293 R	71.7%	28.3%	71.7%	28.3%
24,045	POINTE COUPEE	9,498	2,582	6,916		4,334 D	27.2%	72.8%	27.2%	72.8%
135,282	RAPIDES	38,989	19,472	19,517		45 D	49.9%	50.1%	49.9%	50.1%
10,433	RED RIVER	5,350	2,044	3,306		1,262 D	38.2%	61.8%	38.2%	61.8%
22,187	RICHLAND	7,642	3,856	3,786		70 R	50.5%	49.5%	50.5%	49.5%
25,280	SABINE	8,357	3,655	4,702		1,047 D	43.7%	56.3%	43.7%	56.3%
64,097	ST. BERNARD	29,923	15,215	14,708		507 D	50.8%	49.2%	50.8%	49.2%
37,259	ST. CHARLES	14,445	6,437	8,008		1,571 D	44.6%	55.4%	44.6%	55.4%
9,827	ST. HELENA	5,333	1,404	3,929		2,525 D	26.3%	73.7%	26.3%	73.7%
21,495	ST. JAMES	9,520	2,038	7,482		5,444 D	21.4%	78.6%	21.4%	78.6%
31,924	ST. JOHN THE BAPTIST	14,024	4,331	9,693		5,362 D	30.9%	69.1%	30.9%	69.1%
84,128	ST. LANDRY	30,697	13,424	17,273		3,849 D	43.7%	56.3%	43.7%	56.3%
40,214	ST. MARTIN	15,018	7,665	7,353		312 R	51.0%	49.0%	51.0%	49.0%
64,395	ST. MARY	20,041	11,651	8,390		3,261 R	58.1%	41.9%	58.1%	41.9%
110,554	ST. TAMMANY	35,890	21,527	14,363		7,164 R	60.0%	40.0%	60.0%	40.0%
80,698	TANGIPAHOA	31,360	12,003	19,357		7,354 D	38.3%	61.7%	38.3%	61.7%
8,525	TENSAS	3,439	1,457	1,982		525 D	42.4%	57.6%	42.4%	57.6%
94,393	TERREBONNE	27,708	18,107	9,601		8,506 R	65.3%	34.7%	65.3%	34.7%
21,167	UNION	9,134	4,625	4,509		116 R	50.6%	49.4%	50.6%	49.4%
48,458	VERMILION	21,842	11,934	9,908		2,026 R	54.6%	45.4%	54.6%	45.4%
53,475	VERNON	12,460	5,268	7,192		1,924 D	42.3%	57.7%	42.3%	57.7%
44,207	WASHINGTON	19,851	7,254	12,597		5,343 D	36.5%	63.5%	36.5%	63.5%
43,631	WEBSTER	15,356	6,951	8,405		1,454 D	45.3%	54.7%	45.3%	54.7%
19,086	WEST BATON ROUGE	6,997	1,950	5,047		3,097 D	27.9%	72.1%	27.9%	72.1%
12,922	WEST CARROLL	5,432	2,604	2,828		224 D	47.9%	52.1%	47.9%	52.1%
12,186	WEST FELICIANA	3,923	1,115	2,808		1,693 D	28.4%	71.6%	28.4%	71.6%
17,253	WINN	7,791	3,425	4,366		941 D	44.0%	56.0%	44.0%	56.0%
4,203,972	TOTAL	1,371,825	690,691	681,134		9,557 R	50.3%	49.7%	50.3%	49.7%

LOUISIANA

SENATOR 1980
(Primary Election)

1980 Census Population	Parish	Total Vote	Jenkins	Long	Other	Jenkins-Long Plurality	Percentage Total Vote Jenkins	Total Vote Long	Major Vote Jenkins	Major Vote Long
56,427	ACADIA	10,897	4,187	6,327	383	2,140 L	38.4%	58.1%	39.8%	60.2%
21,390	ALLEN	4,618	1,600	2,910	108	1,310 L	34.6%	63.0%	35.5%	64.5%
50,068	ASCENSION	14,798	4,706	7,487	2,605	2,781 L	31.8%	50.6%	38.6%	61.4%
22,084	ASSUMPTION	4,347	1,516	2,685	146	1,169 L	34.9%	61.8%	36.1%	63.9%
41,393	AVOYELLES	8,496	3,635	4,656	205	1,021 L	42.8%	54.8%	43.8%	56.2%
29,692	BEAUREGARD	5,388	1,683	3,506	199	1,823 L	31.2%	65.1%	32.4%	67.6%
16,387	BIENVILLE	5,503	1,909	3,352	242	1,443 L	34.7%	60.9%	36.3%	63.7%
80,721	BOSSIER	17,835	7,776	9,423	636	1,647 L	43.6%	52.8%	45.2%	54.8%
252,294	CADDO	59,018	21,985	35,261	1,772	13,276 L	37.3%	59.7%	38.4%	61.6%
167,048	CALCASIEU	29,006	12,215	15,907	884	3,692 L	42.1%	54.8%	43.4%	56.6%
10,761	CALDWELL	2,654	1,239	1,340	75	101 L	46.7%	50.5%	48.0%	52.0%
9,336	CAMERON	2,374	870	1,394	110	524 L	36.6%	58.7%	38.4%	61.6%
12,287	CATAHOULA	3,088	1,279	1,732	77	453 L	41.4%	56.1%	42.5%	57.5%
17,095	CLAIBORNE	4,646	1,961	2,486	199	525 L	42.2%	53.5%	44.1%	55.9%
22,981	CONCORDIA	4,786	2,132	2,537	117	405 L	44.5%	53.0%	45.7%	54.3%
25,664	DE SOTO	7,827	2,533	5,055	239	2,522 L	32.4%	64.6%	33.4%	66.6%
366,164	EAST BATON ROUGE	94,401	35,391	56,664	2,346	21,273 L	37.5%	60.0%	38.4%	61.6%
11,772	EAST CARROLL	2,069	642	1,366	61	724 L	31.0%	66.0%	32.0%	68.0%
19,015	EAST FELICIANA	3,233	1,252	1,850	131	598 L	38.7%	57.2%	40.4%	59.6%
33,343	EVANGELINE	11,038	4,777	5,646	615	869 L	43.3%	51.2%	45.8%	54.2%
24,141	FRANKLIN	6,337	2,993	3,196	148	203 L	47.2%	50.4%	48.4%	51.6%
16,703	GRANT	4,920	2,364	2,446	110	82 L	48.0%	49.7%	49.1%	50.9%
63,752	IBERIA	10,806	5,277	5,182	347	95 J	48.8%	48.0%	50.5%	49.5%
32,159	IBERVILLE	6,464	1,732	4,456	276	2,724 L	26.8%	68.9%	28.0%	72.0%
17,321	JACKSON	6,180	2,118	3,874	188	1,756 L	34.3%	62.7%	35.3%	64.7%
454,592	JEFFERSON	71,789	29,465	37,425	4,899	7,960 L	41.0%	52.1%	44.0%	56.0%
32,168	JEFFERSON DAVIS	5,691	2,446	3,052	193	606 L	43.0%	53.6%	44.5%	55.5%
150,017	LAFAYETTE	21,464	9,167	11,689	608	2,522 L	42.7%	54.5%	44.0%	56.0%
82,483	LAFOURCHE	18,909	6,038	12,290	581	6,252 L	31.9%	65.0%	32.9%	67.1%
17,004	LA SALLE	4,077	2,122	1,872	83	250 J	52.0%	45.9%	53.1%	46.9%
39,763	LINCOLN	6,568	2,272	4,099	197	1,827 L	34.6%	62.4%	35.7%	64.3%
58,655	LIVINGSTON	9,681	4,577	4,822	282	245 L	47.3%	49.8%	48.7%	51.3%
14,733	MADISON	3,011	915	1,978	118	1,063 L	30.4%	65.7%	31.6%	68.4%
34,803	MOREHOUSE	5,549	2,503	2,913	133	410 L	45.1%	52.5%	46.2%	53.8%
39,863	NATCHITOCHES	10,198	3,676	6,270	252	2,594 L	36.0%	61.5%	37.0%	63.0%
557,482	ORLEANS	98,909	29,421	64,901	4,587	35,480 L	29.7%	65.6%	31.2%	68.8%
139,241	OUACHITA	21,253	9,339	11,445	469	2,106 L	43.9%	53.9%	44.9%	55.1%
26,049	PLAQUEMINES	7,151	1,680	5,163	308	3,483 L	23.5%	72.2%	24.6%	75.4%
24,045	POINTE COUPEE	4,774	1,449	3,212	113	1,763 L	30.4%	67.3%	31.1%	68.9%
135,282	RAPIDES	29,360	15,966	12,743	651	3,223 J	54.4%	43.4%	55.6%	44.4%
10,433	RED RIVER	3,693	1,172	2,411	110	1,239 L	31.7%	65.3%	32.7%	67.3%
22,187	RICHLAND	6,362	2,615	3,583	164	968 L	41.1%	56.3%	42.2%	57.8%
25,280	SABINE	6,910	2,306	4,437	167	2,131 L	33.4%	64.2%	34.2%	65.8%
64,097	ST. BERNARD	16,893	6,651	9,501	741	2,850 L	39.4%	56.2%	41.2%	58.8%
37,259	ST. CHARLES	6,782	2,538	3,871	373	1,333 L	37.4%	57.1%	39.6%	60.4%
9,827	ST. HELENA	2,948	1,090	1,756	102	666 L	37.0%	59.6%	38.3%	61.7%
21,495	ST. JAMES	6,178	1,685	4,316	177	2,631 L	27.3%	69.9%	28.1%	71.9%
31,924	ST. JOHN THE BAPTIST	6,198	1,942	3,955	301	2,013 L	31.3%	63.8%	32.9%	67.1%
84,128	ST. LANDRY	14,524	5,825	8,157	542	2,332 L	40.1%	56.2%	41.7%	58.3%
40,214	ST. MARTIN	5,384	2,006	3,187	191	1,181 L	37.3%	59.2%	38.6%	61.4%
64,395	ST. MARY	8,902	3,885	4,782	235	897 L	43.6%	53.7%	44.8%	55.2%
110,554	ST. TAMMANY	15,327	7,694	6,652	981	1,042 J	50.2%	43.4%	53.6%	46.4%
80,698	TANGIPAHOA	16,474	7,041	8,808	625	1,767 L	42.7%	53.5%	44.4%	55.6%
8,525	TENSAS	2,324	634	1,633	57	999 L	27.3%	70.3%	28.0%	72.0%
94,393	TERREBONNE	11,500	5,304	5,814	382	510 L	46.1%	50.6%	47.7%	52.3%
21,167	UNION	5,079	2,042	2,893	144	851 L	40.2%	57.0%	41.4%	58.6%
48,458	VERMILION	12,155	5,813	5,951	391	138 L	47.8%	49.0%	49.4%	50.6%
53,475	VERNON	9,929	2,511	7,208	210	4,697 L	25.3%	72.6%	25.8%	74.2%
44,207	WASHINGTON	9,680	3,764	5,624	292	1,860 L	38.9%	58.1%	40.1%	59.9%
43,631	WEBSTER	11,716	4,786	6,516	414	1,730 L	40.9%	55.6%	42.3%	57.7%
19,086	WEST BATON ROUGE	4,956	1,692	3,170	94	1,478 L	34.1%	64.0%	34.8%	65.2%
12,922	WEST CARROLL	3,618	1,659	1,848	111	189 L	45.9%	51.1%	47.3%	52.7%
12,186	WEST FELICIANA	2,430	676	1,687	67	1,011 L	27.8%	69.4%	28.6%	71.4%
17,253	WINN	4,287	1,783	2,398	106	615 L	41.6%	55.9%	42.6%	57.4%
4,203,972	TOTAL	841,013	325,922	484,770	30,321	158,848 L	38.8%	57.6%	40.2%	59.8%

LOUISIANA

CONGRESS

CD	Year	Total Vote	Republican Vote	Republican Candidate	Democratic Vote	Democratic Candidate	Other Vote	Rep.-Dem. Plurality	Percentage Total Vote Rep.	Percentage Total Vote Dem.	Major Vote Rep.	Major Vote Dem.
1	1980			LIVINGSTON, BOB								
1	1978			LIVINGSTON, BOB								
1	1976	130,558	56,679	LIVINGSTON, BOB	61,652	TONRY, RICHARD A.	12,227	4,973 D	43.4%	47.2%	47.9%	52.1%
1	1974	48,452			48,452	HEBERT, F. EDWARD		48,452 D		100.0%		100.0%
1	1972	78,156			78,156	HEBERT, F. EDWARD		78,156 D		100.0%		100.0%
2	1980					BOGGS, LINDY						
2	1978					BOGGS, LINDY						
2	1976	92,827			85,923	BOGGS, LINDY	6,904	85,923 D		92.6%		100.0%
2	1974	65,756	9,632	MORPHOS, DIANE	53,802	BOGGS, LINDY	2,322	44,170 D	14.6%	81.8%	15.2%	84.8%
2	1972	68,093			68,093	BOGGS, HALE		68,093 D		100.0%		100.0%
3	1980					TAUZIN, W. J.						
3	1978			TREEN, DAVID C.								
3	1976	148,863	109,135	TREEN, DAVID C.	39,728	SCHEURMANN, DAVID H.		69,407 R	73.3%	26.7%	73.3%	26.7%
3	1974	94,986	55,574	TREEN, DAVID C.	39,412	GRISBAUM, CHARLES		16,162 R	58.5%	41.5%	58.5%	41.5%
3	1972	131,611	71,090	TREEN, DAVID C.	60,521	WATKINS, J. LOUIS		10,569 R	54.0%	46.0%	54.0%	46.0%
4	1980	162,330			162,330	ROEMER/LEACH		162,330 D		100.0%		100.0%
4	1978	130,900	65,317	WILSON, JIMMY	65,583	LEACH, CLAUDE		266 D	49.9%	50.1%	49.9%	50.1%
4	1976	76,406			76,406	WAGGONNER, JOE D.		76,406 D		100.0%		100.0%
4	1974	47,371			47,371	WAGGONNER, JOE D.		47,371 D		100.0%		100.0%
4	1972	74,397			74,397	WAGGONNER, JOE D.		74,397 D		100.0%		100.0%
5	1980					HUCKABY, JERRY						
5	1978					HUCKABY, JERRY						
5	1976	159,270	75,574	SPOONER, FRANK	83,696	HUCKABY, JERRY		8,122 D	47.5%	52.5%	47.5%	52.5%
5	1974	43,068			43,068	PASSMAN, OTTO E.		43,068 D		100.0%		100.0%
5	1972	64,027			64,027	PASSMAN, OTTO E.		64,027 D		100.0%		100.0%
6	1980			MOORE, W. HENSON								
6	1978			MOORE, W. HENSON								
6	1976	152,992	99,780	MOORE, W. HENSON	53,212	DE BLIEUX, J. D.		46,568 R	65.2%	34.8%	65.2%	34.8%
6	1974	138,168	74,802	MOORE, W. HENSON	63,366	LACAZE, JEFF		11,436 R	54.1%	45.9%	54.1%	45.9%
6	1972	84,275			84,275	RARICK, JOHN R.		84,275 D		100.0%		100.0%
7	1980					BREAUX, JOHN B.						
7	1978					BREAUX, JOHN B.						
7	1976	140,610	23,414	HUFF, CHARLES F.	117,196	BREAUX, JOHN B.		93,782 D	16.7%	83.3%	16.7%	83.3%
7	1974	66,537			59,406	BREAUX, JOHN B.	7,131	59,406 D		89.3%		100.0%
7	1972	71,901			71,901	BREAUX, JOHN B.		71,901 D		100.0%		100.0%
8	1980					LONG, GILLIS W.						
8	1978					LONG, GILLIS W.						
8	1976	112,811			106,285	LONG, GILLIS W.	6,526	106,285 D		94.2%		100.0%
8	1974	41,704			41,704	LONG, GILLIS W.		41,704 D		100.0%		100.0%
8	1972	105,968	15,517	STRICKLAND, ROY C.	72,607	LONG, GILLIS W.	17,844	57,090 D	14.6%	68.5%	17.6%	82.4%

LOUISIANA

1979 GENERAL ELECTION

Governor   The general election run-off was held December 8th.

1980 GENERAL ELECTION

President   Other vote was 26,345 Anderson (Independent); 10,333 Rarick (American Independent); 8,240 Clark (Libertarian); 1,584 Commoner (Citizens); 783 DeBerry (Socialist Workers).

Senator   See primary note section below. Since there was no general election run-off, the data carried in the table for Senator 1980 are for the primary contest between the candidates listed in the primary section. A "J" in the plurality column is a Louis Jenkins plurality and an "L" in that column is a Russell B. Long plurality.

Congress   See primary note section below. Since candidates who receive a majority in the open primary are elected unopposed, there were no candidates names on the general election ballot except in CD 4. In that district both candidates in the run-off general election were Democrats and the vote was 103,625 Charles Roemer and 58,705 Claude Leach. Roemer won the contest with a 44,920 plurality and 63.8% of the vote.

PRIMARIES

Louisiana holds an open-primary election with candidates from all parties running on the same ballot. Any candidate who receives a majority is elected; if no candidate receives 50 percent, there is a run-off election between the top two finishers.

OCTOBER 27, 1979

Governor   297,674 David C. Treen (R); 283,266 Louis Lambert (D); 280,760 James E. Fitzmorris (D); 227,026 Paul Hardy (D); 135,769 E. L. Henry (D); 124,333 Edgar G. Mouton (D); 6,327 Luther D. Knox (D); 5,942 Ken Lewis (D); 4,783 Greg Nelson (no party). There was a court-ordered recount of the votes for the top three candidates. The official recount was as follows:

	Voting Machines	Absentee	Total
Treen	286,144	11,325	297,469
Lambert	278,412	4,296	282,708
Fitzmorris	274,009	6,403	280,412

SEPTEMBER 13, 1980

Senator   484,770 Russell B. Long (D); 325,922 Louis Jenkins (D); 13,739 Jerry C. Bardwell (R); 10,208 Robert M. Ross (R); 6,374 Naomi Bracey (no party).

Congress   Unopposed in CD 7. Contested as follows:

CD 1   81,777 Bob Livingston (R); 8,277 Michael J. Musmeci (D); 2,501 Tristan P. Junius (no party).
CD 2   45,091 Lindy Boggs (D); 25,521 Rob Couhig (R); 3,571 Clyde F. Bel (D).
CD 3   80,455 W. J. Tauzin (D); 14,074 Bob Namer (D).
CD 4   35,847 Claude Leach (D); 33,049 Charles Roemer (D); 29,992 Jimmy Wilson (R); 14,666 Foster Campbell (D); 8,208 Forrest Dunn (D); 1,329 C. Kay Carter (D).
CD 5   93,519 Jerry Huckaby (D); 11,748 L. D. Knox (D).
CD 6   118,540 W. Henson Moore (R); 12,149 Alice Brooks (D).
CD 8   75,433 Gillis W. Long (D); 27,816 Clyde C. Holloway (R); 6,243 Robert H. Mitchell (R).

MAINE

GOVERNOR
Joseph E. Brennan (D). Elected 1978 to a four-year term.

SENATORS
William S. Cohen (R). Elected 1978 to a six-year term.

George J. Mitchell (D). Appointed to the Senate May 1980 on the resignation of Senator Edmund S. Muskie to become Secretary of State. Next election in 1982.

REPRESENTATIVES
1. David F. Emery (R) 2. Olympia J. Snowe (R)

POSTWAR VOTE FOR GOVERNOR

Year	Total Vote	Republican Vote	Candidate	Democratic Vote	Candidate	Other Vote	Rep.-Dem. Plurality	Total Vote Rep.	Total Vote Dem.	Major Vote Rep.	Major Vote Dem.
1978	370,258	126,862	Palmer, Linwood E.	176,493	Brennan, Joseph E.	66,903	49,631 D	34.3%	47.7%	41.8%	58.2%
1974	363,945	84,176	Erwin, James S.	132,219	Mitchell, George J.	147,550	48,043 D	23.1%	36.3%	38.9%	61.1%
1970	325,386	162,248	Erwin, James S.	163,138	Curtis, Kenneth M.	—	890 D	49.9%	50.1%	49.9%	50.1%
1966	323,838	151,802	Reed, John H.	172,036	Curtis, Kenneth M.	—	20,234 D	46.9%	53.1%	46.9%	53.1%
1962	292,725	146,604	Reed, John H.	146,121	Dolloff, Maynard C.	—	483 R	50.1%	49.9%	50.1%	49.9%
1960s	417,315	219,768	Reed, John H.	197,547	Coffin, Frank M.	—	22,221 R	52.7%	47.3%	52.7%	47.3%
1958	280,295	134,572	Hildreth, Horace A.	145,723	Clauson, Clinton A.	—	11,151 D	48.0%	52.0%	48.0%	52.0%
1956	304,649	124,395	Trafton, Willis A.	180,254	Muskie, Edmund S.	—	55,859 D	40.8%	59.2%	40.8%	59.2%
1954	248,971	113,298	Cross, Burton M.	135,673	Muskie, Edmund S.	—	22,375 D	45.5%	54.5%	45.5%	54.5%
1952	248,441	128,532	Cross, Burton M.	82,538	Oliver, James C.	37,371	45,994 R	51.7%	33.2%	60.9%	39.1%
1950	241,177	145,823	Payne, Frederick G.	94,304	Grant, Earl S.	1,050	51,519 R	60.5%	39.1%	60.7%	39.3%
1948	222,500	145,956	Payne, Frederick G.	76,544	Lausier, Louis B.	—	69,412 R	65.6%	34.4%	65.6%	34.4%
1946	179,951	110,327	Hildreth, Horace A.	69,624	Clark, F. Davis	—	40,703 R	61.3%	38.7%	61.3%	38.7%

The term of office of Maine's Governor was increased from two to four years effective with the 1958 election. The election in 1960 was for a short term to fill a vacancy. In 1974 James B. Longley, an Independent candidate, polled 142,464 votes (39.1% of the total vote) and won the election with a 10,245 plurality.

POSTWAR VOTE FOR SENATOR

Year	Total Vote	Republican Vote	Candidate	Democratic Vote	Candidate	Other Vote	Rep.-Dem. Plurality	Total Vote Rep.	Total Vote Dem.	Major Vote Rep.	Major Vote Dem.
1978	375,172	212,294	Cohen, William S.	127,327	Hathaway, William D.	35,551	84,967 R	56.6%	33.9%	62.5%	37.5%
1976	486,254	193,489	Monks, Robert A. G.	292,704	Muskie, Edmund S.	61	99,215 D	39.8%	60.2%	39.8%	60.2%
1972	421,310	197,040	Smith, Margaret Chase	224,270	Hathaway, William D.	—	27,230 D	46.8%	53.2%	46.8%	53.2%
1970	323,860	123,906	Bishop, Neil S.	199,954	Muskie, Edmund S.	—	76,048 D	38.3%	61.7%	38.3%	61.7%
1966	319,535	188,291	Smith, Margaret Chase	131,136	Violette, Elmer H.	108	57,155 R	58.9%	41.0%	58.9%	41.1%
1964	380,551	127,040	McIntire, Clifford	253,511	Muskie, Edmund S.	—	126,471 D	33.4%	66.6%	33.4%	66.6%
1960	416,699	256,890	Smith, Margaret Chase	159,809	Cormier, Lucia M.	—	97,081 R	61.6%	38.4%	61.6%	38.4%
1958	284,226	111,522	Payne, Frederick G.	172,704	Muskie, Edmund S.	—	61,182 D	39.2%	60.8%	39.2%	60.8%
1954	246,605	144,530	Smith, Margaret Chase	102,075	Fullam, Paul A.	—	42,455 R	58.6%	41.4%	58.6%	41.4%
1952	237,164	139,205	Payne, Frederick G.	82,665	Dube, Roger P.	15,294	56,540 R	58.7%	34.9%	62.7%	37.3%
1948	223,256	159,182	Smith, Margaret Chase	64,074	Scolten, Adrian H.	—	95,108 R	71.3%	28.7%	71.3%	28.7%
1946	175,014	111,215	Brewster, Owen	63,799	MacDonald, Peter	—	47,416 R	63.5%	36.5%	63.5%	36.5%

MAINE

Districts Established June 21, 1971

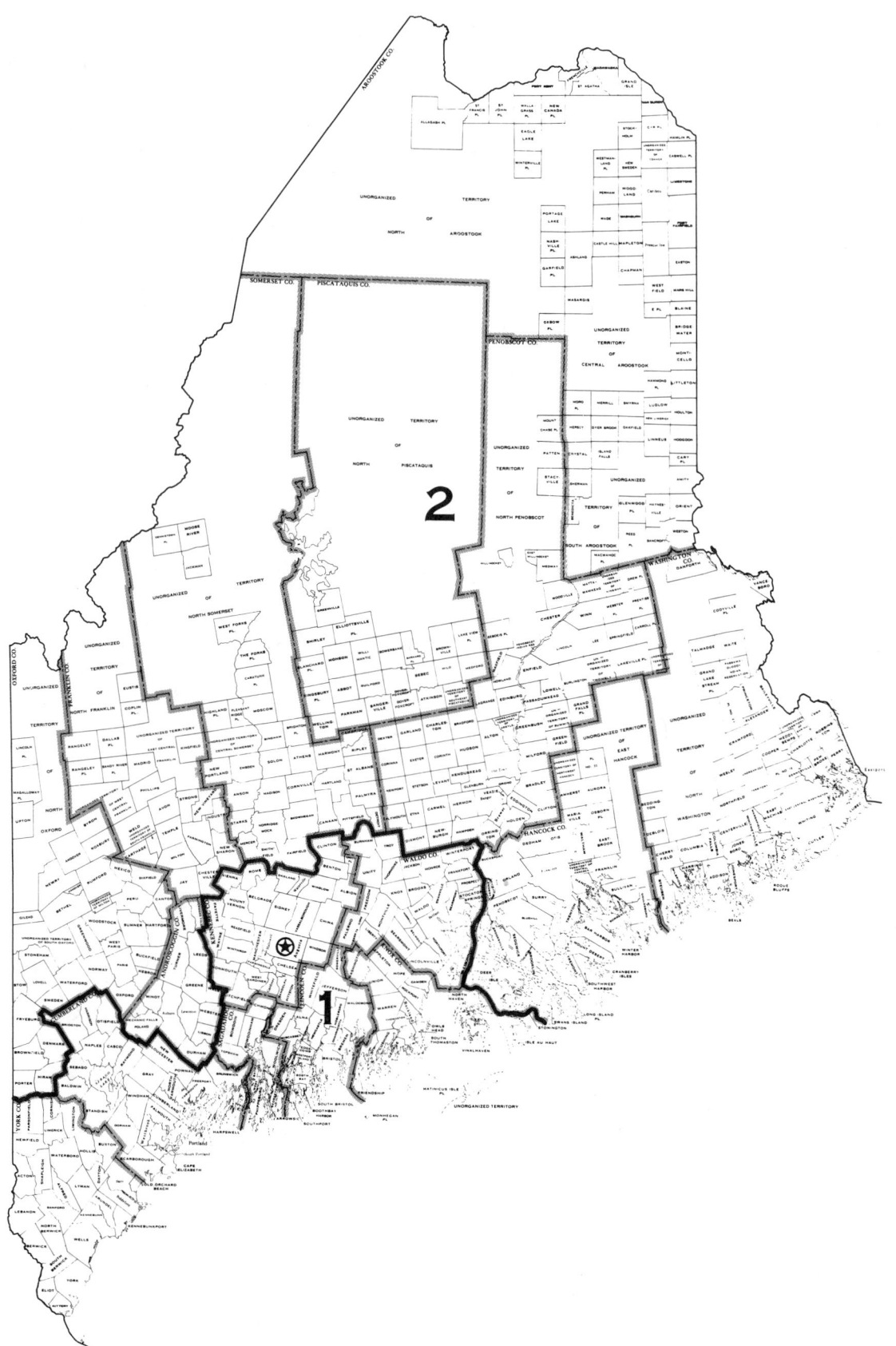

MAINE

PRESIDENT 1980

1980 Census Population	County	Total Vote	Republican	Democratic	Other	Rep.-Dem. Plurality	Percentage			
							Total Vote		Major Vote	
							Rep.	Dem.	Rep.	Dem.
99,657	ANDROSCOGGIN	46,080	18,399	22,715	4,966	4,316 D	39.9%	49.3%	44.8%	55.2%
91,331	AROOSTOOK	33,846	16,343	14,492	3,011	1,851 R	48.3%	42.8%	53.0%	47.0%
215,789	CUMBERLAND	107,461	45,820	47,337	14,304	1,517 D	42.6%	44.1%	49.2%	50.8%
27,098	FRANKLIN	12,128	5,680	4,979	1,469	701 R	46.8%	41.1%	53.3%	46.7%
41,781	HANCOCK	21,334	11,435	7,027	2,872	4,408 R	53.6%	32.9%	61.9%	38.1%
109,889	KENNEBEC	49,077	21,517	20,943	6,617	574 R	43.8%	42.7%	50.7%	49.3%
32,941	KNOX	15,581	7,631	5,732	2,218	1,899 R	49.0%	36.8%	57.1%	42.9%
25,691	LINCOLN	14,259	7,434	4,776	2,049	2,658 R	52.1%	33.5%	60.9%	39.1%
48,968	OXFORD	23,474	11,041	9,914	2,519	1,127 R	47.0%	42.2%	52.7%	47.3%
137,015	PENOBSCOT	62,793	28,869	26,519	7,405	2,350 R	46.0%	42.2%	52.1%	47.9%
17,634	PISCATAQUIS	8,555	4,015	3,550	990	465 R	46.9%	41.5%	53.1%	46.9%
28,795	SAGADAHOC	13,145	5,946	5,663	1,536	283 R	45.2%	43.1%	51.2%	48.8%
45,028	SOMERSET	19,513	9,286	8,115	2,112	1,171 R	47.6%	41.6%	53.4%	46.6%
28,414	WALDO	13,140	6,514	4,883	1,743	1,631 R	49.6%	37.2%	57.2%	42.8%
34,963	WASHINGTON	14,788	7,180	6,050	1,558	1,130 R	48.6%	40.9%	54.3%	45.7%
139,666	YORK	67,837	31,412	28,279	8,146	3,133 R	46.3%	41.7%	52.6%	47.4%
1,124,660	TOTAL	523,011	238,522	220,974	63,515	17,548 R	45.6%	42.3%	51.9%	48.1%

MAINE

PRESIDENT 1980

1980 Census Population	City/Town	Total Vote	Republican	Democratic	Other	Rep.-Dem. Plurality		Percentage Total Vote Rep.	Dem.	Major Vote Rep.	Dem.
23,128	AUBURN	11,289	4,886	5,071	1,332	185	D	43.3%	44.9%	49.1%	50.9%
21,819	AUGUSTA	10,445	4,271	4,740	1,434	469	D	40.9%	45.4%	47.4%	52.6%
31,643	BANGOR	13,937	6,082	6,032	1,823	50	R	43.6%	43.3%	50.2%	49.8%
10,246	BATH	4,638	2,005	2,173	460	168	D	43.2%	46.9%	48.0%	52.0%
6,243	BELFAST	2,700	1,391	1,007	302	384	R	51.5%	37.3%	58.0%	42.0%
19,638	BIDDEFORD	9,537	2,738	5,788	1,011	3,050	D	28.7%	60.7%	32.1%	67.9%
9,017	BREWER	4,775	2,526	1,767	482	759	R	52.9%	37.0%	58.8%	41.2%
17,366	BRUNSWICK	7,572	2,857	3,619	1,096	762	D	37.7%	47.8%	44.1%	55.9%
5,775	BUXTON	2,845	1,343	1,207	295	136	R	47.2%	42.4%	52.7%	47.3%
7,838	CAPE ELIZABETH	4,946	2,710	1,545	691	1,165	R	54.8%	31.2%	63.7%	36.3%
9,916	CARIBOU	3,500	1,694	1,482	324	212	R	48.4%	42.3%	53.3%	46.7%
5,284	CUMBERLAND TOWN	2,929	1,626	900	403	726	R	55.5%	30.7%	64.4%	35.6%
5,179	ELLSWORTH	2,729	1,684	773	272	911	R	61.7%	28.3%	68.5%	31.5%
6,113	FAIRFIELD	2,475	1,083	1,081	311	2	R	43.8%	43.7%	50.0%	50.0%
6,853	FALMOUTH	4,268	2,358	1,337	573	1,021	R	55.2%	31.3%	63.8%	36.2%
6,730	FARMINGTON	2,895	1,274	1,215	406	59	R	44.0%	42.0%	51.2%	48.8%
5,863	FREEPORT	3,074	1,361	1,248	465	113	R	44.3%	40.6%	52.2%	47.8%
6,485	GARDINER	3,055	1,265	1,325	465	60	D	41.4%	43.4%	48.8%	51.2%
10,101	GORHAM	5,455	2,425	2,302	728	123	R	44.5%	42.2%	51.3%	48.7%
5,250	HAMPDEN	2,595	1,361	915	319	446	R	52.4%	35.3%	59.8%	40.2%
6,766	HOULTON	2,874	1,596	1,012	266	584	R	55.5%	35.2%	61.2%	38.8%
5,080	JAY	2,205	794	1,189	222	395	D	36.0%	53.9%	40.0%	60.0%
6,621	KENNEBUNK	3,887	2,236	1,238	413	998	R	57.5%	31.8%	64.4%	35.6%
9,314	KITTERY	3,817	1,942	1,292	583	650	R	50.9%	33.8%	60.0%	40.0%
40,481	LEWISTON	19,707	6,205	11,365	2,137	5,160	D	31.5%	57.7%	35.3%	64.7%
8,719	LIMESTONE	1,168	671	406	91	265	R	57.4%	34.8%	62.3%	37.7%
5,066	LINCOLN TOWN	2,164	1,138	878	148	260	R	52.6%	40.6%	56.4%	43.6%
8,769	LISBON	3,415	1,644	1,475	296	169	R	48.1%	43.2%	52.7%	47.3%
5,282	MADAWASKA	1,989	620	1,213	156	593	D	31.2%	61.0%	33.8%	66.2%
7,567	MILLINOCKET	3,713	1,541	1,806	366	265	D	41.5%	48.6%	46.0%	54.0%
5,162	OAKLAND	1,953	927	821	205	106	R	47.5%	42.0%	53.0%	47.0%
6,291	OLD ORCHARD BEACH	3,327	1,302	1,590	435	288	D	39.1%	47.8%	45.0%	55.0%
8,422	OLD TOWN	4,480	1,480	2,454	546	974	D	33.0%	54.8%	37.6%	62.4%
10,578	ORONO	5,121	1,587	2,269	1,265	682	D	31.0%	44.3%	41.2%	58.8%
61,572	PORTLAND	28,150	9,122	14,815	4,213	5,693	D	32.4%	52.6%	38.1%	61.9%
11,172	PRESQUE ISLE	4,536	2,252	1,694	590	558	R	49.6%	37.3%	57.1%	42.9%
7,919	ROCKLAND	2,830	1,366	1,140	324	226	R	48.3%	40.3%	54.5%	45.5%
8,240	RUMFORD	3,918	1,406	2,074	438	668	D	35.9%	52.9%	40.4%	59.6%
12,921	SACO	6,585	2,583	3,240	762	657	D	39.2%	49.2%	44.4%	55.6%
18,020	SANFORD	7,935	3,124	4,020	791	896	D	39.4%	50.7%	43.7%	56.3%
11,347	SCARBOROUGH	5,717	2,775	2,259	683	516	R	48.5%	39.5%	55.1%	44.9%
8,098	SKOWHEGAN	3,435	1,627	1,449	359	178	R	47.4%	42.2%	52.9%	47.1%
22,712	SOUTH PORTLAND	11,325	4,519	5,371	1,435	852	D	39.9%	47.4%	45.7%	54.3%
5,946	STANDISH	2,796	1,313	1,144	339	169	R	47.0%	40.9%	53.4%	46.6%
6,431	TOPSHAM	2,543	1,107	1,139	297	32	D	43.5%	44.8%	49.3%	50.7%
17,779	WATERVILLE	8,147	2,952	4,125	1,070	1,173	D	36.2%	50.6%	41.7%	58.3%
8,211	WELLS	3,116	1,787	996	333	791	R	57.3%	32.0%	64.2%	35.8%
14,976	WESTBROOK	7,599	2,952	3,882	765	930	D	38.8%	51.1%	43.2%	56.8%
11,282	WINDHAM	5,009	2,389	2,047	573	342	R	47.7%	40.9%	53.9%	46.1%
8,057	WINSLOW	2,001	774	1,026	201	252	D	38.7%	51.3%	43.0%	57.0%
5,889	WINTHROP	2,785	1,404	974	407	430	R	50.4%	35.0%	59.0%	41.0%
6,585	YARMOUTH	3,781	1,859	1,315	607	544	R	49.2%	34.8%	58.6%	41.4%
8,465	YORK TOWN	4,680	2,572	1,367	741	1,205	R	55.0%	29.2%	65.3%	34.7%

MAINE

CONGRESS

CD	Year	Total Vote	Republican Vote	Republican Candidate	Democratic Vote	Democratic Candidate	Other Vote	Rep.-Dem. Plurality	Percentage Total Vote Rep.	Percentage Total Vote Dem.	Major Vote Rep.	Major Vote Dem.
1	1980	275,491	188,667	EMERY, DAVID F.	86,819	PACHIOS, HAROLD C.	5	101,848 R	68.5%	31.5%	68.5%	31.5%
1	1978	196,498	120,791	EMERY, DAVID F.	70,348	QUINN, JOHN	5,359	50,443 R	61.5%	35.8%	63.2%	36.8%
1	1976	253,643	145,523	EMERY, DAVID F.	108,105	BARTON, FREDERICK D.	15	37,418 R	57.4%	42.6%	57.4%	42.6%
1	1974	187,727	94,203	EMERY, DAVID F.	93,524	KYROS, PETER N.		679 R	50.2%	49.8%	50.2%	49.8%
1	1972	217,996	88,588	PORTEOUS, L. ROBERT	129,408	KYROS, PETER N.		40,820 D	40.6%	59.4%	40.6%	59.4%
1	1970	168,154	68,671	SPEERS, RONALD T.	99,483	KYROS, PETER N.		30,812 D	40.8%	59.2%	40.8%	59.2%
1	1968	200,450	86,949	HILDRETH, HORACE, JR.	113,501	KYROS, PETER N.		26,552 D	43.4%	56.6%	43.4%	56.6%
1	1966	161,384	72,984	GARLAND, PETER A.	81,302	KYROS, PETER N.	7,098	8,318 D	45.2%	50.4%	47.3%	52.7%
1	1964	190,593	95,398	TUPPER, STANLEY R.	95,195	CURTIS, KENNETH M.		203 R	50.1%	49.9%	50.1%	49.9%
1	1962	143,993	85,864	TUPPER, STANLEY R.	58,129	KELLAM, RONALD L.		27,735 R	59.6%	40.4%	59.6%	40.4%
2	1980	237,448	186,406	SNOWE, OLYMPIA J.	51,026	SILVERMAN, HAROLD L.	16	135,380 R	78.5%	21.5%	78.5%	21.5%
2	1978	173,054	87,939	SNOWE, OLYMPIA J.	70,691	GARTLEY, MARKHAM L.	14,424	17,248 R	50.8%	40.8%	55.4%	44.6%
2	1976	219,570	169,292	COHEN, WILLIAM S.	43,150	COONEY, LEIGHTON	7,128	126,142 R	77.1%	19.7%	79.7%	20.3%
2	1974	165,553	118,154	COHEN, WILLIAM S.	47,399	GARTLEY, MARKHAM L.		70,755 R	71.4%	28.6%	71.4%	28.6%
2	1972	195,415	106,280	COHEN, WILLIAM S.	89,135	VIOLETTE, ELMER H.		17,145 R	54.4%	45.6%	54.4%	45.6%
2	1970	149,877	53,642	CONNERS, MAYNARD G.	96,235	HATHAWAY, WILLIAM D.		42,593 D	35.8%	64.2%	35.8%	64.2%
2	1968	183,767	81,398	SHUTE, ELDEN H.	102,369	HATHAWAY, WILLIAM D.		20,971 D	44.3%	55.7%	44.3%	55.7%
2	1966	151,432	65,476	FOLEY, HOWARD M.	85,956	HATHAWAY, WILLIAM D.		20,480 D	43.2%	56.8%	43.2%	56.8%
2	1964	178,909	67,978	MACLEOD, KENNETH P.	110,931	HATHAWAY, WILLIAM D.		42,953 D	38.0%	62.0%	38.0%	62.0%
2	1962	141,508	72,349	MCINTIRE, CLIFFORD	69,159	HATHAWAY, WILLIAM D.		3,190 R	51.1%	48.9%	51.1%	48.9%

MAINE

1980 GENERAL ELECTION

In addition to the country-by-county figures, data are presented for selected Maine communities. Since not all jurisdictions of the state are listed in this special tabulation, state-wide totals are shown only with the county-by-county statistics.

President   Other vote was 53,327 Anderson (Independent); 5,119 Clark (Libertarian); 4,394 Commoner (Citizens); 591 Hall (Communist); 84 scattered.

Congress   Other vote was scattered in both CD's.

1980 PRIMARIES

JUNE 10 REPUBLICAN

Congress   Unopposed in both CD's.

JUNE 10 DEMOCRATIC

Congress   Unopposed in both CD's.

MARYLAND

GOVERNOR
Harry Hughes (D). Elected 1978 to a four-year term.

SENATORS
Charles Mathias (R). Re-elected 1980 to a six-year term. Previously elected 1974, 1968.

Paul S. Sarbanes (D). Elected 1976 to a six-year term.

REPRESENTATIVES
1. Roy Dyson (D)
2. Clarence D. Long (D)
3. Barbara A. Mikulski (D)
4. Marjorie S. Holt (R)
5. Gladys N. Spellman (D) (see page 1)
6. Beverly B. Byron (D)
7. Parren J. Mitchell (D)
8. Michael D. Barnes (D)

POSTWAR VOTE FOR GOVERNOR

Year	Total Vote	Republican Vote	Candidate	Democratic Vote	Candidate	Other Vote	Rep.-Dem. Plurality	Total Vote Rep.	Dem.	Major Vote Rep.	Dem.
1978	1,011,963	293,635	Beall, J. Glenn, Jr.	718,328	Hughes, Harry	—	424,693 D	29.0%	71.0%	29.0%	71.0%
1974	949,097	346,449	Gore, Louise	602,648	Mandel, Marvin	—	256,199 D	36.5%	63.5%	36.5%	63.5%
1970	973,099	314,336	Blair, C. Stanley	639,579	Mandel, Marvin	19,184	325,243 D	32.3%	65.7%	33.0%	67.0%
1966	918,761	455,318	Agnew, Spiro T.	373,543	Mahoney, George P.	89,900	81,775 R	49.6%	40.7%	54.9%	45.1%
1962	775,101	343,051	Small, Frank	432,045	Tawes, J. Millard	5	88,994 D	44.3%	55.7%	44.3%	55.7%
1958	763,234	278,173	Devereux, James	485,061	Tawes, J. Millard	—	206,888 D	36.4%	63.6%	36.4%	63.6%
1954	700,484	381,451	McKeldin, Theodore	319,033	Byrd, Harry C.	—	62,418 R	54.5%	45.5%	54.5%	45.5%
1950	645,631	369,807	McKeldin, Theodore	275,824	Lane, William P.	—	93,983 R	57.3%	42.7%	57.3%	42.7%
1946	489,836	221,752	McKeldin, Theodore	268,084	Lane, William P.	—	46,332 D	45.3%	54.7%	45.3%	54.7%

POSTWAR VOTE FOR SENATOR

Year	Total Vote	Republican Vote	Candidate	Democratic Vote	Candidate	Other Vote	Rep.-Dem. Plurality	Total Vote Rep.	Dem.	Major Vote Rep.	Dem.
1980	1,286,088	850,970	Mathias, Charles	435,118	Conroy, Edward T.	—	415,852 R	66.2%	33.8%	66.2%	33.8%
1976	1,365,568	530,439	Beall, J. Glenn, Jr.	772,101	Sarbanes, Paul S.	63,028	241,662 D	38.8%	56.5%	40.7%	59.3%
1974	877,786	503,223	Mathias, Charles	374,563	Mikulski, Barbara A.	—	128,660 R	57.3%	42.7%	57.3%	42.7%
1970	956,370	484,960	Beall, J. Glenn, Jr.	460,422	Tydings, Joseph D.	10,988	24,538 R	50.7%	48.1%	51.3%	48.7%
1968	1,133,727	541,893	Mathias, Charles	443,367	Brewster, Daniel B.	148,467	98,526 R	47.8%	39.1%	55.0%	45.0%
1964	1,081,049	402,393	Beall, J. Glenn	678,649	Tydings, Joseph D.	7	276,256 D	37.2%	62.8%	37.2%	62.8%
1962	714,248	270,312	Miller, Edward T.	443,935	Brewster, Daniel B.	1	173,623 D	37.8%	62.2%	37.8%	62.2%
1958	749,291	382,021	Beall, J. Glenn	367,270	D'Alesandro, Thomas	—	14,751 R	51.0%	49.0%	51.0%	49.0%
1956	892,167	473,059	Butler, John Marshall	419,108	Mahoney, George P.	—	53,951 R	53.0%	47.0%	53.0%	47.0%
1952	856,193	449,823	Beall, J. Glenn	406,370	Mahoney, George P.	—	43,453 R	52.5%	47.5%	52.5%	47.5%
1950	615,614	326,291	Butler, John Marshall	283,180	Tydings, Millard E.	6,143	43,111 R	53.0%	46.0%	53.5%	46.5%
1946	472,232	235,000	Markey, David John	237,232	O'Conor, Herbert R.	—	2,232 D	49.8%	50.2%	49.8%	50.2%

MARYLAND

Districts Established March 21, 1972

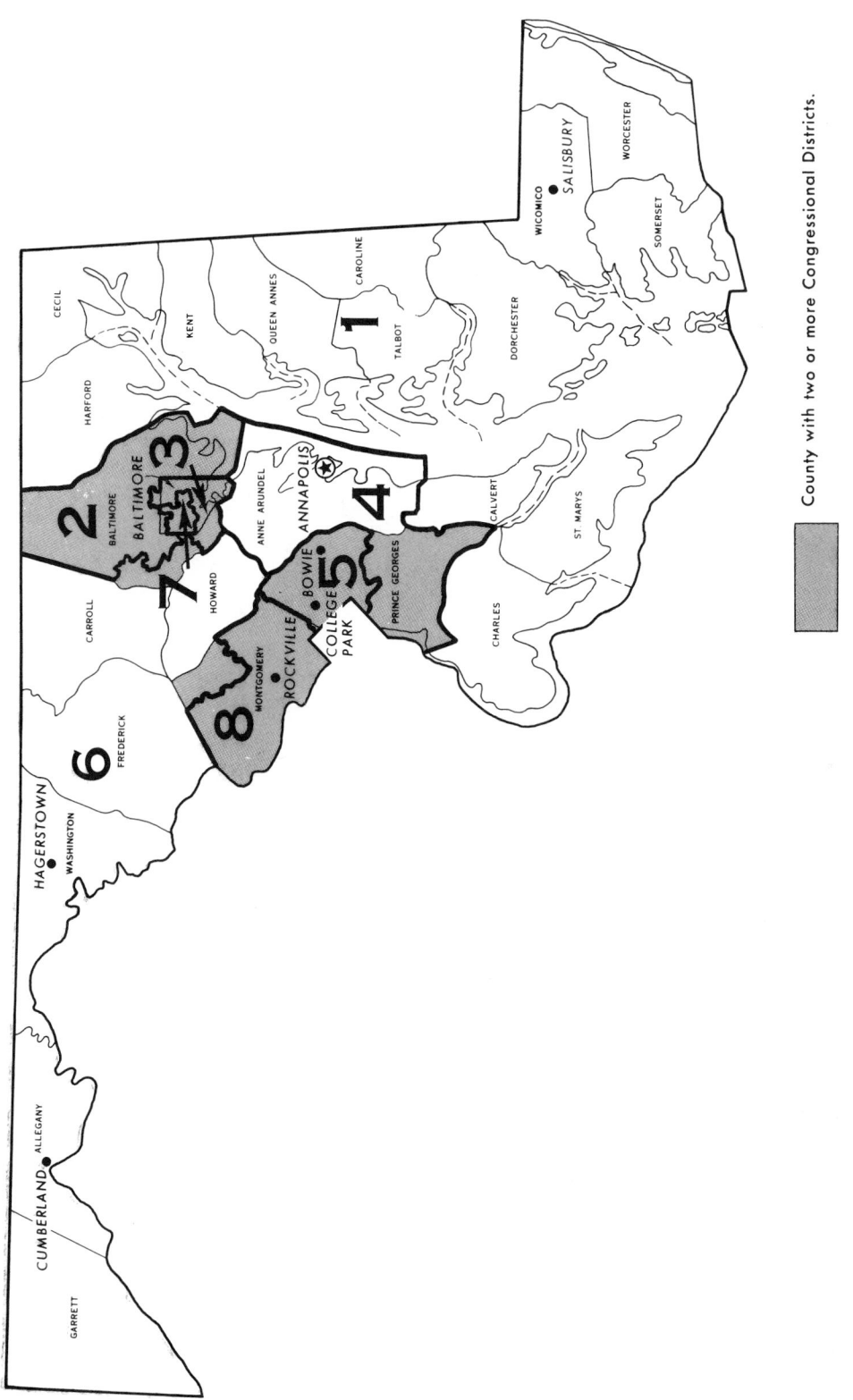

County with two or more Congressional Districts.

MARYLAND

PRESIDENT 1980

1980 Census Population	County	Total Vote	Republican	Democratic	Other	Rep.-Dem. Plurality		Percentage			
								Total Vote		Major Vote	
								Rep.	Dem.	Rep.	Dem.
80,548	ALLEGANY	31,484	17,512	12,167	1,805	5,345	R	55.6%	38.6%	59.0%	41.0%
370,775	ANNE ARUNDEL	131,632	69,443	50,780	11,409	18,663	R	52.8%	38.6%	57.8%	42.2%
786,775	BALTIMORE CITY	264,775	57,902	191,911	14,962	134,009	D	21.9%	72.5%	23.2%	76.8%
655,615	BALTIMORE COUNTY	279,917	132,490	121,280	26,147	11,210	R	47.3%	43.3%	52.2%	47.8%
34,638	CALVERT	10,870	5,440	4,745	685	695	R	50.0%	43.7%	53.4%	46.6%
23,143	CAROLINE	6,765	3,582	2,833	350	749	R	52.9%	41.9%	55.8%	44.2%
96,356	CARROLL	32,940	19,859	10,393	2,688	9,466	R	60.3%	31.6%	65.6%	34.4%
60,430	CECIL	18,846	9,673	7,937	1,236	1,736	R	51.3%	42.1%	54.9%	45.1%
72,751	CHARLES	22,020	11,807	8,887	1,326	2,920	R	53.6%	40.4%	57.1%	42.9%
30,623	DORCHESTER	10,550	5,160	4,908	482	252	R	48.9%	46.5%	51.3%	48.7%
114,263	FREDERICK	39,130	22,033	13,629	3,468	8,404	R	56.3%	34.8%	61.8%	38.2%
26,498	GARRETT	8,545	5,475	2,708	362	2,767	R	64.1%	31.7%	66.9%	33.1%
145,930	HARFORD	50,941	26,713	20,042	4,186	6,671	R	52.4%	39.3%	57.1%	42.9%
118,572	HOWARD	51,599	24,272	20,702	6,625	3,570	R	47.0%	40.1%	54.0%	46.0%
16,695	KENT	6,304	2,889	2,986	429	97	D	45.8%	47.4%	49.2%	50.8%
579,053	MONTGOMERY	266,151	125,515	105,822	34,814	19,693	R	47.2%	39.8%	54.3%	45.7%
665,071	PRINCE GEORGES	193,987	78,977	98,757	16,253	19,780	D	40.7%	50.9%	44.4%	55.6%
25,508	QUEEN ANNES	9,112	4,749	3,820	543	929	R	52.1%	41.9%	55.4%	44.6%
59,895	ST. MARYS	16,056	8,267	6,773	1,016	1,494	R	51.5%	42.2%	55.0%	45.0%
19,188	SOMERSET	6,937	3,312	3,342	283	30	D	47.7%	48.2%	49.8%	50.2%
25,604	TALBOT	10,711	6,044	3,995	672	2,049	R	56.4%	37.3%	60.2%	39.8%
113,086	WASHINGTON	39,083	22,901	14,118	2,064	8,783	R	58.6%	36.1%	61.9%	38.1%
64,540	WICOMICO	21,905	11,229	9,431	1,245	1,798	R	51.3%	43.1%	54.4%	45.6%
30,889	WORCESTER	10,236	5,362	4,195	679	1,167	R	52.4%	41.0%	56.1%	43.9%
4,216,446	TOTAL	1,540,496	680,606	726,161	133,729	45,555	D	44.2%	47.1%	48.4%	51.6%

MARYLAND

SENATOR 1980

1980 Census Population	County	Total Vote	Republican	Democratic	Other	Rep.-Dem. Plurality		Percentage			
								Total Vote		Major Vote	
								Rep.	Dem.	Rep.	Dem.
80,548	ALLEGANY	25,529	18,700	6,829		11,871	R	73.3%	26.7%	73.3%	26.7%
370,775	ANNE ARUNDEL	109,380	76,352	33,028		43,324	R	69.8%	30.2%	69.8%	30.2%
786,775	BALTIMORE CITY	191,227	108,051	83,176		24,875	R	56.5%	43.5%	56.5%	43.5%
655,615	BALTIMORE COUNTY	229,781	151,087	78,694		72,393	R	65.8%	34.2%	65.8%	34.2%
34,638	CALVERT	8,870	5,774	3,096		2,678	R	65.1%	34.9%	65.1%	34.9%
23,143	CAROLINE	5,157	3,586	1,571		2,015	R	69.5%	30.5%	69.5%	30.5%
96,356	CARROLL	26,908	16,623	10,285		6,338	R	61.8%	38.2%	61.8%	38.2%
60,430	CECIL	14,608	9,507	5,101		4,406	R	65.1%	34.9%	65.1%	34.9%
72,751	CHARLES	17,859	11,308	6,551		4,757	R	63.3%	36.7%	63.3%	36.7%
30,623	DORCHESTER	7,983	5,463	2,520		2,943	R	68.4%	31.6%	68.4%	31.6%
114,263	FREDERICK	34,373	26,230	8,143		18,087	R	76.3%	23.7%	76.3%	23.7%
26,498	GARRETT	6,745	5,136	1,609		3,527	R	76.1%	23.9%	76.1%	23.9%
145,930	HARFORD	45,367	32,805	12,562		20,243	R	72.3%	27.7%	72.3%	27.7%
118,572	HOWARD	43,710	31,740	11,970		19,770	R	72.6%	27.4%	72.6%	27.4%
16,695	KENT	4,750	3,331	1,419		1,912	R	70.1%	29.9%	70.1%	29.9%
579,053	MONTGOMERY	257,323	196,817	60,506		136,311	R	76.5%	23.5%	76.5%	23.5%
665,071	PRINCE GEORGES	166,843	87,311	79,532		7,779	R	52.3%	47.7%	52.3%	47.7%
25,508	QUEEN ANNES	6,891	4,730	2,161		2,569	R	68.6%	31.4%	68.6%	31.4%
59,895	ST. MARYS	12,153	7,602	4,551		3,051	R	62.6%	37.4%	62.6%	37.4%
19,188	SOMERSET	4,567	2,986	1,581		1,405	R	65.4%	34.6%	65.4%	34.6%
25,604	TALBOT	8,351	6,439	1,912		4,527	R	77.1%	22.9%	77.1%	22.9%
113,086	WASHINGTON	32,680	22,460	10,220		12,240	R	68.7%	31.3%	68.7%	31.3%
64,540	WICOMICO	17,338	11,675	5,663		6,012	R	67.3%	32.7%	67.3%	32.7%
30,889	WORCESTER	7,695	5,257	2,438		2,819	R	68.3%	31.7%	68.3%	31.7%
4,216,446	TOTAL	1,286,088	850,970	435,118		415,852	R	66.2%	33.8%	66.2%	33.8%

MARYLAND

CONGRESS

CD	Year	Total Vote	Republican Vote	Republican Candidate	Democratic Vote	Democratic Candidate	Other Vote	Rep.-Dem. Plurality	Total Vote Rep.	Total Vote Dem.	Major Vote Rep.	Major Vote Dem.
1	1980	188,886	91,143	BAUMAN, ROBERT E.	97,743	DYSON, ROY		6,600 D	48.3%	51.7%	48.3%	51.7%
1	1978	126,295	80,202	BAUMAN, ROBERT E.	46,093	QUINN, JOSEPH D.		34,109 R	63.5%	36.5%	63.5%	36.5%
1	1976	158,912	85,919	BAUMAN, ROBERT E.	72,993	DYSON, ROY		12,926 R	54.1%	45.9%	54.1%	45.9%
1	1974	112,423	59,570	BAUMAN, ROBERT E.	52,853	HATEM, THOMAS J.		6,717 R	53.0%	47.0%	53.0%	47.0%
1	1972	122,465	86,326	MILLS, WILLIAM O.	36,139	HARGREAVES, JOHN R.		50,187 R	70.5%	29.5%	70.5%	29.5%
2	1980	210,978	89,961	BENTLEY, HELEN D.	121,017	LONG, CLARENCE D.		31,056 D	42.6%	57.4%	42.6%	57.4%
2	1978	148,487	49,886	MCKNIGHT, MALCOLM M.	98,601	LONG, CLARENCE D.		48,715 D	33.6%	66.4%	33.6%	66.4%
2	1976	196,303	35,258	SENEY, JOHN M.	139,196	LONG, CLARENCE D.	21,849	103,938 D	18.0%	70.9%	20.2%	79.8%
2	1974	133,861	30,639	SENEY, JOHN M.	103,222	LONG, CLARENCE D.		72,583 D	22.9%	77.1%	22.9%	77.1%
2	1972	187,465	64,119	BISHOP, JOHN J.	123,346	LONG, CLARENCE D.		59,227 D	34.2%	65.8%	34.2%	65.8%
3	1980	134,367	32,074	SCHAFFER, RUSSELL T.	102,293	MIKULSKI, BARBARA A.		70,219 D	23.9%	76.1%	23.9%	76.1%
3	1978	91,189			91,189	MIKULSKI, BARBARA A.		91,189 D		100.0%		100.0%
3	1976	143,461	36,447	CULOTTA, SAMUEL A.	107,014	MIKULSKI, BARBARA A.		70,567 D	25.4%	74.6%	25.4%	74.6%
3	1974	111,185	17,967	MATHEWS, WILLIAM H.	93,218	SARBANES, PAUL S.		75,251 D	16.2%	83.8%	16.2%	83.8%
3	1972	133,535	40,442	MORROW, ROBERT D.	93,093	SARBANES, PAUL S.		52,651 D	30.3%	69.7%	30.3%	69.7%
4	1980	168,360	120,985	HOLT, MARJORIE S.	47,375	RILEY, JAMES J.		73,610 R	71.9%	28.1%	71.9%	28.1%
4	1978	115,037	71,374	HOLT, MARJORIE S.	43,663	WARD, SUE F.		27,711 R	62.0%	38.0%	62.0%	38.0%
4	1976	165,013	95,158	HOLT, MARJORIE S.	69,855	FORNOS, WERNER H.		25,303 R	57.7%	42.3%	57.7%	42.3%
4	1974	105,267	61,208	HOLT, MARJORIE S.	44,059	WINELAND, FRED L.		17,149 R	58.1%	41.9%	58.1%	41.9%
4	1972	147,411	87,534	HOLT, MARJORIE S.	59,877	FORNOS, WERNER H.		27,657 R	59.4%	40.6%	59.4%	40.6%
5	1980	131,728	25,693	IGOE, KEVIN R.	106,035	SPELLMAN, GLADYS N.		80,342 D	19.5%	80.5%	19.5%	80.5%
5	1978	84,028	19,160	HARRIS, SAUL J.	64,868	SPELLMAN, GLADYS N.		45,708 D	22.8%	77.2%	22.8%	77.2%
5	1976	134,893	57,057	BURCHAM, JOHN B.	77,836	SPELLMAN, GLADYS N.		20,779 D	42.3%	57.7%	42.3%	57.7%
5	1974	86,016	40,805	BURCHAM, JOHN B.	45,211	SPELLMAN, GLADYS N.		4,406 D	47.4%	52.6%	47.4%	52.6%
5	1972	143,065	90,016	HOGAN, LAWRENCE J.	53,049	CONROY, EDWARD T.		36,967 R	62.9%	37.1%	62.9%	37.1%
6	1980	209,014	62,913	BECK, RAYMOND E.	146,101	BYRON, BEVERLY B.		83,188 D	30.1%	69.9%	30.1%	69.9%
6	1978	140,741	14,545	PERKINS, MELVIN	126,196	BYRON, BEVERLY B.		111,651 D	10.3%	89.7%	10.3%	89.7%
6	1976	179,004	52,203	BOND, ARTHUR T.	126,801	BYRON, GOODLOE E.		74,598 D	29.2%	70.8%	29.2%	70.8%
6	1974	123,298	32,416	WAMPLER, ELTON R.	90,882	BYRON, GOODLOE E.		58,466 D	26.3%	73.7%	26.3%	73.7%
6	1972	165,542	58,259	MASON, EDWARD J.	107,283	BYRON, GOODLOE E.		49,024 D	35.2%	64.8%	35.2%	64.8%
7	1980	109,754	12,650	CLARK, VICTOR	97,104	MITCHELL, PARREN J.		84,454 D	11.5%	88.5%	11.5%	88.5%
7	1978	58,622			51,996	MITCHELL, PARREN J.	6,626	51,996 D		88.7%		100.0%
7	1976	100,633			94,991	MITCHELL, PARREN J.	5,642	94,991 D		94.4%		100.0%
7	1974	43,252			43,252	MITCHELL, PARREN J.		43,252 D		100.0%		100.0%
7	1972	104,625	20,876	ADAIR, VERDELL	83,749	MITCHELL, PARREN J.		62,873 D	20.0%	80.0%	20.0%	80.0%
8	1980	249,960	101,659	STEERS, NEWTON I.	148,301	BARNES, MICHAEL D.		46,642 D	40.7%	59.3%	40.7%	59.3%
8	1978	159,658	77,807	STEERS, NEWTON I.	81,851	BARNES, MICHAEL D.		4,044 D	48.7%	51.3%	48.7%	51.3%
8	1976	237,652	111,274	STEERS, NEWTON I.	100,343	DAVIS, LANNY	26,035	10,931 R	46.8%	42.2%	52.6%	47.4%
8	1974	158,787	104,675	GUDE, GILBERT	54,112	KRAMER, SIDNEY		50,563 R	65.9%	34.1%	65.9%	34.1%
8	1972	214,838	137,287	GUDE, GILBERT	77,551	ANASTASI, JOSEPH G.		59,736 R	63.9%	36.1%	63.9%	36.1%

MARYLAND

1980 GENERAL ELECTION

President   Other vote was 119,537 Anderson (Independent); 14,192 Clark (Libertarian).

Senator

Congress

1980 PRIMARIES

MAY 13 REPUBLICAN

Senator   82,430 Charles Mathias; 24,848 John M. Brennan; 23,073 V. Dallas Merrell; 10,970 Roscoe G. Bartlett; 5,176 Jack F. Holden; 3,476 Gerald G. Warren.

Congress   Unopposed in two CD's. Contested as follows:

CD 2   8,179 Helen D. Bentley; 5,681 Malcolm M. McKnight; 1,356 Suzanne Hall; 1,052 Joseph A. Arena.
CD 3   3,173 Russell T. Schaffer; 2,898 Richard L. Andrews.
CD 5   4,894 Kevin R. Igoe; 2,662 William P. Guthrie; 1,631 William A. Albaugh; 993 George W. Benns.
CD 6   20,464 Raymond E. Beck; 5,663 Clifford H. Andrews.
CD 7   1,607 Victor Clark; 1,099 Theodore M. Williams.
CD 8   16,249 Newton I. Steers; 13,106 Constance A. Morella; 7,350 Robin Ficker; 1,632 Phillip Buford.

MAY 13 DEMOCRATIC

Senator   79,033 Edward T. Conroy; 52,803 Victor L. Crawford; 43,035 Robert L. Douglass; 40,510 Dennis C. McCoy; 35,407 R. Spencer Oliver; 20,255 John A. Kennedy; 19,455 Frank J. Broschart; 17,364 James A. Young; 12,375 Richard J. Taranto; 11,461 Mello Cottone; 10,869 David E. Shaw; 9,952 Kurt Summers.

Congress   Unopposed in CD 8. Contested as follows:

CD 1   26,585 Roy Dyson; 11,833 Donald M. DeArmon.
CD 2   44,280 Clarence D. Long; 30,335 Thomas B. Kernan; 3,217 William A. Basil.
CD 3   40,928 Barbara A. Mikulski; 5,026 Michael Baccala; 3,280 Robert B. Lewis; 2,917 Edward J. Eagan; 2,386 Morgan L. Amaimo.
CD 4   10,015 James J. Riley; 7,174 Jaye E. Bauckman; 6,971 James Brianas; 6,388 John E. Sellner; 5,616 Robert G. Bassette; 3,790 Marvin O. Morris.
CD 5   33,244 Gladys N. Spellman; 4,518 Michael I. Sprague.
CD 6   38,842 Beverly B. Byron; 6,388 Thomas H. Hattery; 3,880 William B. McMahon; 2,746 Kent Sullivan; 1,457 Melvin C. Perkins; 1,356 John J. Kubricky.
CD 7   33,747 Parren J. Mitchell; 7,681 Edward J. Makowski.

MASSACHUSETTS

GOVERNOR
Edward J. King (D). Elected 1978 to a four-year term.

SENATORS
Edward M. Kennedy (D). Re-elected 1976 to a six-year term. Previously elected 1970, 1964, and in 1962 to fill out term vacated by the resignation of Senator John F. Kennedy.

Paul E. Tsongas (D). Elected 1978 to a six-year term.

REPRESENTATIVES
1. Silvio O. Conte (R)
2. Edward P. Boland (D)
3. Joseph D. Early (D)
4. Barney Frank (D)
5. James M. Shannon (D)
6. Nicholas Mavroules (D)
7. Edward J. Markey (D)
8. Thomas P. O'Neill (D)
9. John J. Moakley (D)
10. Margaret M. Heckler (R)
11. Brian J. Donnelly (D)
12. Gerry E. Studds (D)

POSTWAR VOTE FOR GOVERNOR

Year	Total Vote	Republican Vote	Republican Candidate	Democratic Vote	Democratic Candidate	Other Vote	Rep.-Dem. Plurality	Total Vote Rep.	Total Vote Dem.	Major Vote Rep.	Major Vote Dem.
1978	1,962,251	926,072	Hatch, Francis W.	1,030,294	King, Edward J.	5,885	104,222 D	47.2%	52.5%	47.3%	52.7%
1974	1,854,798	784,353	Sargent, Francis W.	992,284	Dukakis, Michael S.	78,161	207,931 D	42.3%	53.5%	44.1%	55.9%
1970	1,867,906	1,058,623	Sargent, Francis W.	799,269	White, Kevin H.	10,014	259,354 R	56.7%	42.8%	57.0%	43.0%
1966	2,041,177	1,277,358	Volpe, John A.	752,720	McCormack, Edward J.	11,099	524,638 R	62.6%	36.9%	62.9%	37.1%
1964	2,340,130	1,176,462	Volpe, John A.	1,153,416	Bellotti, Francis X.	10,252	23,046 R	50.3%	49.3%	50.5%	49.5%
1962	2,109,089	1,047,891	Volpe, John A.	1,053,322	Peabody, Endicott	7,876	5,431 D	49.7%	49.9%	49.9%	50.1%
1960	2,417,133	1,269,295	Volpe, John A.	1,130,810	Ward, Joseph D.	17,028	138,485 R	52.5%	46.8%	52.9%	47.1%
1958	1,899,117	818,463	Gibbons, Charles	1,067,020	Furcolo, Foster	13,634	248,557 D	43.1%	56.2%	43.4%	56.6%
1956	2,339,884	1,096,759	Whittier, Sumner G.	1,234,618	Furcolo, Foster	8,507	137,859 D	46.9%	52.8%	47.0%	53.0%
1954	1,903,774	985,339	Herter, Christian A.	910,087	Murphy, Robert F.	8,348	75,252 R	51.8%	47.8%	52.0%	48.0%
1952	2,356,298	1,175,955	Herter, Christian A.	1,161,499	Dever, Paul A.	18,844	14,456 R	49.9%	49.3%	50.3%	49.7%
1950	1,910,180	824,069	Coolidge, Arthur W.	1,074,570	Dever, Paul A.	11,541	250,501 D	43.1%	56.3%	43.4%	56.6%
1948	2,099,250	849,895	Bradford, Robert F.	1,239,247	Dever, Paul A.	10,108	389,352 D	40.5%	59.0%	40.7%	59.3%
1946	1,683,452	911,152	Bradford, Robert F.	762,743	Tobin, Maurice	9,557	148,409 R	54.1%	45.3%	54.4%	45.6%

The term of office of Massachusetts' Governor was increased from two to four years effective with the 1966 election.

POSTWAR VOTE FOR SENATOR

Year	Total Vote	Republican Vote	Republican Candidate	Democratic Vote	Democratic Candidate	Other Vote	Rep.-Dem. Plurality	Total Vote Rep.	Total Vote Dem.	Major Vote Rep.	Major Vote Dem.
1978	1,985,700	890,584	Brooke, Edward W.	1,093,283	Tsongas, Paul E.	1,833	202,699 D	44.8%	55.1%	44.9%	55.1%
1976	2,491,255	722,641	Robertson, Michael	1,726,657	Kennedy, Edward M.	41,957	1,004,016 D	29.0%	69.3%	29.5%	70.5%
1972	2,370,676	1,505,932	Brooke, Edward W.	823,278	Droney, John J.	41,466	682,654 R	63.5%	34.7%	64.7%	35.3%
1970	1,935,607	715,978	Spaulding, Josiah A.	1,202,856	Kennedy, Edward M.	16,773	486,878 D	37.0%	62.1%	37.3%	62.7%
1966	1,999,949	1,213,473	Brooke, Edward W.	774,761	Peabody, Endicott	11,715	438,712 R	60.7%	38.7%	61.0%	39.0%
1964	2,312,028	587,663	Whitmore, Howard	1,716,907	Kennedy, Edward M.	7,458	1,129,244 D	25.4%	74.3%	25.5%	74.5%
1962s	2,097,085	877,669	Lodge, George C.	1,162,611	Kennedy, Edward M.	56,805	284,942 D	41.9%	55.4%	43.0%	57.0%
1960	2,417,813	1,358,556	Saltonstall, Leverett	1,050,725	O'Connor, Thomas J.	8,532	307,831 R	56.2%	43.5%	56.4%	43.6%
1958	1,862,041	488,318	Celeste, Vincent J.	1,362,926	Kennedy, John F.	10,797	874,608 D	26.2%	73.2%	26.4%	73.6%
1954	1,892,710	956,605	Saltonstall, Leverett	927,899	Furcolo, Foster	8,206	28,706 R	50.5%	49.0%	50.8%	49.2%
1952	2,360,425	1,141,247	Lodge, Henry Cabot	1,211,984	Kennedy, John F.	7,194	70,737 D	48.3%	51.3%	48.5%	51.5%
1948	2,055,798	1,088,475	Saltonstall, Leverett	954,398	Fitzgerald, John I.	12,925	134,077 R	52.9%	46.4%	53.3%	46.7%
1946	1,662,063	989,736	Lodge, Henry Cabot	660,200	Walsh, David I.	12,127	329,536 R	59.5%	39.7%	60.0%	40.0%

The 1962 election was for a short term to fill a vacancy.

MASSACHUSETTS

Districts Established November 12, 1971

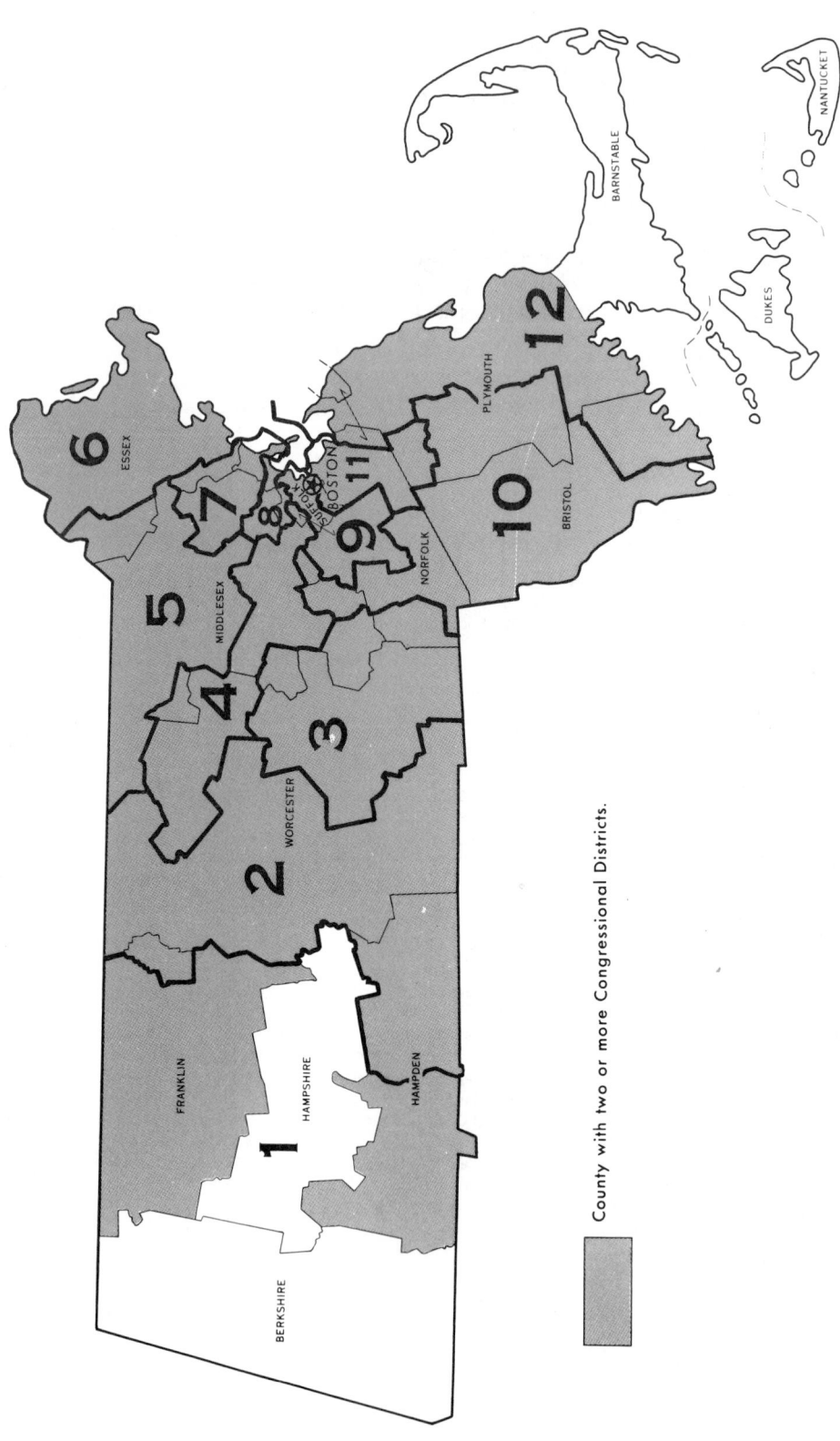

County with two or more Congressional Districts.

MASSACHUSETTS

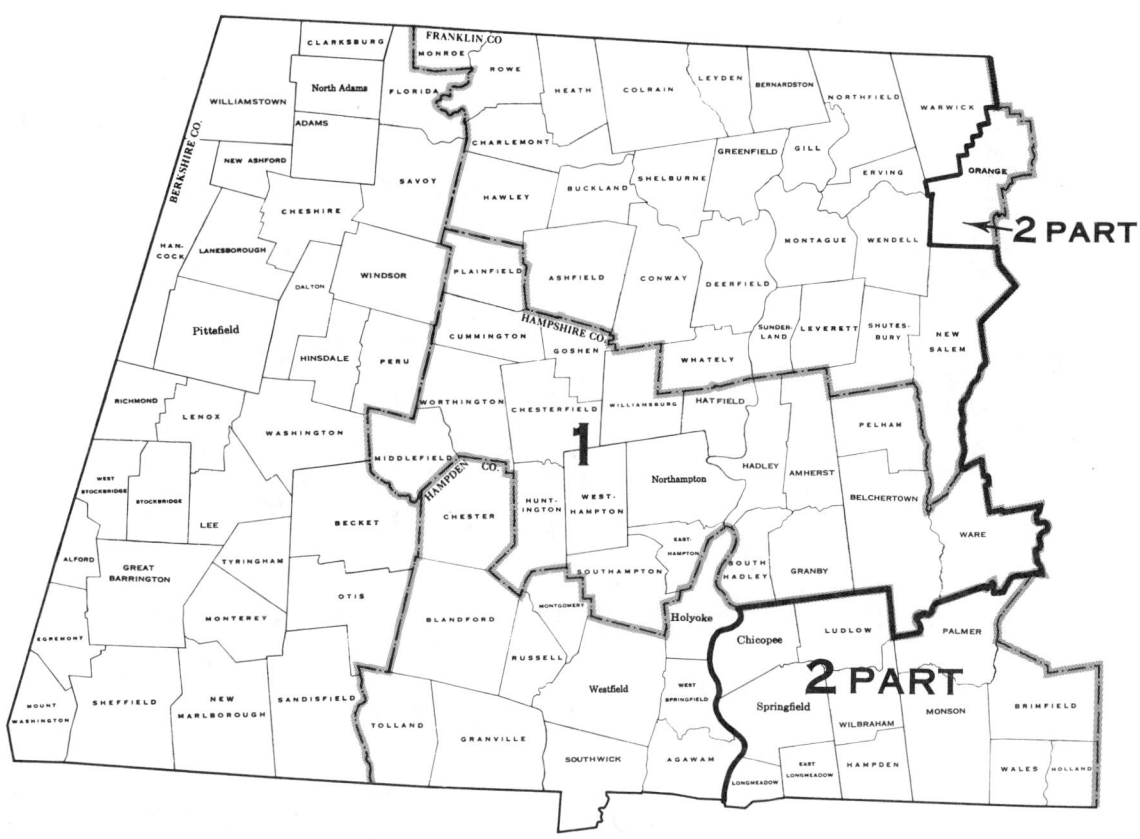

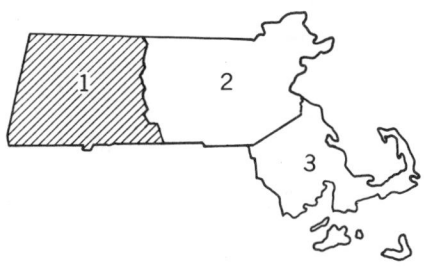

MASSACHUSETTS

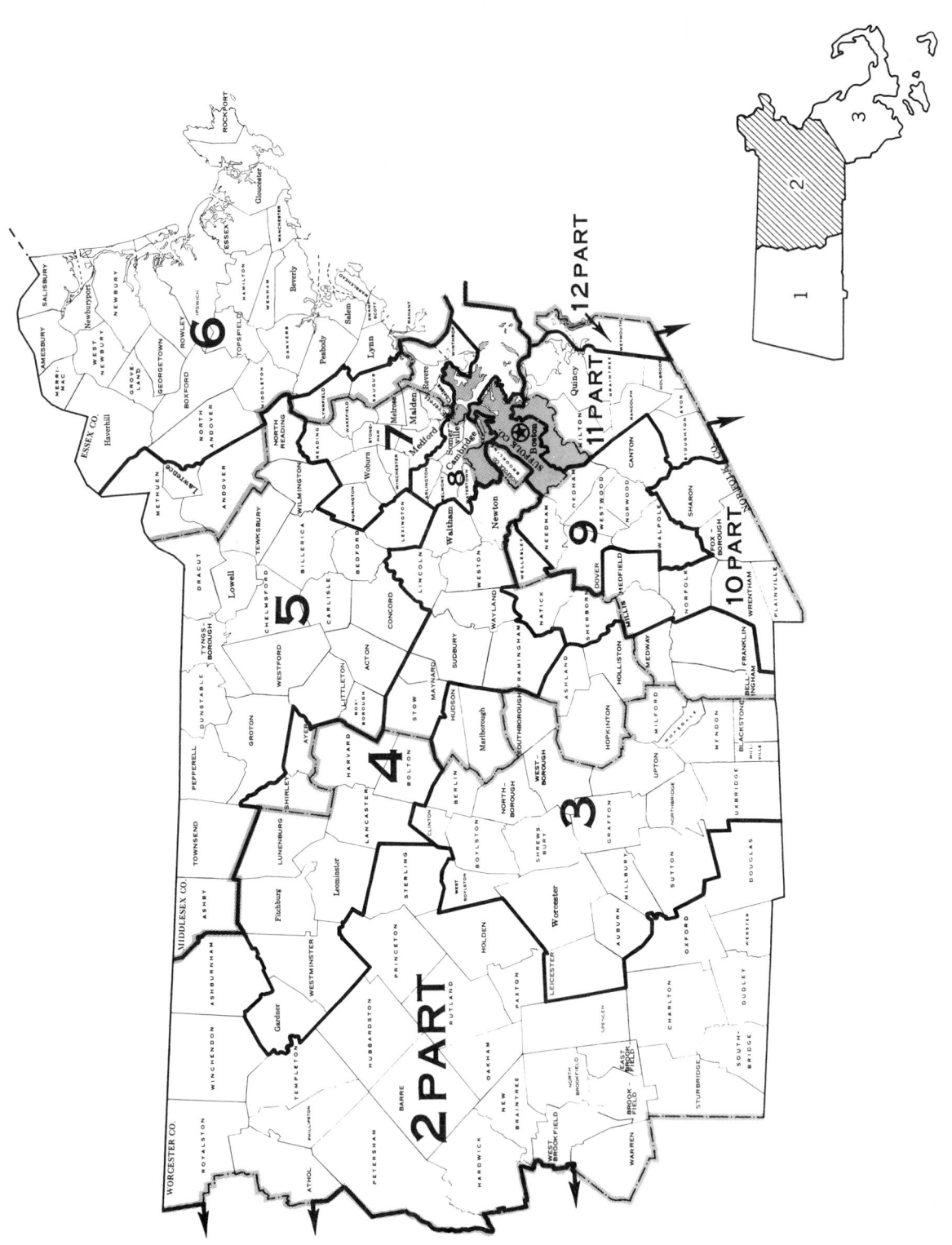

MASSACHUSETTS

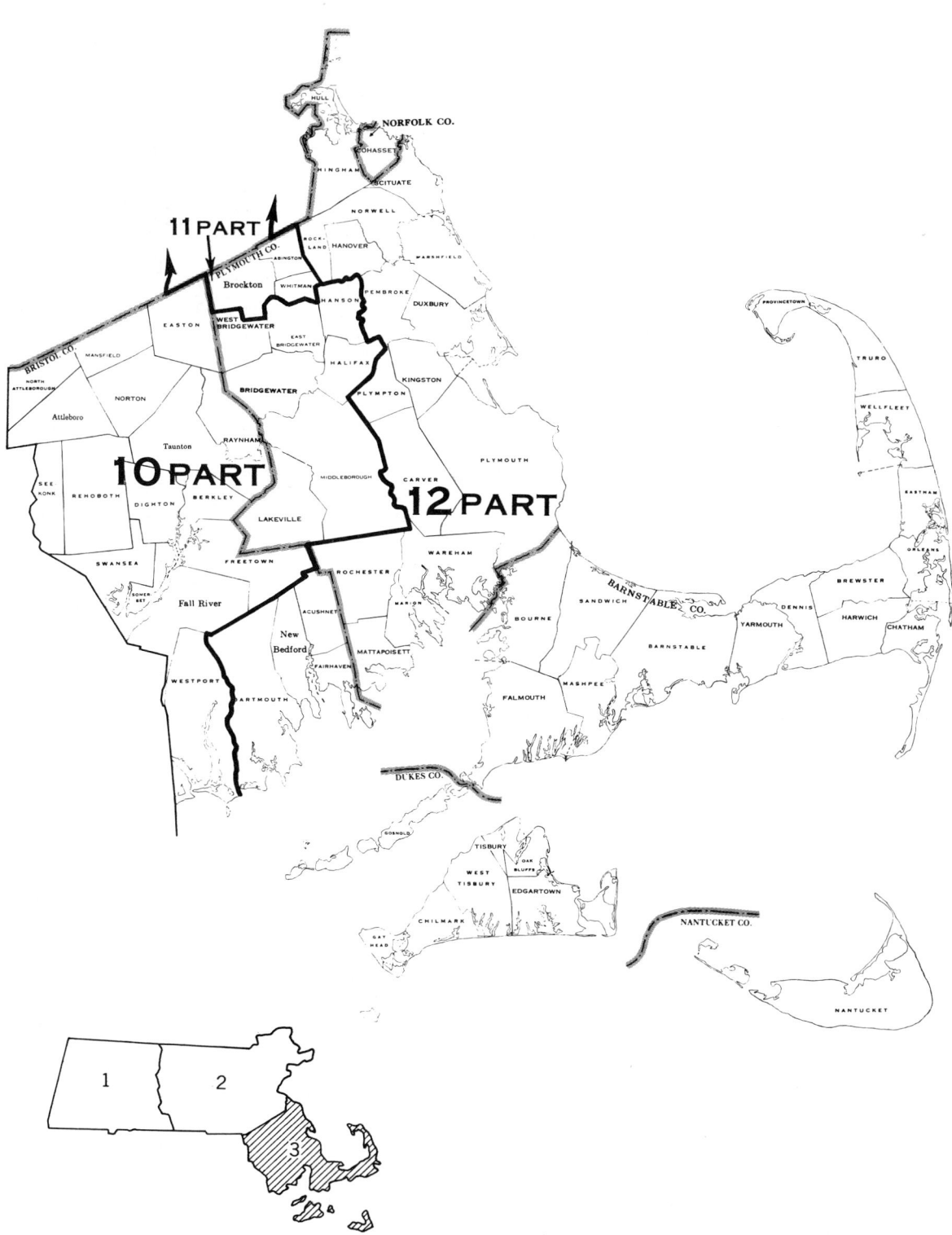

MASSACHUSETTS

PRESIDENT 1980

1980 Census Population	County	Total Vote	Republican	Democratic	Other	Rep.-Dem. Plurality	Percentage Total Vote Rep.	Dem.	Major Vote Rep.	Dem.
147,925	BARNSTABLE	82,273	41,493	23,952	16,828	17,541 R	50.4%	29.1%	63.4%	36.6%
145,110	BERKSHIRE	68,031	27,063	29,458	11,510	2,395 D	39.8%	43.3%	47.9%	52.1%
474,641	BRISTOL	188,605	77,545	83,460	27,600	5,915 D	41.1%	44.3%	48.2%	51.8%
8,942	DUKES	5,397	1,809	2,370	1,218	561 D	33.5%	43.9%	43.3%	56.7%
633,632	ESSEX	297,533	130,252	116,173	51,108	14,079 R	43.8%	39.0%	52.9%	47.1%
64,317	FRANKLIN	30,122	12,528	11,830	5,764	698 R	41.6%	39.3%	51.4%	48.6%
443,018	HAMPDEN	179,720	72,528	80,369	26,823	7,841 D	40.4%	44.7%	47.4%	52.6%
138,813	HAMPSHIRE	60,355	21,117	27,611	11,627	6,494 D	35.0%	45.7%	43.3%	56.7%
1,367,034	MIDDLESEX	637,679	256,999	270,751	109,929	13,752 D	40.3%	42.5%	48.7%	51.3%
5,087	NANTUCKET	2,838	1,149	1,040	649	109 R	40.5%	36.6%	52.5%	47.5%
606,587	NORFOLK	303,729	136,184	117,274	50,271	18,910 R	44.8%	38.6%	53.7%	46.3%
405,437	PLYMOUTH	173,248	85,593	58,772	28,883	26,821 R	49.4%	33.9%	59.3%	40.7%
650,142	SUFFOLK	216,207	73,271	113,416	29,520	40,145 D	33.9%	52.5%	39.2%	60.8%
646,352	WORCESTER	278,561	120,100	117,326	41,135	2,774 R	43.1%	42.1%	50.6%	49.4%
5,737,037	TOTAL	2,524,298	1,057,631	1,053,802	412,865	3,829 R	41.9%	41.7%	50.1%	49.9%

MASSACHUSETTS

PRESIDENT 1980

1980 Census Population	City/Town	Total Vote	Republican	Democratic	Other	Rep.-Dem. Plurality	Total Vote Rep.	Total Vote Dem.	Major Vote Rep.	Major Vote Dem.
26,271	AGAWAM	10,749	4,758	4,215	1,776	543 R	44.3%	39.2%	53.0%	47.0%
33,229	AMHERST	11,739	2,421	6,001	3,317	3,580 D	20.6%	51.1%	28.7%	71.3%
26,370	ANDOVER	13,663	7,122	4,028	2,513	3,094 R	52.1%	29.5%	63.9%	36.1%
48,219	ARLINGTON	26,980	10,726	11,737	4,517	1,011 D	39.8%	43.5%	47.7%	52.3%
34,196	ATTLEBORO	12,473	5,899	4,376	2,198	1,523 R	47.3%	35.1%	57.4%	42.6%
30,898	BARNSTABLE TOWN	16,403	8,335	4,613	3,455	3,722 R	50.8%	28.1%	64.4%	35.6%
26,100	BELMONT	15,268	6,701	5,767	2,800	934 R	43.9%	37.8%	53.7%	46.3%
37,655	BEVERLY	18,334	8,012	6,360	3,962	1,652 R	43.7%	34.7%	55.7%	44.3%
36,727	BILLERICA	14,426	6,607	5,458	2,361	1,149 R	45.8%	37.8%	54.8%	45.2%
562,994	BOSTON	178,493	58,656	95,133	24,704	36,477 D	32.9%	53.3%	38.1%	61.9%
36,337	BRAINTREE	18,595	9,121	6,878	2,596	2,243 R	49.1%	37.0%	57.0%	43.0%
95,172	BROCKTON	33,217	15,350	12,751	5,116	2,599 R	46.2%	38.4%	54.6%	45.4%
55,062	BROOKLINE	27,769	8,441	14,038	5,290	5,597 D	30.4%	50.6%	37.6%	62.4%
23,486	BURLINGTON	11,278	5,265	4,091	1,922	1,174 R	46.7%	36.3%	56.3%	43.7%
95,322	CAMBRIDGE	40,006	7,952	24,337	7,717	16,385 D	19.9%	60.8%	24.6%	75.4%
31,174	CHELMSFORD	15,815	8,198	5,085	2,532	3,113 R	51.8%	32.2%	61.7%	38.3%
25,431	CHELSEA	9,578	3,183	5,292	1,103	2,109 D	33.2%	55.3%	37.6%	62.4%
55,112	CHICOPEE	24,466	8,575	12,745	3,146	4,170 D	35.0%	52.1%	40.2%	59.8%
24,100	DANVERS	11,908	5,831	3,742	2,335	2,089 R	49.0%	31.4%	60.9%	39.1%
23,966	DARTMOUTH	10,606	4,934	4,044	1,628	890 R	46.5%	38.1%	55.0%	45.0%
25,298	DEDHAM	13,622	6,367	5,071	2,184	1,296 R	46.7%	37.2%	55.7%	44.3%
21,249	DRACUT	10,096	4,621	4,211	1,264	410 R	45.8%	41.7%	52.3%	47.7%
37,195	EVERETT	16,607	6,341	8,208	2,058	1,867 D	38.2%	49.4%	43.6%	56.4%
92,574	FALL RIVER	33,603	9,958	19,644	4,001	9,686 D	29.6%	58.5%	33.6%	66.4%
23,640	FALMOUTH	12,480	5,582	4,412	2,486	1,170 R	44.7%	35.4%	55.9%	44.1%
39,580	FITCHBURG	15,085	6,032	7,029	2,024	997 D	40.0%	46.6%	46.2%	53.8%
65,113	FRAMINGHAM	29,412	11,979	12,275	5,158	296 D	40.7%	41.7%	49.4%	50.6%
27,768	GLOUCESTER	12,697	5,530	4,928	2,239	602 R	43.6%	38.8%	52.9%	47.1%
46,865	HAVERHILL	20,073	7,949	9,253	2,871	1,304 D	39.6%	46.1%	46.2%	53.8%
20,339	HINGHAM	10,535	5,503	3,274	1,758	2,229 R	52.2%	31.1%	62.7%	37.3%
44,678	HOLYOKE	17,291	6,268	8,701	2,322	2,433 D	36.3%	50.3%	41.9%	58.1%
63,175	LAWRENCE	22,740	8,020	12,145	2,575	4,125 D	35.3%	53.4%	39.8%	60.2%
34,508	LEOMINSTER	13,909	6,320	5,805	1,784	515 R	45.4%	41.7%	52.1%	47.9%
29,479	LEXINGTON	17,377	6,999	6,557	3,821	442 R	40.3%	37.7%	51.6%	48.4%
92,418	LOWELL	33,131	12,668	16,353	4,110	3,685 D	38.2%	49.4%	43.7%	56.3%
78,471	LYNN	32,066	11,966	15,777	4,323	3,811 D	37.3%	49.2%	43.1%	56.9%
53,386	MALDEN	23,821	8,521	11,659	3,641	3,138 D	35.8%	48.9%	42.2%	57.8%
20,126	MARBLEHEAD	12,313	6,038	3,415	2,860	2,623 R	49.0%	27.7%	63.9%	36.1%
30,617	MARLBOROUGH	13,389	5,345	5,908	2,136	563 D	39.9%	44.1%	47.5%	52.5%
20,916	MARSHFIELD	9,907	4,744	3,330	1,833	1,414 R	47.9%	33.6%	58.8%	41.2%
58,076	MEDFORD	27,734	10,633	13,303	3,798	2,670 D	38.3%	48.0%	44.4%	55.6%
30,055	MELROSE	15,243	7,195	5,340	2,708	1,855 R	47.2%	35.0%	57.4%	42.6%
36,701	METHUEN	17,425	7,950	7,358	2,117	592 R	45.6%	42.2%	51.9%	48.1%
23,390	MILFORD	11,001	4,152	5,392	1,457	1,240 D	37.7%	49.0%	43.5%	56.5%
25,860	MILTON	15,460	7,244	5,881	2,335	1,363 R	46.9%	38.0%	55.2%	44.8%
29,461	NATICK	15,108	6,097	6,067	2,944	30 R	40.4%	40.2%	50.1%	49.9%
27,901	NEEDHAM	16,458	8,331	4,894	3,233	3,437 R	50.6%	29.7%	63.0%	37.0%
98,478	NEW BEDFORD	35,545	13,217	18,014	4,314	4,797 D	37.2%	50.7%	42.3%	57.7%
83,622	NEWTON	44,074	15,621	20,173	8,280	4,552 D	35.4%	45.8%	43.6%	56.4%
29,286	NORTHAMPTON	13,073	4,081	6,629	2,363	2,548 D	31.2%	50.7%	38.1%	61.9%
20,129	NORTH ANDOVER	9,915	4,764	3,570	1,581	1,194 R	48.0%	36.0%	57.2%	42.8%
21,095	NORTH ATTLEBORO	8,330	4,375	2,596	1,359	1,779 R	52.5%	31.2%	62.8%	37.2%
29,711	NORWOOD	14,798	6,479	5,942	2,377	537 R	43.8%	40.2%	52.2%	47.8%
45,976	PEABODY	22,767	9,129	9,749	3,889	620 D	40.1%	42.8%	48.4%	51.6%
51,974	PITTSFIELD	24,422	9,154	11,127	4,141	1,973 D	37.5%	45.6%	45.1%	54.9%
35,913	PLYMOUTH TOWN	15,231	7,183	5,354	2,694	1,829 R	47.2%	35.2%	57.3%	42.7%
84,743	QUINCY	41,882	18,038	17,977	5,867	61 R	43.1%	42.9%	50.1%	49.9%
28,218	RANDOLPH	13,675	5,468	6,037	2,170	569 D	40.0%	44.1%	47.5%	52.5%
22,678	READING	12,203	5,986	3,836	2,381	2,150 R	49.1%	31.4%	60.9%	39.1%
42,423	REVERE	18,685	7,524	8,844	2,317	1,320 D	40.3%	47.3%	46.0%	54.0%
38,220	SALEM	18,083	6,378	8,137	3,568	1,759 D	35.3%	45.0%	43.9%	56.1%
24,746	SAUGUS	11,919	5,376	4,772	1,771	604 R	45.1%	40.0%	53.0%	47.0%
22,674	SHREWSBURY	11,346	5,186	4,255	1,905	931 R	45.7%	37.5%	54.9%	45.1%
77,372	SOMERVILLE	31,158	9,533	16,931	4,694	7,398 D	30.6%	54.3%	36.0%	64.0%
152,319	SPRINGFIELD	50,974	17,694	26,414	6,866	8,720 D	34.7%	51.8%	40.1%	59.9%
21,424	STONEHAM	10,389	4,711	3,937	1,741	774 R	45.3%	37.9%	54.5%	45.5%
26,710	STOUGHTON	11,815	4,979	4,951	1,885	28 R	42.1%	41.9%	50.1%	49.9%
45,001	TAUNTON	16,599	6,610	7,591	2,398	981 D	39.8%	45.7%	46.5%	53.5%
24,635	TEWKSBURY	10,366	4,846	3,987	1,533	859 R	46.7%	38.5%	54.9%	45.1%
24,895	WAKEFIELD	12,896	5,842	4,818	2,236	1,024 R	45.3%	37.4%	54.8%	45.2%

MASSACHUSETTS

PRESIDENT 1980

1980 Census Population	City/Town	Total Vote	Republican	Democratic	Other	Rep.-Dem. Plurality	Percentage			
							Total Vote		Major Vote	
							Rep.	Dem.	Rep.	Dem.
58,200	WALTHAM	23,078	9,450	9,885	3,743	435 D	40.9%	42.8%	48.9%	51.1%
34,384	WATERTOWN	17,125	6,070	8,255	2,800	2,185 D	35.4%	48.2%	42.4%	57.6%
27,209	WELLESLEY	14,441	7,326	4,212	2,903	3,114 R	50.7%	29.2%	63.5%	36.5%
27,042	WEST SPRINGFIELD	12,657	5,702	4,881	2,074	821 R	45.1%	38.6%	53.9%	46.1%
36,465	WESTFIELD	14,711	6,358	5,875	2,478	483 R	43.2%	39.9%	52.0%	48.0%
55,601	WEYMOUTH	25,778	11,692	10,245	3,841	1,447 R	45.4%	39.7%	53.3%	46.7%
20,701	WINCHESTER	11,396	5,429	3,884	2,083	1,545 R	47.6%	34.1%	58.3%	41.7%
19,294	WINTHROP	9,451	3,908	4,147	1,396	239 D	41.4%	43.9%	48.5%	51.5%
36,626	WOBURN	17,090	6,997	7,444	2,649	447 D	40.9%	43.6%	48.5%	51.5%
161,799	WORCESTER CITY	63,361	23,305	31,146	8,910	7,841 D	36.8%	49.2%	42.8%	57.2%

MASSACHUSETTS

CONGRESS

CD	Year	Total Vote	Republican Vote	Republican Candidate	Democratic Vote	Democratic Candidate	Other Vote	Rep.-Dem. Plurality	Total Vote Rep.	Total Vote Dem.	Major Vote Rep.	Major Vote Dem.
1	1980	208,892	156,415	CONTE, SILVIO O.	52,457	DOYLE, HELEN P.	20	103,958 R	74.9%	25.1%	74.9%	25.1%
1	1978	131,918	131,773	CONTE, SILVIO O.			145	131,773 R	99.9%		100.0%	
1	1976	215,870	137,652	CONTE, SILVIO O.	78,181	McCOLGAN, EDWARD A.	37	59,471 R	63.8%	36.2%	63.8%	36.2%
1	1974	150,816	107,285	CONTE, SILVIO O.	43,524	MANNING, THOMAS R.	7	63,761 R	71.1%	28.9%	71.1%	28.9%
1	1972	159,429	159,282	CONTE, SILVIO O.			147	159,282 R	99.9%		100.0%	
2	1980	179,665	38,672	SWANK, THOMAS P.	120,711	BOLAND, EDWARD P.	20,282	82,039 D	21.5%	67.2%	24.3%	75.7%
2	1978	139,479	37,881	SWANK, THOMAS P.	101,570	BOLAND, EDWARD P.	28	63,689 D	27.2%	72.8%	27.2%	72.8%
2	1976	185,755	41,563	SWANK, THOMAS P.	134,408	BOLAND, EDWARD P.	9,784	92,845 D	22.4%	72.4%	23.6%	76.4%
2	1974	105,793			105,763	BOLAND, EDWARD P.	30	105,763 D		100.0%		100.0%
2	1972	137,625			137,616	BOLAND, EDWARD P.	9	137,616 D		100.0%		100.0%
3	1980	195,693	54,123	SKEHAN, DAVID G.	141,560	EARLY, JOSEPH D.	10	87,437 D	27.7%	72.3%	27.7%	72.3%
3	1978	158,730	39,259	MACLEOD, CHARLES K.	119,337	EARLY, JOSEPH D.	134	80,078 D	24.7%	75.2%	24.8%	75.2%
3	1976	168,568			168,520	EARLY, JOSEPH D.	48	168,520 D		100.0%		100.0%
3	1974	158,120	60,717	LIONETT, DAVID J.	78,244	EARLY, JOSEPH D.	19,159	17,527 D	38.4%	49.5%	43.7%	56.3%
3	1972	156,839			156,703	DONOHUE, HAROLD D.	136	156,703 D		99.9%		100.0%
4	1980	199,376	95,898	JONES, RICHARD A.	103,466	FRANK, BARNEY	12	7,568 D	48.1%	51.9%	48.1%	51.9%
4	1978	111,491			111,353	DRINAN, ROBERT F.	138	111,353 D		99.9%		100.0%
4	1976	209,835	100,562	MASON, ARTHUR D.	109,268	DRINAN, ROBERT F.	5	8,706 D	47.9%	52.1%	47.9%	52.1%
4	1974	151,996	21,922	MANDELL, ALVIN	77,286	DRINAN, ROBERT F.	52,788	55,364 D	14.4%	50.8%	22.1%	77.9%
4	1972	205,047	93,927	LINSKY, MARTIN A.	99,977	DRINAN, ROBERT F.	11,143	6,050 D	45.8%	48.8%	48.4%	51.6%
5	1980	207,321	70,547	SAWYER, WILLIAM C.	136,758	SHANNON, JAMES M.	16	66,211 D	34.0%	66.0%	34.0%	66.0%
5	1978	172,681	48,685	BUCKLEY, JOHN J.	90,156	SHANNON, JAMES M.	33,840	41,471 D	28.2%	52.2%	35.1%	64.9%
5	1976	214,263	70,036	DURKIN, ROGER P.	144,217	TSONGAS, PAUL E.	10	74,181 D	32.7%	67.3%	32.7%	67.3%
5	1974	164,117	64,596	CRONIN, PAUL W.	99,518	TSONGAS, PAUL E.	3	34,922 D	39.4%	60.6%	39.4%	60.6%
5	1972	207,623	110,970	CRONIN, PAUL W.	92,847	KERRY, JOHN F.	3,806	18,123 R	53.4%	44.7%	54.4%	45.6%
6	1980	219,257	103,192	TRIMARCO, THOMAS H.	111,393	MAVROULES, NICHOLAS	4,672	8,201 D	47.1%	50.8%	48.1%	51.9%
6	1978	180,645	83,511	BRONSON, WILLIAM E.	97,099	MAVROULES, NICHOLAS	35	13,588 D	46.2%	53.8%	46.2%	53.8%
6	1976	221,813	91,655	BRONSON, WILLIAM E.	121,562	HARRINGTON, MICHAEL J.	8,596	29,907 D	41.3%	54.8%	43.0%	57.0%
6	1974	119,301			119,278	HARRINGTON, MICHAEL J.	23	119,278 D		100.0%		100.0%
6	1972	218,078	78,381	MOSELEY, JAMES B.	139,697	HARRINGTON, MICHAEL J.	61,316 D	61,316 D	35.9%	64.1%	35.9%	64.1%
7	1980	155,783			155,759	MARKEY, EDWARD J.	24	155,759 D		100.0%		100.0%
7	1978	171,646			145,615	MARKEY, EDWARD J.	26,031	145,615 D		84.8%		100.0%
7	1976	210,809	37,063	DALY, RICHARD W.	162,126	MARKEY, EDWARD J.	11,620	125,063 D	17.6%	76.9%	18.6%	81.4%
7	1974	153,127			122,165	MACDONALD, TORBERT	30,962	122,165 D		79.8%		100.0%
7	1972	199,562	64,357	ALIBERTI, JOAN M.	135,193	MACDONALD, TORBERT	12	70,836 D	32.2%	67.7%	32.3%	67.7%
8	1980	164,183	35,477	BARNSTEAD, WILLIAM A.	128,689	O'NEILL, THOMAS P.	17	93,212 D	21.6%	78.4%	21.6%	78.4%
8	1978	136,928	28,566	BARNSTEAD, WILLIAM A.	102,160	O'NEILL, THOMAS P.	6,202	73,594 D	20.9%	74.6%	21.9%	78.1%
8	1976	178,850	33,437	BARNSTEAD, WILLIAM A.	133,131	O'NEILL, THOMAS P.	12,282	99,694 D	18.7%	74.4%	20.1%	79.9%
8	1974	121,845			107,042	O'NEILL, THOMAS P.	14,803	107,042 D		87.9%		100.0%
8	1972	160,687			142,470	O'NEILL, THOMAS P.	18,217	142,470 D		88.7%		100.0%
9	1980	104,046			104,010	MOAKLEY, JOHN J.	36	104,010 D		100.0%		100.0%
9	1978	116,338			106,805	MOAKLEY, JOHN J.	9,533	106,805 D		91.8%		100.0%
9	1976	149,371	34,547	CUNNINGHAM, ROBERT G.	103,901	MOAKLEY, JOHN J.	10,923	69,354 D	23.1%	69.6%	25.0%	75.0%
9	1974	106,158			94,804	MOAKLEY, JOHN J.	11,354	94,804 D		89.3%		100.0%
9	1972	163,288	23,177	MILLER, HOWARD M.	67,143	HICKS, LOUISE DAY	72,968	43,966 D	14.2%	41.1%	25.7%	74.3%
10	1980	217,433	131,794	HECKLER, MARGARET M.	85,629	McCARTHY, ROBERT E.	10	46,165 R	60.6%	39.4%	60.6%	39.4%
10	1978	166,957	102,080	HECKLER, MARGARET M.	64,868	MARINO, JOHN J.	9	37,212 R	61.1%	38.9%	61.1%	38.9%
10	1976	176,691	176,604	HECKLER, MARGARET M.			87	176,604 R	100.0%		100.0%	
10	1974	155,868	99,993	HECKLER, MARGARET M.	55,871	MONAHAN, BARRY F.	4	44,122 R	64.2%	35.8%	64.2%	35.8%
10	1972	161,765	161,708	HECKLER, MARGARET M.			57	161,708 R	100.0%		100.0%	
11	1980	137,122			137,066	DONNELLY, BRIAN J.	56	137,066 D		100.0%		100.0%
11	1978	145,722			133,644	DONNELLY, BRIAN J.	12,078	133,644 D		91.7%		100.0%
11	1976	191,055			131,789	BURKE, JAMES A.	59,266	131,789 D		69.0%		100.0%
11	1974	125,991			125,978	BURKE, JAMES A.	13	125,978 D		100.0%		100.0%
11	1972	154,453			154,397	BURKE, JAMES A.	56	154,397 D		100.0%		100.0%
12	1980	267,421	71,620	DOANE, PAUL V.	195,791	STUDDS, GERRY E.	10	124,171 D	26.8%	73.2%	26.8%	73.2%
12	1978	176,859			176,704	STUDDS, GERRY E.	155	176,704 D		99.9%		100.0%
12	1976	222,504			222,418	STUDDS, GERRY E.	86	222,418 D		100.0%		100.0%
12	1974	185,569	46,787	MACKAY, J. ALAN	138,779	STUDDS, GERRY E.	3	91,992 D	25.2%	74.8%	25.2%	74.8%
12	1972	234,305	116,592	WEEKS, WILLIAM D.	117,710	STUDDS, GERRY E.	3	1,118 D	49.8%	50.2%	49.8%	50.2%

MASSACHUSETTS

1980 GENERAL ELECTION

In addition to the county-by-county figures, data are presented for selected Massachusetts communities. Since not all jurisdictions of the state are listed in this special tabulation, state-wide totals are shown only with the county-by-county statistics.

President   Other vote was 382,539 Anderson (Anderson Coalition); 22,038 Clark (Libertarian); 3,735 DeBerry (Socialist Workers); 2,056 Commoner (write-in); 62 McReynolds (write-in); 34 Bubar (write-in); 19 Griswold (write-in); 2,382 scattered. Early uncorrected returns gave the Reagan (Republican) state-wide total as 1,056,223 and the DeBerry (Socialist Workers) state-wide total vote as 5,143.

Congress   Other vote was 20,247 Aubuchon (Independent) and 35 scattered in CD 2; 3,290 Batchelder (Citizens), 1,304 Gonzalez (Socialist Workers) and 78 scattered in CD 6; scattered in all other CD's.

1980 PRIMARIES

SEPTEMBER 16 REPUBLICAN

Congress   Unopposed in eight CD's. No candidates in CD's 7, 9 and 11. Contested as follows:

  CD 6   9,785 Thomas H. Trimarco; 9,550 William E. Bronson; 26 scattered.

SEPTEMBER 16 DEMOCRATIC

Congress   Unopposed in six CD's. Contested as follows:

  CD 2   38,811 Edward P. Boland; 11,999 Paul M. Kozikowski; 3,784 Alwin E. Hopfmann; 14 scattered.
  CD 4   42,162 Barney Frank; 37,694 Arthur J. Clark; 574 Robert B. Shaffer; 544 David J. Mofenson; 19 scattered.
  CD 5   41,207 James M. Shannon; 34,573 Robert F. Hatem; 5 scattered.
  CD 6   32,177 Nicholas Mavroules; 14,405 Kenneth G. Bellevue; 14 scattered.
  CD 7   29,190 Edward J. Markey; 5,247 James J. Murphy; 3 scattered.
  CD 10 21,006 Robert E. McCarthy; 13,471 M. Earle Gaudette; 2 scattered.

MICHIGAN

GOVERNOR

William G. Milliken (R). Re-elected 1978 to a four-year term. Previously elected 1974, 1970; as Lieutenant-Governor became Governor January 1969 on the resignation of Governor George W. Romney.

SENATORS

Carl Levin (D). Elected 1978 to a six-year term.

Donald W. Riegle (D). Elected 1976 to a six-year term.

REPRESENTATIVES

1. John Conyers (D)
2. Carl D. Pursell (R)
3. Howard Wolpe (D)
4. Dave Stockman (R) (see page 1)
5. Harold S. Sawyer (R)
6. Jim Dunn (R)
7. Dale E. Kildee (D)
8. J. Robert Traxler (D)
9. Guy Vander Jagt (R)
10. Donald J. Albosta (D)
11. Robert W. Davis (R)
12. David E. Bonior (D)
13. George W. Crockett (D)
14. Dennis M. Hertel (D)
15. William D. Ford (D)
16. John D. Dingell, Jr. (D)
17. William M. Brodhead (D)
18. James J. Blanchard (D)
19. William S. Broomfield (R)

POSTWAR VOTE FOR GOVERNOR

Year	Total Vote	Republican Vote	Candidate	Democratic Vote	Candidate	Other Vote	Rep.-Dem. Plurality	Rep.	Dem.	Rep.	Dem.
1978	2,867,212	1,628,485	Milliken, William G.	1,237,256	Fitzgerald, William	1,471	391,229 R	56.8%	43.2%	56.8%	43.2%
1974	2,657,017	1,356,865	Milliken, William G.	1,242,247	Levin, Sander	57,905	114,618 R	51.1%	46.8%	52.2%	47.8%
1970	2,656,162	1,339,047	Milliken, William G.	1,294,638	Levin, Sander	22,477	44,409 R	50.4%	48.7%	50.8%	49.2%
1966	2,461,909	1,490,430	Romney, George W.	963,383	Ferency, Zolton A.	8,096	527,047 R	60.5%	39.1%	60.7%	39.3%
1964	3,158,102	1,764,355	Romney, George W.	1,381,442	Staebler, Neil	12,305	382,913 R	55.9%	43.7%	56.1%	43.9%
1962	2,764,839	1,420,086	Romney, George W.	1,339,513	Swainson, John B.	5,240	80,573 R	51.4%	48.4%	51.5%	48.5%
1960	3,255,991	1,602,022	Bagwell, Paul D.	1,643,634	Swainson, John B.	10,335	41,612 D	49.2%	50.5%	49.4%	50.6%
1958	2,312,184	1,078,089	Bagwell, Paul D.	1,225,533	Williams, G. Mennen	8,562	147,444 D	46.6%	53.0%	46.8%	53.2%
1956	3,049,651	1,376,376	Cobo, Albert E.	1,666,689	Williams, G. Mennen	6,586	290,313 D	45.1%	54.7%	45.2%	54.8%
1954	2,187,027	963,300	Leonard, Donald S.	1,216,308	Williams, G. Mennen	7,419	253,008 D	44.0%	55.6%	44.2%	55.8%
1952	2,865,980	1,423,275	Alger, Fred M.	1,431,893	Williams, G. Mennen	10,812	8,618 D	49.7%	50.0%	49.8%	50.2%
1950	1,879,382	933,998	Kelly, Harry F.	935,152	Williams, G. Mennen	10,232	1,154 D	49.7%	49.8%	50.0%	50.0%
1948	2,113,122	964,810	Sigler, Kim	1,128,664	Williams, G. Mennen	19,648	163,854 D	45.7%	53.4%	46.1%	53.9%
1946	1,665,475	1,003,878	Sigler, Kim	644,540	Van Wagoner, Murray	17,057	359,338 R	60.3%	38.7%	60.9%	39.1%

The term of office of Michigan's Governor was increased from two to four years effective with the 1966 election.

POSTWAR VOTE FOR SENATOR

Year	Total Vote	Republican Vote	Candidate	Democratic Vote	Candidate	Other Vote	Rep.-Dem. Plurality	Rep.	Dem.	Rep.	Dem.
1978	2,846,630	1,362,165	Griffin, Robert P.	1,484,193	Levin, Carl	272	122,028 D	47.9%	52.1%	47.9%	52.1%
1976	3,490,664	1,635,087	Esch, Marvin L.	1,831,031	Riegle, Donald W.	24,546	195,944 D	46.8%	52.5%	47.2%	52.8%
1972	3,406,906	1,781,065	Griffin, Robert P.	1,577,178	Kelley, Frank J.	48,663	203,887 R	52.3%	46.3%	53.0%	47.0%
1970	2,610,839	858,470	Romney, Lenore	1,744,716	Hart, Philip A.	7,653	886,246 D	32.9%	66.8%	33.0%	67.0%
1966	2,439,365	1,363,530	Griffin, Robert P.	1,069,484	Williams, G. Mennen	6,351	294,046 R	55.9%	43.8%	56.0%	44.0%
1964	3,101,667	1,096,272	Peterson, Elly M.	1,996,912	Hart, Philip A.	8,483	900,640 D	35.3%	64.4%	35.4%	64.6%
1960	3,226,647	1,548,873	Bentley, Alvin M.	1,669,179	McNamara, Patrick V.	8,595	120,306 D	48.0%	51.7%	48.1%	51.9%
1958	2,271,644	1,046,963	Potter, Charles E.	1,216,966	Hart, Philip A.	7,715	170,003 D	46.1%	53.6%	46.2%	53.8%
1954	2,144,840	1,049,420	Ferguson, Homer	1,088,550	McNamara, Patrick V.	6,870	39,130 D	48.9%	50.8%	49.1%	50.9%
1952	2,821,133	1,428,352	Potter, Charles E.	1,383,416	Moody, Blair	9,365	44,936 R	50.6%	49.0%	50.8%	49.2%
1948	2,062,097	1,045,156	Ferguson, Homer	1,000,329	Hook, Frank E.	16,612	44,827 R	50.7%	48.5%	51.1%	48.9%
1946	1,618,720	1,085,570	Vandenberg, Arthur	517,923	Lee, James H.	15,227	567,647 R	67.1%	32.0%	67.7%	32.3%

MICHIGAN

Districts Established May 15, 1972

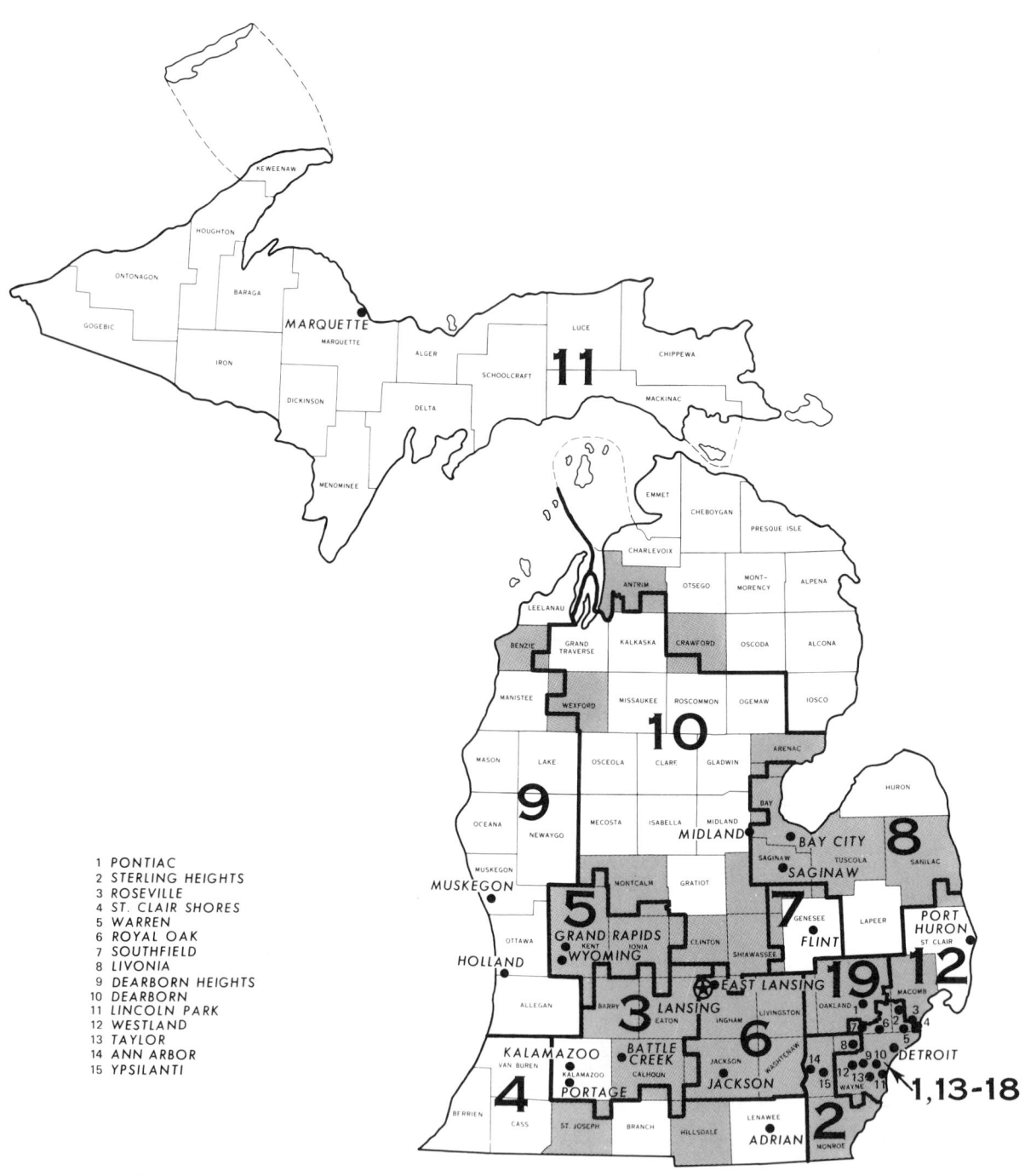

1 PONTIAC
2 STERLING HEIGHTS
3 ROSEVILLE
4 ST. CLAIR SHORES
5 WARREN
6 ROYAL OAK
7 SOUTHFIELD
8 LIVONIA
9 DEARBORN HEIGHTS
10 DEARBORN
11 LINCOLN PARK
12 WESTLAND
13 TAYLOR
14 ANN ARBOR
15 YPSILANTI

County with two or more Congressional Districts.

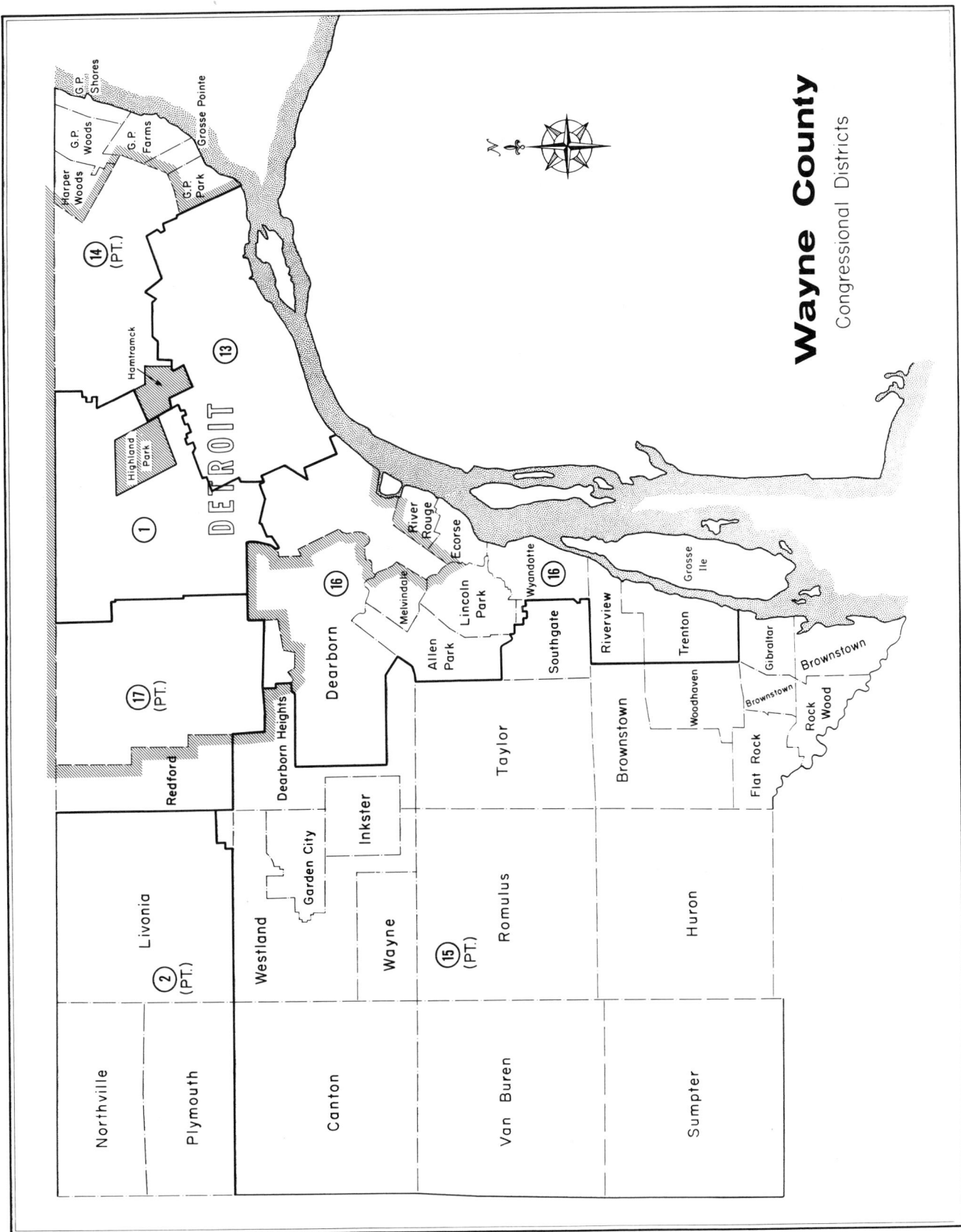

Wayne County
Congressional Districts

206

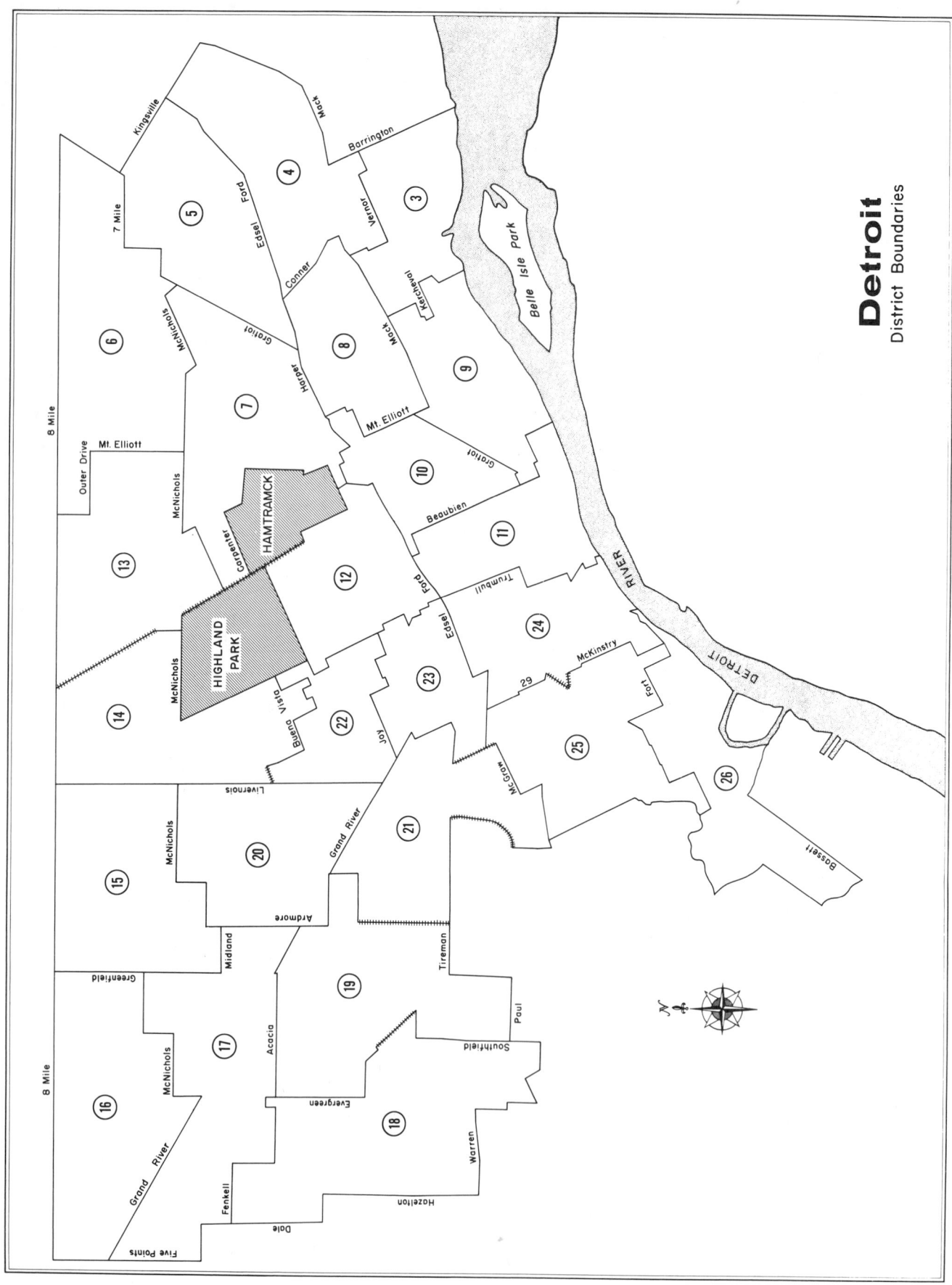

Detroit
District Boundaries

MICHIGAN

PRESIDENT 1980

1980 Census Population	County	Total Vote	Republican	Democratic	Other	Rep.-Dem. Plurality	Percentage Total Vote Rep.	Dem.	Major Vote Rep.	Dem.
9,740	ALCONA	5,062	2,905	1,857	300	1,048 R	57.4%	36.7%	61.0%	39.0%
9,225	ALGER	4,647	2,059	2,242	346	183 D	44.3%	48.2%	47.9%	52.1%
81,555	ALLEGAN	33,031	20,560	9,877	2,594	10,683 R	62.2%	29.9%	67.5%	32.5%
32,315	ALPENA	13,832	6,901	5,834	1,097	1,067 R	49.9%	42.2%	54.2%	45.8%
16,194	ANTRIM	8,364	4,706	2,909	749	1,797 R	56.3%	34.8%	61.8%	38.2%
14,706	ARENAC	6,431	3,436	2,547	448	889 R	53.4%	39.6%	57.4%	42.6%
8,484	BARAGA	3,921	2,046	1,609	266	437 R	52.2%	41.0%	56.0%	44.0%
45,781	BARRY	20,654	12,006	6,857	1,791	5,149 R	58.1%	33.2%	63.6%	36.4%
119,881	BAY	54,592	25,331	24,517	4,744	814 R	46.4%	44.9%	50.8%	49.2%
11,205	BENZIE	5,498	3,054	1,842	602	1,212 R	55.5%	33.5%	62.4%	37.6%
171,276	BERRIEN	67,978	41,458	22,152	4,368	19,306 R	61.0%	32.6%	65.2%	34.8%
40,188	BRANCH	16,230	10,224	4,635	1,371	5,589 R	63.0%	28.6%	68.8%	31.2%
141,557	CALHOUN	59,176	30,912	23,022	5,242	7,890 R	52.2%	38.9%	57.3%	42.7%
49,499	CASS	19,735	11,206	7,058	1,471	4,148 R	56.8%	35.8%	61.4%	38.6%
19,907	CHARLEVOIX	9,796	5,053	3,741	1,002	1,312 R	51.6%	38.2%	57.5%	42.5%
20,649	CHEBOYGAN	9,954	5,221	3,938	795	1,283 R	52.5%	39.6%	57.0%	43.0%
29,029	CHIPPEWA	13,494	7,059	5,268	1,167	1,791 R	52.3%	39.0%	57.3%	42.7%
23,822	CLARE	10,718	5,719	4,164	835	1,555 R	53.4%	38.9%	57.9%	42.1%
55,893	CLINTON	24,691	14,968	7,539	2,184	7,429 R	60.6%	30.5%	66.5%	33.5%
9,465	CRAWFORD	4,964	2,652	1,826	486	826 R	53.4%	36.8%	59.2%	40.8%
38,947	DELTA	17,692	8,146	8,475	1,071	329 D	46.0%	47.9%	49.0%	51.0%
25,341	DICKINSON	13,077	6,614	5,694	769	920 R	50.6%	43.5%	53.7%	46.3%
88,337	EATON	39,977	22,927	12,742	4,308	10,185 R	57.4%	31.9%	64.3%	35.7%
22,992	EMMET	11,006	5,930	3,724	1,352	2,206 R	53.9%	33.8%	61.4%	38.6%
450,449	GENESEE	183,900	78,572	90,393	14,935	11,821 D	42.7%	49.2%	46.5%	53.5%
19,957	GLADWIN	8,825	4,509	3,733	583	776 R	51.1%	42.3%	54.7%	45.3%
19,686	GOGEBIC	10,252	4,388	5,254	610	866 D	42.8%	51.2%	45.5%	54.5%
54,899	GRAND TRAVERSE	24,706	14,484	7,150	3,072	7,334 R	58.6%	28.9%	67.0%	33.0%
40,448	GRATIOT	15,670	9,294	4,916	1,460	4,378 R	59.3%	31.4%	65.4%	34.6%
42,071	HILLSDALE	16,501	10,951	4,375	1,175	6,576 R	66.4%	26.5%	71.5%	28.5%
37,872	HOUGHTON	16,534	7,926	6,858	1,750	1,068 R	47.9%	41.5%	53.6%	46.4%
36,459	HURON	16,167	10,553	4,434	1,180	6,119 R	65.3%	27.4%	70.4%	29.6%
272,437	INGHAM	125,631	56,777	48,278	20,576	8,499 R	45.2%	38.4%	54.0%	46.0%
51,815	IONIA	20,982	12,040	7,039	1,903	5,001 R	57.4%	33.5%	63.1%	36.9%
28,349	IOSCO	11,815	6,680	4,255	880	2,425 R	56.5%	36.0%	61.1%	38.9%
13,635	IRON	7,732	3,507	3,742	483	235 D	45.4%	48.4%	48.4%	51.6%
54,110	ISABELLA	20,715	10,407	7,293	3,015	3,114 R	50.2%	35.2%	58.8%	41.2%
151,495	JACKSON	62,580	33,749	23,685	5,146	10,064 R	53.9%	37.8%	58.8%	41.2%
212,378	KALAMAZOO	95,617	48,669	34,528	12,420	14,141 R	50.9%	36.1%	58.5%	41.5%
10,952	KALKASKA	4,966	2,802	1,807	357	995 R	56.4%	36.4%	60.8%	39.2%
444,506	KENT	206,290	112,604	72,790	20,896	39,814 R	54.6%	35.3%	60.7%	39.3%
1,963	KEWEENAW	1,260	583	570	107	13 R	46.3%	45.2%	50.6%	49.4%
7,711	LAKE	4,003	1,730	2,041	232	311 D	43.2%	51.0%	45.9%	54.1%
70,038	LAPEER	28,069	15,996	9,671	2,402	6,325 R	57.0%	34.5%	62.3%	37.7%
14,007	LEELANAU	7,935	4,585	2,348	1,002	2,237 R	57.8%	29.6%	66.1%	33.9%
89,948	LENAWEE	36,085	20,366	12,935	2,784	7,431 R	56.4%	35.8%	61.2%	38.8%
100,289	LIVINGSTON	41,570	25,012	12,626	3,932	12,386 R	60.2%	30.4%	66.5%	33.5%
6,659	LUCE	2,882	1,659	992	231	667 R	57.6%	34.4%	62.6%	37.4%
10,178	MACKINAC	5,784	3,021	2,262	501	759 R	52.2%	39.1%	57.2%	42.8%
694,600	MACOMB	297,119	154,155	120,125	22,839	34,030 R	51.9%	40.4%	56.2%	43.8%
23,019	MANISTEE	10,702	5,662	4,164	876	1,498 R	52.9%	38.9%	57.6%	42.4%
74,101	MARQUETTE	29,479	13,181	13,312	2,986	131 D	44.7%	45.2%	49.8%	50.2%
26,365	MASON	12,276	7,137	4,134	1,005	3,003 R	58.1%	33.7%	63.3%	36.7%
36,961	MECOSTA	14,528	7,754	5,228	1,546	2,526 R	53.4%	36.0%	59.7%	40.3%
26,201	MENOMINEE	11,749	6,170	4,962	617	1,208 R	52.5%	42.2%	55.4%	44.6%
73,578	MIDLAND	33,610	17,828	12,019	3,763	5,809 R	53.0%	35.8%	59.7%	40.3%
10,009	MISSAUKEE	5,075	3,221	1,563	291	1,658 R	63.5%	30.8%	67.3%	32.7%
134,659	MONROE	49,964	25,612	20,578	3,774	5,034 R	51.3%	41.2%	55.4%	44.6%
47,555	MONTCALM	19,150	10,822	6,706	1,622	4,116 R	56.5%	35.0%	61.7%	38.3%
7,492	MONTMORENCY	4,308	2,400	1,654	254	746 R	55.7%	38.4%	59.2%	40.8%
157,589	MUSKEGON	67,954	36,512	26,645	4,797	9,867 R	53.7%	39.2%	57.8%	42.2%
34,917	NEWAYGO	15,223	8,918	5,236	1,069	3,682 R	58.6%	34.4%	63.0%	37.0%
1,011,793	OAKLAND	463,328	253,211	164,869	45,248	88,342 R	54.7%	35.6%	60.6%	39.4%
22,002	OCEANA	9,564	5,465	3,386	713	2,079 R	57.1%	35.4%	61.7%	38.3%
16,436	OGEMAW	8,128	4,169	3,426	533	743 R	51.3%	42.2%	54.9%	45.1%
9,861	ONTONAGON	5,248	2,569	2,375	304	194 R	49.0%	45.3%	52.0%	48.0%
18,928	OSCEOLA	8,164	4,902	2,650	612	2,252 R	60.0%	32.5%	64.9%	35.1%
6,858	OSCODA	3,466	1,915	1,325	226	590 R	55.3%	38.2%	59.1%	40.9%
14,993	OTSEGO	7,023	3,771	2,666	586	1,105 R	53.7%	38.0%	58.6%	41.4%
157,174	OTTAWA	75,484	51,217	18,435	5,832	32,782 R	67.9%	24.4%	73.5%	26.5%

MICHIGAN

PRESIDENT 1980

1980 Census Population	County	Total Vote	Republican	Democratic	Other	Rep.-Dem. Plurality	Percentage Total Vote Rep.	Dem.	Major Vote Rep.	Dem.
14,267	PRESQUE ISLE	6,912	3,486	2,952	474	534 R	50.4%	42.7%	54.1%	45.9%
16,374	ROSCOMMON	9,659	5,280	3,763	616	1,517 R	54.7%	39.0%	58.4%	41.6%
228,059	SAGINAW	93,800	45,233	41,650	6,917	3,583 R	48.2%	44.4%	52.1%	47.9%
138,802	ST. CLAIR	55,778	31,021	20,410	4,347	10,611 R	55.6%	36.6%	60.3%	39.7%
56,083	ST. JOSEPH	21,570	13,631	6,318	1,621	7,313 R	63.2%	29.3%	68.3%	31.7%
40,789	SANILAC	18,117	12,158	4,898	1,061	7,260 R	67.1%	27.0%	71.3%	28.7%
8,575	SCHOOLCRAFT	4,374	2,097	1,964	313	133 R	47.9%	44.9%	51.6%	48.4%
71,140	SHIAWASSEE	30,470	15,756	11,985	2,729	3,771 R	51.7%	39.3%	56.8%	43.2%
56,961	TUSCOLA	22,505	13,306	7,632	1,567	5,674 R	59.1%	33.9%	63.5%	36.5%
66,814	VAN BUREN	25,824	14,451	9,248	2,125	5,203 R	56.0%	35.8%	61.0%	39.0%
264,748	WASHTENAW	116,179	48,699	51,013	16,467	2,314 D	41.9%	43.9%	48.8%	51.2%
2,337,240	WAYNE	890,844	315,532	522,024	53,288	206,492 D	35.4%	58.6%	37.7%	62.3%
25,102	WEXFORD	11,160	6,027	4,173	960	1,854 R	54.0%	37.4%	59.1%	40.9%
9,258,344	TOTAL	3,909,725	1,915,225	1,661,532	332,968	253,693 R	49.0%	42.5%	53.5%	46.5%

DETROIT

PRESIDENT 1980

1980 Census Population	District	Total Vote	Republican	Democratic	Other	Rep.-Dem. Plurality	Total Vote Rep.	Total Vote Dem.	Major Vote Rep.	Major Vote Dem.
37,383	DISTRICT 3	9,614	607	8,821	186	8,214 D	6.3%	91.8%	6.4%	93.6%
58,491	DISTRICT 4	16,226	5,018	10,143	1,065	5,125 D	30.9%	62.5%	33.1%	66.9%
59,698	DISTRICT 5	17,505	6,708	9,566	1,231	2,858 D	38.3%	54.6%	41.2%	58.8%
56,109	DISTRICT 6	18,620	7,458	9,987	1,175	2,529 D	40.1%	53.6%	42.8%	57.2%
49,876	DISTRICT 7	12,992	2,278	10,291	423	8,013 D	17.5%	79.2%	18.1%	81.9%
43,206	DISTRICT 8	14,220	237	13,890	93	13,653 D	1.7%	97.7%	1.7%	98.3%
37,217	DISTRICT 9	11,747	1,215	10,024	508	8,809 D	10.3%	85.3%	10.8%	89.2%
27,565	DISTRICT 10	7,473	525	6,822	126	6,297 D	7.0%	91.3%	7.1%	92.9%
29,780	DISTRICT 11	6,684	829	5,421	434	4,592 D	12.4%	81.1%	13.3%	86.7%
41,302	DISTRICT 12	11,187	403	10,585	199	10,182 D	3.6%	94.6%	3.7%	96.3%
57,607	DISTRICT 13	17,398	1,587	15,434	377	13,847 D	9.1%	88.7%	9.3%	90.7%
60,103	DISTRICT 14	17,411	1,613	15,003	795	13,390 D	9.3%	86.2%	9.7%	90.3%
70,315	DISTRICT 15	25,130	671	24,089	370	23,418 D	2.7%	95.9%	2.7%	97.3%
65,318	DISTRICT 16	19,303	3,914	14,486	903	10,572 D	20.3%	75.0%	21.3%	78.7%
69,142	DISTRICT 17	20,860	5,091	14,427	1,342	9,336 D	24.4%	69.2%	26.1%	73.9%
56,235	DISTRICT 18	17,409	7,014	9,166	1,229	2,152 D	40.3%	52.7%	43.3%	56.7%
64,920	DISTRICT 19	17,212	2,788	13,821	603	11,033 D	16.2%	80.3%	16.8%	83.2%
63,436	DISTRICT 20	19,119	403	18,550	166	18,147 D	2.1%	97.0%	2.1%	97.9%
59,270	DISTRICT 21	17,482	1,319	15,867	296	14,548 D	7.5%	90.8%	7.7%	92.3%
47,502	DISTRICT 22	14,378	235	14,026	117	13,791 D	1.6%	97.6%	1.6%	98.4%
38,187	DISTRICT 23	12,098	155	11,857	86	11,702 D	1.3%	98.0%	1.3%	98.7%
29,360	DISTRICT 24	7,026	679	6,122	225	5,443 D	9.7%	87.1%	10.0%	90.0%
52,855	DISTRICT 25	11,776	3,770	7,408	598	3,638 D	32.0%	62.9%	33.7%	66.3%
26,003	DISTRICT 26	7,414	889	6,313	212	5,424 D	12.0%	85.1%	12.3%	87.7%
	ABSENTEE	56,470	17,187	37,097	2,186	19,910 D	30.4%	65.7%	31.7%	68.3%
1,203,339	TOTAL	406,754	72,593	319,216	14,945	246,623 D	17.8%	78.5%	18.5%	81.5%

MICHIGAN

CONGRESS

CD	Year	Total Vote	Republican Vote	Republican Candidate	Democratic Vote	Democratic Candidate	Other Vote	Rep.-Dem. Plurality	Total Vote Rep.	Total Vote Dem.	Major Vote Rep.	Major Vote Dem.
1	1980	130,230	6,244	BELL, WILLIAM M.	123,286	CONYERS, JOHN	700	117,042 D	4.8%	94.7%	4.8%	95.2%
1	1978	96,526	6,878	ARNOLD, ROBERT S.	89,646	CONYERS, JOHN	2	82,768 D	7.1%	92.9%	7.1%	92.9%
1	1976	136,585	8,927	HOOD, ISAAC	126,161	CONYERS, JOHN	1,497	117,234 D	6.5%	92.4%	6.6%	93.4%
1	1974	107,573	9,358	GIRARDOT, WALTER F.	97,620	CONYERS, JOHN	595	88,262 D	8.7%	90.7%	8.7%	91.3%
1	1972	148,603	16,096	GIRARDOT, WALTER F.	131,353	CONYERS, JOHN	1,154	115,257 D	10.8%	88.4%	10.9%	89.1%
2	1980	201,801	115,562	PURSELL, CARL D.	83,550	O'REILLY, KATHLEEN F.	2,689	32,012 R	57.3%	41.4%	58.0%	42.0%
2	1978	144,326	97,503	PURSELL, CARL D.	45,631	GREENE, EARL	1,192	51,872 R	67.6%	31.6%	68.1%	31.9%
2	1976	191,746	95,397	PURSELL, CARL D.	95,053	PIERCE, EDWARD C.	1,296	344 R	49.8%	49.6%	50.1%	49.9%
2	1974	138,160	72,245	ESCH, MARVIN L.	62,755	REUTHER, JOHN S.	3,160	9,490 R	52.3%	45.4%	53.5%	46.5%
2	1972	184,396	103,321	ESCH, MARVIN L.	79,762	STEMPIEN, MARVIN R.	1,313	23,559 R	56.0%	43.3%	56.4%	43.6%
3	1980	217,414	102,591	GILMORE, JAMES S.	113,080	WOLPE, HOWARD	1,743	10,489 D	47.2%	52.0%	47.6%	52.4%
3	1978	163,510	79,572	BROWN, GARRY	83,932	WOLPE, HOWARD	6	4,360 D	48.7%	51.3%	48.7%	51.3%
3	1976	196,163	99,231	BROWN, GARRY	95,261	WOLPE, HOWARD	1,671	3,970 R	50.6%	48.6%	51.0%	49.0%
3	1974	137,139	70,157	BROWN, GARRY	65,212	TODD, PAUL H.	1,770	4,945 R	51.2%	47.6%	51.8%	48.2%
3	1972	185,937	110,082	BROWN, GARRY	74,114	BRIGNALL, JAMES T.	1,741	35,968 R	59.2%	39.9%	59.8%	40.2%
4	1980	199,292	148,950	STOCKMAN, DAVE	47,777	FURST, LYNDON G.	2,565	101,173 R	74.7%	24.0%	75.7%	24.3%
4	1978	135,108	95,440	STOCKMAN, DAVE	38,204	HAGER, MORGAN L.	1,464	57,236 R	70.6%	28.3%	71.4%	28.6%
4	1976	179,746	107,881	STOCKMAN, DAVE	69,655	DAUGHERTY, RICHARD E.	2,210	38,226 R	60.0%	38.8%	60.8%	39.2%
4	1974	121,925	64,731	HUTCHINSON, EDWARD	55,469	DAUGHERTY, RICHARD E.	1,725	9,262 R	53.1%	45.5%	53.9%	46.1%
4	1972	165,326	111,185	HUTCHINSON, EDWARD	54,141	JAMESON, CHARLES W.		57,044 R	67.3%	32.7%	67.3%	32.7%
5	1980	222,158	118,061	SAWYER, HAROLD S.	101,737	SPRIK, DALE R.	2,360	16,324 R	53.1%	45.8%	53.7%	46.3%
5	1978	165,446	81,794	SAWYER, HAROLD S.	80,622	SPRIK, DALE R.	3,030	1,172 R	49.4%	48.7%	50.4%	49.6%
5	1976	205,452	109,589	SAWYER, HAROLD S.	94,973	VANDER VEEN, RICHARD F.	890	14,616 R	53.3%	46.2%	53.6%	46.4%
5	1974	153,475	66,659	GOEBEL, PAUL G.	80,778	VANDER VEEN, RICHARD F.	6,038	14,119 D	43.4%	52.6%	45.2%	54.8%
5	1972	193,229	118,027	FORD, GERALD R.	72,782	MCKEE, JEAN	2,420	45,245 R	61.1%	37.7%	61.9%	38.1%
6	1980	219,826	111,272	DUNN, JIM	108,548	CARR, M. ROBERT	6	2,724 R	50.6%	49.4%	50.6%	49.4%
6	1978	172,706	74,718	CONLIN, MIKE	97,971	CARR, M. ROBERT	17	23,253 D	43.3%	56.7%	43.3%	56.7%
6	1976	206,514	96,008	TAYLOR, CLIFFORD W.	108,909	CARR, M. ROBERT	1,597	12,901 D	46.5%	52.7%	46.9%	53.1%
6	1974	149,986	73,309	TAYLOR, CLIFFORD W.	73,956	CARR, M. ROBERT	2,721	647 D	48.9%	49.3%	49.8%	50.2%
6	1972	192,875	97,666	CHAMBERLAIN, C. E.	95,209	CARR, M. ROBERT		2,457 R	50.6%	49.4%	50.6%	49.4%
7	1980	158,803			147,280	KILDEE, DALE E.	11,523	147,280 D		92.7%		100.0%
7	1978	137,540	29,958	CRONK, GALE M.	105,402	KILDEE, DALE E.	2,180	75,444 D	21.8%	76.6%	22.1%	77.9%
7	1976	177,582	50,301	WIDGERY, ROBIN	124,260	KILDEE, DALE E.	3,021	73,959 D	28.3%	70.0%	28.8%	71.2%
7	1974	125,129	41,603	EASTMAN, ROBERT E.	81,014	RIEGLE, DONALD W.	2,512	39,411 D	33.2%	64.7%	33.9%	66.1%
7	1972	163,539	114,656	RIEGLE, DONALD W.	48,883	MATTISON, EUGENE L.		65,773 R	70.1%	29.9%	70.1%	29.9%
8	1980	204,401	77,009	HUGHES, NORMAN R.	124,155	TRAXLER, J. ROBERT	3,237	47,146 D	37.7%	60.7%	38.3%	61.7%
8	1978	155,248	51,900	HUGHES, NORMAN R.	103,346	TRAXLER, J. ROBERT	2	51,446 D	33.4%	66.6%	33.4%	66.6%
8	1976	186,632	75,323	DENTON, E. BRADY	110,127	TRAXLER, J. ROBERT	1,182	34,804 D	40.4%	59.0%	40.6%	59.4%
8	1974	141,854	61,578	SPARLING, JAMES M.	77,795	TRAXLER, J. ROBERT	2,481	16,217 D	43.4%	54.8%	44.2%	55.8%
8	1972	169,750	100,597	HARVEY, JAMES	66,873	HART, JEROME	2,280	33,724 R	59.3%	39.4%	60.1%	39.9%
9	1980	174,776	168,713	VANDER JAGT, GUY			6,063	168,713 R	96.5%		100.0%	
9	1978	175,819	122,363	VANDER JAGT, GUY	53,450	LEROUX, HOWARD M.	6	68,913 R	69.6%	30.4%	69.6%	30.4%
9	1976	209,704	146,712	VANDER JAGT, GUY	61,641	FAWLEY, STEPHEN E.	1,351	85,071 R	70.0%	29.4%	70.4%	29.6%
9	1974	154,811	87,551	VANDER JAGT, GUY	65,235	HALBOWER, NORM	2,025	22,316 R	56.6%	42.1%	57.3%	42.7%
9	1972	190,614	132,268	VANDER JAGT, GUY	56,236	OLSON, LARRY H.	2,110	76,032 R	69.4%	29.5%	70.2%	29.8%
10	1980	242,252	111,496	ALLEN, RICHARD J.	126,962	ALBOSTA, DONALD J.	3,794	15,466 D	46.0%	52.4%	46.8%	53.2%
10	1978	184,389	89,451	CEDERBERG, ELFORD A.	94,913	ALBOSTA, DONALD J.	25	5,462 D	48.5%	51.5%	48.5%	51.5%
10	1976	210,191	118,726	CEDERBERG, ELFORD A.	89,980	ALBOSTA, DONALD J.	1,485	28,746 R	56.5%	42.8%	56.9%	43.1%
10	1974	146,937	78,897	CEDERBERG, ELFORD A.	67,467	MARBLE, SAMUEL D.	573	11,430 R	53.7%	45.9%	53.9%	46.1%
10	1972	181,886	121,368	CEDERBERG, ELFORD A.	56,149	GRAVES, BENNIE D.	4,369	65,219 R	66.7%	30.9%	68.4%	31.6%
11	1980	223,139	146,205	DAVIS, ROBERT W.	75,515	DORRITY, DAN	1,419	70,690 R	65.5%	33.8%	65.9%	34.1%
11	1978	175,435	96,351	DAVIS, ROBERT W.	79,081	MCLEOD, KEITH	3	17,270 R	54.9%	45.1%	54.9%	45.1%
11	1976	217,117	118,871	RUPPE, PHILIP E.	97,325	BROUILLETTE, FRANCIS D.	921	21,546 R	54.7%	44.8%	55.0%	45.0%
11	1974	163,536	83,293	RUPPE, PHILIP E.	79,793	BROUILLETTE, FRANCIS D.	450	3,500 R	50.9%	48.8%	51.1%	48.9%
11	1972	195,609	135,786	RUPPE, PHILIP E.	58,334	MCNAMARA, JAMES E.	1,489	77,452 R	69.4%	29.8%	69.9%	30.1%
12	1980	203,647	90,931	WALSH, KIRK	112,698	BONIOR, DAVID E.	18	21,767 D	44.7%	55.3%	44.7%	55.3%
12	1978	150,956	68,063	HOLMES, KIRBY	82,892	BONIOR, DAVID E.	1	14,829 D	45.1%	54.9%	45.1%	54.9%
12	1976	180,877	85,326	SEROTKIN, DAVID M.	94,815	BONIOR, DAVID E.	736	9,489 D	47.2%	52.4%	47.4%	52.6%
12	1974	124,415	34,293	TYZA, EUGENE J.	89,822	O'HARA, JAMES G.	300	55,529 D	27.6%	72.2%	27.6%	72.4%
12	1972	164,018	80,667	SEROTKIN, DAVID M.	83,351	O'HARA, JAMES G.		2,684 D	49.2%	50.8%	49.2%	50.8%

MICHIGAN

CONGRESS

CD	Year	Total Vote	Republican Vote	Candidate	Democratic Vote	Candidate	Other Vote	Rep.-Dem. Plurality	Total Vote Rep.	Total Vote Dem.	Major Vote Rep.	Major Vote Dem.
13	1980	87,090	6,473	HURD, M. MICHAEL	79,719	CROCKETT, GEORGE W.	898	73,246 D	7.4%	91.5%	7.5%	92.5%
13	1978	56,543	11,749	PICKETT, DOVIE T.	44,771	DIGGS, CHARLES C.	23	33,022 D	20.8%	79.2%	20.8%	79.2%
13	1976	93,690	9,002	GOLDEN, RICHARD A.	83,387	DIGGS, CHARLES C.	1,301	74,385 D	9.6%	89.0%	9.7%	90.3%
13	1974	72,403	8,036	MCCALL, GEORGE E.	63,246	DIGGS, CHARLES C.	1,121	55,210 D	11.1%	87.4%	11.3%	88.7%
13	1972	113,928	15,180	EDWARDS, LEONARD T.	97,562	DIGGS, CHARLES C.	1,186	82,382 D	13.3%	85.6%	13.5%	86.5%
14	1980	169,666	78,395	CAPUTO, VIC	90,362	HERTEL, DENNIS M.	909	11,967 D	46.2%	53.3%	46.5%	53.5%
14	1978	124,756	40,716	GETZ, JOHN E.	84,032	NEDZI, LUCIEN N.	8	43,316 D	32.6%	67.4%	32.6%	67.4%
14	1976	161,668	52,995	GETZ, JOHN E.	107,503	NEDZI, LUCIEN N.	1,170	54,508 D	32.8%	66.5%	33.0%	67.0%
14	1974	131,925	35,723	STEIGER, HERBERT O.	93,973	NEDZI, LUCIEN N.	2,229	58,250 D	27.1%	71.2%	27.5%	72.5%
14	1972	171,196	77,273	MCGRATH, ROBERT V.	93,923	NEDZI, LUCIEN N.		16,650 D	45.1%	54.9%	45.1%	54.9%
15	1980	167,795	53,046	CARLSON, GERALD R.	113,492	FORD, WILLIAM D.	1,257	60,446 D	31.6%	67.6%	31.9%	68.1%
15	1978	119,545	23,177	NIETEN, EDGAR	95,137	FORD, WILLIAM D.	1,231	71,960 D	19.4%	79.6%	19.6%	80.4%
15	1976	158,553	39,177	WALASKAY, JAMES D.	117,313	FORD, WILLIAM D.	2,063	78,136 D	24.7%	74.0%	25.0%	75.0%
15	1974	110,910	23,028	UNDERWOOD, JACK A.	86,601	FORD, WILLIAM D.	1,281	63,573 D	20.8%	78.1%	21.0%	79.0%
15	1972	147,530	48,504	FACKLER, ERNEST C.	97,054	FORD, WILLIAM D.	1,972	48,550 D	32.9%	65.8%	33.3%	66.7%
16	1980	151,465	42,735	SEAY, PAMELLA A.	105,844	DINGELL, JOHN D., JR.	2,886	63,109 D	28.2%	69.9%	28.8%	71.2%
16	1978	122,111	26,827	HEUER, MELVIN E.	93,387	DINGELL, JOHN D., JR.	1,897	66,560 D	22.0%	76.5%	22.3%	77.7%
16	1976	160,351	36,378	ROSTRON, WILLIAM E.	121,682	DINGELL, JOHN D., JR.	2,291	85,304 D	22.7%	75.9%	23.0%	77.0%
16	1974	123,284	25,248	ENGLISH, WALLACE D.	95,834	DINGELL, JOHN D., JR.	2,202	70,586 D	20.5%	77.7%	20.9%	79.1%
16	1972	162,683	48,414	ROSTRON, WILLIAM E.	110,715	DINGELL, JOHN D., JR.	3,554	62,301 D	29.8%	68.1%	30.4%	69.6%
17	1980	174,528	44,313	PATTERSON, ALFRED L.	127,525	BRODHEAD, WILLIAM M.	2,690	83,212 D	25.4%	73.1%	25.8%	74.2%
17	1978	111,654			106,303	BRODHEAD, WILLIAM M.	5,351	106,303 D		95.2%		100.0%
17	1976	175,474	60,476	·BURDICK, JAMES W.	112,746	BRODHEAD, WILLIAM M.	2,252	52,270 D	34.5%	64.3%	34.9%	65.1%
17	1974	135,674	39,856	GALLAGHER, KENNETH C.	94,242	BRODHEAD, WILLIAM M.	1,576	54,386 D	29.4%	69.5%	29.7%	70.3%
17	1972	185,633	60,337	JUDD, RALPH E.	123,331	GRIFFITHS, MARTHA W.	1,965	62,994 D	32.5%	66.4%	32.9%	67.1%
18	1980	207,977	68,575	SUIDA, BETTY J.	135,705	BLANCHARD, JAMES J.	3,697	67,130 D	33.0%	65.3%	33.6%	66.4%
18	1978	151,798	36,913	SALLOUM, ROBERT J.	113,037	BLANCHARD, JAMES J.	1,848	76,124 D	24.3%	74.5%	24.6%	75.4%
18	1976	186,196	60,995	OLSEN, JOHN E.	123,113	BLANCHARD, JAMES J.	2,088	62,118 D	32.8%	66.1%	33.1%	66.9%
18	1974	142,232	57,133	HUBER, ROBERT J.	83,523	BLANCHARD, JAMES J.	1,576	26,390 D	40.2%	58.7%	40.6%	59.4%
18	1972	180,633	95,053	HUBER, ROBERT J.	85,580	COOPER, DANIEL S.		9,473 R	52.6%	47.4%	52.6%	47.4%
19	1980	231,894	168,530	BROOMFIELD, WILLIAM S.	60,100	DANIELS, WAYNE E.	3,264	108,430 R	72.7%	25.9%	73.7%	26.3%
19	1978	164,298	117,122	BROOMFIELD, WILLIAM S.	47,165	COLLIER, BETTY F.	11	69,957 R	71.3%	28.7%	71.3%	28.7%
19	1976	197,649	131,799	BROOMFIELD, WILLIAM S.	64,337	BECKER, DOROTHEA	1,513	67,462 R	66.7%	32.6%	67.2%	32.8%
19	1974	138,052	86,846	BROOMFIELD, WILLIAM S.	50,924	MONTGOMERY, GEORGE F.	282	35,922 R	62.9%	36.9%	63.0%	37.0%
19	1972	175,789	123,697	BROOMFIELD, WILLIAM S.	50,355	MONTGOMERY, GEORGE F.	1,737	73,342 R	70.4%	28.6%	71.1%	28.9%

MICHIGAN

1980 GENERAL ELECTION

President   Other vote was 275,223 Anderson (Anderson Coalition); 41,597 Clark (Libertarian); 11,930 Commoner (Citizens); 3,262 Hall (Independent); 30 Griswold (write-in); 21 Greaves (write-in); 9 Bubar (write-in); 5 Rarick (write-in); 891 scattered.

Congress   Other vote was 699 Jones (Libertarian) and 1 scattered in CD 1; 1,464 Hudler (Libertarian), 1,214 Wagner (American Independent) and 11 scattered in CD 2; 891 Todd (Libertarian), 843 Wells (American Independent) and 9 scattered in CD 3; 1,644 Smith (Libertarian), 915 Drenkhahn (American Independent) and 6 scattered in CD 4; 2,321 Smith (Libertarian) and 39 scattered in CD 5; scattered in CD 6; 11,507 Berry (Libertarian) and 16 scattered in CD 7; 3,230 Hart (Libertarian) and 7 scattered in CD 8; 5,985 Tufts (American Independent) and 78 scattered in CD 9; 2,530 Dechow (Libertarian), 1,254 Isaac (American Independent) and 10 scattered in CD 10; 1,363 Stariha (American Independent) and 56 scattered in CD 11; scattered in CD 12; 886 Roddis (Libertarian) and 12 scattered in CD 13; 904 Little (Libertarian) and 5 scattered in CD 14; 1,175 Fuhrman (American Independent) and 82 scattered in CD 15; 1,810 Davidson (Libertarian), 1,069 Slote (American Independent) and 7 scattered in CD 16; 2,667 Krebaum (Libertarian) and 23 scattered in CD 17; 2,323 Erwin (Libertarian), 1,373 Neal (American Independent) and 1 scattered in CD 18; 3,263 Wright (Libertarian) and 1 scattered in CD 19.

DETROIT

The total of the 1980 population data by districts in Detroit will be some 3,000 short of the stated total as this small portion was not allocated by precinct by the Census Bureau.

President   Other vote was 11,485 Anderson (Anderson Coalition); 1,815 Clark (Libertarian); 1,138 Commoner (Citizens); 507 Hall (Independent).

1980 PRIMARIES

AUGUST 5 REPUBLICAN

Congress   Unopposed in nine CD's. No candidate in CD 7. Contested as follows:

CD 2   11,946 Carl D. Pursell; 1,383 Helen T. Gotowka; 1 scattered.
CD 5   23,970 Harold S. Sawyer; 5,484 Bruce H. Kamps; 19 scattered.
CD 6   21,270 Jim Dunn; 5,063 Aubrey Radcliffe; 3 scattered.
CD 10   30,197 Richard J. Allen; 15,710 Bill Smith; 12,531 John M. Pafford; 6 scattered.
CD 12   10,328 Kirk Walsh; 5,012 Bill Froberg; 2,582 Eugene J. Tyza; 6 scattered.
CD 13   338 M. Michael Hurd; 322 Theodore C. Wallace; 247 Jerome P. Barney; 226 Charlita A. Blair; 1 scattered.
CD 14   11,707 Vic Caputo; 2,031 John Lauve; 759 John J. Cunningham; 449 Mark E. Wise; 1 scattered.
CD 15   3,763 Gerald R. Carlson; 3,078 James A. Caygill.
CD 17   4,468 Alfred L. Patterson; 2,566 Raymond Cochran; 2,059 Arve Bakken.

AUGUST 5 DEMOCRATIC

Congress   Unopposed in ten CD's. No candidate in CD 9. Contested as follows:

CD 5   9,207 Dale R. Sprik; 8,040 Stephen V. Monsma.
CD 6   11,134 M. Robert Carr; 2,082 Russell Severance; 1 scattered.
CD 11   14,864 Dan Dorrity; 11,646 Herbert Stephens; 11,437 Theodore Albert; 20 scattered.
CD 12   20,383 David E. Bonior; 2,399 Owen O. Love; 1,842 Anthony J. Polselli; 95 scattered.
CD 13   8,810 George W. Crockett; 4,187 David S. Holmes; 3,373 Clyde Cleveland; 3,364 Nicholas Houd; 337 Dennis L. Gibson; 328 Henry Stallings; 170 Norville Hendrieth; 150 David Boston; 142 Nathaniel Coakley; 110 Lorenzo Montgomery; 100 James D. Jackson; 98 Andrew J. Ridley; 32 scattered.

MICHIGAN

CD 14   20,595 Dennis M. Hertel; 6,188 John Kelly; 3,389 Walter J. Gajewski; 1,477 Helen M. Irving; 743 Larry Rocca; 323 Richard T. Kuszmar; 201 Peter A. Signorelli; 114 Herbert H. Schebor.
CD 16   21,780 John D. Dingell, Jr.; 2,906 Malcolm F. Beaton.
CD 19   3,880 Wayne E. Daniels; 2,887 L. J. Peterson; 1,303 James M. Pidgeon; 1 scattered.

MINNESOTA

GOVERNOR
Albert H. Quie (R). Elected 1978 to a four-year term.

SENATORS
Rudy Boschwitz (R). Elected 1978 to a six-year term.

David Durenberger (R). Elected 1978 to fill out the remaining four years of the term vacated by the death of Senator Hubert H. Humphrey.

REPRESENTATIVES

1. Arlen Erdahl (R)
2. Tom Hagedorn (R)
3. Bill Frenzel (R)
4. Bruce F. Vento (D)
5. Martin O. Sabo (D)
6. Vin Weber (R)
7. Arlan Stangeland (R)
8. James L. Oberstar (D)

POSTWAR VOTE FOR GOVERNOR

Year	Total Vote	Republican Vote	Candidate	Democratic Vote	Candidate	Other Vote	Rep.-Dem. Plurality	Total Vote Rep.	Dem.	Major Vote Rep.	Dem.
1978	1,585,702	830,019	Quie, Albert H.	718,244	Perpich, Rudy	37,439	111,775 R	52.3%	45.3%	53.6%	46.4%
1974	1,252,898	367,722	Johnson, John W.	786,787	Anderson, Wendell R.	98,389	419,065 D	29.3%	62.8%	31.9%	68.1%
1970	1,365,443	621,780	Head, Douglas M.	737,921	Anderson, Wendell R.	5,742	116,141 D	45.5%	54.0%	45.7%	54.3%
1966	1,295,058	680,593	LeVander, Harold	607,943	Rolvaag, Karl F.	6,522	72,650 R	52.6%	46.9%	52.8%	47.2%
1962	1,246,904	619,751	Andersen, Elmer L.	619,842	Rolvaag, Karl F.	7,311	91 D	49.7%	49.7%	50.0%	50.0%
1960	1,550,265	783,813	Andersen, Elmer L.	760,934	Freeman, Orville L.	5,518	22,879 R	50.6%	49.1%	50.7%	49.3%
1958	1,159,915	490,731	MacKinnon, George	658,326	Freeman, Orville L.	10,858	167,595 D	42.3%	56.8%	42.7%	57.3%
1956	1,422,161	685,196	Nelsen, Ancher	731,180	Freeman, Orville L.	5,785	45,984 D	48.2%	51.4%	48.4%	51.6%
1954	1,151,417	538,865	Anderson, C. Elmer	607,099	Freeman, Orville L.	5,453	68,234 D	46.8%	52.7%	47.0%	53.0%
1952	1,418,869	785,125	Anderson, C. Elmer	624,480	Freeman, Orville L.	9,264	160,645 R	55.3%	44.0%	55.7%	44.3%
1950	1,046,632	635,800	Youngdahl, Luther	400,637	Peterson, Harry H.	10,195	235,163 R	60.7%	38.3%	61.3%	38.7%
1948	1,210,894	643,572	Youngdahl, Luther	545,766	Halsted, Charles L.	21,556	97,806 R	53.1%	45.1%	54.1%	45.9%
1946	880,348	519,067	Youngdahl, Luther	349,565	Barker, Harold H.	11,716	169,502 R	59.0%	39.7%	59.8%	40.2%

The term of office of Minnesota's Governor was increased from two to four years effective with the 1962 election.

POSTWAR VOTE FOR SENATOR

Year	Total Vote	Republican Vote	Candidate	Democratic Vote	Candidate	Other Vote	Rep.-Dem. Plurality	Total Vote Rep.	Dem.	Major Vote Rep.	Dem.
1978	1,580,778	894,092	Boschwitz, Rudy	638,375	Anderson, Wendell R.	48,311	255,717 R	56.6%	40.4%	58.3%	41.7%
1978s	1,560,724	957,908	Durenberger, David	538,675	Short, Robert E.	64,141	419,233 R	61.4%	34.5%	64.0%	36.0%
1976	1,912,068	478,611	Brekke, Gerald W.	1,290,736	Humphrey, Hubert H.	142,721	812,125 D	25.0%	67.5%	27.1%	72.9%
1972	1,731,653	742,121	Hansen, Philip	981,340	Mondale, Walter F.	8,192	239,219 D	42.9%	56.7%	43.1%	56.9%
1970	1,364,887	568,025	MacGregor, Clark	788,256	Humphrey, Hubert H.	8,606	220,231 D	41.6%	57.8%	41.9%	58.1%
1966	1,271,426	574,868	Forsythe, Robert A.	685,840	Mondale, Walter F.	10,718	110,972 D	45.2%	53.9%	45.6%	54.4%
1964	1,543,590	605,933	Whitney, Wheelock	931,353	McCarthy, Eugene J.	6,304	325,420 D	39.3%	60.3%	39.4%	60.6%
1960	1,536,839	648,586	Peterson, P. K.	884,168	Humphrey, Hubert H.	4,085	235,582 D	42.2%	57.5%	42.3%	57.7%
1958	1,150,883	536,629	Thye, Edward J.	608,847	McCarthy, Eugene J.	5,407	72,218 D	46.6%	52.9%	46.8%	53.2%
1954	1,138,952	479,619	Bjornson, Val	642,193	Humphrey, Hubert H.	17,140	162,574 D	42.1%	56.4%	42.8%	57.2%
1952	1,387,419	785,649	Thye, Edward J.	590,011	Carlson, William E.	11,759	195,638 R	56.6%	42.5%	57.1%	42.9%
1948	1,220,250	485,801	Ball, Joseph H.	729,494	Humphrey, Hubert H.	4,955	243,693 D	39.8%	59.8%	40.0%	60.0%
1946	878,731	517,775	Thye, Edward J.	349,520	Jorgenson, Theodore	11,436	168,255 R	58.9%	39.8%	59.7%	40.3%

One of the 1978 elections was for a short term to fill a vacancy.

MINNESOTA

Districts Established June 7, 1971

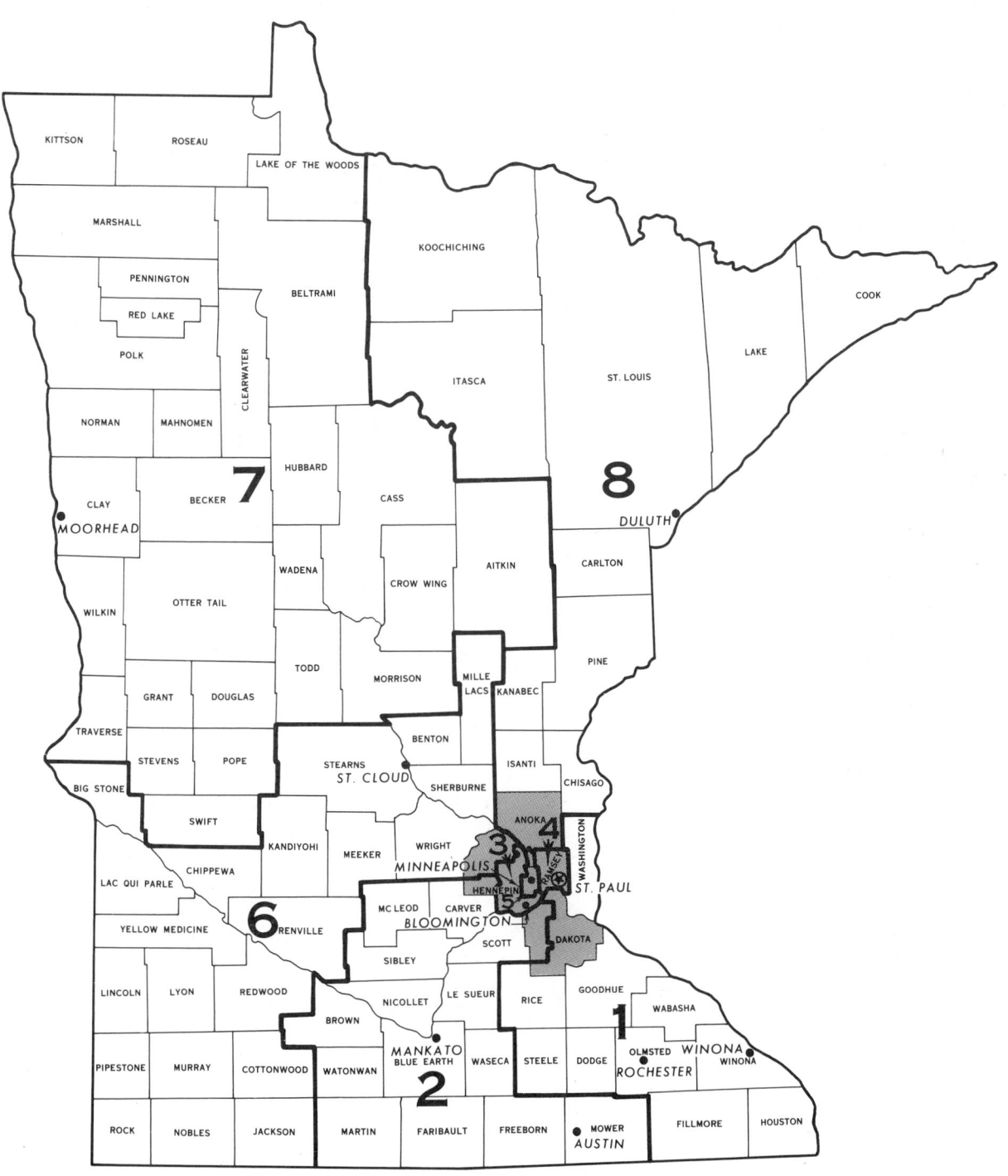

KITTSON
ROSEAU
LAKE OF THE WOODS
MARSHALL
KOOCHICHING
PENNINGTON
RED LAKE
BELTRAMI
POLK
CLEARWATER
COOK
NORMAN MAHNOMEN
LAKE
ST. LOUIS
ITASCA
CLAY
BECKER **7**
HUBBARD
8
MOORHEAD
DULUTH
WADENA
CASS
CARLTON
AITKIN
WILKIN
OTTER TAIL
CROW WING
PINE
TODD
MILLE
LACS KANABEC
MORRISON
GRANT DOUGLAS
TRAVERSE
BENTON
STEVENS POPE
STEARNS
ST. CLOUD
SHERBURNE
ISANTI
CHISAGO
BIG STONE
SWIFT
ANOKA **4**
KANDIYOHI
WRIGHT
WASHINGTON
MEEKER
MINNEAPOLIS **3**
LAC QUI PARLE
CHIPPEWA
ST. PAUL
HENNEPIN **5**
YELLOW MEDICINE
6 RENVILLE
MC LEOD CARVER
BLOOMINGTON
SIBLEY
SCOTT DAKOTA
LINCOLN LYON REDWOOD
NICOLLET LE SUEUR
RICE GOODHUE
BROWN
WABASHA
MANKATO
BLUE EARTH
WASECA STEELE DODGE
OLMSTED WINONA
1
ROCHESTER WINONA
PIPESTONE MURRAY COTTONWOOD WATONWAN
2
ROCK NOBLES JACKSON MARTIN FARIBAULT FREEBORN
MOWER
AUSTIN
FILLMORE HOUSTON

County with two or more Congressional Districts.

MINNESOTA

PRESIDENT 1980

1980 Census Population	County	Total Vote	Republican	Democratic	Other	Rep.-Dem. Plurality		Percentage			
								Total Vote		Major Vote	
								Rep.	Dem.	Rep.	Dem.
13,404	AITKIN	7,670	3,396	3,677	597	281	D	44.3%	47.9%	48.0%	52.0%
195,998	ANOKA	87,843	33,100	45,532	9,211	12,432	D	37.7%	51.8%	42.1%	57.9%
29,336	BECKER	13,134	6,848	5,221	1,065	1,627	R	52.1%	39.8%	56.7%	43.3%
30,982	BELTRAMI	15,537	6,481	7,432	1,624	951	D	41.7%	47.8%	46.6%	53.4%
25,187	BENTON	11,782	5,513	5,272	997	241	R	46.8%	44.7%	51.1%	48.9%
7,716	BIG STONE	4,091	1,950	1,814	327	136	R	47.7%	44.3%	51.8%	48.2%
52,314	BLUE EARTH	26,138	11,966	10,930	3,242	1,036	R	45.8%	41.8%	52.3%	47.7%
28,645	BROWN	14,122	8,051	4,915	1,156	3,136	R	57.0%	34.8%	62.1%	37.9%
29,936	CARLTON	14,850	4,760	8,822	1,268	4,062	D	32.1%	59.4%	35.0%	65.0%
37,046	CARVER	18,481	9,909	6,621	1,951	3,288	R	53.6%	35.8%	59.9%	40.1%
21,050	CASS	11,504	6,119	4,717	668	1,402	R	53.2%	41.0%	56.5%	43.5%
14,941	CHIPPEWA	8,101	4,252	3,164	685	1,088	R	52.5%	39.1%	57.3%	42.7%
25,717	CHISAGO	12,535	5,017	6,240	1,278	1,223	D	40.0%	49.8%	44.6%	55.4%
49,327	CLAY	22,508	10,447	8,940	3,121	1,507	R	46.4%	39.7%	53.9%	46.1%
8,761	CLEARWATER	4,138	1,919	1,955	264	36	D	46.4%	47.2%	49.5%	50.5%
4,092	COOK	2,293	1,174	871	248	303	R	51.2%	38.0%	57.4%	42.6%
14,854	COTTONWOOD	7,847	4,258	2,958	631	1,300	R	54.3%	37.7%	59.0%	41.0%
41,722	CROW WING	21,677	10,844	9,323	1,510	1,521	R	50.0%	43.0%	53.8%	46.2%
194,111	DAKOTA	94,755	40,708	43,433	10,614	2,725	D	43.0%	45.8%	48.4%	51.6%
14,773	DODGE	7,100	3,900	2,698	502	1,202	R	54.9%	38.0%	59.1%	40.9%
27,839	DOUGLAS	14,445	7,778	5,530	1,137	2,248	R	53.8%	38.3%	58.4%	41.6%
19,714	FARIBAULT	10,481	6,206	3,620	655	2,586	R	59.2%	34.5%	63.2%	36.8%
21,930	FILLMORE	11,312	6,452	4,010	850	2,442	R	57.0%	35.4%	61.7%	38.3%
36,329	FREEBORN	17,785	8,475	8,212	1,098	263	R	47.7%	46.2%	50.8%	49.2%
38,749	GOODHUE	20,262	9,329	8,566	2,367	763	R	46.0%	42.3%	52.1%	47.9%
7,171	GRANT	4,272	2,054	1,822	396	232	R	48.1%	42.6%	53.0%	47.0%
941,411	HENNEPIN	505,372	194,898	239,592	70,882	44,694	D	38.6%	47.4%	44.9%	55.1%
19,617	HOUSTON	9,483	5,582	3,218	683	2,364	R	58.9%	33.9%	63.4%	36.6%
14,098	HUBBARD	7,524	4,172	2,840	512	1,332	R	55.4%	37.7%	59.5%	40.5%
23,600	ISANTI	10,809	4,480	5,457	872	977	D	41.4%	50.5%	45.1%	54.9%
43,006	ITASCA	22,256	8,368	12,134	1,754	3,766	D	37.6%	54.5%	40.8%	59.2%
13,690	JACKSON	7,064	3,391	3,062	611	329	R	48.0%	43.3%	52.5%	47.5%
12,161	KANABEC	5,508	2,500	2,654	354	154	D	45.4%	48.2%	48.5%	51.5%
36,763	KANDIYOHI	18,095	8,480	8,038	1,577	442	R	46.9%	44.4%	51.3%	48.7%
6,672	KITTSON	3,577	1,875	1,407	295	468	R	52.4%	39.3%	57.1%	42.9%
17,571	KOOCHICHING	8,250	3,433	4,181	636	748	D	41.6%	50.7%	45.1%	54.9%
10,592	LAC QUI PARLE	5,903	2,981	2,457	465	524	R	50.5%	41.6%	54.8%	45.2%
13,043	LAKE	6,931	2,414	3,864	653	1,450	D	34.8%	55.7%	38.5%	61.5%
3,764	LAKE OF THE WOODS	2,000	1,052	763	185	289	R	52.6%	38.1%	58.0%	42.0%
23,434	LE SUEUR	11,631	5,478	5,161	992	317	R	47.1%	44.4%	51.5%	48.5%
8,207	LINCOLN	4,130	2,122	1,640	368	482	R	51.4%	39.7%	56.4%	43.6%
25,207	LYON	12,911	5,852	5,626	1,433	226	R	45.3%	43.6%	51.0%	49.0%
29,657	MCLEOD	14,040	7,819	4,987	1,234	2,832	R	55.7%	35.5%	61.1%	38.9%
5,535	MAHNOMEN	2,637	1,275	1,175	187	100	R	48.4%	44.6%	52.0%	48.0%
13,027	MARSHALL	6,775	3,638	2,636	501	1,002	R	53.7%	38.9%	58.0%	42.0%
24,687	MARTIN	12,294	7,057	4,301	936	2,756	R	57.4%	35.0%	62.1%	37.9%
20,594	MEEKER	10,095	5,032	4,238	825	794	R	49.8%	42.0%	54.3%	45.7%
18,430	MILLE LACS	9,013	3,860	4,443	710	583	D	42.8%	49.3%	46.5%	53.5%
29,311	MORRISON	14,024	6,296	6,930	798	634	D	44.9%	49.4%	47.6%	52.4%
40,390	MOWER	20,335	7,908	10,538	1,889	2,630	D	38.9%	51.8%	42.9%	57.1%
11,507	MURRAY	6,186	3,004	2,714	468	290	R	48.6%	43.9%	52.5%	47.5%
26,929	NICOLLET	13,643	6,436	5,400	1,807	1,036	R	47.2%	39.6%	54.4%	45.6%
21,840	NOBLES	10,365	4,706	4,703	956	3	R	45.4%	45.4%	50.0%	50.0%
9,379	NORMAN	4,880	2,192	2,253	435	61	D	44.9%	46.2%	49.3%	50.7%
91,971	OLMSTED	40,911	22,704	13,983	4,224	8,721	R	55.5%	34.2%	61.9%	38.1%
51,937	OTTER TAIL	26,138	15,091	9,108	1,939	5,983	R	57.7%	34.8%	62.4%	37.6%
15,258	PENNINGTON	7,416	3,715	3,101	600	614	R	50.1%	41.8%	54.5%	45.5%
19,871	PINE	9,687	3,899	5,121	667	1,222	D	40.2%	52.9%	43.2%	56.8%
11,690	PIPESTONE	6,243	3,207	2,392	644	815	R	51.4%	38.3%	57.3%	42.7%
34,844	POLK	17,644	9,036	7,151	1,457	1,885	R	51.2%	40.5%	55.8%	44.2%
11,657	POPE	6,153	3,159	2,527	467	632	R	51.3%	41.1%	55.6%	44.4%
459,784	RAMSEY	232,744	78,860	124,774	29,110	45,914	D	33.9%	53.6%	38.7%	61.3%
5,471	RED LAKE	2,707	1,223	1,318	166	95	D	45.2%	48.7%	48.1%	51.9%
19,341	REDWOOD	9,699	5,993	2,952	754	3,041	R	61.8%	30.4%	67.0%	33.0%
20,401	RENVILLE	10,444	5,544	4,058	842	1,486	R	53.1%	38.9%	57.7%	42.3%
46,087	RICE	20,677	8,168	9,531	2,978	1,363	D	39.5%	46.1%	46.1%	53.9%
10,703	ROCK	5,713	3,164	2,089	460	1,075	R	55.4%	36.6%	60.2%	39.8%
12,574	ROSEAU	6,317	3,358	2,616	343	742	R	53.2%	41.4%	56.2%	43.8%
222,229	ST. LOUIS	114,757	33,407	69,403	11,947	35,996	D	29.1%	60.5%	32.5%	67.5%
43,784	SCOTT	20,038	9,018	9,115	1,905	97	D	45.0%	45.5%	49.7%	50.3%

MINNESOTA

PRESIDENT 1980

1980 Census Population	County	Total Vote	Republican	Democratic	Other	Rep.-Dem. Plurality	Percentage			
							Total Vote		Major Vote	
							Rep.	Dem.	Rep.	Dem.
29,908	SHERBURNE	13,620	6,035	6,229	1,356	194 D	44.3%	45.7%	49.2%	50.8%
15,448	SIBLEY	7,642	4,460	2,521	661	1,939 R	58.4%	33.0%	63.9%	36.1%
108,161	STEARNS	51,522	24,888	21,862	4,772	3,026 R	48.3%	42.4%	53.2%	46.8%
30,328	STEELE	14,279	7,805	5,095	1,379	2,710 R	54.7%	35.7%	60.5%	39.5%
11,322	STEVENS	6,487	3,283	2,559	645	724 R	50.6%	39.4%	56.2%	43.8%
12,920	SWIFT	6,823	2,943	3,245	635	302 D	43.1%	47.6%	47.6%	52.4%
24,991	TODD	12,111	6,451	4,975	685	1,476 R	53.3%	41.1%	56.5%	43.5%
5,542	TRAVERSE	3,032	1,574	1,258	200	316 R	51.9%	41.5%	55.6%	44.4%
19,335	WABASHA	9,453	4,986	3,712	755	1,274 R	52.7%	39.3%	57.3%	42.7%
14,192	WADENA	7,103	4,089	2,635	379	1,454 R	57.6%	37.1%	60.8%	39.2%
18,448	WASECA	9,303	4,801	3,535	967	1,266 R	51.6%	38.0%	57.6%	42.4%
113,571	WASHINGTON	54,902	22,718	25,634	6,550	2,916 D	41.4%	46.7%	47.0%	53.0%
12,361	WATONWAN	6,587	3,629	2,442	516	1,187 R	55.1%	37.1%	59.8%	40.2%
8,382	WILKIN	4,113	2,224	1,496	393	728 R	54.1%	36.4%	59.8%	40.2%
46,256	WINONA	22,903	10,332	9,814	2,757	518 R	45.1%	42.9%	51.3%	48.7%
58,962	WRIGHT	26,991	12,293	12,383	2,315	90 D	45.5%	45.9%	49.8%	50.2%
13,653	YELLOW MEDICINE	7,427	4,004	2,833	590	1,171 R	53.9%	38.1%	58.6%	41.4%
4,077,148	TOTAL	2,051,980	873,268	954,174	224,538	80,906 D	42.6%	46.5%	47.8%	52.2%

MINNESOTA

CONGRESS

CD	Year	Total Vote	Republican		Democratic		Other Vote	Rep.-Dem. Plurality	Percentage			
			Vote	Candidate	Vote	Candidate			Total Vote		Major Vote	
									Rep.	Dem.	Rep.	Dem.
1	1980	238,380	171,099	ERDAHL, ARLEN	67,279	SMITH, RUSSELL V.	2	103,820 R	71.8%	28.2%	71.8%	28.2%
1	1978	195,929	110,090	ERDAHL, ARLEN	83,271	SIKORSKI, GERRY	2,568	26,819 R	56.2%	42.5%	56.9%	43.1%
1	1976	231,780	158,177	QUIE, ALBERT H.	70,630	OLSON, ROBERT C.	2,973	87,547 R	68.2%	30.5%	69.1%	30.9%
1	1974	152,011	95,138	QUIE, ALBERT H.	56,868	SCOTT, ULRIC	5	38,270 R	62.6%	37.4%	62.6%	37.4%
1	1972	201,804	142,698	QUIE, ALBERT H.	59,106	THOMPSON, CHARLES S.		83,592 R	70.7%	29.3%	70.7%	29.3%
2	1980	260,668	158,082	HAGEDORN, TOM	102,586	BERGQUIST, HAROLD J.		55,496 R	60.6%	39.4%	60.6%	39.4%
2	1978	206,599	145,415	HAGEDORN, TOM	61,173	CONSIDINE, JOHN F.	11	84,242 R	70.4%	29.6%	70.4%	29.6%
2	1976	245,816	148,322	HAGEDORN, TOM	97,488	GRIFFIN, GLORIA	6	50,834 R	60.3%	39.7%	60.3%	39.7%
2	1974	165,920	88,071	HAGEDORN, TOM	77,780	BABCOCK, STEVE	69	10,291 R	53.1%	46.9%	53.1%	46.9%
2	1972	217,783	124,350	NELSEN, ANCHER	93,433	TURNBULL, CHARLES V.		30,917 R	57.1%	42.9%	57.1%	42.9%
3	1980	237,261	179,393	FRENZEL, BILL	57,868	SALITERMAN, JOEL A.		121,525 R	75.6%	24.4%	75.6%	24.4%
3	1978	195,879	128,759	FRENZEL, BILL	67,120	FREEMAN, MICHAEL O.		61,639 R	65.7%	34.3%	65.7%	34.3%
3	1976	225,459	149,013	FRENZEL, BILL	72,044	COUGHLIN, JEROME W.	4,402	76,969 R	66.1%	32.0%	67.4%	32.6%
3	1974	137,955	83,325	FRENZEL, BILL	54,630	RIGGS, ROBERT		28,695 R	60.4%	39.6%	60.4%	39.6%
3	1972	210,942	132,638	FRENZEL, BILL	66,070	BELL, JIM	12,234	66,568 R	62.9%	31.3%	66.8%	33.2%
4	1980	203,712	82,537	BERG, JOHN	119,182	VENTO, BRUCE F.	1,993	36,645 D	40.5%	58.5%	40.9%	59.1%
4	1978	165,385	69,396	BERG, JOHN	95,989	VENTO, BRUCE F.		26,593 D	42.0%	58.0%	42.0%	58.0%
4	1976	200,635	59,767	ENGEBRETSON, ANDREW	133,282	VENTO, BRUCE F.	7,586	73,515 D	29.8%	66.4%	31.0%	69.0%
4	1974	125,529	30,083	RHEINBERGER, JOSEPH A.	95,437	KARTH, JOSEPH E.	9	65,354 D	24.0%	76.0%	24.0%	76.0%
4	1972	191,078	52,786	THOMPSON, STEVE	138,292	KARTH, JOSEPH E.		85,506 D	27.6%	72.4%	27.6%	72.4%
5	1980	180,430	48,200	DOHERTY, JOHN	126,451	SABO, MARTIN O.	5,779	78,251 D	26.7%	70.1%	27.6%	72.4%
5	1978	147,087	55,412	TILL, MIKE	91,673	SABO, MARTIN O.	2	36,261 D	37.7%	62.3%	37.7%	62.3%
5	1976	195,596	50,764	ERDALL, RICHARD M.	138,213	FRASER, DONALD M.	6,619	87,449 D	26.0%	70.7%	26.9%	73.1%
5	1974	122,045	30,146	RATTE, PHIL	90,012	FRASER, DONALD M.	1,887	59,866 D	24.7%	73.8%	25.1%	74.9%
5	1972	205,200	50,014	DAVISSON, ALLAN	135,108	FRASER, DONALD M.	20,078	85,094 D	24.4%	65.8%	27.0%	73.0%
6	1980	266,584	140,402	WEBER, VIN	126,173	BAUMANN, ARCHIE	9	14,229 R	52.7%	47.3%	52.7%	47.3%
6	1978	209,632	93,742	BJORHUS, RUSS	115,880	NOLAN, RICHARD M.	10	22,138 D	44.7%	55.3%	44.7%	55.3%
6	1976	246,710	99,201	ANDERSON, JAMES	147,507	NOLAN, RICHARD M.	2	48,306 D	40.2%	59.8%	40.2%	59.8%
6	1974	174,263	77,797	GRUNSETH, JON	96,465	NOLAN, RICHARD M.	1	18,668 D	44.6%	55.4%	44.6%	55.4%
6	1972	224,492	114,537	ZWACH, JOHN M.	109,955	NOLAN, RICHARD M.		4,582 R	51.0%	49.0%	51.0%	49.0%
7	1980	259,113	135,084	STANGELAND, ARLAN	124,026	WENSTROM, GENE	3	11,058 R	52.1%	47.9%	52.1%	47.9%
7	1978	209,075	109,456	STANGELAND, ARLAN	93,055	WENSTROM, GENE	6,564	16,401 R	52.4%	44.5%	54.0%	46.0%
7	1976	241,664	64,333	LEISETH, BOB	174,080	BERGLAND, BOB	3,251	109,747 D	26.6%	72.0%	27.0%	73.0%
7	1974	172,266	43,054	REBER, DAN	129,207	BERGLAND, BOB	5	86,153 D	25.0%	75.0%	25.0%	75.0%
7	1972	225,350	92,283	HAAVEN, JON O.	133,067	BERGLAND, BOB		40,784 D	41.0%	59.0%	41.0%	59.0%
8	1980	258,765	72,350	FIORE, EDWARD	182,228	OBERSTAR, JAMES L.	4,187	109,878 D	28.0%	70.4%	28.4%	71.6%
8	1978	196,294			171,125	OBERSTAR, JAMES L.	25,169	171,125 D		87.2%		100.0%
8	1976	206,844			206,755	OBERSTAR, JAMES L.	89	206,755 D		100.0%		100.0%
8	1974	169,013	44,298	ARNOLD, JEROME	104,740	OBERSTAR, JAMES L.	19,975	60,442 D	26.2%	62.0%	29.7%	70.3%
8	1972	213,137	51,314	JOHNSON, EDWARD	161,823	BLATNIK, JOHN A.		110,509 D	24.1%	75.9%	24.1%	75.9%

MINNESOTA

1980 GENERAL ELECTION

In Minnesota the Democratic party is known as the Democratic-Farmer-Labor party and the Republican party as the Independent-Republican party; candidates appear on the ballot with these designations. Socialist Labor candidates appear on the ballot with the designation Industrial Government.

President   Other vote was 174,990 Anderson (Anderson Coalition); 31,592 Clark (Libertarian); 8,407 Commoner (Citizens); 6,139 American party with no candidate specified; 1,184 Hall (Communist); 711 DeBerry (Socialist Workers); 698 Griswold (Workers World); 536 McReynolds (Socialist); 281 scattered. Uncorrected returns gave the Carter (Democratic) vote as 954,173; Anderson (Anderson Coalition) vote as 174,997; Clark (Libertarian) vote as 31,593; Commoner (Citizens) vote as 8,406; American party vote as 6,136 and the Hall (Communist) vote as 1,117.

Congress   Other vote was Kendrick (Socialist Workers) in CD 4; 2,552 Miller (New Union), 1,611 Thomas (Socialist Workers) and 1,616 Wallace (Industrial Government) in CD 5; 4,134 Gersh (Socialist Workers) and 53 scattered in CD 8; scattered in CD's 1, 6 and 7.

1980 PRIMARIES

SEPTEMBER 9 REPUBLICAN

Congress   Unopposed in five CD's. Contested as follows:

CD 3   12,111 Bill Frenzel; 1,143 Rodger M. Rose.
CD 5   4,142 John Doherty; 2,424 George Franklin; 1,214 Steve Thewis.
CD 6   18,154 Vin Weber; 2,655 Francis E. S. Brunton.

SEPTEMBER 9 DEMOCRATIC

Congress   Unopposed in four CD's. Contested as follows:

CD 3   3,128 Joel A. Saliterman; 2,417 Harris H. Herman.
CD 6   14,526 Archie Baumann; 5,867 Pat O'Reilly.
CD 7   23,204 Gene Wenstrom; 3,900 Russell R. Ellis.
CD 8   38,450 James L. Oberstar; 30,618 Thomas E. Dougherty.

MISSISSIPPI

GOVERNOR
William F. Winter (D). Elected 1979 to a four-year term.

SENATORS
Thad Cochran (R). Elected 1978 to a six-year term.

John Stennis (D). Re-elected 1976 to a six-year term. Previously elected 1970, 1964, 1958, 1952, and in 1947 to fill out term vacated by the death of Senator Theodore Bilbo.

REPRESENTATIVES
1. Jamie L. Whitten (D)
2. David R. Bowen (D)
3. G. V. Montgomery (D)
4. Jon C. Hinson (R) (see page 1)
5. Trent Lott (R)

POSTWAR VOTE FOR GOVERNOR

Year	Total Vote	Republican Vote	Candidate	Democratic Vote	Candidate	Other Vote	Rep.-Dem. Plurality	Total Vote Rep.	Total Vote Dem.	Major Vote Rep.	Major Vote Dem.
1979	677,322	263,702	Carmichael, Gil	413,620	Winter, William F.	—	149,918 D	38.9%	61.1%	38.9%	61.1%
1975	708,033	319,632	Carmichael, Gil	369,568	Finch, Cliff	18,833	49,936 D	45.1%	52.2%	46.4%	53.6%
1971	780,537	—	—	601,122	Waller, William L.	179,415	601,122 D	—	77.0%	—	100.0%
1967	448,697	133,379	Phillips, Rubel L.	315,318	Williams, John Bell	—	181,939 D	29.7%	70.3%	29.7%	70.3%
1963	363,971	138,515	Phillips, Rubel L.	225,456	Johnson, Paul B.	—	86,941 D	38.1%	61.9%	38.1%	61.9%
1959	57,671	—	—	57,671	Barnett, Ross R.	—	57,671 D	—	100.0%	—	100.0%
1955	40,707	—	—	40,707	Coleman, James P.	—	40,707 D	—	100.0%	—	100.0%
1951	43,422	—	—	43,422	White, Hugh	—	43,422 D	—	100.0%	—	100.0%
1947	166,095	—	—	161,993	Wright, Fielding L.	4,102	161,993 D	—	97.5%	—	100.0%

POSTWAR VOTE FOR SENATOR

Year	Total Vote	Republican Vote	Candidate	Democratic Vote	Candidate	Other Vote	Rep.-Dem. Plurality	Total Vote Rep.	Total Vote Dem.	Major Vote Rep.	Major Vote Dem.
1978	583,936	263,089	Cochran, Thad	185,454	Dantin, Maurice	135,393	77,635 R	45.1%	31.8%	58.7%	41.3%
1976	554,433	—	—	554,433	Stennis, John	—	554,433 D	—	100.0%	—	100.0%
1972	645,746	249,779	Carmichael, Gil	375,102	Eastland, James O.	20,865	125,323 D	38.7%	58.1%	40.0%	60.0%
1970	324,215	—	—	286,622	Stennis, John	37,593	286,622 D	—	88.4%	—	100.0%
1966	393,900	105,150	Walker, Prentiss	258,248	Eastland, James O.	30,502	153,098 D	26.7%	65.6%	28.9%	71.1%
1964	343,364	—	—	343,364	Stennis, John	—	343,364 D	—	100.0%	—	100.0%
1960	266,148	21,807	Moore, Joe A.	244,341	Eastland, James O.	—	222,534 D	8.2%	91.8%	8.2%	91.8%
1958	61,039	—	—	61,039	Stennis, John	—	61,039 D	—	100.0%	—	100.0%
1954	105,526	4,678	White, James A.	100,848	Eastland, James O.	—	96,170 D	4.4%	95.6%	4.4%	95.6%
1952	233,919	—	—	233,919	Stennis, John	—	233,919 D	—	100.0%	—	100.0%
1948	151,478	—	—	151,478	Eastland, James O.	—	151,478 D	—	100.0%	—	100.0%
1947s	193,709	(See note below)									
1946	46,747	—	—	46,747	Bilbo, Theodore	—	46,747 D	—	100.0%	—	100.0%

The 1947 election was for a short term to fill a vacancy and was held without party designation or nomination; John Stennis polled 52,068 votes (26.9% of the total vote) and won the election with a 6,343 plurality.

MISSISSIPPI

Districts Established March 1, 1972

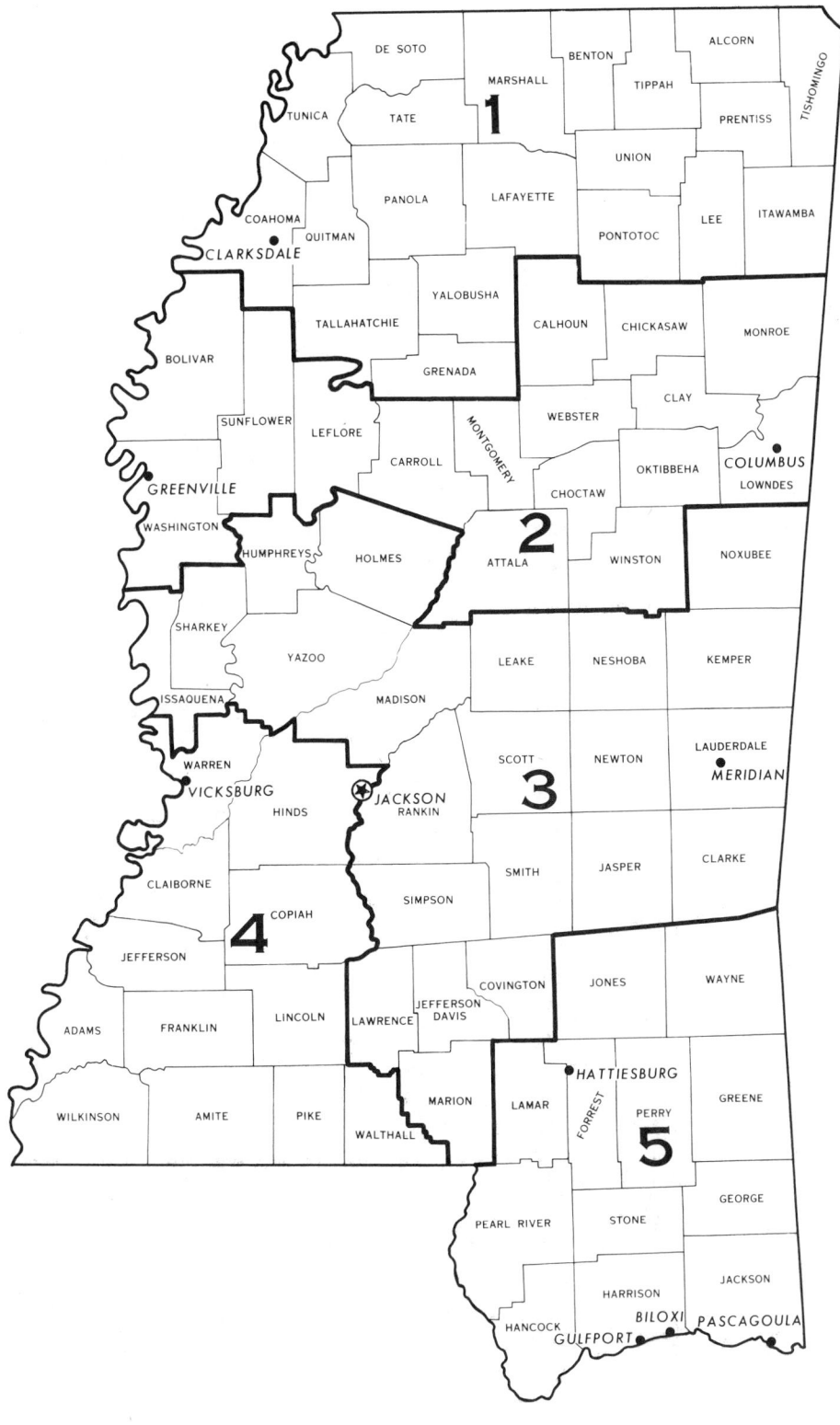

MISSISSIPPI

PRESIDENT 1980

1980 Census Population	County	Total Vote	Republican	Democratic	Other	Rep.-Dem. Plurality		Percentage Total Vote Rep.	Dem.	Major Vote Rep.	Dem.
38,035	ADAMS	15,363	7,523	7,228	612	295	R	49.0%	47.0%	51.0%	49.0%
33,036	ALCORN	12,595	5,196	6,242	1,157	1,046	D	41.3%	49.6%	45.4%	54.6%
13,369	AMITE	5,971	2,653	3,229	89	576	D	44.4%	54.1%	45.1%	54.9%
19,865	ATTALA	8,214	3,975	4,117	122	142	D	48.4%	50.1%	49.1%	50.9%
8,153	BENTON	3,427	1,254	2,094	79	840	D	36.6%	61.1%	37.5%	62.5%
45,965	BOLIVAR	14,491	5,148	8,839	504	3,691	D	35.5%	61.0%	36.8%	63.2%
15,664	CALHOUN	6,019	2,579	3,295	145	716	D	42.8%	54.7%	43.9%	56.1%
9,776	CARROLL	4,228	2,153	2,037	38	116	R	50.9%	48.2%	51.4%	48.6%
17,853	CHICKASAW	6,329	2,540	3,622	167	1,082	D	40.1%	57.2%	41.2%	58.8%
8,996	CHOCTAW	3,695	1,927	1,729	39	198	R	52.2%	46.8%	52.7%	47.3%
12,279	CLAIBORNE	4,228	1,129	3,032	67	1,903	D	26.7%	71.7%	27.1%	72.9%
16,945	CLARKE	6,721	3,303	3,303	115			49.1%	49.1%	50.0%	50.0%
21,082	CLAY	7,964	3,439	4,275	250	836	D	43.2%	53.7%	44.6%	55.4%
36,918	COAHOMA	12,015	4,592	7,030	393	2,438	D	38.2%	58.5%	39.5%	60.5%
26,503	COPIAH	10,140	4,461	5,517	162	1,056	D	44.0%	54.4%	44.7%	55.3%
15,927	COVINGTON	6,531	3,471	2,956	104	515	R	53.1%	45.3%	54.0%	46.0%
53,930	DE SOTO	16,419	9,655	6,344	420	3,311	R	58.8%	38.6%	60.3%	39.7%
66,018	FORREST	21,327	12,656	8,274	397	4,382	R	59.3%	38.8%	60.5%	39.5%
8,208	FRANKLIN	4,109	2,026	2,040	43	14	D	49.3%	49.6%	49.8%	50.2%
15,297	GEORGE	5,932	3,052	2,757	123	295	R	51.4%	46.5%	52.5%	47.5%
9,827	GREENE	3,541	1,772	1,740	29	32	R	50.0%	49.1%	50.5%	49.5%
21,043	GRENADA	8,300	3,993	4,182	125	189	D	48.1%	50.4%	48.8%	51.2%
24,537	HANCOCK	8,915	5,088	3,544	283	1,544	R	57.1%	39.8%	58.9%	41.1%
157,665	HARRISON	42,888	25,175	16,318	1,395	8,857	R	58.7%	38.0%	60.7%	39.3%
250,998	HINDS	90,074	48,135	39,369	2,570	8,766	R	53.4%	43.7%	55.0%	45.0%
22,970	HOLMES	8,336	2,693	5,463	180	2,770	D	32.3%	65.5%	33.0%	67.0%
13,931	HUMPHREYS	5,020	1,841	2,970	209	1,129	D	36.7%	59.2%	38.3%	61.7%
2,513	ISSAQUENA	968	349	598	21	249	D	36.1%	61.8%	36.9%	63.1%
20,518	ITAWAMBA	7,853	2,906	4,852	95	1,946	D	37.0%	61.8%	37.5%	62.5%
118,015	JACKSON	35,958	22,498	12,226	1,234	10,272	R	62.6%	34.0%	64.8%	35.2%
17,265	JASPER	6,673	2,781	3,813	79	1,032	D	41.7%	57.1%	42.2%	57.8%
9,181	JEFFERSON	3,724	751	2,871	102	2,120	D	20.2%	77.1%	20.7%	79.3%
13,846	JEFFERSON DAVIS	6,187	2,280	3,831	76	1,551	D	36.9%	61.9%	37.3%	62.7%
61,912	JONES	24,289	12,900	11,117	272	1,783	R	53.1%	45.8%	53.7%	46.3%
10,148	KEMPER	4,439	1,822	2,601	16	779	D	41.0%	58.6%	41.2%	58.8%
31,030	LAFAYETTE	9,571	4,366	4,887	318	521	D	45.6%	51.1%	47.2%	52.8%
23,821	LAMAR	8,546	5,395	3,005	146	2,390	R	63.1%	35.2%	64.2%	35.8%
77,285	**LAUDERDALE**	26,119	14,727	9,918	1,474	4,809	R	56.4%	38.0%	59.8%	40.2%
12,518	LAWRENCE	5,560	2,781	2,692	87	89	R	50.0%	48.4%	50.8%	49.2%
18,790	LEAKE	7,738	3,624	4,033	81	409	D	46.8%	52.1%	47.3%	52.7%
57,061	LEE	18,889	8,326	10,047	516	1,721	D	44.1%	53.2%	45.3%	54.7%
41,525	LEFLORE	13,675	5,798	7,498	379	1,700	D	42.4%	54.8%	43.6%	56.4%
30,174	LINCOLN	12,610	7,286	5,213	111	2,073	R	57.8%	41.3%	58.3%	41.7%
57,304	LOWNDES	16,355	9,973	6,187	195	3,786	R	61.0%	37.8%	61.7%	38.3%
41,613	MADISON	14,039	6,024	7,621	394	1,597	D	42.9%	54.3%	44.1%	55.9%
25,708	MARION	10,707	5,218	5,366	123	148	D	48.7%	50.1%	49.3%	50.7%
29,296	MARSHALL	10,848	3,455	7,153	240	3,698	D	31.8%	65.9%	32.6%	67.4%
36,404	MONROE	12,239	4,793	6,998	448	2,205	D	39.2%	57.2%	40.6%	59.4%
13,366	MONTGOMERY	5,326	2,479	2,730	117	251	D	46.5%	51.3%	47.6%	52.4%
23,789	NESHOBA	9,149	5,165	3,872	112	1,293	R	56.5%	42.3%	57.2%	42.8%
19,944	NEWTON	7,941	4,317	3,455	169	862	R	54.4%	43.5%	55.5%	44.5%
13,212	NOXUBEE	5,555	1,970	3,434	151	1,464	D	35.5%	61.8%	36.5%	63.5%
36,018	OKTIBBEHA	12,675	6,300	6,039	336	261	R	49.7%	47.6%	51.1%	48.9%
28,164	PANOLA	10,728	4,219	6,179	330	1,960	D	39.3%	57.6%	40.6%	59.4%
33,795	PEARL RIVER	12,141	6,822	5,028	291	1,794	R	56.2%	41.4%	57.6%	42.4%
9,864	PERRY	4,263	2,255	1,957	51	298	R	52.9%	45.9%	53.5%	46.5%
36,173	PIKE	13,716	6,661	6,694	361	33	D	48.6%	48.8%	49.9%	50.1%
20,918	PONTOTOC	7,802	3,198	4,499	105	1,301	D	41.0%	57.7%	41.5%	58.5%
24,025	PRENTISS	8,178	3,264	4,832	82	1,568	D	39.9%	59.1%	40.3%	59.7%
12,636	QUITMAN	4,810	1,691	2,926	193	1,235	D	35.2%	60.8%	36.6%	63.4%
69,427	RANKIN	25,132	16,650	8,047	435	8,603	R	66.3%	32.0%	67.4%	32.6%
24,556	SCOTT	8,832	4,645	4,043	144	602	R	52.6%	45.8%	53.5%	46.5%
7,964	SHARKEY	3,021	996	1,957	68	961	D	33.0%	64.8%	33.7%	66.3%
23,441	SIMPSON	9,334	5,190	4,015	129	1,175	R	55.6%	43.0%	56.4%	43.6%
15,077	SMITH	6,340	3,772	2,474	94	1,298	R	59.5%	39.0%	60.4%	39.6%
9,716	STONE	3,837	1,888	1,821	128	67	R	49.2%	47.5%	50.9%	49.1%
34,844	SUNFLOWER	8,927	3,728	5,035	164	1,307	D	41.8%	56.4%	42.5%	57.5%
17,157	TALLAHATCHIE	5,776	2,183	3,467	126	1,284	D	37.8%	60.0%	38.6%	61.4%
20,119	TATE	7,366	3,343	3,892	131	549	D	45.4%	52.8%	46.2%	53.8%
18,739	TIPPAH	7,423	3,338	3,878	207	540	D	45.0%	52.2%	46.3%	53.7%

MISSISSIPPI

PRESIDENT 1980

1980 Census Population	County	Total Vote	Republican	Democratic	Other	Rep.-Dem. Plurality	Percentage			
							Total Vote		Major Vote	
							Rep.	Dem.	Rep.	Dem.
18,434	TISHOMINGO	7,221	2,489	4,595	137	2,106 D	34.5%	63.6%	35.1%	64.9%
9,652	TUNICA	3,205	954	2,198	53	1,244 D	29.8%	68.6%	30.3%	69.7%
21,741	UNION	8,715	3,545	5,001	169	1,456 D	40.7%	57.4%	41.5%	58.5%
13,761	WALTHALL	5,762	2,703	2,960	99	257 D	46.9%	51.4%	47.7%	52.3%
51,627	WARREN	18,128	10,151	7,489	488	2,662 R	56.0%	41.3%	57.5%	42.5%
72,344	WASHINGTON	20,117	8,978	10,722	417	1,744 D	44.6%	53.3%	45.6%	54.4%
19,135	WAYNE	7,383	3,844	3,494	45	350 R	52.1%	47.3%	52.4%	47.6%
10,300	WEBSTER	4,712	2,386	2,178	148	208 R	50.6%	46.2%	52.3%	47.7%
10,021	WILKINSON	4,500	1,442	2,981	77	1,539 D	32.0%	66.2%	32.6%	67.4%
19,474	WINSTON	8,545	3,998	4,416	131	418 D	46.8%	51.7%	47.5%	52.5%
13,139	YALOBUSHA	5,783	2,224	3,432	127	1,208 D	38.5%	59.3%	39.3%	60.7%
27,349	YAZOO	10,498	4,819	5,468	211	649 D	45.9%	52.1%	46.8%	53.2%
2,520,638	TOTAL	892,620	441,089	429,281	22,250	11,808 R	49.4%	48.1%	50.7%	49.3%

MISSISSIPPI

GOVERNOR 1979

1980 Census Population	County	Total Vote	Republican	Democratic	Other	Rep.-Dem. Plurality	Percentage Total Vote Rep.	Dem.	Major Vote Rep.	Dem.
38,035	ADAMS	11,174	4,268	6,906		2,638 D	38.2%	61.8%	38.2%	61.8%
33,036	ALCORN	8,147	3,521	4,626		1,105 D	43.2%	56.8%	43.2%	56.8%
13,369	AMITE	5,394	1,381	4,013		2,632 D	25.6%	74.4%	25.6%	74.4%
19,865	ATTALA	6,010	2,143	3,867		1,724 D	35.7%	64.3%	35.7%	64.3%
8,153	BENTON	3,040	946	2,094		1,148 D	31.1%	68.9%	31.1%	68.9%
45,965	BOLIVAR	11,147	3,522	7,625		4,103 D	31.6%	68.4%	31.6%	68.4%
15,664	CALHOUN	5,313	1,803	3,510		1,707 D	33.9%	66.1%	33.9%	66.1%
9,776	CARROLL	3,490	1,167	2,323		1,156 D	33.4%	66.6%	33.4%	66.6%
17,853	CHICKASAW	4,330	1,628	2,702		1,074 D	37.6%	62.4%	37.6%	62.4%
8,996	CHOCTAW	2,780	1,067	1,713		646 D	38.4%	61.6%	38.4%	61.6%
12,279	CLAIBORNE	4,379	1,321	3,058		1,737 D	30.2%	69.8%	30.2%	69.8%
16,945	CLARKE	5,624	2,620	3,004		384 D	46.6%	53.4%	46.6%	53.4%
21,082	CLAY	6,241	2,258	3,983		1,725 D	36.2%	63.8%	36.2%	63.8%
36,918	COAHOMA	8,086	2,454	5,632		3,178 D	30.3%	69.7%	30.3%	69.7%
26,503	COPIAH	8,017	2,752	5,265		2,513 D	34.3%	65.7%	34.3%	65.7%
15,927	COVINGTON	5,425	2,100	3,325		1,225 D	38.7%	61.3%	38.7%	61.3%
53,930	DE SOTO	9,447	3,825	5,622		1,797 D	40.5%	59.5%	40.5%	59.5%
66,018	FORREST	16,910	8,008	8,902		894 D	47.4%	52.6%	47.4%	52.6%
8,208	FRANKLIN	3,414	1,153	2,261		1,108 D	33.8%	66.2%	33.8%	66.2%
15,297	GEORGE	3,513	1,541	1,972		431 D	43.9%	56.1%	43.9%	56.1%
9,827	GREENE	3,817	1,505	2,312		807 D	39.4%	60.6%	39.4%	60.6%
21,043	GRENADA	7,964	1,955	6,009		4,054 D	24.5%	75.5%	24.5%	75.5%
24,537	HANCOCK	7,441	3,170	4,271		1,101 D	42.6%	57.4%	42.6%	57.4%
157,665	HARRISON	30,168	15,687	14,481		1,206 R	52.0%	48.0%	52.0%	48.0%
250,998	HINDS	60,869	23,392	37,477		14,085 D	38.4%	61.6%	38.4%	61.6%
22,970	HOLMES	7,299	1,898	5,401		3,503 D	26.0%	74.0%	26.0%	74.0%
13,931	HUMPHREYS	4,037	1,187	2,850		1,663 D	29.4%	70.6%	29.4%	70.6%
2,513	ISSAQUENA	752	200	552		352 D	26.6%	73.4%	26.6%	73.4%
20,518	ITAWAMBA	5,912	2,215	3,697		1,482 D	37.5%	62.5%	37.5%	62.5%
118,015	JACKSON	24,849	12,873	11,976		897 R	51.8%	48.2%	51.8%	48.2%
17,265	JASPER	5,422	1,953	3,469		1,516 D	36.0%	64.0%	36.0%	64.0%
9,181	JEFFERSON	3,471	973	2,498		1,525 D	28.0%	72.0%	28.0%	72.0%
13,846	JEFFERSON DAVIS	4,824	1,502	3,322		1,820 D	31.1%	68.9%	31.1%	68.9%
61,912	JONES	19,750	8,066	11,684		3,618 D	40.8%	59.2%	40.8%	59.2%
10,148	KEMPER	3,884	1,330	2,554		1,224 D	34.2%	65.8%	34.2%	65.8%
31,030	LAFAYETTE	6,718	2,245	4,473		2,228 D	33.4%	66.6%	33.4%	66.6%
23,821	LAMAR	7,070	3,504	3,566		62 D	49.6%	50.4%	49.6%	50.4%
77,285	LAUDERDALE	22,668	11,079	11,589		510 D	48.9%	51.1%	48.9%	51.1%
12,518	LAWRENCE	3,954	1,424	2,530		1,106 D	36.0%	64.0%	36.0%	64.0%
18,790	LEAKE	5,309	1,719	3,590		1,871 D	32.4%	67.6%	32.4%	67.6%
57,061	LEE	12,774	5,482	7,292		1,810 D	42.9%	57.1%	42.9%	57.1%
41,525	LEFLORE	11,975	3,656	8,319		4,663 D	30.5%	69.5%	30.5%	69.5%
30,174	LINCOLN	10,923	4,237	6,686		2,449 D	38.8%	61.2%	38.8%	61.2%
57,304	LOWNDES	10,357	5,081	5,276		195 D	49.1%	50.9%	49.1%	50.9%
41,613	MADISON	11,219	4,614	6,605		1,991 D	41.1%	58.9%	41.1%	58.9%
25,708	MARION	9,795	4,072	5,723		1,651 D	41.6%	58.4%	41.6%	58.4%
29,296	MARSHALL	9,576	2,315	7,261		4,946 D	24.2%	75.8%	24.2%	75.8%
36,404	MONROE	8,792	3,681	5,111		1,430 D	41.9%	58.1%	41.9%	58.1%
13,366	MONTGOMERY	4,078	1,107	2,971		1,864 D	27.1%	72.9%	27.1%	72.9%
23,789	NESHOBA	8,320	2,771	5,549		2,778 D	33.3%	66.7%	33.3%	66.7%
19,944	NEWTON	6,616	2,442	4,174		1,732 D	36.9%	63.1%	36.9%	63.1%
13,212	NOXUBEE	5,171	1,644	3,527		1,883 D	31.8%	68.2%	31.8%	68.2%
36,018	OKTIBBEHA	9,229	3,890	5,339		1,449 D	42.1%	57.9%	42.1%	57.9%
28,164	PANOLA	8,208	2,870	5,338		2,468 D	35.0%	65.0%	35.0%	65.0%
33,795	PEARL RIVER	11,281	4,628	6,653		2,025 D	41.0%	59.0%	41.0%	59.0%
9,864	PERRY	3,545	1,524	2,021		497 D	43.0%	57.0%	43.0%	57.0%
36,173	PIKE	10,452	3,379	7,073		3,694 D	32.3%	67.7%	32.3%	67.7%
20,918	PONTOTOC	6,433	2,479	3,954		1,475 D	38.5%	61.5%	38.5%	61.5%
24,025	PRENTISS	7,288	2,680	4,608		1,928 D	36.8%	63.2%	36.8%	63.2%
12,636	QUITMAN	3,938	1,289	2,649		1,360 D	32.7%	67.3%	32.7%	67.3%
69,427	RANKIN	17,362	8,833	8,529		304 R	50.9%	49.1%	50.9%	49.1%
24,556	SCOTT	6,842	2,677	4,165		1,488 D	39.1%	60.9%	39.1%	60.9%
7,964	SHARKEY	2,548	745	1,803		1,058 D	29.2%	70.8%	29.2%	70.8%
23,441	SIMPSON	7,172	2,558	4,614		2,056 D	35.7%	64.3%	35.7%	64.3%
15,077	SMITH	5,505	2,263	3,242		979 D	41.1%	58.9%	41.1%	58.9%
9,716	STONE	3,365	1,477	1,888		411 D	43.9%	56.1%	43.9%	56.1%
34,844	SUNFLOWER	7,005	1,988	5,017		3,029 D	28.4%	71.6%	28.4%	71.6%
17,157	TALLAHATCHIE	4,394	1,327	3,067		1,740 D	30.2%	69.8%	30.2%	69.8%
20,119	TATE	5,130	1,558	3,572		2,014 D	30.4%	69.6%	30.4%	69.6%
18,739	TIPPAH	5,052	1,666	3,386		1,720 D	33.0%	67.0%	33.0%	67.0%

MISSISSIPPI

GOVERNOR 1979

1980 Census Population	County	Total Vote	Republican	Democratic	Other	Rep.-Dem. Plurality	Percentage Total Vote		Major Vote	
							Rep.	Dem.	Rep.	Dem.
18,434	TISHOMINGO	3,853	1,365	2,488		1,123 D	35.4%	64.6%	35.4%	64.6%
9,652	TUNICA	2,906	770	2,136		1,366 D	26.5%	73.5%	26.5%	73.5%
21,741	UNION	5,699	1,853	3,846		1,993 D	32.5%	67.5%	32.5%	67.5%
13,761	WALTHALL	3,466	1,269	2,197		928 D	36.6%	63.4%	36.6%	63.4%
51,627	WARREN	11,885	5,759	6,126		367 D	48.5%	51.5%	48.5%	51.5%
72,344	WASHINGTON	13,428	5,014	8,414		3,400 D	37.3%	62.7%	37.3%	62.7%
19,135	WAYNE	6,309	2,537	3,772		1,235 D	40.2%	59.8%	40.2%	59.8%
10,300	WEBSTER	3,584	1,386	2,198		812 D	38.7%	61.3%	38.7%	61.3%
10,021	WILKINSON	3,862	683	3,179		2,496 D	17.7%	82.3%	17.7%	82.3%
19,474	WINSTON	6,544	2,190	4,354		2,164 D	33.5%	66.5%	33.5%	66.5%
13,139	YALOBUSHA	4,560	1,643	2,917		1,274 D	36.0%	64.0%	36.0%	64.0%
27,349	YAZOO	8,822	2,945	5,877		2,932 D	33.4%	66.6%	33.4%	66.6%
2,520,638	TOTAL	677,322	263,702	413,620		149,918 D	38.9%	61.1%	38.9%	61.1%

MISSISSIPPI

CONGRESS

CD	Year	Total Vote	Republican Vote	Candidate	Democratic Vote	Candidate	Other Vote	Rep.-Dem. Plurality	Percentage Total Vote Rep.	Dem.	Major Vote Rep.	Dem.
1	1980	165,561	61,292	MOFFETT, T. K.	104,269	WHITTEN, JAMIE L.		42,977 D	37.0%	63.0%	37.0%	63.0%
1	1978	86,151	26,734	MOFFETT, T. K.	57,358	WHITTEN, JAMIE L.	2,059	30,624 D	31.0%	66.6%	31.8%	68.2%
1	1976	93,687			93,687	WHITTEN, JAMIE L.		93,687 D		100.0%		100.0%
1	1974	44,408			39,158	WHITTEN, JAMIE L.	5,250	39,158 D		88.2%		100.0%
1	1972	87,526			87,526	WHITTEN, JAMIE L.		87,526 D		100.0%		100.0%
2	1970	59,781			51,689	WHITTEN, JAMIE L.	8,092	51,689 D		86.5%		100.0%
2	1968	71,260			71,260	WHITTEN, JAMIE L.		71,260 D		100.0%		100.0%
2	1966	64,242	10,622	WISE, S. B.	53,620	WHITTEN, JAMIE L.		42,998 D	16.5%	83.5%	16.5%	83.5%
2	1980	139,050	42,300	DRAKE, FRANK	96,750	BOWEN, DAVID R.		54,450 D	30.4%	69.6%	30.4%	69.6%
2	1978	93,408	35,730	BYRD, ROLAND	57,678	BOWEN, DAVID R.		21,948 D	38.3%	61.7%	38.3%	61.7%
2	1976	119,173	42,601	BYRD, ROLAND	75,092	BOWEN, DAVID R.		32,491 D	35.7%	63.0%	36.2%	63.8%
2	1974	57,358	15,876	HILBUN, BEN F.	37,909	BOWEN, DAVID R.	1,480	22,033 D	27.7%	66.1%	29.5%	70.5%
2	1972	112,837	39,117	BUTLER, CARL	69,892	BOWEN, DAVID R.	3,573	30,775 D	34.7%	61.9%	35.9%	64.1%
3	1980	128,035			128,035	MONTGOMERY, G. V.	3,828	128,035 D		100.0%		100.0%
3	1978	110,093	8,408	CLEVELAND, DOROTHY C.	101,685	MONTGOMERY, G. V.		93,277 D	7.6%	92.4%	7.6%	92.4%
3	1976	137,409	8,321	CLEVELAND, DOROTHY C.	129,088	MONTGOMERY, G. V.		120,767 D	6.1%	93.9%	6.1%	93.9%
3	1974	43,020			43,020	MONTGOMERY, G. V.		43,020 D		100.0%		100.0%
3	1972	105,722			105,722	MONTGOMERY, G. V.		105,722 D		100.0%		100.0%
4	1980	177,896	69,321	HINSON, JON C.	52,303	SINGLETARY, BRITT R.	56,272	17,018 R	39.0%	29.4%	57.0%	43.0%
4	1978	132,132	68,225	HINSON, JON C.	34,837	STENNIS, JOHN H.	29,070	33,388 R	51.6%	26.4%	66.2%	33.8%
4	1976	132,991	101,132	COCHRAN, THAD	28,737	DAVIS, STERLING P.	3,122	72,395 R	76.0%	21.6%	77.9%	22.1%
4	1974	89,201	62,634	COCHRAN, THAD	25,699	DEAN, KENNETH L.	868	36,935 R	70.2%	28.8%	70.9%	29.1%
4	1972	141,374	67,655	COCHRAN, THAD	62,148	BODRON, ELLIS B.	11,571	5,507 R	47.9%	44.0%	52.1%	47.9%
3	1970	79,374	28,847	LEE, RAY	50,527	GRIFFIN, CHARLES H.		21,680 D	36.3%	63.7%	36.3%	63.7%
3	1968	82,896			82,896	GRIFFIN, CHARLES H.		82,896 D		100.0%		100.0%
3	1966	86,595			71,377	WILLIAMS, JOHN BELL	15,218	71,377 D		82.4%		100.0%
5	1980	177,975	131,559	LOTT, TRENT	46,416	MCVEAY, JIMMY		85,143 R	73.9%	26.1%	73.9%	26.1%
5	1978	97,177	97,177	LOTT, TRENT				97,177 R	100.0%		100.0%	
5	1976	153,278	104,554	LOTT, TRENT	48,724	BLESSEY, GERALD		55,830 R	68.2%	31.8%	68.2%	31.8%
5	1974	71,922	52,489	LOTT, TRENT	10,333	MURPHEY, WALTER W.	9,100	42,156 R	73.0%	14.4%	83.6%	16.4%
5	1972	140,614	77,826	LOTT, TRENT	62,101	STONE, BEN	687	15,725 R	55.3%	44.2%	55.6%	44.4%

MISSISSIPPI

1979 GENERAL ELECTION

Governor

1980 GENERAL ELECTION

President   Other vote was 12,036 Anderson (Independent); 5,465 Clark (Independent); 2,402 Griswold (Independent); 2,347 Pulley (Independent).

Congress   Other vote was 52,959 McLemore (Independent) and 3,313 McInerney (Independent) in CD 4.

1979 PRIMARIES

AUGUST 7 REPUBLICAN

Governor   17,216 Gil Carmichael; 15,236 Leon Bramlett.

AUGUST 7 DEMOCRATIC

Governor   224,746 Evelyn Gandy; 183,944 William F. Winter; 143,411 John A. Eaves; 135,812 Jim Herring; 34,700 Charles M. Deaton; 14,550 Richard Barrett.

AUGUST 28 DEMOCRATIC RUN-OFF

Governor   386,174 William F. Winter; 295,835 Evelyn Gandy.

1980 PRIMARIES

JUNE 3 REPUBLICAN

Congress   Unopposed in three CD's. No candidate in CD 3. Contested as follows:

  CD 2   2,315 Frank Drake; 2,131 Charles Yoste.

JUNE 3 DEMOCRATIC

Congress   Unopposed in three CD's. Contested as follows:

  CD 4   11,050 Henry J. Kirksey; 7,190 Britt R. Singletary; 6,376 W. H. Pyron; 1,235 W. B. Cagle.
  CD 5   11,239 Jimmy McVeay; 5,090 James E. Parker; 1,531 Arlon Coate.

JUNE 24 DEMOCRATIC RUN-OFF

Congress

  CD 4   26,303 Britt R. Singletary; 20,051 Henry J. Kirksey.

MISSOURI

GOVERNOR
Christopher Bond (R). Elected 1980 to a four-year term. Previously elected 1972.

SENATORS
John C. Danforth (R). Elected 1976 to a six-year term.

Thomas F. Eagleton (D). Re-elected 1980 to a six-year term. Previously elected 1974, 1968.

REPRESENTATIVES
1. William Clay (D)
2. Robert A. Young (D)
3. Richard A. Gephardt (D)
4. Ike Skelton (D)
5. Richard Bolling (D)
6. E. Thomas Coleman (R)
7. Gene Taylor (R)
8. Wendell Bailey (R)
9. Harold Volkmer (D)
10. Bill Emerson (R)

POSTWAR VOTE FOR GOVERNOR

Year	Total Vote	Republican Vote	Candidate	Democratic Vote	Candidate	Other Vote	Rep.-Dem. Plurality	Total Vote Rep.	Total Vote Dem.	Major Vote Rep.	Major Vote Dem.
1980	2,088,028	1,098,950	Bond, Christopher	981,884	Teasdale, Joseph P.	7,194	117,066 R	52.6%	47.0%	52.8%	47.2%
1976	1,933,575	958,110	Bond, Christopher	971,184	Teasdale, Joseph P.	4,281	13,074 D	49.6%	50.2%	49.7%	50.3%
1972	1,865,683	1,029,451	Bond, Christopher	832,751	Dowd, Edward L.	3,481	196,700 R	55.2%	44.6%	55.3%	44.7%
1968	1,764,602	691,797	Roos, Lawrence K.	1,072,805	Hearnes, Warren E.	—	381,008 D	39.2%	60.8%	39.2%	60.8%
1964	1,789,600	678,949	Shepley, Ethan	1,110,651	Hearnes, Warren E.	—	431,702 D	37.9%	62.1%	37.9%	62.1%
1960	1,887,331	792,131	Farmer, Edward G.	1,095,200	Dalton, John M.	—	303,069 D	42.0%	58.0%	42.0%	58.0%
1956	1,808,338	866,810	Hocker, Lon	941,528	Blair, James T.	—	74,718 D	47.9%	52.1%	47.9%	52.1%
1952	1,871,095	886,370	Elliott, Howard	983,166	Donnelly, Phil M.	1,559	96,796 D	47.4%	52.5%	47.4%	52.6%
1948	1,567,338	670,064	Thompson, Murray	893,092	Smith, Forrest	4,182	223,028 D	42.8%	57.0%	42.9%	57.1%

POSTWAR VOTE FOR SENATOR

Year	Total Vote	Republican Vote	Candidate	Democratic Vote	Candidate	Other Vote	Rep.-Dem. Plurality	Total Vote Rep.	Total Vote Dem.	Major Vote Rep.	Major Vote Dem.
1980	2,066,965	985,399	McNary, Gene	1,074,859	Eagleton, Thomas F.	6,707	89,460 D	47.7%	52.0%	47.8%	52.2%
1976	1,914,777	1,090,067	Danforth, John C.	813,571	Hearnes, Warren E.	11,139	276,496 R	56.9%	42.5%	57.3%	42.7%
1974	1,224,303	480,900	Curtis, Thomas B.	735,433	Eagleton, Thomas F.	7,970	254,533 D	39.3%	60.1%	39.5%	60.5%
1970	1,283,912	617,903	Danforth, John C.	655,431	Symington, Stuart	10,578	37,528 D	48.1%	51.0%	48.5%	51.5%
1968	1,737,958	850,544	Curtis, Thomas B.	887,414	Eagleton, Thomas F.	—	36,870 D	48.9%	51.1%	48.9%	51.1%
1964	1,783,043	596,377	Bradshaw, Jean P.	1,186,666	Symington, Stuart	—	590,289 D	33.4%	66.6%	33.4%	66.6%
1962	1,222,259	555,330	Kemper, Crosby	666,929	Long, Edward V.	—	111,599 D	45.4%	54.6%	45.4%	54.6%
1960s	1,880,232	880,576	Hocker, Lon	999,656	Long, Edward V.	—	119,080 D	46.8%	53.2%	46.8%	53.2%
1958	1,173,903	393,847	Palmer, Hazel	780,056	Symington, Stuart	—	386,209 D	33.6%	66.4%	33.6%	66.4%
1956	1,800,984	785,048	Douglas, Herbert	1,015,936	Hennings, Thomas C.	—	230,888 D	43.6%	56.4%	43.6%	56.4%
1952	1,868,083	858,170	Kem, James P.	1,008,523	Symington, Stuart	1,390	150,353 D	45.9%	54.0%	46.0%	54.0%
1950	1,279,414	592,922	Donnell, Forrest C.	685,732	Hennings, Thomas C.	760	92,810 D	46.3%	53.6%	46.4%	53.6%
1946	1,084,100	572,556	Kem, James P.	511,544	Briggs, Frank P.	—	61,012 R	52.8%	47.2%	52.8%	47.2%

The 1960 election was for a short term to fill a vacancy.

MISSOURI

Districts Established February 22, 1972

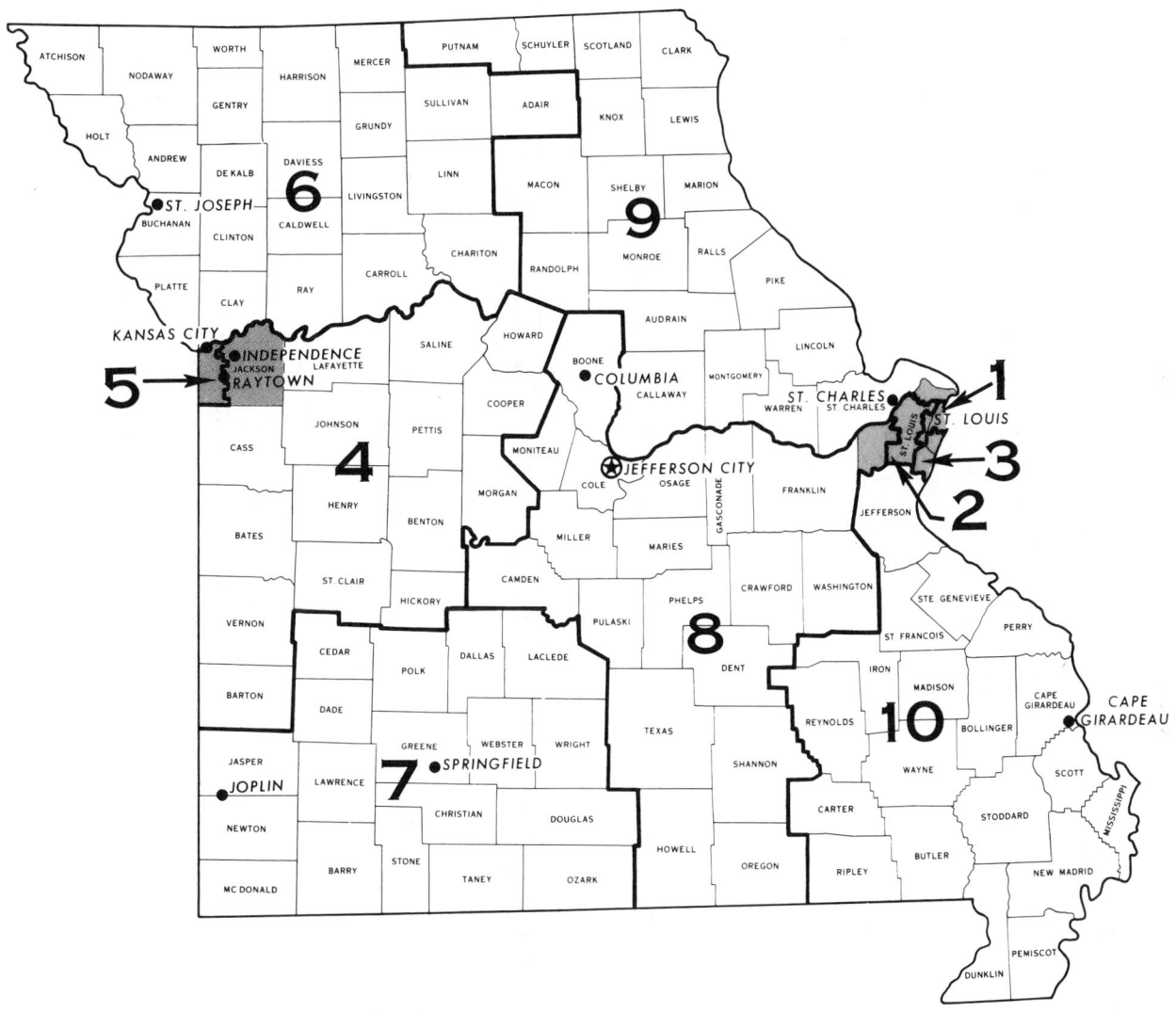

County with two or more Congressional Districts.

MISSOURI

PRESIDENT 1980

1980 Census Population	County	Total Vote	Republican	Democratic	Other	Rep.-Dem. Plurality	Percentage Total Vote Rep.	Dem.	Major Vote Rep.	Dem.
24,870	ADAIR	9,522	5,513	3,507	502	2,006 R	57.9%	36.8%	61.1%	38.9%
13,980	ANDREW	6,573	3,690	2,575	308	1,115 R	56.1%	39.2%	58.9%	41.1%
8,605	ATCHISON	3,556	2,096	1,273	187	823 R	58.9%	35.8%	62.2%	37.8%
26,458	AUDRAIN	11,834	6,347	5,168	319	1,179 R	53.6%	43.7%	55.1%	44.9%
24,408	BARRY	11,458	7,038	4,193	227	2,845 R	61.4%	36.6%	62.7%	37.3%
11,292	BARTON	5,398	3,337	1,901	160	1,436 R	61.8%	35.2%	63.7%	36.3%
15,873	BATES	7,521	4,061	3,297	163	764 R	54.0%	43.8%	55.2%	44.8%
12,183	BENTON	5,852	3,451	2,241	160	1,210 R	59.0%	38.3%	60.6%	39.4%
10,301	BOLLINGER	5,105	2,863	2,160	82	703 R	56.1%	42.3%	57.0%	43.0%
100,376	BOONE	38,837	16,313	18,527	3,997	2,214 D	42.0%	47.7%	46.8%	53.2%
87,888	BUCHANAN	35,150	16,551	16,967	1,632	416 D	47.1%	48.3%	49.4%	50.6%
37,693	BUTLER	14,181	8,342	5,605	234	2,737 R	58.8%	39.5%	59.8%	40.2%
8,660	CALDWELL	4,226	2,551	1,541	134	1,010 R	60.4%	36.5%	62.3%	37.7%
32,252	CALLAWAY	12,835	6,755	5,560	520	1,195 R	52.6%	43.3%	54.9%	45.1%
19,963	CAMDEN	10,246	6,541	3,416	289	3,125 R	63.8%	33.3%	65.7%	34.3%
58,837	CAPE GIRARDEAU	24,549	14,861	8,625	1,063	6,236 R	60.5%	35.1%	63.3%	36.7%
12,131	CARROLL	5,583	3,291	2,130	162	1,161 R	58.9%	38.2%	60.7%	39.3%
5,428	CARTER	2,368	1,218	1,087	63	131 R	51.4%	45.9%	52.8%	47.2%
51,029	CASS	19,134	10,105	8,198	831	1,907 R	52.8%	42.8%	55.2%	44.8%
11,894	CEDAR	5,283	3,469	1,703	111	1,766 R	65.7%	32.2%	67.1%	32.9%
10,489	CHARITON	4,973	2,641	2,250	82	391 R	53.1%	45.2%	54.0%	46.0%
22,402	CHRISTIAN	10,251	6,487	3,502	262	2,985 R	63.3%	34.2%	64.9%	35.1%
8,493	CLARK	3,614	2,042	1,494	78	548 R	56.5%	41.3%	57.7%	42.3%
136,488	CLAY	56,314	28,521	24,250	3,543	4,271 R	50.6%	43.1%	54.0%	46.0%
15,916	CLINTON	6,852	3,599	3,001	252	598 R	52.5%	43.8%	54.5%	45.5%
56,663	COLE	26,423	16,373	9,210	840	7,163 R	62.0%	34.9%	64.0%	36.0%
14,643	COOPER	6,849	3,996	2,687	166	1,309 R	58.3%	39.2%	59.8%	40.2%
18,300	CRAWFORD	7,011	4,081	2,710	220	1,371 R	58.2%	38.7%	60.1%	39.9%
7,383	DADE	3,778	2,410	1,283	85	1,127 R	63.8%	34.0%	65.3%	34.7%
12,096	DALLAS	5,438	3,297	2,011	130	1,286 R	60.6%	37.0%	62.1%	37.9%
8,905	DAVIESS	3,984	2,125	1,770	89	355 R	53.3%	44.4%	54.6%	45.4%
8,222	DE KALB	3,885	2,062	1,677	146	385 R	53.1%	43.2%	55.1%	44.9%
14,517	DENT	6,131	3,477	2,528	126	949 R	56.7%	41.2%	57.9%	42.1%
11,594	DOUGLAS	5,252	3,440	1,677	135	1,763 R	65.5%	31.9%	67.2%	32.8%
36,324	DUNKLIN	11,530	5,253	6,120	157	867 D	45.6%	53.1%	46.2%	53.8%
71,233	FRANKLIN	26,832	15,210	10,480	1,142	4,730 R	56.7%	39.1%	59.2%	40.8%
13,181	GASCONADE	6,203	4,481	1,550	172	2,931 R	72.2%	25.0%	74.3%	25.7%
7,887	GENTRY	3,869	2,005	1,720	144	285 R	51.8%	44.5%	53.8%	46.2%
185,302	GREENE	77,425	43,116	30,498	3,811	12,618 R	55.7%	39.4%	58.6%	41.4%
11,959	GRUNDY	5,106	2,890	2,064	152	826 R	56.6%	40.4%	58.3%	41.7%
9,890	HARRISON	4,655	2,734	1,732	189	1,002 R	58.7%	37.2%	61.2%	38.8%
19,672	HENRY	9,772	4,807	4,648	317	159 R	49.2%	47.6%	50.8%	49.2%
6,367	HICKORY	3,213	1,893	1,248	72	645 R	58.9%	38.8%	60.3%	39.7%
6,882	HOLT	3,190	1,993	1,119	78	874 R	62.5%	35.1%	64.0%	36.0%
10,008	HOWARD	4,554	2,179	2,243	132	64 D	47.8%	49.3%	49.3%	50.7%
28,807	HOWELL	11,903	7,149	4,472	282	2,677 R	60.1%	37.6%	61.5%	38.5%
11,084	IRON	4,551	2,205	2,226	120	21 D	48.5%	48.9%	49.8%	50.2%
629,180	JACKSON	256,687	106,156	135,805	14,726	29,649 D	41.4%	52.9%	43.9%	56.1%
86,958	JASPER	34,666	21,664	11,953	1,049	9,711 R	62.5%	34.5%	64.4%	35.6%
146,814	JEFFERSON	54,882	28,546	24,042	2,294	4,504 R	52.0%	43.8%	54.3%	45.7%
39,059	JOHNSON	12,585	6,449	5,441	695	1,008 R	51.2%	43.2%	54.2%	45.8%
5,508	KNOX	2,710	1,475	1,187	48	288 R	54.4%	43.8%	55.4%	44.6%
24,323	LACLEDE	9,282	5,642	3,443	197	2,199 R	60.8%	37.1%	62.1%	37.9%
29,925	LAFAYETTE	13,468	7,271	5,792	405	1,479 R	54.0%	43.0%	55.7%	44.3%
28,973	LAWRENCE	12,843	7,921	4,670	252	3,251 R	61.7%	36.4%	62.9%	37.1%
10,901	LEWIS	4,789	2,350	2,314	125	36 R	49.1%	48.3%	50.4%	49.6%
22,193	LINCOLN	9,335	4,963	4,110	262	853 R	53.2%	44.0%	54.7%	45.3%
15,495	LINN	7,224	3,585	3,467	172	118 R	49.6%	48.0%	50.8%	49.2%
15,739	LIVINGSTON	7,270	3,654	3,368	248	286 R	50.3%	46.3%	52.0%	48.0%
14,917	MCDONALD	6,783	4,114	2,485	184	1,629 R	60.7%	36.6%	62.3%	37.7%
16,313	MACON	8,187	4,430	3,578	179	852 R	54.1%	43.7%	55.3%	44.7%
10,725	MADISON	4,938	2,618	2,231	89	387 R	53.0%	45.2%	54.0%	46.0%
7,551	MARIES	3,789	1,985	1,732	72	253 R	52.4%	45.7%	53.4%	46.6%
28,638	MARION	12,186	6,036	5,890	260	146 R	49.5%	48.3%	50.6%	49.4%
4,685	MERCER	2,158	1,266	821	71	445 R	58.7%	38.0%	60.7%	39.3%
18,532	MILLER	8,185	5,560	2,469	156	3,091 R	67.9%	30.2%	69.2%	30.8%
15,726	MISSISSIPPI	5,579	2,459	3,040	80	581 D	44.1%	54.5%	44.7%	55.3%
12,068	MONITEAU	5,834	3,430	2,284	120	1,146 R	58.8%	39.1%	60.0%	40.0%
9,716	MONROE	4,555	2,026	2,445	84	419 D	44.5%	53.7%	45.3%	54.7%
11,537	MONTGOMERY	5,225	3,061	2,007	157	1,054 R	58.6%	38.4%	60.4%	39.6%

MISSOURI

PRESIDENT 1980

1980 Census Population	County	Total Vote	Republican	Democratic	Other	Rep.-Dem. Plurality	Percentage Total Vote Rep.	Dem.	Major Vote Rep.	Dem.
13,807	MORGAN	6,182	3,577	2,460	145	1,117 R	57.9%	39.8%	59.3%	40.7%
22,945	NEW MADRID	8,298	4,041	4,171	86	130 D	48.7%	50.3%	49.2%	50.8%
40,555	NEWTON	16,662	10,515	5,621	526	4,894 R	63.1%	33.7%	65.2%	34.8%
21,996	NODAWAY	9,290	4,544	4,257	489	287 R	48.9%	45.8%	51.6%	48.4%
10,238	OREGON	3,898	1,523	2,326	49	803 D	39.1%	59.7%	39.6%	60.4%
12,014	OSAGE	5,822	3,679	2,045	98	1,634 R	63.2%	35.1%	64.3%	35.7%
7,961	OZARK	3,770	2,434	1,242	94	1,192 R	64.6%	32.9%	66.2%	33.8%
24,987	PEMISCOT	7,732	3,519	4,140	73	621 D	45.5%	53.5%	45.9%	54.1%
16,784	PERRY	7,689	5,053	2,416	220	2,637 R	65.7%	31.4%	67.7%	32.3%
36,378	PETTIS	15,841	8,833	6,475	533	2,358 R	55.8%	40.9%	57.7%	42.3%
33,633	PHELPS	13,566	7,366	5,470	730	1,896 R	54.3%	40.3%	57.4%	42.6%
17,568	PIKE	7,591	3,932	3,454	205	478 R	51.8%	45.5%	53.2%	46.8%
46,341	PLATTE	18,756	10,092	7,342	1,322	2,750 R	53.8%	39.1%	57.9%	42.1%
18,822	POLK	8,368	4,842	3,336	190	1,506 R	57.9%	39.9%	59.2%	40.8%
42,011	PULASKI	7,871	3,998	3,707	166	291 R	50.8%	47.1%	51.9%	48.1%
6,092	PUTNAM	2,655	1,722	871	62	851 R	64.9%	32.8%	66.4%	33.6%
8,911	RALLS	4,142	1,968	2,069	105	101 D	47.5%	50.0%	48.7%	51.3%
25,460	RANDOLPH	10,276	5,141	4,884	251	257 R	50.0%	47.5%	51.3%	48.7%
21,378	RAY	8,871	4,064	4,518	289	454 D	45.8%	50.9%	47.4%	52.6%
7,230	REYNOLDS	3,250	1,271	1,919	60	648 D	39.1%	59.0%	39.8%	60.2%
12,458	RIPLEY	4,765	2,524	2,156	85	368 R	53.0%	45.2%	53.9%	46.1%
143,455	ST. CHARLES	59,768	36,050	20,668	3,050	15,382 R	60.3%	34.6%	63.6%	36.4%
8,622	ST. CLAIR	4,210	2,419	1,706	85	713 R	57.5%	40.5%	58.6%	41.4%
42,600	ST. FRANCOIS	16,916	8,914	7,495	507	1,419 R	52.7%	44.3%	54.3%	45.7%
453,085	ST. LOUIS CITY	170,751	50,333	113,697	6,721	63,364 D	29.5%	66.6%	30.7%	69.3%
974,815	ST. LOUIS COUNTY	484,831	263,518	192,796	28,517	70,722 R	54.4%	39.8%	57.7%	42.3%
15,180	STE. GENEVIEVE	6,291	2,768	3,324	199	556 D	44.0%	52.8%	45.4%	54.6%
24,919	SALINE	10,576	5,218	4,943	415	275 R	49.3%	46.7%	51.4%	48.6%
4,979	SCHUYLER	2,559	1,386	1,114	59	272 R	54.2%	43.5%	55.4%	44.6%
5,415	SCOTLAND	2,869	1,592	1,200	77	392 R	55.5%	41.8%	57.0%	43.0%
39,647	SCOTT	15,336	8,227	6,854	255	1,373 R	53.6%	44.7%	54.6%	45.4%
7,885	SHANNON	3,401	1,523	1,818	60	295 D	44.8%	53.5%	45.6%	54.4%
7,826	SHELBY	4,079	2,151	1,849	79	302 R	52.7%	45.3%	53.8%	46.2%
29,009	STODDARD	11,512	6,199	5,128	185	1,071 R	53.8%	44.5%	54.7%	45.3%
15,587	STONE	7,209	4,780	2,210	219	2,570 R	66.3%	30.7%	68.4%	31.6%
7,434	SULLIVAN	4,325	2,412	1,824	89	588 R	55.8%	42.2%	56.9%	43.1%
20,467	TANEY	9,854	6,230	3,389	235	2,841 R	63.2%	34.4%	64.8%	35.2%
21,070	TEXAS	9,309	4,879	4,261	169	618 R	52.4%	45.8%	53.4%	46.6%
19,806	VERNON	8,456	4,391	3,704	361	687 R	51.9%	43.8%	54.2%	45.8%
14,900	WARREN	6,743	4,366	2,132	245	2,234 R	64.7%	31.6%	67.2%	32.8%
17,983	WASHINGTON	6,465	3,439	2,873	153	566 R	53.2%	44.4%	54.5%	45.5%
11,277	WAYNE	5,444	2,823	2,549	72	274 R	51.9%	46.8%	52.6%	47.4%
20,414	WEBSTER	8,719	5,121	3,409	189	1,712 R	58.7%	39.1%	60.0%	40.0%
3,008	WORTH	1,657	833	760	64	73 R	50.3%	45.9%	52.3%	47.7%
16,188	WRIGHT	6,716	4,451	2,182	83	2,269 R	66.3%	32.5%	67.1%	32.9%
4,917,444	TOTAL	2,099,824	1,074,181	931,182	94,461	142,999 R	51.2%	44.3%	53.6%	46.4%

MISSOURI

GOVERNOR 1980

1980 Census Population	County	Total Vote	Republican	Democratic	Other	Rep.-Dem. Plurality	Percentage Total Vote Rep.	Dem.	Major Vote Rep.	Dem.
24,870	ADAIR	9,451	5,656	3,752	43	1,904 R	59.8%	39.7%	60.1%	39.9%
13,980	ANDREW	6,550	3,584	2,959	7	625 R	54.7%	45.2%	54.8%	45.2%
8,605	ATCHISON	3,527	1,928	1,581	18	347 R	54.7%	44.8%	54.9%	45.1%
26,458	AUDRAIN	11,784	5,562	6,209	13	647 D	47.2%	52.7%	47.3%	52.7%
24,408	BARRY	11,379	6,249	5,122	8	1,127 R	54.9%	45.0%	55.0%	45.0%
11,292	BARTON	5,329	3,213	2,109	7	1,104 R	60.3%	39.6%	60.4%	39.6%
15,873	BATES	7,538	3,740	3,788	10	48 D	49.6%	50.3%	49.7%	50.3%
12,183	BENTON	5,835	3,272	2,558	5	714 R	56.1%	43.8%	56.1%	43.9%
10,301	BOLLINGER	5,086	2,641	2,442	3	199 R	51.9%	48.0%	52.0%	48.0%
100,376	BOONE	38,790	23,040	15,129	621	7,911 R	59.4%	39.0%	60.4%	39.6%
87,888	BUCHANAN	35,087	17,838	17,158	91	680 R	50.8%	48.9%	51.0%	49.0%
37,693	BUTLER	14,050	7,471	6,569	10	902 R	53.2%	46.8%	53.2%	46.8%
8,660	CALDWELL	4,198	2,354	1,839	5	515 R	56.1%	43.8%	56.1%	43.9%
32,252	CALLAWAY	12,795	7,298	5,457	40	1,841 R	57.0%	42.6%	57.2%	42.8%
19,963	CAMDEN	10,192	6,470	3,707	15	2,763 R	63.5%	36.4%	63.6%	36.4%
58,837	CAPE GIRARDEAU	24,357	16,197	8,064	96	8,133 R	66.5%	33.1%	66.8%	33.2%
12,131	CARROLL	5,566	3,269	2,292	5	977 R	58.7%	41.2%	58.8%	41.2%
5,428	CARTER	2,353	1,250	1,098	5	152 R	53.1%	46.7%	53.2%	46.8%
51,029	CASS	18,729	9,499	9,172	58	327 R	50.7%	49.0%	50.9%	49.1%
11,894	CEDAR	5,266	3,118	2,144	4	974 R	59.2%	40.7%	59.3%	40.7%
10,489	CHARITON	4,958	2,343	2,611	4	268 D	47.3%	52.7%	47.3%	52.7%
22,402	CHRISTIAN	10,228	5,759	4,453	16	1,306 R	56.3%	43.5%	56.4%	43.6%
8,493	CLARK	3,596	1,729	1,864	3	135 D	48.1%	51.8%	48.1%	51.9%
136,488	CLAY	55,785	30,777	24,729	279	6,048 R	55.2%	44.3%	55.4%	44.6%
15,916	CLINTON	6,770	3,467	3,290	13	177 R	51.2%	48.6%	51.3%	48.7%
56,663	COLE	26,463	17,715	8,686	62	9,029 R	66.9%	32.8%	67.1%	32.9%
14,643	COOPER	6,852	3,890	2,957	5	933 R	56.8%	43.2%	56.8%	43.2%
18,300	CRAWFORD	6,937	3,722	3,183	32	539 R	53.7%	45.9%	53.9%	46.1%
7,383	DADE	3,754	2,099	1,651	4	448 R	55.9%	44.0%	56.0%	44.0%
12,096	DALLAS	5,417	2,920	2,487	10	433 R	53.9%	45.9%	54.0%	46.0%
8,905	DAVIESS	3,989	2,089	1,897	3	192 R	52.4%	47.6%	52.4%	47.6%
8,222	DE KALB	3,874	2,076	1,789	9	287 R	53.6%	46.2%	53.7%	46.3%
14,517	DENT	6,115	3,198	2,908	9	290 R	52.3%	47.6%	52.4%	47.6%
11,594	DOUGLAS	5,186	3,151	2,011	24	1,140 R	60.8%	38.8%	61.0%	39.0%
36,324	DUNKLIN	11,239	5,203	6,026	10	823 D	46.3%	53.6%	46.3%	53.7%
71,233	FRANKLIN	26,744	15,058	11,560	126	3,498 R	56.3%	43.2%	56.6%	43.4%
13,181	GASCONADE	6,158	4,286	1,857	15	2,429 R	69.6%	30.2%	69.8%	30.2%
7,887	GENTRY	3,872	2,121	1,745	6	376 R	54.8%	45.1%	54.9%	45.1%
185,302	GREENE	76,944	44,471	32,161	312	12,310 R	57.8%	41.8%	58.0%	42.0%
11,959	GRUNDY	5,097	2,976	2,118	3	858 R	58.4%	41.6%	58.4%	41.6%
9,890	HARRISON	4,592	2,912	1,677	3	1,235 R	63.4%	36.5%	63.5%	36.5%
19,672	HENRY	9,626	4,557	5,055	14	498 D	47.3%	52.5%	47.4%	52.6%
6,367	HICKORY	3,208	1,690	1,511	7	179 R	52.7%	47.1%	52.8%	47.2%
6,882	HOLT	3,196	1,799	1,390	7	409 R	56.3%	43.5%	56.4%	43.6%
10,008	HOWARD	4,552	2,060	2,489	3	429 D	45.3%	54.7%	45.3%	54.7%
28,807	HOWELL	11,685	6,956	4,711	18	2,245 R	59.5%	40.3%	59.6%	40.4%
11,084	IRON	4,537	2,322	2,206	9	116 R	51.2%	48.6%	51.3%	48.7%
629,180	JACKSON	255,061	116,304	137,494	1,263	21,190 D	45.6%	53.9%	45.8%	54.2%
86,958	JASPER	34,559	20,821	13,709	29	7,112 R	60.2%	39.7%	60.3%	39.7%
146,814	JEFFERSON	54,574	27,691	26,762	121	929 R	50.7%	49.0%	50.9%	49.1%
39,059	JOHNSON	12,635	7,100	5,457	78	1,643 R	56.2%	43.2%	56.5%	43.5%
5,508	KNOX	2,703	1,318	1,381	4	63 D	48.8%	51.1%	48.8%	51.2%
24,323	LACLEDE	9,237	5,408	3,815	14	1,593 R	58.5%	41.3%	58.6%	41.4%
29,925	LAFAYETTE	13,450	7,614	5,821	15	1,793 R	56.6%	43.3%	56.7%	43.3%
28,973	LAWRENCE	12,958	7,295	5,652	11	1,643 R	56.3%	43.6%	56.3%	43.7%
10,901	LEWIS	4,771	2,146	2,625		479 D	45.0%	55.0%	45.0%	55.0%
22,193	LINCOLN	9,287	3,945	5,325	17	1,380 D	42.5%	57.3%	42.6%	57.4%
15,495	LINN	7,257	3,580	3,669	8	89 D	49.3%	50.6%	49.4%	50.6%
15,739	LIVINGSTON	7,210	3,975	3,227	8	748 R	55.1%	44.8%	55.2%	44.8%
14,917	MCDONALD	6,774	3,813	2,955	6	858 R	56.3%	43.6%	56.3%	43.7%
16,313	MACON	8,131	3,942	4,178	11	236 D	48.5%	51.4%	48.5%	51.5%
10,725	MADISON	4,981	2,889	2,088	4	801 R	58.0%	41.9%	58.0%	42.0%
7,551	MARIES	3,796	1,825	1,965	6	140 D	48.1%	51.8%	48.2%	51.8%
28,638	MARION	12,222	5,956	6,261	5	305 D	48.7%	51.2%	48.8%	51.2%
4,685	MERCER	2,142	1,318	822	2	496 R	61.5%	38.4%	61.6%	38.4%
18,532	MILLER	8,154	5,309	2,840	5	2,469 R	65.1%	34.8%	65.1%	34.9%
15,726	MISSISSIPPI	5,452	2,091	3,356	5	1,265 D	38.4%	61.6%	38.4%	61.6%
12,068	MONITEAU	5,813	3,374	2,430	9	944 R	58.0%	41.8%	58.1%	41.9%
9,716	MONROE	4,536	1,582	2,946	8	1,364 D	34.9%	64.9%	34.9%	65.1%
11,537	MONTGOMERY	5,199	2,629	2,566	4	63 R	50.6%	49.4%	50.6%	49.4%

MISSOURI

GOVERNOR 1980

1980 Census Population	County	Total Vote	Republican	Democratic	Other	Rep.-Dem. Plurality		Percentage			
								Total Vote		Major Vote	
								Rep.	Dem.	Rep.	Dem.
13,807	MORGAN	6,179	3,573	2,601	5	972	R	57.8%	42.1%	57.9%	42.1%
22,945	NEW MADRID	8,181	3,176	5,002	3	1,826	D	38.8%	61.1%	38.8%	61.2%
40,555	NEWTON	16,323	9,770	6,487	66	3,283	R	59.9%	39.7%	60.1%	39.9%
21,996	NODAWAY	9,299	4,850	4,427	22	423	R	52.2%	47.6%	52.3%	47.7%
10,238	OREGON	3,843	1,542	2,299	2	757	D	40.1%	59.8%	40.1%	59.9%
12,014	OSAGE	5,819	3,366	2,448	5	918	R	57.8%	42.1%	57.9%	42.1%
7,961	OZARK	3,712	2,287	1,418	7	869	R	61.6%	38.2%	61.7%	38.3%
24,987	PEMISCOT	7,259	3,067	4,181	11	1,114	D	42.3%	57.6%	42.3%	57.7%
16,784	PERRY	7,718	4,333	3,381	4	952	R	56.1%	43.8%	56.2%	43.8%
36,378	PETTIS	15,713	8,075	7,616	22	459	R	51.4%	48.5%	51.5%	48.5%
33,633	PHELPS	13,516	7,701	5,755	60	1,946	R	57.0%	42.6%	57.2%	42.8%
17,568	PIKE	7,566	3,568	3,991	7	423	D	47.2%	52.7%	47.2%	52.8%
46,341	PLATTE	18,766	10,383	8,293	90	2,090	R	55.3%	44.2%	55.6%	44.4%
18,822	POLK	8,298	4,454	3,829	15	625	R	53.7%	46.1%	53.8%	46.2%
42,011	PULASKI	7,872	3,901	3,964	7	63	D	49.6%	50.4%	49.6%	50.4%
6,092	PUTNAM	2,618	1,710	906	2	804	R	65.3%	34.6%	65.4%	34.6%
8,911	RALLS	4,128	1,670	2,454	4	784	D	40.5%	59.4%	40.5%	59.5%
25,460	RANDOLPH	10,223	4,958	5,258	7	300	D	48.5%	51.4%	48.5%	51.5%
21,378	RAY	8,804	3,878	4,912	14	1,034	D	44.0%	55.8%	44.1%	55.9%
7,230	REYNOLDS	3,229	1,389	1,837	3	448	D	43.0%	56.9%	43.1%	56.9%
12,458	RIPLEY	4,714	2,510	2,202	2	308	R	53.2%	46.7%	53.3%	46.7%
143,455	ST. CHARLES	59,514	33,369	25,924	221	7,445	R	56.1%	43.6%	56.3%	43.7%
8,622	ST. CLAIR	4,194	2,126	2,060	8	66	R	50.7%	49.1%	50.8%	49.2%
42,600	ST. FRANCOIS	16,940	8,797	8,113	30	684	R	51.9%	47.9%	52.0%	48.0%
453,085	ST. LOUIS CITY	171,171	56,454	113,908	809	57,454	D	33.0%	66.5%	33.1%	66.9%
974,815	ST. LOUIS COUNTY	481,437	282,313	197,222	1,902	85,091	R	58.6%	41.0%	58.9%	41.1%
15,180	STE. GENEVIEVE	6,195	2,490	3,692	13	1,202	D	40.2%	59.6%	40.3%	59.7%
24,919	SALINE	10,505	5,608	4,872	25	736	R	53.4%	46.4%	53.5%	46.5%
4,979	SCHUYLER	2,550	1,272	1,274	4	2	D	49.9%	50.0%	50.0%	50.0%
5,415	SCOTLAND	2,856	1,486	1,369	1	117	R	52.0%	47.9%	52.0%	48.0%
39,647	SCOTT	15,299	7,619	7,669	11	50	D	49.8%	50.1%	49.8%	50.2%
7,885	SHANNON	3,329	1,530	1,793	6	263	D	46.0%	53.9%	46.0%	54.0%
7,826	SHELBY	4,064	1,701	2,361	2	660	D	41.9%	58.1%	41.9%	58.1%
29,009	STODDARD	11,406	6,093	5,308	5	785	R	53.4%	46.5%	53.4%	46.6%
15,587	STONE	7,047	4,224	2,820	3	1,404	R	59.9%	40.0%	60.0%	40.0%
7,434	SULLIVAN	4,323	2,240	2,082	1	158	R	51.8%	48.2%	51.8%	48.2%
20,467	TANEY	9,805	5,873	3,918	14	1,955	R	59.9%	40.0%	60.0%	40.0%
21,070	TEXAS	9,313	4,932	4,369	12	563	R	53.0%	46.9%	53.0%	47.0%
19,806	VERNON	8,418	4,447	3,950	21	497	R	52.8%	46.9%	53.0%	47.0%
14,900	WARREN	6,757	3,827	2,917	13	910	R	56.6%	43.2%	56.7%	43.3%
17,983	WASHINGTON	6,488	3,278	3,202	8	76	R	50.5%	49.4%	50.6%	49.4%
11,277	WAYNE	5,424	2,769	2,652	3	117	R	51.1%	48.9%	51.1%	48.9%
20,414	WEBSTER	8,727	4,579	4,137	11	442	R	52.5%	47.4%	52.5%	47.5%
3,008	WORTH	1,646	807	837	2	30	D	49.0%	50.9%	49.1%	50.9%
16,188	WRIGHT	6,702	4,035	2,659	8	1,376	R	60.2%	39.7%	60.3%	39.7%
4,917,444	TOTAL	2,088,028	1,098,950	981,884	7,194	117,066	R	52.6%	47.0%	52.8%	47.2%

MISSOURI

SENATOR 1980

1980 Census Population	County	Total Vote	Republican	Democratic	Other	Rep.-Dem. Plurality	Percentage Total Vote Rep.	Total Vote Dem.	Major Vote Rep.	Major Vote Dem.
24,870	ADAIR	9,355	4,475	4,841	39	366 D	47.8%	51.7%	48.0%	52.0%
13,980	ANDREW	6,474	3,105	3,360	9	255 D	48.0%	51.9%	48.0%	52.0%
8,605	ATCHISON	3,414	1,320	2,085	9	765 D	38.7%	61.1%	38.8%	61.2%
26,458	AUDRAIN	11,678	5,849	5,816	13	33 R	50.1%	49.8%	50.1%	49.9%
24,408	BARRY	11,273	6,750	4,509	14	2,241 R	59.9%	40.0%	60.0%	40.0%
11,292	BARTON	5,286	3,042	2,232	12	810 R	57.5%	42.2%	57.7%	42.3%
15,873	BATES	7,470	3,518	3,942	10	424 D	47.1%	52.8%	47.2%	52.8%
12,183	BENTON	5,742	3,078	2,658	6	420 R	53.6%	46.3%	53.7%	46.3%
10,301	BOLLINGER	5,017	2,478	2,535	4	57 D	49.4%	50.5%	49.4%	50.6%
100,376	BOONE	38,598	14,355	23,857	386	9,502 D	37.2%	61.8%	37.6%	62.4%
87,888	BUCHANAN	34,214	13,778	20,352	84	6,574 D	40.3%	59.5%	40.4%	59.6%
37,693	BUTLER	13,704	7,714	5,977	13	1,737 R	56.3%	43.6%	56.3%	43.7%
8,660	CALDWELL	4,161	2,130	2,026	5	104 R	51.2%	48.7%	51.3%	48.7%
32,252	CALLAWAY	12,494	6,098	6,351	45	253 D	48.8%	50.8%	49.0%	51.0%
19,963	CAMDEN	10,012	6,201	3,795	16	2,406 R	61.9%	37.9%	62.0%	38.0%
58,837	CAPE GIRARDEAU	22,983	12,236	10,690	57	1,546 R	53.2%	46.5%	53.4%	46.6%
12,131	CARROLL	5,542	2,869	2,669	4	200 R	51.8%	48.2%	51.8%	48.2%
5,428	CARTER	2,251	1,078	1,167	6	89 D	47.9%	51.8%	48.0%	52.0%
51,029	CASS	18,431	8,251	10,112	68	1,861 D	44.8%	54.9%	44.9%	55.1%
11,894	CEDAR	5,220	3,284	1,931	5	1,353 R	62.9%	37.0%	63.0%	37.0%
10,489	CHARITON	4,900	2,145	2,750	5	605 D	43.8%	56.1%	43.8%	56.2%
22,402	CHRISTIAN	10,052	6,167	3,870	15	2,297 R	61.4%	38.5%	61.4%	38.6%
8,493	CLARK	3,564	1,646	1,913	5	267 D	46.2%	53.7%	46.2%	53.8%
136,488	CLAY	54,359	22,786	31,288	285	8,502 D	41.9%	57.6%	42.1%	57.9%
15,916	CLINTON	6,755	2,831	3,915	9	1,084 D	41.9%	58.0%	42.0%	58.0%
56,663	COLE	26,285	15,880	10,325	80	5,555 R	60.4%	39.3%	60.6%	39.4%
14,643	COOPER	6,772	3,485	3,281	6	204 R	51.5%	48.4%	51.5%	48.5%
18,300	CRAWFORD	6,873	4,134	2,714	25	1,420 R	60.1%	39.5%	60.4%	39.6%
7,383	DADE	3,681	2,221	1,454	6	767 R	60.3%	39.5%	60.4%	39.6%
12,096	DALLAS	5,312	3,189	2,114	9	1,075 R	60.0%	39.8%	60.1%	39.9%
8,905	DAVIESS	3,970	1,790	2,174	6	384 D	45.1%	54.8%	45.2%	54.8%
8,222	DE KALB	3,844	1,769	2,062	13	293 D	46.0%	53.6%	46.2%	53.8%
14,517	DENT	6,034	3,512	2,515	7	997 R	58.2%	41.7%	58.3%	41.7%
11,594	DOUGLAS	4,978	3,362	1,595	21	1,767 R	67.5%	32.0%	67.8%	32.2%
36,324	DUNKLIN	10,781	3,869	6,902	10	3,033 D	35.9%	64.0%	35.9%	64.1%
71,233	FRANKLIN	26,423	14,872	11,414	137	3,458 R	56.3%	43.2%	56.6%	43.4%
13,181	GASCONADE	5,892	4,192	1,677	23	2,515 R	71.1%	28.5%	71.4%	28.6%
7,887	GENTRY	3,844	1,694	2,146	4	452 D	44.1%	55.8%	44.1%	55.9%
185,302	GREENE	76,362	41,396	34,609	357	6,787 R	54.2%	45.3%	54.5%	45.5%
11,959	GRUNDY	5,055	2,626	2,421	8	205 R	51.9%	47.9%	52.0%	48.0%
9,890	HARRISON	4,531	2,401	2,125	5	276 R	53.0%	46.9%	53.0%	47.0%
19,672	HENRY	9,630	3,889	5,723	18	1,834 D	40.4%	59.4%	40.5%	59.5%
6,367	HICKORY	3,155	1,835	1,317	3	518 R	58.2%	41.7%	58.2%	41.8%
6,882	HOLT	3,149	1,726	1,418	5	308 R	54.8%	45.0%	54.9%	45.1%
10,008	HOWARD	4,438	1,720	2,715	3	995 D	38.8%	61.2%	38.8%	61.2%
28,807	HOWELL	11,437	6,874	4,545	18	2,329 R	60.1%	39.7%	60.2%	39.8%
11,084	IRON	4,465	2,013	2,447	5	434 D	45.1%	54.8%	45.1%	54.9%
629,180	JACKSON	253,669	88,385	164,032	1,252	75,647 D	34.8%	64.7%	35.0%	65.0%
86,958	JASPER	34,030	21,114	12,885	31	8,229 R	62.0%	37.9%	62.1%	37.9%
146,814	JEFFERSON	54,367	29,367	24,862	138	4,505 R	54.0%	45.7%	54.2%	45.8%
39,059	JOHNSON	12,464	5,735	6,660	69	925 D	46.0%	53.4%	46.3%	53.7%
5,508	KNOX	2,667	1,184	1,482	1	298 D	44.4%	55.6%	44.4%	55.6%
24,323	LACLEDE	9,087	5,513	3,555	19	1,958 R	60.7%	39.1%	60.8%	39.2%
29,925	LAFAYETTE	13,350	6,250	7,087	13	837 D	46.8%	53.1%	46.9%	53.1%
28,973	LAWRENCE	12,828	7,664	5,151	13	2,513 R	59.7%	40.2%	59.8%	40.2%
10,901	LEWIS	4,656	1,719	2,933	4	1,214 D	36.9%	63.0%	37.0%	63.0%
22,193	LINCOLN	9,206	4,324	4,861	21	537 D	47.0%	52.8%	47.1%	52.9%
15,495	LINN	7,162	3,037	4,122	3	1,085 D	42.4%	57.6%	42.4%	57.6%
15,739	LIVINGSTON	7,196	3,236	3,952	8	716 D	45.0%	54.9%	45.0%	55.0%
14,917	MCDONALD	6,661	3,835	2,819	7	1,016 R	57.6%	42.3%	57.6%	42.4%
16,313	MACON	8,024	3,582	4,431	11	849 D	44.6%	55.2%	44.7%	55.3%
10,725	MADISON	4,964	2,532	2,427	5	105 R	51.0%	48.9%	51.1%	48.9%
7,551	MARIES	3,741	1,916	1,821	4	95 R	51.2%	48.7%	51.3%	48.7%
28,638	MARION	12,001	5,178	6,813	10	1,635 D	43.1%	56.8%	43.2%	56.8%
4,685	MERCER	2,081	1,094	985	2	109 R	52.6%	47.3%	52.6%	47.4%
18,532	MILLER	8,017	5,326	2,684	7	2,642 R	66.4%	33.5%	66.5%	33.5%
15,726	MISSISSIPPI	5,240	1,895	3,341	4	1,446 D	36.2%	63.8%	36.2%	63.8%
12,068	MONITEAU	5,761	3,268	2,487	6	781 R	56.7%	43.2%	56.8%	43.2%
9,716	MONROE	4,503	1,720	2,776	7	1,056 D	38.2%	61.6%	38.3%	61.7%
11,537	MONTGOMERY	5,152	2,757	2,390	5	367 R	53.5%	46.4%	53.6%	46.4%

MISSOURI

SENATOR 1980

1980 Census Population	County	Total Vote	Republican	Democratic	Other	Rep.-Dem. Plurality	Percentage Total Vote Rep.	Dem.	Major Vote Rep.	Dem.
13,807	MORGAN	6,087	3,416	2,664	7	752 R	56.1%	43.8%	56.2%	43.8%
22,945	NEW MADRID	7,914	3,056	4,854	4	1,798 D	38.6%	61.3%	38.6%	61.4%
40,555	NEWTON	15,834	9,759	5,986	89	3,773 R	61.6%	37.8%	62.0%	38.0%
21,996	NODAWAY	9,240	3,638	5,586	16	1,948 D	39.4%	60.5%	39.4%	60.6%
10,238	OREGON	3,752	1,428	2,319	5	891 D	38.1%	61.8%	38.1%	61.9%
12,014	OSAGE	5,774	3,449	2,318	7	1,131 R	59.7%	40.1%	59.8%	40.2%
7,961	OZARK	3,576	2,340	1,227	9	1,113 R	65.4%	34.3%	65.6%	34.4%
24,987	PEMISCOT	6,986	2,245	4,734	7	2,489 D	32.1%	67.8%	32.2%	67.8%
16,784	PERRY	7,527	4,275	3,245	7	1,030 R	56.8%	43.1%	56.8%	43.2%
36,378	PETTIS	15,578	7,016	8,553	9	1,537 D	45.0%	54.9%	45.1%	54.9%
33,633	PHELPS	13,424	7,365	6,005	54	1,360 R	54.9%	44.7%	55.1%	44.9%
17,568	PIKE	7,448	3,600	3,844	4	244 D	48.3%	51.6%	48.4%	51.6%
46,341	PLATTE	18,695	7,937	10,667	91	2,730 D	42.5%	57.1%	42.7%	57.3%
18,822	POLK	8,247	4,435	3,802	10	633 R	53.8%	46.1%	53.8%	46.2%
42,011	PULASKI	7,719	4,136	3,571	12	565 R	53.6%	46.3%	53.7%	46.3%
6,092	PUTNAM	2,586	1,481	1,104	1	377 R	57.3%	42.7%	57.3%	42.7%
8,911	RALLS	4,070	1,642	2,420	8	778 D	40.3%	59.5%	40.4%	59.6%
25,460	RANDOLPH	10,030	4,208	5,820	2	1,612 D	42.0%	58.0%	42.0%	58.0%
21,378	RAY	8,705	3,059	5,633	13	2,574 D	35.1%	64.7%	35.2%	64.8%
7,230	REYNOLDS	3,166	1,167	1,995	4	828 D	36.9%	63.0%	36.9%	63.1%
12,458	RIPLEY	4,603	2,250	2,348	5	98 D	48.9%	51.0%	48.9%	51.1%
143,455	ST. CHARLES	57,309	31,743	25,376	190	6,367 R	55.4%	44.3%	55.6%	44.4%
8,622	ST. CLAIR	4,153	2,199	1,949	5	250 R	52.9%	46.9%	53.0%	47.0%
42,600	ST. FRANCOIS	16,791	8,671	8,100	20	571 R	51.6%	48.2%	51.7%	48.3%
453,085	ST. LOUIS CITY	170,631	48,490	121,383	758	72,893 D	28.4%	71.1%	28.5%	71.5%
974,815	ST. LOUIS COUNTY	482,009	261,298	219,030	1,681	42,268 R	54.2%	45.4%	54.4%	45.6%
15,180	STE. GENEVIEVE	6,138	2,459	3,671	8	1,212 D	40.1%	59.8%	40.1%	59.9%
24,919	SALINE	10,328	4,238	6,076	14	1,838 D	41.0%	58.8%	41.1%	58.9%
4,979	SCHUYLER	2,502	1,126	1,372	4	246 D	45.0%	54.8%	45.1%	54.9%
5,415	SCOTLAND	2,810	1,229	1,577	4	348 D	43.7%	56.1%	43.8%	56.2%
39,647	SCOTT	14,932	6,281	8,641	10	2,360 D	42.1%	57.9%	42.1%	57.9%
7,885	SHANNON	3,227	1,425	1,795	7	370 D	44.2%	55.6%	44.3%	55.7%
7,826	SHELBY	4,024	1,786	2,235	3	449 D	44.4%	55.5%	44.4%	55.6%
29,009	STODDARD	11,073	5,207	5,860	6	653 D	47.0%	52.9%	47.0%	53.0%
15,587	STONE	6,940	4,449	2,484	7	1,965 R	64.1%	35.8%	64.2%	35.8%
7,434	SULLIVAN	4,270	2,114	2,154	2	40 D	49.5%	50.4%	49.5%	50.5%
20,467	TANEY	9,603	5,933	3,661	9	2,272 R	61.8%	38.1%	61.8%	38.2%
21,070	TEXAS	9,179	4,708	4,460	11	248 R	51.3%	48.6%	51.4%	48.6%
19,806	VERNON	8,318	3,938	4,360	20	422 D	47.3%	52.4%	47.5%	52.5%
14,900	WARREN	6,656	4,097	2,546	13	1,551 R	61.6%	38.3%	61.7%	38.3%
17,983	WASHINGTON	6,367	3,393	2,963	11	430 R	53.3%	46.5%	53.4%	46.6%
11,277	WAYNE	5,317	2,570	2,743	4	173 D	48.3%	51.6%	48.4%	51.6%
20,414	WEBSTER	8,553	4,913	3,627	13	1,286 R	57.4%	42.4%	57.5%	42.5%
3,008	WORTH	1,637	638	998	1	360 D	39.0%	61.0%	39.0%	61.0%
16,188	WRIGHT	6,550	4,328	2,213	9	2,115 R	66.1%	33.8%	66.2%	33.8%
4,917,444	TOTAL	2,066,965	985,399	1,074,859	6,707	89,460 D	47.7%	52.0%	47.8%	52.2%

MISSOURI

CONGRESS

CD	Year	Total Vote	Republican Vote	Republican Candidate	Democratic Vote	Democratic Candidate	Other Vote	Rep.-Dem. Plurality	Total Vote Rep.	Total Vote Dem.	Major Vote Rep.	Major Vote Dem.
1	1980	129,939	38,667	WHITE, WILLIAM E.	91,272	CLAY, WILLIAM		52,605 D	29.8%	70.2%	29.8%	70.2%
1	1978	99,010	30,995	WHITE, WILLIAM E.	65,950	CLAY, WILLIAM	2,065	34,955 D	31.3%	66.6%	32.0%	68.0%
1	1976	133,226	45,874	WITHERSPOON, ROBERT L.	87,310	CLAY, WILLIAM	42	41,436 D	34.4%	65.5%	34.4%	65.6%
1	1974	90,640	28,707	MARTIN, ARTHUR O.	61,933	CLAY, WILLIAM		33,226 D	31.7%	68.3%	31.7%	68.3%
1	1972	148,694	53,596	FUNSCH, RICHARD O.	95,098	CLAY, WILLIAM		41,502 D	36.0%	64.0%	36.0%	64.0%
2	1980	229,989	81,762	SHIELDS, JOHN O.	148,227	YOUNG, ROBERT A.		66,465 D	35.6%	64.4%	35.6%	64.4%
2	1978	182,406	79,495	CHASE, BOB	102,911	YOUNG, ROBERT A.		23,416 D	43.6%	56.4%	43.6%	56.4%
2	1976	218,461	106,811	SNYDER, ROBERT O.	111,568	YOUNG, ROBERT A.	82	4,757 D	48.9%	51.1%	48.9%	51.1%
2	1974	141,003	55,026	OHLENDORF, HOWARD C.	85,977	SYMINGTON, JAMES W.		30,951 D	39.0%	61.0%	39.0%	61.0%
2	1972	211,524	77,192	COOPER, JOHN W.	134,332	SYMINGTON, JAMES W.		57,140 D	36.5%	63.5%	36.5%	63.5%
3	1980	184,409	41,277	CEDARBURG, ROBERT A.	143,132	GEPHARDT, RICHARD A.		101,855 D	22.4%	77.6%	22.4%	77.6%
3	1978	148,446	26,881	BUCHSCHACHER, LEE	121,565	GEPHARDT, RICHARD A.		94,684 D	18.1%	81.9%	18.1%	81.9%
3	1976	180,743	65,623	BADARACCO, JOSEPH L.	115,109	GEPHARDT, RICHARD A.	11	49,486 D	36.3%	63.7%	36.3%	63.7%
3	1974	129,541	31,489	RAISCH, JOANN P.	96,201	SULLIVAN, LEONOR K.	1,851	64,712 D	24.3%	74.3%	24.7%	75.3%
3	1972	179,353	54,523	HOLST, ALBERT	124,365	SULLIVAN, LEONOR K.	465	69,842 D	30.4%	69.3%	30.5%	69.5%
4	1980	223,328	71,869	BAKER, WILLIAM D.	151,459	SKELTON, IKE		79,590 D	32.2%	67.8%	32.2%	67.8%
4	1978	165,864	45,116	BAKER, WILLIAM D.	120,748	SKELTON, IKE		75,632 D	27.2%	72.8%	27.2%	72.8%
4	1976	207,562	91,605	KING, RICHARD A.	115,955	SKELTON, IKE	2	24,350 D	44.1%	55.9%	44.1%	55.9%
4	1974	121,502	39,055	PATTERSON, CLAUDE	82,447	RANDALL, WILLIAM J.		43,392 D	32.1%	67.9%	32.1%	67.9%
4	1972	188,359	80,228	BARROWS, RAYMOND E.	108,131	RANDALL, WILLIAM J.		27,903 D	42.6%	57.4%	42.6%	57.4%
5	1980	158,266	47,309	BAKER, VINCENT E.	110,957	BOLLING, RICHARD		63,648 D	29.9%	70.1%	29.9%	70.1%
5	1978	114,131	30,360	WALTER, STEVEN L.	82,140	BOLLING, RICHARD	1,631	51,780 D	26.6%	72.0%	27.0%	73.0%
5	1976	148,302	41,681	COLLINS, JOANNE	100,876	BOLLING, RICHARD	5,745	59,195 D	28.1%	68.0%	29.2%	70.8%
5	1974	82,605	24,669	MCDONOUGH, JOHN J.	57,081	BOLLING, RICHARD	855	32,412 D	29.9%	69.1%	30.2%	69.8%
5	1972	149,450	53,257	RICE, VERNON E.	93,812	BOLLING, RICHARD	2,381	40,555 D	35.6%	62.8%	36.2%	63.8%
6	1980	211,329	149,281	COLEMAN, E. THOMAS	62,048	KING, VERNON		87,233 R	70.6%	29.4%	70.6%	29.4%
6	1978	172,635	96,574	COLEMAN, E. THOMAS	76,061	SNOWDEN, PHIL		20,513 R	55.9%	44.1%	55.9%	44.1%
6	1976	206,707	120,969	COLEMAN, E. THOMAS	83,755	MAXFIELD, MORGAN	1,983	37,214 R	58.5%	40.5%	59.1%	40.9%
6	1974	128,756	27,147	SPEERS, GROVER H.	101,609	LITTON, JERRY		74,462 D	21.1%	78.9%	21.1%	78.9%
6	1972	201,657	91,610	SLOAN, RUSSELL	110,047	LITTON, JERRY		18,437 D	45.4%	54.6%	45.4%	54.6%
7	1980	238,512	161,668	TAYLOR, GENE	76,844	YOUNG, KEN		84,824 R	67.8%	32.2%	67.8%	32.2%
7	1978	170,917	104,566	TAYLOR, GENE	66,351	THOMAS, JIM		38,215 R	61.2%	38.8%	61.2%	38.8%
7	1976	215,515	133,656	TAYLOR, GENE	81,848	HAWKINS, DOLAN G.	11	51,808 R	62.0%	38.0%	62.0%	38.0%
7	1974	152,440	79,787	TAYLOR, GENE	72,653	FRANKS, RICHARD L.		7,134 R	52.3%	47.7%	52.3%	47.7%
7	1972	208,393	132,780	TAYLOR, GENE	75,613	THOMAS, WILLIAM		57,167 R	63.7%	36.3%	63.7%	36.3%
8	1980	223,426	127,675	BAILEY, WENDELL	95,751	GARDNER, STEVE		31,924 R	57.1%	42.9%	57.1%	42.9%
8	1978	159,618	63,109	MEYER, DONALD D.	96,509	ICHORD, RICHARD		33,400 D	39.5%	60.5%	39.5%	60.5%
8	1976	196,650	60,179	LEICK, CHARLES R.	132,386	ICHORD, RICHARD	4,085	72,207 D	30.6%	67.3%	31.3%	68.7%
8	1974	123,964	37,369	NOLAND, JAMES A.	86,595	ICHORD, RICHARD		49,226 D	30.1%	69.9%	30.1%	69.9%
8	1972	181,136	68,580	COUNTIE, DAVID R.	112,556	ICHORD, RICHARD		43,976 D	37.9%	62.1%	37.9%	62.1%
9	1980	240,740	104,835	TURNER, JOHN W.	135,905	VOLKMER, HAROLD		31,070 D	43.5%	56.5%	43.5%	56.5%
9	1978	180,965	45,795	DENT, JERRY A.	135,170	VOLKMER, HAROLD		89,375 D	25.3%	74.7%	25.3%	74.7%
9	1976	215,144	94,816	FRAPPIER, J. H.	120,325	VOLKMER, HAROLD	3	25,509 D	44.1%	55.9%	44.1%	55.9%
9	1974	131,864	44,318	BISCHOF, MILTON	87,546	HUNGATE, WILLIAM L.		43,228 D	33.6%	66.4%	33.6%	66.4%
9	1972	198,678	66,528	PRANGE, ROBERT L.	132,150	HUNGATE, WILLIAM L.		65,622 D	33.5%	66.5%	33.5%	66.5%
10	1980	210,632	116,167	EMERSON, BILL	94,465	BURLISON, BILL D.		21,702 R	55.2%	44.8%	55.2%	44.8%
10	1978	151,835	52,687	WEIR, JAMES A.	99,148	BURLISON, BILL D.		46,461 D	34.7%	65.3%	34.7%	65.3%
10	1976	182,706	51,024	CARRON, JOE	131,675	BURLISON, BILL D.	7	80,651 D	27.9%	72.1%	27.9%	72.1%
10	1974	106,727	29,050	FARROW, TRUMAN	77,677	BURLISON, BILL D.		48,627 D	27.2%	72.8%	27.2%	72.8%
10	1972	165,384	59,083	SVENDROWSKI, FRANK	106,301	BURLISON, BILL D.		47,218 D	35.7%	64.3%	35.7%	64.3%

MISSOURI

1980 GENERAL ELECTION

President Other vote was 77,920 Anderson (Independent); 14,422 Clark (Libertarian); 1,515 DeBerry (Socialist Workers); 573 Commoner (write-in); 26 Hall (write-in); 5 McCormack (write-in). State-wide total for other vote column includes 604 scattered votes not reported by county.

Governor Other vote was 7,193 Salvo (Socialist Workers) and 1 scattered.

Senator Other vote was Pettit (Socialist Workers).

Congress

1980 PRIMARIES

AUGUST 5 REPUBLICAN

Governor 223,678 Christopher Bond; 122,867 William Phelps; 3,532 Troy Spencer; 2,002 Paul Binggeli.

Senator 197,060 Gene McNary; 82,332 David Doctorian; 21,959 Morris Duncan; 18,893 Gregory Hansman.

Congress Unopposed in three CD's. Contested as follows:

CD 1 7,910 William E. White; 1,438 Takuri Tei.
CD 2 12,263 John O. Shields; 10,593 Norman A. Myers; 8,166 Hugh V. Murray; 3,563 Wallace Anderson; 2,451 Joseph J. Rohan.
CD 4 16,173 William D. Baker; 5,701 Gary Dolson; 4,204 John Hovis.
CD 5 11,181 Vincent E. Baker; 4,432 Stella Sollars.
CD 8 17,741 Wendell Bailey; 14,081 Paul Dietrich; 10,017 Larry R. Marshall; 7,735 Don Meyer, 2,475 Janice Noland; 614 Billy Brown.
CD 9 15,636 John W. Turner; 5,396 Arthur L. Martin; 4,269 Ken A. Dudley; 3,306 Terry G. Agler.
CD 10 18,758 Bill Emerson; 5,573 James A. Weir.

AUGUST 5 DEMOCRATIC

Governor 359,263 Joseph P. Teasdale; 294,917 James I. Spainhower; 11,377 Milton Morris.

Senator 553,392 Thomas F. Eagleton; 53,280 Lee C. Sutton; 38,677 Herb Fillmore.

Congress Unopposed in CD 3. Contested as follows:

CD 1 37,611 William Clay; 6,643 Melvin Smotherson; 4,900 Elsa D. Hill; 2,893 David Grace.
CD 2 51,325 Robert A. Young; 8,175 Edward P. Roche.
CD 4 63,567 Ike Skelton; 8,036 William B. Biggs.
CD 5 40,656 Richard Bolling; 9,110 Bert Naberhaus.
CD 6 24,331 Vernon King; 19,130 H. N. Sutherland; 17,694 Gene Schweizer.
CD 7 14,029 Ken Young; 8,262 James W. Roberts; 7,761 Virgil J. Hill.
CD 8 14,764 Steve Gardner; 10,683 Michael J. Lybyer; 9,414 Jim McHugh; 9,277 Tom Rost; 7,118 John L. Woodward; 3,358 Ann Kutcher; 3,041 William D. Kimme; 1,450 George D. Weber; 1,374 Emerald McKay; 1,218 Michael R. Burke; 1,183 Earl C. Grandstaff; 793 James C. Foreman; 733 Louis E. Bredeman; 720 Leonard L. Bade; 307 Francis Welch.
CD 9 73,258 Harold Volkmer; 11,495 Hiram King.
CD 10 50,728 Bill D. Burlison; 37,265 Frank X. Hastings.

MONTANA

GOVERNOR
Ted Schwinden (D). Elected 1980 to a four-year term.

SENATORS
Max S. Baucus (D). Elected 1978 to a six-year term.

John Melcher (D). Elected 1976 to a six-year term.

REPRESENTATIVES
1. Pat Williams (D)   2. Ron Marlenee (R)

POSTWAR VOTE FOR GOVERNOR

Year	Total Vote	Republican Vote	Candidate	Democratic Vote	Candidate	Other Vote	Rep.-Dem. Plurality	Percentage Total Vote Rep.	Dem.	Major Vote Rep.	Dem.
1980	360,466	160,892	Ramirez, Jack	199,574	Schwinden, Ted	—	38,682 D	44.6%	55.4%	44.6%	55.4%
1976	316,720	115,848	Woodahl, Robert	195,420	Judge, Thomas L.	5,452	79,572 D	36.6%	61.7%	37.2%	62.8%
1972	318,754	146,231	Smith, Ed	172,523	Judge, Thomas L.	—	26,292 D	45.9%	54.1%	45.9%	54.1%
1968	278,112	116,432	Babcock, Tim M.	150,481	Anderson, Forrest H.	11,199	34,049 D	41.9%	54.1%	43.6%	56.4%
1964	280,975	144,113	Babcock, Tim M.	136,862	Renne, Roland	—	7,251 R	51.3%	48.7%	51.3%	48.7%
1960	279,881	154,230	Nutter, Donald G.	125,651	Cannon, Paul	—	28,579 R	55.1%	44.9%	55.1%	44.9%
1956	270,366	138,878	Aronson, J. Hugo	131,488	Olsen, Arnold H.	—	7,390 R	51.4%	48.6%	51.4%	48.6%
1952	263,792	134,423	Aronson, J. Hugo	129,369	Bonner, John W.	—	5,054 R	51.0%	49.0%	51.0%	49.0%
1948	222,964	97,792	Ford, Sam C.	124,267	Bonner, John W.	905	26,475 D	43.9%	55.7%	44.0%	56.0%

POSTWAR VOTE FOR SENATOR

Year	Total Vote	Republican Vote	Candidate	Democratic Vote	Candidate	Other Vote	Rep.-Dem. Plurality	Percentage Total Vote Rep.	Dem.	Major Vote Rep.	Dem.
1978	287,942	127,589	Williams, Larry	160,353	Baucus, Max S.	—	32,764 D	44.3%	55.7%	44.3%	55.7%
1976	321,445	115,213	Burger, Stanley C.	206,232	Melcher, John	—	91,019 D	35.8%	64.2%	35.8%	64.2%
1972	314,925	151,316	Hibbard, Henry S.	163,609	Metcalf, Lee	—	12,293 D	48.0%	52.0%	48.0%	52.0%
1970	247,869	97,809	Wallace, Harold E.	150,060	Mansfield, Mike	—	52,251 D	39.5%	60.5%	39.5%	60.5%
1966	259,863	121,697	Babcock, Tim M.	138,166	Metcalf, Lee	—	16,469 D	46.8%	53.2%	46.8%	53.2%
1964	280,010	99,367	Blewett, Alex	180,643	Mansfield, Mike	—	81,276 D	35.5%	64.5%	35.5%	64.5%
1960	276,612	136,281	Fjare, Orvin B.	140,331	Metcalf, Lee	—	4,050 D	49.3%	50.7%	49.3%	50.7%
1958	229,483	54,573	Welch, Lou W.	174,910	Mansfield, Mike	—	120,337 D	23.8%	76.2%	23.8%	76.2%
1954	227,454	112,863	D'Ewart, Wesley A.	114,591	Murray, James E.	—	1,728 D	49.6%	50.4%	49.6%	50.4%
1952	262,297	127,360	Ecton, Zales N.	133,109	Mansfield, Mike	1,828	5,749 D	48.6%	50.7%	48.9%	51.1%
1948	221,003	94,458	David, Tom J.	125,193	Murray, James E.	1,352	30,735 D	42.7%	56.6%	43.0%	57.0%
1946	190,566	101,901	Ecton, Zales N.	86,476	Erickson, Leif	2,189	15,425 R	53.5%	45.4%	54.1%	45.9%

MONTANA

Districts Established March 3, 1971

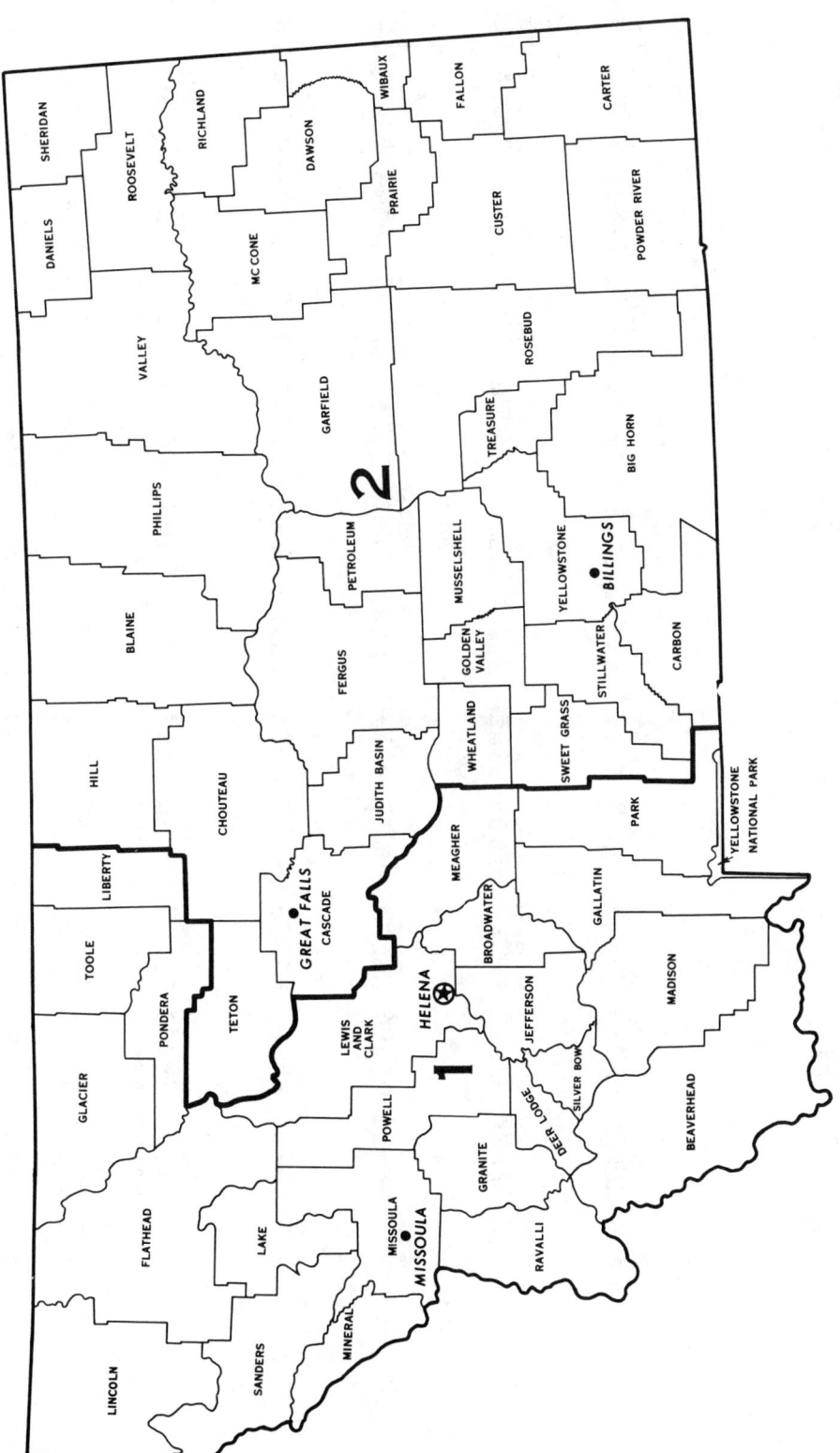

MONTANA

PRESIDENT 1980

1980 Census Population	County	Total Vote	Republican	Democratic	Other	Rep.-Dem. Plurality	Percentage Total Vote Rep.	Dem.	Major Vote Rep.	Dem.
8,186	BEAVERHEAD	4,103	2,955	842	306	2,113 R	72.0%	20.5%	77.8%	22.2%
11,096	BIG HORN	3,735	1,730	1,644	361	86 R	46.3%	44.0%	51.3%	48.7%
6,999	BLAINE	2,995	1,686	1,107	202	579 R	56.3%	37.0%	60.4%	39.6%
3,267	BROADWATER	1,564	1,052	401	111	651 R	67.3%	25.6%	72.4%	27.6%
8,099	CARBON	4,363	2,471	1,468	424	1,003 R	56.6%	33.6%	62.7%	37.3%
1,799	CARTER	1,058	766	237	55	529 R	72.4%	22.4%	76.4%	23.6%
80,696	CASCADE	32,234	17,664	11,105	3,465	6,559 R	54.8%	34.5%	61.4%	38.6%
6,092	CHOUTEAU	3,583	2,448	853	282	1,595 R	68.3%	23.8%	74.2%	25.8%
13,109	CUSTER	5,816	3,533	1,822	461	1,711 R	60.7%	31.3%	66.0%	34.0%
2,835	DANIELS	1,666	1,086	483	97	603 R	65.2%	29.0%	69.2%	30.8%
11,805	DAWSON	5,118	3,045	1,543	530	1,502 R	59.5%	30.1%	66.4%	33.6%
12,518	DEER LODGE	5,638	1,905	3,077	656	1,172 D	33.8%	54.6%	38.2%	61.8%
3,763	FALLON	1,920	1,286	512	122	774 R	67.0%	26.7%	71.5%	28.5%
13,076	FERGUS	6,852	4,455	1,840	557	2,615 R	65.0%	26.9%	70.8%	29.2%
51,966	FLATHEAD	23,767	15,102	6,349	2,316	8,753 R	63.5%	26.7%	70.4%	29.6%
42,865	GALLATIN	21,726	12,738	5,747	3,241	6,991 R	58.6%	26.5%	68.9%	31.1%
1,656	GARFIELD	974	760	169	45	591 R	78.0%	17.4%	81.8%	18.2%
10,628	GLACIER	4,093	2,283	1,394	416	889 R	55.8%	34.1%	62.1%	37.9%
1,026	GOLDEN VALLEY	556	362	155	39	207 R	65.1%	27.9%	70.0%	30.0%
2,700	GRANITE	1,371	811	439	121	372 R	59.2%	32.0%	64.9%	35.1%
17,985	HILL	8,089	4,448	2,875	766	1,573 R	55.0%	35.5%	60.7%	39.3%
7,029	JEFFERSON	3,223	1,841	1,055	327	786 R	57.1%	32.7%	63.6%	36.4%
2,646	JUDITH BASIN	1,627	1,030	480	117	550 R	63.3%	29.5%	68.2%	31.8%
19,056	LAKE	8,532	5,083	2,615	834	2,468 R	59.6%	30.6%	66.0%	34.0%
43,039	LEWIS AND CLARK	21,212	12,128	6,815	2,269	5,313 R	57.2%	32.1%	64.0%	36.0%
2,329	LIBERTY	1,256	872	283	101	589 R	69.4%	22.5%	75.5%	24.5%
17,752	LINCOLN	7,348	4,202	2,422	724	1,780 R	57.2%	33.0%	63.4%	36.6%
2,702	MCCONE	1,471	1,000	349	122	651 R	68.0%	23.7%	74.1%	25.9%
5,448	MADISON	3,145	2,220	676	249	1,544 R	70.6%	21.5%	76.7%	23.3%
2,154	MEAGHER	990	689	247	54	442 R	69.6%	24.9%	73.6%	26.4%
3,675	MINERAL	1,657	800	660	197	140 R	48.3%	39.8%	54.8%	45.2%
76,016	MISSOULA	34,594	16,161	13,115	5,318	3,046 R	46.7%	37.9%	55.2%	44.8%
4,428	MUSSELSHELL	2,204	1,279	784	141	495 R	58.0%	35.6%	62.0%	38.0%
12,660	PARK	6,195	3,929	1,663	603	2,266 R	63.4%	26.8%	70.3%	29.7%
655	PETROLEUM	341	225	90	26	135 R	66.0%	26.4%	71.4%	28.6%
5,367	PHILLIPS	2,653	1,723	745	185	978 R	64.9%	28.1%	69.8%	30.2%
6,731	PONDERA	3,432	2,270	897	265	1,373 R	66.1%	26.1%	71.7%	28.3%
2,520	POWDER RIVER	1,443	985	336	122	649 R	68.3%	23.3%	74.6%	25.4%
6,958	POWELL	2,993	1,770	883	340	887 R	59.1%	29.5%	66.7%	33.3%
1,836	PRAIRIE	927	580	283	64	297 R	62.6%	30.5%	67.2%	32.8%
22,493	RAVALLI	11,404	7,268	3,063	1,073	4,205 R	63.7%	26.9%	70.4%	29.6%
12,243	RICHLAND	5,038	3,348	1,252	438	2,096 R	66.5%	24.9%	72.8%	27.2%
10,467	ROOSEVELT	4,160	2,298	1,504	358	794 R	55.2%	36.2%	60.4%	39.6%
9,899	ROSEBUD	3,443	1,875	1,167	401	708 R	54.5%	33.9%	61.6%	38.4%
8,675	SANDERS	3,999	2,194	1,395	410	799 R	54.9%	34.9%	61.1%	38.9%
5,414	SHERIDAN	2,912	1,658	955	299	703 R	56.9%	32.8%	63.5%	36.5%
38,092	SILVER BOW	19,377	7,301	9,721	2,355	2,420 D	37.7%	50.2%	42.9%	57.1%
5,598	STILLWATER	2,984	1,828	919	237	909 R	61.3%	30.8%	66.5%	33.5%
3,216	SWEET GRASS	1,739	1,169	440	130	729 R	67.2%	25.3%	72.7%	27.3%
6,491	TETON	3,564	2,415	902	247	1,513 R	67.8%	25.3%	72.8%	27.2%
5,559	TOOLE	2,850	2,000	634	216	1,366 R	70.2%	22.2%	75.9%	24.1%
981	TREASURE	554	321	181	52	140 R	57.9%	32.7%	63.9%	36.1%
10,250	VALLEY	5,190	3,242	1,567	381	1,675 R	62.5%	30.2%	67.4%	32.6%
2,359	WHEATLAND	1,230	742	381	107	361 R	60.3%	31.0%	66.1%	33.9%
1,476	WIBAUX	731	450	219	62	231 R	61.6%	30.0%	67.3%	32.7%
108,035	YELLOWSTONE	48,313	27,332	15,272	5,709	12,060 R	56.6%	31.6%	64.2%	35.8%
786,690	TOTAL	363,952	206,814	118,032	39,106	88,782 R	56.8%	32.4%	63.7%	36.3%

MONTANA

GOVERNOR 1980

1980 Census Population	County	Total Vote	Republican	Democratic	Other	Rep.-Dem. Plurality	Percentage Total Vote Rep.	Dem.	Major Vote Rep.	Dem.
8,186	BEAVERHEAD	4,052	2,288	1,764		524 R	56.5%	43.5%	56.5%	43.5%
11,096	BIG HORN	3,607	1,462	2,145		683 D	40.5%	59.5%	40.5%	59.5%
6,999	BLAINE	2,969	1,267	1,702		435 D	42.7%	57.3%	42.7%	57.3%
3,267	BROADWATER	1,587	802	785		17 R	50.5%	49.5%	50.5%	49.5%
8,099	CARBON	4,371	1,909	2,462		553 D	43.7%	56.3%	43.7%	56.3%
1,799	CARTER	1,026	613	413		200 R	59.7%	40.3%	59.7%	40.3%
80,696	CASCADE	31,631	13,532	18,099		4,567 D	42.8%	57.2%	42.8%	57.2%
6,092	CHOUTEAU	3,589	1,650	1,939		289 D	46.0%	54.0%	46.0%	54.0%
13,109	CUSTER	5,855	2,433	3,422		989 D	41.6%	58.4%	41.6%	58.4%
2,835	DANIELS	1,660	492	1,168		676 D	29.6%	70.4%	29.6%	70.4%
11,805	DAWSON	5,140	2,261	2,879		618 D	44.0%	56.0%	44.0%	56.0%
12,518	DEER LODGE	5,394	1,592	3,802		2,210 D	29.5%	70.5%	29.5%	70.5%
3,763	FALLON	1,876	868	1,008		140 D	46.3%	53.7%	46.3%	53.7%
13,076	FERGUS	6,854	3,291	3,563		272 D	48.0%	52.0%	48.0%	52.0%
51,966	FLATHEAD	23,664	11,335	12,329		994 D	47.9%	52.1%	47.9%	52.1%
42,865	GALLATIN	21,650	10,358	11,292		934 D	47.8%	52.2%	47.8%	52.2%
1,656	GARFIELD	973	484	489		5 D	49.7%	50.3%	49.7%	50.3%
10,628	GLACIER	4,052	1,782	2,270		488 D	44.0%	56.0%	44.0%	56.0%
1,026	GOLDEN VALLEY	572	263	309		46 D	46.0%	54.0%	46.0%	54.0%
2,700	GRANITE	1,374	765	609		156 R	55.7%	44.3%	55.7%	44.3%
17,985	HILL	8,099	3,221	4,878		1,657 D	39.8%	60.2%	39.8%	60.2%
7,029	JEFFERSON	3,246	1,398	1,848		450 D	43.1%	56.9%	43.1%	56.9%
2,646	JUDITH BASIN	1,642	798	844		46 D	48.6%	51.4%	48.6%	51.4%
19,056	LAKE	8,538	4,333	4,205		128 R	50.7%	49.3%	50.7%	49.3%
43,039	LEWIS AND CLARK	20,812	7,478	13,334		5,856 D	35.9%	64.1%	35.9%	64.1%
2,329	LIBERTY	1,260	628	632		4 D	49.8%	50.2%	49.8%	50.2%
17,752	LINCOLN	7,236	3,209	4,027		818 D	44.3%	55.7%	44.3%	55.7%
2,702	MCCONE	1,497	565	932		367 D	37.7%	62.3%	37.7%	62.3%
5,448	MADISON	3,142	1,900	1,242		658 R	60.5%	39.5%	60.5%	39.5%
2,154	MEAGHER	990	544	446		98 R	54.9%	45.1%	54.9%	45.1%
3,675	MINERAL	1,660	708	952		244 D	42.7%	57.3%	42.7%	57.3%
76,016	MISSOULA	34,266	14,166	20,100		5,934 D	41.3%	58.7%	41.3%	58.7%
4,428	MUSSELSHELL	2,207	1,074	1,133		59 D	48.7%	51.3%	48.7%	51.3%
12,660	PARK	6,281	2,835	3,446		611 D	45.1%	54.9%	45.1%	54.9%
655	PETROLEUM	337	146	191		45 D	43.3%	56.7%	43.3%	56.7%
5,367	PHILLIPS	2,648	1,298	1,350		52 D	49.0%	51.0%	49.0%	51.0%
6,731	PONDERA	3,434	1,614	1,820		206 D	47.0%	53.0%	47.0%	53.0%
2,520	POWDER RIVER	1,402	767	635		132 R	54.7%	45.3%	54.7%	45.3%
6,958	POWELL	2,967	1,459	1,508		49 D	49.2%	50.8%	49.2%	50.8%
1,836	PRAIRIE	1,014	486	528		42 D	47.9%	52.1%	47.9%	52.1%
22,493	RAVALLI	11,359	6,545	4,814		1,731 R	57.6%	42.4%	57.6%	42.4%
12,243	RICHLAND	5,015	2,297	2,718		421 D	45.8%	54.2%	45.8%	54.2%
10,467	ROOSEVELT	4,151	1,036	3,115		2,079 D	25.0%	75.0%	25.0%	75.0%
9,899	ROSEBUD	3,429	1,686	1,743		57 D	49.2%	50.8%	49.2%	50.8%
8,675	SANDERS	3,970	2,114	1,856		258 R	53.2%	46.8%	53.2%	46.8%
5,414	SHERIDAN	2,887	970	1,917		947 D	33.6%	66.4%	33.6%	66.4%
38,092	SILVER BOW	19,009	6,644	12,365		5,721 D	35.0%	65.0%	35.0%	65.0%
5,598	STILLWATER	2,975	1,331	1,644		313 D	44.7%	55.3%	44.7%	55.3%
3,216	SWEET GRASS	1,745	988	757		231 R	56.6%	43.4%	56.6%	43.4%
6,491	TETON	3,542	1,723	1,819		96 D	48.6%	51.4%	48.6%	51.4%
5,559	TOOLE	2,839	1,388	1,451		63 D	48.9%	51.1%	48.9%	51.1%
981	TREASURE	555	208	347		139 D	37.5%	62.5%	37.5%	62.5%
10,250	VALLEY	5,011	2,023	2,988		965 D	40.4%	59.6%	40.4%	59.6%
2,359	WHEATLAND	1,224	553	671		118 D	45.2%	54.8%	45.2%	54.8%
1,476	WIBAUX	721	331	390		59 D	45.9%	54.1%	45.9%	54.1%
108,035	YELLOWSTONE	47,460	22,981	24,479		1,498 D	48.4%	51.6%	48.4%	51.6%
786,690	TOTAL	360,466	160,892	199,574		38,682 D	44.6%	55.4%	44.6%	55.4%

MONTANA

CONGRESS

CD	Year	Total Vote	Republican		Democratic		Other Vote	Rep.-Dem. Plurality	Percentage			
			Vote	Candidate	Vote	Candidate			Total Vote		Major Vote	
									Rep.	Dem.	Rep.	Dem.
1	1980	183,740	70,874	MCDONALD, JOHN K.	112,866	WILLIAMS, PAT		41,992 D	38.6%	61.4%	38.6%	61.4%
1	1978	150,109	64,093	WALTERMIRE, JIM	86,016	WILLIAMS, PAT		21,923 D	42.7%	57.3%	42.7%	57.3%
1	1976	167,784	56,297	DIEHL, W. D.	111,487	BAUCUS, MAX S.		55,190 D	33.6%	66.4%	33.6%	66.4%
1	1974	135,613	61,309	SHOUP, RICHARD G.	74,304	BAUCUS, MAX S.		12,995 D	45.2%	54.8%	45.2%	54.8%
1	1972	164,446	88,373	SHOUP, RICHARD G.	76,073	OLSEN, ARNOLD H.		12,300 R	53.7%	46.3%	53.7%	46.3%
2	1980	154,801	91,431	MARLENEE, RON	63,370	MONAHAN, THOMAS G.		28,061 R	59.1%	40.9%	59.1%	40.9%
2	1978	133,246	75,766	MARLENEE, RON	57,480	MONAHAN, THOMAS G.		18,286 R	56.9%	43.1%	56.9%	43.1%
2	1976	153,121	84,149	MARLENEE, RON	68,972	TOWE, THOMAS E.		15,177 R	55.0%	45.0%	55.0%	45.0%
2	1974	118,533	43,853	MCDONALD, JOHN K.	74,680	MELCHER, JOHN		30,827 D	37.0%	63.0%	37.0%	63.0%
2	1972	150,587	36,063	FORESTER, RICHARD L.	114,524	MELCHER, JOHN		78,461 D	23.9%	76.1%	23.9%	76.1%

MONTANA

Population total includes 275 persons living in Yellowstone National Park and not under any county jurisdiction.

1980 GENERAL ELECTION

President   Other vote was 29,281 Anderson (Independent) and 9,825 Clark (Libertarian).

Governor

Congress

1980 PRIMARIES

JUNE 3 REPUBLICAN

Governor   48,926 Jack Ramirez; 14,522 Al Bishop; 8,118 Florence Haegen.

Congress   Unopposed in CD 2. Contested as follows:

  CD 1   15,817 John K. McDonald; 9,735 Suzanne Morris; 7,684 Ken Dunham.

JUNE 3 DEMOCRATIC

Governor   69,051 Ted Schwinden; 57,946 Thomas L. Judge; 5,990 Martin J. Beckman; 3,377 Robert C. Kelleher.

Congress   Contested as follows:

  CD 1   56,532 Pat Williams; 18,620 Bill Hand.
  CD 2   26,874 Thomas G. Monahan; 14,027 Larry Pettit; 3,903 James A. Howard; 3,390 Bob Friel.

NEBRASKA

GOVERNOR
Charles Thone (R). Elected 1978 to a four-year term.

SENATORS
J. J. Exon (D). Elected 1978 to a six-year term.

Edward Zorinsky (D). Elected 1976 to a six-year term.

REPRESENTATIVES
1. Douglas K. Bereuter (R) 2. Harold J. Daub (R) 3. Virginia Smith (R)

POSTWAR VOTE FOR GOVERNOR

Year	Total Vote	Republican Vote	Candidate	Democratic Vote	Candidate	Other Vote	Rep.-Dem. Plurality	Rep.	Dem.	Rep.	Dem.
1978	492,423	275,473	Thone, Charles	216,754	Whelan, Gerald T.	196	58,719 R	55.9%	44.0%	56.0%	44.0%
1974	451,306	159,780	Marvel, Richard D.	267,012	Exon, J. J.	24,514	107,232 D	35.4%	59.2%	37.4%	62.6%
1970	461,619	201,994	Tiemann, Norbert T.	248,552	Exon, J. J.	11,073	46,558 D	43.8%	53.8%	44.8%	55.2%
1966	486,396	299,245	Tiemann, Norbert T.	186,985	Sorensen, Philip C.	166	112,260 R	61.5%	38.4%	61.5%	38.5%
1964	578,090	231,029	Burney, Dwight W.	347,026	Morrison, Frank B.	35	115,997 D	40.0%	60.0%	40.0%	60.0%
1962	464,585	221,885	Seaton, Fred A.	242,669	Morrison, Frank B.	31	20,784 D	47.8%	52.2%	47.8%	52.2%
1960	598,971	287,302	Cooper, John R.	311,344	Morrison, Frank B.	325	24,042 D	48.0%	52.0%	48.0%	52.0%
1958	421,067	209,705	Anderson, Victor E.	211,345	Brooks, Ralph G.	17	1,640 D	49.8%	50.2%	49.8%	50.2%
1956	567,933	308,293	Anderson, Victor E.	228,048	Sorrell, Frank	31,592	80,245 R	54.3%	40.2%	57.5%	42.5%
1954	414,841	250,080	Anderson, Victor E.	164,753	Ritchie, William	8	85,327 R	60.3%	39.7%	60.3%	39.7%
1952	595,714	366,009	Crosby, Robert B.	229,700	Raecke, Walter R.	5	136,309 R	61.4%	38.6%	61.4%	38.6%
1950	449,720	247,081	Peterson, Val	202,638	Raecke, Walter R.	1	44,443 R	54.9%	45.1%	54.9%	45.1%
1948	476,352	286,119	Peterson, Val	190,214	Sorrell, Frank	19	95,905 R	60.1%	39.9%	60.1%	39.9%
1946	380,835	249,468	Peterson, Val	131,367	Sorrell, Frank	—	118,101 R	65.5%	34.5%	65.5%	34.5%

The term of office of Nebraska's Governor was increased from two to four years effective with the 1966 election.

POSTWAR VOTE FOR SENATOR

Year	Total Vote	Republican Vote	Candidate	Democratic Vote	Candidate	Other Vote	Rep.-Dem. Plurality	Rep.	Dem.	Rep.	Dem.
1978	494,368	159,806	Shasteen, Donald	334,276	Exon, J. J.	286	174,470 D	32.3%	67.6%	32.3%	67.7%
1976	598,314	284,284	McCollister, John Y.	313,809	Zorinsky, Edward	221	29,525 D	47.5%	52.4%	47.5%	52.5%
1972	568,580	301,841	Curtis, Carl T.	265,922	Carpenter, Terry	817	35,919 R	53.1%	46.8%	53.2%	46.8%
1970	458,966	240,894	Hruska, Roman L.	217,681	Morrison, Frank B.	391	23,213 R	52.5%	47.4%	52.5%	47.5%
1966	485,101	296,116	Curtis, Carl T.	187,950	Morrison, Frank B.	1,035	108,166 R	61.0%	38.7%	61.2%	38.8%
1964	563,401	345,772	Hruska, Roman L.	217,605	Arndt, Raymond W.	24	128,167 R	61.4%	38.6%	61.4%	38.6%
1960	598,743	352,748	Curtis, Carl T.	245,837	Conrad, Robert	158	106,911 R	58.9%	41.1%	58.9%	41.1%
1958	417,385	232,227	Hruska, Roman L.	185,152	Morrison, Frank B.	6	47,075 R	55.6%	44.4%	55.6%	44.4%
1954	418,691	255,695	Curtis, Carl T.	162,990	Neville, Keith	6	92,705 R	61.1%	38.9%	61.1%	38.9%
1954s	411,225	250,341	Hruska, Roman L.	160,881	Green, James F.	3	89,460 R	60.9%	39.1%	60.9%	39.1%
1952	591,749	408,971	Butler, Hugh	164,660	Long, Stanley D.	18,118	244,311 R	69.1%	27.8%	71.3%	28.7%
1952s	581,750	369,841	Griswold, Dwight	211,898	Ritchie, William	11	157,943 R	63.6%	36.4%	63.6%	36.4%
1948	471,895	267,575	Wherry, Kenneth S.	204,320	Carpenter, Terry	—	63,255 R	56.7%	43.3%	56.7%	43.3%
1946	382,958	271,208	Butler, Hugh	111,750	Mekota, John E.	—	159,458 R	70.8%	29.2%	70.8%	29.2%

One each of the 1954 and 1952 elections was for a short term to fill a vacancy.

NEBRASKA

Districts Established January 11, 1968

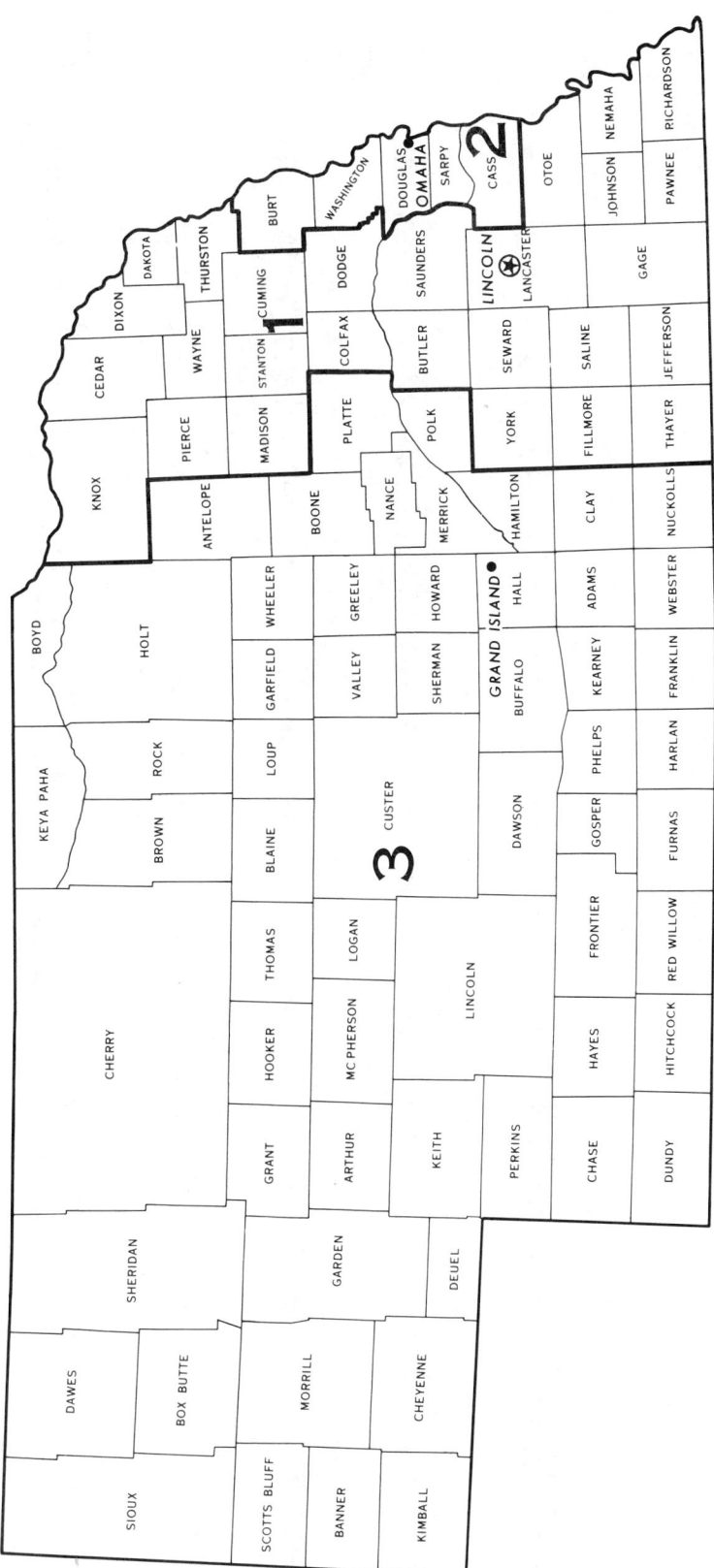

NEBRASKA

PRESIDENT 1980

1980 Census Population	County	Total Vote	Republican	Democratic	Other	Rep.-Dem. Plurality	Percentage Total Vote Rep.	Dem.	Major Vote Rep.	Dem.
30,656	ADAMS	12,973	8,500	3,372	1,101	5,128 R	65.5%	26.0%	71.6%	28.4%
8,675	ANTELOPE	4,057	3,192	659	206	2,533 R	78.7%	16.2%	82.9%	17.1%
513	ARTHUR	319	245	57	17	188 R	76.8%	17.9%	81.1%	18.9%
918	BANNER	532	481	33	18	448 R	90.4%	6.2%	93.6%	6.4%
867	BLAINE	442	361	63	18	298 R	81.7%	14.3%	85.1%	14.9%
7,391	BOONE	3,603	2,598	769	236	1,829 R	72.1%	21.3%	77.2%	22.8%
13,696	BOX BUTTE	5,532	3,912	1,208	412	2,704 R	70.7%	21.8%	76.4%	23.6%
3,331	BOYD	1,733	1,261	376	96	885 R	72.8%	21.7%	77.0%	23.0%
4,377	BROWN	2,087	1,615	341	131	1,274 R	77.4%	16.3%	82.6%	17.4%
34,797	BUFFALO	14,243	9,769	3,167	1,307	6,602 R	68.6%	22.2%	75.5%	24.5%
8,813	BURT	3,893	2,806	814	273	1,992 R	72.1%	20.9%	77.5%	22.5%
9,330	BUTLER	3,929	2,596	1,112	221	1,484 R	66.1%	28.3%	70.0%	30.0%
20,297	CASS	7,818	5,193	2,007	618	3,186 R	66.4%	25.7%	72.1%	27.9%
10,852	CEDAR	4,858	3,259	1,265	334	1,994 R	67.1%	26.0%	72.0%	28.0%
4,758	CHASE	2,103	1,593	324	186	1,269 R	75.7%	15.4%	83.1%	16.9%
6,758	CHERRY	3,155	2,517	489	149	2,028 R	79.8%	15.5%	83.7%	16.3%
10,057	CHEYENNE	4,108	3,073	776	259	2,297 R	74.8%	18.9%	79.8%	20.2%
8,106	CLAY	3,824	2,739	840	245	1,899 R	71.6%	22.0%	76.5%	23.5%
9,890	COLFAX	4,454	3,259	893	302	2,366 R	73.2%	20.0%	78.5%	21.5%
11,664	CUMING	5,131	4,006	803	322	3,203 R	78.1%	15.6%	83.3%	16.7%
13,877	CUSTER	5,934	4,563	1,011	360	3,552 R	76.9%	17.0%	81.9%	18.1%
16,573	DAKOTA	5,488	3,165	1,930	393	1,235 R	57.7%	35.2%	62.1%	37.9%
9,609	DAWES	4,306	3,283	705	318	2,578 R	76.2%	16.4%	82.3%	17.7%
22,162	DAWSON	8,609	6,689	1,463	457	5,226 R	77.7%	17.0%	82.1%	17.9%
2,462	DEUEL	1,220	946	192	82	754 R	77.5%	15.7%	83.1%	16.9%
7,137	DIXON	3,385	2,328	822	235	1,506 R	68.8%	24.3%	73.9%	26.1%
35,847	DODGE	14,250	9,522	3,564	1,164	5,958 R	66.8%	25.0%	72.8%	27.2%
397,884	DOUGLAS	163,930	96,908	51,668	15,354	45,240 R	59.1%	31.5%	65.2%	34.8%
2,861	DUNDY	1,411	1,138	192	81	946 R	80.7%	13.6%	85.6%	14.4%
7,920	FILLMORE	3,746	2,435	1,025	286	1,410 R	65.0%	27.4%	70.4%	29.6%
4,377	FRANKLIN	2,265	1,675	441	149	1,234 R	74.0%	19.5%	79.2%	20.8%
3,647	FRONTIER	1,698	1,346	259	93	1,087 R	79.3%	15.3%	83.9%	16.1%
6,486	FURNAS	3,172	2,483	536	153	1,947 R	78.3%	16.9%	82.2%	17.8%
24,456	GAGE	9,201	6,089	2,259	853	3,830 R	66.2%	24.6%	72.9%	27.1%
2,802	GARDEN	1,580	1,297	202	81	1,095 R	82.1%	12.8%	86.5%	13.5%
2,363	GARFIELD	1,108	811	238	59	573 R	73.2%	21.5%	77.3%	22.7%
2,140	GOSPER	1,029	783	181	65	602 R	76.1%	17.6%	81.2%	18.8%
877	GRANT	465	373	76	16	297 R	80.2%	16.3%	83.1%	16.9%
3,462	GREELEY	1,625	1,028	495	102	533 R	63.3%	30.5%	67.5%	32.5%
47,690	HALL	17,857	12,166	4,422	1,269	7,744 R	68.1%	24.8%	73.3%	26.7%
9,301	HAMILTON	4,271	3,200	778	293	2,422 R	74.9%	18.2%	80.4%	19.6%
4,292	HARLAN	2,317	1,690	486	141	1,204 R	72.9%	21.0%	77.7%	22.3%
1,356	HAYES	730	617	82	31	535 R	84.5%	11.2%	88.3%	11.7%
4,079	HITCHCOCK	1,963	1,474	329	160	1,145 R	75.1%	16.8%	81.8%	18.2%
13,552	HOLT	5,838	4,495	1,016	327	3,479 R	77.0%	17.4%	81.6%	18.4%
990	HOOKER	472	386	63	23	323 R	81.8%	13.3%	86.0%	14.0%
6,773	HOWARD	2,970	1,971	789	210	1,182 R	66.4%	26.6%	71.4%	28.6%
9,817	JEFFERSON	4,572	3,090	1,125	357	1,965 R	67.6%	24.6%	73.3%	26.7%
5,285	JOHNSON	2,565	1,719	626	220	1,093 R	67.0%	24.4%	73.3%	26.7%
7,053	KEARNEY	3,530	2,512	726	292	1,786 R	71.2%	20.6%	77.6%	22.4%
9,364	KEITH	4,354	3,381	710	263	2,671 R	77.7%	16.3%	82.6%	17.4%
1,301	KEYA PAHA	688	526	130	32	396 R	76.5%	18.9%	80.2%	19.8%
4,882	KIMBALL	2,136	1,615	385	136	1,230 R	75.6%	18.0%	80.8%	19.3%
11,457	KNOX	4,789	3,404	1,057	328	2,347 R	71.1%	22.1%	76.3%	23.7%
192,884	LANCASTER	76,233	38,780	27,162	10,291	11,618 R	50.9%	35.6%	58.8%	41.2%
36,455	LINCOLN	14,479	9,643	3,768	1,068	5,875 R	66.6%	26.0%	71.9%	28.1%
983	LOGAN	536	442	71	23	371 R	82.5%	13.2%	86.2%	13.8%
859	LOUP	470	368	74	28	294 R	78.3%	15.7%	83.3%	16.7%
593	MCPHERSON	343	285	49	9	236 R	83.1%	14.3%	85.3%	14.7%
31,382	MADISON	12,329	9,718	1,926	685	7,792 R	78.8%	15.6%	83.5%	16.5%
8,945	MERRICK	3,694	2,710	712	272	1,998 R	73.4%	19.3%	79.2%	20.8%
6,085	MORRILL	2,540	1,893	512	135	1,381 R	74.5%	20.2%	78.7%	21.3%
4,740	NANCE	2,143	1,442	561	140	881 R	67.3%	26.2%	72.0%	28.0%
8,367	NEMAHA	3,911	2,695	930	286	1,765 R	68.9%	23.8%	74.3%	25.7%
6,726	NUCKOLLS	3,282	2,180	899	203	1,281 R	66.4%	27.4%	70.8%	29.2%
15,183	OTOE	6,559	4,611	1,471	477	3,140 R	70.3%	22.4%	75.8%	24.2%
3,937	PAWNEE	1,993	1,418	431	144	987 R	71.1%	21.6%	76.7%	23.3%
3,637	PERKINS	1,762	1,342	313	107	1,029 R	76.2%	17.8%	81.1%	18.9%
9,769	PHELPS	4,445	3,465	734	246	2,731 R	78.0%	16.5%	82.5%	17.5%
8,481	PIERCE	3,639	2,938	517	184	2,421 R	80.7%	14.2%	85.0%	15.0%

NEBRASKA

PRESIDENT 1980

1980 Census Population	County	Total Vote	Republican	Democratic	Other	Rep.-Dem. Plurality	Percentage Total Vote		Major Vote	
							Rep.	Dem.	Rep.	Dem.
28,852	PLATTE	11,975	8,803	2,389	783	6,414 R	73.5%	19.9%	78.7%	21.3%
6,320	POLK	2,936	2,206	538	192	1,668 R	75.1%	18.3%	80.4%	19.6%
12,615	RED WILLOW	5,278	4,050	899	329	3,151 R	76.7%	17.0%	81.8%	18.2%
11,315	RICHARDSON	5,344	3,634	1,350	360	2,284 R	68.0%	25.3%	72.9%	27.1%
2,383	ROCK	1,059	855	146	58	709 R	80.7%	13.8%	85.4%	14.6%
13,131	SALINE	5,416	2,934	1,908	574	1,026 R	54.2%	35.2%	60.6%	39.4%
86,015	SARPY	23,202	15,552	5,689	1,961	9,863 R	67.0%	24.5%	73.2%	26.8%
18,716	SAUNDERS	7,906	5,223	2,034	649	3,189 R	66.1%	25.7%	72.0%	28.0%
38,344	SCOTTS BLUFF	13,249	9,504	2,854	891	6,650 R	71.7%	21.5%	76.9%	23.1%
15,789	SEWARD	5,965	3,527	1,803	635	1,724 R	59.1%	30.2%	66.2%	33.8%
7,544	SHERIDAN	3,271	2,749	370	152	2,379 R	84.0%	11.3%	88.1%	11.9%
4,226	SHERMAN	1,970	1,254	578	138	676 R	63.7%	29.3%	68.4%	31.6%
1,845	SIOUX	932	760	120	52	640 R	81.5%	12.9%	86.4%	13.6%
6,549	STANTON	2,466	1,945	362	159	1,583 R	78.9%	14.7%	84.3%	15.7%
7,582	THAYER	3,650	2,514	926	210	1,588 R	68.9%	25.4%	73.1%	26.9%
973	THOMAS	402	306	65	31	241 R	76.1%	16.2%	82.5%	17.5%
7,186	THURSTON	2,356	1,454	726	176	728 R	61.7%	30.8%	66.7%	33.3%
5,633	VALLEY	2,929	2,101	655	173	1,446 R	71.7%	22.4%	76.2%	23.8%
15,508	WASHINGTON	6,463	4,570	1,454	439	3,116 R	70.7%	22.5%	75.9%	24.1%
9,858	WAYNE	3,921	2,844	733	344	2,111 R	72.5%	18.7%	79.5%	20.5%
4,858	WEBSTER	2,403	1,676	547	180	1,129 R	69.7%	22.8%	75.4%	24.6%
1,060	WHEELER	501	374	93	34	281 R	74.7%	18.6%	80.1%	19.9%
14,798	YORK	6,634	5,089	1,131	414	3,958 R	76.7%	17.0%	81.8%	18.2%
1,570,006	TOTAL	640,854	419,937	166,851	54,066	253,086 R	65.5%	26.0%	71.6%	28.4%

NEBRASKA

CONGRESS

CD	Year	Total Vote	Republican Vote	Republican Candidate	Democratic Vote	Democratic Candidate	Other Vote	Rep.-Dem. Plurality	Percentage Total Vote Rep.	Dem.	Major Vote Rep.	Dem.
1	1980	204,341	160,705	BEREUTER, DOUGLAS K.	43,605	STORY, REX S.	31	117,100 R	78.6%	21.3%	78.7%	21.3%
1	1978	170,329	99,013	BEREUTER, DOUGLAS K.	71,311	DYAS, HESS	5	27,702 R	58.1%	41.9%	58.1%	41.9%
1	1976	200,272	146,558	THONE, CHARLES	53,703	ANDERSON, PAULINE F.	11	92,855 R	73.2%	26.8%	73.2%	26.8%
1	1974	154,454	82,353	THONE, CHARLES	72,099	DYAS, HESS	2	10,254 R	53.3%	46.7%	53.3%	46.7%
1	1972	197,436	126,789	THONE, CHARLES	70,570	BERG, DARREL E.	77	56,219 R	64.2%	35.7%	64.2%	35.8%
1	1970	156,305	79,131	THONE, CHARLES	36,240	BURROWS, GEORGE	40,934	42,891 R	50.6%	23.2%	68.6%	31.4%
1	1968	180,622	97,697	DENNEY, ROBERT V.	78,374	CALLAN, CLAIR A.	4,551	19,323 R	54.1%	43.4%	55.5%	44.5%
2	1980	203,050	107,736	DAUB, HAROLD J.	88,843	FELLMAN, RICHARD M.	6,471	18,893 R	53.1%	43.8%	54.8%	45.2%
2	1978	147,536	70,309	DAUB, HAROLD J.	77,135	CAVANAUGH, JOHN J.	92	6,826 D	47.7%	52.3%	47.7%	52.3%
2	1976	194,775	88,352	TERRY, LEE	106,296	CAVANAUGH, JOHN J.	127	17,944 D	45.4%	54.6%	45.4%	54.6%
2	1974	131,925	72,731	MCCOLLISTER, JOHN Y.	59,142	LYNCH, DANIEL C.	52	13,589 R	55.1%	44.8%	55.2%	44.8%
2	1972	179,387	114,669	MCCOLLISTER, JOHN Y.	64,696	COONEY, PATRICK L.	22	49,973 R	63.9%	36.1%	63.9%	36.1%
2	1970	134,387	69,671	MCCOLLISTER, JOHN Y.	64,620	HLAVACEK, JOHN	96	5,051 R	51.8%	48.1%	51.9%	48.1%
2	1968	158,977	87,683	CUNNINGHAM, GLENN	71,254	MORRISON, MRS. FRANK	40	16,429 R	55.2%	44.8%	55.2%	44.8%
3	1980	217,870	182,887	SMITH, VIRGINIA	34,967	DITUS, STAN	16	147,920 R	83.9%	16.0%	83.9%	16.1%
3	1978	176,973	141,597	SMITH, VIRGINIA	35,371	FOWLER, MARILYN	5	106,226 R	80.0%	20.0%	80.0%	20.0%
3	1976	206,765	150,720	SMITH, VIRGINIA	51,012	HANSEN, JAMES T.	5,033	99,708 R	72.9%	24.7%	74.7%	25.3%
3	1974	161,312	80,992	SMITH, VIRGINIA	80,255	ZIEBARTH, WAYNE W.	65	737 R	50.2%	49.8%	50.2%	49.8%
3	1972	192,023	133,607	MARTIN, DAVE	58,378	FITZGERALD, WARREN	38	75,229 R	69.6%	30.4%	69.6%	30.4%
3	1970	157,407	93,705	MARTIN, DAVE	63,698	SEARCY, DONALD	4	30,007 R	59.5%	40.5%	59.5%	40.5%
3	1968	182,572	123,838	MARTIN, DAVE	58,728	DEAN, J. B.	6	65,110 R	67.8%	32.2%	67.8%	32.2%

NEBRASKA

1980 GENERAL ELECTION

President   Other vote was 44,993 Anderson (Independent); 9,073 Clark (Libertarian). Vote totals by county include new-resident vote canvassed separately.

Congress   Other vote was scattered in CD's 1 and 3; 6,247 Putney (Libertarian) and 224 scattered in CD 2.

1980 PRIMARIES

MAY 13 REPUBLICAN

Congress   Unopposed in two CD's. Contested as follows:

  CD 2   33,306 Harold J. Daub; 17,874 Mike Albert; 2,452 Allen Jones; 839 Paul R. Kaiman; 80 scattered.

MAY 13 DEMOCRATIC

Congress   Unopposed in CD 1. Contested as follows:

  CD 2   29,912 Richard M. Fellman; 8,589 Jay McCarthy; 6,866 Tom Plambeck; 5,765 Bud Morrissy; 367 scattered.
  CD 3   21,879 Stan Ditus; 14,217 Alan Sydow; 89 scattered.

NEVADA

GOVERNOR
Robert F. List (R). Elected 1978 to a four-year term.

SENATORS
Howard W. Cannon (D). Re-elected 1976 to a six-year term. Previously elected 1970, 1964, 1958.

Paul Laxalt (R). Re-elected 1980 to a six-year term. Previously elected 1974.

REPRESENTATIVE
At-Large. James Santini (D)

POSTWAR VOTE FOR GOVERNOR

									Percentage			
	Total	Republican		Democratic		Other	Rep.-Dem.	Total Vote		Major Vote		
Year	Vote	Vote	Candidate	Vote	Candidate	Vote	Plurality	Rep.	Dem.	Rep.	Dem.	
1978	192,445	108,097	List, Robert F.	76,361	Rose, Robert E.	7,987	31,736 R	56.2%	39.7%	58.6%	41.4%	
1974	169,358	28,959	Crumpler, Shirley	114,114	O'Callaghan, Mike	26,285	85,155 D	17.1%	67.4%	20.2%	79.8%	
1970	146,991	64,400	Fike, Ed	70,697	O'Callaghan, Mike	11,894	6,297 D	43.8%	48.1%	47.7%	52.3%	
1966	137,677	71,807	Laxalt, Paul	65,870	Sawyer, Grant	—	5,937 R	52.2%	47.8%	52.2%	47.8%	
1962	96,929	32,145	Gragson, Oran K.	64,784	Sawyer, Grant	—	32,639 D	33.2%	66.8%	33.2%	66.8%	
1958	84,889	34,025	Russell, Charles H.	50,864	Sawyer, Grant	—	16,839 D	40.1%	59.9%	40.1%	59.9%	
1954	78,462	41,665	Russell, Charles H.	36,797	Pittman, Vail	—	4,868 R	53.1%	46.9%	53.1%	46.9%	
1950	61,773	35,609	Russell, Charles H.	26,164	Pittman, Vail	—	9,445 R	57.6%	42.4%	57.6%	42.4%	
1946	49,902	21,247	Jepson, Melvin E.	28,655	Pittman, Vail	—	7,408 D	42.6%	57.4%	42.6%	57.4%	

POSTWAR VOTE FOR SENATOR

									Percentage			
	Total	Republican		Democratic		Other	Rep.-Dem.	Total Vote		Major Vote		
Year	Vote	Vote	Candidate	Vote	Candidate	Vote	Plurality	Rep.	Dem.	Rep.	Dem.	
1980	246,436	144,224	Laxalt, Paul	92,129	Gojack, Mary	10,083	52,095 R	58.5%	37.4%	61.0%	39.0%	
1976	201,980	63,471	Towell, David	127,295	Cannon, Howard W.	11,214	63,824 D	31.4%	63.0%	33.3%	66.7%	
1974	169,473	79,605	Laxalt, Paul	78,981	Reid, Harry	10,887	624 R	47.0%	46.6%	50.2%	49.8%	
1970	147,768	60,838	Raggio, William J.	85,187	Cannon, Howard W.	1,743	24,349 D	41.2%	57.6%	41.7%	58.3%	
1968	152,690	69,068	Fike, Ed	83,622	Bible, Alan	—	14,554 D	45.2%	54.8%	45.2%	54.8%	
1964	134,624	67,288	Laxalt, Paul	67,336	Cannon, Howard W.	—	48 D	50.0%	50.0%	50.0%	50.0%	
1962	97,192	33,749	Wright, William B.	63,443	Bible, Alan	—	29,694 D	34.7%	65.3%	34.7%	65.3%	
1958	84,492	35,760	Malone, George W.	48,732	Cannon, Howard W.	—	12,972 D	42.3%	57.7%	42.3%	57.7%	
1956	96,389	45,712	Young, Clifton	50,677	Bible, Alan	—	4,965 D	47.4%	52.6%	47.4%	52.6%	
1954s	77,513	32,470	Brown, Ernest S.	45,043	Bible, Alan	—	12,573 D	41.9%	58.1%	41.9%	58.1%	
1952	81,090	41,906	Malone, George W.	39,184	Mechling, Thomas B.	—	2,722 R	51.7%	48.3%	51.7%	48.3%	
1950	61,762	25,933	Marshall, George E.	35,829	McCarran, Pat	—	9,896 D	42.0%	58.0%	42.0%	58.0%	
1946	50,354	27,801	Malone, George W.	22,553	Bunker, Berkeley	—	5,248 R	55.2%	44.8%	55.2%	44.8%	

The 1954 election was for a short term to fill a vacancy.

NEVADA

NEVADA

PRESIDENT 1980

1980 Census Population	County	Total Vote	Republican	Democratic	Other	Rep.-Dem. Plurality	Percentage Total Vote Rep.	Dem.	Major Vote Rep.	Dem.
32,022	CARSON CITY	12,556	8,389	2,769	1,398	5,620 R	66.8%	22.1%	75.2%	24.8%
13,917	CHURCHILL	5,273	3,841	1,055	377	2,786 R	72.8%	20.0%	78.5%	21.5%
461,816	CLARK	127,424	76,194	38,313	12,917	37,881 R	59.8%	30.1%	66.5%	33.5%
19,421	DOUGLAS	7,343	5,254	1,352	737	3,902 R	71.6%	18.4%	79.5%	20.5%
17,269	ELKO	6,197	4,393	1,296	508	3,097 R	70.9%	20.9%	77.2%	22.8%
777	ESMERALDA	469	311	110	48	201 R	66.3%	23.5%	73.9%	26.1%
1,198	EUREKA	564	430	103	31	327 R	76.2%	18.3%	80.7%	19.3%
9,434	HUMBOLDT	2,843	1,950	684	209	1,266 R	68.6%	24.1%	74.0%	26.0%
4,082	LANDER	1,425	935	361	129	574 R	65.6%	25.3%	72.1%	27.9%
3,732	LINCOLN	1,586	1,087	396	103	691 R	68.5%	25.0%	73.3%	26.7%
13,594	LYON	5,456	3,709	1,288	459	2,421 R	68.0%	23.6%	74.2%	25.8%
6,217	MINERAL	2,546	1,628	631	287	997 R	63.9%	24.8%	72.1%	27.9%
9,048	NYE	3,720	2,387	973	360	1,414 R	64.2%	26.2%	71.0%	29.0%
3,408	PERSHING	1,282	877	311	94	566 R	68.4%	24.3%	73.8%	26.2%
1,459	STOREY	783	460	222	101	238 R	58.7%	28.4%	67.4%	32.6%
193,623	WASHOE	64,956	41,276	15,621	8,059	25,655 R	63.5%	24.0%	72.5%	27.5%
8,167	WHITE PINE	3,462	1,896	1,181	385	715 R	54.8%	34.1%	61.6%	38.4%
799,184	TOTAL	247,885	155,017	66,666	26,202	88,351 R	62.5%	26.9%	69.9%	30.1%

NEVADA

SENATOR 1980

1980 Census Population	County	Total Vote	Republican	Democratic	Other	Rep.-Dem. Plurality	Percentage Total Vote Rep.	Dem.	Major Vote Rep.	Dem.
32,022	CARSON CITY	12,619	8,264	3,851	504	4,413 R	65.5%	30.5%	68.2%	31.8%
13,917	CHURCHILL	5,279	3,758	1,360	161	2,398 R	71.2%	25.8%	73.4%	26.6%
461,816	CLARK	126,244	69,335	53,081	3,828	16,254 R	54.9%	42.0%	56.6%	43.4%
19,421	DOUGLAS	7,328	4,936	2,052	340	2,884 R	67.4%	28.0%	70.6%	29.4%
17,269	ELKO	6,179	4,369	1,546	264	2,823 R	70.7%	25.0%	73.9%	26.1%
777	ESMERALDA	468	284	161	23	123 R	60.7%	34.4%	63.8%	36.2%
1,198	EUREKA	574	468	80	26	388 R	81.5%	13.9%	85.4%	14.6%
9,434	HUMBOLDT	2,835	1,938	778	119	1,160 R	68.4%	27.4%	71.4%	28.6%
4,082	LANDER	1,477	884	489	104	395 R	59.9%	33.1%	64.4%	35.6%
3,732	LINCOLN	1,576	1,185	356	35	829 R	75.2%	22.6%	76.9%	23.1%
13,594	LYON	5,442	3,507	1,666	269	1,841 R	64.4%	30.6%	67.8%	32.2%
6,217	MINERAL	2,528	1,514	889	125	625 R	59.9%	35.2%	63.0%	37.0%
9,048	NYE	3,693	2,170	1,388	135	782 R	58.8%	37.6%	61.0%	39.0%
3,408	PERSHING	1,269	839	384	46	455 R	66.1%	30.3%	68.6%	31.4%
1,459	STOREY	782	425	322	35	103 R	54.3%	41.2%	56.9%	43.1%
193,623	WASHOE	64,709	38,022	22,725	3,962	15,297 R	58.8%	35.1%	62.6%	37.4%
8,167	WHITE PINE	3,434	2,326	1,001	107	1,325 R	67.7%	29.1%	69.9%	30.1%
799,184	TOTAL	246,436	144,224	92,129	10,083	52,095 R	58.5%	37.4%	61.0%	39.0%

NEVADA

CONGRESS

CD	Year	Total Vote	Republican Vote	Republican Candidate	Democratic Vote	Democratic Candidate	Other Vote	Rep.-Dem. Plurality	Total Vote Rep.	Total Vote Dem.	Major Vote Rep.	Major Vote Dem.
AL	1980	244,587	63,163	SAUNDERS, VINCE	165,107	SANTINI, JAMES	16,317	101,944 D	25.8%	67.5%	27.7%	72.3%
AL	1978	190,643	44,425	O'MARA, BILL	132,513	SANTINI, JAMES	13,705	88,088 D	23.3%	69.5%	25.1%	74.9%
AL	1976	199,863	24,124	EARHART, WALDEN C.	153,996	SANTINI, JAMES	21,743	129,872 D	12.1%	77.1%	13.5%	86.5%
AL	1974	167,966	61,182	TOWELL, DAVID	93,665	SANTINI, JAMES	13,119	32,483 D	36.4%	55.8%	39.5%	60.5%
AL	1972	180,462	94,113	TOWELL, DAVID	86,349	BILBRAY, JAMES H.		7,764 R	52.2%	47.8%	52.2%	47.8%
AL	1970	137,643	24,147	CHARLES, J. ROBERT	113,496	BARING, WALTER S.		89,349 D	17.5%	82.5%	17.5%	82.5%
AL	1968	144,345	40,209	SLATTERY, JAMES M.	104,136	BARING, WALTER S.		63,927 D	27.9%	72.1%	27.9%	72.1%
AL	1966	127,850	41,383	KRAEMER, RALPH L.	86,467	BARING, WALTER S.		45,084 D	32.4%	67.6%	32.4%	67.6%
AL	1964	130,737	47,989	VON TOBEL, GEORGE	82,748	BARING, WALTER S.		34,759 D	36.7%	63.3%	36.7%	63.3%
AL	1962	93,324	26,458	ADAIR, J. CARLTON	66,866	BARING, WALTER S.		40,408 D	28.4%	71.6%	28.4%	71.6%
AL	1960	103,602	43,986	MALONE, GEORGE W.	59,616	BARING, WALTER S.		15,630 D	42.5%	57.5%	42.5%	57.5%
AL	1958	82,328	27,275	HORTON, ROBERT C.	55,053	BARING, WALTER S.		27,778 D	33.1%	66.9%	33.1%	66.9%
AL	1956	94,254	43,154	HORTON, RICHARD W.	51,100	BARING, WALTER S.		7,946 D	45.8%	54.2%	45.8%	54.2%
AL	1954	77,639	42,321	YOUNG, CLIFTON	35,318	BARING, WALTER S.		7,003 R	54.5%	45.5%	54.5%	45.5%
AL	1952	80,595	40,683	YOUNG, CLIFTON	39,912	BARING, WALTER S.		771 R	50.5%	49.5%	50.5%	49.5%
AL	1950	60,328	28,485	MACKENZIE, A. E.	31,843	BARING, WALTER S.		3,358 D	47.2%	52.8%	47.2%	52.8%
AL	1948	58,705	28,972	RUSSELL, CHARLES H.	29,733	BARING, WALTER S.		761 D	49.4%	50.6%	49.4%	50.6%
AL	1946	49,046	28,859	RUSSELL, CHARLES H.	20,187	MCEACHIN, MALCOLM		8,672 R	58.8%	41.2%	58.8%	41.2%

NEVADA

1980 GENERAL ELECTION

President   Other vote was 17,651 Anderson (Independent); 4,358 Clark (Libertarian); 4,193 "None of these Candidates".

Senator   Other vote was 6,920 Hacker (Libertarian) and 3,163 "None of these Candidates".

Congress   Other vote was 7,759 Mangrum (Libertarian) and 8,558 "None of these Candidates".

1980 PRIMARIES

SEPTEMBER 9 REPUBLICAN

Senator   45,857 Paul Laxalt; 2,509 Richard A. Gilster (also ran for the at-large House seat in this primary); 2,401 "None of these Candidates".

Congress   Contested as follows:

AL   26,247 Vince Saunders; 6,134 Richard A. Gilster; 8,721 "None of these Candidates".

SEPTEMBER 9 DEMOCRATIC

Senator   Mary Gojack, unopposed.

Congress   Contested as follows:

AL   54,495 James Santini; 8,407 Lloyd R. Williams; 5,832 "None of these Candidates".

NEW HAMPSHIRE

GOVERNOR
Hugh J. Gallen (D). Re-elected 1980 to a two-year term. Previously elected 1978.

SENATORS
Gordon J. Humphrey (R). Elected 1978 to a six-year term.

Warren Rudman (R). Elected 1980 to a six-year term.

REPRESENTATIVES
1. Norman E. D'Amours (D)   2. Judd Gregg (R)

POSTWAR VOTE FOR GOVERNOR

		Republican		Democratic		Other	Rep.-Dem.	Percentage Total Vote		Major Vote	
Year	Total Vote	Vote	Candidate	Vote	Candidate	Vote	Plurality	Rep.	Dem.	Rep.	Dem.
1980	384,031	156,178	Thomson, Meldrim	226,436	Gallen, Hugh J.	1,417	70,258 D	40.7%	59.0%	40.8%	59.2%
1978	269,587	122,464	Thomson, Meldrim	133,133	Gallen, Hugh J.	13,990	10,669 D	45.4%	49.4%	47.9%	52.1%
1976	342,669	197,589	Thomson, Meldrim	145,015	Spanos, Harry V.	65	52,574 R	57.7%	42.3%	57.7%	42.3%
1974	226,665	115,933	Thomson, Meldrim	110,591	Leonard, Richard W.	141	5,342 R	51.1%	48.8%	51.2%	48.8%
1972	323,102	133,702	Thomson, Meldrim	126,107	Crowley, Roger J.	63,293	7,595 R	41.4%	39.0%	51.5%	48.5%
1970	222,441	102,298	Peterson, Walter R.	98,098	Crowley, Roger J.	22,045	4,200 R	46.0%	44.1%	51.0%	49.0%
1968	285,342	149,902	Peterson, Walter R.	135,378	Bussiere, Emile R.	62	14,524 R	52.5%	47.4%	52.5%	47.5%
1966	233,642	107,259	Gregg, Hugh	125,882	King, John W.	501	18,623 D	45.9%	53.9%	46.0%	54.0%
1964	285,863	94,824	Pillsbury, John	190,863	King, John W.	176	96,039 D	33.2%	66.8%	33.2%	66.8%
1962	230,048	94,567	Pillsbury, John	135,481	King, John W.	—	40,914 D	41.1%	58.9%	41.1%	58.9%
1960	290,527	161,123	Powell, Wesley	129,404	Boutin, Bernard L.	—	31,719 R	55.5%	44.5%	55.5%	44.5%
1958	206,745	106,790	Powell, Wesley	99,955	Boutin, Bernard L.	—	6,835 R	51.7%	48.3%	51.7%	48.3%
1956	258,695	141,578	Dwinell, Lane	117,117	Shaw, John	—	24,461 R	54.7%	45.3%	54.7%	45.3%
1954	194,631	107,287	Dwinell, Lane	87,344	Shaw, John	—	19,943 R	55.1%	44.9%	55.1%	44.9%
1952	265,715	167,791	Gregg, Hugh	97,924	Craig, William H.	—	69,867 R	63.1%	36.9%	63.1%	36.9%
1950	191,239	108,907	Adams, Sherman	82,258	Bingham, Robert P.	74	26,649 R	56.9%	43.0%	57.0%	43.0%
1948	222,571	116,212	Adams, Sherman	105,207	Hill, Herbert W.	1,152	11,005 R	52.2%	47.3%	52.5%	47.5%
1946	163,451	103,204	Dale, Charles M.	60,247	Keefe, F. Clyde	—	42,957 R	63.1%	36.9%	63.1%	36.9%

POSTWAR VOTE FOR SENATOR

		Republican		Democratic		Other	Rep.-Dem.	Percentage Total Vote		Major Vote	
Year	Total Vote	Vote	Candidate	Vote	Candidate	Vote	Plurality	Rep.	Dem.	Rep.	Dem.
1980	375,060	195,559	Rudman, Warren	179,455	Durkin, John A.	46	16,104 R	52.1%	47.8%	52.1%	47.9%
1978	263,779	133,745	Humphrey, Gordon J.	127,945	McIntyre, Thomas J.	2,089	5,800 R	50.7%	48.5%	51.1%	48.9%
1975s	262,682	113,007	Wyman, Louis C.	140,778	Durkin, John A.	8,897	27,771 D	43.0%	53.6%	44.5%	55.5%
1974	223,363	110,926	Wyman, Louis C.	110,924	Durkin, John A.	1,513	2 R	49.7%	49.7%	50.0%	50.0%
1972	324,354	139,852	Powell, Wesley	184,495	McIntyre, Thomas J.	7	44,643 D	43.1%	56.9%	43.1%	56.9%
1968	286,989	170,163	Cotton, Norris	116,816	King, John W.	10	53,347 R	59.3%	40.7%	59.3%	40.7%
1966	229,305	105,241	Thyng, Harrison R.	123,888	McIntyre, Thomas J.	176	18,647 D	45.9%	54.0%	45.9%	54.1%
1962	224,479	134,035	Cotton, Norris	90,444	Catalfo, Alfred	—	43,591 R	59.7%	40.3%	59.7%	40.3%
1962s	224,811	107,199	Bass, Perkins	117,612	McIntyre, Thomas J.	—	10,413 D	47.7%	52.3%	47.7%	52.3%
1960	287,545	173,521	Bridges, Styles	114,024	Hill, Herbert W.	—	59,497 R	60.3%	39.7%	60.3%	39.7%
1956	251,943	161,424	Cotton, Norris	90,519	Pickett, Laurence M.	—	70,905 R	64.1%	35.9%	64.1%	35.9%
1954	194,536	117,150	Bridges, Styles	77,386	Morin, Gerard L.	—	39,764 R	60.2%	39.8%	60.2%	39.8%
1954s	189,558	114,068	Cotton, Norris	75,490	Betley, Stanley J.	—	38,578 R	60.2%	39.8%	60.2%	39.8%
1950	190,573	106,142	Tobey, Charles W.	72,473	Kelley, Emmet J.	11,958	33,669 R	55.7%	38.0%	59.4%	40.6%
1948	222,898	129,600	Bridges, Styles	91,760	Fortin, Alfred E.	1,538	37,840 R	58.1%	41.2%	58.5%	41.5%

One each of the 1962 and 1954 elections were for short terms to fill vacancies. Following the 1974 election, neither candidate was seated and the 1975 special election was held for the remaining years of this term.

NEW HAMPSHIRE

Districts Established March 1, 1972

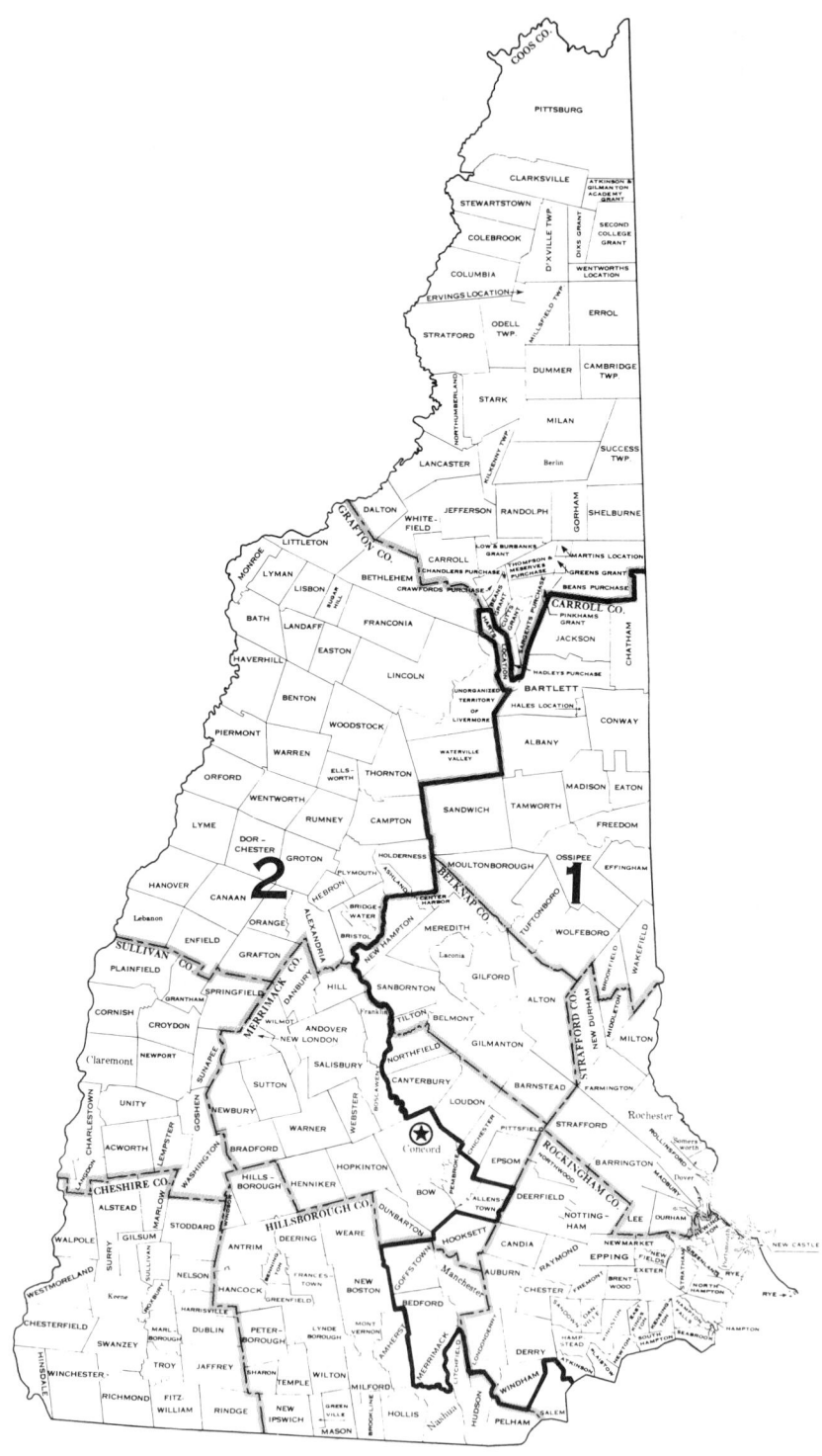

NEW HAMPSHIRE

PRESIDENT 1980

1980 Census Population	County	Total Vote	Republican	Democratic	Other	Rep.-Dem. Plurality	Percentage Total Vote Rep.	Dem.	Major Vote Rep.	Dem.
42,884	BELKNAP	18,558	12,077	4,365	2,116	7,712 R	65.1%	23.5%	73.5%	26.5%
27,931	CARROLL	14,853	9,980	3,119	1,754	6,861 R	67.2%	21.0%	76.2%	23.8%
62,116	CHESHIRE	25,467	13,242	7,835	4,390	5,407 R	52.0%	30.8%	62.8%	37.2%
35,147	COOS	14,520	8,724	4,749	1,047	3,975 R	60.1%	32.7%	64.8%	35.2%
65,806	GRAFTON	27,142	15,273	7,282	4,587	7,991 R	56.3%	26.8%	67.7%	32.3%
276,608	HILLSBOROUGH	115,343	68,994	31,789	14,560	37,205 R	59.8%	27.6%	68.5%	31.5%
98,302	MERRIMACK	41,963	23,584	12,083	6,296	11,501 R	56.2%	28.8%	66.1%	33.9%
190,345	ROCKINGHAM	79,474	45,960	21,712	11,802	24,248 R	57.8%	27.3%	67.9%	32.1%
85,408	STRAFFORD	32,533	16,399	11,041	5,093	5,358 R	50.4%	33.9%	59.8%	40.2%
36,063	SULLIVAN	14,137	7,472	4,889	1,776	2,583 R	52.9%	34.6%	60.4%	39.6%
920,610	TOTAL	383,990	221,705	108,864	53,421	112,841 R	57.7%	28.4%	67.1%	32.9%

NEW HAMPSHIRE

PRESIDENT 1980

1980 Census Population	City/Town	Total Vote	Republican	Democratic	Other	Rep.-Dem. Plurality	Percentage Total Vote Rep.	Dem.	Major Vote Rep.	Dem.
8,243	AMHERST	3,967	2,633	609	725	2,024 R	66.4%	15.4%	81.2%	18.8%
9,481	BEDFORD	4,766	3,400	853	513	2,547 R	71.3%	17.9%	79.9%	20.1%
13,084	BERLIN	5,435	2,847	2,202	386	645 R	52.4%	40.5%	56.4%	43.6%
14,557	CLAREMONT	5,079	2,365	2,171	543	194 R	46.6%	42.7%	52.1%	47.9%
30,400	CONCORD	12,766	6,092	4,330	2,344	1,762 R	47.7%	33.9%	58.5%	41.5%
7,158	CONWAY	3,097	1,910	782	405	1,128 R	61.7%	25.3%	71.0%	29.0%
18,875	DERRY	6,456	4,060	1,519	877	2,541 R	62.9%	23.5%	72.8%	27.2%
22,377	DOVER	9,516	4,497	3,344	1,675	1,153 R	47.3%	35.1%	57.4%	42.6%
10,652	DURHAM	3,230	1,128	1,016	1,086	112 R	34.9%	31.5%	52.6%	47.4%
11,024	EXETER	4,859	2,685	1,375	799	1,310 R	55.3%	28.3%	66.1%	33.9%
7,901	FRANKLIN	3,063	1,760	1,022	281	738 R	57.5%	33.4%	63.3%	36.7%
11,315	GOFFSTOWN	4,723	3,150	1,130	443	2,020 R	66.7%	23.9%	73.6%	26.4%
10,493	HAMPTON	5,265	2,833	1,547	885	1,286 R	53.8%	29.4%	64.7%	35.3%
9,119	HANOVER	3,342	1,108	1,143	1,091	35 D	33.2%	34.2%	49.2%	50.8%
7,303	HOOKSETT	3,115	2,165	677	273	1,488 R	69.5%	21.7%	76.2%	23.8%
14,022	HUDSON	5,802	3,239	1,768	795	1,471 R	55.8%	30.5%	64.7%	35.3%
21,449	KEENE	8,941	4,317	2,875	1,749	1,442 R	48.3%	32.2%	60.0%	40.0%
15,575	LACONIA	5,821	3,529	1,635	657	1,894 R	60.6%	28.1%	68.3%	31.7%
11,134	LEBANON	3,861	1,905	1,068	888	837 R	49.3%	27.7%	64.1%	35.9%
5,558	LITTLETON	2,336	1,527	635	174	892 R	65.4%	27.2%	70.6%	29.4%
13,598	LONDONDERRY	5,036	3,274	1,008	754	2,266 R	65.0%	20.0%	76.5%	23.5%
90,936	MANCHESTER	37,836	23,557	10,919	3,360	12,638 R	62.3%	28.9%	68.3%	31.7%
15,406	MERRIMACK TOWN	5,680	3,555	1,330	795	2,225 R	62.6%	23.4%	72.8%	27.2%
8,685	MILFORD	3,607	2,327	711	569	1,616 R	64.5%	19.7%	76.6%	23.4%
67,865	NASHUA	26,658	13,874	9,156	3,628	4,718 R	52.0%	34.3%	60.2%	39.8%
6,229	NEWPORT	2,227	1,253	748	226	505 R	56.3%	33.6%	62.6%	37.4%
8,090	PELHAM	3,366	1,834	1,058	474	776 R	54.5%	31.4%	63.4%	36.6%
5,609	PLAISTOW	2,210	1,347	558	305	789 R	61.0%	25.2%	70.7%	29.3%
5,094	PLYMOUTH	1,447	874	299	274	575 R	60.4%	20.7%	74.5%	25.5%
26,254	PORTSMOUTH	9,257	4,023	3,666	1,568	357 R	43.5%	39.6%	52.3%	47.7%
5,453	RAYMOND	2,174	1,470	457	247	1,013 R	67.6%	21.0%	76.3%	23.7%
21,560	ROCHESTER	7,749	4,495	2,566	688	1,929 R	58.0%	33.1%	63.7%	36.3%
24,124	SALEM	9,676	5,348	3,047	1,281	2,301 R	55.3%	31.5%	63.7%	36.3%
5,917	SEABROOK	2,507	1,514	729	264	785 R	60.4%	29.1%	67.5%	32.5%
10,350	SOMERSWORTH	3,776	1,687	1,663	426	24 R	44.7%	44.0%	50.4%	49.6%
5,183	SWANZEY	1,975	1,163	530	282	633 R	58.9%	26.8%	68.7%	31.3%
5,664	WINDHAM	2,510	1,563	548	399	1,015 R	62.3%	21.8%	74.0%	26.0%

NEW HAMPSHIRE

GOVERNOR 1980

1980 Census Population	County	Total Vote	Republican	Democratic	Other	Rep.-Dem. Plurality	Percentage Total Vote Rep.	Dem.	Major Vote Rep.	Dem.
42,884	BELKNAP	18,806	8,191	10,578	37	2,387 D	43.6%	56.2%	43.6%	56.4%
27,931	CARROLL	14,993	8,214	6,732	47	1,482 R	54.8%	44.9%	55.0%	45.0%
62,116	CHESHIRE	25,385	7,650	17,644	91	9,994 D	30.1%	69.5%	30.2%	69.8%
35,147	COOS	14,799	6,661	8,126	12	1,465 D	45.0%	54.9%	45.0%	55.0%
65,806	GRAFTON	27,371	11,587	15,726	58	4,139 D	42.3%	57.5%	42.4%	57.6%
276,608	HILLSBOROUGH	113,126	49,647	62,974	505	13,327 D	43.9%	55.7%	44.1%	55.9%
98,302	MERRIMACK	42,433	14,110	28,132	191	14,022 D	33.3%	66.3%	33.4%	66.6%
190,345	ROCKINGHAM	79,730	34,684	44,690	356	10,006 D	43.5%	56.1%	43.7%	56.3%
85,408	STRAFFORD	32,932	10,440	22,397	95	11,957 D	31.7%	68.0%	31.8%	68.2%
36,063	SULLIVAN	14,456	4,994	9,437	25	4,443 D	34.5%	65.3%	34.6%	65.4%
920,610	TOTAL	384,031	156,178	226,436	1,417	70,258 D	40.7%	59.0%	40.8%	59.2%

NEW HAMPSHIRE

GOVERNOR 1980

1980 Census Population	City/Town	Total Vote	Republican	Democratic	Other	Rep.-Dem. Plurality	Percentage Total Vote Rep.	Dem.	Major Vote Rep.	Dem.
8,243	AMHERST	4,051	1,881	2,146	24	265 D	46.4%	53.0%	46.7%	53.3%
9,481	BEDFORD	4,794	2,652	2,131	11	521 R	55.3%	44.5%	55.4%	44.6%
13,084	BERLIN	5,586	1,852	3,731	3	1,879 D	33.2%	66.8%	33.2%	66.8%
14,557	CLAREMONT	5,175	1,504	3,666	5	2,162 D	29.1%	70.8%	29.1%	70.9%
30,400	CONCORD	12,715	2,733	9,895	87	7,162 D	21.5%	77.8%	21.6%	78.4%
7,158	CONWAY	3,144	1,599	1,537	8	62 R	50.9%	48.9%	51.0%	49.0%
18,875	DERRY	6,532	3,342	3,174	16	168 R	51.2%	48.6%	51.3%	48.7%
22,377	DOVER	9,453	2,830	6,601	22	3,771 D	29.9%	69.8%	30.0%	70.0%
10,652	DURHAM	3,243	584	2,641	18	2,057 D	18.0%	81.4%	18.1%	81.9%
11,024	EXETER	4,824	1,766	3,041	17	1,275 D	36.6%	63.0%	36.7%	63.3%
7,901	FRANKLIN	3,117	1,105	1,999	13	894 D	35.5%	64.1%	35.6%	64.4%
11,315	GOFFSTOWN	4,762	2,456	2,300	6	156 R	51.6%	48.3%	51.6%	48.4%
10,493	HAMPTON	5,379	1,713	3,634	32	1,921 D	31.8%	67.6%	32.0%	68.0%
9,119	HANOVER	3,310	543	2,758	9	2,215 D	16.4%	83.3%	16.4%	83.6%
7,303	HOOKSETT	3,174	1,798	1,372	4	426 R	56.6%	43.2%	56.7%	43.3%
14,022	HUDSON	5,776	1,892	3,822	62	1,930 D	32.8%	66.2%	33.1%	66.9%
21,449	KEENE	8,738	2,003	6,710	25	4,707 D	22.9%	76.8%	23.0%	77.0%
15,575	LACONIA	5,894	2,121	3,763	10	1,642 D	36.0%	63.8%	36.0%	64.0%
11,134	LEBANON	4,234	1,111	3,114	9	2,003 D	26.2%	73.5%	26.3%	73.7%
5,558	LITTLETON	2,463	1,085	1,378		293 D	44.1%	55.9%	44.1%	55.9%
13,598	LONDONDERRY	5,086	2,591	2,460	35	131 R	50.9%	48.4%	51.3%	48.7%
90,936	MANCHESTER	36,677	18,520	18,013	144	507 R	50.5%	49.1%	50.7%	49.3%
15,406	MERRIMACK TOWN	5,665	2,390	3,259	16	869 D	42.2%	57.5%	42.3%	57.7%
8,685	MILFORD	3,597	1,872	1,709	16	163 R	52.0%	47.5%	52.3%	47.7%
67,865	NASHUA	25,503	7,594	17,757	152	10,163 D	29.8%	69.6%	30.0%	70.0%
6,229	NEWPORT	2,300	876	1,423	1	547 D	38.1%	61.9%	38.1%	61.9%
8,090	PELHAM	3,412	1,581	1,824	7	243 D	46.3%	53.5%	46.4%	53.6%
5,609	PLAISTOW	2,200	1,180	1,017	3	163 R	53.6%	46.2%	53.7%	46.3%
5,094	PLYMOUTH	1,456	697	749	10	52 D	47.9%	51.4%	48.2%	51.8%
26,254	PORTSMOUTH	9,094	2,130	6,931	33	4,801 D	23.4%	76.2%	23.5%	76.5%
5,453	RAYMOND	2,206	1,376	823	7	553 R	62.4%	37.3%	62.6%	37.4%
21,560	ROCHESTER	8,098	2,850	5,231	17	2,381 D	35.2%	64.6%	35.3%	64.7%
24,124	SALEM	9,519	4,574	4,871	74	297 D	48.1%	51.2%	48.4%	51.6%
5,917	SEABROOK	2,524	1,290	1,217	17	73 R	51.1%	48.2%	51.5%	48.5%
10,350	SOMERSWORTH	3,789	1,083	2,702	4	1,619 D	28.6%	71.3%	28.6%	71.4%
5,183	SWANZEY	2,018	550	1,461	7	911 D	27.3%	72.4%	27.3%	72.7%
5,664	WINDHAM	2,508	1,222	1,277	9	55 D	48.7%	50.9%	48.9%	51.1%

NEW HAMPSHIRE

SENATOR 1980

1980 Census Population	County	Total Vote	Republican	Democratic	Other	Rep.-Dem. Plurality	Total Vote Rep.	Total Vote Dem.	Major Vote Rep.	Major Vote Dem.
42,884	BELKNAP	18,336	10,855	7,477	4	3,378 R	59.2%	40.8%	59.2%	40.8%
27,931	CARROLL	14,402	9,751	4,643	8	5,108 R	67.7%	32.2%	67.7%	32.3%
62,116	CHESHIRE	24,769	11,915	12,852	2	937 D	48.1%	51.9%	48.1%	51.9%
35,147	COOS	14,249	6,671	7,573	5	902 D	46.8%	53.1%	46.8%	53.2%
65,806	GRAFTON	26,221	15,001	11,217	3	3,784 R	57.2%	42.8%	57.2%	42.8%
276,608	HILLSBOROUGH	111,234	60,152	51,076	6	9,076 R	54.1%	45.9%	54.1%	45.9%
98,302	MERRIMACK	41,334	22,284	19,044	6	3,240 R	53.9%	46.1%	53.9%	46.1%
190,345	ROCKINGHAM	77,688	38,729	38,953	6	224 D	49.9%	50.1%	49.9%	50.1%
85,408	STRAFFORD	32,428	13,714	18,710	4	4,996 D	42.3%	57.7%	42.3%	57.7%
36,063	SULLIVAN	14,399	6,487	7,910	2	1,423 D	45.1%	54.9%	45.1%	54.9%
920,610	TOTAL	375,060	195,559	179,455	46	16,104 R	52.1%	47.8%	52.1%	47.9%

NEW HAMPSHIRE

SENATOR 1980

1980 Census Population	City/Town	Total Vote	Republican	Democratic	Other	Rep.-Dem. Plurality	Total Vote Rep.	Total Vote Dem.	Major Vote Rep.	Major Vote Dem.
8,243	AMHERST	4,012	2,883	1,129		1,754 R	71.9%	28.1%	71.9%	28.1%
9,481	BEDFORD	4,739	2,968	1,771		1,197 R	62.6%	37.4%	62.6%	37.4%
13,084	BERLIN	5,435	1,862	3,573		1,711 D	34.3%	65.7%	34.3%	65.7%
14,557	CLAREMONT	5,109	1,931	3,178		1,247 D	37.8%	62.2%	37.8%	62.2%
30,400	CONCORD	12,076	6,089	5,985	2	104 R	50.4%	49.6%	50.4%	49.6%
7,158	CONWAY	3,019	1,910	1,107	2	803 R	63.3%	36.7%	63.3%	36.7%
18,875	DERRY	6,341	3,391	2,950		441 R	53.5%	46.5%	53.5%	46.5%
22,377	DOVER	9,327	3,791	5,535	1	1,744 D	40.6%	59.3%	40.6%	59.4%
10,652	DURHAM	3,153	1,319	1,834		515 D	41.8%	58.2%	41.8%	58.2%
11,024	EXETER	4,751	2,363	2,388		25 D	49.7%	50.3%	49.7%	50.3%
7,901	FRANKLIN	3,054	1,465	1,589		124 D	48.0%	52.0%	48.0%	52.0%
11,315	GOFFSTOWN	4,686	2,505	2,181		324 R	53.5%	46.5%	53.5%	46.5%
10,493	HAMPTON	5,226	2,382	2,844		462 D	45.6%	54.4%	45.6%	54.4%
9,119	HANOVER	3,224	1,423	1,801		378 D	44.1%	55.9%	44.1%	55.9%
7,303	HOOKSETT	3,103	1,796	1,307		489 R	57.9%	42.1%	57.9%	42.1%
14,022	HUDSON	5,705	3,045	2,660		385 R	53.4%	46.6%	53.4%	46.6%
21,449	KEENE	8,640	3,969	4,671		702 D	45.9%	54.1%	45.9%	54.1%
15,575	LACONIA	5,774	2,996	2,775	3	221 R	51.9%	48.1%	51.9%	48.1%
11,134	LEBANON	4,103	1,831	2,272		441 D	44.6%	55.4%	44.6%	55.4%
5,558	LITTLETON	2,302	1,387	915		472 R	60.3%	39.7%	60.3%	39.7%
13,598	LONDONDERRY	4,994	2,987	2,007		980 R	59.8%	40.2%	59.8%	40.2%
90,936	MANCHESTER	36,052	17,373	18,676	3	1,303 D	48.2%	51.8%	48.2%	51.8%
15,406	MERRIMACK TOWN	5,671	3,318	2,352	1	966 R	58.5%	41.5%	58.5%	41.5%
8,685	MILFORD	3,508	2,270	1,238		1,032 R	64.7%	35.3%	64.7%	35.3%
67,865	NASHUA	25,205	12,883	12,321	1	562 R	51.1%	48.9%	51.1%	48.9%
6,229	NEWPORT	2,262	1,047	1,215		168 D	46.3%	53.7%	46.3%	53.7%
8,090	PELHAM	3,251	1,424	1,827		403 D	43.8%	56.2%	43.8%	56.2%
5,609	PLAISTOW	2,084	987	1,097		110 D	47.4%	52.6%	47.4%	52.6%
5,094	PLYMOUTH	1,413	930	483		447 R	65.8%	34.2%	65.8%	34.2%
26,254	PORTSMOUTH	9,034	3,239	5,795		2,556 D	35.9%	64.1%	35.9%	64.1%
5,453	RAYMOND	2,104	1,170	934		236 R	55.6%	44.4%	55.6%	44.4%
21,560	ROCHESTER	7,918	3,488	4,429	1	941 D	44.1%	55.9%	44.1%	55.9%
24,124	SALEM	9,239	4,217	5,022		805 D	45.6%	54.4%	45.6%	54.4%
5,917	SEABROOK	2,374	1,207	1,167		40 R	50.8%	49.2%	50.8%	49.2%
10,350	SOMERSWORTH	3,877	1,221	2,656		1,435 D	31.5%	68.5%	31.5%	68.5%
5,183	SWANZEY	1,982	969	1,012	1	43 D	48.9%	51.1%	48.9%	51.1%
5,664	WINDHAM	2,418	1,361	1,057		304 R	56.3%	43.7%	56.3%	43.7%

NEW HAMPSHIRE

CONGRESS

CD	Year	Total Vote	Republican		Democratic		Other Vote	Rep.-Dem. Plurality	Percentage			
			Vote	Candidate	Vote	Candidate			Total Vote		Major Vote	
									Rep.	Dem.	Rep.	Dem.
1	1980	187,646	73,565	COBLEIGH, MARSHALL W.	114,061	D'AMOURS, NORMAN E.	20	40,496 D	39.2%	60.8%	39.2%	60.8%
1	1978	134,235	49,131	HUGHES, DANIEL M.	82,697	D'AMOURS, NORMAN E.	2,407	33,566 D	36.6%	61.6%	37.3%	62.7%
1	1976	158,465	48,087	ADAMS, JOHN	107,806	D'AMOURS, NORMAN E.	2,572	59,719 D	30.3%	68.0%	30.8%	69.2%
1	1974	112,004	53,610	BANKS, DAVID A.	58,388	D'AMOURS, NORMAN E.	6	4,778 D	47.9%	52.1%	47.9%	52.1%
1	1972	158,749	115,732	WYMAN, LOUIS C.	42,996	MERROW, CHESTER E.	21	72,736 R	72.9%	27.1%	72.9%	27.1%
2	1980	176,679	113,304	GREGG, JUDD	63,350	AREL, MAURICE L.	25	49,954 R	64.1%	35.9%	64.1%	35.9%
2	1978	124,081	84,535	CLEVELAND, JAMES C.	39,546	HELMS, EDGAR J.		44,989 R	68.1%	31.9%	68.1%	31.9%
2	1976	166,709	100,911	CLEVELAND, JAMES C.	65,792	GRANDMAISON, J. JOSEPH	6	35,119 R	60.5%	39.5%	60.5%	39.5%
2	1974	107,538	69,068	CLEVELAND, JAMES C.	38,463	BLISS, HELEN L.	7	30,605 R	64.2%	35.8%	64.2%	35.8%
2	1972	158,285	107,021	CLEVELAND, JAMES C.	51,259	OFFICER, CHARLES B.	5	55,762 R	67.6%	32.4%	67.6%	32.4%

NEW HAMPSHIRE

1980 GENERAL ELECTION

In addition to the county-by-county figures, data are presented for selected New Hampshire communities. Since not all jurisdictions of the state are listed in this special tabulation, state-wide totals are shown only with the county-by-county statistics.

President   Other vote was 49,693 Anderson (Independent); 2,064 Clark (Libertarian); 1,320 Commoner (Citizens); 129 Hall (Communist); 76 Griswold (Workers World); 71 DeBerry (Socialist Workers); 68 scattered.

Governor   Other vote was 1,318 Pinard (Libertarian) and 99 scattered.

Senator   Other vote was scattered.

Congress   Other vote was scattered in both CD's.

1980 PRIMARIES

SEPTEMBER 9 REPUBLICAN

Governor   55,554 Meldrim Thomson; 40,060 Louis C. D'Allesandro; 2,799 Elmer E. Bussey.

Senator   20,206 Warren Rudman; 16,885 John H. Sununu; 14,861 Wesley Powell; 9,821 Edward B. Hager; 9,426 Lawrence J. Brady; 9,361 David H. Bradley; 8,495 Anthony Campaigne; 7,397 George B. Roberts; 1,475 Robert Marvel; 1,166 E. J. Smith; 502 Carmen C. Chimento.

Congress   Contested as follows:

CD 1   11,815 Marshall W. Cobleigh; 10,554 Robert C. Smith; 8,494 John C. Mongan; 5,098 Paul R. Hatch; 2,965 George W. Sanborn; 2,954 Stephen W. Mansfield; 1,800 Walter L. Koenig.

CD 2   16,603 Judd Gregg; 12,064 Susan McLane; 10,689 Charles F. Bass; 3,495 Robert W. Sweet; 1,627 John F. Upton; 1,586 Webster E. Bridges; 1,557 Eric V. Bleicken; 855 Constance M. Mehegan; 682 Albert Kashulines.

SEPTEMBER 9 DEMOCRATIC

Governor   37,786 Hugh J. Gallen; 8,689 Thomas B. Wingate.

Senator   36,933 John A. Durkin; 9,486 William F. Sullivan.

Congress   Unopposed in CD 1. Contested as follows:

CD 2   12,255 Maurice L. Arel; 7,397 Phyllis J. Pucci.

NEW JERSEY

GOVERNOR
Brendan T. Byrne (D). Re-elected 1977 to a four-year term. Previously elected 1973.

SENATORS
Bill Bradley (D). Elected 1978 to a six-year term.

Harrison Williams (D). Re-elected 1976 to a six-year term. Previously elected 1970, 1964, 1958.

REPRESENTATIVES
1. James J. Florio (D)
2. William J. Hughes (D)
3. James J. Howard (D)
4. Christopher H. Smith (R)
5. Millicent Fenwick (R)
6. Edwin B. Forsythe (R)
7. Margaret S. Roukema (R)
8. Robert A. Roe (D)
9. Harold C. Hollenbeck (R)
10. Peter W. Rodino (D)
11. Joseph G. Minish (D)
12. Matthew J. Rinaldo (R)
13. James A. Courter (R)
14. Frank J. Guarini (D)
15. Bernard J. Dwyer (D)

POSTWAR VOTE FOR GOVERNOR

Year	Total Vote	Republican Vote	Candidate	Democratic Vote	Candidate	Other Vote	Rep.-Dem. Plurality	Total Vote Rep.	Total Vote Dem.	Major Vote Rep.	Major Vote Dem.
1977	2,126,264	888,880	Bateman, Raymond H.	1,184,564	Byrne, Brendan T.	52,820	295,684 D	41.8%	55.7%	42.9%	57.1%
1973	2,122,009	676,235	Sandman, Charles W.	1,414,613	Byrne, Brendan T.	31,161	738,378 D	31.9%	66.7%	32.3%	67.7%
1969	2,366,606	1,411,905	Cahill, William T.	911,003	Meyner, Robert B.	43,698	500,902 R	59.7%	38.5%	60.8%	39.2%
1965	2,229,583	915,996	Dumont, Wayne	1,279,568	Hughes, Richard J.	34,019	363,572 D	41.1%	57.4%	41.7%	58.3%
1961	2,152,662	1,049,274	Mitchell, James P.	1,084,194	Hughes, Richard J.	19,194	34,920 D	48.7%	50.4%	49.2%	50.8%
1957	2,018,488	897,321	Forbes, Malcolm S.	1,101,130	Meyner, Robert B.	20,037	203,809 D	44.5%	54.6%	44.9%	55.1%
1953	1,810,812	809,068	Troast, Paul L.	962,710	Meyner, Robert B.	39,034	153,642 D	44.7%	53.2%	45.7%	54.3%
1949	1,718,788	885,882	Driscoll, Alfred	810,022	Wene, Elmer H.	22,884	75,860 R	51.5%	47.1%	52.2%	47.8%
1946	1,414,527	807,378	Driscoll, Alfred	585,960	Hansen, Lewis G.	21,189	221,418 R	57.1%	41.4%	57.9%	42.1%

The term of office of New Jersey's Governor was increased from three to four years effective with the 1949 election.

POSTWAR VOTE FOR SENATOR

Year	Total Vote	Republican Vote	Candidate	Democratic Vote	Candidate	Other Vote	Rep.-Dem. Plurality	Total Vote Rep.	Total Vote Dem.	Major Vote Rep.	Major Vote Dem.
1978	1,957,515	844,200	Bell, Jeffrey	1,082,960	Bradley, Bill	30,355	238,760 D	43.1%	55.3%	43.8%	56.2%
1976	2,771,390	1,054,508	Norcross, David F.	1,681,140	Williams, Harrison	35,742	626,632 D	38.0%	60.7%	38.5%	61.5%
1972	2,791,907	1,743,854	Case, Clifford P.	963,573	Krebs, Paul J.	84,480	780,281 R	62.5%	34.5%	64.4%	35.6%
1970	2,142,105	903,026	Gross, Nelson G.	1,157,074	Williams, Harrison	82,005	254,048 D	42.2%	54.0%	43.8%	56.2%
1966	2,131,188	1,279,343	Case, Clifford P.	788,021	Wilentz, Warren W.	63,824	491,322 R	60.0%	37.0%	61.9%	38.1%
1964	2,710,441	1,011,610	Shanley, Bernard M.	1,678,051	Williams, Harrison	20,780	666,441 D	37.3%	61.9%	37.6%	62.4%
1960	2,664,556	1,483,832	Case, Clifford P.	1,151,385	Lord, Thorn	29,339	332,447 R	55.7%	43.2%	56.3%	43.7%
1958	1,881,329	882,287	Kean, Robert W.	966,832	Williams, Harrison	32,210	84,545 D	46.9%	51.4%	47.7%	52.3%
1954	1,770,557	861,528	Case, Clifford P.	858,158	Howell, Charles R.	50,871	3,370 R	48.7%	48.5%	50.1%	49.9%
1952	2,318,232	1,286,782	Smith, H. Alexander	1,011,187	Alexander, Archibald	20,263	275,595 R	55.5%	43.6%	56.0%	44.0%
1948	1,869,882	934,720	Hendrickson, Robert	884,414	Alexander, Archibald	50,748	50,306 R	50.0%	47.3%	51.4%	48.6%
1946	1,367,155	799,808	Smith, H. Alexander	548,458	Brunner, George E.	18,889	251,350 R	58.5%	40.1%	59.3%	40.7%

NEW JERSEY

Districts Established April 12, 1972

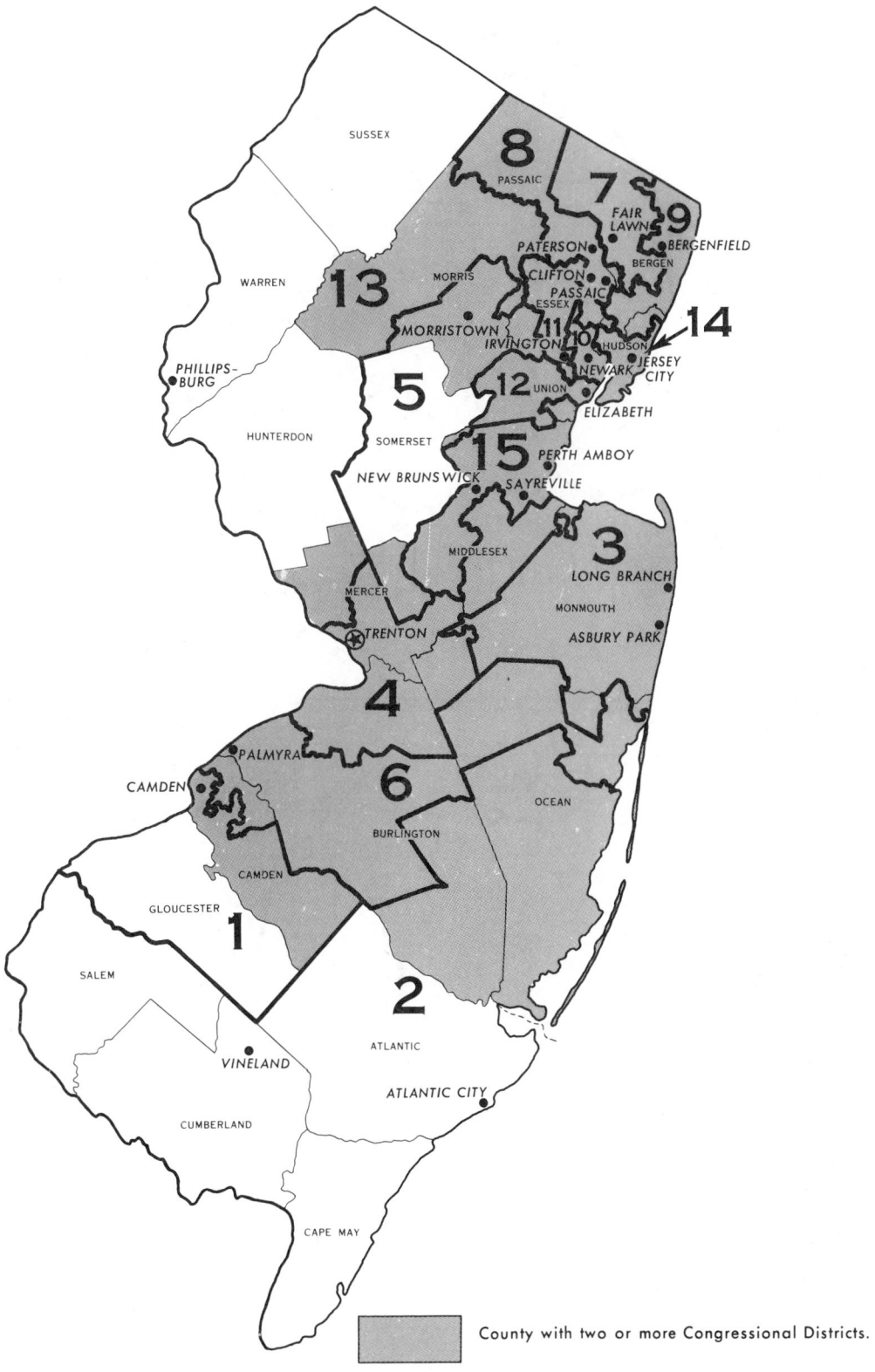

NEW JERSEY

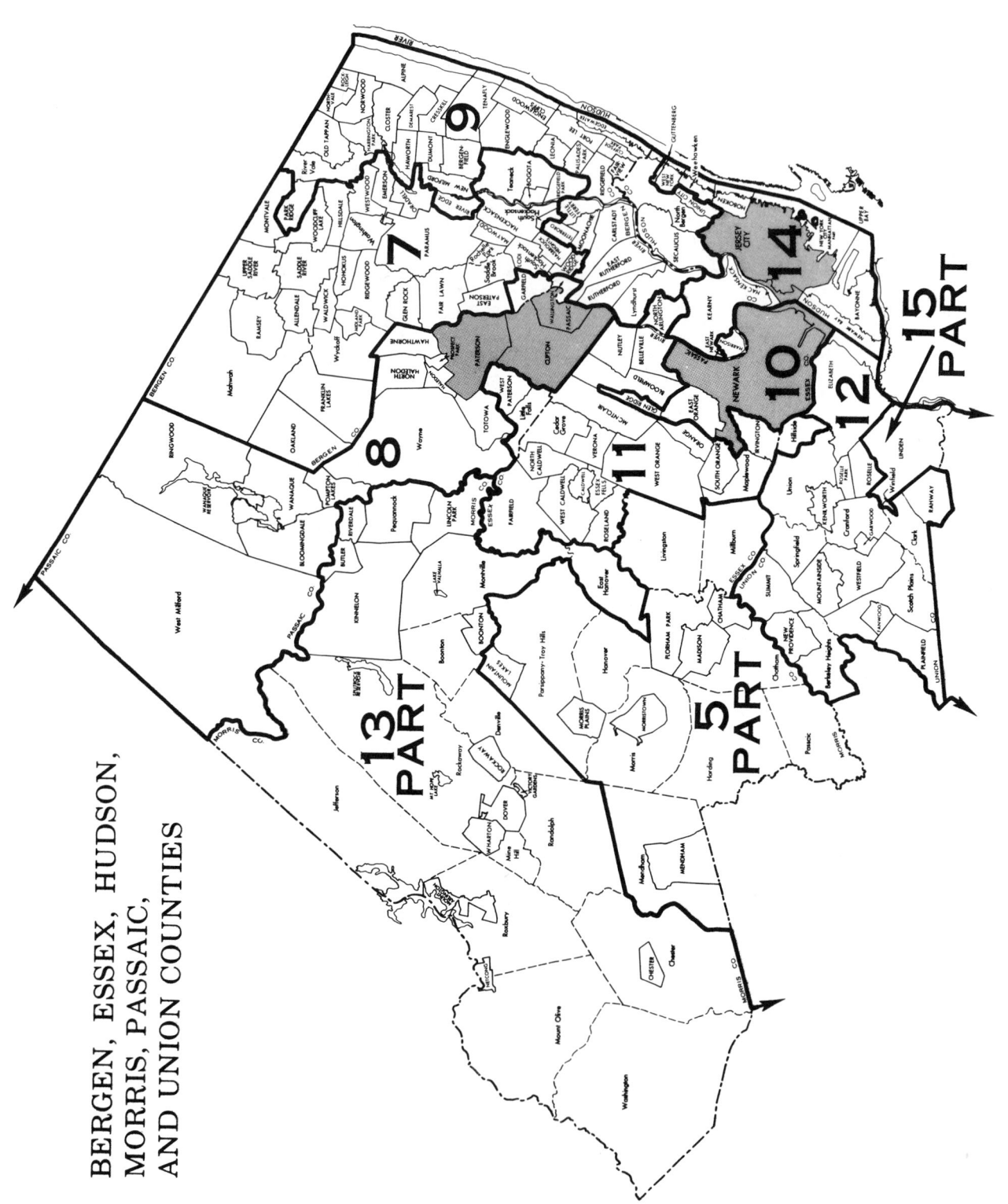

BERGEN, ESSEX, HUDSON,
MORRIS, PASSAIC,
AND UNION COUNTIES

NEW JERSEY

PRESIDENT 1980

1980 Census Population	County	Total Vote	Republican	Democratic	Other	Rep.-Dem. Plurality	Percentage Total Vote Rep.	Dem.	Major Vote Rep.	Dem.
194,119	ATLANTIC	76,202	37,973	31,286	6,943	6,687 R	49.8%	41.1%	54.8%	45.2%
845,385	BERGEN	415,157	232,043	139,474	43,640	92,569 R	55.9%	33.6%	62.5%	37.5%
362,542	BURLINGTON	131,709	68,415	50,083	13,211	18,332 R	51.9%	38.0%	57.7%	42.3%
471,650	CAMDEN	186,808	87,939	80,033	18,836	7,906 R	47.1%	42.8%	52.4%	47.6%
82,266	CAPE MAY	38,471	22,729	12,708	3,034	10,021 R	59.1%	33.0%	64.1%	35.9%
132,866	CUMBERLAND	46,403	23,242	19,356	3,805	3,886 R	50.1%	41.7%	54.6%	45.4%
850,451	ESSEX	287,166	117,222	145,281	24,663	28,059 D	40.8%	50.6%	44.7%	55.3%
199,917	GLOUCESTER	78,903	40,306	29,804	8,793	10,502 R	51.1%	37.8%	57.5%	42.5%
556,972	HUDSON	198,688	91,207	95,622	11,859	4,415 D	45.9%	48.1%	48.8%	51.2%
87,361	HUNTERDON	36,430	21,403	10,029	4,998	11,374 R	58.8%	27.5%	68.1%	31.9%
307,863	MERCER	128,582	53,450	60,888	14,244	7,438 D	41.6%	47.4%	46.7%	53.3%
595,893	MIDDLESEX	241,206	122,354	97,304	21,548	25,050 R	50.7%	40.3%	55.7%	44.3%
503,173	MONMOUTH	211,971	120,173	71,328	20,470	48,845 R	56.7%	33.6%	62.8%	37.2%
407,630	MORRIS	173,604	105,260	48,965	19,379	56,295 R	60.6%	28.2%	68.3%	31.7%
346,038	OCEAN	157,568	98,433	46,923	12,212	51,510 R	62.5%	29.8%	67.7%	32.3%
447,585	PASSAIC	158,951	82,531	61,486	14,934	21,045 R	51.9%	38.7%	57.3%	42.7%
64,676	SALEM	25,474	13,000	10,209	2,265	2,791 R	51.0%	40.1%	56.0%	44.0%
203,129	SOMERSET	91,928	52,591	29,470	9,867	23,121 R	57.2%	32.1%	64.1%	35.9%
116,119	SUSSEX	42,327	27,063	10,531	4,733	16,532 R	63.9%	24.9%	72.0%	28.0%
504,094	UNION	217,339	112,288	86,074	18,977	26,214 R	51.7%	39.6%	56.6%	43.4%
84,429	WARREN	30,797	16,935	10,510	3,352	6,425 R	55.0%	34.1%	61.7%	38.3%
7,364,158	TOTAL	2,975,684	1,546,557	1,147,364	281,763	399,193 R	52.0%	38.6%	57.4%	42.6%

NEW JERSEY

CONGRESS

CD	Year	Total Vote	Republican		Democratic		Other Vote	Rep.-Dem. Plurality	Percentage			
									Total Vote		Major Vote	
			Vote	Candidate	Vote	Candidate			Rep.	Dem.	Rep.	Dem.
1	1980	192,081	42,154	SIBERT, SCOTT L.	147,352	FLORIO, JAMES J.	2,575	105,198 D	21.9%	76.7%	22.2%	77.8%
1	1978	133,620	26,853	DEITCH, ROBERT M.	106,096	FLORIO, JAMES J.	671	79,243 D	20.1%	79.4%	20.2%	79.8%
1	1976	194,898	56,363	MCCULLOUGH, JOSEPH I.	136,624	FLORIO, JAMES J.	1,911	80,261 D	28.9%	70.1%	29.2%	70.8%
1	1974	140,468	54,069	HUNT, JOHN E.	80,768	FLORIO, JAMES J.	5,631	26,699 D	38.5%	57.5%	40.1%	59.9%
1	1972	186,026	97,650	HUNT, JOHN E.	87,492	FLORIO, JAMES J.	884	10,158 R	52.5%	47.0%	52.7%	47.3%
2	1980	235,710	97,072	FOX, BEECH N.	135,437	HUGHES, WILLIAM J.	3,201	38,365 D	41.2%	57.5%	41.7%	58.3%
2	1978	169,765	56,997	BIGGS, JAMES H.	112,768	HUGHES, WILLIAM J.		55,771 D	33.6%	66.4%	33.6%	66.4%
2	1976	229,668	87,915	HURLEY, JAMES R.	141,753	HUGHES, WILLIAM J.		53,838 D	38.3%	61.7%	38.3%	61.7%
2	1974	191,520	79,064	SANDMAN, CHARLES W.	109,763	HUGHES, WILLIAM J.	2,693	30,699 D	41.3%	57.3%	41.9%	58.1%
2	1972	202,470	133,096	SANDMAN, CHARLES W.	69,374	ROSE, JOHN D.		63,722 R	65.7%	34.3%	65.7%	34.3%
3	1980	212,830	104,184	MUHLER, MARIE S.	106,269	HOWARD, JAMES J.	2,377	2,085 D	49.0%	49.9%	49.5%	50.5%
3	1978	148,955	64,730	COE, BRUCE G.	83,349	HOWARD, JAMES J.	876	18,619 D	43.5%	56.0%	43.7%	56.3%
3	1976	204,739	75,934	SICILIANO, RALPH A.	127,164	HOWARD, JAMES J.	1,641	51,230 D	37.1%	62.1%	37.4%	62.6%
3	1974	153,906	45,932	CLARK, KENNETH W.	105,979	HOWARD, JAMES J.	1,995	60,047 D	29.8%	68.9%	30.2%	69.8%
3	1972	196,178	92,285	DOWD, WILLIAM F.	103,893	HOWARD, JAMES J.		11,608 D	47.0%	53.0%	47.0%	53.0%
4	1980	168,504	95,447	SMITH, CHRISTOPHER H.	68,480	THOMPSON, FRANK	4,577	26,967 R	56.6%	40.6%	58.2%	41.8%
4	1978	113,382	41,833	SMITH, CHRISTOPHER H.	69,259	THOMPSON, FRANK	2,290	27,426 D	36.9%	61.1%	37.7%	62.3%
4	1976	170,868	54,789	INDYK, JOSEPH S.	113,281	THOMPSON, FRANK	2,798	58,492 D	32.1%	66.3%	32.6%	67.4%
4	1974	122,992	40,797	KELLER, HENRY J.	82,195	THOMPSON, FRANK		41,398 D	33.2%	66.8%	33.2%	66.8%
4	1972	169,236	71,030	GARIBALDI, PETER P.	98,206	THOMPSON, FRANK		27,176 D	42.0%	58.0%	42.0%	58.0%
5	1980	201,299	156,016	FENWICK, MILLICENT	41,269	PILLION, KIERAN E.	4,014	114,747 R	77.5%	20.5%	79.1%	20.9%
5	1978	138,847	100,739	FENWICK, MILLICENT	38,108	FAHY, JOHN T.		62,631 R	72.6%	27.4%	72.6%	27.4%
5	1976	206,106	137,803	FENWICK, MILLICENT	64,598	NERO, F. R.	3,705	73,205 R	66.9%	31.3%	68.1%	31.9%
5	1974	152,758	81,498	FENWICK, MILLICENT	66,380	BOHEN, FREDERICK M.	4,880	15,118 R	53.4%	43.5%	55.1%	44.9%
5	1972	205,386	127,310	FRELINGHUYSEN, PETER	78,076	BOHEN, FREDERICK M.		49,234 R	62.0%	38.0%	62.0%	38.0%
6	1980	223,254	125,792	FORSYTHE, EDWIN B.	92,227	WEINSTEIN, LEWIS M.	5,235	33,565 R	56.3%	41.3%	57.7%	42.3%
6	1978	148,184	89,446	FORSYTHE, EDWIN B.	56,874	MCGANN, W. THOMAS	1,864	32,572 R	60.4%	38.4%	61.1%	38.9%
6	1976	214,304	125,920	FORSYTHE, EDWIN B.	85,053	COSTA, CATHERINE A.	3,331	40,867 R	58.8%	39.7%	59.7%	40.3%
6	1974	154,712	81,190	FORSYTHE, EDWIN B.	70,353	YATES, CHARLES B.	3,169	10,837 R	52.5%	45.5%	53.6%	46.4%
6	1972	196,821	123,610	FORSYTHE, EDWIN B.	71,113	BRENNAN, FRANCIS P.	2,098	52,497 R	62.8%	36.1%	63.5%	36.5%
7	1980	214,343	108,760	ROUKEMA, MARGARET S.	99,737	MAGUIRE, ANDREW	5,846	9,023 R	50.7%	46.5%	52.2%	47.8%
7	1978	149,118	69,543	ROUKEMA, MARGARET S.	78,358	MAGUIRE, ANDREW	1,217	8,815 D	46.6%	52.5%	47.0%	53.0%
7	1976	213,150	92,624	SHEEHAN, JAMES J.	120,526	MAGUIRE, ANDREW		27,902 D	43.5%	56.5%	43.5%	56.5%
7	1974	160,705	71,377	WIDNALL, WILLIAM B.	79,808	MAGUIRE, ANDREW	9,520	8,431 D	44.4%	49.7%	47.2%	52.8%
7	1972	214,634	124,365	WIDNALL, WILLIAM B.	85,712	LESEMANN, ARTHUR J.	4,557	38,653 R	57.9%	39.9%	59.2%	40.8%
8	1980	142,201	44,625	CLEVELAND, WILLIAM R.	95,493	ROE, ROBERT A.	2,083	50,868 D	31.4%	67.2%	31.8%	68.2%
8	1978	93,338	23,842	MELANI, THOMAS	69,496	ROE, ROBERT A.		45,654 D	25.5%	74.5%	25.5%	74.5%
8	1976	154,196	44,775	DOTY, BESSIE	108,841	ROE, ROBERT A.	580	64,066 D	29.0%	70.6%	29.1%	70.9%
8	1974	113,327	27,839	SCHMIDT, HERMAN	83,724	ROE, ROBERT A.	1,764	55,885 D	24.6%	73.9%	25.0%	75.0%
8	1972	165,454	61,073	JOHNSON, WALTER E.	104,381	ROE, ROBERT A.		43,308 D	36.9%	63.1%	36.9%	63.1%
9	1980	196,504	116,128	HOLLENBECK, HAROLD C.	75,321	AMBROSIO, GABRIEL M.	5,055	40,807 R	59.1%	38.3%	60.7%	39.3%
9	1978	150,155	73,478	HOLLENBECK, HAROLD C.	56,888	MASTORELLI, NICHOLAS S.	19,789	16,590 R	48.9%	37.9%	56.4%	43.6%
9	1976	202,344	107,454	HOLLENBECK, HAROLD C.	89,723	HELSTOSKI, HENRY	5,167	17,731 R	53.1%	44.3%	54.5%	45.5%
9	1974	154,362	50,859	PARETI, HAROLD A.	99,592	HELSTOSKI, HENRY	3,911	48,733 D	32.9%	64.5%	33.8%	66.2%
9	1972	214,290	94,747	SCHIAFFO, ALFRED D.	119,543	HELSTOSKI, HENRY		24,796 D	44.2%	55.8%	44.2%	55.8%
10	1980	89,245	11,778	JENNINGS, EVERETT J.	76,154	RODINO, PETER W.	1,313	64,376 D	13.2%	85.3%	13.4%	86.6%
10	1978	63,777	8,066	PELT, JOHN L.	55,074	RODINO, PETER W.	637	47,008 D	12.6%	86.4%	12.8%	87.2%
10	1976	106,775	17,129	GRANDISON, TONY	88,245	RODINO, PETER W.	1,401	71,116 D	16.0%	82.6%	16.3%	83.7%
10	1974	65,538	9,936	TALIAFERRO, JOHN R.	53,094	RODINO, PETER W.	2,508	43,158 D	15.2%	81.0%	15.8%	84.2%
10	1972	118,257	23,949	MILLER, KENNETH C.	94,308	RODINO, PETER W.		70,359 D	20.3%	79.7%	20.3%	79.7%
11	1980	168,524	57,772	DAVIS, ROBERT A.	106,155	MINISH, JOSEPH G.	4,597	48,383 D	34.3%	63.0%	35.2%	64.8%
11	1978	125,174	35,642	FELD, JULIUS G.	88,294	MINISH, JOSEPH G.	1,238	52,652 D	28.5%	70.5%	28.8%	71.2%
11	1976	190,808	59,397	POEKEL, CHARLES A.	129,026	MINISH, JOSEPH G.	2,385	69,629 D	31.1%	67.6%	31.5%	68.5%
11	1974	142,915	42,036	GRANT, WILLIAM B.	98,957	MINISH, JOSEPH G.	1,922	56,921 D	29.4%	69.2%	29.8%	70.2%
11	1972	209,102	82,957	WALDOR, MILTON A.	120,277	MINISH, JOSEPH G.	5,868	37,320 D	39.7%	57.5%	40.8%	59.2%
12	1980	175,026	134,973	RINALDO, MATTHEW J.	36,577	MONYEK, ROSE Z.	3,476	98,396 R	77.1%	20.9%	78.7%	21.3%
12	1978	129,273	94,850	RINALDO, MATTHEW J.	34,423	MCCORMACK, RICHARD		60,427 R	73.4%	26.6%	73.4%	26.6%
12	1976	187,282	136,973	RINALDO, MATTHEW J.	49,189	BUGGELLI, RICHARD A.	1,120	87,784 R	73.1%	26.3%	73.6%	26.4%
12	1974	142,843	92,829	RINALDO, MATTHEW J.	46,246	LEVIN, ADAM K.	3,768	46,583 R	65.0%	32.4%	66.7%	33.3%
12	1972	201,179	127,690	RINALDO, MATTHEW J.	72,758	ENGLISH, JERRY F.	731	54,932 R	63.5%	36.2%	63.7%	36.3%

NEW JERSEY

CONGRESS

CD	Year	Total Vote	Republican Vote	Candidate	Democratic Vote	Candidate	Other Vote	Rep.-Dem. Plurality	Percentage Total Vote Rep.	Dem.	Major Vote Rep.	Dem.
13	1980	213,373	152,862	COURTER, JAMES A.	56,251	STICKLE, DAVE	4,260	96,611 R	71.6%	26.4%	73.1%	26.9%
13	1978	149,109	77,301	COURTER, JAMES A.	71,808	MEYNER, HELEN S.		5,493 R	51.8%	48.2%	51.8%	48.2%
13	1976	209,051	100,050	SCHLUTER, WILLIAM E.	105,291	MEYNER, HELEN S.	3,710	5,241 D	47.9%	50.4%	48.7%	51.3%
13	1974	150,209	64,166	MARAZITI, JOSEPH J.	86,043	MEYNER, HELEN S.		21,877 D	42.7%	57.3%	42.7%	57.3%
13	1972	196,958	109,640	MARAZITI, JOSEPH J.	84,492	MEYNER, HELEN S.	2,826	25,148 R	55.7%	42.9%	56.5%	43.5%
14	1980	135,430	45,606	TETI, DENNIS	86,921	GUARINI, FRANK J.	2,903	41,315 D	33.7%	64.2%	34.4%	65.6%
14	1978	105,340	21,355	HILL, HENRY J.	67,008	GUARINI, FRANK J.	16,977	45,653 D	20.3%	63.6%	24.2%	75.8%
14	1976	146,768	66,319	CAMPENNI, ANTHONY L.	73,174	LEFANTE, JOSEPH A.	7,275	6,855 D	45.2%	49.9%	47.5%	52.5%
14	1974	106,935	17,231	SHERIDAN, CLAIRE J.	85,438	DANIELS, DOMINICK V.	4,266	68,207 D	16.1%	79.9%	16.8%	83.2%
14	1972	168,363	57,683	BOZZONE, RICHARD T.	103,089	DANIELS, DOMINICK V.	7,591	45,406 D	34.3%	61.2%	35.9%	64.1%
15	1980	173,071	75,812	O'SULLIVAN, WILLIAM J.	92,457	DWYER, BERNARD J.	4,802	16,645 D	43.8%	53.4%	45.1%	54.9%
15	1978	115,886	53,108	WILEY, CHARLES W.	55,944	PATTEN, EDWARD J.	6,834	2,836 D	45.8%	48.3%	48.7%	51.3%
15	1976	179,836	54,487	WILEY, CHARLES W.	106,170	PATTEN, EDWARD J.	19,179	51,683 D	30.3%	59.0%	33.9%	66.1%
15	1974	130,367	35,875	HAMMESFAHR, ERNEST J.	92,593	PATTEN, EDWARD J.	1,899	56,718 D	27.5%	71.0%	27.9%	72.1%
15	1972	187,555	89,400	BROOKS, FULLER H.	98,155	PATTEN, EDWARD J.		8,755 D	47.7%	52.3%	47.7%	52.3%

NEW JERSEY

1980 GENERAL ELECTION

President   Other vote was 234,632 Anderson (The Anderson Alternative); 20,652 Clark (Libertarian); 8,203 Commoner (Citizens); 3,927 McCormack (Right to Life); 3,694 Lynen (Middle Class Candidate); 2,555 Hall (Communist); 2,198 Pulley (Socialist Workers); 1,973 McReynolds (Socialist); 1,718 Gahres (Down with Lawyers); 1,288 Griswold (Workers World); 923 Wendelken (Independent).

Congress   Other vote was 2,262 Rothhouse (Libertarian) and 939 Frisch (Socialist Labor) in CD 2; 2,801 Moyers (Libertarian) and 1,776 Rizzo (no slogan) in CD 4; 2,465 Samson (Libertarian) and 1,549 Gould (Contempt of Court) in CD 5; 1,209 Rabel (Socialist Labor) and 874 Horowitz (Libertarian) in CD 8; 2,358 Jensen (Independent) and 1,118 Vandersteel (Libertarian) in CD 12; Schafer (Libertarian) in CD 13; 1,765 Steele (Libertarian) and 1,138 Famularo (Action Talks) in CD 14; 2,937 Mintz (People's Independent Coalition) and 1,865 Hart (Libertarian) in CD 15; in other CD's as follows:

CD 1   1,327 Watson (Independent); 1,029 Wishart (Libertarian) and 219 Levin (Socialist Labor).
CD 3   1,450 Palven (Libertarian); 643 Erickson (Socialist) and 284 Wilson (J-E-B Party Inc.).
CD 6   2,165 Flynn (Libertarian); 1,848 Kinnevy (Citizens); 666 Smith (Constitution) and 556 Doganiero (Socialist Labor).
CD 7   3,594 Randazzo (Pro-Life Independent); 1,640 Shapiro (Libertarian) and 612 Wendelken (Independent). Mr. Wendelken was also a Presidential candidate in New Jersey.
CD 9   2,290 Koch (Libertarian); 1,588 Shaw (Politicians are Crooks) and 1,177 Davis (Citizens).
CD 10   542 Keno (Human Rights Ratification); 281 Scott (Youth Against Draft); 271 Penque (Libertarian); 219 Hildebrand (Socialist Workers).
CD 11   1,650 Britton (Socialist Workers); 1,630 Trugman (Independent Alternative) and 1,317 Roth (Libertarian).

1980 PRIMARIES

JUNE 3 REPUBLICAN

Congress   Unopposed in nine CD's. Contested as follows:

CD 2   19,143 Beech N. Fox; 11,041 John J. Mahoney.
CD 4   8,121 Christopher H. Smith; 1,676 John D. Scalamonti.
CD 5   23,419 Millicent Fenwick; 10,080 Larry Haverly.
CD 6   18,768 Edwin B. Forsythe; 2,126 Richard D. Amber.
CD 14   3,371 Dennis Teti; 519 Anthony P. Scalcione.
CD 15   4,538 William J. O'Sullivan; 3,836 Charles W. Wiley.

JUNE 3 DEMOCRATIC

Congress   Unopposed in eight CD's. Contested as follows:

CD 5   6,839 Kieran E. Pillion; 6,507 William R. Norris.
CD 6   9,713 Lewis M. Weinstein; 8,535 Bruce MacNaul; 8,357 Alene S. Ammond.
CD 9   16,804 Gabriel M. Ambrosio; 14,417 Burt Ross; 9,359 Henry Helstoski.
CD 10   26,943 Peter W. Rodino; 9,825 Donald M. Payne; 5,316 Golden E. Johnson; 1,251 Russell Fox.
CD 12   9,085 Rose Z. Monyek; 8,120 Charles A. Leary.
CD 13   8,064 Dave Stickle; 4,678 Edward J. Baker; 3,972 Carl A. Mottey; 2,272 Ray Rollinson; 1,160 Roger A. Singerling.
CD 15   16,328 Bernard J. Dwyer; 12,800 David C. Schwartz, 12,329 George Spadoro; 7,720 Richard Pucci; 1,806 Doris Sipos.

NEW MEXICO

GOVERNOR

Bruce King (D). Elected 1978 to a four-year term. Previously elected 1970.

SENATORS

Peter V. Domenici (R). Re-elected 1978 to a six-year term. Previously elected 1972.

Harrison Schmitt (R). Elected 1976 to a six-year term.

REPRESENTATIVES

1. Manual Lujan, Jr. (R)   2. Joseph R. Skeen (R)

POSTWAR VOTE FOR GOVERNOR

Year	Total Vote	Republican Vote	Republican Candidate	Democratic Vote	Democratic Candidate	Other Vote	Rep.-Dem. Plurality	Total Vote Rep.	Total Vote Dem.	Major Vote Rep.	Major Vote Dem.
1978	345,577	170,848	Skeen, Joseph R.	174,631	King, Bruce	98	3,783 D	49.4%	50.5%	49.5%	50.5%
1974	328,742	160,430	Skeen, Joseph R.	164,172	Apodaca, Jerry	4,140	3,742 D	48.8%	49.9%	49.4%	50.6%
1970	290,375	134,640	Domenici, Peter V.	148,835	King, Bruce	6,900	14,195 D	46.4%	51.3%	47.5%	52.5%
1968	318,975	160,140	Cargo, David F.	157,230	Chavez, Fabian	1,605	2,910 R	50.2%	49.3%	50.5%	49.5%
1966	260,232	134,625	Cargo, David F.	125,587	Lusk, Thomas E.	20	9,038 R	51.7%	48.3%	51.7%	48.3%
1964	318,042	126,540	Tucker, Merle H.	191,497	Campbell, Jack M.	5	64,957 D	39.8%	60.2%	39.8%	60.2%
1962	247,135	116,184	Mechem, Edwin L.	130,933	Campbell, Jack M.	18	14,749 D	47.0%	53.0%	47.0%	53.0%
1960	305,542	153,765	Mechem, Edwin L.	151,777	Burroughs, John	—	1,988 R	50.3%	49.7%	50.3%	49.7%
1958	205,048	101,567	Mechem, Edwin L.	103,481	Burroughs, John	—	1,914 D	49.5%	50.5%	49.5%	50.5%
1956	251,751	131,488	Mechem, Edwin L.	120,263	Simms, John F.	—	11,225 R	52.2%	47.8%	52.2%	47.8%
1954	193,956	83,373	Stockton, Alvin	110,583	Simms, John F.	—	27,210 D	43.0%	57.0%	43.0%	57.0%
1952	240,150	129,116	Mechem, Edwin L.	111,034	Grantham, Everett	—	18,082 R	53.8%	46.2%	53.8%	46.2%
1950	180,205	96,846	Mechem, Edwin L.	83,359	Miles, John E.	—	13,487 R	53.7%	46.3%	53.7%	46.3%
1948	189,992	86,023	Lujan, Manuel	103,969	Mabry, Thomas J.	—	17,946 D	45.3%	54.7%	45.3%	54.7%
1946	132,930	62,875	Safford, Edward L.	70,055	Mabry, Thomas J.	—	7,180 D	47.3%	52.7%	47.3%	52.7%

The term of office for New Mexico's Governor was increased from two to four years effective with the 1970 election.

POSTWAR VOTE FOR SENATOR

Year	Total Vote	Republican Vote	Republican Candidate	Democratic Vote	Democratic Candidate	Other Vote	Rep.-Dem. Plurality	Total Vote Rep.	Total Vote Dem.	Major Vote Rep.	Major Vote Dem.
1978	343,554	183,442	Domenici, Peter V.	160,045	Anaya, Toney	67	23,397 R	53.4%	46.6%	53.4%	46.6%
1976	413,141	234,681	Schmitt, Harrison	176,382	Montoya, Joseph M.	2,078	58,299 R	56.8%	42.7%	57.1%	42.9%
1972	378,330	204,253	Domenici, Peter V.	173,815	Daniels, Jack	262	30,438 R	54.0%	45.9%	54.0%	46.0%
1970	289,906	135,004	Carter, Anderson	151,486	Montoya, Joseph M.	3,416	16,482 D	46.6%	52.3%	47.1%	52.9%
1966	258,203	120,988	Carter, Anderson	137,205	Anderson, Clinton P.	10	16,217 D	46.9%	53.1%	46.9%	53.1%
1964	325,774	147,562	Mechem, Edwin L.	178,209	Montoya, Joseph M.	3	30,647 D	45.3%	54.7%	45.3%	54.7%
1960	300,551	109,897	Colwes, William F.	190,654	Anderson, Clinton P.	—	80,757 D	36.6%	63.4%	36.6%	63.4%
1958	203,323	75,827	Atchley, Forrest S.	127,496	Chavez, Dennis	—	51,669 D	37.3%	62.7%	37.3%	62.7%
1954	194,422	83,071	Mechem, Edwin L.	111,351	Anderson, Clinton P.	—	28,280 D	42.7%	57.3%	42.7%	57.3%
1952	239,711	117,168	Hurley, Patrick J.	122,543	Chavez, Dennis	—	5,375 D	48.9%	51.1%	48.9%	51.1%
1948	188,495	80,226	Hurley, Patrick J.	108,269	Anderson, Clinton P.	—	28,043 D	42.6%	57.4%	42.6%	57.4%
1946	133,282	64,632	Hurley, Patrick J.	68,650	Chavez, Dennis	—	4,018 D	48.5%	51.5%	48.5%	51.5%

NEW MEXICO

Districts Established May 15, 1968

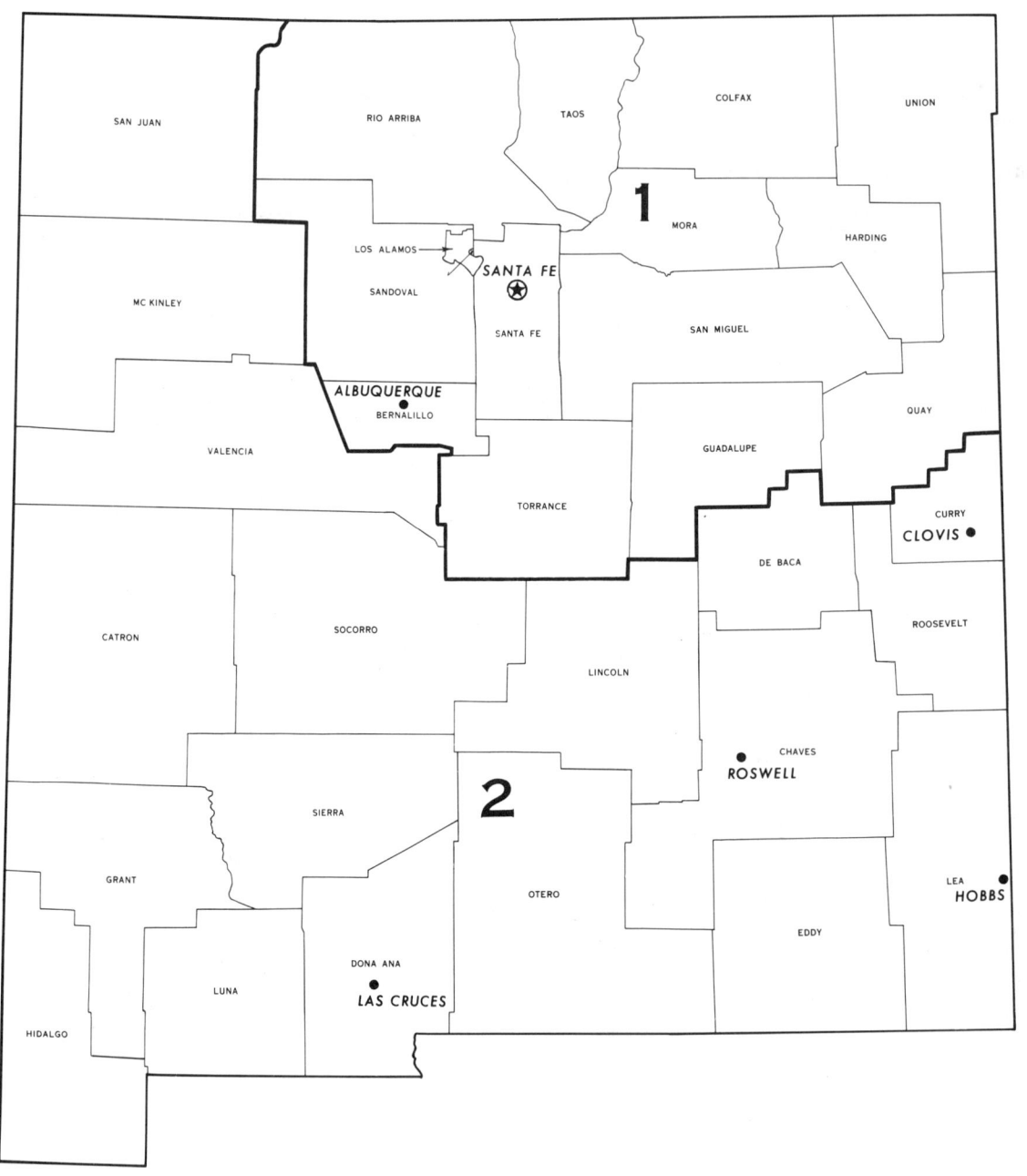

NEW MEXICO

PRESIDENT 1980

1980 Census Population	County	Total Vote	Republican	Democratic	Other	Rep.-Dem. Plurality	Percentage Total Vote Rep.	Dem.	Major Vote Rep.	Dem.
419,700	BERNALILLO	157,284	83,956	54,841	18,487	29,115 R	53.4%	34.9%	60.5%	39.5%
2,720	CATRON	1,448	906	466	76	440 R	62.6%	32.2%	66.0%	34.0%
51,103	CHAVES	18,657	12,502	5,350	805	7,152 R	67.0%	28.7%	70.0%	30.0%
13,706	COLFAX	5,094	2,537	2,266	291	271 R	49.8%	44.5%	52.8%	47.2%
42,019	CURRY	12,070	8,132	3,622	316	4,510 R	67.4%	30.0%	69.2%	30.8%
2,454	DEBACA	1,167	655	484	28	171 R	56.1%	41.5%	57.5%	42.5%
96,340	DONA ANA	28,852	15,539	10,839	2,474	4,700 R	53.9%	37.6%	58.9%	41.1%
47,855	EDDY	17,417	9,817	7,028	572	2,789 R	56.4%	40.4%	58.3%	41.7%
26,204	GRANT	9,778	4,628	4,600	550	28 R	47.3%	47.0%	50.2%	49.8%
4,496	GUADALUPE	2,145	1,065	980	100	85 R	49.7%	45.7%	52.1%	47.9%
1,090	HARDING	601	356	225	20	131 R	59.2%	37.4%	61.3%	38.7%
6,049	HIDALGO	1,993	1,059	840	94	219 R	53.1%	42.1%	55.8%	44.2%
55,634	LEA	16,261	10,727	5,006	528	5,721 R	66.0%	30.8%	68.2%	31.8%
10,997	LINCOLN	4,393	3,009	1,127	257	1,882 R	68.5%	25.7%	72.8%	27.2%
17,599	LOS ALAMOS	9,383	5,460	2,368	1,555	3,092 R	58.2%	25.2%	69.7%	30.3%
15,585	LUNA	6,373	3,636	2,443	294	1,193 R	57.1%	38.3%	59.8%	40.2%
54,950	MCKINLEY	12,934	7,329	4,869	736	2,460 R	56.7%	37.6%	60.1%	39.9%
4,205	MORA	2,385	1,037	1,274	74	237 D	43.5%	53.4%	44.9%	55.1%
44,665	OTERO	11,995	7,210	4,111	674	3,099 R	60.1%	34.3%	63.7%	36.3%
10,577	QUAY	4,026	2,499	1,422	105	1,077 R	62.1%	35.3%	63.7%	36.3%
29,282	RIO ARRIBA	10,594	3,794	6,245	555	2,451 D	35.8%	58.9%	37.8%	62.2%
15,695	ROOSEVELT	6,497	3,950	2,240	307	1,710 R	60.8%	34.5%	63.8%	36.2%
34,799	SANDOVAL	12,597	6,762	4,740	1,095	2,022 R	53.7%	37.6%	58.8%	41.2%
80,833	SAN JUAN	23,556	15,579	6,705	1,272	8,874 R	66.1%	28.5%	69.9%	30.1%
22,751	SAN MIGUEL	8,369	3,292	4,514	563	1,222 D	39.3%	53.9%	42.2%	57.8%
75,306	SANTA FE	28,871	12,361	12,658	3,852	297 D	42.8%	43.8%	49.4%	50.6%
8,454	SIERRA	3,567	2,222	1,169	176	1,053 R	62.3%	32.8%	65.5%	34.5%
12,969	SOCORRO	5,427	2,685	2,226	516	459 R	49.5%	41.0%	54.7%	45.3%
18,862	TAOS	8,603	3,584	4,346	673	762 D	41.7%	50.5%	45.2%	54.8%
7,491	TORRANCE	3,322	1,907	1,261	154	646 R	57.4%	38.0%	60.2%	39.8%
4,725	UNION	2,140	1,407	675	58	732 R	65.7%	31.5%	67.6%	32.4%
60,853	VALENCIA	19,172	11,177	6,886	1,109	4,291 R	58.3%	35.9%	61.9%	38.1%
1,299,968	TOTAL	456,971	250,779	167,826	38,366	82,953 R	54.9%	36.7%	59.9%	40.1%

NEW MEXICO

CONGRESS

CD	Year	Total Vote	Republican Vote	Republican Candidate	Democratic Vote	Democratic Candidate	Other Vote	Rep.-Dem. Plurality	Percentage Total Vote Rep.	Percentage Total Vote Dem.	Percentage Major Vote Rep.	Percentage Major Vote Dem.
1	1980	246,813	125,910	LUJAN, MANUEL, JR.	120,903	RICHARDSON, BILL		5,007 R	51.0%	49.0%	51.0%	49.0%
1	1978	188,885	118,075	LUJAN, MANUEL, JR.	70,761	HAWK, ROBERT M.	49	47,314 R	62.5%	37.5%	62.5%	37.5%
1	1976	225,592	162,587	LUJAN, MANUEL, JR.	61,800	GARCIA, RAYMOND	1,205	100,787 R	72.1%	27.4%	72.5%	27.5%
1	1974	181,334	106,268	LUJAN, MANUEL, JR.	71,968	MONDRAGON, ROBERT A.	3,098	34,300 R	58.6%	39.7%	59.6%	40.4%
1	1972	212,672	118,403	LUJAN, MANUEL, JR.	94,239	GALLEGOS, EUGENE	30	24,164 R	55.7%	44.3%	55.7%	44.3%
1	1970	158,368	91,187	LUJAN, MANUEL, JR.	64,598	CHAVEZ, FABIAN	2,583	26,589 R	57.6%	40.8%	58.5%	41.5%
1	1968	167,488	88,517	LUJAN, MANUEL, JR.	78,117	MORRIS, THOMAS G.	854	10,400 R	52.8%	46.6%	53.1%	46.9%
2	1980	161,992	61,564	SKEEN, JOSEPH R.	55,085	KING, DAVID	45,343	6,479 R	38.0%	34.0%	52.8%	47.2%
2	1978	95,797			95,710	RUNNELS, HAROLD L.	87	95,710 D		99.9%		100.0%
2	1976	175,713	52,131	TRUBEY, DONALD W.	123,563	RUNNELS, HAROLD L.	19	71,432 D	29.7%	70.3%	29.7%	70.3%
2	1974	135,038	43,045	TRUBEY, DONALD W.	90,127	RUNNELS, HAROLD L.	1,866	47,082 D	31.9%	66.7%	32.3%	67.7%
2	1972	160,981	44,784	PRESSON, GEORGE E.	116,152	RUNNELS, HAROLD L.	45	71,368 D	27.8%	72.2%	27.8%	72.2%
2	1970	126,990	61,074	FOREMAN, ED	64,518	RUNNELS, HAROLD L.	1,398	3,444 D	48.1%	50.8%	48.6%	51.4%
2	1968	142,364	71,857	FOREMAN, ED	69,858	WALKER, E. S. JOHNNY	649	1,999 R	50.5%	49.1%	50.7%	49.3%

NEW MEXICO

1980 GENERAL ELECTION

President   Other vote was 29,459 Anderson (Independent); 4,365 Clark (Libertarian); 2,202 Commoner (Citizens); 1,281 Bubar (Statesman); 325 Pulley (Socialist Workers); 734 scattered.

Congress   Other vote was Dorothy Runnels (write-in) in CD 2. In that district the Republican candidate Skeen was also a write-in candidate. Write-in totals for Runnels and Skeen were reported by the state authority. For other scattered write-ins, see detailed state canvass report. No district-wide total for these scattered write-ins is available.

1980 PRIMARIES

JUNE 3 REPUBLICAN

Congress   Unopposed in CD 1. No candidate in CD 2. After the primary Joseph R. Skeen, former Republican Gubernatorial candidate in 1974 and 1978, was nominated by the local party committee as the candidate in CD 2. He was unable to obtain a place on the ballot and ran a write-in campaign for the seat.

JUNE 3 DEMOCRATIC

Congress   Contested as follows:

CD 1   54,032 Bill Richardson; 13,344 William J. Orona; 2 Orlin G. Cole (write-in).
CD 2   56,560 Harold L. Runnels; 14,003 Gil M. Olguin. Mr. Runnels died after the primary and David King was substituted by the local party committee.

NEW YORK

GOVERNOR
Hugh L. Carey (D). Re-elected 1978 to a four-year term. Previously elected 1974.

SENATORS
Alfonse M. D'Amato (R). Elected 1980 to a six-year term.

Daniel P. Moynihan (D). Elected 1976 to a six-year term.

REPRESENTATIVES

1. William Carney (R)
2. Thomas J. Downey (D)
3. Gregory W. Carman (R)
4. Norman F. Lent (R)
5. Raymond J. McGrath (R)
6. John LeBoutillier (R)
7. Joseph P. Addabbo (D)
8. Benjamin Rosenthal (D)
9. Geraldine A. Ferraro (D)
10. Mario Biaggi (D)
11. James H. Scheuer (D)
12. Shirley Chisholm (D)
13. Stephen J. Solarz (D)
14. Frederick W. Richmond (D)
15. Leo C. Zeferetti (D)
16. Charles E. Schumer (D)
17. Guy V. Molinari (R)
18. S. William Green (R)
19. Charles B. Rangel (D)
20. Theodore S. Weiss (D)
21. Robert Garcia (D)
22. Jonathan Bingham (D)
23. Peter A. Peyser (D)
24. Richard L. Ottinger (D)
25. Hamilton Fish (R)
26. Benjamin A. Gilman (R)
27. Matthew F. McHugh (D)
28. Samuel S. Stratton (D)
29. Gerald B. Solomon (R)
30. David O'B. Martin (R)
31. Donald J. Mitchell (R)
32. George C. Wortley (R)
33. Gary A. Lee (R)
34. Frank J. Horton (R)
35. Barber B. Conable (R)
36. John J. LaFalce (D)
37. Henry J. Nowak (D)
38. Jack F. Kemp (R)
39. Stanley N. Lundine (D)

POSTWAR VOTE FOR GOVERNOR

Year	Total Vote	Republican Vote	Candidate	Democratic Vote	Candidate	Other Vote	Rep.-Dem. Plurality	Total Vote Rep.	Total Vote Dem.	Major Vote Rep.	Major Vote Dem.
1978	4,768,820	2,156,404	Duryea, Perry B.	2,429,272	Carey, Hugh L.	183,144	272,868 D	45.2%	50.9%	47.0%	53.0%
1974	5,293,176	2,219,667	Wilson, Malcolm	3,028,503	Carey, Hugh L.	45,006	808,836 D	41.9%	57.2%	42.3%	57.7%
1970	6,013,064	3,151,432	Rockefeller, Nelson A.	2,421,426	Goldberg, Arthur	440,206	730,006 R	52.4%	40.3%	56.5%	43.5%
1966	6,031,585	2,690,626	Rockefeller, Nelson A.	2,298,363	O'Connor, Frank D.	1,042,596	392,263 R	44.6%	38.1%	53.9%	46.1%
1962	5,805,631	3,081,587	Rockefeller, Nelson A.	2,552,418	Morgenthau, Robert M.	171,626	529,169 R	53.1%	44.0%	54.7%	45.3%
1958	5,712,665	3,126,929	Rockefeller, Nelson A.	2,553,895	Harriman, Averell	31,841	573,034 R	54.7%	44.7%	55.0%	45.0%
1954	5,161,942	2,549,613	Ives, Irving M.	2,560,738	Harriman, Averell	51,591	11,125 D	49.4%	49.6%	49.9%	50.1%
1950	5,308,889	2,819,523	Dewey, Thomas E.	2,246,855	Lynch, Walter A.	242,511	572,668 R	53.1%	42.3%	55.7%	44.3%
1946	4,964,552	2,825,633	Dewey, Thomas E.	2,138,482	Mead, James M.	437	687,151 R	56.9%	43.1%	56.9%	43.1%

POSTWAR VOTE FOR SENATOR

Year	Total Vote	Republican Vote	Candidate	Democratic Vote	Candidate	Other Vote	Rep.-Dem. Plurality	Total Vote Rep.	Total Vote Dem.	Major Vote Rep.	Major Vote Dem.
1980	6,014,914	2,699,652	D'Amato, Alfonse M.	2,618,661	Holtzman, Elizabeth	696,601	80,991 R	44.9%	43.5%	50.8%	49.2%
1976	6,319,755	2,836,633	Buckley, James L.	3,422,594	Moynihan, Daniel P.	60,528	585,961 D	44.9%	54.2%	45.3%	54.7%
1974	5,163,600	2,340,188	Javits, Jacob K.	1,973,781	Clark, Ramsey	849,631	366,407 R	45.3%	38.2%	54.2%	45.8%
1970	5,904,782	1,434,472	Goodell, Charles	2,171,232	Ottinger, Richard L.	2,299,078	736,760 D	24.3%	36.8%	39.8%	60.2%
1968	6,581,587	3,269,772	Javits, Jacob K.	2,150,695	O'Dwyer, Paul	1,161,120	1,119,077 R	49.7%	32.7%	60.3%	39.7%
1964	7,151,686	3,104,056	Keating, Kenneth B.	3,823,749	Kennedy, Robert F.	223,881	719,693 D	43.4%	53.5%	44.8%	55.2%
1962	5,700,186	3,269,417	Javits, Jacob K.	2,289,341	Donovan, James B.	141,428	980,076 R	57.4%	40.2%	58.8%	41.2%
1958	5,602,088	2,842,942	Keating, Kenneth B.	2,709,950	Hogan, Frank S.	49,196	132,992 R	50.7%	48.4%	51.2%	48.8%
1956	6,991,136	3,723,933	Javits, Jacob K.	3,265,159	Wagner, Robert F.	2,044	458,774 R	53.3%	46.7%	53.3%	46.7%
1952	6,980,259	3,853,934	Ives, Irving M.	2,521,736	Cashmore, John	604,589	1,332,198 R	55.2%	36.1%	60.4%	39.6%
1950	5,228,403	2,367,353	Hanley, Joe R.	2,632,313	Lehman, Herbert H.	228,737	264,960 D	45.3%	50.3%	47.4%	52.6%
1949s	4,966,878	2,384,381	Dulles, John Foster	2,582,438	Lehman, Herbert H.	59	198,057 D	48.0%	52.0%	48.0%	52.0%
1946	4,867,564	2,559,365	Ives, Irving M.	2,308,112	Lehman, Herbert H.	87	251,253 R	52.6%	47.4%	52.6%	47.4%

The 1949 election was for a short term to fill a vacancy. In 1970 James L. Buckley, the Conservative candidate, polled 2,288,190 votes (38.8% of the total vote) and won the election with a 116,958 plurality.

NEW YORK

Districts Established March 28, 1972

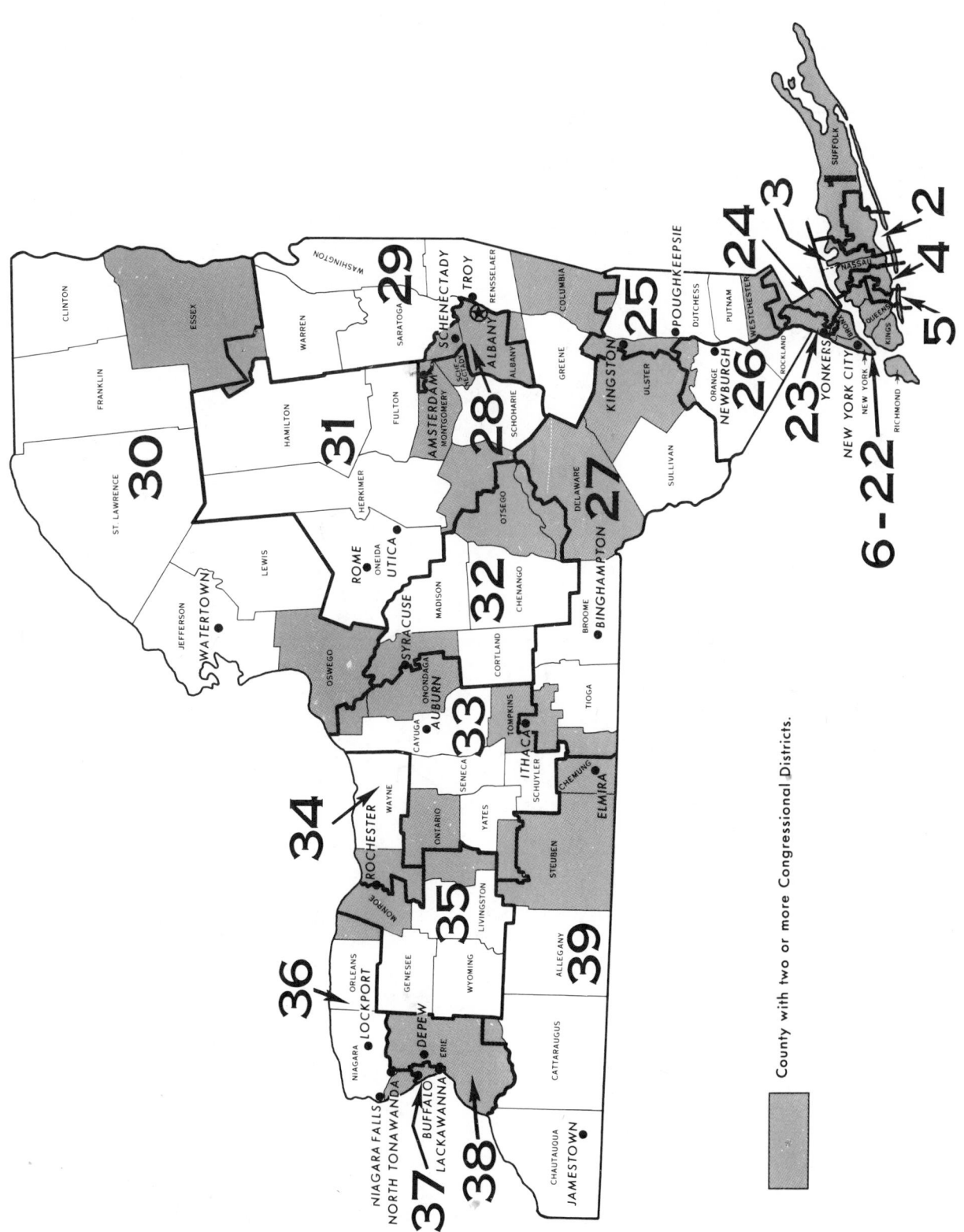

County with two or more Congressional Districts.

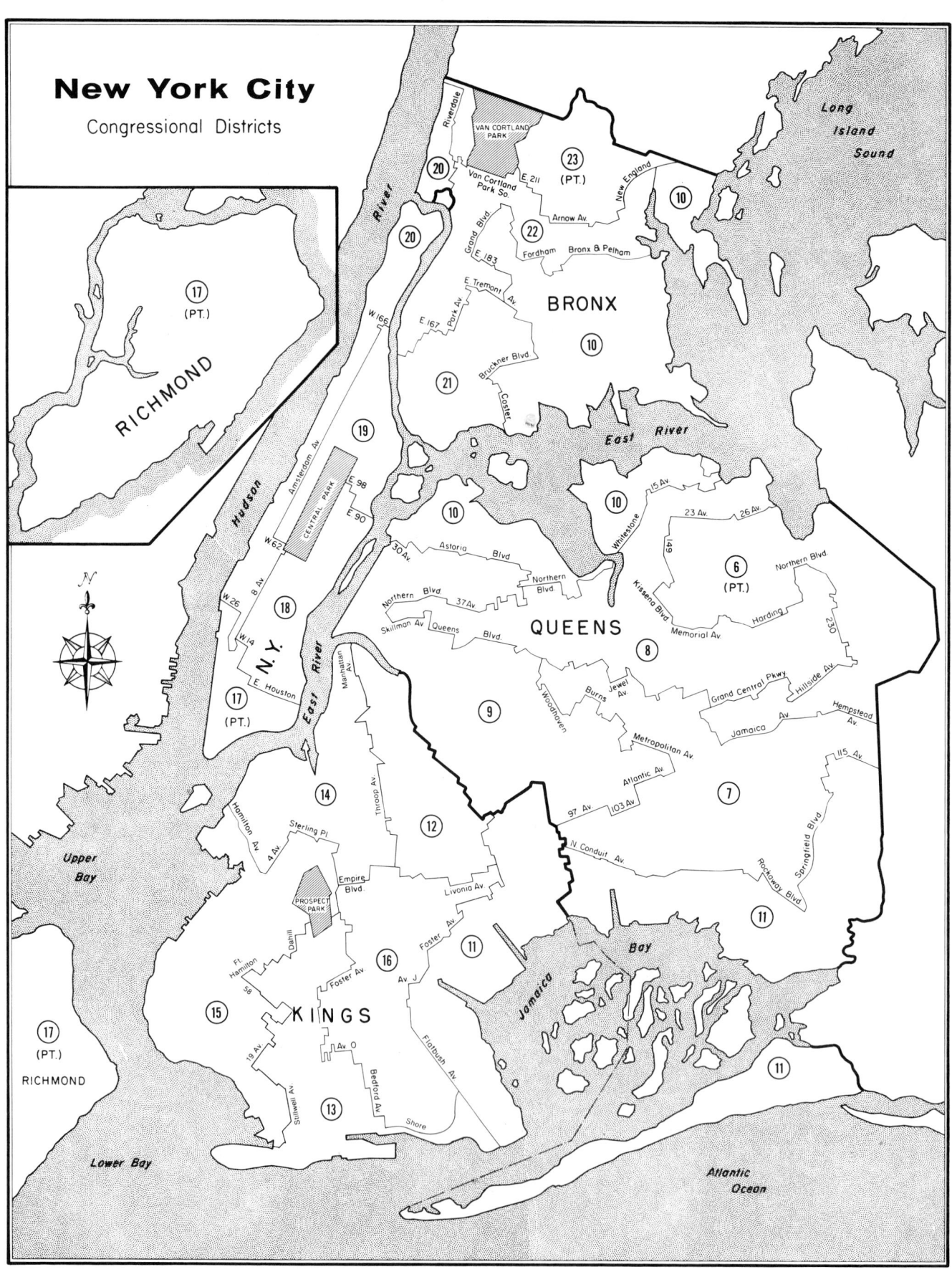

New York City
Congressional Districts

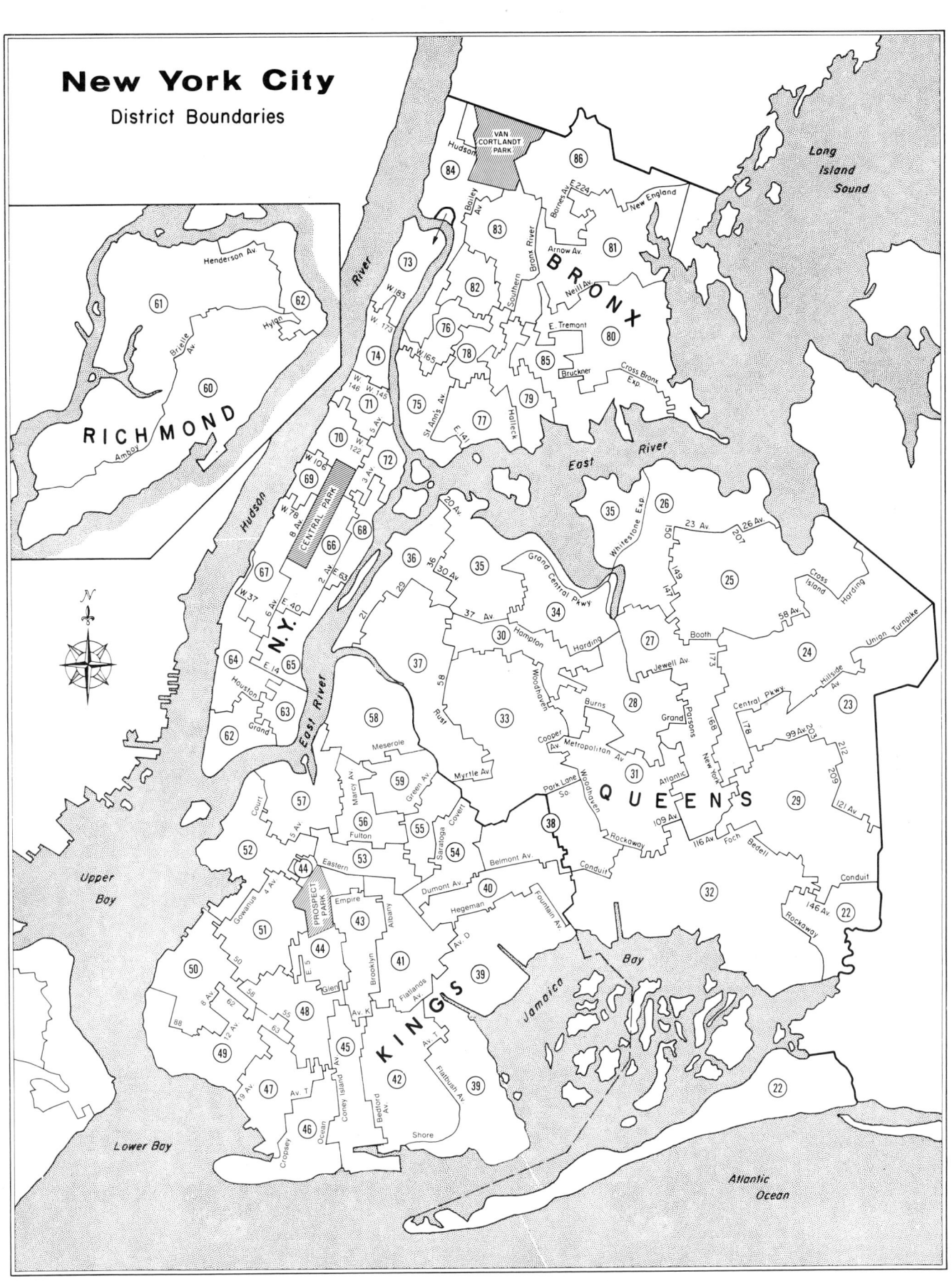

New York City
District Boundaries

NEW YORK

PRESIDENT 1980

1980 Census Population	County	Total Vote	Republican	Democratic	Other	Rep.-Dem. Plurality	Percentage Total Vote Rep.	Dem.	Major Vote Rep.	Dem.
285,909	ALBANY	144,364	52,354	74,429	17,581	22,075 D	36.3%	51.6%	41.3%	58.7%
51,742	ALLEGANY	17,640	10,423	5,879	1,338	4,544 R	59.1%	33.3%	63.9%	36.1%
1,169,115	BRONX	282,847	86,843	181,090	14,914	94,247 D	30.7%	64.0%	32.4%	67.6%
213,648	BROOME	89,280	39,275	37,013	12,992	2,262 R	44.0%	41.5%	51.5%	48.5%
85,697	CATTARAUGUS	32,709	17,222	12,917	2,570	4,305 R	52.7%	39.5%	57.1%	42.9%
79,894	CAYUGA	32,756	17,945	11,708	3,103	6,237 R	54.8%	35.7%	60.5%	39.5%
146,925	CHAUTAUQUA	58,756	30,081	22,871	5,804	7,210 R	51.2%	38.9%	56.8%	43.2%
97,656	CHEMUNG	37,209	19,674	14,565	2,970	5,109 R	52.9%	39.1%	57.5%	42.5%
49,344	CHENANGO	19,592	10,400	6,917	2,275	3,483 R	53.1%	35.3%	60.1%	39.9%
80,750	CLINTON	26,890	13,120	11,498	2,272	1,622 R	48.8%	42.8%	53.3%	46.7%
59,487	COLUMBIA	26,274	13,946	9,500	2,828	4,446 R	53.1%	36.2%	59.5%	40.5%
48,820	CORTLAND	18,048	9,885	6,176	1,987	3,709 R	54.8%	34.2%	61.5%	38.5%
46,931	DELAWARE	19,164	10,609	6,333	2,222	4,276 R	55.4%	33.0%	62.6%	37.4%
245,055	DUTCHESS	93,007	53,616	28,616	10,775	25,000 R	57.6%	30.8%	65.2%	34.8%
1,015,472	ERIE	420,473	169,209	215,283	35,981	46,074 D	40.2%	51.2%	44.0%	56.0%
36,176	ESSEX	16,978	9,025	6,443	1,510	2,582 R	53.2%	37.9%	58.3%	41.7%
44,929	FRANKLIN	16,292	7,620	7,281	1,391	339 R	46.8%	44.7%	51.1%	48.9%
55,153	FULTON	21,522	11,448	8,105	1,969	3,343 R	53.2%	37.7%	58.5%	41.5%
59,400	GENESEE	24,489	11,650	10,677	2,162	973 R	47.6%	43.6%	52.2%	47.8%
40,861	GREENE	19,498	11,286	6,488	1,724	4,798 R	57.9%	33.3%	63.5%	36.5%
5,034	HAMILTON	3,230	2,038	925	267	1,113 R	63.1%	28.6%	68.8%	31.2%
66,714	HERKIMER	27,888	14,105	11,497	2,286	2,608 R	50.6%	41.2%	55.1%	44.9%
88,151	JEFFERSON	33,128	16,455	13,271	3,402	3,184 R	49.7%	40.1%	55.4%	44.6%
2,230,936	KINGS	521,109	200,306	288,893	31,910	88,587 D	38.4%	55.4%	40.9%	59.1%
25,035	LEWIS	9,822	4,937	3,973	912	964 R	50.3%	40.5%	55.4%	44.6%
57,006	LIVINGSTON	22,454	11,193	9,030	2,231	2,163 R	49.8%	40.2%	55.3%	44.7%
65,150	MADISON	23,937	13,369	7,843	2,725	5,526 R	55.9%	32.8%	63.0%	37.0%
702,238	MONROE	306,733	128,615	142,423	35,695	13,808 D	41.9%	46.4%	47.5%	52.5%
53,439	MONTGOMERY	24,088	11,917	9,645	2,526	2,272 R	49.5%	40.0%	55.3%	44.7%
1,321,582	NASSAU	596,154	333,567	207,602	54,985	125,965 R	56.0%	34.8%	61.6%	38.4%
1,427,533	NEW YORK	441,901	115,911	275,742	50,248	159,831 D	26.2%	62.4%	29.6%	70.4%
227,101	NIAGARA	86,409	38,760	40,405	7,244	1,645 D	44.9%	46.8%	49.0%	51.0%
253,466	ONEIDA	104,799	51,968	44,292	8,539	7,676 R	49.6%	42.3%	54.0%	46.0%
463,324	ONONDAGA	193,372	97,887	73,453	22,032	24,434 R	50.6%	38.0%	57.1%	42.9%
88,909	ONTARIO	35,506	17,036	14,477	3,993	2,559 R	48.0%	40.8%	54.1%	45.9%
259,603	ORANGE	90,470	51,268	30,022	9,180	21,246 R	56.7%	33.2%	63.1%	36.9%
38,496	ORLEANS	14,611	7,536	5,767	1,308	1,769 R	51.6%	39.5%	56.6%	43.4%
113,901	OSWEGO	42,541	22,816	15,343	4,382	7,473 R	53.6%	36.1%	59.8%	40.2%
59,075	OTSEGO	23,907	11,814	8,795	3,298	3,019 R	49.4%	36.8%	57.3%	42.7%
77,193	PUTNAM	31,819	20,193	8,691	2,935	11,502 R	63.5%	27.3%	69.9%	30.1%
1,891,325	QUEENS	560,923	251,333	269,147	40,443	17,814 D	44.8%	48.0%	48.3%	51.7%
151,966	RENSSELAER	69,747	32,005	29,880	7,862	2,125 R	45.9%	42.8%	51.7%	48.3%
352,121	RICHMOND	110,651	64,885	37,306	8,460	27,579 R	58.6%	33.7%	63.5%	36.5%
259,530	ROCKLAND	104,995	59,068	35,277	10,650	23,791 R	56.3%	33.6%	62.6%	37.4%
114,254	ST. LAWRENCE	39,624	18,437	17,006	4,181	1,431 R	46.5%	42.9%	52.0%	48.0%
153,759	SARATOGA	65,362	34,184	23,641	7,537	10,543 R	52.3%	36.2%	59.1%	40.9%
149,946	SCHENECTADY	70,534	32,003	29,932	8,599	2,071 R	45.4%	42.4%	51.7%	48.3%
29,710	SCHOHARIE	12,262	6,382	4,715	1,165	1,667 R	52.0%	38.5%	57.5%	42.5%
17,686	SCHUYLER	6,957	3,838	2,514	605	1,324 R	55.2%	36.1%	60.4%	39.6%
33,733	SENECA	13,690	7,174	5,010	1,506	2,164 R	52.4%	36.6%	58.9%	41.1%
99,135	STEUBEN	38,170	22,418	12,826	2,926	9,592 R	58.7%	33.6%	63.6%	36.4%
1,284,231	SUFFOLK	449,655	256,294	149,945	43,416	106,349 R	57.0%	33.3%	63.1%	36.9%
65,155	SULLIVAN	27,218	15,089	9,553	2,576	5,536 R	55.4%	35.1%	61.2%	38.8%
49,812	TIOGA	19,214	10,291	6,690	2,233	3,601 R	53.6%	34.8%	60.6%	39.4%
87,085	TOMPKINS	29,668	12,448	11,970	5,250	478 R	42.0%	40.3%	51.0%	49.0%
158,158	ULSTER	66,726	36,709	22,179	7,838	14,530 R	55.0%	33.2%	62.3%	37.7%
54,854	WARREN	22,377	13,264	6,971	2,142	6,293 R	59.3%	31.2%	65.5%	34.5%
54,795	WASHINGTON	21,906	12,835	7,144	1,927	5,691 R	58.6%	32.6%	64.2%	35.8%
85,230	WAYNE	32,512	16,498	12,590	3,424	3,908 R	50.7%	38.7%	56.7%	43.3%
866,599	WESTCHESTER	365,166	198,552	130,136	36,478	68,416 R	54.4%	35.6%	60.4%	39.6%
39,895	WYOMING	14,552	8,108	5,234	1,210	2,874 R	55.7%	36.0%	60.8%	39.2%
21,459	YATES	8,384	4,694	2,828	862	1,866 R	56.0%	33.7%	62.4%	37.6%
17,557,288	TOTAL	6,201,959	2,893,831	2,728,372	579,756	165,459 R	46.7%	44.0%	51.5%	48.5%

NEW YORK

SENATOR 1980

1980 Census Population	County	Total Vote	Republican	Democratic	Other	Rep.-Dem. Plurality	Percentage Total Vote Rep.	Dem.	Major Vote Rep.	Dem.
285,909	ALBANY	139,401	47,150	72,221	20,030	25,071 D	33.8%	51.8%	39.5%	60.5%
51,742	ALLEGANY	16,968	10,553	4,517	1,898	6,036 R	62.2%	26.6%	70.0%	30.0%
1,169,115	BRONX	262,285	76,602	158,543	27,140	81,941 D	29.2%	60.4%	32.6%	67.4%
213,648	BROOME	85,947	44,266	33,647	8,034	10,619 R	51.5%	39.1%	56.8%	43.2%
85,697	CATTARAUGUS	31,303	18,071	9,559	3,673	8,512 R	57.7%	30.5%	65.4%	34.6%
79,894	CAYUGA	31,705	19,088	9,323	3,294	9,765 R	60.2%	29.4%	67.2%	32.8%
146,925	CHAUTAUQUA	56,809	30,756	19,069	6,984	11,687 R	54.1%	33.6%	61.7%	38.3%
97,656	CHEMUNG	35,705	20,030	12,963	2,712	7,067 R	56.1%	36.3%	60.7%	39.3%
49,344	CHENANGO	18,952	11,330	5,487	2,135	5,843 R	59.8%	29.0%	67.4%	32.6%
80,750	CLINTON	25,256	15,584	7,199	2,473	8,385 R	61.7%	28.5%	68.4%	31.6%
59,487	COLUMBIA	25,473	13,226	8,988	3,259	4,238 R	51.9%	35.3%	59.5%	40.5%
48,820	CORTLAND	17,480	10,264	5,313	1,903	4,951 R	58.7%	30.4%	65.9%	34.1%
46,931	DELAWARE	18,393	10,481	5,682	2,230	4,799 R	57.0%	30.9%	64.8%	35.2%
245,055	DUTCHESS	90,360	46,618	33,725	10,017	12,893 R	51.6%	37.3%	58.0%	42.0%
1,015,472	ERIE	406,136	207,292	144,207	54,637	63,085 R	51.0%	35.5%	59.0%	41.0%
36,176	ESSEX	15,803	10,008	3,971	1,824	6,037 R	63.3%	25.1%	71.6%	28.4%
44,929	FRANKLIN	15,109	8,722	4,422	1,965	4,300 R	57.7%	29.3%	66.4%	33.6%
55,153	FULTON	20,745	10,970	7,146	2,629	3,824 R	52.9%	34.4%	60.6%	39.4%
59,400	GENESEE	23,648	13,831	7,046	2,771	6,785 R	58.5%	29.8%	66.2%	33.8%
40,861	GREENE	19,044	11,076	6,043	1,925	5,033 R	58.2%	31.7%	64.7%	35.3%
5,034	HAMILTON	3,070	1,955	744	371	1,211 R	63.7%	24.2%	72.4%	27.6%
66,714	HERKIMER	25,850	15,583	7,752	2,515	7,831 R	60.3%	30.0%	66.8%	33.2%
88,151	JEFFERSON	30,831	15,652	9,038	6,141	6,614 R	50.8%	29.3%	63.4%	36.6%
2,230,936	KINGS	502,965	153,865	295,406	53,694	141,541 D	30.6%	58.7%	34.2%	65.8%
25,035	LEWIS	9,078	5,366	2,365	1,347	3,001 R	59.1%	26.1%	69.4%	30.6%
57,006	LIVINGSTON	21,662	12,417	6,721	2,524	5,696 R	57.3%	31.0%	64.9%	35.1%
65,150	MADISON	23,023	13,203	7,166	2,654	6,037 R	57.3%	31.1%	64.8%	35.2%
702,238	MONROE	295,051	143,048	114,301	37,702	28,747 R	48.5%	38.7%	55.6%	44.4%
53,439	MONTGOMERY	23,078	11,704	8,804	2,570	2,900 R	50.7%	38.1%	57.1%	42.9%
1,321,582	NASSAU	593,499	295,135	242,581	55,783	52,554 R	49.7%	40.9%	54.9%	45.1%
1,427,533	NEW YORK	428,048	65,685	296,815	65,548	231,130 D	15.3%	69.3%	18.1%	81.9%
227,101	NIAGARA	83,417	43,030	28,913	11,474	14,117 R	51.6%	34.7%	59.8%	40.2%
253,466	ONEIDA	100,405	57,549	33,821	9,035	23,728 R	57.3%	33.7%	63.0%	37.0%
463,324	ONONDAGA	188,444	102,539	62,769	23,136	39,770 R	54.4%	33.3%	62.0%	38.0%
88,909	ONTARIO	34,104	17,891	11,920	4,293	5,971 R	52.5%	35.0%	60.0%	40.0%
259,603	ORANGE	88,066	46,069	32,580	9,417	13,489 R	52.3%	37.0%	58.6%	41.4%
38,496	ORLEANS	13,988	8,114	4,293	1,581	3,821 R	58.0%	30.7%	65.4%	34.6%
113,901	OSWEGO	39,737	23,343	11,080	5,314	12,263 R	58.7%	27.9%	67.8%	32.2%
59,075	OTSEGO	23,070	12,576	7,344	3,150	5,232 R	54.5%	31.8%	63.1%	36.9%
77,193	PUTNAM	31,167	17,914	10,086	3,167	7,828 R	57.5%	32.4%	64.0%	36.0%
1,891,325	QUEENS	548,936	211,255	277,469	60,212	66,214 D	38.5%	50.5%	43.2%	56.8%
151,966	RENSSELAER	66,937	31,777	25,592	9,568	6,185 R	47.5%	38.2%	55.4%	44.6%
352,121	RICHMOND	108,473	61,551	37,555	9,367	23,996 R	56.7%	34.6%	62.1%	37.9%
259,530	ROCKLAND	103,168	46,182	44,236	12,750	1,946 R	44.8%	42.9%	51.1%	48.9%
114,254	ST. LAWRENCE	36,805	19,170	11,410	6,225	7,760 R	52.1%	31.0%	62.7%	37.3%
153,759	SARATOGA	62,799	32,464	21,484	8,851	10,980 R	51.7%	34.2%	60.2%	39.8%
149,946	SCHENECTADY	68,477	31,194	27,684	9,599	3,510 R	45.6%	40.4%	53.0%	47.0%
29,710	SCHOHARIE	11,994	6,551	3,881	1,562	2,670 R	54.6%	32.4%	62.8%	37.2%
17,686	SCHUYLER	6,744	4,014	2,172	558	1,842 R	59.5%	32.2%	64.9%	35.1%
33,733	SENECA	13,039	7,557	4,020	1,462	3,537 R	58.0%	30.8%	65.3%	34.7%
99,135	STEUBEN	36,326	22,774	10,605	2,947	12,169 R	62.7%	29.2%	68.2%	31.8%
1,284,231	SUFFOLK	444,156	240,093	164,598	39,465	75,495 R	54.1%	37.1%	59.3%	40.7%
65,155	SULLIVAN	26,526	12,338	11,216	2,972	1,122 R	46.5%	42.3%	52.4%	47.6%
49,812	TIOGA	18,457	10,552	6,024	1,881	4,528 R	57.2%	32.6%	63.7%	36.3%
87,085	TOMPKINS	28,627	11,894	13,548	3,185	1,654 D	41.5%	47.3%	46.7%	53.3%
158,158	ULSTER	65,153	33,213	25,685	6,255	7,528 R	51.0%	39.4%	56.4%	43.6%
54,854	WARREN	21,196	11,772	6,135	3,289	5,637 R	55.5%	28.9%	65.7%	34.3%
54,795	WASHINGTON	21,052	11,811	6,347	2,894	5,464 R	56.1%	30.1%	65.0%	35.0%
85,230	WAYNE	31,268	18,105	9,488	3,675	8,617 R	57.9%	30.3%	65.6%	34.4%
866,599	WESTCHESTER	357,451	163,342	149,785	44,324	13,557 R	45.7%	41.9%	52.2%	47.8%
39,895	WYOMING	14,143	8,824	3,675	1,644	5,149 R	62.4%	26.0%	70.6%	29.4%
21,459	YATES	8,112	4,663	2,482	967	2,181 R	57.5%	30.6%	65.3%	34.7%
17,557,288	TOTAL	6,014,914	2,699,652	2,618,661	696,601	80,991 R	44.9%	43.5%	50.8%	49.2%

NEW YORK CITY

BRONX COUNTY

PRESIDENT 1980

1980 Census Population	Assembly District	Total Vote	Republican	Democratic	Other	Rep.-Dem. Plurality	Percentage Total Vote		Major Vote	
							Rep.	Dem.	Rep.	Dem.
80,204	DISTRICT 75	15,797	1,577	13,792	428	12,215 D	10.0%	87.3%	10.3%	89.7%
97,787	DISTRICT 76	13,194	1,214	11,625	355	10,411 D	9.2%	88.1%	9.5%	90.5%
59,488	DISTRICT 77	9,114	823	8,089	202	7,266 D	9.0%	88.8%	9.2%	90.8%
53,255	DISTRICT 78	10,706	463	10,059	184	9,596 D	4.3%	94.0%	4.4%	95.6%
50,220	DISTRICT 79	9,590	748	8,604	238	7,856 D	7.8%	89.7%	8.0%	92.0%
118,275	DISTRICT 80	34,444	20,498	12,108	1,838	8,390 R	59.5%	35.2%	62.9%	37.1%
138,383	DISTRICT 81	50,350	15,601	31,349	3,400	15,748 D	31.0%	62.3%	33.2%	66.8%
104,540	DISTRICT 82	14,127	3,126	10,430	571	7,304 D	22.1%	73.8%	23.1%	76.9%
123,539	DISTRICT 83	30,445	11,801	16,600	2,044	4,799 D	38.8%	54.5%	41.6%	58.4%
103,751	DISTRICT 84	32,136	10,606	18,634	2,896	8,028 D	33.0%	58.0%	36.3%	63.7%
125,622	DISTRICT 85	31,579	8,761	21,572	1,246	12,811 D	27.7%	68.3%	28.9%	71.1%
114,051	DISTRICT 86	31,365	11,625	18,228	1,512	6,603 D	37.1%	58.1%	38.9%	61.1%
1,169,115	TOTAL	282,847	86,843	181,090	14,914	94,247 D	30.7%	64.0%	32.4%	67.6%

NEW YORK CITY

KINGS COUNTY

PRESIDENT 1980

1980 Census Population	Assembly District	Total Vote	Republican	Democratic	Other	Rep.-Dem. Plurality	Percentage Total Vote		Major Vote	
							Rep.	Dem.	Rep.	Dem.
59,194	DISTRICT 38 [PART]	7,911	3,267	4,350	294	1,083 D	41.3%	55.0%	42.9%	57.1%
126,303	DISTRICT 39	38,162	16,572	19,135	2,455	2,563 D	43.4%	50.1%	46.4%	53.6%
96,067	DISTRICT 40	12,935	745	11,964	226	11,219 D	5.8%	92.5%	5.9%	94.1%
114,606	DISTRICT 41	25,251	8,710	15,326	1,215	6,616 D	34.5%	60.7%	36.2%	63.8%
105,774	DISTRICT 42	40,539	22,040	15,517	2,982	6,523 R	54.4%	38.3%	58.7%	41.3%
127,450	DISTRICT 43	18,564	3,817	13,785	962	9,968 D	20.6%	74.3%	21.7%	78.3%
122,016	DISTRICT 44	25,681	7,756	15,549	2,376	7,793 D	30.2%	60.5%	33.3%	66.7%
111,042	DISTRICT 45	39,655	17,658	18,472	3,525	814 D	44.5%	46.6%	48.9%	51.1%
112,227	DISTRICT 46	32,294	13,185	16,876	2,233	3,691 D	40.8%	52.3%	43.9%	56.1%
111,529	DISTRICT 47	30,300	15,243	13,269	1,788	1,974 R	50.3%	43.8%	53.5%	46.5%
115,275	DISTRICT 48	31,523	18,862	10,785	1,876	8,077 R	59.8%	34.2%	63.6%	36.4%
107,969	DISTRICT 49	33,049	20,425	10,931	1,693	9,494 R	61.8%	33.1%	65.1%	34.9%
108,910	DISTRICT 50	29,403	16,374	11,027	2,002	5,347 R	55.7%	37.5%	59.8%	40.2%
107,900	DISTRICT 51	24,856	11,543	11,559	1,754	16 D	46.4%	46.5%	50.0%	50.0%
97,532	DISTRICT 52	26,651	7,569	15,988	3,094	8,419 D	28.4%	60.0%	32.1%	67.9%
93,837	DISTRICT 53	14,366	764	13,224	378	12,460 D	5.3%	92.1%	5.5%	94.5%
76,414	DISTRICT 54	10,413	472	9,782	159	9,310 D	4.5%	93.9%	4.6%	95.4%
70,720	DISTRICT 55	10,644	828	9,597	219	8,769 D	7.8%	90.2%	7.9%	92.1%
82,673	DISTRICT 56	15,761	1,490	13,943	328	12,453 D	9.5%	88.5%	9.7%	90.3%
98,453	DISTRICT 57	20,970	3,481	16,239	1,250	12,758 D	16.6%	77.4%	17.7%	82.3%
96,455	DISTRICT 58	18,802	7,701	10,327	774	2,626 D	41.0%	54.9%	42.7%	57.3%
88,590	DISTRICT 59	13,379	1,804	11,248	327	9,444 D	13.5%	84.1%	13.8%	86.2%
2,230,936	TOTAL	521,109	200,306	288,893	31,910	88,587 D	38.4%	55.4%	40.9%	59.1%

NEW YORK CITY

NEW YORK COUNTY
PRESIDENT 1980

1980 Census Population	Assembly District	Total Vote	Republican	Democratic	Other	Rep.-Dem. Plurality	Percentage Total Vote Rep.	Dem.	Major Vote Rep.	Dem.
83,046	DISTRICT 62 [PART]	16,382	4,905	9,709	1,768	4,804 D	29.9%	59.3%	33.6%	66.4%
93,288	DISTRICT 63	22,850	5,663	14,921	2,266	9,258 D	24.8%	65.3%	27.5%	72.5%
122,037	DISTRICT 64	49,362	11,066	30,396	7,900	19,330 D	22.4%	61.6%	26.7%	73.3%
133,106	DISTRICT 65	53,141	20,219	25,807	7,115	5,588 D	38.0%	48.6%	43.9%	56.1%
122,342	DISTRICT 66	49,075	21,852	20,899	6,324	953 R	44.5%	42.6%	51.1%	48.9%
126,697	DISTRICT 67	46,040	12,038	27,237	6,765	15,199 D	26.1%	59.2%	30.7%	69.3%
119,647	DISTRICT 68	45,054	15,788	23,449	5,817	7,661 D	35.0%	52.0%	40.2%	59.8%
118,853	DISTRICT 69	42,992	7,508	29,411	6,073	21,903 D	17.5%	68.4%	20.3%	79.7%
93,621	DISTRICT 70	23,750	2,489	19,170	2,091	16,681 D	10.5%	80.7%	11.5%	88.5%
94,911	DISTRICT 71	23,513	1,000	22,077	436	21,077 D	4.3%	93.9%	4.3%	95.7%
90,369	DISTRICT 72	19,616	1,839	17,195	582	15,356 D	9.4%	87.7%	9.7%	90.3%
119,311	DISTRICT 73	26,529	9,135	15,204	2,190	6,069 D	34.4%	57.3%	37.5%	62.5%
110,305	DISTRICT 74	23,597	2,409	20,267	921	17,858 D	10.2%	85.9%	10.6%	89.4%
1,427,533	TOTAL	441,901	115,911	275,742	50,248	159,831 D	26.2%	62.4%	29.6%	70.4%

NEW YORK CITY

QUEENS COUNTY
PRESIDENT 1980

1980 Census Population	Assembly District	Total Vote	Republican	Democratic	Other	Rep.-Dem. Plurality	Percentage Total Vote Rep.	Dem.	Major Vote Rep.	Dem.
122,302	DISTRICT 22	35,019	15,315	17,250	2,454	1,935 D	43.7%	49.3%	47.0%	53.0%
118,008	DISTRICT 23	36,248	16,519	17,454	2,275	935 D	45.6%	48.2%	48.6%	51.4%
106,859	DISTRICT 24	42,597	17,439	20,957	4,201	3,518 D	40.9%	49.2%	45.4%	54.6%
110,850	DISTRICT 25	42,831	24,283	14,769	3,779	9,514 R	56.7%	34.5%	62.2%	37.8%
121,283	DISTRICT 26	38,862	17,788	17,575	3,499	213 R	45.8%	45.2%	50.3%	49.7%
107,705	DISTRICT 27	34,392	12,188	19,690	2,514	7,502 D	35.4%	57.3%	38.2%	61.8%
108,958	DISTRICT 28	40,496	17,992	18,621	3,883	629 D	44.4%	46.0%	49.1%	50.9%
109,917	DISTRICT 29	31,273	2,670	27,743	860	25,073 D	8.5%	88.7%	8.8%	91.2%
124,056	DISTRICT 30	29,748	13,490	13,742	2,516	252 D	45.3%	46.2%	49.5%	50.5%
122,200	DISTRICT 31	34,225	18,926	12,886	2,413	6,040 R	55.3%	37.7%	59.5%	40.5%
104,550	DISTRICT 32	32,634	9,499	21,700	1,435	12,201 D	29.1%	66.5%	30.4%	69.6%
113,258	DISTRICT 33	36,680	23,485	11,023	2,172	12,462 R	64.0%	30.1%	68.1%	31.9%
126,625	DISTRICT 34	24,806	8,593	14,698	1,515	6,105 D	34.6%	59.3%	36.9%	63.1%
113,599	DISTRICT 35	32,341	17,838	12,110	2,393	5,728 R	55.2%	37.4%	59.6%	40.4%
114,470	DISTRICT 36	26,508	11,053	13,656	1,799	2,603 D	41.7%	51.5%	44.7%	55.3%
114,649	DISTRICT 37	27,098	14,803	10,491	1,804	4,312 R	54.6%	38.7%	58.5%	41.5%
52,009	DISTRICT 38 [PART]	15,165	9,452	4,782	931	4,670 R	62.3%	31.5%	66.4%	33.6%
1,891,325	TOTAL	560,923	251,333	269,147	40,443	17,814 D	44.8%	48.0%	48.3%	51.7%

NEW YORK CITY

RICHMOND COUNTY
PRESIDENT 1980

1980 Census Population	Assembly District	Total Vote	Republican	Democratic	Other	Rep.-Dem. Plurality	Percentage			
							Total Vote		Major Vote	
							Rep.	Dem.	Rep.	Dem.
144,332	DISTRICT 60	49,371	31,209	14,554	3,608	16,655 R	63.2%	29.5%	68.2%	31.8%
155,967	DISTRICT 61	48,147	27,688	16,635	3,824	11,053 R	57.5%	34.6%	62.5%	37.5%
51,740	DISTRICT 62 [PART]	13,133	5,988	6,117	1,028	129 D	45.6%	46.6%	49.5%	50.5%
352,121	TOTAL	110,651	64,885	37,306	8,460	27,579 R	58.6%	33.7%	63.5%	36.5%

NEW YORK CITY

PRESIDENT 1980

1980 Census Population	County	Total Vote	Republican	Democratic	Other	Rep.-Dem. Plurality	Percentage			
							Total Vote		Major Vote	
							Rep.	Dem.	Rep.	Dem.
1,169,115	BRONX	282,847	86,843	181,090	14,914	94,247 D	30.7%	64.0%	32.4%	67.6%
2,230,936	KINGS	521,109	200,306	288,893	31,910	88,587 D	38.4%	55.4%	40.9%	59.1%
1,427,533	NEW YORK	441,901	115,911	275,742	50,248	159,831 D	26.2%	62.4%	29.6%	70.4%
1,891,325	QUEENS	560,923	251,333	269,147	40,443	17,814 D	44.8%	48.0%	48.3%	51.7%
352,121	RICHMOND	110,651	64,885	37,306	8,460	27,579 R	58.6%	33.7%	63.5%	36.5%
7,071,030	TOTAL	1,917,431	719,278	1,052,178	145,975	332,900 D	37.5%	54.9%	40.6%	59.4%

NEW YORK CITY

BRONX COUNTY

SENATOR 1980

1980 Census Population	Assembly District	Total Vote	Republican	Democratic	Other	Rep.-Dem. Plurality	Percentage			
							Total Vote		Major Vote	
							Rep.	Dem.	Rep.	Dem.
80,204	DISTRICT 75	13,196	1,560	10,598	1,038	9,038 D	11.8%	80.3%	12.8%	87.2%
97,787	DISTRICT 76	9,714	1,162	7,668	884	6,506 D	12.0%	78.9%	13.2%	86.8%
59,488	DISTRICT 77	7,077	780	5,726	571	4,946 D	11.0%	80.9%	12.0%	88.0%
53,255	DISTRICT 78	9,109	618	7,961	530	7,343 D	6.8%	87.4%	7.2%	92.8%
50,220	DISTRICT 79	8,034	843	6,638	553	5,795 D	10.5%	82.6%	11.3%	88.7%
118,275	DISTRICT 80	33,460	21,524	9,601	2,335	11,923 R	64.3%	28.7%	69.2%	30.8%
138,383	DISTRICT 81	49,024	10,682	31,891	6,451	21,209 D	21.8%	65.1%	25.1%	74.9%
104,540	DISTRICT 82	12,806	2,735	8,722	1,349	5,987 D	21.4%	68.1%	23.9%	76.1%
123,539	DISTRICT 83	29,296	10,061	15,526	3,709	5,465 D	34.3%	53.0%	39.3%	60.7%
103,751	DISTRICT 84	31,266	6,055	20,411	4,800	14,356 D	19.4%	65.3%	22.9%	77.1%
125,622	DISTRICT 85	29,221	8,552	18,110	2,559	9,558 D	29.3%	62.0%	32.1%	67.9%
114,051	DISTRICT 86	30,082	12,030	15,691	2,361	3,661 D	40.0%	52.2%	43.4%	56.6%
1,169,115	TOTAL	262,285	76,602	158,543	27,140	81,941 D	29.2%	60.4%	32.6%	67.4%

NEW YORK CITY

KINGS COUNTY

SENATOR 1980

1980 Census Population	Assembly District	Total Vote	Republican	Democratic	Other	Rep.-Dem. Plurality	Percentage			
							Total Vote		Major Vote	
							Rep.	Dem.	Rep.	Dem.
59,194	DISTRICT 38 [PART]	7,445	3,434	3,443	568	9 D	46.1%	46.2%	49.9%	50.1%
126,303	DISTRICT 39	37,695	9,006	23,722	4,967	14,716 D	23.9%	62.9%	27.5%	72.5%
96,067	DISTRICT 40	11,786	860	10,392	534	9,532 D	7.3%	88.2%	7.6%	92.4%
114,606	DISTRICT 41	24,779	4,872	17,005	2,902	12,133 D	19.7%	68.6%	22.3%	77.7%
105,774	DISTRICT 42	40,549	15,573	21,302	3,674	5,729 D	38.4%	52.5%	42.2%	57.8%
127,450	DISTRICT 43	17,860	2,476	14,043	1,341	11,567 D	13.9%	78.6%	15.0%	85.0%
122,016	DISTRICT 44	25,106	5,020	17,110	2,976	12,090 D	20.0%	68.2%	22.7%	77.3%
111,042	DISTRICT 45	40,098	7,781	26,289	6,028	18,508 D	19.4%	65.6%	22.8%	77.2%
112,227	DISTRICT 46	32,104	7,379	20,614	4,111	13,235 D	23.0%	64.2%	26.4%	73.6%
111,529	DISTRICT 47	30,035	14,163	13,135	2,737	1,028 R	47.2%	43.7%	51.9%	48.1%
115,275	DISTRICT 48	31,376	9,607	13,633	8,136	4,026 D	30.6%	43.5%	41.3%	58.7%
107,969	DISTRICT 49	32,457	22,101	8,246	2,110	13,855 R	68.1%	25.4%	72.8%	27.2%
108,910	DISTRICT 50	28,181	15,925	10,052	2,204	5,873 R	56.5%	35.7%	61.3%	38.7%
107,900	DISTRICT 51	24,088	10,839	10,861	2,388	22 D	45.0%	45.1%	49.9%	50.1%
97,532	DISTRICT 52	26,082	7,326	16,491	2,265	9,165 D	28.1%	63.2%	30.8%	69.2%
93,837	DISTRICT 53	13,160	904	11,365	891	10,461 D	6.9%	86.4%	7.4%	92.6%
76,414	DISTRICT 54	9,477	661	8,388	428	7,727 D	7.0%	88.5%	7.3%	92.7%
70,720	DISTRICT 55	9,585	1,030	8,028	527	6,998 D	10.7%	83.8%	11.4%	88.6%
82,673	DISTRICT 56	13,502	1,788	10,423	1,291	8,635 D	13.2%	77.2%	14.6%	85.4%
98,453	DISTRICT 57	19,017	3,258	13,848	1,911	10,590 D	17.1%	72.8%	19.0%	81.0%
96,455	DISTRICT 58	16,915	7,878	7,955	1,082	77 D	46.6%	47.0%	49.8%	50.2%
88,590	DISTRICT 59	11,668	1,984	9,061	623	7,077 D	17.0%	77.7%	18.0%	82.0%
2,230,936	TOTAL	502,965	153,865	295,406	53,694	141,541 D	30.6%	58.7%	34.2%	65.8%

NEW YORK CITY

NEW YORK COUNTY
SENATOR 1980

1980 Census Population	Assembly District	Total Vote	Republican	Democratic	Other	Rep.-Dem. Plurality	Percentage Total Vote Rep.	Dem.	Major Vote Rep.	Dem.
83,046	DISTRICT 62 [PART]	15,688	4,114	9,957	1,617	5,843 D	26.2%	63.5%	29.2%	70.8%
93,288	DISTRICT 63	21,355	3,366	14,904	3,085	11,538 D	15.8%	69.8%	18.4%	81.6%
122,037	DISTRICT 64	49,146	7,132	36,069	5,945	28,937 D	14.5%	73.4%	16.5%	83.5%
133,106	DISTRICT 65	52,832	10,495	31,819	10,518	21,324 D	19.9%	60.2%	24.8%	75.2%
122,342	DISTRICT 66	49,239	9,501	27,357	12,381	17,856 D	19.3%	55.6%	25.8%	74.2%
126,697	DISTRICT 67	45,530	5,971	32,340	7,219	26,369 D	13.1%	71.0%	15.6%	84.4%
119,647	DISTRICT 68	44,001	8,638	27,649	7,714	19,011 D	19.6%	62.8%	23.8%	76.2%
118,853	DISTRICT 69	42,257	3,276	32,958	6,023	29,682 D	7.8%	78.0%	9.0%	91.0%
93,621	DISTRICT 70	22,117	1,830	18,172	2,115	16,342 D	8.3%	82.2%	9.1%	90.9%
94,911	DISTRICT 71	21,209	1,472	18,186	1,551	16,714 D	6.9%	85.7%	7.5%	92.5%
90,369	DISTRICT 72	16,795	1,933	13,524	1,338	11,591 D	11.5%	80.5%	12.5%	87.5%
119,311	DISTRICT 73	25,669	5,716	15,883	4,070	10,167 D	22.3%	61.9%	26.5%	73.5%
110,305	DISTRICT 74	22,210	2,241	17,997	1,972	15,756 D	10.1%	81.0%	11.1%	88.9%
1,427,533	TOTAL	428,048	65,685	296,815	65,548	231,130 D	15.3%	69.3%	18.1%	81.9%

NEW YORK CITY

QUEENS COUNTY
SENATOR 1980

1980 Census Population	Assembly District	Total Vote	Republican	Democratic	Other	Rep.-Dem. Plurality	Percentage Total Vote Rep.	Dem.	Major Vote Rep.	Dem.
122,302	DISTRICT 22	34,143	10,659	19,218	4,266	8,559 D	31.2%	56.3%	35.7%	64.3%
118,008	DISTRICT 23	35,586	15,935	16,553	3,098	618 D	44.8%	46.5%	49.0%	51.0%
106,859	DISTRICT 24	42,408	9,609	26,641	6,158	17,032 D	22.7%	62.8%	26.5%	73.5%
110,850	DISTRICT 25	42,434	22,432	15,581	4,421	6,851 R	52.9%	36.7%	59.0%	41.0%
121,283	DISTRICT 26	38,518	12,715	21,010	4,793	8,295 D	33.0%	54.5%	37.7%	62.3%
107,705	DISTRICT 27	33,868	8,893	20,797	4,178	11,904 D	26.3%	61.4%	30.0%	70.0%
108,958	DISTRICT 28	40,212	7,047	24,925	8,240	17,878 D	17.5%	62.0%	22.0%	78.0%
109,917	DISTRICT 29	30,111	3,275	24,832	2,004	21,557 D	10.9%	82.5%	11.7%	88.3%
124,056	DISTRICT 30	29,272	10,170	15,117	3,985	4,947 D	34.7%	51.6%	40.2%	59.8%
122,200	DISTRICT 31	33,308	17,476	12,495	3,337	4,981 R	52.5%	37.5%	58.3%	41.7%
104,550	DISTRICT 32	31,819	8,934	20,436	2,449	11,502 D	28.1%	64.2%	30.4%	69.6%
113,258	DISTRICT 33	36,009	23,364	9,983	2,662	13,381 R	64.9%	27.7%	70.1%	29.9%
126,625	DISTRICT 34	23,767	7,986	13,368	2,413	5,382 D	33.6%	56.2%	37.4%	62.6%
113,599	DISTRICT 35	31,468	17,319	11,365	2,784	5,954 R	55.0%	36.1%	60.4%	39.6%
114,470	DISTRICT 36	25,393	11,473	11,961	1,959	488 D	45.2%	47.1%	49.0%	51.0%
114,649	DISTRICT 37	25,725	14,028	9,306	2,391	4,722 R	54.5%	36.2%	60.1%	39.9%
52,009	DISTRICT 38 [PART]	14,895	9,940	3,881	1,074	6,059 R	66.7%	26.1%	71.9%	28.1%
1,891,325	TOTAL	548,936	211,255	277,469	60,212	66,214 D	38.5%	50.5%	43.2%	56.8%

NEW YORK CITY

RICHMOND COUNTY
SENATOR 1980

1980 Census Population	Assembly District	Total Vote	Republican	Democratic	Other	Rep.-Dem. Plurality	Percentage Total Vote Rep.	Dem.	Major Vote Rep.	Dem.
144,332	DISTRICT 60	48,511	30,596	14,200	3,715	16,396 R	63.1%	29.3%	68.3%	31.7%
155,967	DISTRICT 61	47,237	24,886	17,795	4,556	7,091 R	52.7%	37.7%	58.3%	41.7%
51,740	DISTRICT 62 [PART]	12,725	6,069	5,560	1,096	509 R	47.7%	43.7%	52.2%	47.8%
352,121	TOTAL	108,473	61,551	37,555	9,367	23,996 R	56.7%	34.6%	62.1%	37.9%

NEW YORK CITY

SENATOR 1980

1980 Census Population	County	Total Vote	Republican	Democratic	Other	Rep.-Dem. Plurality	Percentage Total Vote Rep.	Dem.	Major Vote Rep.	Dem.
1,169,115	BRONX	262,285	76,602	158,543	27,140	81,941 D	29.2%	60.4%	32.6%	67.4%
2,230,936	KINGS	502,965	153,865	295,406	53,694	141,541 D	30.6%	58.7%	34.2%	65.8%
1,427,533	NEW YORK	428,048	65,685	296,815	65,548	231,130 D	15.3%	69.3%	18.1%	81.9%
1,891,325	QUEENS	548,936	211,255	277,469	60,212	66,214 D	38.5%	50.5%	43.2%	56.8%
352,121	RICHMOND	108,473	61,551	37,555	9,367	23,996 R	56.7%	34.6%	62.1%	37.9%
7,071,030	TOTAL	1,850,707	568,958	1,065,788	215,961	496,830 D	30.7%	57.6%	34.8%	65.2%

NEW YORK

CONGRESS

CD	Year	Total Vote	Republican Vote	Candidate	Democratic Vote	Candidate	Other Vote	Rep.-Dem. Plurality	Total Vote Rep.	Total Vote Dem.	Major Vote Rep.	Major Vote Dem.
1	1980	204,486	115,213	*CARNEY, WILLIAM	85,629	TWOMEY, THOMAS A.	3,644	29,584 R	56.3%	41.9%	57.4%	42.6%
1	1978	160,204	90,115	*CARNEY, WILLIAM	67,180	RANDOLPH, JOHN F.	2,909	22,935 R	56.3%	41.9%	57.3%	42.7%
1	1976	207,468	61,671	NICOSIA, SALVATORE C.	135,528	*PIKE, OTIS G.	10,269	73,857 D	29.7%	65.3%	31.3%	68.7%
1	1974	155,681	44,513	SALLAH, DONALD R.	101,130	PIKE, OTIS G.	10,038	56,617 D	28.6%	65.0%	30.6%	69.4%
1	1972	195,444	72,133	BOYD, JOSEPH H.	102,628	PIKE, OTIS G.	20,683	30,495 D	36.9%	52.5%	41.3%	58.7%
2	1980	149,141	65,106	*MODICA, LOUIS J.	84,035	DOWNEY, THOMAS J.		18,929 D	43.7%	56.3%	43.7%	56.3%
2	1978	118,129	53,322	*WITHERS, HAROLD J.	64,807	DOWNEY, THOMAS J.		11,485 D	45.1%	54.9%	45.1%	54.9%
2	1976	159,902	67,755	*COHALAN, PETER F.	91,241	*DOWNEY, THOMAS J.	906	23,486 D	42.4%	57.1%	42.6%	57.4%
2	1974	119,451	53,344	GROVER, JAMES R.	58,289	DOWNEY, THOMAS J.	7,818	4,945 D	44.7%	48.8%	47.8%	52.2%
2	1972	151,015	99,348	GROVER, JAMES R.	49,454	DENNISON, FERN C.	2,213	49,894 R	65.8%	32.7%	66.8%	33.2%
3	1980	175,657	87,952	*CARMAN, GREGORY W.	83,389	*AMBRO, JEROME A.	4,316	4,563 R	50.1%	47.5%	51.3%	48.7%
3	1978	138,670	66,458	*CARMAN, GREGORY W.	70,526	AMBRO, JEROME A.	1,686	4,068 D	47.9%	50.9%	48.5%	51.5%
3	1976	181,439	84,824	*HOGAN, HOWARD T.	94,265	AMBRO, JEROME A.	2,350	9,441 D	46.8%	52.0%	47.4%	52.6%
3	1974	147,560	67,986	*RONCALLO, ANGELO D.	76,383	AMBRO, JEROME A.	3,191	8,397 D	46.1%	51.8%	47.1%	52.9%
3	1972	195,160	103,620	RONCALLO, ANGELO D.	73,429	BALES, CARTER F.	18,111	30,191 R	53.1%	37.6%	58.5%	41.5%
4	1980	175,725	117,455	*LENT, NORMAN F.	58,270	*BRENNAN, CHARLES F.		59,185 R	66.8%	33.2%	66.8%	33.2%
4	1978	143,302	94,711	*LENT, NORMAN F.	46,508	ROSENBLUM, EVERETT A.	2,083	48,203 R	66.1%	32.5%	67.1%	32.9%
4	1976	190,029	106,058	*LENT, NORMAN F.	83,971	*HALPERN, GERALD P.		22,087 R	55.8%	44.2%	55.8%	44.2%
4	1974	159,204	85,382	*LENT, NORMAN F.	73,822	*ORENSTEIN, FRANKLIN H.		11,560 R	53.6%	46.4%	53.6%	46.4%
4	1972	201,034	125,422	LENT, NORMAN F.	72,280	HOROWITZ, ELAINE B.	3,332	53,142 R	62.4%	36.0%	63.4%	36.6%
5	1980	182,368	105,140	*MCGRATH, RAYMOND J.	77,228	*BURSTEIN, KAREN S.		27,912 R	57.7%	42.3%	57.7%	42.3%
5	1978	145,383	84,864	*WYDLER, JOHN W.	60,519	*MATTHEWS, JOHN W.		24,345 R	58.4%	41.6%	58.4%	41.6%
5	1976	198,234	110,366	*WYDLER, JOHN W.	87,868	*LOWENSTEIN, ALLARD K.		22,498 R	55.7%	44.3%	55.7%	44.3%
5	1974	169,033	91,677	*WYDLER, JOHN W.	77,356	*LOWENSTEIN, ALLARD K.		14,321 R	54.2%	45.8%	54.2%	45.8%
5	1972	213,542	133,332	WYDLER, JOHN W.	67,709	STECKLER, FERNE M.	12,501	65,623 R	62.4%	31.7%	66.3%	33.7%
6	1980	169,971	89,762	*LEBOUTILLIER, JOHN	80,209	*WOLFF, LESTER L.		9,553 R	52.8%	47.2%	52.8%	47.2%
6	1978	134,606	44,304	AIN, STUART L.	80,799	*WOLFF, LESTER L.	9,503	36,495 D	32.9%	60.0%	35.4%	64.6%
6	1976	181,947	60,567	BALLETTA, VINCENT	112,422	*WOLFF, LESTER L.	8,958	51,855 D	33.3%	61.8%	35.0%	65.0%
6	1974	151,765	50,528	LAYNE, EDYTHE	101,237	*WOLFF, LESTER L.		50,709 D	33.3%	66.7%	33.3%	66.7%
6	1972	212,658	103,038	*GALLAGHER, JOHN T.	109,620	*WOLFF, LESTER L.		6,582 D	48.5%	51.5%	48.5%	51.5%
7	1980	100,840			96,137	*ADDABBO, JOSEPH P.	4,703	96,137 D		95.3%		100.0%
7	1978	77,001			73,066	*ADDABBO, JOSEPH P.	3,935	73,066 D		94.9%		100.0%
7	1976	113,373			107,312	*ADDABBO, JOSEPH P.	6,061	107,312 D		94.7%		100.0%
7	1974	83,972			83,972	*ADDABBO, JOSEPH P.		83,972 D		100.0%		100.0%
7	1972	137,459	28,296	HALL, JOHN E.	103,110	*ADDABBO, JOSEPH P.	6,053	74,814 D	20.6%	75.0%	21.5%	78.5%
8	1980	111,429	27,156	*LEMISHOW, ALBERT	84,273	*ROSENTHAL, BENJAMIN		57,117 D	24.4%	75.6%	24.4%	75.6%
8	1978	95,202	15,165	LEMISHOW, ALBERT	74,872	*ROSENTHAL, BENJAMIN	5,165	59,707 D	15.9%	78.6%	16.8%	83.2%
8	1976	137,861	30,191	*LEMISHOW, ALBERT	107,295	*ROSENTHAL, BENJAMIN	375	77,104 D	21.9%	77.8%	22.0%	78.0%
8	1974	114,180	23,980	*LEMISHOW, ALBERT	90,200	*ROSENTHAL, BENJAMIN		66,220 D	21.0%	79.0%	21.0%	79.0%
8	1972	170,459	60,166	*LA PINA, FRANK	110,293	*ROSENTHAL, BENJAMIN		50,127 D	35.3%	64.7%	35.3%	64.7%
9	1980	109,360	44,473	*BATTISTA, VITO P.	63,796	FERRARO, GERALDINE A.	1,091	19,323 D	40.7%	58.3%	41.1%	58.9%
9	1978	94,787	42,108	*DELLIBOVI, ALFRED A.	51,350	FERRARO, GERALDINE A.	1,329	9,242 D	44.4%	54.2%	45.1%	54.9%
9	1976	115,195			109,552	*DELANEY, JAMES J.	5,643	109,552 D		95.1%		100.0%
9	1974	99,155			92,231	*DELANEY, JAMES J.	6,924	92,231 D		93.0%		100.0%
9	1972	151,288			141,323	*DELANEY, JAMES J.	9,965	141,323 D		93.4%		100.0%
10	1980	100,918			95,322	*BIAGGI, MARIO	5,596	95,322 D		94.5%		100.0%
10	1978	82,061			77,979	*BIAGGI, MARIO	4,082	77,979 D		95.0%		100.0%
10	1976	115,962			106,222	*BIAGGI, MARIO	9,740	106,222 D		91.6%		100.0%
10	1974	91,422			75,375	*BIAGGI, MARIO	16,047	75,375 D		82.4%		100.0%
10	1972	138,597			130,200	*BIAGGI, MARIO	8,397	130,200 D		93.9%		100.0%
11	1980	98,222	25,424	*CARLAN, ANDREW E.	72,798	*SCHEUER, JAMES H.		47,374 D	25.9%	74.1%	25.9%	74.1%
11	1978	75,203	16,206	*HUHN, KENNETH	58,997	*SCHEUER, JAMES H.		42,791 D	21.5%	78.5%	21.5%	78.5%
11	1976	114,458	19,203	CUCCIA, ARTHUR	84,770	SCHEUER, JAMES H.	10,485	65,567 D	16.8%	74.1%	18.5%	81.5%
11	1974	86,351	12,297	DESBOROUGH, EDWARD G.	62,388	SCHEUER, JAMES H.	11,666	50,091 D	14.2%	72.2%	16.5%	83.5%
11	1972	137,546	43,105	*SOLOMON, MELVIN	87,869	BRASCO, FRANK J.	6,572	44,764 D	31.3%	63.9%	32.9%	67.1%
12	1980	40,689	3,372	GIBBS, CHARLES	35,446	*CHISHOLM, SHIRLEY	1,871	32,074 D	8.3%	87.1%	8.7%	91.3%
12	1978	29,277	3,580	GIBBS, CHARLES	25,697	*CHISHOLM, SHIRLEY		22,117 D	12.2%	87.8%	12.2%	87.8%
12	1976	49,632	5,336	MORANCIE, HORACE L.	43,203	*CHISHOLM, SHIRLEY	1,093	37,867 D	10.8%	87.0%	11.0%	89.0%
12	1974	32,979	4,577	VOYTICKY, FRANCIS J.	26,446	*CHISHOLM, SHIRLEY	1,956	21,869 D	13.9%	80.2%	14.8%	85.2%

NEW YORK

CONGRESS

CD	Year	Total Vote	Republican Vote	Candidate	Democratic Vote	Candidate	Other Vote	Rep.-Dem. Plurality	Total Vote Rep.	Dem.	Major Vote Rep.	Dem.
13	1980	103,156	19,536	*DEMELL, HARRY	81,954	*SOLARZ, STEPHEN J.	1,666	62,418 D	18.9%	79.4%	19.2%	80.8%
13	1978	84,839	16,002	*CARASSO, MAX	68,837	*SOLARZ, STEPHEN J.		52,835 D	18.9%	81.1%	18.9%	81.1%
13	1976	132,224	21,600	*DOBOSH, JACK N.	110,624	*SOLARZ, STEPHEN J.		89,024 D	16.3%	83.7%	16.3%	83.7%
13	1974	111,237	20,229	*DOBOSH, JACK N.	91,008	*SOLARZ, STEPHEN J.		70,779 D	18.2%	81.8%	18.2%	81.8%
14	1980	59,162	8,257	*LOVELL, CHRISTOPHER	45,029	*RICHMOND, FREDERICK W.	5,876	36,772 D	14.0%	76.1%	15.5%	84.5%
14	1978	40,745	7,516	BRAMWELL, ARTHUR	31,339	*RICHMOND, FREDERICK W.	1,890	23,823 D	18.4%	76.9%	19.3%	80.7%
14	1976	65,591	8,977	*GARGIULO, FRANK X.	55,723	*RICHMOND, FREDERICK W.	891	46,746 D	13.7%	85.0%	13.9%	86.1%
14	1974	46,551	5,360	CARBAJAL, MICHAEL	33,195	RICHMOND, FREDERICK W.	7,996	27,835 D	11.5%	71.3%	13.9%	86.1%
15	1980	98,976	46,467	*ATANASIO, PAUL M.	49,684	ZEFERETTI, LEO C.	2,825	3,217 D	46.9%	50.2%	48.3%	51.7%
15	1978	72,331	20,508	WHELAN, ROBERT P.	49,272	*ZEFERETTI, LEO C.	2,551	28,764 D	28.4%	68.1%	29.4%	70.6%
15	1976	109,487	33,641	D'ANGELO, RONALD J.	69,242	*ZEFERETTI, LEO C.	6,604	35,601 D	30.7%	63.2%	32.7%	67.3%
15	1974	91,922	34,814	CANADE, AUSTEN D.	53,733	*ZEFERETTI, LEO C.	3,375	18,919 D	37.9%	58.5%	39.3%	60.7%
16	1980	86,926	17,050	*SILVERMAN, THEODORE	67,343	*SCHUMER, CHARLES E.	2,533	50,293 D	19.6%	77.5%	20.2%	79.8%
16	1978	72,890	9,405	*PENNER, LARRY	59,703	*HOLTZMAN, ELIZABETH	3,782	50,298 D	12.9%	81.9%	13.6%	86.4%
16	1976	113,418	19,423	PEMBERTON, GLADYS	93,995	*HOLTZMAN, ELIZABETH		74,572 D	17.1%	82.9%	17.1%	82.9%
16	1974	93,816	19,806	*GENTILI, JOSEPH L.	74,010	*HOLTZMAN, ELIZABETH		54,204 D	21.1%	78.9%	21.1%	78.9%
16	1972	147,892	33,828	MACCHIO, NICHOLAS R.	96,984	HOLTZMAN, ELIZABETH	17,080	63,156 D	22.9%	65.6%	25.9%	74.1%
17	1980	145,645	69,573	*MOLINARI, GUY V.	50,954	*MURPHY, JOHN M.	25,118	18,619 R	47.8%	35.0%	57.7%	42.3%
17	1978	99,961	33,071	*PETERS, JOHN M.	54,228	MURPHY, JOHN M.	12,662	21,157 D	33.1%	54.2%	37.9%	62.1%
17	1976	135,915	27,734	GROSSBERGER, KENNETH	89,126	MURPHY, JOHN M.	19,055	61,392 D	20.4%	65.6%	23.7%	76.3%
17	1974	110,504	28,269	BIONDOLILLO, FRANK J.	63,805	MURPHY, JOHN M.	18,430	35,536 D	25.6%	57.7%	30.7%	69.3%
17	1972	153,064	60,812	*BELARDINO, MARIO D.	92,252	MURPHY, JOHN M.		31,440 D	39.7%	60.3%	39.7%	60.3%
18	1980	161,200	91,341	*GREEN, S. WILLIAM	68,786	*GREEN, MARK J.	1,073	22,555 R	56.7%	42.7%	57.0%	43.0%
18	1978	114,301	60,867	*GREEN, S. WILLIAM	53,434	*BURDEN, CARTER		7,433 R	53.3%	46.7%	53.3%	46.7%
18	1976	149,422	29,728	LANDAU, SONIA	112,187	*KOCH, EDWARD I.	7,507	82,459 D	19.9%	75.1%	20.9%	79.1%
18	1974	119,903	22,560	BOOGAERTS, JOHN	91,985	*KOCH, EDWARD I.	5,358	69,425 D	18.8%	76.7%	19.7%	80.3%
18	1972	178,894	52,379	*LANGLEY, JANE P.	125,117	*KOCH, EDWARD I.	1,398	72,738 D	29.3%	69.9%	29.5%	70.5%
19	1980	87,376			84,062	*RANGEL, CHARLES B.	3,314	84,062 D		96.2%		100.0%
19	1978	61,991			59,731	*RANGEL, CHARLES B.	2,260	59,731 D		96.4%		100.0%
19	1976	94,481			91,672	*RANGEL, CHARLES B.	2,809	91,672 D		97.0%		100.0%
19	1974	65,185			63,146	*RANGEL, CHARLES B.	2,039	63,146 D		96.9%		100.0%
19	1972	108,769			104,427	*RANGEL, CHARLES B.	4,342	104,427 D		96.0%		100.0%
20	1980	104,929	15,350	GREENE, JAMES E.	86,454	*WEISS, THEODORE S.	3,125	71,104 D	14.6%	82.4%	15.1%	84.9%
20	1978	75,936	11,661	TORCZYNER, HARRY	64,275	*WEISS, THEODORE S.		52,614 D	15.4%	84.6%	15.4%	84.6%
20	1976	110,490	14,114	WEISEMAN, DENISE T.	91,977	*WEISS, THEODORE S.	4,399	77,863 D	12.8%	83.2%	13.3%	86.7%
20	1974	96,638	15,053	POSNER, STEPHEN	76,074	*ABZUG, BELLA S.	5,511	61,021 D	15.6%	78.7%	16.5%	83.5%
20	1972	153,492	18,024	LEVY, ANNETTE F.	85,558	ABZUG, BELLA S.	49,910	67,534 D	11.7%	55.7%	17.4%	82.6%
21	1980	32,758			32,173	*GARCIA, ROBERT	585	32,173 D		98.2%		100.0%
21	1978	24,449			23,950	*GARCIA, ROBERT	499	23,950 D		98.0%		100.0%
21	1976	41,883			41,285	*BADILLO, HERMAN	598	41,285 D		98.6%		100.0%
21	1974	28,984			28,025	*BADILLO, HERMAN	959	28,025 D		96.7%		100.0%
21	1972	55,744	6,366	RAMOS, MANUEL A.	48,441	*BADILLO, HERMAN	937	42,075 D	11.4%	86.9%	11.6%	88.4%
22	1980	79,015	9,943	BLACK, ROBERT	66,301	*BINGHAM, JONATHAN	2,771	56,358 D	12.6%	83.9%	13.0%	87.0%
22	1978	69,837	11,110	*GEIDEL, ANTHONY J.	58,727	*BINGHAM, JONATHAN		47,617 D	15.9%	84.1%	15.9%	84.1%
22	1976	106,592	11,130	SLOTKIN, PAUL	92,044	*BINGHAM, JONATHAN	3,418	80,914 D	10.4%	86.4%	10.8%	89.2%
22	1974	90,632	8,142	BLACK, ROBERT	77,157	*BINGHAM, JONATHAN	5,333	69,015 D	9.0%	85.1%	9.5%	90.5%
22	1972	140,493	33,045	*AVARELLO, CHARLES A.	107,448	*BINGHAM, JONATHAN		74,403 D	23.5%	76.5%	23.5%	76.5%
23	1980	152,520	66,771	*ALBANESE, ANDREW	85,749	PEYSER, PETER A.		18,978 D	43.8%	56.2%	43.8%	56.2%
23	1978	128,572	59,455	*MARTINELLI, ANGELO R.	66,354	PEYSER, PETER A.	2,763	6,899 D	46.2%	51.6%	47.3%	52.7%
23	1976	173,430	93,006	*CAPUTO, BRUCE F.	80,424	*MEYER, J. EDWARD		12,582 R	53.6%	46.4%	53.6%	46.4%
23	1974	139,469	80,361	*PEYSER, PETER A.	59,108	*GREENAWALT, WILLIAM S.		21,253 R	57.6%	42.4%	57.6%	42.4%
23	1972	198,072	99,737	*PEYSER, PETER A.	98,335	*OTTINGER, RICHARD L.		1,402 R	50.4%	49.6%	50.4%	49.6%
24	1980	168,553	66,689	*CHRISTIANA, JOSEPH W.	100,182	OTTINGER, RICHARD L.	1,682	33,493 D	39.6%	59.4%	40.0%	60.0%
24	1978	134,463	57,451	*EDELMAN, MICHAEL R.	75,397	OTTINGER, RICHARD L.	1,615	17,946 D	42.7%	56.1%	43.2%	56.8%
24	1976	183,012	81,111	*HICKS, DAVID V.	99,761	OTTINGER, RICHARD L.	2,140	18,650 D	44.3%	54.5%	44.8%	55.2%
24	1974	142,722	60,180	*STEPHENS, CHARLES J.	82,542	OTTINGER, RICHARD L.		22,362 D	42.2%	57.8%	42.2%	57.8%
24	1972	206,797	98,818	*VERGARI, CARL A.	107,979	*REID, OGDEN R.		9,161 D	47.8%	52.2%	47.8%	52.2%

NEW YORK

CONGRESS

CD	Year	Total Vote	Republican Vote	Republican Candidate	Democratic Vote	Democratic Candidate	Other Vote	Rep.-Dem. Plurality	Total Vote Rep.	Total Vote Dem.	Major Vote Rep.	Major Vote Dem.
25	1980	196,305	158,936	*FISH, HAMILTON	37,369	OZOLS, GUNARS M.		121,567 R	81.0%	19.0%	81.0%	19.0%
25	1978	146,533	114,641	FISH, HAMILTON	31,213	OZOLS, GUNARS M.	679	83,428 R	78.2%	21.3%	78.6%	21.4%
25	1976	197,650	139,434	*FISH, HAMILTON	58,216	PEYSER, MINNA P.		81,218 R	70.5%	29.5%	70.5%	29.5%
25	1974	159,037	103,799	*FISH, HAMILTON	53,357	ANGELL, NICHOLAS B.	1,881	50,442 R	65.3%	33.6%	66.0%	34.0%
25	1972	201,536	144,386	*FISH, HAMILTON	54,271	BURNS, JOHN M.	2,879	90,115 R	71.6%	26.9%	72.7%	27.3%
26	1980	184,692	137,159	GILMAN, BENJAMIN A.	37,475	*VICTOR, EUGENE R.	10,058	99,684 R	74.3%	20.3%	78.5%	21.5%
26	1978	139,637	87,059	GILMAN, BENJAMIN A.	41,870	*HOLBROOK, CHARLES E.	10,708	45,189 R	62.3%	30.0%	67.5%	32.5%
26	1976	183,981	120,049	GILMAN, BENJAMIN A.	60,511	MALONEY, JOHN R.	3,421	59,538 R	65.3%	32.9%	66.5%	33.5%
26	1974	151,068	81,562	GILMAN, BENJAMIN A.	58,161	*DOW, JOHN G.	11,345	23,401 R	54.0%	38.5%	58.4%	41.6%
26	1972	190,424	90,922	GILMAN, BENJAMIN A.	74,906	DOW, JOHN G.	24,596	16,016 R	47.7%	39.3%	54.8%	45.2%
27	1980	188,678	83,096	*WALLACE, NEIL T.	103,863	MCHUGH, MATTHEW F.	1,719	20,767 D	44.0%	55.0%	44.4%	55.6%
27	1978	149,590	66,177	*WALLACE, NEIL T.	83,413	MCHUGH, MATTHEW F.		17,236 D	44.2%	55.8%	44.2%	55.8%
27	1976	190,674	63,626	*HARTER, WILLIAM H.	127,048	*MCHUGH, MATTHEW F.		63,422 D	33.4%	66.6%	33.4%	66.6%
27	1974	158,361	68,273	LIBOUS, ALFRED J.	83,562	*MCHUGH, MATTHEW F.	6,526	15,289 D	43.1%	52.8%	45.0%	55.0%
27	1972	184,828	114,902	ROBISON, HOWARD W.	55,076	BLAZER, DAVID H.	14,850	59,826 R	62.2%	29.8%	67.6%	32.4%
28	1980	210,655	37,504	WICKS, FRANK	164,088	STRATTON, SAMUEL S.	9,063	126,584 D	17.8%	77.9%	18.6%	81.4%
28	1978	182,945	36,017	*TOCKER, PAUL H.	139,575	STRATTON, SAMUEL S.	7,353	103,558 D	19.7%	76.3%	20.5%	79.5%
28	1976	215,162	44,053	*BRADT, MARY	170,034	STRATTON, SAMUEL S.	1,075	125,981 D	20.5%	79.0%	20.6%	79.4%
28	1974	193,982	33,493	WAGNER, WAYNE E.	156,439	STRATTON, SAMUEL S.	4,050	122,946 D	17.3%	80.6%	17.6%	82.4%
28	1972	228,018	45,623	*RYAN, JOHN F.	182,395	STRATTON, SAMUEL S.		136,772 D	20.0%	80.0%	20.0%	80.0%
29	1980	212,328	141,631	*SOLOMON, GERALD B.	70,697	*HURLEY, RODGER L.		70,934 R	66.7%	33.3%	66.7%	33.3%
29	1978	184,223	99,518	*SOLOMON, GERALD B.	84,705	*PATTISON, EDWARD W.		14,813 R	54.0%	46.0%	54.0%	46.0%
29	1976	214,222	96,476	MARTINO, JOSEPH A.	100,663	*PATTISON, EDWARD W.	17,083	4,187 D	45.0%	47.0%	48.9%	51.1%
29	1974	184,092	83,768	*KING, CARLETON	100,324	*PATTISON, EDWARD W.		16,556 D	45.5%	54.5%	45.5%	54.5%
29	1972	212,090	148,170	*KING, CARLETON	63,920	*GORDON, HAROLD B.		84,250 R	69.9%	30.1%	69.9%	30.1%
30	1980	173,889	111,008	*MARTIN, DAVID O'B.	54,896	*KRUPSAK, MARY ANNE	7,985	56,112 R	63.8%	31.6%	66.9%	33.1%
30	1978	141,263	85,478	*MCEWEN, ROBERT C.	55,785	*BARTLE, NORMA A.		29,693 R	60.5%	39.5%	60.5%	39.5%
30	1976	171,515	95,564	*MCEWEN, ROBERT C.	75,951	BARTLE, NORMA A.		19,613 R	55.7%	44.3%	55.7%	44.3%
30	1974	142,010	78,117	*MCEWEN, ROBERT C.	63,893	*TUBBY, ROGER W.		14,224 R	55.0%	45.0%	55.0%	45.0%
30	1972	172,981	114,193	*MCEWEN, ROBERT C.	58,788	*LABAFF, ERNEST J.		55,405 R	66.0%	34.0%	66.0%	34.0%
31	1980	175,565	135,976	*MITCHELL, DONALD J.	39,589	*SCHWARTZ, IRVING A.		96,387 R	77.5%	22.5%	77.5%	22.5%
31	1978	107,791	107,791	*MITCHELL, DONALD J.				107,791 R	100.0%		100.0%	
31	1976	185,175	123,143	*MITCHELL, DONALD J.	62,032	MAXWELL, ANITA		61,111 R	66.5%	33.5%	66.5%	33.5%
31	1974	158,239	94,319	*MITCHELL, DONALD J.	59,639	REILE, DONALD J.	4,281	34,680 R	59.6%	37.7%	61.3%	38.7%
31	1972	193,221	98,454	*MITCHELL, DONALD J.	75,513	CASTLE, ROBERT	19,254	22,941 R	51.0%	39.1%	56.6%	43.4%
32	1980	178,957	108,128	*WORTLEY, GEORGE C.	56,535	*BROOKS, JEFFREY S.	14,294	51,593 R	60.4%	31.6%	65.7%	34.3%
32	1978	145,471	67,071	*DEL GIORNO, PETER J.	76,251	HANLEY, JAMES M.	2,149	9,180 D	46.1%	52.4%	46.8%	53.2%
32	1976	185,140	81,597	*WORTLEY, GEORGE C.	101,419	HANLEY, JAMES M.	2,124	19,822 D	44.1%	54.8%	44.6%	55.4%
32	1974	150,039	61,379	*BUSH, WILLIAM E.	88,660	HANLEY, JAMES M.		27,281 D	40.9%	59.1%	40.9%	59.1%
32	1972	194,932	83,451	*KOLDIN, LEONARD C.	111,481	HANLEY, JAMES M.		28,030 D	42.8%	57.2%	42.8%	57.2%
33	1980	175,271	132,831	*LEE, GARY A.	39,542	*REED, DOLORES M.	2,898	93,289 R	75.8%	22.6%	77.1%	22.9%
33	1978	147,454	82,501	LEE, GARY A.	58,286	BERNARDI, ROY A.	6,667	24,215 R	56.0%	39.5%	58.6%	41.4%
33	1976	182,755	125,163	WALSH, WILLIAM F.	48,855	WELCH, CHARLES R.	8,737	76,308 R	68.5%	26.7%	71.9%	28.1%
33	1974	149,091	97,380	WALSH, WILLIAM F.	45,043	BOCKMAN, ROBERT H.	6,668	52,337 R	65.3%	30.2%	68.4%	31.6%
33	1972	185,178	132,139	*WALSH, WILLIAM F.	53,039	KADYS, CLARENCE		79,100 R	71.4%	28.6%	71.4%	28.6%
34	1980	182,795	133,278	HORTON, FRANK J.	37,883	TOOLE, JAMES	11,634	95,395 R	72.9%	20.7%	77.9%	22.1%
34	1978	140,912	122,785	*HORTON, FRANK J.			18,127	122,785 R	87.1%		100.0%	
34	1976	192,196	126,566	HORTON, FRANK J.	58,247	LARSEN, WILLIAM C.	7,383	68,319 R	65.9%	30.3%	68.5%	31.5%
34	1974	156,365	105,585	HORTON, FRANK J.	45,408	GOSSIN, IRENE	5,372	60,177 R	67.5%	29.0%	69.9%	30.1%
34	1972	198,003	142,803	HORTON, FRANK J.	46,509	RUBENS, JACK	8,691	96,294 R	72.1%	23.5%	75.4%	24.6%
35	1980	176,774	127,623	CONABLE, BARBER B.	44,754	*OWENS, JOHN M.	4,397	82,869 R	72.2%	25.3%	74.0%	26.0%
35	1978	138,593	96,119	CONABLE, BARBER B.	36,428	REPICCI, FRANCIS C.	6,046	59,691 R	69.4%	26.3%	72.5%	27.5%
35	1976	187,915	120,738	CONABLE, BARBER B.	67,177	*MACALUSO, MICHAEL		53,561 R	64.3%	35.7%	64.3%	35.7%
35	1974	159,058	90,269	CONABLE, BARBER B.	63,012	COSTANZA, MARGARET	5,777	27,257 R	56.8%	39.6%	58.9%	41.1%
35	1972	187,580	127,298	CONABLE, BARBER B.	53,321	SPENCER, TERENCE J.	6,961	73,977 R	67.9%	28.4%	70.5%	29.5%
36	1980	171,357	48,428	*FEDER, H. WILLIAM	122,929	*LAFALCE, JOHN J.		74,501 D	28.3%	71.7%	28.3%	71.7%
36	1978	134,257	31,527	*CARTONIA, FRANCINA J.	99,497	*LAFALCE, JOHN J.	3,233	67,970 D	23.5%	74.1%	24.1%	75.9%
36	1976	184,947	61,701	*ARGEN, RALPH J.	123,246	*LAFALCE, JOHN J.		61,545 D	33.4%	66.6%	33.4%	66.6%
36	1974	151,940	61,442	*ROURKE, RUSSELL A.	90,498	*LAFALCE, JOHN J.		29,056 D	40.4%	59.6%	40.4%	59.6%
36	1972	192,333	110,238	*SMITH, HENRY P.	82,095	*MCCARTHY, MAX		28,143 R	57.3%	42.7%	57.3%	42.7%

NEW YORK

CONGRESS

CD	Year	Total Vote	Republican Vote	Republican Candidate	Democratic Vote	Democratic Candidate	Other Vote	Rep.-Dem. Plurality	Total Vote Rep.	Total Vote Dem.	Major Vote Rep.	Major Vote Dem.
37	1980	114,337	16,560	*HEYMANOWSKI, ROGER	94,890	*NOWAK, HENRY J.	2,887	78,330 D	14.5%	83.0%	14.9%	85.1%
37	1978	90,271	17,585	ROTH, CHARLES	70,911	*NOWAK, HENRY J.	1,775	53,326 D	19.5%	78.6%	19.9%	80.1%
37	1976	127,951	23,660	KIMBOROUGH, CALVIN	100,042	*NOWAK, HENRY J.	4,249	76,382 D	18.5%	78.2%	19.1%	80.9%
37	1974	112,116	27,531	*BALA, JOSEPH R.	84,064	*NOWAK, HENRY J.	521	56,533 D	24.6%	75.0%	24.7%	75.3%
37	1972	158,708	44,103	*MCLAUGHLIN, WILLIAM F.	114,605	*DULSKI, THADDEUS J.		70,502 D	27.8%	72.2%	27.8%	72.2%
38	1980	205,309	167,434	*KEMP, JACK F.	37,875	*DENN, GALE A.		129,559 R	81.6%	18.4%	81.6%	18.4%
38	1978	120,132	113,928	*KEMP, JACK F.			6,204	113,928 R	94.8%		100.0%	
38	1976	212,009	165,702	*KEMP, JACK F.	46,307	*GERACI, PETER J.		119,395 R	78.2%	21.8%	78.2%	21.8%
38	1974	175,616	126,687	*KEMP, JACK F.	48,929	*WICKS, BARBARA C.		77,758 R	72.1%	27.9%	72.1%	27.9%
38	1972	214,552	156,967	*KEMP, JACK F.	57,585	*LORUSSO, ANTHONY P.		99,382 R	73.2%	26.8%	73.2%	26.8%
39	1980	171,432	75,039	*ABDELLA, JAMES	93,839	LUNDINE, STANLEY N.	2,554	18,800 D	43.8%	54.7%	44.4%	55.6%
39	1978	135,816	56,431	*MAGUIRE, CRISPIN M.	79,385	LUNDINE, STANLEY N.		22,954 D	41.5%	58.5%	41.5%	58.5%
39	1976	178,004	68,018	*SNOWDEN, RICHARD A.	109,986	LUNDINE, STANLEY N.		41,968 D	38.2%	61.8%	38.2%	61.8%
39	1974	145,019	87,321	HASTINGS, JAMES F.	53,866	*PARMENT, WILLIAM L.	3,832	33,455 R	60.2%	37.1%	61.8%	38.2%
39	1972	175,400	126,147	*HASTINGS, JAMES F.	49,253	WHITE, WILBUR		76,894 R	71.9%	28.1%	71.9%	28.1%

NEW YORK

1980 GENERAL ELECTION

President   The Republican candidate was also the Conservative nominee and 256,131 of his votes were received as the Conservative candidate. Other vote was 467,801 Anderson (Liberal); 52,648 Clark (Free Libertarian); 24,159 McCormack (Right to Life); 23,186 Commoner (Citizens); 7,414 Hall (Communist); 2,068 DeBerry (Socialist Workers); 1,416 Griswold (Workers World); 1,064 scattered. Original uncorrected canvass gave the Republican vote in Oswego county as 31,151.

Senator   The Republican candidate was also the Conservative and Right to Life nominee and 275,100 of his votes were received as the Conservative candidate and 152,470 of his votes as the Right to Life candidate. Other vote was 664,544 Javits (Liberal); 21,465 Savadel (Free Libertarian); 4,161 Scott (Communist); 3,643 Soto (Workers World); 2,715 Nieto (Socialist Workers); 73 scattered.

Congress   An asterisk in the Congressional vote table indicates a candidate received votes from another party endorsing his/her candidacy. Other vote was Cummings (Liberal) in CD 1; Meehan (Liberal) in CD 3; Lees (3,303 Conservative and 1,400 Right to Life) in CD 7; Geniale (Liberal) in CD 9; 3,942 Cavanna (Conservative) and 1,654 Mari (Right to Life) in CD 10; 1,344 Carrano (Conservative) and 527 Caesar (Right to Life) in CD 12; Connolly (Right to Life) in CD 13; 4,151 Harris (New Alliance), 1,086 Jones (Socialist Workers) and 639 McKenzie (Right to Life) in CD 14; McNeill (Liberal) in CD 15; Spalding (Right to Life) in CD 16; Codd (Liberal) in CD 17; Washburn (Right to Life) in CD 18; Garvey (1,940 Conservative and 682 Right to Life) and 692 Dixon (Socialist Workers) in CD 19; 2,240 Caplan (Conservative) and 885 Massi (Socialist Labor) in CD 20; 313 Cordero (Right to Life) and 272 Aceto (Conservative) in CD 21; Whalen (Conservative) in CD 22; Reyes (Liberal) in CD 24; 8,766 Farrell (Right to Life) and 1,292 Goonan (Free Libertarian) in CD 26; Muenkel (Right to Life) in CD 27; Bradt (4,970 Conservative and 2,897 Right to Life) and 1,196 Mayberry (Socialist Workers) in CD 28; Zagame (Right to Life) in CD 30; 11,978 DelGiorno (Right to Life) and 2,316 Northrop (Free Libertarian) in CD 32; Jones (Right to Life) in CD 33; 5,829 Benoy (Conservative), 3,178 Bastuk (Right to Life) and 2,627 Hoestly (Free Libertarian) in CD 34; 3,772 Bernard M. O'Connor (Right to Life) and 625 Bayoneta (Workers World) in CD 35; Thomas A. O'Connor (Right to Life) in CD 37; Ronan (Right to Life) in CD 39.

NEW YORK CITY

The city is composed of five counties, each of which for municipal government purposes is known as a borough. Names of the counties and boroughs are the same save in the case of New York county (Manhattan borough) and Kings county (Brooklyn borough). The boundaries of the 38th and 62nd Assembly Districts cross county lines. The 38th District is part in Kings and part in Queens; the 62nd District part in Richmond, part in New York.

President   The Republican vote includes 69,933 votes cast for Reagan as the Conservative candidate. Other vote was 113,845 Anderson (Liberal); 10,426 Commoner (Citizens); 8,791 Clark (Free Libertarian); 6,217 McCormack (Right to Life); 4,892 Hall (Communist); 1,224 DeBerry (Socialist Workers); 556 Griswold (Workers World); 24 scattered.

Senator   The Republican vote includes 69,595 votes cast for D'Amato as the Conservative candidate and 34,097 as the Right to Life candidate. Other vote was 208,731 Javits (Liberal); 3,148 Savadel (Free Libertarian); 1,518 Soto (Workers World); 1,331 Scott (Communist); 1,230 Nieto (Socialist Workers); 3 scattered.

1980 PRIMARIES

SEPTEMBER 9 REPUBLICAN

Senator   323,468 Alfonse M. D'Amato; 257,433 Jacob K. Javits.

Congress   Unopposed in thirty CD's. Democratic candidates were endorsed in CD's 10, 19, and 21. No candidates filed in CD 28. Contested as follows:

NEW YORK

CD 1   15,210 William Carney; 11,102 John J. Hart; 2 scattered.
CD 7   2,805 Joseph P. Addabbo (the unopposed Democratic candidate); 1,160 Francis A. Lees.
CD 9   4,032 Vito P. Battista; 3,080 James E. Eagan.
CD 28   No candidate names appeared on the ballot. Write-in votes were 105 Frank Wicks; 45 Samuel S. Stratton.
CD 30   31,661 David O'B. Martin; 13,358 John R. Zagame.
CD 32   11,521 George C. Wortley; 8,649 Peter J. DelGiorno; 4,459 Pat R. Bombard; 4,084 Herbert D. Brewer.

SEPTEMBER 9 DEMOCRATIC

Senator   378,567 Elizabeth Holtzman; 292,767 Bess Myerson; 146,815 John V. Lindsay; 111,129 John Santucci.

Congress   Unopposed in thirty CD's. Contested as follows:

CD 5   12,214 Karen S. Burstein; 3,286 James Corcoran.
CD 12   9,514 Shirley Chisholm; 2,976 Louis Hernandez; 2,846 David R. Miller.
CD 14   17,474 Frederick W. Richmond; 6,023 Moses S. Harris.
CD 15   16,961 Leo C. Zeferetti; 6,811 Peter A. McNeill.
CD 16   23,260 Charles E. Schumer; 7,385 Susan Alter; 6,041 Theodore Silverman; 2,842 Edward Hayes.
CD 17   14,607 John M. Murphy; 10,797 Mary T. Codd; 9,744 Robert J. Gigante; 7,118 Thomas H. Stokes.
CD 18   29,494 Mark J. Green; 4,817 George T. McDonald; 2,165 William Bryk.
CD 30   10,672 Mary Anne Krupsak; 4,525 William B. Inglee.
CD 32   5,729 Jeffrey S. Brooks; 4,746 Gary L. Nicholson.

SEPTEMBER 9 CONSERVATIVE

Senator   Alfonse M. D'Amato, unopposed.

Congress   Major party candidates endorsed or nominees unopposed in all CD's in which a candidate was named.

SEPTEMBER 9 LIBERAL

Senator   Jacob K. Javits, unopposed.

Congress   Major party candidates endorsed or nominees unopposed in all CD's in which a candidate was named. There was a write-in contest as follows:

CD 29   50 Rodger L. Hurley; 5 Ned Pattison; 4 Bess Myerson; 1 Alfonse M. D'Amato.

SEPTEMBER 9 RIGHT TO LIFE

Senator   Alfonse M. D'Amato, unopposed.

Congress   Major party candidates endorsed or nominees unopposed in all CD's in which a candidate was named. There was a write-in contest as follows:

CD 3   89 Jerome A. Ambro (the unopposed Democratic candidate); 78 Gregory W. Carman.

NORTH CAROLINA

GOVERNOR
James B. Hunt (D). Re-elected 1980 to a four-year term. Previously elected 1976.

SENATORS
John P. East (R). Elected 1980 to a six-year term.

Jesse Helms (R). Re-elected 1978 to a six-year term. Previously elected 1972.

REPRESENTATIVES
1. Walter B. Jones (D)
2. L. H. Fountain (D)
3. Charles Whitley (D)
4. Ike F. Andrews (D)
5. Stephen L. Neal (D)
6. Eugene Johnston (R)
7. Charles G. Rose (D)
8. W. G. Hefner (D)
9. James G. Martin (R)
10. James T. Broyhill (R)
11. William M. Hendon (R)

POSTWAR VOTE FOR GOVERNOR

Year	Total Vote	Republican Vote	Republican Candidate	Democratic Vote	Democratic Candidate	Other Vote	Rep.-Dem. Plurality	Total Vote Rep.	Total Vote Dem.	Major Vote Rep.	Major Vote Dem.
1980	1,847,432	691,449	Lake, Beverly	1,143,145	Hunt, James B.	12,838	451,696 D	37.4%	61.9%	37.7%	62.3%
1976	1,663,824	564,102	Flaherty, David T.	1,081,293	Hunt, James B.	18,429	517,191 D	33.9%	65.0%	34.3%	65.7%
1972	1,504,785	767,470	Holshouser, James E.	729,104	Bowles, Hargrove	8,211	38,366 R	51.0%	48.5%	51.3%	48.7%
1968	1,558,308	737,075	Gardner, James C.	821,233	Scott, Robert W.	—	84,158 D	47.3%	52.7%	47.3%	52.7%
1964	1,396,508	606,165	Gavin, Robert L.	790,343	Moore, Dan K.	—	184,178 D	43.4%	56.6%	43.4%	56.6%
1960	1,350,360	613,975	Gavin, Robert L.	735,248	Sanford, Terry	1,137	121,273 D	45.5%	54.4%	45.5%	54.5%
1956	1,135,859	375,379	Hayes, Kyle	760,480	Hodges, Luther H.	—	385,101 D	33.0%	67.0%	33.0%	67.0%
1952	1,179,635	383,329	Seawell, H. F.	796,306	Umstead, William B.	—	412,977 D	32.5%	67.5%	32.5%	67.5%
1948	780,525	206,166	Pritchard, George	570,995	Scott, William Kerr	3,364	364,829 D	26.4%	73.2%	26.5%	73.5%

POSTWAR VOTE FOR SENATOR

Year	Total Vote	Republican Vote	Republican Candidate	Democratic Vote	Democratic Candidate	Other Vote	Rep.-Dem. Plurality	Total Vote Rep.	Total Vote Dem.	Major Vote Rep.	Major Vote Dem.
1980	1,797,665	898,064	East, John P.	887,653	Morgan, Robert	11,948	10,411 R	50.0%	49.4%	50.3%	49.7%
1978	1,135,814	619,151	Helms, Jesse	516,663	Ingram, John	—	102,488 R	54.5%	45.5%	54.5%	45.5%
1974	1,020,367	377,618	Stevens, William E.	633,775	Morgan, Robert	8,974	256,157 D	37.0%	62.1%	37.3%	62.7%
1972	1,472,541	795,248	Helms, Jesse	677,293	Galifianakis, Nick	—	117,955 R	54.0%	46.0%	54.0%	46.0%
1968	1,437,340	566,934	Somers, Robert V.	870,406	Ervin, Sam J.	—	303,472 D	39.4%	60.6%	39.4%	60.6%
1966	901,978	400,502	Shallcross, John S.	501,440	Jordan, B. Everett	36	100,938 D	44.4%	55.6%	44.4%	55.6%
1962	813,155	321,635	Greene, Claude L.	491,520	Ervin, Sam J.	—	169,885 D	39.6%	60.4%	39.6%	60.4%
1960	1,291,485	497,964	Hayes, Kyle	793,521	Jordan, B. Everett	—	295,557 D	38.6%	61.4%	38.6%	61.4%
1958s	616,469	184,977	Clarke, Richard C.	431,492	Jordan, B. Everett	—	246,515 D	30.0%	70.0%	30.0%	70.0%
1956	1,098,828	367,475	Johnson, Joel A.	731,353	Ervin, Sam J.	—	363,878 D	33.4%	66.6%	33.4%	66.6%
1954	619,634	211,322	West, Paul C.	408,312	Scott, William Kerr	—	196,990 D	34.1%	65.9%	34.1%	65.9%
1954s	410,574	—	—	410,574	Ervin, Sam J.	—	410,574 D	—	100.0%	—	100.0%
1950	548,276	171,804	Leavitt, Halsey B.	376,472	Hoey, Clyde R.	—	204,668 D	31.3%	68.7%	31.3%	68.7%
1950s	544,924	177,753	Gavin, E. L.	364,912	Smith, Willis	2,259	187,159 D	32.6%	67.0%	32.8%	67.2%
1948	764,559	220,307	Wilkinson, John A.	540,762	Broughton, J. M.	3,490	320,455 D	28.8%	70.7%	28.9%	71.1%

The election in 1958, and one each in 1954 and 1950 were for short terms to fill vacancies.

NORTH CAROLINA

Districts Established April 29, 1971

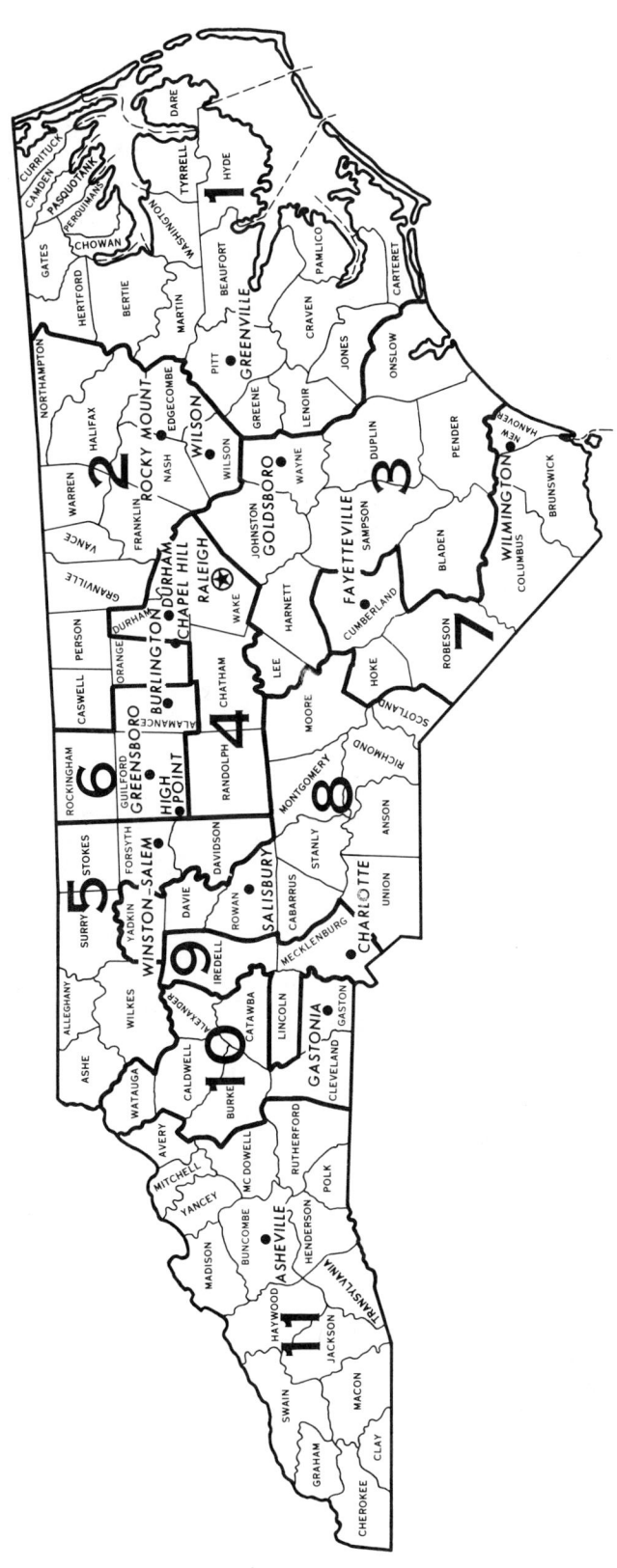

NORTH CAROLINA

PRESIDENT 1980

1980 Census Population	County	Total Vote	Republican	Democratic	Other	Rep.-Dem. Plurality	Percentage Total Vote Rep.	Dem.	Major Vote Rep.	Dem.
99,136	ALAMANCE	34,066	18,077	15,042	947	3,035 R	53.1%	44.2%	54.6%	45.4%
24,999	ALEXANDER	11,109	6,376	4,546	187	1,830 R	57.4%	40.9%	58.4%	41.6%
9,587	ALLEGHANY	4,310	1,995	2,198	117	203 D	46.3%	51.0%	47.6%	52.4%
25,562	ANSON	7,087	1,968	4,973	146	3,005 D	27.8%	70.2%	28.4%	71.6%
22,325	ASHE	10,312	5,643	4,461	208	1,182 R	54.7%	43.3%	55.8%	44.2%
14,409	AVERY	5,182	3,480	1,527	175	1,953 R	67.2%	29.5%	69.5%	30.5%
40,266	BEAUFORT	13,037	6,773	6,024	240	749 R	52.0%	46.2%	52.9%	47.1%
21,024	BERTIE	5,632	1,695	3,863	74	2,168 D	30.1%	68.6%	30.5%	69.5%
30,448	BLADEN	8,941	2,745	6,104	92	3,359 D	30.7%	68.3%	31.0%	69.0%
35,767	BRUNSWICK	13,003	5,897	6,761	345	864 D	45.4%	52.0%	46.6%	53.4%
160,934	BUNCOMBE	53,530	26,124	24,837	2,569	1,287 R	48.8%	46.4%	51.3%	48.7%
72,504	BURKE	25,417	12,956	11,680	781	1,276 R	51.0%	46.0%	52.6%	47.4%
85,895	CABARRUS	25,585	15,143	9,768	674	5,375 R	59.2%	38.2%	60.8%	39.2%
67,746	CALDWELL	22,310	12,965	8,738	607	4,227 R	58.1%	39.2%	59.7%	40.3%
5,829	CAMDEN	2,088	813	1,212	63	399 D	38.9%	58.0%	40.1%	59.9%
41,092	CARTERET	14,767	7,733	6,485	549	1,248 R	52.4%	43.9%	54.4%	45.6%
20,705	CASWELL	5,777	2,156	3,529	92	1,373 D	37.3%	61.1%	37.9%	62.1%
105,208	CATAWBA	37,878	22,873	13,873	1,132	9,000 R	60.4%	36.6%	62.2%	37.8%
33,415	CHATHAM	13,205	5,414	7,144	647	1,730 D	41.0%	54.1%	43.1%	56.9%
18,933	CHEROKEE	7,079	3,849	3,114	116	735 R	54.4%	44.0%	55.3%	44.7%
12,558	CHOWAN	3,660	1,424	2,146	90	722 D	38.9%	58.6%	39.9%	60.1%
6,619	CLAY	3,547	2,136	1,324	87	812 R	60.2%	37.3%	61.7%	38.3%
83,435	CLEVELAND	23,498	10,828	12,219	451	1,391 D	46.1%	52.0%	47.0%	53.0%
51,037	COLUMBUS	15,940	5,522	10,212	206	4,690 D	34.6%	64.1%	35.1%	64.9%
71,043	CRAVEN	16,783	8,554	7,781	448	773 R	51.0%	46.4%	52.4%	47.6%
247,160	CUMBERLAND	45,228	21,540	22,073	1,615	533 D	47.6%	48.8%	49.4%	50.6%
11,089	CURRITUCK	3,786	1,668	1,980	138	312 D	44.1%	52.3%	45.7%	54.3%
13,377	DARE	5,615	2,794	2,497	324	297 R	49.8%	44.5%	52.8%	47.2%
113,162	DAVIDSON	38,269	22,794	14,579	896	8,215 R	59.6%	38.1%	61.0%	39.0%
24,599	DAVIE	9,880	6,302	3,289	289	3,013 R	63.8%	33.3%	65.7%	34.3%
40,952	DUPLIN	13,069	5,403	7,524	142	2,121 D	41.3%	57.6%	41.8%	58.2%
152,785	DURHAM	47,901	19,276	24,969	3,656	5,693 D	40.2%	52.1%	43.6%	56.4%
55,988	EDGECOMBE	14,056	5,916	7,945	195	2,029 D	42.1%	56.5%	42.7%	57.3%
243,683	FORSYTH	84,798	42,389	38,870	3,539	3,519 R	50.0%	45.8%	52.2%	47.8%
30,055	FRANKLIN	9,081	3,508	5,427	146	1,919 D	38.6%	59.8%	39.3%	60.7%
162,568	GASTON	45,204	25,139	19,016	1,049	6,123 R	55.6%	42.1%	56.9%	43.1%
8,875	GATES	3,467	957	2,435	75	1,478 D	27.6%	70.2%	28.2%	71.8%
7,217	GRAHAM	3,615	1,961	1,608	46	353 R	54.2%	44.5%	54.9%	45.1%
33,995	GRANVILLE	9,246	3,513	5,556	177	2,043 D	38.0%	60.1%	38.7%	61.3%
16,117	GREENE	5,113	2,221	2,835	57	614 D	43.4%	55.4%	43.9%	56.1%
317,154	GUILFORD	102,622	53,291	44,516	4,815	8,775 R	51.9%	43.4%	54.5%	45.5%
55,286	HALIFAX	14,648	6,033	8,364	251	2,331 D	41.2%	57.1%	41.9%	58.1%
59,570	HARNETT	16,295	7,284	8,791	220	1,507 D	44.7%	53.9%	45.3%	54.7%
46,495	HAYWOOD	17,462	7,217	9,814	431	2,597 D	41.3%	56.2%	42.4%	57.6%
58,580	HENDERSON	22,181	13,573	7,578	1,030	5,995 R	61.2%	34.2%	64.2%	35.8%
23,368	HERTFORD	6,060	1,854	4,102	104	2,248 D	30.6%	67.7%	31.1%	68.9%
20,383	HOKE	4,628	1,168	3,376	84	2,208 D	25.2%	72.9%	25.7%	74.3%
5,873	HYDE	2,072	807	1,221	44	414 D	38.9%	58.9%	39.8%	60.2%
82,538	IREDELL	27,794	14,926	12,067	801	2,859 R	53.7%	43.4%	55.3%	44.7%
25,811	JACKSON	9,310	4,140	4,857	313	717 D	44.5%	52.2%	46.0%	54.0%
70,599	JOHNSTON	20,376	10,444	9,601	331	843 R	51.3%	47.1%	52.1%	47.9%
9,705	JONES	3,630	1,401	2,198	31	797 D	38.6%	60.6%	38.9%	61.1%
36,718	LEE	10,574	4,847	5,426	301	579 D	45.8%	51.3%	47.2%	52.8%
59,819	LENOIR	17,714	9,832	7,546	336	2,286 R	55.5%	42.6%	56.6%	43.4%
42,372	LINCOLN	17,196	9,009	7,796	391	1,213 R	52.4%	45.3%	53.6%	46.4%
35,135	MCDOWELL	10,606	5,680	4,703	223	977 R	53.6%	44.3%	54.7%	45.3%
20,178	MACON	9,031	4,727	4,105	199	622 R	52.3%	45.5%	53.5%	46.5%
16,827	MADISON	5,972	2,629	3,202	141	573 D	44.0%	53.6%	45.1%	54.9%
25,948	MARTIN	7,412	2,564	4,750	98	2,186 D	34.6%	64.1%	35.1%	64.9%
404,270	MECKLENBURG	143,058	68,384	66,995	7,679	1,389 R	47.8%	46.8%	50.5%	49.5%
14,428	MITCHELL	6,270	4,322	1,765	183	2,557 R	68.9%	28.1%	71.0%	29.0%
22,469	MONTGOMERY	7,842	3,587	4,129	126	542 D	45.7%	52.7%	46.5%	53.5%
50,505	MOORE	18,911	10,158	8,084	669	2,074 R	53.7%	42.7%	55.7%	44.3%
67,153	NASH	19,601	11,043	8,184	374	2,859 R	56.3%	41.8%	57.4%	42.6%
103,471	NEW HANOVER	32,244	17,243	13,670	1,331	3,573 R	53.5%	42.4%	55.8%	44.2%
22,584	NORTHAMPTON	6,861	1,847	4,933	81	3,086 D	26.9%	71.9%	27.2%	72.8%
112,784	ONSLOW	16,736	8,861	7,371	504	1,490 R	52.9%	44.0%	54.6%	45.4%
77,055	ORANGE	28,589	9,261	15,226	4,102	5,965 D	32.4%	53.3%	37.8%	62.2%
10,398	PAMLICO	3,803	1,504	2,224	75	720 D	39.5%	58.5%	40.3%	59.7%
28,462	PASQUOTANK	7,698	3,340	4,128	230	788 D	43.4%	53.6%	44.7%	55.3%

NORTH CAROLINA

PRESIDENT 1980

1980 Census Population	County	Total Vote	Republican	Democratic	Other	Rep.-Dem. Plurality		Percentage Total Vote Rep.	Dem.	Major Vote Rep.	Dem.
22,215	PENDER	7,536	3,018	4,382	136	1,364	D	40.0%	58.1%	40.8%	59.2%
9,486	PERQUIMANS	2,854	1,210	1,560	84	350	D	42.4%	54.7%	43.7%	56.3%
29,164	PERSON	7,534	3,281	4,111	142	830	D	43.5%	54.6%	44.4%	55.6%
83,651	PITT	26,371	12,816	12,590	965	226	R	48.6%	47.7%	50.4%	49.6%
12,984	POLK	5,609	3,021	2,375	213	646	R	53.9%	42.3%	56.0%	44.0%
91,861	RANDOLPH	30,717	19,881	10,107	729	9,774	R	64.7%	32.9%	66.3%	33.7%
45,481	RICHMOND	11,609	3,911	7,416	282	3,505	D	33.7%	63.9%	34.5%	65.5%
101,577	ROBESON	25,030	6,982	17,618	430	10,636	D	27.9%	70.4%	28.4%	71.6%
83,426	ROCKINGHAM	23,522	11,205	11,708	609	503	D	47.6%	49.8%	48.9%	51.1%
99,186	ROWAN	31,109	18,566	11,671	872	6,895	R	59.7%	37.5%	61.4%	38.6%
53,787	RUTHERFORD	16,966	8,363	8,315	288	48	R	49.3%	49.0%	50.1%	49.9%
49,687	SAMPSON	17,578	8,097	9,090	391	993	D	46.1%	51.7%	47.1%	52.9%
32,273	SCOTLAND	6,782	2,133	4,446	203	2,313	D	31.5%	65.6%	32.4%	67.6%
48,517	STANLY	17,846	9,734	7,784	328	1,950	R	54.5%	43.6%	55.6%	44.4%
33,086	STOKES	13,245	7,275	5,764	206	1,511	R	54.9%	43.5%	55.8%	44.2%
59,449	SURRY	19,408	10,065	8,987	356	1,078	R	51.9%	46.3%	52.8%	47.2%
10,283	SWAIN	3,520	1,457	1,987	76	530	D	41.4%	56.4%	42.3%	57.7%
23,417	TRANSYLVANIA	9,175	4,826	4,008	341	818	R	52.6%	43.7%	54.6%	45.4%
3,975	TYRRELL	1,370	466	887	17	421	D	34.0%	64.7%	34.4%	65.6%
70,380	UNION	19,688	9,012	10,073	603	1,061	D	45.8%	51.2%	47.2%	52.8%
36,748	VANCE	9,774	4,217	5,415	142	1,198	D	43.1%	55.4%	43.8%	56.2%
300,833	WAKE	105,193	49,768	49,003	6,422	765	R	47.3%	46.6%	50.4%	49.6%
16,232	WARREN	5,430	1,582	3,750	98	2,168	D	29.1%	69.1%	29.7%	70.3%
14,801	WASHINGTON	5,037	1,943	3,008	86	1,065	D	38.6%	59.7%	39.2%	60.8%
31,678	WATAUGA	11,958	6,149	5,022	787	1,127	R	51.4%	42.0%	55.0%	45.0%
97,054	WAYNE	22,836	12,860	9,586	390	3,274	R	56.3%	42.0%	57.3%	42.7%
58,657	WILKES	23,049	14,462	8,184	403	6,278	R	62.7%	35.5%	63.9%	36.1%
63,132	WILSON	16,704	8,329	8,042	333	287	R	49.9%	48.1%	50.9%	49.1%
28,439	YADKIN	11,570	7,530	3,850	190	3,680	R	65.1%	33.3%	66.2%	33.8%
14,934	YANCEY	7,546	3,363	4,010	173	647	D	44.6%	53.1%	45.6%	54.4%
5,874,429	TOTAL	1,855,833	915,018	875,635	65,180	39,383	R	49.3%	47.2%	51.1%	48.9%

NORTH CAROLINA

GOVERNOR 1980

1980 Census Population	County	Total Vote	Republican	Democratic	Other	Rep.-Dem. Plurality	Percentage Total Vote Rep.	Dem.	Major Vote Rep.	Dem.
99,136	ALAMANCE	34,005	15,116	18,612	277	3,496 D	44.5%	54.7%	44.8%	55.2%
24,999	ALEXANDER	10,880	5,407	5,456	17	49 D	49.7%	50.1%	49.8%	50.2%
9,587	ALLEGHANY	4,255	1,696	2,553	6	857 D	39.9%	60.0%	39.9%	60.1%
25,562	ANSON	6,975	1,419	5,534	22	4,115 D	20.3%	79.3%	20.4%	79.6%
22,325	ASHE	10,227	5,083	5,115	29	32 D	49.7%	50.0%	49.8%	50.2%
14,409	AVERY	4,947	3,011	1,917	19	1,094 R	60.9%	38.8%	61.1%	38.9%
40,266	BEAUFORT	12,581	5,028	7,532	21	2,504 D	40.0%	59.9%	40.0%	60.0%
21,024	BERTIE	5,491	1,108	4,356	27	3,248 D	20.2%	79.3%	20.3%	79.7%
30,448	BLADEN	8,500	2,066	6,349	85	4,283 D	24.3%	74.7%	24.6%	75.4%
35,767	BRUNSWICK	13,016	5,159	7,758	99	2,599 D	39.6%	59.6%	39.9%	60.1%
160,934	BUNCOMBE	54,181	21,707	32,035	439	10,328 D	40.1%	59.1%	40.4%	59.6%
72,504	BURKE	25,005	11,900	12,978	127	1,078 D	47.6%	51.9%	47.8%	52.2%
85,895	CABARRUS	25,901	11,620	14,135	146	2,515 D	44.9%	54.6%	45.1%	54.9%
67,746	CALDWELL	21,602	11,238	10,283	81	955 R	52.0%	47.6%	52.2%	47.8%
5,829	CAMDEN	2,035	445	1,584	6	1,139 D	21.9%	77.8%	21.9%	78.1%
41,092	CARTERET	14,770	6,518	8,177	75	1,659 D	44.1%	55.4%	44.4%	55.6%
20,705	CASWELL	5,618	1,615	3,985	18	2,370 D	28.7%	70.9%	28.8%	71.2%
105,208	CATAWBA	36,826	18,056	18,628	142	572 D	49.0%	50.6%	49.2%	50.8%
33,415	CHATHAM	12,905	4,097	8,687	121	4,590 D	31.7%	67.3%	32.0%	68.0%
18,933	CHEROKEE	7,466	3,553	3,844	69	291 D	47.6%	51.5%	48.0%	52.0%
12,558	CHOWAN	3,743	789	2,900	54	2,111 D	21.1%	77.5%	21.4%	78.6%
6,619	CLAY	3,564	1,975	1,567	22	408 R	55.4%	44.0%	55.8%	44.2%
83,435	CLEVELAND	23,150	7,958	15,091	101	7,133 D	34.4%	65.2%	34.5%	65.5%
51,037	COLUMBUS	16,057	4,429	11,523	105	7,094 D	27.6%	71.8%	27.8%	72.2%
71,043	CRAVEN	16,848	6,115	10,658	/5	4,543 D	36.3%	63.3%	36.5%	63.5%
247,160	CUMBERLAND	44,897	15,378	29,107	412	13,729 D	34.3%	64.8%	34.6%	65.4%
11,089	CURRITUCK	3,607	928	2,667	12	1,739 D	25.7%	73.9%	25.8%	74.2%
13,377	DARE	5,390	1,521	3,822	47	2,301 D	28.2%	70.9%	28.5%	71.5%
113,162	DAVIDSON	39,677	20,069	19,414	194	655 R	50.6%	48.9%	50.8%	49.2%
24,599	DAVIE	9,707	5,220	4,455	32	765 R	53.8%	45.9%	54.0%	46.0%
40,952	DUPLIN	12,734	3,960	8,743	31	4,783 D	31.1%	68.7%	31.2%	68.8%
152,785	DURHAM	47,251	12,409	34,284	558	21,875 D	26.3%	72.6%	26.6%	73.4%
55,988	EDGECOMBE	13,767	4,076	9,635	56	5,559 D	29.6%	70.0%	29.7%	70.3%
243,683	FORSYTH	85,137	31,781	52,684	672	20,903 D	37.3%	61.9%	37.6%	62.4%
30,055	FRANKLIN	8,793	2,711	6,052	30	3,341 D	30.8%	68.8%	30.9%	69.1%
162,568	GASTON	45,512	18,494	26,775	243	8,281 D	40.6%	58.8%	40.9%	59.1%
8,875	GATES	3,297	346	2,940	11	2,594 D	10.5%	89.2%	10.5%	89.5%
7,217	GRAHAM	3,569	1,743	1,820	6	77 D	48.8%	51.0%	48.9%	51.1%
33,995	GRANVILLE	8,932	2,336	6,558	38	4,222 D	26.2%	73.4%	26.3%	73.7%
16,117	GREENE	5,129	1,537	3,584	8	2,047 D	30.0%	69.9%	30.0%	70.0%
317,154	GUILFORD	103,310	39,257	63,138	915	23,881 D	38.0%	61.1%	38.3%	61.7%
55,286	HALIFAX	14,012	4,181	9,802	29	5,621 D	29.8%	70.0%	29.9%	70.1%
59,570	HARNETT	16,690	5,796	10,819	75	5,023 D	34.7%	64.8%	34.9%	65.1%
46,495	HAYWOOD	17,076	6,562	10,456	58	3,894 D	38.4%	61.2%	38.6%	61.4%
58,580	HENDERSON	21,824	10,645	11,051	128	406 D	48.8%	50.6%	49.1%	50.9%
23,368	HERTFORD	5,954	1,011	4,920	23	3,909 D	17.0%	82.6%	17.0%	83.0%
20,383	HOKE	4,425	840	3,559	26	2,719 D	19.0%	80.4%	19.1%	80.9%
5,873	HYDE	2,029	562	1,459	8	897 D	27.7%	71.9%	27.8%	72.2%
82,538	IREDELL	27,402	11,235	16,032	135	4,797 D	41.0%	58.5%	41.2%	58.8%
25,811	JACKSON	9,600	3,661	5,892	47	2,231 D	38.1%	61.4%	38.3%	61.7%
70,599	JOHNSTON	20,406	7,598	12,709	99	5,111 D	37.2%	62.3%	37.4%	62.6%
9,705	JONES	3,534	1,057	2,470	7	1,413 D	29.9%	69.9%	30.0%	70.0%
36,718	LEE	10,681	3,365	7,256	60	3,891 D	31.5%	67.9%	31.7%	68.3%
59,819	LENOIR	17,143	6,779	10,320	44	3,541 D	39.5%	60.2%	39.6%	60.4%
42,372	LINCOLN	16,948	7,400	9,491	57	2,091 D	43.7%	56.0%	43.8%	56.2%
35,135	MCDOWELL	11,017	4,917	6,048	52	1,131 D	44.6%	54.9%	44.8%	55.2%
20,178	MACON	8,834	3,996	4,800	38	804 D	45.2%	54.3%	45.4%	54.6%
16,827	MADISON	5,983	2,261	3,692	30	1,431 D	37.8%	61.7%	38.0%	62.0%
25,948	MARTIN	7,455	1,855	5,561	39	3,706 D	24.9%	74.6%	25.0%	75.0%
404,270	MECKLENBURG	140,431	42,662	96,365	1,404	53,703 D	30.4%	68.6%	30.7%	69.3%
14,428	MITCHELL	6,029	3,866	2,130	33	1,736 R	64.1%	35.3%	64.5%	35.5%
22,469	MONTGOMERY	7,855	2,926	4,916	13	1,990 D	37.3%	62.6%	37.3%	62.7%
50,505	MOORE	18,624	8,150	10,405	69	2,255 D	43.8%	55.9%	43.9%	56.1%
67,153	NASH	19,731	7,791	11,838	102	4,047 D	39.5%	60.0%	39.7%	60.3%
103,471	NEW HANOVER	31,776	11,391	20,099	286	8,708 D	35.8%	63.3%	36.2%	63.8%
22,584	NORTHAMPTON	6,920	1,158	5,722	40	4,564 D	16.7%	82.7%	16.8%	83.2%
112,784	ONSLOW	16,885	6,564	10,173	148	3,609 D	38.9%	60.2%	39.2%	60.8%
77,055	ORANGE	27,756	6,216	20,925	615	14,709 D	22.4%	75.4%	22.9%	77.1%
10,398	PAMLICO	3,690	1,204	2,464	22	1,260 D	32.6%	66.8%	32.8%	67.2%
28,462	PASQUOTANK	7,594	1,748	5,819	27	4,071 D	23.0%	76.6%	23.1%	76.9%

NORTH CAROLINA

GOVERNOR 1980

1980 Census Population	County	Total Vote	Republican	Democratic	Other	Rep.-Dem. Plurality		Percentage Total Vote Rep.	Dem.	Major Vote Rep.	Dem.
22,215	PENDER	7,270	2,361	4,877	32	2,516	D	32.5%	67.1%	32.6%	67.4%
9,486	PERQUIMANS	2,617	503	2,106	8	1,603	D	19.2%	80.5%	19.3%	80.7%
29,164	PERSON	7,531	2,305	5,165	61	2,860	D	30.6%	68.6%	30.9%	69.1%
83,651	PITT	24,877	7,312	17,442	123	10,130	D	29.4%	70.1%	29.5%	70.5%
12,984	POLK	6,201	2,755	3,400	46	645	D	44.4%	54.8%	44.8%	55.2%
91,861	RANDOLPH	31,098	16,283	14,668	147	1,615	R	52.4%	47.2%	52.6%	47.4%
45,481	RICHMOND	11,533	3,034	8,427	72	5,393	D	26.3%	73.1%	26.5%	73.5%
101,577	ROBESON	25,691	6,270	19,169	252	12,899	D	24.4%	74.6%	24.6%	75.4%
83,426	ROCKINGHAM	21,777	8,376	13,250	151	4,874	D	38.5%	60.8%	38.7%	61.3%
99,186	ROWAN	31,727	15,052	16,495	180	1,443	D	47.4%	52.0%	47.7%	52.3%
53,787	RUTHERFORD	17,086	6,662	10,326	98	3,664	D	39.0%	60.4%	39.2%	60.8%
49,687	SAMPSON	17,283	6,609	10,618	56	4,009	D	38.2%	61.4%	38.4%	61.6%
32,273	SCOTLAND	6,669	1,445	5,178	46	3,733	D	21.7%	77.6%	21.8%	78.2%
48,517	STANLY	18,348	8,656	9,634	58	978	D	47.2%	52.5%	47.3%	52.7%
33,086	STOKES	13,089	6,209	6,833	47	624	D	47.4%	52.2%	47.6%	52.4%
59,449	SURRY	20,078	8,385	11,608	85	3,223	D	41.8%	57.8%	41.9%	58.1%
10,283	SWAIN	3,895	1,449	2,430	16	981	D	37.2%	62.4%	37.4%	62.6%
23,417	TRANSYLVANIA	9,201	3,876	5,205	120	1,329	D	42.1%	56.6%	42.7%	57.3%
3,975	TYRRELL	1,315	264	1,048	3	784	D	20.1%	79.7%	20.1%	79.9%
70,380	UNION	19,093	6,390	12,619	84	6,229	D	33.5%	66.1%	33.6%	66.4%
36,748	VANCE	10,160	2,944	7,156	60	4,212	D	29.0%	70.4%	29.1%	70.9%
300,833	WAKE	106,795	33,629	71,896	1,270	38,267	D	31.5%	67.3%	31.9%	68.1%
16,232	WARREN	5,219	1,440	3,751	28	2,311	D	27.6%	71.9%	27.7%	72.3%
14,801	WASHINGTON	4,906	1,356	3,536	14	2,180	D	27.6%	72.1%	27.7%	72.3%
31,678	WATAUGA	12,233	5,470	6,565	198	1,095	D	44.7%	53.7%	45.5%	54.5%
97,054	WAYNE	22,729	8,393	14,193	143	5,800	D	36.9%	62.4%	37.2%	62.8%
58,657	WILKES	23,593	13,267	10,219	107	3,048	R	56.2%	43.3%	56.5%	43.5%
63,132	WILSON	16,971	4,611	12,243	117	7,632	D	27.2%	72.1%	27.4%	72.6%
28,439	YADKIN	11,440	6,612	4,803	25	1,809	R	57.8%	42.0%	57.9%	42.1%
14,934	YANCEY	7,446	3,260	4,157	29	897	D	43.8%	55.8%	44.0%	56.0%
5,874,429	TOTAL	1,847,432	691,449	1,143,145	12,838	451,696	D	37.4%	61.9%	37.7%	62.3%

NORTH CAROLINA

SENATOR 1980

1980 Census Population	County	Total Vote	Republican	Democratic	Other	Rep.-Dem. Plurality	Percentage			
							Total Vote		Major Vote	
							Rep.	Dem.	Rep.	Dem.
99,136	ALAMANCE	32,685	18,838	13,632	215	5,206 R	57.6%	41.7%	58.0%	42.0%
24,999	ALEXANDER	10,739	6,399	4,324	16	2,075 R	59.6%	40.3%	59.7%	40.3%
9,587	ALLEGHANY	4,172	1,915	2,251	6	336 D	45.9%	54.0%	46.0%	54.0%
25,562	ANSON	6,817	1,779	5,021	17	3,242 D	26.1%	73.7%	26.2%	73.8%
22,325	ASHE	10,149	5,527	4,598	24	929 R	54.5%	45.3%	54.6%	45.4%
14,409	AVERY	4,748	3,218	1,512	18	1,706 R	67.8%	31.8%	68.0%	32.0%
40,266	BEAUFORT	12,602	6,339	6,241	22	98 R	50.3%	49.5%	50.4%	49.6%
21,024	BERTIE	4,888	1,458	3,406	24	1,948 D	29.8%	69.7%	30.0%	70.0%
30,448	BLADEN	8,020	2,510	5,433	77	2,923 D	31.3%	67.7%	31.6%	68.4%
35,767	BRUNSWICK	12,252	5,865	6,285	102	420 D	47.9%	51.3%	48.3%	51.7%
160,934	BUNCOMBE	52,836	27,038	25,374	424	1,664 R	51.2%	48.0%	51.6%	48.4%
72,504	BURKE	24,206	13,604	10,533	69	3,071 R	56.2%	43.5%	56.4%	43.6%
85,895	CABARRUS	25,614	15,495	9,963	156	5,532 R	60.5%	38.9%	60.9%	39.1%
67,746	CALDWELL	21,119	12,902	8,156	61	4,746 R	61.1%	38.6%	61.3%	38.7%
5,829	CAMDEN	1,977	505	1,467	5	962 D	25.5%	74.2%	25.6%	74.4%
41,092	CARTERET	14,636	7,619	6,938	79	681 R	52.1%	47.4%	52.3%	47.7%
20,705	CASWELL	5,442	1,969	3,452	21	1,483 D	36.2%	63.4%	36.3%	63.7%
105,208	CATAWBA	36,175	22,609	13,452	114	9,157 R	62.5%	37.2%	62.7%	37.3%
33,415	CHATHAM	12,699	5,426	7,188	85	1,762 D	42.7%	56.6%	43.0%	57.0%
18,933	CHEROKEE	7,146	3,661	3,431	54	230 R	51.2%	48.0%	51.6%	48.4%
12,558	CHOWAN	3,415	1,104	2,270	41	1,166 D	32.3%	66.5%	32.7%	67.3%
6,619	CLAY	3,536	2,011	1,513	12	498 R	56.9%	42.8%	57.1%	42.9%
83,435	CLEVELAND	22,467	11,480	10,877	110	603 R	51.1%	48.4%	51.3%	48.7%
51,037	COLUMBUS	16,463	6,083	10,281	99	4,198 D	36.9%	62.4%	37.2%	62.8%
71,043	CRAVEN	16,223	8,158	7,974	91	184 R	50.3%	49.2%	50.6%	49.4%
247,160	CUMBERLAND	43,811	20,601	22,810	400	2,209 D	47.0%	52.1%	47.5%	52.5%
11,089	CURRITUCK	3,507	934	2,565	8	1,631 D	26.6%	73.1%	26.7%	73.3%
13,377	DARE	5,262	1,921	3,302	39	1,381 D	36.5%	62.8%	36.8%	63.2%
113,162	DAVIDSON	39,326	23,731	15,362	233	8,369 R	60.3%	39.1%	60.7%	39.3%
24,599	DAVIE	9,566	6,115	3,425	26	2,690 R	63.9%	35.8%	64.1%	35.9%
40,952	DUPLIN	12,581	5,124	7,447	10	2,323 D	40.7%	59.2%	40.8%	59.2%
152,785	DURHAM	45,636	18,861	26,112	663	7,251 D	41.3%	57.2%	41.9%	58.1%
55,988	EDGECOMBE	13,380	5,470	7,867	43	2,397 D	40.9%	58.8%	41.0%	59.0%
243,683	FORSYTH	84,139	43,156	40,309	674	2,847 R	51.3%	47.9%	51.7%	48.3%
30,055	FRANKLIN	8,622	3,626	4,977	19	1,351 D	42.1%	57.7%	42.1%	57.9%
162,568	GASTON	44,276	26,017	17,998	261	8,019 R	58.8%	40.6%	59.1%	40.9%
8,875	GATES	3,129	381	2,742	6	2,361 D	12.2%	87.6%	12.2%	87.8%
7,217	GRAHAM	3,523	1,816	1,701	6	115 R	51.5%	48.3%	51.6%	48.4%
33,995	GRANVILLE	8,699	3,282	5,393	24	2,111 D	37.7%	62.0%	37.8%	62.2%
16,117	GREENE	4,946	2,014	2,928	4	914 D	40.7%	59.2%	40.8%	59.2%
317,154	GUILFORD	102,123	54,183	47,090	850	7,093 R	53.1%	46.1%	53.5%	46.5%
55,286	HALIFAX	13,954	5,695	8,231	28	2,536 D	40.8%	59.0%	40.9%	59.1%
59,570	HARNETT	16,453	6,540	9,863	50	3,323 D	39.7%	59.9%	39.9%	60.1%
46,495	HAYWOOD	16,873	7,557	9,276	40	1,719 D	44.8%	55.0%	44.9%	55.1%
58,580	HENDERSON	21,052	12,851	8,070	131	4,781 R	61.0%	38.3%	61.4%	38.6%
23,368	HERTFORD	5,234	1,252	3,951	31	2,699 D	23.9%	75.5%	24.1%	75.9%
20,383	HOKE	4,395	1,166	3,217	12	2,051 D	26.5%	73.2%	26.6%	73.4%
5,873	HYDE	2,013	711	1,295	7	584 D	35.3%	64.3%	35.4%	64.6%
82,538	IREDELL	26,875	14,988	11,775	112	3,213 R	55.8%	43.8%	56.0%	44.0%
25,811	JACKSON	9,340	4,119	5,154	67	1,035 D	44.1%	55.2%	44.4%	55.6%
70,599	JOHNSTON	19,622	10,109	9,434	79	675 R	51.5%	48.1%	51.7%	48.3%
9,705	JONES	3,462	1,327	2,134	1	807 D	38.3%	61.6%	38.3%	61.7%
36,718	LEE	9,928	4,950	4,905	73	45 R	49.9%	49.4%	50.2%	49.8%
59,819	LENOIR	16,889	8,938	7,912	39	1,026 R	52.9%	46.8%	53.0%	47.0%
42,372	LINCOLN	16,826	8,855	7,924	47	931 R	52.6%	47.1%	52.8%	47.2%
35,135	MCDOWELL	10,992	5,934	5,009	49	925 R	54.0%	45.6%	54.2%	45.8%
20,178	MACON	8,732	4,457	4,247	28	210 R	51.0%	48.6%	51.2%	48.8%
16,827	MADISON	5,740	2,399	3,302	39	903 D	41.8%	57.5%	42.1%	57.9%
25,948	MARTIN	7,166	2,443	4,694	29	2,251 D	34.1%	65.5%	34.2%	65.8%
404,270	MECKLENBURG	131,987	64,309	66,396	1,282	2,087 D	48.7%	50.3%	49.2%	50.8%
14,428	MITCHELL	5,938	4,156	1,762	20	2,394 R	70.0%	29.7%	70.2%	29.8%
22,469	MONTGOMERY	7,708	3,467	4,234	7	767 D	45.0%	54.9%	45.0%	55.0%
50,505	MOORE	18,347	10,043	8,251	53	1,792 R	54.7%	45.0%	54.9%	45.1%
67,153	NASH	19,042	10,656	8,311	75	2,345 R	56.0%	43.6%	56.2%	43.8%
103,471	NEW HANOVER	29,267	15,475	13,524	268	1,951 R	52.9%	46.2%	53.4%	46.6%
22,584	NORTHAMPTON	6,214	1,453	4,739	22	3,286 D	23.4%	76.3%	23.5%	76.5%
112,784	ONSLOW	16,835	9,288	7,396	151	1,892 R	55.2%	43.9%	55.7%	44.3%
77,055	ORANGE	27,283	9,320	17,377	586	8,057 D	34.2%	63.7%	34.9%	65.1%
10,398	PAMLICO	3,567	1,361	2,194	12	833 D	38.2%	61.5%	38.3%	61.7%
28,462	PASQUOTANK	6,569	2,206	4,319	44	2,113 D	33.6%	65.7%	33.8%	66.2%

NORTH CAROLINA

SENATOR 1980

1980 Census Population	County	Total Vote	Republican	Democratic	Other	Rep.-Dem. Plurality	Percentage			
							Total Vote		Major Vote	
							Rep.	Dem.	Rep.	Dem.
22,215	PENDER	7,039	2,784	4,242	13	1,458 D	39.6%	60.3%	39.6%	60.4%
9,486	PERQUIMANS	2,702	705	1,980	17	1,275 D	26.1%	73.3%	26.3%	73.7%
29,164	PERSON	6,806	3,471	3,260	75	211 R	51.0%	47.9%	51.6%	48.4%
83,651	PITT	24,341	11,657	12,604	80	947 D	47.9%	51.8%	48.0%	52.0%
12,984	POLK	6,012	3,086	2,884	42	202 R	51.3%	48.0%	51.7%	48.3%
91,861	RANDOLPH	30,551	19,575	10,822	154	8,753 R	64.1%	35.4%	64.4%	35.6%
45,481	RICHMOND	10,973	4,106	6,815	52	2,709 D	37.4%	62.1%	37.6%	62.4%
101,577	ROBESON	24,668	7,484	17,003	181	9,519 D	30.3%	68.9%	30.6%	69.4%
83,426	ROCKINGHAM	21,359	10,294	10,918	147	624 D	48.2%	51.1%	48.5%	51.5%
99,186	ROWAN	31,531	19,302	12,015	214	7,287 R	61.2%	38.1%	61.6%	38.4%
53,787	RUTHERFORD	16,951	8,564	8,272	115	292 R	50.5%	48.8%	50.9%	49.1%
49,687	SAMPSON	17,081	7,494	9,546	41	2,052 D	43.9%	55.9%	44.0%	56.0%
32,273	SCOTLAND	6,265	2,151	4,079	35	1,928 D	34.3%	65.1%	34.5%	65.5%
48,517	STANLY	18,286	10,415	7,809	62	2,606 R	57.0%	42.7%	57.1%	42.9%
33,086	STOKES	12,962	7,114	5,807	41	1,307 R	54.9%	44.8%	55.1%	44.9%
59,449	SURRY	19,539	10,055	9,398	86	657 R	51.5%	48.1%	51.7%	48.3%
10,283	SWAIN	3,797	1,673	2,110	14	437 D	44.1%	55.6%	44.2%	55.8%
23,417	TRANSYLVANIA	8,811	4,646	4,076	89	570 R	52.7%	46.3%	53.3%	46.7%
3,975	TYRRELL	1,266	357	906	3	549 D	28.2%	71.6%	28.3%	71.7%
70,380	UNION	18,767	8,984	9,726	57	742 D	47.9%	51.8%	48.0%	52.0%
36,748	VANCE	10,094	4,332	5,708	54	1,376 D	42.9%	56.5%	43.1%	56.9%
300,833	WAKE	104,148	48,663	54,343	1,142	5,680 D	46.7%	52.2%	47.2%	52.8%
16,232	WARREN	4,903	1,590	3,296	17	1,706 D	32.4%	67.2%	32.5%	67.5%
14,801	WASHINGTON	4,895	1,858	3,033	4	1,175 D	38.0%	62.0%	38.0%	62.0%
31,678	WATAUGA	12,115	6,353	5,527	235	826 R	52.4%	45.6%	53.5%	46.5%
97,054	WAYNE	22,009	11,758	10,120	131	1,638 R	53.4%	46.0%	53.7%	46.3%
58,657	WILKES	23,431	14,604	8,724	103	5,880 R	62.3%	37.2%	62.6%	37.4%
63,132	WILSON	15,815	7,524	8,182	109	658 D	47.6%	51.7%	47.9%	52.1%
28,439	YADKIN	11,281	7,347	3,919	15	3,428 R	65.1%	34.7%	65.2%	34.8%
14,934	YANCEY	7,412	3,349	4,033	30	684 D	45.2%	54.4%	45.4%	54.6%
5,874,429	TOTAL	1,797,665	898,064	887,653	11,948	10,411 R	50.0%	49.4%	50.3%	49.7%

NORTH CAROLINA

CONGRESS

CD	Year	Total Vote	Republican Vote	Republican Candidate	Democratic Vote	Democratic Candidate	Other Vote	Rep.-Dem. Plurality	Total Vote Rep.	Total Vote Dem.	Major Vote Rep.	Major Vote Dem.
1	1980	108,738			108,738	JONES, WALTER B.		108,738 D		100.0%		100.0%
1	1978	84,530	16,814	NEWCOMB, JAMES M.	67,716	JONES, WALTER B.		50,902 D	19.9%	80.1%	19.9%	80.1%
1	1976	129,964	29,295	WARD, JOSEPH M.	98,611	JONES, WALTER B.	2,058	69,316 D	22.5%	75.9%	22.9%	77.1%
1	1974	71,420	16,097	MCMULLAN, HARRY	55,323	JONES, WALTER B.		39,226 D	22.5%	77.5%	22.5%	77.5%
1	1972	112,501	35,063	BONNER, J. JORDAN	77,438	JONES, WALTER B.		42,375 D	31.2%	68.8%	31.2%	68.8%
2	1980	135,243	35,946	GARDNER, BARRY L.	99,297	FOUNTAIN, L. H.		63,351 D	26.6%	73.4%	26.6%	73.4%
2	1978	79,053	15,988	GARDNER, BARRY L.	61,851	FOUNTAIN, L. H.	1,214	45,863 D	20.2%	78.2%	20.5%	79.5%
2	1976	113,561			113,368	FOUNTAIN, L. H.	193	113,368 D		99.8%		100.0%
2	1974	52,786			52,786	FOUNTAIN, L. H.		52,786 D		100.0%		100.0%
2	1972	123,991	35,193	LITTLE, ERICK P.	88,798	FOUNTAIN, L. H.		53,605 D	28.4%	71.6%	28.4%	71.6%
3	1980	124,255	39,393	PARKER, LARRY J.	84,862	WHITLEY, CHARLES		45,469 D	31.7%	68.3%	31.7%	68.3%
3	1978	76,602	22,150	BLANCHARD, WILLARD J.	54,452	WHITLEY, CHARLES		32,302 D	28.9%	71.1%	28.9%	71.1%
3	1976	112,286	35,089	BLANCHARD, WILLARD J.	77,193	WHITLEY, CHARLES	4	42,104 D	31.2%	68.7%	31.3%	68.7%
3	1974	50,931			50,931	HENDERSON, DAVID N.		50,931 D		100.0%		100.0%
3	1972	56,968			56,968	HENDERSON, DAVID N.		56,968 D		100.0%		100.0%
4	1980	184,631	84,631	HOGAN, THURMAN	97,167	ANDREWS, IKE F.	2,833	12,536 D	45.8%	52.6%	46.6%	53.4%
4	1978	78,685			74,249	ANDREWS, IKE F.	4,436	74,249 D		94.4%		100.0%
4	1976	152,100	59,917	GALLEMORE, JOHNNIE L.	92,165	ANDREWS, IKE F.	18	32,248 D	39.4%	60.6%	39.4%	60.6%
4	1974	96,791	33,521	PURRINGTON, WARD	62,600	ANDREWS, IKE F.	670	29,079 D	34.6%	64.7%	34.9%	65.1%
4	1972	145,044	71,972	HAWKE, JIM	73,072	ANDREWS, IKE F.		1,100 D	49.6%	50.4%	49.6%	50.4%
5	1980	194,338	94,894	BAGNAL, ANNE	99,117	NEAL, STEPHEN L.	327	4,223 D	48.8%	51.0%	48.9%	51.1%
5	1978	126,939	58,161	HORTON, HAMILTON C.	68,778	NEAL, STEPHEN L.		10,617 D	45.8%	54.2%	45.8%	54.2%
5	1976	182,166	83,129	MIZELL, WILMER D.	98,789	NEAL, STEPHEN L.	248	15,660 D	45.6%	54.2%	45.7%	54.3%
5	1974	124,241	59,182	MIZELL, WILMER D.	64,634	NEAL, STEPHEN L.	425	5,452 D	47.6%	52.0%	47.8%	52.2%
5	1972	156,361	101,375	MIZELL, WILMER D.	54,986	HAYS, BROOKS		46,389 R	64.8%	35.2%	64.8%	35.2%
6	1980	157,232	80,275	JOHNSTON, EUGENE	76,957	PREYER, L. RICHARDSON		3,318 R	51.1%	48.9%	51.1%	48.9%
6	1978	85,075	26,882	BEMUS, GEORGE H.	58,193	PREYER, L. RICHARDSON		31,311 D	31.6%	68.4%	31.6%	68.4%
6	1976	107,812			103,851	PREYER, L. RICHARDSON	3,961	103,851 D		96.3%		100.0%
6	1974	88,764	31,906	RITCHIE, R. S.	56,507	PREYER, L. RICHARDSON	351	24,601 D	35.9%	63.7%	36.1%	63.9%
6	1972	87,489			82,158	PREYER, L. RICHARDSON	5,331	82,158 D		93.9%		100.0%
7	1980	128,834	40,270	WRIGHT, VIVIAN S.	88,564	ROSE, CHARLES G.		48,294 D	31.3%	68.7%	31.3%	68.7%
7	1978	76,842	23,146	SCHRUMP, RAYMOND C.	53,696	ROSE, CHARLES G.		30,550 D	30.1%	69.9%	30.1%	69.9%
7	1976	117,419	21,955	VAUGHAN, M. H.	95,463	ROSE, CHARLES G.	1	73,508 D	18.7%	81.3%	18.7%	81.3%
7	1974	49,780			49,780	ROSE, CHARLES G.		49,780 D		100.0%		100.0%
7	1972	94,937	36,726	SCOTT, JERRY C.	57,348	ROSE, CHARLES G.	863	20,622 D	38.7%	60.4%	39.0%	61.0%
8	1980	162,330	67,317	HARRIS, LARRY E.	95,013	HEFNER, W. G.		27,696 D	41.5%	58.5%	41.5%	58.5%
8	1978	107,110	43,942	AUSTIN, ROGER L.	63,168	HEFNER, W. G.		19,226 D	41.0%	59.0%	41.0%	59.0%
8	1976	151,081	49,094	EAGLE, CARL	99,296	HEFNER, W. G.	2,691	50,202 D	32.5%	65.7%	33.1%	66.9%
8	1974	108,091	46,500	RUTH, EARL B.	61,591	HEFNER, W. G.		15,091 D	43.0%	57.0%	43.0%	57.0%
8	1972	136,258	82,060	RUTH, EARL B.	54,198	CLARK, RICHARD		27,862 R	60.2%	39.8%	60.2%	39.8%
9	1980	172,660	101,156	MARTIN, JAMES G.	71,504	KINCAID, RANDALL R.		29,652 R	58.6%	41.4%	58.6%	41.4%
9	1978	96,824	66,157	MARTIN, JAMES G.	29,761	MAXWELL, CHARLES K.	906	36,396 R	68.3%	30.7%	69.0%	31.0%
9	1976	153,796	82,297	MARTIN, JAMES G.	70,847	GOODMAN, ARTHUR	652	11,450 R	53.5%	46.1%	53.7%	46.3%
9	1974	93,877	51,032	MARTIN, JAMES G.	41,387	SHORT, MILTON	1,458	9,645 R	54.4%	44.1%	55.2%	44.8%
9	1972	136,527	80,356	MARTIN, JAMES G.	56,171	BEATTY, JAMES		24,185 R	58.9%	41.1%	58.9%	41.1%
10	1980	173,262	120,777	BROYHILL, JAMES T.	52,485	ICENHOUR, JAMES O.		68,292 R	69.7%	30.3%	69.7%	30.3%
10	1978	67,004	67,004	BROYHILL, JAMES T.				67,004 R	100.0%		100.0%	
10	1976	167,072	99,882	BROYHILL, JAMES T.	67,190	HUNT, JOHN J.		32,692 R	59.8%	40.2%	59.8%	40.2%
10	1974	116,513	63,382	BROYHILL, JAMES T.	53,131	RHYNE, JACK L.		10,251 R	54.4%	45.6%	54.4%	45.6%
10	1972	142,144	103,119	BROYHILL, JAMES T.	39,025	BECK, PAUL L.		64,094 R	72.5%	27.5%	72.5%	27.5%
11	1980	195,274	104,485	HENDON, WILLIAM M.	90,789	GUDGER, LAMAR		13,696 R	53.5%	46.5%	53.5%	46.5%
11	1978	141,292	65,832	RATCLIFF, R. CURTIS	75,460	GUDGER, LAMAR		9,628 D	46.6%	53.4%	46.6%	53.4%
11	1976	184,421	88,752	BRIGGS, BRUCE	93,857	GUDGER, LAMAR	1,812	5,105 D	48.1%	50.9%	48.6%	51.4%
11	1974	135,146	45,983	GILMAN, ALBERT F.	89,163	TAYLOR, ROY A.		43,180 D	34.0%	66.0%	34.0%	66.0%
11	1972	158,527	64,062	LEDBETTER, JESSE I.	94,465	TAYLOR, ROY A.		30,403 D	40.4%	59.6%	40.4%	59.6%

NORTH CAROLINA

1980 GENERAL ELECTION

President   Other vote was 52,800 Anderson (Independent); 9,677 Clark (Libertarian); 2,287 Commoner (Citizens); 416 DeBerry (Socialist Workers).

Governor   Other vote was 9,951 Emory (Libertarian); 2,887 Cooper (Socialist Workers).

Senator   Other vote was 7,602 Pasotto (Libertarian); 4,346 Finch (Socialist Workers).

Congress   Other vote was Cunningham (Libertarian) in CD 4; Miller (Socialist Workers) in CD 5.

1980 PRIMARIES

MAY 6 REPUBLICAN

Governor   119,255 Beverly Lake; 28,354 C. J. Carstens.

Senator   John P. East, unopposed.

Congress   Unopposed in ten CD's. No candidate in CD 1.

MAY 6 DEMOCRATIC

Governor   524, 844 James B. Hunt; 217,289 Robert W. Scott; 11,551 Harry J. Welsh.

Senator   Robert Morgan, unopposed.

Congress   Unopposed in five CD's. Contested as follows:

CD 1   66,382 Walter B. Jones; 17,170 Joseph B. Hollowell.
CD 3   53,337 Charles Whitley; 7,127 Larry Turlington; 6,578 Jimmy Hatcher.
CD 4   58,370 Ike F. Andrews; 10,008 Geoffrey E. Gadsden; 7,809 Joseph R. Overby.
CD 6   44,278 L. Richardson Preyer; 11,105 J. R. Washington.
CD 7   56,749 Charles G. Rose; 14,029 Lynn Batson.
CD 8   45,794 W. G. Hefner; 11,156 Edward Sweet; 5,085 John E. Gray.

NORTH DAKOTA

GOVERNOR
Allen I. Olson (R). Elected 1980 to a four-year term.

SENATORS
Mark Andrews (R). Elected 1980 to a six-year term.

Quentin N. Burdick (D). Re-elected 1976 to a six-year term. Previously elected 1970, 1964, and in June 1960 to fill out term vacated by the death of Senator William Langer.

REPRESENTATIVE
At-Large. Byron L. Dorgan (D)

POSTWAR VOTE FOR GOVERNOR

| | | Republican | | Democratic | | | | Percentage | | | |
| | Total | | | | | Other | Rep.-Dem. | Total Vote | | Major Vote | |
Year	Vote	Vote	Candidate	Vote	Candidate	Vote	Plurality	Rep.	Dem.	Rep.	Dem.
1980	302,621	162,230	Olson, Allen I.	140,391	Link, Arthur A.	—	21,839 R	53.6%	46.4%	53.6%	46.4%
1976	297,249	138,321	Elkin, Richard	153,309	Link, Arthur A.	5,619	14,988 D	46.5%	51.6%	47.4%	52.6%
1972	281,931	138,032	Larsen, Richard	143,899	Link, Arthur A.	—	5,867 D	49.0%	51.0%	49.0%	51.0%
1968	248,000	108,382	McCarney, Robert P.	135,955	Guy, William L.	3,663	27,573 D	43.7%	54.8%	44.4%	55.6%
1964	262,661	116,247	Halcrow, Donald M.	146,414	Guy, William L.	—	30,167 D	44.3%	55.7%	44.3%	55.7%
1962	228,509	113,251	Andrews, Mark	115,258	Guy, William L.	—	2,007 D	49.6%	50.4%	49.6%	50.4%
1960	275,375	122,486	Dahl, C. P.	136,148	Guy, William L.	16,741	13,662 D	44.5%	49.4%	47.4%	52.6%
1958	210,599	111,836	Davis, John E.	98,763	Lord, John F.	—	13,073 R	53.1%	46.9%	53.1%	46.9%
1956	252,435	147,566	Davis, John E.	104,869	Warner, Wallace E.	—	42,697 R	58.5%	41.5%	58.5%	41.5%
1954	193,501	124,253	Brunsdale, C. Norman	69,248	Bymers, Cornelius	—	55,005 R	64.2%	35.8%	64.2%	35.8%
1952	253,934	199,944	Brunsdale, C. Norman	53,990	Johnson, Ole C.	—	145,954 R	78.7%	21.3%	78.7%	21.3%
1950	183,772	121,822	Brunsdale, C. Norman	61,950	Byerly, Clyde G.	—	59,872 R	66.3%	33.7%	66.3%	33.7%
1948	214,858	131,764	Aandahl, Fred G.	80,555	Henry, Howard	2,539	51,209 R	61.3%	37.5%	62.1%	37.9%
1946	169,391	116,672	Aandahl, Fred G.	52,719	Burdick, Quentin N.	—	63,953 R	68.9%	31.1%	68.9%	31.1%

The term of office of North Dakota's Governor was increased from two to four years effective with the 1964 election.

POSTWAR VOTE FOR SENATOR

| | | Republican | | Democratic | | | | Percentage | | | |
| | Total | | | | | Other | Rep.-Dem. | Total Vote | | Major Vote | |
Year	Vote	Vote	Candidate	Vote	Candidate	Vote	Plurality	Rep.	Dem.	Rep.	Dem.
1980	299,272	210,347	Andrews, Mark	86,658	Johanneson, Kent	2,267	123,689 R	70.3%	29.0%	70.8%	29.2%
1976	283,062	103,466	Stroup, Richard	175,772	Burdick, Quentin N.	3,824	72,306 D	36.6%	62.1%	37.1%	62.9%
1974	235,661	114,117	Young, Milton R.	113,931	Guy, William L.	7,613	186 R	48.4%	48.3%	50.0%	50.0%
1970	219,560	82,996	Kleppe, Tom	134,519	Burdick, Quentin N.	2,045	51,523 D	37.8%	61.3%	38.2%	61.8%
1968	239,776	154,968	Young, Milton R.	80,815	Lashkowitz, Herschel	3,993	74,153 R	64.6%	33.7%	65.7%	34.3%
1964	258,945	109,681	Kleppe, Tom	149,264	Burdick, Quentin N.	—	39,583 D	42.4%	57.6%	42.4%	57.6%
1962	223,737	135,705	Young, Milton R.	88,032	Lanier, William	—	47,673 R	60.7%	39.3%	60.7%	39.3%
1960s	210,349	103,475	Davis, John E.	104,593	Burdick, Quentin N.	2,281	1,118 D	49.2%	49.7%	49.7%	50.3%
1958	204,635	117,070	Langer, William	84,892	Vendsel, Raymond	2,673	32,178 R	57.2%	41.5%	58.0%	42.0%
1956	244,161	155,305	Young, Milton R.	87,919	Burdick, Quentin N.	937	67,386 R	63.6%	36.0%	63.9%	36.1%
1952	237,995	157,907	Langer, William	55,347	Morrison, Harold A.	24,741	102,560 R	66.3%	23.3%	74.0%	26.0%
1950	186,716	126,209	Young, Milton R.	60,507	O'Brien, Harry	—	65,702 R	67.6%	32.4%	67.6%	32.4%
1946	165,382	88,210	Langer, William	38,368	Larson, Abner B.	38,804	49,842 R	53.3%	23.2%	69.7%	30.3%
1946s	136,852	75,998	Young, Milton R.	37,507	Lanier, William	23,347	38,491 R	55.5%	27.4%	67.0%	33.0%

The 1960 and 1946 special elections were held in June for short terms to fill vacancies.

NORTH DAKOTA

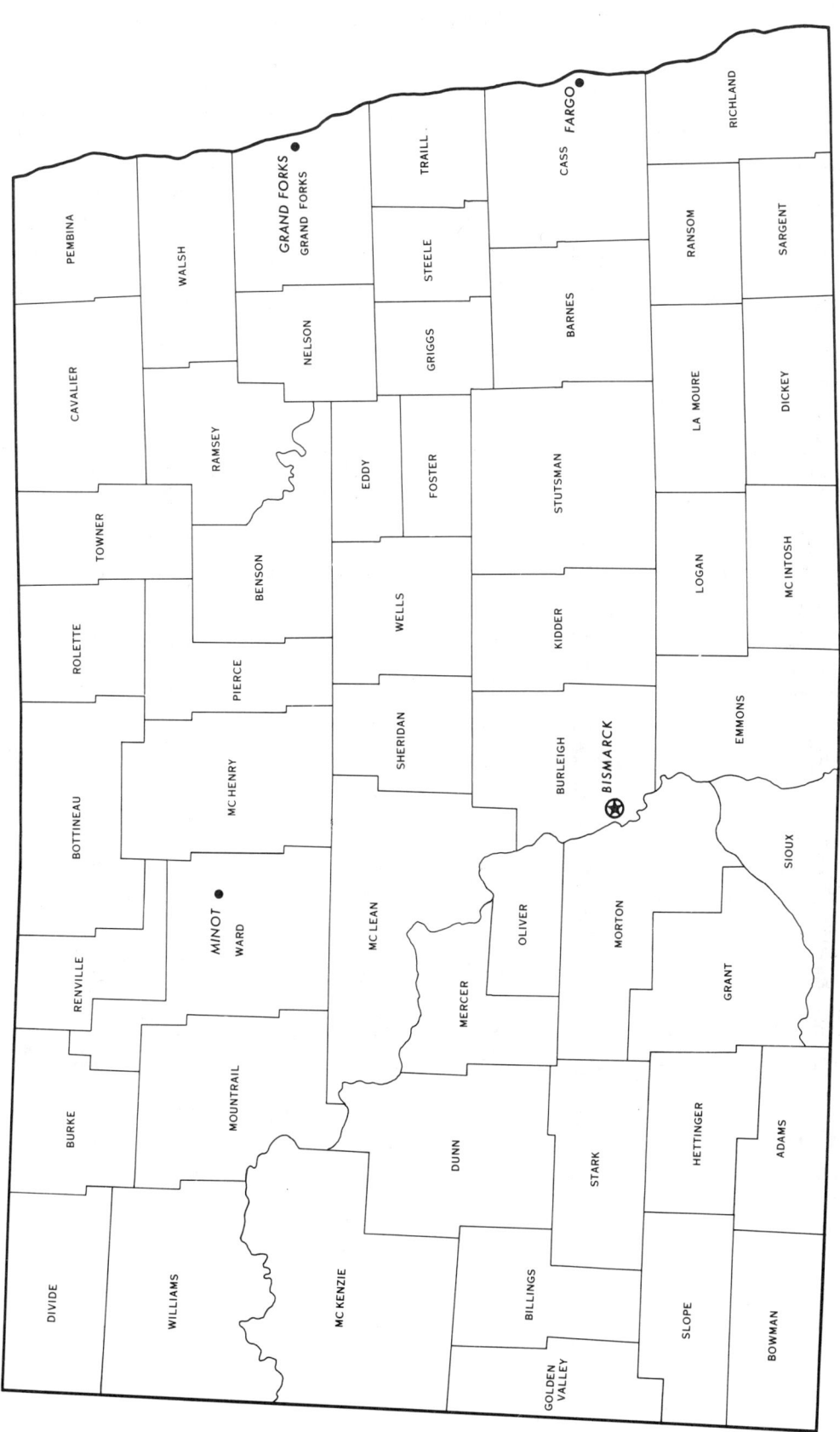

NORTH DAKOTA

PRESIDENT 1980

1980 Census Population	County	Total Vote	Republican	Democratic	Other	Rep.-Dem. Plurality	Percentage			
							Total Vote		Major Vote	
							Rep.	Dem.	Rep.	Dem.
3,584	ADAMS	1,941	1,334	470	137	864 R	68.7%	24.2%	73.9%	26.1%
13,960	BARNES	7,346	4,392	2,128	826	2,264 R	59.8%	29.0%	67.4%	32.6%
7,944	BENSON	3,587	2,149	1,119	319	1,030 R	59.9%	31.2%	65.8%	34.2%
1,138	BILLINGS	689	524	122	43	402 R	76.1%	17.7%	81.1%	18.9%
9,338	BOTTINEAU	4,828	3,394	1,090	344	2,304 R	70.3%	22.6%	75.7%	24.3%
4,229	BOWMAN	2,138	1,507	454	177	1,053 R	70.5%	21.2%	76.8%	23.2%
3,822	BURKE	1,968	1,442	418	108	1,024 R	73.3%	21.2%	77.5%	22.5%
54,811	BURLEIGH	27,137	18,437	6,129	2,571	12,308 R	67.9%	22.6%	75.1%	24.9%
88,247	CASS	43,620	23,886	13,562	6,172	10,324 R	54.8%	31.1%	63.8%	36.2%
7,636	CAVALIER	3,977	2,582	1,105	290	1,477 R	64.9%	27.8%	70.0%	30.0%
7,207	DICKEY	3,574	2,455	917	202	1,538 R	68.7%	25.7%	72.8%	27.2%
3,494	DIVIDE	1,918	1,267	509	142	758 R	66.1%	26.5%	71.3%	28.7%
4,627	DUNN	2,386	1,706	532	148	1,174 R	71.5%	22.3%	76.2%	23.8%
3,554	EDDY	1,883	1,153	539	191	614 R	61.2%	28.6%	68.1%	31.9%
5,877	EMMONS	3,054	2,369	502	183	1,867 R	77.6%	16.4%	82.5%	17.5%
4,611	FOSTER	2,303	1,534	586	183	948 R	66.6%	25.4%	72.4%	27.6%
2,391	GOLDEN VALLEY	1,349	1,006	259	84	747 R	74.6%	19.2%	79.5%	20.5%
66,100	GRAND FORKS	24,731	14,257	6,997	3,477	7,260 R	57.6%	28.3%	67.1%	32.9%
4,274	GRANT	2,339	1,891	317	131	1,574 R	80.8%	13.6%	85.6%	14.4%
3,714	GRIGGS	2,170	1,342	636	192	706 R	61.8%	29.3%	67.8%	32.2%
4,275	HETTINGER	2,257	1,699	434	124	1,265 R	75.3%	19.2%	79.7%	20.3%
3,833	KIDDER	1,913	1,474	326	113	1,148 R	77.1%	17.0%	81.9%	18.1%
6,473	LA MOURE	3,292	2,136	850	306	1,286 R	64.9%	25.8%	71.5%	28.5%
3,493	LOGAN	1,865	1,474	283	108	1,191 R	79.0%	15.2%	83.9%	16.1%
7,858	MCHENRY	4,104	2,922	939	243	1,983 R	71.2%	22.9%	75.7%	24.3%
4,800	MCINTOSH	2,873	2,471	308	94	2,163 R	86.0%	10.7%	88.9%	11.1%
7,132	MCKENZIE	3,368	2,265	867	236	1,398 R	67.3%	25.7%	72.3%	27.7%
12,288	MCLEAN	6,246	4,234	1,613	399	2,621 R	67.8%	25.8%	72.4%	27.6%
9,378	MERCER	4,741	3,224	1,209	308	2,015 R	68.0%	25.5%	72.7%	27.3%
25,177	MORTON	11,458	7,659	2,861	938	4,798 R	66.8%	25.0%	72.8%	27.2%
7,679	MOUNTRAIL	3,587	2,165	1,183	239	982 R	60.4%	33.0%	64.7%	35.3%
5,233	NELSON	2,595	1,611	726	258	885 R	62.1%	28.0%	68.9%	31.1%
2,495	OLIVER	1,316	966	270	80	696 R	73.4%	20.5%	78.2%	21.8%
10,399	PEMBINA	4,718	3,101	1,239	378	1,862 R	65.7%	26.3%	71.5%	28.5%
6,166	PIERCE	2,988	2,273	517	198	1,756 R	76.1%	17.3%	81.5%	18.5%
13,048	RAMSEY	6,285	4,078	1,607	600	2,471 R	64.9%	25.6%	71.7%	28.3%
6,698	RANSOM	3,142	1,883	974	285	909 R	59.9%	31.0%	65.9%	34.1%
3,608	RENVILLE	1,842	1,154	570	118	584 R	62.6%	30.9%	66.9%	33.1%
19,207	RICHLAND	9,337	5,711	2,698	928	3,013 R	61.2%	28.9%	67.9%	32.1%
12,177	ROLETTE	3,566	1,599	1,660	307	61 D	44.8%	46.6%	49.1%	50.9%
5,512	SARGENT	2,823	1,565	1,048	210	517 R	55.4%	37.1%	59.9%	40.1%
2,819	SHERIDAN	1,607	1,326	208	73	1,118 R	82.5%	12.9%	86.4%	13.6%
3,620	SIOUX	1,090	620	383	87	237 R	56.9%	35.1%	61.8%	38.2%
1,157	SLOPE	647	462	128	57	334 R	71.4%	19.8%	78.3%	21.7%
23,697	STARK	9,003	6,312	2,016	675	4,296 R	70.1%	22.4%	75.8%	24.2%
3,106	STEELE	1,870	997	617	256	380 R	53.3%	33.0%	61.8%	38.2%
24,154	STUTSMAN	10,249	6,545	2,573	1,131	3,972 R	63.9%	25.1%	71.8%	28.2%
4,052	TOWNER	2,119	1,375	568	176	807 R	64.9%	26.8%	70.8%	29.2%
9,624	TRAILL	5,076	3,092	1,428	556	1,664 R	60.9%	28.1%	68.4%	31.6%
15,371	WALSH	6,938	4,488	1,850	600	2,638 R	64.7%	26.7%	70.8%	29.2%
58,392	WARD	22,189	14,997	5,554	1,638	9,443 R	67.6%	25.0%	73.0%	27.0%
6,979	WELLS	3,599	2,660	746	193	1,914 R	73.9%	20.7%	78.1%	21.9%
22,237	WILLIAMS	9,904	6,530	2,545	829	3,985 R	65.9%	25.7%	72.0%	28.0%
652,695	TOTAL	301,545	193,695	79,189	28,661	114,506 R	64.2%	26.3%	71.0%	29.0%

NORTH DAKOTA

GOVERNOR 1980

1980 Census Population	County	Total Vote	Republican	Democratic	Other	Rep.-Dem. Plurality		Percentage Total Vote Rep.	Dem.	Major Vote Rep.	Dem.
3,584	ADAMS	1,973	1,139	834		305	R	57.7%	42.3%	57.7%	42.3%
13,960	BARNES	7,412	3,811	3,601		210	R	51.4%	48.6%	51.4%	48.6%
7,944	BENSON	3,670	1,734	1,936		202	D	47.2%	52.8%	47.2%	52.8%
1,138	BILLINGS	712	415	297		118	R	58.3%	41.7%	58.3%	41.7%
9,338	BOTTINEAU	4,833	2,776	2,057		719	R	57.4%	42.6%	57.4%	42.6%
4,229	BOWMAN	2,173	1,233	940		293	R	56.7%	43.3%	56.7%	43.3%
3,822	BURKE	2,043	1,160	883		277	R	56.8%	43.2%	56.8%	43.2%
54,811	BURLEIGH	27,568	16,473	11,095		5,378	R	59.8%	40.2%	59.8%	40.2%
88,247	CASS	42,475	22,546	19,929		2,617	R	53.1%	46.9%	53.1%	46.9%
7,636	CAVALIER	4,001	2,250	1,751		499	R	56.2%	43.8%	56.2%	43.8%
7,207	DICKEY	3,622	2,027	1,595		432	R	56.0%	44.0%	56.0%	44.0%
3,494	DIVIDE	2,000	1,038	962		76	R	51.9%	48.1%	51.9%	48.1%
4,627	DUNN	2,411	1,221	1,190		31	R	50.6%	49.4%	50.6%	49.4%
3,554	EDDY	1,967	936	1,031		95	D	47.6%	52.4%	47.6%	52.4%
5,877	EMMONS	3,105	1,916	1,189		727	R	61.7%	38.3%	61.7%	38.3%
4,611	FOSTER	2,329	1,289	1,040		249	R	55.3%	44.7%	55.3%	44.7%
2,391	GOLDEN VALLEY	1,366	782	584		198	R	57.2%	42.8%	57.2%	42.8%
66,100	GRAND FORKS	23,874	13,095	10,779		2,316	R	54.9%	45.1%	54.9%	45.1%
4,274	GRANT	2,394	1,521	873		648	R	63.5%	36.5%	63.5%	36.5%
3,714	GRIGGS	2,205	1,091	1,114		23	D	49.5%	50.5%	49.5%	50.5%
4,275	HETTINGER	2,352	1,334	1,018		316	R	56.7%	43.3%	56.7%	43.3%
3,833	KIDDER	1,977	1,105	872		233	R	55.9%	44.1%	55.9%	44.1%
6,473	LA MOURE	3,401	1,834	1,567		267	R	53.9%	46.1%	53.9%	46.1%
3,493	LOGAN	2,004	1,189	815		374	R	59.3%	40.7%	59.3%	40.7%
7,858	MCHENRY	4,189	2,339	1,850		489	R	55.8%	44.2%	55.8%	44.2%
4,800	MCINTOSH	2,963	2,070	893		1,177	R	69.9%	30.1%	69.9%	30.1%
7,132	MCKENZIE	3,330	1,759	1,571		188	R	52.8%	47.2%	52.8%	47.2%
12,288	MCLEAN	6,434	3,262	3,172		90	R	50.7%	49.3%	50.7%	49.3%
9,378	MERCER	4,814	2,473	2,341		132	R	51.4%	48.6%	51.4%	48.6%
25,177	MORTON	11,760	6,156	5,604		552	R	52.3%	47.7%	52.3%	47.7%
7,679	MOUNTRAIL	3,758	1,523	2,235		712	D	40.5%	59.5%	40.5%	59.5%
5,233	NELSON	2,648	1,292	1,356		64	D	48.8%	51.2%	48.8%	51.2%
2,495	OLIVER	1,363	709	654		55	R	52.0%	48.0%	52.0%	48.0%
10,399	PEMBINA	4,811	2,669	2,142		527	R	55.5%	44.5%	55.5%	44.5%
6,166	PIERCE	3,043	1,824	1,219		605	R	59.9%	40.1%	59.9%	40.1%
13,048	RAMSEY	6,335	3,551	2,784		767	R	56.1%	43.9%	56.1%	43.9%
6,698	RANSOM	3,201	1,631	1,570		61	R	51.0%	49.0%	51.0%	49.0%
3,608	RENVILLE	1,913	882	1,031		149	D	46.1%	53.9%	46.1%	53.9%
19,207	RICHLAND	9,498	4,550	4,948		398	D	47.9%	52.1%	47.9%	52.1%
12,177	ROLETTE	3,604	1,322	2,282		960	D	36.7%	63.3%	36.7%	63.3%
5,512	SARGENT	2,912	1,296	1,616		320	D	44.5%	55.5%	44.5%	55.5%
2,819	SHERIDAN	1,658	1,135	523		612	R	68.5%	31.5%	68.5%	31.5%
3,620	SIOUX	1,112	467	645		178	D	42.0%	58.0%	42.0%	58.0%
1,157	SLOPE	670	354	316		38	R	52.8%	47.2%	52.8%	47.2%
23,697	STARK	8,771	4,924	3,847		1,077	R	56.1%	43.9%	56.1%	43.9%
3,106	STEELE	1,881	844	1,037		193	D	44.9%	55.1%	44.9%	55.1%
24,154	STUTSMAN	10,207	5,317	4,890		427	R	52.1%	47.9%	52.1%	47.9%
4,052	TOWNER	2,172	1,286	886		400	R	59.2%	40.8%	59.2%	40.8%
9,624	TRAILL	5,064	2,587	2,477		110	R	51.1%	48.9%	51.1%	48.9%
15,371	WALSH	7,094	3,652	3,442		210	R	51.5%	48.5%	51.5%	48.5%
58,392	WARD	21,886	10,940	10,946		6	D	50.0%	50.0%	50.0%	50.0%
6,979	WELLS	3,814	2,269	1,545		724	R	59.5%	40.5%	59.5%	40.5%
22,237	WILLIAMS	9,849	5,232	4,617		615	R	53.1%	46.9%	53.1%	46.9%
652,695	TOTAL	302,621	162,230	140,391		21,839	R	53.6%	46.4%	53.6%	46.4%

NORTH DAKOTA

SENATOR 1980

1980 Census Population	County	Total Vote	Republican	Democratic	Other	Rep.-Dem. Plurality	Percentage Total Vote Rep.	Dem.	Major Vote Rep.	Dem.
3,584	ADAMS	1,982	1,396	585	1	811 R	70.4%	29.5%	70.5%	29.5%
13,960	BARNES	7,456	5,261	2,131	64	3,130 R	70.6%	28.6%	71.2%	28.8%
7,944	BENSON	3,658	2,456	1,197	5	1,259 R	67.1%	32.7%	67.2%	32.8%
1,138	BILLINGS	702	493	206	3	287 R	70.2%	29.3%	70.5%	29.5%
9,338	BOTTINEAU	4,824	3,358	1,456	10	1,902 R	69.6%	30.2%	69.8%	30.2%
4,229	BOWMAN	2,155	1,603	547	5	1,056 R	74.4%	25.4%	74.6%	25.4%
3,822	BURKE	2,038	1,510	525	3	985 R	74.1%	25.8%	74.2%	25.8%
54,811	BURLEIGH	26,914	18,681	7,901	332	10,780 R	69.4%	29.4%	70.3%	29.7%
88,247	CASS	42,264	29,111	12,815	338	16,296 R	68.9%	30.3%	69.4%	30.6%
7,636	CAVALIER	3,997	2,716	1,279	2	1,437 R	68.0%	32.0%	68.0%	32.0%
7,207	DICKEY	3,637	2,655	974	8	1,681 R	73.0%	26.8%	73.2%	26.8%
3,494	DIVIDE	1,976	1,399	571	6	828 R	70.8%	28.9%	71.0%	29.0%
4,627	DUNN	2,407	1,730	674	3	1,056 R	71.9%	28.0%	72.0%	28.0%
3,554	EDDY	1,973	1,279	691	3	588 R	64.8%	35.0%	64.9%	35.1%
5,877	EMMONS	3,037	2,199	824	14	1,375 R	72.4%	27.1%	72.7%	27.3%
4,611	FOSTER	2,301	1,709	586	6	1,123 R	74.3%	25.5%	74.5%	25.5%
2,391	GOLDEN VALLEY	1,360	980	375	5	605 R	72.1%	27.6%	72.3%	27.7%
66,100	GRAND FORKS	23,640	16,660	6,476	504	10,184 R	70.5%	27.4%	72.0%	28.0%
4,274	GRANT	2,379	1,766	602	11	1,164 R	74.2%	25.3%	74.6%	25.4%
3,714	GRIGGS	2,203	1,551	649	3	902 R	70.4%	29.5%	70.5%	29.5%
4,275	HETTINGER	2,348	1,705	638	5	1,067 R	72.6%	27.2%	72.8%	27.2%
3,833	KIDDER	1,954	1,417	531	6	886 R	72.5%	27.2%	72.7%	27.3%
6,473	LA MOURE	3,358	2,427	910	21	1,517 R	72.3%	27.1%	72.7%	27.3%
3,493	LOGAN	1,998	1,532	463	3	1,069 R	76.7%	23.2%	76.8%	23.2%
7,858	MCHENRY	4,169	2,907	1,255	7	1,652 R	69.7%	30.1%	69.8%	30.2%
4,800	MCINTOSH	2,975	2,497	472	6	2,025 R	83.9%	15.9%	84.1%	15.9%
7,132	MCKENZIE	3,353	2,377	968	8	1,409 R	70.9%	28.9%	71.1%	28.9%
12,288	MCLEAN	6,381	4,336	2,023	22	2,313 R	68.0%	31.7%	68.2%	31.8%
9,378	MERCER	4,805	3,239	1,553	13	1,686 R	67.4%	32.3%	67.6%	32.4%
25,177	MORTON	11,303	7,269	3,903	131	3,366 R	64.3%	34.5%	65.1%	34.9%
7,679	MOUNTRAIL	3,730	2,396	1,322	12	1,074 R	64.2%	35.4%	64.4%	35.6%
5,233	NELSON	2,615	1,879	725	11	1,154 R	71.9%	27.7%	72.2%	27.8%
2,495	OLIVER	1,362	934	425	3	509 R	68.6%	31.2%	68.7%	31.3%
10,399	PEMBINA	4,779	3,546	1,199	34	2,347 R	74.2%	25.1%	74.7%	25.3%
6,166	PIERCE	3,035	2,279	745	11	1,534 R	75.1%	24.5%	75.4%	24.6%
13,048	RAMSEY	6,337	4,564	1,735	38	2,829 R	72.0%	27.4%	72.5%	27.5%
6,698	RANSOM	3,174	2,287	874	13	1,413 R	72.1%	27.5%	72.4%	27.6%
3,608	RENVILLE	1,848	973	873	2	100 R	52.7%	47.2%	52.7%	47.3%
19,207	RICHLAND	9,364	6,813	2,486	65	4,327 R	72.8%	26.5%	73.3%	26.7%
12,177	ROLETTE	3,643	2,273	1,332	38	941 R	62.4%	36.6%	63.1%	36.9%
5,512	SARGENT	2,871	1,942	921	8	1,021 R	67.6%	32.1%	67.8%	32.2%
2,819	SHERIDAN	1,658	1,379	276	3	1,103 R	83.2%	16.6%	83.3%	16.7%
3,620	SIOUX	1,111	637	467	7	170 R	57.3%	42.0%	57.7%	42.3%
1,157	SLOPE	665	471	193	1	278 R	70.8%	29.0%	70.9%	29.1%
23,697	STARK	8,481	6,142	2,284	55	3,858 R	72.4%	26.9%	72.9%	27.1%
3,106	STEELE	1,876	1,293	579	4	714 R	68.9%	30.9%	69.1%	30.9%
24,154	STUTSMAN	10,272	7,263	2,871	138	4,392 R	70.7%	27.9%	71.7%	28.3%
4,052	TOWNER	2,182	1,612	568	2	1,044 R	73.9%	26.0%	73.9%	26.1%
9,624	TRAILL	5,122	3,818	1,272	32	2,546 R	74.5%	24.8%	75.0%	25.0%
15,371	WALSH	7,050	5,227	1,801	22	3,426 R	74.1%	25.5%	74.4%	25.6%
58,392	WARD	20,960	14,737	6,064	159	8,673 R	70.3%	28.9%	70.8%	29.2%
6,979	WELLS	3,821	2,817	998	6	1,819 R	73.7%	26.1%	73.8%	26.2%
22,237	WILLIAMS	9,769	6,846	2,868	55	3,978 R	70.1%	29.4%	70.5%	29.5%
652,695	TOTAL	299,272	210,347	86,658	2,267	123,689 R	70.3%	29.0%	70.8%	29.2%

NORTH DAKOTA

CONGRESS

CD	Year	Total Vote	Republican Vote	Republican Candidate	Democratic Vote	Democratic Candidate	Other Vote	Rep.-Dem. Plurality	Total Vote Rep.	Total Vote Dem.	Major Vote Rep.	Major Vote Dem.
AL	1980	293,076	124,707	SMYKOWSKI, JIM	166,437	DORGAN, BYRON L.	1,932	41,730 D	42.6%	56.8%	42.8%	57.2%
AL	1978	220,348	147,746	ANDREWS, MARK	68,016	HAGEN, BRUCE	4,586	79,730 R	67.1%	30.9%	68.5%	31.5%
AL	1976	289,881	181,018	ANDREWS, MARK	104,263	OMDAHL, LLOYD B.	4,600	76,755 R	62.4%	36.0%	63.5%	36.5%
AL	1974	233,688	130,184	ANDREWS, MARK	103,504	DORGAN, BYRON L.		26,680 R	55.7%	44.3%	55.7%	44.3%
AL	1972	268,721	195,360	ANDREWS, MARK	72,850	ISTA, RICHARD	511	122,510 R	72.7%	27.1%	72.8%	27.2%

NORTH DAKOTA

1980 GENERAL ELECTION

President   Other vote was 23,640 Anderson (Independent); 3,743 Clark (Libertarian); 429 Commoner (Citizens); 296 McLain (Natural Peoples League); 235 Greaves (American); 93 Hall (Communist); 89 DeBerry (Socialist Workers); 82 McReynolds (Socialist); 54 Bubar (Statesman).

Governor

Senator   Other vote was 1,625 McLain (Chemical Farming Banned); 642 Klingensmith (Statesman).

Congress   Other vote was 1,004 Langenfelder (Academic Christian Freedom, Prolife, Profamily); 928 Teigen (Independent).

1980 PRIMARIES

SEPTEMBER 2 REPUBLICAN

Governor   60,016 Allen I. Olson; 19,306 Orville W. Hagen.

Senator   Mark Andrews, unopposed.

Congress   Contested as follows:

AL   42,400 Jim Smykowski; 38,321 Lee Christoferson.

SEPTEMBER 2 DEMOCRATIC

Governor   Arthur A. Link, unopposed.

Senator   30,789 Kent Johanneson; 9,013 Michael P. Saba.

Congress   Unopposed at-large.

OHIO

GOVERNOR
James A. Rhodes (R). Re-elected 1978 to a four-year term. Previously elected 1974, 1966, 1962.

SENATORS
John H. Glenn (D). Re-elected 1980 to a six-year term. Previously elected 1974.

Howard Metzenbaum (D). Elected 1976 to a six-year term.

REPRESENTATIVES
1. Willis D. Gradison (R)
2. Thomas A. Luken (D)
3. Tony P. Hall (D)
4. Tennyson Guyer (R) (see page 1)
5. Delbert L. Latta (R)
6. Bob McEwen (R)
7. Clarence Brown, Jr. (R)
8. Thomas N. Kindness (R)
9. Ed Weber (R)
10. Clarence E. Miller (R)
11. J. William Stanton (R)
12. Bob Shamansky (D)
13. Donald J. Pease (D)
14. John F. Seiberling (D)
15. Chalmers P. Wylie (R)
16. Ralph S. Regula (R)
17. John M. Ashbrook (R)
18. Douglas Applegate (D)
19. Lyle Williams (R)
20. Mary Rose Oakar (D)
21. Louis Stokes (D)
22. Dennis E. Eckart (D)
23. Ronald M. Mottl (D)

POSTWAR VOTE FOR GOVERNOR

Year	Total Vote	Republican Vote	Republican Candidate	Democratic Vote	Democratic Candidate	Other Vote	Rep.-Dem. Plurality	Total Vote Rep.	Total Vote Dem.	Major Vote Rep.	Major Vote Dem.
1978	2,843,351	1,402,167	Rhodes, James A.	1,354,631	Celeste, Richard F.	86,553	47,536 R	49.3%	47.6%	50.9%	49.1%
1974	3,072,010	1,493,679	Rhodes, James A.	1,482,191	Gilligan, John J.	96,140	11,488 R	48.6%	48.2%	50.2%	49.8%
1970	3,184,133	1,382,659	Cloud, Roger	1,725,560	Gilligan, John J.	75,914	342,901 D	43.4%	54.2%	44.5%	55.5%
1966	2,887,331	1,795,277	Rhodes, James A.	1,092,054	Reams, Frazier, Jr.	—	703,223 R	62.2%	37.8%	62.2%	37.8%
1962	3,116,711	1,836,190	Rhodes, James A.	1,280,521	DiSalle, Michael V.	—	555,669 R	58.9%	41.1%	58.9%	41.1%
1958	3,284,134	1,414,874	O'Neill, C. William	1,869,260	DiSalle, Michael V.	—	454,386 D	43.1%	56.9%	43.1%	56.9%
1956	3,542,091	1,984,988	O'Neill, C. William	1,557,103	DiSalle, Michael V.	—	427,885 R	56.0%	44.0%	56.0%	44.0%
1954	2,597,790	1,192,528	Rhodes, James A.	1,405,262	Lausche, Frank J.	—	212,734 D	45.9%	54.1%	45.9%	54.1%
1952	3,605,168	1,590,058	Taft, Charles P.	2,015,110	Lausche, Frank J.	—	425,052 D	44.1%	55.9%	44.1%	55.9%
1950	2,892,819	1,370,570	Ebright, Don H.	1,522,249	Lausche, Frank J.	—	151,679 D	47.4%	52.6%	47.4%	52.6%
1948	3,018,289	1,398,514	Herbert, Thomas J.	1,619,775	Lausche, Frank J.	—	221,261 D	46.3%	53.7%	46.3%	53.7%
1946	2,303,750	1,166,550	Herbert, Thomas J.	1,125,997	Lausche, Frank J.	11,203	40,553 R	50.6%	48.9%	50.9%	49.1%

The term of office of Ohio's Governor was increased from two to four years effective with the 1958 election.

POSTWAR VOTE FOR SENATOR

Year	Total Vote	Republican Vote	Republican Candidate	Democratic Vote	Democratic Candidate	Other Vote	Rep.-Dem. Plurality	Total Vote Rep.	Total Vote Dem.	Major Vote Rep.	Major Vote Dem.
1980	4,027,303	1,137,695	Betts, James E.	2,770,786	Glenn, John H.	118,822	1,633,091 D	28.2%	68.8%	29.1%	70.9%
1976	3,920,613	1,823,774	Taft, Robert A., Jr.	1,941,113	Metzenbaum, Howard	155,726	117,339 D	46.5%	49.5%	48.4%	51.6%
1974	2,987,951	918,133	Perk, Ralph J.	1,930,670	Glenn, John H.	139,148	1,012,537 D	30.7%	64.6%	32.2%	67.8%
1970	3,151,274	1,565,682	Taft, Robert A., Jr.	1,495,262	Metzenbaum, Howard	90,330	70,420 R	49.7%	47.4%	51.2%	48.8%
1968	3,743,121	1,928,964	Saxbe, William B.	1,814,152	Gilligan, John J.	5	114,812 R	51.5%	48.5%	51.5%	48.5%
1964	3,830,389	1,906,781	Taft, Robert A., Jr.	1,923,608	Young, Stephen M.	—	16,827 D	49.8%	50.2%	49.8%	50.2%
1962	2,994,986	1,151,173	Briley, John M.	1,843,813	Lausche, Frank J.	—	692,640 D	38.4%	61.6%	38.4%	61.6%
1958	3,149,410	1,497,199	Bricker, John W.	1,652,211	Young, Stephen M.	—	155,012 D	47.5%	52.5%	47.5%	52.5%
1956	3,525,499	1,660,910	Bender, George H.	1,864,589	Lausche, Frank J.	—	203,679 D	47.1%	52.9%	47.1%	52.9%
1954s	2,512,778	1,257,874	Bender, George H.	1,254,904	Burke, Thomas A.	—	2,970 R	50.1%	49.9%	50.1%	49.9%
1952	3,442,291	1,878,961	Bricker, John W.	1,563,330	DiSalle, Michael V.	—	315,631 R	54.6%	45.4%	54.6%	45.4%
1950	2,860,102	1,645,643	Taft, Robert A.	1,214,459	Ferguson, Joseph T.	—	431,184 R	57.5%	42.5%	57.5%	42.5%
1946	2,237,269	1,275,774	Bricker, John W.	947,610	Huffman, James W.	13,885	328,164 R	57.0%	42.4%	57.4%	42.6%

The 1954 election was for a short term to fill a vacancy.

OHIO

Districts Established January 20, 1972

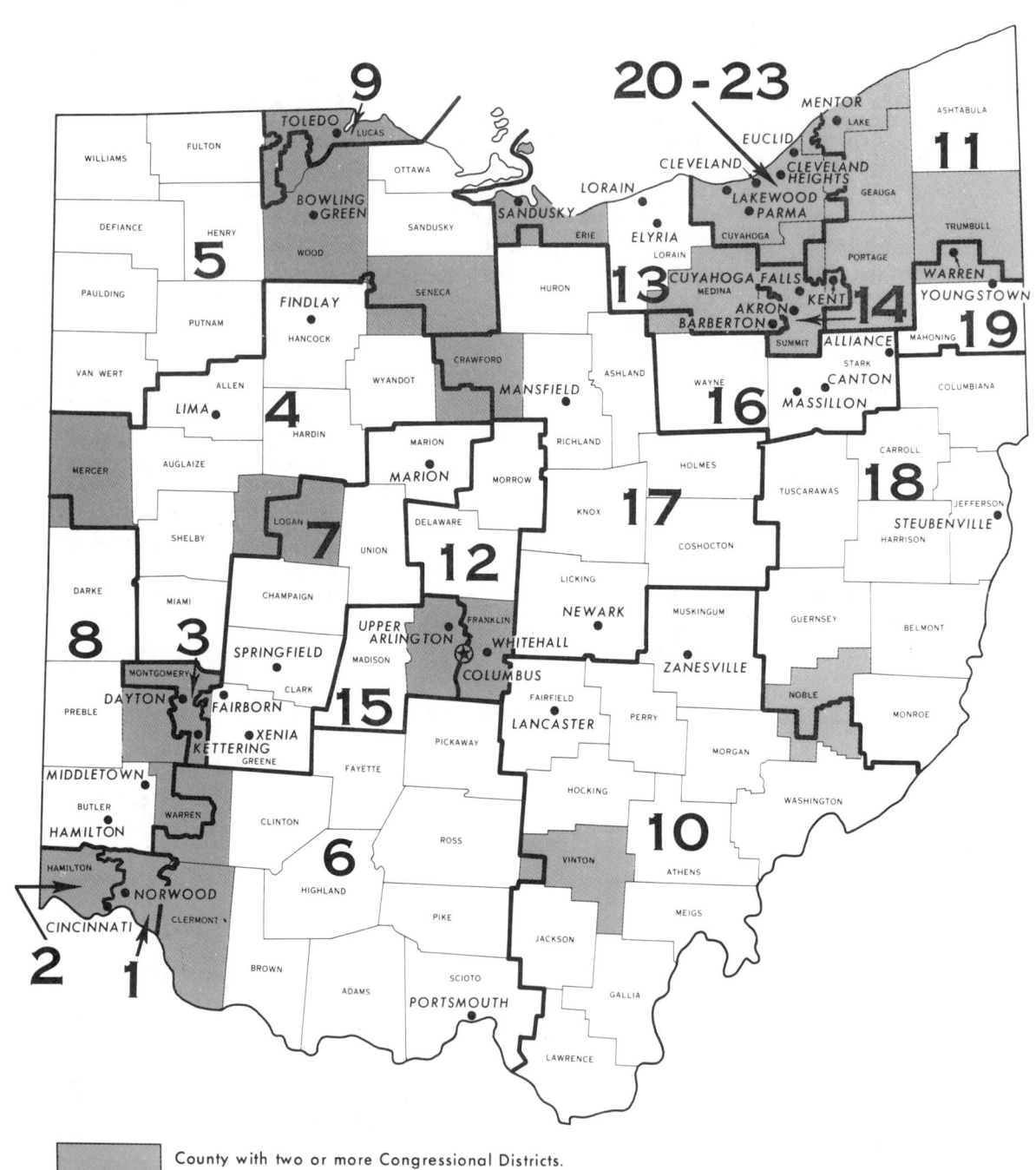

County with two or more Congressional Districts.

OHIO

PRESIDENT 1980

1980 Census Population	County	Total Vote	Republican	Democratic	Other	Rep.-Dem. Plurality	Percentage Total Vote Rep.	Dem.	Major Vote Rep.	Dem.
24,328	ADAMS	9,928	5,336	4,161	431	1,175 R	53.7%	41.9%	56.2%	43.8%
112,241	ALLEN	44,154	29,070	13,140	1,944	15,930 R	65.8%	29.8%	68.9%	31.1%
46,178	ASHLAND	18,689	11,691	5,142	1,856	6,549 R	62.6%	27.5%	69.5%	30.5%
104,215	ASHTABULA	40,467	19,847	17,363	3,257	2,484 R	49.0%	42.9%	53.3%	46.7%
56,399	ATHENS	19,801	8,170	9,514	2,117	1,344 D	41.3%	48.0%	46.2%	53.8%
42,554	AUGLAIZE	17,657	11,537	5,022	1,098	6,515 R	65.3%	28.4%	69.7%	30.3%
82,569	BELMONT	32,024	13,601	16,653	1,770	3,052 D	42.5%	52.0%	45.0%	55.0%
31,920	BROWN	11,337	6,065	4,706	566	1,359 R	53.5%	41.5%	56.3%	43.7%
258,787	BUTLER	98,901	61,231	31,796	5,874	29,435 R	61.9%	32.1%	65.8%	34.2%
25,598	CARROLL	9,851	5,806	3,476	569	2,330 R	58.9%	35.3%	62.6%	37.4%
33,649	CHAMPAIGN	12,225	7,356	4,109	760	3,247 R	60.2%	33.6%	64.2%	35.8%
150,236	CLARK	54,015	27,237	22,630	4,148	4,607 R	50.4%	41.9%	54.6%	45.4%
128,483	CLERMONT	42,091	26,674	13,199	2,218	13,475 R	63.4%	31.4%	66.9%	33.1%
34,603	CLINTON	12,400	7,675	3,967	758	3,708 R	61.9%	32.0%	65.9%	34.1%
113,572	COLUMBIANA	41,143	20,798	17,459	2,886	3,339 R	50.6%	42.4%	54.4%	45.6%
36,024	COSHOCTON	13,856	8,359	4,725	772	3,634 R	60.3%	34.1%	63.9%	36.1%
50,075	CRAWFORD	19,755	12,424	6,058	1,273	6,366 R	62.9%	30.7%	67.2%	32.8%
1,498,295	CUYAHOGA	614,682	254,883	307,448	52,351	52,565 D	41.5%	50.0%	45.3%	54.7%
55,096	DARKE	21,958	12,773	7,635	1,550	5,138 R	58.2%	34.8%	62.6%	37.4%
39,987	DEFIANCE	15,639	9,358	5,096	1,185	4,262 R	59.8%	32.6%	64.7%	35.3%
53,840	DELAWARE	22,861	14,740	6,417	1,704	8,323 R	64.5%	28.1%	69.7%	30.3%
79,655	ERIE	30,470	15,628	12,343	2,499	3,285 R	51.3%	40.5%	55.9%	44.1%
93,678	FAIRFIELD	39,515	24,096	13,144	2,275	10,952 R	61.0%	33.3%	64.7%	35.3%
27,467	FAYETTE	9,068	5,827	2,810	431	3,017 R	64.3%	31.0%	67.5%	32.5%
869,109	FRANKLIN	373,045	200,948	143,932	28,165	57,016 R	53.9%	38.6%	58.3%	41.7%
37,751	FULTON	14,707	9,519	3,972	1,216	5,547 R	64.7%	27.0%	70.6%	29.4%
30,098	GALLIA	11,404	6,469	4,406	529	2,063 R	56.7%	38.6%	59.5%	40.5%
74,474	GEAUGA	30,204	17,762	9,542	2,900	8,220 R	58.8%	31.6%	65.1%	34.9%
129,769	GREENE	48,842	24,922	20,068	3,852	4,854 R	51.0%	41.1%	55.4%	44.6%
42,024	GUERNSEY	14,084	8,180	5,121	783	3,059 R	58.1%	36.4%	61.5%	38.5%
873,136	HAMILTON	358,541	206,979	129,114	22,448	77,865 R	57.7%	36.0%	61.6%	38.4%
64,581	HANCOCK	27,010	18,264	6,843	1,903	11,421 R	67.6%	25.3%	72.7%	27.3%
32,719	HARDIN	12,123	7,457	3,863	803	3,594 R	61.5%	31.9%	65.9%	34.1%
18,152	HARRISON	6,916	3,639	2,848	429	791 R	52.6%	41.2%	56.1%	43.9%
28,383	HENRY	11,489	7,584	3,059	846	4,525 R	66.0%	26.6%	71.3%	28.7%
33,477	HIGHLAND	12,400	7,359	4,363	678	2,996 R	59.3%	35.2%	62.8%	37.2%
24,304	HOCKING	8,819	4,588	3,765	466	823 R	52.0%	42.7%	54.9%	45.1%
29,416	HOLMES	6,394	3,860	2,094	440	1,766 R	60.4%	32.7%	64.8%	35.2%
54,608	HURON	19,159	11,173	6,537	1,449	4,636 R	58.3%	34.1%	63.1%	36.9%
30,592	JACKSON	10,719	5,902	4,409	408	1,493 R	55.1%	41.1%	57.2%	42.8%
91,564	JEFFERSON	38,491	15,777	20,382	2,332	4,605 D	41.0%	53.0%	43.6%	56.4%
46,309	KNOX	18,195	10,384	6,586	1,225	3,798 R	57.1%	36.2%	61.2%	38.8%
212,801	LAKE	86,428	43,485	35,246	7,697	8,239 R	50.3%	40.8%	55.2%	44.8%
63,849	LAWRENCE	26,194	13,799	11,366	1,029	2,433 R	52.7%	43.4%	54.8%	45.2%
120,981	LICKING	48,769	28,425	17,208	3,136	11,217 R	58.3%	35.3%	62.3%	37.7%
39,155	LOGAN	14,994	9,727	4,319	948	5,408 R	64.9%	28.8%	69.3%	30.7%
274,909	LORAIN	103,084	51,034	40,919	11,131	10,115 R	49.5%	39.7%	55.5%	44.5%
471,741	LUCAS	191,298	86,653	85,341	19,304	1,312 R	45.3%	44.6%	50.4%	49.6%
33,004	MADISON	11,350	7,166	3,565	619	3,601 R	63.1%	31.4%	66.8%	33.2%
289,487	MAHONING	125,161	50,153	63,677	11,331	13,524 D	40.1%	50.9%	44.1%	55.9%
67,974	MARION	25,631	14,605	9,419	1,607	5,186 R	57.0%	36.7%	60.8%	39.2%
113,150	MEDINA	42,050	24,723	13,573	3,754	11,150 R	58.8%	32.3%	64.6%	35.4%
23,641	MEIGS	9,170	4,911	3,827	432	1,084 R	53.6%	41.7%	56.2%	43.8%
38,334	MERCER	15,339	8,673	5,506	1,160	3,167 R	56.5%	35.9%	61.2%	38.8%
90,381	MIAMI	35,808	19,928	12,893	2,987	7,035 R	55.7%	36.0%	60.7%	39.3%
17,382	MONROE	6,373	2,870	3,166	337	296 D	45.0%	49.7%	47.5%	52.5%
571,697	MONTGOMERY	223,009	101,443	105,110	16,456	3,667 D	45.5%	47.1%	49.1%	50.9%
14,241	MORGAN	5,366	3,236	1,875	255	1,361 R	60.3%	34.9%	63.3%	36.7%
26,480	MORROW	9,972	6,179	3,239	554	2,940 R	62.0%	32.5%	65.6%	34.4%
83,340	MUSKINGUM	32,688	17,921	12,584	2,183	5,337 R	54.8%	38.5%	58.7%	41.3%
11,310	NOBLE	5,272	3,025	1,944	303	1,081 R	57.4%	36.9%	60.9%	39.1%
40,076	OTTAWA	16,883	8,641	6,753	1,489	1,888 R	51.2%	40.0%	56.1%	43.9%
21,302	PAULDING	8,494	4,971	2,778	745	2,193 R	58.5%	32.7%	64.2%	35.8%
31,032	PERRY	10,648	5,725	4,383	540	1,342 R	53.8%	41.2%	56.6%	43.4%
43,662	PICKAWAY	15,170	9,289	5,052	829	4,237 R	61.2%	33.3%	64.8%	35.2%
22,802	PIKE	9,818	4,426	4,938	454	512 D	45.1%	50.3%	47.3%	52.7%
135,856	PORTAGE	48,190	22,829	20,570	4,791	2,259 R	47.4%	42.7%	52.6%	47.4%
38,223	PREBLE	14,723	8,376	5,416	931	2,960 R	56.9%	36.8%	60.7%	39.3%
32,991	PUTNAM	14,193	9,752	3,742	699	6,010 R	68.7%	26.4%	72.3%	27.7%
131,205	RICHLAND	50,824	29,213	18,253	3,358	10,960 R	57.5%	35.9%	61.5%	38.5%

OHIO

PRESIDENT 1980

1980 Census Population	County	Total Vote	Republican	Democratic	Other	Rep.-Dem. Plurality	Percentage			
							Total Vote		Major Vote	
							Rep.	Dem.	Rep.	Dem.
65,004	ROSS	23,859	13,251	9,355	1,253	3,896 R	55.5%	39.2%	58.6%	41.4%
63,267	SANDUSKY	24,166	13,420	8,482	2,264	4,938 R	55.5%	35.1%	61.3%	38.7%
84,545	SCIOTO	32,568	15,881	15,552	1,135	329 R	48.8%	47.8%	50.5%	49.5%
61,901	SENECA	23,259	14,172	7,303	1,784	6,869 R	60.9%	31.4%	66.0%	34.0%
43,089	SHELBY	16,544	8,988	6,425	1,131	2,563 R	54.3%	38.8%	58.3%	41.7%
378,823	STARK	157,106	87,769	59,005	10,332	28,764 R	55.9%	37.6%	59.8%	40.2%
524,472	SUMMIT	212,919	92,299	102,459	18,161	10,160 D	43.3%	48.1%	47.4%	52.6%
241,863	TRUMBULL	93,002	41,056	44,366	7,580	3,310 D	44.1%	47.7%	48.1%	51.9%
84,614	TUSCARAWAS	30,086	15,708	12,117	2,261	3,591 R	52.2%	40.3%	56.5%	43.5%
29,536	UNION	11,186	7,576	3,038	572	4,538 R	67.7%	27.2%	71.4%	28.6%
30,458	VAN WERT	12,872	7,866	4,070	936	3,796 R	61.1%	31.6%	65.9%	34.1%
11,584	VINTON	5,064	2,484	2,381	199	103 R	49.1%	47.0%	51.1%	48.9%
99,276	WARREN	35,522	22,430	11,306	1,786	11,124 R	63.1%	31.8%	66.5%	33.5%
64,266	WASHINGTON	23,971	14,310	7,936	1,725	6,374 R	59.7%	33.1%	64.3%	35.7%
97,408	WAYNE	33,942	18,962	12,129	2,851	6,833 R	55.9%	35.7%	61.0%	39.0%
36,369	WILLIAMS	14,221	9,146	4,015	1,060	5,131 R	64.3%	28.2%	69.5%	30.5%
107,372	WOOD	42,213	23,315	14,139	4,759	9,176 R	55.2%	33.5%	62.2%	37.8%
22,651	WYANDOT	9,175	5,786	2,757	632	3,029 R	63.1%	30.0%	67.7%	32.3%
10,797,419	TOTAL	4,283,603	2,206,545	1,752,414	324,644	454,131 R	51.5%	40.9%	55.7%	44.3%

OHIO

SENATOR 1980

1980 Census Population	County	Total Vote	Republican	Democratic	Other	Rep.-Dem. Plurality		Percentage			
								Total Vote		Major Vote	
								Rep.	Dem.	Rep.	Dem.
24,328	ADAMS	9,502	3,207	6,151	144	2,944	D	33.8%	64.7%	34.3%	65.7%
112,241	ALLEN	43,716	20,264	22,755	697	2,491	D	46.4%	52.1%	47.1%	52.9%
46,178	ASHLAND	17,912	7,299	10,073	540	2,774	D	40.7%	56.2%	42.0%	58.0%
104,215	ASHTABULA	39,904	9,887	29,298	719	19,411	D	24.8%	73.4%	25.2%	74.8%
56,399	ATHENS	18,785	5,586	12,833	366	7,247	D	29.7%	68.3%	30.3%	69.7%
42,554	AUGLAIZE	17,225	7,340	9,521	364	2,181	D	42.6%	55.3%	43.5%	56.5%
82,569	BELMONT	30,903	6,269	23,931	703	17,662	D	20.3%	77.4%	20.8%	79.2%
31,920	BROWN	10,859	2,501	8,133	225	5,632	D	23.0%	74.9%	23.5%	76.5%
258,787	BUTLER	95,565	30,944	62,563	2,058	31,619	D	32.4%	65.5%	33.1%	66.9%
25,598	CARROLL	9,679	3,494	5,900	285	2,406	D	36.1%	61.0%	37.2%	62.8%
33,649	CHAMPAIGN	11,910	3,996	7,686	228	3,690	D	33.6%	64.5%	34.2%	65.8%
150,236	CLARK	52,641	13,390	38,466	785	25,076	D	25.4%	73.1%	25.8%	74.2%
128,483	CLERMONT	40,877	14,888	25,398	591	10,510	D	36.4%	62.1%	37.0%	63.0%
34,603	CLINTON	11,913	3,408	8,324	181	4,916	D	28.6%	69.9%	29.0%	71.0%
113,572	COLUMBIANA	40,525	13,416	26,410	699	12,994	D	33.1%	65.2%	33.7%	66.3%
36,024	COSHOCTON	11,656	4,226	6,550	880	2,324	D	36.3%	56.2%	39.2%	60.8%
50,075	CRAWFORD	19,555	7,976	11,293	286	3,317	D	40.8%	57.7%	41.4%	58.6%
1,498,295	CUYAHOGA	504,311	107,090	374,282	22,939	267,192	D	21.2%	74.2%	22.2%	77.8%
55,096	DARKE	21,532	6,821	14,279	432	7,458	D	31.7%	66.3%	32.3%	67.7%
39,987	DEFIANCE	15,349	6,802	8,329	218	1,527	D	44.3%	54.3%	45.0%	55.0%
53,840	DELAWARE	22,143	8,334	13,390	419	5,056	D	37.6%	60.5%	38.4%	61.6%
79,655	ERIE	27,828	8,935	17,432	1,461	8,497	D	32.1%	62.6%	33.9%	66.1%
93,678	FAIRFIELD	39,025	12,126	26,195	704	14,069	D	31.1%	67.1%	31.6%	68.4%
27,467	FAYETTE	8,776	3,239	5,428	109	2,189	D	36.9%	61.9%	37.4%	62.6%
869,109	FRANKLIN	350,620	99,840	229,028	21,752	129,188	D	28.5%	65.3%	30.4%	69.6%
37,751	FULTON	14,346	6,579	7,556	211	977	D	45.9%	52.7%	46.5%	53.5%
30,098	GALLIA	10,579	3,687	6,609	283	2,922	D	34.9%	62.5%	35.8%	64.2%
74,474	GEAUGA	28,768	8,530	18,884	1,354	10,354	D	29.7%	65.6%	31.1%	68.9%
129,769	GREENE	47,370	11,763	34,919	688	23,156	D	24.8%	73.7%	25.2%	74.8%
42,024	GUERNSEY	13,619	4,494	8,880	245	4,386	D	33.0%	65.2%	33.6%	66.4%
873,136	HAMILTON	343,471	111,535	226,939	4,997	115,404	D	32.5%	66.1%	33.0%	67.0%
64,581	HANCOCK	23,634	10,849	11,324	1,461	475	D	45.9%	47.9%	48.9%	51.1%
32,719	HARDIN	11,815	4,786	6,845	184	2,059	D	40.5%	57.9%	41.1%	58.9%
18,152	HARRISON	6,672	1,913	4,592	167	2,679	D	28.7%	68.8%	29.4%	70.6%
28,383	HENRY	11,244	5,029	6,102	113	1,073	D	44.7%	54.3%	45.2%	54.8%
33,477	HIGHLAND	12,069	4,022	7,920	127	3,898	D	33.3%	65.6%	33.7%	66.3%
24,304	HOCKING	8,683	2,445	6,109	129	3,664	D	28.2%	70.4%	28.6%	71.4%
29,416	HOLMES	6,201	1,959	4,132	110	2,173	D	31.6%	66.6%	32.2%	67.8%
54,608	HURON	18,796	7,825	10,555	416	2,730	D	41.6%	56.2%	42.6%	57.4%
30,592	JACKSON	9,738	3,544	6,033	161	2,489	D	36.4%	62.0%	37.0%	63.0%
91,564	JEFFERSON	36,352	7,098	28,087	1,167	20,989	D	19.5%	77.3%	20.2%	79.8%
46,309	KNOX	17,163	4,889	10,537	1,737	5,648	D	28.5%	61.4%	31.7%	68.3%
212,801	LAKE	73,882	15,347	54,894	3,641	39,547	D	20.8%	74.3%	21.8%	78.2%
63,849	LAWRENCE	24,293	7,538	16,196	559	8,658	D	31.0%	66.7%	31.8%	68.2%
120,981	LICKING	47,760	15,815	30,945	1,000	15,130	D	33.1%	64.8%	33.8%	66.2%
39,155	LOGAN	14,801	5,509	9,045	247	3,536	D	37.2%	61.1%	37.9%	62.1%
274,909	LORAIN	98,601	21,781	74,345	2,475	52,564	D	22.1%	75.4%	22.7%	77.3%
471,741	LUCAS	177,515	53,039	116,465	8,011	63,426	D	29.9%	65.6%	31.3%	68.7%
33,004	MADISON	11,218	3,655	7,340	223	3,685	D	32.6%	65.4%	33.2%	66.8%
289,487	MAHONING	114,953	20,050	91,784	3,119	71,734	D	17.4%	79.8%	17.9%	82.1%
67,974	MARION	25,267	7,981	16,929	357	8,948	D	31.6%	67.0%	32.0%	68.0%
113,150	MEDINA	41,771	11,970	29,116	685	17,146	D	28.7%	69.7%	29.1%	70.9%
23,641	MEIGS	8,446	2,945	5,303	198	2,358	D	34.9%	62.8%	35.7%	64.3%
38,334	MERCER	14,965	5,627	8,948	390	3,321	D	37.6%	59.8%	38.6%	61.4%
90,381	MIAMI	35,228	10,087	24,630	511	14,543	D	28.6%	69.9%	29.1%	70.9%
17,382	MONROE	6,249	1,082	5,026	141	3,944	D	17.3%	80.4%	17.7%	82.3%
571,697	MONTGOMERY	220,285	48,870	168,770	2,645	119,900	D	22.2%	76.6%	22.5%	77.5%
14,241	MORGAN	5,087	2,073	2,916	98	843	D	40.8%	57.3%	41.6%	58.4%
26,480	MORROW	9,783	3,596	6,027	160	2,431	D	36.8%	61.6%	37.4%	62.6%
83,340	MUSKINGUM	31,811	10,644	20,466	701	9,822	D	33.5%	64.3%	34.2%	65.8%
11,310	NOBLE	5,054	1,737	3,209	108	1,472	D	34.4%	63.5%	35.1%	64.9%
40,076	OTTAWA	16,574	5,619	10,674	281	5,055	D	33.9%	64.4%	34.5%	65.5%
21,302	PAULDING	8,275	4,272	3,817	186	455	R	51.6%	46.1%	52.8%	47.2%
31,032	PERRY	10,333	3,000	7,118	215	4,118	D	29.0%	68.9%	29.7%	70.3%
43,662	PICKAWAY	13,963	3,953	8,562	1,448	4,609	D	28.3%	61.3%	31.6%	68.4%
22,802	PIKE	9,415	2,709	6,613	93	3,904	D	28.8%	70.2%	29.1%	70.9%
135,856	PORTAGE	47,168	11,032	34,935	1,201	23,903	D	23.4%	74.1%	24.0%	76.0%
38,223	PREBLE	14,344	4,059	9,979	306	5,920	D	28.3%	69.6%	28.9%	71.1%
32,991	PUTNAM	13,745	5,927	7,474	344	1,547	D	43.1%	54.4%	44.2%	55.8%
131,205	RICHLAND	50,162	16,801	32,392	969	15,591	D	33.5%	64.6%	34.2%	65.8%

OHIO

SENATOR 1980

1980 Census Population	County	Total Vote	Republican	Democratic	Other	Rep.-Dem. Plurality	Percentage Total Vote Rep.	Dem.	Major Vote Rep.	Dem.
65,004	ROSS	21,453	6,624	13,393	1,436	6,769 D	30.9%	62.4%	33.1%	66.9%
63,267	SANDUSKY	23,668	8,430	14,761	477	6,331 D	35.6%	62.4%	36.4%	63.6%
84,545	SCIOTO	31,508	8,373	22,697	438	14,324 D	26.6%	72.0%	26.9%	73.1%
61,901	SENECA	22,864	10,983	11,403	478	420 D	48.0%	49.9%	49.1%	50.9%
43,089	SHELBY	16,134	4,338	11,486	310	7,148 D	26.9%	71.2%	27.4%	72.6%
378,823	STARK	156,111	46,653	106,738	2,720	60,085 D	29.9%	68.4%	30.4%	69.6%
524,472	SUMMIT	208,020	40,673	162,035	5,312	121,362 D	19.6%	77.9%	20.1%	79.9%
241,863	TRUMBULL	90,650	17,236	71,657	1,757	54,421 D	19.0%	79.0%	19.4%	80.6%
84,614	TUSCARAWAS	30,199	8,913	20,532	754	11,619 D	29.5%	68.0%	30.3%	69.7%
29,536	UNION	10,944	4,382	6,373	189	1,991 D	40.0%	58.2%	40.7%	59.3%
30,458	VAN WERT	12,610	5,976	6,393	241	417 D	47.4%	50.7%	48.3%	51.7%
11,584	VINTON	4,865	1,740	3,030	95	1,290 D	35.8%	62.3%	36.5%	63.5%
99,276	WARREN	34,497	10,600	23,152	745	12,552 D	30.7%	67.1%	31.4%	68.6%
64,266	WASHINGTON	21,942	9,106	12,207	629	3,101 D	41.5%	55.6%	42.7%	57.3%
97,408	WAYNE	33,357	8,290	24,477	590	16,187 D	24.9%	73.4%	25.3%	74.7%
36,369	WILLIAMS	13,809	6,786	6,811	212	25 D	49.1%	49.3%	49.9%	50.1%
107,372	WOOD	41,483	15,692	25,182	609	9,490 D	37.8%	60.7%	38.4%	61.6%
22,651	WYANDOT	9,010	3,957	4,870	183	913 D	43.9%	54.1%	44.8%	55.2%
10,797,419	TOTAL	4,027,303	1,137,695	2,770,786	118,822	1,633,091 D	28.2%	68.8%	29.1%	70.9%

OHIO

CONGRESS

CD	Year	Total Vote	Republican Vote	Republican Candidate	Democratic Vote	Democratic Candidate	Other Vote	Rep.-Dem. Plurality	Total Vote Rep.	Total Vote Dem.	Major Vote Rep.	Major Vote Dem.
1	1980	166,180	124,080	GRADISON, WILLIS D.	38,529	ZWICK, DONALD J.	3,571	85,551 R	74.7%	23.2%	76.3%	23.7%
1	1978	114,169	73,593	GRADISON, WILLIS D.	38,669	BURKE, TIMOTHY M.	1,907	34,924 R	64.5%	33.9%	65.6%	34.4%
1	1976	169,516	109,789	GRADISON, WILLIS D.	56,995	BOWEN, WILLIAM F.	2,732	52,794 R	64.8%	33.6%	65.8%	34.2%
1	1974	137,991	70,284	GRADISON, WILLIS D.	67,685	LUKEN, THOMAS A.	22	2,599 R	50.9%	49.1%	50.9%	49.1%
1	1972	170,044	119,469	KEATING, WILLIAM J.	50,575	HEISER, KARL F.		68,894 R	70.3%	29.7%	70.3%	29.7%
2	1980	176,116	72,693	ATKINS, THEARON O.	103,423	LUKEN, THOMAS A.		30,730 D	41.3%	58.7%	41.3%	58.7%
2	1978	123,238	58,716	ARONOFF, STANLEY J.	64,522	LUKEN, THOMAS A.		5,806 D	47.6%	52.4%	47.6%	52.4%
2	1976	171,637	83,459	CLANCY, DONALD D.	88,178	LUKEN, THOMAS A.		4,719 D	48.6%	51.4%	48.6%	51.4%
2	1974	134,042	71,512	CLANCY, DONALD D.	62,530	WOLTERMAN, E. W.		8,982 R	53.4%	46.6%	53.4%	46.6%
2	1972	175,198	109,961	CLANCY, DONALD D.	65,237	MANES, PENNY		44,724 R	62.8%	37.2%	62.8%	37.2%
3	1980	166,869	66,698	SEALY, ALBERT H.	95,558	HALL, TONY P.	4,613	28,860 D	40.0%	57.3%	41.1%	58.9%
3	1978	116,804	51,833	KIRCHER, DUDLEY P.	62,849	HALL, TONY P.	2,122	11,016 D	44.4%	53.8%	45.2%	54.8%
3	1976	145,374	100,871	WHALEN, CHARLES W.	33,873	STUBBS, LEONARD	10,630	66,998 R	69.4%	23.3%	74.9%	25.1%
3	1974	82,159	82,159	WHALEN, CHARLES W.				82,159 R	100.0%		100.0%	
3	1972	146,072	111,253	WHALEN, CHARLES W.	34,819	LELAK, JOHN W.		76,434 R	76.2%	23.8%	76.2%	23.8%
4	1980	184,945	133,795	GUYER, TENNYSON	51,150	TEBBEN, GERRY		82,645 R	72.3%	27.7%	72.3%	27.7%
4	1978	124,935	85,575	GUYER, TENNYSON	39,360	GRIFFIN, JOHN W.		46,215 R	68.5%	31.5%	68.5%	31.5%
4	1976	172,957	121,173	GUYER, TENNYSON	51,784	DORSEY, CLINTON G.		69,389 R	70.1%	29.9%	70.1%	29.9%
4	1974	132,739	81,674	GUYER, TENNYSON	51,065	GEHRLICH, JAMES L.		30,609 R	61.5%	38.5%	61.5%	38.5%
4	1972	174,828	109,612	GUYER, TENNYSON	65,216	NICHOLAS, DIMITRI		44,396 R	62.7%	37.3%	62.7%	37.3%
5	1980	194,707	137,003	LATTA, DELBERT L.	57,704	SHERCK, JAMES R.		79,299 R	70.4%	29.6%	70.4%	29.6%
5	1978	136,618	85,547	LATTA, DELBERT L.	51,071	SHERCK, JAMES R.		34,476 R	62.6%	37.4%	62.6%	37.4%
5	1976	185,214	124,910	LATTA, DELBERT L.	60,304	EDWARDS, BRUCE		64,606 R	67.4%	32.6%	67.4%	32.6%
5	1974	142,552	89,161	LATTA, DELBERT L.	53,391	EDWARDS, BRUCE		35,770 R	62.5%	37.5%	62.5%	37.5%
5	1972	181,497	132,032	LATTA, DELBERT L.	49,465	EDWARDS, BRUCE		82,567 R	72.7%	27.3%	72.7%	27.3%
6	1980	185,523	101,288	MCEWEN, BOB	84,235	STRICKLAND, TED		17,053 R	54.6%	45.4%	54.6%	45.4%
6	1978	131,910	85,592	HARSHA, WILLIAM H.	46,318	STRICKLAND, TED		39,274 R	64.9%	35.1%	64.9%	35.1%
6	1976	174,131	107,064	HARSHA, WILLIAM H.	67,067	STRICKLAND, TED		39,997 R	61.5%	38.5%	61.5%	38.5%
6	1974	135,716	93,400	HARSHA, WILLIAM H.	42,316	WOOD, LLOYD A.		51,084 R	68.8%	31.2%	68.8%	31.2%
6	1972	128,394	128,394	HARSHA, WILLIAM H.				128,394 R	100.0%		100.0%	
7	1980	163,089	124,137	BROWN, CLARENCE, JR.	38,952	HOLLISTER, DONALD		85,185 R	76.1%	23.9%	76.1%	23.9%
7	1978	92,507	92,507	BROWN, CLARENCE, JR.				92,507 R	100.0%		100.0%	
7	1976	155,782	101,027	BROWN, CLARENCE, JR.	54,755	FRANKE, DOROTHY		46,272 R	64.9%	35.1%	64.9%	35.1%
7	1974	121,419	73,503	BROWN, CLARENCE, JR.	34,828	NELSON, PATRICK L.	13,088	38,675 R	60.5%	28.7%	67.9%	32.1%
7	1972	153,295	112,350	BROWN, CLARENCE, JR.			40,945	112,350 R	73.3%		100.0%	
8	1980	183,752	139,590	KINDNESS, THOMAS N.	44,162	GRIFFIN, JOHN W.		95,428 R	76.0%	24.0%	76.0%	24.0%
8	1978	113,652	81,156	KINDNESS, THOMAS N.	32,493	SCHROEDER, LOU	3	48,663 R	71.4%	28.6%	71.4%	28.6%
8	1976	161,357	110,775	KINDNESS, THOMAS N.	46,424	GRIFFIN, JOHN W.	4,158	64,351 R	68.7%	28.8%	70.5%	29.5%
8	1974	120,415	51,097	KINDNESS, THOMAS N.	45,701	STRINKO, T. EDWARD	23,617	5,396 R	42.4%	38.0%	52.8%	47.2%
8	1972	153,394	80,050	POWELL, WALTER E.	73,344	RUPPERT, JAMES D.		6,706 R	52.2%	47.8%	52.2%	47.8%
9	1980	172,423	96,927	WEBER, ED	68,728	ASHLEY, THOMAS L.	6,768	28,199 R	56.2%	39.9%	58.5%	41.5%
9	1978	113,128	34,326	HOYT, JOHN C.	71,709	ASHLEY, THOMAS L.	7,093	37,383 D	30.3%	63.4%	32.4%	67.6%
9	1976	167,969	73,919	FINKBEINER, C. S.	91,040	ASHLEY, THOMAS L.	3,010	17,121 D	44.0%	54.2%	44.8%	55.2%
9	1974	122,775	57,892	FINKBEINER, C. S.	64,831	ASHLEY, THOMAS L.	52	6,939 D	47.2%	52.8%	47.2%	52.8%
9	1972	159,838	49,388	RICHARDS, JOSEPH C.	110,450	ASHLEY, THOMAS L.		61,062 D	30.9%	69.1%	30.9%	69.1%
10	1980	192,836	143,403	MILLER, CLARENCE E.	49,433	STECHER, JACK E.		93,970 R	74.4%	25.6%	74.4%	25.6%
10	1978	134,368	99,329	MILLER, CLARENCE E.	35,039	PLUMMER, JAMES A.		64,290 R	73.9%	26.1%	73.9%	26.1%
10	1976	184,904	127,147	MILLER, CLARENCE E.	57,757	PLUMMER, JAMES A.		69,390 R	68.8%	31.2%	68.8%	31.2%
10	1974	142,854	100,521	MILLER, CLARENCE E.	42,333	BUMPASS, H. KENT		58,188 R	70.4%	29.6%	70.4%	29.6%
10	1972	177,139	129,683	MILLER, CLARENCE E.	47,456	WHEALEY, ROBERT H.		82,227 R	73.2%	26.8%	73.2%	26.8%
11	1980	185,473	128,507	STANTON, J. WILLIAM	51,224	DONLIN, PATRICK J.	5,742	77,283 R	69.3%	27.6%	71.5%	28.5%
11	1978	131,181	89,327	STANTON, J. WILLIAM	37,131	DONLIN, PATRICK J.	4,723	52,196 R	68.1%	28.3%	70.6%	29.4%
11	1976	168,264	120,716	STANTON, J. WILLIAM	47,548	WEST, THOMAS R.		73,168 R	71.7%	28.3%	71.7%	28.3%
11	1974	131,857	79,756	STANTON, J. WILLIAM	52,017	COFFEY, MICHAEL D.	84	27,739 R	60.5%	39.4%	60.5%	39.5%
11	1972	156,732	106,841	STANTON, J. WILLIAM	49,891	CALLAHAN, DENNIS M.		56,950 R	68.2%	31.8%	68.2%	31.8%
12	1980	206,804	98,110	DEVINE, SAMUEL L.	108,690	SHAMANSKY, BOB	4	10,580 D	47.4%	52.6%	47.4%	52.6%
12	1978	143,271	81,573	DEVINE, SAMUEL L.	61,698	BAUMANN, JAMES L.		19,875 R	56.9%	43.1%	56.9%	43.1%
12	1976	195,840	90,987	DEVINE, SAMUEL L.	89,424	RYAN, FRAN	15,429	1,563 R	46.5%	45.7%	50.4%	49.6%
12	1974	144,121	73,303	DEVINE, SAMUEL L.	70,818	RYAN, FRAN		2,485 R	50.9%	49.1%	50.9%	49.1%
12	1972	184,729	103,655	DEVINE, SAMUEL L.	81,074	GOODRICH, JAMES W.		22,581 R	56.1%	43.9%	56.1%	43.9%

OHIO

CONGRESS

CD	Year	Total Vote	Republican Vote	Republican Candidate	Democratic Vote	Democratic Candidate	Other Vote	Rep.-Dem. Plurality	Total Vote Rep.	Total Vote Dem.	Major Vote Rep.	Major Vote Dem.
13	1980	177,735	64,296	ARMSTRONG, DAVID E.	113,439	PEASE, DONALD J.		49,143 D	36.2%	63.8%	36.2%	63.8%
13	1978	124,144	43,269	WHITFIELD, MARK W.	80,875	PEASE, DONALD J.		37,606 D	34.9%	65.1%	34.9%	65.1%
13	1976	163,683	49,828	MATHNA, WOODROW W.	108,061	PEASE, DONALD J.	5,794	58,233 D	30.4%	66.0%	31.6%	68.4%
13	1974	126,647	72,881	MOSHER, CHARLES A.	53,766	RITENAUER, FRED M.		19,115 R	57.5%	42.5%	57.5%	42.5%
13	1972	163,233	111,242	MOSHER, CHARLES A.	51,991	RYAN, JOHN M.		59,251 R	68.1%	31.9%	68.1%	31.9%
14	1980	159,298	55,962	MANGELS, LOUIS A.	103,336	SEIBERLING, JOHN F.		47,374 D	35.1%	64.9%	35.1%	64.9%
14	1978	113,667	31,311	VOGEL, WALTER J.	82,356	SEIBERLING, JOHN F.		51,045 D	27.5%	72.5%	27.5%	72.5%
14	1976	164,188	39,917	HOUSTON, JAMES E.	121,652	SEIBERLING, JOHN F.	2,619	81,735 D	24.3%	74.1%	24.7%	75.3%
14	1974	124,534	30,603	FIGETAKIS, MARK	93,931	SEIBERLING, JOHN F.		63,328 D	24.6%	75.4%	24.6%	75.4%
14	1972	181,558	46,490	HOLT, NORMAN W.	135,068	SEIBERLING, JOHN F.		88,578 D	25.6%	74.4%	25.6%	74.4%
15	1980	177,733	129,025	WYLIE, CHALMERS P.	48,708	FREEMAN, TERRY		80,317 R	72.6%	27.4%	72.6%	27.4%
15	1978	128,023	91,023	WYLIE, CHALMERS P.	37,000	ECKHART, HENRY W.		54,023 R	71.1%	28.9%	71.1%	28.9%
15	1976	167,371	109,630	WYLIE, CHALMERS P.	57,741	MCGEE, MANLEY L.		51,889 R	65.5%	34.5%	65.5%	34.5%
15	1974	129,059	79,376	WYLIE, CHALMERS P.	49,683	MCGEE, MANLEY L.		29,693 R	61.5%	38.5%	61.5%	38.5%
15	1972	175,913	115,779	WYLIE, CHALMERS P.	55,314	MCGEE, MANLEY L.	4,820	60,465 R	65.8%	31.4%	67.7%	32.3%
16	1980	189,179	149,960	REGULA, RALPH S.	39,219	SLAGLE, LARRY V.		110,741 R	79.3%	20.7%	79.3%	20.7%
16	1978	134,792	105,152	REGULA, RALPH S.	29,640	HAND, OWEN S.		75,512 R	78.0%	22.0%	78.0%	22.0%
16	1976	174,091	116,374	REGULA, RALPH S.	55,671	FREEDOM, JOHN G.	2,046	60,703 R	66.8%	32.0%	67.6%	32.4%
16	1974	141,740	92,986	REGULA, RALPH S.	48,754	FREEDOM, JOHN G.		44,232 R	65.6%	34.4%	65.6%	34.4%
16	1972	177,942	102,013	REGULA, RALPH S.	75,929	MUSSER, VIRGIL L.		26,084 R	57.3%	42.7%	57.3%	42.7%
17	1980	176,770	128,870	ASHBROOK, JOHN M.	47,900	YUNKER, DONALD E.		80,970 R	72.9%	27.1%	72.9%	27.1%
17	1978	129,127	87,010	ASHBROOK, JOHN M.	42,117	GRIER, KENNETH R.		44,893 R	67.4%	32.6%	67.4%	32.6%
17	1976	167,042	94,874	ASHBROOK, JOHN M.	72,168	MCDONALD, JOHN C.		22,706 R	56.8%	43.2%	56.8%	43.2%
17	1974	134,053	70,708	ASHBROOK, JOHN M.	63,342	NOBLE, DAVID D.	3	7,366 R	52.7%	47.3%	52.7%	47.3%
17	1972	161,554	92,666	ASHBROOK, JOHN M.	62,512	BECK, RAYMOND C.	6,376	30,154 R	57.4%	38.7%	59.7%	40.3%
18	1980	177,189	42,354	HAMMERSLEY, GARY L.	134,835	APPLEGATE, DOUGLAS		92,481 D	23.9%	76.1%	23.9%	76.1%
18	1978	120,825	48,931	RESS, BILL	71,894	APPLEGATE, DOUGLAS		22,963 D	40.5%	59.5%	40.5%	59.5%
18	1976	185,834	45,735	MCCOY, RALPH R.	116,901	APPLEGATE, DOUGLAS	23,198	71,166 D	24.6%	62.9%	28.1%	71.9%
18	1974	137,832	47,385	ROMIG, RALPH H.	90,447	HAYS, WAYNE L.		43,062 D	34.4%	65.6%	34.4%	65.6%
18	1972	183,235	54,572	STEWART, ROBERT	128,663	HAYS, WAYNE L.		74,091 D	29.8%	70.2%	29.8%	70.2%
19	1980	184,304	107,032	WILLIAMS, LYLE	77,272	MESHEL, HARRY		29,760 R	58.1%	41.9%	58.1%	41.9%
19	1978	141,867	71,890	WILLIAMS, LYLE	69,977	CARNEY, CHARLES J.		1,913 R	50.7%	49.3%	50.7%	49.3%
19	1976	179,895	86,162	HUNTER, JACK C.	90,386	CARNEY, CHARLES J.	3,347	4,224 D	47.9%	50.2%	48.8%	51.2%
19	1974	134,358	36,649	RIPPLE, JAMES L.	97,709	CARNEY, CHARLES J.		61,060 D	27.3%	72.7%	27.3%	72.7%
19	1972	171,913	61,934	PARR, NORMAN M.	109,979	CARNEY, CHARLES J.		48,045 D	36.0%	64.0%	36.0%	64.0%
20	1980	96,217			96,217	OAKAR, MARY ROSE		96,217 D		100.0%		100.0%
20	1978	76,973			76,973	OAKAR, MARY ROSE		76,973 D		100.0%		100.0%
20	1976	121,976			98,785	OAKAR, MARY ROSE	23,191	98,785 D		81.0%		100.0%
20	1974	99,396	12,991	FRANTZ, ROBERT A.	86,405	STANTON, JAMES V.		73,414 D	13.1%	86.9%	13.1%	86.9%
20	1972	139,219	16,624	VILT, THOMAS E.	117,302	STANTON, JAMES V.	5,293	100,678 D	11.9%	84.3%	12.4%	87.6%
21	1980	94,291	11,103	WOODALL, ROBERT L.	83,188	STOKES, LOUIS		72,085 D	11.8%	88.2%	11.8%	88.2%
21	1978	68,467	9,533	MACK, BILL	58,934	STOKES, LOUIS		49,401 D	13.9%	86.1%	13.9%	86.1%
21	1976	109,626	12,434	SPARKS, BARBARA	91,903	STOKES, LOUIS	5,289	79,469 D	11.3%	83.8%	11.9%	88.1%
21	1974	71,955	12,986	MACK, BILL	58,969	STOKES, LOUIS		45,983 D	18.0%	82.0%	18.0%	82.0%
21	1972	122,339	13,861	JOHNSON, JAMES D.	99,190	STOKES, LOUIS	9,288	85,329 D	11.3%	81.1%	12.3%	87.7%
22	1980	195,869	80,836	NAHRA, JOSEPH J.	108,137	ECKART, DENNIS E.	6,896	27,301 D	41.3%	55.2%	42.8%	57.2%
22	1978	132,572	30,935	SANDER, RICHARD W.	87,551	VANIK, CHARLES A.	14,086	56,616 D	23.3%	66.0%	26.1%	73.9%
22	1976	176,723	42,727	HANNA, HARRY A.	128,535	VANIK, CHARLES A.	5,461	85,808 D	24.2%	72.7%	24.9%	75.1%
22	1974	143,256	30,585	FRANZ, WILLIAM J.	112,671	VANIK, CHARLES A.		82,086 D	21.3%	78.7%	21.3%	78.7%
22	1972	197,844	64,577	GROPP, DONALD W.	126,462	VANIK, CHARLES A.	6,805	61,885 D	32.6%	63.9%	33.8%	66.2%
23	1980	144,377			144,371	MOTTL, RONALD M.	6	144,371 D		100.0%		100.0%
23	1978	133,707	33,732	TAFT, HOMER S.	99,975	MOTTL, RONALD M.		66,243 D	25.2%	74.8%	25.2%	74.8%
23	1976	178,380	47,804	SCANLON, MICHAEL T.	130,576	MOTTL, RONALD M.		82,772 D	26.8%	73.2%	26.8%	73.2%
23	1974	153,455	46,810	MASTICS, GEORGE E.	53,338	MOTTL, RONALD M.	53,307	6,528 D	30.5%	34.8%	46.7%	53.3%
23	1972	199,631	98,594	MINSHALL, WILLIAM E.	94,366	KUCINICH, DENNIS J.	6,671	4,228 R	49.4%	47.3%	51.1%	48.9%

OHIO

1980 GENERAL ELECTION

President   Other vote was 254,472 Anderson (Independent); 49,033 Clark (Independent); 8,564 Commoner (Independent); 4,729 Hall (Independent); 4,029 Congress (Independent); 3,790 Griswold (Independent); 27 Bubar (write-in). Vote for Congress was with Zimmermann for Vice President, the Socialist Workers candidate in other states.

Senator   Other vote was 76,412 Powers (Independent); 42,410 Nagin (Independent).

Congress   Other vote was Breen (Independent) in CD 1; 2,903 Righter (Independent) and 1,710 Tharpe (Independent) in CD 3; 4,357 Emery (Independent) and 2,411 Emmerich (Independent) in CD 9; Richard (Independent) in CD 11; Smith (write-in) in CD 12; Gleisser (Independent) in CD 22; Clendenan (write-in) in CD 23.

1980 PRIMARIES

JUNE 3 REPUBLICAN

Senator   James E. Betts, unopposed.

Congress   Unopposed in fourteen CD's. No candidates in CD's 20 and 23. In CD 20 Guy M. Connors received the nomination with 107 write-in votes, but withdrew after the primary and no substitution was made. Contested as follows:

CD 2   28,197 Thearon O. Atkins; 7,870 Spencer S. Reibman.
CD 6   21,360 Bob McEwen; 8,221 James T. Christy; 6,545 Don Gingerich; 3,746 James A. Murray; 2,601 Ralph Vanzant; 2,249 Leonard L. Toft; 1,466 Joseph J. Walker; 1,233 Gregory J. Vetter.
CD 9   16,322 Ed Weber; 5,153 Vernon W. Wagner.
CD 13   16,599 David E. Armstrong; 10,586 Anthony J. DePaola.
CD 14   12,653 Louis A. Mangels; 10,155 Walter J. Vogel.
CD 21   1,705 Robert L. Woodall; 1,183 Bill Mack.
CD 22   17,924 Joseph J. Nahra; 15,574 Ruth R. Miller.

JUNE 3 DEMOCRATIC

Senator   934,230 John H. Glenn; 88,506 Frances A. Waterman; 64,270 Francis Hunstiger.

Congress   Unopposed in seventeen CD's. Contested as follows:

CD 6   32,997 Ted Strickland; 6,091 Robert M. Smith; 2,468 Fred S. Porginski.
CD 8   22,045 John W. Griffin; 6,947 Philip B. Handler.
CD 10   20,858 Jack E. Stecher; 14,097 William Safranek.
CD 11   22,756 Patrick J. Donlin; 9,583 Ralph A. Swanson; 9,436 Raymond K. Smith; 8,323 Hugo Bouse.
CD 13   41,632 Donald J. Pease; 7,194 John M. Ryan; 6,697 Peter W. Vander Wyden; 5,192 Norbert G. Dennerll.
CD 22   27,854 Dennis E. Eckart; 16,067 J. Timothy McCormack; 12,313 Anthony O. Calabrese; 7,325 Sheldon D. Schecter; 2,575 Thomas W. Lippitt; 1,488 Frank J. Soltis; 810 Edward L. Viets.

OKLAHOMA

GOVERNOR

George Nigh (D). Elected 1978 to a four-year term.

SENATORS

David L. Boren (D). Elected 1978 to a six-year term.

Don Nickles (R). Elected 1980 to a six-year term.

REPRESENTATIVES

1. James R. Jones (D)   3. Wes Watkins (D)   5. M. H. Edwards (R)
2. Mike Synar (D)   4. Dave McCurdy (D)   6. Glenn English (D)

POSTWAR VOTE FOR GOVERNOR

Year	Total Vote	Republican Vote	Candidate	Democratic Vote	Candidate	Other Vote	Rep.-Dem. Plurality	Percentage Total Vote Rep.	Dem.	Major Vote Rep.	Dem.
1978	777,414	367,055	Shotts, Ron	402,240	Nigh, George	8,119	35,185 D	47.2%	51.7%	47.7%	52.3%
1974	804,848	290,459	Inhofe, James M.	514,389	Boren, David L.	—	223,930 D	36.1%	63.9%	36.1%	63.9%
1970	698,790	336,157	Bartlett, Dewey F.	338,338	Hall, David	24,295	2,181 D	48.1%	48.4%	49.8%	50.2%
1966	677,258	377,078	Bartlett, Dewey F.	296,328	Moore, Preston J.	3,852	80,750 R	55.7%	43.8%	56.0%	44.0%
1962	709,763	392,316	Bellmon, Henry	315,357	Atkinson, W. P.	2,090	76,959 R	55.3%	44.4%	55.4%	44.6%
1958	538,839	107,495	Ferguson, Phil	399,504	Edmondson, J. Howard	31,840	292,009 D	19.9%	74.1%	21.2%	78.8%
1954	609,194	251,808	Sparks, Reuben K.	357,386	Gary, Raymond	—	105,578 D	41.3%	58.7%	41.3%	58.7%
1950	644,276	313,205	Ferguson, Jo O.	329,308	Murray, Johnston	1,763	16,103 D	48.6%	51.1%	48.7%	51.3%
1946	494,599	227,426	Flynn, Olney F.	259,491	Turner, Roy J.	7,682	32,065 D	46.0%	52.5%	46.7%	53.3%

POSTWAR VOTE FOR SENATOR

Year	Total Vote	Republican Vote	Candidate	Democratic Vote	Candidate	Other Vote	Rep.-Dem. Plurality	Percentage Total Vote Rep.	Dem.	Major Vote Rep.	Dem.
1980	1,098,294	587,252	Nickles, Don	478,283	Coats, Andrew	32,759	108,969 R	53.5%	43.5%	55.1%	44.9%
1978	754,264	247,857	Kamm, Robert B.	493,953	Boren, David L.	12,454	246,096 D	32.9%	65.5%	33.4%	66.6%
1974	791,809	390,997	Bellmon, Henry	387,162	Edmondson, Ed	13,650	3,835 R	49.4%	48.9%	50.2%	49.8%
1972	1,005,148	516,934	Bartlett, Dewey F.	478,212	Edmondson, Ed	10,002	38,722 R	51.4%	47.6%	51.9%	48.1%
1968	909,119	470,120	Bellmon, Henry	419,658	Monroney, A. S. Mike	19,341	50,462 R	51.7%	46.2%	52.8%	47.2%
1966	638,742	295,585	Patterson, Pat J.	343,157	Harris, Fred R.	—	47,572 D	46.3%	53.7%	46.3%	53.7%
1964s	912,174	445,392	Wilkinson, Bud	466,782	Harris, Fred R.	—	21,390 D	48.8%	51.2%	48.8%	51.2%
1962	664,712	307,966	Crawford, B. Hayden	353,890	Monroney, A. S. Mike	2,856	45,924 D	46.3%	53.2%	46.5%	53.5%
1960	864,475	385,646	Crawford, B. Hayden	474,116	Kerr, Robert S.	4,713	88,470 D	44.6%	54.8%	44.9%	55.1%
1956	831,142	371,146	McKeever, Douglas	459,996	Monroney, A. S. Mike	—	88,850 D	44.7%	55.3%	44.7%	55.3%
1954	600,120	262,013	Mock, Fred M.	335,127	Kerr, Robert S.	2,980	73,114 D	43.7%	55.8%	43.9%	56.1%
1950	631,177	285,224	Alexander, W. H.	345,953	Monroney, A. S. Mike	—	60,729 D	45.2%	54.8%	45.2%	54.8%
1948	708,931	265,169	Rizley, Ross	441,654	Kerr, Robert S.	2,108	176,485 D	37.4%	62.3%	37.5%	62.5%

The 1964 election was for a short term to fill a vacancy.

OKLAHOMA

Districts Established April 3, 1972

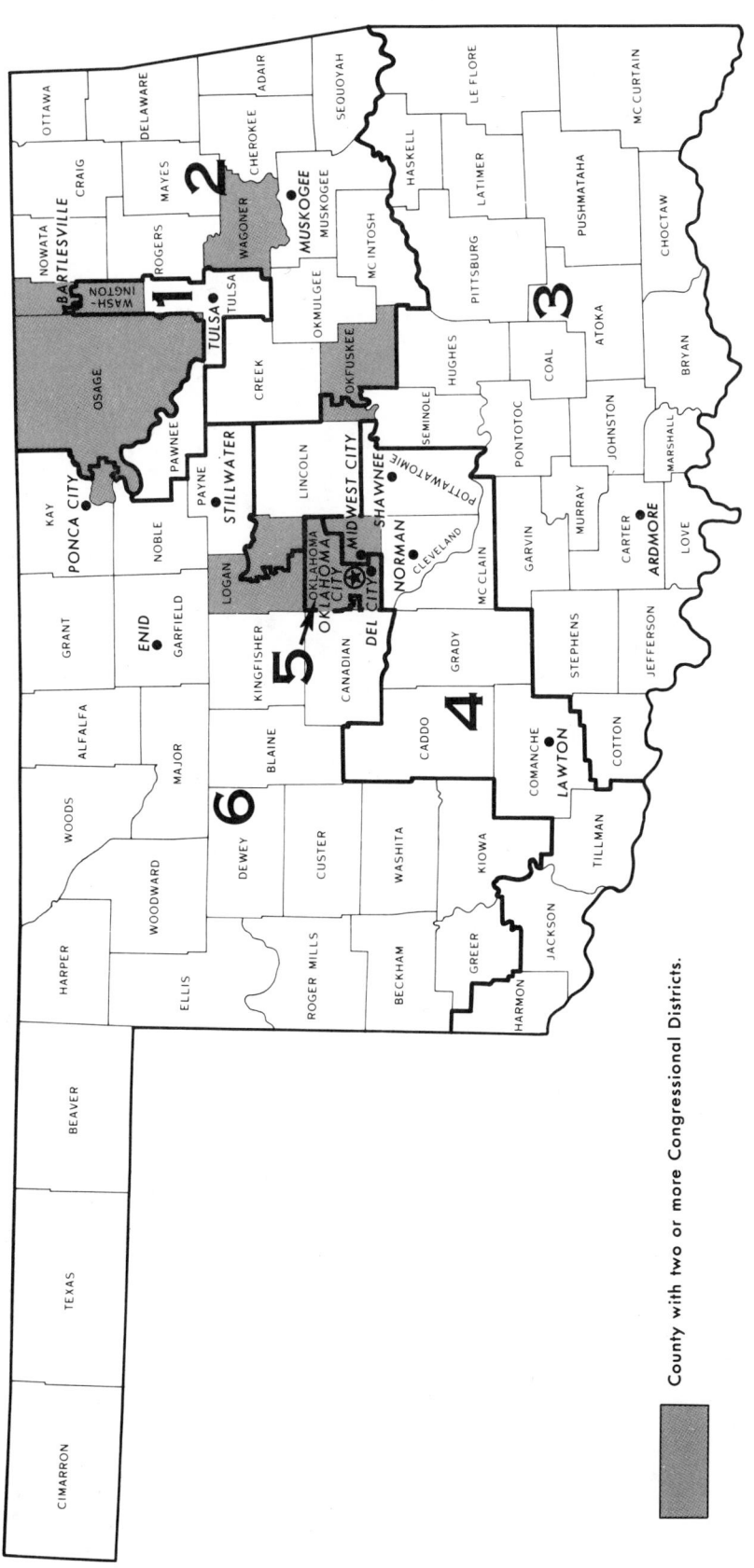

County with two or more Congressional Districts.

OKLAHOMA

PRESIDENT 1980

1980 Census Population	County	Total Vote	Republican	Democratic	Other	Rep.-Dem. Plurality	Percentage Total Vote Rep.	Dem.	Major Vote Rep.	Dem.
18,575	ADAIR	6,341	3,429	2,761	151	668 R	54.1%	43.5%	55.4%	44.6%
7,077	ALFALFA	3,642	2,628	899	115	1,729 R	72.2%	24.7%	74.5%	25.5%
12,748	ATOKA	4,216	1,613	2,505	98	892 D	38.3%	59.4%	39.2%	60.8%
6,806	BEAVER	3,218	2,430	696	92	1,734 R	75.5%	21.6%	77.7%	22.3%
19,243	BECKHAM	7,113	3,637	3,298	178	339 R	51.1%	46.4%	52.4%	47.6%
13,443	BLAINE	5,264	3,708	1,399	157	2,309 R	70.4%	26.6%	72.6%	27.4%
30,535	BRYAN	10,582	3,980	6,410	192	2,430 D	37.6%	60.6%	38.3%	61.7%
30,905	CADDO	10,995	5,945	4,695	355	1,250 R	54.1%	42.7%	55.9%	44.1%
56,452	CANADIAN	21,041	15,272	4,889	880	10,383 R	72.6%	23.2%	75.8%	24.2%
43,610	CARTER	16,154	9,262	6,509	383	2,753 R	57.3%	40.3%	58.7%	41.3%
30,684	CHEROKEE	11,308	5,594	5,215	499	379 R	49.5%	46.1%	51.8%	48.2%
17,203	CHOCTAW	6,009	2,394	3,507	108	1,113 D	39.8%	58.4%	40.6%	59.4%
3,648	CIMARRON	1,821	1,404	373	44	1,031 R	77.1%	20.5%	79.0%	21.0%
133,173	CLEVELAND	50,401	31,178	14,536	4,687	16,642 R	61.9%	28.8%	68.2%	31.8%
6,041	COAL	2,431	926	1,442	63	516 D	38.1%	59.3%	39.1%	60.9%
112,456	COMANCHE	27,910	16,609	9,972	1,329	6,637 R	59.5%	35.7%	62.5%	37.5%
7,338	COTTON	3,206	1,702	1,410	94	292 R	53.1%	44.0%	54.7%	45.3%
15,014	CRAIG	5,952	2,956	2,801	195	155 R	49.7%	47.1%	51.3%	48.7%
59,210	CREEK	19,729	11,749	7,339	641	4,410 R	59.6%	37.2%	61.6%	38.4%
25,995	CUSTER	9,854	6,469	3,008	377	3,461 R	65.6%	30.5%	68.3%	31.7%
23,946	DELAWARE	9,819	5,302	4,244	273	1,058 R	54.0%	43.2%	55.5%	44.5%
5,922	DEWEY	2,876	1,943	826	107	1,117 R	67.6%	28.7%	70.2%	29.8%
5,596	ELLIS	2,550	1,908	561	81	1,347 R	74.8%	22.0%	77.3%	22.7%
62,820	GARFIELD	24,828	17,989	5,718	1,121	12,271 R	72.5%	23.0%	75.9%	24.1%
27,856	GARVIN	10,860	5,520	5,033	307	487 R	50.8%	46.3%	52.3%	47.7%
39,490	GRADY	13,971	8,131	5,330	510	2,801 R	58.2%	38.2%	60.4%	39.6%
6,518	GRANT	3,472	2,411	927	134	1,484 R	69.4%	26.7%	72.2%	27.8%
6,877	GREER	3,099	1,535	1,492	72	43 R	49.5%	48.1%	50.7%	49.3%
4,519	HARMON	1,670	676	961	33	285 D	40.5%	57.5%	41.3%	58.7%
4,715	HARPER	2,230	1,652	517	61	1,135 R	74.1%	23.2%	76.2%	23.8%
11,010	HASKELL	5,011	2,024	2,874	113	850 D	40.4%	57.4%	41.3%	58.7%
14,338	HUGHES	5,515	2,170	3,211	134	1,041 D	39.3%	58.2%	40.3%	59.7%
30,356	JACKSON	8,554	4,327	4,031	196	296 R	50.6%	47.1%	51.8%	48.2%
8,183	JEFFERSON	3,332	1,440	1,812	80	372 D	43.2%	54.4%	44.3%	55.7%
10,356	JOHNSTON	3,857	1,701	2,066	90	365 D	44.1%	53.6%	45.2%	54.8%
49,852	KAY	22,337	15,004	6,449	884	8,555 R	67.2%	28.9%	69.9%	30.1%
14,187	KINGFISHER	6,418	4,962	1,282	174	3,680 R	77.3%	20.0%	79.5%	20.5%
12,711	KIOWA	5,124	2,636	2,372	116	264 R	51.4%	46.3%	52.6%	47.4%
9,840	LATIMER	3,966	1,737	2,105	124	368 D	43.8%	53.1%	45.2%	54.8%
40,698	LE FLORE	13,759	6,807	6,668	284	139 R	49.5%	48.5%	50.5%	49.5%
26,601	LINCOLN	9,585	6,064	3,231	290	2,833 R	63.3%	33.7%	65.2%	34.8%
26,881	LOGAN	9,992	6,311	3,246	435	3,065 R	63.2%	32.5%	66.0%	34.0%
7,469	LOVE	3,075	1,449	1,578	48	129 D	47.1%	51.3%	47.9%	52.1%
20,291	MCCLAIN	7,533	4,284	2,990	259	1,294 R	56.9%	39.7%	58.9%	41.1%
36,151	MCCURTAIN	11,372	5,189	5,953	230	764 D	45.6%	52.3%	46.6%	53.4%
15,495	MCINTOSH	6,763	2,925	3,654	184	729 D	43.3%	54.0%	44.5%	55.5%
8,772	MAJOR	3,739	3,059	584	96	2,475 R	81.8%	15.6%	84.0%	16.0%
10,550	MARSHALL	4,195	1,961	2,157	77	196 D	46.7%	51.4%	47.6%	52.4%
32,261	MAYES	12,358	6,633	5,344	381	1,289 R	53.7%	43.2%	55.4%	44.6%
12,147	MURRAY	5,067	2,494	2,384	189	110 R	49.2%	47.0%	51.1%	48.9%
66,939	MUSKOGEE	25,715	11,511	13,341	863	1,830 D	44.8%	51.9%	46.3%	53.7%
11,573	NOBLE	5,240	3,663	1,398	179	2,265 R	69.9%	26.7%	72.4%	27.6%
11,486	NOWATA	4,470	2,640	1,694	136	946 R	59.1%	37.9%	60.9%	39.1%
11,125	OKFUSKEE	4,401	2,126	2,177	98	51 D	48.3%	49.5%	49.4%	50.6%
568,933	OKLAHOMA	211,273	139,538	58,765	12,970	80,773 R	66.0%	27.8%	70.4%	29.6%
39,169	OKMULGEE	14,285	6,652	7,236	397	584 D	46.6%	50.7%	47.9%	52.1%
39,327	OSAGE	14,246	8,044	5,687	515	2,357 R	56.5%	39.9%	58.6%	41.4%
32,870	OTTAWA	12,919	6,362	6,143	414	219 R	49.2%	47.6%	50.9%	49.1%
15,310	PAWNEE	6,151	3,902	2,020	229	1,882 R	63.4%	32.8%	65.9%	34.1%
62,435	PAYNE	25,691	15,955	7,466	2,270	8,489 R	62.1%	29.1%	68.1%	31.9%
40,524	PITTSBURG	15,857	7,062	8,292	503	1,230 D	44.5%	52.3%	46.0%	54.0%
32,598	PONTOTOC	12,631	6,232	5,942	457	290 R	49.3%	47.0%	51.2%	48.8%
55,239	POTTAWATOMIE	21,850	12,466	8,526	858	3,940 R	57.1%	39.0%	59.4%	40.6%
11,773	PUSHMATAHA	4,775	1,989	2,666	120	677 D	41.7%	55.8%	42.7%	57.3%
4,799	ROGER MILLS	2,171	1,221	877	73	344 R	56.2%	40.4%	58.2%	41.8%
46,436	ROGERS	18,642	11,581	6,399	662	5,182 R	62.1%	34.3%	64.4%	35.6%
27,473	SEMINOLE	10,145	5,067	4,726	352	341 R	49.9%	46.6%	51.7%	48.3%
30,749	SEQUOYAH	11,246	5,987	4,983	276	1,004 R	53.2%	44.3%	54.6%	45.4%
43,419	STEPHENS	17,852	10,199	7,191	462	3,008 R	57.1%	40.3%	58.6%	41.4%
17,727	TEXAS	7,099	5,503	1,451	145	4,052 R	77.5%	20.4%	79.1%	20.9%

OKLAHOMA

PRESIDENT 1980

1980 Census Population	County	Total Vote	Republican	Democratic	Other	Rep.-Dem. Plurality	Percentage Total Vote Rep.	Dem.	Major Vote Rep.	Dem.
12,398	TILLMAN	4,687	2,450	2,144	93	306 R	52.3%	45.7%	53.3%	46.7%
470,593	TULSA	188,148	124,643	53,438	10,067	71,205 R	66.2%	28.4%	70.0%	30.0%
41,801	WAGONER	14,727	8,969	5,235	523	3,734 R	60.9%	35.5%	63.1%	36.9%
48,113	WASHINGTON	23,503	16,563	5,854	1,086	10,709 R	70.5%	24.9%	73.9%	26.1%
13,798	WASHITA	5,373	3,206	2,044	123	1,162 R	59.7%	38.0%	61.1%	38.9%
10,923	WOODS	5,208	3,592	1,364	252	2,228 R	69.0%	26.2%	72.5%	27.5%
21,172	WOODWARD	7,289	5,318	1,703	268	3,615 R	73.0%	23.4%	75.7%	24.3%
3,025,266	TOTAL	1,149,708	695,570	402,026	52,112	293,544 R	60.5%	35.0%	63.4%	36.6%

OKLAHOMA

SENATOR 1980

1980 Census Population	County	Total Vote	Republican	Democratic	Other	Rep.-Dem. Plurality	Total Vote Rep.	Dem.	Major Vote Rep.	Dem.
18,575	ADAIR	5,835	2,878	2,892	65	14 D	49.3%	49.6%	49.9%	50.1%
7,077	ALFALFA	3,387	2,315	1,022	50	1,293 R	68.3%	30.2%	69.4%	30.6%
12,748	ATOKA	4,186	1,366	2,739	81	1,373 D	32.6%	65.4%	33.3%	66.7%
6,806	BEAVER	2,886	2,061	779	46	1,282 R	71.4%	27.0%	72.6%	27.4%
19,243	BECKHAM	6,588	3,200	3,292	96	92 D	48.6%	50.0%	49.3%	50.7%
13,443	BLAINE	5,025	3,396	1,546	83	1,850 R	67.6%	30.8%	68.7%	31.3%
30,535	BRYAN	10,252	2,783	7,290	179	4,507 D	27.1%	71.1%	27.6%	72.4%
30,905	CADDO	10,214	4,800	5,206	208	406 D	47.0%	51.0%	48.0%	52.0%
56,452	CANADIAN	20,497	13,498	6,516	483	6,982 R	65.9%	31.8%	67.4%	32.6%
43,610	CARTER	16,116	7,837	8,000	279	163 D	48.6%	49.6%	49.5%	50.5%
30,684	CHEROKEE	10,657	4,636	5,815	206	1,179 D	43.5%	54.6%	44.4%	55.6%
17,203	CHOCTAW	5,974	1,757	4,128	89	2,371 D	29.4%	69.1%	29.9%	70.1%
3,648	CIMARRON	1,664	1,195	444	25	751 R	71.8%	26.7%	72.9%	27.1%
133,173	CLEVELAND	48,194	26,328	19,448	2,418	6,880 R	54.6%	40.4%	57.5%	42.5%
6,041	COAL	2,421	720	1,641	60	921 D	29.7%	67.8%	30.5%	69.5%
112,456	COMANCHE	25,171	12,141	12,421	609	280 D	48.2%	49.3%	49.4%	50.6%
7,338	COTTON	3,168	1,373	1,728	67	355 D	43.3%	54.5%	44.3%	55.7%
15,014	CRAIG	5,419	2,377	2,943	99	566 D	43.9%	54.3%	44.7%	55.3%
59,210	CREEK	18,380	9,886	8,161	333	1,725 R	53.8%	44.4%	54.8%	45.2%
25,995	CUSTER	9,456	5,286	3,957	213	1,329 R	55.9%	41.8%	57.2%	42.8%
23,946	DELAWARE	8,992	4,395	4,460	137	65 D	48.9%	49.6%	49.6%	50.4%
5,922	DEWEY	2,685	1,618	1,013	54	605 R	60.3%	37.7%	61.5%	38.5%
5,596	ELLIS	2,418	1,670	711	37	959 R	69.1%	29.4%	70.1%	29.9%
62,820	GARFIELD	23,831	16,061	7,265	505	8,796 R	67.4%	30.5%	68.9%	31.1%
27,856	GARVIN	10,802	4,826	5,672	304	846 D	44.7%	52.5%	46.0%	54.0%
39,490	GRADY	13,299	6,797	6,185	317	612 R	51.1%	46.5%	52.4%	47.6%
6,518	GRANT	3,297	2,298	964	35	1,334 R	69.7%	29.2%	70.4%	29.6%
6,877	GREER	2,880	1,186	1,616	78	430 D	41.2%	56.1%	42.3%	57.7%
4,519	HARMON	1,640	628	1,002	10	374 D	38.3%	61.1%	38.5%	61.5%
4,715	HARPER	2,125	1,477	615	33	862 R	69.5%	28.9%	70.6%	29.4%
11,010	HASKELL	4,898	1,658	3,168	72	1,510 D	33.9%	64.7%	34.4%	65.6%
14,338	HUGHES	5,506	1,928	3,473	105	1,545 D	35.0%	63.1%	35.7%	64.3%
30,356	JACKSON	7,710	3,231	4,347	132	1,116 D	41.9%	56.4%	42.6%	57.4%
8,183	JEFFERSON	3,281	1,253	1,972	56	719 D	38.2%	60.1%	38.9%	61.1%
10,356	JOHNSTON	3,809	1,347	2,383	79	1,036 D	35.4%	62.6%	36.1%	63.9%
49,852	KAY	21,874	15,037	6,603	234	8,434 R	68.7%	30.2%	69.5%	30.5%
14,187	KINGFISHER	6,164	4,361	1,683	120	2,678 R	70.7%	27.3%	72.2%	27.8%
12,711	KIOWA	4,860	2,275	2,529	56	254 D	46.8%	52.0%	47.4%	52.6%
9,840	LATIMER	3,949	1,533	2,329	87	796 D	38.8%	59.0%	39.7%	60.3%
40,698	LE FLORE	13,607	5,611	7,834	162	2,223 D	41.2%	57.6%	41.7%	58.3%
26,601	LINCOLN	9,505	5,476	3,800	229	1,676 R	57.6%	40.0%	59.0%	41.0%
26,881	LOGAN	9,973	5,747	3,880	346	1,867 R	57.6%	38.9%	59.7%	40.3%
7,469	LOVE	3,006	1,284	1,669	53	385 D	42.7%	55.5%	43.5%	56.5%
20,291	MCCLAIN	7,000	3,470	3,373	157	97 R	49.6%	48.2%	50.7%	49.3%
36,151	MCCURTAIN	11,152	3,056	7,865	231	4,809 D	27.4%	70.5%	28.0%	72.0%
15,495	MCINTOSH	6,121	2,401	3,604	116	1,203 D	39.2%	58.9%	40.0%	60.0%
8,772	MAJOR	3,609	2,790	771	48	2,019 R	77.3%	21.4%	78.3%	21.7%
10,550	MARSHALL	4,165	1,551	2,546	68	995 D	37.2%	61.1%	37.9%	62.1%
32,261	MAYES	11,386	5,693	5,504	189	189 R	50.0%	48.3%	50.8%	49.2%
12,147	MURRAY	5,062	2,060	2,857	145	797 D	40.7%	56.4%	41.9%	58.1%
66,939	MUSKOGEE	23,580	9,845	13,383	352	3,538 D	41.8%	56.8%	42.4%	57.6%
11,573	NOBLE	5,134	3,510	1,530	94	1,980 R	68.4%	29.8%	69.6%	30.4%
11,486	NOWATA	4,015	2,214	1,713	88	501 R	55.1%	42.7%	56.4%	43.6%
11,125	OKFUSKEE	4,120	1,864	2,171	85	307 D	45.2%	52.7%	46.2%	53.8%
568,933	OKLAHOMA	196,975	112,271	74,524	10,180	37,747 R	57.0%	37.8%	60.1%	39.9%
39,169	OKMULGEE	13,369	5,662	7,519	188	1,857 D	42.4%	56.2%	43.0%	57.0%
39,327	OSAGE	13,274	7,027	5,994	253	1,033 R	52.9%	45.2%	54.0%	46.0%
32,870	OTTAWA	11,687	4,713	6,676	298	1,963 D	40.3%	57.1%	41.4%	58.6%
15,310	PAWNEE	5,784	3,516	2,155	113	1,361 R	60.8%	37.3%	62.0%	38.0%
62,435	PAYNE	25,148	15,275	8,803	1,070	6,472 R	60.7%	35.0%	63.4%	36.6%
40,524	PITTSBURG	15,900	6,336	9,227	337	2,891 D	39.8%	58.0%	40.7%	59.3%
32,598	PONTOTOC	12,633	5,104	7,252	277	2,148 D	40.4%	57.4%	41.3%	58.7%
55,239	POTTAWATOMIE	20,498	10,106	9,867	525	239 R	49.3%	48.1%	50.6%	49.4%
11,773	PUSHMATAHA	4,757	1,533	3,115	109	1,582 D	32.2%	65.5%	33.0%	67.0%
4,799	ROGER MILLS	1,990	1,036	922	32	114 R	52.1%	46.3%	52.9%	47.1%
46,436	ROGERS	17,470	9,783	7,354	333	2,429 R	56.0%	42.1%	57.1%	42.9%
27,473	SEMINOLE	10,087	4,133	5,675	279	1,542 D	41.0%	56.3%	42.1%	57.9%
30,749	SEQUOYAH	9,876	4,249	5,477	150	1,228 D	43.0%	55.5%	43.7%	56.3%
43,419	STEPHENS	17,877	9,016	8,543	318	473 R	50.4%	47.8%	51.3%	48.7%
17,727	TEXAS	6,584	4,586	1,915	83	2,671 R	69.7%	29.1%	70.5%	29.5%

OKLAHOMA

SENATOR 1980

1980 Census Population	County	Total Vote	Republican	Democratic	Other	Rep.-Dem. Plurality	Percentage			
							Total Vote		Major Vote	
							Rep.	Dem.	Rep.	Dem.
12,398	TILLMAN	4,145	1,687	2,402	56	715 D	40.7%	57.9%	41.3%	58.7%
470,593	TULSA	186,425	108,130	71,569	6,726	36,561 R	58.0%	38.4%	60.2%	39.8%
41,801	WAGONER	13,646	7,607	5,775	264	1,832 R	55.7%	42.3%	56.8%	43.2%
48,113	WASHINGTON	22,189	14,542	7,296	351	7,246 R	65.5%	32.9%	66.6%	33.4%
13,798	WASHITA	5,064	2,788	2,199	77	589 R	55.1%	43.4%	55.9%	44.1%
10,923	WOODS	4,957	3,304	1,537	116	1,767 R	66.7%	31.0%	68.3%	31.7%
21,172	WOODWARD	7,014	4,864	2,029	121	2,835 R	69.3%	28.9%	70.6%	29.4%
3,025,266	TOTAL	1,098,294	587,252	478,283	32,759	108,969 R	53.5%	43.5%	55.1%	44.9%

OKLAHOMA

CONGRESS

CD	Year	Total Vote	Republican Vote	Republican Candidate	Democratic Vote	Democratic Candidate	Other Vote	Rep.-Dem. Plurality	Total Vote Rep.	Total Vote Dem.	Major Vote Rep.	Major Vote Dem.
1	1980	197,674	82,293	FREEMAN, RICHARD C.	115,381	JONES, JAMES R.		33,088 D	41.6%	58.4%	41.6%	58.4%
1	1978	123,290	49,404	UNRUH, PAULA	73,886	JONES, JAMES R.		24,482 D	40.1%	59.9%	40.1%	59.9%
1	1976	187,044	84,374	INHOFE, JAMES M.	100,945	JONES, JAMES R.	1,725	16,571 D	45.1%	54.0%	45.5%	54.5%
1	1974	129,856	41,697	MIZER, GEORGE A.	88,159	JONES, JAMES R.		46,462 D	32.1%	67.9%	32.1%	67.9%
1	1972	168,652	73,786	HEWGLEY, J. M.	91,864	JONES, JAMES R.	3,002	18,078 D	43.8%	54.5%	44.5%	55.5%
2	1980	188,060	86,544	RICHARDSON, GARY	101,516	SYNAR, MIKE		14,972 D	46.0%	54.0%	46.0%	54.0%
2	1978	132,436	59,853	RICHARDSON, GARY	72,583	SYNAR, MIKE		12,730 D	45.2%	54.8%	45.2%	54.8%
2	1976	189,743	87,341	STEWART, E. L.	102,402	RISENHOOVER, TED M.		15,061 D	46.0%	54.0%	46.0%	54.0%
2	1974	132,156	54,110	KEEN, RALPH F.	78,046	RISENHOOVER, TED M.		23,936 D	40.9%	59.1%	40.9%	59.1%
2	1972	147,742	42,632	TOLIVER, EMERY H.	105,110	MCSPADDEN, CLEM R.		62,478 D	28.9%	71.1%	28.9%	71.1%
3	1980					WATKINS, WES						
3	1978					WATKINS, WES						
3	1976	184,565	31,732	BEASLEY, GERALD	151,271	WATKINS, WES	1,562	119,539 D	17.2%	82.0%	17.3%	82.7%
3	1974					ALBERT, CARL						
3	1972	108,974			101,732	ALBERT, CARL	7,242	101,732 D		93.4%		100.0%
4	1980	145,584	71,339	RUTLEDGE, HOWARD	74,245	MCCURDY, DAVE		2,906 D	49.0%	51.0%	49.0%	51.0%
4	1978	104,414	41,421	ROBB, SCOTTY	62,993	STEED, TOM		21,572 D	39.7%	60.3%	39.7%	60.3%
4	1976	155,357	34,170	STANLEY, M. C.	116,425	STEED, TOM	4,762	82,255 D	22.0%	74.9%	22.7%	77.3%
4	1974					STEED, TOM						
4	1972	120,062	34,484	CROZIER, WILLIAM E.	85,578	STEED, TOM		51,094 D	28.7%	71.3%	28.7%	71.3%
5	1980	131,590	90,053	EDWARDS, M. H.	36,815	HOOD, DAVID	4,722	53,238 R	68.4%	28.0%	71.0%	29.0%
5	1978	89,429	71,451	EDWARDS, M. H.	17,978	KNIPP, JESSE D.		53,473 R	79.9%	20.1%	79.9%	20.1%
5	1976	157,764	78,651	EDWARDS, M. H.	74,752	DUNLAP, TOM	4,361	3,899 R	49.9%	47.4%	51.3%	48.7%
5	1974	100,812	48,705	EDWARDS, M. H.	52,107	JARMAN, JOHN		3,402 D	48.3%	51.7%	48.3%	51.7%
5	1972	115,421	45,711	KELLER, LLEWELLYN L.	69,710	JARMAN, JOHN		23,999 D	39.6%	60.4%	39.6%	60.4%
6	1980	172,674	60,980	MCCURLEY, CAROL	111,694	ENGLISH, GLENN		50,714 D	35.3%	64.7%	35.3%	64.7%
6	1978	139,543	36,031	HUNTER, HAROLD	103,512	ENGLISH, GLENN		67,481 D	25.8%	74.2%	25.8%	74.2%
6	1976	193,451	55,953	MCCURLEY, CAROL	137,498	ENGLISH, GLENN		81,545 D	28.9%	71.1%	28.9%	71.1%
6	1974	143,488	63,731	CAMP, JOHN N.	76,392	ENGLISH, GLENN	3,365	12,661 D	44.4%	53.2%	45.5%	54.5%
6	1972	156,230	113,567	CAMP, JOHN N.	42,663	SCHMITT, WILLIAM P.		70,904 R	72.7%	27.3%	72.7%	27.3%

OKLAHOMA

1980 GENERAL ELECTION

President   Other vote was 38,284 Anderson (Independent); 13,828 Clark (Libertarian).

Senator   Other vote was 21,179 Nesbitt (Independent); 9,757 Murphy (Libertarian); 1,823 Trent (Independent).

Congress   Under present legislation, votes are not tallied in unopposed elections, so no total vote or candidate vote is available for unopposed Congressional districts. Other vote was Rushing (Libertarian) in CD 5.

1980 PRIMARIES

AUGUST 26 REPUBLICAN

Senator   47,879 Don Nickles; 45,914 John Zink; 39,839 Ed Noble; 2,781 Thorne Stallings; 1,442 Billy Joe Clegg.

Congress   Unopposed in three CD's. No candidate in CD 3. Contested as follows:

CD 4   8,196 Howard Rutledge; 3,710 David Hopper.
CD 6   16,479 Carol McCurley; 15,943 Stephen Jones.

AUGUST 26 DEMOCRATIC

Senator   156,666 Robert S. Kerr, Jr.; 154,762 Andrew Coats; 55,503 Gene Howard; 49,369 James E. Hamilton; 20,074 Paul English; 8,017 John Zelnick; 4,988 Gar Graham; 2,892 Richard W. Klabzuba; 2,762 Johnny Borders; 2,587 Howard W. Joplin; 2,532 Gil Burk.

Congress   Unopposed in three CD's. Contested as follows:

CD 3   108,478 Wes Watkins; 11,373 Leland Kelly.
CD 4   31,104 James B. Townsend; 26,173 Dave McCurdy; 10,722 Cuffie Waid; 7,035 Clifford O. Marshall; 1,781 Rosella P. Saker.
CD 5   19,664 David Hood; 10,298 John Dawson; 3,269 Jesse D. Knipp; 2,494 Art Adams.

AUGUST 26 LIBERTARIAN

Senator   Robert Murphy, unopposed.

Congress   No candidate in five CD's. Contested as follows:

CD 5   24 James F. Rushing; 20 D. Frank Robinson.

SEPTEMBER 16 REPUBLICAN RUN-OFF

Senator   81,697 Don Nickles; 42,818 John Zink.

SEPTEMBER 16 DEMOCRATIC RUN-OFF

Senator   209,952 Andrew Coats; 185,814 Robert S. Kerr, Jr.

Congress

CD 4   33,520 Dave McCurdy; 31,940 James B. Townsend.

OREGON

GOVERNOR
Victor Atiyeh (R). Elected 1978 to a four-year term.

SENATORS
Mark Hatfield (R). Re-elected 1978 to a six-year term. Previously elected 1972, 1966.

Robert W. Packwood (R). Re-elected 1980 to a six-year term. Previously elected 1974, 1968.

REPRESENTATIVES
1. Les AuCoin (D)
2. Denny Smith (R)
3. Ron Wyden (D)
4. James Weaver (D)

POSTWAR VOTE FOR GOVERNOR

Year	Total Vote	Republican Vote	Candidate	Democratic Vote	Candidate	Other Vote	Rep.-Dem. Plurality	Total Vote Rep.	Total Vote Dem.	Major Vote Rep.	Major Vote Dem.
1978	911,143	498,452	Atiyeh, Victor	409,411	Straub, Robert W.	3,280	89,041 R	54.7%	44.9%	54.9%	45.1%
1974	770,574	324,751	Atiyeh, Victor	444,812	Straub, Robert W.	1,011	120,061 D	42.1%	57.7%	42.2%	57.8%
1970	666,394	369,964	McCall, Tom	293,892	Straub, Robert W.	2,538	76,072 R	55.5%	44.1%	55.7%	44.3%
1966	682,862	377,346	McCall, Tom	305,008	Straub, Robert W.	508	72,338 R	55.3%	44.7%	55.3%	44.7%
1962	637,407	345,497	Hatfield, Mark	265,359	Thornton, Robert Y.	26,551	80,138 R	54.2%	41.6%	56.6%	43.4%
1958	599,994	331,900	Hatfield, Mark	267,934	Holmes, Robert D.	160	63,966 R	55.3%	44.7%	55.3%	44.7%
1956s	731,279	361,840	Smith, Elmo E.	369,439	Holmes, Robert D.	—	7,599 D	49.5%	50.5%	49.5%	50.5%
1954	566,701	322,522	Patterson, Paul	244,179	Carson, Joseph K.	—	78,343 R	56.9%	43.1%	56.9%	43.1%
1950	505,910	334,160	McKay, Douglas	171,750	Flegel, Austin F.	—	162,410 R	66.1%	33.9%	66.1%	33.9%
1948s	509,633	271,295	McKay, Douglas	226,958	Wallace, Lew	11,380	44,337 R	53.2%	44.5%	54.4%	45.6%
1946	344,155	237,681	Snell, Earl	106,474	Donaugh, Carl C.	—	131,207 R	69.1%	30.9%	69.1%	30.9%

The elections in 1956 and 1948 were for short terms to fill vacancies.

POSTWAR VOTE FOR SENATOR

Year	Total Vote	Republican Vote	Candidate	Democratic Vote	Candidate	Other Vote	Rep.-Dem. Plurality	Total Vote Rep.	Total Vote Dem.	Major Vote Rep.	Major Vote Dem.
1980	1,140,494	594,290	Packwood, Robert W.	501,963	Kulongoski, Ted	44,241	92,327 R	52.1%	44.0%	54.2%	45.8%
1978	892,518	550,165	Hatfield, Mark	341,616	Cook, Vernon	737	208,549 R	61.6%	38.3%	61.7%	38.3%
1974	766,414	420,984	Packwood, Robert W.	338,591	Roberts, Betty	6,839	82,393 R	54.9%	44.2%	55.4%	44.6%
1972	920,833	494,671	Hatfield, Mark	425,036	Morse, Wayne L.	1,126	69,635 R	53.7%	46.2%	53.8%	46.2%
1968	814,176	408,646	Packwood, Robert W.	405,353	Morse, Wayne L.	177	3,293 R	50.2%	49.8%	50.2%	49.8%
1966	685,067	354,391	Hatfield, Mark	330,374	Duncan, Robert B.	302	24,017 R	51.7%	48.2%	51.8%	48.2%
1962	636,558	291,587	Unander, Sig	344,716	Morse, Wayne L.	255	53,129 D	45.8%	54.2%	45.8%	54.2%
1960	755,875	343,009	Smith, Elmo E.	412,757	Neuberger, Maurine	109	69,748 D	45.4%	54.6%	45.4%	54.6%
1956	732,254	335,405	McKay, Douglas	396,849	Morse, Wayne L.	—	61,444 D	45.8%	54.2%	45.8%	54.2%
1954	569,088	283,313	Cordon, Guy	285,775	Neuberger, Richard L.	—	2,462 D	49.8%	50.2%	49.8%	50.2%
1950	503,455	376,510	Morse, Wayne L.	116,780	Latourette, Howard	10,165	259,730 R	74.8%	23.2%	76.3%	23.7%
1948	498,570	299,295	Cordon, Guy	199,275	Wilson, Manley J.	—	100,020 R	60.0%	40.0%	60.0%	40.0%

OREGON

Districts Established July 2, 1971

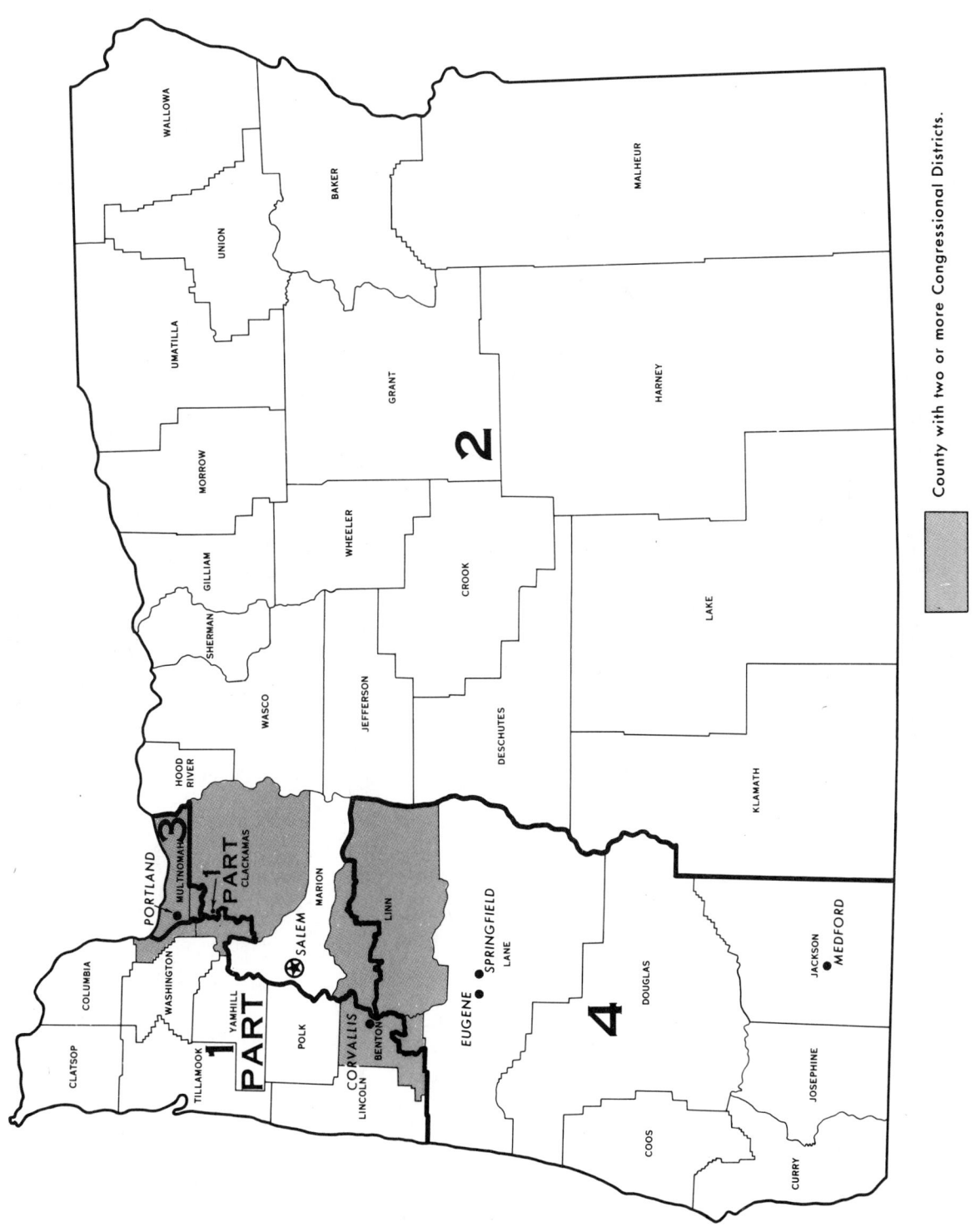

County with two or more Congressional Districts.

OREGON

PRESIDENT 1980

1980 Census Population	County	Total Vote	Republican	Democratic	Other	Rep.-Dem. Plurality	Percentage Total Vote Rep.	Dem.	Major Vote Rep.	Dem.
16,134	BAKER	8,013	4,747	2,515	751	2,232 R	59.2%	31.4%	65.4%	34.6%
68,211	BENTON	34,507	14,982	13,150	6,375	1,832 R	43.4%	38.1%	53.3%	46.7%
241,919	CLACKAMAS	109,483	54,111	40,462	14,910	13,649 R	49.4%	37.0%	57.2%	42.8%
32,489	CLATSOP	14,959	6,124	6,482	2,353	358 D	40.9%	43.3%	48.6%	51.4%
35,646	COLUMBIA	15,505	6,623	7,124	1,758	501 D	42.7%	45.9%	48.2%	51.8%
64,047	COOS	28,176	13,041	11,817	3,318	1,224 R	46.3%	41.9%	52.5%	47.5%
13,091	CROOK	5,862	3,113	2,162	587	951 R	53.1%	36.9%	59.0%	41.0%
16,992	CURRY	8,488	4,910	2,656	922	2,254 R	57.8%	31.3%	64.9%	35.1%
62,142	DESCHUTES	28,715	15,186	9,641	3,888	5,545 R	52.9%	33.6%	61.2%	38.8%
93,748	DOUGLAS	39,516	23,101	12,564	3,851	10,537 R	58.5%	31.8%	64.8%	35.2%
2,057	GILLIAM	1,140	622	394	124	228 R	54.6%	34.6%	61.2%	38.8%
8,210	GRANT	4,187	2,519	1,274	394	1,245 R	60.2%	30.4%	66.4%	33.6%
8,314	HARNEY	3,785	2,313	1,110	362	1,203 R	61.1%	29.3%	67.6%	32.4%
15,835	HOOD RIVER	7,092	3,450	2,924	718	526 R	48.6%	41.2%	54.1%	45.9%
132,456	JACKSON	58,740	32,879	19,903	5,958	12,976 R	56.0%	33.9%	62.3%	37.7%
11,599	JEFFERSON	4,737	2,523	1,654	560	869 R	53.3%	34.9%	60.4%	39.6%
58,820	JOSEPHINE	26,336	16,827	7,116	2,393	9,711 R	63.9%	27.0%	70.3%	29.7%
59,117	KLAMATH	25,592	16,060	7,371	2,161	8,689 R	62.8%	28.8%	68.5%	31.5%
7,532	LAKE	3,689	2,234	1,147	308	1,087 R	60.6%	31.1%	66.1%	33.9%
275,226	LANE	125,604	54,750	52,240	18,614	2,510 R	43.6%	41.6%	51.2%	48.8%
35,264	LINCOLN	17,127	7,637	7,009	2,481	628 R	44.6%	40.9%	52.1%	47.9%
89,495	LINN	36,293	18,943	13,516	3,834	5,427 R	52.2%	37.2%	58.4%	41.6%
26,896	MALHEUR	11,364	7,705	2,937	722	4,768 R	67.8%	25.8%	72.4%	27.6%
204,692	MARION	85,449	42,191	32,134	11,124	10,057 R	49.4%	37.6%	56.8%	43.2%
7,519	MORROW	3,141	1,728	1,077	336	651 R	55.0%	34.3%	61.6%	38.4%
562,640	MULTNOMAH	258,968	101,606	120,487	36,875	18,881 D	39.2%	46.5%	45.7%	54.3%
45,203	POLK	20,531	10,006	7,833	2,692	2,173 R	48.7%	38.2%	56.1%	43.9%
2,172	SHERMAN	1,170	677	389	104	288 R	57.9%	33.2%	63.5%	36.5%
21,164	TILLAMOOK	9,903	4,123	4,521	1,259	398 D	41.6%	45.7%	47.7%	52.3%
58,861	UMATILLA	22,414	12,950	7,382	2,082	5,568 R	57.8%	32.9%	63.7%	36.3%
23,921	UNION	11,272	6,514	3,677	1,081	2,837 R	57.8%	32.6%	63.9%	36.1%
7,273	WALLOWA	3,792	2,485	995	312	1,490 R	65.5%	26.2%	71.4%	28.6%
21,732	WASCO	10,235	4,703	4,336	1,196	367 R	46.0%	42.4%	52.0%	48.0%
245,401	WASHINGTON	111,355	57,165	37,915	16,275	19,250 R	51.3%	34.0%	60.1%	39.9%
1,513	WHEELER	808	442	282	84	160 R	54.7%	34.9%	61.0%	39.0%
55,332	YAMHILL	23,568	12,054	8,694	2,820	3,360 R	51.1%	36.9%	58.1%	41.9%
2,632,663	TOTAL	1,181,516	571,044	456,890	153,582	114,154 R	48.3%	38.7%	55.6%	44.4%

OREGON

SENATOR 1980

1980 Census Population	County	Total Vote	Republican	Democratic	Other	Rep.-Dem. Plurality	Percentage			
							Total Vote		Major Vote	
							Rep.	Dem.	Rep.	Dem.
16,134	BAKER	7,897	4,720	2,813	364	1,907 R	59.8%	35.6%	62.7%	37.3%
68,211	BENTON	33,542	19,600	12,612	1,330	6,988 R	58.4%	37.6%	60.8%	39.2%
241,919	CLACKAMAS	102,569	52,020	46,558	3,991	5,462 R	50.7%	45.4%	52.8%	47.2%
32,489	CLATSOP	12,380	6,476	5,500	404	976 R	52.3%	44.4%	54.1%	45.9%
35,646	COLUMBIA	15,442	7,311	7,577	554	266 D	47.3%	49.1%	49.1%	50.9%
64,047	COOS	27,381	12,387	13,989	1,005	1,602 D	45.2%	51.1%	47.0%	53.0%
13,091	CROOK	5,831	3,350	2,328	153	1,022 R	57.5%	39.9%	59.0%	41.0%
16,992	CURRY	8,249	5,134	2,666	449	2,468 R	62.2%	32.3%	65.8%	34.2%
62,142	DESCHUTES	28,435	17,102	10,434	899	6,668 R	60.1%	36.7%	62.1%	37.9%
93,748	DOUGLAS	39,164	19,184	17,938	2,042	1,246 R	49.0%	45.8%	51.7%	48.3%
2,057	GILLIAM	1,134	731	365	38	366 R	64.5%	32.2%	66.7%	33.3%
8,210	GRANT	4,165	2,636	1,393	136	1,243 R	63.3%	33.4%	65.4%	34.6%
8,314	HARNEY	3,749	2,152	1,435	162	717 R	57.4%	38.3%	60.0%	40.0%
15,835	HOOD RIVER	6,933	3,945	2,551	437	1,394 R	56.9%	36.8%	60.7%	39.3%
132,456	JACKSON	56,217	34,016	19,685	2,516	14,331 R	60.5%	35.0%	63.3%	36.7%
11,599	JEFFERSON	4,711	2,707	1,824	180	883 R	57.5%	38.7%	59.7%	40.3%
58,820	JOSEPHINE	22,673	14,512	6,860	1,301	7,652 R	64.0%	30.3%	67.9%	32.1%
59,117	KLAMATH	25,380	14,312	10,059	1,009	4,253 R	56.4%	39.6%	58.7%	41.3%
7,532	LAKE	3,630	2,116	1,379	135	737 R	58.3%	38.0%	60.5%	39.5%
275,226	LANE	123,908	54,022	64,473	5,413	10,451 D	43.6%	52.0%	45.6%	54.4%
35,264	LINCOLN	16,879	8,485	7,549	845	936 R	50.3%	44.7%	52.9%	47.1%
89,495	LINN	36,060	19,717	15,221	1,122	4,496 R	54.7%	42.2%	56.4%	43.6%
26,896	MALHEUR	10,808	6,941	3,291	576	3,650 R	64.2%	30.4%	67.8%	32.2%
204,692	MARION	83,661	45,669	35,447	2,545	10,222 R	54.6%	42.4%	56.3%	43.7%
7,519	MORROW	3,091	1,987	945	159	1,042 R	64.3%	30.6%	67.8%	32.2%
562,640	MULTNOMAH	249,956	117,276	124,084	8,596	6,808 D	46.9%	49.6%	48.6%	51.4%
45,203	POLK	19,751	11,111	7,928	712	3,183 R	56.3%	40.1%	58.4%	41.6%
2,172	SHERMAN	1,166	720	408	38	312 R	61.7%	35.0%	63.8%	36.2%
21,164	TILLAMOOK	10,026	5,285	4,406	335	879 R	52.7%	43.9%	54.5%	45.5%
58,861	UMATILLA	21,229	13,671	6,779	779	6,892 R	64.4%	31.9%	66.9%	33.1%
23,921	UNION	11,043	6,834	3,786	423	3,048 R	61.9%	34.3%	64.4%	35.6%
7,273	WALLOWA	3,598	2,009	1,362	227	647 R	55.8%	37.9%	59.6%	40.4%
21,732	WASCO	10,137	5,277	4,510	350	767 R	52.1%	44.5%	53.9%	46.1%
245,401	WASHINGTON	109,196	59,487	45,646	4,063	13,841 R	54.5%	41.8%	56.6%	43.4%
1,513	WHEELER	804	546	239	19	307 R	67.9%	29.7%	69.6%	30.4%
55,332	YAMHILL	19,699	10,842	7,923	934	2,919 R	55.0%	40.2%	57.8%	42.2%
2,632,663	TOTAL	1,140,494	594,290	501,963	44,241	92,327 R	52.1%	44.0%	54.2%	45.8%

OREGON

CONGRESS

CD	Year	Total Vote	Republican Vote	Candidate	Democratic Vote	Candidate	Other Vote	Rep.-Dem. Plurality	Percentage Total Vote Rep.	Dem.	Major Vote Rep.	Dem.
1	1980	308,635	105,083	ENGDAHL, LYNN	203,532	AUCOIN, LES	20	98,449 D	34.0%	65.9%	34.0%	66.0%
1	1978	252,378	93,640	BUNICK, NICK	158,706	AUCOIN, LES	32	65,066 D	37.1%	62.9%	37.1%	62.9%
1	1976	264,000	109,140	BLADINE, PHIL	154,844	AUCOIN, LES	16	45,704 D	41.3%	58.7%	41.3%	58.7%
1	1974	204,592	89,848	O SCANNLAIN, DIARMUID	114,629	AUCOIN, LES	115	24,781 D	43.9%	56.0%	43.9%	56.1%
1	1972	242,798	166,476	WYATT, WENDELL	76,307	BUNCH, RALPH E.	15	90,169 R	68.6%	31.4%	68.6%	31.4%
2	1980	290,748	141,854	SMITH, DENNY	138,089	ULLMAN, ALBERT C.	10,805	3,765 R	48.8%	47.5%	50.7%	49.3%
2	1978	220,019	67,547	HICKS, TERRY L.	152,099	ULLMAN, ALBERT C.	373	84,552 D	30.7%	69.1%	30.8%	69.2%
2	1976	240,761	67,431	MERCER, THOMAS H.	173,313	ULLMAN, ALBERT C.	17	105,882 D	28.0%	72.0%	28.0%	72.0%
2	1974	180,449	39,441	BROWN, KENNETH A.	140,963	ULLMAN, ALBERT C.	45	101,522 D	21.9%	78.1%	21.9%	78.1%
2	1972	178,728			178,537	ULLMAN, ALBERT C.	191	178,537 D		99.9%		100.0%
3	1980	217,423	60,940	CONGER, DARRELL R.	156,371	WYDEN, RON	112	95,431 D	28.0%	71.9%	28.0%	72.0%
3	1978	179,460			151,895	DUNCAN, ROBERT B.	27,565	151,895 D		84.6%		100.0%
3	1976	177,051			148,503	DUNCAN, ROBERT B.	28,548	148,503 D		83.9%		100.0%
3	1974	183,537	54,080	PIACENTINI, JOHN	129,290	DUNCAN, ROBERT B.	167	75,210 D	29.5%	70.4%	29.5%	70.5%
3	1972	226,030	84,697	WALSH, MIKE	141,046	GREEN, EDITH	287	56,349 D	37.5%	62.4%	37.5%	62.5%
4	1980	289,634	130,861	FITZGERALD, MICHAEL	158,745	WEAVER, JAMES	28	27,884 D	45.2%	54.8%	45.2%	54.8%
4	1978	221,766	96,953	LAUSMANN, JERRY	124,745	WEAVER, JAMES	68	27,792 D	43.7%	56.3%	43.7%	56.3%
4	1976	244,852	85,943	LAUSMANN, JERRY	122,475	WEAVER, JAMES	36,434	36,532 D	35.1%	50.0%	41.2%	58.8%
4	1974	184,617	86,950	DELLENBACK, JOHN R.	97,580	WEAVER, JAMES	87	10,630 D	47.1%	52.9%	47.1%	52.9%
4	1972	222,174	138,965	DELLENBACK, JOHN R.	83,134	PORTER, CHARLES O.	75	55,831 R	62.5%	37.4%	62.6%	37.4%

OREGON

1980 GENERAL ELECTION

President Other vote was 112,389 Anderson (Independent); 25,838 Clark (Libertarian); 13,642 Commoner (Independent); 1,713 scattered.

Senator Other vote was 43,686 Nathan (Libertarian); 555 scattered.

Congress Other vote was scattered in CD's 1, 3 and 4; 10,787 Marbet (Independent) and 18 scattered in CD 2.

1980 PRIMARIES

MAY 20 REPUBLICAN

Senator 191,127 Robert W. Packwood; 45,973 Brenda Jose; 23,599 Kenneth A. Brown; 22,929 Rosalie Huss; 22,281 Willard D. Severn; 227 scattered.

Congress Unopposed in CD 3. Contested as follows:

CD 1 46,920 Lynn Engdahl; 27,906 Bert Miller; 173 scattered.
CD 2 56,718 Denny Smith; 16,884 Leonard G. Roth; 196 scattered.
CD 4 48,294 Michael Fitzgerald; 14,801 Rutledge Jay; 98 scattered.

MAY 20 DEMOCRATIC

Senator 161,153 Ted Kulongoski; 69,649 Charles O. Porter; 46,107 Jack Sumner; 39,691 John Sweeney; 20,548 Gene Arvidson; 692 scattered.

Congress Unopposed in CD 1. Contested as follows:

CD 2 49,250 Albert C. Ullman; 40,507 Steve Anderson; 413 scattered.
CD 3 55,818 Ron Wyden; 37,132 Robert B. Duncan; 43 scattered.
CD 4 71,388 James Weaver; 23,758 John D. Newkirk; 58 scattered.

PENNSYLVANIA

GOVERNOR
Richard L. Thornburgh (R). Elected 1978 to a four-year term.

SENATORS
H. John Heinz (R). Elected 1976 to a six-year term.

Arlen Specter (R). Elected 1980 to a six-year term.

REPRESENTATIVES
1. Thomas M. Foglietta (I) (see note section)
2. William H. Gray (D)
3. Raymond F. Lederer (see page 1)
4. Charles F. Dougherty (R)
5. Richard T. Schulze (R)
6. Gus Yatron (D)
7. Robert W. Edgar (D)
8. James K. Coyne (R)
9. E. G. Shuster (R)
10. Joseph M. McDade (R)
11. James L. Nelligan (R)
12. John P. Murtha (D)
13. R. Lawrence Coughlin (R)
14. William J. Coyne (D)
15. Donald L. Ritter (R)
16. Robert S. Walker (R)
17. Allen E. Ertel (D)
18. Douglas Walgren (D)
19. William F. Goodling (R)
20. Joseph M. Gaydos (D)
21. Donald Bailey (D)
22. Austin J. Murphy (D)
23. William F. Clinger (R)
24. Marc L. Marks (R)
25. Eugene V. Atkinson (D)

POSTWAR VOTE FOR GOVERNOR

Year	Total Vote	Republican Vote	Candidate	Democratic Vote	Candidate	Other Vote	Rep.-Dem. Plurality	Rep.	Dem.	Rep.	Dem.
1978	3,741,969	1,966,042	Thornburgh, Richard L.	1,737,888	Flaherty, Peter	38,039	228,154 R	52.5%	46.4%	53.1%	46.9%
1974	3,491,234	1,578,917	Lewis, Andrew L.	1,878,252	Shapp, Milton	34,065	299,335 D	45.2%	53.8%	45.7%	54.3%
1970	3,700,060	1,542,854	Broderick, Raymond	2,043,029	Shapp, Milton	114,177	500,175 D	41.7%	55.2%	43.0%	57.0%
1966	4,050,668	2,110,349	Shafer, Raymond P.	1,868,719	Shapp, Milton	71,600	241,630 R	52.1%	46.1%	53.0%	47.0%
1962	4,378,042	2,424,918	Scranton, William W.	1,938,627	Dilworth, Richardson	14,497	486,291 R	55.4%	44.3%	55.6%	44.4%
1958	3,986,918	1,948,769	McGonigle, A. T.	2,024,852	Lawrence, David	13,297	76,083 D	48.9%	50.8%	49.0%	51.0%
1954	3,720,457	1,717,070	Wood, Lloyd H.	1,996,266	Leader, George M.	7,121	279,196 D	46.2%	53.7%	46.2%	53.8%
1950	3,540,059	1,796,119	Fine, John S.	1,710,355	Dilworth, Richardson	33,585	85,764 R	50.7%	48.3%	51.2%	48.8%
1946	3,123,994	1,828,462	Duff, James H.	1,270,947	Rice, John S.	24,585	557,515 R	58.5%	40.7%	59.0%	41.0%

POSTWAR VOTE FOR SENATOR

Year	Total Vote	Republican Vote	Candidate	Democratic Vote	Candidate	Other Vote	Rep.-Dem. Plurality	Rep.	Dem.	Rep.	Dem.
1980	4,418,042	2,230,404	Specter, Arlen	2,122,391	Flaherty, Peter	65,247	108,013 R	50.5%	48.0%	51.2%	48.8%
1976	4,546,353	2,381,891	Heinz, H. John	2,126,977	Green, William J., III	37,485	254,914 R	52.4%	46.8%	52.8%	47.2%
1974	3,477,812	1,843,317	Schweiker, Richard S.	1,596,121	Flaherty, Peter	38,374	247,196 R	53.0%	45.9%	53.6%	46.4%
1970	3,644,305	1,874,106	Scott, Hugh	1,653,774	Sesler, William G.	116,425	220,332 R	51.4%	45.4%	53.1%	46.9%
1968	4,624,218	2,399,762	Schweiker, Richard S.	2,117,662	Clark, Joseph S.	106,794	282,100 R	51.9%	45.8%	53.1%	46.9%
1964	4,803,835	2,429,858	Scott, Hugh	2,359,223	Blatt, Genevieve	14,754	70,635 R	50.6%	49.1%	50.7%	49.3%
1962	4,383,475	2,134,649	Van Zandt, James E.	2,238,383	Clark, Joseph S.	10,443	103,734 D	48.7%	51.1%	48.8%	51.2%
1958	3,988,622	2,042,586	Scott, Hugh	1,929,821	Leader, George M.	16,215	112,765 R	51.2%	48.4%	51.4%	48.6%
1956	4,529,874	2,250,671	Duff, James H.	2,268,641	Clark, Joseph S.	10,562	17,970 D	49.7%	50.1%	49.8%	50.2%
1952	4,519,761	2,331,034	Martin, Edward	2,168,546	Bard, Guy Kurtz	20,181	162,488 R	51.6%	48.0%	51.8%	48.2%
1950	3,548,703	1,820,400	Duff, James H.	1,694,076	Myers, Francis J.	34,227	126,324 R	51.3%	47.7%	51.8%	48.2%
1946	3,127,860	1,853,458	Martin, Edward	1,245,338	Guffey, Joseph F.	29,064	608,120 R	59.3%	39.8%	59.8%	40.2%

PENNSYLVANIA

Districts Established January 25, 1972

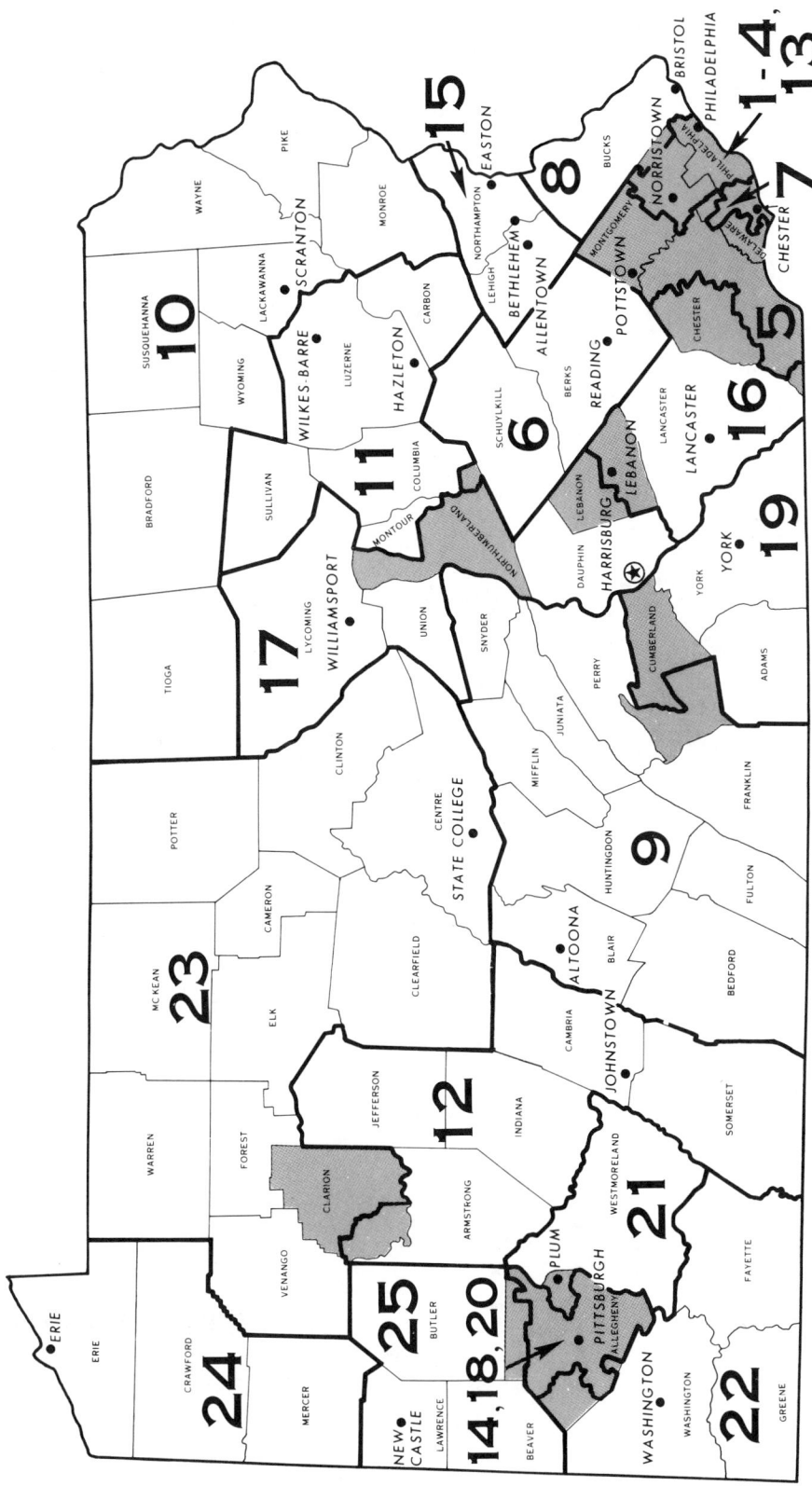

County with two or more Congressional Districts.

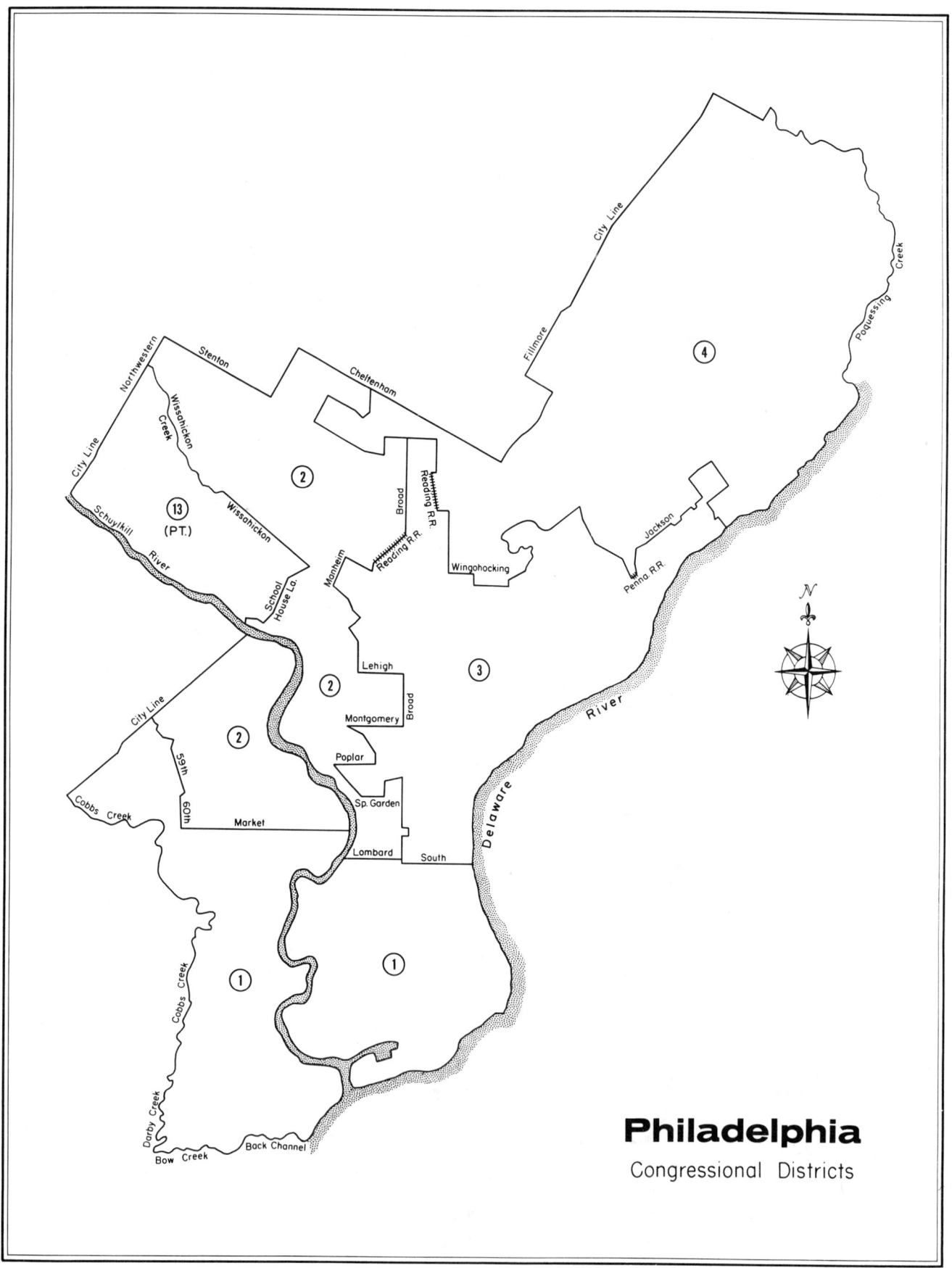

Philadelphia

Congressional Districts

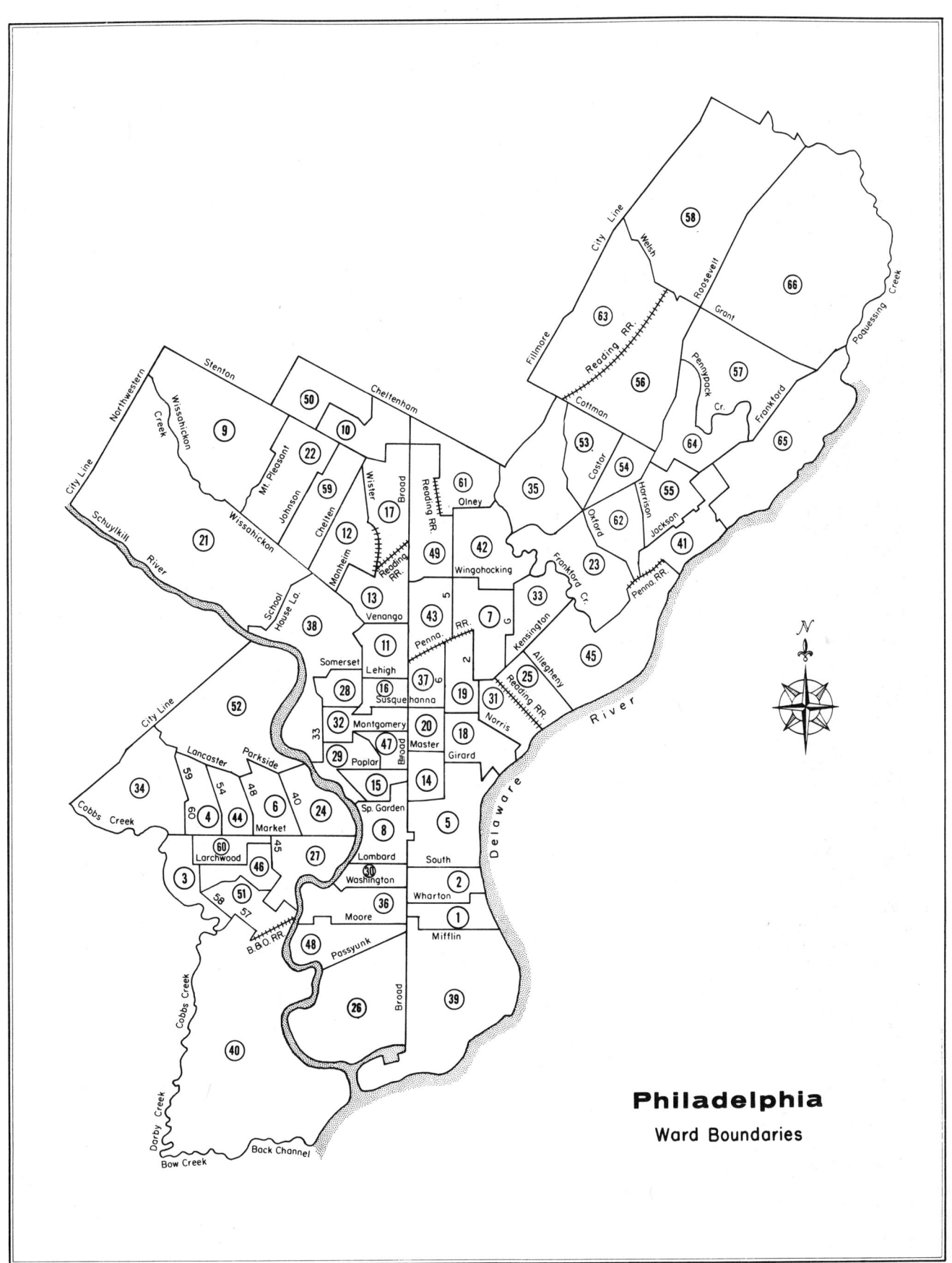

Philadelphia

Ward Boundaries

PENNSYLVANIA

PRESIDENT 1980

1980 Census Population	County	Total Vote	Republican	Democratic	Other	Rep.-Dem. Plurality	Percentage Total Vote Rep.	Dem.	Major Vote Rep.	Dem.
68,292	ADAMS	22,404	13,760	7,266	1,378	6,494 R	61.4%	32.4%	65.4%	34.6%
1,450,085	ALLEGHENY	621,418	271,850	297,464	52,104	25,614 D	43.7%	47.9%	47.8%	52.2%
77,768	ARMSTRONG	27,104	12,955	12,718	1,431	237 R	47.8%	46.9%	50.5%	49.5%
204,441	BEAVER	79,765	30,496	43,955	5,314	13,459 D	38.2%	55.1%	41.0%	59.0%
46,784	BEDFORD	16,419	10,930	4,950	539	5,980 R	66.6%	30.1%	68.8%	31.2%
312,509	BERKS	107,385	60,576	36,449	10,360	24,127 R	56.4%	33.9%	62.4%	37.6%
136,621	BLAIR	46,359	28,931	15,014	2,414	13,917 R	62.4%	32.4%	65.8%	34.2%
62,919	BRADFORD	20,865	13,139	6,439	1,287	6,700 R	63.0%	30.9%	67.1%	32.9%
479,211	BUCKS	181,164	100,536	59,120	21,508	41,416 R	55.5%	32.6%	63.0%	37.0%
147,912	BUTLER	52,689	28,821	19,711	4,157	9,110 R	54.7%	37.4%	59.4%	40.6%
183,263	CAMBRIA	72,131	33,072	36,121	2,938	3,049 D	45.8%	50.1%	47.8%	52.2%
6,674	CAMERON	3,030	1,795	1,112	123	683 R	59.2%	36.7%	61.7%	38.3%
53,285	CARBON	19,329	10,042	8,009	1,278	2,033 R	52.0%	41.4%	55.6%	44.4%
112,760	CENTRE	42,631	20,605	15,987	6,039	4,618 R	48.3%	37.5%	56.3%	43.7%
316,660	CHESTER	119,896	73,046	34,307	12,543	38,739 R	60.9%	28.6%	68.0%	32.0%
43,362	CLARION	15,101	8,812	5,472	817	3,340 R	58.4%	36.2%	61.7%	38.3%
83,578	CLEARFIELD	28,192	15,299	11,647	1,246	3,652 R	54.3%	41.3%	56.8%	43.2%
38,971	CLINTON	12,010	6,288	4,842	880	1,446 R	52.4%	40.3%	56.5%	43.5%
61,967	COLUMBIA	23,313	12,426	9,449	1,438	2,977 R	53.3%	40.5%	56.8%	43.2%
88,869	CRAWFORD	30,909	16,552	11,778	2,579	4,774 R	53.6%	38.1%	58.4%	41.6%
178,037	CUMBERLAND	67,260	41,152	19,789	6,319	21,363 R	61.2%	29.4%	67.5%	32.5%
232,317	DAUPHIN	78,387	44,039	27,252	7,096	16,787 R	56.2%	34.8%	61.8%	38.2%
555,007	DELAWARE	256,859	143,282	88,314	25,263	54,968 R	55.8%	34.4%	61.9%	38.1%
38,338	ELK	13,669	7,175	5,898	596	1,277 R	52.5%	43.1%	54.9%	45.1%
279,780	ERIE	103,162	48,918	45,946	8,298	2,972 R	47.4%	44.5%	51.6%	48.4%
160,395	FAYETTE	49,383	19,252	27,963	2,168	8,711 D	39.0%	56.6%	40.8%	59.2%
5,072	FOREST	2,149	1,206	819	124	387 R	56.1%	38.1%	59.6%	40.4%
113,629	FRANKLIN	36,741	22,716	12,061	1,964	10,655 R	61.8%	32.8%	65.3%	34.7%
12,842	FULTON	4,222	2,740	1,342	140	1,398 R	64.9%	31.8%	67.1%	32.9%
40,355	GREENE	14,121	5,336	8,193	592	2,857 D	37.8%	58.0%	39.4%	60.6%
42,253	HUNTINGDON	13,928	8,140	5,094	694	3,046 R	58.4%	36.6%	61.5%	38.5%
92,281	INDIANA	31,451	15,607	13,828	2,016	1,779 R	49.6%	44.0%	53.0%	47.0%
48,303	JEFFERSON	16,778	9,628	6,296	854	3,332 R	57.4%	37.5%	60.5%	39.5%
19,188	JUNIATA	7,161	4,139	2,696	326	1,443 R	57.8%	37.6%	60.6%	39.4%
227,908	LACKAWANNA	95,447	44,242	45,257	5,948	1,015 D	46.4%	47.4%	49.4%	50.6%
362,346	LANCASTER	118,897	79,963	30,026	8,908	49,937 R	67.3%	25.3%	72.7%	27.3%
107,150	LAWRENCE	40,213	18,404	19,506	2,303	1,102 D	45.8%	48.5%	48.5%	51.5%
109,829	LEBANON	35,507	24,495	8,281	2,731	16,214 R	69.0%	23.3%	74.7%	25.3%
273,582	LEHIGH	95,985	50,782	34,827	10,376	15,955 R	52.9%	36.3%	59.3%	40.7%
343,079	LUZERNE	135,080	67,822	59,976	7,282	7,846 R	50.2%	44.4%	53.1%	46.9%
118,416	LYCOMING	40,553	23,415	14,609	2,529	8,806 R	57.7%	36.0%	61.6%	38.4%
50,635	MCKEAN	15,166	9,229	5,064	873	4,165 R	60.9%	33.4%	64.6%	35.4%
128,299	MERCER	46,090	22,372	19,716	4,002	2,656 R	48.5%	42.8%	53.2%	46.8%
46,908	MIFFLIN	13,520	7,541	5,226	753	2,315 R	55.8%	38.7%	59.1%	40.9%
69,409	MONROE	22,289	12,357	7,551	2,381	4,806 R	55.4%	33.9%	62.1%	37.9%
643,621	MONTGOMERY	271,553	156,996	84,289	30,268	72,707 R	57.8%	31.0%	65.1%	34.9%
16,675	MONTOUR	6,096	3,399	2,272	425	1,127 R	55.8%	37.3%	59.9%	40.1%
225,418	NORTHAMPTON	76,037	35,787	31,920	8,330	3,867 R	47.1%	42.0%	52.9%	47.1%
100,381	NORTHUMBERLAND	36,290	20,608	13,750	1,932	6,858 R	56.8%	37.9%	60.0%	40.0%
35,718	PERRY	12,599	8,026	3,681	892	4,345 R	63.7%	29.2%	68.6%	31.4%
1,688,210	PHILADELPHIA	718,100	244,108	421,253	52,739	177,145 D	34.0%	58.7%	36.7%	63.3%
18,271	PIKE	7,973	5,249	2,132	592	3,117 R	65.8%	26.7%	71.1%	28.9%
17,726	POTTER	6,669	4,073	2,299	297	1,774 R	61.1%	34.5%	63.9%	36.1%
160,630	SCHUYLKILL	64,969	36,273	24,968	3,728	11,305 R	55.8%	38.4%	59.2%	40.8%
33,584	SNYDER	10,591	7,634	2,418	539	5,216 R	72.1%	22.8%	75.9%	24.1%
81,243	SOMERSET	30,455	17,729	11,695	1,031	6,034 R	58.2%	38.4%	60.3%	39.7%
6,349	SULLIVAN	2,902	1,676	1,074	152	602 R	57.8%	37.0%	60.9%	39.1%
37,876	SUSQUEHANNA	14,689	8,994	4,660	1,035	4,334 R	61.2%	31.7%	65.9%	34.1%
40,973	TIOGA	13,849	8,770	4,273	806	4,497 R	63.3%	30.9%	67.2%	32.8%
32,870	UNION	10,256	6,798	2,687	771	4,111 R	66.3%	26.2%	71.7%	28.3%
64,444	VENANGO	20,604	11,547	7,800	1,257	3,747 R	56.0%	37.9%	59.7%	40.3%
47,449	WARREN	15,974	9,165	5,560	1,249	3,605 R	57.4%	34.8%	62.2%	37.8%
217,074	WASHINGTON	82,018	32,532	45,295	4,191	12,763 D	39.7%	55.2%	41.8%	58.2%
35,237	WAYNE	12,548	8,468	3,375	705	5,093 R	67.5%	26.9%	71.5%	28.5%
392,294	WESTMORELAND	140,139	63,140	68,627	8,372	5,487 D	45.1%	49.0%	47.9%	52.1%
26,433	WYOMING	9,167	5,919	2,766	482	3,153 R	64.6%	30.2%	68.2%	31.8%
312,963	YORK	101,891	61,098	33,406	7,387	27,692 R	60.0%	32.8%	64.7%	35.3%
11,866,728	TOTAL	4,561,501	2,261,872	1,937,540	362,089	324,332 R	49.6%	42.5%	53.9%	46.1%

PENNSYLVANIA

SENATOR 1980

1980 Census Population	County	Total Vote	Republican	Democratic	Other	Rep.-Dem. Plurality	Percentage Total Vote Rep.	Dem.	Major Vote Rep.	Dem.
68,292	ADAMS	22,194	13,585	8,307	302	5,278 R	61.2%	37.4%	62.1%	37.9%
1,450,085	ALLEGHENY	604,108	220,216	371,710	12,182	151,494 D	36.5%	61.5%	37.2%	62.8%
77,768	ARMSTRONG	26,885	9,810	16,936	139	7,126 D	36.5%	63.0%	36.7%	63.3%
204,441	BEAVER	79,662	21,040	58,006	616	36,966 D	26.4%	72.8%	26.6%	73.4%
46,784	BEDFORD	16,500	9,728	6,699	73	3,029 R	59.0%	40.6%	59.2%	40.8%
312,509	BERKS	103,044	58,182	43,545	1,317	14,637 R	56.5%	42.3%	57.2%	42.8%
136,621	BLAIR	46,186	23,590	22,185	411	1,405 R	51.1%	48.0%	51.5%	48.5%
62,919	BRADFORD	20,413	13,027	7,073	313	5,954 R	63.8%	34.6%	64.8%	35.2%
479,211	BUCKS	176,920	110,260	64,062	2,598	46,198 R	62.3%	36.2%	63.3%	36.7%
147,912	BUTLER	51,556	20,038	30,894	624	10,856 D	38.9%	59.9%	39.3%	60.7%
183,263	CAMBRIA	71,948	24,693	46,853	402	22,160 D	34.3%	65.1%	34.5%	65.5%
6,674	CAMERON	3,018	1,621	1,371	26	250 R	53.7%	45.4%	54.2%	45.8%
53,285	CARBON	18,710	9,369	9,096	245	273 R	50.1%	48.6%	50.7%	49.3%
112,760	CENTRE	42,176	21,481	19,618	1,077	1,863 R	50.9%	46.5%	52.3%	47.7%
316,660	CHESTER	118,134	81,205	35,352	1,577	45,853 R	68.7%	29.9%	69.7%	30.3%
43,362	CLARION	15,163	6,445	8,580	138	2,135 D	42.5%	56.6%	42.9%	57.1%
83,578	CLEARFIELD	27,909	12,890	14,828	191	1,938 D	46.2%	53.1%	46.5%	53.5%
38,971	CLINTON	11,745	6,357	5,223	165	1,134 R	54.1%	44.5%	54.9%	45.1%
61,967	COLUMBIA	22,865	12,240	10,401	224	1,839 R	53.5%	45.5%	54.1%	45.9%
88,869	CRAWFORD	30,023	15,432	14,120	471	1,312 R	51.4%	47.0%	52.2%	47.8%
178,037	CUMBERLAND	64,072	42,335	20,956	781	21,379 R	66.1%	32.7%	66.9%	33.1%
232,317	DAUPHIN	73,924	46,777	26,237	910	20,540 R	63.3%	35.5%	64.1%	35.9%
555,007	DELAWARE	247,805	154,255	90,400	3,150	63,855 R	62.2%	36.5%	63.1%	36.9%
38,338	ELK	13,701	5,281	8,337	83	3,056 D	38.5%	60.8%	38.8%	61.2%
279,780	ERIE	98,843	39,037	57,822	1,984	18,785 D	39.5%	58.5%	40.3%	59.7%
160,395	FAYETTE	47,991	13,061	34,112	818	21,051 D	27.2%	71.1%	27.7%	72.3%
5,072	FOREST	2,141	1,061	1,069	11	8 D	49.6%	49.9%	49.8%	50.2%
113,629	FRANKLIN	36,076	21,934	13,763	379	8,171 R	60.8%	38.2%	61.4%	38.6%
12,842	FULTON	4,071	2,165	1,852	54	313 R	53.2%	45.5%	53.9%	46.1%
40,355	GREENE	14,266	4,239	9,909	118	5,670 D	29.7%	69.5%	30.0%	70.0%
42,253	HUNTINGDON	13,807	8,030	5,633	144	2,397 R	58.2%	40.8%	58.8%	41.2%
92,281	INDIANA	31,306	13,880	17,180	246	3,300 D	44.3%	54.9%	44.7%	55.3%
48,303	JEFFERSON	16,826	7,736	8,966	124	1,230 D	46.0%	53.3%	46.3%	53.7%
19,188	JUNIATA	7,058	4,502	2,525	31	1,977 R	63.8%	35.8%	64.1%	35.9%
227,908	LACKAWANNA	91,478	40,179	50,061	1,238	9,882 D	43.9%	54.7%	44.5%	55.5%
362,346	LANCASTER	116,517	83,254	32,008	1,255	51,246 R	71.5%	27.5%	72.2%	27.8%
107,150	LAWRENCE	39,674	13,490	25,843	341	12,353 D	34.0%	65.1%	34.3%	65.7%
109,829	LEBANON	34,550	24,237	9,864	449	14,373 R	70.2%	28.5%	71.1%	28.9%
273,582	LEHIGH	92,852	51,590	39,780	1,482	11,810 R	55.6%	42.8%	56.5%	43.5%
343,079	LUZERNE	127,334	60,412	64,768	2,154	4,356 D	47.4%	50.9%	48.3%	51.7%
118,416	LYCOMING	39,540	22,223	16,831	486	5,392 R	56.2%	42.6%	56.9%	43.1%
50,635	MCKEAN	14,471	8,753	5,519	199	3,234 R	60.5%	38.1%	61.3%	38.7%
128,299	MERCER	43,153	19,098	23,260	795	4,162 D	44.3%	53.9%	45.1%	54.9%
46,908	MIFFLIN	13,112	7,344	5,570	198	1,774 R	56.0%	42.5%	56.9%	43.1%
69,409	MONROE	21,480	12,473	8,583	424	3,890 R	58.1%	40.0%	59.2%	40.8%
643,621	MONTGOMERY	265,251	178,632	83,131	3,488	95,501 R	67.3%	31.3%	68.2%	31.8%
16,675	MONTOUR	6,039	3,398	2,596	45	802 R	56.3%	43.0%	56.7%	43.3%
225,418	NORTHAMPTON	72,641	35,473	35,574	1,594	101 D	48.8%	49.0%	49.9%	50.1%
100,381	NORTHUMBERLAND	34,384	18,350	15,515	519	2,835 R	53.4%	45.1%	54.2%	45.8%
35,718	PERRY	12,393	8,125	4,105	163	4,020 R	65.6%	33.1%	66.4%	33.6%
1,688,210	PHILADELPHIA	675,127	337,516	325,593	12,018	11,923 R	50.0%	48.2%	50.9%	49.1%
18,271	PIKE	7,661	4,821	2,704	136	2,117 R	62.9%	35.3%	64.1%	35.9%
17,726	POTTER	6,573	4,061	2,421	91	1,640 R	61.8%	36.8%	62.7%	37.3%
160,630	SCHUYLKILL	64,919	36,692	27,637	590	9,055 R	56.5%	42.6%	57.0%	43.0%
33,584	SNYDER	10,477	7,343	3,058	76	4,285 R	70.1%	29.2%	70.6%	29.4%
81,243	SOMERSET	30,432	12,835	17,460	137	4,625 D	42.2%	57.4%	42.4%	57.6%
6,349	SULLIVAN	2,780	1,637	1,121	22	516 R	58.9%	40.3%	59.4%	40.6%
37,876	SUSQUEHANNA	15,385	9,908	5,264	213	4,644 R	64.4%	34.2%	65.3%	34.7%
40,973	TIOGA	13,624	8,862	4,563	199	4,299 R	65.0%	33.5%	66.0%	34.0%
32,870	UNION	10,210	6,697	3,338	175	3,359 R	65.6%	32.7%	66.7%	33.3%
64,444	VENANGO	20,617	10,159	10,294	164	135 D	49.3%	49.9%	49.7%	50.3%
47,449	WARREN	15,315	8,827	6,229	259	2,598 R	57.6%	40.7%	58.6%	41.4%
217,074	WASHINGTON	82,310	22,986	58,732	592	35,746 D	27.9%	71.4%	28.1%	71.9%
35,237	WAYNE	11,897	7,806	3,916	175	3,890 R	65.6%	32.9%	66.6%	33.4%
392,294	WESTMORELAND	136,507	41,224	93,219	2,064	51,995 D	30.2%	68.3%	30.7%	69.3%
26,433	WYOMING	8,923	5,865	2,953	105	2,912 R	65.7%	33.1%	66.5%	33.5%
312,963	YORK	99,370	60,632	37,261	1,477	23,371 R	61.0%	37.5%	61.9%	38.1%
11,866,728	TOTAL	4,418,042	2,230,404	2,122,391	65,247	108,013 R	50.5%	48.0%	51.2%	48.8%

PHILADELPHIA

PRESIDENT 1980

1980 Census Population	Ward	Total Vote	Republican	Democratic	Other	Rep.-Dem. Plurality	Total Vote Rep.	Total Vote Dem.	Major Vote Rep.	Major Vote Dem.
20,177	WARD 1	10,165	5,031	4,533	601	498 R	49.5%	44.6%	52.6%	47.4%
22,751	WARD 2	10,163	3,933	5,404	826	1,471 D	38.7%	53.2%	42.1%	57.9%
24,119	WARD 3	10,240	474	9,560	206	9,086 D	4.6%	93.4%	4.7%	95.3%
22,303	WARD 4	9,750	409	9,159	182	8,750 D	4.2%	93.9%	4.3%	95.7%
21,593	WARD 5	9,995	3,154	5,263	1,578	2,109 D	31.6%	52.7%	37.5%	62.5%
18,520	WARD 6	6,480	336	6,037	107	5,701 D	5.2%	93.2%	5.3%	94.7%
22,651	WARD 7	7,471	3,418	3,451	602	33 D	45.8%	46.2%	49.8%	50.2%
28,580	WARD 8	14,517	4,942	7,456	2,119	2,514 D	34.0%	51.4%	39.9%	60.1%
16,994	WARD 9	9,027	3,731	4,151	1,145	420 D	41.3%	46.0%	47.3%	52.7%
29,871	WARD 10	11,557	794	10,465	298	9,671 D	6.9%	90.6%	7.1%	92.9%
18,921	WARD 11	6,654	387	6,139	128	5,752 D	5.8%	92.3%	5.9%	94.1%
25,839	WARD 12	9,380	1,121	7,652	607	6,531 D	12.0%	81.6%	12.8%	87.2%
24,273	WARD 13	8,904	942	7,601	361	6,659 D	10.6%	85.4%	11.0%	89.0%
12,560	WARD 14	3,389	219	3,072	98	2,853 D	6.5%	90.6%	6.7%	93.3%
16,990	WARD 15	7,587	2,592	4,153	842	1,561 D	34.2%	54.7%	38.4%	61.6%
18,656	WARD 16	7,393	180	6,982	231	6,802 D	2.4%	94.4%	2.5%	97.5%
27,667	WARD 17	11,104	796	9,985	323	9,189 D	7.2%	89.9%	7.4%	92.6%
17,121	WARD 18	5,723	2,235	2,997	491	762 D	39.1%	52.4%	42.7%	57.3%
19,150	WARD 19	4,309	726	3,376	207	2,650 D	16.8%	78.3%	17.7%	82.3%
11,680	WARD 20	3,332	129	3,070	133	2,941 D	3.9%	92.1%	4.0%	96.0%
48,965	WARD 21	21,820	11,849	7,908	2,063	3,941 R	54.3%	36.2%	60.0%	40.0%
26,193	WARD 22	12,360	1,351	10,157	852	8,806 D	10.9%	82.2%	11.7%	88.3%
23,829	WARD 23	9,689	4,501	4,326	862	175 R	46.5%	44.6%	51.0%	49.0%
17,473	WARD 24	5,664	437	4,949	278	4,512 D	7.7%	87.4%	8.1%	91.9%
22,200	WARD 25	9,061	4,294	4,040	727	254 R	47.4%	44.6%	51.5%	48.5%
27,679	WARD 26	10,944	6,409	3,886	649	2,523 R	58.6%	35.5%	62.3%	37.7%
25,228	WARD 27	8,555	1,599	5,537	1,419	3,938 D	18.7%	64.7%	22.4%	77.6%
17,501	WARD 28	7,107	365	6,623	119	6,258 D	5.1%	93.2%	5.2%	94.8%
16,538	WARD 29	6,354	308	5,813	233	5,505 D	4.8%	91.5%	5.0%	95.0%
14,225	WARD 30	5,692	692	4,642	358	3,950 D	12.2%	81.6%	13.0%	87.0%
18,277	WARD 31	7,137	3,285	3,198	654	87 R	46.0%	44.8%	50.7%	49.3%
30,101	WARD 32	10,335	537	9,603	195	9,066 D	5.2%	92.9%	5.3%	94.7%
22,916	WARD 33	10,702	5,189	4,498	1,015	691 R	48.5%	42.0%	53.6%	46.4%
39,985	WARD 34	18,855	5,695	12,115	1,045	6,420 D	30.2%	64.3%	32.0%	68.0%
32,175	WARD 35	16,038	8,997	5,518	1,523	3,479 R	56.1%	34.4%	62.0%	38.0%
35,472	WARD 36	15,946	3,051	12,277	618	9,226 D	19.1%	77.0%	19.9%	80.1%
20,306	WARD 37	5,998	421	5,466	111	5,045 D	7.0%	91.1%	7.2%	92.8%
23,399	WARD 38	8,854	2,052	6,240	562	4,188 D	23.2%	70.5%	24.7%	75.3%
47,439	WARD 39	21,506	12,018	8,176	1,312	3,842 R	55.9%	38.0%	59.5%	40.5%
50,806	WARD 40	19,925	8,483	10,114	1,328	1,631 D	42.6%	50.8%	45.6%	54.4%
23,528	WARD 41	10,595	5,666	3,914	1,015	1,752 R	53.5%	36.9%	59.1%	40.9%
29,145	WARD 42	11,439	5,765	4,581	1,093	1,184 R	50.4%	40.0%	55.7%	44.3%
27,147	WARD 43	7,566	1,484	5,769	313	4,285 D	19.6%	76.2%	20.5%	79.5%
17,276	WARD 44	7,223	435	6,658	130	6,223 D	6.0%	92.2%	6.1%	93.9%
24,576	WARD 45	11,035	5,311	4,780	944	531 R	48.1%	43.3%	52.6%	47.4%
24,939	WARD 46	10,121	814	8,539	768	7,725 D	8.0%	84.4%	8.7%	91.3%
11,264	WARD 47	4,216	160	3,911	145	3,751 D	3.8%	92.8%	3.9%	96.1%
22,391	WARD 48	9,702	4,711	4,381	610	330 R	48.6%	45.2%	51.8%	48.2%
33,401	WARD 49	9,761	2,054	7,118	589	5,064 D	21.0%	72.9%	22.4%	77.6%
31,271	WARD 50	13,013	1,243	11,320	450	10,077 D	9.6%	87.0%	9.9%	90.1%
28,662	WARD 51	9,861	572	9,049	240	8,477 D	5.8%	91.8%	5.9%	94.1%
28,926	WARD 52	14,393	2,735	10,734	924	7,999 D	19.0%	74.6%	20.3%	79.7%
21,786	WARD 53	12,841	6,111	5,392	1,338	719 R	47.6%	42.0%	53.1%	46.9%
19,800	WARD 54	12,275	4,921	6,080	1,274	1,159 D	40.1%	49.5%	44.7%	55.3%
27,590	WARD 55	14,875	8,090	5,404	1,381	2,686 R	54.4%	36.3%	60.0%	40.0%
35,662	WARD 56	19,902	9,344	8,596	1,962	748 R	47.0%	43.2%	52.1%	47.9%
29,362	WARD 57	14,522	7,963	5,143	1,416	2,820 R	54.8%	35.4%	60.8%	39.2%
47,404	WARD 58	22,354	12,322	7,742	2,290	4,580 R	55.1%	34.6%	61.4%	38.6%
24,998	WARD 59	10,072	1,198	8,372	502	7,174 D	11.9%	83.1%	12.5%	87.5%
21,070	WARD 60	9,247	417	8,628	202	8,211 D	4.5%	93.3%	4.6%	95.4%
27,764	WARD 61	13,341	6,779	5,167	1,395	1,612 R	50.8%	38.7%	56.7%	43.3%
26,749	WARD 62	13,146	6,854	5,024	1,268	1,830 R	52.1%	38.2%	57.7%	42.3%
24,050	WARD 63	12,981	7,362	4,222	1,397	3,140 R	56.7%	32.5%	63.6%	36.4%
16,800	WARD 64	9,406	5,245	3,308	853	1,937 R	55.8%	35.2%	61.3%	38.7%
27,290	WARD 65	10,703	5,555	4,236	912	1,319 R	51.9%	39.6%	56.7%	43.3%
54,236	WARD 66	22,332	13,359	6,850	2,123	6,509 R	59.8%	30.7%	66.1%	33.9%
	SPECIAL BALLOTS	1,496	556	743	197	187 D	37.2%	49.7%	42.8%	57.2%
1,688,210	TOTAL	718,100	244,108	421,253	52,739	177,145 D	34.0%	58.7%	36.7%	63.3%

PHILADELPHIA

SENATOR 1980

1980 Census Population	Ward	Total Vote	Republican	Democratic	Other	Rep.-Dem. Plurality		Percentage Total Vote Rep.	Dem.	Major Vote Rep.	Dem.
20,177	WARD 1	9,663	4,745	4,790	128	45	D	49.1%	49.6%	49.8%	50.2%
22,751	WARD 2	9,391	4,798	4,360	233	438	R	51.1%	46.4%	52.4%	47.6%
24,119	WARD 3	9,399	3,519	5,712	168	2,193	D	37.4%	60.8%	38.1%	61.9%
22,303	WARD 4	8,902	3,047	5,703	152	2,656	D	34.2%	64.1%	34.8%	65.2%
21,593	WARD 5	9,463	5,393	3,710	360	1,683	R	57.0%	39.2%	59.2%	40.8%
18,520	WARD 6	6,049	1,732	4,229	88	2,497	D	28.6%	69.9%	29.1%	70.9%
22,651	WARD 7	6,974	3,297	3,569	108	272	D	47.3%	51.2%	48.0%	52.0%
28,580	WARD 8	13,841	8,499	4,786	556	3,713	R	61.4%	34.6%	64.0%	36.0%
16,994	WARD 9	8,817	5,477	3,055	285	2,422	R	62.1%	34.6%	64.2%	35.8%
29,871	WARD 10	10,500	4,435	5,883	182	1,448	D	42.2%	56.0%	43.0%	57.0%
18,921	WARD 11	6,281	1,955	4,201	125	2,246	D	31.1%	66.9%	31.8%	68.2%
25,839	WARD 12	8,365	3,533	4,473	359	940	D	42.2%	53.5%	44.1%	55.9%
24,273	WARD 13	8,185	2,958	4,993	234	2,035	D	36.1%	61.0%	37.2%	62.8%
12,560	WARD 14	3,167	993	2,091	83	1,098	D	31.4%	66.0%	32.2%	67.8%
16,990	WARD 15	7,033	3,740	3,058	235	682	R	53.2%	43.5%	55.0%	45.0%
18,656	WARD 16	6,608	1,674	4,774	160	3,100	D	25.3%	72.2%	26.0%	74.0%
27,667	WARD 17	10,402	3,573	6,645	184	3,072	D	34.3%	63.9%	35.0%	65.0%
17,121	WARD 18	5,272	2,243	2,960	69	717	D	42.5%	56.1%	43.1%	56.9%
19,150	WARD 19	4,032	1,001	2,962	69	1,961	D	24.8%	73.5%	25.3%	74.7%
11,680	WARD 20	3,041	838	2,116	87	1,278	D	27.6%	69.6%	28.4%	71.6%
48,965	WARD 21	20,984	12,592	8,139	253	4,453	R	60.0%	38.8%	60.7%	39.3%
26,193	WARD 22	11,941	5,729	5,828	384	99	D	48.0%	48.8%	49.6%	50.4%
23,829	WARD 23	9,078	4,971	3,945	162	1,026	R	54.8%	43.5%	55.8%	44.2%
17,473	WARD 24	5,251	1,688	3,362	201	1,674	D	32.1%	64.0%	33.4%	66.6%
22,200	WARD 25	8,722	4,328	4,285	109	43	R	49.6%	49.1%	50.2%	49.8%
27,679	WARD 26	10,159	5,918	4,136	105	1,782	R	58.3%	40.7%	58.9%	41.1%
25,228	WARD 27	7,966	4,025	3,514	427	511	R	50.5%	44.1%	53.4%	46.6%
17,501	WARD 28	6,241	2,074	4,073	94	1,999	D	33.2%	65.3%	33.7%	66.3%
16,538	WARD 29	5,865	1,100	4,627	138	3,527	D	18.8%	78.9%	19.2%	80.8%
14,225	WARD 30	5,287	1,956	3,149	182	1,193	D	37.0%	59.6%	38.3%	61.7%
18,277	WARD 31	6,743	3,266	3,393	84	127	D	48.4%	50.3%	49.0%	51.0%
30,101	WARD 32	9,089	3,001	5,822	266	2,821	D	33.0%	64.1%	34.0%	66.0%
22,916	WARD 33	10,182	5,383	4,678	121	705	R	52.9%	45.9%	53.5%	46.5%
39,985	WARD 34	17,104	8,127	8,754	223	627	D	47.5%	51.2%	48.1%	51.9%
32,175	WARD 35	15,366	9,206	6,027	133	3,179	R	59.9%	39.2%	60.4%	39.6%
35,472	WARD 36	14,357	4,821	9,267	269	4,446	D	33.6%	64.5%	34.2%	65.8%
20,306	WARD 37	5,498	1,375	4,042	81	2,667	D	25.0%	73.5%	25.4%	74.6%
23,399	WARD 38	8,201	3,685	4,364	152	679	D	44.9%	53.2%	45.8%	54.2%
47,439	WARD 39	19,766	11,361	8,155	250	3,206	R	57.5%	41.3%	58.2%	41.8%
50,806	WARD 40	18,431	9,015	9,249	167	234	D	48.9%	50.2%	49.4%	50.6%
23,528	WARD 41	10,190	5,636	4,438	116	1,198	R	55.3%	43.6%	55.9%	44.1%
29,145	WARD 42	10,931	6,161	4,635	135	1,526	R	56.4%	42.4%	57.1%	42.9%
27,147	WARD 43	7,000	2,207	4,678	115	2,471	D	31.5%	66.8%	32.1%	67.9%
17,276	WARD 44	6,633	2,121	4,425	87	2,304	D	32.0%	66.7%	32.4%	67.6%
24,576	WARD 45	10,561	5,236	5,160	165	76	R	49.6%	48.9%	50.4%	49.6%
24,939	WARD 46	9,448	3,462	5,538	448	2,076	D	36.6%	58.6%	38.5%	61.5%
11,264	WARD 47	3,645	650	2,893	102	2,243	D	17.8%	79.4%	18.3%	81.7%
22,391	WARD 48	8,922	4,788	4,007	127	781	R	53.7%	44.9%	54.4%	45.6%
33,401	WARD 49	9,170	3,781	5,142	247	1,361	D	41.2%	56.1%	42.4%	57.6%
31,271	WARD 50	12,294	5,312	6,807	175	1,495	D	43.2%	55.4%	43.8%	56.2%
28,662	WARD 51	8,819	2,924	5,709	186	2,785	D	33.2%	64.7%	33.9%	66.1%
28,926	WARD 52	13,585	6,792	6,565	228	227	R	50.0%	48.3%	50.8%	49.2%
21,786	WARD 53	12,591	8,598	3,875	118	4,723	R	68.3%	30.8%	68.9%	31.1%
19,800	WARD 54	11,927	7,669	4,127	131	3,542	R	64.3%	34.6%	65.0%	35.0%
27,590	WARD 55	14,443	8,228	6,088	127	2,140	R	57.0%	42.2%	57.5%	42.5%
35,662	WARD 56	19,391	13,216	5,989	186	7,227	R	68.2%	30.9%	68.8%	31.2%
29,362	WARD 57	14,239	8,874	5,249	116	3,625	R	62.3%	36.9%	62.8%	37.2%
47,404	WARD 58	21,948	15,461	6,306	181	9,155	R	70.4%	28.7%	71.0%	29.0%
24,998	WARD 59	9,278	4,027	4,987	264	960	D	43.4%	53.8%	44.7%	55.3%
21,070	WARD 60	8,546	2,841	5,570	135	2,729	D	33.2%	65.2%	33.8%	66.2%
27,764	WARD 61	12,916	7,702	4,999	215	2,703	R	59.6%	38.7%	60.6%	39.4%
26,749	WARD 62	12,885	7,373	5,368	144	2,005	R	57.2%	41.7%	57.9%	42.1%
24,050	WARD 63	12,765	8,642	3,944	179	4,698	R	67.7%	30.9%	68.7%	31.3%
16,800	WARD 64	9,190	5,370	3,737	83	1,633	R	58.4%	40.7%	59.0%	41.0%
27,290	WARD 65	10,422	5,884	4,421	117	1,463	R	56.5%	42.4%	57.1%	42.9%
54,236	WARD 66	21,772	13,490	8,057	225	5,433	R	62.0%	37.0%	62.6%	37.4%
1,688,210	TOTAL	675,127	337,516	325,593	12,018	11,923	R	50.0%	48.2%	50.9%	49.1%

PENNSYLVANIA

CONGRESS

CD	Year	Total Vote	Republican Vote	Republican Candidate	Democratic Vote	Democratic Candidate	Other Vote	Rep.-Dem. Plurality	Total Vote Rep.	Total Vote Dem.	Major Vote Rep.	Major Vote Dem.
1	1980	155,451	37,893	BURKE, ROBERT R.	52,956	MYERS, MICHAEL	64,602	15,063 D	24.4%	34.1%	41.7%	58.3%
1	1978	145,162	37,913	FANELLI, SAMUEL N.	104,412	MYERS, MICHAEL	2,837	66,499 D	26.1%	71.9%	26.6%	73.4%
1	1976	159,205	40,191	FANELLI, SAMUEL N.	117,087	MYERS, MICHAEL	1,927	76,896 D	25.2%	73.5%	25.6%	74.4%
1	1974	127,901	29,772	NIGRO, RUSSELL M.	96,988	BARRETT, WILLIAM A.	1,141	67,216 D	23.3%	75.8%	23.5%	76.5%
1	1972	179,932	59,807	PEDICONE, GUS A.	118,953	BARRETT, WILLIAM A.	1,172	59,146 D	33.2%	66.1%	33.5%	66.5%
2	1980	131,828			127,106	GRAY, WILLIAM H.	4,722	127,106 D		96.4%		100.0%
2	1978	161,759	25,785	ATKINS, ROLAND J.	132,594	GRAY, WILLIAM H.	3,380	106,809 D	15.9%	82.0%	16.3%	83.7%
2	1976	149,369	37,907	WOODS, JESSE W.	109,855	NIX, ROBERT N. C.	1,607	71,948 D	25.4%	73.5%	25.7%	74.3%
2	1974	101,386	26,353	WOODS, JESSE W.	75,033	NIX, ROBERT N. C.		48,680 D	26.0%	74.0%	26.0%	74.0%
2	1972	153,262	45,753	BRYANT, FREDERICK D.	107,509	NIX, ROBERT N. C.		61,756 D	29.9%	70.1%	29.9%	70.1%
3	1980	124,608	40,866	PHILLIPS, WILLIAM J.	67,942	LEDERER, RAYMOND F.	15,800	27,076 D	32.8%	54.5%	37.6%	62.4%
3	1978	119,765	33,750	KAUFFMAN, RAYMOND S.	86,015	LEDERER, RAYMOND F.		52,265 D	28.2%	71.8%	28.2%	71.8%
3	1976	134,818	35,491	SHADE, TERRENCE J.	98,627	LEDERER, RAYMOND F.	700	63,136 D	26.3%	73.2%	26.5%	73.5%
3	1974	112,367	27,692	COLBERT, RICHARD P.	84,675	GREEN, WILLIAM J., III		56,983 D	24.6%	75.4%	24.6%	75.4%
3	1972	159,704	57,787	MARROLETTI, ALFRED	101,144	GREEN, WILLIAM J., III	773	43,357 D	36.2%	63.3%	36.4%	63.6%
4	1980	201,370	127,475	DOUGHERTY, CHARLES F.	73,895	MAGRANN, THOMAS J.		53,580 R	63.3%	36.7%	63.3%	36.7%
4	1978	198,000	110,445	DOUGHERTY, CHARLES F.	87,555	EILBERG, JOSHUA		22,890 R	55.8%	44.2%	55.8%	44.2%
4	1976	214,590	69,700	MUGFORD, JAMES E.	144,890	EILBERG, JOSHUA		75,190 D	32.5%	67.5%	32.5%	67.5%
4	1974	174,640	50,688	EINHORN, ISADORE	123,952	EILBERG, JOSHUA		73,264 D	29.0%	71.0%	29.0%	71.0%
4	1972	231,118	102,013	PFENDER, WILLIAM	129,105	EILBERG, JOSHUA		27,092 D	44.1%	55.9%	44.1%	55.9%
5	1980	198,235	148,898	SCHULZE, RICHARD T.	47,092	BRICKHOUSE, GRADY G.	2,245	101,806 R	75.1%	23.8%	76.0%	24.0%
5	1978	147,269	110,565	SCHULZE, RICHARD T.	36,704	ZEALOR, MURRAY P.		73,861 R	75.1%	24.9%	75.1%	24.9%
5	1976	200,981	119,682	SCHULZE, RICHARD T.	81,299	CAMPOLO, ANTHONY		38,383 R	59.5%	40.5%	59.5%	40.5%
5	1974	140,152	83,526	SCHULZE, RICHARD T.	56,626	MCDERMOTT, LEO D.		26,900 R	59.6%	40.4%	59.6%	40.4%
5	1972	187,675	121,346	WARE, JOHN H.	66,329	YERGER, BROWER B.		55,017 R	64.7%	35.3%	64.7%	35.3%
6	1980	175,809	57,844	HULSHART, GEORGE	117,965	YATRON, GUS		60,121 D	32.9%	67.1%	32.9%	67.1%
6	1978	144,177	37,746	MAZUR, STEPHEN	106,431	YATRON, GUS		68,685 D	26.2%	73.8%	26.2%	73.8%
6	1976	180,998	46,103	POSTUPACK, STEPHEN	133,624	YATRON, GUS	1,271	87,521 D	25.5%	73.8%	25.7%	74.3%
6	1974	148,952	35,805	POSTUPACK, STEPHEN	111,127	YATRON, GUS	2,020	75,322 D	24.0%	74.6%	24.4%	75.6%
6	1972	185,408	64,076	HUBLER, EUGENE W.	119,557	YATRON, GUS	1,775	55,481 D	34.6%	64.5%	34.9%	65.1%
7	1980	187,024	87,643	ROCHFORD, DENNIS J.	99,381	EDGAR, ROBERT W.		11,738 D	46.9%	53.1%	46.9%	53.1%
7	1978	158,714	78,403	KANE, EUGENE D.	79,771	EDGAR, ROBERT W.	540	1,368 D	49.4%	50.3%	49.6%	50.4%
7	1976	202,351	92,788	KENNEY, JOHN M.	109,436	EDGAR, ROBERT W.	127	16,648 D	45.9%	54.1%	45.9%	54.1%
7	1974	162,295	70,894	MCEWEN, STEPHEN J.	89,680	EDGAR, ROBERT W.	1,721	18,786 D	43.7%	55.3%	44.2%	55.8%
7	1972	202,200	122,622	WILLIAMS, LAWRENCE	79,578	BOWIE, STUART S.		43,044 R	60.6%	39.4%	60.6%	39.4%
8	1980	204,345	103,585	COYNE, JAMES K.	99,593	KOSTMAYER, PETER H.	1,167	3,992 R	50.7%	48.7%	51.0%	49.0%
8	1978	146,052	56,776	BOWERS, G. ROGER	89,276	KOSTMAYER, PETER H.		32,500 D	38.9%	61.1%	38.9%	61.1%
8	1976	189,623	92,543	RENNINGER, JOHN S.	93,855	KOSTMAYER, PETER H.	3,225	1,312 D	48.8%	49.5%	49.6%	50.4%
8	1974	133,891	75,313	BIESTER, EDWARD G.	54,815	MOYER, WILLIAM B.	3,763	20,498 R	56.2%	40.9%	57.9%	42.1%
8	1972	179,881	115,799	BIESTER, EDWARD G.	64,069	WILLIAMS, ALAN	13	51,730 R	64.4%	35.6%	64.4%	35.6%
9	1980	157,241	157,241	*SHUSTER, E. G.				157,241 R	100.0%		100.0%	
9	1978	135,033	101,151	SHUSTER, E. G.	33,882	HAVICE, BLAINE L.		67,269 R	74.9%	25.1%	74.9%	25.1%
9	1976	154,359	154,359	*SHUSTER, E. G.				154,359 R	100.0%		100.0%	
9	1974	130,725	73,881	SHUSTER, E. G.	56,844	FORD, ROBERT D.		17,037 R	56.5%	43.5%	56.5%	43.5%
9	1972	155,341	95,913	SHUSTER, E. G.	59,386	COLLINS, EARL P.	42	36,527 R	61.7%	38.2%	61.8%	38.2%
10	1980	190,319	145,703	MCDADE, JOSEPH M.	43,152	BASALYGA, GENE	1,464	102,551 R	76.6%	22.7%	77.2%	22.8%
10	1978	151,724	116,003	MCDADE, JOSEPH M.	35,721	BASALYGA, GENE		80,282 R	76.5%	23.5%	76.5%	23.5%
10	1976	200,143	125,218	MCDADE, JOSEPH M.	74,925	MITCHELL, EDWARD		50,293 R	62.6%	37.4%	62.6%	37.4%
10	1974	155,194	100,793	MCDADE, JOSEPH M.	54,401	HANLON, THOMAS J.		46,392 R	64.9%	35.1%	64.9%	35.1%
10	1972	195,221	143,670	MCDADE, JOSEPH M.	51,550	COVELESKIE, STANLEY R.	1	92,120 R	73.6%	26.4%	73.6%	26.4%
11	1980	180,324	93,621	NELLIGAN, JAMES L.	86,703	MUSTO, RAPHAEL		6,918 R	51.9%	48.1%	51.9%	48.1%
11	1978	148,566	69,395	HUDOCK, ROBERT P.	79,171	FLOOD, DANIEL J.		9,776 D	46.7%	53.3%	46.7%	53.3%
11	1976	183,796	53,621	WILLIAMS, HOWARD G.	130,175	FLOOD, DANIEL J.		76,554 D	29.2%	70.8%	29.2%	70.8%
11	1974	149,678	38,106	MAZYKA, RICHARD A.	111,572	FLOOD, DANIEL J.		73,466 D	25.5%	74.5%	25.5%	74.5%
11	1972	182,146	57,809	AYERS, DONALD B.	124,336	FLOOD, DANIEL J.	1	66,527 D	31.7%	68.3%	31.7%	68.3%
12	1980	179,749	72,999	GETTY, CHARLES A.	106,750	MURTHA, JOHN P.		33,751 D	40.6%	59.4%	40.6%	59.4%
12	1978	151,658	47,442	ELKINS, LUTHER V.	104,216	MURTHA, JOHN P.		56,774 D	31.3%	68.7%	31.3%	68.7%
12	1976	180,993	58,489	HUMES, TED	122,504	MURTHA, JOHN P.		64,015 D	32.3%	67.7%	32.3%	67.7%
12	1974	153,619	64,416	FOX, HARRY M.	89,193	MURTHA, JOHN P.	10	24,777 D	41.9%	58.1%	41.9%	58.1%
12	1972	179,947	122,628	SAYLOR, JOHN P.	57,314	MURPHY, JOSEPH	5	65,314 R	68.1%	31.9%	68.1%	31.9%

PENNSYLVANIA

CONGRESS

CD	Year	Total Vote	Republican Vote	Republican Candidate	Democratic Vote	Democratic Candidate	Other Vote	Rep.-Dem. Plurality	Total Vote Rep.	Total Vote Dem.	Major Vote Rep.	Major Vote Dem.
13	1980	197,584	138,212	COUGHLIN, R. LAWRENCE	57,745	SLAWEK, PAUL P.	1,627	80,467 R	70.0%	29.2%	70.5%	29.5%
13	1978	159,862	112,711	COUGHLIN, R. LAWRENCE	47,151	RUBENSTEIN, ALAN B.		65,560 R	70.5%	29.5%	70.5%	29.5%
13	1976	206,140	130,705	COUGHLIN, R. LAWRENCE	75,435	STRICK, GERTRUDE		55,270 R	63.4%	36.6%	63.4%	36.6%
13	1974	158,418	98,985	COUGHLIN, R. LAWRENCE	59,433	CURRY, LAWRENCE H.		39,552 R	62.5%	37.5%	62.5%	37.5%
13	1972	208,818	139,085	COUGHLIN, R. LAWRENCE	69,728	CAMP, KATHERINE L.	5	69,357 R	66.6%	33.4%	66.6%	33.4%
14	1980	149,624	44,071	THOMAS, STAN	102,545	COYNE, WILLIAM J.	3,008	58,474 D	29.5%	68.5%	30.1%	69.9%
14	1978	119,202	49,992	THOMAS, STAN	68,004	MOORHEAD, WILLIAM S.	1,206	18,012 D	41.9%	57.0%	42.4%	57.6%
14	1976	159,644	43,308	BRADLEY, JOHN F.	114,472	MOORHEAD, WILLIAM S.	1,864	71,164 D	27.1%	71.7%	27.4%	72.6%
14	1974	120,332	27,116	DAVIS, ZACHARY T.	93,169	MOORHEAD, WILLIAM S.	47	66,053 D	22.5%	77.4%	22.5%	77.5%
14	1972	178,907	72,275	CATARINELLA, ROLAND S.	106,158	MOORHEAD, WILLIAM S.	474	33,883 D	40.4%	59.3%	40.5%	59.5%
15	1980	167,725	99,874	RITTER, DONALD L.	66,626	REIBMAN, JEANETTE	1,225	33,248 R	59.5%	39.7%	60.0%	40.0%
15	1978	124,063	65,986	RITTER, DONALD L.	58,077	ROONEY, FRED B.		7,909 R	53.2%	46.8%	53.2%	46.8%
15	1976	166,890	57,616	SIVULICH, ALICE B.	108,844	ROONEY, FRED B.	430	51,228 D	34.5%	65.2%	34.6%	65.4%
15	1974	85,905			85,905	ROONEY, FRED B.		85,905 D		100.0%		100.0%
15	1972	164,500	64,560	STEIGERWALT, WARDELL F.	99,937	ROONEY, FRED B.	3	35,377 D	39.2%	60.8%	39.2%	60.8%
16	1980	168,656	129,765	WALKER, ROBERT S.	38,891	WOODCOCK, JAMES A.		90,874 R	76.9%	23.1%	76.9%	23.1%
16	1978	119,296	91,910	WALKER, ROBERT S.	27,386	BOOHAR, CHARLES W.		64,524 R	77.0%	23.0%	77.0%	23.0%
16	1976	156,455	97,527	WALKER, ROBERT S.	57,836	MINNEY, MICHAEL J.	1,092	39,691 R	62.3%	37.0%	62.8%	37.2%
16	1974	115,168	73,130	ESHLEMAN, EDWIN D.	40,273	MINNEY, MICHAEL J.	1,765	32,857 R	63.5%	35.0%	64.5%	35.5%
16	1972	152,827	112,292	ESHLEMAN, EDWIN D.	40,534	GARRETT, SHIRLEY S.	1	71,758 R	73.5%	26.5%	73.5%	26.5%
17	1980	161,785	63,790	SEIVERLING, DANIEL S.	97,995	ERTEL, ALLEN E.		34,205 D	39.4%	60.6%	39.4%	60.6%
17	1978	132,847	53,613	RIPPON, THOMAS	79,234	ERTEL, ALLEN E.		25,621 D	40.4%	59.6%	40.4%	59.6%
17	1976	169,864	82,370	HEPFORD, H. JOSEPH	86,158	ERTEL, ALLEN E.	1,336	3,788 D	48.5%	50.7%	48.9%	51.1%
17	1974	134,850	70,274	SCHNEEBELI, HERMAN	64,576	WAMBACH, PETER C.		5,698 R	52.1%	47.9%	52.1%	47.9%
17	1972	166,494	120,214	SCHNEEBELI, HERMAN	44,202	RIPPON, DONALD J.	2,078	76,012 R	72.2%	26.5%	73.1%	26.9%
18	1980	186,462	58,821	SNYDER, STEVEN R.	127,641	WALGREN, DOUGLAS		68,820 D	31.5%	68.5%	31.5%	68.5%
18	1978	154,671	65,088	JACOB, TED	88,299	WALGREN, DOUGLAS	1,284	23,211 D	42.1%	57.1%	42.4%	57.6%
18	1976	191,381	77,594	CASEY, ROBERT J.	113,787	WALGREN, DOUGLAS		36,193 D	40.5%	59.5%	40.5%	59.5%
18	1974	149,471	107,723	HEINZ, H. JOHN	41,706	MCARDLE, FRANCIS J.	42	66,017 R	72.1%	27.9%	72.1%	27.9%
18	1972	198,472	144,521	HEINZ, H. JOHN	53,929	WALGREN, DOUGLAS	22	90,592 R	72.8%	27.2%	72.8%	27.2%
19	1980	180,002	136,873	GOODLING, WILLIAM F.	41,584	NOLL, RICHARD P.	1,545	95,289 R	76.0%	23.1%	76.7%	23.3%
19	1978	134,001	105,424	GOODLING, WILLIAM F.	28,577	KUMAR, RAJESHWAR		76,847 R	78.7%	21.3%	78.7%	21.3%
19	1976	175,784	124,098	GOODLING, WILLIAM F.	51,686	NOLL, RICHARD P.		72,412 R	70.6%	29.4%	70.6%	29.4%
19	1974	129,158	66,417	GOODLING, WILLIAM F.	61,414	BERGER, ARTHUR L.	1,327	5,003 R	51.4%	47.5%	52.0%	48.0%
19	1972	162,587	93,536	GOODLING, GEORGE A.	67,018	NOLL, RICHARD P.	2,033	26,518 R	57.5%	41.2%	58.3%	41.7%
20	1980	168,413	46,313	MEYER, KATHLEEN M.	122,100	GAYDOS, JOSEPH M.		75,787 D	27.5%	72.5%	27.5%	72.5%
20	1978	135,490	37,745	MEYER, KATHLEEN M.	97,745	GAYDOS, JOSEPH M.		60,000 D	27.9%	72.1%	27.9%	72.1%
20	1976	180,055	44,432	KOSTELAC, JOHN P.	134,961	GAYDOS, JOSEPH M.	662	90,529 D	24.7%	75.0%	24.8%	75.2%
20	1974	137,393	25,129	ANDERKO, JOSEPH J.	112,237	GAYDOS, JOSEPH M.	27	87,108 D	18.3%	81.7%	18.3%	81.7%
20	1972	191,764	73,817	HUNT, WILLIAM R.	117,933	GAYDOS, JOSEPH M.	14	44,116 D	38.5%	61.5%	38.5%	61.5%
21	1980	164,248	51,821	MATSON, DIRK	112,427	BAILEY, DONALD		60,606 D	31.6%	68.4%	31.6%	68.4%
21	1978	139,334	65,622	MILLER, ROBERT H.	73,712	BAILEY, DONALD		8,090 D	47.1%	52.9%	47.1%	52.9%
21	1976	166,923	67,763	MILLER, ROBERT H.	99,160	DENT, JOHN H.		31,397 D	40.6%	59.4%	40.6%	59.4%
21	1974	126,822	38,111	SCONING, CHARLES L.	88,701	DENT, JOHN H.	10	50,590 D	30.1%	69.9%	30.1%	69.9%
21	1972	168,032	63,812	YOUNG, THOMAS H.	104,203	DENT, JOHN H.	17	40,391 D	38.0%	62.0%	38.0%	62.0%
22	1980	169,768	50,020	ECOFF, MARILYN C.	118,084	MURPHY, AUSTIN J.	1,664	68,064 D	29.5%	69.6%	29.8%	70.2%
22	1978	139,077	39,518	ECOFF, MARILYN C.	99,559	MURPHY, AUSTIN J.		60,041 D	28.4%	71.6%	28.4%	71.6%
22	1976	175,416	77,030	FISCHER, ROGER	97,036	MURPHY, AUSTIN J.	1,350	20,006 D	43.9%	55.3%	44.3%	55.7%
22	1974	131,628	41,706	MONTGOMERY, JAMES R.	83,654	MORGAN, THOMAS E.	6,268	41,948 D	31.7%	63.6%	33.3%	66.7%
22	1972	165,934	65,005	MONTGOMERY, JAMES R.	100,918	MORGAN, THOMAS E.	11	35,913 D	39.2%	60.8%	39.2%	60.8%
23	1980	167,046	122,855	CLINGER, WILLIAM F.	41,033	ATIGAN, PETER	3,158	81,822 R	73.5%	24.6%	75.0%	25.0%
23	1978	134,851	73,194	CLINGER, WILLIAM F.	61,657	AMMERMAN, JOSEPH S.		11,537 R	54.3%	45.7%	54.3%	45.7%
23	1976	169,462	73,641	JOHNSON, ALBERT W.	95,821	AMMERMAN, JOSEPH S.		22,180 D	43.5%	56.5%	43.5%	56.5%
23	1974	127,403	67,192	JOHNSON, ALBERT W.	60,211	MAST, YATES		6,981 R	52.7%	47.3%	52.7%	47.3%
23	1972	160,428	90,615	JOHNSON, ALBERT W.	69,813	KASSAB, ERNEST A.		20,802 R	56.5%	43.5%	56.5%	43.5%

PENNSYLVANIA

CONGRESS

CD	Year	Total Vote	Republican Vote	Republican Candidate	Democratic Vote	Democratic Candidate	Other Vote	Rep.-Dem. Plurality		Total Vote Rep.	Total Vote Dem.	Major Vote Rep.	Major Vote Dem.
24	1980	174,555	86,687	MARKS, MARC L.	86,567	DICARLO, DAVID C.	1,301	120	R	49.7%	49.6%	50.0%	50.0%
24	1978	135,935	87,041	MARKS, MARC L.	48,894	VIGORITO, JOSEPH P.		38,147	R	64.0%	36.0%	64.0%	36.0%
24	1976	182,526	101,048	MARKS, MARC L.	79,937	VIGORITO, JOSEPH P.	1,541	21,111	R	55.4%	43.8%	55.8%	44.2%
24	1974	131,197	54,277	SCALZITTI, CLEMENT R.	76,920	VIGORITO, JOSEPH P.		22,643	D	41.4%	58.6%	41.4%	58.6%
24	1972	177,498	55,406	LEVENHAGEN, ALVIN W.	122,092	VIGORITO, JOSEPH P.		66,686	D	31.2%	68.8%	31.2%	68.8%
24	1970	140,848	44,395	MERRICK, WAYNE R.	94,029	VIGORITO, JOSEPH P.	2,424	49,634	D	31.5%	66.8%	32.1%	67.9%
24	1968	174,958	66,429	EDWARDS, JOHN V.	106,869	VIGORITO, JOSEPH P.	1,660	40,440	D	38.0%	61.1%	38.3%	61.7%
24	1966	154,148	68,955	WEAVER, JAMES D.	85,193	VIGORITO, JOSEPH P.		16,238	D	44.7%	55.3%	44.7%	55.3%
24	1964	182,440	89,828	WEAVER, JAMES D.	92,612	VIGORITO, JOSEPH P.		2,784	D	49.2%	50.8%	49.2%	50.8%
24	1962	159,962	82,213	WEAVER, JAMES D.	77,749	JOYCE, PETER J.		4,464	R	51.4%	48.6%	51.4%	48.6%
24	1960	186,647	95,149	KEARNS, CARROLL D.	91,498	HAMPTON, CHESTER C.		3,651	R	51.0%	49.0%	51.0%	49.0%
24	1958	142,807	76,870	KEARNS, CARROLL D.	65,937	O'BRIEN, JAMES P.		10,933	R	53.8%	46.2%	53.8%	46.2%
24	1956	162,449	93,824	KEARNS, CARROLL D.	68,625	THOMAS, WILLIAM D.		25,199	R	57.8%	42.2%	57.8%	42.2%
24	1954	126,847	66,005	KEARNS, CARROLL D.	60,842	ROGERS, EDMUND T.		5,163	R	52.0%	48.0%	52.0%	48.0%
24	1952	158,066	90,276	KEARNS, CARROLL D.	67,790	BEBELL, CLINTON J.		22,486	R	57.1%	42.9%	57.1%	42.9%
28	1950	118,664	67,604	KEARNS, CARROLL D.	51,060	FILIPKOWSKI, STEVE		16,544	R	57.0%	43.0%	57.0%	43.0%
28	1948	119,678	65,276	KEARNS, CARROLL D.	54,402	KENNEDY, JAMES A.		10,874	R	54.5%	45.5%	54.5%	45.5%
28	1946	89,001	56,835	KEARNS, CARROLL D.	32,166	WEBB, CHARLES W.		24,669	R	63.9%	36.1%	63.9%	36.1%
25	1980	178,585	58,768	MORRIS, ROBERT H.	119,817	ATKINSON, EUGENE V.		61,049	D	32.9%	67.1%	32.9%	67.1%
25	1978	146,948	62,160	SHAFFER, TIM	68,293	ATKINSON, EUGENE V.	16,495	6,133	D	42.3%	46.5%	47.6%	52.4%
25	1976	182,489	103,632	MYERS, GARY A.	78,857	ATKINSON, EUGENE V.		24,775	R	56.8%	43.2%	56.8%	43.2%
25	1974	138,732	74,645	MYERS, GARY A.	64,049	CLARK, FRANK M.	38	10,596	R	53.8%	46.2%	53.8%	46.2%
25	1972	174,693	77,123	MYERS, GARY A.	97,549	CLARK, FRANK M.	21	20,426	D	44.1%	55.8%	44.2%	55.8%

PENNSYLVANIA

1980 GENERAL ELECTION

President   Other vote was 292,921 Anderson (Anderson Coalition); 33,263 Clark (Libertarian); 20,291 DeBerry (Socialist Workers); 10,430 Commoner (Consumer); 5,184 Hall (Communist).

Senator   Other vote was 27,229 Mohrbacher (Socialist Workers); 18,595 Walter (Libertarian); 16,089 Frissell (Consumer); 3,334 Kinces (Communist).

Congress   An asterisk in the Congressional vote table indicates a candidate received votes from another party endorsing his/her candidacy. In CD 11, the 1978 figures have been corrected from data that appeared in AMERICA VOTES 13. Other vote was Hoffman (Libertarian) in CD 5; Schroeder (Libertarian) in CD 8; Fallon (Libertarian) in CD 10; Houser (Libertarian) in CD 13; Hughes (Consumer) in CD 14; Karkutt (Libertarian) in CD 15; Davies (Libertarian) in CD 19; Krayer (Libertarian) in CD 22; Mason (Consumer) in CD 23; Hammer (Independent) in CD 24; in other CD's as follows:

   CD 1   58,737 Foglietta (Foglietta); 3,161 Steinberg (Libertarian); 2,704 Haqq (Consumer). Thomas M. Foglietta ran against the incumbent Democrat and the Republican nominee. In the organization of the House, Mr. Foglietta declared himself a Democrat.

   CD 2   2,396 Dempsey (Consumer); 2,326 Buckman (Independent).

   CD 3   11,849 Weiner (Consumer); 3,951 Morris (Morris).

PHILADELPHIA

Philadelphia city and county are coterminous.

President   Other vote was 42,967 Anderson (Anderson Coalition); 4,380 Clark (Libertarian); 2,667 Commoner (Consumer); 1,734 DeBerry (Socialist Workers); 991 Hall (Communist). Special Ballots were Federal ballots limited to those voting for President only.

Senator   Other votes was 5,145 Frissell (Consumer); 3,382 Mohrbacher (Socialist Workers); 2,354 Walter (Libertarian); 1,137 Kinces (Communist).

1980 PRIMARIES

APRIL 22 REPUBLICAN

Senator   419,372 Arlen Specter; 382,281 Bud Haabestad; 148,200 Edward L. Howard; 52,408 Norman W. Bertasavage; 43,992 Andrew J. Watson; 38,164 Warren R. Williams; 36,982 Lewis C. Richards; 30,660 Francis Worley.

Congress   Unopposed in fourteen CD's. No candidate in CD 2. No candidates filed in CD 25. David L. Robinson, the unopposed candidate in CD 21, withdrew after the primary and Dirk Matson was substituted by the local party committee. Contested as follows:

   CD 4   21,923 Charles F. Dougherty; 21,440 Dennis M. O'Brien.

   CD 6   21,918 George Hulshart; 20,707 Harry B. Martin.

   CD 7   41,609 Dennis J. Rochford; 10,180 Nicholas C. Itri; 9,904 Harry F. Nuss; 3,972 William J. Fili.

   CD 11   26,974 James L. Nelligan; 13,299 Robert P. Hudock; 5,746 Howard G. Williams; 3,069 Joseph E. Zukowsky; 680 James T. Lesho.

   CD 12   16,400 Charles A. Getty; 15,528 Allan N. Campbell; 12,100 Luther V. Elkin; 9,764 Eleanor J. Thomas.

   CD 13   60,081 R. Lawrence Coughlin; 10,243 Edward H. Johnson.

   CD 17   35,023 Daniel S. Seiverling; 16,295 David J. Lu.

   CD 18   21,662 Steven R. Snyder; 21,369 Anthony C. Purcell.

   CD 22   14,935 Marilyn C. Ecoff; 14,333 Kevin B. O'Rourke.

   CD 25   No candidates names appeared on the ballot; Robert H. Morris received 6,025 write-in votes and became the nominee.

PENNSYLVANIA

APRIL 22 DEMOCRATIC

Senator 771,119 Peter Flaherty; 179,107 Joseph Rhodes; 116,975 Peter Liacouras; 107,483 C. Delores Tucker; 100,841 Ed Mezvinsky; 89,656 Tom Anderson; 69,701 Craig Lewis; 13,752 John J. Logue.

Congress Unopposed in fifteen CD's. No candidates filed in CD 9. Contested as follows:

CD 1 24,030 Michael Myers; 21,143 Hardy Williams; 8,406 Bernard J. Avellino; 4,170 Andrew DiAntonio; 3,582 Walt Palmer; 3,426 Dante Mattioni; 2,586 Joseph L. Della Guardia; 1,780 Robert G. Allman; 1,648 Mariam Grimes; 1,337 John F. Bonner; 1,119 A. Charles Peruto; 759 Natale F. Carabello; 678 Bernard J. Salera; 664 Gene Bivins; 491 C. Douglas Clark.

CD 3 20,093 Raymond F. Lederer; 10,195 Dennis Waterman; 7,257 Donald P. Sullivan; 4,335 John F. Hohenstein; 3,698 Richard I. Torpey; 1,292 Gilbert Sojo; 924 Harry R. Comer.

CD 4 22,580 Thomas J. Magrann; 22,241 Mike Mustokoff; 21,361 Wendell W. Young; 12,909 Edward S. Goldstein; 8,668 John R. Fitzpatrick; 1,574 Charles McAndrew.

CD 9 No candidates names appeared on the ballot; E. G. Shuster, the unopposed Republican candidate, received 2,194 write-in votes and became the nominee.

CD 11 33,394 Raphael Musto; 23,680 Frank Harrison; 12,022 Paul E. Kanjorski; 6,403 Ed Mitchell; 2,839 Charles J. Demko; 1,444 Douglas H. Hess; 1,035 Richard P. Adams; 544 Samuel W. Daley; 487 Stephen L. Flood.

CD 14 44,142 William J. Coyne; 24,209 William S. Moorhead, III; 8,668 Richard E. Caligiuri.

CD 15 22,839 Jeanette Reibman; 15,646 J. Michael Schweder; 13,227 Michael Krajsa; 6,576 Paul F. McHale.

CD 19 22,935 Richard P. Noll; 11,302 Jess Mays.

CD 21 48,337 Donald Bailey; 27,007 Bernard F. Scherer; 5,376 Eugene G. Saloom.

CD 25 50,767 Eugene V. Atkinson; 8,706 William Kovolenko; 8,041 Gloriann Burick.

RHODE ISLAND

GOVERNOR

J. Joseph Garrahy (D). Re-elected 1980 to a two-year term. Previously elected 1978, 1976.

SENATORS

John H. Chafee (R). Elected 1976 to a six-year term.

Claiborne Pell (D). Re-elected 1978 to a six-year term. Previously elected 1972, 1966, 1960.

REPRESENTATIVES

1. Fernand St. Germain (D)   2. Claudine Schneider (R)

POSTWAR VOTE FOR GOVERNOR

Year	Total Vote	Republican Vote	Candidate	Democratic Vote	Candidate	Other Vote	Rep.-Dem. Plurality	Total Vote Rep.	Total Vote Dem.	Major Vote Rep.	Major Vote Dem.
1980	405,916	106,729	Cianci, Vincent A.	299,174	Garrahy, J. Joseph	13	192,445 D	26.3%	73.7%	26.3%	73.7%
1978	314,363	96,596	Almond, Lincoln	197,386	Garrahy, J. Joseph	20,381	100,790 D	30.7%	62.8%	32.9%	67.1%
1976	398,683	178,254	Taft, James L.	218,561	Garrahy, J. Joseph	1,868	40,307 D	44.7%	54.8%	44.9%	55.1%
1974	321,660	69,224	Nugent, James W.	252,436	Noel, Philip W.	—	183,212 D	21.5%	78.5%	21.5%	78.5%
1972	412,866	194,315	DeSimone, Herbert F.	216,953	Noel, Philip W.	1,598	22,638 D	47.1%	52.5%	47.2%	52.8%
1970	346,342	171,549	DeSimone, Herbert F.	173,420	Licht, Frank	1,373	1,871 D	49.5%	50.1%	49.7%	50.3%
1968	383,725	187,958	Chafee, John H.	195,766	Licht, Frank	1	7,808 R	49.0%	51.0%	49.0%	51.0%
1966	332,064	210,202	Chafee, John H.	121,862	Hobbs, Horace E.	—	88,340 R	63.3%	36.7%	63.3%	36.7%
1964	391,668	239,501	Chafee, John H.	152,165	Gallogly, Edward P.	2	87,336 R	61.1%	38.9%	61.1%	38.9%
1962	327,506	163,952	Chafee, John H.	163,554	Notte, John A.	—	398 R	50.1%	49.9%	50.1%	49.9%
1960	401,362	174,044	Del Sesto, Christopher	227,318	Notte, John A.	—	53,274 D	43.4%	56.6%	43.4%	56.6%
1958	346,780	176,505	Del Sesto, Christopher	170,275	Roberts, Dennis J.	—	6,230 R	50.9%	49.1%	50.9%	49.1%
1956	383,919	191,604	Del Sesto, Christopher	192,315	Roberts, Dennis J.	—	711 D	49.9%	50.1%	49.9%	50.1%
1954	328,670	137,131	Lewis, Dean J.	189,595	Roberts, Dennis J.	1,944	52,464 D	41.7%	57.7%	42.0%	58.0%
1952	409,689	194,102	Archambault, Raoul	215,587	Roberts, Dennis J.	—	21,485 D	47.4%	52.6%	47.4%	52.6%
1950	296,809	120,684	Lachapelle, E. T.	176,125	Roberts, Dennis J.	—	55,441 D	40.7%	59.3%	40.7%	59.3%
1948	323,863	124,441	Ruerat, Albert P.	198,056	Pastore, John O.	1,366	73,615 D	38.4%	61.2%	38.6%	61.4%
1946	275,341	126,456	Murphy, John G.	148,885	Pastore, John O.	—	22,429 D	45.9%	54.1%	45.9%	54.1%

POSTWAR VOTE FOR SENATOR

Year	Total Vote	Republican Vote	Candidate	Democratic Vote	Candidate	Other Vote	Rep.-Dem. Plurality	Total Vote Rep.	Total Vote Dem.	Major Vote Rep.	Major Vote Dem.
1978	305,618	76,061	Reynolds, James G.	229,557	Pell, Claiborne	—	153,496 D	24.9%	75.1%	24.9%	75.1%
1976	398,906	230,329	Chafee, John H.	167,665	Lorber, Richard P.	912	62,664 R	57.7%	42.0%	57.9%	42.1%
1972	413,432	188,990	Chafee, John H.	221,942	Pell, Claiborne	2,500	32,952 D	45.7%	53.7%	46.0%	54.0%
1970	341,222	107,351	McLaughlin, John	230,469	Pastore, John O.	3,402	123,118 D	31.5%	67.5%	31.8%	68.2%
1966	324,173	104,838	Briggs, Ruth M.	219,331	Pell, Claiborne	4	114,493 D	32.3%	67.7%	32.3%	67.7%
1964	386,322	66,715	Lagueux, Ronald R.	319,607	Pastore, John O.	—	252,892 D	17.3%	82.7%	17.3%	82.7%
1960	399,983	124,408	Archambault, Raoul	275,575	Pell, Claiborne	—	151,167 D	31.1%	68.9%	31.1%	68.9%
1958	344,519	122,353	Ewing, Bayard	222,166	Pastore, John O.	—	99,813 D	35.5%	64.5%	35.5%	64.5%
1954	326,624	132,970	Sundlun, Walter I.	193,654	Green, Theodore F.	—	60,684 D	40.7%	59.3%	40.7%	59.3%
1952	410,978	185,850	Ewing, Bayard	225,128	Pastore, John O.	—	39,278 D	45.2%	54.8%	45.2%	54.8%
1950s	297,909	114,184	Levy, Austin T.	183,725	Pastore, John O.	—	69,541 D	48.3%	61.7%	38.3%	61.7%
1948	320,420	130,262	Hazard, Thomas P.	190,158	Green, Theodore F.	—	59,896 D	40.7%	59.3%	40.7%	59.3%
1946	273,528	122,780	Dyer, W. Gurnee	150,748	McGrath, J. Howard	—	27,968 D	44.9%	55.1%	44.9%	55.1%

The election in 1950 was for a short term to fill a vacancy.

RHODE ISLAND

Districts Established January 31, 1972

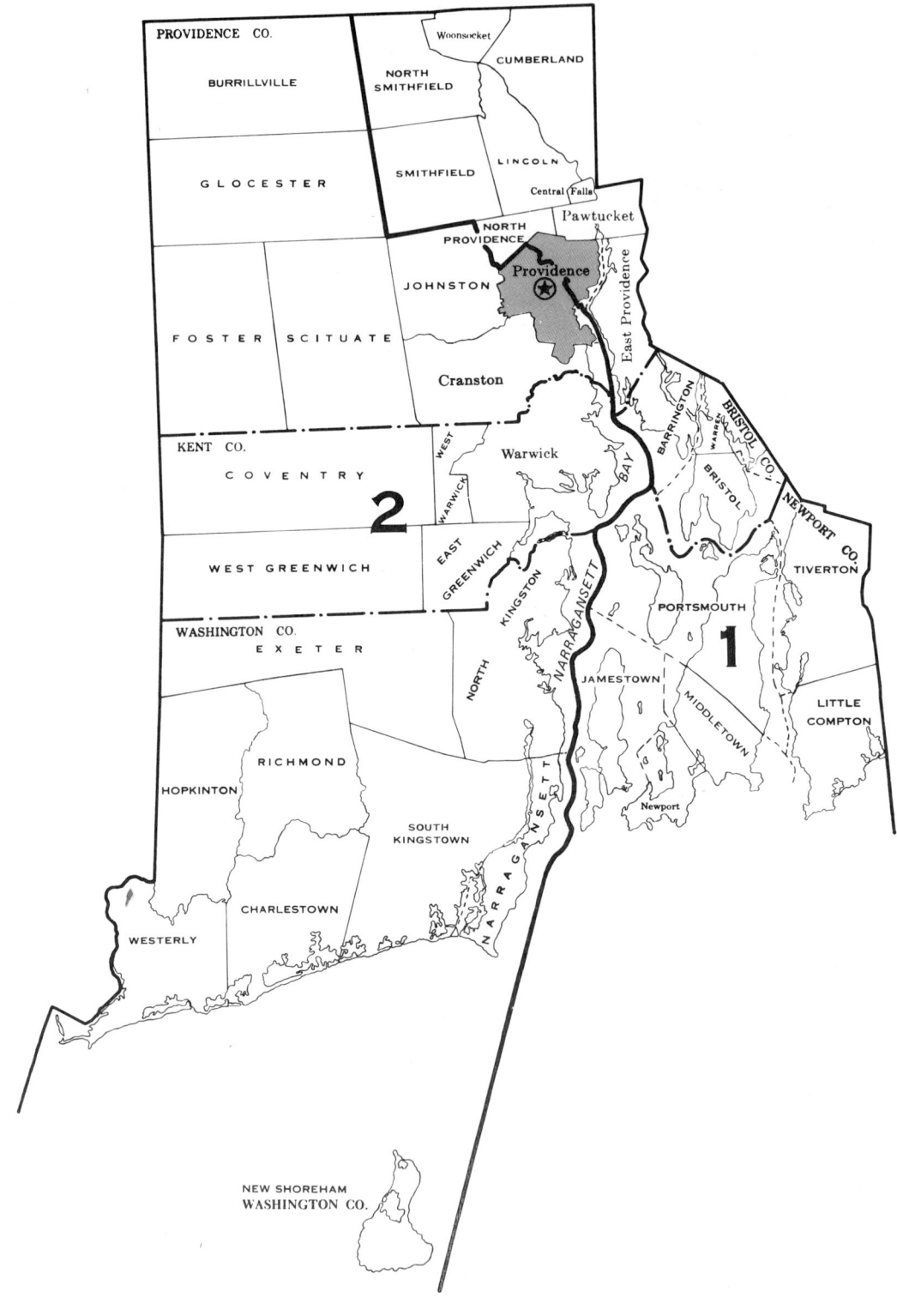

RHODE ISLAND

PRESIDENT 1980

1980 Census Population	County	Total Vote	Republican	Democratic	Other	Rep.-Dem. Plurality		Percentage Total Vote Rep.	Dem.	Major Vote Rep.	Dem.
46,942	BRISTOL	21,852	8,508	9,851	3,493	1,343	D	38.9%	45.1%	46.3%	53.7%
154,163	KENT	71,005	28,331	31,350	11,324	3,019	D	39.9%	44.2%	47.5%	52.5%
81,383	NEWPORT	34,356	14,555	13,904	5,897	651	R	42.4%	40.5%	51.1%	48.9%
571,349	PROVIDENCE	247,927	86,467	126,808	34,652	40,341	D	34.9%	51.1%	40.5%	59.5%
93,317	WASHINGTON	40,827	16,932	16,429	7,466	503	R	41.5%	40.2%	50.8%	49.2%
947,154	TOTAL	416,072	154,793	198,342	62,937	43,549	D	37.2%	47.7%	43.8%	56.2%

RHODE ISLAND

PRESIDENT 1980

1980 Census Population	City/Town	Total Vote	Republican	Democratic	Other	Rep.-Dem. Plurality		Percentage Total Vote Rep.	Dem.	Major Vote Rep.	Dem.
16,174	BARRINGTON	9,030	4,116	3,146	1,768	970	R	45.6%	34.8%	56.7%	43.3%
20,128	BRISTOL TOWN	8,182	2,726	4,305	1,151	1,579	D	33.3%	52.6%	38.8%	61.2%
13,164	BURRILLVILLE	4,744	1,908	2,208	628	300	D	40.2%	46.5%	46.4%	53.6%
16,995	CENTRAL FALLS	5,938	1,907	3,439	592	1,532	D	32.1%	57.9%	35.7%	64.3%
4,800	CHARLESTOWN	2,409	1,100	906	403	194	R	45.7%	37.6%	54.8%	45.2%
27,065	COVENTRY	11,380	4,712	4,756	1,912	44	D	41.4%	41.8%	49.8%	50.2%
71,992	CRANSTON	37,719	14,781	17,293	5,645	2,512	D	39.2%	45.8%	46.1%	53.9%
27,069	CUMBERLAND	13,396	5,556	5,915	1,925	359	D	41.5%	44.2%	48.4%	51.6%
10,211	EAST GREENWICH	5,463	2,726	1,770	967	956	R	49.9%	32.4%	60.6%	39.4%
50,980	EAST PROVIDENCE	22,224	7,566	11,440	3,218	3,874	D	34.0%	51.5%	39.8%	60.2%
4,453	EXETER	1,560	667	606	287	61	R	42.8%	38.8%	52.4%	47.6%
3,370	FOSTER	1,619	739	597	283	142	R	45.6%	36.9%	55.3%	44.7%
7,550	GLOCESTER	3,345	1,471	1,359	515	112	R	44.0%	40.6%	52.0%	48.0%
6,406	HOPKINTON	2,472	1,162	962	348	200	R	47.0%	38.9%	54.7%	45.3%
4,040	JAMESTOWN	1,778	693	675	410	18	R	39.0%	38.0%	50.7%	49.3%
24,907	JOHNSTON	11,651	4,280	5,918	1,453	1,638	D	36.7%	50.8%	42.0%	58.0%
16,949	LINCOLN	9,241	4,016	3,851	1,374	165	R	43.5%	41.7%	51.0%	49.0%
3,085	LITTLE COMPTON	1,817	845	660	312	185	R	46.5%	36.3%	56.1%	43.9%
17,216	MIDDLETOWN	6,345	2,985	2,299	1,061	686	R	47.0%	36.2%	56.5%	43.5%
12,088	NARRAGANSETT	5,860	2,190	2,504	1,166	314	D	37.4%	42.7%	46.7%	53.3%
29,259	NEWPORT CITY	11,886	4,449	5,072	2,365	623	D	37.4%	42.7%	46.7%	53.3%
620	NEW SHOREHAM	738	280	290	168	10	D	37.9%	39.3%	49.1%	50.9%
21,938	NORTH KINGSTOWN	9,908	4,412	3,541	1,955	871	R	44.5%	35.7%	55.5%	44.5%
29,188	NORTH PROVIDENCE	15,108	5,281	7,855	1,972	2,574	D	35.0%	52.0%	40.2%	59.8%
9,972	NORTH SMITHFIELD	5,180	2,310	2,092	778	218	R	44.6%	40.4%	52.5%	47.5%
71,204	PAWTUCKET	26,704	8,402	14,455	3,847	6,053	D	31.5%	54.1%	36.8%	63.2%
14,257	PORTSMOUTH	6,579	3,012	2,547	1,020	465	R	45.8%	38.7%	54.2%	45.8%
156,804	PROVIDENCE CITY	61,367	16,689	36,249	8,429	19,560	D	27.2%	59.1%	31.5%	68.5%
4,018	RICHMOND	1,659	703	679	277	24	R	42.4%	40.9%	50.9%	49.1%
8,405	SCITUATE	4,375	2,269	1,373	733	896	R	51.9%	31.4%	62.3%	37.7%
16,886	SMITHFIELD	7,432	3,034	3,240	1,158	206	D	40.8%	43.6%	48.4%	51.6%
20,414	SOUTH KINGSTOWN	7,859	3,000	3,222	1,637	222	D	38.2%	41.0%	48.2%	51.8%
13,526	TIVERTON	5,951	2,571	2,651	729	80	D	43.2%	44.5%	49.2%	50.8%
10,640	WARREN	4,640	1,666	2,400	574	734	D	35.9%	51.7%	41.0%	59.0%
87,123	WARWICK	41,094	15,890	18,424	6,780	2,534	D	38.7%	44.8%	46.3%	53.7%
18,580	WESTERLY	8,362	3,418	3,719	1,225	301	D	40.9%	44.5%	47.9%	52.1%
2,738	WEST GREENWICH	1,473	702	597	174	105	R	47.7%	40.5%	54.0%	46.0%
27,026	WEST WARWICK	11,595	4,301	5,803	1,491	1,502	D	37.1%	50.0%	42.6%	57.4%
45,914	WOONSOCKET	17,884	6,258	9,524	2,102	3,266	D	35.0%	53.3%	39.7%	60.3%
947,154	TOTAL	416,072	154,793	198,342	62,937	43,549	D	37.2%	47.7%	43.8%	56.2%

RHODE ISLAND

GOVERNOR 1980

1980 Census Population	County	Total Vote	Republican	Democratic	Other	Rep.-Dem. Plurality	Percentage Total Vote Rep.	Dem.	Major Vote Rep.	Dem.
46,942	BRISTOL	21,141	5,881	15,260		9,379 D	27.8%	72.2%	27.8%	72.2%
154,163	KENT	70,098	16,606	53,492		36,886 D	23.7%	76.3%	23.7%	76.3%
81,383	NEWPORT	32,969	7,633	25,336		17,703 D	23.2%	76.8%	23.2%	76.8%
571,349	PROVIDENCE	242,206	66,571	175,635		109,064 D	27.5%	72.5%	27.5%	72.5%
93,317	WASHINGTON	39,489	10,038	29,451		19,413 D	25.4%	74.6%	25.4%	74.6%
947,154	TOTAL	405,916	106,729	299,174	13	192,445 D	26.3%	73.7%	26.3%	73.7%

RHODE ISLAND

GOVERNOR 1980

1980 Census Population	City/Town	Total Vote	Republican	Democratic	Other	Rep.-Dem. Plurality	Percentage Total Vote Rep.	Dem.	Major Vote Rep.	Dem.
16,174	BARRINGTON	8,725	2,530	6,195		3,665 D	29.0%	71.0%	29.0%	71.0%
20,128	BRISTOL TOWN	7,903	2,138	5,765		3,627 D	27.1%	72.9%	27.1%	72.9%
13,164	BURRILLVILLE	4,670	1,090	3,580		2,490 D	23.3%	76.7%	23.3%	76.7%
16,995	CENTRAL FALLS	5,559	984	4,575		3,591 D	17.7%	82.3%	17.7%	82.3%
4,800	CHARLESTOWN	2,345	737	1,608		871 D	31.4%	68.6%	31.4%	68.6%
27,065	COVENTRY	11,259	2,639	8,620		5,981 D	23.4%	76.6%	23.4%	76.6%
71,992	CRANSTON	37,357	11,913	25,444		13,531 D	31.9%	68.1%	31.9%	68.1%
27,069	CUMBERLAND	13,211	2,877	10,334		7,457 D	21.8%	78.2%	21.8%	78.2%
10,211	EAST GREENWICH	5,374	1,517	3,857		2,340 D	28.2%	71.8%	28.2%	71.8%
50,980	EAST PROVIDENCE	21,709	5,219	16,490		11,271 D	24.0%	76.0%	24.0%	76.0%
4,453	EXETER	1,517	427	1,090		663 D	28.1%	71.9%	28.1%	71.9%
3,370	FOSTER	1,629	522	1,107		585 D	32.0%	68.0%	32.0%	68.0%
7,550	GLOCESTER	3,301	898	2,403		1,505 D	27.2%	72.8%	27.2%	72.8%
6,406	HOPKINTON	2,373	644	1,729		1,085 D	27.1%	72.9%	27.1%	72.9%
4,040	JAMESTOWN	1,707	406	1,301		895 D	23.8%	76.2%	23.8%	76.2%
24,907	JOHNSTON	11,602	4,192	7,410		3,218 D	36.1%	63.9%	36.1%	63.9%
16,949	LINCOLN	9,144	2,429	6,715		4,286 D	26.6%	73.4%	26.6%	73.4%
3,085	LITTLE COMPTON	1,774	512	1,262		750 D	28.9%	71.1%	28.9%	71.1%
17,216	MIDDLETOWN	6,143	1,655	4,488		2,833 D	26.9%	73.1%	26.9%	73.1%
12,088	NARRAGANSETT	5,534	1,192	4,342		3,150 D	21.5%	78.5%	21.5%	78.5%
29,259	NEWPORT CITY	11,143	2,249	8,894		6,645 D	20.2%	79.8%	20.2%	79.8%
620	NEW SHOREHAM	729	184	545		361 D	25.2%	74.8%	25.2%	74.8%
21,938	NORTH KINGSTOWN	9,850	2,363	7,487		5,124 D	24.0%	76.0%	24.0%	76.0%
29,188	NORTH PROVIDENCE	15,099	4,836	10,263		5,427 D	32.0%	68.0%	32.0%	68.0%
9,972	NORTH SMITHFIELD	5,018	1,494	3,524		2,030 D	29.8%	70.2%	29.8%	70.2%
71,204	PAWTUCKET	25,778	5,584	20,194		14,610 D	21.7%	78.3%	21.7%	78.3%
14,257	PORTSMOUTH	6,342	1,512	4,830		3,318 D	23.8%	76.2%	23.8%	76.2%
156,804	PROVIDENCE CITY	59,206	17,605	41,601		23,996 D	29.7%	70.3%	29.7%	70.3%
4,018	RICHMOND	1,631	404	1,227		823 D	24.8%	75.2%	24.8%	75.2%
8,405	SCITUATE	4,309	1,561	2,748		1,187 D	36.2%	63.8%	36.2%	63.8%
16,886	SMITHFIELD	7,303	1,907	5,396		3,489 D	26.1%	73.9%	26.1%	73.9%
20,414	SOUTH KINGSTOWN	7,522	1,842	5,680		3,838 D	24.5%	75.5%	24.5%	75.5%
13,526	TIVERTON	5,860	1,299	4,561		3,262 D	22.2%	77.8%	22.2%	77.8%
10,640	WARREN	4,513	1,213	3,300		2,087 D	26.9%	73.1%	26.9%	73.1%
87,123	WARWICK	40,519	9,197	31,322		22,125 D	22.7%	77.3%	22.7%	77.3%
18,580	WESTERLY	7,988	2,245	5,743		3,498 D	28.1%	71.9%	28.1%	71.9%
2,738	WEST GREENWICH	1,444	415	1,029		614 D	28.7%	71.3%	28.7%	71.3%
27,026	WEST WARWICK	11,502	2,838	8,664		5,826 D	24.7%	75.3%	24.7%	75.3%
45,914	WOONSOCKET	17,311	3,460	13,851		10,391 D	20.0%	80.0%	20.0%	80.0%
947,154	TOTAL	405,916	106,729	299,174	13	192,445 D	26.3%	73.7%	26.3%	73.7%

RHODE ISLAND

CONGRESS

CD	Year	Total Vote	Republican Vote	Republican Candidate	Democratic Vote	Democratic Candidate	Other Vote	Rep.-Dem. Plurality	Total Vote Rep.	Total Vote Dem.	Major Vote Rep.	Major Vote Dem.
1	1980	178,603	57,844	MONTGOMERY, WILLIAM P.	120,756	ST. GERMAIN, FERNAND	3	62,912 D	32.4%	67.6%	32.4%	67.6%
1	1978	141,680	54,912	SLOCUM, JOHN J.	86,768	ST. GERMAIN, FERNAND		31,856 D	38.8%	61.2%	38.8%	61.2%
1	1976	187,002	68,080	SLOCUM, JOHN J.	116,674	ST. GERMAIN, FERNAND	2,248	48,594 D	36.4%	62.4%	36.8%	63.2%
1	1974	144,384	39,096	BARONE, ERNEST	105,288	ST. GERMAIN, FERNAND		66,192 D	27.1%	72.9%	27.1%	72.9%
1	1972	193,592	67,125	FEELEY, JOHN M.	120,705	ST. GERMAIN, FERNAND	5,762	53,580 D	34.7%	62.4%	35.7%	64.3%
2	1980	208,030	115,057	SCHNEIDER, CLAUDINE	92,970	BEARD, EDWARD P.	3	22,087 R	55.3%	44.7%	55.3%	44.7%
2	1978	166,122	78,725	SCHNEIDER, CLAUDINE	87,397	BEARD, EDWARD P.		8,672 D	47.4%	52.6%	47.4%	52.6%
2	1976	201,912	45,438	IANNITTI, THOMAS V.	154,453	BEARD, EDWARD P.	2,021	109,015 D	22.5%	76.5%	22.7%	77.3%
2	1974	159,487	34,728	ROTONDO, VINCENT J.	124,759	BEARD, EDWARD P.		90,031 D	21.8%	78.2%	21.8%	78.2%
2	1972	194,400	71,661	RYAN, DONALD P.	122,739	TIERNAN, ROBERT O.		51,078 D	36.9%	63.1%	36.9%	63.1%

RHODE ISLAND

1980 GENERAL ELECTION

In addition to the county-by-county figures, data are presented by cities and towns.

President   Other vote was 59,819 Anderson (Independent); 2,458 Clark (Libertarian); 218 Hall (Communist); 170 McReynolds (Socialist); 90 DeBerry (Socialist Workers); 77 Griswold (Workers World); 67 Commoner (write-in); 1 McCormack (write-in); 37 scattered. State-wide total for other vote column includes these 105 scattered votes not reported by county or city/town.

Governor   Other vote was scattered, and not reported by county or city/town.

Congress   Other vote in both CD's was scattered.

1980 PRIMARIES

SEPTEMBER 9 REPUBLICAN

Governor   Vincent A. Cianci, unopposed.

Congress   Unopposed in CD 2. Contested as follows:

   CD 1   1,589 William P. Montgomery; 332 Louis D. Gingras-O'Hara.

SEPTEMBER 9 DEMOCRATIC

Governor   J. Joseph Garrahy, unopposed.

Congress   Contested as follows:

   CD 1   23,105 Fernand St. Germain; 6,121 Alfred F. Rocha.
   CD 2   22,383 Edward P. Beard; 15,555 Stephen J. Fortunato; 1,671 Geoffrey A. Schoos.

SOUTH CAROLINA

GOVERNOR
Richard W. Riley (D). Elected 1978 to a four-year term.

SENATORS
Ernest F. Hollings (D). Re-elected 1980 to a six-year term. Previously elected 1974, 1968, and in 1966 to fill out term vacated by the death of Senator Olin D. Johnston.

Strom Thurmond (R). Re-elected 1978 to a six-year term. Previously elected 1972, 1966, 1960 and in 1956 to fill out term vacated by his own resignation in April 1956; had been elected to this term in 1954 as an Independent Democrat. Changed party affiliation from Democrat to Republican in September 1964.

REPRESENTATIVES
1. Thomas F. Hartnett (R)
2. Floyd Spence (R)
3. Butler Derrick (D)
4. Carroll Campbell (R)
5. Kenneth L. Holland (D)
6. John L. Napier (R)

POSTWAR VOTE FOR GOVERNOR

		Republican		Democratic		Other	Rep.-Dem.	Total Vote		Major Vote	
	Total							Percentage			
Year	Vote	Vote	Candidate	Vote	Candidate	Vote	Plurality	Rep.	Dem.	Rep.	Dem.
1978	627,182	236,946	Young, Edward L.	384,898	Riley, Richard W.	5,338	147,952 D	37.8%	61.4%	38.1%	61.9%
1974	523,199	266,109	Edwards, James B.	248,938	Dorn, W. J. Bryan	8,152	17,171 R	50.9%	47.6%	51.7%	48.3%
1970	484,857	221,233	Watson, Albert W.	250,551	West, John C.	13,073	29,318 D	45.6%	51.7%	46.9%	53.1%
1966	439,942	184,088	Rogers, Joseph O.	255,854	McNair, Robert E.	—	71,766 D	41.8%	58.2%	41.8%	58.2%
1962	253,721	—	—	253,704	Russell, Donald S.	17	253,704 D	—	100.0%	—	100.0%
1958	77,740	—	—	77,714	Hollings, Ernest F.	26	77,714 D	—	100.0%	—	100.0%
1954	214,212	—	—	214,204	Timmerman, George B.	8	214,204 D	—	100.0%	—	100.0%
1950	50,642	—	—	50,633	Byrnes, James F.	9	50,633 D	—	100.0%	—	100.0%
1946	26,520	—	—	26,520	Thurmond, Strom	—	26,520 D	—	100.0%	—	100.0%

POSTWAR VOTE FOR SENATOR

		Republican		Democratic		Other	Rep.-Dem.	Total Vote		Major Vote	
	Total							Percentage			
Year	Vote	Vote	Candidate	Vote	Candidate	Vote	Plurality	Rep.	Dem.	Rep.	Dem.
1980	870,594	257,946	Mays, Marshall T.	612,554	Hollings, Ernest F.	94	354,608 D	29.6%	70.4%	29.6%	70.4%
1978	632,852	351,733	Thurmond, Strom	281,119	Ravenel, Charles D.	—	70,614 R	55.6%	44.4%	55.6%	44.4%
1974	512,397	146,645	Bush, Gwenyfred	356,126	Hollings, Ernest F.	9,626	209,481 D	28.6%	69.5%	29.2%	70.8%
1972	672,246	426,601	Thurmond, Strom	245,457	Zeigler, Eugene N.	188	181,144 R	63.5%	36.5%	63.5%	36.5%
1968	652,855	248,780	Parker, Marshall	404,060	Hollings, Ernest F.	15	155,280 D	38.1%	61.9%	38.1%	61.9%
1966	436,252	271,297	Thurmond, Strom	164,955	Morrah, Bradley	—	106,342 R	62.2%	37.8%	62.2%	37.8%
1966s	435,822	212,032	Parker, Marshall	223,790	Hollings, Ernest F.	—	11,758 D	48.7%	51.3%	48.7%	51.3%
1962	312,647	133,930	Workman, W. D.	178,712	Johnston, Olin D.	5	44,782 D	42.8%	57.2%	42.8%	57.2%
1960	330,266	—	—	330,164	Thurmond, Strom	102	330,164 D	—	100.0%	—	100.0%
1956	279,845	49,695	Crawford, Leon P.	230,150	Johnston, Olin D.	—	180,455 D	17.8%	82.2%	17.8%	82.2%
1956s	251,907	—	—	251,907	Thurmond, Strom	—	251,907 D	—	100.0%	—	100.0%
1954	227,232	—	—	83,525	Brown, Edgar A.	143,707	83,525 D	—	36.8%	—	100.0%
1950	50,277	—	—	50,240	Johnston, Olin D.	37	50,240 D	—	99.9%	—	100.0%
1948	141,006	5,008	Gerald, J. Bates	135,998	Maybank, Burnet R.	—	130,990 D	3.6%	96.4%	3.6%	96.4%

One each of the 1966 and 1956 elections was for a short term to fill a vacancy. In 1954, Strom Thurmond polled 143,444 votes as an Independent Democratic write-in candidate (63.1% of the total vote) and won the election with a 59,919 plurality.

SOUTH CAROLINA

Districts Established November 11, 1971

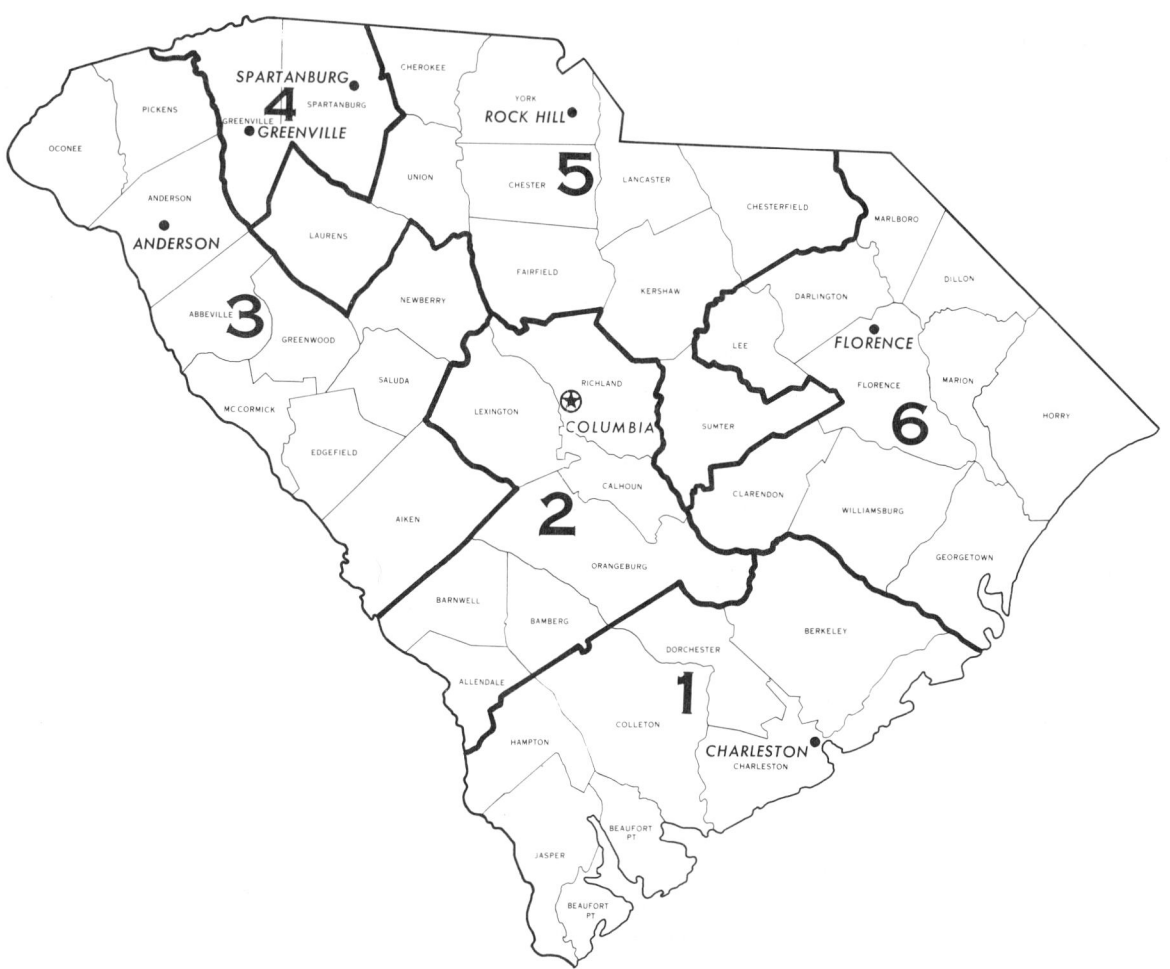

SOUTH CAROLINA

PRESIDENT 1980

1980 Census Population	County	Total Vote	Republican	Democratic	Other	Rep.-Dem. Plurality	Percentage Total Vote Rep.	Dem.	Major Vote Rep.	Dem.
22,627	ABBEVILLE	6,530	2,261	4,049	220	1,788 D	34.6%	62.0%	35.8%	64.2%
105,625	AIKEN	32,369	18,570	13,014	785	5,556 R	57.4%	40.2%	58.8%	41.2%
10,700	ALLENDALE	3,991	1,184	2,775	32	1,591 D	29.7%	69.5%	29.9%	70.1%
133,235	ANDERSON	35,300	15,667	18,801	832	3,134 D	44.4%	53.3%	45.5%	54.5%
18,118	BAMBERG	5,422	2,099	3,294	29	1,195 D	38.7%	60.8%	38.9%	61.1%
19,868	BARNWELL	6,705	3,228	3,399	78	171 D	48.1%	50.7%	48.7%	51.3%
65,364	BEAUFORT	16,684	8,620	7,415	649	1,205 R	51.7%	44.4%	53.8%	46.2%
94,727	BERKELEY	23,024	12,790	9,850	384	2,940 R	55.6%	42.8%	56.5%	43.5%
12,206	CALHOUN	3,850	1,767	2,044	39	277 D	45.9%	53.1%	46.4%	53.6%
277,308	CHARLESTON	81,260	44,833	33,057	3,370	11,776 R	55.2%	40.7%	57.6%	42.4%
40,983	CHEROKEE	12,437	5,392	6,894	151	1,502 D	43.4%	55.4%	43.9%	56.1%
30,148	CHESTER	8,363	3,104	5,145	114	2,041 D	37.1%	61.5%	37.6%	62.4%
38,161	CHESTERFIELD	9,973	3,479	6,393	101	2,914 D	34.9%	64.1%	35.2%	64.8%
27,464	CLARENDON	10,203	4,162	5,983	58	1,821 D	40.8%	58.6%	41.0%	59.0%
31,676	COLLETON	10,543	4,719	5,745	79	1,026 D	44.8%	54.5%	45.1%	54.9%
62,717	DARLINGTON	17,650	8,290	9,011	349	721 D	47.0%	51.1%	47.9%	52.1%
31,083	DILLON	7,998	3,385	4,520	93	1,135 D	42.3%	56.5%	42.8%	57.2%
58,266	DORCHESTER	18,298	10,893	7,237	168	3,656 R	59.5%	39.6%	60.1%	39.9%
17,528	EDGEFIELD	5,945	2,422	3,464	59	1,042 D	40.7%	58.3%	41.1%	58.9%
20,700	FAIRFIELD	6,323	2,098	4,153	72	2,055 D	33.2%	65.7%	33.6%	66.4%
110,163	FLORENCE	33,992	17,069	16,391	532	678 R	50.2%	48.2%	51.0%	49.0%
42,461	GEORGETOWN	12,041	5,151	6,701	189	1,550 D	42.8%	55.7%	43.5%	56.5%
287,913	GREENVILLE	80,415	46,168	32,135	2,112	14,033 R	57.4%	40.0%	59.0%	41.0%
57,847	GREENWOOD	16,886	7,291	9,285	310	1,994 D	43.2%	55.0%	44.0%	56.0%
18,159	HAMPTON	6,612	2,220	4,332	60	2,112 D	33.6%	65.5%	33.9%	66.1%
101,419	HORRY	28,871	14,331	13,897	643	434 R	49.6%	48.1%	50.8%	49.2%
14,504	JASPER	4,977	1,618	3,316	43	1,698 D	32.5%	66.6%	32.8%	67.2%
39,015	KERSHAW	11,970	6,652	5,103	215	1,549 R	55.6%	42.6%	56.6%	43.4%
53,361	LANCASTER	15,166	6,410	8,283	473	1,873 D	42.3%	54.6%	43.6%	56.4%
52,214	LAURENS	14,100	6,041	7,862	197	1,821 D	42.8%	55.8%	43.5%	56.5%
18,929	LEE	7,795	2,952	4,816	27	1,864 D	37.9%	61.8%	38.0%	62.0%
140,353	LEXINGTON	41,711	28,313	12,334	1,064	15,979 R	67.9%	29.6%	69.7%	30.3%
7,797	MCCORMICK	2,610	800	1,775	35	975 D	30.7%	68.0%	31.1%	68.9%
34,179	MARION	8,816	3,323	5,389	104	2,066 D	37.7%	61.1%	38.1%	61.9%
31,634	MARLBORO	8,040	2,585	5,378	77	2,793 D	32.2%	66.9%	32.5%	67.5%
31,111	NEWBERRY	10,508	5,568	4,825	115	743 R	53.0%	45.9%	53.6%	46.4%
48,611	OCONEE	13,588	5,652	7,678	258	2,026 D	41.6%	56.5%	42.4%	57.6%
82,276	ORANGEBURG	27,733	11,313	16,178	242	4,865 D	40.8%	58.3%	41.2%	58.8%
79,292	PICKENS	17,919	9,575	7,789	555	1,786 R	53.4%	43.5%	55.1%	44.9%
267,823	RICHLAND	73,911	36,450	33,916	3,545	2,534 R	49.3%	45.9%	51.8%	48.2%
16,150	SALUDA	5,173	2,450	2,653	70	203 D	47.4%	51.3%	48.0%	52.0%
201,553	SPARTANBURG	60,027	29,979	28,414	1,634	1,565 R	49.9%	47.3%	51.3%	48.7%
88,243	SUMTER	20,126	10,557	9,205	364	1,352 R	52.5%	45.7%	53.4%	46.6%
30,751	UNION	10,450	4,035	6,274	141	2,239 D	38.6%	60.0%	39.1%	60.9%
38,226	WILLIAMSBURG	13,347	5,110	8,138	99	3,028 D	38.3%	61.0%	38.6%	61.4%
106,720	YORK	24,043	11,265	12,075	703	810 D	46.9%	50.2%	48.3%	51.7%
3,119,208	TOTAL	894,071	441,841	430,385	21,845	11,456 R	49.4%	48.1%	50.7%	49.3%

SOUTH CAROLINA

SENATOR 1980

1980 Census Population	County	Total Vote	Republican	Democratic	Other	Rep.-Dem. Plurality	Percentage Total Vote Rep.	Total Vote Dem.	Major Vote Rep.	Major Vote Dem.
22,627	ABBEVILLE	6,226	1,206	5,020		3,814 D	19.4%	80.6%	19.4%	80.6%
105,625	AIKEN	34,180	12,322	21,858		9,536 D	36.1%	63.9%	36.1%	63.9%
10,700	ALLENDALE	3,779	594	3,185		2,591 D	15.7%	84.3%	15.7%	84.3%
133,235	ANDERSON	33,712	10,244	23,468		13,224 D	30.4%	69.6%	30.4%	69.6%
18,118	BAMBERG	5,186	946	4,240		3,294 D	18.2%	81.8%	18.2%	81.8%
19,868	BARNWELL	6,456	1,567	4,889		3,322 D	24.3%	75.7%	24.3%	75.7%
65,364	BEAUFORT	16,346	6,322	10,024		3,702 D	38.7%	61.3%	38.7%	61.3%
94,727	BERKELEY	22,599	7,633	14,966		7,333 D	33.8%	66.2%	33.8%	66.2%
12,206	CALHOUN	3,730	1,047	2,683		1,636 D	28.1%	71.9%	28.1%	71.9%
277,308	CHARLESTON	78,631	33,091	45,540		12,449 D	42.1%	57.9%	42.1%	57.9%
40,983	CHEROKEE	12,048	2,140	9,908		7,768 D	17.8%	82.2%	17.8%	82.2%
30,148	CHESTER	8,186	1,276	6,910		5,634 D	15.6%	84.4%	15.6%	84.4%
38,161	CHESTERFIELD	9,747	1,451	8,296		6,845 D	14.9%	85.1%	14.9%	85.1%
27,464	CLARENDON	9,974	2,088	7,886		5,798 D	20.9%	79.1%	20.9%	79.1%
31,676	COLLETON	10,242	2,618	7,624		5,006 D	25.6%	74.4%	25.6%	74.4%
62,717	DARLINGTON	16,314	3,974	12,340		8,366 D	24.4%	75.6%	24.4%	75.6%
31,083	DILLON	7,323	1,288	6,035		4,747 D	17.6%	82.4%	17.6%	82.4%
58,266	DORCHESTER	17,996	6,063	11,933		5,870 D	33.7%	66.3%	33.7%	66.3%
17,528	EDGEFIELD	5,529	1,294	4,235		2,941 D	23.4%	76.6%	23.4%	76.6%
20,700	FAIRFIELD	6,131	903	5,228		4,325 D	14.7%	85.3%	14.7%	85.3%
110,163	FLORENCE	31,646	7,656	23,990		16,334 D	24.2%	75.8%	24.2%	75.8%
42,461	GEORGETOWN	12,448	2,220	10,228		8,008 D	17.8%	82.2%	17.8%	82.2%
287,913	GREENVILLE	80,397	27,783	52,614		24,831 D	34.6%	65.4%	34.6%	65.4%
57,847	GREENWOOD	16,547	4,338	12,209		7,871 D	26.2%	73.8%	26.2%	73.8%
18,159	HAMPTON	6,308	1,072	5,236		4,164 D	17.0%	83.0%	17.0%	83.0%
101,419	HORRY	27,877	7,747	20,130		12,383 D	27.8%	72.2%	27.8%	72.2%
14,504	JASPER	4,710	930	3,780		2,850 D	19.7%	80.3%	19.7%	80.3%
39,015	KERSHAW	12,419	3,656	8,763		5,107 D	29.4%	70.6%	29.4%	70.6%
53,361	LANCASTER	14,666	2,206	12,460		10,254 D	15.0%	85.0%	15.0%	85.0%
52,214	LAURENS	13,639	2,979	10,660		7,681 D	21.8%	78.2%	21.8%	78.2%
18,929	LEE	7,335	1,597	5,738		4,141 D	21.8%	78.2%	21.8%	78.2%
140,353	LEXINGTON	41,194	16,879	24,315		7,436 D	41.0%	59.0%	41.0%	59.0%
7,797	MCCORMICK	2,504	393	2,111		1,718 D	15.7%	84.3%	15.7%	84.3%
34,179	MARION	8,103	1,289	6,814		5,525 D	15.9%	84.1%	15.9%	84.1%
31,634	MARLBORO	7,475	981	6,494		5,513 D	13.1%	86.9%	13.1%	86.9%
31,111	NEWBERRY	10,329	3,186	7,143		3,957 D	30.8%	69.2%	30.8%	69.2%
48,611	OCONEE	13,113	3,537	9,576		6,039 D	27.0%	73.0%	27.0%	73.0%
82,276	ORANGEBURG	26,905	5,965	20,940		14,975 D	22.2%	77.8%	22.2%	77.8%
79,292	PICKENS	18,428	6,717	11,711		4,994 D	36.4%	63.6%	36.4%	63.6%
267,823	RICHLAND	74,797	22,845	51,952		29,107 D	30.5%	69.5%	30.5%	69.5%
16,150	SALUDA	4,987	1,382	3,605		2,223 D	27.7%	72.3%	27.7%	72.3%
201,553	SPARTANBURG	56,296	19,293	37,003		17,710 D	34.3%	65.7%	34.3%	65.7%
88,243	SUMTER	16,070	4,451	11,619		7,168 D	27.7%	72.3%	27.7%	72.3%
30,751	UNION	10,241	1,506	8,735		7,229 D	14.7%	85.3%	14.7%	85.3%
38,226	WILLIAMSBURG	12,511	2,415	10,096		7,681 D	19.3%	80.7%	19.3%	80.7%
106,720	YORK	25,220	6,856	18,364		11,508 D	27.2%	72.8%	27.2%	72.8%
3,119,208	TOTAL	870,594	257,946	612,554	94	354,608 D	29.6%	70.4%	29.6%	70.4%

SOUTH CAROLINA

CONGRESS

CD	Year	Total Vote	Republican Vote	Republican Candidate	Democratic Vote	Democratic Candidate	Other Vote	Rep.-Dem. Plurality	Total Vote Rep.	Total Vote Dem.	Major Vote Rep.	Major Vote Dem.
1	1980	158,741	81,988	HARTNETT, THOMAS F.	76,743	RAVENEL, CHARLES D.	10	5,245 R	51.6%	48.3%	51.7%	48.3%
1	1978	108,646	42,811	WANNAMAKER, C. C.	65,835	DAVIS, MENDEL J.		23,024 D	39.4%	60.6%	39.4%	60.6%
1	1976	130,503	40,598	ROWELL, LONNIE	89,891	DAVIS, MENDEL J.	14	49,293 D	31.1%	68.9%	31.1%	68.9%
1	1974	86,777	22,450	RAST, GEORGE B.	63,111	DAVIS, MENDEL J.	1,216	40,661 D	25.9%	72.7%	26.2%	73.8%
1	1972	113,094	51,469	LIMEHOUSE, J. SIDI	61,625	DAVIS, MENDEL J.		10,156 D	45.5%	54.5%	45.5%	54.5%
2	1980	165,678	92,306	SPENCE, FLOYD	73,353	TURNIPSEED, TOM	19	18,953 R	55.7%	44.3%	55.7%	44.3%
2	1978	124,229	71,208	SPENCE, FLOYD	53,021	BASS, JACK		18,187 R	57.3%	42.7%	57.3%	42.7%
2	1976	144,995	83,426	SPENCE, FLOYD	60,602	LIVINGSTON, CLYDE B.	967	22,824 R	57.5%	41.8%	57.9%	42.1%
2	1974	105,091	58,936	SPENCE, FLOYD	45,205	PERRY, MATTHEW J.	950	13,731 R	56.1%	43.0%	56.6%	43.4%
2	1972	83,590	83,543	SPENCE, FLOYD			47	83,543 R	99.9%		100.0%	
3	1980	146,642	57,840	PARKER, MARSHALL	87,680	DERRICK, BUTLER	1,122	29,840 D	39.4%	59.8%	39.7%	60.3%
3	1978	99,611	17,973	PANUCCIO, ANTHONY J.	81,638	DERRICK, BUTLER		63,665 D	18.0%	82.0%	18.0%	82.0%
3	1976	117,855			117,740	DERRICK, BUTLER	115	117,740 D		99.9%		100.0%
3	1974	89,166	34,046	PARKER, MARSHALL	55,120	DERRICK, BUTLER		21,074 D	38.2%	61.8%	38.2%	61.8%
3	1972	109,757	27,173	ETHRIDGE, ROY	82,579	DORN, W. J. BRYAN	5	55,406 D	24.8%	75.2%	24.8%	75.2%
3	1970	80,689	19,981	BALLARD, H. GRADY	60,708	DORN, W. J. BRYAN		40,727 D	24.8%	75.2%	24.8%	75.2%
3	1968	112,057	35,463	GRISSO, JOHN	74,104	DORN, W. J. BRYAN	2,490	38,641 D	31.6%	66.1%	32.4%	67.6%
3	1966	74,205	31,331	GRISSO, JOHN	42,874	DORN, W. J. BRYAN		11,543 D	42.2%	57.8%	42.2%	57.8%
4	1980	98,173	90,941	CAMPBELL, CARROLL			7,232	90,941 R	92.6%		100.0%	
4	1978	98,554	51,377	CAMPBELL, CARROLL	45,484	HELLER, MAX M.	1,693	5,893 R	52.1%	46.2%	53.0%	47.0%
4	1976	124,765	32,983	WATKINS, ROBERT L.	91,721	MANN, JAMES R.	61	58,738 D	26.4%	73.5%	26.4%	73.6%
4	1974	71,255	26,185	WATKINS, ROBERT L.	45,070	MANN, JAMES R.		18,885 D	36.7%	63.3%	36.7%	63.3%
4	1972	98,389	33,363	WHATLEY, WAYNE N.	64,989	MANN, JAMES R.	37	31,626 D	33.9%	66.1%	33.9%	66.1%
5	1980	114,038			99,773	HOLLAND, KENNETH L.	14,265	99,773 D		87.5%		100.0%
5	1978	76,789			63,538	HOLLAND, KENNETH L.	13,251	63,538 D		82.7%		100.0%
5	1976	128,510	62,095	RICHARDSON, BOBBY	66,073	HOLLAND, KENNETH L.	342	3,978 D	48.3%	51.4%	48.4%	51.6%
5	1974	77,545	29,294	PHILLIPS, B. LEONARD	47,614	HOLLAND, KENNETH L.	637	18,320 D	37.8%	61.4%	38.1%	61.9%
5	1972	108,968	42,620	PHILLIPS, B. LEONARD	66,343	GETTYS, TOM S.	5	23,723 D	39.1%	60.9%	39.1%	60.9%
6	1980	146,797	75,964	NAPIER, JOHN L.	70,747	JENRETTE, JOHN W.	86	5,217 R	51.7%	48.2%	51.8%	48.2%
6	1978	69,372			69,372	JENRETTE, JOHN W.		69,372 D		100.0%		100.0%
6	1976	136,896	60,288	YOUNG, EDWARD L.	75,916	JENRETTE, JOHN W.	692	15,628 D	44.0%	55.5%	44.3%	55.7%
6	1974	87,378	41,982	YOUNG, EDWARD L.	45,396	JENRETTE, JOHN W.		3,414 D	48.0%	52.0%	48.0%	52.0%
6	1972	116,859	63,527	YOUNG, EDWARD L.	53,324	JENRETTE, JOHN W.	8	10,203 R	54.4%	45.6%	54.4%	45.6%

SOUTH CAROLINA

1980 GENERAL ELECTION

President Other vote was 14,153 Anderson (Independent); 5,139 Clark (Libertarian); 2,177 Rarick (Independent); 376 scattered. State-wide total for other vote column includes these 376 scattered votes not reported by county.

Senator Other vote was scattered. State-wide total for the other vote column represents scattered votes not reported by county.

Congress Other vote was scattered in CD's 1, 2 and 6; 1,118 Muller (Libertarian) and 4 scattered in CD 3; 6,984 Waldenfels (Libertarian) and 248 scattered in CD 4; 14,252 Campbell (Libertarian) and 13 scattered in CD 5.

1980 PRIMARIES

JUNE 10 REPUBLICAN

Senator 14,075 Marshall T. Mays; 11,395 Charles F. Rhodes; 7,575 Robert K. Carley.

Congress Unopposed in three CD's. No candidate in CD 5. Contested as follows:

CD 1 10,510 Thomas F. Hartnett; 3,428 Thomas G. Moore.
CD 6 3,735 John L. Napier; 2,491 Edward L. Young.

JUNE 10 DEMOCRATIC

Senator 266,796 Ernest F. Hollings; 34,720 Nettie DuR. Dickerson; 27,049 William P. Kreml.

Congress Unopposed in three CD's. John B. Culbertson, the unopposed candidate in CD 4, withdrew after the primary and no substitution was made. Contested as follows:

CD 1 30,966 Charles D. Ravenel; 17,070 Wheeler M. Tillman; 3,838 Charley B. Brasser; 3,786 Benjamin Frasier.
CD 2 28,490 Tom Turnipseed; 11,303 Leigh J. Leventis.
CD 6 38,565 John W. Jenrette; 22,251 Hicks Harwell; 11,346 John W. Brassington; 8,061 Erick B. Ficken; 4,887 William T. McElveen.

JUNE 24 REPUBLICAN RUN-OFF

Senator 6,853 Marshall T. Mays; 3,717 Charles F. Rhodes.

JUNE 24 DEMOCRATIC RUN-OFF

Congress

CD 6 42,759 John W. Jenrette; 38,621 Hicks Harwell.

SOUTH DAKOTA

GOVERNOR
William J. Janklow (R). Elected 1978 to a four-year term.

SENATORS
James Abdnor (R). Elected 1980 to a six-year term.

Larry Pressler (R). Elected 1978 to a six-year term.

REPRESENTATIVES
1. Thomas A. Daschle (D)   2. Clint Roberts (R)

POSTWAR VOTE FOR GOVERNOR

| | | | | | | | | | Percentage | | | |
| | Total | Republican | | Democratic | | Other | Rep.-Dem. | Total Vote | | Major Vote | |
Year	Vote	Vote	Candidate	Vote	Candidate	Vote	Plurality	Rep.	Dem.	Rep.	Dem.
1978	259,795	147,116	Janklow, William J.	112,679	McKellips, Roger	—	34,437 R	56.6%	43.4%	56.6%	43.4%
1974	278,228	129,077	Olson, John E.	149,151	Kneip, Richard F.	—	20,074 D	46.4%	53.6%	46.4%	53.6%
1972	308,177	123,165	Thompson, Carveth	185,012	Kneip, Richard F.	—	61,847 D	40.0%	60.0%	40.0%	60.0%
1970	239,963	108,347	Farrar, Frank	131,616	Kneip, Richard F.	—	23,269 D	45.2%	54.8%	45.2%	54.8%
1968	276,906	159,646	Farrar, Frank	117,260	Chamberlin, Robert	—	42,386 R	57.7%	42.3%	57.7%	42.3%
1966	228,214	131,710	Boe, Nils A.	96,504	Chamberlin, Robert	—	35,206 R	57.7%	42.3%	57.7%	42.3%
1964	290,570	150,151	Boe, Nils A.	140,419	Lindley, John F.	—	9,732 R	51.7%	48.3%	51.7%	48.3%
1962	256,120	143,682	Gubbrud, Archie M.	112,438	Herseth, Ralph	—	31,244 R	56.1%	43.9%	56.1%	43.9%
1960	304,625	154,530	Gubbrud, Archie M.	150,095	Herseth, Ralph	—	4,435 R	50.7%	49.3%	50.7%	49.3%
1958	258,281	125,520	Saunders, Phil	132,761	Herseth, Ralph	—	7,241 D	48.6%	51.4%	48.6%	51.4%
1956	292,017	158,819	Foss, Joe J.	133,198	Herseth, Ralph	—	25,621 R	54.4%	45.6%	54.4%	45.6%
1954	236,255	133,878	Foss, Joe J.	102,377	Martin, Ed. C.	—	31,501 R	56.7%	43.3%	56.7%	43.3%
1952	289,515	203,102	Anderson, Sigurd	86,413	Iverson, Sherman A.	—	116,689 R	70.2%	29.8%	70.2%	29.8%
1950	253,316	154,254	Anderson, Sigurd	99,062	Robbie, Joseph	—	55,192 R	60.9%	39.1%	60.9%	39.1%
1948	245,372	149,883	Mickelson, George	95,489	Volz, Harold J.	—	54,394 R	61.1%	38.9%	61.1%	38.9%
1946	162,292	108,998	Mickelson, George	53,294	Haeder, Richard	—	55,704 R	67.2%	32.8%	67.2%	32.8%

The term of office of South Dakota's Governor was increased from two to four years effective with the 1974 election.

POSTWAR VOTE FOR SENATOR

| | | | | | | | | | Percentage | | | |
| | Total | Republican | | Democratic | | Other | Rep.-Dem. | Total Vote | | Major Vote | |
Year	Vote	Vote	Candidate	Vote	Candidate	Vote	Plurality	Rep.	Dem.	Rep.	Dem.
1980	327,478	190,594	Abdnor, James	129,018	McGovern, George S.	7,866	61,576 R	58.2%	39.4%	59.6%	40.4%
1978	255,599	170,832	Pressler, Larry	84,767	Barnett, Don	—	86,065 R	66.8%	33.2%	66.8%	33.2%
1974	278,884	130,955	Thorsness, Leo K.	147,929	McGovern, George S.	—	16,974 D	47.0%	53.0%	47.0%	53.0%
1972	306,386	131,613	Hirsch, Robert W.	174,773	Abourezk, James	—	43,160 D	43.0%	57.0%	43.0%	57.0%
1968	279,912	120,951	Gubbrud, Archie M.	158,961	McGovern, George S.	—	38,010 D	43.2%	56.8%	43.2%	56.8%
1966	227,080	150,517	Mundt, Karl E.	76,563	Wright, Donn H.	—	73,954 R	66.3%	33.7%	66.3%	33.7%
1962	254,319	126,861	Bottum, Joe H.	127,458	McGovern, George S.	—	597 D	49.9%	50.1%	49.9%	50.1%
1960	305,442	160,181	Mundt, Karl E.	145,261	McGovern, George S.	—	14,920 R	52.4%	47.6%	52.4%	47.6%
1956	290,622	147,621	Case, Francis	143,001	Holum, Kenneth	—	4,620 R	50.8%	49.2%	50.8%	49.2%
1954	235,745	135,071	Mundt, Karl E.	100,674	Holum, Kenneth	—	34,397 R	57.3%	42.7%	57.3%	42.7%
1950	251,362	160,670	Case, Francis	90,692	Engel, John A.	—	69,978 R	63.9%	36.1%	63.9%	36.1%
1948	242,833	144,084	Mundt, Karl E.	98,749	Engel, John A.	—	45,335 R	59.3%	40.7%	59.3%	40.7%

SOUTH DAKOTA

Districts Established March 25, 1971

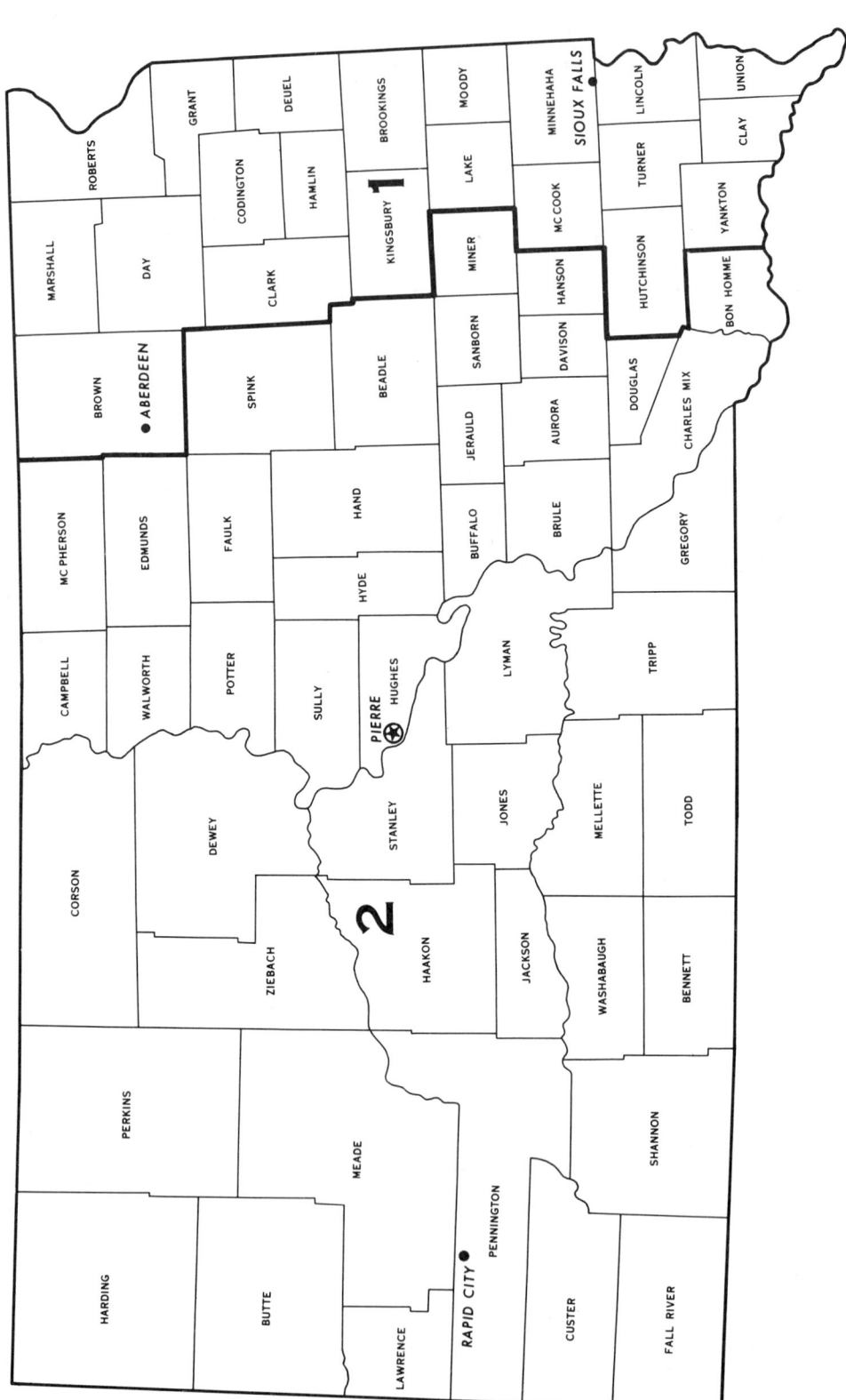

SOUTH DAKOTA

PRESIDENT 1980

1980 Census Population	County	Total Vote	Republican	Democratic	Other	Rep.-Dem. Plurality	Percentage Total Vote Rep.	Dem.	Major Vote Rep.	Dem.
3,628	AURORA	2,123	1,251	709	163	542 R	58.9%	33.4%	63.8%	36.2%
19,195	BEADLE	10,104	5,921	3,521	662	2,400 R	58.6%	34.8%	62.7%	37.3%
3,236	BENNETT	1,324	919	350	55	569 R	69.4%	26.4%	72.4%	27.6%
8,059	BON HOMME	4,239	2,794	1,191	254	1,603 R	65.9%	28.1%	70.1%	29.9%
24,332	BROOKINGS	10,981	5,727	3,934	1,320	1,793 R	52.2%	35.8%	59.3%	40.7%
36,962	BROWN	17,999	10,550	6,050	1,399	4,500 R	58.6%	33.6%	63.6%	36.4%
5,245	BRULE	2,800	1,674	925	201	749 R	59.8%	33.0%	64.4%	35.6%
1,795	BUFFALO	456	272	147	37	125 R	59.6%	32.2%	64.9%	35.1%
8,372	BUTTE	3,898	2,850	843	205	2,007 R	73.1%	21.6%	77.2%	22.8%
2,243	CAMPBELL	1,498	1,271	182	45	1,089 R	84.8%	12.1%	87.5%	12.5%
9,680	CHARLES MIX	4,599	2,608	1,741	250	867 R	56.7%	37.9%	60.0%	40.0%
4,894	CLARK	2,911	1,963	774	174	1,189 R	67.4%	26.6%	71.7%	28.3%
13,135	CLAY	6,316	3,004	2,271	1,041	733 R	47.6%	36.0%	56.9%	43.1%
20,885	CODINGTON	9,990	5,903	3,353	734	2,550 R	59.1%	33.6%	63.8%	36.2%
5,196	CORSON	1,855	1,233	522	100	711 R	66.5%	28.1%	70.3%	29.7%
6,000	CUSTER	2,955	2,057	708	190	1,349 R	69.6%	24.0%	74.4%	25.6%
17,820	DAVISON	8,512	4,743	3,107	662	1,636 R	55.7%	36.5%	60.4%	39.6%
8,133	DAY	4,543	2,507	1,720	316	787 R	55.2%	37.9%	59.3%	40.7%
5,289	DEUEL	2,744	1,657	891	196	766 R	60.4%	32.5%	65.0%	35.0%
5,366	DEWEY	1,767	1,045	600	122	445 R	59.1%	34.0%	63.5%	36.5%
4,181	DOUGLAS	2,463	1,855	508	100	1,347 R	75.3%	20.6%	78.5%	21.5%
5,159	EDMUNDS	2,914	1,881	883	150	998 R	64.6%	30.3%	68.1%	31.9%
8,439	FALL RIVER	4,067	2,831	982	254	1,849 R	69.6%	24.1%	74.2%	25.8%
3,327	FAULK	1,945	1,300	520	125	780 R	66.8%	26.7%	71.4%	28.6%
9,013	GRANT	4,594	2,691	1,602	301	1,089 R	58.6%	34.9%	62.7%	37.3%
6,015	GREGORY	3,340	2,283	883	174	1,400 R	68.4%	26.4%	72.1%	27.9%
2,794	HAAKON	1,465	1,162	255	48	907 R	79.3%	17.4%	82.0%	18.0%
5,261	HAMLIN	3,007	1,885	903	219	982 R	62.7%	30.0%	67.6%	32.4%
4,948	HAND	3,066	2,066	803	197	1,263 R	67.4%	26.2%	72.0%	28.0%
3,415	HANSON	1,725	1,015	598	112	417 R	58.8%	34.7%	62.9%	37.1%
1,700	HARDING	974	727	205	42	522 R	74.6%	21.0%	78.0%	22.0%
14,220	HUGHES	7,048	4,652	1,751	645	2,901 R	66.0%	24.8%	72.7%	27.3%
9,350	HUTCHINSON	5,180	3,789	1,145	246	2,644 R	73.1%	22.1%	76.8%	23.2%
2,069	HYDE	1,221	864	273	84	591 R	70.8%	22.4%	76.0%	24.0%
3,437	JACKSON	1,352	929	354	69	575 R	68.7%	26.2%	72.4%	27.6%
2,929	JERAULD	1,729	1,018	595	116	423 R	58.9%	34.4%	63.1%	36.9%
1,463	JONES	919	689	189	41	500 R	75.0%	20.6%	78.5%	21.5%
6,679	KINGSBURY	3,807	2,376	1,132	299	1,244 R	62.4%	29.7%	67.7%	32.3%
10,724	LAKE	5,852	3,093	2,207	552	886 R	52.9%	37.7%	58.4%	41.6%
18,339	LAWRENCE	8,403	5,306	2,259	838	3,047 R	63.1%	26.9%	70.1%	29.9%
13,942	LINCOLN	6,698	3,848	2,261	589	1,587 R	57.4%	33.8%	63.0%	37.0%
3,864	LYMAN	1,878	1,256	486	136	770 R	66.9%	25.9%	72.1%	27.9%
6,444	MCCOOK	3,544	2,014	1,223	307	791 R	56.8%	34.5%	62.2%	37.8%
4,027	MCPHERSON	2,402	2,056	287	59	1,769 R	85.6%	11.9%	87.8%	12.2%
5,404	MARSHALL	3,001	1,710	1,120	171	590 R	57.0%	37.3%	60.4%	39.6%
20,717	MEADE	7,541	5,349	1,721	471	3,628 R	70.9%	22.8%	75.7%	24.3%
2,249	MELLETTE	963	624	279	60	345 R	64.8%	29.0%	69.1%	30.9%
3,739	MINER	2,171	1,172	833	166	339 R	54.0%	38.4%	58.5%	41.5%
109,435	MINNEHAHA	51,478	26,256	20,008	5,214	6,248 R	51.0%	38.9%	56.8%	43.2%
6,692	MOODY	3,480	1,807	1,364	309	443 R	51.9%	39.2%	57.0%	43.0%
70,133	PENNINGTON	28,204	18,991	7,121	2,092	11,870 R	67.3%	25.2%	72.7%	27.3%
4,700	PERKINS	2,655	1,931	595	129	1,336 R	72.7%	22.4%	76.4%	23.6%
3,674	POTTER	2,169	1,633	436	100	1,197 R	75.3%	20.1%	78.9%	21.1%
10,911	ROBERTS	5,009	2,904	1,829	276	1,075 R	58.0%	36.5%	61.4%	38.6%
3,213	SANBORN	1,932	1,178	628	126	550 R	61.0%	32.5%	65.2%	34.8%
11,323	SHANNON	1,687	438	1,132	117	694 D	26.0%	67.1%	27.9%	72.1%
9,201	SPINK	4,834	2,915	1,572	347	1,343 R	60.3%	32.5%	65.0%	35.0%
2,533	STANLEY	1,299	892	339	68	553 R	68.7%	26.1%	72.5%	27.5%
1,990	SULLY	1,149	852	220	77	632 R	74.2%	19.1%	79.5%	20.5%
7,328	TODD	1,923	803	972	148	169 D	41.8%	50.5%	45.2%	54.8%
7,268	TRIPP	3,776	2,669	947	160	1,722 R	70.7%	25.1%	73.8%	26.2%
9,255	TURNER	5,032	3,343	1,369	320	1,974 R	66.4%	27.2%	70.9%	29.1%
10,938	UNION	5,054	2,788	1,830	436	958 R	55.2%	36.2%	60.4%	39.6%
7,011	WALWORTH	3,588	2,675	753	160	1,922 R	74.6%	21.0%	78.0%	22.0%
18,952	YANKTON	8,747	5,355	2,698	694	2,657 R	61.2%	30.8%	66.5%	33.5%
2,308	ZIEBACH	804	523	246	35	277 R	65.0%	30.6%	68.0%	32.0%
690,178	TOTAL	327,703	198,343	103,855	25,505	94,488 R	60.5%	31.7%	65.6%	34.4%

SOUTH DAKOTA

SENATOR 1980

1980 Census Population	County	Total Vote	Republican	Democratic	Other	Rep.-Dem. Plurality	Percentage			
							Total Vote		Major Vote	
							Rep.	Dem.	Rep.	Dem.
3,628	AURORA	2,138	1,164	895	79	269 R	54.4%	41.9%	56.5%	43.5%
19,195	BEADLE	10,202	5,829	4,103	270	1,726 R	57.1%	40.2%	58.7%	41.3%
3,236	BENNETT	1,334	925	385	24	540 R	69.3%	28.9%	70.6%	29.4%
8,059	BON HOMME	4,144	2,483	1,603	58	880 R	59.9%	38.7%	60.8%	39.2%
24,332	BROOKINGS	11,022	5,745	5,043	234	702 R	52.1%	45.8%	53.3%	46.7%
36,962	BROWN	18,074	9,850	7,855	369	1,995 R	54.5%	43.5%	55.6%	44.4%
5,245	BRULE	2,801	1,694	999	108	695 R	60.5%	35.7%	62.9%	37.1%
1,795	BUFFALO	454	219	197	38	22 R	48.2%	43.4%	52.6%	47.4%
8,372	BUTTE	3,913	2,996	827	90	2,169 R	76.6%	21.1%	78.4%	21.6%
2,243	CAMPBELL	1,470	1,151	293	26	858 R	78.3%	19.9%	79.7%	20.3%
9,680	CHARLES MIX	4,638	2,645	1,914	79	731 R	57.0%	41.3%	58.0%	42.0%
4,894	CLARK	2,850	1,742	1,042	66	700 R	61.1%	36.6%	62.6%	37.4%
13,135	CLAY	6,345	2,882	3,363	100	481 D	45.4%	53.0%	46.1%	53.9%
20,885	CODINGTON	10,186	5,775	4,197	214	1,578 R	56.7%	41.2%	57.9%	42.1%
5,196	CORSON	1,843	1,172	575	96	597 R	63.6%	31.2%	67.1%	32.9%
6,000	CUSTER	2,958	2,073	814	71	1,259 R	70.1%	27.5%	71.8%	28.2%
17,820	DAVISON	8,541	4,280	4,096	165	184 R	50.1%	48.0%	51.1%	48.9%
8,133	DAY	4,517	2,308	2,139	70	169 R	51.1%	47.4%	51.9%	48.1%
5,289	DEUEL	2,715	1,481	1,163	71	318 R	54.5%	42.8%	56.0%	44.0%
5,366	DEWEY	1,766	940	724	102	216 R	53.2%	41.0%	56.5%	43.5%
4,181	DOUGLAS	2,453	1,780	616	57	1,164 R	72.6%	25.1%	74.3%	25.7%
5,159	EDMUNDS	2,885	1,653	1,142	90	511 R	57.3%	39.6%	59.1%	40.9%
8,439	FALL RIVER	4,090	2,807	1,174	109	1,633 R	68.6%	28.7%	70.5%	29.5%
3,327	FAULK	1,948	1,167	707	74	460 R	59.9%	36.3%	62.3%	37.7%
9,013	GRANT	4,606	2,630	1,895	81	735 R	57.1%	41.1%	58.1%	41.9%
6,015	GREGORY	3,360	2,106	1,108	146	998 R	62.7%	33.0%	65.5%	34.5%
2,794	HAAKON	1,468	1,199	221	48	978 R	81.7%	15.1%	84.4%	15.6%
5,261	HAMLIN	2,972	1,731	1,167	74	564 R	58.2%	39.3%	59.7%	40.3%
4,948	HAND	3,073	1,873	929	271	944 R	61.0%	30.2%	66.8%	33.2%
3,415	HANSON	1,733	914	748	71	166 R	52.7%	43.2%	55.0%	45.0%
1,700	HARDING	982	738	220	24	518 R	75.2%	22.4%	77.0%	23.0%
14,220	HUGHES	6,981	4,579	2,190	212	2,389 R	65.6%	31.4%	67.6%	32.4%
9,350	HUTCHINSON	5,098	3,432	1,574	92	1,858 R	67.3%	30.9%	68.6%	31.4%
2,069	HYDE	1,236	716	315	205	401 R	57.9%	25.5%	69.4%	30.6%
3,437	JACKSON	1,351	920	370	61	550 R	68.1%	27.4%	71.3%	28.7%
2,929	JERAULD	1,716	946	701	69	245 R	55.1%	40.9%	57.4%	42.6%
1,463	JONES	926	717	193	16	524 R	77.4%	20.8%	78.8%	21.2%
6,679	KINGSBURY	3,802	2,181	1,507	114	674 R	57.4%	39.6%	59.1%	40.9%
10,724	LAKE	5,868	3,102	2,634	132	468 R	52.9%	44.9%	54.1%	45.9%
18,339	LAWRENCE	8,433	5,587	2,604	242	2,983 R	66.3%	30.9%	68.2%	31.8%
13,942	LINCOLN	6,745	3,625	2,946	174	679 R	53.7%	43.7%	55.2%	44.8%
3,864	LYMAN	1,907	1,369	485	53	884 R	71.8%	25.4%	73.8%	26.2%
6,444	MCCOOK	3,631	1,900	1,663	68	237 R	52.3%	45.8%	53.3%	46.7%
4,027	MCPHERSON	2,438	1,997	412	29	1,585 R	81.9%	16.9%	82.9%	17.1%
5,404	MARSHALL	3,004	1,645	1,329	30	316 R	54.8%	44.2%	55.3%	44.7%
20,717	MEADE	7,560	5,317	1,962	281	3,355 R	70.3%	26.0%	73.0%	27.0%
2,249	MELLETTE	964	630	313	21	317 R	65.4%	32.5%	66.8%	33.2%
3,739	MINER	2,177	1,109	991	77	118 R	50.9%	45.5%	52.8%	47.2%
109,435	MINNEHAHA	51,265	25,506	25,164	595	342 R	49.8%	49.1%	50.3%	49.7%
6,692	MOODY	3,473	1,701	1,697	75	4 R	49.0%	48.9%	50.1%	49.9%
70,133	PENNINGTON	27,765	18,825	8,377	563	10,448 R	67.8%	30.2%	69.2%	30.8%
4,700	PERKINS	2,659	1,845	741	73	1,104 R	69.4%	27.9%	71.3%	28.7%
3,674	POTTER	2,184	1,513	586	85	927 R	69.3%	26.8%	72.1%	27.9%
10,911	ROBERTS	5,005	2,860	2,073	72	787 R	57.1%	41.4%	58.0%	42.0%
3,213	SANBORN	1,898	1,015	831	52	184 R	53.5%	43.8%	55.0%	45.0%
11,323	SHANNON	1,724	358	1,343	23	985 D	20.8%	77.9%	21.0%	79.0%
9,201	SPINK	4,802	2,726	1,918	158	808 R	56.8%	39.9%	58.7%	41.3%
2,533	STANLEY	1,296	877	372	47	505 R	67.7%	28.7%	70.2%	29.8%
1,990	SULLY	1,142	767	277	98	490 R	67.2%	24.3%	73.5%	26.5%
7,328	TODD	1,944	728	1,193	23	465 D	37.4%	61.4%	37.9%	62.1%
7,268	TRIPP	3,783	2,458	1,198	127	1,260 R	65.0%	31.7%	67.2%	32.8%
9,255	TURNER	5,006	3,153	1,761	92	1,392 R	63.0%	35.2%	64.2%	35.8%
10,938	UNION	5,041	2,528	2,413	100	115 R	50.1%	47.9%	51.2%	48.8%
7,011	WALWORTH	3,590	2,414	988	188	1,426 R	67.2%	27.5%	71.0%	29.0%
18,952	YANKTON	8,775	5,126	3,436	213	1,690 R	58.4%	39.2%	59.9%	40.1%
2,308	ZIEBACH	808	470	307	31	163 R	58.2%	38.0%	60.5%	39.5%
690,178	TOTAL	327,478	190,594	129,018	7,866	61,576 R	58.2%	39.4%	59.6%	40.4%

SOUTH DAKOTA

CONGRESS

CD	Year	Total Vote	Republican Vote	Republican Candidate	Democratic Vote	Democratic Candidate	Other Vote	Rep.-Dem. Plurality	Total Vote Rep.	Total Vote Dem.	Major Vote Rep.	Major Vote Dem.
1	1980	167,065	57,155	KULL, BART	109,910	DASCHLE, THOMAS A.		52,755 D	34.2%	65.8%	34.2%	65.8%
1	1978	129,227	64,544	THORSNESS, LEO K.	64,683	DASCHLE, THOMAS A.		139 D	49.9%	50.1%	49.9%	50.1%
1	1976	152,402	121,587	PRESSLER, LARRY	29,533	GUFFEY, JAMES V.	1,282	92,054 R	79.8%	19.4%	80.5%	19.5%
1	1974	141,605	78,266	PRESSLER, LARRY	63,339	DENHOLM, FRANK E.		14,927 R	55.3%	44.7%	55.3%	44.7%
1	1972	156,031	61,589	VICKERMAN, JOHN	94,442	DENHOLM, FRANK E.		32,853 D	39.5%	60.5%	39.5%	60.5%
2	1980	152,438	88,991	ROBERTS, CLINT	63,447	STOFFERAHN, KENNETH D.		25,544 R	58.4%	41.6%	58.4%	41.6%
2	1978	126,296	70,780	ABDNOR, JAMES	55,516	SAMUELSON, BOB		15,264 R	56.0%	44.0%	56.0%	44.0%
2	1976	142,569	99,601	ABDNOR, JAMES	42,968	MICKELSON, GRACE		56,633 R	69.9%	30.1%	69.9%	30.1%
2	1974	130,865	88,746	ABDNOR, JAMES	42,119	WEILAND, JACK		46,627 R	67.8%	32.2%	67.8%	32.2%
2	1972	144,961	79,546	ABDNOR, JAMES	65,415	MCKEEVER, PATRICK		14,131 R	54.9%	45.1%	54.9%	45.1%

SOUTH DAKOTA

1980 GENERAL ELECTION

In 1978 Jackson and Washabaugh counties were combined and are now called Jackson.

President   Other vote was 21,431 Anderson (Independent); 3,824 Clark (Independent); 250 Pulley (Independent).

Senator   Other vote was Peterson (Independent).

Congress

1980 PRIMARIES

JUNE 3 REPUBLICAN

Senator   68,196 James Abdnor; 25,314 Dale Bell.

Congress   Contested as follows:

CD 1   28,424 Bart Kull; 10,563 Bert Tollefson.
CD 2   32,984 Clint Roberts; 17,970 Don Ham.

JUNE 3 DEMOCRATIC

Senator   44,822 George S. McGovern; 26,958 Larry Schumaker.

Congress   Unopposed in CD 1. Contested as follows:

CD 2   23,901 Kenneth D. Stofferahn; 11,544 Thomas M. Katus.

TENNESSEE

GOVERNOR
Lamar Alexander (R). Elected 1978 to a four-year term.

SENATORS
Howard H. Baker, Jr. (R). Re-elected 1978 to a six-year term. Previously elected 1972, 1966.

James R. Sasser (D). Elected 1976 to a six-year term.

REPRESENTATIVES
1. James H. Quillen (R)
2. John J. Duncan (R)
3. Marilyn Lloyd Bouquard (D)
4. Albert Gore, Jr. (D)
5. Bill Boner (D)
6. Robin L. Beard (R)
7. Ed Jones (D)
8. Harold E. Ford (D)

POSTWAR VOTE FOR GOVERNOR

| | | | | | | | | | Percentage | | | |
| | | | | | | | | | Total Vote | | Major Vote | |
Year	Total Vote	Vote	Republican Candidate	Vote	Democratic Candidate	Other Vote	Rep.-Dem. Plurality		Rep.	Dem.	Rep.	Dem.
1978	1,189,695	661,959	Alexander, Lamar	523,495	Butcher, Jake	4,241	138,464 R		55.6%	44.0%	55.8%	44.2%
1974	1,040,714	455,467	Alexander, Lamar	576,833	Blanton, Ray	8,414	121,366 D		43.8%	55.4%	44.1%	55.9%
1970	1,108,247	575,777	Dunn, Winfield	509,521	Hooker, John J.	22,949	66,256 R		52.0%	46.0%	53.1%	46.9%
1966	656,566	—	—	532,998	Ellington, Buford	123,568	532,998 D		—	81.2%	—	100.0%
1962	621,064	100,190	Patty, Hubert D.	315,648	Clement, Frank G.	205,226	215,458 D		16.1%	50.8%	24.1%	75.9%
1958	432,545	35,938	Wall, Thomas P.	248,874	Ellington, Buford	147,733	212,936 D		8.3%	57.5%	12.6%	87.4%
1954	322,586	—	—	281,291	Clement, Frank G.	41,295	281,291 D		—	87.2%	—	100.0%
1952	806,771	166,377	Witt, R. Beecher	640,290	Clement, Frank G.	104	473,913 D		20.6%	79.4%	20.6%	79.4%
1950	236,194	—	—	184,437	Browning, Gordon	51,757	184,437 D		—	78.1%	—	100.0%
1948	543,881	179,957	Acuff, Roy	363,903	Browning, Gordon	21	183,946 D		33.1%	66.9%	33.1%	66.9%
1946	229,456	73,222	Lowe, W. O.	149,937	McCord, Jim Nance	6,297	76,715 D		31.9%	65.3%	32.8%	67.2%

The term of office of Tennessee's Governor was increased from two to four years effective with the 1954 election.

POSTWAR VOTE FOR SENATOR

| | | | | | | | | | Percentage | | | |
| | | | | | | | | | Total Vote | | Major Vote | |
Year	Total Vote	Vote	Republican Candidate	Vote	Democratic Candidate	Other Vote	Rep.-Dem. Plurality		Rep.	Dem.	Rep.	Dem.
1978	1,157,094	642,644	Baker, Howard H., Jr.	466,228	Eskind, Jane	48,222	176,416 R		55.5%	40.3%	58.0%	42.0%
1976	1,432,046	673,231	Brock, William E.	751,180	Sasser, James R.	7,635	77,949 D		47.0%	52.5%	47.3%	52.7%
1972	1,164,195	716,539	Baker, Howard H., Jr.	440,599	Blanton, Ray	7,057	275,940 R		61.5%	37.8%	61.9%	38.1%
1970	1,097,041	562,645	Brock, William E.	519,858	Gore, Albert	14,538	42,787 R		51.3%	47.4%	52.0%	48.0%
1966	866,961	483,063	Baker, Howard H., Jr.	383,843	Clement, Frank G.	55	99,220 R		55.7%	44.3%	55.7%	44.3%
1964	1,064,018	493,475	Kuykendall, Daniel H.	570,542	Gore, Albert	1	77,067 D		46.4%	53.6%	46.4%	53.6%
1964s	1,091,093	517,330	Baker, Howard H., Jr.	568,905	Bass, Ross	4,858	51,575 D		47.4%	52.1%	47.6%	52.4%
1960	828,519	234,053	Frazier, A. Bradley	594,460	Kefauver, Estes	6	360,407 D		28.2%	71.7%	28.2%	71.8%
1958	401,666	76,371	Atkins, Hobart F.	317,324	Gore, Albert	7,971	240,953 D		19.0%	79.0%	19.4%	80.6%
1954	356,094	106,971	Wall, Thomas P.	249,121	Kefauver, Estes	2	142,150 D		30.0%	70.0%	30.0%	70.0%
1952	735,219	153,479	Atkins, Hobart F.	545,432	Gore, Albert	36,308	391,953 D		20.9%	74.2%	22.0%	78.0%
1948	499,218	166,947	Reece, B. Carroll	326,142	Kefauver, Estes	6,129	159,195 D		33.4%	65.3%	33.9%	66.1%
1946	218,714	57,238	Ladd, William B.	145,654	McKellar, Kenneth	15,822	88,416 D		26.2%	66.6%	28.2%	71.8%

One of the 1964 elections was for a short term to fill a vacancy.

TENNESSEE

Districts Established April 13, 1972

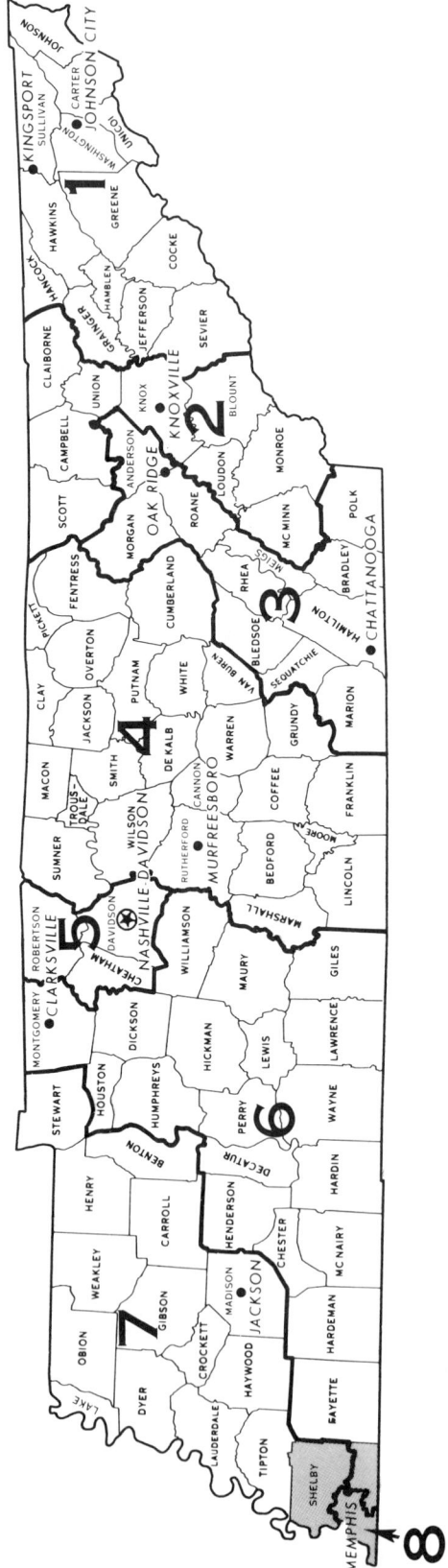

County with two or more Congressional Districts.

TENNESSEE

PRESIDENT 1980

1980 Census Population	County	Total Vote	Republican	Democratic	Other	Rep.-Dem. Plurality	Percentage Total Vote Rep.	Dem.	Major Vote Rep.	Dem.
67,346	ANDERSON	25,736	14,235	10,194	1,307	4,041 R	55.3%	39.6%	58.3%	41.7%
27,916	BEDFORD	9,583	3,377	5,987	219	2,610 D	35.2%	62.5%	36.1%	63.9%
14,901	BENTON	6,193	2,281	3,811	101	1,530 D	36.8%	61.5%	37.4%	62.6%
9,478	BLEDSOE	3,586	1,970	1,585	31	385 R	54.9%	44.2%	55.4%	44.6%
77,770	BLOUNT	28,144	17,959	9,412	773	8,547 R	63.8%	33.4%	65.6%	34.4%
67,547	BRADLEY	19,905	11,869	7,638	398	4,231 R	59.6%	38.4%	60.8%	39.2%
34,841	CAMPBELL	10,450	5,537	4,752	161	785 R	53.0%	45.5%	53.8%	46.2%
10,234	CANNON	3,817	1,403	2,351	63	948 D	36.8%	61.6%	37.4%	62.6%
28,285	CARROLL	11,143	5,681	5,277	185	404 R	51.0%	47.4%	51.8%	48.2%
50,205	CARTER	18,077	11,648	6,006	423	5,642 R	64.4%	33.2%	66.0%	34.0%
21,616	CHEATHAM	6,201	2,296	3,771	134	1,475 D	37.0%	60.8%	37.8%	62.2%
12,727	CHESTER	4,940	2,751	2,123	66	628 R	55.7%	43.0%	56.4%	43.6%
24,595	CLAIBORNE	7,263	4,289	2,844	130	1,445 R	59.1%	39.2%	60.1%	39.9%
7,676	CLAY	2,765	1,344	1,376	45	32 D	48.6%	49.8%	49.4%	50.6%
28,792	COCKE	9,144	6,802	2,139	203	4,663 R	74.4%	23.4%	76.1%	23.9%
38,311	COFFEE	13,393	5,454	7,612	327	2,158 D	40.7%	56.8%	41.7%	58.3%
14,941	CROCKETT	4,588	2,117	2,422	49	305 D	46.1%	52.8%	46.6%	53.4%
28,676	CUMBERLAND	10,436	6,354	3,775	307	2,579 R	60.9%	36.2%	62.7%	37.3%
477,811	DAVIDSON	175,606	65,772	103,741	6,093	37,969 D	37.5%	59.1%	38.8%	61.2%
10,857	DECATUR	4,280	2,095	2,139	46	44 D	48.9%	50.0%	49.5%	50.5%
13,589	DE KALB	4,868	1,841	2,948	79	1,107 D	37.8%	60.6%	38.4%	61.6%
30,037	DICKSON	10,467	3,636	6,622	209	2,986 D	34.7%	63.3%	35.4%	64.6%
34,663	DYER	11,407	5,475	5,713	219	238 D	48.0%	50.1%	48.9%	51.1%
25,305	FAYETTE	7,195	2,944	4,141	110	1,197 D	40.9%	57.6%	41.6%	58.4%
14,826	FENTRESS	4,103	2,493	1,543	67	950 R	60.8%	37.6%	61.8%	38.2%
31,983	FRANKLIN	11,090	3,995	6,760	335	2,765 D	36.0%	61.0%	37.1%	62.9%
49,467	GIBSON	16,923	6,792	9,829	302	3,037 D	40.1%	58.1%	40.9%	59.1%
24,625	GILES	7,537	2,757	4,653	127	1,896 D	36.6%	61.7%	37.2%	62.8%
16,751	GRAINGER	4,848	3,254	1,495	99	1,759 R	67.1%	30.8%	68.5%	31.5%
54,406	GREENE	16,956	10,704	5,822	430	4,882 R	63.1%	34.3%	64.8%	35.2%
13,787	GRUNDY	4,019	1,139	2,837	43	1,698 D	28.3%	70.6%	28.6%	71.4%
49,300	HAMBLEN	16,073	9,741	5,890	442	3,851 R	60.6%	36.6%	62.3%	37.7%
287,740	HAMILTON	102,092	57,575	41,913	2,604	15,662 R	56.4%	41.1%	57.9%	42.1%
6,887	HANCOCK	2,487	1,734	704	49	1,030 R	69.7%	28.3%	71.1%	28.9%
23,873	HARDEMAN	7,205	2,931	4,153	121	1,222 D	40.7%	57.6%	41.4%	58.6%
22,280	HARDIN	7,435	4,152	3,164	119	988 R	55.8%	42.6%	56.8%	43.2%
43,751	HAWKINS	13,529	7,836	5,283	410	2,553 R	57.9%	39.0%	59.7%	40.3%
20,318	HAYWOOD	5,943	2,435	3,445	63	1,010 D	41.0%	58.0%	41.4%	58.6%
21,390	HENDERSON	7,926	5,108	2,702	116	2,406 R	64.4%	34.1%	65.4%	34.6%
28,656	HENRY	11,168	4,299	6,601	268	2,302 D	38.5%	59.1%	39.4%	60.6%
15,151	HICKMAN	5,230	1,903	3,225	102	1,322 D	36.4%	61.7%	37.1%	62.9%
6,871	HOUSTON	2,541	738	1,757	46	1,019 D	29.0%	69.1%	29.6%	70.4%
15,957	HUMPHREYS	5,966	1,897	3,974	95	2,077 D	31.8%	66.6%	32.3%	67.7%
9,398	JACKSON	3,535	995	2,480	60	1,485 D	28.1%	70.2%	28.6%	71.4%
31,284	JEFFERSON	10,392	6,944	3,180	268	3,764 R	66.8%	30.6%	68.6%	31.4%
13,745	JOHNSON	4,955	3,716	1,141	98	2,575 R	75.0%	23.0%	76.5%	23.5%
319,694	KNOX	117,585	66,153	45,634	5,798	20,519 R	56.3%	38.8%	59.2%	40.8%
7,455	LAKE	2,563	823	1,718	22	895 D	32.1%	67.0%	32.4%	67.6%
24,555	LAUDERDALE	7,235	2,818	4,318	99	1,500 D	38.9%	59.7%	39.5%	60.5%
34,110	LAWRENCE	13,477	6,532	6,082	863	450 R	48.5%	45.1%	51.8%	48.2%
9,700	LEWIS	3,309	1,076	2,190	43	1,114 D	32.5%	66.2%	32.9%	67.1%
26,483	LINCOLN	8,409	2,856	5,387	166	2,531 D	34.0%	64.1%	34.6%	65.4%
28,553	LOUDON	10,376	6,382	3,699	295	2,683 R	61.5%	35.6%	63.3%	36.7%
41,878	MCMINN	13,547	7,825	5,460	262	2,365 R	57.8%	40.3%	58.9%	41.1%
22,525	MCNAIRY	8,514	4,603	3,801	110	802 R	54.1%	44.6%	54.8%	45.2%
15,700	MACON	4,961	2,925	1,947	89	978 R	59.0%	39.2%	60.0%	40.0%
74,546	MADISON	27,187	13,667	12,986	534	681 R	50.3%	47.8%	51.3%	48.7%
24,416	MARION	8,651	3,902	4,623	126	721 D	45.1%	53.4%	45.8%	54.2%
19,698	MARSHALL	6,666	2,282	4,277	107	1,995 D	34.2%	64.2%	34.8%	65.2%
51,095	MAURY	15,030	6,637	7,957	436	1,320 D	44.2%	52.9%	45.5%	54.5%
7,431	MEIGS	2,316	1,278	999	39	279 R	55.2%	43.1%	56.1%	43.9%
28,700	MONROE	11,065	6,246	4,612	207	1,634 R	56.4%	41.7%	57.5%	42.5%
83,342	MONTGOMERY	20,698	8,503	11,573	622	3,070 D	41.1%	55.9%	42.4%	57.6%
4,510	MOORE	1,595	551	993	51	442 D	34.5%	62.3%	35.7%	64.3%
16,604	MORGAN	5,015	2,823	2,094	98	729 R	56.3%	41.8%	57.4%	42.6%
32,781	OBION	11,365	5,397	5,766	202	369 D	47.5%	50.7%	48.3%	51.7%
17,575	OVERTON	5,267	1,869	3,343	55	1,474 D	35.5%	63.5%	35.9%	64.1%
6,111	PERRY	2,232	783	1,401	48	618 D	35.1%	62.8%	35.9%	64.1%
4,358	PICKETT	2,102	1,319	758	25	561 R	62.7%	36.1%	63.5%	36.5%
13,602	POLK	4,960	2,414	2,470	76	56 D	48.7%	49.8%	49.4%	50.6%

TENNESSEE

PRESIDENT 1980

1980 Census Population	County	Total Vote	Republican	Democratic	Other	Rep.-Dem. Plurality	Percentage			
							Total Vote		Major Vote	
							Rep.	Dem.	Rep.	Dem.
47,601	PUTNAM	14,753	6,235	8,084	434	1,849 D	42.3%	54.8%	43.5%	56.5%
24,235	RHEA	7,889	4,689	3,070	130	1,619 R	59.4%	38.9%	60.4%	39.6%
48,425	ROANE	18,182	11,096	6,473	613	4,623 R	61.0%	35.6%	63.2%	36.8%
37,021	ROBERTSON	11,126	3,560	7,381	185	3,821 D	32.0%	66.3%	32.5%	67.5%
84,058	RUTHERFORD	27,350	11,208	15,213	929	4,005 D	41.0%	55.6%	42.4%	57.6%
19,259	SCOTT	4,832	3,014	1,724	94	1,290 R	62.4%	35.7%	63.6%	36.4%
8,605	SEQUATCHIE	3,052	1,512	1,509	31	3 R	49.5%	49.4%	50.0%	50.0%
41,418	SEVIER	14,439	10,576	3,450	413	7,126 R	73.2%	23.9%	75.4%	24.6%
777,113	SHELBY	308,517	140,157	159,240	9,120	19,083 D	45.4%	51.6%	46.8%	53.2%
14,935	SMITH	5,531	1,755	3,674	102	1,919 D	31.7%	66.4%	32.3%	67.7%
8,665	STEWART	3,318	985	2,274	59	1,289 D	29.7%	68.5%	30.2%	69.8%
143,968	SULLIVAN	50,470	25,963	22,341	2,166	3,622 R	51.4%	44.3%	53.7%	46.3%
85,790	SUMNER	26,735	11,876	14,150	709	2,274 D	44.4%	52.9%	45.6%	54.4%
32,747	TIPTON	9,401	4,339	4,934	128	595 D	46.2%	52.5%	46.8%	53.2%
6,137	TROUSDALE	2,354	629	1,674	51	1,045 D	26.7%	71.1%	27.3%	72.7%
16,362	UNICOI	5,844	3,828	1,880	136	1,948 R	65.5%	32.2%	67.1%	32.9%
11,707	UNION	3,951	2,453	1,435	63	1,018 R	62.1%	36.3%	63.1%	36.9%
4,728	VAN BUREN	1,404	499	886	19	387 D	35.5%	63.1%	36.0%	64.0%
32,653	WARREN	9,904	3,680	6,021	203	2,341 D	37.2%	60.8%	37.9%	62.1%
88,755	WASHINGTON	30,249	17,457	11,599	1,193	5,858 R	57.7%	38.3%	60.1%	39.9%
13,946	WAYNE	5,297	3,418	1,633	246	1,785 R	64.5%	30.8%	67.7%	32.3%
32,896	WEAKLEY	11,771	5,668	5,910	193	242 D	48.2%	50.2%	49.0%	51.0%
19,567	WHITE	5,613	2,100	3,415	98	1,315 D	37.4%	60.8%	38.1%	61.9%
58,108	WILLIAMSON	21,095	11,597	8,815	683	2,782 R	55.0%	41.8%	56.8%	43.2%
56,064	WILSON	19,274	7,535	11,248	491	3,713 D	39.1%	58.4%	40.1%	59.9%
4,590,750	TOTAL	1,617,616	787,761	783,051	46,804	4,710 R	48.7%	48.4%	50.1%	49.9%

TENNESSEE

CONGRESS

CD	Year	Total Vote	Republican Vote	Republican Candidate	Democratic Vote	Democratic Candidate	Other Vote	Rep.-Dem. Plurality	Total Vote Rep.	Total Vote Dem.	Major Vote Rep.	Major Vote Dem.
1	1980	151,129	130,296	QUILLEN, JAMES H.			20,833	130,296 R	86.2%		100.0%	
1	1978	142,841	92,143	QUILLEN, JAMES H.	50,694	BALL, GORDON	4	41,449 R	64.5%	35.5%	64.5%	35.5%
1	1976	168,734	97,781	QUILLEN, JAMES H.	69,507	BLEVINS, LLOYD	1,446	28,274 R	57.9%	41.2%	58.5%	41.5%
1	1974	118,917	76,394	QUILLEN, JAMES H.	42,523	BLEVINS, LLOYD		33,871 R	64.2%	35.8%	64.2%	35.8%
1	1972	139,608	110,868	QUILLEN, JAMES H.	28,736	CANTOR, BERNARD	4	82,132 R	79.4%	20.6%	79.4%	20.6%
2	1980	194,527	147,947	DUNCAN, JOHN J.	46,578	DUNNAWAY, DAVID H.	2	101,369 R	76.1%	23.9%	76.1%	23.9%
2	1978	152,833	125,082	DUNCAN, JOHN J.	27,745	FRANCIS, MARGARET	6	97,337 R	81.8%	18.2%	81.8%	18.2%
2	1976	186,707	117,256	DUNCAN, JOHN J.	69,449	ROWLAND, MIKE	2	47,807 R	62.8%	37.2%	62.8%	37.2%
2	1974	123,339	87,419	DUNCAN, JOHN J.	35,920	BROWN, JESSE B.		51,499 R	70.9%	29.1%	70.9%	29.1%
2	1972	109,925	109,925	DUNCAN, JOHN J.				109,925 R	100.0%		100.0%	
3	1980	192,156	74,761	BYERS, GLEN	117,355	BOUQUARD, MARILYN LLOYD	40	42,594 D	38.9%	61.1%	38.9%	61.1%
3	1978	121,838			108,282	LLOYD, MARILYN	13,556	108,282 D		88.9%		100.0%
3	1976	183,569	57,116	BAKER, LAMAR	123,872	LLOYD, MARILYN	2,581	66,756 D	31.1%	67.5%	31.6%	68.4%
3	1974	121,198	55,580	BAKER, LAMAR	61,926	LLOYD, MARILYN	3,692	6,346 D	45.9%	51.1%	47.3%	52.7%
3	1972	149,443	82,561	BAKER, LAMAR	62,536	SOMPAYRAC, HOWARD	4,346	20,025 R	55.2%	41.8%	56.9%	43.1%
4	1980	173,570	35,954	SEIGNEUR, JAMES B.	137,612	GORE, ALBERT, JR.	4	101,658 D	20.7%	79.3%	20.7%	79.3%
4	1978	108,701			108,695	GORE, ALBERT, JR.	6	108,695 D		100.0%		100.0%
4	1976	122,723			115,392	GORE, ALBERT, JR.	7,331	115,392 D		94.0%		100.0%
4	1974	94,918			94,847	EVINS, JOE L.	71	94,847 D		99.9%		100.0%
4	1972	114,731	21,689	FINNEY, BILLY JO	93,042	EVINS, JOE L.		71,353 D	18.9%	81.1%	18.9%	81.1%
5	1980	181,262	62,746	ADAMS, MIKE	118,506	BONER, BILL	10	55,760 D	34.6%	65.4%	34.6%	65.4%
5	1978	133,608	47,288	GOODWIN, BILL	68,608	BONER, BILL	17,712	21,320 D	35.4%	51.4%	40.8%	59.2%
5	1976	136,151			125,830	ALLEN, CLIFFORD	10,321	125,830 D		92.4%		100.0%
5	1974	88,350			88,206	FULTON, RICHARD	144	88,206 D		99.8%		100.0%
5	1972	149,464	55,067	ADAMS, ALFRED	93,555	FULTON, RICHARD	842	38,488 D	36.8%	62.6%	37.1%	62.9%
6	1980	128,511	127,945	BEARD, ROBIN L.			566	127,945 R	99.6%		100.0%	
6	1978	153,591	114,630	BEARD, ROBIN L.	38,954	ARLINE, RON	7	75,676 R	74.6%	25.4%	74.6%	25.4%
6	1976	181,375	116,905	BEARD, ROBIN L.	64,462	BASS, ROSS	8	52,443 R	64.5%	35.5%	64.5%	35.5%
7	1980	172,835	39,227	CAMPBELL, DANIEL	133,606	JONES, ED	2	94,379 D	22.7%	77.3%	22.7%	77.3%
7	1978	132,866	36,003	COOK, ROSS E.	96,863	JONES, ED		60,860 D	27.1%	72.9%	27.1%	72.9%
7	1976	105,847			105,832	JONES, ED	15	105,832 D		100.0%		100.0%
8	1980	110,207			110,139	FORD, HAROLD E.	68	110,139 D		99.9%		100.0%
8	1978	115,917	33,679	RAGSDALE, DUNCAN	80,776	FORD, HAROLD E.	1,462	47,097 D	29.1%	69.7%	29.4%	70.6%
8	1976	165,954	63,819	ALISSANDRATOS, A. D.	100,683	FORD, HAROLD E.	1,452	36,864 D	38.5%	60.7%	38.8%	61.2%

TENNESSEE

1980 GENERAL ELECTION

President   Other vote was 35,991 Anderson (Independent); 7,116 Clark (Independent); 1,112 Commoner (Independent); 521 Bubar (Independent); 519 McReynolds (Independent); 503 Hall (Independent); 490 DeBerry (Independent); 400 Griswold (Independent); 152 scattered.

Congress   Other vote was 20,816 Curtis (Independent) and 17 scattered in CD 1; scattered in all other CD's.

1980 PRIMARIES

AUGUST 7 REPUBLICAN

Congress   Unopposed in three CD's. Contested as follows:

CD 1   43,649 James H. Quillen; 12,679 Bill Bays; 4 scattered.
CD 3   14,719 Glen Byers; 7,839 Patrick E. Lloyd; 1 scattered.
CD 5   9,057 Mike Adams; 1,892 Laurel Steinhice; 1 scattered.
CD 7   5,717 Daniel Campbell; 3,850 Lewis Millet; 1 scattered.
CD 8   4,259 William V. Lawson; 3,191 William B. Thompson. Mr. Lawson withdrew after the primary and no substitution was made.

AUGUST 7 DEMOCRATIC

Congress   Unopposed in four CD's. No candidates in CD's 1 and 6. Contested as follows:

CD 4   65,886 Albert Gore, Jr.; 5,533 John L. Welker.
CD 8   40,825 Harold E. Ford; 11,337 Minerva Johnican; 2,982 Mark F. Flanagan; 996 Jack W. Theobald; 1 scattered.

TEXAS

GOVERNOR
William P. Clements (R). Elected 1978 to a four-year term.

SENATORS
Lloyd Bentsen (D). Re-elected 1976 to a six-year term. Previously elected 1970.

John G. Tower (R). Re-elected 1978 to a six-year term. Previously elected 1972, 1966, and in May 1961 to fill out term vacated by the resignation of Senator Lyndon B. Johnson.

REPRESENTATIVES
1. Sam B. Hall (D)
2. Charles Wilson (D)
3. James M. Collins (R)
4. Ralph M. Hall (D)
5. Jim Mattox (D)
6. Phil Gramm (D)
7. W. R. Archer (R)
8. Jack Fields (R)
9. Jack B. Brooks (D)
10. Jake Pickle (D)
11. J. Marvin Leath (D)
12. James C. Wright (D)
13. John Hightower (D)
14. William N. Patman (D)
15. Eligio de la Garza (D)
16. Richard C. White (D)
17. Charles W. Stenholm (D)
18. Mickey Leland (D)
19. Kent Hance (D)
20. Henry B. Gonzalez (D)
21. Tom Loeffler (R)
22. Ron Paul (R)
23. Abraham Kazen (D)
24. Martin Frost (D)

POSTWAR VOTE FOR GOVERNOR

Year	Total Vote	Republican Vote	Republican Candidate	Democratic Vote	Democratic Candidate	Other Vote	Rep.-Dem. Plurality	Total Vote Rep.	Total Vote Dem.	Major Vote Rep.	Major Vote Dem.
1978	2,369,764	1,183,839	Clements, William P.	1,166,979	Hill, John	18,946	16,860 R	50.0%	49.2%	50.4%	49.6%
1974	1,654,984	514,725	Granberry, Jim	1,016,334	Briscoe, Dolph	123,925	501,609 D	31.1%	61.4%	33.6%	66.4%
1972	3,410,128	1,534,060	Grover, Henry C.	1,633,970	Briscoe, Dolph	242,098	99,910 D	45.0%	47.9%	48.4%	51.6%
1970	2,235,847	1,037,723	Eggers, Paul W.	1,197,726	Smith, Preston	398	160,003 D	46.4%	53.6%	46.4%	53.6%
1968	2,916,509	1,254,333	Eggers, Paul W.	1,662,019	Smith, Preston	157	407,686 D	43.0%	57.0%	43.0%	57.0%
1966	1,425,861	368,025	Kennerly, T. E.	1,037,517	Connally, John B.	20,319	669,492 D	25.8%	72.8%	26.2%	73.8%
1964	2,544,753	661,675	Crichton, Jack	1,877,793	Connally, John B.	5,285	1,216,118 D	26.0%	73.8%	26.1%	73.9%
1962	1,569,181	715,025	Cox, Jack	847,036	Connally, John B.	7,120	132,011 D	45.6%	54.0%	45.8%	54.2%
1960	2,250,718	612,963	Steger, William M.	1,637,755	Daniel, Price	—	1,024,792 D	27.2%	72.8%	27.2%	72.8%
1958	789,133	94,098	Mayer, Edwin S.	695,035	Daniel, Price	—	600,937 D	11.9%	88.1%	11.9%	88.1%
1956	1,828,161	271,088	Bryant, William R.	1,433,051	Daniel, Price	124,022	1,161,963 D	14.8%	78.4%	15.9%	84.1%
1954	636,892	66,154	Adams, Tod R.	569,533	Shivers, Allan	1,205	503,379 D	10.4%	89.4%	10.4%	89.6%
1952	1,881,202	—	—	1,844,530	Shivers, Allan	36,672	1,844,530 D	—	98.1%	—	100.0%
1950	394,747	39,737	Currie, Ralph W.	355,010	Shivers, Allan	—	315,273 D	10.1%	89.9%	10.1%	89.9%
1948	1,208,860	177,399	Lane, Alvin H.	1,024,160	Jester, Beauford	7,301	846,761 D	14.7%	84.7%	14.8%	85.2%
1946	378,744	33,231	Nolte, Eugene	345,513	Jester, Beauford	—	312,282 D	8.8%	91.2%	8.8%	91.2%

The term of office of Texas' Governor was increased from two to four years effective with the 1974 election.

POSTWAR VOTE FOR SENATOR

Year	Total Vote	Republican Vote	Republican Candidate	Democratic Vote	Democratic Candidate	Other Vote	Rep.-Dem. Plurality	Total Vote Rep.	Total Vote Dem.	Major Vote Rep.	Major Vote Dem.
1978	2,312,540	1,151,376	Tower, John G.	1,139,149	Krueger, Robert	22,015	12,227 R	49.8%	49.3%	50.3%	49.7%
1976	3,874,516	1,636,370	Steelman, Alan	2,199,956	Bentsen, Lloyd	38,190	563,586 D	42.2%	56.8%	42.7%	57.3%
1972	3,413,903	1,822,877	Tower, John G.	1,511,985	Sanders, Barefoot	79,041	310,892 R	53.4%	44.3%	54.7%	45.3%
1970	2,231,671	1,035,794	Bush, George	1,194,069	Bentsen, Lloyd	1,808	158,275 D	46.4%	53.5%	46.5%	53.5%
1966	1,493,182	842,501	Tower, John G.	643,855	Carr, Waggoner	6,826	198,646 R	56.4%	43.1%	56.7%	43.3%
1964	2,603,856	1,134,337	Bush, George	1,463,958	Yarborough, Ralph	5,561	329,621 D	43.6%	56.2%	43.7%	56.3%
1961s	886,091	448,217	Tower, John G.	437,874	Blakley, William A.	—	10,343 R	50.6%	49.4%	50.6%	49.4%
1960	2,253,784	926,653	Tower, John G.	1,306,625	Johnson, Lyndon B.	20,506	379,972 D	41.1%	58.0%	41.5%	58.5%
1958	787,128	185,926	Whittenburg, Roy	587,030	Yarborough, Ralph	14,172	401,104 D	23.6%	74.6%	24.1%	75.9%
1957s	957,298		(See note below)								
1954	636,475	94,131	Watson, Carlos G.	539,319	Johnson, Lyndon B.	3,025	445,188 D	14.8%	84.7%	14.9%	85.1%
1952	1,895,192	—	—	1,895,192	Daniel, Price	—	1,895,192 D	—	100.0%	—	100.0%
1948	1,061,563	349,665	Porter, Jack	702,985	Johnson, Lyndon B.	8,913	353,320 D	32.9%	66.2%	33.2%	66.8%
1946	380,681	43,750	Sells, Murray C.	336,931	Connally, Tom	—	293,181 D	11.5%	88.5%	11.5%	88.5%

The 1961 election (May) and the 1957 election (April) were for short terms to fill vacancies. Though neither vote was held with official party designations, the 1961 vote above was a run-off contest between unofficial party candidates. In 1957 there was a single ballot without run-off and Ralph Yarborough polled 364,605 votes (38.1% of the total vote) and won the election with a 73,802 plurality.

TEXAS

Districts Established October 17, 1973

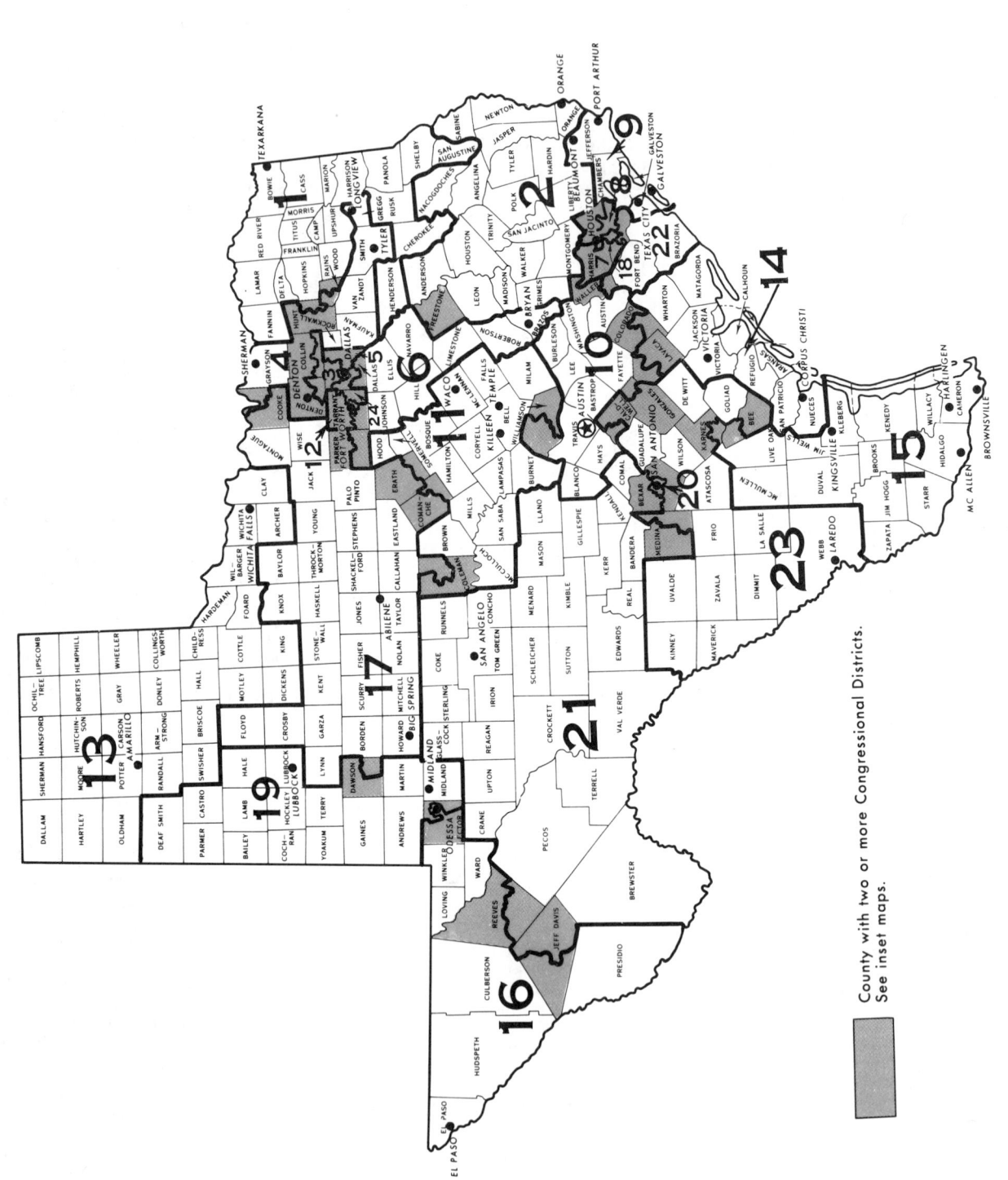

County with two or more Congressional Districts.
See inset maps.

TEXAS

PRESIDENT 1980

1980 Census Population	County	Total Vote	Republican	Democratic	Other	Rep.-Dem. Plurality	Percentage Total Vote Rep.	Dem.	Major Vote Rep.	Dem.
38,381	ANDERSON	11,330	5,970	5,163	197	807 R	52.7%	45.6%	53.6%	46.4%
13,323	ANDREWS	4,013	2,800	1,155	58	1,645 R	69.8%	28.8%	70.8%	29.2%
64,172	ANGELINA	20,394	9,900	10,140	354	240 D	48.5%	49.7%	49.4%	50.6%
14,260	ARANSAS	5,068	3,081	1,800	187	1,281 R	60.8%	35.5%	63.1%	36.9%
7,266	ARCHER	3,289	1,804	1,444	41	360 R	54.8%	43.9%	55.5%	44.5%
1,994	ARMSTRONG	1,065	709	333	23	376 R	66.6%	31.3%	68.0%	32.0%
25,055	ATASCOSA	8,469	4,364	3,980	125	384 R	51.5%	47.0%	52.3%	47.7%
17,726	AUSTIN	5,753	3,734	1,893	126	1,841 R	64.9%	32.9%	66.4%	33.6%
8,168	BAILEY	2,655	1,809	800	46	1,009 R	68.1%	30.1%	69.3%	30.7%
7,084	BANDERA	3,360	2,373	894	93	1,479 R	70.6%	26.6%	72.6%	27.4%
24,726	BASTROP	8,748	3,768	4,716	264	948 D	43.1%	53.9%	44.4%	55.6%
4,919	BAYLOR	2,306	1,098	1,183	25	85 D	47.6%	51.3%	48.1%	51.9%
26,030	BEE	7,931	4,171	3,606	154	565 R	52.6%	45.5%	53.6%	46.4%
157,889	BELL	37,885	20,729	15,823	1,333	4,906 R	54.7%	41.8%	56.7%	43.3%
988,800	BEXAR	308,474	159,578	137,729	11,167	21,849 R	51.7%	44.6%	53.7%	46.3%
4,681	BLANCO	2,301	1,434	794	73	640 R	62.3%	34.5%	64.4%	35.6%
859	BORDEN	415	279	131	5	148 R	67.2%	31.6%	68.0%	32.0%
13,401	BOSQUE	5,437	2,908	2,431	98	477 R	53.5%	44.7%	54.5%	45.5%
75,301	BOWIE	25,650	13,942	11,339	369	2,603 R	54.4%	44.2%	55.1%	44.9%
169,587	BRAZORIA	47,544	27,614	18,253	1,677	9,361 R	58.1%	38.4%	60.2%	39.8%
93,588	BRAZOS	29,539	17,798	9,856	1,885	7,942 R	60.3%	33.4%	64.4%	35.6%
7,573	BREWSTER	2,892	1,496	1,271	125	225 R	51.7%	43.9%	54.1%	45.9%
2,579	BRISCOE	1,150	562	561	27	1 R	48.9%	48.8%	50.0%	50.0%
8,428	BROOKS	3,333	780	2,488	65	1,708 D	23.4%	74.6%	23.9%	76.1%
33,057	BROWN	11,549	6,515	4,867	167	1,648 R	56.4%	42.1%	57.2%	42.8%
12,313	BURLESON	4,609	1,943	2,615	51	672 D	42.2%	56.7%	42.6%	57.4%
17,803	BURNET	7,933	4,033	3,711	189	322 R	50.8%	46.8%	52.1%	47.9%
23,637	CALDWELL	6,184	2,879	3,155	150	276 D	46.6%	51.0%	47.7%	52.3%
19,574	CALHOUN	6,549	3,312	3,034	203	278 R	50.6%	46.3%	52.2%	47.8%
10,992	CALLAHAN	4,331	2,284	2,002	45	282 R	52.7%	46.2%	53.3%	46.7%
209,680	CAMERON	46,285	22,041	23,200	1,044	1,159 D	47.6%	50.1%	48.7%	51.3%
9,275	CAMP	3,618	1,531	2,052	35	521 D	42.3%	56.7%	42.7%	57.3%
6,672	CARSON	2,942	1,888	1,006	48	882 R	64.2%	34.2%	65.2%	34.8%
29,430	CASS	10,672	4,993	5,578	101	585 D	46.8%	52.3%	47.2%	52.8%
10,556	CASTRO	3,218	1,955	1,199	64	756 R	60.8%	37.3%	62.0%	38.0%
18,538	CHAMBERS	5,806	3,140	2,517	149	623 R	54.1%	43.4%	55.5%	44.5%
38,127	CHEROKEE	11,486	5,629	5,726	131	97 D	49.0%	49.9%	49.6%	50.4%
6,950	CHILDRESS	2,713	1,443	1,222	48	221 R	53.2%	45.0%	54.1%	45.9%
9,582	CLAY	4,109	1,824	2,233	52	409 D	44.4%	54.3%	45.0%	55.0%
4,825	COCHRAN	1,607	1,064	513	30	551 R	66.2%	31.9%	67.5%	32.5%
3,196	COKE	1,558	708	838	12	130 D	45.4%	53.8%	45.8%	54.2%
10,439	COLEMAN	3,994	2,228	1,719	47	509 R	55.8%	43.0%	56.4%	43.6%
144,490	COLLIN	53,861	36,559	15,187	2,115	21,372 R	67.9%	28.2%	70.7%	29.3%
4,648	COLLINGSWORTH	1,851	1,020	798	33	222 R	55.1%	43.1%	56.1%	43.9%
18,823	COLORADO	5,991	3,520	2,377	94	1,143 R	58.8%	39.7%	59.7%	40.3%
36,446	COMAL	13,714	9,758	3,554	402	6,204 R	71.2%	25.9%	73.3%	26.7%
12,617	COMANCHE	4,588	1,977	2,550	61	573 D	43.1%	55.6%	43.7%	56.3%
2,915	CONCHO	1,417	700	702	15	2 D	49.4%	49.5%	49.9%	50.1%
27,656	COOKE	10,802	6,760	3,842	200	2,918 R	62.6%	35.6%	63.8%	36.2%
56,767	CORYELL	9,920	5,494	4,097	329	1,397 R	55.4%	41.3%	57.3%	42.7%
2,947	COTTLE	1,266	511	732	23	221 D	40.4%	57.8%	41.1%	58.9%
4,600	CRANE	1,951	1,310	607	34	703 R	67.1%	31.1%	68.3%	31.7%
4,608	CROCKETT	1,494	885	595	14	290 R	59.2%	39.8%	59.8%	40.2%
8,859	CROSBY	2,806	1,361	1,408	37	47 D	48.5%	50.2%	49.2%	50.8%
3,315	CULBERSON	976	541	423	12	118 R	55.4%	43.3%	56.1%	43.9%
6,531	DALLAM	1,639	965	632	42	333 R	58.9%	38.6%	60.4%	39.6%
1,556,549	DALLAS	518,213	306,682	190,459	21,072	116,223 R	59.2%	36.8%	61.7%	38.3%
16,184	DAWSON	5,205	3,267	1,867	71	1,400 R	62.8%	35.9%	63.6%	36.4%
21,165	DEAF SMITH	5,864	4,073	1,666	125	2,407 R	69.5%	28.4%	71.0%	29.0%
4,839	DELTA	2,142	767	1,347	28	580 D	35.8%	62.9%	36.3%	63.7%
143,126	DENTON	49,908	29,908	17,381	2,619	12,527 R	59.9%	34.8%	63.2%	36.8%
18,903	DE WITT	5,580	3,450	2,044	86	1,406 R	61.8%	36.6%	62.8%	37.2%
3,539	DICKENS	1,481	554	912	15	358 D	37.4%	61.6%	37.8%	62.2%
11,367	DIMMIT	3,323	1,173	2,102	48	929 D	35.3%	63.3%	35.8%	64.2%
4,075	DONLEY	1,888	1,106	751	31	355 R	58.6%	39.8%	59.6%	40.4%
12,517	DUVAL	4,757	1,012	3,706	39	2,694 D	21.3%	77.9%	21.4%	78.6%
19,480	EASTLAND	6,877	3,442	3,346	89	96 R	50.1%	48.7%	50.7%	49.3%
115,374	ECTOR	36,179	26,188	9,069	922	17,119 R	72.4%	25.1%	74.3%	25.7%
2,033	EDWARDS	824	575	237	12	338 R	69.8%	28.8%	70.8%	29.2%
59,743	ELLIS	19,580	10,046	9,219	315	827 R	51.3%	47.1%	52.1%	47.9%

TEXAS

PRESIDENT 1980

1980 Census Population	County	Total Vote	Republican	Democratic	Other	Rep.-Dem. Plurality	Percentage Total Vote Rep.	Dem.	Major Vote Rep.	Dem.
479,899	EL PASO	99,526	53,276	40,082	6,168	13,194 R	53.5%	40.3%	57.1%	42.9%
22,560	ERATH	8,306	3,981	4,156	169	175 D	47.9%	50.0%	48.9%	51.1%
17,946	FALLS	6,007	2,606	3,328	73	722 D	43.4%	55.4%	43.9%	56.1%
24,285	FANNIN	8,611	3,196	5,284	131	2,088 D	37.1%	61.4%	37.7%	62.3%
18,832	FAYETTE	6,804	4,104	2,590	110	1,514 R	60.3%	38.1%	61.3%	38.7%
5,891	FISHER	2,437	838	1,564	35	726 D	34.4%	64.2%	34.9%	65.1%
9,834	FLOYD	3,556	2,043	1,477	36	566 R	57.5%	41.5%	58.0%	42.0%
2,158	FOARD	978	349	617	12	268 D	35.7%	63.1%	36.1%	63.9%
130,846	FORT BEND	38,286	25,366	11,583	1,337	13,783 R	66.3%	30.3%	68.7%	31.3%
6,893	FRANKLIN	2,633	1,105	1,487	41	382 D	42.0%	56.5%	42.6%	57.4%
14,830	FREESTONE	5,265	2,468	2,739	58	271 D	46.9%	52.0%	47.4%	52.6%
13,785	FRIO	4,668	1,753	2,849	66	1,096 D	37.6%	61.0%	38.1%	61.9%
13,150	GAINES	3,656	2,390	1,182	84	1,208 R	65.4%	32.3%	66.9%	33.1%
195,940	GALVESTON	63,297	29,527	30,778	2,992	1,251 D	46.6%	48.6%	49.0%	51.0%
5,336	GARZA	1,897	1,188	677	32	511 R	62.6%	35.7%	63.7%	36.3%
13,532	GILLESPIE	6,018	4,736	1,170	112	3,566 R	78.7%	19.4%	80.2%	19.8%
1,304	GLASSCOCK	535	416	116	3	300 R	77.8%	21.7%	78.2%	21.8%
5,193	GOLIAD	2,287	1,170	1,081	36	89 R	51.2%	47.3%	52.0%	48.0%
16,883	GONZALES	5,922	2,931	2,896	95	35 R	49.5%	48.9%	50.3%	49.7%
26,386	GRAY	10,149	7,187	2,786	176	4,401 R	70.8%	27.5%	72.1%	27.9%
89,796	GRAYSON	31,326	16,811	13,807	708	3,004 R	53.7%	44.1%	54.9%	45.1%
99,487	GREGG	34,190	23,399	10,219	572	13,180 R	68.4%	29.9%	69.6%	30.4%
13,580	GRIMES	4,602	2,087	2,440	75	353 D	45.3%	53.0%	46.1%	53.9%
46,708	GUADALUPE	15,428	9,901	5,049	478	4,852 R	64.2%	32.7%	66.2%	33.8%
37,592	HALE	11,050	7,277	3,610	163	3,667 R	65.9%	32.7%	66.8%	33.2%
5,594	HALL	2,220	1,141	1,057	22	84 R	51.4%	47.6%	51.9%	48.1%
8,297	HAMILTON	3,267	1,683	1,526	58	157 R	51.5%	46.7%	52.4%	47.6%
6,209	HANSFORD	2,596	2,046	518	32	1,528 R	78.8%	20.0%	79.8%	20.2%
6,368	HARDEMAN	2,273	1,056	1,174	43	118 D	46.5%	51.6%	47.4%	52.6%
40,721	HARDIN	13,732	6,087	7,358	287	1,271 D	44.3%	53.6%	45.3%	54.7%
2,409,544	HARRIS	720,014	416,655	274,061	29,298	142,594 R	57.9%	38.1%	60.3%	39.7%
52,265	HARRISON	17,493	9,328	7,746	419	1,582 R	53.3%	44.3%	54.6%	45.4%
3,987	HARTLEY	1,757	1,248	470	39	778 R	71.0%	26.8%	72.6%	27.4%
7,725	HASKELL	3,436	1,447	1,951	38	504 D	42.1%	56.8%	42.6%	57.4%
40,594	HAYS	13,289	6,517	6,013	759	504 R	49.0%	45.2%	52.0%	48.0%
5,304	HEMPHILL	1,780	1,152	592	36	560 R	64.7%	33.3%	66.1%	33.9%
42,606	HENDERSON	16,305	7,903	8,199	203	296 D	48.5%	50.3%	49.1%	50.9%
283,229	HIDALGO	61,717	25,808	34,542	1,367	8,734 D	41.8%	56.0%	42.8%	57.2%
25,024	HILL	8,936	4,113	4,688	135	575 D	46.0%	52.5%	46.7%	53.3%
23,230	HOCKLEY	7,183	4,599	2,447	137	2,152 R	64.0%	34.1%	65.3%	34.7%
17,714	HOOD	6,940	3,755	3,001	184	754 R	54.1%	43.2%	55.6%	44.4%
25,247	HOPKINS	8,318	3,834	4,344	140	510 D	46.1%	52.2%	46.9%	53.1%
22,299	HOUSTON	7,144	2,889	4,181	74	1,292 D	40.4%	58.5%	40.9%	59.1%
33,142	HOWARD	11,312	6,658	4,451	203	2,207 R	58.9%	39.3%	59.9%	40.1%
2,728	HUDSPETH	884	471	394	19	77 R	53.3%	44.6%	54.5%	45.5%
55,248	HUNT	18,501	9,283	8,773	445	510 R	50.2%	47.4%	51.4%	48.6%
26,304	HUTCHINSON	10,632	7,439	2,935	258	4,504 R	70.0%	27.6%	71.7%	28.3%
1,386	IRION	670	427	239	4	188 R	63.7%	35.7%	64.1%	35.9%
7,408	JACK	2,877	1,482	1,349	46	133 R	51.5%	46.9%	52.3%	47.7%
13,352	JACKSON	4,463	2,540	1,826	97	714 R	56.9%	40.9%	58.2%	41.8%
30,781	JASPER	10,257	4,396	5,707	154	1,311 D	42.9%	55.6%	43.5%	56.5%
1,647	JEFF DAVIS	729	409	300	20	109 R	56.1%	41.2%	57.7%	42.3%
250,938	JEFFERSON	84,602	36,763	45,642	2,197	8,879 D	43.5%	53.9%	44.6%	55.4%
5,168	JIM HOGG	1,997	535	1,437	25	902 D	26.8%	72.0%	27.1%	72.9%
36,498	JIM WELLS	12,013	4,606	7,267	140	2,661 D	38.3%	60.5%	38.8%	61.2%
67,649	JOHNSON	22,454	11,411	10,542	501	869 R	50.8%	46.9%	52.0%	48.0%
17,268	JONES	5,874	2,765	3,043	66	278 D	47.1%	51.8%	47.6%	52.4%
13,593	KARNES	5,074	2,719	2,284	71	435 R	53.6%	45.0%	54.3%	45.7%
39,015	KAUFMAN	12,287	5,852	6,266	169	414 D	47.6%	51.0%	48.3%	51.7%
10,635	KENDALL	5,086	3,890	1,075	121	2,815 R	76.5%	21.1%	78.3%	21.7%
543	KENEDY	187	76	106	5	30 D	40.6%	56.7%	41.8%	58.2%
1,145	KENT	694	339	351	4	12 D	48.8%	50.6%	49.1%	50.9%
28,780	KERR	12,855	9,090	3,387	378	5,703 R	70.7%	26.3%	72.9%	27.1%
4,063	KIMBLE	1,651	1,011	608	32	403 R	61.2%	36.8%	62.4%	37.6%
425	KING	205	144	55	6	89 R	70.2%	26.8%	72.4%	27.6%
2,279	KINNEY	1,046	543	472	31	71 R	51.9%	45.1%	53.5%	46.5%
33,358	KLEBERG	10,053	4,608	5,125	320	517 D	45.8%	51.0%	47.3%	52.7%
5,329	KNOX	1,968	783	1,163	22	380 D	39.8%	59.1%	40.2%	59.8%
42,156	LAMAR	13,490	6,094	7,178	218	1,084 D	45.2%	53.2%	45.9%	54.1%
18,669	LAMB	5,933	3,723	2,132	78	1,591 R	62.8%	35.9%	63.6%	36.4%

TEXAS

PRESIDENT 1980

1980 Census Population	County	Total Vote	Republican	Democratic	Other	Rep.-Dem. Plurality	Total Vote Rep.	Dem.	Major Vote Rep.	Dem.
12,005	LAMPASAS	4,381	2,323	1,979	79	344 R	53.0%	45.2%	54.0%	46.0%
5,514	LA SALLE	2,248	773	1,442	33	669 D	34.4%	64.1%	34.9%	65.1%
19,004	LAVACA	5,999	3,254	2,678	67	576 R	54.2%	44.6%	54.9%	45.1%
10,952	LEE	3,462	1,803	1,581	78	222 R	52.1%	45.7%	53.3%	46.7%
9,594	LEON	4,053	1,821	2,190	42	369 D	44.9%	54.0%	45.4%	54.6%
47,088	LIBERTY	13,561	6,470	6,810	281	340 D	47.7%	50.2%	48.7%	51.3%
20,224	LIMESTONE	6,319	2,835	3,403	81	568 D	44.9%	53.9%	45.4%	54.6%
3,766	LIPSCOMB	1,733	1,343	338	52	1,005 R	77.5%	19.5%	79.9%	20.1%
9,606	LIVE OAK	3,618	2,193	1,380	45	813 R	60.6%	38.1%	61.4%	38.6%
10,144	LLANO	5,097	2,866	2,130	101	736 R	56.2%	41.8%	57.4%	42.6%
91	LOVING	72	50	22	—	28 R	69.4%	30.6%	69.4%	30.6%
211,651	LUBBOCK	67,867	46,711	18,732	2,424	27,979 R	68.8%	27.6%	71.4%	28.6%
8,605	LYNN	2,874	1,603	1,236	35	367 R	55.8%	43.0%	56.5%	43.5%
8,735	MCCULLOCH	3,366	1,572	1,750	44	178 D	46.7%	52.0%	47.3%	52.7%
170,755	MCLENNAN	59,515	31,968	26,305	1,242	5,663 R	53.7%	44.2%	54.9%	45.1%
789	MCMULLEN	398	271	122	5	149 R	68.1%	30.7%	69.0%	31.0%
10,649	MADISON	3,018	1,389	1,583	46	194 D	46.0%	52.5%	46.7%	53.3%
10,360	MARION	3,730	1,666	2,015	49	349 D	44.7%	54.0%	45.3%	54.7%
4,684	MARTIN	1,716	1,093	605	18	488 R	63.7%	35.3%	64.4%	35.6%
3,683	MASON	1,621	966	630	25	336 R	59.6%	38.9%	60.5%	39.5%
37,828	MATAGORDA	10,382	5,545	4,585	252	960 R	53.4%	44.2%	54.7%	45.3%
31,398	MAVERICK	4,367	1,370	2,932	65	1,562 D	31.4%	67.1%	31.8%	68.2%
23,164	MEDINA	7,888	4,742	3,034	112	1,708 R	60.1%	38.5%	61.0%	39.0%
2,346	MENARD	1,050	548	489	13	59 R	52.2%	46.6%	52.8%	47.2%
82,636	MIDLAND	32,692	25,027	6,839	826	18,188 R	76.6%	20.9%	78.5%	21.5%
22,732	MILAM	7,627	3,251	4,230	146	979 D	42.6%	55.5%	43.5%	56.5%
4,477	MILLS	2,059	985	1,028	46	43 D	47.8%	49.9%	48.9%	51.1%
9,088	MITCHELL	2,926	1,455	1,446	25	9 R	49.7%	49.4%	50.2%	49.8%
17,410	MONTAGUE	6,472	3,143	3,233	96	90 D	48.6%	50.0%	49.3%	50.7%
128,487	MONTGOMERY	39,971	26,237	12,593	1,141	13,644 R	65.6%	31.5%	67.6%	32.4%
16,575	MOORE	5,583	3,736	1,743	104	1,993 R	66.9%	31.2%	68.2%	31.8%
14,629	MORRIS	5,280	2,133	3,105	42	972 D	40.4%	58.8%	40.7%	59.3%
1,950	MOTLEY	929	573	341	15	232 R	61.7%	36.7%	62.7%	37.3%
46,786	NACOGDOCHES	15,150	8,626	5,981	543	2,645 R	56.9%	39.5%	59.1%	40.9%
35,323	NAVARRO	12,591	5,400	6,988	203	1,588 D	42.9%	55.5%	43.6%	56.4%
13,254	NEWTON	4,714	1,379	3,284	51	1,905 D	29.3%	69.7%	29.6%	70.4%
17,359	NOLAN	5,695	2,781	2,796	118	15 D	48.8%	49.1%	49.9%	50.1%
268,215	NUECES	86,644	40,586	43,424	2,634	2,838 D	46.8%	50.1%	48.3%	51.7%
9,588	OCHILTREE	3,702	3,032	594	76	2,438 R	81.9%	16.0%	83.6%	16.4%
2,283	OLDHAM	874	557	290	27	267 R	63.7%	33.2%	65.8%	34.2%
83,838	ORANGE	27,887	12,389	14,928	570	2,539 D	44.4%	53.5%	45.4%	54.6%
24,062	PALO PINTO	8,484	4,068	4,244	172	176 D	47.9%	50.0%	48.9%	51.1%
20,724	PANOLA	7,747	4,022	3,637	88	385 R	51.9%	46.9%	52.5%	47.5%
44,609	PARKER	16,155	8,505	7,336	314	1,169 R	52.6%	45.4%	53.7%	46.3%
11,038	PARMER	3,398	2,640	707	51	1,933 R	77.7%	20.8%	78.9%	21.1%
14,618	PECOS	4,395	2,723	1,602	70	1,121 R	62.0%	36.5%	63.0%	37.0%
24,407	POLK	8,108	3,771	4,213	124	442 D	46.5%	52.0%	47.2%	52.8%
98,637	POTTER	26,831	16,327	9,633	871	6,694 R	60.9%	35.9%	62.9%	37.1%
5,188	PRESIDIO	1,799	723	1,039	37	316 D	40.2%	57.8%	41.0%	59.0%
4,839	RAINS	2,022	813	1,174	35	361 D	40.2%	58.1%	40.9%	59.1%
75,062	RANDALL	31,382	23,136	7,323	923	15,813 R	73.7%	23.3%	76.0%	24.0%
4,135	REAGAN	1,351	917	414	20	503 R	67.9%	30.6%	68.9%	31.1%
2,469	REAL	1,453	832	603	18	229 R	57.3%	41.5%	58.0%	42.0%
16,101	RED RIVER	5,773	2,225	3,501	47	1,276 D	38.5%	60.6%	38.9%	61.1%
15,801	REEVES	4,544	2,315	2,138	91	177 R	50.9%	47.1%	52.0%	48.0%
9,289	REFUGIO	4,251	1,944	2,224	83	280 D	45.7%	52.3%	46.6%	53.4%
1,187	ROBERTS	642	482	150	10	332 R	75.1%	23.4%	76.3%	23.7%
14,653	ROBERTSON	5,310	1,661	3,572	77	1,911 D	31.3%	67.3%	31.7%	68.3%
14,528	ROCKWALL	6,184	4,036	1,985	163	2,051 R	65.3%	32.1%	67.0%	33.0%
11,872	RUNNELS	4,233	2,532	1,648	53	884 R	59.8%	38.9%	60.6%	39.4%
41,382	RUSK	14,467	8,705	5,582	180	3,123 R	60.2%	38.6%	60.9%	39.1%
8,702	SABINE	3,398	1,387	1,983	28	596 D	40.8%	58.4%	41.2%	58.8%
8,785	SAN AUGUSTINE	3,091	1,397	1,674	20	277 D	45.2%	54.2%	45.5%	54.5%
11,434	SAN JACINTO	4,193	1,726	2,376	91	650 D	41.2%	56.7%	42.1%	57.9%
58,013	SAN PATRICIO	17,494	8,326	8,627	541	301 D	47.6%	49.3%	49.1%	50.9%
5,693	SAN SABA	2,385	948	1,405	32	457 D	39.7%	58.9%	40.3%	59.7%
2,820	SCHLEICHER	1,131	672	444	15	228 R	59.4%	39.3%	60.2%	39.8%
18,192	SCURRY	5,846	3,745	2,003	98	1,742 R	64.1%	34.3%	65.2%	34.8%
3,915	SHACKELFORD	1,581	959	606	16	353 R	60.7%	38.3%	61.3%	38.7%
23,084	SHELBY	7,804	3,500	4,215	89	715 D	44.8%	54.0%	45.4%	54.6%

TEXAS

PRESIDENT 1980

1980 Census Population	County	Total Vote	Republican	Democratic	Other	Rep.-Dem. Plurality	Percentage			
							Total Vote		Major Vote	
							Rep.	Dem.	Rep.	Dem.
3,174	SHERMAN	1,456	1,128	286	42	842 R	77.5%	19.6%	79.8%	20.2%
128,366	SMITH	43,700	28,236	14,838	626	13,398 R	64.6%	34.0%	65.6%	34.4%
4,154	SOMERVELL	1,852	792	1,015	45	223 D	42.8%	54.8%	43.8%	56.2%
27,266	STARR	6,253	1,389	4,782	82	3,393 D	22.2%	76.5%	22.5%	77.5%
9,926	STEPHENS	3,608	2,161	1,372	75	789 R	59.9%	38.0%	61.2%	38.8%
1,206	STERLING	586	364	218	4	146 R	62.1%	37.2%	62.5%	37.5%
2,406	STONEWALL	1,219	488	719	12	231 D	40.0%	59.0%	40.4%	59.6%
5,130	SUTTON	1,511	1,000	485	26	515 R	66.2%	32.1%	67.3%	32.7%
9,723	SWISHER	3,366	1,450	1,854	62	404 D	43.1%	55.1%	43.9%	56.1%
860,880	TARRANT	305,066	173,466	121,068	10,532	52,398 R	56.9%	39.7%	58.9%	41.1%
110,932	TAYLOR	37,032	22,961	13,245	826	9,716 R	62.0%	35.8%	63.4%	36.6%
1,595	TERRELL	686	411	260	15	151 R	59.9%	37.9%	61.3%	38.7%
14,581	TERRY	5,195	3,178	1,945	72	1,233 R	61.2%	37.4%	62.0%	38.0%
2,053	THROCKMORTON	908	444	455	9	11 D	48.9%	50.1%	49.4%	50.6%
21,442	TITUS	7,700	3,747	3,872	81	125 D	48.7%	50.3%	49.2%	50.8%
84,784	TOM GREEN	27,271	16,555	9,892	824	6,663 R	60.7%	36.3%	62.6%	37.4%
419,335	TRAVIS	160,093	73,151	75,028	11,914	1,877 D	45.7%	46.9%	49.4%	50.6%
9,450	TRINITY	4,068	1,503	2,510	55	1,007 D	36.9%	61.7%	37.5%	62.5%
16,223	TYLER	6,195	2,545	3,540	110	995 D	41.1%	57.1%	41.8%	58.2%
28,595	UPSHUR	9,852	4,836	4,894	122	58 D	49.1%	49.7%	49.7%	50.3%
4,619	UPTON	1,684	1,169	485	30	684 R	69.4%	28.8%	70.7%	29.3%
22,441	UVALDE	6,366	3,887	2,402	77	1,485 R	61.1%	37.7%	61.8%	38.2%
35,910	VAL VERDE	9,353	5,055	4,116	182	939 R	54.0%	44.0%	55.1%	44.9%
31,426	VAN ZANDT	11,340	5,495	5,707	138	212 D	48.5%	50.3%	49.1%	50.9%
68,807	VICTORIA	21,269	13,392	7,382	495	6,010 R	63.0%	34.7%	64.5%	35.5%
41,789	WALKER	10,906	5,657	4,869	380	788 R	51.9%	44.6%	53.7%	46.3%
19,798	WALLER	6,463	3,019	3,329	115	310 D	46.7%	51.5%	47.6%	52.4%
13,976	WARD	4,396	2,912	1,405	79	1,507 R	66.2%	32.0%	67.5%	32.5%
21,998	WASHINGTON	7,495	4,821	2,518	156	2,303 R	64.3%	33.6%	65.7%	34.3%
99,258	WEBB	17,593	5,421	11,856	316	6,435 D	30.8%	67.4%	31.4%	68.6%
40,242	WHARTON	11,958	6,598	5,138	222	1,460 R	55.2%	43.0%	56.2%	43.8%
7,137	WHEELER	2,743	1,626	1,090	27	536 R	59.3%	39.7%	59.9%	40.1%
121,082	WICHITA	41,625	22,884	17,657	1,084	5,227 R	55.0%	42.4%	56.4%	43.6%
15,931	WILBARGER	5,463	3,031	2,347	85	684 R	55.5%	43.0%	56.4%	43.6%
17,495	WILLACY	5,108	1,995	3,047	66	1,052 D	39.1%	59.7%	39.6%	60.4%
76,521	WILLIAMSON	26,661	15,035	10,408	1,218	4,627 R	56.4%	39.0%	59.1%	40.9%
16,756	WILSON	6,632	3,443	3,097	92	346 R	51.9%	46.7%	52.6%	47.4%
9,944	WINKLER	3,232	2,160	1,021	51	1,139 R	66.8%	31.6%	67.9%	32.1%
26,575	WISE	9,205	4,350	4,674	181	324 D	47.3%	50.8%	48.2%	51.8%
24,697	WOOD	8,671	4,515	4,033	123	482 R	52.1%	46.5%	52.8%	47.2%
8,299	YOAKUM	2,694	1,937	715	42	1,222 R	71.9%	26.5%	73.0%	27.0%
19,001	YOUNG	7,022	4,153	2,740	129	1,413 R	59.1%	39.0%	60.2%	39.8%
6,628	ZAPATA	2,131	874	1,218	39	344 D	41.0%	57.2%	41.8%	58.2%
11,666	ZAVALA	3,538	831	2,621	86	1,790 D	23.5%	74.1%	24.1%	75.9%
14,228,383	TOTAL	4,541,636	2,510,705	1,881,147	149,784	629,558 R	55.3%	41.4%	57.2%	42.8%

TEXAS

CONGRESS

CD	Year	Total Vote	Republican Vote	Republican Candidate	Democratic Vote	Democratic Candidate	Other Vote	Rep.-Dem. Plurality	Total Vote Rep.	Total Vote Dem.	Major Vote Rep.	Major Vote Dem.
1	1980	137,665			137,665	HALL, SAM B.		137,665 D		100.0%		100.0%
1	1978	94,408	20,700	HUDSON, FRED	73,708	HALL, SAM B.		53,008 D	21.9%	78.1%	21.9%	78.1%
1	1976	161,745	26,334	HOGAN, JAMES	135,384	HALL, SAM B.	27	109,050 D	16.3%	83.7%	16.3%	83.7%
1	1974	72,050	22,619	FARRIS, JAMES W.	49,426	PATMAN, WRIGHT	5	26,807 D	31.4%	68.6%	31.4%	68.6%
2	1980	205,768	60,742	PANNILL, F. H.	142,496	WILSON, CHARLES	2,530	81,754 D	29.5%	69.3%	29.9%	70.1%
2	1978	95,570	28,584	DILLION, JIM	66,986	WILSON, CHARLES		38,402 D	29.9%	70.1%	29.9%	70.1%
2	1976	140,971			133,910	WILSON, CHARLES	7,061	133,910 D		95.0%		100.0%
2	1974	57,132			57,096	WILSON, CHARLES	36	57,096 D		99.9%		100.0%
3	1980	275,234	218,228	COLLINS, JAMES M.	49,667	PORTER, EARLE S.	7,339	168,561 R	79.3%	18.0%	81.5%	18.5%
3	1978	96,406	96,406	COLLINS, JAMES M.				96,406 R	100.0%		100.0%	
3	1976	231,430	171,343	COLLINS, JAMES M.	60,070	SHACKELFORD, LES E.	17	111,273 R	74.0%	26.0%	74.0%	26.0%
3	1974	98,130	63,489	COLLINS, JAMES M.	34,623	COLLUM, HAROLD	18	28,866 R	64.7%	35.3%	64.7%	35.3%
4	1980	196,702	93,915	WRIGHT, JOHN	102,787	HALL, RALPH M.		8,872 D	47.7%	52.3%	47.7%	52.3%
4	1978	94,918	36,582	GLENN, FRANK S.	58,336	ROBERTS, RAY		21,754 D	38.5%	61.5%	38.5%	61.5%
4	1976	168,038	62,641	GLENN, FRANK S.	105,394	ROBERTS, RAY	3	42,753 D	37.3%	62.7%	37.3%	62.7%
4	1974	64,329	16,113	LETOURNEAU, DICK	48,209	ROBERTS, RAY	7	32,096 D	25.0%	74.9%	25.1%	74.9%
5	1980	139,035	67,848	PAUKEN, TOM	70,892	MATTOX, JIM	295	3,044 D	48.8%	51.0%	48.9%	51.1%
5	1978	70,593	34,672	PAUKEN, TOM	35,524	MATTOX, JIM	397	852 D	49.1%	50.3%	49.4%	50.6%
5	1976	125,778	56,056	JUDY, NANCY	67,871	MATTOX, JIM	1,851	11,815 D	44.6%	54.0%	45.2%	54.8%
5	1974	54,637	28,446	STEELMAN, ALAN	26,190	MCKOOL, MIKE	1	2,256 R	52.1%	47.9%	52.1%	47.9%
6	1980	204,319	59,503	HASKINS, DAVE	144,816	GRAMM, PHIL		85,313 D	29.1%	70.9%	29.1%	70.9%
6	1978	101,418	35,393	MOWERY, WES	66,025	GRAMM, PHIL		30,632 D	34.9%	65.1%	34.9%	65.1%
6	1976	180,549	60,316	MOWERY, WES	119,025	TEAGUE, OLIN E.	1,208	58,709 D	33.4%	65.9%	33.6%	66.4%
6	1974	64,256	10,908	NIGLIAZZO, CARL	53,345	TEAGUE, OLIN E.	3	42,437 D	17.0%	83.0%	17.0%	83.0%
7	1980	295,684	242,810	ARCHER, W. R.	48,594	HUTCHINGS, ROBERT L.	4,280	194,216 R	82.1%	16.4%	83.3%	16.7%
7	1978	150,629	128,214	ARCHER, W. R.	22,415	HUTCHINGS, ROBERT L.		105,799 R	85.1%	14.9%	85.1%	14.9%
7	1976	193,127	193,127	ARCHER, W. R.				193,127 R	100.0%		100.0%	
7	1974	88,887	70,363	ARCHER, W. R.	18,524	BRADY, JIM		51,839 R	79.2%	20.8%	79.2%	20.8%
8	1980	140,777	72,856	FIELDS, JACK	67,921	ECKHARDT, BOB		4,935 R	51.8%	48.2%	51.8%	48.2%
8	1978	64,102	24,673	GEARHART, NICK	39,429	ECKHARDT, BOB		14,756 D	38.5%	61.5%	38.5%	61.5%
8	1976	139,163	54,566	GEARHART, NICK	84,404	ECKHARDT, BOB	193	29,838 D	39.2%	60.7%	39.3%	60.7%
8	1974	41,763	11,605	WHITEFIELD, DONALD D.	30,158	ECKHARDT, BOB		18,553 D	27.8%	72.2%	27.8%	72.2%
9	1980	103,574			103,225	BROOKS, JACK B.	349	103,225 D		99.7%		100.0%
9	1978	80,265	29,473	EVANS, RANDY	50,792	BROOKS, JACK B.		21,319 D	36.7%	63.3%	36.7%	63.3%
9	1976	113,016			112,945	BROOKS, JACK B.	71	112,945 D		99.9%		100.0%
9	1974	60,210	22,935	FERGUSON, COLEMAN R.	37,275	BROOKS, JACK B.		14,340 D	38.1%	61.9%	38.1%	61.9%
10	1980	229,424	88,940	BIGGAR, JOHN	135,618	PICKLE, JAKE	4,866	46,678 D	38.8%	59.1%	39.6%	60.4%
10	1978	123,857	29,328	HUDSPETH, EMMETT	94,529	PICKLE, JAKE		65,201 D	23.7%	76.3%	23.7%	76.3%
10	1976	209,172	48,482	MCCLURE, PAUL	160,683	PICKLE, JAKE	7	112,201 D	23.2%	76.8%	23.2%	76.8%
10	1974	94,814	18,560	WEISS, PAUL A.	76,240	PICKLE, JAKE	14	57,680 D	19.6%	80.4%	19.6%	80.4%
11	1980	128,520			128,520	LEATH, J. MARVIN		128,520 D		100.0%		100.0%
11	1978	103,319	49,965	BURGESS, JACK	53,354	LEATH, J. MARVIN		3,389 D	48.4%	51.6%	48.4%	51.6%
11	1976	160,563	68,373	BURGESS, JACK	92,142	POAGE, W. R.	48	23,769 D	42.6%	57.4%	42.6%	57.4%
11	1974	57,411	9,883	CLEMENTS, DON	46,828	POAGE, W. R.	700	36,945 D	17.2%	81.6%	17.4%	82.6%
12	1980	165,390	65,005	BRADSHAW, JIM	99,104	WRIGHT, JAMES C.	1,281	34,099 D	39.3%	59.9%	39.6%	60.4%
12	1978	67,820	21,364	BROWN, CLAUDE K.	46,456	WRIGHT, JAMES C.		25,092 D	31.5%	68.5%	31.5%	68.5%
12	1976	134,259	31,941	DURHAM, W. R.	101,814	WRIGHT, JAMES C.	504	69,873 D	23.8%	75.8%	23.9%	76.1%
12	1974	54,175	11,543	GARVEY, JAMES S.	42,632	WRIGHT, JAMES C.		31,089 D	21.3%	78.7%	21.3%	78.7%
13	1980	179,598	80,819	SLOVER, RON	98,779	HIGHTOWER, JOHN		17,960 D	45.0%	55.0%	45.0%	55.0%
13	1978	100,546	25,275	JONES, CLIFFORD A.	75,271	HIGHTOWER, JOHN		49,996 D	25.1%	74.9%	25.1%	74.9%
13	1976	171,682	69,328	PRICE, ROBERT	101,798	HIGHTOWER, JOHN	556	32,470 D	40.4%	59.3%	40.5%	59.5%
13	1974	92,182	39,087	PRICE, ROBERT	53,094	HIGHTOWER, JOHN	1	14,007 D	42.4%	57.6%	42.4%	57.6%
14	1980	165,379	71,495	CONCKLIN, C. L.	93,884	PATMAN, WILLIAM N.		22,389 D	43.2%	56.8%	43.2%	56.8%
14	1978	88,278	24,325	YATES, JOY	63,953	WYATT, JOE		39,628 D	27.6%	72.4%	27.6%	72.4%
14	1976	152,416	58,788	HOLFORD, L. DEAN	93,589	YOUNG, JOHN	39	34,801 D	38.6%	61.4%	38.6%	61.4%
14	1974	41,076			41,066	YOUNG, JOHN	10	41,066 D		100.0%		100.0%

TEXAS

CONGRESS

CD	Year	Total Vote	Republican Vote	Republican Candidate	Democratic Vote	Democratic Candidate	Other Vote	Rep.-Dem. Plurality	Total Vote Rep.	Total Vote Dem.	Major Vote Rep.	Major Vote Dem.
15	1980	150,415	45,090	MCDONALD, R. L.	105,325	DE LA GARZA, ELIGIO		60,235 D	30.0%	70.0%	30.0%	70.0%
15	1978	82,413	27,853	MCDONALD, R. L.	54,560	DE LA GARZA, ELIGIO		26,707 D	33.8%	66.2%	33.8%	66.2%
15	1976	138,285	35,446	MCDONALD, R. L.	102,837	DE LA GARZA, ELIGIO	2	67,391 D	25.6%	74.4%	25.6%	74.4%
15	1974	42,568			42,567	DE LA GARZA, ELIGIO	1	42,567 D		100.0%		100.0%
16	1980	123,744			104,734	WHITE, RICHARD C.	19,010	104,734 D		84.6%		100.0%
16	1978	75,833	22,743	GIERE, MICHAEL	53,090	WHITE, RICHARD C.		30,347 D	30.0%	70.0%	30.0%	70.0%
16	1976	124,448	52,499	SHACKELFORD, VIC	71,876	WHITE, RICHARD C.	73	19,377 D	42.2%	57.8%	42.2%	57.8%
16	1974	42,897			42,880	WHITE, RICHARD C.	17	42,880 D		100.0%		100.0%
17	1980	130,465			130,465	STENHOLM, CHARLES W.		130,465 D		100.0%		100.0%
17	1978	101,332	32,302	FISHER, BILL	69,030	STENHOLM, CHARLES W.		36,728 D	31.9%	68.1%	31.9%	68.1%
17	1976	127,683			127,613	BURLESON, OMAR	70	127,613 D		99.9%		100.0%
17	1974	64,969			64,959	BURLESON, OMAR	10	64,959 D		100.0%		100.0%
18	1980	90,096	16,128	KENNEDY, C. L.	71,985	LELAND, MICKEY	1,983	55,857 D	17.9%	79.9%	18.3%	81.7%
18	1978	38,018			36,783	LELAND, MICKEY	1,235	36,783 D		96.8%		100.0%
18	1976	109,876	15,381	WRIGHT, SAM H.	93,953	JORDAN, BARBARA	542	78,572 D	14.0%	85.5%	14.1%	85.9%
18	1974	43,168	6,053	MITCHELL, ROBBINS	36,597	JORDAN, BARBARA	518	30,544 D	14.0%	84.8%	14.2%	85.8%
19	1980	135,424			126,632	HANCE, KENT	8,792	126,632 D		93.5%		100.0%
19	1978	102,799	48,070	BUSH, GEORGE W.	54,729	HANCE, KENT		6,659 D	46.8%	53.2%	46.8%	53.2%
19	1976	160,901	72,991	REESE, JIM	87,908	MAHON, GEORGE H.	2	14,917 D	45.4%	54.6%	45.4%	54.6%
19	1974	49,634			49,619	MAHON, GEORGE H.	15	49,619 D		100.0%		100.0%
20	1980	102,685	17,725	NASH, MERLE	84,113	GONZALEZ, HENRY B.	847	66,388 D	17.3%	81.9%	17.4%	82.6%
20	1978	51,584			51,584	GONZALEZ, HENRY B.		51,584 D		100.0%		100.0%
20	1976	90,181			90,173	GONZALEZ, HENRY B.	8	90,173 D		100.0%		100.0%
20	1974	39,358			39,358	GONZALEZ, HENRY B.		39,358 D		100.0%		100.0%
21	1980	256,744	196,424	LOEFFLER, TOM	58,425	SULLIVAN, JOE	1,895	137,999 R	76.5%	22.8%	77.1%	22.9%
21	1978	147,837	84,336	LOEFFLER, TOM	63,501	WOLFF, NELSON W.		20,835 R	57.0%	43.0%	57.0%	43.0%
21	1976	210,315	56,211	LOCKE, BOBBY A.	149,395	KRUEGER, ROBERT	4,709	93,184 D	26.7%	71.0%	27.3%	72.7%
21	1974	101,761	45,959	HARLAN, DOUG	53,543	KRUEGER, ROBERT	2,259	7,584 D	45.2%	52.6%	46.2%	53.8%
22	1980	209,251	106,797	PAUL, RON	101,094	ANDREWS, MIKE	1,360	5,703 R	51.0%	48.3%	51.4%	48.6%
22	1978	108,086	54,643	PAUL, RON	53,443	GAMMAGE, BOB		1,200 R	50.6%	49.4%	50.6%	49.4%
22	1976	192,802	96,267	PAUL, RON	96,535	GAMMAGE, BOB		268 D	49.9%	50.1%	49.9%	50.1%
22	1974	68,718	19,483	PAUL, RON	47,783	CASEY, ROBERT R.	1,452	28,300 D	28.4%	69.5%	29.0%	71.0%
23	1980	149,780	45,139	LOCKE, BOBBY A.	104,595	KAZEN, ABRAHAM	46	59,456 D	30.1%	69.8%	30.1%	69.9%
23	1978	69,834			62,649	KAZEN, ABRAHAM	7,185	62,649 D		89.7%		100.0%
23	1976	96,524			96,481	KAZEN, ABRAHAM	43	96,481 D		100.0%		100.0%
23	1974	47,257			47,249	KAZEN, ABRAHAM	8	47,249 D		100.0%		100.0%
24	1980	152,862	59,172	SMOTHERS, CLAY	93,690	FROST, MARTIN		34,518 D	38.7%	61.3%	38.7%	61.3%
24	1978	72,515	33,314	BERMAN, LEO	39,201	FROST, MARTIN		5,887 D	45.9%	54.1%	45.9%	54.1%
24	1976	130,531	47,075	BERMAN, LEO	82,743	MILFORD, DALE	713	35,668 D	36.1%	63.4%	36.3%	63.7%
24	1974	47,437	9,698	BEAMAN, JOSEPH	36,085	MILFORD, DALE	1,654	26,387 D	20.4%	76.1%	21.2%	78.8%

TEXAS

1980 GENERAL ELECTION

President   Other vote was 111,613 Anderson (Independent); 37,643 Clark (Libertarian); 453 Commoner (write-in); 49 Hall (write-in); 15 Perkins (write-in); 11 Griswold (write-in). There is a discrepancy of one vote in the other vote column.

Congress   Other vote was Sorrells (Libertarian) in CD 2; Briggs (Libertarian) in CD 3; Jackson (write-in) in CD 5; 4,278 Ward (Libertarian) and 2 Newton (write-in) in CD 7; Allen (write-in) in CD 9; Grossberg (Libertarian) in CD 10; Mauldin (Libertarian) in CD 12; McDivitt (Libertarian) in CD 16; Fraser (Libertarian) in CD 18; Webster (Libertarian) in CD 19; 846 Burnham (Libertarian) and 1 McRee (write-in) in CD 20; Rice (Libertarian) in CD 21; Nance (Independent) in CD 22; Webster (write-in) in CD 23.

1980 PRIMARIES

MAY 3 REPUBLICAN

Congress   Unopposed in twelve CD's. No candidates in CD's 1, 9, 11, 16, 17 and 19. Contested as follows:

CD 4   8,836 John Wright; 7,988 J. L. Gulley.
CD 6   9,252 Dave Haskins; 8,171 Darla H. Mortensen.
CD 10   8,308 John Biggar; 7,151 Jack Bower; 1,585 Radcliffe J. Finley.
CD 12   14,102 Jim Bradshaw; 3,105 Jim Ryan.
CD 14   5,312 C. L. Concklin; 2,340 Russ Baird; 1,415 Gerald D'Unger.
CD 23   4,099 Bobby A. Locke; 3,535 Martin P. Ross.

MAY 3 DEMOCRATIC

Congress   Unopposed in fourteen CD's. Contested as follows:

CD 2   88,557 Charles Wilson; 25,338 Allen Sumners.
CD 4   36,874 Ralph M. Hall; 27,341 Jerdy Gary.
CD 8   16,241 Bob Eckhardt; 12,147 Larry C. Washburn.
CD 9   26,343 Jack B. Brooks; 22,188 W. L. Pate; 3,600 Jack Brookshire.
CD 10   65,409 Jake Pickle; 21,271 Greg Stallings.
CD 12   21,186 James C. Wright; 5,424 C. R. Silcox.
CD 14   32,258 William N. Patman; 28,660 Robert N. Barnes; 21,974 Joe Salem; 8,600 Jason Luby.
CD 21   36,151 Joe Sullivan; 24,143 Marilyn Jones.
CD 22   21,208 Bob Gammage; 17,986 Mike Andrews; 7,209 Joe Pentony.
CD 23   59,210 Abraham Kazen; 18,275 Paul Rich.

JUNE 7 REPUBLICAN RUN-OFF

Congress

CD 10   2,352 John Biggar; 899 Jack Bower.

JUNE 7 DEMOCRATIC RUN-OFF

Congress

CD 14   25,480 William N. Patman; 23,923 Robert N. Barnes.
CD 22   14,259 Mike Andrews; 10,983 Bob Gammage.

UTAH

GOVERNOR
Scott M. Matheson (D). Re-elected 1980 to a four-year term. Previously elected 1976.

SENATORS
E. J. Garn (R). Re-elected 1980 to a six-year term. Previously elected 1974.

Orrin G. Hatch (R). Elected 1976 to a six-year term.

REPRESENTATIVES
1. James V. Hansen (R)   2. Dan Marriott (R)

POSTWAR VOTE FOR GOVERNOR

Year	Total Vote	Republican Vote	Candidate	Democratic Vote	Candidate	Other Vote	Rep.-Dem. Plurality	Total Vote Rep.	Total Vote Dem.	Major Vote Rep.	Major Vote Dem.
1980	600,019	266,578	Wright, Bob	330,974	Matheson, Scott M.	2,467	64,396 D	44.4%	55.2%	44.6%	55.4%
1976	539,649	248,027	Romney, Vernon B.	280,706	Matheson, Scott M.	10,916	32,679 D	46.0%	52.0%	46.9%	53.1%
1972	476,447	144,449	Strike, Nicholas L.	331,998	Rampton, Calvin L.	—	187,549 D	30.3%	69.7%	30.3%	69.7%
1968	421,012	131,729	Buehner, Carl W.	289,283	Rampton, Calvin L.	—	157,554 D	31.3%	68.7%	31.3%	68.7%
1964	398,256	171,300	Melich, Mitchell	226,956	Rampton, Calvin L.	—	55,656 D	43.0%	57.0%	43.0%	57.0%
1960	371,489	195,634	Clyde, George D.	175,855	Barlocker, W. A.	—	19,779 R	52.7%	47.3%	52.7%	47.3%
1956	332,889	127,164	Clyde, George D.	111,297	Romney, L. C.	94,428	15,867 R	38.2%	33.4%	53.3%	46.7%
1952	327,704	180,516	Lee, J. Bracken	147,188	Glade, Earl J.	—	33,328 R	55.1%	44.9%	55.1%	44.9%
1948	275,067	151,253	Lee, J. Bracken	123,814	Maw, Herbert B.	—	27,439 R	55.0%	45.0%	55.0%	45.0%

POSTWAR VOTE FOR SENATOR

Year	Total Vote	Republican Vote	Candidate	Democratic Vote	Candidate	Other Vote	Rep.-Dem. Plurality	Total Vote Rep.	Total Vote Dem.	Major Vote Rep.	Major Vote Dem.
1980	594,298	437,675	Garn, E. J.	151,454	Berman, Dan	5,169	286,221 R	73.6%	25.5%	74.3%	25.7%
1976	540,108	290,221	Hatch, Orrin G.	241,948	Moss, Frank E.	7,939	48,273 R	53.7%	44.8%	54.5%	45.5%
1974	420,642	210,299	Garn, E. J.	185,377	Owens, Wayne	24,966	24,922 R	50.0%	44.1%	53.1%	46.9%
1970	374,303	159,004	Burton, Laurence J.	210,207	Moss, Frank E.	5,092	51,203 D	42.5%	56.2%	43.1%	56.9%
1968	419,262	225,075	Bennett, Wallace F.	192,168	Weilenmann, Milton	2,019	32,907 R	53.7%	45.8%	53.9%	46.1%
1964	397,384	169,562	Wilkinson, Ernest L.	227,822	Moss, Frank E.	—	58,260 D	42.7%	57.3%	42.7%	57.3%
1962	318,411	166,755	Bennett, Wallace F.	151,656	King, David S.	—	15,099 R	52.4%	47.6%	52.4%	47.6%
1958	291,311	101,471	Watkins, Arthur V.	112,827	Moss, Frank E.	77,013	11,356 D	34.8%	38.7%	47.4%	52.6%
1956	330,381	178,261	Bennett, Wallace F.	152,120	Hopkin, Alonzo F.	—	26,141 R	54.0%	46.0%	54.0%	46.0%
1952	327,033	177,435	Watkins, Arthur V.	149,598	Granger, Walter K.	—	27,837 R	54.3%	45.7%	54.3%	45.7%
1950	264,440	142,427	Bennett, Wallace F.	121,198	Thomas, Elbert D.	815	21,229 R	53.9%	45.8%	54.0%	46.0%
1946	197,399	101,142	Watkins, Arthur V.	96,257	Murdock, Abe	—	4,885 R	51.2%	48.8%	51.2%	48.8%

UTAH

Districts Established February 6, 1971

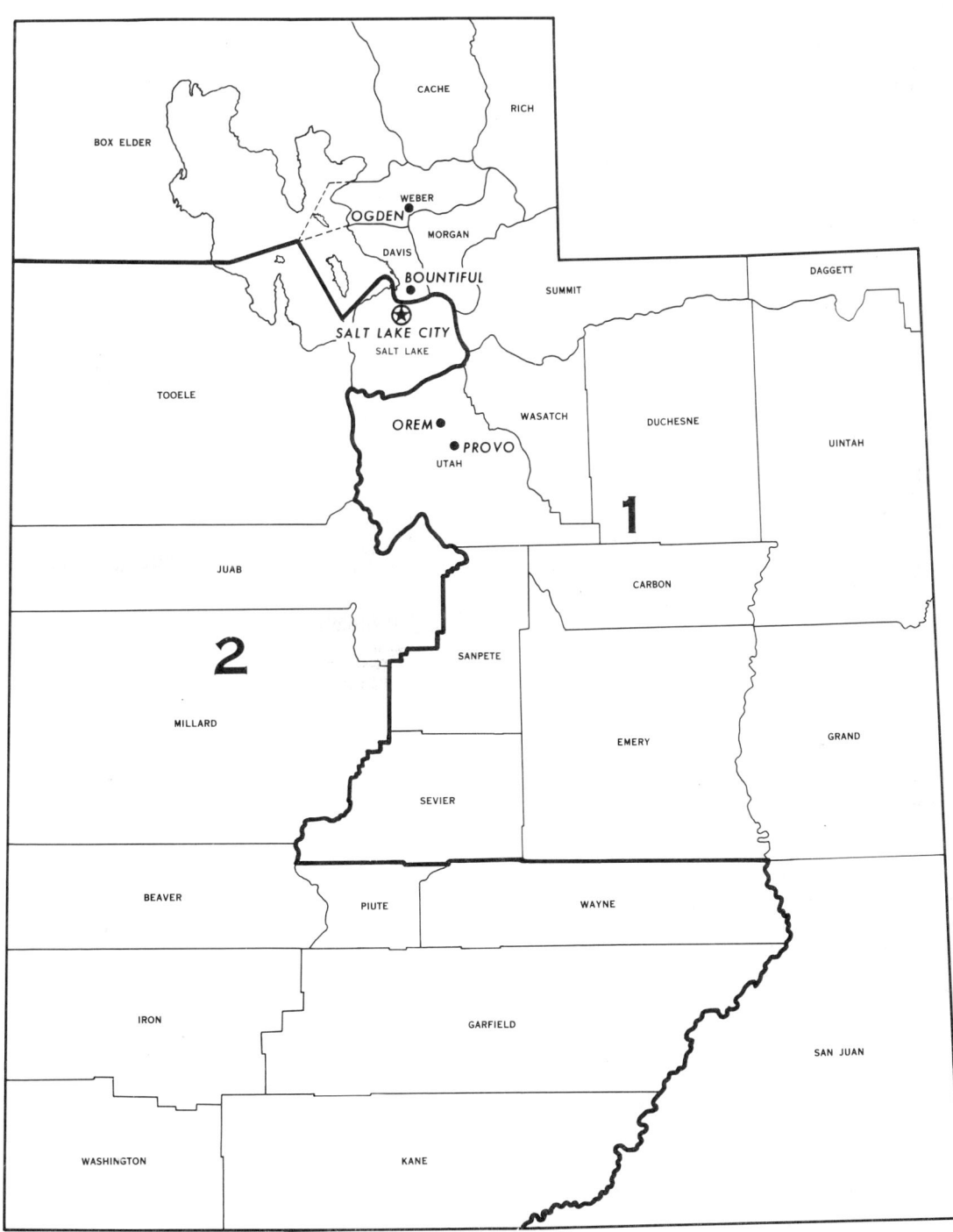

UTAH

PRESIDENT 1980

1980 Census Population	County	Total Vote	Republican	Democratic	Other	Rep.-Dem. Plurality		Percentage			
								Total Vote		Major Vote	
								Rep.	Dem.	Rep.	Dem.
4,378	BEAVER	2,157	1,477	621	59	856	R	68.5%	28.8%	70.4%	29.6%
33,222	BOX ELDER	15,111	12,500	2,142	469	10,358	R	82.7%	14.2%	85.4%	14.6%
57,176	CACHE	25,735	20,251	3,639	1,845	16,612	R	78.7%	14.1%	84.8%	15.2%
22,179	CARBON	9,063	4,320	4,317	426	3	R	47.7%	47.6%	50.0%	50.0%
769	DAGGETT	415	290	109	16	181	R	69.9%	26.3%	72.7%	27.3%
146,540	DAVIS	57,859	45,695	9,065	3,099	36,630	R	79.0%	15.7%	83.4%	16.6%
12,565	DUCHESNE	4,819	3,827	854	138	2,973	R	79.4%	17.7%	81.8%	18.2%
11,451	EMERY	4,579	3,076	1,315	188	1,761	R	67.2%	28.7%	70.1%	29.9%
3,673	GARFIELD	2,015	1,578	375	62	1,203	R	78.3%	18.6%	80.8%	19.2%
8,241	GRAND	3,354	2,362	703	289	1,659	R	70.4%	21.0%	77.1%	22.9%
17,349	IRON	7,804	6,207	1,242	355	4,965	R	79.5%	15.9%	83.3%	16.7%
5,530	JUAB	2,701	1,872	720	109	1,152	R	69.3%	26.7%	72.2%	27.8%
4,024	KANE	1,834	1,492	256	86	1,236	R	81.4%	14.0%	85.4%	14.6%
8,970	MILLARD	4,537	3,620	795	122	2,825	R	79.8%	17.5%	82.0%	18.0%
4,917	MORGAN	2,435	1,985	373	77	1,612	R	81.5%	15.3%	84.2%	15.8%
1,329	PIUTE	719	551	157	11	394	R	76.6%	21.8%	77.8%	22.2%
2,100	RICH	939	762	143	34	619	R	81.2%	15.2%	84.2%	15.8%
619,066	SALT LAKE	252,835	169,411	58,472	24,952	110,939	R	67.0%	23.1%	74.3%	25.7%
12,253	SAN JUAN	3,650	2,774	763	113	2,011	R	76.0%	20.9%	78.4%	21.6%
14,620	SANPETE	6,614	5,143	1,260	211	3,883	R	77.8%	19.1%	80.3%	19.7%
14,727	SEVIER	6,949	5,614	1,112	223	4,502	R	80.8%	16.0%	83.5%	16.5%
10,198	SUMMIT	5,093	3,330	1,184	579	2,146	R	65.4%	23.2%	73.8%	26.2%
26,033	TOOELE	9,712	6,024	3,132	556	2,892	R	62.0%	32.2%	65.8%	34.2%
20,506	UINTAH	7,332	6,045	1,049	238	4,996	R	82.4%	14.3%	85.2%	14.8%
218,106	UTAH	86,121	71,859	12,166	2,096	59,693	R	83.4%	14.1%	85.5%	14.5%
8,523	WASATCH	3,946	2,799	994	153	1,805	R	70.9%	25.2%	73.8%	26.2%
26,065	WASHINGTON	12,197	10,181	1,678	338	8,503	R	83.5%	13.8%	85.9%	14.1%
1,911	WAYNE	1,098	835	226	37	609	R	76.0%	20.6%	78.7%	21.3%
144,616	WEBER	62,599	43,807	15,404	3,388	28,403	R	70.0%	24.6%	74.0%	26.0%
1,461,037	TOTAL	604,222	439,687	124,266	40,269	315,421	R	72.8%	20.6%	78.0%	22.0%

UTAH

GOVERNOR 1980

1980 Census Population	County	Total Vote	Republican	Democratic	Other	Rep.-Dem. Plurality		Percentage Total Vote Rep.	Dem.	Major Vote Rep.	Dem.
4,378	BEAVER	2,149	683	1,464	2	781	D	31.8%	68.1%	31.8%	68.2%
33,222	BOX ELDER	15,010	8,009	6,963	38	1,046	R	53.4%	46.4%	53.5%	46.5%
57,176	CACHE	25,494	14,202	11,192	100	3,010	R	55.7%	43.9%	55.9%	44.1%
22,179	CARBON	9,018	2,143	6,867	8	4,724	D	23.8%	76.1%	23.8%	76.2%
769	DAGGETT	412	136	276		140	D	33.0%	67.0%	33.0%	67.0%
146,540	DAVIS	57,576	28,521	28,763	292	242	D	49.5%	50.0%	49.8%	50.2%
12,565	DUCHESNE	4,868	2,807	2,055	6	752	R	57.7%	42.2%	57.7%	42.3%
11,451	EMERY	4,548	1,640	2,897	11	1,257	D	36.1%	63.7%	36.1%	63.9%
3,673	GARFIELD	1,985	810	1,173	2	363	D	40.8%	59.1%	40.8%	59.2%
8,241	GRAND	3,266	1,410	1,849	7	439	D	43.2%	56.6%	43.3%	56.7%
17,349	IRON	7,741	2,926	4,795	20	1,869	D	37.8%	61.9%	37.9%	62.1%
5,530	JUAB	2,682	1,049	1,627	6	578	D	39.1%	60.7%	39.2%	60.8%
4,024	KANE	1,805	886	914	5	28	D	49.1%	50.6%	49.2%	50.8%
8,970	MILLARD	4,457	1,921	2,529	7	608	D	43.1%	56.7%	43.2%	56.8%
4,917	MORGAN	2,453	1,255	1,195	3	60	R	51.2%	48.7%	51.2%	48.8%
1,329	PIUTE	717	320	393	4	73	D	44.6%	54.8%	44.9%	55.1%
2,100	RICH	931	418	511	2	93	D	44.9%	54.9%	45.0%	55.0%
619,066	SALT LAKE	251,219	99,691	149,985	1,543	50,294	D	39.7%	59.7%	39.9%	60.1%
12,253	SAN JUAN	3,508	1,864	1,625	19	239	R	53.1%	46.3%	53.4%	46.6%
14,620	SANPETE	6,577	3,006	3,546	25	540	D	45.7%	53.9%	45.9%	54.1%
14,727	SEVIER	6,897	3,209	3,654	34	445	D	46.5%	53.0%	46.8%	53.2%
10,198	SUMMIT	5,000	1,859	3,135	6	1,276	D	37.2%	62.7%	37.2%	62.8%
26,033	TOOELE	9,694	4,614	5,051	29	437	D	47.6%	52.1%	47.7%	52.3%
20,506	UINTAH	7,219	4,064	3,145	10	919	R	56.3%	43.6%	56.4%	43.6%
218,106	UTAH	85,619	44,693	40,804	122	3,889	R	52.2%	47.7%	52.3%	47.7%
8,523	WASATCH	3,938	1,635	2,299	4	664	D	41.5%	58.4%	41.6%	58.4%
26,065	WASHINGTON	11,881	6,365	5,465	51	900	R	53.6%	46.0%	53.8%	46.2%
1,911	WAYNE	1,094	599	492	3	107	R	54.8%	45.0%	54.9%	45.1%
144,616	WEBER	62,261	25,843	36,310	108	10,467	D	41.5%	58.3%	41.6%	58.4%
1,461,037	TOTAL	600,019	266,578	330,974	2,467	64,396	D	44.4%	55.2%	44.6%	55.4%

UTAH

SENATOR 1980

1980 Census Population	County	Total Vote	Republican	Democratic	Other	Rep.-Dem. Plurality		Percentage Total Vote		Major Vote	
								Rep.	Dem.	Rep.	Dem.
4,378	BEAVER	2,134	1,553	578	3	975	R	72.8%	27.1%	72.9%	27.1%
33,222	BOX ELDER	14,816	12,312	2,444	60	9,868	R	83.1%	16.5%	83.4%	16.6%
57,176	CACHE	25,433	20,743	4,416	274	16,327	R	81.6%	17.4%	82.4%	17.6%
22,179	CARBON	8,904	4,039	4,848	17	809	D	45.4%	54.4%	45.4%	54.6%
769	DAGGETT	399	280	117	2	163	R	70.2%	29.3%	70.5%	29.5%
146,540	DAVIS	57,481	45,278	11,529	674	33,749	R	78.8%	20.1%	79.7%	20.3%
12,565	DUCHESNE	4,584	3,754	820	10	2,934	R	81.9%	17.9%	82.1%	17.9%
11,451	EMERY	4,511	3,026	1,471	14	1,555	R	67.1%	32.6%	67.3%	32.7%
3,673	GARFIELD	1,949	1,632	313	4	1,319	R	83.7%	16.1%	83.9%	16.1%
8,241	GRAND	3,204	2,397	794	13	1,603	R	74.8%	24.8%	75.1%	24.9%
17,349	IRON	7,652	6,260	1,374	18	4,886	R	81.8%	18.0%	82.0%	18.0%
5,530	JUAB	2,648	1,923	715	10	1,208	R	72.6%	27.0%	72.9%	27.1%
4,024	KANE	1,771	1,487	282	2	1,205	R	84.0%	15.9%	84.1%	15.9%
8,970	MILLARD	4,437	3,490	932	15	2,558	R	78.7%	21.0%	78.9%	21.1%
4,917	MORGAN	2,208	1,744	453	11	1,291	R	79.0%	20.5%	79.4%	20.6%
1,329	PIUTE	705	566	137	2	429	R	80.3%	19.4%	80.5%	19.5%
2,100	RICH	914	757	154	3	603	R	82.8%	16.8%	83.1%	16.9%
619,066	SALT LAKE	249,933	171,123	75,386	3,424	95,737	R	68.5%	30.2%	69.4%	30.6%
12,253	SAN JUAN	3,441	2,691	726	24	1,965	R	78.2%	21.1%	78.8%	21.2%
14,620	SANPETE	6,489	5,113	1,353	23	3,760	R	78.8%	20.9%	79.1%	20.9%
14,727	SEVIER	6,804	5,549	1,223	32	4,326	R	81.6%	18.0%	81.9%	18.1%
10,198	SUMMIT	4,867	3,313	1,531	23	1,782	R	68.1%	31.5%	68.4%	31.6%
26,033	TOOELE	9,632	6,474	3,122	36	3,352	R	67.2%	32.4%	67.5%	32.5%
20,506	UINTAH	7,135	5,747	1,368	20	4,379	R	80.5%	19.2%	80.8%	19.2%
218,106	UTAH	84,686	69,801	14,721	164	55,080	R	82.4%	17.4%	82.6%	17.4%
8,523	WASATCH	3,854	2,862	985	7	1,877	R	74.3%	25.6%	74.4%	25.6%
26,065	WASHINGTON	11,805	10,130	1,624	51	8,506	R	85.8%	13.8%	86.2%	13.8%
1,911	WAYNE	1,081	867	212	2	655	R	80.2%	19.6%	80.4%	19.6%
144,616	WEBER	60,821	42,764	17,826	231	24,938	R	70.3%	29.3%	70.6%	29.4%
1,461,037	TOTAL	594,298	437,675	151,454	5,169	286,221	R	73.6%	25.5%	74.3%	25.7%

UTAH

CONGRESS

CD	Year	Total Vote	Republican Vote	Candidate	Democratic Vote	Candidate	Other Vote	Rep.-Dem. Plurality	Percentage Total Vote Rep.	Dem.	Major Vote Rep.	Dem.
1	1980	301,570	157,111	HANSEN, JAMES V.	144,459	MCKAY, K. GUNN		12,652 R	52.1%	47.9%	52.1%	47.9%
1	1978	183,994	85,028	RICHARDSON, JED	93,892	MCKAY, K. GUNN	5,074	8,864 D	46.2%	51.0%	47.5%	52.5%
1	1976	267,531	106,542	FERGUSON, JOE H.	155,631	MCKAY, K. GUNN	5,358	49,089 D	39.8%	58.2%	40.6%	59.4%
1	1974	199,264	62,807	INKLEY, RON W.	124,793	MCKAY, K. GUNN	11,664	61,986 D	31.5%	62.6%	33.5%	66.5%
1	1972	229,366	96,296	WOLTHUIS, ROBERT K.	127,027	MCKAY, K. GUNN	6,043	30,731 D	42.0%	55.4%	43.1%	56.9%
2	1980	290,765	194,885	MARRIOTT, DAN	87,967	MONSON, ARTHUR L.	7,913	106,918 R	67.0%	30.3%	68.9%	31.1%
2	1978	195,166	121,492	MARRIOTT, DAN	68,899	FIRMAGE, EDWIN B.	4,775	52,593 R	62.3%	35.3%	63.8%	36.2%
2	1976	276,300	144,861	MARRIOTT, DAN	110,931	HOWE, ALLAN T.	20,508	33,930 R	52.4%	40.1%	56.6%	43.4%
2	1974	213,698	100,259	HARMSEN, STEPHEN M.	105,739	HOWE, ALLAN T.	7,700	5,480 D	46.9%	49.5%	48.7%	51.3%
2	1972	243,702	107,185	LLOYD, SHERMAN P.	132,832	OWENS, WAYNE	3,685	25,647 D	44.0%	54.5%	44.7%	55.3%

UTAH

1980 GENERAL ELECTION

President   Other vote was 30,284 Anderson (Independent); 7,226 Clark (Libertarian); 1,009 Commoner (Independent); 965 Greaves (American); 522 Rarick (Independent American); 139 Hall (Independent); 124 DeBerry (Socialist Workers). Original uncorrected canvass gave the Clark (Libertarian) state-wide total vote as 7,156.

Governor   Other vote was Topham (American).

Senator   Other vote was 3,186 Bangerter (Independent); 1,983 Batchelor (American).

Congress   Other vote was 5,411 Larsen (Independent); 1,520 Montgomery (American) and 982 Hurst (Socialist Workers) in CD 2.

1980 PRIMARIES

SEPTEMBER 9 REPUBLICAN

Governor   Bob Wright, nominated by convention.

Senator   E. J. Garn, nominated by convention.

Congress   Candidates nominated by convention in both CD's.

SEPTEMBER 9 DEMOCRATIC

Governor   Scott M. Matheson, nominated by convention.

Senator   28,930 Dan Berman; 28,643 A. Stephen Dirks.

Congress   Candidates nominated by convention in both CD's.

SEPTEMBER 9 AMERICAN

Governor   Jack J. Lambson, nominated by convention. Mr. Lambson withdrew and Larry Topham was substituted by the state committee.

Senator   675 George M. Batchelor; 563 Larry Topham.

Congress   No candidate in CD 1; candidate nominated by convention in CD 2.

VERMONT

GOVERNOR
Richard A. Snelling (R). Re-elected 1980 to a two-year term. Previously elected 1978, 1976.

SENATORS
Patrick J. Leahy (D). Re-elected 1980 to a six-year term. Previously elected 1974.

Robert T. Stafford (R). Re-elected 1976 to a six-year term. Previously elected January 1972 to fill out term vacated by the death of Senator Winston L. Prouty; had been appointed September 1971 to fill this same vacancy.

REPRESENTATIVE
At-Large. James M. Jeffords (R)

POSTWAR VOTE FOR GOVERNOR

Year	Total Vote	Republican Vote	Republican Candidate	Democratic Vote	Democratic Candidate	Other Vote	Rep.-Dem. Plurality	Total Vote Rep.	Total Vote Dem.	Major Vote Rep.	Major Vote Dem.
1980	210,381	123,229	Snelling, Richard A.	77,363	Diamond, M. Jerome	9,789	45,866 R	58.6%	36.8%	61.4%	38.6%
1978	124,482	78,181	Snelling, Richard A.	42,482	Granai, Edwin C.	3,819	35,699 R	62.8%	34.1%	64.8%	35.2%
1976	185,929	99,268	Snelling, Richard A.	75,262	Hackel, Stella B.	11,399	24,006 R	53.4%	40.5%	56.9%	43.1%
1974	141,156	53,672	Kennedy, Walter L.	79,842	Salmon, Thomas P.	7,642	26,170 D	38.0%	56.6%	40.2%	59.8%
1972	189,237	82,491	Hackett, Luther F.	104,533	Salmon, Thomas P.	2,213	22,042 D	43.6%	55.2%	44.1%	55.9%
1970	153,528	87,458	Davis, Deane C.	66,028	O'Brien, Leo	42	21,430 R	57.0%	43.0%	57.0%	43.0%
1968	161,089	89,387	Davis, Deane C.	71,656	Daley, John J.	46	17,731 R	55.5%	44.5%	55.5%	44.5%
1966	136,262	57,577	Snelling, Richard A.	78,669	Hoff, Philip H.	16	21,092 D	42.3%	57.7%	42.3%	57.7%
1964	164,199	57,576	Foote, Ralph A.	106,611	Hoff, Philip H.	12	49,035 D	35.1%	64.9%	35.1%	64.9%
1962	121,422	60,035	Keyser, F. Ray	61,383	Hoff, Philip H.	4	1,348 D	49.4%	50.6%	49.4%	50.6%
1960	164,632	92,861	Keyser, F. Ray	71,755	Niquette, Russell F.	16	21,106 R	56.4%	43.6%	56.4%	43.6%
1958	123,728	62,222	Stafford, Robert T.	61,503	Leddy, Bernard J.	3	719 R	50.3%	49.7%	50.3%	49.7%
1956	153,809	88,379	Johnson, Joseph B.	65,420	Branon, E. Frank	10	22,959 R	57.5%	42.5%	57.5%	42.5%
1954	114,360	59,778	Johnson, Joseph B.	54,554	Branon, E. Frank	28	5,224 R	52.3%	47.7%	52.3%	47.7%
1952	150,862	78,338	Emerson, Lee E.	60,051	Larrow, Robert W.	12,473	18,287 R	51.9%	39.8%	56.6%	43.4%
1950	87,155	64,915	Emerson, Lee E.	22,227	Moran, J. Edward	13	42,688 R	74.5%	25.5%	74.5%	25.5%
1948	120,183	86,394	Gibson, Ernest W., Jr.	33,588	Ryan, Charles F.	201	52,806 R	71.9%	27.9%	72.0%	28.0%
1946	72,044	57,849	Gibson, Ernest W., Jr.	14,096	Coburn, Berthold	99	43,753 R	80.3%	19.6%	80.4%	19.6%

POSTWAR VOTE FOR SENATOR

Year	Total Vote	Republican Vote	Republican Candidate	Democratic Vote	Democratic Candidate	Other Vote	Rep.-Dem. Plurality	Total Vote Rep.	Total Vote Dem.	Major Vote Rep.	Major Vote Dem.
1980	209,124	101,421	Ledbetter, Stewart M.	104,176	Leahy, Patrick J.	3,527	2,755 D	48.5%	49.8%	49.3%	50.7%
1976	189,060	94,481	Stafford, Robert T.	85,682	Salmon, Thomas P.	8,897	8,799 R	50.0%	45.3%	52.4%	47.6%
1974	142,772	66,223	Mallary, Richard W.	70,629	Leahy, Patrick J.	5,920	4,406 D	46.4%	49.5%	48.4%	51.6%
1972s	71,348	45,888	Stafford, Robert T.	23,842	Major, Randolph T.	1,618	22,046 R	64.3%	33.4%	65.8%	34.2%
1970	154,899	91,198	Prouty, Winston L.	62,271	Hoff, Philip H.	1,430	28,927 R	58.9%	40.2%	59.4%	40.6%
1968	157,375	157,154	Aiken, George D.	—	—	221	157,154 R	99.9%	—	100.0%	—
1964	164,350	87,879	Prouty, Winston L.	76,457	Fayette, Frederick J.	14	11,422 R	53.5%	46.5%	53.5%	46.5%
1962	121,571	81,241	Aiken, George D.	40,134	Johnson, W. Robert	196	41,107 R	66.8%	33.0%	66.9%	33.1%
1958	124,442	64,900	Prouty, Winston L.	59,536	Fayette, Frederick J.	6	5,364 R	52.2%	47.8%	52.2%	47.8%
1956	155,289	103,101	Aiken, George D.	52,184	O'Shea, Bernard G.	4	50,917 R	66.4%	33.6%	66.4%	33.6%
1952	154,052	111,406	Flanders, Ralph E.	42,630	Johnston, Allan R.	16	68,776 R	72.3%	27.7%	72.3%	27.7%
1950	89,171	69,543	Aiken, George D.	19,608	Bigelow, James E.	20	49,935 R	78.0%	22.0%	78.0%	22.0%
1946	73,340	54,729	Flanders, Ralph E.	18,594	McDevitt, Charles P.	17	36,135 R	74.6%	25.4%	74.6%	25.4%

In 1968 the Republican candidate won both major party nominations. The 1972 election was held in January for a short term to fill a vacancy.

VERMONT

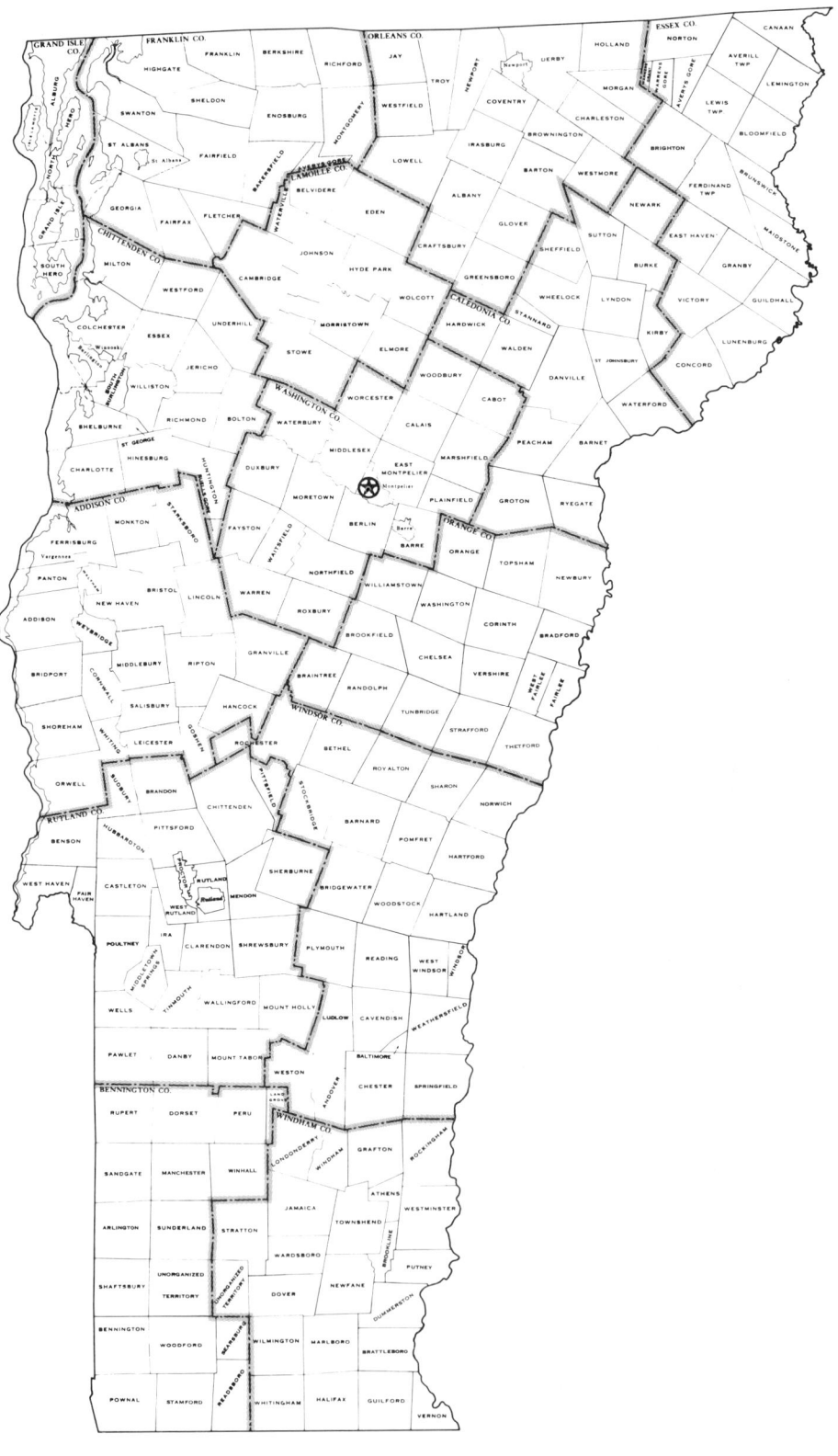

VERMONT

PRESIDENT 1980

1980 Census Population	County	Total Vote	Republican	Democratic	Other	Rep.-Dem. Plurality		Percentage			
								Total Vote		Major Vote	
								Rep.	Dem.	Rep.	Dem.
29,406	ADDISON	11,630	5,216	4,351	2,063	865	R	44.8%	37.4%	54.5%	45.5%
33,345	BENNINGTON	13,721	6,091	5,361	2,269	730	R	44.4%	39.1%	53.2%	46.8%
25,808	CALEDONIA	10,523	5,986	3,284	1,253	2,702	R	56.9%	31.2%	64.6%	35.4%
115,534	CHITTENDEN	47,003	18,310	19,027	9,666	717	D	39.0%	40.5%	49.0%	51.0%
6,313	ESSEX	2,340	1,305	799	236	506	R	55.8%	34.1%	62.0%	38.0%
34,788	FRANKLIN	13,445	5,998	5,914	1,533	84	R	44.6%	44.0%	50.4%	49.6%
4,613	GRAND ISLE	2,240	947	999	294	52	D	42.3%	44.6%	48.7%	51.3%
16,767	LAMOILLE	6,890	3,228	2,414	1,248	814	R	46.9%	35.0%	57.2%	42.8%
22,739	ORANGE	9,402	4,656	3,079	1,667	1,577	R	49.5%	32.7%	60.2%	39.8%
23,440	ORLEANS	9,217	4,503	3,671	1,043	832	R	48.9%	39.8%	55.1%	44.9%
58,347	RUTLAND	24,236	11,142	9,597	3,497	1,545	R	46.0%	39.6%	53.7%	46.3%
52,393	WASHINGTON	23,151	9,714	9,559	3,878	155	R	42.0%	41.3%	50.4%	49.6%
36,933	WINDHAM	16,598	7,062	5,830	3,706	1,232	R	42.5%	35.1%	54.8%	45.2%
51,030	WINDSOR	22,903	10,470	8,067	4,366	2,403	R	45.7%	35.2%	56.5%	43.5%
511,456	TOTAL	213,299	94,628	81,952	36,719	12,676	R	44.4%	38.4%	53.6%	46.4%

VERMONT

PRESIDENT 1980

1980 Census Population	City/Town	Total Vote	Republican	Democratic	Other	Rep.-Dem. Plurality		Percentage			
								Total Vote		Major Vote	
								Rep.	Dem.	Rep.	Dem.
9,824	BARRE CITY	3,975	1,603	1,857	515	254	D	40.3%	46.7%	46.3%	53.7%
7,090	BARRE TOWN	3,061	1,459	1,264	338	195	R	47.7%	41.3%	53.6%	46.4%
15,815	BENNINGTON TOWN	5,528	2,029	2,528	971	499	D	36.7%	45.7%	44.5%	55.5%
11,886	BRATTLEBORO	4,948	1,890	1,877	1,181	13	R	38.2%	37.9%	50.2%	49.8%
37,712	BURLINGTON	14,682	4,506	6,752	3,424	2,246	D	30.7%	46.0%	40.0%	60.0%
12,629	COLCHESTER	4,115	1,717	1,664	734	53	R	41.7%	40.4%	50.8%	49.2%
14,392	ESSEX TOWN	5,414	2,528	1,859	1,027	669	R	46.7%	34.3%	57.6%	42.4%
7,963	HARTFORD	2,935	1,373	981	581	392	R	46.8%	33.4%	58.3%	41.7%
7,574	MIDDLEBURY	2,789	1,119	1,109	561	10	R	40.1%	39.8%	50.2%	49.8%
6,829	MILTON	2,492	1,104	992	396	112	R	44.3%	39.8%	52.7%	47.3%
8,241	MONTPELIER	4,193	1,824	1,575	794	249	R	43.5%	37.6%	53.7%	46.3%
5,435	NORTHFIELD	2,147	965	873	309	92	R	44.9%	40.7%	52.5%	47.5%
5,538	ROCKINGHAM	2,172	874	919	379	45	D	40.2%	42.3%	48.7%	51.3%
18,436	RUTLAND CITY	7,257	2,921	3,284	1,052	363	D	40.3%	45.3%	47.1%	52.9%
7,308	ST. ALBANS CITY	3,108	1,381	1,395	332	14	D	44.4%	44.9%	49.7%	50.3%
7,938	ST. JOHNSBURY	3,309	1,918	1,055	336	863	R	58.0%	31.9%	64.5%	35.5%
5,000	SHELBURNE	2,548	1,202	781	565	421	R	47.2%	30.7%	60.6%	39.4%
10,679	SOUTH BURLINGTON	5,470	2,324	2,044	1,102	280	R	42.5%	37.4%	53.2%	46.8%
10,190	SPRINGFIELD	4,572	2,048	1,725	799	323	R	44.8%	37.7%	54.3%	45.7%
5,141	SWANTON	1,636	761	739	136	22	R	46.5%	45.2%	50.7%	49.3%
6,318	WINOOSKI	2,434	686	1,425	323	739	D	28.2%	58.5%	32.5%	67.5%

VERMONT

GOVERNOR 1980

1980 Census Population	County	Total Vote	Republican	Democratic	Other	Rep.-Dem. Plurality	Percentage Total Vote		Percentage Major Vote	
							Rep.	Dem.	Rep.	Dem.
29,406	ADDISON	11,505	6,933	4,128	444	2,805 R	60.3%	35.9%	62.7%	37.3%
33,345	BENNINGTON	13,269	8,661	4,062	546	4,599 R	65.3%	30.6%	68.1%	31.9%
25,808	CALEDONIA	10,382	5,601	4,207	574	1,394 R	53.9%	40.5%	57.1%	42.9%
115,534	CHITTENDEN	46,357	26,720	17,880	1,757	8,840 R	57.6%	38.6%	59.9%	40.1%
6,313	ESSEX	2,311	1,248	1,003	60	245 R	54.0%	43.4%	55.4%	44.6%
34,788	FRANKLIN	13,308	5,722	6,380	1,206	658 D	43.0%	47.9%	47.3%	52.7%
4,613	GRAND ISLE	2,288	1,176	999	113	177 R	51.4%	43.7%	54.1%	45.9%
16,767	LAMOILLE	6,813	4,076	2,205	532	1,871 R	59.8%	32.4%	64.9%	35.1%
22,739	ORANGE	9,301	5,865	3,047	389	2,818 R	63.1%	32.8%	65.8%	34.2%
23,440	ORLEANS	9,138	4,676	4,067	395	609 R	51.2%	44.5%	53.5%	46.5%
58,347	RUTLAND	23,990	14,636	8,145	1,209	6,491 R	61.0%	34.0%	64.2%	35.8%
52,393	WASHINGTON	22,797	12,565	9,124	1,108	3,441 R	55.1%	40.0%	57.9%	42.1%
36,933	WINDHAM	16,352	10,616	5,005	731	5,611 R	64.9%	30.6%	68.0%	32.0%
51,030	WINDSOR	22,570	14,734	7,111	725	7,623 R	65.3%	31.5%	67.4%	32.6%
511,456	TOTAL	210,381	123,229	77,363	9,789	45,866 R	58.6%	36.8%	61.4%	38.6%

VERMONT

GOVERNOR 1980

1980 Census Population	City/Town	Total Vote	Republican	Democratic	Other	Rep.-Dem. Plurality	Percentage Total Vote		Percentage Major Vote	
							Rep.	Dem.	Rep.	Dem.
9,824	BARRE CITY	3,962	2,008	1,833	121	175 R	50.7%	46.3%	52.3%	47.7%
7,090	BARRE TOWN	3,049	1,790	1,171	88	619 R	58.7%	38.4%	60.5%	39.5%
15,815	BENNINGTON TOWN	5,218	3,198	1,757	263	1,441 R	61.3%	33.7%	64.5%	35.5%
11,886	BRATTLEBORO	4,892	3,202	1,481	209	1,721 R	65.5%	30.3%	68.4%	31.6%
37,712	BURLINGTON	14,498	7,484	6,286	728	1,198 R	51.6%	43.4%	54.4%	45.6%
12,629	COLCHESTER	4,029	2,275	1,622	132	653 R	56.5%	40.3%	58.4%	41.6%
14,392	ESSEX TOWN	5,258	3,491	1,592	175	1,899 R	66.4%	30.3%	68.7%	31.3%
7,963	HARTFORD	2,909	2,023	813	73	1,210 R	69.5%	27.9%	71.3%	28.7%
7,574	MIDDLEBURY	2,694	1,720	902	72	818 R	63.8%	33.5%	65.6%	34.4%
6,829	MILTON	2,471	1,265	1,121	85	144 R	51.2%	45.4%	53.0%	47.0%
8,241	MONTPELIER	3,990	2,358	1,366	266	992 R	59.1%	34.2%	63.3%	36.7%
5,435	NORTHFIELD	2,105	1,247	786	72	461 R	59.2%	37.3%	61.3%	38.7%
5,538	ROCKINGHAM	2,164	1,203	883	78	320 R	55.6%	40.8%	57.7%	42.3%
18,436	RUTLAND CITY	7,184	4,246	2,478	460	1,768 R	59.1%	34.5%	63.1%	36.9%
7,308	ST. ALBANS CITY	3,004	1,350	1,495	159	145 D	44.9%	49.8%	47.5%	52.5%
7,938	ST. JOHNSBURY	3,292	1,859	1,309	124	550 R	56.5%	39.8%	58.7%	41.3%
5,000	SHELBURNE	2,542	1,916	563	63	1,353 R	75.4%	22.1%	77.3%	22.7%
10,679	SOUTH BURLINGTON	5,424	3,411	1,876	137	1,535 R	62.9%	34.6%	64.5%	35.5%
10,190	SPRINGFIELD	4,464	2,641	1,684	139	957 R	59.2%	37.7%	61.1%	38.9%
5,141	SWANTON	1,632	789	773	70	16 R	48.3%	47.4%	50.5%	49.5%
6,318	WINOOSKI	2,328	898	1,334	96	436 D	38.6%	57.3%	40.2%	59.8%

VERMONT

SENATOR 1980

1980 Census Population	County	Total Vote	Republican	Democratic	Other	Rep.-Dem. Plurality	Percentage			
							Total Vote		Major Vote	
							Rep.	Dem.	Rep.	Dem.
29,406	ADDISON	11,464	5,724	5,610	130	114 R	49.9%	48.9%	50.5%	49.5%
33,345	BENNINGTON	13,080	6,777	5,896	407	881 R	51.8%	45.1%	53.5%	46.5%
25,808	CALEDONIA	10,324	5,874	4,325	125	1,549 R	56.9%	41.9%	57.6%	42.4%
115,534	CHITTENDEN	46,040	20,071	25,305	664	5,234 D	43.6%	55.0%	44.2%	55.8%
6,313	ESSEX	2,259	1,227	994	38	233 R	54.3%	44.0%	55.2%	44.8%
34,788	FRANKLIN	13,257	6,143	6,944	170	801 D	46.3%	52.4%	46.9%	53.1%
4,613	GRAND ISLE	2,209	981	1,205	23	224 D	44.4%	54.5%	44.9%	55.1%
16,767	LAMOILLE	6,765	3,636	3,005	124	631 R	53.7%	44.4%	54.8%	45.2%
22,739	ORANGE	9,198	4,920	4,129	149	791 R	53.5%	44.9%	54.4%	45.6%
23,440	ORLEANS	9,004	4,711	4,142	151	569 R	52.3%	46.0%	53.2%	46.8%
58,347	RUTLAND	23,865	11,793	11,668	404	125 R	49.4%	48.9%	50.3%	49.7%
52,393	WASHINGTON	22,878	10,129	12,439	310	2,310 D	44.3%	54.4%	44.9%	55.1%
36,933	WINDHAM	16,307	7,833	8,025	449	192 D	48.0%	49.2%	49.4%	50.6%
51,030	WINDSOR	22,474	11,602	10,489	383	1,113 R	51.6%	46.7%	52.5%	47.5%
511,456	TOTAL	209,124	101,421	104,176	3,527	2,755 D	48.5%	49.8%	49.3%	50.7%

VERMONT

SENATOR 1980

1980 Census Population	City/Town	Total Vote	Republican	Democratic	Other	Rep.-Dem. Plurality	Percentage			
							Total Vote		Major Vote	
							Rep.	Dem.	Rep.	Dem.
9,824	BARRE CITY	3,950	1,622	2,291	37	669 D	41.1%	58.0%	41.5%	58.5%
7,090	BARRE TOWN	3,025	1,418	1,577	30	159 D	46.9%	52.1%	47.3%	52.7%
15,815	BENNINGTON TOWN	5,117	2,454	2,459	204	5 D	48.0%	48.1%	49.9%	50.1%
11,886	BRATTLEBORO	4,873	2,153	2,605	115	452 D	44.2%	53.5%	45.3%	54.7%
37,712	BURLINGTON	14,207	4,979	8,943	285	3,964 D	35.0%	62.9%	35.8%	64.2%
12,629	COLCHESTER	4,029	1,965	2,026	38	61 D	48.8%	50.3%	49.2%	50.8%
14,392	ESSEX TOWN	5,281	2,720	2,492	69	228 R	51.5%	47.2%	52.2%	47.8%
7,963	HARTFORD	2,884	1,506	1,340	38	166 R	52.2%	46.5%	52.9%	47.1%
7,574	MIDDLEBURY	2,718	1,223	1,468	27	245 D	45.0%	54.0%	45.4%	54.6%
6,829	MILTON	2,452	1,235	1,197	20	38 R	50.4%	48.8%	50.8%	49.2%
8,241	MONTPELIER	4,143	1,886	2,187	70	301 D	45.5%	52.8%	46.3%	53.7%
5,435	NORTHFIELD	2,101	1,085	992	24	93 R	51.6%	47.2%	52.2%	47.8%
5,538	ROCKINGHAM	2,144	971	1,138	35	167 D	45.3%	53.1%	46.0%	54.0%
18,436	RUTLAND CITY	7,228	3,159	3,943	126	784 D	43.7%	54.6%	44.5%	55.5%
7,308	ST. ALBANS CITY	3,057	1,444	1,584	29	140 D	47.2%	51.8%	47.7%	52.3%
7,938	ST. JOHNSBURY	3,249	1,840	1,370	39	470 R	56.6%	42.2%	57.3%	42.7%
5,000	SHELBURNE	2,531	1,279	1,224	28	55 R	50.5%	48.4%	51.1%	48.9%
10,679	SOUTH BURLINGTON	5,428	2,424	2,960	44	536 D	44.7%	54.5%	45.0%	55.0%
10,190	SPRINGFIELD	4,483	2,264	2,150	69	114 R	50.5%	48.0%	51.3%	48.7%
5,141	SWANTON	1,617	737	877	3	140 D	45.6%	54.2%	45.7%	54.3%
6,318	WINOOSKI	2,307	839	1,391	77	552 D	36.4%	60.3%	37.6%	62.4%

VERMONT

CONGRESS

CD	Year	Total Vote	Republican Vote	Republican Candidate	Democratic Vote	Democratic Candidate	Other Vote	Rep.-Dem. Plurality	Total Vote Rep.	Total Vote Dem.	Major Vote Rep.	Major Vote Dem.
AL	1980	194,697	154,274	JEFFORDS, JAMES M.			40,423	154,274 R	79.2%		100.0%	
AL	1978	120,502	90,688	JEFFORDS, JAMES M.	23,228	DIETZ, S. MARIE	6,586	67,460 R	75.3%	19.3%	79.6%	20.4%
AL	1976	184,783	124,458	JEFFORDS, JAMES M.	60,202	*BURGESS, JOHN A.	123	64,256 R	67.4%	32.6%	67.4%	32.6%
AL	1974	140,899	74,561	JEFFORDS, JAMES M.	56,342	*CAIN, FRANCIS J.	9,996	18,219 R	52.9%	40.0%	57.0%	43.0%
AL	1972	186,028	120,924	MALLARY, RICHARD W.	65,062	MEYER, WILLIAM H.	42	55,862 R	65.0%	35.0%	65.0%	35.0%
AL	1970	152,557	103,806	*STAFFORD, ROBERT T.	44,415	O'SHEA, BERNARD G.	4,336	59,391 R	68.0%	29.1%	70.0%	30.0%
AL	1968	157,133	156,956	*STAFFORD, ROBERT T.			177	156,956 R	99.9%		100.0%	
AL	1966	135,748	89,097	STAFFORD, ROBERT T.	46,643	RYAN, WILLIAM J.	8	42,454 R	65.6%	34.4%	65.6%	34.4%
AL	1964	163,452	92,252	STAFFORD, ROBERT T.	71,193	O'SHEA, BERNARD G.	7	21,059 R	56.4%	43.6%	56.4%	43.6%
AL	1962	121,381	68,822	STAFFORD, ROBERT T.	52,535	RAYNOLDS, HAROLD	24	16,287 R	56.7%	43.3%	56.7%	43.3%
AL	1960	166,035	94,905	STAFFORD, ROBERT T.	71,111	MEYER, WILLIAM H.	19	23,794 R	57.2%	42.8%	57.2%	42.8%
AL	1958	122,702	59,536	ARTHUR, HAROLD J.	63,131	MEYER, WILLIAM H.	35	3,595 D	48.5%	51.5%	48.5%	51.5%
AL	1956	154,536	103,736	PROUTY, WINSTON L.	50,797	ST. AMOUR, CAMILLE	3	52,939 R	67.1%	32.9%	67.1%	32.9%
AL	1954	114,289	70,143	PROUTY, WINSTON L.	44,141	BOYLAN, JOHN J.	5	26,002 R	61.4%	38.6%	61.4%	38.6%
AL	1952	153,060	109,871	PROUTY, WINSTON L.	43,187	COMINGS, HERBERT B.	2	66,684 R	71.8%	28.2%	71.8%	28.2%
AL	1950	88,851	65,248	PROUTY, WINSTON L.	22,709	COMINGS, HERBERT B.	894	42,539 R	73.4%	25.6%	74.2%	25.8%
AL	1948	121,968	74,076	PLUMLEY, CHARLES A.	47,767	READY, ROBERT W.	125	26,309 R	60.7%	39.2%	60.8%	39.2%
AL	1946	73,066	46,985	PLUMLEY, CHARLES A.	26,056	CALDBECK, MATTHEW J.	25	20,929 R	64.3%	35.7%	64.3%	35.7%

VERMONT

1980 GENERAL ELECTION

In addition to the county-by-county figures, data are presented for selected Vermont communities. Since not all jurisdictions of the state are listed in this tabulation, state-wide totals are shown only with the county-by-county statistics.

President   Other vote was 31,761 Anderson (Independent); 2,316 Commoner (Citizens); 1,900 Clark (Libertarian); 136 McReynolds (Liberty Union); 118 Hall (Communist); 75 DeBerry (Socialist Workers); 413 scattered.

Governor   Other vote was 5,323 Woodward (Independent); 2,263 Cullen (Independent); 1,952 Potthast (Liberty Union); 251 scattered.

Senator   Other vote was 1,776 Doria (Independent); 1,629 Gardner (Liberty Union); 122 scattered.

Congress   An asterisk in the Congressional vote table indicates a candidate received votes from another party endorsing his/her candidacy. Other vote was 24,758 Lloyd (Citizens); 15,218 Diamondstone (Liberty Union); 447 scattered.

1980 PRIMARIES

SEPTEMBER 9 REPUBLICAN

Governor   38,228 Richard A. Snelling; 3,432 Clifford Thompson; 2,273 Kirk E. Faryniasz; 1,059 scattered.

Senator   16,518 Stewart M. Ledbetter; 12,256 James E. Mullin; 8,575 Tom Evslin; 5,209 T. Garry Buckley; 3,450 Robert Schuettinger; 496 Anthony N. Doria; 316 scattered.

Congress   Unopposed at-large.

SEPTEMBER 9 DEMOCRATIC

Governor   15,738 M. Jerome Diamond; 14,857 Timothy J. O'Connor; 406 John Potthast; 255 scattered.

Senator   Patrick J. Leahy, unopposed.

Congress   No candidates names appeared on the ballot; there were 2,794 write-in votes of which James M. Jeffords, the Republican candidate, received 2,180. He refused the nomination.

SEPTEMBER 9 LIBERTY UNION

Governor   No candidate in the primary. John Potthast nominated by the party after the primary.

Senator   Earl S. Gardner, unopposed.

Congress   Unopposed at-large.

VIRGINIA

GOVERNOR
John Dalton (R). Elected 1977 to a four-year term.

SENATORS
Harry Flood Byrd, Jr. (I). Re-elected 1976 to a six-year term. Previously elected 1970 as an Independent and 1966 as a Democrat to fill out term vacated by the resignation of Senator Harry Flood Byrd; had been appointed November 1965 to fill this same vacancy.

John Warner (R). Elected 1978 to a six-year term.

REPRESENTATIVES
1. Paul Trible (R)
2. G. W. Whitehurst (R)
3. Thomas J. Bliley (R)
4. Robert W. Daniel (R)
5. W. C. Daniel (D)
6. M. Caldwell Butler (R)
7. J. Kenneth Robinson (R)
8. Stanford E. Parris (R)
9. William C. Wampler (R)
10. Frank R. Wolf (R)

POSTWAR VOTE FOR GOVERNOR

Year	Total Vote	Republican Vote	Candidate	Democratic Vote	Candidate	Other Vote	Rep.-Dem. Plurality	Total Vote Rep.	Dem.	Major Vote Rep.	Dem.
1977	1,250,940	699,302	Dalton, John	541,319	Howell, Henry	10,319	157,983 R	55.9%	43.3%	56.4%	43.6%
1973	1,035,495	525,075	Godwin, Mills E.	—	—	510,420	525,075 R	50.7%	—	100.0%	—
1969	915,764	480,869	Holton, Linwood	415,695	Battle, William C.	19,200	65,174 R	52.5%	45.4%	53.6%	46.4%
1965	562,789	212,207	Holton, Linwood	269,526	Godwin, Mills E.	81,056	57,319 D	37.7%	47.9%	44.1%	55.9%
1961	394,490	142,567	Pearson, H. Clyde	251,861	Harrison, Albertis	62	109,294 D	36.1%	63.8%	36.1%	63.9%
1957	517,655	188,628	Dalton, Ted	326,921	Almond, J. Lindsay	2,106	138,293 D	36.4%	63.2%	36.6%	63.4%
1953	414,025	183,328	Dalton, Ted	226,998	Stanley, Thomas B.	3,699	43,670 D	44.3%	54.8%	44.7%	55.3%
1949	262,350	71,991	Johnson, Walter	184,772	Battle, John S.	5,587	112,781 D	27.4%	70.4%	28.0%	72.0%
1945	168,783	52,386	Landreth, S. Floyd	112,355	Tuck, William M.	4,042	59,969 D	31.0%	66.6%	31.8%	68.2%

In 1973, other vote was 510,103 Henry Howell (Independent) and 317 scattered.

POSTWAR VOTE FOR SENATOR

Year	Total Vote	Republican Vote	Candidate	Democratic Vote	Candidate	Other Vote	Rep.-Dem. Plurality	Total Vote Rep.	Dem.	Major Vote Rep.	Dem.
1978	1,222,256	613,232	Warner, John	608,511	Miller, Andrew P.	513	4,721 R	50.2%	49.8%	50.2%	49.8%
1976	1,557,500	—	—	596,009	Zumwalt, Elmo R.	961,491	596,009 D	—	38.3%	—	100.0%
1972	1,396,268	718,337	Scott, William L.	643,963	Spong, William B.	33,968	74,374 R	51.4%	46.1%	52.7%	47.3%
1970	946,751	145,031	Garland, Ray	295,057	Rawlings, George C.	506,663	150,026 D	15.3%	31.2%	33.0%	67.0%
1966	733,879	245,681	Ould, James P.	429,855	Spong, William B.	58,343	184,174 D	33.5%	58.6%	36.4%	63.6%
1966s	729,839	272,804	Traylor, Lawrence M.	389,028	Byrd, Harry Flood, Jr.	68,007	116,224 D	37.4%	53.3%	41.2%	58.8%
1964	928,363	176,624	May, Richard A.	592,260	Byrd, Harry Flood	159,479	415,636 D	19.0%	63.8%	23.0%	77.0%
1960	622,820	—	—	506,169	Robertson, A. Willis	116,651	506,169 D	—	81.3%	—	100.0%
1958	457,640	—	—	317,221	Byrd, Harry Flood	140,419	317,221 D	—	69.3%	—	100.0%
1954	306,510	—	—	244,844	Robertson, A. Willis	61,666	244,844 D	—	79.9%	—	100.0%
1952	543,516	—	—	398,677	Byrd, Harry Flood	144,839	398,677 D	—	73.4%	—	100.0%
1948	386,178	118,546	Woods, Robert	253,865	Robertson, A. Willis	13,767	135,319 D	30.7%	65.7%	31.8%	68.2%
1946	252,863	77,005	Parsons, Lester S.	163,960	Byrd, Harry Flood	11,898	86,955 D	30.5%	64.8%	32.0%	68.0%
1946s	248,962	72,253	Woods, Robert	169,680	Robertson, A. Willis	7,029	97,427 D	29.0%	68.2%	29.9%	70.1%

One each of the 1966 and 1946 elections was for a short term to fill a vacancy. In 1970 Harry Flood Byrd, Jr., the Independent candidate, polled 506,633 votes (53.5% of the total vote) and won the election with a 211,576 plurality. In 1976 Harry Flood Byrd, Jr., polled 890,778 votes as an Independent candidate (57.2% of the total vote) and won the election with a 294,769 plurality.

393

VIRGINIA

Districts Established March 11, 1972

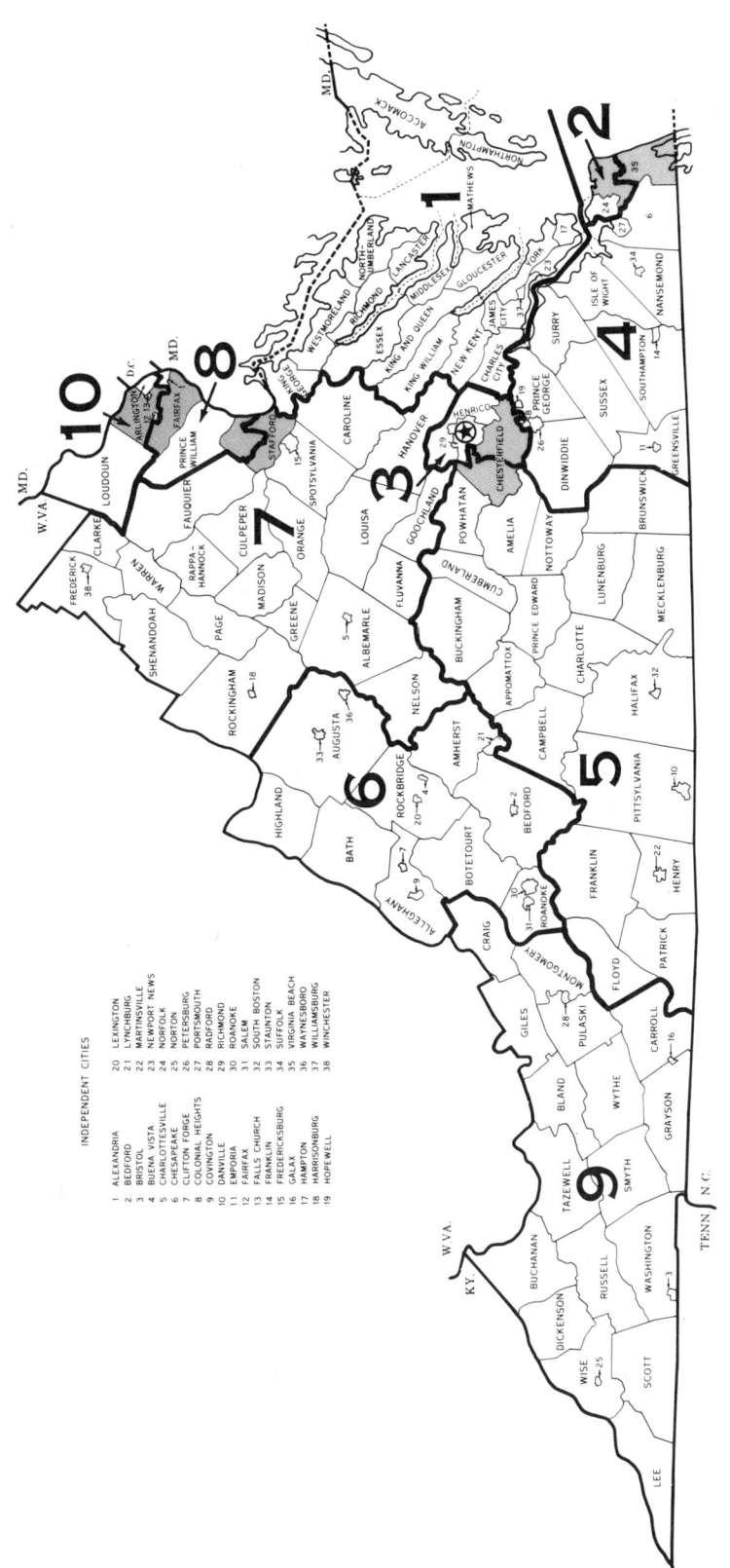

County with two or more Congressional Districts.

VIRGINIA

PRESIDENT 1980

1980 Census Population	County	Total Vote	Republican	Democratic	Other	Rep.-Dem. Plurality	Percentage Total Vote Rep.	Dem.	Percentage Major Vote Rep.	Dem.
31,268	ACCOMACK	10,698	5,371	4,872	455	499 R	50.2%	45.5%	52.4%	47.6%
50,689	ALBEMARLE	19,582	10,424	7,293	1,865	3,131 R	53.2%	37.2%	58.8%	41.2%
14,333	ALLEGHANY	4,756	2,185	2,411	160	226 D	45.9%	50.7%	47.5%	52.5%
8,405	AMELIA	3,701	1,969	1,643	89	326 R	53.2%	44.4%	54.5%	45.5%
29,122	AMHERST	8,840	5,088	3,476	276	1,612 R	57.6%	39.3%	59.4%	40.6%
11,971	APPOMATTOX	4,217	2,548	1,492	177	1,056 R	60.4%	35.4%	63.1%	36.9%
152,599	ARLINGTON	66,861	30,854	26,502	9,505	4,352 R	46.1%	39.6%	53.8%	46.2%
53,732	AUGUSTA	17,120	11,011	5,202	907	5,809 R	64.3%	30.4%	67.9%	32.1%
5,860	BATH	2,007	921	999	87	78 D	45.9%	49.8%	48.0%	52.0%
34,927	BEDFORD COUNTY	11,840	6,608	4,721	511	1,887 R	55.8%	39.9%	58.3%	41.7%
6,349	BLAND	2,345	1,278	1,002	65	276 R	54.5%	42.7%	56.1%	43.9%
23,270	BOTETOURT	8,602	4,408	3,698	496	710 R	51.2%	43.0%	54.4%	45.6%
15,632	BRUNSWICK	5,864	2,310	3,430	124	1,120 D	39.4%	58.5%	40.2%	59.8%
37,989	BUCHANAN	10,629	4,554	5,768	307	1,214 D	42.8%	54.3%	44.1%	55.9%
11,751	BUCKINGHAM	3,923	1,864	1,933	126	69 D	47.5%	49.3%	49.1%	50.9%
45,424	CAMPBELL	14,721	9,592	4,473	656	5,119 R	65.2%	30.4%	68.2%	31.8%
17,904	CAROLINE	5,154	2,071	2,924	159	853 D	40.2%	56.7%	41.5%	58.5%
27,270	CARROLL	9,634	5,905	3,437	292	2,468 R	61.3%	35.7%	63.2%	36.8%
6,692	CHARLES CITY	2,131	506	1,564	61	1,058 D	23.7%	73.4%	24.4%	75.6%
12,266	CHARLOTTE	4,530	2,322	2,108	100	214 R	51.3%	46.5%	52.4%	47.6%
141,372	CHESTERFIELD	53,613	37,908	13,060	2,645	24,848 R	70.7%	24.4%	74.4%	25.6%
9,965	CLARKE	3,266	1,876	1,156	234	720 R	57.4%	35.4%	61.9%	38.1%
3,948	CRAIG	1,779	768	946	65	178 D	43.2%	53.2%	44.8%	55.2%
22,620	CULPEPER	7,255	4,312	2,519	424	1,793 R	59.4%	34.7%	63.1%	36.9%
7,881	CUMBERLAND	3,024	1,515	1,355	154	160 R	50.1%	44.8%	52.8%	47.2%
19,806	DICKENSON	7,995	3,687	4,177	131	490 D	46.1%	52.2%	46.9%	53.1%
22,602	DINWIDDIE	7,018	3,369	3,475	174	106 D	48.0%	49.5%	49.2%	50.8%
8,864	ESSEX	2,987	1,581	1,280	126	301 R	52.9%	42.9%	55.3%	44.7%
596,901	FAIRFAX COUNTY	239,705	137,620	73,734	28,351	63,886 R	57.4%	30.8%	65.1%	34.9%
35,889	FAUQUIER	11,670	6,782	4,119	769	2,663 R	58.1%	35.3%	62.2%	37.8%
11,563	FLOYD	4,323	2,447	1,642	234	805 R	56.6%	38.0%	59.8%	40.2%
10,244	FLUVANNA	3,184	1,605	1,424	155	181 R	50.4%	44.7%	53.0%	47.0%
35,740	FRANKLIN COUNTY	11,090	4,993	5,685	412	692 D	45.0%	51.3%	46.8%	53.2%
34,150	FREDERICK	10,787	7,293	2,948	546	4,345 R	67.6%	27.3%	71.2%	28.8%
17,810	GILES	6,940	2,978	3,627	335	649 D	42.9%	52.3%	45.1%	54.9%
20,107	GLOUCESTER	7,897	4,261	3,138	498	1,123 R	54.0%	39.7%	57.6%	42.4%
11,761	GOOCHLAND	4,877	2,423	2,290	164	133 R	49.7%	47.0%	51.4%	48.6%
16,579	GRAYSON	6,547	3,494	2,875	178	619 R	53.4%	43.9%	54.9%	45.1%
7,625	GREENE	2,811	1,702	925	184	777 R	60.5%	32.9%	64.8%	35.2%
10,903	GREENSVILLE	3,800	1,583	2,142	75	559 D	41.7%	56.4%	42.5%	57.5%
30,418	HALIFAX	9,836	5,088	4,528	220	560 R	51.7%	46.0%	52.9%	47.1%
50,398	HANOVER	20,368	14,262	5,383	723	8,879 R	70.0%	26.4%	72.6%	27.4%
180,735	HENRICO	75,551	50,505	21,023	4,023	29,482 R	66.8%	27.8%	70.6%	29.4%
57,654	HENRY	17,783	8,258	8,800	725	542 D	46.4%	49.5%	48.4%	51.6%
2,937	HIGHLAND	1,278	751	487	40	264 R	58.8%	38.1%	60.7%	39.3%
21,603	ISLE OF WIGHT	7,784	3,526	3,951	307	425 D	45.3%	50.8%	47.2%	52.8%
22,763	JAMES CITY	8,048	4,289	3,068	691	1,221 R	53.3%	38.1%	58.3%	41.7%
5,968	KING AND QUEEN	2,150	949	1,128	73	179 D	44.1%	52.5%	45.7%	54.3%
10,543	KING GEORGE	3,332	1,784	1,318	230	466 R	53.5%	39.6%	57.5%	42.5%
9,327	KING WILLIAM	3,601	2,036	1,446	119	590 R	56.5%	40.2%	58.5%	41.5%
10,129	LANCASTER	4,557	2,780	1,567	210	1,213 R	61.0%	34.4%	64.0%	36.0%
25,956	LEE	9,377	4,417	4,758	202	341 D	47.1%	50.7%	48.1%	51.9%
57,427	LOUDOUN	20,492	12,076	6,694	1,722	5,382 R	58.9%	32.7%	64.3%	35.7%
17,825	LOUISA	5,706	2,633	2,809	264	176 D	46.1%	49.2%	48.4%	51.6%
12,124	LUNENBURG	4,136	2,045	1,958	133	87 R	49.4%	47.3%	51.1%	48.9%
10,232	MADISON	3,521	1,959	1,351	211	608 R	55.6%	38.4%	59.2%	40.8%
7,995	MATHEWS	3,716	2,204	1,300	212	904 R	59.3%	35.0%	62.9%	37.1%
29,444	MECKLENBURG	8,913	4,853	3,790	270	1,063 R	54.4%	42.5%	56.1%	43.9%
7,719	MIDDLESEX	3,344	1,810	1,395	139	415 R	54.1%	41.7%	56.5%	43.5%
63,516	MONTGOMERY	17,344	8,222	7,455	1,667	767 R	47.4%	43.0%	52.4%	47.6%
12,204	NELSON	4,496	1,866	2,410	220	544 D	41.5%	53.6%	43.6%	56.4%
8,781	NEW KENT	3,035	1,739	1,204	92	535 R	57.3%	39.7%	59.1%	40.9%
14,625	NORTHAMPTON	4,743	2,165	2,363	215	198 D	45.6%	49.8%	47.8%	52.2%
9,828	NORTHUMBERLAND	4,330	2,598	1,551	181	1,047 R	60.0%	35.8%	62.6%	37.4%
14,666	NOTTOWAY	5,611	2,813	2,593	205	220 R	50.1%	46.2%	52.0%	48.0%
17,827	ORANGE	6,158	3,381	2,420	357	961 R	54.9%	39.3%	58.3%	41.7%
19,401	PAGE	7,138	4,297	2,607	234	1,690 R	60.2%	36.5%	62.2%	37.8%
17,585	PATRICK	6,123	3,436	2,382	305	1,054 R	56.1%	38.9%	59.1%	40.9%
66,147	PITTSYLVANIA	20,280	12,022	7,653	605	4,369 R	59.3%	37.7%	61.1%	38.9%
13,062	POWHATAN	4,570	2,933	1,484	153	1,449 R	64.2%	32.5%	66.4%	33.6%

VIRGINIA

PRESIDENT 1980

1980 Census Population	County	Total Vote	Republican	Democratic	Other	Rep.-Dem. Plurality		Percentage Total Vote Rep.	Dem.	Major Vote Rep.	Dem.
16,456	PRINCE EDWARD	5,598	2,774	2,553	271	221	R	49.6%	45.6%	52.1%	47.9%
25,733	PRINCE GEORGE	5,888	3,389	2,310	189	1,079	R	57.6%	39.2%	59.5%	40.5%
144,703	PRINCE WILLIAM	39,119	23,061	12,787	3,271	10,274	R	59.0%	32.7%	64.3%	35.7%
35,229	PULASKI	12,040	5,747	5,769	524	22	D	47.7%	47.9%	49.9%	50.1%
6,093	RAPPAHANNOCK	2,367	1,179	1,055	133	124	R	49.8%	44.6%	52.8%	47.2%
6,952	RICHMOND COUNTY	2,495	1,567	854	74	713	R	62.8%	34.2%	64.7%	35.3%
72,945	ROANOKE COUNTY	30,814	17,182	12,114	1,518	5,068	R	55.8%	39.3%	58.6%	41.4%
17,911	ROCKBRIDGE	5,677	2,784	2,475	418	309	R	49.0%	43.6%	52.9%	47.1%
57,038	ROCKINGHAM	17,859	11,397	5,294	1,168	6,103	R	63.8%	29.6%	68.3%	31.7%
31,761	RUSSELL	10,874	4,778	5,764	332	986	D	43.9%	53.0%	45.3%	54.7%
25,068	SCOTT	9,387	4,744	4,314	329	430	R	50.5%	46.0%	52.4%	47.6%
27,559	SHENANDOAH	11,203	7,517	3,137	549	4,380	R	67.1%	28.0%	70.6%	29.4%
33,366	SMYTH	11,861	6,033	5,335	493	698	R	50.9%	45.0%	53.1%	46.9%
18,731	SOUTHAMPTON	6,587	2,997	3,347	243	350	D	45.5%	50.8%	47.2%	52.8%
34,435	SPOTSYLVANIA	10,005	5,385	4,039	581	1,346	R	53.8%	40.4%	57.1%	42.9%
40,470	STAFFORD	12,075	7,106	4,211	758	2,895	R	58.8%	34.9%	62.8%	37.2%
6,046	SURRY	2,821	962	1,756	103	794	D	34.1%	62.2%	35.4%	64.6%
10,874	SUSSEX	4,273	1,664	2,447	162	783	D	38.9%	57.3%	40.5%	59.5%
50,511	TAZEWELL	14,425	7,021	7,003	401	18	R	48.7%	48.5%	50.1%	49.9%
21,200	WARREN	6,920	3,861	2,597	462	1,264	R	55.8%	37.5%	59.8%	40.2%
46,487	WASHINGTON	15,597	8,402	6,390	805	2,012	R	53.9%	41.0%	56.8%	43.2%
14,041	WESTMORELAND	4,989	2,510	2,271	208	239	R	50.3%	45.5%	52.5%	47.5%
43,863	WISE	13,141	5,767	6,779	595	1,012	D	43.9%	51.6%	46.0%	54.0%
25,522	WYTHE	8,766	4,758	3,677	331	1,081	R	54.3%	41.9%	56.4%	43.6%
35,463	YORK	12,133	6,744	4,532	857	2,212	R	55.6%	37.4%	59.8%	40.2%
	City										
103,217	ALEXANDRIA	40,388	17,865	17,134	5,389	731	R	44.2%	42.4%	51.0%	49.0%
5,991	BEDFORD CITY	2,423	1,145	1,149	129	4	D	47.3%	47.4%	49.9%	50.1%
19,042	BRISTOL	6,515	3,432	2,889	194	543	R	52.7%	44.3%	54.3%	45.7%
6,717	BUENA VISTA	2,089	942	1,031	116	89	D	45.1%	49.4%	47.7%	52.3%
45,010	CHARLOTTESVILLE	14,562	5,907	6,866	1,789	959	D	40.6%	47.2%	46.2%	53.8%
114,226	CHESAPEAKE	36,904	17,888	17,155	1,861	733	R	48.5%	46.5%	51.0%	49.0%
5,046	CLIFTON FORGE	1,825	716	1,012	97	296	D	39.2%	55.5%	41.4%	58.6%
16,509	COLONIAL HEIGHTS	7,063	5,012	1,692	359	3,320	R	71.0%	24.0%	74.8%	25.2%
9,063	COVINGTON	3,150	1,187	1,813	150	626	D	37.7%	57.6%	39.6%	60.4%
45,642	DANVILLE	17,362	10,665	6,138	559	4,527	R	61.4%	35.4%	63.5%	36.5%
4,840	EMPORIA	1,902	988	855	59	133	R	51.9%	45.0%	53.6%	46.4%
19,390	FAIRFAX CITY	8,004	4,475	2,614	915	1,861	R	55.9%	32.7%	63.1%	36.9%
9,515	FALLS CHURCH	4,758	2,485	1,703	570	782	R	52.2%	35.8%	59.3%	40.7%
7,308	FRANKLIN CITY	2,456	1,045	1,324	87	279	D	42.5%	53.9%	44.1%	55.9%
15,322	FREDERICKSBURG	4,968	2,502	2,174	292	328	R	50.4%	43.8%	53.5%	46.5%
6,524	GALAX	2,293	1,188	1,061	44	127	R	51.8%	46.3%	52.8%	47.2%
122,617	HAMPTON	37,765	17,023	18,517	2,225	1,494	R	45.1%	49.0%	47.9%	52.1%
19,671	HARRISONBURG	5,796	3,388	1,896	512	1,492	R	58.5%	32.7%	64.1%	35.9%
23,397	HOPEWELL	7,872	4,423	3,102	347	1,321	R	56.2%	39.4%	58.8%	41.2%
7,292	LEXINGTON	2,083	956	963	164	7	D	45.9%	46.2%	49.8%	50.2%
66,743	LYNCHBURG	24,417	15,245	7,783	1,389	7,462	R	62.4%	31.9%	66.2%	33.8%
15,438	MANASSAS	4,952	3,009	1,565	378	1,444	R	60.8%	31.6%	65.8%	34.2%
6,524	MANASSAS PARK	1,254	729	447	78	282	R	58.1%	35.6%	62.0%	38.0%
18,149	MARTINSVILLE	7,032	3,433	3,337	262	96	R	48.8%	47.5%	50.7%	49.3%
144,903	NEWPORT NEWS	46,982	22,423	22,066	2,493	357	R	47.7%	47.0%	50.4%	49.6%
266,979	NORFOLK	67,200	27,506	35,118	4,576	7,612	D	40.9%	52.3%	43.9%	56.1%
4,757	NORTON	1,400	572	762	66	190	D	40.9%	54.4%	42.9%	57.1%
41,055	PETERSBURG	13,277	5,001	7,931	345	2,930	D	37.7%	59.7%	38.7%	61.3%
8,726	POQUOSON	3,399	2,338	877	184	1,461	R	68.8%	25.8%	72.7%	27.3%
104,577	PORTSMOUTH	35,949	13,660	20,900	1,389	7,240	D	38.0%	58.1%	39.5%	60.5%
13,225	RADFORD	4,463	1,964	2,225	274	261	D	44.0%	49.9%	46.9%	53.1%
219,214	RICHMOND CITY	87,106	34,629	47,975	4,502	13,346	D	39.8%	55.1%	41.9%	58.1%
100,427	ROANOKE CITY	34,946	15,164	18,139	1,643	2,975	D	43.4%	51.9%	45.5%	54.5%
23,958	SALEM	9,389	4,862	4,091	436	771	R	51.8%	43.6%	54.3%	45.7%
7,093	SOUTH BOSTON	2,649	1,615	971	63	644	R	61.0%	36.7%	62.5%	37.5%
21,857	STAUNTON	7,927	4,819	2,658	450	2,161	R	60.8%	33.5%	64.5%	35.5%
47,621	SUFFOLK	16,765	7,179	9,064	522	1,885	D	42.8%	54.1%	44.2%	55.8%
262,199	VIRGINIA BEACH	79,235	47,936	24,895	6,404	23,041	R	60.5%	31.4%	65.8%	34.2%
15,329	WAYNESBORO	5,978	3,697	1,926	355	1,771	R	61.8%	32.2%	65.7%	34.3%
9,870	WILLIAMSBURG	2,953	1,344	1,199	410	145	R	45.5%	40.6%	52.9%	47.1%
20,217	WINCHESTER	6,623	4,240	2,006	377	2,234	R	64.0%	30.3%	67.9%	32.1%
5,346,279	**TOTAL**	1,866,032	989,609	752,174	124,249	237,435	R	53.0%	40.3%	56.8%	43.2%

VIRGINIA

CONGRESS

CD	Year	Total Vote	Republican Vote	Candidate	Democratic Vote	Candidate	Other Vote	Rep.-Dem. Plurality	Total Vote Rep.	Total Vote Dem.	Major Vote Rep.	Major Vote Dem.
1	1980	143,839	130,130	TRIBLE, PAUL			13,709	130,130 R	90.5%		100.0%	
1	1978	123,741	89,158	TRIBLE, PAUL	34,578	PULLER, LEWIS B.	5	54,580 R	72.1%	27.9%	72.1%	27.9%
1	1976	147,850	71,789	TRIBLE, PAUL	70,159	QUINN, ROBERT E.	5,902	1,630 R	48.6%	47.5%	50.6%	49.4%
1	1974	58,474			58,338	DOWNING, THOMAS N.	136	58,338 D		99.8%		100.0%
1	1972	129,218	28,310	WELLS, KENNETH D.	100,901	DOWNING, THOMAS N.	7	72,591 D	21.9%	78.1%	21.9%	78.1%
2	1980	108,328	97,319	WHITEHURST, G. W.			11,009	97,319 R	89.8%		100.0%	
2	1978	63,530	63,512	WHITEHURST, G. W.			18	63,512 R	100.0%		100.0%	
2	1976	120,847	79,381	WHITEHURST, G. W.	41,464	WASHINGTON, ROBERT E.	2	37,917 R	65.7%	34.3%	65.7%	34.3%
2	1974	82,299	49,369	WHITEHURST, G. W.	32,923	RICHARDS, ROBERT R.	7	16,446 R	60.0%	40.0%	60.0%	40.0%
2	1972	108,482	79,672	WHITEHURST, G. W.	28,803	BURLAGE, L. CHARLES	7	50,869 R	73.4%	26.6%	73.4%	26.6%
3	1980	186,912	96,524	BLILEY, THOMAS J.	60,962	MAPP, JOHN A.	29,426	35,562 R	51.6%	32.6%	61.3%	38.7%
3	1978	119,217			104,550	SATTERFIELD, DAVID	14,667	104,550 D		87.7%		100.0%
3	1976	146,788			129,066	SATTERFIELD, DAVID	17,722	129,066 D		87.9%		100.0%
3	1974	72,996			64,627	SATTERFIELD, DAVID	8,369	64,627 D		88.5%		100.0%
3	1972	102,679			102,523	SATTERFIELD, DAVID	156	102,523 D		99.8%		100.0%
4	1980	152,494	92,557	DANIEL, ROBERT W.	59,930	JENKINS, CECIL Y.	7	32,627 R	60.7%	39.3%	60.7%	39.3%
4	1978	77,873	77,827	DANIEL, ROBERT W.			46	77,827 R	99.9%		100.0%	
4	1976	140,480	74,495	DANIEL, ROBERT W.	65,982	O'BRIEN, J. W.	3	8,513 R	53.0%	47.0%	53.0%	47.0%
4	1974	101,748	48,032	DANIEL, ROBERT W.	36,489	SCHLITZ, LESTER E.	17,227	11,543 R	47.2%	35.9%	56.8%	43.2%
4	1972	122,159	57,520	DANIEL, ROBERT W.	45,776	GIBSON, ROBERT E.	18,863	11,744 R	47.1%	37.5%	55.7%	44.3%
5	1980	112,218			112,143	DANIEL, W. C.	75	112,143 D		99.9%		100.0%
5	1978	83,619			83,575	DANIEL, W. C.	44	83,575 D		99.9%		100.0%
5	1976	101,079			101,038	DANIEL, W. C.	41	101,038 D		100.0%		100.0%
5	1974	52,751			52,459	DANIEL, W. C.	292	52,459 D		99.4%		100.0%
5	1972	83,819			83,772	DANIEL, W. C.	47	83,772 D		99.9%		100.0%
6	1980	124,143	123,125	BUTLER, M. CALDWELL			1,018	123,125 R	99.2%		100.0%	
6	1978	88,803	88,647	BUTLER, M. CALDWELL			156	88,647 R	99.8%		100.0%	
6	1976	145,976	90,830	BUTLER, M. CALDWELL			55,146	90,830 R	62.2%		100.0%	
6	1974	101,463	45,805	BUTLER, M. CALDWELL	27,350	PUCKETT, PAUL	28,308	18,455 R	45.1%	27.0%	62.6%	37.4%
6	1972	137,650	75,189	BUTLER, M. CALDWELL	53,928	ANDERSON, WILLIS M.	8,533	21,261 R	54.6%	39.2%	58.2%	41.8%
7	1980	140,396	139,957	ROBINSON, J. KENNETH			439	139,957 R	99.7%		100.0%	
7	1978	131,476	84,517	ROBINSON, J. KENNETH	46,950	FICKETT, LEWIS P.	9	37,567 R	64.3%	35.7%	64.3%	35.7%
7	1976	141,482	115,508	ROBINSON, J. KENNETH			25,974	115,508 R	81.6%		100.0%	
7	1974	103,100	54,267	ROBINSON, J. KENNETH	48,611	GILLIAM, GEORGE H.	222	5,656 R	52.6%	47.1%	52.7%	47.3%
7	1972	134,634	89,120	ROBINSON, J. KENNETH	45,513	WILLIAMS, MURAT	1	43,607 R	66.2%	33.8%	66.2%	33.8%
8	1980	195,897	95,624	PARRIS, STANFORD E.	94,530	HARRIS, HERBERT E.	5,743	1,094 R	48.8%	48.3%	50.3%	49.7%
8	1978	111,170	52,396	HERRITY, JOHN F.	56,137	HARRIS, HERBERT E.	2,637	3,741 D	47.1%	50.5%	48.3%	51.7%
8	1976	161,327	68,729	TATE, JAMES R.	83,245	HARRIS, HERBERT E.	9,353	14,516 D	42.6%	51.6%	45.2%	54.8%
8	1974	92,082	38,997	PARRIS, STANFORD E.	53,074	HARRIS, HERBERT E.	11	14,077 D	42.4%	57.6%	42.4%	57.6%
8	1972	136,099	60,446	PARRIS, STANFORD E.	51,444	HORAN, ROBERT F.	24,209	9,002 R	44.4%	37.8%	54.0%	46.0%
9	1980	171,864	119,196	WAMPLER, WILLIAM C.	52,636	FERGUSON, ROOSEVELT	32	66,560 R	69.4%	30.6%	69.4%	30.6%
9	1978	124,254	76,877	WAMPLER, WILLIAM C.	47,367	CLARK, C. CHAMP	10	29,510 R	61.9%	38.1%	61.9%	38.1%
9	1976	167,504	96,052	WAMPLER, WILLIAM C.	71,439	HORNE, CHARLES J.	13	24,613 R	57.3%	42.6%	57.3%	42.7%
9	1974	133,969	68,183	WAMPLER, WILLIAM C.	65,783	HORNE, CHARLES J.	3	2,400 R	50.9%	49.1%	50.9%	49.1%
9	1972	136,470	98,178	WAMPLER, WILLIAM C.	36,000	CHRISTIAN, ZANE DALE	2,292	62,178 R	71.9%	26.4%	73.2%	26.8%
10	1980	216,744	110,840	WOLF, FRANK R.	105,883	FISHER, JOSEPH L.	21	4,957 R	51.1%	48.9%	51.1%	48.9%
10	1978	132,882	61,981	WOLF, FRANK R.	70,892	FISHER, JOSEPH L.	9	8,911 D	46.6%	53.3%	46.6%	53.4%
10	1976	189,489	73,616	CALLAHAN, VINCENT F.	103,689	FISHER, JOSEPH L.	12,184	30,073 D	38.8%	54.7%	41.5%	58.5%
10	1974	125,304	56,649	BROYHILL, JOEL T.	67,184	FISHER, JOSEPH L.	1,471	10,535 D	45.2%	53.6%	45.7%	54.3%
10	1972	179,778	101,138	BROYHILL, JOEL T.	78,638	MILLER, HAROLD O.	2	22,500 R	56.3%	43.7%	56.3%	43.7%

VIRGINIA

Under Virginia's local government system a number of urban areas — 41 since 1977 — are organized as cities independent of county authority. The number of these cities is subject to change and their boundaries alter from year to year.

1980 GENERAL ELECTION

President   Other vote was 95,418 Anderson (Independent); 14,024 Commoner (Independent); 12,821 Clark (Libertarian); 1,986 DeBerry (Independent).

Congress   Other vote was 13,688 Grant (Independent) and 21 scattered in CD 1; 11,003 Morrison (Independent) and 6 scattered in CD 2; 19,549 Carwile (Independent), 9,852 Turney (Independent) and 25 scattered in CD 3; 5,729 Frantz (Independent) and 14 scattered in CD 8; scattered in all other CD's.

1980 PRIMARIES

JUNE 10 REPUBLICAN

Congress   Candidates nominated by convention in CD's 1, 2, 3, 4, 6, 7 and 9. No candidate in CD 5. Contested as follows:

CD 8   9,930 Stanford E. Parris; 6,564 Robert L. Thoburn.
CD 10   13,782 Frank R. Wolf; 3,182 Martin H. Perper; 1,384 Harold L. Miller.

JUNE 10 DEMOCRATIC

Congress   Unopposed in CD's 3, 5 and 10. Candidates nominated by convnetion in CD's 4, 8 and 9. No candidates in CD's 1, 2, 6 and 7.

WASHINGTON

GOVERNOR
John D. Spellman (R). Elected 1980 to a four-year term.

SENATORS
Slade Gorton (R). Elected 1980 to a six-year term.

Henry M. Jackson (D). Re-elected 1976 to a six-year term. Previously elected 1970, 1964, 1958, 1952.

REPRESENTATIVES
1. Joel Pritchard (R)
2. Al Swift (D)
3. Don Bonker (D)
4. Sid Morrison (R)
5. Thomas S. Foley (D)
6. Norman D. Dicks (D)
7. Mike Lowry (D)

POSTWAR VOTE FOR GOVERNOR

Year	Total Vote	Republican Vote	Candidate	Democratic Vote	Candidate	Other Vote	Rep.-Dem. Plurality	Total Vote Rep.	Total Vote Dem.	Major Vote Rep.	Major Vote Dem.
1980	1,730,896	981,083	Spellman, John D.	749,813	McDermott, James A.	—	231,270 R	56.7%	43.3%	56.7%	43.3%
1976	1,546,382	687,039	Spellman, John D.	821,797	Ray, Dixy Lee	37,546	134,758 D	44.4%	53.1%	45.5%	54.5%
1972	1,472,542	747,825	Evans, Daniel J.	630,613	Rosellini, Albert D.	94,104	117,212 R	50.8%	42.8%	54.3%	45.7%
1968	1,265,355	692,378	Evans, Daniel J.	560,262	O'Connell, John J.	12,715	132,116 R	54.7%	44.3%	55.3%	44.7%
1964	1,250,274	697,256	Evans, Daniel J.	548,692	Rosellini, Albert D.	4,326	148,564 R	55.8%	43.9%	56.0%	44.0%
1960	1,215,748	594,122	Andrews, Lloyd J.	611,987	Rosellini, Albert D.	9,639	17,865 D	48.9%	50.3%	49.3%	50.7%
1956	1,128,977	508,041	Anderson, Emmett T.	616,773	Rosellini, Albert D.	4,163	108,732 D	45.0%	54.6%	45.2%	54.8%
1952	1,078,497	567,822	Langlie, Arthur B.	510,675	Mitchell, Hugh B.	—	57,147 R	52.6%	47.4%	52.6%	47.4%
1948	883,141	445,958	Langlie, Arthur B.	417,035	Wallgren, Mon C.	20,148	28,923 R	50.5%	47.2%	51.7%	48.3%

POSTWAR VOTE FOR SENATOR

Year	Total Vote	Republican Vote	Candidate	Democratic Vote	Candidate	Other Vote	Rep.-Dem. Plurality	Total Vote Rep.	Total Vote Dem.	Major Vote Rep.	Major Vote Dem.
1980	1,728,369	936,317	Gorton, Slade	792,052	Magnuson, Warren G.	—	144,265 R	54.2%	45.8%	54.2%	45.8%
1976	1,491,111	361,546	Brown, George M.	1,071,219	Jackson, Henry M.	58,346	709,673 D	24.2%	71.8%	25.2%	74.8%
1974	1,007,847	363,626	Metcalf, Jack	611,811	Magnuson, Warren G.	32,410	248,185 D	36.1%	60.7%	37.3%	62.7%
1970	1,066,807	170,790	Elicker, Charles W.	879,385	Jackson, Henry M.	16,632	708,595 D	16.0%	82.4%	16.3%	83.7%
1968	1,236,063	435,894	Metcalf, Jack	796,183	Magnuson, Warren G.	3,986	360,289 D	35.3%	64.4%	35.4%	64.6%
1964	1,213,088	337,138	Andrews Lloyd J.	875,950	Jackson, Henry M.	—	538,812 D	27.8%	72.2%	27.8%	72.2%
1962	943,229	446,204	Christensen, Richard G.	491,365	Magnuson, Warren G.	5,660	45,161 D	47.3%	52.1%	47.6%	52.4%
1958	886,822	278,271	Bantz, William B.	597,040	Jackson, Henry M.	11,511	318,769 D	31.4%	67.3%	31.8%	68.2%
1956	1,122,217	436,652	Langlie, Arthur B.	685,565	Magnuson, Warren G.	—	248,913 D	38.9%	61.1%	38.9%	61.1%
1952	1,058,735	460,884	Cain, Harry P.	595,288	Jackson, Henry M.	2,563	134,404 D	43.5%	56.2%	43.6%	56.4%
1950	744,783	342,464	Williams, Walter	397,719	Magnuson, Warren G.	4,600	55,255 D	46.0%	53.4%	46.3%	53.7%
1946	660,342	358,847	Cain, Harry P.	298,683	Mitchell, Hugh B.	2,812	60,164 R	54.3%	45.2%	54.6%	45.4%

WASHINGTON

Districts Established April 21, 1972

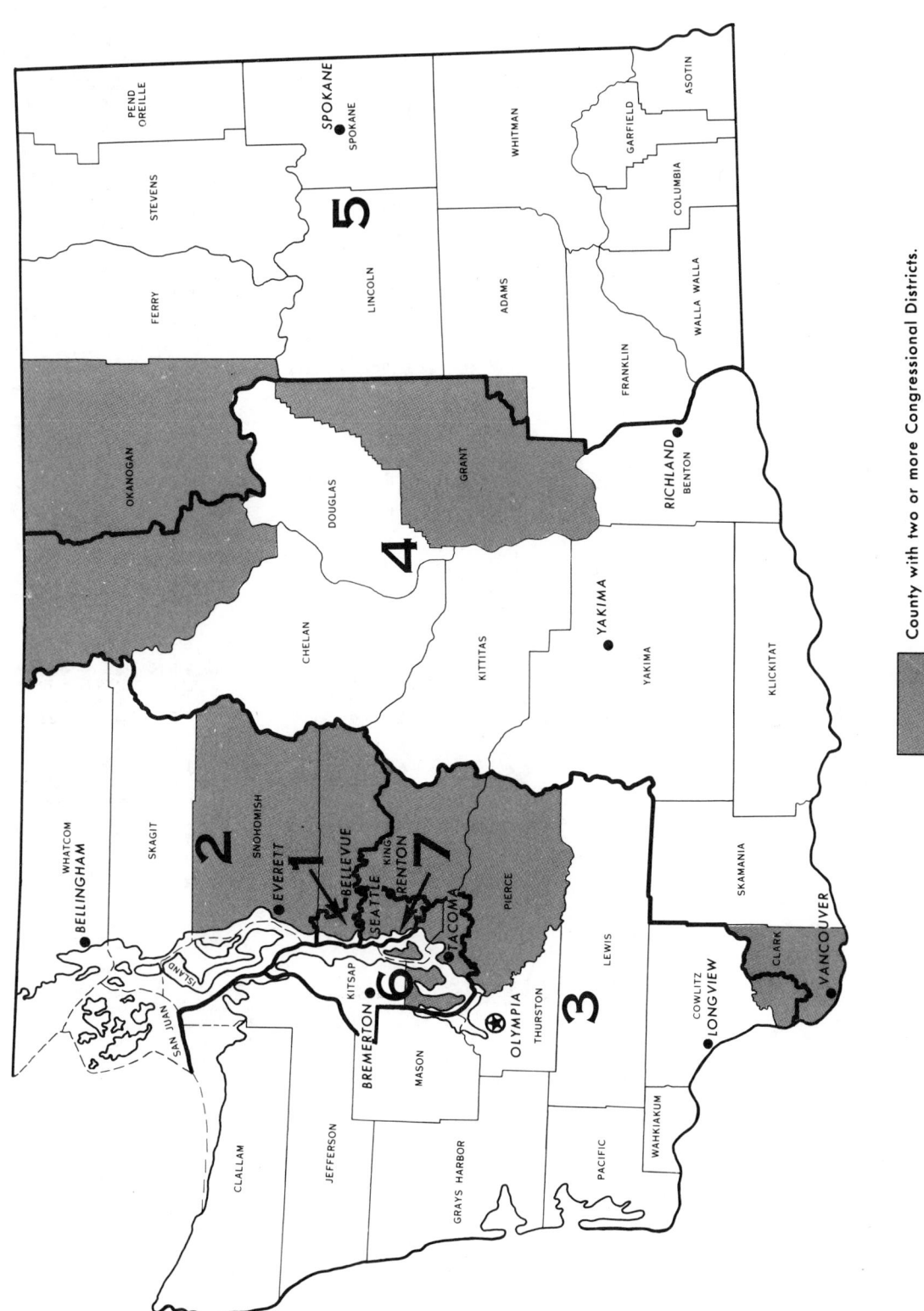

County with two or more Congressional Districts.

WASHINGTON

PRESIDENT 1980

1980 Census Population	County	Total Vote	Republican	Democratic	Other	Rep.-Dem. Plurality	Percentage Total Vote Rep.	Dem.	Major Vote Rep.	Dem.
13,267	ADAMS	4,776	3,248	1,223	305	2,025 R	68.0%	25.6%	72.6%	27.4%
16,823	ASOTIN	6,659	3,275	2,724	660	551 R	49.2%	40.9%	54.6%	45.4%
109,444	BENTON	44,413	28,728	11,561	4,124	17,167 R	64.7%	26.0%	71.3%	28.7%
45,061	CHELAN	19,850	11,299	6,483	2,068	4,816 R	56.9%	32.7%	63.5%	36.5%
51,648	CLALLAM	22,296	11,515	8,029	2,752	3,486 R	51.6%	36.0%	58.9%	41.1%
192,227	CLARK	72,075	33,223	30,584	8,268	2,639 R	46.1%	42.4%	52.1%	47.9%
4,057	COLUMBIA	2,086	1,349	587	150	762 R	64.7%	28.1%	69.7%	30.3%
79,548	COWLITZ	28,639	13,154	12,560	2,925	594 R	45.9%	43.9%	51.2%	48.8%
22,144	DOUGLAS	8,709	5,171	2,833	705	2,338 R	59.4%	32.5%	64.6%	35.4%
5,811	FERRY	2,100	1,108	802	190	306 R	52.8%	38.2%	58.0%	42.0%
35,025	FRANKLIN	11,961	7,327	3,719	915	3,608 R	61.3%	31.1%	66.3%	33.7%
2,468	GARFIELD	1,519	875	509	135	366 R	57.6%	33.5%	63.2%	36.8%
48,522	GRANT	18,196	11,152	5,673	1,371	5,479 R	61.3%	31.2%	66.3%	33.7%
66,314	GRAYS HARBOR	25,444	10,226	11,290	3,928	1,064 D	40.2%	44.4%	47.5%	52.5%
44,048	ISLAND	18,559	10,926	5,422	2,211	5,504 R	58.9%	29.2%	66.8%	33.2%
15,965	JEFFERSON	8,170	3,645	3,279	1,246	366 R	44.6%	40.1%	52.6%	47.4%
1,269,749	KING	600,157	272,567	235,046	92,544	37,521 R	45.4%	39.2%	53.7%	46.3%
146,609	KITSAP	60,296	29,420	20,893	9,983	8,527 R	48.8%	34.7%	58.5%	41.5%
24,877	KITTITAS	10,748	5,359	4,075	1,314	1,284 R	49.9%	37.9%	56.8%	43.2%
15,822	KLICKITAT	6,284	3,113	2,596	575	517 R	49.5%	41.3%	54.5%	45.5%
55,279	LEWIS	22,749	13,636	6,962	2,151	6,674 R	59.9%	30.6%	66.2%	33.8%
9,604	LINCOLN	5,337	3,324	1,597	416	1,727 R	62.3%	29.9%	67.5%	32.5%
31,184	MASON	13,737	6,745	5,241	1,751	1,504 R	49.1%	38.2%	56.3%	43.7%
30,639	OKANOGAN	12,493	6,460	4,634	1,399	1,826 R	51.7%	37.1%	58.2%	41.8%
17,237	PACIFIC	8,012	3,132	3,727	1,153	595 D	39.1%	46.5%	45.7%	54.3%
8,580	PEND OREILLE	3,835	2,136	1,399	300	737 R	55.7%	36.5%	60.4%	39.6%
485,643	PIERCE	176,511	90,247	64,444	21,820	25,803 R	51.1%	36.5%	58.3%	41.7%
7,838	SAN JUAN	5,031	2,363	1,666	1,002	697 R	47.0%	33.1%	58.6%	41.4%
64,138	SKAGIT	30,623	15,520	11,299	3,804	4,221 R	50.7%	36.9%	57.9%	42.1%
7,919	SKAMANIA	3,095	1,416	1,373	306	43 R	45.8%	44.4%	50.8%	49.2%
337,016	SNOHOMISH	135,907	66,153	52,003	17,751	14,150 R	48.7%	38.3%	56.0%	44.0%
341,835	SPOKANE	140,685	78,096	49,263	13,326	28,833 R	55.5%	35.0%	61.3%	38.7%
28,979	STEVENS	11,530	7,094	3,584	852	3,510 R	61.5%	31.1%	66.4%	33.6%
124,264	THURSTON	54,823	26,369	20,508	7,946	5,861 R	48.1%	37.4%	56.3%	43.7%
3,832	WAHKIAKUM	1,778	828	751	199	77 R	46.6%	42.2%	52.4%	47.6%
47,435	WALLA WALLA	18,977	11,223	5,825	1,929	5,398 R	59.1%	30.7%	65.8%	34.2%
106,701	WHATCOM	46,057	21,371	18,430	6,256	2,941 R	46.4%	40.0%	53.7%	46.3%
40,103	WHITMAN	17,024	8,636	5,726	2,662	2,910 R	50.7%	33.6%	60.1%	39.9%
172,508	YAKIMA	61,253	33,815	21,873	5,565	11,942 R	55.2%	35.7%	60.7%	39.3%
4,130,163	TOTAL	1,742,394	865,244	650,193	226,957	215,051 R	49.7%	37.3%	57.1%	42.9%

WASHINGTON

GOVERNOR 1980

1980 Census Population	County	Total Vote	Republican	Democratic	Other	Rep.-Dem. Plurality	Total Vote Rep.	Total Vote Dem.	Major Vote Rep.	Major Vote Dem.
13,267	ADAMS	4,787	3,259	1,528		1,731 R	68.1%	31.9%	68.1%	31.9%
16,823	ASOTIN	6,676	3,817	2,859		958 R	57.2%	42.8%	57.2%	42.8%
109,444	BENTON	44,347	30,710	13,637		17,073 R	69.2%	30.8%	69.2%	30.8%
45,061	CHELAN	19,404	11,734	7,670		4,064 R	60.5%	39.5%	60.5%	39.5%
51,648	CLALLAM	22,296	12,729	9,567		3,162 R	57.1%	42.9%	57.1%	42.9%
192,227	CLARK	71,589	39,225	32,364		6,861 R	54.8%	45.2%	54.8%	45.2%
4,057	COLUMBIA	2,022	1,352	670		682 R	66.9%	33.1%	66.9%	33.1%
79,548	COWLITZ	28,070	14,160	13,910		250 R	50.4%	49.6%	50.4%	49.6%
22,144	DOUGLAS	8,710	5,248	3,462		1,786 R	60.3%	39.7%	60.3%	39.7%
5,811	FERRY	2,023	956	1,067		111 D	47.3%	52.7%	47.3%	52.7%
35,025	FRANKLIN	11,703	7,249	4,454		2,795 R	61.9%	38.1%	61.9%	38.1%
2,468	GARFIELD	1,476	974	502		472 R	66.0%	34.0%	66.0%	34.0%
48,522	GRANT	17,828	10,839	6,989		3,850 R	60.8%	39.2%	60.8%	39.2%
66,314	GRAYS HARBOR	26,069	12,971	13,098		127 R	49.8%	50.2%	49.8%	50.2%
44,048	ISLAND	18,283	11,285	6,998		4,287 R	61.7%	38.3%	61.7%	38.3%
15,965	JEFFERSON	8,066	3,961	4,105		144 D	49.1%	50.9%	49.1%	50.9%
1,269,749	KING	595,159	327,941	267,218		60,723 R	55.1%	44.9%	55.1%	44.9%
146,609	KITSAP	60,522	36,372	24,150		12,222 R	60.1%	39.9%	60.1%	39.9%
24,877	KITTITAS	10,605	5,783	4,822		961 R	54.5%	45.5%	54.5%	45.5%
15,822	KLICKITAT	6,096	2,944	3,152		208 D	48.3%	51.7%	48.3%	51.7%
55,279	LEWIS	22,810	14,230	8,580		5,650 R	62.4%	37.6%	62.4%	37.6%
9,604	LINCOLN	5,380	3,471	1,909		1,562 R	64.5%	35.5%	64.5%	35.5%
31,184	MASON	13,771	7,414	6,357		1,057 R	53.8%	46.2%	53.8%	46.2%
30,639	OKANOGAN	12,451	6,710	5,741		969 R	53.9%	46.1%	53.9%	46.1%
17,237	PACIFIC	8,029	3,379	4,650		1,271 D	42.1%	57.9%	42.1%	57.9%
8,580	PEND OREILLE	3,733	2,045	1,688		357 R	54.8%	45.2%	54.8%	45.2%
485,643	PIERCE	173,594	98,289	75,305		22,984 R	56.6%	43.4%	56.6%	43.4%
7,838	SAN JUAN	4,902	2,587	2,315		272 R	52.8%	47.2%	52.8%	47.2%
64,138	SKAGIT	30,686	17,003	13,683		3,320 R	55.4%	44.6%	55.4%	44.6%
7,919	SKAMANIA	2,964	1,361	1,603		242 D	45.9%	54.1%	45.9%	54.1%
337,016	SNOHOMISH	135,790	75,203	60,587		14,616 R	55.4%	44.6%	55.4%	44.6%
341,835	SPOKANE	141,227	84,400	56,827		27,573 R	59.8%	40.2%	59.8%	40.2%
28,979	STEVENS	11,500	7,178	4,322		2,856 R	62.4%	37.6%	62.4%	37.6%
124,264	THURSTON	54,925	31,803	23,122		8,681 R	57.9%	42.1%	57.9%	42.1%
3,832	WAHKIAKUM	1,693	767	926		159 D	45.3%	54.7%	45.3%	54.7%
47,435	WALLA WALLA	18,947	11,993	6,954		5,039 R	63.3%	36.7%	63.3%	36.7%
106,701	WHATCOM	45,937	23,722	22,215		1,507 R	51.6%	48.4%	51.6%	48.4%
40,103	WHITMAN	16,968	9,773	7,195		2,578 R	57.6%	42.4%	57.6%	42.4%
172,508	YAKIMA	59,858	36,246	23,612		12,634 R	60.6%	39.4%	60.6%	39.4%
4,130,163	TOTAL	1,730,896	981,083	749,813		231,270 R	56.7%	43.3%	56.7%	43.3%

WASHINGTON

SENATOR 1980

1980 Census Population	County	Total Vote	Republican	Democratic	Other	Rep.-Dem. Plurality	Percentage			
							Total Vote		Major Vote	
							Rep.	Dem.	Rep.	Dem.
13,267	ADAMS	4,783	3,272	1,511		1,761 R	68.4%	31.6%	68.4%	31.6%
16,823	ASOTIN	6,658	3,441	3,217		224 R	51.7%	48.3%	51.7%	48.3%
109,444	BENTON	44,492	24,837	19,655		5,182 R	55.8%	44.2%	55.8%	44.2%
45,061	CHELAN	19,237	12,054	7,183		4,871 R	62.7%	37.3%	62.7%	37.3%
51,648	CLALLAM	22,249	12,676	9,573		3,103 R	57.0%	43.0%	57.0%	43.0%
192,227	CLARK	71,481	36,593	34,888		1,705 R	51.2%	48.8%	51.2%	48.8%
4,057	COLUMBIA	2,010	1,279	731		548 R	63.6%	36.4%	63.6%	36.4%
79,548	COWLITZ	27,594	12,261	15,333		3,072 D	44.4%	55.6%	44.4%	55.6%
22,144	DOUGLAS	8,745	5,562	3,183		2,379 R	63.6%	36.4%	63.6%	36.4%
5,811	FERRY	1,995	1,025	970		55 R	51.4%	48.6%	51.4%	48.6%
35,025	FRANKLIN	11,755	6,579	5,176		1,403 R	56.0%	44.0%	56.0%	44.0%
2,468	GARFIELD	1,458	903	555		348 R	61.9%	38.1%	61.9%	38.1%
48,522	GRANT	17,717	10,812	6,905		3,907 R	61.0%	39.0%	61.0%	39.0%
66,314	GRAYS HARBOR	26,057	11,861	14,196		2,335 D	45.5%	54.5%	45.5%	54.5%
44,048	ISLAND	18,119	10,871	7,248		3,623 R	60.0%	40.0%	60.0%	40.0%
15,965	JEFFERSON	8,023	3,855	4,168		313 D	48.0%	52.0%	48.0%	52.0%
1,269,749	KING	594,146	308,050	286,096		21,954 R	51.8%	48.2%	51.8%	48.2%
146,609	KITSAP	60,713	27,797	32,916		5,119 D	45.8%	54.2%	45.8%	54.2%
24,877	KITTITAS	10,503	6,122	4,381		1,741 R	58.3%	41.7%	58.3%	41.7%
15,822	KLICKITAT	5,947	3,097	2,850		247 R	52.1%	47.9%	52.1%	47.9%
55,279	LEWIS	22,829	15,020	7,809		7,211 R	65.8%	34.2%	65.8%	34.2%
9,604	LINCOLN	5,375	3,451	1,924		1,527 R	64.2%	35.8%	64.2%	35.8%
31,184	MASON	13,737	7,525	6,212		1,313 R	54.8%	45.2%	54.8%	45.2%
30,639	OKANOGAN	12,458	7,160	5,298		1,862 R	57.5%	42.5%	57.5%	42.5%
17,237	PACIFIC	8,030	3,694	4,336		642 D	46.0%	54.0%	46.0%	54.0%
8,580	PEND OREILLE	3,714	2,197	1,517		680 R	59.2%	40.8%	59.2%	40.8%
485,643	PIERCE	173,177	89,286	83,891		5,395 R	51.6%	48.4%	51.6%	48.4%
7,838	SAN JUAN	4,819	2,916	1,903		1,013 R	60.5%	39.5%	60.5%	39.5%
64,138	SKAGIT	30,787	17,150	13,637		3,513 R	55.7%	44.3%	55.7%	44.3%
7,919	SKAMANIA	2,928	1,376	1,552		176 D	47.0%	53.0%	47.0%	53.0%
337,016	SNOHOMISH	136,117	74,862	61,255		13,607 R	55.0%	45.0%	55.0%	45.0%
341,835	SPOKANE	141,797	86,210	55,587		30,623 R	60.8%	39.2%	60.8%	39.2%
28,979	STEVENS	11,529	7,643	3,886		3,757 R	66.3%	33.7%	66.3%	33.7%
124,264	THURSTON	54,896	30,900	23,996		6,904 R	56.3%	43.7%	56.3%	43.7%
3,832	WAHKIAKUM	1,672	816	856		40 D	48.8%	51.2%	48.8%	51.2%
47,435	WALLA WALLA	18,857	11,944	6,913		5,031 R	63.3%	36.7%	63.3%	36.7%
106,701	WHATCOM	45,863	25,148	20,715		4,433 R	54.8%	45.2%	54.8%	45.2%
40,103	WHITMAN	17,015	9,896	7,119		2,777 R	58.2%	41.8%	58.2%	41.8%
172,508	YAKIMA	59,087	36,176	22,911		13,265 R	61.2%	38.8%	61.2%	38.8%
4,130,163	TOTAL	1,728,369	936,317	792,052		144,265 R	54.2%	45.8%	54.2%	45.8%

WASHINGTON

CONGRESS

CD	Year	Total Vote	Republican Vote	Republican Candidate	Democratic Vote	Democratic Candidate	Other Vote	Rep.-Dem. Plurality	Total Vote Rep.	Total Vote Dem.	Major Vote Rep.	Major Vote Dem.
1	1980	230,534	180,475	PRITCHARD, JOEL	41,830	DRAKE, ROBIN	8,229	138,645 R	78.3%	18.1%	81.2%	18.8%
1	1978	156,193	99,942	PRITCHARD, JOEL	52,706	NIEMI, JANICE	3,545	47,236 R	64.0%	33.7%	65.5%	34.5%
1	1976	224,561	161,354	PRITCHARD, JOEL	58,006	WOOD, DAVE	5,201	103,348 R	71.9%	25.8%	73.6%	26.4%
1	1974	156,021	108,391	PRITCHARD, JOEL	44,655	KNEDLIK, W. R.	2,975	63,736 R	69.5%	28.6%	70.8%	29.2%
1	1972	213,941	107,581	PRITCHARD, JOEL	104,959	HEMPELMANN, JOHN	1,401	2,622 R	50.3%	49.1%	50.6%	49.4%
2	1980	253,688	82,639	SNIDER, NEAL	162,002	SWIFT, AL	9,047	79,363 D	32.6%	63.9%	33.8%	66.2%
2	1978	137,413	66,793	GARNER, JOHN N.	70,620	SWIFT, AL		3,827 D	48.6%	51.4%	48.6%	51.4%
2	1976	217,858	106,786	GARNER, JOHN N.	107,328	MEEDS, LLOYD	3,744	542 D	49.0%	49.3%	49.9%	50.1%
2	1974	136,544	53,157	REED, RONALD C.	81,565	MEEDS, LLOYD	1,822	28,408 D	38.9%	59.7%	39.5%	60.5%
2	1972	190,081	75,181	REAMS, BILL	114,900	MEEDS, LLOYD		39,719 D	39.6%	60.4%	39.6%	60.4%
3	1980	248,778	92,872	CULP, ROD	155,906	BONKER, DON		63,034 D	37.3%	62.7%	37.3%	62.7%
3	1978	140,886	58,270	BENNETT, RICK	82,616	BONKER, DON		24,346 D	41.4%	58.6%	41.4%	58.6%
3	1976	205,072	57,517	ELHART, CHUCK	145,198	BONKER, DON	2,357	87,681 D	28.0%	70.8%	28.4%	71.6%
3	1974	154,270	58,774	KRAMER, A. LUDLOW	93,980	BONKER, DON	1,516	35,206 D	38.1%	60.9%	38.5%	61.5%
3	1972	185,497	62,564	MCCONKEY, R. C.	122,933	HANSEN, JULIA BUTLER		60,369 D	33.7%	66.3%	33.7%	66.3%
4	1980	234,805	134,691	MORRISON, SID	100,114	MCCORMACK, MIKE		34,577 R	57.4%	42.6%	57.4%	42.6%
4	1978	139,991	54,389	ROYLANCE, SUSAN	85,602	MCCORMACK, MIKE		31,213 D	38.9%	61.1%	38.9%	61.1%
4	1976	199,664	81,813	GRANGER, DICK	115,364	MCCORMACK, MIKE	2,487	33,551 D	41.0%	57.8%	41.5%	58.5%
4	1974	144,198	59,249	PAXTON, FLOYD	84,949	MCCORMACK, MIKE		25,700 D	41.1%	58.9%	41.1%	58.9%
4	1972	187,405	89,812	BLEDSOE, STEWART	97,593	MCCORMACK, MIKE		7,781 D	47.9%	52.1%	47.9%	52.1%
5	1980	232,235	111,705	SONNELAND, JOHN E.	120,530	FOLEY, THOMAS S.		8,825 D	48.1%	51.9%	48.1%	51.9%
5	1978	160,849	68,761	ALTON, DUANE	77,201	FOLEY, THOMAS S.	14,887	8,440 D	42.7%	48.0%	47.1%	52.9%
5	1976	207,571	84,262	ALTON, DUANE	120,415	FOLEY, THOMAS S.	2,894	36,153 D	40.6%	58.0%	41.2%	58.8%
5	1974	136,698	48,739	GAGE, GARY G.	87,959	FOLEY, THOMAS S.		39,220 D	35.7%	64.3%	35.7%	64.3%
5	1972	185,322	34,742	PRIVETTE, CLARICE	150,580	FOLEY, THOMAS S.		115,838 D	18.7%	81.3%	18.7%	81.3%
6	1980	229,139	106,236	BEAVER, JAMES E.	122,903	DICKS, NORMAN D.		16,667 D	46.4%	53.6%	46.4%	53.6%
6	1978	116,740	43,640	BEAVER, JAMES E.	71,057	DICKS, NORMAN D.	2,043	27,417 D	37.4%	60.9%	38.0%	62.0%
6	1976	187,754	47,539	REYNOLDS, ROBERT M.	137,964	DICKS, NORMAN D.	2,251	90,425 D	25.3%	73.5%	25.6%	74.4%
6	1974	132,754	37,400	NALLEY, GEORGE M.	95,354	HICKS, FLOYD V.		57,954 D	28.2%	71.8%	28.2%	71.8%
6	1972	175,263	48,914	LOWRY, THOMAS C.	126,349	HICKS, FLOYD V.		77,435 D	27.9%	72.1%	27.9%	72.1%
7	1980	197,066	84,218	DUNLAP, RON	112,848	LOWRY, MIKE		28,630 D	42.7%	57.3%	42.7%	57.3%
7	1978	126,502	59,052	CUNNINGHAM, JOHN E.	67,450	LOWRY, MIKE		8,398 D	46.7%	53.3%	46.7%	53.3%
7	1976	183,122	46,448	PRITCHARD, RAYMOND	133,673	ADAMS, BROCK	3,001	87,225 D	25.4%	73.0%	25.8%	74.2%
7	1974	120,440	34,847	PRITCHARD, RAYMOND	85,593	ADAMS, BROCK		50,746 D	28.9%	71.1%	28.9%	71.1%
7	1972	164,324	19,889	FREEMAN, J. J.	140,307	ADAMS, BROCK	4,128	120,418 D	12.1%	85.4%	12.4%	87.6%

WASHINGTON

1980 GENERAL ELECTION

President Other vote was 185,073 Anderson (Independent); 29,213 Clark (Libertarian); 9,403 Commoner (Citizens); 1,137 DeBerry (Socialist Workers); 956 McReynolds (Socialist); 834 Hall (Communist); 341 Griswold (Workers World).

Governor

Senator

Congress Other vote was Willey (Libertarian) in CD 1; McCord (Libertarian) in CD 2.

1980 PRIMARIES

SEPTEMBER 16 REPUBLICAN

Governor 162,426 John D. Spellman; 154,724 Duane Berentson; 70,875 Bruce Chapman; 7,324 Patrick S. McGowan; 2,622 Louise A. Saluteen; 1,606 Rabbine M. Sutich.

Senator 313,560 Slade Gorton; 229,178 Lloyd E. Cooney; 13,736 William McCallum; 7,112 Barry W. McClain.

Congress Unopposed in two CD's. Contested as follows:

CD 2 26,260 Neal Snider; 16,320 J. Eric Brown.
CD 3 16,380 Rod Culp; 11,802 Harold Engelbertson; 9,667 Henry L. Adams; 5,254 John VanVessem; 5,157 Ed Gerrick; 2,991 H. W. VanVlack.
CD 4 39,673 Sid Morrison; 27,547 Claude L. Oliver.
CD 5 42,520 John E. Sonneland; 12,690 Mel Tonasket; 6,294 I. E. McCray; 5,582 George W. Bible.
CD 7 30,947 Ron Dunlap; 7,513 Bob Dorse; 3,348 Chun Y. Gee.

SEPTEMBER 16 DEMOCRATIC

Governor 321,256 James A. McDermott; 234,252 Dixy Lee Ray; 4,184 Caroline Diamond; 3,578 Robert L. Baldwin; 2,723 Lloyd G. Isley; 2,481 Douglas P. Bestle; 1,476 Jef Jaisun.

Senator 348,471 Warren G. Magnuson; 18,348 James S. Stokes; 10,157 John Patric.

Congress Unopposed in three CD's. Contested as follows:

CD 2 84,552 Al Swift; 7,736 Zell A. Young.
CD 3 88,001 Don Bonker; 8,332 Dan Jones.
CD 6 71,407 Norman D. Dicks; 7,059 Robert Satiacum.
CD 7 66,209 Mike Lowry; 4,092 Arthur Bauder.

WEST VIRGINIA

GOVERNOR
John D. Rockefeller (D). Re-elected 1980 to a four-year term. Previously elected 1976.

SENATORS
Robert C. Byrd (D). Re-elected 1976 to a six-year term. Previously elected 1970, 1964, 1958.

Jennings Randolph (D). Re-elected 1978 to a six-year term. Previously elected 1972, 1966, 1960, and in 1958 to fill out term vacated by the death of Senator Matthew M. Neely.

REPRESENTATIVES
1. Robert H. Mollohan (D)
2. Cleveland K. Benedict (R)
3. David M. Staton (R)
4. Nick J. Rahall (D)

POSTWAR VOTE FOR GOVERNOR

		Republican		Democratic		Other	Rep.-Dem.	Percentage Total Vote		Major Vote	
Year	Total Vote	Vote	Candidate	Vote	Candidate	Vote	Plurality	Rep.	Dem.	Rep.	Dem.
1980	742,150	337,240	Moore, Arch A.	401,863	Rockefeller, John D.	3,047	64,623 D	45.4%	54.1%	45.6%	54.4%
1976	749,270	253,420	Underwood, Cecil H.	495,661	Rockefeller, John D.	189	242,241 D	33.8%	66.2%	33.8%	66.2%
1972	774,279	423,817	Moore, Arch A.	350,462	Rockefeller, John D.	–	73,355 R	54.7%	45.3%	54.7%	45.3%
1968	743,845	378,315	Moore, Arch A.	365,530	Sprouse, James M.	–	12,785 R	50.9%	49.1%	50.9%	49.1%
1964	788,582	355,559	Underwood, Cecil H.	433,023	Smith, Hulett C.	–	77,464 D	45.1%	54.9%	45.1%	54.9%
1960	827,420	380,665	Neely, Harold E.	446,755	Barron, W. W.	--	66,090 D	46.0%	54.0%	46.0%	54.0%
1956	817,623	440,502	Underwood, Cecil H.	377,121	Mollohan, Robert H.	–	63,381 R	53.9%	46.1%	53.9%	46.1%
1952	882,527	427,629	Holt, Rush D.	454,898	Marland, William C.	–	27,269 D	48.5%	51.5%	48.5%	51.5%
1948	768,061	329,309	Boreman, Herbert	438,752	Patteson, Okey L.	–	109,443 D	42.9%	57.1%	42.9%	57.1%

POSTWAR VOTE FOR SENATOR

		Republican		Democratic		Other	Rep.-Dem.	Percentage Total Vote		Major Vote	
Year	Total Vote	Vote	Candidate	Vote	Candidate	Vote	Plurality	Rep.	Dem.	Rep.	Dem.
1978	493,351	244,317	Moore, Arch A.	249,034	Randolph, Jennings	–	4,717 D	49.5%	50.5%	49.5%	50.5%
1976	566,790	–	–	566,423	Byrd, Robert C.	367	566,423 D	–	99.9%	–	100.0%
1972	731,841	245,531	Leonard, Louise	486,310	Randolph, Jennings	–	240,779 D	33.5%	66.5%	33.5%	66.5%
1970	445,623	99,658	Dodson, Elmer H.	345,965	Byrd, Robert C.	–	246,307 D	22.4%	77.6%	22.4%	77.6%
1966	491,216	198,891	Love, Francis J.	292,325	Randolph, Jennings	–	93,434 D	40.5%	59.5%	40.5%	59.5%
1964	761,087	246,072	Benedict, Cooper P.	515,015	Byrd, Robert C.	–	268,943 D	32.3%	67.7%	32.3%	67.7%
1960	828,292	369,935	Underwood, Cecil H.	458,355	Randolph, Jennings	2	88,420 D	44.7%	55.3%	44.7%	55.3%
1958	644,917	263,172	Revercomb, Chapman	381,745	Byrd, Robert C.	–	118,573 D	40.8%	59.2%	40.8%	59.2%
1958s	630,677	256,510	Hoblitzell, John D.	374,167	Randolph, Jennings	–	117,657 D	40.7%	59.3%	40.7%	59.3%
1956s	805,174	432,123	Revercomb, Chapman	373,051	Marland, William C.	–	59,072 R	53.7%	46.3%	53.7%	46.3%
1954	593,329	268,066	Sweeney, Tom	325,263	Neely, Matthew M.	–	57,197 D	45.2%	54.8%	45.2%	54.8%
1952	876,573	406,554	Revercomb, Chapman	470,019	Kilgore, Harley M.	–	63,465 D	46.4%	53.6%	46.4%	53.6%
1948	763,888	328,534	Revercomb, Chapman	435,354	Neely, Matthew M.	–	106,820 D	43.0%	57.0%	43.0%	57.0%
1946	542,768	269,617	Sweeney, Tom	273,151	Kilgore, Harley M.	–	3,534 D	49.7%	50.3%	49.7%	50.3%

One of the elections in 1958 and that in 1956 were for short terms to fill vacancies.

WEST VIRGINIA

Districts Established March 6, 1971

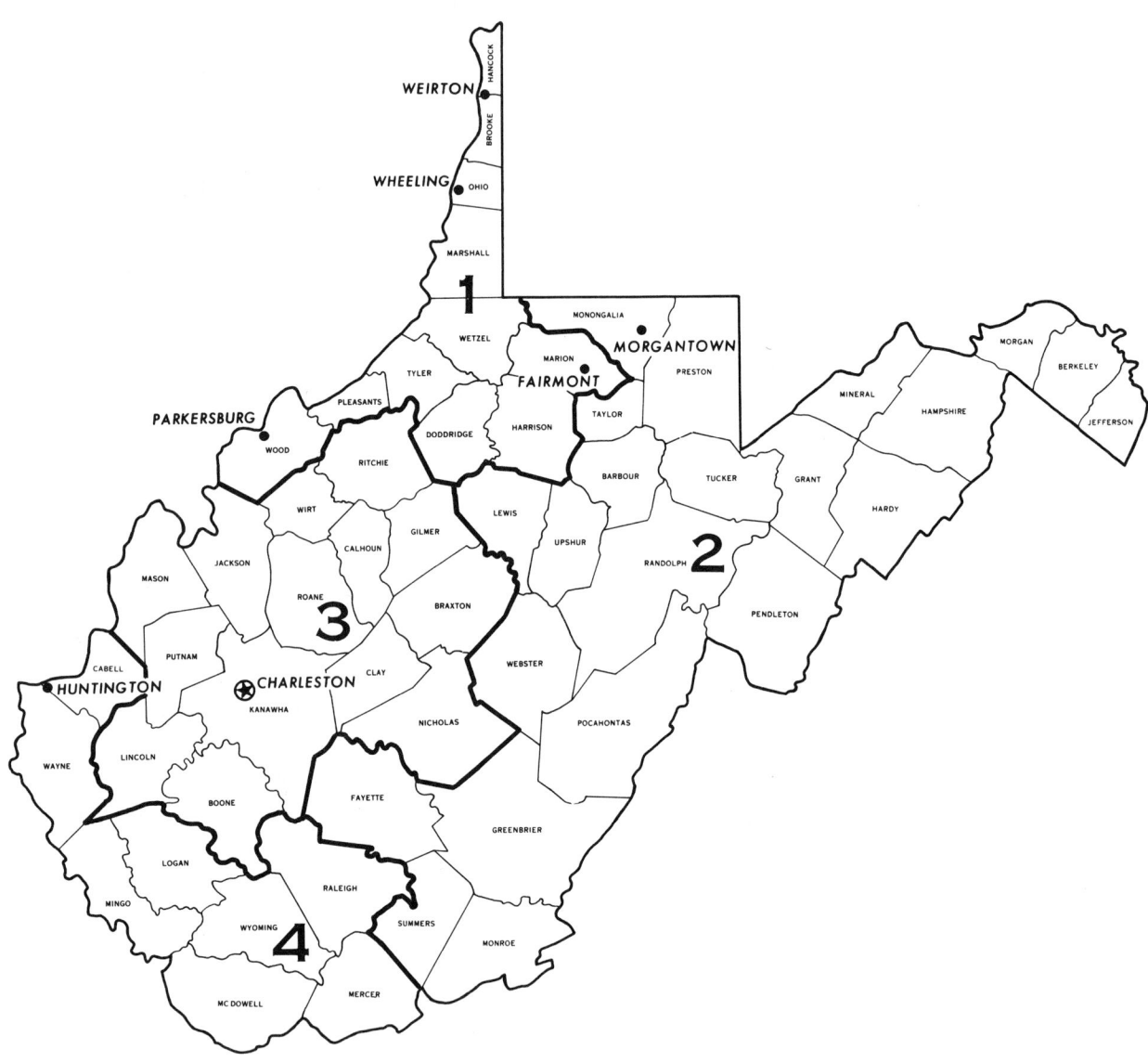

WEST VIRGINIA

PRESIDENT 1980

1980 Census Population	County	Total Vote	Republican	Democratic	Other	Rep.-Dem. Plurality	Percentage Total Vote Rep.	Dem.	Major Vote Rep.	Dem.
16,639	BARBOUR	7,086	3,311	3,451	324	140 D	46.7%	48.7%	49.0%	51.0%
46,775	BERKELEY	17,454	9,955	6,783	716	3,172 R	57.0%	38.9%	59.5%	40.5%
30,447	BOONE	12,000	4,164	7,515	321	3,351 D	34.7%	62.6%	35.7%	64.3%
13,894	BRAXTON	6,408	2,403	3,795	210	1,392 D	37.5%	59.2%	38.8%	61.2%
31,117	BROOKE	11,795	4,622	6,430	743	1,808 D	39.2%	54.5%	41.8%	58.2%
106,835	CABELL	39,588	19,482	17,732	2,374	1,750 R	49.2%	44.8%	52.4%	47.6%
8,250	CALHOUN	3,441	1,606	1,717	118	111 D	46.7%	49.9%	48.3%	51.7%
11,265	CLAY	3,762	1,452	2,185	125	733 D	38.6%	58.1%	39.9%	60.1%
7,433	DODDRIDGE	3,051	1,888	1,043	120	845 R	61.9%	34.2%	64.4%	35.6%
57,863	FAYETTE	19,774	5,784	13,175	815	7,391 D	29.3%	66.6%	30.5%	69.5%
8,334	GILMER	3,486	1,452	1,854	180	402 D	41.7%	53.2%	43.9%	56.1%
10,210	GRANT	4,591	3,452	1,041	98	2,411 R	75.2%	22.7%	76.8%	23.2%
37,665	GREENBRIER	14,004	6,221	7,128	655	907 D	44.4%	50.9%	46.6%	53.4%
14,867	HAMPSHIRE	5,585	2,879	2,522	184	357 R	51.5%	45.2%	53.3%	46.7%
40,418	HANCOCK	16,475	6,610	8,784	1,081	2,174 D	40.1%	53.3%	42.9%	57.1%
10,030	HARDY	4,499	2,329	2,050	120	279 R	51.8%	45.6%	53.2%	46.8%
77,710	HARRISON	34,602	14,251	18,813	1,538	4,562 D	41.2%	54.4%	43.1%	56.9%
25,794	JACKSON	10,581	6,041	4,120	420	1,921 R	57.1%	38.9%	59.5%	40.5%
30,302	JEFFERSON	9,818	4,454	4,679	685	225 D	45.4%	47.7%	48.8%	51.2%
231,414	KANAWHA	91,760	42,604	42,829	6,327	225 D	46.4%	46.7%	49.9%	50.1%
18,813	LEWIS	7,611	3,747	3,455	409	292 R	49.2%	45.4%	52.0%	48.0%
23,675	LINCOLN	9,490	4,009	5,317	164	1,308 D	42.2%	56.0%	43.0%	57.0%
50,679	LOGAN	17,428	4,945	12,024	459	7,079 D	28.4%	69.0%	29.1%	70.9%
49,899	MCDOWELL	13,943	3,862	9,822	259	5,960 D	27.7%	70.4%	28.2%	71.8%
65,789	MARION	26,471	10,952	14,189	1,330	3,237 D	41.4%	53.6%	43.6%	56.4%
41,608	MARSHALL	15,916	7,252	7,832	832	580 D	45.6%	49.2%	48.1%	51.9%
27,045	MASON	12,108	6,040	5,683	385	357 R	49.9%	46.9%	51.5%	48.5%
73,942	MERCER	24,741	12,273	11,804	664	469 R	49.6%	47.7%	51.0%	49.0%
27,234	MINERAL	11,274	6,125	4,671	478	1,454 R	54.3%	41.4%	56.7%	43.3%
37,336	MINGO	13,280	3,716	9,328	236	5,612 D	28.0%	70.2%	28.5%	71.5%
75,024	MONONGALIA	27,826	11,972	12,883	2,971	911 D	43.0%	46.3%	48.2%	51.8%
12,873	MONROE	6,072	2,999	2,877	196	122 R	49.4%	47.4%	51.0%	49.0%
10,711	MORGAN	4,627	2,833	1,594	200	1,239 R	61.2%	34.4%	64.0%	36.0%
28,126	NICHOLAS	9,516	3,885	5,265	366	1,380 D	40.8%	55.3%	42.5%	57.5%
61,389	OHIO	23,873	11,414	10,973	1,486	441 R	47.8%	46.0%	51.0%	49.0%
7,910	PENDLETON	3,504	1,677	1,724	103	47 D	47.9%	49.2%	49.3%	50.7%
8,236	PLEASANTS	3,447	1,852	1,494	101	358 R	53.7%	43.3%	55.3%	44.7%
9,919	POCAHONTAS	4,355	2,011	2,170	174	159 D	46.2%	49.8%	48.1%	51.9%
30,460	PRESTON	10,746	5,828	4,317	601	1,511 R	54.2%	40.2%	57.4%	42.6%
38,181	PUTNAM	14,686	7,561	6,409	716	1,152 R	51.5%	43.6%	54.1%	45.9%
86,821	RALEIGH	28,831	10,713	16,955	1,163	6,242 D	37.2%	58.8%	38.7%	61.3%
28,734	RANDOLPH	10,921	4,374	5,937	610	1,563 D	40.1%	54.4%	42.4%	57.6%
11,442	RITCHIE	4,691	3,081	1,450	160	1,631 R	65.7%	30.9%	68.0%	32.0%
15,952	ROANE	5,953	3,219	2,498	236	721 R	54.1%	42.0%	56.3%	43.7%
15,875	SUMMERS	5,797	2,456	3,114	227	658 D	42.4%	53.7%	44.1%	55.9%
16,584	TAYLOR	6,487	3,010	3,216	261	206 D	46.4%	49.6%	48.3%	51.7%
8,675	TUCKER	3,855	1,798	1,862	195	64 D	46.6%	48.3%	49.1%	50.9%
11,320	TYLER	4,382	2,707	1,482	193	1,225 R	61.8%	33.8%	64.6%	35.4%
23,427	UPSHUR	8,099	4,751	2,867	481	1,884 R	58.7%	35.4%	62.4%	37.6%
46,021	WAYNE	16,719	7,541	8,687	491	1,146 D	45.1%	52.0%	46.5%	53.5%
12,245	WEBSTER	3,974	1,262	2,578	134	1,316 D	31.8%	64.9%	32.9%	67.1%
21,874	WETZEL	8,015	3,588	4,035	392	447 D	44.8%	50.3%	47.1%	52.9%
4,922	WIRT	2,293	1,176	1,058	59	118 R	51.3%	46.1%	52.6%	47.4%
93,648	WOOD	35,512	20,080	13,622	1,810	6,458 R	56.5%	38.4%	59.6%	40.4%
35,993	WYOMING	11,512	4,537	6,624	351	2,087 D	39.4%	57.5%	40.7%	59.3%
1,949,644	TOTAL	737,715	334,206	367,462	36,047	33,256 D	45.3%	49.8%	47.6%	52.4%

WEST VIRGINIA

GOVERNOR 1980

1980 Census Population	County	Total Vote	Republican	Democratic	Other	Rep.-Dem. Plurality	Total Vote Rep.	Total Vote Dem.	Major Vote Rep.	Major Vote Dem.
16,639	BARBOUR	7,171	3,768	3,378	25	390 R	52.5%	47.1%	52.7%	47.3%
46,775	BERKELEY	17,591	8,729	8,842	20	113 D	49.6%	50.3%	49.7%	50.3%
30,447	BOONE	12,011	4,500	7,480	31	2,980 D	37.5%	62.3%	37.6%	62.4%
13,894	BRAXTON	6,406	2,919	3,462	25	543 D	45.6%	54.0%	45.7%	54.3%
31,117	BROOKE	11,820	3,839	7,911	70	4,072 D	32.5%	66.9%	32.7%	67.3%
106,835	CABELL	39,630	18,421	21,018	191	2,597 D	46.5%	53.0%	46.7%	53.3%
8,250	CALHOUN	3,454	1,994	1,437	23	557 R	57.7%	41.6%	58.1%	41.9%
11,265	CLAY	3,816	1,683	2,124	9	441 D	44.1%	55.7%	44.2%	55.8%
7,433	DODDRIDGE	3,113	2,191	906	16	1,285 R	70.4%	29.1%	70.7%	29.3%
57,863	FAYETTE	19,701	6,359	13,281	61	6,922 D	32.3%	67.4%	32.4%	67.6%
8,334	GILMER	3,498	1,934	1,544	20	390 R	55.3%	44.1%	55.6%	44.4%
10,210	GRANT	4,617	3,466	1,141	10	2,325 R	75.1%	24.7%	75.2%	24.8%
37,665	GREENBRIER	13,956	6,654	7,191	111	537 D	47.7%	51.5%	48.1%	51.9%
14,867	HAMPSHIRE	5,664	2,474	3,168	22	694 D	43.7%	55.9%	43.8%	56.2%
40,418	HANCOCK	16,347	5,100	11,167	80	6,067 D	31.2%	68.3%	31.4%	68.6%
10,030	HARDY	4,512	2,226	2,284	2	58 D	49.3%	50.6%	49.4%	50.6%
77,710	HARRISON	34,936	15,850	19,017	69	3,167 D	45.4%	54.4%	45.5%	54.5%
25,794	JACKSON	11,180	6,640	4,540		2,100 R	59.4%	40.6%	59.4%	40.6%
30,302	JEFFERSON	9,800	4,067	5,652	81	1,585 D	41.5%	57.7%	41.8%	58.2%
231,414	KANAWHA	91,818	45,627	45,707	484	80 D	49.7%	49.8%	50.0%	50.0%
18,813	LEWIS	7,679	4,400	3,279		1,121 R	57.3%	42.7%	57.3%	42.7%
23,675	LINCOLN	9,615	4,298	5,298	19	1,000 D	44.7%	55.1%	44.8%	55.2%
50,679	LOGAN	17,682	5,048	12,594	40	7,546 D	28.5%	71.2%	28.6%	71.4%
49,899	MCDOWELL	13,977	3,700	10,248	29	6,548 D	26.5%	73.3%	26.5%	73.5%
65,789	MARION	26,920	12,283	14,582	55	2,299 D	45.6%	54.2%	45.7%	54.3%
41,608	MARSHALL	15,629	8,286	7,281	62	1,005 R	53.0%	46.6%	53.2%	46.8%
27,045	MASON	12,225	5,846	6,355	24	509 D	47.8%	52.0%	47.9%	52.1%
73,942	MERCER	24,729	11,125	13,544	60	2,419 D	45.0%	54.8%	45.1%	54.9%
27,234	MINERAL	11,331	5,909	5,422		487 R	52.1%	47.9%	52.1%	47.9%
37,336	MINGO	13,318	3,065	10,232	21	7,167 D	23.0%	76.8%	23.1%	76.9%
75,024	MONONGALIA	27,989	12,096	15,694	199	3,598 D	43.2%	56.1%	43.5%	56.5%
12,873	MONROE	6,142	2,926	3,203	13	277 D	47.6%	52.1%	47.7%	52.3%
10,711	MORGAN	4,634	2,409	2,213	12	196 R	52.0%	47.8%	52.1%	47.9%
28,126	NICHOLAS	9,476	4,066	5,382	28	1,316 D	42.9%	56.8%	43.0%	57.0%
61,389	OHIO	23,944	10,568	13,244	132	2,676 D	44.1%	55.3%	44.4%	55.6%
7,910	PENDLETON	3,522	1,617	1,896	9	279 D	45.9%	53.8%	46.0%	54.0%
8,236	PLEASANTS	3,453	1,798	1,642	13	156 R	52.1%	47.6%	52.3%	47.7%
9,919	POCAHONTAS	4,406	2,090	2,301	15	211 D	47.4%	52.2%	47.6%	52.4%
30,460	PRESTON	10,793	6,066	4,682	45	1,384 R	56.2%	43.4%	56.4%	43.6%
38,181	PUTNAM	14,656	7,749	6,840	67	909 R	52.9%	46.7%	53.1%	46.9%
86,821	RALEIGH	28,760	7,812	20,860	88	13,048 D	27.2%	72.5%	27.2%	72.8%
28,734	RANDOLPH	10,899	4,880	5,921	98	1,041 D	44.8%	54.3%	45.2%	54.8%
11,442	RITCHIE	4,715	3,199	1,481	35	1,718 R	67.8%	31.4%	68.4%	31.6%
15,952	ROANE	6,288	3,733	2,513	42	1,220 R	59.4%	40.0%	59.8%	40.2%
15,875	SUMMERS	5,792	2,663	3,101	28	438 D	46.0%	53.5%	46.2%	53.8%
16,584	TAYLOR	6,565	3,383	3,163	19	220 R	51.5%	48.2%	51.7%	48.3%
8,675	TUCKER	3,891	2,297	1,579	15	718 R	59.0%	40.6%	59.3%	40.7%
11,320	TYLER	4,425	2,712	1,686	27	1,026 R	61.3%	38.1%	61.7%	38.3%
23,427	UPSHUR	8,109	4,916	3,140	53	1,776 R	60.6%	38.7%	61.0%	39.0%
46,021	WAYNE	16,679	7,674	8,977	28	1,303 D	46.0%	53.8%	46.1%	53.9%
12,245	WEBSTER	3,982	1,526	2,441	15	915 D	38.3%	61.3%	38.5%	61.5%
21,874	WETZEL	8,045	3,385	4,605	55	1,220 D	42.1%	57.2%	42.4%	57.6%
4,922	WIRT	2,307	1,241	1,066		175 R	53.8%	46.2%	53.8%	46.2%
93,648	WOOD	36,910	19,537	17,044	329	2,493 R	52.9%	46.2%	53.4%	46.6%
35,993	WYOMING	11,622	4,496	7,104	22	2,608 D	38.7%	61.1%	38.8%	61.2%
1,949,644	TOTAL	742,150	337,240	401,863	3,047	64,623 D	45.4%	54.1%	45.6%	54.4%

WEST VIRGINIA

CONGRESS

CD	Year	Total Vote	Republican Vote	Republican Candidate	Democratic Vote	Democratic Candidate	Other Vote	Rep.-Dem. Plurality	Total Vote Rep.	Total Vote Dem.	Major Vote Rep.	Major Vote Dem.
1	1980	168,909	61,438	BARTLETT, JOE	107,471	MOLLOHAN, ROBERT H.		46,033 D	36.4%	63.6%	36.4%	63.6%
1	1978	120,434	44,062	HAYNES, GENE A.	76,372	MOLLOHAN, ROBERT H.		32,310 D	36.6%	63.4%	36.6%	63.4%
1	1976	186,263	78,159	MCCUSKEY, JOHN F.	108,103	MOLLOHAN, ROBERT H.	1	29,944 D	42.0%	58.0%	42.0%	58.0%
1	1974	121,423	48,966	LAURITA, JOE	72,457	MOLLOHAN, ROBERT H.		23,491 D	40.3%	59.7%	40.3%	59.7%
1	1972	187,336	57,274	KAPNICKY, GEORGE E.	130,062	MOLLOHAN, ROBERT H.		72,788 D	30.6%	69.4%	30.6%	69.4%
2	1980	183,745	102,805	BENEDICT, CLEVELAND K.	80,940	HAMILTON, PAT R.		21,865 R	55.9%	44.1%	55.9%	44.1%
2	1978	125,955	56,272	BENEDICT, CLEVELAND K.	69,683	STAGGERS, HARLEY O.		13,411 D	44.7%	55.3%	44.7%	55.3%
2	1976	186,832	50,079	SLOAN, JIM	136,749	STAGGERS, HARLEY O.	4	86,670 D	26.8%	73.2%	26.8%	73.2%
2	1974	114,462	40,779	LOY, WILLIAM H.	73,683	STAGGERS, HARLEY O.		32,904 D	35.6%	64.4%	35.6%	64.4%
2	1972	183,235	54,949	DIX, DAVID	128,286	STAGGERS, HARLEY O.		73,337 D	30.0%	70.0%	30.0%	70.0%
3	1980	179,563	94,583	STATON, DAVID M.	84,980	HUTCHINSON, JOHN G.		9,603 R	52.7%	47.3%	52.7%	47.3%
3	1978	126,421	51,584	STATON, DAVID M.	74,837	SLACK, JOHN M.		23,253 D	40.8%	59.2%	40.8%	59.2%
3	1976	128,479			128,086	SLACK, JOHN M.	393	128,086 D		99.7%		100.0%
3	1974	113,209	35,623	LARCAMP, WILLIAM L.	77,586	SLACK, JOHN M.		41,963 D	31.5%	68.5%	31.5%	68.5%
3	1972	185,787	67,441	HIGGINS, T. DAVID	118,346	SLACK, JOHN M.		50,905 D	36.3%	63.7%	36.3%	63.7%
4	1980	153,615	36,020	COVEY, WINTON G.	117,595	RAHALL, NICK J.		81,575 D	23.4%	76.6%	23.4%	76.6%
4	1978	70,035			70,035	RAHALL, NICK J.		70,035 D		100.0%		100.0%
4	1976	161,520	28,825	GOODMAN, E. S.	73,626	RAHALL, NICK J.	59,069	44,801 D	17.8%	45.6%	28.1%	71.9%
4	1974	66,420			66,420	HECHLER, KEN		66,420 D		100.0%		100.0%
4	1972	164,842	64,242	NEAL, JOE	100,600	HECHLER, KEN		36,358 D	39.0%	61.0%	39.0%	61.0%

WEST VIRGINIA

1980 GENERAL ELECTION

President   Other vote was 31,691 Anderson (Independent); 4,356 Clark (Libertarian).

Governor   Other vote was Kelley (Libertarian).

Congress

1980 PRIMARIES

JUNE 3 REPUBLICAN

Governor   Arch A. Moore, unopposed.

Congress   Unopposed in CD 4. Contested as follows:

CD 1   17,967 Joe Bartlett; 16,040 Robert L. Levenson.
CD 2   24,593 Cleveland K. Benedict; 14,778 Edgar Heiskell.
CD 3   28,259 David M. Staton; 7,457 Richie Robb; 2,435 Tom R. Williams.

JUNE 3 DEMOCRATIC

Governor   250,550 John D. Rockefeller; 70,452 H. John Rogers.

Congress   Unopposed in two CD's. Contested as follows:

CD 2   36,513 Pat R. Hamilton; 35,265 Harley O. Staggers, Jr.; 11,282 Joe Caudle; 2,481 Patricia Rodinoff-Peck; 1,415 Si Allen.
CD 3   38,274 John G. Hutchinson; 19,501 Si Galperin; 17,912 Jack L. Pauley; 2,676 Paul E. Lawrence.

WISCONSIN

GOVERNOR
Lee S. Dreyfus (R). Elected 1978 to a four-year term.

SENATORS
Robert W. Kasten (R). Elected 1980 to a six-year term.

William Proxmire (D). Re-elected 1976 to a six-year term. Previously elected 1970, 1964, 1958, and in August 1957 to fill out term vacated by the death of Senator Joseph R. McCarthy.

REPRESENTATIVES
1. Les Aspin (D)
2. Robert Kastenmeier (D)
3. Steven Gunderson (R)
4. Clement J. Zablocki (D)
5. Henry S. Reuss (D)
6. Thomas E. Petri (R)
7. David R. Obey (D)
8. Toby Roth (R)
9. F. James Sensenbrenner (R)

POSTWAR VOTE FOR GOVERNOR

Year	Total Vote	Republican Vote	Candidate	Democratic Vote	Candidate	Other Vote	Rep.-Dem. Plurality	Rep.	Dem.	Rep.	Dem.
1978	1,500,996	816,056	Dreyfus, Lee S.	673,813	Schreiber, Martin J.	11,127	142,243 R	54.4%	44.9%	54.8%	45.2%
1974	1,181,976	497,195	Dyke, William D.	628,639	Lucey, Patrick J.	56,142	131,444 D	42.1%	53.2%	44.2%	55.8%
1970	1,343,160	602,617	Olson, Jack B.	728,403	Lucey, Patrick J.	12,140	125,786 D	44.9%	54.2%	45.3%	54.7%
1968	1,689,738	893,463	Knowles, Warren P.	791,100	LaFollette, Bronson C.	5,175	102,363 R	52.9%	46.8%	53.0%	47.0%
1966	1,170,173	626,041	Knowles, Warren P.	539,258	Lucey, Patrick J.	4,874	86,783 R	53.5%	46.1%	53.7%	46.3%
1964	1,694,887	856,779	Knowles, Warren P.	837,901	Reynolds, John W.	207	18,878 R	50.6%	49.4%	50.6%	49.4%
1962	1,265,900	625,536	Kuehn, Philip G.	637,491	Reynolds, John W.	2,873	11,955 D	49.4%	50.4%	49.5%	50.5%
1960	1,728,009	837,123	Kuehn, Philip G.	890,868	Nelson, Gaylord A.	18	53,745 D	48.4%	51.6%	48.4%	51.6%
1958	1,202,219	556,391	Thomson, Vernon W.	644,296	Nelson, Gaylord A.	1,532	87,905 D	46.3%	53.6%	46.3%	53.7%
1956	1,557,788	808,273	Thomson, Vernon W.	749,421	Proxmire, William	94	58,852 R	51.9%	48.1%	51.9%	48.1%
1954	1,158,666	596,158	Kohler, Walter J.	560,747	Proxmire, William	1,761	35,411 R	51.5%	48.4%	51.5%	48.5%
1952	1,615,214	1,009,171	Kohler, Walter J.	601,844	Proxmire, William	4,199	407,327 R	62.4%	37.3%	62.6%	37.4%
1950	1,138,148	605,649	Kohler, Walter J.	525,319	Thompson, Carl W.	7,180	80,330 R	53.2%	46.2%	53.6%	46.4%
1948	1,266,139	684,839	Rennebohm, Oscar	558,497	Thompson, Carl W.	22,803	126,342 R	54.1%	44.1%	55.1%	44.9%
1946	1,040,444	621,970	Goodland, Walter	406,499	Hoan, Daniel W.	11,975	215,471 R	59.8%	39.1%	60.5%	39.5%

The term of office for Wisconsin's Governor was increased from two to four years effective with the 1970 election.

POSTWAR VOTE FOR SENATOR

Year	Total Vote	Republican Vote	Candidate	Democratic Vote	Candidate	Other Vote	Rep.-Dem. Plurality	Rep.	Dem.	Rep.	Dem.
1980	2,204,202	1,106,311	Kasten, Robert W.	1,065,487	Nelson, Gaylord A.	32,404	40,824 R	50.2%	48.3%	50.9%	49.1%
1976	1,935,183	521,902	York, Stanley	1,396,970	Proxmire, William	16,311	875,068 D	27.0%	72.2%	27.2%	72.8%
1974	1,199,495	429,327	Petri, Thomas E.	740,700	Nelson, Gaylord A.	29,468	311,373 D	35.8%	61.8%	36.7%	63.3%
1970	1,338,967	381,297	Erickson, John E.	948,445	Proxmire, William	9,225	567,148 D	28.5%	70.8%	28.7%	71.3%
1968	1,654,861	633,910	Leonard, Jerris	1,020,931	Nelson, Gaylord A.	20	387,021 D	38.3%	61.7%	38.3%	61.7%
1964	1,673,776	780,116	Renk, Wilbur N.	892,013	Proxmire, William	1,647	111,897 D	46.6%	53.3%	46.7%	53.3%
1962	1,260,168	594,846	Wiley, Alexander	662,342	Nelson, Gaylord A.	2,980	67,496 D	47.2%	52.6%	47.3%	52.7%
1958	1,194,678	510,398	Steinle, Roland J.	682,440	Proxmire, William	1,840	172,042 D	42.7%	57.1%	42.8%	57.2%
1957s	772,620	312,931	Kohler, Walter J.	435,985	Proxmire, William	23,704	123,054 D	40.5%	56.4%	41.8%	58.2%
1956	1,523,356	892,473	Wiley, Alexander	627,903	Maier, Henry W.	2,980	264,570 R	58.6%	41.2%	58.7%	41.3%
1952	1,605,228	870,444	McCarthy, Joseph R.	731,402	Fairchild, Thomas E.	3,382	139,042 R	54.2%	45.6%	54.3%	45.7%
1950	1,116,135	595,283	Wiley, Alexander	515,539	Fairchild, Thomas E.	5,313	79,744 R	53.3%	46.2%	53.6%	46.4%
1946	1,014,594	620,430	McCarthy, Joseph R.	378,772	McMurray, Howard J.	15,392	241,658 R	61.2%	37.3%	62.1%	37.9%

The 1957 election was held in August for a short term to fill a vacancy.

WISCONSIN

Districts Established November 20, 1971

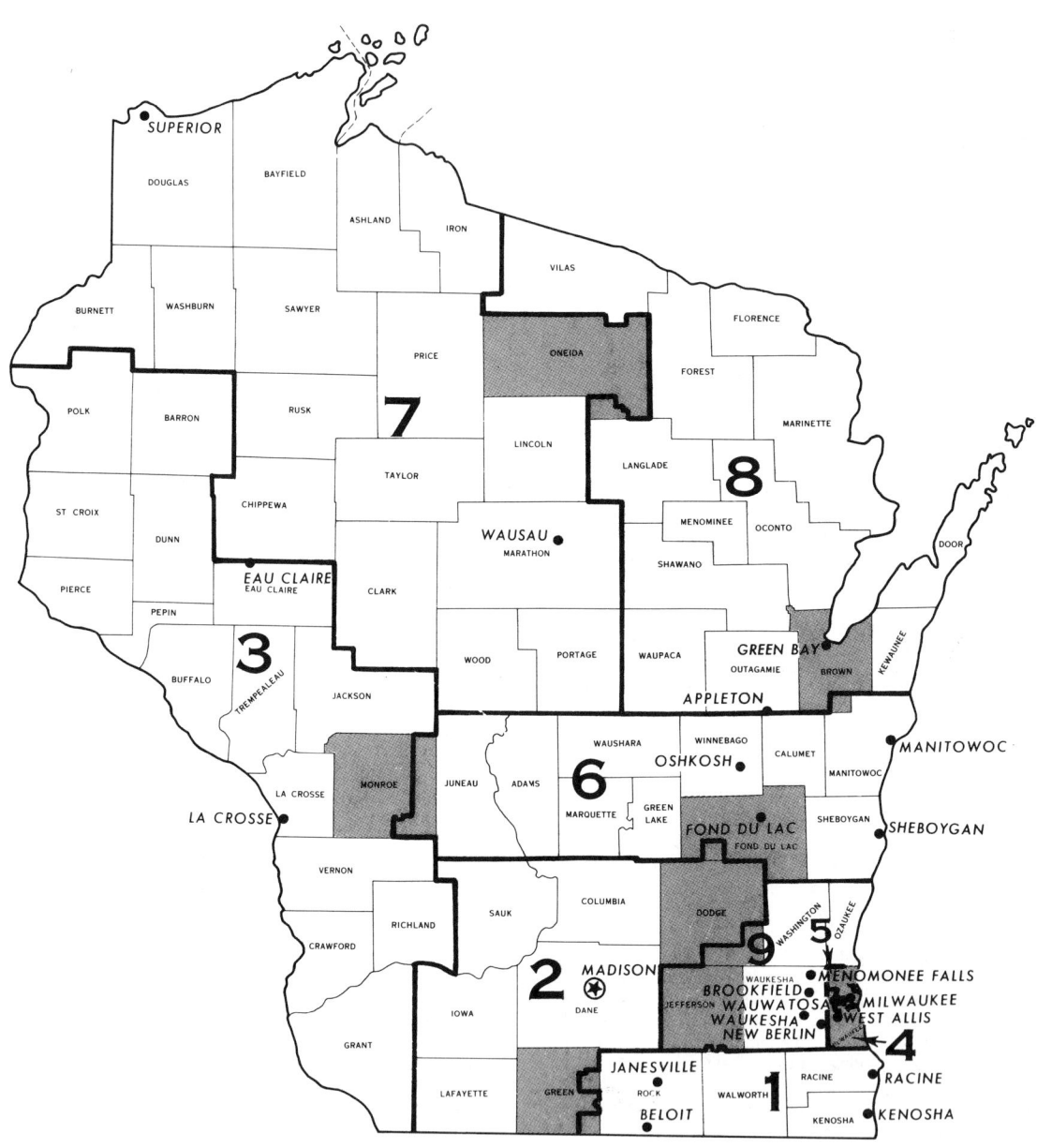

County with two or more Congressional Districts.

WISCONSIN

PRESIDENT 1980

1980 Census Population	County	Total Vote	Republican	Democratic	Other	Rep.-Dem. Plurality	Percentage Total Vote Rep.	Dem.	Major Vote Rep.	Dem.
13,457	ADAMS	6,527	3,304	2,773	450	531 R	50.6%	42.5%	54.4%	45.6%
16,783	ASHLAND	8,685	3,262	4,469	954	1,207 D	37.6%	51.5%	42.2%	57.8%
38,730	BARRON	18,698	8,791	8,654	1,253	137 D	47.0%	46.3%	50.4%	49.6%
13,822	BAYFIELD	7,802	3,278	3,705	819	427 D	42.0%	47.5%	46.9%	53.1%
175,280	BROWN	82,997	47,067	29,796	6,134	17,271 R	56.7%	35.9%	61.2%	38.8%
14,309	BUFFALO	7,428	3,569	3,276	583	293 R	48.0%	44.1%	52.1%	47.9%
12,340	BURNETT	6,757	3,027	3,200	530	173 D	44.8%	47.4%	48.6%	51.4%
30,867	CALUMET	14,321	7,885	5,036	1,400	2,849 R	55.1%	35.2%	61.0%	39.0%
51,702	CHIPPEWA	21,921	10,531	9,836	1,554	695 R	48.0%	44.9%	51.7%	48.3%
32,910	CLARK	15,039	7,921	6,091	1,027	1,830 R	52.7%	40.5%	56.5%	43.5%
43,222	COLUMBIA	21,031	10,478	8,715	1,838	1,763 R	49.8%	41.4%	54.6%	45.4%
16,556	CRAWFORD	7,861	3,934	3,392	535	542 R	50.0%	43.1%	53.7%	46.3%
323,545	DANE	168,563	57,545	85,609	25,409	28,064 D	34.1%	50.8%	40.2%	59.8%
74,747	DODGE	33,682	19,435	11,966	2,281	7,469 R	57.7%	35.5%	61.9%	38.1%
25,029	DOOR	13,006	7,170	4,961	875	2,209 R	55.1%	38.1%	59.1%	40.9%
44,421	DOUGLAS	21,219	7,258	11,703	2,258	4,445 D	34.2%	55.2%	38.3%	61.7%
34,314	DUNN	17,095	7,428	7,743	1,924	315 D	43.5%	45.3%	49.0%	51.0%
78,805	EAU CLAIRE	38,943	17,304	17,602	4,037	298 D	44.4%	45.2%	49.6%	50.4%
4,172	FLORENCE	2,261	1,187	943	131	244 R	52.5%	41.7%	55.7%	44.3%
88,952	FOND DU LAC	42,497	24,196	15,293	3,008	8,903 R	56.9%	36.0%	61.3%	38.7%
9,044	FOREST	4,680	2,070	2,402	208	332 D	44.2%	51.3%	46.3%	53.7%
51,736	GRANT	23,830	13,298	8,406	2,126	4,892 R	55.8%	35.3%	61.3%	38.7%
30,012	GREEN	14,296	7,714	5,336	1,246	2,378 R	54.0%	37.3%	59.1%	40.9%
18,370	GREEN LAKE	9,262	5,868	2,851	543	3,017 R	63.4%	30.8%	67.3%	32.7%
19,802	IOWA	9,001	4,068	4,154	779	86 D	45.2%	46.2%	49.5%	50.5%
6,730	IRON	4,021	1,811	1,941	269	130 D	45.0%	48.3%	48.3%	51.7%
16,831	JACKSON	8,524	4,327	3,629	568	698 R	50.8%	42.6%	54.4%	45.6%
66,152	JEFFERSON	30,016	16,174	11,335	2,507	4,839 R	53.9%	37.8%	58.8%	41.2%
21,039	JUNEAU	10,146	5,591	3,884	671	1,707 R	55.1%	38.3%	59.0%	41.0%
123,137	KENOSHA	55,893	24,481	26,738	4,674	2,257 D	43.8%	47.8%	47.8%	52.2%
19,539	KEWAUNEE	9,794	5,577	3,706	511	1,871 R	56.9%	37.8%	60.1%	39.9%
91,056	LA CROSSE	45,293	23,427	17,304	4,562	6,123 R	51.7%	38.2%	57.5%	42.5%
17,412	LAFAYETTE	8,597	4,421	3,598	578	823 R	51.4%	41.9%	55.1%	44.9%
19,978	LANGLADE	9,883	4,866	4,498	519	368 R	49.2%	45.5%	52.0%	48.0%
26,311	LINCOLN	12,755	6,473	5,438	844	1,035 R	50.7%	42.6%	54.3%	45.7%
82,918	MANITOWOC	38,754	18,591	17,330	2,833	1,261 R	48.0%	44.7%	51.8%	48.2%
111,270	MARATHON	53,549	25,868	23,281	4,400	2,587 R	48.3%	43.5%	52.6%	47.4%
39,314	MARINETTE	19,182	10,444	7,718	1,020	2,726 R	54.4%	40.2%	57.5%	42.5%
11,672	MARQUETTE	5,789	3,166	2,180	443	986 R	54.7%	37.7%	59.2%	40.8%
3,373	MENOMINEE	936	302	544	90	242 D	32.3%	58.1%	35.7%	64.3%
964,988	MILWAUKEE	464,160	183,450	240,174	40,536	56,724 D	39.5%	51.7%	43.3%	56.7%
35,074	MONROE	15,689	8,136	6,521	1,032	1,615 R	51.9%	41.6%	55.5%	44.5%
28,947	OCONTO	14,314	8,292	5,352	670	2,940 R	57.9%	37.4%	60.8%	39.2%
31,216	ONEIDA	16,867	8,602	7,008	1,257	1,594 R	51.0%	41.5%	55.1%	44.9%
128,726	OUTAGAMIE	59,456	31,500	21,284	6,672	10,216 R	53.0%	35.8%	59.7%	40.3%
66,981	OZAUKEE	35,040	21,371	10,779	2,890	10,592 R	61.0%	30.8%	66.5%	33.5%
7,477	PEPIN	3,473	1,541	1,673	259	132 D	44.4%	48.2%	47.9%	52.1%
31,149	PIERCE	15,662	6,209	7,312	2,141	1,103 D	39.6%	46.7%	45.9%	54.1%
32,351	POLK	16,313	7,207	7,607	1,499	400 D	44.2%	46.6%	48.6%	51.4%
57,420	PORTAGE	30,708	10,465	16,443	3,800	5,978 D	34.1%	53.5%	38.9%	61.1%
15,788	PRICE	8,172	4,028	3,595	549	433 R	49.3%	44.0%	52.8%	47.2%
173,132	RACINE	79,775	39,683	33,565	6,527	6,118 R	49.7%	42.1%	54.2%	45.8%
17,476	RICHLAND	8,594	4,601	3,413	580	1,188 R	53.5%	39.7%	57.4%	42.6%
139,420	ROCK	61,218	30,960	24,740	5,518	6,220 R	50.6%	40.4%	55.6%	44.4%
15,589	RUSK	7,800	3,704	3,584	512	120 R	47.5%	45.9%	50.8%	49.2%
43,872	ST. CROIX	21,792	9,265	10,203	2,324	938 D	42.5%	46.8%	47.6%	52.4%
43,469	SAUK	20,208	9,992	8,456	1,760	1,536 R	49.4%	41.8%	54.2%	45.8%
12,843	SAWYER	7,089	3,548	3,065	476	483 R	50.0%	43.2%	53.7%	46.3%
35,928	SHAWANO	16,283	9,922	5,410	951	4,512 R	60.9%	33.2%	64.7%	35.3%
100,935	SHEBOYGAN	48,600	23,036	20,974	4,590	2,062 R	47.4%	43.2%	52.3%	47.7%
18,817	TAYLOR	8,972	4,596	3,739	637	857 R	51.2%	41.7%	55.1%	44.9%
26,158	TREMPEALEAU	12,133	5,992	5,390	751	602 R	49.4%	44.4%	52.6%	47.4%
25,642	VERNON	12,774	6,528	5,501	745	1,027 R	51.1%	43.1%	54.3%	45.7%
16,535	VILAS	9,932	6,034	3,293	605	2,741 R	60.8%	33.2%	64.7%	35.3%
71,507	WALWORTH	33,730	19,194	11,344	3,192	7,850 R	56.9%	33.6%	62.9%	37.1%
13,174	WASHBURN	6,887	3,193	3,172	522	21 R	46.4%	46.1%	50.2%	49.8%
84,848	WASHINGTON	39,493	23,213	12,944	3,336	10,269 R	58.8%	32.8%	64.2%	35.8%
280,326	WAUKESHA	139,236	81,059	46,612	11,565	34,447 R	58.2%	33.5%	63.5%	36.5%
42,831	WAUPACA	20,397	12,568	6,401	1,428	6,167 R	61.6%	31.4%	66.3%	33.7%
18,526	WAUSHARA	9,077	5,576	2,987	514	2,589 R	61.4%	32.9%	65.1%	34.9%

WISCONSIN

PRESIDENT 1980

1980 Census Population	County	Total Vote	Republican	Democratic	Other	Rep.-Dem. Plurality	Percentage			
							Total Vote		Major Vote	
							Rep.	Dem.	Rep.	Dem.
131,732	WINNEBAGO	64,360	34,286	24,203	5,871	10,083 R	53.3%	37.6%	58.6%	41.4%
72,799	WOOD	34,483	17,987	13,804	2,692	4,183 R	52.2%	40.0%	56.6%	43.4%
4,705,335	TOTAL	2,273,221	1,088,845	981,584	202,792	107,261 R	47.9%	43.2%	52.6%	47.4%

WISCONSIN

SENATOR 1980

1980 Census Population	County	Total Vote	Republican	Democratic	Other	Rep.-Dem. Plurality	Percentage Total Vote Rep.	Dem.	Major Vote Rep.	Dem.
13,457	ADAMS	6,229	3,077	2,996	156	81 R	49.4%	48.1%	50.7%	49.3%
16,783	ASHLAND	8,065	3,331	4,616	118	1,285 D	41.3%	57.2%	41.9%	58.1%
38,730	BARRON	17,462	8,121	9,239	102	1,118 D	46.5%	52.9%	46.8%	53.2%
13,822	BAYFIELD	7,475	2,929	4,473	73	1,544 D	39.2%	59.8%	39.6%	60.4%
175,280	BROWN	80,490	43,475	35,747	1,268	7,728 R	54.0%	44.4%	54.9%	45.1%
14,309	BUFFALO	6,842	3,279	3,522	41	243 D	47.9%	51.5%	48.2%	51.8%
12,340	BURNETT	6,378	2,412	3,888	78	1,476 D	37.8%	61.0%	38.3%	61.7%
30,867	CALUMET	13,838	7,856	5,716	266	2,140 R	56.8%	41.3%	57.9%	42.1%
51,702	CHIPPEWA	21,768	9,883	11,477	408	1,594 D	45.4%	52.7%	46.3%	53.7%
32,910	CLARK	14,610	7,966	6,175	469	1,791 R	54.5%	42.3%	56.3%	43.7%
43,222	COLUMBIA	20,268	10,646	9,361	261	1,285 R	52.5%	46.2%	53.2%	46.8%
16,556	CRAWFORD	7,248	3,615	3,605	28	10 R	49.9%	49.7%	50.1%	49.9%
323,545	DANE	164,837	52,855	109,070	2,912	56,215 D	32.1%	66.2%	32.6%	67.4%
74,747	DODGE	33,041	21,129	11,557	355	9,572 R	63.9%	35.0%	64.6%	35.4%
25,029	DOOR	12,369	7,106	5,203	60	1,903 R	57.5%	42.1%	57.7%	42.3%
44,421	DOUGLAS	20,386	5,438	14,432	516	8,994 D	26.7%	70.8%	27.4%	72.6%
34,314	DUNN	16,379	6,920	9,206	253	2,286 D	42.2%	56.2%	42.9%	57.1%
78,805	EAU CLAIRE	37,690	17,123	19,909	658	2,786 D	45.4%	52.8%	46.2%	53.8%
4,172	FLORENCE	2,001	1,092	896	13	196 R	54.6%	44.8%	54.9%	45.1%
88,952	FOND DU LAC	40,861	24,287	15,997	577	8,290 R	59.4%	39.1%	60.3%	39.7%
9,044	FOREST	4,355	1,965	2,310	80	345 D	45.1%	53.0%	46.0%	54.0%
51,736	GRANT	21,997	12,679	9,170	148	3,509 R	57.6%	41.7%	58.0%	42.0%
30,012	GREEN	13,506	7,468	5,979	59	1,489 R	55.3%	44.3%	55.5%	44.5%
18,370	GREEN LAKE	8,806	6,006	2,692	108	3,314 R	68.2%	30.6%	69.1%	30.9%
19,802	IOWA	8,574	4,159	4,346	69	187 D	48.5%	50.7%	48.9%	51.1%
6,730	IRON	3,678	1,432	2,215	31	783 D	38.9%	60.2%	39.3%	60.7%
16,831	JACKSON	7,973	4,165	3,689	119	476 R	52.2%	46.3%	53.0%	47.0%
66,152	JEFFERSON	29,198	17,516	11,441	241	6,075 R	60.0%	39.2%	60.5%	39.5%
21,039	JUNEAU	9,788	5,628	4,020	140	1,608 R	57.5%	41.1%	58.3%	41.7%
123,137	KENOSHA	51,955	21,243	29,872	840	8,629 D	40.9%	57.5%	41.6%	58.4%
19,539	KEWAUNEE	9,300	5,251	3,982	67	1,269 R	56.5%	42.8%	56.9%	43.1%
91,056	LA CROSSE	43,798	23,247	19,980	571	3,267 R	53.1%	45.6%	53.8%	46.2%
17,412	LAFAYETTE	8,110	4,222	3,859	29	363 R	52.1%	47.6%	52.2%	47.8%
19,978	LANGLADE	9,494	5,547	3,799	148	1,748 R	58.4%	40.0%	59.4%	40.6%
26,311	LINCOLN	12,499	7,116	5,110	273	2,006 R	56.9%	40.9%	58.2%	41.8%
82,918	MANITOWOC	36,976	19,060	16,988	928	2,072 R	51.5%	45.9%	52.9%	47.1%
111,270	MARATHON	51,490	28,447	21,223	1,820	7,224 R	55.2%	41.2%	57.3%	42.7%
39,314	MARINETTE	18,377	10,498	7,691	188	2,807 R	57.1%	41.9%	57.7%	42.3%
11,672	MARQUETTE	5,379	3,053	2,188	138	865 R	56.8%	40.7%	58.3%	41.7%
3,373	MENOMINEE	778	200	566	12	366 D	25.7%	72.8%	26.1%	73.9%
964,988	MILWAUKEE	458,829	197,380	255,756	5,693	58,376 D	43.0%	55.7%	43.6%	56.4%
35,074	MONROE	14,791	8,671	6,001	119	2,670 R	58.6%	40.6%	59.1%	40.9%
28,947	OCONTO	13,630	8,017	5,531	82	2,486 R	58.8%	40.6%	59.2%	40.8%
31,216	ONEIDA	16,363	9,276	6,792	295	2,484 R	56.7%	41.5%	57.7%	42.3%
128,726	OUTAGAMIE	56,742	33,649	22,018	1,075	11,631 R	59.3%	38.8%	60.4%	39.6%
66,981	OZAUKEE	34,808	23,399	11,150	259	12,249 R	67.2%	32.0%	67.7%	32.3%
7,477	PEPIN	3,228	1,385	1,804	39	419 D	42.9%	55.9%	43.4%	56.6%
31,149	PIERCE	14,465	5,847	8,469	149	2,622 D	40.4%	58.5%	40.8%	59.2%
32,351	POLK	15,446	5,905	9,414	127	3,509 D	38.2%	60.9%	38.5%	61.5%
57,420	PORTAGE	29,419	12,570	16,020	829	3,450 D	42.7%	54.5%	44.0%	56.0%
15,788	PRICE	7,873	4,404	3,285	184	1,119 R	55.9%	41.7%	57.3%	42.7%
173,132	RACINE	77,672	39,695	36,497	1,480	3,198 R	51.1%	47.0%	52.1%	47.9%
17,476	RICHLAND	8,073	4,925	3,088	60	1,837 R	61.0%	38.3%	61.5%	38.5%
139,420	ROCK	58,585	29,008	28,457	1,120	551 R	49.5%	48.6%	50.5%	49.5%
15,589	RUSK	7,513	3,537	3,772	204	235 D	47.1%	50.2%	48.4%	51.6%
43,872	ST. CROIX	20,344	8,042	12,183	119	4,141 D	39.5%	59.9%	39.8%	60.2%
43,469	SAUK	19,746	10,267	9,268	211	999 R	52.0%	46.9%	52.6%	47.4%
12,843	SAWYER	6,611	3,246	3,276	89	30 D	49.1%	49.6%	49.8%	50.2%
35,928	SHAWANO	15,563	9,715	5,528	320	4,187 R	62.4%	35.5%	63.7%	36.3%
100,935	SHEBOYGAN	48,481	24,618	23,440	423	1,178 R	50.8%	48.3%	51.2%	48.8%
18,817	TAYLOR	8,616	4,704	3,620	292	1,084 R	54.6%	42.0%	56.5%	43.5%
26,158	TREMPEALEAU	11,397	5,571	5,745	81	174 D	48.9%	50.4%	49.2%	50.8%
25,642	VERNON	12,271	7,160	5,021	90	2,139 R	58.3%	40.9%	58.8%	41.2%
16,535	VILAS	9,587	5,986	3,463	138	2,523 R	62.4%	36.1%	63.4%	36.6%
71,507	WALWORTH	32,490	19,839	12,315	336	7,524 R	61.1%	37.9%	61.7%	38.3%
13,174	WASHBURN	6,485	2,721	3,714	50	993 D	42.0%	57.3%	42.3%	57.7%
84,848	WASHINGTON	39,585	26,304	12,900	381	13,404 R	66.4%	32.6%	67.1%	32.9%
280,326	WAUKESHA	137,717	87,406	48,958	1,353	38,448 R	63.5%	35.5%	64.1%	35.9%
42,831	WAUPACA	19,647	12,945	6,512	190	6,433 R	65.9%	33.1%	66.5%	33.5%
18,526	WAUSHARA	8,697	5,693	2,870	134	2,823 R	65.5%	33.0%	66.5%	33.5%

WISCONSIN

SENATOR 1980

1980 Census Population	County	Total Vote	Republican	Democratic	Other	Rep.-Dem. Plurality	Percentage Total Vote Rep.	Dem.	Major Vote Rep.	Dem.
131,732	WINNEBAGO	61,725	34,510	26,183	1,032	8,327 R	55.9%	42.4%	56.9%	43.1%
72,799	WOOD	33,535	18,474	14,232	829	4,242 R	55.1%	42.4%	56.5%	43.5%
4,705,335	TOTAL	2,204,202	1,106,311	1,065,487	32,404	40,824 R	50.2%	48.3%	50.9%	49.1%

WISCONSIN

CONGRESS

CD	Year	Total Vote	Republican Vote	Republican Candidate	Democratic Vote	Democratic Candidate	Other Vote	Rep.-Dem. Plurality	Total Vote Rep.	Total Vote Dem.	Major Vote Rep.	Major Vote Dem.
1	1980	224,442	96,047	CANARY, KATHRYN H.	126,222	ASPIN, LES	2,173	30,175 D	42.8%	56.2%	43.2%	56.8%
1	1978	141,585	64,437	PETRIE, WILLIAM W.	77,146	ASPIN, LES	2	12,709 D	45.5%	54.5%	45.5%	54.5%
1	1976	209,807	71,427	PETRIE, WILLIAM W.	136,162	ASPIN, LES	2,218	64,735 D	34.0%	64.9%	34.4%	65.6%
1	1974	116,191	34,288	SMITH, LEONARD W.	81,902	ASPIN, LES	1	47,614 D	29.5%	70.5%	29.5%	70.5%
1	1972	190,937	66,665	STALBAUM, MERRILL E.	122,973	ASPIN, LES	1,299	56,308 D	34.9%	64.4%	35.2%	64.8%
2	1980	263,138	119,514	WRIGHT, JAMES A.	142,037	KASTENMEIER, ROBERT	1,587	22,523 D	45.4%	54.0%	45.7%	54.3%
2	1978	172,762	71,412	WRIGHT, JAMES A.	99,631	KASTENMEIER, ROBERT	1,719	28,219 D	41.3%	57.7%	41.8%	58.2%
2	1976	236,545	81,350	MILLER, ELIZABETH T.	155,158	KASTENMEIER, ROBERT	37	73,808 D	34.4%	65.6%	34.4%	65.6%
2	1974	144,453	50,890	MILLER, ELIZABETH T.	93,561	KASTENMEIER, ROBERT	2	42,671 D	35.2%	64.8%	35.2%	64.8%
2	1972	217,318	68,167	KELLY, J. MICHAEL	148,136	KASTENMEIER, ROBERT	1,015	79,969 D	31.4%	68.2%	31.5%	68.5%
3	1980	258,868	132,001	GUNDERSON, STEVEN	126,859	BALDUS, ALVIN	8	5,142 R	51.0%	49.0%	51.0%	49.0%
3	1978	153,412	57,060	ELLIS, MICHAEL S.	96,326	BALDUS, ALVIN	26	39,266 D	37.2%	62.8%	37.2%	62.8%
3	1976	239,311	100,218	GUNDERSEN, ADOLF L.	139,083	BALDUS, ALVIN	10	38,865 D	41.9%	58.1%	41.9%	58.1%
3	1974	150,028	71,171	THOMSON, VERNON W.	76,668	BALDUS, ALVIN	2,189	5,497 D	47.4%	51.1%	48.1%	51.9%
3	1972	206,356	112,905	THOMSON, VERNON W.	91,953	THORESEN, WALTER	1,498	20,952 R	54.7%	44.6%	55.1%	44.9%
4	1980	209,139	61,027	HONADEL, ELROY C.	146,437	ZABLOCKI, CLEMENT J.	1,675	85,410 D	29.2%	70.0%	29.4%	70.6%
4	1978	153,703	52,125	HONADEL, ELROY C.	101,575	ZABLOCKI, CLEMENT J.	3	49,450 D	33.9%	66.1%	33.9%	66.1%
4	1976	172,243			172,166	ZABLOCKI, CLEMENT J.	77	172,166 D		100.0%		100.0%
4	1974	116,995	27,818	COLLISON, LEWIS D.	84,768	ZABLOCKI, CLEMENT J.	4,409	56,950 D	23.8%	72.5%	24.7%	75.3%
4	1972	197,072	45,003	MROZINSKI, PHILLIP D.	149,078	ZABLOCKI, CLEMENT J.	2,991	104,075 D	22.8%	75.6%	23.2%	76.8%
5	1980	168,218	37,267	BATHKE, DAVID	129,574	REUSS, HENRY S.	1,377	92,307 D	22.2%	77.0%	22.3%	77.7%
5	1978	116,420	30,185	MEDINA, JAMES R.	85,067	REUSS, HENRY S.	1,168	54,882 D	25.9%	73.1%	26.2%	73.8%
5	1976	173,511	36,413	HICKS, ROBERT L.	134,935	REUSS, HENRY S.	2,163	98,522 D	21.0%	77.8%	21.3%	78.7%
5	1974	81,361	16,293	MORRIES, MILDRED A.	65,060	REUSS, HENRY S.	8	48,767 D	20.0%	80.0%	20.0%	80.0%
5	1972	164,654	33,627	VAN HECKE, FREDERICK	127,273	REUSS, HENRY S.	3,754	93,646 D	20.4%	77.3%	20.9%	79.1%
6	1980	242,611	143,980	PETRI, THOMAS E.	98,628	GOYKE, GARY R.	3	45,352 R	59.3%	40.7%	59.3%	40.7%
6	1978	164,817	114,742	STEIGER, WILLIAM A.	48,785	STEFFES, ROBERT J.	1,290	65,957 R	69.6%	29.6%	70.2%	29.8%
6	1976	220,271	139,541	STEIGER, WILLIAM A.	80,715	SMITH, JOSEPH C.	15	58,826 R	63.3%	36.6%	63.4%	36.6%
6	1974	145,660	86,652	STEIGER, WILLIAM A.	51,571	SIMENZ, NANCY J.	7,437	35,081 R	59.5%	35.4%	62.7%	37.3%
6	1972	198,610	130,701	STEIGER, WILLIAM A.	63,643	ADAMS, JAMES A.	4,266	67,058 R	65.8%	32.0%	67.3%	32.7%
7	1980	254,107	89,745	VESTA, VINTON A.	164,340	OBEY, DAVID R.	22	74,595 D	35.3%	64.7%	35.3%	64.7%
7	1978	178,304	65,750	VESTA, VINTON A.	110,874	OBEY, DAVID R.	1,680	45,124 D	36.9%	62.2%	37.2%	62.8%
7	1976	233,937	60,952	SAVINO, FRANK A.	171,366	OBEY, DAVID R.	1,619	110,414 D	26.1%	73.3%	26.2%	73.8%
7	1974	148,172	43,558	BURGER, JOSEF	104,468	OBEY, DAVID R.	146	60,910 D	29.4%	70.5%	29.4%	70.6%
7	1972	215,612	80,207	O'KONSKI, ALVIN E.	135,385	OBEY, DAVID R.	20	55,178 D	37.2%	62.8%	37.2%	62.8%
8	1980	250,726	169,664	ROTH, TOBY	81,043	MONFILS, MICHAEL R.	19	88,621 R	67.7%	32.3%	67.7%	32.3%
8	1978	175,791	101,856	ROTH, TOBY	73,925	CORNELL, ROBERT J.	10	27,931 R	57.9%	42.1%	57.9%	42.1%
8	1976	228,106	107,048	FROEHLICH, HAROLD V.	115,996	CORNELL, ROBERT J.	5,062	8,948 D	46.9%	50.9%	48.0%	52.0%
8	1974	146,840	66,889	FROEHLICH, HAROLD V.	79,923	CORNELL, ROBERT J.	28	13,034 D	45.6%	54.4%	45.6%	54.4%
8	1972	201,643	101,634	FROEHLICH, HAROLD V.	97,795	CORNELL, ROBERT J.	2,214	3,839 R	50.4%	48.5%	51.0%	49.0%
9	1980	263,079	206,227	SENSENBRENNER, F. JAMES	56,838	BENEDICT, GARY C.	14	149,389 R	78.4%	21.6%	78.4%	21.6%
9	1978	193,688	118,386	SENSENBRENNER, F. JAMES	75,207	FLYNN, MATTHEW J.	95	43,179 R	61.1%	38.8%	61.2%	38.8%
9	1976	248,524	163,791	KASTEN, ROBERT W.	84,706	MCDONALD, LYNN M.	27	79,085 R	65.9%	34.1%	65.9%	34.1%
9	1974	146,871	77,733	KASTEN, ROBERT W.	66,071	ADELMAN, LYNN S.	3,067	11,662 R	52.9%	45.0%	54.1%	45.9%
9	1972	208,892	128,230	DAVIS, GLENN R.	76,585	FINE, RALPH A.	4,077	51,645 R	61.4%	36.7%	62.6%	37.4%

WISCONSIN

1980 GENERAL ELECTION

President   Other vote was 160,657 Anderson (Independent); 29,135 Clark (Libertarian); 7,767 Commoner (Citizens); 1,519 Rarick (Constitution); 808 McReynolds (Socialist); 772 Hall (Communist); 414 Griswold (Workers World); 383 DeBerry (Socialist Workers); 1,337 scattered.

Senator   Other vote was 16,156 Wickstrom (Constitution); 9,679 Larson (Libertarian); 6,502 Hagen (Socialist Workers); 67 scattered.

Congress   Other vote was 2,168 Jackson (Libertarian) and 5 scattered in CD 1; 1,582 Key (Libertarian) and 5 scattered in CD 2; 1,670 Rashkind (Independent) and 5 scattered in CD 4; 1,371 Forrestal (Independent) and 6 scattered in CD 5; scattered in all other CD's.

1980 PRIMARIES

SEPTEMBER 9 REPUBLICAN

Senator   134,586 Robert W. Kasten; 106,270 Terry J. Kohler; 84,355 Douglass Cofrin; 40,823 Russell A. Olson; 46 scattered.

Congress   Unopposed in four CD's. Contested as follows:

CD 1   10,558 Kathryn H. Canary; 9,795 Donald Walsh; 7,807 Edward J. Huck; 3,922 George M. Knuckles; 8 scattered.
CD 2   30,732 James A. Wright; 5,470 Herbert F. Hoover; 12 scattered.
CD 3   35,710 Steven Gunderson; 11,515 Gary K. Madson; 4,487 Ward W. Repp; 9 scattered.
CD 5   8,281 David Bathke; 3,457 Walter G. Beach.
CD 7   15,594 Vinton A. Vesta; 10,399 Eugene F. Barrett; 8,686 Delmar F. Drumm; 7 scattered.

SEPTEMBER 9 DEMOCRATIC

Senator   Gaylord A. Nelson, unopposed.

Congress   Unopposed in six CD's. Contested as follows:

CD 4   29,411 Clement J. Zablocki; 3,489 Roman R. Blenski; 1 scattered.
CD 5   20,977 Henry S. Reuss; 2,842 Rajababu Kilaru; 1 scattered.
CD 8   10,708 Michael R. Monfils; 5,407 Michael R. Janczy; 3 scattered.

SEPTEMBER 9 CONSTITUTION

Senator   James P. Wickstrom, unopposed.

Congress   None. No candidates.

SEPTEMBER 9 LIBERTARIAN

Senator   Bervin J. Larson, unopposed.

Congress   Unopposed in the two CD's in which a candidate was nominated. No candidates in other CD's.

WYOMING

GOVERNOR
Ed Herschler (D). Re-elected 1978 to a four-year term. Previously elected 1974.

SENATORS
Alan K. Simpson (R). Elected 1978 to a six-year term.

Malcolm Wallop (R). Elected 1976 to a six-year term.

REPRESENTATIVE
At-Large. Richard Cheney (R)

POSTWAR VOTE FOR GOVERNOR

Year	Total Vote	Republican Vote	Candidate	Democratic Vote	Candidate	Other Vote	Rep.-Dem. Plurality	Total Vote Rep.	Total Vote Dem.	Major Vote Rep.	Major Vote Dem.
1978	137,567	67,595	Ostlund, John C.	69,972	Herschler, Ed	—	2,377 D	49.1%	50.9%	49.1%	50.9%
1974	128,386	56,645	Jones, Dick	71,741	Herschler, Ed	—	15,096 D	44.1%	55.9%	44.1%	55.9%
1970	118,257	74,249	Hathaway, Stan	44,008	Rooney, John J.	—	30,241 R	62.8%	37.2%	62.8%	37.2%
1966	120,873	65,624	Hathaway, Stan	55,249	Wilkerson, Ernest	—	10,375 R	54.3%	45.7%	54.3%	45.7%
1962	119,268	64,970	Hansen, Clifford P.	54,298	Gage, Jack R.	—	10,672 R	54.5%	45.5%	54.5%	45.5%
1958	112,537	52,488	Simpson, Milward L.	55,070	Hickey, J. J.	4,979	2,582 D	46.6%	48.9%	48.8%	51.2%
1954	111,438	56,275	Simpson, Milward L.	55,163	Jack, William	—	1,112 R	50.5%	49.5%	50.5%	49.5%
1950	96,959	54,441	Barrett, Frank A.	42,518	McIntyre, John J.	—	11,923 R	56.1%	43.9%	56.1%	43.9%
1946	81,353	38,333	Wright, Earl	43,020	Hunt, Lester C.	—	4,687 D	47.1%	52.9%	47.1%	52.9%

POSTWAR VOTE FOR SENATOR

Year	Total Vote	Republican Vote	Candidate	Democratic Vote	Candidate	Other Vote	Rep.-Dem. Plurality	Total Vote Rep.	Total Vote Dem.	Major Vote Rep.	Major Vote Dem.
1978	133,364	82,908	Simpson, Alan K.	50,456	Whitaker, Raymond B.	—	32,452 R	62.2%	37.8%	62.2%	37.8%
1976	155,368	84,810	Wallop, Malcolm	70,558	McGee, Gale	—	14,252 R	54.6%	45.4%	54.6%	45.4%
1972	142,067	101,314	Hansen, Clifford P.	40,753	Vinich, Mike	—	60,561 R	71.3%	28.7%	71.3%	28.7%
1970	120,486	53,279	Wold, John S.	67,207	McGee, Gale	—	13,928 D	44.2%	55.8%	44.2%	55.8%
1966	122,689	63,548	Hansen, Clifford P.	59,141	Roncalio, Teno	—	4,407 R	51.8%	48.2%	51.8%	48.2%
1964	141,670	65,185	Wold, John S.	76,485	McGee, Gale	—	11,300 D	46.0%	54.0%	46.0%	54.0%
1962s	119,372	69,043	Simpson, Milward L.	50,329	Hickey, J. J.	—	18,714 R	57.8%	42.2%	57.8%	42.2%
1960	138,550	78,103	Thomson, E. Keith	60,447	Whitaker, Ray	—	17,656 R	56.4%	43.6%	56.4%	43.6%
1958	114,157	56,122	Barrett, Frank A.	58,035	McGee, Gale	—	1,913 D	49.2%	50.8%	49.2%	50.8%
1954	112,252	54,407	Harrison, William H.	57,845	O'Mahoney, Joseph C.	—	3,438 D	48.5%	51.5%	48.5%	51.5%
1952	130,097	67,176	Barrett, Frank A.	62,921	O'Mahoney, Joseph C.	—	4,255 R	51.6%	48.4%	51.6%	48.4%
1948	101,480	43,527	Robertson, Edward V.	57,953	Hunt, Lester C.	—	14,426 D	42.9%	57.1%	42.9%	57.1%
1946	81,557	35,714	Henderson, Harry B.	45,843	O'Mahoney, Joseph C.	—	10,129 D	43.8%	56.2%	43.8%	56.2%

The election in 1962 was for a short term to fill a vacancy.

WYOMING

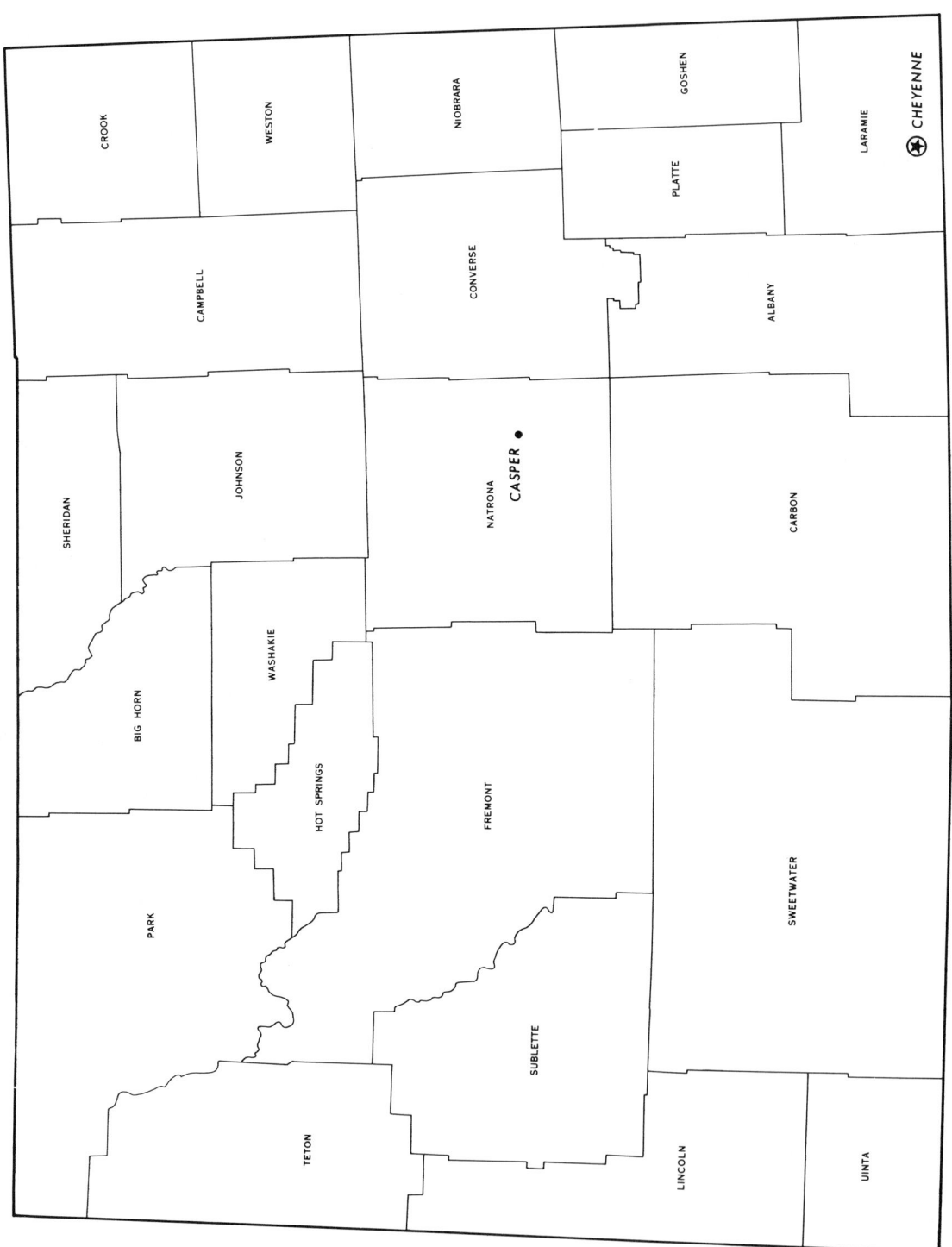

WYOMING

PRESIDENT 1980

1980 Census Population	County	Total Vote	Republican	Democratic	Other	Rep.-Dem. Plurality	Percentage			
							Total Vote		Major Vote	
							Rep.	Dem.	Rep.	Dem.
29,062	ALBANY	11,527	5,830	3,772	1,925	2,058 R	50.6%	32.7%	60.7%	39.3%
11,896	BIG HORN	5,223	3,709	1,212	302	2,497 R	71.0%	23.2%	75.4%	24.6%
24,367	CAMPBELL	7,669	5,613	1,400	656	4,213 R	73.2%	18.3%	80.0%	20.0%
21,896	CARBON	7,283	4,337	2,272	674	2,065 R	59.5%	31.2%	65.6%	34.4%
14,069	CONVERSE	4,229	2,987	922	320	2,065 R	70.6%	21.8%	76.4%	23.6%
5,308	CROOK	2,416	1,909	413	94	1,496 R	79.0%	17.1%	82.2%	17.8%
40,251	FREMONT	13,403	9,077	3,307	1,019	5,770 R	67.7%	24.7%	73.3%	26.7%
12,040	GOSHEN	5,315	3,572	1,373	370	2,199 R	67.2%	25.8%	72.2%	27.8%
5,710	HOT SPRINGS	2,555	1,602	745	208	857 R	62.7%	29.2%	68.3%	31.7%
6,700	JOHNSON	3,148	2,291	635	222	1,656 R	72.8%	20.2%	78.3%	21.7%
68,649	LARAMIE	27,713	15,361	9,512	2,840	5,849 R	55.4%	34.3%	61.8%	38.2%
12,177	LINCOLN	4,694	3,412	1,063	219	2,349 R	72.7%	22.6%	76.2%	23.8%
71,856	NATRONA	26,672	16,801	7,111	2,760	9,690 R	63.0%	26.7%	70.3%	29.7%
2,924	NIOBRARA	1,412	1,075	270	67	805 R	76.1%	19.1%	79.9%	20.1%
21,639	PARK	8,811	6,435	1,718	658	4,717 R	73.0%	19.5%	78.9%	21.1%
11,975	PLATTE	4,618	2,642	1,555	421	1,087 R	57.2%	33.7%	62.9%	37.1%
25,048	SHERIDAN	9,646	5,649	3,034	963	2,615 R	58.6%	31.5%	65.1%	34.9%
4,548	SUBLETTE	2,082	1,538	357	187	1,181 R	73.9%	17.1%	81.2%	18.8%
41,723	SWEETWATER	12,067	6,265	4,728	1,074	1,537 R	51.9%	39.2%	57.0%	43.0%
9,355	TETON	5,212	3,004	1,361	847	1,643 R	57.6%	26.1%	68.8%	31.2%
13,021	UINTA	4,151	2,738	1,138	275	1,600 R	66.0%	27.4%	70.6%	29.4%
9,496	WASHAKIE	3,897	2,634	945	318	1,689 R	67.6%	24.2%	73.6%	26.4%
7,106	WESTON	2,970	2,219	584	167	1,635 R	74.7%	19.7%	79.2%	20.8%
470,816	TOTAL	176,713	110,700	49,427	16,586	61,273 R	62.6%	28.0%	69.1%	30.9%

WYOMING

CONGRESS

CD	Year	Total Vote	Republican Vote	Republican Candidate	Democratic Vote	Democratic Candidate	Other Vote	Rep.-Dem. Plurality	Total Vote Rep.	Total Vote Dem.	Major Vote Rep.	Major Vote Dem.
AL	1980	169,699	116,361	CHENEY, RICHARD	53,338	ROGERS, JIM		63,023 R	68.6%	31.4%	68.6%	31.4%
AL	1978	129,377	75,855	CHENEY, RICHARD	53,522	BAGLEY, BILL		22,333 R	58.6%	41.4%	58.6%	41.4%
AL	1976	151,868	66,147	HART, LARRY	85,721	RONCALIO, TENO		19,574 D	43.6%	56.4%	43.6%	56.4%
AL	1974	126,933	57,499	STROOCK, TOM	69,434	RONCALIO, TENO		11,935 D	45.3%	54.7%	45.3%	54.7%
AL	1972	146,299	70,667	KIDD, WILLIAM	75,632	RONCALIO, TENO		4,965 D	48.3%	51.7%	48.3%	51.7%
AL	1970	116,304	57,848	ROBERTS, HARRY	58,456	RONCALIO, TENO		608 D	49.7%	50.3%	49.7%	50.3%
AL	1968	123,313	77,363	WOLD, JOHN S.	45,950	LINFORD, VELMA		31,413 R	62.7%	37.3%	62.7%	37.3%
AL	1966	119,426	62,984	HARRISON, WILLIAM H.	56,442	CHRISTIAN, AL		6,542 R	52.7%	47.3%	52.7%	47.3%
AL	1964	139,175	68,482	HARRISON, WILLIAM H.	70,693	RONCALIO, TENO		2,211 D	49.2%	50.8%	49.2%	50.8%
AL	1962	116,474	71,489	HARRISON, WILLIAM H.	44,985	MANKUS, LOUIS A.		26,504 R	61.4%	38.6%	61.4%	38.6%
AL	1960	134,331	70,241	HARRISON, WILLIAM H.	64,090	ARMSTRONG, H. T.		6,151 R	52.3%	47.7%	52.3%	47.7%
AL	1958	111,780	59,894	THOMSON, E. KEITH	51,886	WHITAKER, RAY		8,008 R	53.6%	46.4%	53.6%	46.4%
AL	1956	120,128	69,903	THOMSON, E. KEITH	50,225	O'CALLAGHAN, JERRY		19,678 R	58.2%	41.8%	58.2%	41.8%
AL	1954	108,771	61,111	THOMSON, E. KEITH	47,660	TULLY, SAM		13,451 R	56.2%	43.8%	56.2%	43.8%
AL	1952	126,720	76,161	HARRISON, WILLIAM H.	50,559	ROSE, ROBERT R.		25,602 R	60.1%	39.9%	60.1%	39.9%
AL	1950	93,348	50,865	HARRISON, WILLIAM H.	42,483	CLARK, JOHN B.		8,382 R	54.5%	45.5%	54.5%	45.5%
AL	1948	97,464	50,218	BARRETT, FRANK A.	47,246	FLANNERY, L. G.		2,972 R	51.5%	48.5%	51.5%	48.5%
AL	1946	79,438	44,482	BARRETT, FRANK A.	34,956	MCINTYRE, JOHN J.		9,526 R	56.0%	44.0%	56.0%	44.0%

WYOMING

1980 GENERAL ELECTION

President   Other vote was 12,072 Anderson (Independent); 4,514 Clark (Independent).

Congress

1980 PRIMARIES

SEPTEMBER 9 REPUBLICAN

Congress   Unopposed at-large.

SEPTEMBER 9 DEMOCRATIC

Congress   Contested as follows:

AL   19,448 Jim Rogers; 8,450 Al Hamburg; 5,398 Theodore H. Hommel; 3,343 Sid Kornegay.

DISTRICT OF COLUMBIA

GOVERNMENT
The District of Columbia is governed by a Mayor and a City Council of thirteen.

MAYOR
Marion Barry (D). Elected 1978 to a four-year term.

DELEGATE
Walter E. Fauntroy (D)

POSTWAR VOTE FOR MAYOR

Year	Total Vote	Republican Vote	Candidate	Democratic Vote	Candidate	Other Vote	Rep.-Dem. Plurality	Total Vote Rep.	Total Vote Dem.	Major Vote Rep.	Major Vote Dem.
1978	100,861	28,032	Fletcher, Arthur	69,888	Barry, Marion	2,941	41,856 D	27.8%	69.3%	28.6%	71.4%
1974	105,183	3,703	Champion, Jackson R.	84,676	Washington, Walter E.	16,804	80,973 D	3.5%	80.5%	4.2%	95.8%

POSTWAR VOTE FOR DELEGATE

Year	Total Vote	Republican Vote	Candidate	Democratic Vote	Candidate	Other Vote	Rep.-Dem. Plurality	Total Vote Rep.	Total Vote Dem.	Major Vote Rep.	Major Vote Dem.
1980	151,046	21,245	Roehr, Robert J.	112,339	Fauntroy, Walter E.	17,462	91,094 D	14.1%	74.4%	15.9%	84.1%
1978	96,306	11,677	Champion, Jackson R.	76,557	Fauntroy, Walter E.	8,072	64,880 D	12.1%	79.5%	13.2%	86.8%
1976	159,790	21,699	Hall, Daniel L.	123,464	Fauntroy, Walter E.	14,627	101,765 D	13.6%	77.3%	14.9%	85.1%
1974	104,014	9,166	Phillips, William R.	66,337	Fauntroy, Walter E.	28,511	57,171 D	8.8%	63.8%	12.1%	87.9%
1972	159,612	39,487	Chin-Lee, William	95,300	Fauntroy, Walter E.	24,825	55,813 D	24.7%	59.7%	29.3%	70.7%
1971	116,635	29,249	Nevius, John A.	68,166	Fauntroy, Walter E.	19,220	38,917 D	25.1%	58.4%	30.0%	70.0%

The 1971 election was for a short term to the end of the 92nd Congress.

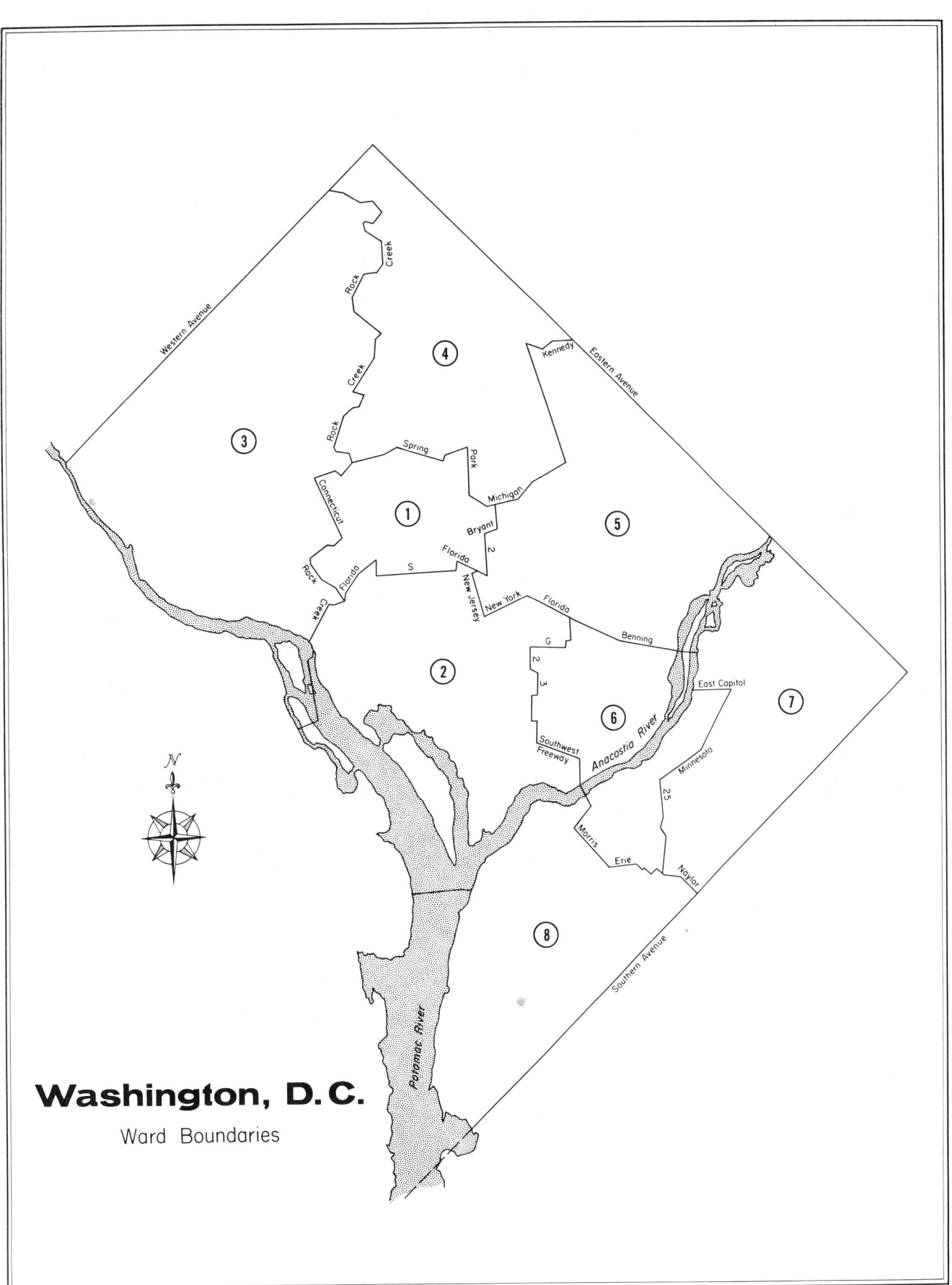

Washington, D.C.

Ward Boundaries

DISTRICT OF COLUMBIA

PRESIDENT 1980

1980 Census Population	Ward	Total Vote	Republican	Democratic	Other	Rep.-Dem. Plurality	Percentage Total Vote Rep.	Dem.	Major Vote Rep.	Dem.
77,400	WARD 1	18,804	1,870	14,060	2,874	12,190 D	9.9%	74.8%	11.7%	88.3%
72,700	WARD 2	20,194	3,409	13,156	3,629	9,747 D	16.9%	65.1%	20.6%	79.4%
88,300	WARD 3	35,759	12,654	15,258	7,847	2,604 D	35.4%	42.7%	45.3%	54.7%
82,900	WARD 4	27,273	1,734	23,993	1,546	22,259 D	6.4%	88.0%	6.7%	93.3%
81,700	WARD 5	22,562	1,040	20,497	1,025	19,457 D	4.6%	90.8%	4.8%	95.2%
73,400	WARD 6	19,064	1,550	15,022	2,492	13,472 D	8.1%	78.8%	9.4%	90.6%
83,400	WARD 7	20,857	935	19,138	784	18,203 D	4.5%	91.8%	4.7%	95.3%
77,900	WARD 8	10,622	336	9,918	368	9,582 D	3.2%	93.4%	3.3%	96.7%
	SPECIAL BALLOTS	102	17	71	14	54 D	16.7%	69.6%	19.3%	80.7%
637,700	TOTAL	175,237	23,545	131,113	20,579	107,568 D	13.4%	74.8%	15.2%	84.8%

DISTRICT OF COLUMBIA

DELEGATE 1980

1980 Census Population	Ward	Total Vote	Republican	Democratic	Other	Rep.-Dem. Plurality	Percentage Total Vote Rep.	Dem.	Major Vote Rep.	Dem.
77,400	WARD 1	16,035	1,937	11,438	2,660	9,501 D	12.1%	71.3%	14.5%	85.5%
72,700	WARD 2	17,431	3,622	11,273	2,536	7,651 D	20.8%	64.7%	24.3%	75.7%
88,300	WARD 3	29,892	10,745	14,377	4,770	3,632 D	35.9%	48.1%	42.8%	57.2%
82,900	WARD 4	23,833	1,327	20,467	2,039	19,140 D	5.6%	85.9%	6.1%	93.9%
81,700	WARD 5	19,745	779	17,464	1,502	16,685 D	3.9%	88.4%	4.3%	95.7%
73,400	WARD 6	16,641	1,925	12,694	2,022	10,769 D	11.6%	76.3%	13.2%	86.8%
83,400	WARD 7	18,019	686	16,074	1,259	15,388 D	3.8%	89.2%	4.1%	95.9%
77,900	WARD 8	9,370	214	8,497	659	8,283 D	2.3%	90.7%	2.5%	97.5%
	SPECIAL BALLOTS	80	10	55	15	45 D	12.5%	68.8%	15.4%	84.6%
637,700	TOTAL	151,046	21,245	112,339	17,462	91,094 D	14.1%	74.4%	15.9%	84.1%

DISTRICT OF COLUMBIA

Population data for wards are from the Office of Planning and Development of the District of Columbia and represent rounded-off figures.

1980 GENERAL ELECTION

President   Other vote was 16,337 Anderson (Independent); 1,840 Commoner (Citizens); 1,114 Clark (Libertarian); 371 Hall (Communist); 173 DeBerry (Socialist Workers); 52 Griswold (Workers World); 692 scattered. Uncorrected returns gave the vote for the following candidates as: 23,313 Reagan; 130,231 Carter; 16,131 Anderson; 1,826 Commoner; 1,104 Clark; 369 Hall; 690 scattered. Special ballots are those classed by District election authorities as Federal Voters.

Delegate   Other vote was 14,467 Butler (D.C. Statehood); 2,995 scattered. Uncorrected returns gave the vote as 111,631 Fauntroy; 21,021 Roehr; 14,325 Butler; 2,979 scattered. Special ballots are those classed by District election authorities as Federal Voters.

1980 PRIMARIES

MAY 6 REPUBLICAN

Delegate   No candidate names appeared on the ballot; there were 894 write-in votes and Robert J. Roehr received the nomination by write-in.

MAY 6 DEMOCRATIC

Delegate   Walter E. Fauntroy, unopposed.

MAY 6 STATEHOOD

Delegate   No candidate names appeared on the ballot; there were 130 write-in votes and Josephine D. Butler received the nomination by write-in.